ENGLAND

THE COMPLETE
POST-WAR RECORD

First published in Great Britain by
The Breedon Books Publishing Company Limited
44 Friar Gate, Derby, DE1 1DA
1993

ISBN 1 873626 39 8

Printed and bound by Hillmans Printers, Frome, Somerset.
Covers printed by BDC Printing Services Limited of Derby.

ENGLAND

THE COMPLETE POST-WAR RECORD

MIKE PAYNE

The Breedon Books
Publishing Company
Derby

Foreword

AS I penned these notes the news came through of the sad passing of England's greatest ever captain, Bobby Moore. Finding words at such a time is never easy but I take some comfort that Bobby's supreme contribution to English football is more than demonstrated in the pages of this book. He will never be forgotten.

There is no greater honour for any footballer than to represent his country . . .it is the ultimate. I was fortunate enough to play for England 76 times in those glory years after the war and every occasion was a memorable experience.

England appearances took me to all corners of the world, to some imposing stadiums, in front of some of the most partisan crowds. Brazil in Rio, Scotland at Hampden Park and so many thrill-a-minute encounters at wonderful Wembley. I enjoyed it all, even though there were occasional

disappointments like the shock defeat by the USA. I took part in three World Cup finals and figured both alongside and against some legendary footballers — not bad for a young plumber from Preston.

This book, painstakingly researched by Mike Payne, has brought the memories flooding back. The detail is quite remarkable with match accounts from all of England's full internationals since the war. It is a book for every English soccer enthusiast to treasure; a step-by-step guide to close on half a century of international action.

I feel privileged to have been asked to pen this short introduction — a small contribution to a fine book on a glorious game.

Tom Finney

Introduction

WHEN I first sat down to look back over England's international history I found it fascinating, but regarded it as nothing more than a browse through just one aspect of my favourite hobby of football. But the more I researched the more hooked I became. Thus, over the past seven years, I have browsed through countless newspapers, magazines, programmes, books and articles in an effort to piece together the amazing story of England's progress since the war.

I purposely began in 1946 because I felt that the giants of the English game would be more familiar to the younger reader than perhaps the stars of the pre-war period would be. And I hope you will agree that the careers of the Finney's, Matthews' and Lofthouse's etc are vividly highlighted in the match reports. They were truly great players who carried the game to many a far off foreign field, always showing the same stature that made them such wonderful ambassadors for our country. Thankfully, that respect has been handed down over the years, and today's stars carry on the traditions.

The memories are many. Twelve World Cup campaigns, eight European Championships and countless friendlies have produced a million moments of magic to be savoured. Over the years the England

team has received much criticism, some justified, but for the most part the country should be proud of our achievements. In fact, England's record in the 470 matches recorded in this book is tremendous and, in some quarters, not appreciated. For such a small country we have an enviable record and we have deservedly held a place in the world's list of top ten teams for every one of the 47 years since 1946. England still remain the team every other nation wants to beat the most. That is something we all should be very proud of and remembered when criticism is being thrown around, as it sometimes is.

As you will see I have tried to emphasise the actual way the game was played when writing my match reports and I have avoided all the off the field waffling that tends to accompany every England game these days. By doing this I hope the reader will obtain a true feeling of being there and savouring the occasion. Relive all the glorious moments, remember the fine players and enjoy the many marvellous goals that have graced our international football.

Come with me on a memorable journey through time.

Mike Payne
May 1993

Photographic Acknowledgements
Photographs have been supplied by Empics and the Hulton-Deutsch Picture Library.

Northern Ireland v England Home Championship

Played on Saturday 28 September 1946 at Windsor Park, Belfast.

Northern Ireland: A.Russell (Linfield); W.C.Gorman (Brentford), T.Ahearne (Belfast Celtic), J.J.Carey (Man Utd), J.Vernon (Belfast Celtic), J.P.Douglas (Belfast Celtic), D.Cochran (Leeds Utd), J.McAlinden (Portsmouth), E.J.McMorran (Belfast Celtic), P.D.Doherty (Derby Co), N.Lockhart (Linfield).

England: F.V.Swift (Man City); L.Scott (Arsenal), G.F.M.Hardwick (Middlesbrough, captain), W.A.Wright (Wolves), C.F.Franklin (Stoke C), H.Cockburn (Man Utd), T.Finney (Preston NE), H.S.Carter (Derby Co), T.Lawton (Chelsea), W.J.Mannion (Middlesbrough), R.Langton (Blackburn R).

Half-time 0-3   Full-time 2-7

Ref: W.Webb (Scotland)   Att: 57,000

A RECORD 57,000 people attended the first official full Home International football match since 1939 and the huge swirling crowd threatened to cancel the game as the spectators spilled on to the pitch. Thankfully, common sense and good humour prevailed and order was restored in time for the kick-off.

The match got off to a sensational start with England taking the lead in the first minute. George Hardwick sent the ball into the Irish penalty area and after Ahearne had made a weak attempt at a clearance, Raich Carter pounced to open the scoring.

Although Ireland tried desperately to recover they could not stop the eager England forwards. In the seventh minute it was 2-0. Henry Cockburn found Tommy Lawton with a lovely pass and the centre-forward found some space brilliantly to set up an easy goal for Wilf Mannion. Middlesbrough's Mannion scored again before half-time after Lawton's ferocious shot rebounded off the crossbar and England went in with a commanding lead.

Carter and Mannion continued to perform brilliantly after the break to completely destroy Ireland's already shattered defences. Time and again their fine passing set up more goal chances. Within 15 minutes England had scored two more goals through Tom Finney and Mannion, who thus completed his hat-trick.

Finney was doing just as he pleased on the right wing and by this time Mannion and Carter were walking through the demoralised Irish ranks. Lockhart gave

Tom Finney, the Preston winger who had his debut against Northern Ireland and marked it with a goal. Finney went on to win 76 full caps in a glorious career which stretched until 1959.

54th match v Northern Ireland.
Debut for Swift, Scott, Hardwick, Wright, Franklin, Cockburn, Finney, Mannion and Langton.
Debut goals for Finney, Mannion (hat-trick) and Langton.
Lawton was winning his ninth cap (he had played eight times before the war) and Carter his seventh. Hardwick was the first post-war captain.
"It was wonderful to make my debut and every player's ambition. I was so pleased for my father who gave me so much encouragement."
Tom Finney.

the eerily silent crowd something to cheer with a goal from the left, but Lawton and then Bobby Langton underlined England's superiority with goals six and seven. Just before the end Lockhart gave the Irish another consolation goal but it was a very dejected set of green-shirted footballers who left the field at the final whistle.

England's display had been very impressive and Carter's link up with Finney was outstanding, much better than at anytime with Stanley Matthews; Mannion's performance was also memorable.

Republic of Ireland v England Friendly

Played on Monday, 30 September 1946 at Dalymount Park, Dublin.

Republic of Ireland: T.Breen (Shamrock R); W.C.Gorman (Brentford), W.E.Hayes (Huddersfield T), J.J.Carey (Man Utd), C.J.Martin (Glentoran), W.Walsh (Man City), Dr K.P.O'Flanagan (Arsenal), P.Coad (Shamrock R), M.O'Flanagan (Bohemians), A.E.Stevenson (Everton), T.J.Eglington (Everton).

England: F.V.Swift (Man City); L.Scott (Arsenal), G.F.M.Hardwick (Middlesbrough, captain) W.A.Wright (Wolves), C.F.Franklin (Stoke C), H.Cockburn (Man Utd), T.Finney (Preston NE), H.S.Carter (Derby Co), T.Lawton (Chelsea), W.J.Mannion (Middlesbrough), R.Langton (Blackburn R).

Half-time 0-0   Full-time 0-1
Ref: W.Webb (Scotland)   Att: 23,000

THE first-ever meeting between the two nations was played in persistent drizzle and the difficult pitch made life awkward for the players. Throughout the match, the Republic put up a terrific fight and made the England team fight all the way to gain their eventual undeserved win. Indeed, had it not been for the fact that Frank Swift was in inspired form, then the visitors could have been well beaten.

The Irish won the toss but England were soon on the attack, winning two early corners. On 15 minutes, Tom Finney set off on a brilliant dribble only to see Raich Carter's first-time shot from his pass saved well by Tommy Breen. However, the Republic were always in contention and they forced Swift into a fine save and also forced corners on both wings.

The strong tackling home defenders were upsetting the rhythm of the sometimes delightful play of the England forwards. Only a brave save by Swift at the feet of Kevin O'Flannagan saved a difficult situation before Carter, Wilf Mannion and Tommy Lawton all went close for England. At half-time the score was 0-0 with Ireland more than holding their own.

Hayes was suffering from a pulled muscle as the second half began and moved to the wing position. England were soon on the attack with Carey heading an early Bobby Langton effort off the goal-line. After 59 minutes, Stevenson was desperately unlucky not to give the Irish the lead. He beat two players in a fine run but saw his shot crash against the bar with Swift beaten.

The next 15 minutes saw the Irishmen in control. Twice Swift saved magnificently from Eglington and Coad and only a brilliant tackle by Billy Wright averted one dangerous situation. Somehow, England held on and recovered their poise.

With only nine minutes remaining they stole victory with a fine goal. Langton gave Mannion a through pass down the left. The 'Boro man cut in and unleashed an angled shot which Breen could only parry. The ball ran loose and Finney dashed in to slot it home. England had won by the skin of their teeth.

1st match v the Republic of Ireland.

England v Wales   Home Championship

Played on Wednesday, 13 November 1946 at Maine Road, Manchester.

England: F.V.Swift (Man City); L.Scott (Arsenal), G.F.M.Hardwick (Middlesbrough, captain), W.A.Wright (Wolves), C.F.Franklin (Stoke C), H.Cockburn (Man Utd), T.Finney (Preston NE), H.S.Carter (Derby Co), T.Lawton (Chelsea), W.J.Mannion (Middlesbrough), R.Langton (Blackburn R).
Wales: C.Sidlow (Liverpool); A.T.Sherwood (Cardiff C), W.M.Hughes (Birmingham C), D.F.Witcomb (West Brom), T.G.Jones Everton), W.A.R.Burgess (Spurs), W.E.A.Jones (Swansea T), A.Powell (Leeds Utd), S.V.Richards (Cardiff C), I.V.Powell (QPR), G.Edwards (Birmingham C).

Half-time 2-0   Full-time 3-0
Ref: W.Webb (Scotland)   Att: 59,250

ENGLAND fought off the spirited challenge of the Welsh to gain at least a share of the Home International Championship for 1946-47. Several times the crowd were treated to the smooth rythmic understanding of a team with so many outstanding talents, although the typical Welsh tenacity made sure that they knew that they had been in a very tough game.

An early goal is welcome in any game and it took England only eight minutes to take the lead. Tommy Lawton sent a long raking pass out to Bobby Langton on the left wing and Langton's cross was met by Raich Carter, who scrambled it towards goal. Wilf Mannion was also in the area and helped the ball on its way with a touch through Sidlow's legs. Although the ball was cleared by Hughes,

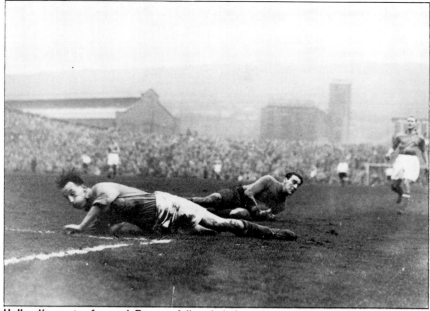
Holland's centre-forward Roozen falls winded to the ground after Frank Swift has bravely dropped on the ball during the game at Huddersfield in November 1946.

the referee had decided that it had already crossed the goal-line.

Two good efforts by Ivor Powell then went close for Wales as they hit back strongly. The first shot went over and the second was superbly saved by Frank Swift. Then, with five minutes to go before half-time, England scored a second goal to set Wales back on their heels. Fine work and passing by Billy Wright, Carter and Mannion set up Lawton. The centre-forward needed no second bidding and Sidlow was soon picking the ball out of his net.

In the second half, Wales tried everything they knew to get back into the game. They threw everything at the home defence. Richards shot wide and Swift again saved well, this time from a header by Aubrey Powell. For 15 minutes it was all Wales but England weathered the storm and on 76 minutes they produced another flash of brilliance to finally kill off the Welsh Dragons.

Tom Finney found Henry Cockburn with a pass in midfield and he, in turn, found Lawton. Mannion then came from nowhere to speed through a gap to take the final pass and settle the match with a good shot.

57th match v Wales.

England v Holland   Friendly

Played on Wednesday, 27 November 1946 at Leeds Road, Huddersfield.

England: F.V.Swift (Man City); L.Scott (Arsenal), G.F.M.Hardwick (Middlesbrough, captain), W.A.Wright (Wolves), C.F.Franklin (Stoke C), H.Johnston (Blackpool), T.Finney (Preston NE), H.S.Carter (Derby Co), T.Lawton (Chelsea), W.J.Mannion (Middlesbrough), R.Langton (Blackburn R).
Holland: P.C.Kraak (Stormvogels); J.H.Potharst (Ajax Amsterdam), H.Van der Linden (Ajax Amsterdam), B.J.Paauwe (Feyenoord), A.Vermeer (Excelsior), A.De Vroet (Feyenoord), G.K.Dräger (Ajax Amsterdam), S.Wilkes (Xerxes), W.G.V.Roozen (FC Haarlem), J.C.Smit (FC Haarlem), J.F.T.Bergman (Bleuw Wit).

Half-time 6-1   Full-time 8-2
Ref: J.M.Martin (Scotland)   Att: 32,500

ENGLAND totally outplayed Holland from start to finish in this one-sided match. The pitch was heavy and slippery after much rain had fallen and in the opening quarter the Dutch side gave a good account of themselves. Their number-eight, Wilkes, caught the eye but, alas, he seemed the only man who could match the England ball players.

Raich Carter, first capped with Sunderland before the war and now a Derby County star.

In the 24th minute, England took the lead and from that moment there was only ever going to be one outcome. Raich Carter and Wilf Mannion had already taken a firm grip on the game with their immaculate passing and it came as no real surprise when Tommy Lawton scored with a shot from the edge of the area. Four minutes later the same player headed a

Raich Carter rounds off an excellent move to level the scores against Scotland at Wembley in April 1947.

second and in the next seven minutes there were an incredible four more goals, three to England and one to Holland.

First Carter notched number three before Mannion and Lawton, his own third, made it 5-0. Bergman did manage to pull one back for the visitors but just before the interval there was more drama as George Hardwick missed a penalty and then Tom Finney scored a sixth goal. Holland trooped off at half-time in a daze, not knowing which way to turn next.

The pace, quite naturally after that onslaught, slackened after the restart and much of the play was scrappy. England went through the motions for most of the half but towards the end they livened up again creating more chances. From one excellent move Carter scored his second and then Lawton scored his fourth and England's eighth. In a late rally, Smit netted a second goal for Holland but it was, in the true sense of the word, only a consolation.

> 2nd match v Holland.
> Debut for Johnston.
> Lawton scored four goals and Hardwick missed a penalty.

England v Scotland Home Championship

Played on Saturday, 12 April 1947 at Wembley Stadium.

England: F.V.Swift (Man City); L.Scott (Arsenal), G.F.M.Hardwick (Middlesbrough, captain), W.A.Wright (Wolves), C.F.Franklin (Stoke C), H.Johnston (Blackpool), S.Matthews (Stoke C), H.S.Carter (Derby Co), T.Lawton (Chelsea), W.J.Mannion (Middlesbrough), J.Mullen (Wolves).
Scotland: W.Miller (Celtic); G.K.Young (Rangers), J.Shaw (Rangers), A.R.Macauley (Brentford), W.A.Woodburn (Rangers), A.R.Forbes (Sheffield Utd), G.Smith (Hibernian), A.McLaren (Preston NE), J.Delaney (Man Utd), W.Steel (Morton), T.Pearson (Newcastle Utd).

Half-time 0-1   **Full-time 1-1**
Ref: C.Delasalle (France)   Att: 98,250

THE Home International Championship went to England after their draw in this final match of the season against Scotland. It was not a very good display and it was the Scots who gained most of the credit.

Over 98,000 spectators packed into Wembley on a glorious sunny day. The pitch looked superb and it was a very colourful scene especially when decorated by the pipes and drums of the Scots Guards. The teams were presented to the Prime Minister, Clement Atlee, before the kick-off.

The first-half belonged to Scotland. Driven on by marvellous displays from Macauley and Forbes in the midfield, they tore England apart. The rhythm that had been seen in England's previous games was completely upset and the usual inspirational pair, Raich Carter and Wilf Mannion, just could not get going against their Scottish counterparts.

After 15 minutes Scotland took the lead their play had deserved. The move typified their native quality. Shaw found Pearson with a good pass. The winger dribbled down the left before laying on a perfect pass for McLaren, bursting through the middle, to shoot home a fine goal past the helpless Frank Swift.

England went from bad to worse. Pearson saw a shot blocked. Swift twice dropped the ball under pressure and there was a vociferous appeal for handball against Laurie Scott. Somehow though, England held on until half-time although at this stage they should have been out of the game completely.

To their eternal credit the half-time break was used to good effect by England and they restarted with a much more determined look about them. Within minutes a sparkling move involving Tommy Lawton, Jimmy Mullen and Carter ended with a shot into the side netting.

Two other similar moves lingered in the memory before, on 56 minutes, England equalized. A superb quick passing move-

ment between Lawton, Mannion and Carter ended with the latter shooting an excellent goal. At last England were something like their old selves again. They forced three corners in as many minutes as they searched for a winner but the Scots were not going to let that happen and they gave as good as they got, rising above themselves in a thriller.

There had been some interesting individual battles on the day with Scott doing well against Pearson, Smith worrying George Hardwick and Delaney having Neil Franklin in two minds for much of the game. Mullen, meanwhile, had a quiet but promising debut. In the end, though, the two sides shared the points and, reluctantly, settled for the draw.

> 64th match v Scotland.
> First post-war Wembley international. Debut for Mullen; Matthews was making his 18th appearance, the other 17 caps being pre-war.

England v France Friendly

Played on Saturday, 3 May 1947 at Arsenal Stadium, London.

England: F.V.Swift (Man City); L.Scott (Arsenal), G.F.M.Hardwick (Middlesbrough, captain), W.A.Wright (Wolves), C.F.Franklin (Stoke C), E.Lowe (Aston Villa), T.Finney (Preston NE), H.S.Carter (Derby Co), T.Lawton (Chelsea), W.J.Mannion (Middlesbrough), R.Langton (Blackburn R).
France: J.Da Rui (CO Roubaix Toucoing); J.Swiatek (Girondins), R.Marche (Stade de Reims), A.Cuissard (AS St-Etienne), J.Grégoire (Stade Francais), J.Prouff (Stade de Reims), E.Vaast (RC de Paris), B.Tempowski (Lille OSC), E.Bongiorni (RC de Paris), O.Hesserer (RC Strasbourg), J.Lechantre (Lille OSC).

Half-time 0-0   **Full-time 3-0**
Ref: L.Baert (Belgium)   Att: 54,500

England skipper George Hardwick and France's Hesserer with Belgian referee L.Baert before the game at Highbury in May 1947.

Frank Swift collects the ball at the feet of French centre-forward Bongiorni.

FRANCE were totally outclassed by England in an interesting international at Highbury, home of Arsenal FC. The fact that the visitors held out until after half-time was mainly due to Da Rui's acrobatics in the French goal.

England were soon pressing forward and enjoyed virtually all the possession in the first 45 minutes. They tended to spoil their approach play, though, by over elaborating in midfield. This gave the French the time to regroup in defence and the visitors did this well.

Da Rui saved well from Tommy Lawton and Tom Finney from England's best efforts of the half, whilst France's only worthwhile shot flew over Frank Swift's crossbar from Lechantre. It was remarkable that the scoreline was still blank at the break, as England had been so much on top.

After the interval, however, England were much more sensible about their passing. Raich Carter and Wilf Mannion began to release the ball much earlier and holes soon began to appear in the French rearguard.

After 51 minutes, the breakthrough arrived. A sparkling move involving high-speed passing between Bobby Langton, Carter, Lawton and Mannion ended with Finney taking the final pass in his stride to shoot home a fine goal. It was significant that not one Frenchman had touched the ball in 50 yards.

France hit back briefly when Tempowski forced Swift into a full-length save, but Mannion soon underlined England's superiority with a second goal. Swiatek made a poor clearance and the England number-ten expertly lobbed the ball over the goalkeeper and into the net.

Fifteen minutes from the end, Lowe, on a satisfying debut, capped a fine second half for his team by selling the whole French defence a dummy before putting Carter through with a glorious pass for England's third goal.

By this time France were all at sea and only some desperate tackling prevented further goals. Once again, a European challenge had failed on English soil.

10th match v France.
Debut for Lowe.

Switzerland v England   Friendly

Played on Sunday, 18 May 1947 at the Hardturm Sportsplatz, Zürich.

Switzerland: E.Ballabio (FC Grenchen); R.Gyger (FC Cantonal), W.Steffen (FC Cantonal), A.Belli (Servette FC), O.Eggimann (Lausanne-Sports), R.Bocquet (Lausanne-Sports), J.Tamini (Servette FC), W.Fink (Young Fellows), A.Bickel (Grasshoppers), L.Amadò (Grasshoppers), J.Fatton (Servette FC).

England: F.Swift (Man City); L.Scott (Arsenal), G.F.M.Hardwick (Middlesbrough, captain), W.A.Wright (Wolves), C.F.Franklin (Stoke C), E.Lowe (Aston Villa), S.Matthews (Blackpool), H.S.Carter (Derby Co), T.Lawton (Chelsea), W.J.Mannion (Middlesbrough), R.Langton (Blackburn R).

Half-time 1-0   **Full-time 1-0**

Ref: V.Sdez (France)   Att: 30,000

Cyger, the Swiss defender, performs acrobatics watched by Wilf Mannion and Willi Steffen in England's 1-0 defeat in Zurich in May 1947.

OVER 30,000 people watched this Sunday afternoon international in what was the first of two England games in a European tour. The superior teamwork of the Swiss eventually won the game against a strangely subdued England side.

England never reproduced any of the exciting play of their previous post-war encounters and on this day even the defence looked well below its best against the speedy Swiss forwards.

What proved to be the deciding goal came in the 27th minute. A pass by Amado found Fatton completely unmarked to score from close range. The crowd went wild with delight as England struggled to get their game together. In one incident Tommy Lawton did get the ball into the Swiss net but the referee ruled it out for offside.

The second half was much the same pattern with the Swiss showing a lot of confidence and England desperately trying to improve. Fatton and Fink were particularly dangerous for Switzerland and Laurie Scott had his hands full with the lively winger.

It was not until the final 15 minutes that England came into the game. Lawton, easily England's most dangerous attacker, twice forced Ballabio into excellent saves but try as they might they could not force an equalizer.

3rd match v Switzerland.
England's first post-war defeat.

Portugal v England
Friendly

Played on Sunday, 25 May 1947 at the National Stadium, Lisbon.

Portugal: J.Azevedo (Sporting Lisbon); A.Cordoso (Sporting Lisbon), A.Feliciano (Belenenses), M.Amoro (Belenenses), F.Moreira (Benfica), F.Ferreira (Belenenses), J.Correia (Sporting Lisbon), A.Arajúo (FC Porto), F.Peyroteo (Sporting Lisbon), J.Travaços (Sporting Lisbon), R.de Carvalho (Benfica).

Subs: M.Capela (Belenenses) for Azevedo; V.de Oliveira (Belenenses) for Cordoso.

England: F.V.Swift (Man City); L.Scott (Arsenal), G.F.M.Hardwick (Middlesbrough, captain), W.A.Wright (Wolves), C.F.Franklin (Stoke C), E.Lowe (Aston Villa), S.Matthews (Blackpool), S.H.Mortensen (Blackpool), T.Lawton (Chelsea), W.J.Mannion (Middlesbrough), T.Finney (Preston NE).

Half-time 0-5   Full-time 0-10
Ref: C.Delasalle (France)   Att: 62,000

ENGLAND overwhelmed Portugal in this, the very first meeting between the two countries. It was a hot and sunny day and the superb pitch was perfectly suited to the fine ball players in the England side. They tore into the beleagured Portuguese defence from the start and on the day were in a completely different class.

After only two minutes, England were already two goals up. Both Stan Mortensen and Tommy Lawton crashed the ball past Azevedo in a devastating opening. Immediately, Portugal tried to bend the rules. Before the match, it was agreed that a normal full-size ball would be used. Somehow, the Portuguese officials managed to swap it for a lighter, smaller version which they preferred. Later they illegally made two substitutions.

All this made no difference to the superior and highly experienced England players. With Stanley Matthews and Tom Finney in exquisite form, they ripped Portugal apart. Lawton notched their third and fifth goals and, sandwiched between them, Finney scored a cracker. Picking the ball up on the half-way line, he beat one man, then another before reaching the by-line. As he turned towards goal, a third opponent came at him only to be beaten as well. Finney then shot past the goalkeeper from the narrowest of angles.

Half-time came and Portugal looked demoralised. But there was no let up for them after the break as the game continued in the same pattern. Lawton scored his fourth and this was followed by three more

goals from Mortensen. The icing on the cake came when Matthews scored a rare goal to put the total in double figures.

It was little wonder that the unhappy, bewildered Portuguese team missed the official after match banquet.

First match v Portugal.
Debut goal for Mortensen, who went on to score four.
Four goals also for Lawton (the second time he had achieved that for England).
Fourth time England had scored ten goals or more in a match.
First time Finney and Matthews had been in the same side.
Portugal's de Carvalho also known as 'Rogerio' and de Oliveira also known as 'Vasco'.

Belgium v England
Friendly

Played on Sunday, 21 September 1947 in the Heysel Stadium, Brussels.

Belgium: F.Daenen (FC Tillew); L.Aernoudts (Berchem Sport), J.Pannaye (FC Tillew), H.Coppens (KV Mechelen), J.Henriet (RSC Charleroi), F.Massay (Standard Liège), V.Lemberecht (KV Mechelen), J.Mermans (RSC Anderlecht), A.De Cleyn (KV Mechelen), L.Anoul (FC Liège), R.Thirifays (RSC Charleroi).

England: F.V.Swift (Man City); L.Scott (Arsenal), G.F.M.Hardwick (Middlesbrough, captain), T.V.Ward (Derby Co), C.F.Franklin (Stoke C), W.A.Wright (Wolves), S.Matthews (Blackpool), S.H.Mortensen (Blackpool), T.Lawton (Chelsea), W.J.Mannion (Middlesbrough), T.Finney (Preston NE).

Half-time 1-3   Full-time 2-5
Ref: J.M.Martin (Scotland)   Att: 62,500

MOST of Belgium's political VIPs were amongst the spectators in the Heysel Stadium to witness a fine performance by an England side inspired by the magic of Stanley Matthews.

Rain threatened at the start but it took England only one minute to take the lead. A lovely move, in which all the forwards featured, ended with Tommy Lawton scoring from Matthews' pass.

By now the rain was lashing down but more delightful play soon gave England their second goal. Again Matthews was involved. His cross was headed down into some space by Lawton and Stan Mortensen burst through to beat Daenen with a good shot.

That goal had come after 15 minutes and, almost at once, Matthews set up another goal. This time his cross to the far post was met by Tom Finney, who made it 3-0.

Belgium hit back before half-time when Mermans put in a fine header that was well saved by Frank Swift. The inside-right was not to be denied though and shortly afterwards he took a pass from De Cleyn and shot home via a deflection off George Hardwick's legs. The goal ended an eventful first 45 minutes.

After the break the rain stopped and the sun came out. It spurred Belgium on and ten minutes into the second half, they really opened up the game with a second goal. Swift was drawn badly out of position and Lemberecht was able to head into an empty net.

The Belgians then threw everything at England trying desperately to find an equalizer. But Matthews had other ideas. A superb dribble, in which he beat man after man, ended with him setting up Finney with the easiest of chances for the goal that settled the issue.

Before the end, England underlined their superiority with a fifth goal. The incredible Matthews again made the running before Lawton headed past the goalkeeper.

11th match v Belgium.
Debut for Ward.

Wales v England Home Championship

Played on Saturday, 18 October 1947 at Ninian Park, Cardiff.

Wales: C.Sidlow (Liverpool); R.Lambert (Liverpool), W.Barnes (Arsenal), I.V.Powell (QPR), T.G.Jones (Everton), W.A.R.Burgess (Spurs), D.S.Thomas (Fulham), A.Powell (Leeds Utd), G.Lowrie (Coventry C), B.Jones (Arsenal), G.Edwards (Birmingham C).
England: F.V.Swift (Man City); L.Scott (Arsenal), G.F.M.Hardwick (Middlesbrough, captain), P.H.Taylor (Liverpool), C.F.Franklin (Stoke C), W.A.Wright (Wolves), S.Matthews (Blackpool), S.H.Mortensen (Blackpool), T.Lawton (Chelsea), W.J.Mannion (Middlesbrough), T.Finney (Preston NE).

Half-time 0-3   Full-time 0-3
Ref: J.M.Martin (Scotland)   Att: 55,000

IT was case of 'genius defeating talent' when these two sides met in 1947. The match was decided in the first 15 minutes as the England side put together some superb football to score three times.

After only 30 seconds, the Welsh goalkeeper Cyril Sidlow had parried a fierce shot from Stan Mortensen and then saved Tommy Lawton's follow-up header.

England were moving brilliantly. Stanley Matthews and Tom Finney were already casting their spells down the wings and after six minutes they took the lead. A fine quick-passing movement sent the ball from Phil Taylor to Matthews, to Wilf Mannion and on to Finney, who scored with his left foot. Finney had failed to score in only one of his internationals so far, a marvellous testament to his finishing skills.

After 11 minutes, Matthews left Barnes in a daze before laying on goal number-two for Mortensen. That was bad enough for Wales, but all too soon their defence was again caught flat-footed. Matthews and Mannion had Jones and Barnes in a right old tangle before Mannion's diagonal pass found Lawton travelling at speed. Sidlow probably no more than heard the centre-forward's shot as it whizzed past him. There might have been more goals for England before half-time as they had the Welsh defence running in circles.

The second half was much more evenly contested as England, with Mortensen and Scott both suffering from pulled muscles, eased up. Lawton and Mortensen shot

Neil Franklin of Stoke City, the classy centre-half who won 27 caps for England.

wide for England and as Wales fought back, Lowrie missed a good chance close in and Aubrey Powell twice forced Frank Swift into diving saves.

With Taylor having a fine debut and Billy Wright outstanding, Wales could find little change from the English defence. Ronnie Burgess had a good game but Ray Lambert and Walley Barnes had a torrid time. Right until the end, that man Matthews was leaving a trail of red shirts in his wake as England registered their first win on Welsh soil for 13 years.

58th match v Wales.
Debut for Taylor.

England v Home Championship Northern Ireland

Played on Wednesday, 5 November 1947 at Goodison Park, Liverpool.

England: F.V.Swift (Man City); L.Scott (Arsenal), G.F.M.Hardwick (Middlesbrough, captain), P.H.Taylor (Liverpool), C.F.Franklin (Stoke C), W.A.Wright (Wolves), S.Matthews (Blackpool), S.H.Mortensen (Blackpool), T.Lawton (Notts Co), W.J.Mannion (Middlesbrough), T.Finney (Preston NE).
Northern Ireland: E.Hinton (Fulham); C.J.Martin (Leeds Utd), J.J.Carey (Man Utd), W.Walsh (Man City), J.Vernon (West Brom), P.D.Farrell (Everton), D.Cochrane (Leeds Utd), S.Smyth (Wolves), D.J.Walsh (West Brom), P.D.Doherty (Huddersfield T), T.J.Eglington (Everton).

Half-time 0-0   Full-time 2-2
Ref: P.Fitzpatrick (Scotland)   Att: 68,000

APPROPRIATELY, there were plenty of fireworks in this explosive match which saw Northern Ireland almost pull off an astonishing victory. During the first half hour of the game, England were well on top and a couple of fine chances went begging. But although England had the edge, they were not firing on all cylinders.

Stanley Matthews was not as prominent as usual but Tom Finney was playing well and gave Martin a troublesome afternoon. Wilf Mannion was also performing well and was consistently the best of the England forwards. However, Ireland came more into the game as the first half wore on, playing with their customary passion. A lot of effort was put into the half by both sides but, alas, no goals.

Nine minutes into the second half came the almost unbelievable — Ireland took the lead! Dave Walsh, taking a pass from Doherty, upset the form book by putting Ireland 1-0 up with a good shot past Frank Swift. It could have been worse for England shortly afterwards as Ireland nearly went two up. First Eglington and then Smyth came very close to breaching the shaky England defence.

Ireland were playing like men inspired but, with 20 minutes left, it seemed that all their good work was for nothing as Matthews was sent sprawling in the area. Mannion took the penalty kick but Hinton saved.

Ireland, everyone thought, now surely had to win; but England also knew how to fight and they rose to the challenge superbly. With only seven minutes left they equalized. Billy Wright, up with his forwards, gave Mannion the chance to make amends for his penalty miss and this time the 'Boro man made no mistake.

Amazingly, the match then took a new twist. Mannion sent Matthews away down the right. Over came a perfect cross and Tommy Lawton volleyed a magnificent shot past Hinton from 15 yards.

It would have been a travesty if Ireland's spirited display had ended with nothing to show for it. Happily, justice was done in the dying seconds. Indeed it was the last kick of the game when Eglington put over a superb cross to find Doherty throwing himself at the ball. The former Glentoran man was injured in the process but the important thing was that the ball nestled in the bottom of the net. The final whistle sounded immediately and Doherty was carried from the field by jubilant Irish supporters, the hero of the day.

Vernon, Doherty, Farrell and Bill Walsh were the cornerstones of a fine team performance by the Irish.

55th match v Northern Ireland.
First time the Irish had avoided defeat in 13 games against England.
Penalty miss by Mannion.

England v Sweden Friendly

Played on Wednesday, 19 November 1947 at Arsenal Stadium, London.

England: F.V.Swift (Man City); L.Scott (Arsenal), G.Hardwick (Middlesbrough,

Top: The Crown Prince of Sweden shakes hands with Frank Swift before the game at Highbury in November 1947. *Bottom:* Stan Mortensen watches as Lindberg, the Swedish goalkeeper, gathers the ball.

captain), P.H.Taylor (Liverpool), C.F. Franklin (Stoke C), W.A.Wright (Wolves), T.Finney (Preston NE), S.H.Mortensen (Blackpool), T.Lawton (Notts Co), W.J.Mannion (Middlesbrough), R.Langton (Blackburn R).

Sweden: T.Lindberg (IFK Norrköping); K.Nordahl (IFK Norrköping), E.Nilsson (Malmö FF), S.Andersson (AIK Stockholm), B.Nordahl (Degerfors IF), R.Emanuelsson (IFK Göteborg), M.Mårtensson (Helsingborgs IF), G.Gren (IFK Göteborg), G.Nordahl (IFK Norrköping), N.Liedholm (IFK Norrköping), S.Nilsson (Malmö FF).

Half-time 3-1   Full-time 4-2

Ref: W.Webb (Scotland)   Att: 44,250

ENGLAND dominated the first half of this match at Highbury and would have won by more goals had they not faded so badly after the interval to allow Sweden to come right back into the game.

England were quickly into their stride and after 13 minutes, brilliant work by Wilf Mannion set up their first goal. He dribbled out to the right before splitting the Swedish defence with a brilliant reverse pass which let in Stan Mortensen to score.

After 20 minutes, England added a second from the penalty spot. Mortensen burst through to take Tommy Lawton's headed pass but was brought down in the box. Lawton scored from the spot-kick.

Sweden then hit back and Gunnar Nordahl scored after a free-kick had caught England badly positioned. This was only a momentary lapse by the home side and they were soon back on top. Lindberg made some fine saves but was powerless to stop Mortensen making it 3-1 after another pass by Lawton.

The midfield mastery of Mannion, Mortensen, Billy Wright and Phil Taylor was superb during the first half and, but for Lindberg's brilliance, especially in two saves from Mannion, England would have been in an unassailable position.

As it was, the second half was a much different story. The edge went from England's play and the half had barely started when George Hardwick was desperately heading a shot off his goal-line. Sweden were beginning to take control as England faded and they really put the pressure on when Gren scored from a penalty to make it 3-2.

For a while it seemed as though they

might equalize but England withstood the pressure well and near the end a piece of sheer brilliance by Mortensen clinched the match. He picked up the ball and set off on a magnificent 40-yard run before ending it with a deadly left-foot shot.

After the break England were certainly made to think by the gutsy Swedish display.

> 4th match v Sweden.
> Hat-trick by Mortensen.
> Lawton scored England's first penalty since the war to be converted. Sweden also scored from a penalty (Gren).

Scotland v England Home Championship

Played on Saturday, 10 April 1948 at Hampden Park, Glasgow.

Scotland: I.H.Black (Southampton); J.Govan (Hibernian), D.Shaw (Hibernian), W.Campbell (Morton), G.L.Young (Rangers), A.R.Macauley (Arsenal), J.Delaney (Man Utd), J.R.Combe (Hibernian), W.Thornton (Rangers), W.Steel (Derby Co), W.Liddell (Liverpool).

England: F.V.Swift (Man City); L.Scott (Arsenal), G.F.M.Hardwick (Middlesbrough, captain), W.A.Wright (Wolves), C.F.Franklin (Stoke C), H.Cockburn (Man Utd), S.Matthews (Blackpool), S.H.Mortensen (Blackpool), T.Lawton (Notts Co), S.C.Pearson (Man Utd), T.Finney (Preston NE).

Half-time 0-1   Full-time 0-2

Ref: L.J.Dates (Scotland)   Att: 135,376

OVER 135,000 people saw England retain the Home International Championship but most of the crowd went away very disappointed at Scotland's performance. From the start the Scots employed some pretty robust tactics and resorted to some ruthless tackling to upset the usual England rhythm. But in the end their destructive tactics proved their own undoing as it was far too negative.

Early on George Hardwick and, to a lesser degree, Lionel Scott were given a hard time by the pacey Scottish wingers. Billy Wright was constantly pulled out of position by Steel's ability, but Scotland lacked the necessary thrust up front. Neil Franklin was playing the game of his life at the heart of the England defence and gradually they began to repel the frequent Scottish raids.

Thornton missed two easy opportunities to give Scotland the lead their early play had deserved and it wasted the good work of Govan, Shaw, Young and Macauley who had given them the upper hand. Thornton especially missed badly when he headed a perfect Steel centre wide from close in.

The England attack was occasionally breaking dangerously and Stan Mortensen showed some electric pace but generally their forward line was mostly starved of service. But, after spending most of the first half with their backs to the wall, England suddenly produced a touch of magic a minute before half-time.

A superb move began with Frank Swift's clearance finding Tommy Lawton. The centre-forward flicked the ball to Stan Pearson who, in turn, found Tom Finney with a perfect through ball. The 'Preston Plumber' took the ball in his stride, beat Young and Govan by balance and footwork, to shoot magnificently past Black. The ball had gone from England's penalty area to the back of the Scottish net without a home player getting near it. It was a goal out of the text book and out of the blue.

For the first ten minutes after the break Scotland, urged on by the mighty Hampden Roar, fought to get on terms. Twice Swift received severe buffetings on his goal-line — he was later found to have suffered a cracked rib — but, he held firm. Scott blocked a shot from Steel on the line and Neil Franklin and Henry Cockburn continued to defend magnificently.

On 64 minutes, England conjured up a second and decisive goal. Lawton was the architect, robbing MacAuley and putting a brilliant ball through for Mortensen to score easily.

Scotland fought desperately to salvage something. Delaney gave Liddell a clear chance but Hardwick saved his shot on the line and then blocked Thornton's rebound shot.

After that, Scotland faded and towards the end, with Wright now containing Steel, England became more controlled and comfortable. The robust tackling had left its mark, though. Stanley Matthews had been continually brought down by Macauley and Hardwick ended the match limping on the left wing.

> 65th match v Scotland.
> Debut goal for Pearson.

Italy v England Friendly

Played on Sunday, 16 May 1948 at the Stadio Comunale, Turin.

Italy: V.Bacigalupo (Torino); A.Ballarin (Torino), A.Eliani (Fiorentina), C.Annovazzi (Milan AC), SC Parola (Juventus), G.Grezar (Torino), R.Menti (Torino), E.Loik (Torino), G.Gabetto (Torino), V.Mazzola (Torino), R.Carapallese (Milan AC).

England: F.V.Swift (Man City, captain);

Mortensen's scores England's first in Turin.

Tom Finney volleys the last in a 4-0 win over the Italians.

L.Scott (Arsenal), J.R.Howe (Derby Co), W.A.Wright (Wolves), C.F.Franklin (Stoke C), H.Cockburn (Man Utd), S.Matthews (Blackpool), S.H.Mortensen (Blackpool), T.Lawton (Notts Co), W.J.Mannion (Middlesbrough), T.Finney (Preston NE).

Half-time 0-2   Full-time 0-4
Ref: P.Escartin (Spain)   Att: 58,000

THE scoreline does not reflect the closeness of this contest. A huge crowd, mostly white-shirted and dotted with black umbrellas under a blazing sun, gave the teams a tremendous welcome as they came out.

England won the toss but Carapallese and Mazzola were soon worrying their defenders. After four minutes, though, it was England who took the lead. Stan Mortensen took a clever through pass from Stanley Matthews, cut past the Italian left flank and shot home from an unbelievable angle. It was a great goal, typical of such a great player.

For the next 20 minutes England were rocked back on their heels. The Italian forwards and wing-halves pressed forward with methodical precision. Yet on 24 minutes, and completely out of the blue, England suddenly increased their lead.

This time Neil Franklin found Matthews. Again, a through-ball reached Mortensen, who then changed pace twice to leave Grezar and Parola floundering before hooking the ball back for Tommy Lawton to shoot home a thunderbolt.

Before that goal, Menti twice had goals ruled out for offside and Swift had saved brilliantly from a Gabetto close-range header. Lionel Scott also had to save a shot from Carapallese on the goal-line and then, after the second England goal, the same Italian forced Frank Swift into another fine save.

Immediately after the interval, Mazzola was clean through and had a golden opportunity but he shot straight at Swift. On 59 minutes a header by Gabetto rebounded from the crossbar and then Swift made yet another brilliant save, diving full-length to stop the rebound from going over the line.

Alhough England were now moving more comfortably with Henry Cockburn coming into the picture more, Italy were still very dangerous up front. Billy Wright was playing magnificently for the visitors and he did particularly well to stop Mazzola and Carapallese, Italy's best players.

With 19 minutes remaining, England settled the match with two more fine goals in as many minutes. A clever lobbed pass by Wilf Mannion was volleyed home by Tom Finney; and the Preston player then netted again after good work by Cockburn and Mortensen.

It was all over now and the game ended with England giving Italy a football lesson. Their superior tactics, individual brilliance and lethal finishing had won the day.

Swift, Wright, Franklin, Scott and Mortensen had all been outstanding.

> 4th match v Italy.
> Debut for Howe.
> Swift captained England for the first time.

Denmark v England   Friendly
Played on Sunday, 26 September 1948 at the Idraetspark, Copenhagen.

Denmark: E.Nielson (KB København); P.Peterson (AB København), V.Jensen (EfB Esbjerg), A.Pilmark (KB København), D.Ørnvold (KB København), I.Jensen (AB København), J.Pløeger (BK Frem), K.A.Hansen (AB København), C.A.Praest (ØB København), J.Hansen (BK Frem), H.Seebach (AB København).
England: F.V.Swift (Man City, captain); L.Scott (Arsenal), J.Aston (Man Utd), W.A.Wright (Wolves), C.F.Franklin (Stoke C), H.Cockburn (Man Utd), S.Matthews (Blackpool), J.Hagan (Sheffield Utd), T.Lawton (Notts Co), L.F.Shackleton (Sunderland), R.Langton (Preston NE).

Half-time 0-0   Full-time 0-0
Ref: K.Van Der Meer (Holland) Att: 41,000

THE King and Queen of Denmark and our own Duke and Duchess of Gloucester were amongst the spectators to see England surprisingly held by the amateurs of Denmark.

On a rain-soaked ground, a much-changed England side featured in its first goalless draw since the war. There was no doubt that they were the better side but on the day they were woefully weak up front.

Although the sun was shining at the start, the pitch was sodden after heavy rain and water lay on at least one part of the playing area.

England should have scored after only two minutes but Len Shackleton with only the goalkeeper to beat, dallied too long and the defenders were able to clear. Nielson then did well to save a stinging shot from Tommy Lawton six minutes later but had no chance when the same player crashed the ball past him on 20 minutes. Fortunately for Denmark, the goal was disallowed for an earlier infringement by Shackleton. At the time, all the crowd seemed convinced that it was a wrong decision by the referee.

Denmark were defending stubbornly and the occasional break they made was dangerous. Indeed, only a fine save by Frank Swift stopped the embarrassment of I.Jensen scoring. England had the better of the first half, but sadly had left their shooting boots at home.

Denmark twice went close early in the second half when first K.Hansen headed over and then when Pløeger's cross-cum-shot hit the top of the England crossbar. However, England continued to have most of the possession but they were badly missing the power of Stan Mortensen and Tom Finney in front of goal.

In the end, Denmark's crowd was absolutely delighted with the result and thoroughly enjoyed the whole experience of entertaining the mighty England team.

> First match v Denmark.
> Debuts for Aston, Hagan and Shackleton.
> England's first goalless draw since the war.

Manchester City goalkeeper Frank Swift, skippered England for a spell.

Northern Ireland v England   Home Championship
Played on Saturday, 9 October 1948 at Windsor Park, Belfast.

Northern Ireland: W.Smyth (Distillery); J.J.Carey (Man Utd), C.J.Martin (Aston Villa), W.Walsh (Man City), J.Vernon (West Brom), P.D.Farrell (Everton), J.F.O'Driscoll (Swansea T), J.McAlinden (Southend Utd), D.J.Walsh (West Brom), C.P.Tully (Celtic), T.J.Eglington (Everton).
England: F.V.Swift (Man City); L.Scott (Arsenal), J.R.Howe (Derby Co), W.A.Wright (Wolves, captain), C.F.Franklin (Stoke C), H.Cockburn (Man Utd), S.Matthews (Blackpool), S.H.Mortensen (Blackpool), J.E.T.Milburn (Newcastle Utd), S.C.Pearson (Man Utd), T.Finney (Preston NE).

Manchester United defender John Aston, made his debut in Copenhagen.

Half-time 0-1   Full-time 2-6

Ref: W.Webb (Scotland)   Att: 53,000

SOME 53,000 people packed into Windsor Park to see this match. The result went against the home side but in no way did the final scoreline tell the full story. Indeed, only in the last 30 minutes did England finally get on top.

The game had begun with Ireland pressing forward in their usual passionate style. Frank Swift, Lionel Scott and Jack Howe all showed hesitancy in the English defence and the Irish should really have pressed home the advantage that their early play had given them. As it was, they were punished by a freak goal by Stanley Matthews after 27 minutes which gave England a lead they barely deserved.

Taking a throw-in on Tom Finney's wing, Matthews received a return pass from Jackie Milburn. He then swung across a curling centre which ricocheted off the far post, hit Smyth on the back and went into the net. It was an amazing goal and cruel luck for the Irish. England's only other worthwhile attack of the first half came just before the break when, following a brilliant five man move, Mortensen had Smyth at full stretch to save.

Five minutes into the second half, Northern Ireland equalized. O'Driscoll beat Howe for speed and Dave Walsh headed home his cross in fine style. For a few moments it seemed that the now rampant home team might forge ahead. But suddenly and unexpectedly, England and especially Matthews came to life. Within ten minutes it was 4-1 to the visitors!

First Milburn headed in Matthews' cross. Then Mortensen headed in a pass from Billy Wright after more good work by the Blackpool winger, before finally Mortensen got on the end of a fine cross by Stan Pearson to cleverly lob the ball over the advancing Smyth. Quite suddenly it was all over and the crowd, so excited a few minutes earlier, were dazed into a stunned silence.

Finney now began to lose Carey, after previously having been well held by the full-back. Milburn showed dash and spirit and England at last were now moving as a team.

Two more headers added to the goals tally. First Mortensen scored his third goal by heading a Henry Cockburn free-kick; then Pearson added number-six with a header from yet another Matthews cross. England had thus scored five goals in a little over 30 minutes. With the last kick of the game, Dave Walsh scored his and Northern Ireland's second, only to leave everyone wondering just what an earth had gone wrong.

56th match v Northern Ireland.
Debut goal for Milburn.
Hat-trick by Mortensen.
Wright captained England for the first time.

England v Wales   Home Championship

Played on Wednesday, 10 November 1948 at Villa Park, Birmingham.

England: F.V.Swift (Man City); L.Scott (Arsenal), J.Aston (Man Utd), T.V.Ward (Derby Co), C.F.Franklin (Stoke C), W.A.Wright (Wolves, captain), S.Matthews (Blackpool), S.H.Mortensen (Blackpool), J.E.T.Milburn (Newcastle Utd), L.F.Shackleton (Sunderland), T.Finney (Preston NE).

Wales: W.A.Hughes (Blackburn R); W.Barnes (Arsenal), A.T.Sherwood (Cardiff C), R.Paul (Swansea T), T.G.Jones (Everton), W.A.R.Burgess (Spurs), W.E.A.Jones (Spurs), A.Powell (Everton), T.Ford (Aston Villa), W.Morris (Burnley), R.J.Clarke (Man City).

Half-time 1-0   Full-time 1-0

Ref: J.A.Mowat (Scotland)   Att: 68,750

IN a disappointing match at Villa Park, neither side reached a particularly high standard of play. True, England were disorganised when they were reduced to ten men after 25 minutes when Lionel Scott suffered a ligament injury in his right knee, but they never really got into their usual rhythm.

After the injury, Stan Mortensen went back to right-half and Tim Ward replaced Scott at full-back. It seemed a wrong decision by England as they badly missed

Mortensen's qualities up front. Wales, meanwhile, never really impressed. They showed plenty of typical Welsh fervour but their limitations were there for all to see. The fact that England won with ten men says it all.

The vital goal came after 39 minutes. Jackie Milburn, lively throughout, made a strong run down the middle and, as he was desperately challenged by the Welsh defenders, the ball ran loose to Tom Finney and the winger did the rest, giving Hughes no chance. Before the goal, Ford missed two excellent chances for Wales; had he taken one of them, it might have been a different story.

In the second half, Wales' attacks usually petered out on the edge of the England penalty area, although they had a good deal of the game. England were relying on Milburn, Matthews and Finney to breakaway and relieve the pressure. Billy Wright and Neil Franklin had storming games in the heart of the England defence and comfortably held a poor Welsh attack.

Near the end, the England fans had their hearts in their mouths as Frank Swift missed two crosses in quick succession but the luck went the way of England and they held on to their lead.

59th match v Wales.
"This was the first international I ever commentated on and although my memory is faded, what a forward line: Matthews, Mortensen, Milburn, Shackleton and Finney!"
TV commentator Kenneth Wolstenholme.

England v Switzerland   Friendly

Played on Thursday, 2 December 1948 at Arsenal Stadium, London.

England: E.G.Ditchburn (Spurs); A.E.Ramsey (Southampton), J.Aston (Man Utd), W.A.Wright (Wolves, captain), C.F.Franklin (Stoke C), H.Cockburn (Man Utd), S.Matthews (Blackpool), J.F.Rowley (Man Utd), J.E.T.Milburn (Newcastle Utd), J.T.W.Haines (West Brom), J.Hancocks (Wolves).

Switzerland: E.Corrodi (FC Lugano); R.Gyger (FC Cantonal), R.Bocquet (Lausanne-Sports), B.Lanz (Lausanne-Sports), O.Eggimann (Servette FC), G.Lusenti (AC Bellinzona), A.Bickel (Grasshoppers), L.Amadò (Grasshoppers), J.Tamini (Servette FC), R.Bader (FC Basel), J.Fatton (Servette FC).

Half-time 3-0   Full-time 6-0

Ref: K.Van Der Meer (Holland)

Att: 35,000

THIS match, postponed from the previous day because of dense fog, saw the defeat of yet another European challenge to England's unbeaten home record against Continental sides. In fact, Switzerland were annihilated!

Before the kick-off, several question-marks had been put against an unfamilar England line-up. Six changes had been made from the previous match but all of the newcomers came out of the game well. Ted Ditchburn had little to do, but Alf

The Swiss Prime Minister meets the England team before his country's 6-0 drubbing at Highbury in December 1948.

Ramsey looked perfectly at home in his first appearance. Johnny Hancocks was a success and Jack Rowley moved smoothly and dangerously.

The biggest success of the new boys, though, was John Haines. England, still searching for a replacement for Wilf Mannion, seemed to have found an answer as the inside-left made a very impressive debut, showing plenty of imagination and flair.

Despite the fact that all these new players did well, it was the magic of the irrepressible Stanley Matthews that once again stood out. The mercurial winger enjoyed the freedom of Highbury as he ran the poor Swiss defenders ragged. Every time he received the ball he left a trail of wreckage behind him with his superb artistry.

Ramsey cleared early on from his own goal-line, but after that it was virtual one-way traffic. After five minutes, England opened the scoring when Jackie Milburn robbed Bader in the area and crossed for Haines to head home.

After 25 minutes of continuous pressure, Matthews waltzed towards the middle and sent in a low cross from which Hancocks scored with a good shot. A minute later, Haines headed in a Hancocks corner as the whole Swiss defence stood and watched.

The second half opened with Switzerland trying vainly to fight back. Tamini, Bickel and Fatton all made gallant efforts but England soon regained control and scored further goals to increase their lead. Rowley produced a thunderbolt from outside the box before Hancocks, from a cross by Matthews, and finally Milburn ended the contest in style. Switzerland had no answer to England's power and especially could do nothing to stop Matthews and Hancocks.

4th match v Switzerland
Debuts for Ditchburn, Ramsey, Rowley, Haines and Hancocks.
Debut goals for Rowley, Haines (2) and Hancocks (2).

Left: Johnny Hancocks of Wolves (out of picture) marks his England debut with the first of two goals against Switzerland. Right: Swiss goalkeeper Corrodi watches helplessly as West Brom's Haines heads one of his two goals in his only international appearance.

Billy Wright leads out England to play Scotland at Wembley in April 1949. England lost the game, their first home defeat since the war.

Scotland's goalkeeper Jimmy Cowan, who had a fine game, takes the ball cleanly as the Scots march towards a famous victory.

England v Scotland Home Championship

Played on Saturday, 9 April 1949 at Wembley Stadium.

England: F.V.Swift (Man City); J.Aston (Man Utd), J.R.Howe (Derby Co), W.A.Wright (Wolves, captain), C.F.Franklin (Stoke C), H.Cockburn (Man Utd), S.Matthews (Blackpool), S.H.Mortensen (Blackpool), J.E.T.Milburn (Newcastle Utd), S.C.Pearson (Man Utd), T.Finney (Preston NE).

Scotland: J.Cowan (Morton); G.L.Young (Rangers), S.Cox (Rangers), R.Evans (Celtic), W.A.Woodburn (Rangers), G.G.Aitken (East Fife), W.Waddell (Rangers), J.Mason (Third Lanark), W.Houliston (Queen of the South), W.Steel (Derby Co), L.Reilly (Hibernian).

Half-time 0-1   **Full-time 1-3**
Ref: B.M.Griffiths (Wales)   Att: 98,188

ENGLAND lost their first Home International since the war in a game watched by nearly 100,000 people. Princess Elizabeth and the Duke of Edinburgh joined the spectators under blue skies and a warm April sun.

For the first 25 minutes England tore into the Scottish defence with some brilliant football. Unfortunately, they found Cowan in unbeatable form and the goalkeeper virtually took England on single-handedly in this spell. Two saves from Stan Mortensen will live long in the memory as he continually kept Scotland in the match.

At the end of that period of England pressure, Cowan blocked Stan Pearson's shot after Tom Finney had centred. Mortensen followed up to flash the rebound towards the empty net, only to see Cox come from nowhere to clear from the goal-line. Twice Jackie Milburn went close and Cowan then saved brilliantly again, this time from Mortensen.

That final save brought England's superiority to an end and the Scots then hit back hard. On 29 minutes they took the lead. A throw-in by Houliston found Steel, who gave Reilly a clever pass which took John Aston out of the game. Reilly's cross was met by Mason and it was 1-0 as the ball went in off the far post.

After the interval Scotland inspired by the goal, were a changed side. Now moving quickly and effectively they were winning all of the loose balls and most of the tackles. Only Neil Franklin stood firm for England as Steel and Mason took control of the game.

In the first 15 minutes of the second-half, Scotland scored two more goals to virtually settle the result. Swift inter-passing between Mason and Steel found Houliston. The centre-forward back-heeled out of a ruck of English defenders and Steel was left with the easy task of walking the ball into the net. When Reilly headed home Waddell's perfect cross a few minutes later, the England defence was again caught flat-footed.

The home side, devastated by these two goals, manfully tried to fight back and in the last quarter of an hour came close to sensationally saving the game. Milburn pulled one goal back when he diverted a Mortensen shot and then Stanley Matthews saw a goalbound shot blocked by Milburn. Finally, in a rousing finish, a Pearson header hit the bar.

Over all, Scotland had deserved their win, but had it not been for the superb early work of Cowan, then it might have been a different story.

> 66th match v Scotland
> First home defeat since the war.

Sweden v England   Friendly

Played on Friday, 13 May 1949 at the Råsunda Stadium, Solna.

Sweden: K.Svensson (Helsingborgs IF); K.Nordahl (IFK Norrköping), E.Nilsson (Malmö FF), K.Rosén (Malmö FF), B.Leander (AIK Stockholm), S.Andersson (AIK Stockholm), E.Johnsson (GAIS Göteborg), G.Gren (IFK Göteborg), H.Jeppson (Djurgårdens IF), H.Carlsson (AIK Stockholm), B.Bäckvall (AIK Stockholm).
England: E.G.Ditchburn (Spurs); E.Shimwell (Blackpool), J.Aston (Man Utd), W.A.Wright (Wolves, captain), C.F.Franklin (Stoke C), H.Cockburn (Man Utd), T.Finney (Preston NE), S.H.Mortensen (Blackpool), R.T.F.Bentley (Chelsea), J.F.Rowley (Man Utd), R.Langton (Preston NE).

Half-time 3-0   Full-time 3-1

Ref: G.Galeati (Italy)   Att: 37,500

IT really was a case of unlucky 'Friday the thirteenth' when England met Sweden in Stockholm in the first game of their summer tour of Scandinavia. The Swedes dished out quite a football lesson to their illustrious visitors and fully realised the potential they had shown at Highbury two years ago.

The first two minutes contained two of the games important moments. After 90 seconds, Roy Bentley all but scored when he followed on to a bad back-pass by Leander and lobbed the ball over Svensson. The goalkeeper, though, somewhat luckily, managed to keep it out of his net.

It was a crucial miss as Sweden then went straight up to the other end and opened their scoring. Gren, lively throughout, caught England out with a fine pass for Carlsson to run on to and score a good goal.

England were stunned and it showed in their play. On 35 minutes Gren was again the playmaker as a brilliant four-man move ended with Jeppson crashing home a shot on the run. Then, three minutes from half-time, Johnsson volleyed home spectacularly after receiving yet another cross from Gren. That goal brought the near 40,000 crowd to their feet and they gave their players a standing ovation at the break. Mortensen had hit a post just before the end of the half, but England trooped off bemused and bewildered.

To their eternal credit, England rallied after the restart and in the last 25 minutes controlled the play. When, after 67 minutes, Tom Finney scored to round off a fine dribble and pass by Bentley it seemed that a miracle may be possible.

However, it was at this stage of the game that the ball began to run very unkindly for England. Bentley saw a shot cannon off a post and Finney was twice dispossessed when seemingly about to score.

Then, in the last minute, Svensson saved bravely at Mortensen's feet when a goal seemed certain as the inside-right strode clear.

> 5th match v Sweden.
> Debuts for Shimwell and Bentley.

Norway v England   Friendly

Played on Wednesday, 18 May 1949 at the Ulleval Stadium, Oslo.

Norway: T.Torgersen (IL Viking); B.Spydevold (Fredrikstad FK), H.B.Karlsen (Ørn Horten), T.Svensen (Sandefjord BK), K.Anderssen (Skeid), O.Andersen (Fredrikstad FK), T.Arnesen (Vålerengens IF), G.Thoresen (Larvik T), W.Andresen (Sarpsborg FK), H.Nordahl (Skeid), G.Dahlen (Freidig).
England: F.V.Swift (Man City); W.Ellerington (Southampton), J.Aston (Man Utd), W.A.Wright(Wolves, captain), C.F.Franklin (Stoke C), J.W.Dickinson (Portsmouth), T.Finney (Preston NE), J.Morris (Derby Co), S.H.Mortensen (Blackpool), W.J.Mannion (Middlesbrough), J.Mullen (Wolves).

Half-time 0-2   Full-time 1-4

Ref: J.E.Andersson (Sweden)   Att: 36,000

UNDER overcast skies and with one or two sharp downpours of rain, England continued their tour by beating Norway easily. However, although it was a clear win, it was far from convincing.

It took only six minutes for England to take the lead. Billy Wright sent a crossfield pass towards Johnny Morris, who guided it on to Jimmy Mullen for the winger to score with a crisp left-foot shot.

After taking command so early it seemed only a question of how many goals England would score. Unfortunately, for most of the rest of the first half all the visiting players tended to overdo the ball skills and as a result showed little finishing power. Morris was making an enterprising debut, though, and quickly struck up a good partnership with Wilf Mannion. Tom Finney and Mullen however were not at their best and they were both guilty of dallying too long before shooting.

Norway worked hard and after 30 minutes produced their best move of the match. It gave the England defence a few awkward moments before they eventually cleared the danger. With seven minutes of the half remaining, England produced a thrilling goal.

A superb move involving Wright, Morris, Mannion, Stan Mortensen and Finney ended with the latter shooting home to score a beauty. From then on it was largely an exhibition game for England, although their were still a few question-marks over certain positions. Both Frank Swift and Billy Ellerington looked uncomfortable and some felt that they had seen the last of 'Big Swifty', who had graced the goalkeeping position for so long.

Wright, Neil Franklin and Jimmy Dickinson looked powerful enough, though, and Dickinson certainly seemed the perfect foil for Wright in the midfield.

With eight minutes of the second half gone, W.Andresen headed a centre from Arnesen on to the bar but quickly latched on to the rebound to shoot past Swift. This opened the game up considerably for a few minutes and England were forced back as Norway pressed for an equalizer. Twice Thoresen caused Swift to fumble the ball but England escaped and the fight-back was short-lived. In, fact the visitors soon increased their lead when Spydevold had the misfortune to divert a long job by Mannion wide of his own goalkeeper.

With 20 minutes of the game remaining, man of the match Morris gained his reward for a fine display with a piece of high speed thinking as he shot home over a crowd of players into the unguarded net.

> 3rd match v Norway.
> Debuts for Ellerington, Dickinson and Morris.
> Debut goal for Morris.

France v England   Friendly

Played on Sunday, 22 May 1949 at the Colombes Stadium, Paris.

France: R.Vignal (RC de Paris); A.Grillon (RC de Paris), M.Salva (RC de Paris), R.Jonquet (Stade de Reims), R.Mindonnet (OGC Nice), L.Hon (Stade Francais), R.Gabet (RC de Paris), A.Cuissard (AS St-Etienne), R.Quenolle (RC de Paris), A.Batteux (Stade de Reims), G.Moreel (RC de Paris).
England: B.F.Williams (Wolves); W.Ellerington (Southampton), J.Aston (Man Utd), W.A.Wright (Wolves, captain), C.F.Franklin (Stoke C), J.W.Dickinson (Portsmouth), T.Finney (Preston NE), J.Morris (Derby Co), J.F.Rowley (Man Utd), W.J.Mannion (Middlesbrough), J.Mullen (Wolves).

Half-time 1-2   Full-time 1-3

Ref: K.Van Der Meer (Holland)

Att: 61,500

ENGLAND completed their summer tour with a splendid win in Paris, recovering from a disastrous start. On a very hot, sunny afternoon and on a pitch like concrete, the visitors made a terrible start. Within 30 seconds France were ahead. A couple of mistakes by Bert Williams and Neil Franklin let Moreel in to score. It was a real dagger-thrust to the heart for England and it inspired the passionate crowd of over 61,000 people.

A lesser team would have crumbled under such pressure but as it was the England players knuckled down and fought back magnificently. Overcoming some fierce 'continental tackling' they gradually got to grips with the midfield battle.

It took only eight minutes for them to find an equalizer. Johnny Morris found Jimmy Dickinson with a neat flick. Dickinson then sent Jack Rowley clear down the left with a lovely through-ball. When the cross came over fast and low into the box, there was Morris, up with the attack, to finish off the move he had started back in his own half.

It was a memorable goal and for the next 15 minutes fast counter-attacking by

England and France line up at the Colombes Stadium in Paris before the start of the international in May 1949. England won 3-1 with goals by Johnny Morris (2) and Billy Wright.

both sides, a feature of the match, tested the defences as each team strove for the upper hand. Dickinson was an inspiration with a powerful display and Williams also did well, especially considering his shaky start. After 26 minutes England snatched the lead.

Morris, Jimmy Mullen, Wilf Mannion and Rowley all took part in a fine move down the left flank. At the end of it, Rowley placed a pass diagonally into space some 12 yards from goal. Suddenly, from nowhere, came Billy Wright speeding in to shoot past Vignal. Shortly afterwards the goalkeeper made a superb save from Morris as England ended the half in a much better frame of mind than they had started it.

France fought hard for a 20-minute spell at the start of the second half. They strung together some excellent moves and Moreel missed one particularly good chance. But by now England were looking much more solid with Franklin in complete command. With Morris and, especially, Mannion dominating the midfield England always looked capable of scoring again and this they did with four minutes to go, when Morris put the result beyond doubt.

Tom Finney, who had been the best forward on view with his play doing as much as anyone to open up the French defence, was in great form and Rowley, too, was impressive and he added life to the centre of the attack. Altogether it was a very satisfying result for England.

11th match v France.
Debut for Williams.
First England goal for Wright and the first by a non-forward since the war.

England v
Friendly
Republic of Ireland

Played on Wednesday, 21 September 1949 at Goodison Park, Liverpool.

England: B.F.Williams (Wolves); B.Mozley (Derby Co), J.Aston (Man Utd), W.A.Wright (Wolves, captain), C.F.Franklin (Stoke C), J.W.Dickinson (Portsmouth), P.P.Harris (Portsmouth), J.Morris (Derby Co), J.Pye (Wolves), W.J.Mannion (Middlesbrough), T.Finney (Preston NE).
Republic of Ireland: T.F.Godwin (Shamrock R); J.J.Carey (Man Utd), T.Ahearne (Luton T), W.Walsh (Man City), C.J.Martin (Aston Villa), T.Moroney (West Ham), P.J.Corr (Everton), P.D.Farrell (Everton), D.J.Walsh (West Brom), P.Desmond (Middlesbrough), T.O'Connor (Shamrock R).

Half-time 0-1   Full-time 0-2
Ref: J.A.Mowat (Scotland)   Att: 52,000

THIS was truly an amazing victory by the plucky Irishmen on their first visit to English soil. Every one of their team was a hero as they defied all of England's efforts.

Yet at the start, there was no inkling as to the drama that was to follow. Indeed, England could have scored after only 20 seconds. Straight from the kick-off, Wilf Mannion sent Tom Finney away and from the winger's centre, Jesse Pye headed just wide.

England immediately took hold of the game. A move between Johnny Morris, Billy Wright and Pye ended with the centre-forward having his shot blocked. Finney then shot straight at Godwin when it seemed he must score.

This early dominance encouraged England but the Irish defended well and they were dangerous when they broke quickly. Dave Walsh and Farrell provided their main threat and they caused England some problems with Jimmy Dickinson particularly suspect.

After 32 minutes there came the first hint of what lay ahead. A quick pass by Moroney sent Desmond free inside the box. Bert Mozley, trying to recover, succeeded only in bringing the number-ten down from behind for an obvious penalty. It was Martin who scored from the spot to give Eire a sensational lead.

Before the break Dave Walsh saw a flashing shot just miss and England ended the half with the pressure on them.

The second half was one-way traffic. With a swirling wind at their backs, England threw everything at the beleaguered Irish defence. They had 90 per cent of the possession and a whole series of amazing escapes somehow left Eire's lead intact.

Pye, Morris and Finney all hesitated when in good positions, Morris shot straight at Godwin from ten yards and then Pye did the same. Twice the inside-forwards dawdled with the goal at their mercy and Godwin made flying saves from both Peter Harris and Wright; and when the goalkeeper was beaten, Bill Walsh and Martin both cleared shots from the goal-line.

So, in rising excitement the Irish clung on. Then, with only five minutes to go, the unbelievable happened. With England pushing everyone forward, Desmond's pass put Farrell through and suddenly the match was all over as the number-eight shot past Bert Williams.

2nd match v Republic of Ireland.
Debuts for Mozley, Harris and Pye.
Technically, the first home defeat by 'foreign' opposition.

Wales v
England Home Championship

Played on Saturday, 15 October 1949 at Ninian Park, Cardiff.

Wales: C.Sidlow (Liverpool); W.Barnes

(Arsenal), A.T.Sherwood (Cardiff C), R.Paul (Swansea T), T.G.Jones (Everton), W.A.R.Burgess (Spurs), M.W.Griffiths (Leicester C), W.H.Lucas (Swansea T), T.Ford (Aston Villa), F.H.Scrine (Swansea T), G.Edwards (Cardiff C).

England: B.F.Williams (Wolves); B.Mozley (Derby Co), J.Aston (Man Utd), W.A.Wright (Wolves, captain), C.F.Franklin (Stoke C), J.W.Dickinson (Portsmouth), T.Finney (Preston NE), S.H.Mortensen (Blackpool), J.E.T.Milburn (Newcastle Utd), L.F.Shackleton (Sunderland), J.Hancocks (Wolves).

Half-time 0-3   Full-time 1-4

Ref: J.A.Mowat (Scotland)   Att: 61,000

ANXIOUS to get back to winning ways after their humiliating defeat by the Republic of Ireland the previous month, England went to Cardiff to face Wales in front of 61,000 passionate home supporters packed into Ninian Park.

A rousing version of *Men of Harlech* greeted the two teams and for the first 20 minutes Wales put the England defence under extreme pressure. Bert Mozley and John Aston both made slight errors but quickly recovered before any damage was done.

Neil Franklin and Bert Williams both had treatment after severe buffetings from the powerful Ford, and when Griffiths cut inside Aston to shoot just over, Wales scented victory. However, within the space of 12 hectic minutes, a breathtaking burst by England saw them take a 3-0 lead.

After 22 minutes Jackie Milburn, taking a pass from Billy Wright, brought Sidlow to a full-length save. From the resultant corner, taken by Tom Finney, the ball was brilliantly headed back by Milburn for Stan Mortensen to head into the net.

Seconds later, England were celebrating another goal. This time a clever move between Mortensen and Johnny Hancocks ended with Sidlow clawing away the winger's centre untidily. Finney quickly lobbed the ball back into the middle, where Milburn glided it into the net.

Almost at once it was 3-0. Milburn, who was looking better than any England number-nine since Tommy Lawton, strode through the hesitant Welsh defence to score after a well-timed pass from Len Shackleton. The crowd were well and truly silenced, and although territorially the scoreline was unrepresentative of the play, there was no disputing England's finishing power.

An early second-half injury to Wright upset England's rhythm and the skipper spent much of this half hobbling out on the left wing. This meant several positional changes for the visitors and, as a result, Wales had most of the play. They attacked for long spells. Burgess almost scored with a 30-yard blockbuster and Mozley cleared off the line from Ford.

Yet amazingly, and ironically it was England who scored again.

Good work by Shackleton and Finney, (who cut out the over-elaboration to produce one of his best games), set up Milburn to once again beat Sidlow with a header. With Williams also now hobbling and able only to throw the ball, it seemed odds-on that Wales would score. But it was not until ten minutes from the end that they did. This time it was Griffiths who finally beat Williams after the goalkeeper had saved brilliantly from Ford.

It was unfortunate that Wright's injury had disrupted the England forward line as their first-half performance had shown considerable promise.

60th match v Wales.

England v Home Championship
Northern Ireland

Played on Wednesday, 16 November 1949 at Maine Road, Manchester.

England: B.R.Streten (Luton T.); B.Mozley (Derby Co), J.Aston (Man Utd), W.Watson (Sunderland), C.F.Franklin (Stoke C), W.A.Wright (Wolves, captain), T.Finney (Preston NE), S.H.Mortensen (Blackpool), J.F.Rowley (Man Utd), S.C.Pearson (Man Utd), J.Froggatt (Portsmouth).

Northern Ireland: H.R.Kelly (Fulham); J.M.Feeney (Swansea T), A.McMichael (Newcastle Utd), G.C.Bowler (Hull C), J.Vernon (West Brom), J.J.McCabe (Leeds Utd), D.Cochrane (Leeds Utd), S.Smyth (Wolves), R.A.Brennan (Birmingham C),

C.P.Tully (Celtic), J.McKenna (Huddersfield T).

Half-time 4-0   Full-time 9-2

Ref: B.M.Griffiths (Wales)   Att: 70,000

GREY sky and persistent drizzle could not dampen the Manchester crowd's enthusiasm for one of England's most impressive and fluent performances. They completely overwhelmed the Northern Ireland side with a display of football that was pure delight.

The Irish offered plenty of pluck and never gave up but really there was only one team in it. The goals simply rained into the Irish net and poor Kelly in goal did not know what hit him.

After five minutes Jack Rowley sent Jack Froggatt away and then followed up to meet the centre smoothly to shoot home. Although Smyth and Tully set the England defence a few problems, when Tom Finney took a hold of the match in the 25th minute, the landslide began.

Playing one of his best-ever games he conjured up some sheer magic as he teased the whole Irish defence with the balance,

England goalkeeper Bernard Streten punches clear from an Irish attack in the 9-2 drubbing at Maine Road. in November 1949.

Top: Jack Rowley walks the ball over the Irish line for England's eighth goal. *Bottom left:* England team pictured whilst training at Brighton in November 1949. Back row (left to right): Watson, Franklin, Williams, Streten, Ramsey, Aston. Front row: Finney, Rowley, Wright, Pearson, R.Froggatt.

poise, speed and footwork. Poor McMichael did not know which way to turn next. In that 25th minute, perfect footwork and controlled speed took Finney past three defenders on the right and Froggatt headed in the cross as clean as a whistle.

Within minutes the ball was off again, moving swiftly between Willie Watson, Finney, Billy Wright and Stan Mortensen before Stan Pearson joined in to add the finishing touch.

Hardly had the crowd had time to enjoy that little gem before they looked up to see Mortensen flying through the air to meet Finney's centre with a glorious header to make it 4-0 at half-time.

Rowley made it five a minute into the second half and shortly afterwards Kelly could only hear Mortensen's shot whizz past him. Smyth did pull one goal back for the Irish, but England were at full steam now, doing exactly what they liked, when they liked. Rowley scored two more

goals, both of which had all the forwards helping in the build-up. The first 13 minutes of the second half had seen five goals.

A Finney headed pass to Pearson gave the England number nine the chance to score, appropriately, their ninth goal. Finally, a goal by Brennan, after a mistake by Neil Franklin, ended the scoring and an altogether extraordinary afternoon.

57th match v Northern Ireland.
Debuts for Streten, Watson and J.Froggatt.
Debut goal for J.Froggatt.
Four goals for Rowley.

England v Italy
Friendly

Played on Wednesday, 30 November 1949 at White Hart Lane, Tottenham.

England: B.F.Williams (Wolves); A.E.Ramsey (Spurs), J.Aston (Man Utd), W.Watson (Sunderland), C.F.Franklin (Stoke C), W.A.Wright (Wolves, captain), T.Finney (Preston NE), S.H.Mortensen (Blackpool), J.F.Rowley (Man Utd), S.C.Pearson (Man Utd), J.Froggatt (Portsmouth).

Italy: G.Moro (Torino); A.Bertucelli (Juventus), A.Giovannini (Inter-Milan), C.Annovazzi (AC Milan), C.Parola (Juventus), A.Piccinini, (Juventus) G.Boniperti (Juventus), B.Lorenzi (Inter-Milan), A.Amadei (Inter-Milan), R.Martino (Juventus), R.Carapallese (Torino).

Half-time 0-0   Full-time 2-0

Ref: J.A.Mowat (Scotland)   Att: 60,000

THERE were over 60,000 people packed into White Hart Lane to see the latest challenge from a European country to

England's unbeaten home record. They went away satisfied with the scoreline but not so happy with their team's performance. Only a superb display in goal from Bert Williams kept the eager Italian forward line at bay and it was certainly a narrow shave for England.

However, the home side could have been ahead in the first minute. Right from the kick-off, a clever back-heel by Jack Rowley set up Stan Mortensen for a flashing shot which was brilliantly saved by Moro at full stretch.

Gradually, though, Italy's powerful forwards put England under increasing pressure. Lorenzi was particularly dangerous although all the forwards gave their markers a hard time. How Williams saved at point-blank range from Carapallese and Martino only he could tell you and he bettered even those saves with another brilliant effort from Lorenzi's shot.

This pattern carried on for two-thirds of the match. Mortensen's header did bring another fine save out of Moro following Tom Finney's cross, but Italy were pressing for much of the time. Finney was England's main hope and he was always troubling Giovannini with his neat footwork. With 14 minutes to go, England gained a vital breakthrough.

Willie Watson sent Jack Froggatt away and the winger cut inside before passing to Stan Pearson. His centre was then crashed home by a rocket shot from Rowley's left foot. It was a magnificent goal and one that was cruel luck for Italy, especially after having dominated the game for so long.

If that was cruel luck, then the second, killer goal was pure fluke. A hopeful 40-yard punt forward by England skipper Billy Wright was hopelessly misjudged by Moro and the ball somehow ended up in the back of the net.

It had been a narrow squeak for a disjointed England display. Neil Franklin and Watson always looked uncomfortable and Pearson and Froggatt never got their play together. In the end, England were thankful for Williams' mighty saves.

| 5th match v Italy. |

Scotland v
England   Home Championship

Played on Saturday, 15 April 1950 at Hampden Park, Glasgow.

Scotland: J.Cowan (Morton); G.L.Young (Rangers), S.Cox (Rangers), I.M.McColl (Rangers), W.A.Woodburn (Rangers), A.R.Forbes (Arsenal), W.Waddell (Rangers), W.Moir (Bolton W), W.Bauld (Hearts), W.Steel (Derby Co), W.Liddell (Liverpool).
England: B.F.Williams (Wolves); A.E.Ramsey (Spurs), J.Aston (Man Utd), W.A.Wright (Wolves, captain), C.F. Franklin (Stoke C), J.W.Dickinson (Portsmouth), T.Finney (Preston NE), W.J.Mannion (Middlesbrough), S.H.Mortensen (Blackpool), R.T.F.Bentley (Chelsea), R.Langton (Bolton W).

Half-time 0-0   Full-time 0-1
Ref: R.Leafe (England)   Att: 133,250

ENGLAND once again clinched the Home International Championship —

and with it a place in the World Cup finals — with this hard-fought win in front of a massive crowd of 133,250 spectators. It was a very close game with both sides grappling for supremacy.

Scotland began by missing a great chance as early as the second minute. Centre-forward Bauld, who, although missing chances throughout, gave Neil Franklin a tough time, beat the England defender on a headed pass from Steel and broke clear. He seemed certain to score but shot straight at Bert Williams from 15 yards. If he had been on target, then the outcome would probably have been much different.

That was not the only near-miss of an exciting and eventful first half. Indeed, it might have been 2-2 at the interval.

The England forwards began to move the ball about beautifully along the ground and at times they had Young, Cox and Woodburn at full stretch.

After 27 minutes Scotland had their first escape when Wilf Mannion volleyed Stan Mortensen's headed pass just wide. Shortly afterwards it was Mannion again going close when he took a clever flick from Tom Finney before volleying another shot. This time Young saved his side brilliantly with a spectacular goal-line clearance.

Play then swung straight to the other end, where it was England's turn to escape. Bauld sent Waddell away and, in his efforts to scramble the ball away, Williams ended up prostrate as Liddell lobbed over the bar to miss an open goal.

Six minutes into the second half, Mortensen had a goal disallowed for offside after Mannion had set him up. The Scottish crowd began to get behind their favourites and the home pressure increased. Bauld shot wide after a good shot on the turn and Williams saved twice low down from Steel and Liddell.

England stood firm though especially at full-back and centre-half. Midway through the half came what proved to be the decisive goal.

It came out of the blue. Jimmy Dickinson began the move with a pass to the left, Mannion dummied the pass and it ran on to Bobby Langton. The winger ran and held the ball well before releasing the perfect pass to Roy Bentley. Before Woodburn or Forbes could react, the England number-nine shot past Cowan.

The goal gave England much more freedom. Bentley began to roam more happily, Mannion, Billy Wright and Dickinson fed the forwards with a stream of good passes and Finney, Mortensen and Langton responded to them well.

Scotland kept battling though and 15 minutes from the end Liddell, always a danger, took a headed pass from Forbes and hit a magnificent right-foot volley which arrowed its way to the top corner. Nine times out of ten it would have been a goal, but this time Williams leapt across goal to make the save of a lifetime.

Scotland increased the pressure and after 84 minutes Bauld saw an effort strike the crossbar. Then a rare mistake by John Aston let in Waddell who shot wide from a good position. But England held on, having just about deserved the result.

Individually, England had the better of the game. Wright and Dickinson were outstanding, Williams faultless, Alf Ramsey cool and calculated, and Mannion and Finney excelled up front. Indeed,

Mannion, with his splendid vision was the best forward on view. For Scotland, Forbes was the outstanding player.

| 67th match v Scotland. |

Portugal v
England   Friendly

Played on Sunday, 14 May 1950 at the National Stadium, Lisbon.

Portugal: E.de Oliveira (Atlético Lisbon); V.Mendes (FC Porto), A.Carvalho (FC Porto), S.Baptista (Boavista), F.Antunes (Benfica), F.Ferreira (Benfica), R.de Carvalho (Benfica), M.Vasques (Sporting Lisbon), H.Ben David (Atlético Lisbon), J.Travacos (Sporting Lisbon), A.Pereira (Sporting Lisbon).
Subs: O.Barrosa (Sporting Lisbon) for Mendes; C.Canario (Sporting Lisbon) for Ferreira.
England: B.F.Williams (Wolves); A.E.Ramsey (Spurs), J.Aston (Man Utd), W.A.Wright (Wolves, captain), W.H.Jones (Liverpool), J.W.Dickinson (Portsmouth), J.E.T.Milburn (Newcastle Utd), S.H.Mortensen (Blackpool), R.T.F.Bentley (Chelsea), W.J.Mannion (Middlesbrough), T.Finney (Preston NE).

Half-time 0-3   Full-time 3-5
Ref: G.Carpani (Italy)   Att: 70,000

ENGLAND began a two-match Continental tour in preparation for their first appearance in the World Cup finals starting the following month. In Lisbon they gave a thrilling first-half exhibition and romped into a 3-0 interval lead with some scintillating football. The man who inspired them was Tom Finney, who was in brilliant form scoring four times in a superb display.

The tightly packed crowd of 70,000 saw Roy Bentley kick-off and immediately a third-minute shot by Finney skimmed the crossbar. Two minutes later, the winger was pulled down in the box. He took the penalty himself and calmly scored.

As England continued to dominate, Jackie Milburn fired in a blockbuster which the goalkeeper never saw but was relieved when it again skimmed the bar. After 15 minutes, England went two up with a beautiful goal from Stan Mortensen. He took a through-pass from Wilf Mannion and deftly strode past several Portuguese defenders before unleashing a fierce shot to score.

Portugal at this stage had been restricted to long-range efforts to test Bert Williams. They made a substitution but straight away it was England who scored again. Milburn and Bentley were involved in the approach work but Finney came in to finish the move off.

The home side improved before half-time after a further substitution and it showed early in the second half when they pulled a goal back. Vasques moved out to the right wing and put over a perfect centre which their big coloured striker David headed home. It gave the crowd a lift and they really got behind their team. England began to feel the pressure.

Some of the steam was taken out of the situation in the 55th minute when that man Finney scored a fabulous fourth goal. A lovely dribble took him through the defence and he finished with a marvellous shot wide of Ernesto. Portugal hit back and Alf Ramsey saved one effort on the goal-line before David again scored, this time getting the vital touch after a terrific scramble.

That made it 4-2 and in the 67th minute Portugal had a golden opportunity to pull another goal back, but Albano missed an open goal. However the same player atoned for that miss shortly afterwards by sending over a lovely centre for Vasques to head home. With the score at 4-3 and the crowd delirious with excitement, England had to show all their character and experience to keep the Portuguese at bay.

They fought like tigers relying on breakaways to relieve the pressure. From one of these breakaways, England clinched the match.

Mortensen broke clear only for his legs to be whipped away from under him in the penalty area by Barrosa. Imagine the pressure on Finney as he stepped up to take the spot-kick. The crowd were howling their derision but Finney remained ice-cool and calmly slotted the ball past the goalkeeper.

> 2nd match v Portugal
> Debut for Jones.
> Four goals for Finney (2 penalties).
> Portugal's de Oliveira also known as 'Ernesto'; Mendes as 'Virgilio'; Carvalho as 'Angelo'; Antunes as 'Felix'; de Carvalho as 'Rogerio'; Pereira as 'Albano'.

Belgium v England
Friendly

Played on Thursday, 18 May 1950 at the Heysel Stadium, Brussels.

Belgium: H.Meert (RSC Anderlecht); A.Vaillant (RSC Anderlecht), L.Anoul (FC Liège), J.Van der Auwera (KV Mechelen), V.Mees (FC Antwerp), L.Carré (FC Liège), J. Van Looy (La Ghantoise), F.Chavès (La Ghantoise), J.Mermans (RSC Anderlecht), A. De Hert (Berchem Sport), G.Mordant (Olympic Charleroi).

England: B.F.Williams (Wolves); A.E.Ramsey (Spurs), J.Aston (Man Utd), W.A.Wright (Wolves, captain), W.H.Jones (Liverpool), J.W.Dickinson (Portsmouth), J.E.T.Milburn (Newcastle Utd), S.H.Mortensen (Blackpool), R.T.F.Bentley (Chelsea), W.J.Mannion (Middlesbrough), T.Finney (Preston NE), Sub: J.Mullen (Wolves) for Milburn.

Half-time 1-0   Full-time 1-4
R.Vincenti (France)   Att: 55,750

AFTER being a goal down at half-time, England produced a spectacular second-half comeback to give themselves a marvellous boost before they left for the World Cup in Brazil.

From being a disjointed and unhappy side before the interval, England were transformed into a superb fighting unit afterwards. An injury to Jackie Milburn, who was forced to go off after 15 minutes to be replaced by Jimmy Mullen, meant that they had to reorganise with Tom Finney moving to the right wing and Mullen taking up the left-wing position.

For a while it had no real effect. Belgium

John Aston is too late to stop a Belgian forward getting in a cross at the Heysel Stadium in May 1950.

had the better of the first-half and took the lead in the 44th minute. A pass from Mees found Mermans completely unmarked in front of goal and in the area. He made no mistake and scored with a terrific right-foot shot.

Straight after the break though England equalized. Only a minute of the half had gone when Mullen picked up the ball and dribbled down the left before cutting inside to shoot neatly wide of Meert.

From that moment, England gradually got better and better. The attack was more thrustful and the defence tightened up considerably. On 66 minutes it appeared that a Belgium defender handled the ball well inside the area, but the referee awarded a free-kick outside the box. Justice appeared to be done, though as Finney placed the kick perfectly for Mortensen to head home.

A minute later England scored again. This time a brilliant move involving Mortensen and Roy Bentley ended with Wilf Mannion scoring.

By now the visitors were totally dominating the game and Meert was called upon to make some fine saves, but two minutes from the end he was beaten again when Bentley scored England's fourth.

> 12th match v Belgium.
> Mullen first substitute for England and, thus, the first to score.

World Cup Finals

Chile v England
Pool Two

Played on Sunday, 25 June 1950 at the Maracana Stadium, Rio de Janeiro, Brazil.

Chile: S.Livingstone (Universidad Catolica); A.Farias (Colo Colo), F.Roldan (Santiago W), M.Alvarez (Santiago W), M.Busquet (Universidad de Chile), H.Carvalho (Santiago W), L.Mayanes (Santiago W), A.Cremaschi (Union Española), J.Robledo (Newcastle Utd), M.Muñoz (Colo Colo), G.Diaz (Santiago W).

England: B.F.Williams (Wolves); A.E.Ramsey (Spurs), J.Aston (Man Utd), W.A.Wright (Wolves, captain), L.Hughes (Liverpool), J.W.Dickinson (Portsmouth), T.Finney (Preston NE), W.J.Mannion (Middlesbrough), R.T.F.Bentley (Chelsea), S.H.Mortensen (Blackpool), J.Mullen (Wolves).

Half-time 0-1   Full-time 0-2
K.Van Der Meer (Holland)   Att: 29,703

THIS long-awaited first World Cup finals match for the England team was played in pouring rain in front of an estimated crowd of 50,000 — although the official attendance given by the Brazilian FA was much less than that.

England sprung a surprise by selecting Laurie Hughes of Liverpool to win his first cap. It was a tough match in which to make an international debut but Hughes acquitted himself well.

The football was disappointing. The England attack never really got going and the defence found the Chilean forward line lively, albeit weak in front of goal.

It was England who went ahead in the 38th minute. A centre by Jimmy Mullen found Stan Mortensen and he gave Livingstone no chance with a firm header.

England enjoyed territorial advantage for most of the first half but Chile were unlucky when Carvalho hit the bar and again when Robledo, the Newcastle centre-forward who led the Chilean side, hit the post with a 30-yard free-kick.

Chile employed some robust tactics in the second half and the England players found it difficult to get into any sort of rhythm. Billy Wright and Wilf Mannion strove manfully, though, and England still remained in a comfortable position.

It was their turn for some bad luck in this half as they hit the bar twice. Roy Bentley and Mortensen both went close with headers and the two England forwards had looked sharp.

Robledo was Chile's main threat, but midway through the second half, England scored their decisive second goal. Mortensen sent Finney away down the right and his cross was put neatly inside the post with a low shot by Mannion.

First match v Chile and first World Cup finals match.
Debut for Hughes.
Mortensen was England's first World Cup finals goalscorer.

USA v England Pool Two

Played on Thursday, 29 June 1950 at the Mineiro Stadium, Belo Horizonte, Brazil.

USA: F.Borghi (Simpkins FC, St Louis); H.Keough (McMahons FC, St Louis), J.Macca (Brooklyn Hispano, New York), E.McIlvenny (Philadelphia Nationals), C.Colombo (Simpkins FC, St Louis), W.A.Bahr (Philadelphia Nationals), F.Wallace (Simpkins FC, St Louis), G.Pariani (Simpkins FC, St Louis), J.E.Gaetjens (Brook-Haltan, New York), J.B.Souza (Ponte Delgada, River Falls), E.Souza (Ponte Delgada, River Falls).

England: B.F.Williams (Wolves); A.E.Ramsey (Spurs), J.Aston (Man Utd), W.A.Wright (Wolves, captain), L.Hughes (Liverpool), J.W.Dickinson (Portsmouth), T.Finney (Preston NE), W.Mannion (Middlesbrough), R.T.F. Bentley (Chelsea), S.H.Mortensen (Blackpool), J.Mullen (Wolves).

Half-time 1-0   Full-time 1-0
Ref: G.Dattilo (Italy)   Att: 10,151

THIS match will probably go down as the most infamous and humiliating defeat ever suffered by an England international side. It seems that never before had the team played so badly, although it must be said that never before had the team suffered such appalling bad luck.

The first half was almost exclusively played in the American half with only a rare breakaway relieving the pressure on Borghi's goal. The goalkeeper worked overtime as the England forwards repeatedly had the goal at their mercy. Time after time though the ball went narrowly wide of the post, just over the bar, hit the woodwork or brought a fine save from Borghi.

After all this pressure the unbelievable happened in the 38th minute. A throw-in by Scotsman Ted McIlvenny — soon to sign for Manchester United — found Bahr and he hit a 25-yard shot, more in hope than anything else. Imagine his surprise when the ball struck Gaetjens on the head to deflect over a stunned Bert Williams and into the England net.

Jimmy Mullen, Tom Finney, Wilf Mannion and Stan Mortensen all missed from good positions as England became more and more frustrated at their inability to score. Simple chances went begging and it appeared that the American goal had a charmed life.

The second half was just as one-sided. The woodwork kept on being rattled and Borghi continued to be his side's saviour, although he was very lucky to save one Mortensen header which he appeared to haul back from behind the line. That was one of several errors of judgement on the part of the Italian referee and there were at least two strong penalty claims by England which went unheeded.

England became ragged as the game

Bert Williams looks behind him in disbelief as the ball enters the net after Bahr's hopeful shot struck Gaetjens on the head to give the USA a sensational victory.

slipped away from them but the chances still came and went. Mortensen shot over, Roy Bentley had the ball taken off his toes when a goal seemed certain and Mannion also missed a fine chance after he shot over when unmarked right in front of goal. Finally, Alf Ramsey forced the save of the match out of hero Borghi.

At the final whistle Larry Gaetjens — who in 1970 was to disappear during political unrest in his native Haiti — was hoisted shoulder-high and the crowd went wild. The small ground and close-marking had a bad effect on England but no amount of excuses could hide the fact that this had been a day of total disaster for the team. Everything had gone wrong and at the final count they had hit the woodwork no less than 11 times!

Needless to say, England's chances of qualifying for the next stages of the competition had suffered a severe blow.

1st match v USA.

Spain v England Pool Two

Played on Sunday, 2 July 1950 at the Maracana Stadium, Rio de Janeiro, Brazil.

Spain: A.Ramallets (FC Barcelona); J.Parra (Español), G.Alonzo (Real Madrid), J.Gonzalvo (FC Barcelona), S.M. Gonzalvo (FC Barcelona), A.Puchades (Valencia CF), E.Basora (FC Barcelona), S.Igoa (Valencia CF), T.Zarraonandia (Athletic Bilbao), J.L.Panizo (Athletic Bilbao), A.Gainza (Athletic Bilbao).

England: B.F.Williams (Wolves); A.E.Ramsey (Spurs), W.Eckersley (Blackburn R), W.A.Wright (Wolves, captain), L.Hughes (Liverpool), J.W.Dickinson (Portsmouth), S.Matthews (Blackpool), S.H.Mortensen (Blackpool), J.E.T. Milburn (Newcastle Utd), E.F.Baily (Spurs), T.Finney (Preston NE).

Half-time 0-0   Full-time 1-0
Ref: G.Galeati (Italy)   Att: 74,462

DESPERATELY needing to recover from the devastating defeat by the USA, England gave their all against Spain and produced a tremendous performance which lacked only one ingredient — goals. The team knew they had to beat the Spaniards to qualify for the next stage of the tournament, but sadly 'Lady Luck' refused to smile on them.

England brought Stan Matthews, flown in from the FA's tour of Canada, and Jackie Milburn into a reorganised forward line and gave debuts to Eddie Baily and Bill Eckersley.

The new-look front line was a constant danger to the Spanish defence and with just a hint of good fortune they could easily have had two or three goals. A big crowd watched the game and saw a fine performance from the English. Spain seemed obsessed with underhand tactics and they continually felled the England players. Alas, the Italian referee preferred to turn a blind eye to all that went on and offered no punishment.

England could and should have had two penalties when Tom Finney was twice sent sprawling in the area. Again the referee gave nothing. Stan Mortensen, Milburn and Baily all showed up well as England put together some neat passing movements, whilst Finney and Matthews showed all their ball skills on the wings. All the time though the main stumbling block for England was Ramallets in the Spanish goal. He was outstanding and time and again he thwarted the eager England attack.

As the match entered the second half the crowd became more and more frustrated by Spain's dubious tactics and they certainly sided with the England players. But five minutes into the half Spain went ahead. Their outside-left made a fine run and centred for the number-nine Zarraonandia to beat Bert Williams and score.

England continued to give everything and were desperately unlucky not to pull the goal back. Their only consolation was the winning back of their self respect and the ovation from the crowd as they trooped off at the end.

3rd match v Spain.
Debuts for Eckersley and Baily.

Northern Ireland v England Home Championship

Played on Saturday, 7 October 1950 at Windsor Park, Belfast.

Northern Ireland: H.R.Kelly (Southampton); C.Galloghy (Huddersfield T), A.McMichael (Newcastle Utd), R.D.Blanchflower (Barnsley), J.Vernon (West Brom), W.W.Cush (Glenavon), J.P.Campbell (Fulham), E.Crossan (Blackburn R), E.J.McMorran (Barnsley), R.A.Brennan (Fulham), J.McKenna (Huddersfield T).
England: B.F.Williams (Wolves); A.E.Ramsey (Spurs), J.Aston (Man Utd), W.A.Wright (Wolves, captain), A.C.Chilton (Man Utd), J.W.Dickinson (Portsmouth), S.Matthews (Blackpool), W.J.Mannion (Middlesbrough), J.Lee (Derby Co), E.F.Baily (Spurs), R.Langton (Bolton W).

Half-time 0-1   Full-time 1-4

Ref: G.Mitchell (Scotland)   Att: 46,000

FOUR missed chances in the first 30 minutes cost Northern Ireland dearly in a game that was never as clear-cut as the score suggests. If the Irish had not squandered those chances the story might have been different.

In that first half-hour, Ireland, urged on by their traditional passion and dedicated followers, put the England defence under extreme pressure. The visitors made a very tentative opening and McMorran twice missed with the simplest of headers from point-blank range. Soon afterwards Campbell and Crossan also failed to hit the target from clear positions.

The crisis passed as England gradually clawed themselves into the game. They started to search for openings in the Irish defence. Vernon, Cush and McMichael were outstanding for them and although the balance of attacks was now swinging England's way the Irish battled for everything.

The conditions were a little bit different from England's previous match, against Spain in the World Cup, and the cold October wind blowing down from Mount Colin brought some drizzle with it. The half seemed destined to end goalless but just before half-time the sun came out and with it England broke the deadlock by conjuring up a goal.

Not surprisingly the move developed down the left wing where Bobby Langton was giving Galloghy a torrid time. A swift inter-change with Eddie Baily set up the chance which the inside-left took gratefully, shooting past Kelly's left hand. The lead gave England time to rethink during the interval and they came out with a new strategy and a new determination. Suddenly Wilf Mannion became the focal point of their improvement.

The 63rd minute saw a decisive moment at both ends. First the referee refused an appeal for hands against Alf Ramsey, and then, 60 seconds later, following a swift counter-attack, Kelly failed to clear Baily's lob into the goalmouth and Jack Lee pounced to head the loose ball into the net.

Everyone thought that that was the end, but Ireland refused to lie down. Within six minutes the issue was wide open again as they pulled a goal back.

McMorran, an eager beaver all afternoon, chased a long clearance down wind and beat Allenby Chilton to the ball and shot on the turn to flick it over the advancing Bert Williams. Urged on by their crowd, the Irish threw everything at England and McMorran was unlucky with a shot that skimmed the bar.

England, however, met the challenge bravely. Inspired by the powerful Jimmy Dickinson, Billy Wright and Ramsey they weathered the storm and began to mount more positive raids. Stanley Matthews came into the game at last and gradually the Irish began to wilt.

In the last five minutes, England scored two more goals. First Wright shot home through a crowd of players following a corner by Langton, and within a minute of that goal, Baily scored the best goal of the match with a clever hooked shot.

The match, although full of incident, had never reached the high standards of most internationals but England's performance was nonetheless satisfactory.

58th match v Northern Ireland.
Debut for Chilton and Lee.
Debut goal for Lee.

England v Wales Home Championship

Played on Wednesday, 15 November 1950 at Roker Park, Sunderland.

England: B.F.Williams (Wolves); A.E.Ramsey (Spurs, captain), L.Smith (Arsenal), W.Watson (Sunderland), L.H.Compton (Arsenal), J.W.Dickinson (Portsmouth), T.Finney (Preston NE), W.J.Mannion (Middlesbrough), J.E.T.Milburn (Newcastle Utd), E.F.Baily (Spurs), L.D.Medley (Spurs).
Wales: I.Hughes (Luton T); W.Barnes (Arsenal), A.T.Sherwood (Cardiff C), R.Paul (Man City), R.W.Daniel (Arsenal), W.H.Lucas (Swansea T), M.W.Griffiths (Leicester C), B.W.Allen (Coventry C), T.Ford (Sunderland), I.J.Allchurch (Swansea T), R.J.Clarke (Man City).

Half-time 2-0   Full-time 4-2

Ref: J.A.Mowat (Scotland)   Att: 50,250

THIS was undoubtedly the best Welsh performance against England since the war and the fact that England, at times, had to be at their most brilliant best says it all. On a treacherous surface and on a bitterly cold day, the football served up warmed the crowd to fever pitch as the excitement grew.

Excellent precision passing by Wilf Mannion, Eddie Baily, Jackie Milburn, Les Medley and Tom Finney had given England a bright opening. However, the Welsh terriers were continually snapping at their heels with Daniel, Paul and Lucas working tirelessly in the midfield battle. Gradually though the extra class began to show and three of the four England goals were pure genius.

Wales had the ball in the net on the half-hour but Clarke's shot was ruled out for offside. A few seconds later, England took the lead as a long controlled clearance by Lionel Smith, who had a good game, reached Baily on the edge of the Welsh penalty area. The Spurs player flicked the ball up with his right foot and crashed it into the net with his left for a wonderful goal.

The England attack, well prompted by Willie Watson and Jimmy Dickinson, then began to flow superbly. The ball was moving forward quickly and smoothly.

Five minutes before half-time England scored their second. Again it was a shot by Baily that did the trick when he finished off a splendid round of passing by Finney, Mannion, Watson and Mannion again. It seemed that the 2-0 interval lead had put England clear but with Allchurch and Ford showing some tremendous play it was far from over.

Indeed, with only three minutes of the second half gone Wales pulled a goal back. Griffiths put over a fine centre which landed between Leslie Compton and Bert Williams, and before either could react, Ford nipped in smartly to flick the ball in with his head.

It was end to end stuff now as both sides searched for another goal. Ford forced two brilliant saves out of Williams and then Bailey saw his 20-yard shot strike the Welsh crossbar. A scramble on the England goal-line almost produced an equalizer before, on 66 minutes, the home side engineered the next crucial goal. Again it was a super strike. Mannion was the man on target this time, cleverly flicking the ball past Hughes after Watson and Milburn had created the opening.

Still Wales refused to lie down and five minutes later it was 3-2. Once more the combination of Griffiths and Ford gave the centre-forward the chance to touch the ball past Williams with the other England defenders off balance. So the excitement continued until the dying seconds, after another flowing move between Finney, Mannion, Baily and Milburn, the England number-nine shot home from an acute angle. That put the final stamp on England's extra quality and authority and was the last action of a magnificent afternoon's football.

61st match v Wales.
Debuts for Smith, Compton and Medley.
Ramsey captained England for the first time.

England v Yugoslavia Friendly

Played on Wednesday, 22 November 1950 at Arsenal Stadium, London.

England: B.F.Williams (Wolves); A.E.Ramsey (Spurs, captain), W.Eckersley (Blackburn R), W.Watson (Sunderland), L.H.Compton (Arsenal), J.W.Dickinson (Portsmouth), J.Hancocks (Wolves), W.J.Mannion (Middlesbrough), N.Lofthouse (Bolton W), E.F.Baily (Spurs), L.D.Medley (Spurs).
Yugoslavia: V.Beara (Hajduk Split); B.Stanković (Red Star Belgrade), R.Colić (Partizan Belgrade), Z.Cajkovski (Partizan Belgrade), I.Horvat (Dinamo Zagreb), P.Djajić (Red Star Belgrade), T.Orgjanon (Red Star Belgrade), R.Mitić (Red Star Belgrade), T.Živanović (OFK Belgrade), S.Bobek (Partizan Belgrade), B.Vukas (Hajduk Split).

Half-time 2-1   Full-time 2-2

Ref: K.Van Der Meer (Holland) Att: 62,000

ENGLAND'S unbeaten home record against continental opposition remained intact, but they all but threw away this game after, at one time, being in a commanding position.

After a slow start, the big crowd was lulled into a false sense of security as England worked themselves into a convincing 2-0 lead after 35 minutes.

The home forwards forced the Yugoslav defenders into errors with their positive play and both Johnny Hancocks and Les Medley had the beating of their markers. The Yugoslavian goalkeeper, Beara, once a ballet dancer, was soon showing his agility.

In the 28th minute he made an unbelievable point-blank save from the debutant Nat Lofthouse after Medley had just previously hit the far post, but a minute later England deservedly took the lead. A long pass by Eddie Baily bounced beyond Stanković for Medley to sweep the ball into the middle where Lofthouse left Beara helpless.

Five minutes later it was 2-0. Jimmy Dickinson fed Hancocks on the right and there was Lofthouse again to play his part with a glorious header into the far corner from a perfect cross. It seemed all over at this stage but how wrong that assumption was.

Nat Lofthouse, the Bolton centre-forward whose 33 goals was a record for England.

With only five minutes of the second half gone, the first hint of what lay ahead arrived. Willie Watson, dallying with the ball on his own goal-line, was robbed by Orgjanon. His cross seemed harmless enough but alas Leslie Compton, in trying to shield Bert Williams, only succeeded in diverting the ball into his own net for an unnecessary goal which unfortunately was to completely change the course of the game.

In the next minute Živanović forced Williams into a fine diving save. England then tried desperately to reaffirm their first-half superiority and but for Beara's performance in goal they would have done. Three times in as many minutes he made flying saves from Wilf Mannion and how he kept out Lofthouse's header from a Hancocks centre defied belief.

With half an hour to play, the England team faded. Inspired by Beara's saves the Yugoslavia side suddenly took control. With the outstanding Bobek pulling all the strings and good support coming from

Cajkovski and Djajić they were making full use of their fine footwork.

In the 78th minute they finally scored their deserved equalizer. Again England's defence was badly at fault with Bobek's first shot needlessly blocked by Alf Ramsey when Williams was in position behind him. The rebound went straight to Živanović and in a flash it was 2-2.

Only Dickinson, Bill Eckersley, Hancocks and the impressive Lofthouse looked their true selves and the second half had been a real struggle for England. To their credit, though, they almost snatched victory near the end only to find man-of-the-match Beara once again barring the way.

2nd match v Yugoslavia.
Two debut goals for Lofthouse.
"My debut gave me a feeling you can't describe or buy."
Nat Lofthouse

England v Scotland Home Championship

Played on Saturday, 14 April 1951 at Wembley Stadium.

England: B.F.Williams (Wolves); A.E.Ramsey (Spurs), W.Eckersley (Blackburn R), H.Johnston (Blackpool), J.Froggatt (Portsmouth), W.A.Wright (Wolves, captain), S.Matthews (Black-

pool), W.J.Mannion (Middlesbrough), S.H.Mortensen (Blackpool), H.W.Hassall (Huddersfield T), T.Finney (Preston NE).
Scotland: J.Cowan (Morton); G.L.Young (Rangers), S.Cox (Rangers), R.Evans (Celtic), W.A.Woodburn (Rangers), W.Redpath (Motherwell), W.Waddell (Rangers), R.Johnstone (Hibernian), L.Reilly (Hibernian), W.Steel (Dundee), W.Liddell (Liverpool).

Half-time 1-1   Full-time 2-3
Ref: T.Mitchell (Northern Ireland)
                              Att: 98,750

SCOTLAND once again scored a famous victory on the hallowed turf of Wembley to win the Home International Championship but both sides came out of this magnificent match with a great deal of credit, especially since England spent 80 minutes playing with only ten men.

Unbeaten at Wembley in the Championship since 1934, Scotland began the game purposefully and were already imposing their skills before Wilf Mannion left the arena with a fractured cheekbone. He had been involved in an aerial duel with Liddell on 11 minutes and went off in agony. Bert Williams had already twice saved brilliantly from Johnstone and the limitations of the shaky England defence were soon showing up. After Mannion's loss England looked understandably disjointed as they struggled to reorganise.

Scotland began to play on Jack Froggatt who did not have the happiest of games

The Duke of Gloucester shakes hands with Blackburn full-back Bill Eckersley before the Scotland game at Wembley in April 1951. Billy Wright looks on.

at centre-half. The other defenders also struggled and for once even Billy Wright was not on his game. But England did have one quality in abundance and that was courage. The ten men fought manfully and the marvellous skills of Tom Finney, Stanley Matthews, Stan Mortensen and Harold Hassall made sure that Scotland would not have things all their own way.

The Froggatt cousins, Jack (left) and Redfern, training at Stamford Bridge.

Scotland increased the pressure though and Williams had to save well from Liddell. Johnstone then missed two more clear chances before, on 26 minutes, and totally out of the blue, England took the lead. It was a gem of a goal too. Alf Ramsey and Harry Johnston began the move by combining to find Finney out on the right. The winger showed controlled dribbling skills before passing to Mortensen. He, in turn, pulled the ball square to Hassall who conjured up some sheer inspiration to deceive Young and shoot a glorious angled drive into the roof of the Scottish net.

It seemed like 1949 in reverse, but with 33 minutes gone Johnstone gained a further chance for Scotland when good work by Reilly and Liddell opened up a gap for the inside-right to score.

For a short time after the interval England were down to nine men whilst Mortensen had treatment for a facial injury, but he soon returned to the action. Shortly though it was Scotland who swept into a decisive lead. In the space of seven minutes they scored twice. First a glorious passing movement between Evans, Johnstone and Reilly ended with the centre-forward making it 2-1 by beating Froggatt and picking his spot. Then Williams tragically dropped a long cross by Steel and Liddell, with a low shot, fired the ball into the unguarded net.

All over? Not a bit of it! Driven on by the stylish Johnston, Finney, Matthews, Mortensen and Hassall, England captured the last half-hour with some superlative play. It brought the Wembley crowd to a crescendo of noise and passion and it almost brought the Scots to their knees.

On 80 minutes, a passing duet between Finney and Mortensen ended with Finney streaking clear to lob a superb goal over the advancing Cowan to make it 3-2. Matthews tormented Cox, Finney all but got through again and then Mortensen, taking a pass from Hassall, shot inches wide raising a puff of chalk as it went past the post. The desperate Scots almost conceded a penalty when Mortensen was bundled over unceremoniously, but then, amongst all the excitement the referee blew the final whistle on an extraordinary afternoon.

> 68th match v Scotland.
> Debut goal for Hassall.

England v Argentina

Friendly

Played on Wednesday, 9 May 1951 at Wembley Stadium.

England: B.F.Williams (Wolves); A.E.Ramsey (Spurs), W.Eckersley (Blackburn R), W.A.Wright (Wolves, captain), J.G.Taylor (Fulham), H.Cockburn (Man Utd), T.Finney (Preston NE), S.H.Mortensen (Blackpool), J.E.T.Milburn (Newcastle Utd), H.W.Hassall (Huddersfield T), V.Metcalfe (Huddersfield T).

Argentina: M.A.Rugilo (Velez); J.C.Colman (Boca Juniors), R.Filgueiras (Huracán), N.Iácono (River Plate), M.Faina (Newell's Old Boys), N.Pescia (Boca Juniors), M.Boyé (Racing Club), N.Mendez (Racing Club), R.Bravo (Racing Club), A.Labruna (River Plate), F.Loustau (River Plate).
Sub: F.Allegri (Newell's Old Boys) for Colman.

Half-time 0-1   Full-time 2-1
Ref: B.M.Griffiths (Wales)   Att: 99,000

IN a match helping to celebrate the Festival of Britain, England came so close to losing their precious unbeaten home record against foreign opposition. Playing in red shirts, they began with a determined burst but struggled later.

Henry Cockburn quickly asserted his authority and soon Rugilo was making athletic saves from Stan Mortensen and Jackie Milburn. Clearly the goalkeeper was an eccentric, as he showed in his exaggerated play, but he was effective and kept England at bay. Argentina built their game around short, sharp passes and Pescia was outstanding.

The visitors first serious attack incredibly brought them a goal. It came in the 18th minute and began after a mistake by Billy Wright in midfield. From there the Argentinians worked the ball brilliantly. Labruna, killing Rugilo's long clearance perfectly, sent Loustau away. He beat Alf Ramsey for pace before crossing for Boyé to head past Bert Williams. Boyé was so taken with the excitement of scoring that one would have been mistaken to think that the goal had won the World Cup.

From that moment until half-time it was all England. Milburn latched on to a Mortensen pass but was thwarted by a brave dive by Rugilo at his feet. Harold Hassall, with a flashing drive and two searching headers forced the goalkeeper

Jackie Milburn in action against Argentina at Wembley in May 1951.

into three more saves as the pressure increased. At the end of the first 45 minutes though England were still searching for the equalizer. They went off to have a re-think.

It was soon noticeable that they were releasing their passes quicker when they restarted and as a result began to create more chances. Wright was supporting Tom Finney better now and Milburn was finding gaps at last in the tough tackling Argentine defence. For 15 minutes England laid seige on the visitor's goal. Once, Allegri, who had come on as substitute for Colman, cleared off the line with an acrobatic scissors kick and then Milburn twice hit Rugilo's right hand post.

And so it went on. Time drained away and still no England goal. Williams had been a virtual spectator for 95 per cent of the game and it was all England. A huge Wembley roar built up to urge England forward and with only 11 minutes to go, they finally gained their long overdue reward. Mortensen was the hero as he rose to head in a corner by Finney. It was England's 14th corner and that was some measure of their domi-nance. With only four minutes left the game was transformed with the winning goal.

This time Mortensen turned provider when he headed Ramsey's free-kick across the goalmouth for Milburn to ram the ball in from close range. This ruined Rugilo's day but his antics, although raising quite a few laughs amongst the crowd, in the end got their just desserts.

It was a spectacular ending to a spec-tacular match.

1st match v Argentina.
Debuts for Taylor and Metcalfe.
Argentina became the first country other than Scotland to play at Wembley.

England v Portugal
Friendly

Played on Saturday, 19 May 1951 at Goodison Park, Liverpool.

England: B.F.Williams (Wolves); A.E.Ramsey (Spurs, captain), W.Eckersley (Blackburn R), W.E.Nicholson (Spurs), J.G.Taylor (Fulham), H.Cockburn (Man Utd), T.Finney (Preston NE), S.C.Pearson (Man Utd), J.E.T.Milburn (Newcastle Utd), H.W.Hassall (Huddersfield T), V.Metcalfe (Huddersfield T).
Portugal: E.de Oliveira (Atlético Lisbon); V.Mendes (FC Porto), S.des Neves (Bele-nenses), C.Canário (Sporting Lisbon), F.Antunes (Benfica), F.Ferreira (Benfica), D.Demétrio (Elvas), J.Travaços (Sporting Lisbon), H.Ben David (Atlético Lisbon), F.Caiado (Boavista), A.Pereira (Sporting Lisbon).
Sub: C.Martinho (Atlético Lisbon) for Demétrio.

Half-time 2-1   Full-time 5-2
Ref: L.Baert (Belgium)   Att: 52,750

ENGLAND brought the Festival of Britain football programme to a close with a spectacular finish to a game evenly contested for 75 minutes.

Nearly 53,000 people packed into Goodison Park and they were soon on their feet cheering a first-minute goal for England. Only 19 seconds had gone on the stop-watch when a close passing movement straight from the kick-off enabled Henry Cockburn, Vic Metcalf and Stan Pearson to give Billy Nicholson a dream debut when he scored with a magnificent 18-yard shot with his first touch.

This would have knocked the stuffing out of most sides but within a minute Portugal drew level. A counter-thrust by Caiado, Travaços and David set up the chance for Patalino to shoot past Wil-liams. It had been a remarkable opening and ten minutes later the dashing Jackie Milburn, who had a fine game, put England back into the lead with a swift low shot after receiving a pass from Pearson.

That lead lasted until just after half-time. Hesitancy between Alf Ramsey and Jim Taylor allowed Albano to slip the ball past Bert Williams to once again level the scores. This really set the game alight and with the Portuguese tails well and truly up they began to ask severe questions of the English defence.

Then suddenly with 15 minutes left the England side changed completely. Gone was the tired and lethargic look. It was replaced by the much more normal look of the England team. They then proceeded to produce an appropriate festival of goals to end the match.

Tom Finney, in one of his most devastating moods, scored the decisive and killer goal in the 76th minute. It came with a superb swerving left-foot shot from the touch-line. It really was a match-winning goal and it finally broke the stubborn resistance of the brave Portu-guese. The goals that followed from Milburn and Hassall were mere formal-ities and simply entertained the crowd still further. In the end the extra power of the English team finally saw off another continental challenge.

3rd match v Portugal.
Debut goal for Nicholson.
Portugal's de Oliveria also known as 'Ernesto'; Mendes as 'Virgilio'; des Neves as 'Serafim'; Antunes as 'Felix'; Demétrio as 'Patalino'; Pereira as 'Albano'.

England v France
Friendly

Played on Wednesday, 3 October 1951 at Arsenal Stadium, London.

England: B.F.Williams (Wolves); A.E.Ramsey (Spurs), A.Willis (Spurs), W.A.Wright (Wolves, captain), A.C.Chilton (Man Utd), H.Cockburn (Man Utd), T.Finney (Preston NE), W.J.Mannion (Middlesbrough), J.E.T.Milburn (Newcastle Utd), H.W.Hassall (Huddersfield T), L.D.Medley (Spurs).
France: R.Vignal (RC de Paris); A.Grillon (RC de Paris), M.Salva (RC de Paris), K.Firoud (OGC Nice), R.Jonquet (Stade de Reims), A.Bonifaci (OGC Nice), R.Alpsteg (AS St-Etienne), J.Baratte (Lille OSC), J.Grumellon (Stade Rennes), P.Flamion (Olympique Lyonnais), A.Doye (Girondins).

Half-time 2-2   Full-time 2-2
Ref: J.A.Mowatt (Scotland)   Att: 57,500

THIS result defied all the odds as France gained a draw that they deserved but never expected. England gave a very indifferent display and would quickly want to forget this match. At least they managed to retain their proud unbeaten record against continental teams but they were lucky to come away with a draw and could easily have lost.

The success France obtained was built largely on a defensive display and they won few friends amongst the crowd with their tactics.

England had an excellent start, scoring in the fourth minute. A firm cross pass by Tom Finney was unfortunately diverted beyond his own goalkeeper by Firoud. Then they should have had a second when Harold Hassall was put clear by Henry Cockburn's throw-in. Vignal did well to save Hassall's shot but a square pass to the unmarked Jackie Milburn would probably have brought a more positive result.

In the next 20 minutes, France hit back hard. Inspired by Doye, their best player, they hit the crossbar with a cracker from Baratte. The warning was there for England and shortly afterwards France turned the game around with two goals in two minutes.

First Allenby Chilton, who struggled throughout, failed to clear a corner taken by Alpsteg and Doye was on hand to shoot home from close range. Almost at once Doye, with some clever footwork and a quick pass, sent Arthur Willis and Cockburn the wrong way and left Alpsteg with a clear chance. He shot from an acute angle and the ball flew into the England net with the aid of a deflection. England were stunned and watched as Grummel-lon and Alpsteg tested Bert Williams. But gradually they began to fight back. Billy Wright's long pass sent Milburn away only for the centre-forward's shot to go just wide.

Just before half-time England equal-ized. A fine move involving Alf Ramsey and Wilf Mannion ended with Les Medley cutting through at inside-right to score.

That was the end of the scoring and the second half was one of England battling against a well organised and uncompromising French defence without any success. There was one other dramatic moment in the half and it almost brought that record to an end. Sloppy work by Willis and Cockburn gave Grumelon the chance to gain possession and speed off towards goal unchallenged. Williams came out and, although he went to his left, he somehow managed to reach back to his right to parry the shot.

12th match v France.
Debut for Willis.

Wales v England
Home Championship

Played on Saturday, 20 October 1951 at Ninian Park, Cardiff.

Wales: W.W.Shortt (Plymouth A); W.Barnes (Arsenal), A.T.Sherwood (Cardiff C), R.Paul (Man City), R.W.Daniel (Arsenal), W.A.R.Burgess (Spurs), W.I.Foulkes (Newcastle Utd), N.Kinsey (Norwich C), T.Ford (Sunderland), I.J.Allchurch (Swansea T), R.J.Clarke (Man City).

England: B.F.Williams (Wolves); A.E.Ramsey (Spurs), L.Smith (Arsenal), W.A.Wright (Wolves, captain), M.W.Barrass (Bolton W), J.W.Dickinson (Portsmouth), T.Finney (Preston NE), T.Thompson (Aston Villa), N.Lofthouse (Bolton W), E.F.Baily (Spurs), L.D.Medley (Spurs).

Half-time 1-1   Full-time 1-1

Ref: D.Gerrard (Scotland)   Att: 51,500

WALES managed to avoid defeat against England for the first time since the war when the sides met in Cardiff in this 1951 clash. What is more, if they had taken more care in front of goal, they may have celebrated a win.

The home side scored after only three minutes. A foul by Malcolm Barrass gave Wales a free-kick on the right-hand corner of the penalty box. Paul took the kick and his low cross was met by Foulkes with his first touch in international football. He left Lionel Smith flat-footed before going on to shoot past Bert Williams.

England quickly pulled themselves together and were soon back on level terms. Tom Finney, taking a pass from Billy Wright, moved through the inside-right channel before laying the ball square to Les Medley. He quickly lobbed the ball into the middle where Eddie Baily was on hand for an easy headed goal.

The game then gradually drifted into a scrappy affair with Wales relying on their strong midfield players creating their most dangerous moves. Daniel, Paul and Burgess always had control and their tigerish tackling was causing England to struggle. Barrass at centre-half, although neat in distribution, always came off second best in his battle with the powerful Ford. Some good play by Jimmy Dickinson, Medley and Baily promised something for England before half-time but there were no really clear chances created.

England never functioned on all cylinders and their weakness at inside-forward was very obvious. Tommy Thompson, on his debut, never got into the match at all and Baily only flitted in and out of proceedings. The tough-tackling Burgess was prominent for Wales and with Ford a constant threat they came very close to forcing a win. Foulkes and Clarke sent in a stream of crosses towards the big centre-forward and from one Ford missed a sitter. Paul sent Foulkes away on an attack and he left the ponderous Smith in a fine run to centre from the left. Once again, though, Ford contrived to miss a golden chance to take the match. England were somewhat fortunate to come away from Cardiff with a draw.

> 62nd match v Wales.
> Debuts for Barrass and Thompson.

England v Home Championship
Northern Ireland

Played on Wednesday, 14 November 1951 at Villa Park, Birmingham.

England: G.H.Merrick (Birmingham C); A.E.Ramsey (Spurs), L.Smith (Arsenal), W.A.Wright (Wolves, captain), M.W.Barrass (Bolton W), J.W.Dickinson (Portsmouth), T.Finney (Preston NE), J.Sewell (Sheffield Wed), N.Lofthouse (Bolton W), L.H.Phillips (Portsmouth), L.D.Medley (Spurs).

Northern Ireland: W.N.M.C.Uprichard (Swindon T); W.G.L.Graham (Doncaster R), A.McMichael (Newcastle Utd), W.Dickson (Chelsea), J.Vernon (West Brom), F.J.McCourt (Man City), W.L.Bingham (Sunderland), S.Smyth (Stoke C), E.J.McMorran (Barnsley), J.McIlroy (Burnley), J.McKenna (Huddersfield T).

Half-time 1-0   Full-time 2-0

Ref: B.M.Griffiths (Wales)   Att: 58,000

WITH Scotland surprisingly losing at home to Wales this win proved very important in the race for the Home International Championship. Once again, though, it was a poor performance by England and indeed, a poor game overall.

With both defences well-organised all the forwards found it hard to make headway. Nat Lofthouse was the most dangerous of the England players and in one of the rare first-half attacking moves he almost scored. A fine crossfield pass by Len Phillips sent Tom Finney away and split the Irish defence wide open. Finney's pass found Lofthouse and only a desperate dive by Uprichard at the big centre-forward's feet saved the day. England's only other worthwhile attack of the half brought them a goal.

A fine move from Phillips to Lofthouse, square to Jackie Sewell, back to Lofthouse, on to Finney, and a centre into the middle met by a crashing header from Lofthouse again.

Nat Lofthouse dives full length to score England's first goal against Northern Ireland at Villa Park in November 1951.

The goal brought hope for a better second half but, alas, the game never got any better. Both Sewell and Phillips were a little predictable in their play and only three moments in the second-half warranted a mention. McMorran was unlucky with Northern Ireland's best effort of the match when his tremendous 25-yard shot crashed against the angle of the post and crossbar after he beat Malcolm Barrass, not for the first time.

The second moment was when a firework went off surprising a touch-line photographer, much to the crowd's amusement. The final highlight gave England their second and decisive goal. It came thanks to a bad mistake by Uprichard seven minutes from the end. A harmless looking centre from Sewell was dropped by the goalkeeper straight to the feet of the lurking Lofthouse and before you could say his name the ball was in the back of the net to make it 2-0.

> 59th match v Northern Ireland.
> Debuts for Merrick, Sewell and Phillips.

England v Austria
Friendly

Played on Wednesday, 28 November 1951 at Wembley Stadium.

England: G.H.Merrick (Birmingham C); A.E.Ramsey (Spurs), W.Eckersley (Sou- thampton), W.A.Wright (Wolves, cap- tain), J.Froggatt (Portsmouth), J.W.Dickinson (Portsmouth), C.A.Milton (Arsenal), I.A.Broadis (Man City), N.Lofthouse (Bolton), E.F.Baily (Spurs), L.D.Medley (Spurs).

Austria: W.Zeman (Rapid Wien); R.Röckl (SK Wien), E.Happel (Rapid Wien), G.Hanappi (Rapid Wien), E.Ocwirk (FK Austria), T.Brenek (Wacker Wien), E.Melchior (FK Austria), L.Gernhardt (Rapid Wien), A.Huber (FK Austria), E.Stojaspal (FK Austria), A.Körner (Rapid Wien).

Half-time 0-0   Full-time 2-2
Ref: J.A.Mowat (Scotland)   Att: 98,000

AT last England produced a much betterperformance than of late against a very good Austrian side. It made for an excellent international match and notable for two very different styles. England, quick and incisive, did everything at top speed. Austria, meanwhile, remained slow, precise and deliberate in their build up before producing some dangerous through balls.

But this was undoubtedly England's best display for some time and they could and should have won. Unfortunately they failed to punish some bad defensive errors by the Austrian defence although it must be said that the ball did not run too kindly at times for the England players.

Shining brightest amongst all the talent on show was a remarkable performance by the Austrian goalkeeper Zeman. His agility and handling was superb and he continually thwarted the eager home forwards. As early as the fourth minute he made a brilliant save from Ivor Broadis after Arthur Milton had put the Manches- ter City man through. The fact that England did not get that early goal, so vital against the Continental sides, probably had a large bearing on the final result as Austria improved as the game went on.

England certainly had the better chan- ces in the first half. Billy Wright, Jack Froggatt and Jimmy Dickinson worked tirelessly for them and the impressive Stojaspal and Ocwirk did the same for the visitors. Broadis had that early chance quickly followed by another, and then Milton and Nat Lofthouse, twice, saw good efforts saved. At the other end Huber forced Gil Merrick into an excellent save before Bill Eckersley did well to block another Huber effort. Despite this good football producing umpteen goal attempts the scoreline was still blank at the interval.

Only two minutes into the second half England suffered a shock when the Austrians took the lead. Ocwirk placed a deep free-kick into the penalty area and caught the home defence flat-footed. In a flash Melchior cut in from the left to leave Merrick helpless with a fine shot.

Now it really was a test for England but they rose to the challenge splendidly. Wave after wave of relentless attacks swept forward and after 70 minutes they gained their reward. Eddie Baily was sent spra- wling in the area by Ocwirk's tackle and the referee awarded a penalty which the ice-cool Alf Ramsey calmly slotted past Zeman. The Wembley crowd really got behind England at this stage and they went wild with excitement when their team took the lead with 14 minutes to go.

England skipper Billy Wright exchanges pennants with Austria's Gernhardt before the match at Wembley in November 1951.

Left: England and Austria march out at Wembley. *Right:* Nat Lofthouse is foiled by the Austrian defence.

Left: Lofthouse heads England into the lead from Ramsey's free-kick. *Right:* Ramsey scores England's first from the penalty spot.

Left: Ivor Broadis watches as Zeman blocks his shot. *Right:* Gil Merrick is beaten by Stojaspal's penalty as Austria snatch a draw.

The English and Austrian players shake hands after the 2-2 Wembley draw.

This time Ramsey took a free-kick and placed the ball perfectly for Lofthouse to run in and head home.

The action never let up and in the 88th minute Huber fired in a header which beat Merrick but was pushed away by Eckersley's hand. Another penalty! Stojaspal capped a fine personal display by showing Ramsey's coolness by tucking away the spot-kick. It was no less than Austria deserved for a thrilling display.

It was ironic that despite such a fine football match all the goals had come from set situations.

7th match v Austria.
Debuts for Milton and Broadis.

Scotland v England Home Championship

Played on Saturday, 5 April 1952 at Hampden Park, Glasgow.

Scotland: R.Brown (Rangers); G.L.Young (Rangers), W.McNaught (Raith R), J.Scoular (Portsmouth), W.A.Woodburn (Rangers), W.Redpath (Motherwell), G.Smith (Hibernian), R.Johnstone (Hibernian), L.Reilly (Hibernian), J.L.McMillan (Airdrieonians), W.Liddell (Liverpool).

England: G.H.Merrick (Birmingham C); A.E.Ramsey (Spurs), T.H.Garrett (Blackpool), W.A.Wright (Wolves, captain), J.Froggatt (Portsmouth), J.W.Dickinson (Portsmouth), T.Finney (Preston NE), I.A.Broadis (Man City), N.Lofthouse (Bolton W), S.C.Pearson (Man Utd), J.F.Rowley (Man Utd).

Zeman, Austria's acrobatic goalkeeper, in action against England at Wembley in November 1951.

Half-time 0-2 **Full-time 1-2**

Ref: P.Morris (Northern Ireland)

Att: 134,504

THE pattern of England doing well at Hampden whilst Scotland do better at Wembley continued in this latest meeting leaving England unbeaten in Scotland since 1937. The new Press box was open for the game and the two teams took the field in very wet conditions.

England made a bright start and quickly forged their way in front with an eighth minute goal from Stan Pearson. Keeping the ball on the ground, good passes from Billy Wright to Nat Lofthouse and on to Jack Rowley down the left ended with the winger centring low into the middle. Redpath's deflection caused the ball to fly upwards and when it came down, Pearson met it on the full to crash home a superb rising shot with his left foot. It was a goal typical of the Manchester United player and one that will be long remembered, as well as giving him great confidence.

Despite the overall superiority of the England team Scotland were able to create three clear chances which should have been taken in the first half. On ten minutes Reilly missed Liddell's header after it landed at his feet, then ten minutes later the roles were reversed when Liddell missed a golden opportunity after Reilly had set him up with a backheeled pass. He could only shoot straight at Gil Merrick when it seemed he must score. Finally, Liddell again missed the target with a diving header from point-blank range after Scoular had lobbed the ball in from the left.

But don't get the impression that Scotland had it all their own way. Far from it as Tom Finney and Ivor Broadis combined magnificently to carve gaping holes in the home defence. Only the finishing let them down, although with a minute left of the first-half Pearson confirmed his value to the side with his second goal. He pounced on a terrible mix-up between Redpath and Woodburn to shoot just inside Brown's left-hand post.

Scotland began to rue their missed chances as England turned on the style after the break. Broadis and Finney, twice, should have scored and Rowley was very unlucky to see his ferocious shot rebound from a post. Scoular worked overtime during this spell to repel the eager English raiders and towards the end he inspired more passion from his teammates. The improvement culminated in a goal after 75 minutes.

McMillan put pressure on a hesitant Alf Ramsey and was able to centre for Reilly to score Scotland's first home goal against the Auld Enemy since the war. The crowd then tried to lift Scotland for the last quarter of an hour but England held firm, survived two corners in the last minute, and deservedly clinched victory.

Tom Garrett made an impressive debut whilst Wright, Dickinson, Broadis and Finney were outstanding for England.

> 69th match v Scotland.
> Debut for Garrett.

Italy v England
Friendly

Played on Sunday, 18 May 1952 at the Stadio Comunale, Florence.

Italy: G.Moro (Sampdoria); A.Giavannini (Inter-Milan), S.Manentes (Juventus), G.Mari (Juventus), R.Ferrario (Juventus), A.Piccinini (Juventus), G.Boniperti (Juventus), E.Pandolfini (Fiorentina), S.Piola (Novara), A.Amadei (Napoli), G.Cappello (Bologna).

England: G.H.Merrick (Birmingham C); A.E.Ramsey (Spurs), T.H.Garrett (Blackpool), W.A.Wright (Wolves, captain), J.Froggatt (Portsmouth), J.W.Dickinson (Portsmouth), T.Finney (Preston NE), I.A.Broadis (Man City), N.Lofthouse (Bolton W), S.C.Pearson (Man Utd), W.H.Elliott (Burnley).

Gil Merrick and Bill Eckersley combine to keep out an Austrian attack in Vienna in May 1952.

Half-time 0-1   **Full-time 1-1**
Ref: A.Beranek (Austria)   Att: 93,000

THIS first match of England's summer tour turned out to be a very disappointing game with Italy looking the more likely winners. England started well enough and took the lead after only four minutes with a well-taken goal by Ivor Broadis. For the next 25 minutes the visitors bombarded the Italian goal, only to be totally frustrated by an outstanding performance from goalkeeper Moro.

He defied all that England could throw at him and made particularly good saves from Nat Lofthouse and Tom Finney. If England could have added to their early score in this period of intense pressure then they would surely have gone on to a convincing victory.

As it was their missed chances enabled Italy to fight their way back into the game. A minute before half-time Piola missed a golden opportunity to net an equalizer and England still held their lead at the break.

Before the change of ends, Italy had shown their capabilities and in the second half they dominated the game. The England defenders worked overtime to repel the eager Italians and Billy Wright and Jack Froggatt were in outstanding form. However, in the 63rd minute Italy's pressure paid off with Amadei scoring to put his side level.

For the remainder of the match, urged on by their passionate crowd, the home side continually pressed forward. England did make one or two dangerous breakaway raids but neither side could force a winner. For Piola it was the last chance at international level as he made his 34th and last appearance. At 39 years old he had been especially recalled for this game and that missed chance just before half-time ruined the possibility of a glorious ending to his career.

> 6th match v Italy.
> Debut for Elliott.

Austria v England
Friendly

Played on Sunday, 25 May 1952 at the Prater Stadium, Vienna.

Austria: J.Musil (Rapid Wien); R.Röckl (1. Vienna FC), E.Happel (Rapid Wien), W.Schleger (FK Austria), E.Ocwirk (FK Austria), T.Brinek (Wacker Wien), E.Melchior (FK Austria), G.Hanappi (Rapid Wien), R.Dienst (Rapid Wien), A.Huber (FK Austria), W.Haummer (Wacker Wien).

England: G.H.Merrick (Birmingham C); A.E.Ramsey (Spurs), W.Eckersley (Blackburn R), W.A.Wright (Wolves, captain), J.Froggatt (Portsmouth), J.W.Dickinson (Portsmouth), T.Finney (Preston NE), J.Sewell (Sheffield Wed), N.Lofthouse (Bolton W), E.F.Baily (Spurs), W.H. Elliott (Burnley).

Half-time 2-2   **Full-time 2-3**
Ref: G.Carpani (Italy)   65,500

THIS match against probably the best of the current European sides, gave England a famous victory. The game was a personal triumph for their centre-forward Nat Lofthouse. He was outstanding and his performance earned him the nickname of 'The Lion of Vienna'.

A crowd of over 65,000, considerably boosted by the presence of many British soldiers stationed in Austria, saw a thrilling match that often became very rough, especially in the latter stages.

England decided on a tactical plan that allowed the Austrians to attack them continually. They defended in numbers and relied on a positive breakaway or two. From the first such breakaway England scored a fine goal. In a flowing move the ball sped from Eddie Baily to Billy Elliott, on to Jackie Sewell whose centre was met by Nat Lofthouse who thumped it past Musil.

England's joy lasted barely a minute as Austria were then awarded a rather fortunate penalty after Jack Froggatt's

England players discuss tactics during a training session at Eastbourne cricket ground in May 1952, before embarking on their summer tour. From left to right are Eddie Baily, Gil Merrick, Ivor Broadis and Billy Wright.

shoulder charge on Dienst was seen as a foul by the referee. Huber made no mistake with the spot-kick. This sent the crowd wild with delight and the home attacks grew even more fierce.

But the England players held their nerve and on 31 minutes another excellent break gave them a second goal. This time it was Froggatt who set the move going, slipping the ball to Billy Wright. Wright moved forward and released a fine pass through to Sewell who sold a marvellous dummy to the whole Austrian defence before cracking in a fine right-foot shot which left Musil helpless.

Austria were stunned but came back strongly and with only three minutes of the first-half left they scored a superb equalizer. It came from Dienst and was the result of a glorious run and shot giving Gil Merrick no chance.

What followed after the break was probably one of the toughest halves England have ever faced. The Austrians tried to power their way through and the visitors needed all their experience to keep them out.

Then on 82 minutes came a wonderful moment for the English fans present. Once again a swift break paid off as Merrick's kick was flicked on by Tom Finney's head to send Lofthouse scampering away from the half-way line. With the

entire Austrian defence bearing down on him from behind the Bolton star kept his nerve and slipped the ball past Musil as the goalkeeper came out of his goal.

Lofthouse never saw the goal as the defenders had clattered into him as he shot and he had to go off for treatment. But the great-hearted player was soon back and in the last few seconds he came desperately close to a hat-trick when another shot crashed against the bar.

The British soldiers went berserk at the end of the match and chaired the brilliant Lofthouse from the field in their delight. For Lofthouse it was a game he will never forget.

> 8th match v Austria.
> *"The Austria game is the game I remember most, scoring two with one the winner".*
> Nat Lofthouse.

Switzerland v England   Friendly

Played on Wednesday, 28 May 1952 at the Hardturm Sportplatz, Zürich.

Switzerland: T.Priezz (Grasshoppers); W.Kernen (La Chaux de Fonds),

R.Bocquet (Lausanne-Sports), H.Neukom (FC Locarno), O.Eggimann (Servette FC), W.Neukom (Grasshoppers), R.Ballaman (Grasshoppers), J.Hügi (FC Basel), R.Bader (FC Basel), L.Pasteur (Servette FC), J.Fatton (Servette FC).

England: G.H.Merrick (Birmingham C); A.E.Ramsey (Spurs), W.Eckersley (Blackburn R), W.A.Wright (Wolves, captain), J.Froggatt (Portsmouth), J.W.Dickinson (Portsmouth), R.Allen (West Brom), J.Sewell (Sheffield Wed), N.Lofthouse (Bolton W), E.F.Baily (Spurs), T.Finney (Preston NE).

Half-time 0-1   Full-time 0-3

Ref: L.Baert (Belgium)   Att: 32,000

FOR the last match of their 1952 summer tour, England travelled to the beautiful city of Zürich. Here they gained another good result to round off a very successful trip.

On a sultry day, 32,000 people were present to see these two sides meet and they did not have to wait long for the first goal. This came in the 13th minute when new cap Ronnie Allen took a right-wing corner. The ball reached Jackie Sewell, who cleverly lobbed it over Preizz and into the Swiss net. That was the only goal of the first half and England, in control, looked in no mood to surrender their lead.

In fact, six minutes into the second period they increased that lead when Nat Lofthouse followed up his success in Vienna by netting number two.

To round off a competent display by England, the Bolton star added his second and England's third before the end just to emphasise the purple patch he was enjoying.

> 5th match v Switzerland.
> Debut for Allen.

Northern Ireland v England Home Championship

Played on Saturday, 4 October 1952 at Windsor Park, Belfast.

Northern Ireland: W.N.M.C.Uprichard (Swindon T); W.E.Cunningham (St Mirren), A.McMichael (Newcastle Utd), R.D.Blanchflower (Aston Villa), W.Dickson (Chelsea), F.J.McCourt (Man City), W.L.Bingham (Sunderland), S.D.D'Arcy (Chelsea), E.J.McMorran (Barnsley), J.McIlroy (Burnley), C.P.Tully (Celtic).

England: G.H.Merrick (Birmingham C); A.E.Ramsey (Spurs), W.Eckersley (Blackburn R), W.A.Wright (Wolves, captain), J.Froggatt (Portsmouth), J.W.Dickinson (Portsmouth), T.Finney (Preston NE), J.Sewell (Sheffield Wed), N.Lofthouse (Bolton W), E.F.Baily (Spurs), W.H.Elliott (Burnley).

Half-time 1-1   Full-time 2-2
Ref: D.Gerrard (Scotland)   Att: 60,000

AFTER England had done so well on their summer tour, the match in Northern Ireland seemed to be only a formality for their experienced players. But, if that was what they were thinking, they were in for a rude awakening.

Indeed, Ireland came so desperately close to pulling off a famous victory and only a very late goal saved England.

There had been no hint of the impending drama when the record crowd of 60,000 saw England snatch the lead after only ninety seconds. Billy Wright split the Irish defence with a superb long through ball which found Nat Lofthouse, the current 'Golden Boy' of English football. He hit a firm shot wide of the advancing Uprichard to open the scoring.

It set the match up for its seemingly inevitable defeat for the Irish. After all, they had not beaten England since 1927 and results between the countries had taken on a somewhat monotonous similarity.

But this day was somehow different. Soon the powerful Blanchflower and McCourt began to impose their superiority on to the likes of Jackie Sewell and Eddie Baily and suddenly England found the going somewhat tricky.

Bingham and Tully were giving the England full-backs a torrid time with their speed and trickery and it was no more than Ireland deserved when they gained an equalizer on 15 minutes.

Tully, whose footwork kept causing England problems, forced a corner on the left. He took the kick and it curled wickedly in towards Alf Ramsey, who was stood at the near post. The Spurs full-back ducked under the ball, fully expecting Gil Merrick to gather safely. Unfortunately, by the time the goalkeeper reacted, the ball was in the net. It was Ireland's first goal for 18 months and, although bizarre, it was none the less very welcome.

Three nasty injuries added to the list of incidents gradually building up. First Uprichard was injured following a collision with Billy Elliott but he bravely carried on after treatment. Then a nasty clash of heads between McMorran and Jimmy Dickinson ended with both players going off for stitches.

Dickinson was back ten minutes afterwards but McMorran was off until well into the second half. But Ireland were undaunted and a minute after half-time they took the lead amidst unparalleled excitement.

A free-kick by McMichael was flicked on by Blanchflower's head straight to Tully, again, who made no mistake shooting past the partially unsighted Merrick. The crowd sensed that a victory was really possible. McMorran bravely came back on, typifying the Irish spirit and he very nearly wrapped the game up, only to be foiled by a fine save from Merrick.

To England's credit they refused to go completely under and, with Wright and Dickinson once again working tirelessly, they clawed their way back as the game reached its climax. Sewell, Lofthouse and Elliott all went close before, with only three minutes left, they found an equalizer.

Jack Froggatt decided to push his weight forward to help his attack. His pass found Tom Finney, a flick on to Wright and back to Froggatt. The Portsmouth player powerfully beat McCourt before putting over a perfect centre which Elliott headed home firmly.

The drama had been incredible and, although the match was never a classic, it certainly had plenty of incident.

> 60th match v Northern Ireland.

England v Wales Home Championship

Played on Wednesday, 12 November 1952 at Wembley Stadium.

England: G.H.Merrick (Birmingham C); A.E.Ramsey (Spurs), L.Smith (Arsenal), W.A.Wright (Wolves, captain), J.Froggatt (Portsmouth), J.W.Dickinson (Portsmouth), T.Finney (Preston NE), R.Froggatt (Sheffield Wed), N.Lofthouse (Bolton W), R.T.F.Bentley (Chelsea), W.H.Elliott (Burnley).

Wales: W.W.Shortt (Plymouth A); R.F.Stitfall (Cardiff C), A.T.Sherwood (Cardiff C), R.Paul (Man City), R.W.Daniel (Arsenal), W.A.R.Burgess (Spurs), W.I.Foulkes (Newcastle Utd), E.R.Davies (Newcastle Utd), T.Ford (Sunderland), I.J.Allchurch (Swansea T), R.J.Clarke (Man City).

Half-time 3-1   Full-time 5-2
Ref: D.Gerrard (Scotland)   Att: 93,500

FOR the first time, England took their home match with Wales to Wembley. The teams celebrated this event by providing the stadium with a memorable game and a magnificent spectacle for the crowd.

Some 93,500 people paid a record £43,600 and greeted the sides with a tremendous cheer as they strode on to the lush green grass which was bathed in warm sunshine. The white and scarlet jerseys made for a colourful scene and amongst the crowd was the Duke of Edinburgh.

From the start both teams played attacking football. England quickly moved into a smooth flowing rhythm and all their forwards looked dangerous. The passing was swift and accurate and the home side's teamwork became the outstanding feature of the game.

Soon the Welsh defence was struggling and, within ten minutes, England were 2-0 up. The first goal was as a result of a lovely move. Redfern Froggatt began the move with a pass to Nat Lofthouse. He quickly moved it on to Tom Finney, whose centre was touched on by Roy Bentley to Billy Elliott on the left. The Burnley star quickly turned the ball back across goal to find Finney, now in the middle, who shot a fine goal past Shortt.

Shortly afterwards came the second goal. Elliott took a corner on the left and, as the cross came over, Redfern Froggatt cleverly flicked the ball to Lofthouse and the number nine scored from close range.

It looked as though England were going to run up a cricket score but, quite unexpectedly, Wales pulled a goal back after 15 minutes.

Ford, always a real handful for Jack Froggatt, found himself competing with the centre half for a high bouncing ball in the area. Ford won the duel and latched on to it nodding it down with his head before crashing a low shot past Gil Merrick with his right foot.

This put a different complexion on the scoreline and on the half-hour another incident seemed to offer Wales further hope. Again Jack Froggatt and Ford clashed for a 50-50 ball but this time the England player was injured. As he was carried off the crowd thought that it was the last they would see of him in this game. How wrong they all were.

Within ten minutes, he came back on to the field to a tumultuous welcome. His injury meant that he would have to line-up on the left wing, a position he used to play and England reorganised completely to accommodate him. It was quickly obvious the changes were not going to affect their general play.

Redfern Froggatt, Finney and especially Lofthouse were magnificent in restoring England's superiority. Mere words cannot convey the superb contribution of Finney to England's cause and Lofthouse gave his best performance so far in the purple patch that he is in. He gave Daniel a torrid time both in the air and on the ground. Just before half-time, England took a 3-1 lead through an unlikely source.

Finney, turning brilliantly, fired in a shot which was going wide of the far post, that is, until the large figure of Jack Froggatt came from nowhere to dive forward to head home. The roar that greeted the goal must surely have been heard in Cardiff. Incredibly before the break he nearly added another only to be foiled by the legs of Shortt.

England continued with their magical play after half-time. Almost immediately it was 4-1. Another superb Finney,

England players meet the Duke of Gloucester before the game against Belgium at Wembley in November 1952.

Lofthouse combination gave Bentley the chance to shoot a fine goal from twenty yards.

Wales, who all the time played open attractive football, showed their character a minute later by pulling a goal back. Again Ford was on target latching on to a Foulkes shot that bounced off Lionel Smith.

England continued to turn on the style, though, and with 15 minutes left, Lofthouse capped a marvellous performance with a fifth and final goal. His fierce shot from 25 yards was far too hot for Shortt to handle and the ball went in despite the goalkeeper's attempted save.

It had been a memorable match with outstanding performances from many, if not all, of the 22 players.

63rd match v Wales.
First visit to Wembley for Wales.

England v Belgium
Friendly

Played on Wednesday, 26 November 1952 at Wembley Stadium.

England: G.H.Merrick (Birmingham C); A.E.Ramsey (Spurs), L.Smith (Arsenal), W.A.Wright (Wolves, captain), J.Froggatt (Portsmouth), J.W.Dickinson (Portsmouth), T.Finney (Preston NE), R.T.F.Bentley (Chelsea), N.Lofthouse (Bolton W), R.Froggatt (Sheffield Wed), W.H.Elliott (Burnley).

Belgium: F.Boogaerts (Standard Liège); H.Dirickx (Union Bruxelles), A.VanBrandt (SK Lierse), V.Mees (FC Antwerp), L.Carré (FC Liège), R.Maertens (FC Antwerp), V.Lemberechts (KV Mechelen), J.Van der Auwera (RC Mechelen), J.Mermans (RSC Anderlecht), R.Coppens (FC Beerschot), J.Straetmans (White Star Bruxelles).

Half-time 2-0   Full-time 5-0
Ref: L.Horn (Holland)   Att: 65,000

ON a bitterly cold day and, with a pitch covered in icy patches, England produced another fine performance to continue their good run. Belgium became the latest victims of the unbeaten home record against continental sides and they ended the match well beaten.

England's recent good form has coincided with the excellent play of two players in particular. Redfern Froggatt and Nat Lofthouse have been superb with Lofthouse especially the outstanding star of the England side.

The Duke of Gloucester was the VIP guest and he, and the rest of the disappointing crowd of 65,000, enjoyed some sparkling football.

England took the lead early on, a familiar pattern, when Tom Finney fed a lovely pass to Lofthouse. He nodded it down to his right foot before crashing a thunderous drive against the Belgium crossbar. When the rebound came out, Billy Elliott was on hand to hit a firm shot wide of Boogaerts.

From that moment, England rarely lost control. Playing neat and constructive football they continually split the Belgium defence to set up many chances. Roy Bentley missed, so did Finney but, shortly before half-time, the deserved second goal

duly arrived. It was a real beauty.

Redfern Froggatt made another good break, this time down the left. When his centre came over, Finney and Bentley combined well to set up Lofthouse. Again, he fired in a fierce shot, which this time, went in off the crossbar.

Six minutes into the second half, England emphasised their dominance with a third goal. This time Finney sent Bentley away down the left. He carefully measured a lovely cross into the middle where Lofthouse's challenge forced Boogaerts to fumble, allowing Elliott the chance to shoot home from close range as the ball fell loose.

It was all England now and on the hour they scored again. Redfern Froggatt, who had already missed several good chances including a sitter just previously, this time made no mistake when he headed home Finney's free-kick perfectly.

Apart from the occasional break from the hard working Coppens and Mermans, Belgium had little to offer although it must be said that England's defence held together brilliantly to emphasise what a good team performance it had been.

With the second half being played in driving sleet, the conditions were awful but nonetheless the football certainly warmed the crowd. Belgium did make a spirited rally towards the end and at last gave Gil Merrick something to warm him up. But the final word had to come from that man Lofthouse.

He rose superbly to head in Bentley's precise cross to round off a fine performance and another excellent result.

13th match v Belgium.

Nat Lofthouse's shot goes in off the crossbar for England's second goal at Wembley and the Belgian defence can do nothing about it.

England v Scotland Home Championship

Played on Saturday, 18 April 1953 at Wembley Stadium.

England: G.H.Merrick (Birmingham C); A.E.Ramsey (Spurs), L.Smith (Arsenal), W.A.Wright (Wolves, captain), M.W.Barrass (Bolton W), J.W.Dickinson (Portsmouth), T.Finney (Preston NE), I.A.Broadis (Newcastle Utd), N.Lofthouse (Bolton W), R.Froggatt (Sheffield Wed), J.Froggatt (Portsmouth).

Scotland: G.N.Farm (Blackpool); G.L.Young (Rangers), S.Cox (Rangers), T.H.Docherty (Preston NE), F.Brennan (Newcastle Utd), D.Cowie (Dundee), T.Wright (Sunderland), R.Johnstone (Hibernian), L.Reilly (Hibernian), W.Steel (Dundee), W.Liddell (Liverpool).

Half-time 1-0   **Full-time 2-2**

Ref: T.Mitchell (Northern Ireland)

Att: 97,000

THE run of Scottish success at Wembley has now stretched for 19 years continuing with this highly deserved draw. Ever since 1934, Scotland had been able to pride themselves at not being beaten at England's premier stadium. Certainly an England win would have been a travesty. For, although they always created the more clear-cut openings, Scotland's courage and spirit deserved nothing less than a draw. Let the story unfold.

The early exchanges had seen both sides push forward. Docherty and Cowie were setting a high standard with their industry in midfield and Billy Wright and Jimmy Dickinson were having to battle hard. Tom Finney was weaving some good runs

Billy Wright introduces Alf Ramsey to Lord Alexander of Tunis before the game against Scotland at Wembley in April 1953.

Scotland skipper George Young and goalkeeper George Farm are helpless to prevent Ivor Broadis regaining England's lead.

on the right but the visitors were having slightly the better of things in this spell. It therefore came as a big surprise when England scored in the 19th minute.

Finney conjured up some wonderful magic as he twisted his way infield past Steel, Cowie and Cox before sending Ivor Broadis through the middle with an inch perfect pass. The number-eight switched the ball from right foot to left foot under pressure from Brennan before unleashing a thunderbolt wide of the diving Farm.

Although Redfern Froggatt could twice have increased England's lead, both times missing when in a one against one situation, Scotland, too, had their moments.

One amazing escape came when Malcolm Barrass and Lionel Smith somehow kept Johnstone's shot out after Gil Merrick had dropped a free-kick from Young. It was in fact the long leg of Smith that retrieved the danger. Then, a minute before the interval, Steel's cross-shot hit the bar and bounced down for Barrass to, once again, come to the rescue.

Barrass had held Reilly well in the first half but, with Steel's increasing influence beginning to stretch the home defence, the England centre-half began to struggle later on.

In the 55th minute, Scotland at last gained that elusive equalizer. The England defence was all at sea as Johnstone's powerful shot again hit the bar but this time Reilly was quickly on to the rebound to crash the ball home. The goal was no more than Scotland deserved and had come from a splendid move involving Cox, Cowie, Docherty and Steel.

Cowie was having a tremendous match and after the goal the tempo of the whole game began to rise. England still created chances though. Soon Jack Froggatt joined his cousin in missing a good chance, allowing Farm to save his shot after he raced clear on to a Nat Lofthouse pass. Broadis, too, missed a fine chance but made up for it in the 17th minute when he scored a superb goal.

Wright sent Broadis away just inside his own half. A long dribble ended with a square pass to Finney. The Preston player

suddenly moved into second gear and with a breathtaking piece of footwork, a slight feint and a change of pace, left Cox in his wake before finally pulling back a diagonal pass to Broadis again who hit home a low first-time shot. Cox was left writhing in agony after his attempted tackle on Finney and, sadly, his injury meant he had to leave the field.

Losing 2-1 and a man short, it seemed curtains for Scotland. But their national pride and passion would not allow them to give in. Docherty, Cowie, Steel and Young rolled up their sleeves and worked even harder to inspire their colleagues to greater heights. Steel and Liddell forced full-length saves from Merrick as England wavered under the onslaught. But with only 30 seconds remaining, the tide of the blue shirts finally gained their reward.

Good passing between Johnstone and Reilly split the English defence wide open and it ended with the centre-forward hitting the roof of the home net with a fierce shot. It was no more than Scotland deserved.

70th match v Scotland.

Argentina v England
Friendly

Played on Sunday, 17 May 1953 at the Estadio Antonio Liberti 'Monumental', Buenos Aires (abandoned (0-0) after 25 minutes due to torrential rain).

Argentina: J.Musimessi (Boca Juniors); P.Dellacha (Racing Club), G.Perez (Racing Club), E.Mouriño (Boca Juniors), F.Lombardo (Boca Juniors), E.Guttierez (Racing Club), C.Michelli (Independiente), R.Cecconato (Independiente), C.Lacasa (Independiente), E.Grillo (Independiente), O.Cruz (Independiente).

England: G.H.Merrick (Birmingham C); A.E.Ramsey (Spurs), W.Eckersley (Blackburn), W.A.Wright (Wolves, captain), H.Johnston (Blackpool), J.W.Dickinson (Portsmouth), T.Finney (Preston NE), I.A.Broadis (Newcastle Utd), N.Lofthouse (Bolton W), T.Taylor (Man Utd), J.J.Berry (Man Utd).

Ref: A.Ellis (England)   Att: 85,000

THE summer tour of 1953 saw England venture to the far off lands of South America but in their first match they experienced a monsoon! Torrential rain forced the referee to end proceedings in the 25th minute after the pitch became unplayable.

The England officials tried desperately to rearrange the game, asking if they could replay it in the next three days. Unfortunately, their Argentine counterparts would not agree, stating that the pitch 'would not be ready for at least five days'. So, England moved on to Chile.

For two England debutants, Tommy Taylor and Johnny Berry, it had certainly been a memorable first game but, for all the wrong reasons!

2nd match v Argentina.
Debuts for Taylor and Berry.

Chile v England
Friendly

Played on Sunday, 24 May 1953 in the National Stadium, Santiago.

Chile: S.Livingstone (Universidad Catolica); M.Alvarez (Santiago W), G.Nuñez (Everton, Viña del Mar), P.Cortez (Colo Colo), A.Farias (Colo Colo), C.Rojas (Universidad Catolica), H.Carrasco (Colo Colo), A.Cremaschi (Union Española), J.Melendez (Colo Colo), M.Muñoz (Colo Colo), G.Diaz (Santiago W).

England: G.H.Merrick (Birmingham C); A.E.Ramsey (Spurs), W.Eckersley (Blackburn R), W.A.Wright (Wolves), H.Johnston (Blackpool), J.W.Dickinson (Portsmouth), T.Finney (Preston NE), I.A.Broadis (Newcastle Utd), N.Lofthouse (Bolton W), T.Taylor (Man Utd), J.J.Berry (Man Utd).

Half-time 0-0   **Full-time 1-2**

Ref: A.Ellis (England)   Att: 70,000

FULLY two hours before the start of this eagerly awaited clash, 70,000 people were

England's line-up for the game against Uruguay in Montevideo in May 1953. Back row (left to right): Ramsey, Johnston, Wright (making his 50th appearance), Merrick, Dickinson, Eckersley. Front row: Finney, Broadis, Lofthouse, Taylor, Berry.

packed into the National Stadium, Santiago to see their favourites take on the mighty England.

As anticipated, Chile began well as their crowd got behind them but there was little punch in their attack. England, on the other hand, were dangerous on the break, although the blank scoresheet at half-time reflected a poorish game.

Chile had Rojas injured before the interval and he did not reappear immediately when the game restarted. He had still not appeared when, in the 48th minute, Tommy Taylor opened his England scoring account to give his team the lead.

Rojas then came back on the field but, after 68 minutes, England increased their lead with a goal by Nat Lofthouse. Chile came back and, with 12 minutes to go, Rojas completed an eventful match for him by pulling a goal back. His shot took a deflection off of Alf Ramsey leaving Gil Merrick helpless.

There were no more real scares for England before the end and they were able to celebrate a good victory.

2nd match v Chile.
First full match for Taylor, so arguably a debut goal.

Uruguay v England
Friendly

Played on Sunday, 31 May 1953 at the Centenary Stadium, Montevideo.

Uruguay: R.Máspoli (Peñarol);
M.Gonzáles (Cerro), W.Martínez (Rampla Juniors), R.Andrade (Peñarol), N.Carballo (Nacional), L.Cruz (Nacional), J.Abbadie (Peñarol), J.Schiaffino (Peñarol), O.Miguez (Peñarol), J.Pérez (Nacional), B.Cabrera (Rampla Juniors).
England: G.H.Merrick (Birmingham C); A.E.Ramsey (Spurs), W.Eckersley (Blackburn R), W.A.Wright (Wolves, captain), H.Johnston (Blackpool), J.W.Dickinson (Portsmouth), T.Finney (Preston NE), I.A.Broadis (Newcastle Utd), N.Lofthouse (Bolton W), T.Taylor (Man Utd), J.J.Berry (Man Utd).

Half-time 1-0 Full-time 2-1
Ref: A.Ellis (England)   Att: 80,000

ENGLAND faced a formidable match on the last leg of their South American tour when they took on the current World Champions, Uruguay. Having won the trophy in 1950 they were now eagerly building a side to defend it in Switzerland the following year and emphasised their power.

England were desperately unlucky before the match. After the Chile game many of the party were struck down by stomach upsets and some of the players looked barely fit enough to play. Nevertheless they battled bravely and to only lose by the odd goal in three was no disgrace.

Uruguay took the lead after 27 minutes. Abbadie cut in from the right wing to fire low, hard and accurately from 20 yards leaving Gil Merrick well beaten. The crowd went wild with delight and fireworks were let off all around the stadium, a frighteningly new experience for some

of the younger players of this England team.

The England attack was always struggling and never really got going. Nat Lofthouse, especially, was a pale shadow of his normal self. Having said that England did have their moments. Tommy Taylor and Tom Finney almost got through and Uruguay occasionally had to hang on desperately to their lead. England had no luck at all especially when both Lofthouse and Ivor Broadis hit the inside of the Uruguayans' upright with shots that deserved a better reward.

In the 60th minute, Uruguay stretched their lead. Cabrera, out on the left, centred perfectly for Miguez to head wide of the despairing Merrick. Five minutes later Abbadie missed a sitter, shooting over from close range.

At this stage Uruguay were in control, continually beating England for possession. But all credit to the tiring visitors as they refused to give up and they gained some deserved consolation in the last minute when Taylor pulled a goal back.

1st match v Uruguay.
50th cap for Wright.

USA v England
Friendly

Played on Monday, 8 June 1953 at the Yankee Stadium, New York City.

USA: I.I.Moore (New York Americans); R.Milne (New York Americans), H.Keough (St Louis FC), T.Springthorpe

(New York Americans), R.Decker (New York Hakoah), W.Bahr (Philadelphia Nationals), T.Schultz (St Louis FC), M.Connolly (Brook-Halton, New York), G.Atheneos (Eintracht, New York), B.McLaughlin (Philadelphia Nationals), I.Chakhuryan (Swiss FC, New York).
Sub: O.Decker (New York Hakoah) for Schultz.
England: E.G.Ditchburn (Spurs); A.E.Ramsey (Spurs), W.Eckersley (Blackburn R), W.A.Wright (Wolves, captain), H.Johnston (Blackpool), J.W.Dickinson (Portsmouth), T.Finney (Preston NE), I.A.Broadis (Newcastle Utd), N.Lofthouse (Bolton W), R.Froggatt (Sheffield Wed), J.Froggatt (Portsmouth).

Half-time 0-1   Full-time 3-6

Ref: S.Gallin (USA)   Att: 10,000

THE last match of England's 1953 summer tour was scheduled to be played on Sunday the 7th of June but due to a spell of torrential rain, the game was postponed. It was rearranged for the following night and was played under the floodlights of the Yankee Stadium. This was a new experience for the England players and may have had something to do with the fact that they took so long to break down a stubborn home defence.

There were shades of the infamous 1950 World Cup game between the two sides as England, always far superior in technique and skills, missed chance after chance. Goalkeeper Moore worked overtime and the American goal led a charmed life. Finally though with two minutes of the first-half left Ivor Broadis broke the deadlock by hooking home a pass from Tom Finney.

The second half was a different story as England relaxed to play some controlled football. Within minutes of the restart Nat Lofthouse scored number two and Finney quickly added a third to build up a commanding lead. The Americans gamely fought on and their side, which included several players who had had English League experience, pulled a goal back when the lively substitute O.Decker, who came on for the injured Schultz, shot past Ted Ditchburn. That goal came in the 61st minute but a minute later Lofthouse scored again to quash the fightback, or at least, so England thought.

To everyone's astonishment the referee then gave the USA another chance by awarding them a penalty for a highly dubious handball against Harry Johnston. Atheneos converted the gift and three minutes later O.Decker scored again to really set the game alight.

But England were in no mood to allow a repeat of that 1950 fiasco and they quickly regained control. Finney, who had been much more direct in this half, scored England's fifth goal and with ten minutes to go Redfern Froggatt sealed victory with number six.

The tour of the Americas had certainly been an eventful trip with many things learned. It was an experience that the players would never forget.

> 2nd match v USA.

Wales v England   Home Championship

Played on Saturday, 10 October 1953 at Ninian Park, Cardiff.

Wales: R.G.Howells (Cardiff C); W.Barnes (Arsenal), A.T.Sherwood (Cardiff C), R.Paul (Man City), R.W.Daniel (Sunderland), W.A.R. Burgess (Spurs), W.I.Foulkes (Newcastle Utd), E.R.Davies (Newcastle Utd), W.N.Charles (Leeds Utd), I.J.Allchurch (Swansea T), R.J.Clarke (Man City).
England: G.H.Merrick (Birmingham C); T.Garrett (Blackpool), W.Eckersley (Blackburn R), W.A.Wright (Wolves, captain), H.Johnston (Blackpool), J.W.Dickinson (Portsmouth), T.Finney (Preston NE), A.Quixall (Sheffield Wed), N.Lofthouse (Bolton W), D.J.Wilshaw (Wolves), J.J.Mullen (Wolves).

Half-time 1-1   Full-time 1-4

Ref: C.Faultless (Scotland)   Att: 61,000

SO often since the war, England have received adverse criticism after a clear win. Once again they found themselves in that situation after this visit to Cardiff, for although the scoreline looks healthy enough, the England performance in getting there was far from convincing.

With the Home Championship being used to determine Great Britain's entry for the following year's World Cup, there was extra importance on this match. Ninian Park was bulging at the seams as 61,000 people packed into the ground. Before the play started they set the atmosphere tingling by singing their hearts out as only Welshmen can.

For the first half-hour it was one-way traffic towards Gil Merrick's goal. Wales put in a storming start and at the heart of all their good play was the mighty Charles. He was magnificent! Three times he forced superb saves from the England goalkeeper with bullet-like headers and he continually had the England defenders struggling. The pressure had to tell eventually and in the 23rd minute it did.

More good play by Charles set up the goal. Combining well with Davies he sent the ball in for Allchurch to fire a good shot past Merrick, who for once was well beaten. Things looked good for the Welsh but just before the end of the first half the tide suddenly, and undeservedly, began to turn against them. First they lost Sherwood with an injury and then, in the last minute of the half, conceded an equalizer. A free-kick, given against Burgess, was curled into the box by Albert Quixall and Dennis Wilshaw popped up to head home.

The half-time score was a total travesty of the events of the half and Wales could hardly believe it. Within seven minutes after the restart they were stunned into defeat!

With England having been kept in the match by Merrick's saves in the first 45 minutes, they now turned to the lively Jimmy Mullen to spark the response at the other end. The Wolves winger began to tease Barnes with his pace and body swerve.

Four minutes into the second period he took a pass from Bill Eckersley and centred for Wilshaw to score his and England's second goal. A minute later Mullen again was involved, linking well with Wilshaw before the latter's cross was headed in by Nat Lofthouse.

Sherwood then came back on to a huge roar but hardly had the cheers died down when England amazingly scored a fourth goal. Again Lofthouse was the scorer and

again Mullen was the provider. So, in the space of nine minutes either side of the interval, England had completely sewn up the result.

The Welsh crowd were stunned into an eerie silence now and England comfortably controlled most of the remaining time. However, the visitors still had some obvious problems and large question-marks still hung over the inside-forwards, full-backs and centre-half. Quixall often looked bemused in his first game and Wilshaw also struggled despite his two goals which probably earned him another chance. Even Tom Finney looked well below par and England must surely have looked for an improvement in their next match.

> 64th match v Wales.
> Debuts for Quixall and Wilshaw and two debut goals for Wilshaw.

England v Rest of Europe   Friendly

Played on Wednesday, 21 October 1953 at Wembley Stadium.

England: G.H.Merrick (Birmingham C); A.E.Ramsey (Spurs), W.Eckersley (Blackburn R), W.A.Wright (Wolves, captain), D.G.Ufton (Charlton A), J.W.Dickinson (Portsmouth), S.Matthews (Blackpool), S.H.Mortensen (Blackpool), N.Lofthouse (Bolton W), A.Quixall (Sheffield Wed), J.Mullen (Wolves).
Rest of Europe: W.Zeman (Rapid Wien & Austria); J.Navarro (Real Madrid & Spain), G.Hanappi (Rapid Wein & Austria), Z.Čajkovski (Partizan Belgrade & Yugoslavia), J.Posipal (Hamburger SV & West Germany), E.Ocwirk (FK Austria Wein & Austria), G.Boniperti (Juventus & Italy), L.Kubala (FC Barcelona & Spain), G.Nordahl (Milan AC & Sweden), B.Vukas (Hajduk Split & Yugoslavia), B.Zebec (Partizan Belgrade & Yugoslavia).
Sub: V.Beara (Hadjuk Split & Yugoslavia) for Zeman.

Half-time 2-3   Full-time 4-4

Ref: B.M.Griffiths (Wales)   Att: 97,000

THIS superb match was arranged to celebrate the 90th anniversary of the Football Association and although the Rest of Europe side was somewhat of a makeshift eleven, the two teams produced a suitably memorable occasion. In fact the visitors almost ended England's proud record of never losing to a continental side on home soil. It was magnificent entertainment and the 97,000 crowd thrilled to the superior skills of the Europe team.

They were also thrilled by the never-say-die spirit of the England lads. Three times they came back from being behind and it all culminated in one of the most exciting climaxes that this famous old stadium had ever seen.

From the start it was obvious that England were going to struggle. The silky skills of Kubala, Vukas and Zebec constantly exposed the home defenders. Alf Ramsey and Bill Eckersley looked particularly vulnerable and the FIFA team should have done more with their superiority. The different styles quickly gelled and the Europeans pushed the ball around

England pictured at Stamford Bridge on the eve of the game against the Rest of Europe in October 1953. Back row (left to right): Mullen, Ramsey, Ufton, Merrick, Dickinson, Eckersley. Front row: Matthews, Mortensen, Wright, Lofthouse, Quixall.

Lord Montgomery meets the England team before they take on the Rest of Europe.

in short sharp bursts, creating many openings and spreading panic through the England ranks.

England got off to a dreadful start by conceding a first-minute penalty. Hanappi sent a lovely through pass for Vukas who was clear of the defence. Eckersley, chased back but his despairing tackle succeeded only in giving Kubala the chance to score from the resultant spot-kick.

Three minutes later England hit back.

Playing their usual long ball game they put together a fine move as a lovely reverse pass by Nat Lofthouse sent Stan Mortensen galloping clear through the middle. The Blackpool star moved forward confidently before hitting a great cross shot wide of Zeman to equalize. Although that goal levelled the scores, the Rest of Europe side were putting some tremendous play together and on 15 minutes deservedly regained the lead.

This time superb play between Ocwirk

and Nordahl gave Zebec the chance to get past Ramsey and then centre for Boniperti to cut inside and crash home number two. The same player then repeated his strike in the 39th minute cutting in past Eckersley to fire home after another good pass from Vukas.

England, 3-1 down and fighting for their lives, were then given a gift two minutes before half-time. A terrible mix-up between Navarro and Zeman gave Jimmy Mullen the chance to pull a goal back. Zeman had struggled against the England crosses and was once saved by his crossbar after a Stan Matthews centre had beaten him.

After the break the goalkeeper was replaced by Beara of Yugoslavia, much to the annoyance of the England players. Matthews had been England's star of the half and although Hanappi contributed much to the visitor's attack, defensively he never lived with the Blackpool star.

The undoubted fighting spirit of the England players shone through brightly early in the second half when they forced another equalizer. A splendid dribble and centre by the irrepressible Matthews found Mullen running in at the far post to shoot home. Mortensen then hit a post as play swung from end to end and the Rest of Europe missed several good chances before both Mortensen and Lofthouse inexplicably missed with headers. The match was on a knife edge.

With 25 minutes to go Zebec popped up on the right wing. His centre was met by a tremendous Kubala left-foot shot which flew into the top corner with Gil

Stan Mortensen scores England's first goal against the Rest of Europe.

Jimmy Mullen beats a stranded Zeman to hit England's second against the FIFA team.

Alf Ramsey's last-minute penalty which earned England a 4-4 draw.

Merrick groping helplessly. It looked all over with only Matthews and occasionally Mortensen looking likely to pull the game out of the fire. Only a desperate dive by Merrick prevented Kubala adding another goal with the 'keeper just managing to get a touch on to the post after a fierce cross shot.

But then, just as it seemed that the record had gone, England summoned up one last determined effort. With only seconds remaining, a burst by Mortensen was ended by Čajkovski's clumsy challenge and the referee awarded a penalty. Imagine what must have been going through Ramsey's mind as he stepped up to take the kick. He showed no nerves though and he confidently crashed the ball into the net to end a tremendous afternoon's football.

> 2nd match v a FIFA XI (England beat the Rest of Europe 3-0 at Arsenal Stadium in October 1938, in a match to celebrate the 75th anniversary of the FA).
> Debut for Ufton.
> Penalty for Ramsey.

England v Home Championship
Northern Ireland

Played on Wednesday, 11 November 1953 at Goodison Park, Everton.

England: G.H.Merrick (Birmingham C); S.Rickaby (West Brom) W.Eckersley (Blackburn R), W.A.Wright (Wolves, captain), H.Johnston (Blackpool), J.W.Dickinson (Portsmouth), S.Matthews (Blackpool), A.Quixall (Sheffield Wed), N.Lofthouse (Bolton W), H.W.Hassall (Bolton W), J.Mullen (Wolves).
Northern Ireland: W.Smyth (Distillery); W.G.L.Graham (Doncaster R), A.McMichael (Newcastle Utd), R.D.Blanchflower (Aston Villa), W.Dickson (Arsenal), W.W.Cush (Glenavon), W.L.Bingham (Sunderland), J.McIlroy (Burnley), W.J.Simpson (Rangers), E.J.McMorran (Doncaster R), N.Lockhart (Aston Villa).

Half-time 1-0   Full-time 3-1
Ref: R.Smith (Wales)   Att: 70,000

BY winning this match England duly qualified for the World Cup finals to be held in June of the following year in Switzerland, but their performance on the day would not send too many fears to the other competing nations.

It was a poor game with the Irish showing up better than England for long spells. With their wing-halves, Blanchflower and Cush, dominating the midfield battle, they should have capitalised on their superiority. As it was, they were given a lesson in finishing.

Even a gift goal for England after only 30 seconds could not inspire the home side. A cross shot by Harold Hassall seemed easy for Smyth but the goalkeeper unaccountably allowed the ball to squirm under his body and into the net. Having been given that terrific start, it was disappointing to see England fail to build on it. Their team play was non-existent and there was no cohesion in their performance. Not so Northern Ireland!

With Blanchflower outstanding and McIlroy, Cush and Bingham working

tirelessly, they came back strongly. Alas, their finishing was poor although credit must go to the excellent defensive play of Harry Johnston, Jimmy Dickinson and Gil Merrick. At the other end, Smyth made up for his earlier blunder by pulling off a thrilling point-blank save from Hassall. But that was an isolated raid by England and they were somewhat fortunate to see their lead still intact at the half-time whistle.

Nine minutes after the interval, though, Northern Ireland deservedly equalized. Bingham sent over a right-wing cross and McMorran headed past Merrick. The goalkeeper was a little unlucky as the ball rebounded off his body and into the net but it was no more than the Irish deserved.

From that moment, England had to turn to the one saving grace of their day. Once again it was the incomparable Stanley Matthews who shone like a beacon on the dull afternoon's proceedings. His footwork was superb and he wandered into the middle to test all the Irish defenders.

It was Matthews who began the move on the hour that gave England the lead again. A lovely piece of trickery ended with a pass to Billy Wright. The captain moved down the right wing before crossing for Hassall to head a fine goal from 15 yards into the top corner.

A quarter of an hour later England made the game safe with a third goal. This time Jimmy Mullen was the provider as his long centre was crashed into the net by the head of Nat Lofthouse. After the goal, both Lofthouse and Smyth left the field injured. Lofthouse, already limping, had hurt his head and Smyth left the action with a broken nose.

Dickson took over in goal for the Irish but was not seriously troubled in the remaining minutes. It was a case for Ireland to reflect on their missed chances of the first half especially, whilst for England only Matthews, Johnston, Dickinson and Merrick could be satisfied with their display.

> 61st match v Northern Ireland.
> Debut for Rickaby.

England v
Hungary   Friendly

Played on Wednesday, 25 November 1953 at Wembley Stadium.

England: G.H.Merrick (Birmingham C); A.E.Ramsey (Spurs), W.Eckersley (Blackburn R), W.A.Wright (Wolves, captain), H.Johnston (Blackpool), J.W.Dickinson (Portsmouth), S.Matthews (Blackpool), E.Taylor (Blackpool), S.H.Mortensen (Blackpool), J.Sewell (Sheffield Wed), G.Robb (Spurs).
Hungary: G.Grosics (Honvéd); J.Buzánszky (Dorogi), M.Lantos (MTK Budapest), J.Bozsik (Honvéd), G.Lóránt (Honvéd), J.Zakariás (MTK Budapest), L.Budai (Honvéd), S.Kocsis (Honvéd), N.Hidegkuti (MTK Budapest), F.Puskás (Honvéd), Z.Czibor (Honvéd).
Sub: Gellér (MTK Budapest) for Grosics.

Half-time 2-4   Full-time 3-6
Ref: L.Horn (Holland)   Att: 100,000
THERE can be no words to adequately describe the feelings of the 100,000 people

present at Wembley Stadium on this dull and grey November afternoon. The game, which will be talked about for as long as football is played, produced one of the most exciting and breathtaking team performances the world has ever seen.

The disappointment that was felt by England, at last losing their long and distinguished unbeaten home record against foreign opposition, was certainly tempered by the knowledge that the record was finally taken by such a superb team. The current Olympic champions were simply magnificent!

Hungary tore through the home defence almost at will and the goal tally in no way flattered them. Indeed, England had a rude awakening to the true realities of world football. Many regular supporters had realised before the game that the writing had been on the wall for some time. Recent performances had not been good but the sheer devastation of this result will take some getting over.

Hungary scored after only 60 seconds. A forceful burst by Bozsik, Zakariás and Hidegkuti ended with the centre-forward selling the England defence a perfect dummy before crashing home a fierce shot.

England were stunned and never fully recovered. To be fair they did have their moments and they equalized after 15 minutes play. Just before that goal, though, Hungary produced a brilliant move between Czibor and the marvellous Puskás which was finished off by Hidegkuti. Thankfully, from England's point of view, it was disallowed by the Dutch referee for offside, but if it had counted it would have been one of the greatest goals ever. As it was, England came away and somehow snatched an equalizer.

This too came following a splendid move. Harry Johnston picked the ball up in his own half and fed a good pass forward for Stan Mortensen to run on to. He, in turn, found Jackie Sewell and the inside-left scored with a lovely left-foot shot wide of the diving Grosics. Any thoughts England had of victory were soon nipped in the bud as within 13 devastating minutes Hungary had forged a 4-1 lead.

They ripped open the heart of the England defence with some scintillating football. On 20 minutes superb play by Puskás, Czibor and Kocsis gave Hidegkuti the chance to score from close range. Straight after that, Kocsis sent Czibor away down the right. Bill Eckersley had no answer to his skills and the winger passed inside to Puskás. The podgy inside-forward then produced a piece of sheer magic, a drag back that totally fooled Billy Wright, and enabled him to drill home a ferocious left-foot shot into the roof of the net between Gil Merrick and the near post.

Minutes later, Bozsik took a free-kick and the ball flew past Merrick off of Puskás' heel. England were in total disarray, having no answer to the cherry red shirted marvels. To their credit and mainly due to the skills of Stanley Matthews and Mortensen they managed a slight rally which brought them a second goal. George Robb forced Grosics into a spectacular save and then Mortensen sped through after receiving a throw-in to score with a glorious shot. The crowd rose to that goal and it was reminiscent of earlier glory days of English football.

Top: Billy Wright and Ferenc Puskás lead out the teams for the game against Hungary at Wembley in November 1953. *Bottom left:* Grosics watches the ball enter his net after Jackie Sewell's equalizer. *Bottom right:* Grosics is again unhappy after Mortensen scores England's second, but the Hungarians still romped home.

Alas, it was the only glimpse the crowd would get this day of England at their best as after the break the Hungarians put the finishing touch to their famous victory. Only ten minutes of the second-half had gone when the score was 6-2. First Boszik hit a tremendous rising shot for number five and then Hidegkuti completed his personal treble when he volleyed home after a lob by Puskás.

Although England had the last say in the goalscoring they never looked like producing the miracle they needed to come back from such a scoreline. The final goal came from the penalty spot after

Mortensen was brought down on the hour. Alf Ramsey was the scorer.

England's proud record was shattered. They were beaten in every aspect of the game and history must now be rewritten. Hungary had everything and their game was made up of long and short passing with absolutely lethal finishing. The capacity crowd would never forget them.

6th match v Hungary.
Debuts for Taylor and Robb.
Penalty by Ramsey.
First home defeat by Continental opposition.

Scotland v England Home Championship

Played on Saturday, 3 April 1954 at Hampden Park, Glasgow.

Scotland: G.N.Farm (Blackpool); M.Haughney (Celtic), S.Cox (Rangers), R.Evans (Celtic), F.Brennan (Newcastle Utd), G.G.Aitken (Sunderland), J.A.McKenzie (Partick T), R.Johnstone (Hibernian, J.G.Henderson (Portsmouth), A.D.Brown (Blackpool), W.E.Ormond (Hibernian).

England: G.H.Merrick (Birmingham C);

R.Staniforth (Huddersfield), R.W.Byrne (Man Utd), W.A.Wright (Wolves, captain), H.A.Clarke (Spurs), J.W.Dickinson (Portsmouth), T.Finney (Preston NE), I.A.Broadis (Newcastle Utd), R.Allen (West Brom), J.Nicholls (West Brom), J.Mullen (Wolves).

Half-time 1-1   Full-time 2-4
Ref: T.Mitchell (Northern Ireland)

Att: 134,554

ONCE again the incredible sequence of results between these countries continued with England winning at Hampden. With Scotland's record at Wembley almost as good as England's was in Glasgow, perhaps there was a case for the two sides swapping grounds!

England, still reeling from the devastating defeat at the hands of Hungary at Wembley the previous November, made eight changes for this game. Four new caps were brought in and there were other changes, too. There was an awful lot at stake as the winners of this match gained automatic entry into the 1954 World Cup finals to be held in Switzerland.

The big difference between the sides on this day was in the taking of chances. In this department England gave Scotland a lesson.

A massive crowd of over 134,000 people roared Scotland on in the early stages and the England defenders clung on desperately as chance after chance went begging for the Scots. After three minutes Gil Merrick made a superb save from a point-blank shot by Johnstone. Then Jimmy Dickinson was very relieved to see his attempted clearance slice just wide of his own goal.

Shortly afterwards, Brown missed a golden opportunity, shooting tamely at Merrick after breaking clear of the England defence. The pressure eventually told, though, and after seven minutes Scotland took the lead.

McKenzie sent over a corner which found Brown and, with the aid of a deflection off Ron Staniforth, his shot found the net. The crowd went wild and were baying for the heads of the Auld Enemy. But amongst the new faces in the England side there was also the experience of Billy Wright and Dickinson. Between them they coolly went about steadying the ship.

They were given a boost in the 15th minute when England equalized, and a real gem it was too. Staniforth found Wright with a good pass. The captain moved the ball on to Tom Finney, who was beginning to get the better of Cox. The Preston player sent an inch-perfect pass forward right into the stride of Ivor Broadis. The inside-forward drew Farm from goal before firing a good shot wide of the goalkeeper.

For the remainder of the half Scotland had the better of things but continued to miss chances. They were missing the lively Reilly up front and failed to exploit Harry Clarke's obvious weaknesses to the full. The fact that the scores were still level at the break flattered England somewhat but after half-time the visitors made Scotland pay for their lack of finishing.

Five minutes after the restart England gained the lead they were not to lose. Again Finney was the star of the move. Wright again found the winger with his pass from defence and Finney set off on

a mazy dribble that left Cox chasing shadows. When the cross came over Johnny Nicholls dived full length to head home.

Cox was now being given the run-around and the link up that Finney had with Broadis was beginning to dominate. Ronnie Allen too, looked very good with his deep-lying role and sharp pace. Nicholls though was not as promising despite his goal. He missed two good chances before England increased their lead in the 70th minute. This time a deep free-kick by Jimmy Mullen was fiercely headed in by Allen. Near the end England wrapped up the result with a goal which typified the way the game had gone.

Scotland, once again, were pressing hard. A corner from the right was cleared by Nicholls to Finney, who set off on another superb run. Poor Cox was sent in many different directions before Finney crossed for Mullen to head number four. Scotland, bewildered but battling to the end, did score again in the dying seconds. A swirling cross by Ormond completely deceived both Merrick and Roger Byrne on the goal-line to drop into the net.

So, a win for England and although the game was never a classic, it had many memorable moments.

> 71st match v Scotland.
> Debuts for Staniforth, Byrne, Clarke and Nicholls.
> Debut goal for Nicholls.

Yugoslavia v England   Friendly

Played on Sunday, 16 May 1954 at the Partisan Stadium, Belgrade.

Yugoslavia: V.Beara (Hajduk Split); B.Stankovič (Red Star Belgrade), T.Crnkovič (Dinamo Zagreb), Z.Čajkovski (Partizan Belgrade), S.Milovanov (Vojvodina Novi Sad), B.Boškov (Vojvodina Novi Sad), M.Milutinovič (Partizan Belgrade), R.Mitič (Red Star Belgrade), B.Vukas (Hajduk Split), S.Bobek (Partizan Belgrade),

D.Dvornič (Dinamo Zagreb). Sub: Zebec (Partizan Belgrade) for Dvornič.
England: G.H.Merrick (Birmingham C); R.Staniforth (Huddersfield T), R.W.Byrne (Man Utd), W.A.Wright (Wolves, captain), S.W.Owen (Luton T), J.W.Dickinson (Portsmouth), T.Finney (Preston NE), I.A.Broadis (Newcastle Utd), R.Allen (West Brom), J.Nicholls (West Brom), J.Mullen (Wolves).

Half-time 0-0   Full-time 1-0
Ref: E.Steiner (Austria)   Att: 59,000

AS a build-up for the forthcoming World Cup, England embarked on a short continental tour with games against formidable opponents Yugoslavia and Hungary.

The first of these games took place in front of a capacity crowd who saw a desperate defensive performance by England which almost succeeded but was dealt a bitter blow just three minutes from the end.

It was certainly a day of celebrations for the Yugoslavs. They won both this game plus a 'B' international played in Ljubljana. That match was won by 2-1 with Bedford Jezzard scoring England's consolation goal.

The match here was virtually dominated by the home side throughout with England relying on the occasional swift breakaway to try and catch out the Yugoslav defenders. The England honours were almost totally confined to the defenders. Billy Wright was an inspirational skipper who worked tirelessly and defended magnificently.

Roger Byrne, Ron Staniforth, Jimmy Dickinson and especially Sid Owen also came out with much credit but for the rest it was a disappointing story.

Ivor Broadis tried hard to get his forwards moving as a unit but too often Ronnie Allen was left to plough a lonely furrow down the middle. Always he met the daunting figure of Milovanov who was outstanding and dominated at the heart of the Yugoslav defence. Most of England's best efforts came in the first half

Players take a stroll along the front at Eastbourne in May 1954, before England's close-season tour. From left to right: Barry Mansell (Portsmouth), Johnny Haynes (Fulham), Jimmy Mullen (Wolves), Ray King (Port Vale), Ted Burgin (Sheffield United) and Bedford Jezzard (Fulham). Mansell, King and Burgin were attending the England camp but never played senior international football.

and in one particular spell midway through the half they were on top.

Beara made a brilliant tip over save to deny Jimmy Mullen's header after Broadis and Tom Finney had set up the chance. The goalkeeper also had to save well from both Allen and Johnny Nicholls.

Unfortunately, this spell of pressure was to last for only a short while as Yugoslavia, playing a typical continental style of game, began to move very sweetly. Luckily for England their finishing did not match their approach play and when Dvornić missed a simple chance he was quickly substituted, a decision that puzzled the England contingent as the new FIFA rule was to allow substitutes for injuries only.

The second half saw wave after wave of Yugoslav attacks. Bobek, Vukas and Mitić all saw shots graze the uprights as the pressure increased. Čajkovski inspired most of Yugoslavia's best moves and little was seen of England's attack in this half. Indeed, their defence was sometimes forced into desperate measures with Byrne, Owen and Wright all saving Gil Merrick with goal-saving clearances.

It looked as if all this valiant defending would earn England an honourable draw but, right at the end, the Yugoslavs snatched victory. Only three minutes remained when the Austrian referee awarded a dubious free-kick against the unlucky Byrne.

It was a decision which cost England the match. Stanković fired the free-kick low and hard into the packed penalty area and the ball rebounded off a defender straight to the feet of Mitić standing only six yards from goal. He could hardly miss . . .and he didn't! The crowd went wild with delight and although it was a cruel twist for England nobody could deny Yugoslavia's right to the result.

34th match v Yugoslavia.
Debut for Owen.
50th cap for Finney.

Hungary v England   Friendly

Played on Sunday, 23 May 1954 at the Nep Stadium, Budapest.

Hungary: G.Grosics (Honvéd); J.Buzánsky (Dorogi), M.Lantos (MTK Budapest), J.Bozsik (Honvéd), G.Lóránt (Honvéd), J.Zakariás (MTK Budapest), J.Tóth (Csepel), S.Kocsis (Honvéd), N.Hidegkuti (MTK Budapest), F.Puskás (Honvéd), Z.Czibor (Honvéd).
Sub: Gellér (MTK Budapest) for Groscis.

England: G.H.Merrick (Birmingham C); R.Staniforth (Huddersfield), R.W.Byrne (Man Utd), W.A.Wright (Wolves, captain), S.W.Owen (Luton T), J.W. Dickinson (Portsmouth), P.P.Harris (Portsmouth), J.Sewell (Sheffield Wed), B.A.G.Jezzard (Fulham), I.A.Broadis (Newcastle Utd), T.Finney (Preston NE).

Half-time 3-0   Full-time 7-1
Ref: G.Bernardi (Italy)   Att: 92,000

SIX months earlier at Wembley, England were given a football lesson by the magnificent Hungarian side. It was the first time they had been beaten on home soil by a continental team and it was hoped that many lessons would be learned

England's Sid Owen tries to clear as goalkeeper Gil Merrick is beaten in Budapest during England's 7-1 humiliation in May 1954.

Merrick is well beaten for the Hungarians' fifth goal, scored by Tóth.

from the experience. Sadly, on this performance against that same Hungarian side, few would believe that they have learned any.

England were once again totally out-classed. Hungary simply tore them apart with some devastating football and scored virtually at will. The old fashioned tactics that England employed were shown up to be woefully inadequate by the slick pattern of the Hungarian formation. Quick, accurate short passing was coupled with lethal long passes which totally bemused overworked defenders. One of the most obvious differences between the two sides was in the teamwork. Whereas England played as a group of individuals doing their own jobs the Hungarians moved as one unit with Puskás, especially, pulling the strings.

The trouble began in the tenth minute when Jimmy Dickinson was somewhat harshly penalised for a foul on Hidegkuti 20 yards from goal. Puskás summoned up the powerful Lantos from the back to take the free-kick and before you could say 'Hidegkuti' the ball crashed into the England net. It was the beginning of the end for the visitors and 12 minutes later they went 2-0 down when Puskás lashed home a rebound from close range after Ron Staniforth had blocked a sharp cross by Kocsis.

The lean and skilful inside-right Kocsis was having a fine game and on the half-hour he scored a brilliant goal volleying home a pass from Puskás. Kocsis had just come back on to the field after having running repairs to an injury. How England had wished he had stayed off!

Belgium goalkeeper Gernaey gets to the ball before Nat Lofthouse in the World Cup game at Basle in June 1954.

For the remainder of the half Hungary turned on the full exhibition of their skills and it was a bemused and bedraggled bunch of England players that trooped off at half-time 3-0 down. Only a good shot by Ivor Broadis which brought the best out of Grosics had given them any encouragement.

At the start of the second half England made a brief spirited reply when Peter Harris saw a shot blocked on the Hungarian goal-line but alas it was only a token gesture as within 20 minutes of the restart Hungary had conjured up some more magic to score three more goals. Kocsis, Tóth and the incomparable Hidegkuti all added to the goal tally with splendid strikes rounding off marvellous passing movements. Gil Merrick hardly knew what had hit him and he had little chance.

The 92,000 crowd loved every minute of this superb performance and watched in delight as each of the goals were created following some super play.

England battled gamely on. Billy Wright, Dickinson and Staniforth all worked themselves into the ground but Roger Byrne was their best player with a cultured display despite all that went on around him. Jackie Sewell and Tom Finney also worked hard although Finney in fact missed a sitter in one attack. In the end, though, the England players were willing the referee to end their misery. Before the final whistle though they did manage to salvage some pride when Broadis met a Dickinson free-kick to pull a goal back. Hungary were not amused

by this and immediately struck again with goal number seven.

This time, appropriately perhaps, it was Puskás who advanced on to a defence splitting pass by Hidegkuti to fire home the last humiliating nail into the England coffin. In the remaining minutes Hungary totally dominated and even a substitution of Grosics in goal had little effect on an England display which is best forgotten. Unfortunately, the fact that this ranks as England's biggest-ever defeat will probably mean that it will never be forgotten.

7th match v Hungary.
Debut for Jezzard.
Heaviest international defeat.

World Cup Finals

Belgium v England   Pool Four

Played on Thursday, 17 June 1954 at the St Jakob Stadium, Basle, Switzerland.

Belgium: L.Gernaey (AS Ostend); M.Dries (Berchem Sport), A.Van Brandt (Lierse SK), C.Huysmans (FC Beerschot), L.Carré (FC Liège), V.Mees (FC Antwerp), J.Mermans (RSC Anderlecht), L.Anoul (FC Liège), R.Coppens (FC Beerschot), D.Houf (Standard Liège), P.Van Den Bosch (RSC Anderlecht).

England: G.H.Merrick (Birmingham C); R.Staniforth (Huddersfield T), R.W.Byrne (Man Utd), W.A.Wright

(Wolves, captain), S.W.Owen (Luton T), J.W.Dickinson (Portsmouth), S.Matthews (Blackpool), I.A.Broadis (Newcastle Utd), N.Lofthouse (Bolton W), T.Taylor (Man Utd), T.Finney (Preston NE).

Half-time 1-2   Full-time 4-4 aet (90 minutes, 3-3)

Ref: E.Schmetzer (West Germany)

Att: 14,000

SO, at last, the 1954 World Cup Finals are under way for England, and surely this match will rank as one of the most eventful of the whole tournament, no matter whatever else happens. For an hour England were magnificent.

Playing fast, purposeful football they stretched Belgium to the limit and only a tremendous display by Gernaey in goal saved them from an embarrassing defeat. Learning a good deal from their Hungarian experience, England employed much of the style of the magnificent Magyars. They overcame a shock early goal by Anoul for Belgium to quickly equalize when Ivor Broadis scored after good work by Billy Wright and Tommy Taylor had created the opening.

That goal came in the 25th minute and seven minutes later a Taylor through-pass sent Tom Finney away. The Preston winger sent over a lovely centre and Nat Lofthouse roared in to dive horizontally to head a magnificient goal.

When Broadis added a third goal shortly after half-time following a piece of typical Stanley Matthews magic it seemed all over bar the shouting. But instead of pressing home their advantage England tended to over-elaborate their passing movements and in the last 15 minutes they were made to pay for this approach. In a sudden five minute burst from Belgium the scores, remarkably, were level. First Houf and then Coppens pounced on loose defensive work to give Belgium a reward they barely deserved, extra-time.

This, too, was full of drama. Lofthouse restored the England lead when fine work by Broadis and Taylor set up the chance. However their joy was short-lived as two minutes later a tragic own-goal ended the scoring. A long hopeful cross by Dries was met by Jimmy Dickinson's head and the ball flew past Gil Merrick to the dismay of all English fans present.

This was a very frustrating result for England and particularly annoying because they should have won the match convincingly.

14th match v Belgium.
Own-goal by Dickinson.

Switzerland v England   Pool Four

Played on Sunday, 20 June 1954 at the Wankdorf Stadium, Berne, Switzerland.

Switzerland: E.Parlier (Servette FC); A.Neury (Servette FC), R.Bocquet (Lausanne-Sports), W.Kernen (La Chaux de Fonds), O.Eggimann (La Chaux de Fonds), H.Bigler (Young Boys), C.Antenen (La Chaux de Fonds), R.Vonlanthen (Grasshoppers), E.Meier (Young Boys), R.Ballaman (Grasshoppers), J.Fatton (Servette FC).

England: G.H.Merrick (Birmingham C); R.Staniforth (Huddersfield T), R.W.Byrne (Man Utd), W.H.McGarry (Huddersfield T), W.A.Wright (Wolves, captain), J.W.Dickinson (Portsmouth), T.Finney (Preston NE), I.A.Broadis (Newcastle Utd), T.Taylor (Man Utd), D.J.Wilshaw (Wolves), J.Mullen (Wolves).

Half-time 0-1   Full-time 0-2
Ref: I.Zsolt (Hungary)   Att: 60,000

INJURIES to Stanley Matthews and Nat Lofthouse caused England to make several changes to their team for this vital World Cup match against the host nation. The Wankdorf Stadium looked very impressive under a cloudless blue sky and it soon warmed to a cauldron-like atmosphere as the shirt-sleeved crowd, reminiscent of a Test match, basked in the conditions. Sadly, the football match, understandably perhaps, never rose above the mediocre.

England, looking disjointed, never really got to grips with the game and far too often moves broke down before reaching the danger zone. The Swiss fared little better and it was hard to believe that they had already beaten Italy in these finals. On the plus side Billy Wright looked superb in his new role of centre-half and perhaps he will now settle down into a position that has been beckoning for some time.

Thirty minutes into the match, Tom Finney began to cause some flutters in the Swiss defence by moving to inside-right. Tommy Taylor also looked good and gave his marker, Neury, a hard time. Five minutes before the break England broke

Switzerland's Parlier gathers cleanly, despite the attentions of Tommy Taylor (10) and Dennis Wilshaw (15) at the Wankdorf Stadium during the 1954 World Cup finals.

the deadlock. Taylor headed a long through-pass in to space and Jimmy Mullen moved in to slide the ball past Parlier. It was a much-needed boost for England.

The second half was very poor with the seering heat taking its toll on all the players, so, when midway through the half England settled the result with a second goal, the relief could be felt everywhere. The chance came with Bill McGarry finding Dennis Wilshaw with a ground pass. The inside-left sold two dummies before dribbling past Neury, Bigler and Bocquet to shoot a brilliant goal beyond Parlier. It was a fine effort by the Wolves player and effectively ended the contest.

There was only one other noteworthy moment when Switzerland almost set up a grandstand finish. With 15 minutes to go Ballaman flicked his shot past Gil Merrick, only to see Ron Staniforth save a certain goal by running back to clear off the line to safety.

So England moved into the next round as Britain's only survivors but they would have to improve on this performance to have any chance of progressing any further.

6th match v Switzerland.
Debut for McGarry.

Uruguay v England   Quarter-final

Played on Saturday, 26 June 1954 at the St Jakob Stadium, Basle, Switzerland.

Uruguay: R.Máspoli (Peñarol);

W.Martínez (Rampla Juniors), J.Santamaria (Nacional), R.Andrade (Peñarol), O.Varela (Peñarol), L.Cruz (Nacional), J.Abbadíe (Peñarol), J.Ambrois (Nacional), O.Míguez (Peñarol), J.Schiaffino (Peñarol), C.Borges (Peñarol).

England: G.H.Merrick (Birmingham C); R.Staniforth (Huddersfield T), R.W.Byrne (Man Utd), W.H.McGarry (Huddersfield T), W.A.Wright (Wolves, captain), J.W.Dickinson (Portsmouth), S.Matthews (Blackpool), I.A.Broadis (Newcastle Utd), N.Lofthouse (Bolton W), D.J.Wilshaw (Wolves), T.Finney (Preston NE).

Half-time 2-1   Full-time 4-2
Ref: E.Steiner (Austria)   Att: 50,000

ENGLAND finally made their exit from the 1954 World Cup when they lost to the current holders of the trophy, Uruguay, in the sweltering heat of the St Jakob Stadium in Basle. Ironically, though, the crowd witnessed England's best performance of the tournament by far and the players could leave Switzerland with their heads held high.

Courage and determination has never been a characteristic lacking in an Englishman and the players had to draw on all their experience to do battle against the intimidating South Americans. Led by their captain Billy Wright, England pushed forward at every opportunity, feeding the mercurial Stanley Matthews as often as possible. The winger was used in a roving role and always seemed available when his fierce-tackling defenders fed the ball out of defence.

The histrionics of the Uruguayans quickly turned the crowd against them, so England enjoyed valuable support, but there was no disputing Uruguay's skill and after only five minutes they took the lead.

Superb interpassing between Abbadíe, Schiaffino and Borges ended with the latter brilliantly shooting past Gil Merrick. At that moment visions of Uruguay's 7-0 thrashing of Scotland earlier in the tournament came flooding back. But England were made of sterner stuff and they quickly got back into the game.

Fifteen minutes had gone when Matthews picked the ball up in midfield and brilliantly sent Dennis Wilshaw clear. In turn, the inside-left gave Nat Lofthouse the perfect pass and the Bolton player did the rest. From then on the game boiled up into a frenzy as the excitement reached fever pitch. Lofthouse was denied only by the fingertips of Máspoli as the goalkeeper produced a dazzling save following a good pass by Ivor Broadis.

Wright then sent Wilshaw away again and when Lofthouse received another pass from the number-ten he was once more thwarted by Máspoli. This time the ball ran loose though and Wilshaw followed up to flick it agonisingly the wrong side of the post.

Ironically, after all those narrow escapes, it was Uruguay who stole the lead again with six minutes of the half remaining. Roger Byrne, who had a torrid time throughout, up-ended Abbadie and from the free-kick by Santamaria, Varella hit a tremendous 25-yarder wide of Merrick's right hand. The 'keeper might have done better but there was no denying the power of the shot. By half-time

Ivor Broadis gets over the outstretched leg of a Uruguayan defender in England's 4-2 defeat in the 1954 World Cup quarter-finals in Basle.

Uruguay had Varela, Abbadíe and Andrade all struggling with injuries.

The last thing England wanted straight after the break was an early goal against them. Unfortunately that is exactly what happened. Yet another foul by Byrne, one of many by him, gave Uruguay a free-kick. The ball was quickly moved between Ambrois and Míguez before the superb Schiaffino came through a gap to shoot past Merrick, who again was slow to react.

The goal stunned England but they refused to surrender. Urged on by Wright, Matthews, Dickinson, Staniforth and Wilshaw, they tried everything they knew to break down the clever defending by the Uruguayans. Ever-watchful of the danger of a breakaway, Ambrois once hit the bar from such an attack, they pushed forward relentlessly. With 25 minutes remaining, the game was once more put into the melting pot.

Yet another purposeful attack again saw Lofthouse shoot at goal. This time, when the ball bounced out, Tom Finney was on the spot to push it over the line. Suddenly it was 3-2 and everything to play for.

England gave everything in those last minutes and Matthews twice came within a whisker of equalizing, once when his shot struck the back stanchion and again when Máspoli produced another excellent save.

With the crowd willing for an equalizer, Uruguay then did what was least expected of them by breaking away to score a fourth, killer, goal. Lovely passing between Martínez and Míguez set up the chance for Ambrois to fire a diagonal shot from the right beating Merrick again, although this time the goalkeeper may have been unsighted.

The goal came ten minutes from the end and was a cruel blow and poor reward for England's sterling efforts. The end of England's World Cup campaign had at least given them a share of respect from all who saw the game.

2nd match v Uruguay.

Northern Ireland v England Home Championship

Played on Saturday, 2 October 1954 at Windsor Park, Belfast.

Northern Ireland: W.N.M.C.Uprichard (Portsmouth); F.J.Montgomery (Coleraine), A.McMichael (Newcastle Utd), R.D.Blanchflower (Spurs), W.Dickson (Arsenal), R.Peacock (Celtic), W.L.Bingham (Sunderland), J.Blanchflower (Man Utd), W.J.Simpson (Rangers), J.McIlroy (Burnley), P.J.McParland (Aston Villa).

England: R.E.Wood (Man Utd); W.A.Foulkes (Man Utd), R.W.Byrne (Man Utd), J.E.Wheeler (Bolton W), W.A.Wright (Wolves, captain), R.J.Barlow (West Brom), S.Matthews (Blackpool), D.G.Revie (Man City), N.Lofthouse (Bolton W), J.N.Haynes (Fulham), B.Pilkington (Burnley).

Half-time 0-0   Full-time 0-2

Ref: C.Faultless (Scotland)   Att: 50,000

ENGLAND, home from a crushing defeat by Hungary and failure in the World Cup, travelled across the Irish Sea for their match against Northern Ireland. The result followed the usual pattern of previous clashes between the two sides with England, once again, coming out on top. Every game they have played in Ireland since 1927, apart from a solitary draw in 1952, had ended the same way and the fixture now had a monotonous ring about it. With all the problems of the summer now hopefully behind them, England were now looking to begin a new era.

With seven new caps in the side they were hoping to open their season with an encouraging performance. Alas, what followed proved to be a total anticlimax as England produced a mediocre display.

There had been lots of words both written and spoken since the summer all suggesting ideas and tactics that England could use to climb back up the world football tree. Indeed, get togethers had been arranged in both Manchester and Liverpool during last week to emphasise the concern everyone felt for improving the side.

But all the talking came to nothing as Northern Ireland pinned England back for long periods. It, in fact, took England 75 minutes to produce a worthwhile moment.

Ireland were not convincing or strong enough and despite all their possession they showed little up front. They missed their chance of victory mainly in the 20-minute spell leading up to half-time.

Stan Matthews, one of only four men who had been capped before as England picked up the pieces against Northern Ireland.

Simpson was put through by Jackie Blanchflower and, with England standing vainly appealing for offside, the centre-forward missed a golden chance, shooting tamely at Ray Wood.

Then, two minutes before the break, Simpson missed another opening when he headed Bingham's centre straight at Wood's body when it seemed easier to score. Surely, Ireland would have gone on to win had they taken either of those two fine chances?

A tremendous shot by Swansea Town's Ivor Allchurch whistles past Ray Wood's far post at Wembley in November 1954.

Immediately after half-time, Ray Wood became the hero for England when he did well to save efforts from McIlroy, Jackie Blanchflower and McParland. Showing anticipation and agility, the goalkeeper did all that was asked of him on his debut.

Billy Wright, Ray Barlow and Wood all showed up well in this period with Wright outstanding in his new role of centre-half. He was rarely beaten, both in the air and on the ground and showed true world class. He was the shining beacon in the dullest of dull games.

The other new players all struggled for England. Johnny Wheeler, Bill Foulkes and Roger Byrne all looked vulnerable and Don Revie and Johnny Haynes often failed with their passing.

Despite the criticism of this England performance they did have the satisfaction of the win. This came thanks to a couple of minutes of inspired play a quarter of an hour from the end.

Stanley Matthews, who had begun to wander in search of the ball, set up the first goal. Picking it up in the inside-left channel, he found Brian Pilkington with a good pass. The winger's touch gave Haynes the chance to at last get in a defence-splitting pass which found Revie. Haynes then did well to move into a position to receive Revie's return pass before side-stepping a defender and shooting past Uprichard.

Within seconds it was 2-0. Wright again sent Matthews free and swift passing between Matthews, Revie, Lofthouse and Haynes ended with Revie firmly shooting the second goal.

So, amazingly, England had transformed the match with their only moments of worthwhile football. It failed, however to hide all the problems that the team must face up to. The referee was Mr

Faultless of Scotland! Oh for an England performance of the same name.

62nd match v Northern Ireland.
Debuts for Wood, Foulkes, Wheeler, Barlow, Revie, Haynes and Pilkington.
Debut goals for Revie and Haynes.

England v Wales   Home Championship

Played on Wednesday, 10 November 1954 at Wembley Stadium.

England: R.E.Wood (Man Utd); R.Staniforth (Huddersfield), R.W.Byrne (Man Utd), L.H.Phillips (Portsmouth), W.A.Wright (Wolves, captain), W.J.Slater (Wolves), S.Matthews (Blackpool), R.T.F.Bentley (Chelsea), R.Allen (West Brom), L.F.Shackleton (Sunderland), F.Blunstone (Chelsea).

Wales: J.King (Swansea T); S.G.Williams (West Brom), A.T.Sherwood (Cardiff C), R.Paul (Man City), R.W.Daniel (Sunderland), D.Sullivan (Cardiff C), D.R. Tapscott (Arsenal), T.Ford (Cardiff C), W.J.Charles (Leeds Utd), I.J.Allchurch (Swansea T), R.J.Clarke (Man City).

Half-time 0-1   Full-time 3-2
Ref: C.Faultless (Scotland)   Att: 91,112

WHAT A difference a month makes! After their abysmal performance in Belfast, England came back to Wembley to produce a tremendous display which augered well for the future. It was a stirring game from start to finish which built up to a thrilling climax with England's late flurry deciding the issue.

On a dismal, rain-soaked November day, the two sides served up some lovely football. Wales contributed much to the game and can consider themselves unlucky not to gain some reward out of it. Over 91,000 people soaked up the atmosphere — and the rain — and they really enjoyed this game.

England soon moved into a smooth rhythm. With some much improved passing they put together some sparkling moves and, but for Ronnie Allen missing a couple of chances, might have taken the lead. As it was, Wales were to do just that in the 35th minute.

Ford, who sold a clever dummy to Billy Wright, allowed the ball to run on to Allchurch. The inside-forward hit a low cross into the middle which Ray Wood failed to cut out. Before anyone could clear the danger, the mighty Charles roared in to score. The Welsh number-nine was magnificent and his duel with Wright was probably the highlight of the game. To the England skipper's credit he contained him well, calling upon all his skill and experience.

Despite the Welsh lead, England continued with their excellent football. The visiting defenders held on doggedly, though, and at half-time they still had their lead.

England's new inspiration was coming from their wing-halves. Len Phillips and Bill Slater gave fine performances with Phillips always seeming to have that extra yard on the ball. Having played so badly in Belfast, it was also heartening to see the forwards play with so much more conviction. Although they missed chances, they all contributed well with Stanley Matthews, Frank Blunstone and Len Shackleton particularly impressive.

Billy Wright and West Germany's Posipal exchange banners before the friendly at Wembley in December 1954.

Both goalkeepers made fingertip saves as the game continued after the break and it was obvious that England's pressure must bring its reward. It came with 20 minutes left. Good work by Shackleton and Blunstone gave Matthews the chance to run at Sullivan. A typical burst by the mercurial winger ended with a lovely cross which Roy Bentley met superbly with a firm header.

At last England were level and they sensed that they were in with a chance of victory. Four minutes later Roger Byrne lobbed the ball into the middle, King misjudged it, and Bentley outjumped him to head England in front.

Wales were down but by no means out and a few moments later their fans went wild when they saw Charles once again emphasise his power. This time he declined the obvious pass to Tapscott and elected to swivel and fire in a thunderous shot low past the startled Wood from the edge of the box to make it 2-2.

England were not to be denied, though, and just before the end Phillips found Blunstone with a pass and the winger, capped a promising debut to send a fine

low centre into the middle where, once again, Bentley's strength saw him run the ball into the net. The England number-eight thus completed a memorable hat-trick.

Although Ford and Allchurch only just failed with shots at the other end before the final whistle, England had won an excellent victory. To the lasting pleasure of their fans it was the way their team played that was more important. Their football, at times, was a delight.

> 65th match v Wales.
> Debuts for Slater and Blunstone.
> Hat-trick by Bentley.

England v West Germany   Friendly

Played on Wednesday, 1 December 1954 at Wembley Stadium.

England: B.F.Williams (Wolves); R.Staniforth (Huddersfield T), R.W.Byrne (Man Utd), L.H.Phillips (Portsmouth), W.A.Wright (Wolves, cap-

tain), W.J.Slater (Wolves), S.Matthews (Blackpool), R.T.F.Bentley (Chelsea), R.Allen (West Brom), L.F.Shackleton (Sunderland), T.Finney (Preston NE).

West Germany: F.Herkenrath (Rot-Weiss Essen); J.Posipal (Hamburger SV), W.Kohlmeyer (1.FC Kaiserslautern), H.Erhardt (Sp Vgg Fürth 49), W.Liebrich (1.FC Kaiserslautern), G.Harpers (SV Sodingen), G.Kaufhold (Kickers Offenbach), M.Pfeiffer (Alemania), U.Seeler (Hamburger SV), J.Derwall (Fortuna Düsseldorf), A.Beck (St Pauli).

Half-time 1-0   Full-time 3-1

Ref: V.Orlandini (Italy)   Att: 100,000

ENGLAND, in front of a full house (and again the 100,000 crowd broke the receipts record by paying £51,716), entertained West Germany at Wembley. The Germans, who were now World Champions thanks to their memorable win over Hungary in the summer of 1954, had never won in England and again they went home empty-handed. The Germans fielded only three players that had appeared in the World Cup Final, but none the less still proved formidable opposition.

The heavy storms of the previous few days had given way to a lovely sunny, cloudless sky. The Wembley surface was pretty sodden but the ball playing forwards of England revelled in the conditions. Nobody more so than the evergreen Stanley Matthews. He was once again superb. It was hard to imagine that when he made his debut against Germany in 1935, the current German centre-forward, Uwe Seeler, had not even been born.

England were quickly into their stride and Herkenrath was soon in action. Time and time again he denied England with thrilling saves. Twice Tom Finney had shots blocked and Ronnie Allen also saw the same fate befall two of his efforts.

Finally, though, the pressure told. In the 27th minute more good work by the lively Allen set Matthews on his way. When the winger's centre reached the far post, Roy Bentley carried on where he had left off against Wales by scoring with another fine header.

Play was almost totally confined to the German half. Liebrich was outstanding, as he was in that memorable Final against Hungary, and it was solely due to him that the Germans were held together. Bert Williams was called upon to make a superb point-blank save from Seeler, but generally the English 'keeper was merely a spectator for long spells. With Len Phillips and Len Shackleton showing up very well, England continued with their forceful play until half-time and the measure of their lead did them no justice at all.

Deservedly, within three minutes of the restart, England went 2-0 ahead. Shackleton chipped a lovely ball over the German defence for Finney to run on to. Again his run was blocked by Herkenrath's brave dive but this time the ball ran loose for Allen to follow up and score. At this stage England's wingers were outstanding. Matthews once again carved trails of wreckage down the right flank and set up chance after chance. Finney, meanwhile, preferred to cut inside to create havoc. Unfortunately, England failed to capitalise on their superiority. They should have had many goals as the new-look German line-up understandably lacked cohesion.

Shackleton produced one dazzling moment when he set off on a tremendous dribble that took him through the whole German defence, bringing the crowd to its feet. He then dribbled around Herkenrath, only to push the ball too far forward at the vital moment and it ran out of play. It would have been a stupendous goal; as it was, it still brought a huge roar of approval from the spectators.

England, by now, were coasting. Their play became sloppy due to their dominance and the Germans, typically, made them pay for their casualness by suddenly pulling a goal back. Only 15 minutes remained when Seeler, who for once beat the majestic Billy Wright, passed the ball to Beck, who calmly beat Williams with a low shot.

This succeeded in waking England up again and although for a few seconds Germany threatened, the match was finally settled in the 80th minute. A brilliant reverse pass by Allen gave Shackleton a half-chance and as Herkenrath came to challenge, the Sunderland

West Brom's Ronnie Allen is celebrating but Roy Bentley's effort against the West Germans was disallowed.

Roger Byrne gets the ball off West Germany's Uwe Seeler.

West Germany's stranded goalkeeper Herkenrath looks back as Len Shackleton chases the ball. The England man was unable to turn it into the net, however.

Roy Bentley (8) turns away as even this acrobatic effort cannot deny England a goal. Ronnie Allen is about to lead the celebrations.

star produced the perfect chip to score a delightful third goal. Other chances were missed by England in the remaining minutes and Matthews continued, to the end, to be the scourge of the German defenders.

4th match v West Germany.

England v Scotland Home Championship

Played on Saturday, 2 April 1955 at Wembley Stadium.

England: B.F.Williams (Wolves); J.Meadows (Man City), R.W.Byrne (Man Utd), K.Armstrong (Chelsea), W.A. Wright (Wolves, captain), D.Edwards (Man Utd), S.Matthews (Blackpool), D.G.Revie (Man City), N.Lofthouse (Bolton W), D.J.Wilshaw (Wolves), F.Blunstone (Chelsea).

Scotland: F.Martin (Aberdeen); W.C.Cunningham (Preston NE), H.Haddock (Clyde), T.H.Docherty (Preston NE), J.A.Davidson (Partick T), J.Cumming (Hearts), J.A.McKenzie (Partick T), R.Johnstone (Man City), L.Reilly (Hibernian), J.L.McMillan (Airdrieonians), T.Ring (Clyde).

Half-time 4-1   Full-time 7-2
Ref: B.M.Griffiths (Wales)   Att: 96,847

Don Revie slides the ball into the Scottish net for England's third goal at Wembley in April 1955.

NOT since 1934 had England managed to beat Scotland at Wembley and in this, the 72nd international between the two countries, they finally broke the hoodoo with a vengeance.

Cunningham won the toss for Scotland and the teams kicked-off in glorious sunshine with the full tartan flavour on the terraces. Within seconds though the Scots were a goal down. Martin, who

endured a nightmare throughout, inexplicably dropped a cross from Frank Blunstone. Don Revie was in there quickly to get a touch on to Dennis Wilshaw, who rammed in the loose ball.

Duncan Edwards, making an immediate and impressive impact, was at the heart of all of England's early play. On seven minutes they increased their lead. A perfect centre by the incomparable

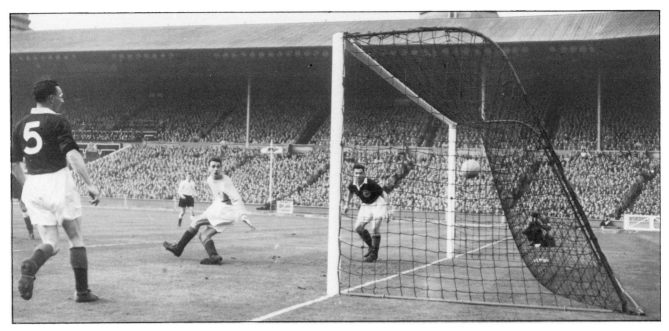

Above and below: **Scotland goalkeeper Fred Martin is beaten all ends up as England establish a commanding lead that would live forever as one of the darker days of Scottish football.**

Stanley Matthews was snapped up by Nat Lofthouse's head and it was 2-0. Matthews, now 40, was superb and his teasing play gave Haddock a torrid time.

Scotland still worked hard, though, with Docherty a driving force. They found that when they put pressure on the England defenders then they too, looked vulnerable. In the tenth minute good work by Johnstone set up a chance well-taken by Reilly and it was now 2-1.

The pace of the game was relentless and the crowd could not look away for a moment for fear of missing something. England's attacking play was often exhilarating with Matthews going close and Wilshaw hitting a post. The pressure had to tell and in the 24th minute, good passing by the forwards was finally rounded off by Revie's cross-shot finding the net.

Cumming moved across to try to help Haddock stem the danger from Matthews but three minutes later the winger carved yet another goal with his superb footwork. This time he pulled the ball back for Lofthouse to score his second and England's fourth. It was not all one-way traffic and McMillan, Johnstone and Reilly all

showed up well, but there was no denying England's convincing half-time lead.

In the second half Scotland continued to match their rivals in ball skills but alas their finishing let them down. This was highlighted when McKenzie missed a fine chance after 47 minutes. Understandably perhaps, the game went through a scrappy and lifeless spell for awhile. Docherty impressed with his energy and tenacity for Scotland as did his counterpart Edwards for England. At 18 years old, this young colossus looked to have a tremendous future.

Matthews went close and then further attempts by Matthews, again, and Lofthouse brought the game back to life. Matthews then set up another chance for Wilshaw to head number five on 70 minutes. Three minutes later the same pair combined again for Wilshaw to crash home an unstoppable drive in the far corner, thus completing his hat-trick. By this time, Scotland were demoralised and with seven minutes left Wilshaw scored yet again following a Matthews centre.

Docherty did salvage something for Scotland when he hammered home a free-kick. The power and accuracy of his kick

left Bert Williams helpless, but that goal in no way detracted from the superiority of a marvellous display from England.

> 72nd match v Scotland.
> Debuts for Meadows, Armstrong and Edwards.
> Wilshaw scored four goals (sixth time since the war that feat had been achieved).

France v England   Friendly

Played on Sunday, 15 May 1955 at the Colombes Stadium, Paris.

France: F.Remetter (FC Sochaux); G.Bieganski (Lille OSC), R.Marche (RC de Paris), A.Penverne (Stade de Reims), R.Jonquet (Stade de Reims), X.Louis (RC Lens), J.Ujlacki (OGC Nice), L.Glovacki (Stade de Reims), R.Kopa (Stade de Reims), R.Bliard (Stade de Reims), J.Vincent (Lille OSC).

England: B.F.Williams (Wolves); R.P.T.Sillett (Chelsea), R.W.Byrne (Man

Bert Williams claws at the ball as France's Bliard comes racing in at the Colombes Stadium in May 1955.

Utd), R.Flowers (Wolves), W.A.Wright (Wolves, captain), D.Edwards (Man Utd), S.Matthews (Blackpool), D.G.Revie (Man City), N.Lofthouse (Bolton W), D.J.Wilshaw (Wolves), F.Blunstone (Chelsea).

Half-time 1-0   Full-time 1-0
Ref: E.Schmetzer (West Germany)
Att: 54,750

AFTER the euphoria of the magnificent win against Scotland, England were brought back down to earth by France on this the first leg of their 1955 summer tour. It was a very disappointing performance by England and the Union Jacks in the crowd were waving in a rather forlorn way at the end. Once again the continental style of play contrasted greatly to England's and the gap in class seemed to widen again.

Nearly 55,000 people packed into the Colombes Stadium to see France quickly move into their stride. Marche, their captain, soon latched on to Stan Matthews and subdued the great man in a better way than many defenders before him. It was also obvious why France had had such a good season. Wins against Sweden, Germany and Spain, combined with a good draw against Belgium, had boosted their confidence and now they were looking to add the biggest scalp of all.

England looked sluggish and for long spells the quick and delightful football of the French stole the honours. Kopa, Glovacki, Bliard and the long-legged coloured player Louis showed some super skills. Alas, the English challenge never really got going. Matthews was marked out of it by Marche and with Ron Flowers having a quiet debut, thus making Don Revie ineffective, they rarely threatened.

Only Dennis Wilshaw looked dangerous for the visitors and he put in some spirited attempts. Ironically, despite the quality of France's football, the goal that

settled the match came from a penalty. Indeed, some questionable refereeing decisions had a big say in the outcome.

In the 21st minute, Blunstone was sent sprawling by a reckless challenge in the French penalty area. To England's disgust the German official waved play on. It was a different story some 15 minutes later, though. This time Peter Sillett brought down the elusive Vincent in the England box and the referee showed no hesitation in awarding the spot-kick. There was no doubting his decision but this foul was no less obvious than the one against Blunstone. Kopa stepped up calmly to beat Bert Williams with his shot and the French fans went wild with delight.

After the interval, Kopa, who was outstanding throughout, and Vincent, both crashed fierce shots against the England goalposts and the writing was on the wall. Bliard featured in one amazing incident when he found himself clean through. Believing he was offside he simply tapped the ball to Williams, only afterwards realising the whistle had not blown. Williams, always the busier of the two goalkeepers, then made flying saves from Bliard and Vincent. Despite all of this French pressure, England could still have won the match. On 62 minutes they began an eight-minute spell when they might easily have scored three times.

First Wilshaw sent Nat Lofthouse clean through, only for his shot to strike Remetter's body as the 'keeper came out. Then, England's best move of the game involving Duncan Edwards, Revie and Wilshaw ended with the latter also finding his shot somewhat fortuitously blocked by Remetter's body. Finally, Matthews, with a marvellous piece of skill, killed a high pass superbly to set up Lofthouse. This time the centre-forward did beat Remetter, only to see Penverne appear from nowhere to clear off the goal-line.

That was the end of England's efforts and at the end France did a lap of honour

to celebrate their famous victory. As for England, only Billy Wright and Edwards could be totally happy with their performances and the party now moved on to Spain.

13th match v France.
Debuts for Sillett and Flowers.
Penalty by Kopa (full name Kopaszewski) for France.

Spain v England   Friendly

Played on Wednesday, 18 May 1955 at the Chamartin Stadium, Madrid.

Spain: A.Ramallets (FC Barcelona); R.Matito (Real Valladolid), M.Gonzalez (Seville FC), M.Ugartemendia (Athletic Bilbao), J.Garay (Athletic Bilbao), J.M.Zarraga (Real Madrid), D.Maño (Valencia CF), J.L.Perez-Paya (Real Madrid), L.Kubala (FC Barcelona), J.H.Rial (Real Madrid), F.Gento (Real Madrid).

England: B.F.Williams (Wolves); R.P.T.Sillett (Chelsea), R.W.Byrne (Man Utd), J.W.Dickinson (Portsmouth), W.A.Wright (Wolves, captain), D.Edwards (Man Utd), S.Matthews (Blackpool), R.T.F.Bentley (Chelsea), N.Lofthouse (Bolton W), A.Quixall (Sheffield Wed), D.J.Wilshaw (Wolves).

Half-time 0-1   Full-time 1-1
Ref: R.Pieri (Italy)   Att: 125,000

THIS game will be remembered for all the wrong reasons. On a beautiful sunny day, in front of 125,000 people in a magnificent stadium, the scene was set for a classic confrontation. Sadly, by the end, it had degenerated into nothing short of a brawl.

Spain had looked forward to this match and the air of expectancy was much in evidence around this lovely city prior to the kick-off. England withstood a passionate opening by the Spaniards. Kubala was instrumental in all the good things his team produced and they forced England back on their heels for long spells. Bert Williams was looking very safe in goal, though, and Billy Wright marshalled his defenders superbly, drawing on all his vast experience.

As the first half progressed, the visitors began to come into things a little more and with Stanley Matthews roaming inside to gain more of the possession some chances were beginning to appear. After 25 minutes, Ramallets saved at Albert Quixall's feet bravely after the Sheffield Wednesday player had been put through by Roy Bentley. Then Nat Lofthouse had the goalkeeper diving full length to save a screamer before, amazingly, with six minutes of the half remaining England took the lead.

A good move between Dennis Wilshaw, Quixall and Lofthouse set up Bentley. The number eight continued with his impressive goal tally by shooting home a beauty from 20 yards out. Three minutes after the goal came the incident that, more than any other, lowered the tone of the game.

In a breakaway attack, Bentley hit a long pass forward. It dropped in front of Lofthouse, who for once was clear of his marker, Garay. The big centre-forward strode clear and seemed certain to score, but two yards from the edge of the Spanish penalty area Garay dived forward, rugby style, to grab Lofthouse and end the attack in the most callous way possible. From that moment England's dander was up and the second half was 'fought' out in a most uncompromising manner.

The Italian referee struggled to keep control and all the rhythm went from the play as his whistle constantly interrupted the proceedings. For the most part of the second half, England were under heavy pressure as Spain searched for an opening. With 25 minutes left, the impressive debutant Ugartemendia dribbled hard at the England defence. As the ball fell between Sillett and Duncan Edwards, Rial nipped in smartly to finish off the attack to equalize.

Neither side impressed during the remainder of the match and some players seemed more intent on kicking each other rather than the ball.

> 4th match v Spain.
> Spain's Gonzalez also known as 'Campanal'; Ugartemendia also known as 'Mauri'.

Portugal v England
Friendly

Played on Sunday, 22 May 1955 at the Antas Stadium, Oporto.

Portugal: A.Costa-Pereira (Benfica); M.Caldeira (Sporting Lisbon), A.Carvalho (FC Porto), J.M.Pedroto (FC Porto), M.Passos-Fernandes (Sporting Lisbon), J.Pereira (Sporting Lisbon), J.Dimas (Belenenses), L.de Fonseca (Belenenses), J.Águas (Benfica), J.Travaços (Sporting Lisbon), J.P.Biléll (Lusitano). Sub: J.Martin (Sporting Lisbon) for Biléll.
England: B.F.Williams (Wolves); R.P.T.Sillett (Chelsea), R.W.Byrne (Man

Utd), J.W.Dickinson (Portsmouth), W.A.Wright (Wolves, captain), D.Edwards (Man Utd), S.Matthews (Blackpool), R.T.F.Bentley (Chelsea), N.Lofthouse (Bolton W), D.J.Wilshaw (Wolves), F.Blunstone (Chelsea). Sub: A.Quixall (Sheffield Wed) for Lofthouse.

Half-time 1-1   Full-time 3-1

Ref: G.Bernardi (Italy)   Att: 55,000

ENGLAND, with a defeat in Paris and a draw in Madrid, tried to end their 1955 summer tour on a higher note against Portugal. But the dismal run continued after Portugal registered their first victory over them.

To be fair, England should never have lost this match. They had most of the possession but failed miserably in front of goal, showing a distinct, and annoying reluctance to shoot. Coupled with this they then made two terrible blunders in defence in the last ten minutes and consequently lost the game.

Yet it had all started brightly enough. In the 19th minute Roy Bentley gave England the lead with a good shot following a delightful move involving Bentley, Jimmy Dickinson and Dennis Wilshaw. Sadly, that turned out to be their only worthwhile goal attempt of the opening half. After 24 minutes England's defence was caught dreaming and the lapse enabled Portugal to level the scores with a 25-yard screamer by Águas which flew into the top left-hand corner of Bert William's goal.

De Fonseca, always dangerous, and Travaços both went close afterwards but on the whole the half continued to favour England. But despite their long periods of possession it could not be turned into goals. Passos was a tower of strength for the home side and the England forwards, although showing their undoubted skill, could find little to encourage them.

There was a distinctly lethargic look about the England players, although the irrepressible Billy Wright was the exception. He was his usual immaculate self, inspiring his colleagues with a fine performance. Wright covered the many errors of his teammates with the minimum of fuss and yet still found time to urge on his forwards. The rest of the team did not respond to their skipper's example as they should have done.

The opening 25 minutes of the second half saw England surging forward and in this spell they should have put the result out of Portugal's reach. First Bentley and Wilshaw combined to create an opening, but Bentley tried one pass too many and the chance was lost. Then Albert Quixall, who had substituted for Nat Lofthouse, missed a sitter from close in when he ought to have scored. Finally, Wilshaw saw a header rebound off the crossbar when, again, he ought to have done better. Stanley Matthews had set up that last chance with a typical piece of skill but, apart from that, the Blackpool wizard was largely subdued by the hard-working Portuguese defence.

With ten minutes to go, England made a fatal error. They were pressing hard for a winner when Portugal made a rare break from defence. When Roger Byrne gathered the ball to clear it seemed the attack had broken down. But the ever-alert de Fonseca chased Byrne and challenged for the ball. In a flash the coloured striker

Duncan Edwards, the magnificent young Manchester United player who lost his life in the Munich air disaster.

robbed the full-back before striding on to shoot past Williams. The crowd went wild with delight as the possibility of a famous victory was sensed.

Four minutes later they were even more ecstatic as that possibility became fact. This time, Wright, making his only mistake of the game, tried a back-header that fell short of Williams. Águas nipped in smartly and once again the goalkeeper was helpless.

At the end of the game the scenes at the stadium were reminiscent of a team winning the World Cup!

> 4th match v Portugal.
> Portugal's Pereira also known as 'Juca'; de Fonseca also known as 'Matateu'.

Denmark v England
Friendly

Played on Sunday, 2 October 1955 at the Idraetspark, Copenhagen.

Denmark: P.Henriksen (BK Frem);

P.Andersen (Skovshoved), V.Nielsen (AB København), E.Jensen (AB København), C.Brøgger (A.B.København), J.Olesen (Aarhus GF), J.Hansen (Naestved IF), J.Jacobsen (B.93 København), O.Andersen (Brønshøj), K.Lundberg (AB København), P.Pedersen (AIA Aarhus). Sub: J.Jørgensen (Skovshoved) for Brøgger.

England: R.L.Baynham (Luton T); J.J.Hall (Birmingham C), R.W.Byrne (Man Utd), W.H.McGarry (Wolves), W.A.Wright (Wolves, captain), J.W.Dickinson (Portsmouth), J.E.T.Milburn (Newcastle Utd), D.G.Revie (Man City), N.Lofthouse (Bolton W), G.R.W.Bradford (Bristol R), T.Finney (Preston NE).

Half-time 0-3   Full-time 1-5

Ref: G.Bernardi (Italy)   Att: 53,000

A RECORD crowd packed into the Idraetspark Stadium to see this match which was arranged as part of the promotion of the British Exhibition which was in full swing in the Danish capital. Even the King and Queen of Denmark were there to see the stars of the English side. Alas, the game did not live up to the occasion, only bursting into life now and again.

For the first 20 minutes Denmark largely controlled the proceedings. Urged on by an enthusiastic crowd they went at England and the visitors, without several leading players, for varying reasons, struggled to get going. Billy Wright spent most of this early part of the match covering the mistakes of his nervous colleagues and even he looked nervous at times. As a result the Danes created several openings.

A fine move at the start between Hansen, O.Andersen and Jacobsen ended with Olesen bursting through a gap to fire a shot just over the England crossbar. The lively Lundberg also gave England's defence some problems and he went very close with one effort.

But in the 26th minute, the game dramatically changed its course. Tom Finney gained possession and set off on a mazy dribble. As he beat a defender to dart into the penalty area another defender bundled the Preston winger off the ball for an obvious penalty. Don Revie coolly sent the goalkeeper the wrong way from the spot and after that England settled down. Just after the goal Brøgger left the field injured to be replaced by Jørgensen and within the space of the next 15 minutes, England killed off the remaining Danish challenge.

First, a clever lob by Jeff Hall into the goalmouth found Henriksen wanting as he was challenged and the ball ran loose. Geoff Bradford's shot was then blocked, but Lofthouse was on hand to latch on to the second rebound to score from close range.

Then, shortly before half-time, England scored the best goal of the match. Wright and Bill McGarry sent Bradford off on a long run down the left. When he centred, Finney cleverly dummied the defence to allow Lofthouse the easiest of chances from close in.

So, after a shaky start, England had moved into an unassailable lead by half-time, although in truth it was hardly deserved on their overall display.

The second half was equally unimpressive. England, three up and coasting, and Denmark, struggling to get their part-time players to raise their game a level, failed

to lift the match out of its mediocrity. However, one player did stand out in the gloom and that was Revie. His positional play, passing and general all round contribution always caught the eye. The rest of the attack failed to gell, though, and moved in fits and starts.

Finney, when he played on the left, often seemed to over-elaborate and his left foot dribbling style seemed better suited to the right wing. Jackie Milburn never reproduced the speed and dash of his club form, and Bradford, hard though he worked, did not seem international class.

Having said all that, England still created all the chances and added goal number four just after the turn round. This came when Revie fired in a super shot on the run from 20 yards after a clever flick by Milburn.

England missed many more chances as the Danes tired but Lundberg did bring the crowd back to life when he headed past Ron Baynham for a consolation goal. Just before the end Bradford rounded off the scoring when he ran on to a long forward pass by Milburn which split the defence to shoot past the hapless Henriksen.

> 2nd match v Denmark
> Debuts for Baynham, Hall and Bradford.
> Debut goal for Bradford.
> Penalty by Revie.

Wales v England Home Championship

Played on Saturday, 22 October 1955 at Ninian Park, Cardiff.

Wales: A.J.Kelsey (Arsenal); S.G.Williams (West Brom), A.T.Sherwood (Cardiff C), M.Charles (Swansea T), W.J.Charles (Leeds Utd), R.Paul (Man City), D.R.Tapscott (Arsenal), N.Kinsey (Birmingham C), T.Ford (Cardiff C), I.J.Allchurch (Swansea T), C.Jones (Swansea T).

England: B.F.Williams (Wolves); J.J.Hall (Birmingham), R.W.Byrne (Man Utd), W.H.McGarry (Wolves), W.A.Wright (Wolves, captain), J.W.Dickinson (Portsmouth), S.Matthews (Blackpool),

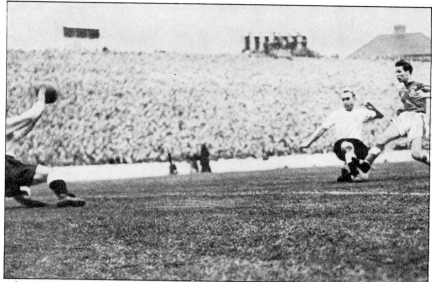

Arsenal's Derek Tapscott scores Wales' first goal at Ninian Park in October 1955.

D.G.Revie (Man City), N.Lofthouse (Bolton W), D.J.Wilshaw (Wolves), T.Finney (Preston NE).

Half-time 2-0   Full-time 2-1

Ref: T.Mitchell (Northern Ireland)

Att: 60,000

IT WAS 17 years to the day that Wales last tasted victory against the old enemy from England and when this game began there seemed to be no hint that that record would be improved.

Stan Matthews and Tom Finney quickly got into their stride, causing Sherwood and S.Williams several anxious moments. In one incident even Ford was seen to tackle Matthews deep in the Welsh half, such was the pressure. Gradually, though, the home defenders began to take control and, as the game progressed, less was seen of the two English wingers. Mel Charles began to dominate in midfield and, with his brother John Charles showing immense stature at the back, Wales looked more and more composed.

Ford almost scored when he headed just over and then the centre-forward was caught narrowly offside after Kinsey delayed his pass a fraction too long. The Welsh pressure was increasing all the time now and Kelsey was often the only man in his own half. Eventually the attacking paid off explosively with Wales scoring two goals within sixty seconds.

Thirty-eight minutes had gone when hesitancy in the England defence allowed Tapscott to run on to Kinsey's through pass before striking a rising shot high into Bert Williams' net.

The ecstatic crowd hardly had time to settle before the England goalkeeper was again picking the ball out of the net. This time Cliff Jones met a centre by Paul perfectly to head home a stunning goal. The noise from the crowd was deafening and at half-time they gave their team a wonderful ovation as they left the pitch. Even the dogs that performed for the crowd during the break seemed to have an extra spring in their step.

Six minutes after the restart that same crowd were stunned into silence as England pulled a goal back in the strangest of circumstances. A long, harmless-looking lob by Roger Byrne into the Welsh penalty area seemed to be of no danger to their defence, but inexplicably John Charles leapt and planted a superb header wide of his own startled 'keeper. The strange thing was that it looked so intentional.

Luckily, from Charles' viewpoint, the goal did not matter in the final analysis. England had most of the play during this half but lacked the necessary thrust up front. Wales were hampered by an injury to Paul but only once did England nearly score. That came when Don Revie brilliantly back-heeled on the volley a centre by Finney, only for the ball to rebound off of the crossbar. The last quarter of an hour was untidy and full of niggling incidents, but in the end Wales just about deserved their famous victory.

> 66th match v Wales.
> Own-goal by John Charles for England.

England v Home Championship
Northern Ireland

Played on Wednesday, 2 November 1955 at Wembley Stadium.

England: R.L.Baynham (Luton T); J.J.Hall (Birmingham C), R.W.Byrne (Man Utd), R.Clayton (Blackburn R), W.A.Wright (Wolves, captain), J.W.Dickinson (Portsmouth), T.Finney (Preston NE), J.N.Haynes (Fulham), B.A.G.Jezzard (Fulham), D.J.Wilshaw (Wolves), W.Perry (Blackpool).

Northern Ireland: W.N.M.C.Uprichard (Portsmouth); W.E.Cunningham (Leicester C), W.G.L.Graham (Doncaster R), R.D.Blanchflower (Spurs), W.T.McCavana (Coleraine), R.Peacock (Celtic), W.L.Bingham (Sunderland), J.McIlroy (Burnley), F.Coyle (Coleraine), C.P.Tully (Celtic), P.J.McParland (Aston Villa).

Half-time 0-0   Full-time 3-0
Ref: B.M.Griffiths (Wales)   Att: 62,000

TO help celebrate the 75th anniversary of the Irish FA, England decided, for the first time, to play them at Wembley. Alas, the game did not live up to the extra prestige of the venue and it will be quickly forgotten. The football matched the greyness of the day and the first half was dull and unimaginative. Ireland had a good deal of the play but neither side threatened much in front of goal.

The one shining light in all this gloom was the youthful Johnny Haynes. Here was a player of real class, who showed a maturity well beyond his years. His superb passing and two footed skills were the main features of the match.

Ireland looked out of place at Wembley. One of the smallest crowds ever assembled for an important international, only 62,000, had little to warm their hearts. True, there was plenty of effort but the general play fell well short of what is expected at this level. The only memorable incident of the first-half came when one of many passes by Haynes found Bedford Jezzard who beat Uprichard with a shot, only for Graham to save the day with a goal-line clearance.

At the other end, Ron Baynham looked decidedly shaky on crosses and the wing-halves, Ronnie Clayton and Jimmy Dickinson, never imposed themselves on the play. Up front Tom Finney never made the impact that Stan Matthews might have done, despite making several good runs. Finney seemed to find it difficult at times to raise his game on the big occasions as Matthews does.

Predictably, the half ended goalless, but five minutes into the second period the match suddenly burst into life. Baynham made a superb point-blank save from Tully and then play swung brilliantly to the other end via a fine triangular move involving Haynes, Dennis Wilshaw and Jezzard. Haynes finally delivered a defence-splitting reverse diagonal pass for Wilshaw to take possession, side-step Uprichard and shoot into the empty net.

If ever a pass won a match, it was Haynes' at that moment. Ireland were now down, and two minutes later they were out as England scored again. This time Jezzard sent Finney away. The winger sent over a deep centre which was lobbed back into the middle by Bill Perry. It dropped under the crossbar and Wilshaw was on the spot to head home. It was ironic in some ways as the Wolves striker had been largely anonymous, and yet here he was with two goals under his belt.

The victory was rounded off by Finney in the 88th minute. Haynes was again at the heart of the move and when Finney received Jezzard's square pass, his change of direction and acceleration took him inside Graham before a diagonal shot beat Uprichard and found the far corner. It was Finney's first goal since the World Cup match against Uruguay.

It was a disappointing performance from England who needed to improve for the forthcoming visit of Spain.

> 63rd match v Northern Ireland.
> Debuts for Clayton and Perry.
> *"Before the start I was anxious, nervous and pacing up and down hoping the game would hurry up and get started."*
> Ronnie Clayton

England v
Spain   Friendly

Played on Wednesday, 30 November 1955 at Wembley Stadium.

England R.L.Baynham (Luton T); J.J.Hall (Birmingham C), R.W.Byrne (Man Utd), R.Clayton (Blackburn R), W.A.Wright (Wolves, captain), J.W.Dickinson (Portsmouth), T.Finney (Preston NE), P.J.W.Atyeo (Bristol C), N.Lofthouse (Bolton W), J.N.Haynes (Fulham), W.Perry (Blackpool).

Spain: C.Cedrun (Athletic Bilbao); J.Segarra (FC Barcelona), M.Gonzalez (Sevilla FC), M.Ugartemendia (Athletic Bilbao), J.Garay (Athletic Bilbao), J.M.Magureghi (Athletic Bilbao), M.Gonzalez (Atlético Madrid), J.L.Perez-Paya (Real Madrid), I.Arieta-Araunabena (Athletic Bilbao), M.Domenech (Sevilla FC), E.Collar (Atlético Madrid).

Half-time 2-0   Full-time 4-1
Ref: M.Guigue (France)   Att: 85,000

ON a cold, murky November day, Wembley seems a million miles from the Spanish summer sunshine. Thus these two sides were meeting each other in far different circumstances to the match played in the sweltering heat of Madrid the previous May.

The scoreline does not reflect the pattern of play but it does emphasise that the team which takes its chances will win the day. Both sides produced some good football with Spain having a great deal of the possession. Unfortunately for them they lacked the ability to finish off the fine approach play.

England began at a brisk pace and after only seven minutes were awarded a penalty. A lovely through-ball by Johnny Haynes sent Tom Finney clear, but as the winger entered the penalty area he was fouled by a Spanish defender for an obvious spot-kick. The Preston player took the penalty himself but his kick was

England manager Walter Winterbottom with his charges at Stamford Bridge in November 1955, before a trial match against a Chelsea XI. England were set to meet Spain at Wembley Stadium the following week and Winterbottom was having a last look before the team was selected, although an FA committee helped out with that job.

Left: Tom Finney's penalty is saved by Cedrun in the game against Spain. *Right:* Cedrun misses this shot from debutant John Atyeo and England are ahead.

Left: England's third goal, scored by Finney. *Right:* Arieta heads home Miguel's cross for Spain's consolation goal.

far too timid and Carmelo saved with ease. Luckily for England they did not have to wait too long for a goal to wipe out the memory of that penalty miss.

On 12 minutes, a splendid move involving Ronnie Clayton, Haynes, Nat Lofthouse and Finney ended with John Atyeo taking Bill Perry's touched pass to shoot home. Sixty seconds later, England scored again. This time the goal owed much to the long pass which was to dominate their style on the day. Haynes was the architect again, sending Atyeo away. Atyeo moved the ball on to Lofthouse who then found Bill Perry who scored with a good shot following a 30-yard run. Before half-time Perry hit the Spanish post with another good effort and England were well worth their 2-0 interval lead.

Spain saw plenty of the ball and in Magureghi they had a superb player urging them on. But always the tendancy of the visitors to overdo the ball skills gave England and especially Billy Wright the chance to clear. The England captain was magnificent and must surely rank as one of the world's truly great players. His anticipation, tackling and heading were an inspiration to his colleagues. With Jeff Hall and Roger Byrne also having splendid matches, the home defence looked very secure.

The pattern continued throughout the

second half with Spain having plenty of possession and England countering with the searching long pass and some lethal finishing. Before the hour was up, England had made the game safe. A slight slip by Garay gave Finney the chance to make ground before cutting inside and planting a lovely diagonal shot just inside the far post. As Finney went to shoot, a crunching Gonzalez tackle stopped him.

Shortly afterwards, and with half an hour to go England hit their fourth goal. Once again the Preston Plumber was the instigator of the attack as his pass found Clayton who centred from the right for Perry to head home perfectly.

Despite several shortcomings in their overall play, one could certainly not criticise the England finishing and all four goals had been expertly taken.

Spain continued, to their great credit, to dominate the midfield with their short passing game and they deserved better

---

5th match v Spain.
Debut goal for Atyeo.
Penalty miss by Finney.
Spain's Cedrun also known as 'Carmelo'; M.Gonzalez (Sevilla FC) also known as 'Campanal'; Ugartemendia as 'Mauri'; M.Gonzalez (Atlético Madrid) as 'Miguel'; Arieta-Araunabena as 'Arieta'.

---

when Arieta's shot hit a post. Then, only a desperate Jimmy Dickinson block prevented Miguel netting the rebound. The visitors did gain some consolation when in the 80th minute Arieta headed home a Miguel cross.

Scotland v England Home Championship

Played on Saturday, 14 April 1956 at Hampden Park, Glasgow.

Scotland: T.Younger (Hibernian); A.H.Parker (Falkirk), J.D.Hewie (Charlton A), R.Evans (Celtic), G.L.Young (Rangers), A.Glen (Aberdeen), G.Leggatt (Aberdeen), R.Johnstone (Man City), L.Reilly (Hibernian), J.L.McMillan (Airdrieonians), G.Smith (Hibernian).

England: R.D.Matthews (Coventry C); J.J.Hall (Birmingham C), R.W.Byrne (Man Utd), J.W.Dickinson (Portsmouth), W.A. Wright (Wolves, captain), D.Edwards (Man Utd), T.Finney (Preston NE), T.Taylor (Man Utd), N.Lofthouse (Bolton W), J.N.Haynes (Fulham), W.Perry (Blackpool).

Half-time 0-0   Full-time 1-1

Ref: L.Callaghan (Wales)   Att: 132,817

IT WAS in 1937 that England had last

lost to Scotland at Hampden Park and the run continued after this latest match between these old rivals. This time, though, Scotland came so very close to ending the sequence. It is always a special occasion when these two sides meet and it came as quite a surprise when England chose Reg Matthews in goal. The selection of a Third Division player raised a few eyebrows, but by the end of the game it was most gratifying to see how well the lad from Coventry performed.

Despite having much less of the possession, England always created the better chances. This was due mainly to the superb play of Johnny Haynes, who really looked a class above the rest. His passing was a delight, although his forward line colleagues tended to waste his best moments. Scotland, with Parker, Hewie and Young outstanding in defence, rarely created a worthwhile goalscoring attempt and they lacked someone of Haynes's ability to take advantage of their greater possession. Even with a massive 132,000 crowd behind them, they still struggled to find the target.

In the first half Scotland managed only one decent attempt. This came in the 15th minute when Matthews made a brilliant diving save low down from Johnstone. This gave the goalkeeper confidence and he went on to show the calm authority that belied his inexperience. Evans was an inspiring worker in midfield for Scotland and much of the play revolved around him. But England could and should have scored twice in the opening period. Both Nat Lofthouse and Bill Perry squandered golden chances, the second one coming from a rare burst of skill from Tom Finney.

The second half began with both sides striving for the breakthrough. It finally came after 60 minutes and it was the Scots who went ahead. Johnstone began the move down the right with a pass to McMillan. He, in turn, found Leggatt advancing down the left. The winger centred and quickly moved into the middle to receive a return pass from Smith. Leggatt then lobbed the ball over a crowd of players and into the net with Matthews stranded.

The 'keeper had some excuse as Leggatt partially mishit his shot although it did not matter to the massive crowd how the goal was scored as it was the first time in nearly 20 years that Scotland had taken the lead against the Auld Enemy at Hampden.

The goal stirred England into life, though and, at last, they began to move more fluently. Wright, Dickinson, Edwards and especially Haynes began to impose themselves on to the game and in the last half-hour England stepped up a gear. They won a stream of corners and Younger excelled when making fine saves twice from Taylor. Berry and Taylor then missed when well placed and Haynes threw away a good chance when his effort struck a post.

With the time ticking away the excitement grew and at times only desperate clearances saved Scotland. Finally, with the home side within seconds of that elusive Hampden victory, England bravely snatched their deserved equalizer. Byrne moved forward to add weight to the attack and put in a good cross to the head of Taylor. His nod down dropped per-

fectly for man-of-the-match, Haynes to sweep the ball past Younger.

The crowd were stunned into almost total silence, not quite believing what had happened. The result also left a unique situation in the Home Championship as all four countries finished level on three points thus sharing the title.

> 73rd match v Scotland.
> Debut for R.Matthews.

England v Brazil
Friendly

Played on Wednesday, 9 May 1956 at Wembley Stadium.

England: R.D.Matthews (Coventry C); J.J.Hall (Birmingham C), R.W.Byrne (Man Utd), R.Clayton (Blackburn), W.A. Wright (Wolves, captain), D.Edwards (Man Utd), S.Matthews (Blackpool), P.J.W.Atyeo (Bristol C), T.Taylor (Man Utd), J.N.Haynes (Fulham), C.Grainger (Sheffield Utd).
Brazil: G.dos Santos (Corinthians); D.Santos (Portuguese), N.Santos (Botafogo), Z.Alves (Bangu), J.Pavão (Bangu), J.Mendonca (Flamengo), P.de Almeida (Flamengo), A.J.Rodrigues (Santos), G.Orlando (São Paulo), W.Pereira (Botafogo), J.Ribamar (São Paulo).

Half-time 2-0   **Full-time 4-2**
Ref: M.Guigue (France)   Att: 100,000

John Atyeo (8) heads the ball on for Tommy Taylor to restore England's lead against Brazil at Wembley in May 1956.

Colin Grainger heads one of his two debut goals against the Brazilians with Stan Matthews, who laid on the cross, in the background.

THIS international had just about everything and the 100,000 people who were privileged to be present enjoyed every minute of an occasion that was pulsating from first whistle to last. Two early goals gave England a tremendous start and the exciting incidents came one after the other. Superlatives are frequent in this report and that just about sums up a superb game.

England began with a devastating burst and in the opening seconds Tommy Taylor found himself clean through, only to shoot just too high with the crowd already celebrating a goal. They did not have to wait much longer, though, as after two minutes Taylor had redeemed himself with a lovely goal. A fine move began with a pass from Duncan Edwards to Stanley Matthews. The 41-year-old genius put a lovely square pass inside to Johnny Haynes who, in turn, pushed the ball forward. Taylor was on to it like a flash and crashed the ball into the roof of the Brazilian net.

Amazingly, within three minutes of that goal England went 2-0 up. Stan Matthews was again heavily involved, picking the ball up near the corner-flag at England's end, he cheekily flicked it between Canhoteiro's legs to find Jeff Hall. The full-back's long, raking pass forward found Taylor again beating Pavão, and, after Haynes had got a touch, Colin Grainger was there to slam home number two.

Incidents galore followed, notably when Canhoteiro struck a shot against an England post, but the home side held on to their lead although realising only too well that Brazil were far from out of the game.

The first half had been superb, surely the second half could not live up to that standard? It did! And not only that the entertainment surpassed the first 45 minutes. Within ten minutes of the restart Brazil had suddenly pulled level. With the wind now behind them and with rain now falling they began the half with a renewed appetite.

Nilton Santos, a superb player, made a break down the left. His cross found Paulinho on the right. The winger seemingly had nowhere to go but suddenly unleashed a shot which struck Roger Byrne and deflected up and over Reg Matthews to spin wickedly over the line. Two minutes later, Brazil were level. A rare mistake by Billy Wright gave Didí possession. The wonderfully gifted player then surprised England's goalkeeper with a vicious 20-yard shot which Matthews could only help into the net.

With Brazil now having their tails well and truly up they proceeded to push the ball around Wembley's lush turf confidently and with great skill. It was now, though, that their South American temperament came into the story. On the hour, the Brazilian tendency for over excitement gave England a penalty when a defender inexplicably handled the ball following Haynes' free-kick.

The referee unhesitatingly gave the spot-kick but in so doing sent the Brazilians wild with rage. For a while the French referee struggled to regain control of a volatile situation but eventually the kick could be taken. Somewhat surprisingly the responsibility was given to John Atyeo, who had not had a particularly inspired game. The crowd groaned as

Atyeo's kick was saved by Gilmar. However it was not long before those groans turned to cheers.

Stan Matthews took a lovely pass from Haynes and centred for Atyeo to head the ball back for Taylor to head England back into the lead. Soon afterwards, in this breathless match, England were awarded another penalty for handball. Again there was pandemonium in the Brazilian ranks and again England missed the kick. This time Byrne's shot was saved by Gilmar.

But, with ten minutes to go, England, with Stan Matthews again to the fore, scored their fourth and most decisive goal. Hall found the Blackpool winger and once again the maestro served up a perfect centre for Grainger to celebrate a fine debut by heading past Gilmar in style.

The teams left the arena to tremendous and deserved applause, it had all been wonderful entertainment.

1st match v Brazil.
Two debut goals for Grainger.
Penalty misses by both Atyeo and Byrne.
Brazil's dos Santos also known as 'Gilmar'; Alves as 'Zozimo'; Mendonca as 'Dequinha'; Almeida as 'Paulinho'; Rodrigues as 'Alvaro'; Orlando as 'Gino'; Pereira as 'Didí'; Ribamar as 'Canhoteiro'.

Sweden v England
Friendly

Played on Wednesday, 16 May 1956 at the Råsunda Stadium, Solna.

Sweden: K.Svensson (Helsingborgs IF); A.Johansson (IFK Norrköping), S.Axbom (IFK Norrköping), S.O.Svensson (Helsingborgs IF), B.Gustavsson (Åtvidabergs FF), S.Parling (Djurgårdens IF), B.Berndtsson (IFK Göteborg), G.Löfgren (Motala AIF), J.Ekström (Malmö FF), B.Lindskog (Malmö FF), G.Sandberg (Djurgårdens IF).

England: R.D.Matthews (Coventry C); J.J.Hall (Birmingham C), R.W.Byrne (Man Utd), R.Clayton (Blackburn R), W.A.Wright (Wolves, captain), D.Edwards (Man Utd), J.J.Berry (Man Utd), P.J.W.Atyeo (Bristol C), T.Taylor (Man Utd), J.N.Haynes (Fulham), C.Grainger (Sheffield Utd).

Half-time 0-0   Full-time 0-0
Ref: L.Horn (Holland)   Att: 38,000

IT WAS a case of 'after the Lord Mayor's Show' as England travelled to Sweden for the first match of their summer tour fresh from the memory of that scintillating game against the Brazilians the previous week.

A strong, blustery wind was blowing around the stadium and Sweden kicked-off with the elements in their favour. Playing determined and uncompromising football, they soon had England pinned back in their own half. The visitors were virtually totally committed to defending as Sweden pressed forward.

Luckily for England, Sweden's finishing was very poor and they missed all their best chances. Lindskog and Sandberg both shot high and wide when well placed and Reg Matthews made super diving saves from both of those players as well as from another effort by S.Svensson.

Two other attempts could easily have opened the scoring. First Ekström hit a post and then Berndtsson lobbed over the bar from a great position. There was also a lucky let-off for England when Duncan Edwards clearly appeared to handle in the penalty area as Sweden exerted yet more pressure. The referee ignored the frantic appeals of the Swedes and waved play on.

England seldom threatened to score themselves and made only a few sorties upfield. Two powerhouse runs by Edwards promised much but then fizzled out, and England's best chances fell to John Atyeo, who twice wasted good opportunities.

After the change of ends, and with the wind now at their backs, it was England's turn to lay siege on the Swedish goal. They forced five corners in as many minutes early on but were frustrated by both Sweden's resolute defending and the unpredictable conditions. Time and again the ball ran out of control as they attacked and all too often the England players chased balls out of play. Edwards again made a strong burst and Taylor fired a good shot just over the angle of post and crossbar from 20 yards.

Unfortunately, these moments grew rarer as the game went on and when the referee blew the final whistle it came as somewhat of a relief to everyone. England had missed the other Matthews in this poor match but if he had had the same sort of service that Johnny Berry had received, then even he would have found it difficult to inject the much-needed boost to England's play.

6th match v Sweden.
First goalless draw since 1948.

Finland v England
Friendly

Played on Sunday, 20 May 1956 at the Olympic Stadium, Helsinki.

Finland: K.Hurri (KuPS Kuopio); V.Pajunen (Haka Valkeakosken), A.Sommarberg (KPT Kotka), A.Lintamo (HPS Helsinki), L.Lehtinen (HJK Helsinki), R.Jalava (HJK Helsinki), J.Peltonen (Haka Valkeakosken), M.Hiltunen (KIF Kronohagen), K.Pahlman (HPS Helsinki), O.Lahtinen (HJK Helsinki), O.Forsgren (KIF Kronohagen).
Sub: A.Klinga (KIF Kronshagen) for Hurri.

England: R.E.Wood (Man Utd); J.J.Hall (Birmingham C), R.W.Byrne (Man Utd), R.Clayton (Blackburn R), W.A.Wright (Wolves, captain), D.Edwards (Man Utd), G.Astall (Birmingham C), J.N.Haynes (Fulham), T.Taylor (Man Utd), D.J.Wilshaw (Wolves), C.Grainger (Sheffield Utd).
Sub: N.Lofthouse (Bolton W) for Taylor.

Half-time 1-3   Full-time 1-5
Ref: J.F.Jörgensen (Denmark) Att: 20,250

SOMETIMES it can seem very unfair to criticise our national team when they gain a convincing win on some foreign field, but this win against mediocre opposition was one of England's worst performances for a long time. True, the standard of opponents can drag any team down to their level, but there was no excuse for this inept display. The game, in all honesty, was awful!

To be fair, England were never stretched and long before the end it became little more than a training exercise. After a scrappy opening 20 minutes, England took the lead. A long through-ball by Duncan Edwards found the speedy Dennis Wilshaw and the Wolves player continued his excellent England scoring record with a fierce cross shot which flew past Hurri in the Finland goal. Two minutes later it was Edwards again, this time setting up Johnny Haynes who scored with another good shot.

Before the half-hour was up, England scored a third goal, the best of the match. A flowing move involving Billy Wright, Colin Grainger, Edwards, Tommy Taylor and Haynes ended with Gordon Astall cutting in to meet the pass from Haynes and shooting home from the narrowest of angles.

After this flurry of activity Taylor collided with Hurri and the goalkeeper was replaced by Klinga. Then, before the break, Finland pulled a goal back when sloppiness in England's defence allowed Forsgren a header past the previously unemployed Ray Woods.

In the second half the game slipped more and more into mediocrity. The lead which England had built up had taken the urgency from their game and only a few moments of the half were worth recording. Taylor also had to leave the field injured, he had damaged his stomach muscles, and he was replaced by Nat Lofthouse.

It was Lofthouse who scored England's other two goals, the first of which equalled Steve Bloomer's long-standing total and the second equalling Vivian Woodward's record of 29 goals for England.

The goal which finally put Lofthouse into the record books was a scrappy one to say the least. It came eight minutes from time when Grainger's corner was headed on by Lofthouse. Wilshaw swung a boot at it and missed, and then two defenders on the line left the clearance to each other before watching horrified as the ball crept between them and over the line for a bizarre goal.

The goal was not really worthy of such stature but definitely summed up this particular game. Astall, Grainger, Haynes and Edwards could be pleased with their efforts but Taylor and Jeff Hall, who dislocated a shoulder, looked doubtful for England's next match.

> 2nd match v Finland.
> Debut goal for Astall.
> Lofthouse scored two goals as substitute.

West Germany v England Friendly

Played on Saturday, 26 May 1956 at the Olympic Stadium, Berlin.

West Germany: I.F.Herkenrath (Rot-Weiss Essen); E.Retter (VfB Stuttgart), E.Juskowiak (Fortuna Düsseldorf), R.Schlienz (VfB Stuttgart), H.Wewers (Rot-Weiss Essen), K.Mai (SpVgg Fürth), F.Waldner (VfB Stuttgart), M.Morlock (1.FC Nuremberg), O.Walter (1.FC Kaiserslautern), F.Walter (1.FC Kaiserslautern), H.Schäfer (1.FC Cologne). Sub: A.Pfaff (Eintracht Frankfurt) for Morlock.
England: R.D.Matthews (Coventry C); J.J.Hall (Birmingham C), R.W.Byrne (Man Utd), R.Clayton (Blackburn R), W.A. Wright (Wolves, captain), D.Edwards (Man Utd), G.Astall (Birmingham C), J.N.Haynes (Fulham), T.Taylor (Man Utd), D.J.Wilshaw (Wolves), C.Grainger (Sheffield Utd).

Half-time 0-1   Full-time 1-3
Ref: I.Zsolt (Hungary)

AFTER two lacklustre displays England completed their summer tour with a magnificent victory against the current World Champions West Germany in Berlin. The visitors produced a superb team performance, just when it mattered and now they can start to look forward to the 1958 World Cup with some optimism.

As early as the first 20 seconds it became apparent that England could do well. At that moment Dennis Wilshaw burst through on to a Johnny Haynes pass to shoot inches wide. It was an early warning for the Germans and one that they did not heed. Playing the ball around confidently, England swept forward in search of goals. They won most of the tackles and supported each other superbly.

In the 25th minute the goal their early play deserved duly arrived, and what a cracker it was! Colin Grainger's corner was cleared to be met by Ron Clayton and Morlock together. As the ball ran loose from their challenge Duncan Edwards pounced, and with that characteristic power, he swept past three tackles with consummate ease before crashing an unstoppable shot past Herkenrath's right hand. The youngster, in that one moment, demonstrated to the world what an awesome sight he is when he is in full flight.

The England half-backs dominated the German forwards and only a glancing header by Ottmar Walter forced Reg Matthews into the action. The goalkeeper was more than equal to the task, though, and produced a marvellous save to keep England's lead intact.

The visitors could well have added to their lead and some of their football was quite outstanding. Unfortunately they could not finish off their fine approach play, although on the half-hour they came very close. A brilliant six-man attack down the left finally ended when Tommy Taylor's shot was superbly blocked by Herkenrath and Grainger's follow up effort struck the 'keeper again with the England fans already celebrating what they thought would be a certain goal.

But the Germans held on and just before half-time Morlock stretched to send a shot just over. In so doing the inside-right injured himself and had to leave the field to be replaced by Pfaff.

At the half-time whistle, the many British servicemen in the crowd cheered their team off. They knew that if England continued to play as well, they would surely be celebrating a famous victory.

Not unexpectedly West Germany came hard at England after the restart but Billy Wright and his fellow defenders were in immaculate form. Jeff Hall and Roger Byrne stifled the danger from the wingers and when England countered they always looked likely to score.

In the 63rd and 69th minutes, England at last made the game safe with two deadly strikes. Haynes, who started quietly but gradually took control of the play, threaded a superb pass through for

Gordon Astall to collect. The winger slipped the ball inside to where Grainger showed pace and skill before shooting home an excellent goal.

Six minutes later came goal number-three. Taylor, who oozed class in all that he did, worked the ball in from the right to find Wilshaw. The hard-working Wolves player glanced it into space and Haynes latched on to it to coolly beat Herkenrath with a well-placed shot. The England fans were delirious and they made their presence felt with some tremendous and much appreciated support.

The West Germans, characteristically, never gave up and although three goals down they pressed forward to put more pressure on England. Reg Matthews made another fine stop to deny the dangerous Pfaff but was powerless, five minutes from time, to prevent Fritz Walter from finishing off a delightful move featuring himself, Mai and Schaeffer. It was to be the Germans' only consolation and at the final whistle there were jubilant scenes amongst the visiting fans celebrating a memorable triumph.

> 5th match v West Germany.

Northern Ireland v England Home Championship

Played on Saturday, 6 October 1956 at Windsor Park, Belfast.

Northern Ireland: H.Gregg (Doncaster R); W.E.Cunningham (Leicester C), A.McMichael (Newcastle Utd), R.D.Blanchflower (Spurs), J.Blanchflower (Man Utd), T.Casey (Newcastle Utd), W.L.Bingham (Sunderland), J.McIlory (Burnley), J.Jones (Glenavon), W.J.McAdams (Man City), P.J.McParland (Aston Villa).
England: R.D.Matthews (Coventry C); J.J.Hall (Birmingham C), R.W.Byrne (Man Utd), R.Clayton (Blackburn R), W.A.Wright (Wolves, captain), D.Edwards (Man Utd), S.Matthews (Blackpool), D.G.Revie (Man City), T.Taylor (Man Utd), D.J.Wilshaw (Wolves), C.Grainger (Sheffield Utd).

Half-time 1-1   Full-time 1-1
Ref: H.Phillips (Scotland)   Att: 58,500

ENGLAND had nearly always been assured of victory in Northern Ireland but on this occasion they came so very close to losing. Despite an inspired opening burst, they ended the match hanging on for dear life to the draw.

The visitors began with a devastating first nine minutes. With the magnificent win in Germany still fresh in their memory, England played some superb football. They pushed the ball around with arrogance and confidence and twice in the opening seconds, Ronnie Clayton and Don Revie set up Stan Matthews to provide tantalising centres to fully test the Irish rearguard.

This was followed up in the third minute with a glorious goal. Fine inter-passing between Duncan Edwards, Revie and Tommy Taylor ended with the centre-forward putting a square pass inside to Revie. Revie flicked it to his right and Stan Matthews came in to shoot a lovely, low left-foot shot into the far corner. It was his first international goal for eight years and, coincidentally, his last one was also against the Irish at Windsor Park.

The goal signalled a five-minute spell of intense pressure by England. Brilliant football, sometimes involving six or seven players, carved open the Irish defence. At this stage only the immaculate Gregg stood between England and a hatfull of goals. Twice he saved superbly from Colin Grainger and Taylor as England served up some vintage play.

But in the tenth minute came the moment that totally and inexplicably changed the pattern of the game.

Northern Ireland equalized with a goal right out of the blue and one that came straight off their training ground. A well-rehearsed long throw to the near post by McParland was flicked on by McAdams as he was challenged by a defender, and the ball dropped perfectly for the incoming McIlroy to volley past Reg Matthews. The goal was joyfully received by the home crowd and there was a cup-tie atmosphere.

The turn round was unbelievable as Danny Blanchflower and Casey powerfully subdued Revie and Edwards to take control of the midfield. McParland helped McMichael in curbing the threat from Stan Matthews and the England winger was forced inside in search of the ball making him less effective. McIlroy was also prominent now and several times his passes split the England defence. But despite this change in fortunes, Ireland could not turn their advantage into goals.

The same pattern continued into the second half with England restricted to only the occasional spasmodic raid. Stan Matthews was by now almost exclusively playing down the middle and was never again allowed to operate in his more favoured right-wing position. Having said that he was still England's best player.

Reg Matthews made some fine saves but he also had some hair-raising moments as Ireland pressed hard. In the last five minutes the home side almost snatched that long-awaited victory. Both McIlroy and McParland suffered desperately bad luck when they saw good efforts cannon back off the woodwork. It was a sad end for the Irish and there were few people present who would have begrudged them that extra glory of winning.

64th match v Northern Ireland.

England v Wales Home Championship

Played on Wednesday, 14 November 1956 at Wembley Stadium.

England: E.G.Ditchburn (Spurs); J.J.Hall (Birmingham C), R.W.Byrne (Man Utd), R.Clayton (Blackburn R), W.A.Wright (Wolves, captain), J.W.Dickinson (Portsmouth), S.Matthews (Blackpool), J.Brooks (Spurs), T.Finney (Preston NE), J.N.Haynes (Fulham), C.Grainger (Sheffield Utd).

Wales: A.J.Kelsey (Arsenal); A.T.Sherwood (Newport Co), M.Hopkins (Spurs), A.C.Harrington (Cardiff C), R.W.Daniel (Sunderland), D.Sullivan (Cardiff C), T.C.Medwin (Spurs), M.Charles (Swansea T), W.J.Charles (Leeds Utd), I.J.Allchurch (Swansea T), C.W.Jones (Swansea T).

Half-time 0-1   Full-time 3-1

Ref: H.Phillips (Scotland)   Att: 95,000

Tom Finney scores England's third goal in the 75th minute against Wales at Wembley in November 1956.

ENGLAND'S recent good run at Wembley was stretched to seven consecutive victories after they beat Wales by three goals to one. The match was far from memorable though and was too often interrupted by a succession of injuries.

Wales began in their usual fervent fashion and the awesome J.Charles was soon showing his power. After only eight minutes they produced a shock by taking the lead. An infringement by Roger Byrne gave Allchurch the chance to send a free-kick to the far post from a position just outside the right-hand edge of the penalty area. The kick was perfectly judged and it was met by the incoming J.Charles who outjumped the defenders to head firmly past Ted Ditchburn's despairing left hand.

The Welsh supporters were delighted but their joy was soon replaced by concern as Jack Kelsey was injured diving at Tom Finney's feet. The goalkeeper was badly hurt and had to be stretchered off. Sherwood went in goal and immediately impressed with some confident handling. However, the rhythm of the game was upset and England, although not convincingly, began to take control.

With tenacious defending though the Welsh held on to their lead with Daniel holding Finney expertly and Hopkins outstanding at full-back. Finney was struggling in his new roll of a ball playing centre-forward and even when Mel Charles had to go off for treatment five minutes from the break England could still find no way past the resolute defending of the Welsh.

Indeed, Wales almost snatched another goal on a couple of breakaway occasions and Ronnie Clayton was very fortunate to see his foul on Allchurch only produce a free-kick just outside the box when a penalty looked likely. John Charles almost broke through again, only for Billy Wright to make a brilliant saving tackle.

England, meanwhile, came very close when first Finney headed a Colin Grainger cross against a post, and then Grainger himself hit the same post with a header

from a Stan Matthews cross. The Welshmen in the 95,000 crowd kept cheering their players on and their team miraculously held out until half-time. After the break M.Charles returned fully fit to the fray and Kelsey took up a position on the left wing to provide, perhaps, a nuisance to the England defenders. Unfortunately it was not to be and the goalkeeper soon hobbled off again, this time for good.

The pressure increased from England and in seven minutes after half-time they forged a lead they were not to lose. First, a corner by Grainger on the left was headed back across goal by Finney and Johnny Haynes was on hand to hit a low, hard left-foot volley past Sherwood to equalize.

Shortly afterwards England took the lead when an excellent passing movement between Haynes, Clayton, Matthews and Johnny Brooks ended with the latter latching on to a rebound off of a defender to hit home an angled shot wide of the unfortunate Sherwood.

Ironically, Grainger then had to leave the field injured, thus making the sides level in numbers again, but then Haynes began to hobble too. This did not seem to stop England from retaining control though and, with Wright now stifling the threat from John Charles, there was little danger from the Welsh attack.

Brooks was enjoying much more freedom now and with 15 minutes left he and Matthews set up goal number three. Combining at a short corner, the ball ran for Matthews to centre from the right. In came Finney to delicately flick the ball wide of Sherwood to score the decisive goal.

The game was now well and truly over and the feeling was left that the injuries had had a bad effect on the pattern of the match. Also there was a question-mark over Finney as the new centre-forward as his ball-playing style seemed a little lost as the natural tendancy of the wingers to cross the ball did not suit such a tactical move.

67th match v Wales.
Debut goal for Brooks.

England v Yugoslavia Friendly

Played on Wednesday, 28 November 1956 at Wembley Stadium.

England: E.G.Ditchburn (Spurs); J.J.Hall (Birmingham C), R.W.Byrne (Man Utd), R.Clayton (Blackburn R), W.Wright (Wolves, captain), J.W.Dickinson (Portsmouth), S.Matthews (Blackpool), J.Brooks (Spurs), T.Finney (Preston NE), J.N.Haynes (Fulham), F.Blunstone (Chelsea). Sub: T.Taylor (Man Utd) for Haynes.

Yugoslavia: V.Beara (Red Star Belgrade); B.Belin (Partizan Belgrade), B.Stanković (Red Star Belgrade), L.Tasić (Red Star Belgrade), I.Horvat (Dinamo Zagreb), V.Boškov (Vojvodina Novi Sad), Z.Rajkov (Vojvodina Novi Sad), V.Čonč (Dinamo Zagreb), I.Toplak (Red Star Belgrade), B.Vukas (Hajduk Split), B.Zebec (Partizan Belgrade).

Half-time 1-0   Full-time 3-0

Ref: E.Harzic (France)   Att: 78,500

THIS was England's fourth meeting with Yugoslavia, the first had come some 17 years earlier, and at last, on a rain-soaked Wembley pitch, they finally gained their first victory. And what an impressive win it turned out to be. But for Beara in the visitors' goal, the score might have been doubled.

Right from the start England set about the Yugoslavs with an abundance of attacking flair. At the centre of the inspired play was Stanley Matthews. The England maestro had played in that first meeting in Belgrade all those years ago and by the end of this match he had more than exacted revenge for the 2-1 defeat then. The Yugoslav defenders tried everything they knew to stop him and resorted to many variations of the 'tackle'. Sometimes it was more suited to Twickenham than Wembley!

In the first half-hour England put together some lovely football. With Matthews and Tom Finney at their brilliant best and Johnny Haynes and Johnny Brooks setting up some lovely moves, goalkeeper Beara had every opportunity to show his class and agility. He made a breathtaking one-handed save from a Haynes thunderbolt after some brilliant play by Matthews and Finney. Then a Ronnie Clayton through ball sent Brooks racing clear, only for Beara to make another fine save from the final shot.

On 13 minutes, though, England took a deserved lead. A goal-kick by Ted Ditchburn gave Matthews and Finney the chance to combine down the left. Matthews passed to Haynes, who immediately turned the ball square for Brooks to ghost in and crash his shot into the roof of the net.

Straight after the goal Beara again produced heroics to deny Matthews a goal after another brilliant burst. Sadly for England their rhythm was upset on the half-hour when Haynes had to go off injured after being tackled in the act of shooting. Tommy Taylor came on to replace him and Finney moved to inside-right with Brooks moving over to partner Frank Blunstone.

For a quarter of an hour either side of half-time, England lost control of the midfield, but during this stage of the game their half-back line was magnificent. With

Bukas showing all his undoubted skills and Zebec showing tremendous pace, England had to hold steady. But Billy Wright, Clayton and Jimmy Dickinson controlled things so superbly that Ditchburn was rarely troubled.

With 25 minutes left the result was finally put beyond doubt. Finney, who continually left Horvat stranded, set off on a longer run, holding the ball and evading desperate tackles. He weaved his way to the right-hand by-line before turning the ball neatly inside where Taylor was left with the simple task of firing into the empty net.

By this time the rain was lashing down and in the last 15 minutes it was all England. Matthews, for the umpteenth time, was scythed down by Stanković. This time though it was in the penalty area and Roger Byrne stepped up for the spot-kick. Once again it was Beara to the rescue as he leapt like a salmon to save the ball a foot inside the post. But England were not to be denied and they kept up the pressure. The floodlights came on five minutes from the end to lift the gloom and soon Frank Blunstone was heading just wide from yet another Matthews cross.

Then, with the last minute ticking away, Matthews again passed to Blunstone and this time the Chelsea winger gave Taylor a second chance to fire into an empty net.

It was an excellent victory with Matthews brilliant throughout and Finney outstanding. The only blot came with the news that Haynes' injury looked like keeping him out of the side for the following week's World Cup match against Denmark at Molineux.

> 4th match v Yugoslavia.
> 50th cap for Matthews.
> Penalty miss by Byrne.
> Two goals for Taylor as a substitute.

England v Denmark World Cup Qualifier

Played on Wednesday, 5 December 1956 at Molineux, Wolverhampton.

England: E.G.Ditchburn (Spurs); J.J.Hall (Birmingham C), R.W.Byrne (Man Utd), R.Clayton (Blackburn R), W.A.Wright (Wolves, captain), J.W.Dickinson (Portsmouth), S.Matthews (Blackpool), J.Brooks (Spurs), T.Taylor (Man Utd), D.Edwards (Man Utd), T.Finney (Preston NE).

Denmark: T.Drensgård (Skovshoved); V.Nielsen (AB København), E.L.Larsen (Odense BKØ9), F.Nielsen (B93 København), O.Hansen (Esbjerg BK), J.Olesen (Aarhus GF), J.Hansen (Naestved IF), B.Petersen (Horsens fs), O.B.Nielsen (AB København), A.R.Jensen (Aarhus GF), J.P.Hansen (Esbjerg BK).

Half-time 2-1   Full-time 5-2

Ref: M.Guigue (France)   Att: 53,000

ENGLAND made their first strides towards the 1958 World Cup Finals with this hard-fought win against the gallant amateurs of Denmark. But the home side certainly made hard work of it even though they got off to the perfect start.

Only two minutes had gone when Tom Finney made a superb darting run inside

Tom Finney, restored to the wing for the World Cup qualifier against Denmark.

before a slide rule pass gave Tommy Taylor a simple goal. The expected pattern of England domination continued for awhile and after 20 minutes they increased their lead. Again Finney was the goalmaker. His clever body swerves and electric pace left Larsen groping and Taylor was again on the end of the final pass.

Not unnaturally England tended to relax after this opening but they were almost made to pay by a spirited fight-back by Denmark. Their tricky wingers J.Hansen and P.Hansen gave Roger Byrne and Jeff Hall a difficult time and Billy Wright saw his defenders pinned back on their heels by a brave effort from the Danes.

One splendid move involving all their forwards ended with O.Nielsen hitting a shot against Ted Ditchburn's crossbar. On the half-hour the visitors gained their due reward by scoring a fine goal. P.Hansen sent J.Hansen away on the right and this time O.Nielsen ended the move by striking a good shot just inside a post.

So, at half-time it was 2-1, but eight minutes after the turnround Taylor completed a fine hat-trick when he latched on to a mistake by O.Hansen after a long clearance by Byrne. That put England back in command but, to their credit, Denmark stubbornly refused to give in and after 73 minutes they again pulled a goal

Lord Rosebery meets England's Stanley Matthews before the game against Scotland at Wembley in April 1957. Waiting in line are Jeff Hall and Tommy Thompson.

back. Petersen seized on a mistake in midfield by Duncan Edwards and put a lovely pass through for O.Nielsen to once more shoot past Ditchburn.

That put the game back in the melting pot but by this time the extra power and fitness of England began to show and Denmark's challenge was finally killed off by a wonderful goal by Edwards. Stan Matthews, largely anonymous up to now, suddenly produced one of his typical runs before hitting a crossfield pass into the path of Edwards. The powerful midfield player met it brilliantly to unleash a ferocious shot which almost burst through the net.

That goal came in the 75th minute and almost immediately Edwards again showed his powerhouse shooting when he nearly uprooted a post with another blockbuster from a free-kick.

Towards the end of the game Edwards

completed the scoring with yet another fierce shot after a clever flick by Matthews. The crowd gave the Danes some generous applause at the end, though, as they realised what a lot of effort they had put in to their play. It seemed a shame that they would not be competing in the 1956 Melbourne Olympics, withdrawing because they felt they might be outclassed.

Finney, in the first-half especially, Taylor and Edwards were the pick of the England side, with Ronnie Clayton and Matthews coming on strong at the end.

3rd match v Denmark.
Hat-trick by Taylor.

England v Scotland Home Championship

Played on Saturday, 6 April 1957 at Wembley Stadium.

England: A.Hodgkinson (Sheffield Utd); J.J.Hall (Birmingham C), R.W.Byrne (Man Utd), R.Clayton (Blackburn R), W.A. Wright (Wolves, captain), D.Edwards (Man Utd), S.Matthews (Blackpool), T.Thompson (Preston NE), T.Finney (Preston NE), D.T.Kevan (West Brom), C.Grainger (Sheffield Utd).

Scotland: T.Younger (Liverpool); E.Caldow (Rangers), J.D.Hewie (Charlton A), I.M.McColl (Rangers), G.L.Young (Rangers), T.H.Docherty (Preston NE), R.Y.Collins (Celtic), W.Fernie (Celtic), L.Reilly (Hibernian), J.K.Mudie (Blackpool), T.Ring (Clyde).

Half-time 0-1   **Full-time 2-1**

Ref: P.P.Roomer (Holland)   Att: 97,520

SCOTLAND had a dream start to this international match at Wembley. Within 60 seconds of the opening whistle they were a goal in front. Ring, intercepting a pass from Jeff Hall intended for Stan Matthews, burst past Billy Wright into a huge space before easily beating Alan Hodgkinson with a good shot — not the best of starts for England's new goalkeeper on his debut.

For the next 25 minutes Scotland had a good deal of the play and the pressure and could easily have wrapped up the result during that spell. That they didn't was due mainly to Wright, who drew on all his experience and skill to snuff out any attack that threatened his goal. He was always there to help his fellow defenders when they were in trouble, especially Hall, who had a difficult time with the lively Ring.

Despite Wright's fine form, the Scots created several clear chances. Docherty, a tigerish wing-half, and McColl, had a firm grip on the midfield and three times Hodgkinson, who lacks inches, was struggling with high crosses. However, the goalkeeper lacks nothing in bravery and dived at both Reilly and Ring's feet

to avert dangerous situations.

As the half wore on, Wright's influence began to rub off on his teammates, Hall worked hard to subdue Ring, and Mudie and Fernie lost the impetus of their early play and it allowed England to come more into the game, perhaps that was the crucial factor in the final outcome.

There was a dramatic moment straight after half-time when Scotland had a goal disallowed by the Dutch referee. Hodgkinson, challenged by Reilly, dropped a cross at the feet of Fernie, who promptly shot home, but the referee ordered a free-kick, adjudging Reilly's challenge unfair. That would have made it 2-0 but as it was England then took control for the rest of the match and gradually turned the result around.

Things did not flow that freely for them, though, and their disjointed forward line did not look a combined unit. Tommy Thompson was far too easily shackled by his Preston clubmate Docherty and Derek Kevan, too, looked a little below international class.

However, Kevan did not appear to be afraid to shoot and it was he who equalized in the 63rd minute. Indeed, it was Kevan who started the move as passes flowed between him, Thompson, Kevan again, Tom Finney and Colin Grainger, who took it down the left to centre. Kevan, who was following up, met the cross as he dived headlong to finish off the move he had started.

Stanley Matthews, who had had a quiet game up to now, suddenly began to turn on the style. With six minutes left he set up Duncan Edwards to score one of the best goals ever seen at Wembley. A typical dribble by the Blackpool winger ended with a square pass inside. The ball was some 25 yards from goal when Edwards came steaming in. The youngster hit it with ferocious power and the ball was in the net before Younger could move. It was a goal fit to win a much better match than this one and will be remembered long after the game is forgotten.

> 74th match v Scotland.
> Debuts for Hodgkinson and Kevan.
> Debut goal for Kevan.

England v World Cup Qualifier
Republic of Ireland

Played on Wednesday, 8 May 1957 at Wembley Stadium.

England: A.Hodgkinson (Sheffield Utd); J.J.Hall (Birmingham C), R.W.Byrne (Man Utd), R.Clayton (Blackburn R), W.A.Wright (Wolves, captain), D.Edwards (Man Utd), S.Matthews (Blackpool), P.J.W.Atyeo (Bristol C), T.Taylor (Man Utd), J.N.Haynes (Fulham), T.Finney (Preston NE).

Republic of Ireland: J.A.Kelly (Drumcondra); D.C.Donovan (Everton), N.Cantwell (West Ham), P.D.Farrell (Everton), G.Mackey (Shamrock R), P.Saward (Aston Villa), A.Ringstead (Sheffield Utd), W.A.Whelan (Man Utd), D.P.Curtis (Bristol C), A.G.Fitzsimons (Middlesbrough), J.Haverty (Arsenal).

Half-time 4-0   **Full-time 5-1**
Ref: H.Phillips (Scotland)   Att: 52,000

ENGLAND moved a step nearer to the 1958 World Cup finals in Sweden as they beat off the challenge of the Republic of Ireland. Although the scoreline looks convincing enough, the actual performance by the home side was not entirely inspiring. For long periods in the second half, Eire were on top, producing a clever brand of football that at times was reminiscent of Hungary or Austria at their best. Alas, for the Irish, they could find no finish to this attractive approach play.

England did all the damage in the first half and their star was undoubtedly Johnny Haynes. He really looked the part and his all-round contribution was once again the key. With John Atyeo being used in a twin-pronged attack alongside Tommy Taylor, the home side took the lead in the ninth minute.

Stan Matthews showed some skilful footwork before laying the ball inside to Ronnie Clayton. The wing-half then produced a lovely through pass and Taylor raced in, sold a dummy to the defence, and hit a good shot past Kelly.

Just after the quarter-hour, England

The Republic of Ireland defence concede a goal during the World Cup qualifier at Wembley in May 1957.

John Atyeo heads home another goal for England as the Irish go crashing out at Wembley.

made it 2-0 when Haynes fed Tom Finney. When the winger's pass came inside Taylor was there again to fire an 18-yard shot past a strangely flat-footed Kelly. England attacked at will and before the interval they added two more goals.

Many of their best attacks had involved the in-form Finney. His influence on the first half was enormous and it was the Preston player who set up number three. Receiving possession from Duncan Edwards, he cut inside and hit a fierce shot at goal. Kelly could only parry the ball upwards and before the goalkeeper could recover, Atyeo pounced to head home.

Almost immediately poor Kelly was again fishing the ball out of the back of his net, this time after Taylor had soared gloriously to head in Finney's corner. The scoreline was emphatic to say the least with Taylor having scored his eighth goal in only three and a half internationals. It is often difficult for a team to raise their game in the second half when they are so far in front and that is just how it proved as England gave a lethargic display after the break.

All credit to the Irish, though, as they refused to give up and, indeed, came back at them strongly.

England looked jaded with Edwards, particularly, looking very tired after his many games in the season just ended. The Irish put some excellent football together at this stage and scored a deserved goal when Curtis headed in a left-wing centre from little Joe Haverty. They continually pressed forward and Farrell shot high over when well placed. Shortly after that incident Alan Hodgkinson was relieved to see Whelan's close-range shot crash against the crossbar.

Those missed chances did not help Ireland's cause at all and just to rub salt into the wound, England snatched a fifth goal in the last minute. Haynes and Finney again combined and from Finney's pass Atyeo was again the man in the right position to beat Kelly.

Now England faced two difficult return games in Copenhagen and Dublin to see who goes to Sweden. It would not be easy for them.

> 3rd match v Republic of Ireland.
> Hat-trick by Taylor (his second for England).

Denmark v England World Cup Qualifier

Played on Wednesday, 15 May 1957 at the Idraetspark, Copenhagen.

Denmark: T.Drensgård (Skovshoved); J.Amdisen (Aarhus GF), V.Nielsen (AB København), F.Nielsen (B 93 København), O.Hansen (Esbjerg BK), J.Olesen (Aarhus GF), J.Hansen (Naestved IF), J.Jensen (Aarhus GF), E.Jensen (Aarhus GF), A.R.Jensen (Aarhus GF), J.P.Hansen (Esbjerg BK).

England: A.Hodgkinson (Sheffield Utd); J.J.Hall (Birmingham C), R.W.Byrne (Man Utd), R.Clayton (Blackburn R), W.A. Wright (Wolves, captain), D.Edwards (Man Utd), S.Matthews (Blackpool), P.J.W.Atyeo (Bristol C), T.Taylor (Man Utd), J.N.Haynes (Fulham), T.Finney (Preston NE).

Half-time 1-1   **Full-time 1-4**
Ref: A.Dusch (West Germany) Att: 45,000

WHEN England play away from home they invariably have to face inspired opposition. Teams seem to raise their game several levels when the former masters of the game visit their shores. This match was no exception. The added spice of a World Cup final place at stake gave Denmark all the encouragement they needed and they stretched England to the limits. With two Nielsens, three Hansens and three Jensens in their side it was also a commentator's nightmare!

It is easy to forget, when reporting on England's internationals, that other countries have an extra determination to beat us, therefore we sometimes underestimate and over-criticise some of their performances. This was just such a game. There was an awful lot wrong with England's display with several players well below par. Having said that, they went a goal down yet still ended worthy winners, something of which they can be justly proud.

For the first quarter of an hour England looked in command. Johnny Haynes and Tom Finney were producing some lovely play and all looked set for a comfortable win. But in the 26th minute, a defence-splitting pass by A.Jensen, Denmark's captain, set up a fine chance for J.Jensen, who fired a fierce shot into the roof of Alan Hodgkinson's net.

The crowd went wild but hardly had time to celebrate before England equalized. Haynes, Finney and Duncan Edwards weaved a delightful pattern down the left before Haynes ended the move with a good shot low under Drengsgård's desperate dive.

O.Hansen twice had to save his side by heading away goalbound efforts and he was outstanding at the heart of the Danish defence. His efforts were largely responsible for his team still being on level terms at the break.

England could do nothing special early in the second half, although a Tommy Taylor blockbuster crashed against Denmark's crossbar in one attack. In fact, midway through the half it was the home side who were well on top. They missed a wonderful chance when J.Olsen's long pass caught England out only for J.Jensen, despite being clean through, to miss a golden opening by chipping just over as Hodgkinson challenged.

With 20 minutes to go there was a vital turning point. O.Hansen, Denmark's star player was badly injured in a collision with Taylor, and whilst he was off the field receiving treatment England suddenly and clinically took full advantage of the situation. Jeff Hall passed to John Atyeo and when the next pass came inside, there was Taylor, now unmarked, to shoot home.

In the 75th minute England made it 3-1 when Haynes centred from the right to find Atyeo at the far post to head in off the crossbar.

Finally, Finney, taking yet another super pass from Haynes, had the chance to centre from the left. He found Taylor's head as the centre-forward continued his rich scoring vein.

> 4th match v Denmark.
> Stanley Matthews' last international appearance.

Republic of Ireland v England World Cup Qualifier

Played on Sunday, 19 May 1957 at Dalymount Park, Dublin.

Republic of Ireland T.F.Godwin (Bournemouth); S.Dunne (Luton T), N.Cantwell (West Ham), R.Nolan (Shamrock R), C.J.Hurley (Millwall), P.Saward (Aston Villa), A.Ringstead (Sheffield Utd), W.A.Whelan (Man Utd), D.P.Curtis (Britol R), A.G.Fitzsimons (Middlesbrough), J.Haverty (Arsenal).

England: A.Hodgkinson (Sheffield Utd); J.J.Hall (Birmingham C), R.W.Byrne (Man Utd), R.Clayton (Blackburn R), W.A.Wright (Wolves, captain), D.Edwards (Man Utd), T.Finney (Preston NE), P.J.W.Atyeo (Bristol C), T.Taylor (Man Utd), J.N.Haynes (Fulham), D.Pegg (Man Utd).

Half-time 1-0   **Full-time 1-1**
Ref: H.Phillips (Scotland)   Att: 47,000

ENGLAND had made it! By virtue of this hard-won point in Dublin, they now qualify for next June's World Cup finals in Sweden. But oh, what a narrow squeak they had in getting that conclusive point.

This was one of the most stirring internationals since the war. With so much at stake, and with a fervent and excited 47,000-strong crowd right behind the Irishmen, it was also one of England's most difficult games. That they won a point at all says a lot for their character. Let the story unfold.

Only three minutes had gone and the crowd were hardly settled, when the Irish set the stadium alight by taking the lead. Fitzsimons began the move by creating an opening for Haverty down the left. He whipped in a cross and although Alan Hodgkinson partially saved, the ball ran loose for Ringstead to crash home a shot amid great excitement from the crowd.

They knew that a win here and victory over Denmark later would see them through to Sweden at England's expense.

Ireland were inspired by the goal and with their half-backs looking magnificent they were formidable opposition. On 15 minutes a very important incident occured. A superb move by the Republic began with Whelan and was carried on by Ringstead and Curtis. At the end of the attack Haverty was left with an open goal. It looked curtains for England at that moment but somehow Haverty's shot struck Hodgkinson as the goalkeeper made a despairing dive. A goal then and the game would probably have been all over.

Ireland's dominance at this stage was emphasised by the fact that they won most of the tackles and the loose balls. Whelan, at inside-right, was outstanding and easily the best midfield player on view. Despite all this, the Republic still had only the one-goal lead at half-time to show for their efforts.

After the break, England really rolled their sleeves up. They realised they had a very difficult match and knuckled down bravely to their challenge. Gradually, Ronnie Clayton and Duncan Edwards imposed their powerful presence on the midfield battle. But the Republic's defence gave nothing away with Godwin and Hurley outstanding. Tommy Taylor did produce some danger with his determined running, but England, with Johnny Haynes strangely subdued, had no cool head to finish off the improved approach play. They forced many corners, on both flanks, but always the final touch was missing.

The Irish were dangerous when given the chance to break from defence with Whelan shooting just wide and Haverty seeing his shot headed off the line by Billy Wright. But by now it was nearly all England, possession wise, and with 15 minutes to go Taylor missed a sitter after he turned sharply to sieze on to Godwin's only mistake under the Irish crossbar. That looked to be a costly miss.

To their credit though England continued to throw everything forward and they forced corner after corner. With the 90 minutes up and injury time fast disappearing, the visitors looked destined for defeat. The crowd were at fever pitch with victory so close. But then, in virtually the last attack of the game, came the last dramatic moment of a pulsating game. Tom Finney, who up until then had had a quiet match, picked up a fine pass from Jeff Hall and set off for one last run down the right wing. He cut inside Saward's tackle and then swerved outside Cantwell. Saward ran back for another go but was beaten on the by-line. Finney then produced a perfect centre for John Atyeo to head home.

The England players jumped for joy as the Irish crowd looked on in disbelief. A truly dramatic end to an exhilarating afternoon.

4th match v Republic of Ireland.
Debut for Pegg.

Wales v
England Home Championship

Played on Saturday, 19 October 1957 at Ninian Park, Cardiff.

Wales: A.J.Kelsey (Arsenal); S.G.Williams (West Brom), M.Hopkins (Spurs), W.C.Harris (Middlesbrough), M.Charles (Swansea T), D.L.Bowen (Arsenal), T.C.Medwin (Spurs), E.R.Davis (Newcastle Utd), D.F.Palmer (Swansea T), T.R.Vernon (Blackburn R), C.W.Jones (Swansea T.

England: E.Hopkinson (Bolton W); D.Howe (West Brom), R.W.Byrne (Man Utd), R.Clayton (Blackburn R), W.A. Wright (Wolves, captain), D.Edwards (Man Utd), B.Douglas (Blackburn R), D.T.Kevan (West Brom), T.Taylor (Man Utd), J.N.Haynes (Fulham), T.Finney (Preston NE).

Half-time 0-2   Full-time 0-4
Ref: T.Mitchell (Northern Ireland)
Att: 58,000

ENGLAND stretched their unbeaten run to 16 games with this easy victory over the Welsh in Cardiff. Ironically, it was Wales who were the last team to beat England, two years earlier, but there was never any chance of a repeat result this time. Without the likes of John Charles, Tapscott and Allchurch in their ranks Wales were a pale shadow of some of their previous sides and they had little to offer. Indeed, it must be said that this was the poorest Welsh team for many years.

A gift goal, right at the beginning, sent England on their way. Johnny Haynes,

so often the instigator of the visitors' attacks, threaded a strong through ball for Derek Kevan to chase. Hopkins intercepted and turned to roll the ball back to Kelsey, unaware that his goalkeeper had advanced from his goal. The ball trickled agonisingly over the line to give England a very fortunate lead.

That poor start seemed to upset the Welsh and for long periods there was only one side in it. Tom Finney, Haynes and Duncan Edwards combined well down the left and repeatedly tore large holes in the home defence. England should really have finished off the game in the first half but some scrappy play meant few clear chances especially as the forwards tended to bunch up. The second goal was long overdue but when it did come it was a real beauty.

Billy Wright sent a long pass forward and Tommy Taylor cleverly flicked it to Haynes. The inside-left took it brilliantly in his stride, advanced a few paces, and then hit a low, hard shot into the far corner from the edge of the area. Almost immediately the half-time whistle blew with only the solid performances of Hopkins, despite his own-goal, and Bowen keeping the score down to 2-0. The rain-soaked crowd had little to cheer.

The second half continued with the same pattern and on 64 minutes England scored the best goal of the match. Wright found Haynes and once again the schemer-in-chief set up a chance. This time he sent Finney away. Finney approached the defenders and, as Haynes made a decoy run outside him, the winger dummied his markers before cutting inside to hit a screamer into the far corner of Kelsey's net.

Soon afterwards it was 4-0. Kevan's square pass was again picked up by Haynes and he once more quickly despatched a firm shot into the corner. It was a clinical piece of finishing and already the Welsh fans began to sadly drift away from the stadium knowing their side had been well beaten.

England's three new caps, Eddie Hopkinson, Don Howe and Bryan Douglas, all had their moments although Douglas had little chance to shine as most of the England play was channelled down the left side. To succeed in following the legendary Stanley Matthews, Douglas would need better service from inside than Kevan gave him on this occasion.

68th match v Wales.
Debut for Hopkinson, Howe and Douglas.
Own-goal by Hopkins for England.
"I was excited and proud about my debut but also nervous, especially as I was taking over from Stanley Matthews, my boyhood hero, and was playing alongside the great Tom Finney."
Bryan Douglas

England v Home Championship
Northern Ireland

Played on Wednesday, 6 November 1957 at Wembley Stadium.

England: E.Hopkinson (Bolton W); D.Howe (West Brom), R.W.Byrne (Man Utd), R.Clayton (Blackburn R), W.A. Wright (Wolves, captain), D.Edwards

(Man Utd), B.Douglas (Blackburn R), D.T.Kevan (West Brom), T.Taylor (Man Utd), J.N.Haynes (Fulham), A.A'Court (Liverpool).

Northern Ireland: H.Gregg (Doncaster R); R.M.Keith (Newcastle Utd), A. McMichael (Newcastle Utd) R.D.Blanchflower (Spurs), J.Blanchflower (Man Utd), R.Peacock (Celtic), W.L.Bingham (Sunderland), S.McCrory (Southend Utd), W.J.Simpson (Rangers), J.McIlroy (Burnley), P.J.McParland (Aston Villa).

Half-time 0-1   Full-time 2-3
Ref: B.M.Griffiths (Wales)   Att: 42,000

MATCHES between England and Northern Ireland had been taking place on English soil for some 65 years and in all that time Northern Ireland had only ever won once before. That was at Middlesbrough in 1914, so the chances of the Irish celebrating victory at Wembley on this Wednesday afternoon seemed very remote. But sure enough, at 4.15pm the green shirts of this latest challenge stood proudly as victors with the sound of their fans cheering ringing in their ears.

Sadly, only 42,000 were at Wembley for this historic game but the ones that stayed away were the losers after a thrilling encounter. The play was won and lost in the midfield. Northern Ireland's half-back line of the two Blanchflowers and Peacock controlled almost all that England could muster and these three players, more than most, were responsible for the eventual outcome.

England began well enough and Johnny Haynes was soon spraying some typically accurate passes to his colleagues. It looked for a while that England would soon be ahead, but on the half-hour it was Ireland who took a surprise lead.

Danny Blanchflower's fine through-ball sent McCrory galloping away and as he entered the penalty area, Billy Wright sent him crashing to the ground with a fierce tackle. Too fierce a challenge in the referee's eyes, it was a penalty. McIlroy was given the job and his kick beat Eddie Hopkinson in a somewhat fortuitous fashion. The ball struck the post and rebounded against the diving Hopkinson's back and into the net . . .Were the Leprechauns at work today, one thought?

It certainly seemed that way as England hit back. They had no luck at all as Duncan Edwards and Ronnie Clayton both shot narrowly over. Then Bryan Douglas saw an effort hit the bar after a lovely pass by Roger Byrne. Peacock then cleared a Tommy Taylor header off the line and finally Alan A'Court saw his centre run along the crossbar before being cleared.

So the half ended with Ireland clinging on to their lead but it was very noticeable by now that Danny Blanchflower had curbed the flow of passes from Haynes and that Jackie Blanchflower and Peacock were also having an increasing influence. However, 15 minutes into the second half England at last equalized. Derek Kevan passed to A'Court and the winger marked his debut by squeezing a shot between Gregg and the near post. This really ignited the crowd and the excitement began to build up.

The Irish were playing with great determination and within a minute they were sensationally ahead again. A mix-up between Edwards and Wright gave

Harry Gregg almost punches Tommy Taylor on the nose as the Irish score an historic victory at Wembley in November 1957.

McCrory the chance to pounce and his shot went in off the far post which emphasised the difference in luck between Hopkinson and Gregg.

In the 71st minute the match was virtually settled by another Irish goal. This time Bingham's centre was met by Simpson diving at full length to head home. That fully punished an initial poor clearance by Byrne and although the England defenders appealed for an offside decision, it was to no avail.

And so, the unbelievable was now almost a certainty, but England refused to give up and with ten minutes to go they really set the Irish nerves jangling by pulling back another goal. It was a beauty, too. Hopkinson began the move which went the whole length of the field via Clayton, Haynes, Taylor and Douglas. Suddenly the ball was in the net as Edwards moved in swiftly to hammer a low right-foot shot past Gregg.

At this point Gregg became the Irish saviour with two magnificent saves. First he denied Kevan's header and then brought the house down when he somehow reached Clayton's screamer to the top corner with a back-breaking leap. The English players and fans alike threw their heads in their hands in disbelief. The last

desperate attempt saw Kevan's shot blocked by a headlong dive by full-back McMichael.

The final whistle put the Irish out of their misery and brought ecstatic scenes of joy from 11 green shirted heroes. How they had deserved their famous victory.

> 65th match v Northern Ireland.
> Debut goal for A'Court.
> Penalty by McIlroy for Ireland.

England v France
Friendly

Played on Wednesday, 27 November 1957 at Wembley Stadium.

England: E.Hopkinson (Bolton W); D.Howe (West Brom), R.W.Byrne (Man Utd), R.Clayton (Blackburn R), W.A. Wright (Wolves, captain), D.Edwards (Man Utd), B.Douglas (Blackburn R), R.W.Robson (West Brom), T.Taylor (Man Utd), J.N.Haynes (Fulham), T.Finney (Preston NE).

France: C.Abbes (AS St-Etienne); M.Zitouni (AS Monaco), R.Kaelbel (AS Monaco), R.Domingo (AS St-Etienne), R.Tylinski (AS St-Etienne), B.Bollini (RC Paris), M.Wisnieski (RC Lens), J.Ujlaki (OGC Nice), Y.Douis (Lille OSC), R.Piantoni (Stade de Reims), J.Vincent (Stade de Reims).

Half-time 3-0   **Full-time 4-0**
Ref: N.Latychev (USSR)   Att: 60,000

ENGLAND came back from their home defeat against the Irish with a superb victory over France which sowed the seeds of promise for the following year's World Cup finals in Sweden. Everyone felt that this England team must surely provide the nucleus of the squad for that tournament unless there was a major lapse in fitness or form.

The big success in this game was the outstanding play of Bryan Douglas. Since the great Stanley Matthews left the international arena there had been a void which nobody had yet been able to fill. But the great man himself would have been proud of Douglas' performance against the French. He teased and tormented the visiting defenders from the start and in the first half England were able to build up an impregnable 3-0 lead, thanks mainly to the wing wizardry of the Blackburn star.

It was worth recording that for the first time Douglas had a proper inside-forward alongside him and Bobby Robson's performance was almost as impressive. The partnership certainly promised a great deal.

The rout began as early as the third minute. Robson fed Douglas and the winger cleverly went round Kaelbel to centre. Tommy Taylor, under pressure from Tylinski, timed his jump perfectly at the near post to beat Abbes superbly with a looping header to the far corner.

In the 24th minute England notched a second. Again it was Douglas the provider as he received a good pass from Don Howe and then jinked his way past several challenges before only Abbes blocked his path to goal. The 'keeper dived one way and Douglas went the other before pulling the ball square, giving Robson the easiest of chances to score.

Johnny Haynes was also in top form and he sprayed passes all over the lush Wembley turf. On the half-hour he sent a glorious through-ball for Taylor to run on to and the game was virtually all over at 3-0 to England.

The French tried bravely to rally themselves early in the second half and Wisnieski was unlucky with one effort which struck the base of Eddie Hopkinson's post. This attempt at a revival was short-lived, though, and England soon regained control to dominate the rest of the game.

They missed many glorious chances and Abbes leapt across his goal like a demented frog, getting in the way of several close-range attempts. Taylor, Haynes, Tom Finney, Robson and Douglas all missed straight forward chances and Abbes was by far the busiest player on the field. In the last 23 minutes, no less than 18 shots rained in on the French goal but miraculously for them only one more counted.

That came with five minutes to go and was the icing on the cake. A superb seven-man move began with Duncan Edwards. Eventually, and inevitably, Douglas made the final pass, once again setting up

Duncan Edwards (left) and Bobby Robson in training at White Hart Lane before the game against France at Wembley in November 1957.

England's fourth goal against the French, scored by Robson after Bryan Douglas laid on the pass.

Robson for goal number four. A damp and grey November day had definitely been brightened up by a splendid England performance that augered well for the future and excited the crowd.

> 14th match v France.
> Two debut goals for Robson.

Scotland v England Home Championship

Played on Saturday, 19 April 1958 at Hampden Park, Glasgow.

Scotland: T.Younger (Liverpool); A.H.Parker (Falkirk), H.Haddock (Clyde), I.M.McColl (Rangers), R.Evans (Celtic), T.H.Docherty (Preston NE), G.Herd (Clyde), J.Murray (Hearts), J.K.Mudie (Blackpool), J.Forrest (Motherwell), T.Ewing (Partick T).

England: E.Hopkinson (Bolton W); D.Howe (West Brom), E.J.Langley (Fulham), R.Clayton (Blackburn R), W.A.Wright (Wolves, captain), W.J.Slater (Wolves), B.Douglas (Blackburn R), R.Charlton (Man Utd), D.T.Kevan (West Brom), J.N.Haynes (Fulham), T.Finney (Preston NE).

Half-time 0-3   Full-time 0-4

Ref: A.Dusch (West Germany) Att: 127,874

THIS was the first England international since that dreadful day in February 1958 when the country lost so many talented players through the Munich air disaster. Gone forever were Roger Byrne, Tommy Taylor, David Pegg and, probably one of the finest players England has ever produced, Duncan Edwards. We would now never know what heights that lad would have reached and, indeed, the England side with those great stars included.

And so, it was with a saddened heart and not without a tear or two that Billy Wright led his team out for his 89th international. Into the side for the first time came Bobby Charlton, a survivor of that terrible tragedy and now seeking to emulate his illustrious predecessors in the white shirt of England. The 19-year-old went into the game knowing many eyes were upon him, but he need not have worried as the guiding words of Billy Wright and Tom Finney saw him through magnificently. Now his talents were set before the rest of the world.

England's recent record at Hampden has been phenomenal and a whole generation of Scots has grown up without seeing a home victory against the Auld Enemy. There was never a chance of that changing in this match as England dominated from start to finish.

Bryan Douglas was again in fine form and gave his marker, Haddock a torrid time. The full-back must have cursed his luck because in 1955 the same player had been given the runaround by Stanley Matthews at Wembley. It was Douglas who made the breakthrough in the 12th minute. A free-kick taken by Charlton on the right was met superbly by Douglas and his header flashed past the startled Younger. Eleven minutes later, Derek Kevan made it 2-0 to England with a firm shot after another splendid run by Douglas had set up the chance.

England, with Johnny Haynes in another of his dominant moods, swept forward relentlessly and shortly afterwards came the goal of the match. Tom Finney picked up the ball and attacked Parker down the left flank. The full-back was totally bemused by the pace and skill of the Preston winger. A shimmy of the hips and a shrug of the shoulders gave Finney the opening to get past his marker and to the goal-line. His brilliant cross then swept into the middle, where it was met by the young Charlton full on the volley on the penalty spot. Poor Younger never even saw it. Even the partisan Scottish crowd rose to that goal and it will be long remembered by all who were there.

So, at half-time, as against France, the game was effectively over. The Hampden Roar had been silenced and the mood of the crowd sank even further into depression when Mudie's header struck the England crossbar. That incident drained any last remaining fight from the Scotland players and their usual passion was certainly missing from their game.

The second half was practically a non-event and by the time Kevan scored his second and England's fourth goal 15 minutes from the end many of the crowd had begun to make their way home. The goal was a good one ending a lovely move involving Haynes, Charlton and Bill Slater.

It was another impressive performance by England, whilst Scotland were left with many problems to solve before the World Cup in Sweden the following June.

> 75th match v Scotland.
> Debuts for Langley and Charlton.
> Debut goal from Charlton.
> *"A very proud moment for me and a lifetime ambition realised. Mind you, but for the Munich accident I certainly wouldn't have been picked."*
> Bobby Charlton

England v Portugal
Friendly

Played on Wednesday, 7 May 1958 at Wembley Stadium.

England: E.Hopkinson (Bolton W); D.Howe (West Brom), E.J.Langley (Fulham), R.Clayton (Blackburn R), W.A. Wright (Wolves, captain), W.J.Slater (Wolves), B.Douglas (Blackburn R), R.Charlton (Man Utd), D.T.Kevan (West Brom), J.N.Haynes (Fulham), T.Finney (Preston NE).
Portugal: C.Gomes (Sporting Lisbon); V.Mendes (FC Porto), A.Martins (Benfica), E.Graça (Vitória Setúbal), M.A.Oliveira (FC Porto), M.Torres (Académica Coimbra), C.Duarte (FC Porto), M.Coluña (Benfica), J.A.Almeida (Barreirense), A.Rocha (Académica Coimbra), H.da Silva (FC Porto).
Sub: Travaços (Sporting Lisbon) for Almeida.

Half-time 1-0   Full-time 2-1
Ref: A.Alsteen (Belgium)   Att: 65,000

WITH the World Cup fast approaching, England were looking for a good performance to give them the encouragement they need for the coming weeks. Unfortunately, Portugal came to Wembley determined to prove that they were unlucky not to qualify from their group and on this display they had every reason

Portugal's Gomes saves from Johnny Haynes at Wembley in May 1958.

to feel disappointed at not making it to Sweden.

England lacked consistency, struggling in the first half but picking up after the interval. With Johnny Haynes failing to control the game in his usual manner, the midfield never came to grips with the job at hand. The strong point of Haynes' play was his passing, but the accuracy just was not there on this day.

But even though Haynes was off his game England still had Bobby Charlton. He proved that his auspicious debut at Hampden Park was no fluke and his shooting was the highlight of the game. Every time he received possession a buzz went around the ground, just as it had the previous Saturday in the FA Cup Final for Manchester United against Bolton.

In the 25th minute, Charlton brought the crowd to its feet with a tremendous goal. Latching on to a Haynes pass, he hit a fierce, low shot past Gomes from 20 yards. It was made all the better by the fact that he was falling off balance as he shot after a strong challenge by Torres.

The goal was a bit unfair on Portugal, as with a little luck they could have been ahead themselves. Right at the start, Augusto missed an open goal when Rocha's clever flick set the centre-forward up. Also, only a last-ditch tackle by Jim Langley saved the situation as Torres burst through. Towards the end of the half, Don Howe made a goal-line clearance after a mistake by Eddie Hopkinson and then, right on the half-time whistle, Rocha saw a shot skim along the crossbar before being cleared. Also around this time, Augusto left the field, apparently injured, and so we saw another of those strange continental substitutions as the veteran Travaços came on.

After all this Portuguese pressure it was only justice when they deservedly equalized just after the restart. Da Silva made the goal with some super play, splitting Howe and Ronnie Clayton with his burst of speed before setting up Duarte. Strangely, the goal seemed to signal an end to Portugal's attacking play and they rarely threatened the England goal again.

England spent the rest of the game peppering shots at the visitor's goal. They regained the lead midway through the half with another memorable effort by Charlton. Again he received a pass from Haynes before moving swiftly forward. He brought Bryan Douglas into play on the right and then moved into position anticipating a cross. When the centre duly arrived, Charlton met the ball brilliantly to hit a left-footed half volley from 20 yards which flew past Gomes. It brought the house down and the Manchester United star was already building a huge reputation for himself with his power shooting.

The rest of the story belonged to England. Haynes hit the crossbar, and then Haynes and Charlton combined to set Tom Finney up. The winger was unceremoniously floored by a defender to give England a penalty. The kick was entrusted to Langley but his shot struck the post before being scrambled clear. It was the fourth penalty miss in a row at Wembley in an international.

In the last quarter of an hour, Derek Kevan missed three fine chances and his display added fuel to the argument from his many critics that he was not international class.

> 5th match v Portugal.
> Penalty miss by Langley.
> Portugal's Mendes also known as 'Virgilio'; Martins as 'Angelo'; Oliveira as 'Arcanja'; Almeida as 'José Augusto'; Travaços as 'Hernani'.

Yugoslavia v England
Friendly

Played on Sunday, 11 May 1958 at the JNA Stadium, Belgrade.

Yugoslavia: V.Beara (Red Star Belgrade); Šijaković (OFK Belgrade), T.Crnković (Dinamo Zagreb), D.Kristić (Vojvodina Novi Sad), B.Zebec (Partizan Belgrade), V.Boškov (Vojvodina Novi Sad), A.Petaković (Rad Belgrade),

T.Veselinović (Vojvodina Novi Sad), M.Milutinović (Partizan Belgrade), D.Šekularac (Red Star Belgrade), I.Pašić (FK Željezničar).
England: E.Hopkinson (Bolton W); D.Howe (West Brom), E.J.Langley (Fulham), R.Clayton (Blackburn R), W.A.Wright (Wolves, captain), W.J.Slater (Wolves), B.Douglas (Blackburn R), R.Charlton (Man Utd), D.T.Kevan (West Brom), J.N.Haynes (Fulham), T.Finney (Preston NE).

Half-time 1-0　　Full-time 5-0
Ref: I.Zsolt (Hungary)　　Att: 58,000

TEMPERATURES were in the 90s as the teams took to the field for this match and England, trying to establish a side capable of winning the forthcoming World Cup tournament, had a disastrous day. They were well and truly beaten by a Yugoslav side that, on the day, was in a different class.

Everything went wrong from the start and Yugoslavia took a deserved lead in the 23rd minute. Milutinović gained possession, sold Billy Wright a dummy, and then let fly a shot from some 25 yards. The ball hit the ground just in front of Eddie Hopkinson's dive and hit the goalkeeper on the shoulder before flying into the net. It was a good shot but Hopkinson could have perhaps done better.

From then on Yugoslavia dominated the play. Three times before half-time they beat Hopkinson again, but each time the goal was disallowed for offside. On another occasion a screamer from Šekularac crashed against the England crossbar.

The visitors were struggling. Wright was being given a torrid time by Milutinović, Ronnie Clayton could not get into the game, and Johnny Haynes and Bobby Charlton looked jaded and ineffective. Jim Langley battled well and Wright, despite his difficulties, was still England's best defender. However, his side were fortunate to only be the one goal down at the break especially as they had not put in one worthwhile effort of their own.

After the interval the England crossbar was again nearly broken in two when a fierce shot by Boškov bounced back into play off it. The visitors probably had their best spell of the match in the opening ten minutes of the half and actually applied some pressure on Yugoslavia. But on 56 minutes any hope that England had of gaining anything from the game was shattered by a brilliant goal by Petaković. A superb move involving Kristić, Veselinović, Šekularac and Pašić ended with Petaković lashing home the cross.

England were now out of the contest and the Slavs produced some brilliant play as the game progressed. For some strange reason little went beyond the England penalty area, though as the home side showed a reluctance to shoot. But with 15 minutes left all that changed. Šekularac put through and his fierce shot flew past Hopkinson. Moments later the right-winger completed his hat-trick when he scored following a pass from Veselinović.

To complete England's misery a brilliant run by Šekularac ended with him setting up Veselinović for number five.

The crowd were ecstatic by now and fires were burning on the terraces with their team showing everyone just what

they were capable of. Milutinović and Kristić were absolutely outstanding.

As for England, Hopkinson had a miserable afternoon and although he made some fine saves he had to be faulted for the crucial first goal. Up front England put in only two goal attempts in the whole 90 minutes, one from Ron Clayton and a typical Bobby Charlton effort. Bryan Douglas and Derek Kevan never threatened and Tom Finney was totally stifled by the cynical tackling of the Yugoslav defenders. Countless free-kicks were given after tackles on Finney but England could create nothing from those kicks.

After this display, thoughts of England winning the World Cup seemed a million miles away.

> 5th match v Yugoslavia.

USSR v England　　Friendly
Played on Sunday, 18 May 1958 in the Lenin Stadium, Moscow.

USSR: L.Yashin (Dinamo Moscow); M.Ogon'kov (Spartak Moscow), B.Kuznetsov (Dinamo Moscow), Y.Voinov (Dinamo Kiev), K.K.Krijevski (Dinamo Moscow), I.Netto (Spartak Moscow), G.Apukhtin (CSKA Moscow), V.Ivanov (Torpedo Moscow), E.Strel'tsov (Torpedo Moscow), Y.Falin (Torpedo Moscow), A.Ilyin (Dinamo Moscow).
England: C.A.McDonald (Burnley); D.Howe (West Brom), T.Banks (Bolton W), H.E.Clamp (Wolves), W.A.Wright (Wolves, captain), W.J.Slater (Wolves), B.Douglas (Blackburn R), R.W.Robson (West Brom), D.T.Kevan (West Brom), J.N.Haynes (Fulham), T.Finney (Preston NE).

Half-time 0-1　　Full-time 1-1
Ref: F.Seipelt (Austria)　　Att: 105,000

THE third stage of England's summer tour and pre-World Cup build up took them to Moscow in a game which also marked the 60th anniversary of the Soviet FA. England almost ruined the celebrations and could have won handsomely but in the end they had to be content with a draw as bad luck and some inspired goalkeeping by Yashin saved the day for the Soviets.

After the previous week's thrashing at the hands of the Yugoslavs, England were anxious to regain some confidence for the following month's tournament. They certainly managed that with a very impressive display. Right from the start they moved forward confidently. Within 20 minutes they had put in at least six goalworthy attempts and could have had the game sewn up.

New midfield man Eddie Clamp made a very impressive debut and his club colleagues completed a dominating Wolverhampton half-back line. Billy Wright was his usual immaculate self and Bill Slater was the best player on view with his poise, artistry and speed of thought really making an impact with everyone watching.

Derek Kevan also hit back at his critics with a powerhouse showing. The Soviet central defenders found him a real handful and his battering ram style upset their normal composure. Four times the West

Brom man came close to scoring in the first half only to be denied by Yashin or wayward shooting. Johnny Haynes and Tom Finney both shot narrowly wide and England's 200 travelling supporters could hardly understand why their team was not comfortably ahead.

Tommy Banks showed fire and solidity at left-back and Colin McDonald also looked the part in goal.

On the left wing, Finney was at his brilliant best. The form, so seldom seen at Wembley but loved by the Deepdale fans was now here for all to see. The Soviets had little answer to him and three, sometimes four, defenders were sent to challenge in some attacks. Finney was desperately unlucky when he met a Bryan Douglas corner only for his header to strike Yashin's post.

Then Finney took a corner and this time Bobby Robson saw his header also thud against a post. With only seconds of the half remaining, England at last scored the goal they so richly deserved. More fine work by the tireless Clamp sent Douglas away. The winger sent over a perfect cross to the far post and there was Kevan to head down and under Yashin's despairing dive. Kevan, more than most, had earned that goal.

After the break Russia came back briefly and McDonald saved well from Strel'tsov who was easily their most dangerous attacker. He gave Wright a tough time of it throughout. But England soon regained control and on the hour forced Yashin into the save of the match. Finney and Haynes combined again and, as Kevan made a decoy run, taking defenders with him, Finney cut inside to fire in a fierce shot. It looked a goal all the way but somehow Yashin extended one of his seemingly telescopic arms to turn the ball away for a wonderful save.

Kevan went close on two more occasions and with Wright and his fellow defenders comfortably holding the Soviet attack, it seemed odds on a memorable win. But with only 12 minutes left, the Soviets scored an equalizer they barely deserved. A swift move begun by Voinov was carried on by Falin. His long, high pass forward cleared Banks and found Ivanov, who brilliantly brought the ball under control before he hooked it past McDonald.

It was a bitter blow for England, although Clamp, still going strong at the end, almost restored the lead with a good shot which flew just over with Yashin groping.

> 1st match v USSR.
> Debuts for McDonald, Banks and Clamp.
> *"I'll never forget the sight of Tommy Banks of Bolton chasing the Russian number seven all over the field at the end of the match. He only wanted to shake hands, but the Russian thought he wanted to thump him!"*
> Bryan Douglas

World Cup Finals

USSR v England　　Pool Four
Played on Sunday, 8 June 1958 at the Nya Ullevi Stadium, Gothenburg, Sweden.

England's squad at Roehampton before the 1958 World Cup. Back row (left to right): Hopkinson, Howe, Clayton, Clamp, Finney, Robson, Douglas, McDonald, Kevan, Brabrook, Smith, Haynes. Front row: A'Court, Norman, Slater, Wright, Charlton, Sillett, Broadbent, Banks.

England's Derek Kevan leaps high to a cross from Douglas against the Soviet Union in Gothenburg in the opening game of the 1958 World Cup finals.

USSR: L.Yashin (Dinamo Moscow); V.Kesarev (Dinamo Moscow), B.Kuznetsov (Dinamo Moscow), Y.Voinov (Dinamo Kiev), K.Krijevski (Dinamo Moscow), V.Tsarev (Dinamo Moscow), A.Ivanov (Zenit Leningrad), V.Ivanov (Torpedo Moscow), N.Simonian (Spartak Moscow), S.Salnikov (Spartak Moscow), A.Ilyin (Spartak Moscow).

England: C.A.McDonald (Burnley); D.Howe (West Brom), T.Banks (Bolton W), H.E.Clamp (Wolves), W.A.Wright (Wolves, captain), W.J.Slater (Wolves), B.Douglas (Blackburn R), R.W.Robson (West Brom), D.T.Kevan (West Brom), J.N.Haynes (Fulham), T.Finney (Preston NE).

Half-time 1-0   Full-time 2-2
Ref: I.Zsolt (Hungary)   Att: 49,348

WITH the host country, Sweden, opening

the 1958 World Cup earlier in the day by beating Mexico, the competition was well and truly under way by the time England and the Soviet Union took to the field early in the evening. By the end of this match, the crowd were jumping up and down with excitement as the two sides fought out a thriller.

Having met only three weeks before in a friendly, both sides were familiar with each other's style. It was the Soviets who were quickly into their stride as England struggled to get going. Indeed, England's first-half display was very disappointing and the Soviets had much more of the play. It was a hard, physical game with Russia having the edge up front. Valentin Ivanov, Simonian and Salnikov were particularly impressive and it came as no real surprise when the Soviets took the lead after a quarter of an hour.

Alexander Ivanov fired in a low cross shot which Colin McDonald could only parry. The ball ran loose and Simonian nipped in to flick it home. England were now up against it and for a while Billy Wright and his players could not respond. McDonald made one superb save and there were several other near misses before half-time arrived.

One hoped that the break would give England time to regroup but ten minutes into the second half the Soviets made it 2-0 and the writing seemed to be on the wall. Kesarev began the move with a strong run from full-back. He then put Alexander Ivanov through in the inside-left channel and the winger evaded Bill Slater's attempted interception before shooting past the goalkeeper.

England at this stage looked out of it as Salnikov and Valentin Ivanov turned on the style. The England defence looked at sixes and sevens for much of the time although Don Howe was outstanding at right-back. Wright and Eddie Clamp worked hard but Tom Finney was too often left on his own in attack to battle against the tough-tackling Russian defenders. The free-kicks they conceded were testament to the ferocity of their tackles. Bobby Robson tried hard to create some sort of pattern in England's play but had little joy. Until, that is, only 30 minutes were left on the referee's watch.

Robson had just seen a goal disallowed after Derek Kevan was penalised for a foul on Yashin. Although England were obviously disappointed with that decision, the incident had a profound effect on the final outcome. Suddenly the Soviets became jittery and nervous. Players, who for the first hour had looked confident and composed, were now being forced into errors by a rejuvenated England team. England were in fact unrecognisable from the first half and now, with their tails up, they threw everything at the Soviets.

Within seconds of the disallowed goal, England at last pulled one back. A long free-kick by Wright sent alarm bells running through the Soviet defence. Bryan Douglas caused panic by nipping in and when the ball bounced up and free Kevan pounced to score.

From then on it was all England as wave after wave of attacks swept forward. The crowd roared their approval as the forward line found space that had previously been denied them earlier. Finney, especially, was the key and one of many near misses came when Robson shot just wide when it seemed he must score.

With 15 minutes left, Finney was again prominent as he combined well with Kevan and Haynes to set up a return pass which Kevan crashed against Yashin's body. When the rebound came out Robson reacted first to flick the ball home. The jubilation was quickly curtailed as once again the goal was ruled out by the Hungarian referee for a foul on Yashin.

England were not to be denied, though, and as the excitement reached a crescendo with five minutes to go, they found their equalizer. A lovely pass by Finney sent Haynes through, only for the number ten to be unceremoniously upended. Penalty!

What a situation for Finney. In an atmosphere of edge of the seat tension and almost total silence the ice-cool Preston man slotted the ball past even Yashin's vast reach to score. The relief of the crowd was felt to the full in a tremendous cheer. So, England, in the end, deserved their draw but one could not forget that for two-thirds of the match they had not played well at all. But with the other game in their group ending Brazil 3 Austria 0, they still had everything to play for.

> 2nd match v USSR.
> Penalty by Finney.
> *"The worst moment of my international career was having to accept that you were coming to the end of your time in the side, getting injured in the 1958 World Cup and playing only one game, having to watch the rest from the side-lines."*
> Tom Finney

Brazil v England Pool Four

Played on Wednesday, 11 June 1958 at the Nya Ullevi Stadium, Gothenburg, Sweden.

Brazil: G.dos Santos (Corinthians); N.De Sordi (São Paulo), N.Santos (Botafogo), D.Sani (São Paulo), H.L.Bellini (Vasco da Gama), O.Pecanha (Vasco da Gama), J.A.Martins (Flamengo), W.Pereira (Botafogo), J.J.Altafini (Palmeiras), E.I.Neto (Vasco da Gama), M.J.L.Zagalo (Flamengo).

England: C.A.McDonald (Burnley); D.Howe (West Brom), T.Banks (Bolton W), H.E.Clamp (Wolves), W.A.Wright (Wolves, captain), W.J.Slater (Wolves), B.Douglas (Blackburn R), R.W.Robson (West Brom), D.T.Kevan (West Brom), J.N.Haynes (Fulham), A.A'Court (Liverpool).

Half-time 0-0   Full-time 0-0

Ref: A.Dusch (West Germany) Att: 40,895

ENGLAND suffered a devastating blow before the kick-off in this vital match when Tom Finney was ruled out because of injury. Alan A'Court came into the side for a game where it was very important that England did not lose. The mighty Brazilians were already showing all the signs of being a fine team.

Despite the final scoreline the game was a thriller. Full of open and attacking football it was very much a case of contrasting styles with the subtle skills of the silky smooth Brazilians pitched against the typical English game of hard tackling and swift counter-attacks. The control of the South Americans was breathtaking at times with Didí and

Altafini outstanding. The ease at which they killed the ball from any angle and then laid off accurate passes was beautiful to watch.

England, meanwhile, battled like tigers. A'Court proved a capable deputy and although he did not have the extra class of Finney, he more than held his own. On 11 minutes, A'Court put Derek Kevan through, only for Gilmar to make a fine diving save. Then Colin McDonald, superb throughout, made an equally good save when he sprang to catch a header from Altafini. The end to end action was continuous and Gilmar then made an even better save when he touched a tremendous shot from Johnny Haynes around the post.

The big crowd were delighted at the excitement on the pitch with the England lads enjoying the full vocal backing of a contingent from the British Navy. The player who stood out for England was, once again, Billy Wright. The captain was magnificent and he spurred his colleagues on with an immaculate display. Don Howe, Eddie Clamp and Bill Slater gave him admirable support in what was a very good team effort.

After half an hour, England had an escape when a brilliant 20-yard shot by the impressive Vavá crashed back into play off the crossbar. But the swift tackling of the whole England side began to have its effect on Brazil and soon Wright and his men were controlling the game. For most of the second half the match belonged to them as the pressure on Gilmar's goal intensified all through the half.

Kevan was only stopped at the expense of a corner. A superb move between Haynes and Bobby Robson produced another corner and then A'Court, Slater and Kevan combined for Robson to just miss again. Yet another corner.

It was great stuff and England deserved a goal. However, Brazil also had their moments, a side as skilful as they are can never be totally subdued. Didí and Vavá both tested the faultless McDonald to the full. It was a pulsating game which only lacked one thing and that was a goal.

Each of the England players were heroes with Howe in fine form. Clamp and Slater showed everyone the form they displayed every week at Molineux and Wright was inspiration personified. And one other thing. Kevan had put up with a good deal of criticism during his England career but in this match he gave an excellent display of powerhouse centre-forward play. But for the agility and skill of Gilmar, the West Brom player could have been the hero of a nation.

England now had a great chance of reaching the next round provided they could beat Austria in their final group match.

> 2nd match v Brazil.
> Brazil's dos Santos also known as 'Gilmar'; Pecanha as 'Orlando'; Martins as 'Joel'; Pereira as 'Didí'; Altafini as 'Mazzola'; Neto as 'Vavá'.

Austria v England Pool Four

Played on Sunday, 15 June 1958 at the Ryavallen Stadium, Borås, Sweden.

Austria: R.Szanwald (SK Wien); W.Kollmann (Wacker Wien), F.Swoboda (FK Austria, Wien), G.Hanappi (Rapid Wien), E.Happel (Rapid Wien), K.Koller (1.Vienna FC), E.Kozlicek (Wacker Wien), P.Kozlicek (Wacker Wien), H.Buzek (1.Vienna FC), A.Körner (Rapid Wien), H.Senekowitsch (Sturm Graz).

England: C.A.McDonald (Burnley); D.Howe (West Brom), T.Banks (Bolton), H.E.Clamp (Wolves), W.A.Wright (Wolves, captain), W.J.Slater (Wolves), B.Douglas (Blackburn R), R.W.Robson (West Brom), D.T.Kevan (West Brom), J.N.Haynes (Fulham), A A'Court (Liverpool),

Half-time 1-0   Full-time 2-2

Ref: A.Asmussen (Denmark)   Att: 16,800

ENGLAND knew exactly what they had to do against the Austrians in this crucial World Cup game but at half-time the victory they needed seemed a million miles away. What a dismal performance they put up! It was even harder to take and doubly disappointing after their brilliant display against Brazil. Nothing went right in that opening half. There was no cohesion, no thrust and only some desperate defending prevented an even worse disaster.

The crowd, once again, was boosted by the presence of around 300 British sailors and their white hats made an interesting sight. But they must have been very frustrated by England's performance, there was plenty of effort but no real pattern emerged. Johnny Haynes tried hard to lift his colleagues but when Austria scored after 15 minutes nobody in the stadium was particularly surprised.

It was a cracking goal too with Koller firing in a brilliant 25-yard shot which gave Colin McDonald no chance. England continually struggled and before half-time Austria had several other near misses. Two more thunderbolts by Koller and an open goal missed chance from the tall Buzek threatened to finish off England. In this spell McDonald, Billy Wright and Tommy Banks strove manfully to repel the eager Austrian attack and McDonald particularly was again in top form. He made some fine saves and effectively kept England in the match.

As against both the Soviet Union and Brazil, though, England proved themselves very much a second-half side and they were thankfully a very different proposition after the break. Within five minutes of the restart Haynes had fired in three fierce shots, all just off target. Shortly afterwards Alan A'Court saw a good effort diverted for a corner. This brought the strains of the *Last Post* from a bugler amongst the navy lads, but suddenly their spirits were lifted by an England equalizer.

Bill Slater planted a free-kick into the area where Derek Kevan headed it on to A'Court who immediately hit a right foot shot at goal. Szanwald blocked that effort but Haynes moved in smartly to hit home the rebound.

The game had changed dramatically and from then on it was nearly all England as the ball playing Austrians faded. All of the England forwards put in goal attempts although usually off target. This was where Tom Finney was sorely missed as his coolness in finishing would surely have paid dividends. Despite their new-

England goalkeeper Colin McDonald under pressure against Brazil in Gothenburg. Skipper Billy Wright doesn't seem to be making things any easier.

Johnny Haynes takes the ball through against Austria in Borås but the referee is about to blow for a free-kick.

found dominance, England's build-up was slow and their finishing was poor as they searched desperately for the winner. One wondered how the two-footed power shooting of young Bobby Charlton might have used some of the chances that came England's way.

With 20 minutes remaining, disaster struck. Austria, in a rare attack, regained the lead. Once more it was a long-range shot this time from Körner. McDonald moved late for the ball and could have been unsighted, it was his only blemish on another fine display of goalkeeping. Unfortunately, at this level players can be severely punished for even the slightest mistake.

England now had to dig deep into their reserves of energy to get out of trouble but they showed great character by swiftly coming back at Austria. A speedy interchange of passes between Haynes and Bobby Robson allowed Haynes to put Kevan through for a second, and well taken, equalizer. For the remainder of the game England pushed forward to try and snatch the winner but bad luck and bad finishing combined to prevent them gaining the win that would have seen them automatically go on to the next stage.

It now remained that England must play-off against the Soviet Union to see who finally qualified from the group.

> 9th match v Austria.

USSR v England   Pool Four Play-off

Played on Tuesday, 17 June 1958 at the Nya Ullevi Stadium, Gothenburg, Sweden.

USSR: L.Yashin (Dinamo Moscow); V.Kesarev (Dinamo Moscow), B.Kuznetsov (Dinamo Moscow), Y.Voinov (Dinamo Kiev), K.Krijevski (Dinamo Moscow), V.Tsarev (Dinamo Moscow), G.Apoukhtin (CSKA Moscow), V.Ivanov (Torpedo Moscow), N.Simonian (Spartak Moscow), Y.Falin (Torpedo Moscow), A.Ilyin (Spartak Moscow).

England: C.A.McDonald (Burnley); D.Howe (West Brom), T.Banks (Bolton W), R.Clayton (Blackburn R), W.A. Wright (Wolves, captain), W.J.Slater (Wolves), P.Brabrook (Chelsea), P.F.Broadbent (Wolves), D.T.Kevan (West Brom), J.N.Haynes (Fulham), A A'Court (Liverpool).

Half-time 0-0   Full-time 1-0

Ref: A.Dusch (West Germany)   Att: 23,182

THIS was the third meeting of these two sides in the space of five weeks but this time there was far more at stake. The winners would progress to the World Cup quarter-finals as runners-up in their group behind Brazil. England made three changes to the team held by Austria with Ronnie Clayton returning and Peter Brabrook and Peter Broadbent coming in for their first caps. The new right-wing partnership quickly established itself with some excellent work.

England played well but lacked the one ingredient they needed . . .good fortune. Nothing went right for them on this day. The match was evenly contested for the first half-hour but from the moment

Haynes in a tussle with Lev Yashin during the World Cup play-off game in Gothenburg.

Broadbent forced Yashin into a fine diving save low to his right England were on top. Yashin showed all his marvellous talents as he and his defenders worked overtime to keep the English attack at bay. The Soviet Union were almost on their knees but, alas, England could not find the knock-out blow.

Seven minutes before the interval they missed a fine chance. Broadbent, showing some silky skills, carved his way down the right before laying off a perfect pass to Brabrook. It seemed the Chelsea man must score, but the winger succeeded only in stabbing his shot straight at Yashin.

It was not all England, however, as the Soviets, too, had their moments. Don Howe kicked one effort from Apoukhtin off the line and then saw Simonian miss an open goal from close in. Colin McDonald had to be alert at all times and showed plenty of confidence. Billy Wright and his co-defenders gradually gained a grip on the Soviet attack and by the end of the first half their goal chances evaporated.

Clayton, Bill Slater, Howe and Tommy Banks all tackled like lions but up front

England lacked the necessary class they needed to break through. Haynes looked tired, and A'Court and Derek Kevan, although showing they had big hearts, were often found to be struggling.

Broadbent was the big hope for England. After that 35th minute effort he showed magnificent form. His display lifted everyone and England were eventually well on top. At the end of the first half the shot ratio had been Soviet Union 8 and England 3, but after the break the pattern was reversed with England having ten shots to the Soviets' three.

Twice in the second half, England were desperately unlucky. Both times Brabrook hit the right-hand post of Yashin's goal and then the winger had the ball in the net only to be penalised for handball. It was all very frustrating as the Soviets were down and almost out.

But, as so often happens, the one clear chance that came Russia's way after the break was clinically tucked away. Ironically, having played so well throughout the tournament, it was a mistake by McDonald which led to the winning goal. His poor goal-kick in the 65th minute was intercepted by Ilyin. Voinov came into the action and flicked the ball to Simonian. A return pass to Ilyin and the winger raced through to shoot past the luckless McDonald. Just to rub salt into the wound, the ball went in off the post, thus highlighting the small margin between success and failure.

England's best effort in the remaining minutes came from Kevan. He once powered his way through only for Yashin to pull off a wonderful save diving low to his right.

At the referee's final whistle the England players trooped off looking very dejected. The whole team had played their hearts out and, for effort, could not be faulted. Looking back over their four matches, one could point to several 'if only's'. But at the end of the day the long-term question was whether some of the England players were up to the standard required of modern-day international football? Only time would tell.

> 3rd match v USSR.
> Debuts for Brabrook and Broadbent.

Northern Ireland v England Home Championship

Played on Saturday, 4 October 1958 at Windsor Park, Belfast.

Northern Ireland: H.Gregg (Man Utd); R.M.Keith (Newcastle Utd), W.G.L. Graham (Doncaster R), R.D.Blanchflower (Spurs), W.E.Cunningham (Leicester C), R.Peacock (Celtic), W.L.Bingham (Luton T), W.W.Cush (Leeds Utd), T.Casey (Portsmouth), J.McIlroy (Burnley), P.J.McParland (Aston Villa).
England: C.A.McDonald (Burnley); D.Howe (West Brom), T.Banks (Bolton W), R.Clayton (Blackburn R), W.A. Wright (Wolves, captain), W.McGuinness (Man Utd), P.Brabrook (Chelsea), P.F.Broadbent (Wolves), R.Charlton (Man Utd), J.N.Haynes (Fulham), T.Finney (Preston NE).

Half-time 1-1   Full-time 3-3
Ref: R.H.Davidson (Scotland) Att: 58,000

WHAT a spectacular match! This was the closest Northern Ireland have come to beating England on Irish soil since 1927. Three times they led and twice they hit the woodwork. In driving rain and cloying mud, both sides served up a feast of entertainment and seldom has a game had so many talking points.

Some 58,000 people crammed into Windsor Park and they were soon getting right behind their favourites as Ireland produced their usual passionate start to the game. This style always gave England a hard time although the extra skill factor remained with the visitors. Bobby Charlton, (why, oh why had he not been given a game in Sweden?), looked in sparkling form. His pedigree was there for all to see and his roving centre-forward role worked a treat.

The Irish were driven on by Blanch-flower and McIlroy. They held the midfield together quickly shutting down on England's space and making them work for everything. Peacock, Cush and the lively Bingham gave them good support and on the half-hour Ireland deservedly took the lead. Good work by Blanchflower down the middle ended with a fine pass to Cush who crashed home an excellent shot for the first goal.

England, though, were quickly level. Charlton, who kept popping up everywhere eagerly wanting the ball, received a short pass from Johnny Haynes, turned sharply and fired in a rocket shot which flew into the top corner of Gregg's goal from just outside the area. It was a magnificent goal.

The rain had been incessant throughout the first half and England had done well to share the honours at half-time. But 15 minutes after the restart, Ireland once again sent their fans wild with delight. Blanchflower sent Bingham away down the right and the winger found McParland. When the deep centre came over, Peacock was there to hit home a fine goal.

No sooner had the crowd celebrated that goal than England were level again. This time Tom Finney burst through on to a Charlton pass before cleverly sliding the ball under the advancing Gregg's body. A slip by Cunningham had given the Preston winger the chance to create a new scoring record for England with his 30th international goal.

The excitement continued unabated and with 20 minutes left, Ireland forced themselves into the lead yet again. Another cross from McParland was caught by Colin McDonald, only for Casey to come in and barge the 'keeper and the ball over the line. It was shades of Nat Lofthouse's effort in the previous season's FA Cup Final for Bolton against Manchester United. How ruefully Gregg, in the Irish goal, must have viewed Casey's copy-cat goal.

Still England were not finished and it was Charlton who once again produced a stunning goal to equalize for a third time. Surging past two defenders on the left, he took Haynes' pass inside Keith and unleashed yet another of those awesome shots from long range. Once more Gregg was left clutching only raindrops as the ball thudded into the net to stifle any thoughts the home side had of victory.

> 66th match v Northern Ireland.
> Debut for McGuinness.
> 30th goal for Finney, an England record.

England v USSR Friendly

Played on Wednesday, 22 October 1958 at Wembley Stadium.

England: C.A.McDonald (Burnley); D.Howe (West Brom), G.L.Shaw (Sheffield Utd), R.Clayton (Blackburn R), W.A.Wright (Wolves, captain), W.J.Slater (Wolves), B.Douglas (Blackburn R), R.Charlton (Man Utd), N.Lofthouse (Bolton W), J.N.Haynes (Fulham), T.Finney (Preston NE).
USSR: V.Belaev (Dinamo Moscow); V.Kesarev (Dinamo Moscow), B.Kuznetsov (Dinamo Moscow), Y.Voinov (Dinamo Kiev), A.Maslenkin (Spartak Moscow), V.Tsarev (Dinamo Moscow), S.Metreveli (Torpedo Moscow), V.Ivanov (Torpedo Moscow), N.Simonian (Spartak Moscow), A.Mamedov (Dinamo Moscow), A.Ilyin (Spartak Moscow).

Half-time 1-0   Full-time 5-0
Ref: M.Guigue (France)   Att: 100,000

ENGLAND met the Soviet Union at Wembley still smarting from the painful memory of Sweden and the World Cup the previous June. For obvious reasons they had a desire to gain revenge over their opponents and, at the end of the day, they managed a result far beyond their dreams.

In a largely uneventful first half, both sides carefully tested each other out without showing any real threat. Powerful running by Nat Lofthouse, recalled for the first time since 1956, did cause some anxious moments for the visitors but neither goalkeeper was severely tested. Play was mostly confined to the midfield area where England gradually gained control. Ronnie Clayton, Johnny Haynes and Bobby Charlton were particularly impressive with Clayton having probably his best game in an England shirt.

The Soviet's best scoring opportunity came on the half-hour and Mamedov surely rued the simple chance he missed. It could well have been the most crucial turning point in the game. Charlton tried a few shots, usually off target, but deservedly just before the interval England gained their breakthrough. The half was almost over when Charlton, Tom Finney and Brian Douglas combined down the left to send Haynes in to shoot low and hard past Belaev.

That was a body-blow to the Soviets, going in one down at half-time instead of being on level terms. Indeed, after the break England completely took over, swamping their opponents with some fine play. Despite the fact that Voinov and Simonian showed some lovely touches, Clayton's driving performance kept his side pushing forward relentlessly. Haynes continued in his role as an extra front man and the home side, after completely dominating the second half, reaped the benefit as the goals came later on.

A header by Lofthouse brought a desperate and untidy clearance by Kesarev and Haynes was on hand to punish the error by crashing the ball into the net. With eight minutes to go, Haynes and Finney worked a short corner and Haynes burst through the defence to complete a memorable hat-trick with a good shot.

The pressure continued right to the end with the Soviets fading and Bryan Douglas then made another goal. His wing play had caused problems all through and when he burst through on a run through the middle he was unceremoniously hauled down by Kuznetsov whilst in full flight. Penalty! Up stepped Charlton and it was 4-0. The final, and probably the loudest cheer, was reserved for Lofthouse. The game was into the last minute when Charlton found the big man with a good pass. The Bolton forward seized the opportunity with both hands and he

> 4th match v USSR.
> Debut for Shaw.
> Hat-trick by Haynes.
> Finney's last international appearance.
> Penalty by Charlton.
> Lofthouse's goal was his 30th, thus equalling Finney's record.
> *"It was sad playing my last international but I was grateful for a wonderful host of happy memories, the satisfaction of having played with so many good players and making so many friends."*
> Tom Finney

England's Colin McDonald gathers the ball from Metreveli, the Soviet winger, as Ronnie Clayton looks on.

quickly fired in a splendid shot which gave Belaev no chance to save. The delight of the crowd was obvious and it was a just reward for a typical performance by the gutsy number nine.

This was the first victory in eight internationals for England and the convincing nature of the win gave everyone a boost after the summer's disappointments. Graham Shaw's debut was full of promise and, despite Haynes' goals, Clayton was undoubtedly man-of-the-match.

England v Wales Home Championship

Played on Wednesday, 26 November 1958 at Villa Park, Birmingham.

England: C.A.McDonald (Burnley); D.Howe (West Brom), G.L.Shaw (Sheffield Utd), R.Clayton (Blackburn R), W.A.Wright (Wolves, captain), R.Flowers (Wolves), D.R.Clapton (Arsenal), P.F.Broadbent (Wolves), N.Lofthouse (Bolton W), R.Charlton (Man Utd), A.A'Court (Liverpool).
Wales: A.J.Kelsey (Arsenal); S.G.Williams (West Brom), M.Hopkins (Spurs), V.H.Crowe (Aston Villa), M.Charles (Swansea T), D.L.Bowen (Arsenal), T.C.Medwin (Spurs), D.Ward (Bristol R), D.R.Tapscott (Cardiff C), I.J.Allchurch (Newcastle Utd), A.P.Woosnam (West Ham).

Half-time 1-1   Full-time 2-2
Ref: A.Dusch (West Germany) Att: 40,500

THIS was a very disjointed performance by England in this Home International against Wales. The Welsh, showing much of the form so evident in Sweden, put up a fine display and England had to fight all the way for a draw.

Johnny Haynes was badly missed and although his deputy, Peter Broadbent, showed some admirable skills, he did not command the midfield in the manner that Haynes can. Also, Billy Wright had an unusually shaky game in what was his 99th international.

From the first minute, when his mistake almost let in Woosnam, the England captain showed a most uncharacteristic nervousness. Perhaps it was a case of the 'nervous nineties'. Whatever it was, Tapscott's mobility gave Wright a torrid time.

Ronnie Clayton was also a disappointment especially after his magnificent display against the Soviet Union at Wembley, but to be fair he was given little support from Ron Flowers in what was a ragged England midfield.

Wales took the lead after 15 minutes. Medwin fired in a cross shot and when Colin McDonald failed to hold the ball Tapscott nipped in smartly to drive the loose ball home. But 15 minutes after the goal Wales suffered a cruel blow when their captain, Dave Bowen, picked up a nasty arm injury. He bravely continued on the left wing but he was virtually a passenger. This gave England the chance to exert some pressure and Bobby Charlton was able to reveal his awesome shooting power.

Several times he had the crowd on their feet with some spectacular shots after splendid dribbles. For 25 minutes up to half-time, Charlton was rampant, although he failed to find the net. In fact England had no luck at all and Broadbent was particularly unlucky to see his header from Danny Clapton's centre strike the bar, rebound down and then to be cleared from the line by a possee of Welsh defenders.

Next, Clayton burst through to seize on to a clever Charlton, Nat Lofthouse worked opening. His 20-yard shot crashed against Kelsey's post. The goalkeeper then made two fine saves from Charlton rockets and then Charles managed to get in the way of another goal-bound Charlton shot.

Just when it seemed that England would go in at the break a goal down, Broadbent produced a marvellous equalizer. Graham Shaw fed through a delightful pass and although Broadbent was quickly hemmed in by defenders, he spotted Kelsey off his line and coolly and cleverly lobbed the ball over the 'keeper and into the net.

After the interval Wales came at England throwing everything forward. Ivor Allchurch was magnificent in this spell and inspired his colleagues. He was well supported by Woosnam and Tapscott. England, meanwhile faded badly. Clapton saw little of the ball and Alan A'Court achieved little on the left wing. Charlton's shots all but dried up and only Broadbent posed a threat of any kind.

With 20 minutes remaining, the underdogs grabbed the lead again. Allchurch picked up a pass from Ward, turned on the proverbial sixpence, and fired in a shot which went in off the far post. The Welshmen in the crowd were now at fever pitch as they sensed that their side were within sight of their first victory in England for some 23 years.

Soon, however, England drew level again. It needed something special and it came when a fine accurate cross by A'Court was met by a leaping Broadbent. The England number-eight rose superbly to send a brilliant header into the top corner of Kelsey's goal. That ended the scoring in what had been an interesting contest.

69th match v Wales.
Debut for Clapton.
Lofthouse's last international appearance.
"How did I feel when I realised I had played my last international? Bloody awful!"
Nat Lofthouse

England v Scotland Home Championship

Played on Saturday, 11 April 1959 at Wembley Stadium.

England: E.Hopkinson (Bolton W); D.Howe (West Brom), G.L.Shaw (Sheffield Utd), R.Clayton (Blackburn R), W.A.Wright (Wolves, captain), R.Flowers (Wolves), B.Douglas (Blackburn R), P.F.Broadbent (Wolves), R.Charlton (Man Utd), J.N.Haynes (Fulham), A.D.Holden (Bolton W).
Scotland: W.D.F.Brown (Dundee); D.McKay (Celtic), E.Caldow (Rangers), T.H.Docherty (Arsenal), R.Evans (Celtic), D.C.Mackay (Spurs), G.Leggatt (Fulham), R.Y.Collins (Everton), D.G.Herd (Arsenal), J.Dick (West Ham), E.Ormond (Hibernian).

Half-time 0-0   Full-time 1-0
Ref: J.F.Campos (Portugal) Att: 98,329

THE magnificent Billy Wright led England out against the Auld Enemy in what was an appropriate fixture to gain his 100th international cap. The packed Wembley fans stood as one to give the England captain a tumultuous welcome on what was a very special day for him. The Wolverhampton Wanderers player had been a tremendous ambassador for both club and country, and there has rarely been a more deserving honour in the history of the game.

England skipper Billy Wright shakes hands with Prime Minister Harold Macmillan before the game against Scotland at Wembley in April 1959. It was Wright's 100th appearance for England.

Bobby Charlton scores the only goal of the 1959 England-Scotland match with a superb diving header that gave Brown no chance.

The match was always going to play second fiddle to Wright's achievement, but as it happened it turned out to be a close and well-contested affair. Scotland, with Evans and Brown in sparkling form, held on for an hour, withstanding some fierce England pressure. The first half saw Peter Broadbent and Bobby Charlton showing some lovely skills with Charlton's power shooting once more to the fore.

On 20 minutes, a fine move involving Johnny Haynes and Charlton saw the Manchester United man hit a tremendous long pass out to the impressive Doug Holden on the left wing. It split the Scottish defence wide open but when Holden's cross found Broadbent on the six yard line, Brown charged from his line to brilliantly smother the danger.

During the first half it became apparent that England manager Walter Winterbottom was using a new plan. Instead of a big bustling centre-forward of old, he was now putting Charlton in the middle, instructing him to take on a roving role alternating with the other two inside-men, Haynes and Broadbent. It worked well and failed only in the respect of goals. Meanwhile, in defence, Wright and Ronnie Clayton snuffed out the Scottish threat by giving Collins and Dick no room to manoeuvre.

After the interval Charlton was again the main thorn in Scotland's side and on the hour, England finally gained the breakthrough they richly deserved, scoring a goal that was fit to win any match.

Clayton found Broadbent down the right and he, in turn, cleverly sent Bryan Douglas away. The winger sent over a long, tantalising cross and Charlton, roaring in, met it with an unstoppable downward header. His momentum carried him into a forward roll and Brown, this time, had no chance to save.

Brown saved his side shortly afterwards following another Charlton special. Holden, showing some lovely touches on the left wing, put the number-nine through. Charlton ghosted past two blue shirts as though they weren't there, before hitting a tremendous right-footer, knee-high. At the last second, Brown leapt across goal brilliantly to turn the ball aside. It was a super save and Brown, alone at times, denied England their deserved bigger victory margin.

Wright, Clayton and the other defenders kept Herd and Dick totally in check and Scotland had only one real chance to score. That came 12 minutes from the end and exposed Eddie Hopkinson's lack of inches. The goalkeeper failed to gather Docherty's deep cross and when the ball ran loose, Herd was left with a free shot at an empty goal. Unfortunately for him and for Scotland the ball struck Leggatt and was eventually cleared.

It would have been unfair on England had Scotland equalized but, having said that, if a team does not emphasise its superiority with goals, then they leave themselves wide open to that sort of thing happening.

To be fair, had Brown not been in such splendid form the victory would have been far more clear cut, but if Brown was Scotland's hero, then Charlton was undoubtedly England's. Superbly backed up by Broadbent and Haynes, this trio made sure that Wright had a double celebration at the end of the day.

76th match v Scotland.
Debut for Holden.
Wright's 100th cap.

England v Italy
Friendly

Played on Wednesday, 6 May 1959 at Wembley Stadium.

England: E.Hopkinson (Bolton W); D.Howe (West Brom), G.L.Shaw (Sheffield Utd), R.Clayton (Blackburn R), W.A.Wright (Wolves, captain), R.Flowers (Wolves), W.Bradley (Man Utd), P.F.Broadbent (Wolves), R.Charlton (Man Utd), J.N.Haynes (Fulham), A.D.Holden (Bolton W).

Italy: L.Buffon (Milan AC); E.Robotti

Billy Wright exchanges pennants with Italy's skipper before the game at Wembley in May 1959.

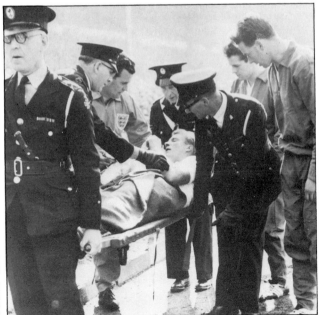

Left: Italy's Brighenti is already celebrating as his goal, the result of a mix-up between Hopkinson and Shaw. *Right:* Ron Flowers is stretchered off early in the second half.

(Fiorentina), S.Castelletti (Fiorentina), F.Zaglio (AS Roma), G.Bernasconi (Sampdoria), A.Segato (Fiorentina), A.Mariani (Padova CS), G.Gratton (Fiorentina), S.Brighenti (Padova CS), C.Galli (Milan AC), G.Petris (Fiorentina)

Half-time 2-0   Full-time 2-2
Ref: A.Dusch (West Germany) Att: 91,000

WEMBLEY Stadium was packed with 91,000 people to see an entertaining match, albeit with an indifferent display by England. Sometimes they were brilliant, other times dismal, too often the latter for the home fans. In the end the Italians deserved their draw, delighting the huge following that England provided them with. Indeed, every Italian restaurant in London must have been deserted as the afternoon was turned into a Roman holiday.

England began brightly and the inside trio of Peter Broadbent, Bobby Charlton and Johnny Haynes were quickly into their stride. However, it was the Italians who had the first two dangerous strikes at goal. Don Howe and Graham Shaw both came to England's rescue with goal-line clearances after Eddie Hopkinson was beaten by shots from Mariani and Galli. Immediately, though, Charlton struck back. A superb side-step and a thunderous left-foot shot was brilliantly tipped away by Buffon. Seconds later, in the 26th minute, Charlton gave England the lead with a real beauty.

Picking up a pass from Broadbent, he cleverly skipped around Bernasconi, moved forward and hit a superb low left-foot shot just inside the post from the edge of the penalty area. It was typical Charlton.

By this time England were moving well and five minutes before the break they increased their lead with another splendid goal. A lovely interpassing movement involving Haynes, Charlton and Haynes again, then brought Doug Holden into the move down the right. His deep cross was met on the volley by Haynes and although the shot was blocked, Warren Bradley did some clever poaching to turn sharply before hitting home the rebound.

Despite holding a comfortable lead, the game had certainly not been all England's and several times Hopkinson's goal was put under extreme pressure by the eager Italian forwards. Indeed, even in those remaining minutes of the first half, Betris missed two golden chances.

Early in the second half Ron Flowers was stretchered off, after a collision left him with a suspected broken nose. Although he managed to return to the action, patched up, about 15 minutes later, by then the damage had been done as Italy rocked England with two goals.

A long through-ball produced a terrible misunderstanding between Hopkinson and Shaw. The ball ran loose and Brighenti accepted the free gift with glee to pull one goal back. Then within minutes, it was 2-2. Gratton, taking advantage of some poor defensive play put Mariani through to shoot home the equalizer. Again Hopkinson might have done better with his attempted save.

After this burst of activity, Flowers returned to the fray and the game settled down again to an even pattern. Bradley and Charlton both saw efforts cleared off the line but by the end of the 90 minutes it was England who seemed more relieved to hear the final whistle. After their long, hard season the forthcoming summer tour seemed to be something that the players did not really want and their current form was such that a trip to visit the current World Champions, Brazil, was the last thing they need. But that is exactly what England had to do the following Wednesday.

> 7th match v Italy.
> Debut goal for Bradley.

Brazil v England   Friendly
Played on Wednesday, 13 May 1959 at the Maracana Stadium, Rio de Janeiro.

Brazil: G.dos Santos (Santos); D.Santos (Palmeiras), N.Santos (Botafogo), D.Sani (São Paulo), H.L.Bellini (Vasco da Gama), O.Pecanha (Santos), J.Botelho (Palmeiras), W.Pereira (Botafogo), H.Oliveira (Palmeiras), E.Arantes (Santos), J.Ribamar (São Paulo).
Sub: F.Fidelis (Santos) for Pecanha

England: E.Hopkinson (Bolton W); D.Howe (West Brom), J.C.Armfield (Blackpool), R.Clayton (Blackburn R), W.A.Wright (Wolves, captain), R.Flowers (Wolves), N.V.Deeley (Wolves), P.F.Broadbent (Wolves), R.Charlton (Man Utd), J.N.Haynes (Fulham), A.D.Holden (Bolton W).

Half-time 2-0   Full-time 2-0
Ref: J.Brozzi (Argentina)   Att: 200,000

A DULL overcast day gave England a much better chance of a result when they took on the reigning World Champions, Brazil in the magnificent Maracana Stadium. The usual hot baking sun had relented just in time for this, the first of four tour games of the Americas.

Brazil made a late change, bringing in Julinho in place of the legendary Garrincha. It was a controversial choice but one that was entirely vindicated after only three minutes play. For it was at that moment that Julinho opened the scoring after splendid approach play by Canho-teiro and Henrique down the left. The goal had come before England even had time to settle and it took them until the eighth minute to manage their first attack.

Brazil showed plenty of the magical skills now so world famous and their build up was a joy to watch. The huge crowd were soon cheering their favourites passionately and Julinho earned more applause when another good effort struck the England post.

England, slow and ragged, only managed the occasional raid. Peter Broadbent and Norman Deeley both shot over, but their attacks were rare and Brazil emphasised their superiority with a second goal on 28 minutes. Julinho was again prominent in the move and his dazzling skill spread-eagled the England defence. Eventually his pass inside found Henrique completely unmarked and the centre-forward easily beat Eddie Hopkinson from close range.

The visitors managed two other efforts before the break: in the 37th minute when Johnny Haynes failed to get any real power behind his shot; four minutes later, Bobby Charlton hit a typical long-range effort which crashed against Gilmar's post. To complete an eventful end to the half, Orlando, Brazil's left-half, left the field, apparently uninjured, to be replaced by Fidelis in the 43rd minute.

An incredible miss by Pelé in the 53rd minute, when he shot wide of an open goal, kept England in the game, but the visitors were continually outplayed and even when they mounted a rare attack, they were thwarted by the strong Brazilian defence. The full-back pairing of Nilton Santos and Delmar Santos was particularly impressive.

On the hour, Haynes put in a worthy attempt, only to be foiled by a marvellous save by Gilmar. That shot ended one of the few good moves by England.

As the game petered out, the floodlights came on. The crowd had by now lost interest in the game as the result was not in question, but in the 73rd minute a fierce tackle by Ronnie Clayton on Pelé ended with the Brazilian star being carried off. Pelé returned to the action after a couple of minutes but the Blackburn Rovers player again incurred the wrath of the spectators after another fearsome challenge, this time on Canhoteiro.

Brazil's Pelé challenges Eddie Hopkinson in the huge Maracana Stadium where England went down 2-0 in May 1959.

Towards the end, England showed some improvement, although it was mainly due to the Brazilians easing off. Nevertheless, Haynes was unlucky to see another good drive pushed on to a post by Gilmar. This stung Brazil into more urgency and in the final minutes Julinho, twice, and Canhoteiro put in shots that fizzed past Hopkinson's posts. At the end of the day England, although fighting hard, were well beaten.

3rd match v Brazil.
Debuts for Armfield and Deeley.
Brazil's dos Santos also known as Gilmar; Pecanha as 'Orlando'; Botelho as 'Julinho'; Pereira as 'Didí'; Oliveira as 'Henrique'; Arantes as 'Pelé'; Ribamar as 'Canhoteiro'; Fidelis as 'Formiga'.
"Pelé was the most difficult opponent I ever came up against. You couldn't get near him to tackle!"
Ronnie Clayton

Peru v England   Friendly

Played on Sunday, 17 May 1959 in the National Stadium, Lima.

Peru: P.Azca (Sport Boys); W.Fleming (Alianza), E.Andrade (Universitario), V.Benitez (Universitario), J.Fernandez (Universitario), J.Delavega (Alienza), H.Montalvo (Universitario), M.Loyaza (Sport Boys), J.L.Joya (Sporting Cristal), J.Carrasco (Universitario), J.Seminario (Municipal).
England: E.Hopkinson (Bolton W); D.Howe (West Brom), J.C.Armfield (Blackpool), R.Clayton (Blackburn R), W.A.Wright (Wolves, captain), R.Flowers (Wolves), N.V.Deeley (Wolves), J.P.Greaves (Chelsea), R.Charlton (Man Utd), J.N.Haynes (Fulham), A.D.Holden (Bolton W).

Half-time 2-0   Full-time 4-1
Ref: E.Hieger (Austria)   Att: 54,000

FOR the second time in five days, England were totally outclassed by a South American team. For the second leg of their summer tour they journeyed to the ancient city of Lima to take on Peru and ended up well beaten.

England made only one change from the side beaten in Brazil, bringing in Chelsea's prolific goalscorer Jimmy Greaves for his first game and leaving out Peter Broadbent. They wore unfamiliar blue shirts and white shorts and kicked off facing a bright sun.

Bobby Charlton was soon hitting a screamer just over the bar, but Peru gradually settled and began to take a firm grip on the play. Eddie Hopkinson was tested by Loyaza and Seminario before the latter opened the scoring after ten minutes.

If Julinho had been Brazil's star, then Seminario was certainly Peru's, and the tricky winger's goal was a real beauty, a 20-yard cracker, a-la-Charlton!

Peru went close on several other occasions and Carrasco wasted a fine opportunity by shooting wildly over the bar from five yards. But with five minutes to go before half-time, Peru scored a second goal. This time Hopkinson failed

Jimmy Greaves, scored on his England debut against Peru.

to hold a fierce drive from Loyaza and when the ball ran free, Seminario nipped in to flick it into the net.

That goal did stir some response from England after the break. Ron Flowers hit a shot against a post and Charlton saw an effort cleared off the line. Although Peru were quicker and passed more accurately, the extra England determination brought its reward when Greaves pulled a goal back. He combined well with Johnny Haynes and Charlton before shooting in off the post to beat Azca. It was some consolation that Greaves had scored the goal which emphasised a promising debut.

However, it was not too long before Peru had regained the initiative and in fact they were soon dominating play against the tiring England players. Seminario continued to be the danger man and twice he almost scored again.

Hopkinson did very well on the second occasion, just getting his fingertips to the ball. Shortly afterwards, though, the goalkeeper was powerless to stop Joya from making it 3-1 following a goalmouth scramble.

With ten minutes to go the win was completed when Peru added a fourth goal through the ever-dangerous Seminario. He clinched a brilliant hat-trick with another good shot past the bewildered Hopkinson.

1st match v Peru.
Debut goal for Greaves.
Hat-trick by Seminario for Peru.

Mexico v England   Friendly

Played on Sunday, 24 May 1959 at the CU Stadium, Mexico City.

Mexico: A.Carbajal (León); J.Bosco (América), I.Jáuregui (Atlas), R.Cardenas (Zacatepec), J.Del Muro (Atlas), F.Flores (Guadalajara), A.Del Aguila (Toluca), S.Reyes (Guadalajara), C.Gonzalez (Tampico), S.Ponce (Guadalajara), R.Arellano (Guadalajara).
Subs: Jasso (Zacatepec) for Ponce and Hernández (Guadalajara) for Gonzalez.
England: E.Hopkinson (Bolton W); D.Howe (West Brom), J.C.Armfield (Blackpool), R.Clayton (Blackburn R), W.A.Wright (Wolves, captain), W.McGuinness (Man Utd), A.D.Holden (Bolton W), J.P.Greaves (Chelsea), D.T.Kevan (West Brom), J.N.Haynes (Fulham), R.Charlton (Man Utd).
Subs: R.Flowers (Wolves) for McGuinness and W.Bradley (Man Utd) for Holden.

Half-time 1-1   Full-time 2-1
Ref: E.de Queiroz (Brazil)   Att: 82,000

ENGLAND suffered their third defeat in a row on this tour with this match in Mexico probably the most disappointing result of all. Having been well beaten in Brazil and Peru, they were looking to do better against a Mexican side not generally considered one of South America's strongest.

England kicked-off under a blazing sun and in the rarified air of Mexico City. Bobby Charlton was quickly in the action forcing a good save from Carbajal low down. The Mexicans who favoured a square passing style made little headway against the England defence despite enjoying most of the possession. After ten minutes, Billy Wright was forced into heading a dangerous Mexican centre over his own crossbar to rescue his side whilst at the other end, Derek Kevan put in a header which was well held by the goalkeeper.

Then after 17 minutes, England took the lead. A corner was swung over and this time Kevan made his header count. This stung Mexico into retaliation and Reyes shot wide in one attack. England always looked likely to break dangerously though and Charlton almost added a second goal with a typical effort which flew just past Carbajal's post.

In the 23rd minute, Mexico made a change in their line-up when they brought on Jasso as substitute for Ponce. This move soon paid handsome dividends as three minutes later the home side equalized. Again the goal stemmed from a corner and this time it was Cardenas who ran in to beat Eddie Hopkinson from eight yards with a header.

In the 31st minute, England also made a substitution with Ron Flowers replacing Wilf McGuinness and later in the half two fine saves by Carbajal foiled two more England goal attempts. In the opening seconds of the second half, Jimmy Greaves netted following a pass from Kevan but unfortunately the referee disallowed the goal for offside.

That was crucial because a minute after that incident, Mexico took the lead. Gonzalez had the England defence all over the place and his final pass found the unmarked Reyes who had an easy task to score from close range. The earlier poise of the visitors' defence was now gone and Mexico had most of the play in the remaining period.

Warren Bradley replaced Doug Holden in the 57th minute but it was Wright who saved England again with another timely intervention of a dangerous Mexico attack. At this stage the Mexicans were well on top and missed several fine opportunities to add to their score.

So, in the end it was another disappointing display from a very jaded England team. They had now won only two of their last 14 games.

> 1st match v Mexico.

USA v England
Friendly

Played on Thursday, 28 May 1959 at Wrigley Field, Los Angeles.

USA: V.Ottobini (San Francisco Vikings); D.Farquhar (New York Hakoah), B.Cinowitz (New York Hakoah), A.Bachmeier (Chicago Kickers), B.Evans (Los Angeles McIlwain), J.Traina (St Louis Kutis), E.Murphy (Chicago Slovaks), F.Cameron (Los Angeles Kickers), B.Carson (Los Angeles Kickers), W.Looby (St Louis Kutis), A.Zerhusen (Los Angeles Kickers).
Subs: P.Kulitschenko (Ukranians, Philadelphia) for Bachmeier.
England: E.Hopkinson (Bolton W); D.Howe (West Brom), J.C.Armfield (Blackpool), R.Clayton (Blackburn R), W.A.Wright (Wolves, captain), R.Flowers (Wolves), W.Bradley (Man Utd), J.P.Greaves (Chelsea), D.T.Kevan (West Brom), J.N.Haynes (Fulham), R.Charlton (Man Utd).

Half-time 1-1   **Full-time 1-8**
R.Morgan (Canada)   Att: 13,000

ENGLAND'S disastrous summer tour of the America's finally came to an end in Los Angeles where a victory over the USA gave them some consolation for the earlier disappointment in South America. Even in this match, though, their poor form made them struggle for a long spell before finally coming to terms with the opposition and then overpowering them.

All the vivid memories of that infamous 1950 World Cup humiliation came flooding back when in the 18th minute the USA took a shock lead. They had already had a goal disallowed five minutes earlier, but this time Murphy's effort counted. Needless to say the 13,000 crowd went wild with delight and they grew even more confident as the half wore on with England seemingly unable to string any worthwhile attacks together. It was a real struggle but gradually the American challenge wilted and before half-time England at last found a goal.

A long, curling throw-in by Ron Flowers landed in the home goalmouth and as the USA defenders hesitated, Warren Bradley nipped in to head home from four yards. There was almost tangible relief coming from the England team and at last they began to settle down to the job in hand. By half-time the American attacks had dwindled down to nothing and after the break it was one-way traffic from start to finish.

Ron Flowers, one of Wolves' incredible half-back strength which served England so well.

On 52 minutes, Flowers gave England the lead with a tremendous left-foot drive from fully 30 yards. Twelve minutes later, Bobby Charlton increased the total with another thunderbolt from 20 yards. His left-foot shot whizzed in off the post.

Long-range shooting now seemed to be the order of the day as Ottobini was beaten all ends up by another long-distance shot by Flowers. That goal came in the 69th minute and five minutes later, Derek Kevan added number five with a glorious 30 yarder. With eight minutes to go, England were awarded a penalty which Charlton duly hammered home and then three minutes later the Manchester United man completed his hat-trick with goal number seven.

Johnny Haynes had the final say in the scoring when his goal in the 87th minute made it 8-1 much to the dismay of the exhausted Americans. The England team manager Walter Winterbottom said afterwards that the first half had been almost a replica of that 1950 game, but added that he thought the Americans had improved considerably.

The match marked the end of an era too, as Billy Wright left the international arena for the last time, having announced his intention to retire. He had been a magnificent servant to English football and would be sadly missed.

> 3rd match v USA.
> Hat-trick for Charlton including a penalty.
> Wright's 105th and last international. It was also his 70th consecutive appearance and his 90th as captain, both records.

Wales v England
Home Championship

Played on Saturday, 17 October 1959 at Ninian Park, Cardiff.

Wales: A.J.Kelsey (Arsenal); S.G.Williams (West Brom), M.Hopkins (Spurs), V.H.Crowe (Aston Villa), M.T.G.Nurse (Swansea T), D.Sullivan (Cardiff C), T.C.Medwin (Spurs), A.P.Woosnam (West Ham), G.Moore (Cardiff C), I.J.Allchurch (Newcastle Utd), C.W.Jones (Spurs).
England: E.Hopkinson (Bolton W); D.Howe (West Brom), A.Allen (Stoke C), R.Clayton (Blackburn R, captain), T.Smith (Birmingham C), R.Flowers (Wolves), J.M.Connelly (Burnley), J.P.Greaves (Chelsea), B.H.Clough (Middlesbrough), R.Charlton (Man Utd), E.Holliday (Middlesbrough).

Half-time 0-1   **Full-time 1-1**
Ref: T.Mitchell (Northern Ireland)
                                 Att: 60,000

IT was an appalling day's weather at Ninian Park for this international and the big crowd had to endure a driving wind and heavy rain as well as a poor performance from the Welsh side. Before the match, Wales were hot favourites as England with five new caps seeked to rebuild a team able to challenge the best again. It fell to Ronnie Clayton to succeed the inimitable Billy Wright as captain and it was with immense pride that the Blackburn Rovers player led his side out at the start.

His teammates then responded well to the task and in the first half especially the game gave England hope for a brighter future. All the new faces settled quickly with Tony Allen the pick of them with a cultured display at left-back. Wales, meanwhile, retained their usual style but alas for them the way they play is beginning to look more and more outdated.

England attacked from the start and they were soon threatening Kelsey's goal. Unfortunately for the visitors, the Arsenal goalkeeper was in fine form and his saves were vital as England pushed for the early breakthrough. Brian Clough, who had made his name as a big scorer with Second Division Middlesbrough, saw an effort cleared by Williams from the Welsh goal-line after good work by Edwin Holliday.

Then Kelsey made a superb save from Bobby Charlton, England's star player. The Manchester United man was everywhere and he tried all he knew to conjure up a goal. He and Holliday both put in good attempts and then Jimmy Greaves missed a great chance when he shot over following a lovely cross by John Connelly.

At last England finally scored the goal their play deserved when Greaves netted in the 25th minute. He was brilliantly put through by Charlton and although Kelsey blocked his first shot, the inside-right, typically, followed up to score from the rebound. Half-time arrived with England still one goal up but regretting the fact that it could, and should, have been more.

After all this first-half promise from England, the second half came as a bitter disappointment and fell way below the standard one expects from an international football match. Only the occasional glimpses of class from Woosnam

John Connelly flicks home England's first goal against Sweden at Wembley in October 1959.

of Wales and Charlton from England brightened the gloom. The bad weather never relented and there were precious few moments of note in an uninspiring second 45 minutes.

England had some plusses, though, and all the newcomers did quite well. Allen continued his good start and although Trevor Smith looked a little cumbersome at times, Clough, Holliday and Connelly all showed promise. The visitors did not seem in too much trouble from the poor Welsh attack and all looked set for a narrow but comfortable victory. But with barely a minute left the red-shirted Welsh Dragons suddenly produced a goal out of nothing.

Jones, who had been largely anonymous up until then, summoned up his first positive run of the game. At the end of it he sent over a perfect cross to the far post and there was Moore to head home.

It was a bitter blow for England and they looked back ruefully on their first half dominance and many missed chances.

> 70th match v Wales.
> Debuts for Allen, Smith, Connelly, Clough and Holliday.
> Clayton captain for the first time.

England v Sweden
Friendly

Played on Wednesday, 28 October 1959 at Wembley Stadium.

England: E.Hopkinson (Bolton W); D.Howe (West Brom), A.Allen (Stoke C), R.Clayton (Blackburn R, captain), T.Smith (Birmingham C), R.Flowers (Wolves), J.M.Connelly (Burnley), J.P.Greaves (Chelsea), B.H.Clough (Mid-

dlesbrough), R.Charlton (Man Utd), E.Holliday (Middlesbrough).

Sweden: B.Nyholm (IFK Norrköping); O.Bergmark (Örebro SK), S.Axbom (IFK Norrköping), T.Jönsson (IFK Norrköping), A.Johansson (IFK Norrköping), S.Parling (Djurgårdens IF), B.Berntdsson (IFK Göteborg), H.Thillberg (Malmö FF), A.Simonsson (Örgryte IS), R.Börjesson (Örgryte IS), B.Salomonsson (Helsingborgs IF).

Half-time 1-0   Full-time 2-3

Ref: R.H.Davidson (Scotland) Att: 72,000

AS in 1953, when Hungary were the never-to-be-forgotten visitors, England were once again taught a football lesson by an emerging power in the game. Whereas the home side employed the traditional game, the Swedes strolled effortlessly through the proceedings with an air of authority not born out by the final scoreline. All through the match there was much to admire in the deft touches of the talented Swedish team, but for England there must be many question-marks in their attempts to build a side capable of mounting a serious challenge on the 1962 World Cup in Chile.

On a dull, grey afternoon, 72,000 people gathered to see a game that was full of incident. It started well enough for England, who settled quickly. In fact for the opening 20 minutes they controlled the play and during that time they scored an excellent goal. It was on eight minutes that a move involving Don Howe, John Connelly, Jimmy Greaves and Brian Clough, worked its way down the right nicely. When the final pass came in, Connelly met the ball to flick it past Nyholm.

However, as the half wore on Sweden began to find their feet and by the half-hour they could easily have been level. Twice Berntdsson met Simonsson passes

but succeeded only in rattling each of Eddie Hopkinson's posts. Simonsson, by now, was stamping his undoubted class on the game and he gave Trevor Smith a torrid afternoon at the heart of England's defence. Smith looked slow and ponderous as the balance and skill of Simonsson weaved patterns around him.

For England, Bobby Charlton was struggling in his role of midfield provider and all the forwards were guilty of holding on to the ball too long. Clough almost added a second for England before half-time when he intercepted a sloppy backpass by Johansson, but he too was thwarted by a goalpost.

After the break, the Swedes stepped up a gear. Superbly marshalled by Jönsson at right-half, they began to make their extra skills count. The inside trio of Thillberg, Simonsson and Börjesson were constantly in the action.

In the 52nd minute, Sweden finally gained a deserved equalizer. Charlton's attempted pass was lost by Ron Flowers and Berndtsson nipped in smartly to set up an easy header for Simonsson to make it 1-1. The Scandinavians now had their tails up and eight minutes later they took the lead.

A fast interchange of passes between Simonsson and Börjesson ended with a rebound falling just right for Simonsson to shoot home from the narrowest of angles with great accuracy. The Swedes were delighted but the crowd began to barrack the England players. Hopkinson bore the brunt of their frustration as he mixed some brave saves with inexplicable errors. Smith, too, was struggling and England were now really up against it. Clough did hit the bar with a header, from a Connelly centre, but that was an isolated raid.

With 15 minutes to go, the result was settled by a third Swedish goal. A clever move

Brian Clough, who also hit the post and the bar, this time sees Swedish goalkeeper Nyholm block his shot.

down the right drew the whole England defence over and the ever-dangerous Simonsson, spotting Salomonsson unmarked in the middle, flicked the ball inside for the number-ten to shoot home.

England, to their credit, rallied strongly towards the end and Greaves contributed his best moment by cleverly putting Charlton through to reduce the arrears with a well-taken goal. Alas, the fightback was too late and Sweden, with Jonsson and Simonsson outstanding, ended worthy winners.

7th match v Sweden.

England v Northern Ireland Home

Championship

Played on Wednesday, 18 November 1959 at Wembley Stadium.

England: R.D.G.Springett (Sheffield Wed); D.Howe (West Brom), A.Allen (Stoke C), R.Clayton (Blackburn R, captain), K.Brown (West Ham), R.Flowers (Wolves), J.M.Connelly (Burnley), J.N.Haynes (Fulham), J.H.Baker (Hibernian), R.A.Parry (Bolton W), E.Holliday (Middlesbrough).

Northern Ireland: H.Gregg (Man Utd); R.M.Keith (Newcastle Utd), A.McMichael (Newcastle Utd), R.D.Blanchflower (Spurs), W.E.Cunningham (Leicester C), R.Peacock (Celtic), W.L.Bingham (Luton T), J.A.Crossan (Sparta Rotterdam), W.W.Cush (Leeds Utd), J.McIlroy (Burnley), P.J.McParland (Aston Villa).

Half-time 1-0   Full-time 2-1
Ref: L.Callaghan (Wales)   Att: 60,000

ENGLAND, desperately searching for a win, brought in four more new caps for the visit of Northern Ireland in the Home Championship. Only three victories in their previous 16 matches was testament to the depressing spell that the side was going through. Not since before the Munich air crash had the England team looked to be mounting a serious challenge to world football and this side did not look likely to improve things.

This game began slowly before ending with a flourish but there was some hope for the England selectors with the form of new centre-forward, Joe Baker. At last England seem to have found a number-nine of real quality and despite the fact that he played for Hibernian in the Scottish League and spoke with a broad Scottish accent, Baker gave a performance which suggested that he would serve England well. His skill and speed were a joy to watch and this, coupled with his intelligent running, was a real handful for his marker, Cunningham for the whole 90 minutes.

Baker quickly adapted to his new surroundings and early on he set up chances for both Johnny Haynes and Ray Parry. Both shots were cleared from the line but on 16 minutes Baker himself got into the act with a superb opening strike. Tony Allen took a free-kick which Baker cleverly allowed to run and after one bounce a flashing right-foot shot found the top corner. It was a stunning goal and the number-nine had already won over the crowd.

Unfortunately the rest of the game did not match up to Baker's contribution and for a long spell the play became as tedious and intricate as a chess game with both sides drawing long-winded patterns in midfield. For Ireland, the workload fell heavily on Blanchflower and McIlroy, whereas England looked to Haynes and Parry for inspiration.

It was all very negative stuff, although the Irish should have been level at half-time. McIlroy set off on an effortless run which took him past three England defenders. It all ended abruptly, though, when he was sandwiched between Ken Brown and Don Howe. The referee saw it as a foul and awarded Ireland a penalty.

McIlroy himself took the spot-kick but stroked it all too gently towards the corner of the goal, enabling Ron Springett to anticipate well and save at full stretch. Ironically, McIlroy had missed a penalty against Scotland earlier this season after having previously gone three years without failure. The save by Springett was one of several very confident moments for England's new goalkeeper, who gave an excellent display throughout.

The second half began with the Irish surging forward, and in one incredible attack four shots by McParland, McIlroy, twice, and Cush were all blocked by a wall of English defenders. As the pace of the game increased then so did the number of goalmouth incidents. A lovely run by John Connelly left McMichael sprawling before a cross from the by-line was headed inches wide by the diving Baker. Then, at the other end, McParland and Cush both shot only just off target before Baker came roaring in to shoot wide from a good

Joe Baker scores a brilliant goal give England the lead against Northern Ireland at Wembley in November 1959.

position as England retaliated. He really should have scored from that one.

All of a sudden, with the sky darkening and the match into the last two minutes, there was pandemonium. McParland, always a threat when he pulled on that green shirt, made a good run down the left before hitting over a low centre to the near post. Springett's dive appeared to have done enough but before the ball could roll out for a corner, Bingham nipped in to hook it back and into the net. Needless to say, his colleagues swarmed round the diminutive winger with their congratulations.

Alas, their joy was premature as within seconds of the end England came back to snatch victory with a dramatic winner. Gregg had already saved brilliantly from Connelly when England regained possession through Edwin Holliday. He fed Baker a good pass and the centre-forward moved to the left-hand by-line before sending a diagonal pass into the path of Parry. The Bolton player calmly stroked the ball wide of Gregg and England had won the match.

> 67th match v Northern Ireland.
> Debuts for Springett, Brown, Baker and Parry.
> Debut goals for Baker and Parry.

Scotland v England Home Championship

Played on Saturday, 9 April 1960 at Hampden Park, Glasgow.

Scotland: F.Haffey (Celtic); D.McKay (Celtic), E.Caldow (Rangers), J.Cumming (Hearts), R.Evans (Celtic), R.J.McCann (Motherwell), G.Leggatt (Fulham), A.Young (Hearts), I.St John (Motherwell), D.Law (Man City), A.Weir (Motherwell).
England: R.D.G.Springett (Sheffield Wed); J.C.Armfield (Blackpool),

R.Wilson (Huddersfield T), R.Clayton (Blackburn R, captain), W.J.Slater (Wolves), R.Flowers (Wolves), J.M.Connelly (Burnley), P.F.Broadbent (Wolves), J.H.Baker (Hibernian), R.A.Parry (Bolton W), R.Charlton (Man Utd).

Half-time 1-0   Full-time 1-1
Ref: G.E.Szranko (Hungary) Att: 129,193

A STRONG wind and some inconsistent refereeing decisions made for a very disappointing match at Hampden Park in this annual game between two old adversaries. Scotland, seeking their first victory on home soil against England since 1937, should have won handsomely and but for some woeful finishing would have done. At the end of the day, though, they were lucky to escape with a draw.

St John was a real livewire at centre-forward and gave Bill Slater a torrid time throughout the game. The Wolves defender suffered a nightmare. Four excellent chances were created down the middle for Scotland and each one of them stemmed from an inexplicable error by Slater.

In the 17th minute, one of them was punished by Leggatt. Ron Flowers had just thundered a free-kick against the Scottish crossbar before Scotland broke quickly into attack. Slater lost the ball in the air to St John, but recovered to regain possession, only to then set up Leggatt with a disastrously short back-pass. The winger sped forward to plant a splendid shot wide of Ron Springett's dive.

Immediately after the goal, Baker scrambled the ball into the Scottish net after challenging Haffey. It was reminiscent of Nat Lofthouse's goal in the 1958 Cup Final, but this time the referee ruled out the effort. So at half-time, Scotland led, for the first time since the war, much to the delight of the crowd. But England, now with the wind at their backs, were soon level after the interval.

Baker, who received little support from

his inside-forwards Ray Parry and Peter Broadbent, sent a fine pass to Bobby Charlton. The winger strode into the penalty area and was brought down by a trip from full-back McKay. Not for the first time in the match, the Bulgarian referee's decision was not entirely agreed upon. However, a penalty it was and Charlton himself took it, sending Haffey the wrong way with his spot-kick.

Later, the other chances courtesy of Mr Slater duly presented themselves. Three times, errors on the ground left St John free, but each time the number-nine lost his composure and Springett out-thought him to make the save.

Springett was undoubtedly England's main saviour and he again gave a very assured performance. Twice more he made brave saves at the feet of Leggatt and St John. Flowers, too, had a fine game and was full of tireless effort. For Ray Wilson it was an eventful match. He looked composed and confident and enjoyed an excellent debut, all this after the full-back had broken his nose in the second minute!

For Scotland, Haffey looked decidedly shaky at times but their star was the red-haired Evans, who was outstanding and rock-like in defence. The other impressive Scot was the tireless Law at inside-left. He covered every inch of Hampden in supporting both his defence and his attack, showing immense stamina and true Scottish fire. Ronnie Clayton could not get near him and the blond-haired will-o'-the-wisp enjoyed every moment of it.

An amazing incident could easily have swung the match England's way near the end. After showing a distinct lack of thrust all through, they were suddenly awarded a second penalty. Charlton again took the kick, only to shoot straight at Haffey. The referee then ordered a retake as Caldow had encroached into the penalty area and amid deafening boos, Charlton had another chance. This time he made a total hash of it, shooting well wide.

Perhaps that was justice in a way as Scotland, at the very least, deserved their draw.

> 77th match v Scotland.
> Debut for Wilson.
> Penalty by Charlton but then he missed a twice-taken second penalty.

England v Yugoslavia Friendly

Played on Wednesday, 11 May 1960 at Wembley Stadium.

England: R.D.G.Springett (Sheffield Wed); J.C.Armfield (Blackpool), R.Wilson (Huddersfield T), R.Clayton (Blackburn R, captain), P.Swan (Sheffield Wed), R.Flowers (Wolves), B.Douglas (Blackburn R), J.N.Haynes (Fulham), J.H.Baker (Hibernian), J.P.Greaves (Chelsea), R.Charlton (Man Utd).
Yugoslavia: M.Šoškić (Partizan Belgrade); V.Durković (Red Star Belgrade), F.Jusufi (Partizan Belgrade), A.Žanetić (Hajduk Split), B.Zebec (Red Star Belgrade), Z.Perušić (Dinamo Zagreb), L.Lipošinović (Dinamo Zagreb), D.Jerković (Dinamo Zagreb), D.Šekularac (Red Star Belgrade), M.Galić (Red Star Belgrade), B.Kostić (Red Star Begrade).
Sub: M.Mujić (Velež Mostar) for Jerković.

England XI in Bolton Wanderers shirts, pictured during training at Burnden Park before the game against Scotland at Hampden Park in April 1960. Back row (left to right): Armfield, Slater, Flowers, Springett, Parry, Wilson. Front row: Connelly, Broadbent, Clayton, Baker, Charlton.

Bryan Douglas draws England level against Yugoslavia at Wembley in May 1960, flicking home Joe Baker's header.

Half-time 1-1   Full-time 3-3

Ref: R.H.Davidson (Scotland) Att: 70,000

A CROWD of 70,000 saw this thrilling international at Wembley and enjoyed a late England revival which saw them draw level and all but snatch victory. Once again, though, an Iron Curtain country came to this stadium and produced a typical brand of close-passing football which, at times, had the home side tied up in knots.

Both teams had early chances. Jimmy Greaves and Bobby Charlton for England and Lipošinović for the Slavs all failed to take advantage when well placed in front of goal. With Šekularac the main tormentor, ably assisted by Perušić, Galić and Kostić, Yugoslavia began to take control and on the half-hour they took the lead. Zebec took a free-kick and Jerković outjumped Peter Swan to glance the ball sideways for Galić to shoot home.

Just before half-time, Yugoslavia brought on a substitute when Mujic replaced Jerković but it did them little good as even nearer the break England found an equalizer. It was a similar goal to the earlier one, this time Joe Baker heading down Ray Wilson's free-kick for Brian Douglas to flick the ball past Šoškić.

After the interval, England had their best spell. For 15 minutes, with Johnny Haynes pulling all the strings, they controlled proceedings. In the 48th minute, Greaves latched on to a fine pass by Charlton and made for goal. Baker played his part by pulling defenders out of position with some unselfish running, whilst Greaves continued to run on before shooting a fine goal wide of the goalkeeper.

At this stage it looked as though England would go on to win, but it was not to be as the Yugoslavs suddenly stepped up a gear. With half an hour to go, Perušić set up Galić with a lovely through pass and the inside-left scored his second to square things up at 2-2. That goal was the cue for the visitors to turn on the style and it was keep-ball play for several minutes. This frustrated the home fans and they were drawn into the slow hand-clap.

In the 80th minute, a fine goal by Kostić, after a cheeky back-heel by Galić gave the Slavs the lead again, and it looked all over for the England team. Other chances were created by the talented Yugoslavian players but solid work by the excellent full-back pairing of Jimmy Armfield and Wilson held the team together and enabled England to make a barnstorming finish.

Greaves put in a cross from the left and Baker hit a tremendous volley against the crossbar. Before the disappointment of that could hit the crowd, Haynes popped up to head home the rebound to equalize yet again. Then in the final seconds, Baker was desperately unlucky to see his header from Charlton's centre strike the Yugoslav upright and bounce clear.

That could so easily have given England a sensational victory in a match that they could just as easily have lost.

6th match v Yugoslavia.
Debut for Swan.

Spain v England   Friendly

Played on Sunday, 15 May 1960 at the Bernabeu Stadium, Madrid.

Spain: A.Ramallets (FC Barcelona); E.Pérez-Diaz (Real Madrid), S.Gracia (FC Barcelona), M.Verges (FC Barcelona), J.Garay (Athletic Bilbao), J.Segarra (FC Barcelona), J.M.Pereda (Sevilla FC), E.Martinez (FC Barcelona), A.Di Stefano (Real Madrid), J.Peiro (Atlético Madrid), F.Gento (Real Madrid).

England: R.D.G.Springett (Sheffield Wed); J.C.Armfield (Blackpool), R.Wilson (Huddersfield T), R.Robson (West Brom), P.Swan (Sheffield Wed), R.Flowers (Wolves), P.Brabrook (Chelsea), J.N.Haynes (Fulham, captain), J.H.Baker (Hibernian), J.P.Greaves (Chelsea), R.Charlton (Man Utd).

Half-time 1-0   Full-time 3-0

Ref: A.Dusch (West Germany) Att: 87,250

ENGLAND'S three matches in May continued with a visit to the magnificent Bernabeu Stadium, home of Real Madrid, taking with them one of the youngest sides they have ever fielded. But they had the daunting task of facing one of the best international sides in the world. The ground was well short of capacity but still held over 87,000 people at the start. They were soon passionately voicing their opinions, generating a cauldron of noise and a terrific atmosphere.

The Spaniards immediately showed their marvellous skills, attacking from the first whistle. But one thing that England have never lacked is a combative spirit and they made Spain fight for every ball. Ron Flowers carried out the tactical plan of man-marking the irrepressible Di Stefano, leaving Peter Swan the task of covering the central area. Swan did well against the probings of Peiro and Martinez and

Martinez beats Armfield's challenge to hit home Spain's second goal in Madrid in May 1960.

Flowers, Bobby Robson and especially Jimmy Armfield gave sterling service to the England cause.

Spain had most of the first-half possession and chances were created at regular intervals. In the 38th minute they scored the goal their play deserved. Pereda found Gento with a long cross-field pass. The winger made ground before splitting the England defence wide open with a wonderful pass which gave Peiro the chance to score, a chance he gleefully took.

Johnny Haynes, revelling in his new role of captain, gave Jimmy Greaves the best England chance of the first half. A glorious through ball sent Greaves away but the Chelsea player just overran it allowing Ramellets the chance to block. That opportunity had come just before Spain's goal and if Greaves had taken it, then maybe a different story would have to be told. As it was, Peiro's goal was enough to give the Spanish their half-time lead.

After the break, England continued to work hard and create some chances. With Haynes prompting well, they were still in there with a real chance of saving the game. Joe Baker almost forced an equalizer 15 minutes into the second half when he intercepted an attempted back-pass by Garay. Alas, he too, overran the ball and again Ramallets was able to save.

England then had another fine chance when a short corner was worked by Peter Brabrook and Armfield before the full-back put in a centre which Greaves headed over when it seemed easier for him to score. These were crucial misses by the visitors and they were to rue them as, with ten minutes to go, Spain scored a decisive second goal.

A superb move involving Di Stefano, Peiro and Diaz ended with Diaz's cross finding Martinez. The number-eight controlled the ball well, moved to the left of goal and then drilled a shot past Ron Springett from a tight angle.

The crowd went wild with delight and Spain ended the match in full control as they turned on the style. They tormented the England defenders with some keep-ball passing movements and then rubbed salt into the wound by adding a third goal. Again Martinez was the scorer, showing clever skills and finishing with an arrogant strike inside the far post. Although

the win was merited, that last goal did give a slightly flattering look to the scoreline.

Finally, a word of praise for Armfield. Faced with one of the world's fastest wingers in Gento, the full-back was rarely beaten for pace and had a tremendous game against the dangerous Spaniard.

> 6th match v Spain.
> Haynes captain for the first time.
> Spain's Pérez-Diaz also known as 'Pachin'.

Hungary v England   Friendly

Played on Sunday, 22 May 1960 in the Nep Stadium, Budapest.

Hungary: G.Grosics (Tatabánya); S.Mátrai (Ferencváros), J.Dalnoki (Ferencváros), D.Bundzsák (Vasas), F.Sipos (MTK Budapest), A.Kotász (Honvéd), K.Sándor (MTK Budapest), J.Görőcs (Újpesti Dózsa), F.Albert (Ferencváros), J.Dunai (Pecs Dózsa), G.Rákosi (Ferencváros).

England: R.D.G.Springett (Sheffield Wed); J.C.Armfield (Blackpool), R.Wilson (Huddersfield T), R.W.Robson (West Brom), P.Swan (Sheffield Wed), R.Flowers (Wolves), B.Douglas (Blackburn R), J.N.Haynes (Fulham, captain), J.H.Baker (Hibernian), D.S.Viollet (Man Utd), R.Charlton (Man Utd).

Half-time 0-0   Full-time 2-0

Ref: C.Lo Bello (Italy)   Att: 90,000

THE late afternoon sun shone down as England continued their tour with a visit to Budapest. Hungary's side of 1960 did not live up to the level of their magnificent predecessors of the early '50s but another gem of a player has been produced in the shape of the tall, lean form of Albert at centre-forward. At 18 years, old the youngster gave a thrilling display in a good match which also saw England have their moments.

Indeed, England played quite well although once again their lack of thrust up front let them down. But they made an excellent start and dominated the first 25 minutes. Bobby Charlton saw his flashing shot saved by Grosics and then Bryan Douglas had an effort pushed away

by the goalkeeper following a good move involving Johnny Haynes, Joe Baker, Douglas himself and Charlton.

England kept up the pressure and Douglas again made a good run, going outside his marker before shooting just wide of the far post. Then in the 25th minute, another good attack involving Charlton, Haynes, Dennis Viollet and Douglas ended with a free-kick that Ron Flowers fired just wide.

It was at this point that Albert began to show his pedigree. First of all, he forced Ron Springett into a brilliant save with a header; then a superb flowing run took him past Peter Swan, Jimmy Armfield and Ray Wilson, only for his shot to be blocked. Soon afterwards, following good work by Sándor and Dunai, Albert hit a tremendous volley which crashed against England's crossbar. Despite these anxious moments England were still very much in the match at half-time.

The turning point of this particular game probably came three minutes into the second half. Flowers sent Charlton streaking away down the left-wing. Over came his centre and Haynes jumped with Grosics and other defenders. Everyone missed the ball and with Grosics grovelling around on the floor, Baker was left with an open goal some eight yards out. Incredibly, he managed to shoot over the bar and the chance was gone.

It was doubly disappointing as within three minutes of that incident, the Hungarians swept forward to take the lead. A long through pass was picked up by Albert, who beat Swan before firing an unstoppable shot into the top corner of England's net.

England tried to hit back and a lovely pass by Viollet sent Charlton away again. With the winger cutting in at great speed an equalizer looked a distinct possibility. But right at the death, a brilliant saving tackle by Mátrai kept Charlton out.

As the action continued in this entertaining game, Springett made another fine save, this time from Sándor. Then Armfield kicked off the goal-line a shot by Albert, whilst at the other end Charlton was narrowly wide with another fierce effort.

With 15 minutes to go, the decisive moment duly arrived to settle the result. Dunai put Albert through the centre and again the superb youngster cleverly outwitted Swan and Bobby Robson to shoot home left footed. And that, as they say, was that!

Some good performances for England, had come out of this tour, notably in a defence which seemed to be taking shape nicely, but there were still some obvious problems which must be overcome if they were, once again, to make a serious world challenge.

> 8th match v Hungary.
> Debut for Viollet.

Northern Ireland v England   Home Championship

Played on Saturday, 8 October 1960 at Windsor Park, Belfast.

Northern Ireland: H.Gregg (Man Utd); R.M.Keith (Newcastle Utd), A.R.Elder (Burnley), R.D.Blanchflower (Spurs), J.T.Forde (Ards), R.Peacock (Celtic), W.L.Bingham (Luton T), J.McIlroy

(Burnley), W.J.McAdams (Bolton W), A.D.Dougan (Blackburn R), P.J.McParland (Aston Villa).

England: R.D.G.Springett (Sheffield Wed); J.C.Armfield (Blackpool), M.McNeil (Middlesbrough), R.W.Robson (West Brom), P.Swan (Sheffield Wed), R.Flowers (Wolves), B.Douglas (Blackburn R), J.P.Greaves (Chelsea), R.A.Smith (Spurs), J.N.Haynes (Fulham, captain), R.Charlton (Man Utd).

Half-time 1-2   Full-time 2-5

Ref: H.Phillips (Scotland)   Att: 59,000

THE proverbial 'Luck of the Irish' had nearly always been missing when these teams met in Belfast and this day saw no exception. In fact, it was England who enjoyed the lion's share of any luck that was going and although they deserved to win, the margin of victory was a little flattering.

It was England who took the lead after a quarter of an hour. Johnny Haynes flicked a short free-kick to Bobby Smith and the big centre-forward thundered a 20-yard shot into the top corner of Gregg's net. Smith was full of powerful running and he constantly gave the Irish defence much to think about. He continually pulled Forde, Elder and Keith out of position which created openings for his colleagues.

However the Irish were soon back on level terms as the pace hotted up. Dougan's overhead flick was met by McAdams, who hit home a fine goal. Almost immediately the Northern Ireland side went close to taking the lead. It seemed certain that Bingham's shot would go in, but it hit McParland who was standing almost on the goal-line. That was typical of the bad luck that Ireland had, but worse was to come.

Nearly 60,000 people had crammed into this famous ground and they were watching an excellent game. Before half-time, though, they were to be very disappointed as England regained the lead. This time Haynes put in a cross from the right and Jimmy Greaves hit the ball past Gregg from 18 yards for another well-struck goal.

Overall, England deserved their half-time lead, their plan to have Ron Flowers alongside Peter Swan was working well against the twin aerial threat of Dougan and McAdams. Although Swan struggled at times, Flowers was always there to mop up any problems. Haynes, Greaves and especially Bobby Charlton were all in tip-top form and Charlton was a particular delight with his long, raking passes stretching the Irish to the limits.

Blanchflower's usual skilful contribution in midfield was somewhat stifled by the Irish tactic of pumping high balls to the big men up front, so, with Bobby Robson supporting Haynes superbly, England had the edge in midfield.

Immediately after the interval, England scored again. The alert and dangerous Brian Douglas centred from the right and goalkeeper Gregg came a long way out of his goal in trying to palm the ball clear. Greaves, once again the man for the situation, punished the mistake with a clever looping header which dropped just under the crossbar.

It seemed all over bar the shouting but back came the battling Irish. McIlroy crossed and there was McAdams, again, to thump home a powerful header. The

Bobby Charlton, won his 19th cap against Northern Ireland at Windsor Park, on his way to 106 full appearances for England.

crowd were at fever pitch now but alas for them, the leprechauns refused to help their green-shirted countrymen at this stage. Dougan and McParland both struck the goalposts with good efforts and England could count themselves very lucky that they held on to their lead. Just as it seemed that the Irish must equalize they suddenly faded, allowing England the chance to reassert themselves.

Towards the end, they gained complete control again and promptly added two more goals to their tally. First, a fine move involving Charlton, Greaves and Haynes let in Douglas for the fourth goal; then, just before the final whistle, the same quartet combined again with this time Charlton the man in at the kill. Those perfectly-executed goals finally ended the brave Irish challenge.

68th match v Northern Ireland.
Debuts for McNeil and Smith.
Debut goal for Smith.

Luxembourg v England World Cup Qualifier

Played on Wednesday, 19 October 1960 at the Stade de Ville, Luxembourg City.

Luxembourg: T.Stendebach (Stade Dudelange); E.Brenner (Stade Dudelange), N.Hoffmann (CS Grevenmacher), J.P.Mertl (US Luxembourg), F.Brosius (Spora Luxembourg), E.Jann (Jeunesse Esch), A.Schmit (Fola Esch), H.Cirelli (Alliance Dudelange), P.May (Jeunesse Esch), F.Konter (Chiers Rodange), G.Bauer (US Luxembourg).

England: R.D.G.Springett (Sheffield Wed); J.C.Armfield (Blackpool), M.McNeil (Middlesbrough), R.W.Robson (West Brom), P.Swan (Sheffield Wed), R.Flowers (Wolves), B.Douglas (Blackburn R), J.P.Greaves (Chelsea), R.Smith (Spurs), J.N.Haynes (Fulham, captain), R.Charlton (Man Utd).

Half-time 0-4 Full-time 0-9 (Nine)

Ref: J.H.Martens (Holland)   Att: 6,750

ENGLAND took the field in Luxembourg eager to make a winning start to their World Cup group matches. A place in the finals in Chile in 1962 was up for grabs and nothing short of a win would do. Some British soldiers had come down on leave from Brussels, so the team did not lack vociferous support. What followed was a simple, devastating and thoroughly professional job. The television coverage and the weakness of the home nation kept the crowd down to only less than 7,000, who were soon witnessing a goal.

As early as the third minute, Johnny Haynes, masterful throughout, split the defence with a superb long through pass. Jimmy Greaves got a touch and then, as the ball ran loose, in came Bobby Charlton to hit a fierce left-foot shot inside the far post with his first touch of the game.

Four minutes later, his third touch brought the second England goal. It was probably the best of the match and followed a scintillating move involving Haynes, Bobby Smith, Greaves and Brian Douglas. When Douglas's centre came over, there was Charlton leaping to head home.

Play continued to flow only one way and poor Luxembourg hardly managed a touch. After 15 minutes it was 3-0. Haynes again was the architect and, not for the last time, he cleverly switched the direction of play to set up Greaves, who hit a shot in off the underside of the bewildered Stendebach's crossbar. Smith was the next player to get in on the scoring act. Twenty-two minutes had elapsed when Greaves and Charlton combined on the left before Smith headed in Charlton's centre.

For a while England became over-eager in attack as players queued up to have

a pot at the beleaguered Stendebach's goal. Too often they wanted to take the ball that one yard too many and chances were lost. However, it was obviously noticed as after the half-time break the forwards self-control returned.

Within seconds of the restart, Greaves beat three men in a lightning dash before giving Smith the chance to hit a rocket of a shot past Stendebach. Skipper Haynes was the next to score, picking his spot after a fine move between Ron Flowers and Charlton.

Charlton was continually catching the eye and he hit a peach of a goal for number seven. Jimmy Armfield hit a cross-field pass to the Manchester United ace, who gratefully glided through on the left before hitting a screamer with his right foot which swerved into the top corner.

The almost telepathic combination of Haynes and Greaves produced both of the last two goals, with Greaves twice darting through on to long passes to score.

For Luxembourg there was little consolation, although for a while Brenner had to switch to the right wing because of injury. Even when he returned, the pressure on him and Hoffmann was unrelenting with this rampant England display.

> 2nd match v Luxembourg.
> Hat-tricks by Greaves and Charlton.
> Biggest win since 1947 against Portugal.

England v Spain   Friendly

Played on Wednesday, 26 October 1960 at Wembley Stadium.

England: R.D.G.Springett (Sheffield Wed); J.C.Armfield (Blackpool), M.McNeil (Middlesbrough), R.W.Robson (West Brom), P.Swan (Sheffield Wed), R.Flowers (Wolves), B.Douglas (Blackburn R), J.P.Greaves (Chelsea), R.A.Smith (Spurs), J.N.Haynes (Fulham, captain), R.Charlton (Man Utd).
Spain: A.Ramallets (FC Barcelona); M.Alonso (Real Madrid), S.Gracia (FC Barcelona), M.Ruiz-Sosa (Sevilla FC),

J.E.Santamaria (Real Madrid), M.Verges (FC Barcelona), E.Mateos (Real Madrid), L.Del Sol (Real Madrid), A.Di Stefano (Real Madrid), L.Suarez (FC Barcelona), F.Gento (Real Madrid).

Half-time 2-1   Full-time 4-2

Ref: M.Guigue (France)   Att: 80,000

WHAT A magnificent match, magnificent victory and magnificent performance by this new, rejuvenated England team.

On an appalling day with the wind and rain driving down across Wembley from first to last, two splendid sides produced a thriller for the 80,000 spectators. With two fine wins behind them, England were looking for an even bigger confidence booster and they took on the Spaniards determined to show them all that is best about English football.

Within 30 seconds of the start England were granted the wish that they wanted when they scored a precious early goal. A fine move down the right between Bryan Douglas and Bobby Smith ended with a diagonal pass across the face of the penalty area. Before the Spanish defenders could react, Jimmy Greaves burst through the rain, took the ball at top speed, slid through the gap and guided home a low shot past Ramallets. That was just the start England needed and both sides were soon producing some sparkling football.

In the 14th minute, Spain gained a superb equalizer. Fabulous play by Suarez began the move which was carried on by Di Stefano and Mateos. Then, in came Del Sol to finish off the attack with a clinical strike.

With Peter Swan and Ron Flowers holding the middle together well, England's 4-2-4 formation looked effective. Bobby Robson, who got through a mountain of work keeping tabs on Di Stefano as well as supporting Johnny Haynes in midfield, had an excellent game. Bobby Charlton and Greaves were sharp and dangerous up front and the whole side was an impressive unit.

Just before the interval, England regained the lead. A short free-kick by Robson to Jimmy Armfield enabled the full-back to put in a lovely centre. On the end of it, of all people, was Douglas,

Johnny Haynes (right) leads out England alongside Spain at Wembley in 1960.

Left: **Jimmy Greaves scores England's first goal against Spain.** *Right:* **Ron Springett gathers a cross during England's 4-2 win.**

popping up in the centre-forward position to glance home a brilliant header. It was old fashioned but very effective, indeed the English game at its best.

The lead was certainly deserved and England must have been well satisfied with their first-half display. However, immediately after the break Spain levelled the scores again. A good run by the speedy Gento ended with him pulling the ball back for Suarez to sweep it wide of Ron Springett's dive.

The game was buzzing at this stage with the crowd revelling in the skills on show and forgetting the atrocious weather. The best was yet to come as in the last half-hour England's challenge reached a new peak. Charlton suddenly found extra venom as he cut the Spaniards' defence repeatedly to set up chances for his forward colleagues. From one such run, England regained the lead for a third time. This time Charlton's pass found Smith unmarked to head home and then ten minutes from the end England wrapped it all up with an exquisite fourth goal.

Robson began the move and when Smith took his pass, the centre-forward looked up and chipped in a perfect shot over the advancing Ramallets from some 25 yards.

It was a dream come true for the fans and the final icing on the cake came in the closing minutes when England treated the Spaniards to some of their own medicine, cleverly keeping possession with numerous passes which the visitors could not get near. It was poetic justice as England had suffered the same fate in Madrid last May.

It was also a lovely feeling, seeing England get their own back in such style.

7th match v Spain.
Spain's Alonso also known as 'Marquitos'.
"I remember the game against Spain well, not only because at the time they were considered a world force, but also because I scored a headed goal — which was a rare occasion for me!"
Bryan Douglas.

England v Wales   Home Championship

Played on Wednesday, 23 November 1960 at Wembley Stadium.

England: A.Hodgkinson (Sheffield Utd); J.C.Armfield (Blackpool), M.McNeil (Middlesbrough), R.Robson (West Brom), P.Swan (Sheffield Wed), R.W.Flowers (Wolves), B.Douglas (Blackburn R), J.P.Greaves (Chelsea), R.A.Smith (Spurs), J.N.Haynes (Fulham, captain), R.Charlton (Man Utd).

Wales: A.J.Kelsey (Arsenal); A.C. Harrington (Cardiff C), G.E. Williams (West Brom), V.H.Crowe (Aston Villa), M.T.G.Nurse (Swansea T), C.W.Baker (Cardiff C), T.C.Medwin (Spurs), A.P.Woosnam (West Ham), K.Leek (Leicester C), T.R.Vernon (Everton), C.W.Jones (Spurs).

Half-time 3-0   Full-time 5-1

Ref: R.H.Davidson (Scotland) Att: 65,000

ENGLAND'S march continued! This was their fourth consecutive high-scoring victory and was achieved with an ease which suggested that there were more to come.

As against Spain a month earlier, England got off to a flyer with an early goal. Two minutes had gone when a good move down the middle involving Johnny Haynes, Bobby Robson and Bobby Smith ended with Jimmy Greaves shooting past Kelsey to put his team one goal up.

After that, although Wales enjoyed their fair share of possession, England calmly and methodically took the match by the throat. Haynes was always at the heart of the action, keeping things moving swiftly. Robson, too, did some fine work and with Greaves, Smith, Bobby Charlton and Bryan Douglas always dangerous, England stayed well in control.

Their finishing, as so often in recent matches, was lethal and after 16 minutes they added a second goal. Another flowing move preceded it, with Robson, Ron

This time Greaves is on target against the Welsh at Wembley in November 1960, hitting England's fifth after a devastating run.

Flowers and Douglas all prominent. When Douglas set up Flowers 20 yards out, the Wolves man hit a screamer which crashed down off the crossbar. Charlton was first to react and quickly dispatched the rebound into Kelsey's net.

The 4-2-4 formation used by England was again working perfectly and whilst Haynes and Robson were in such great form, it would remain very effective. Soon the home side were adding a third goal. This time the move went the whole length of the field with Mick McNeil feeding Charlton from his own penalty area. Charlton moved the ball on to Greaves, who made ground down the left before centring for Smith to crash home an unstoppable header.

Wales were now virtually out of the game and at half-time they could only reflect that Woosnam had shown a lot of class in all that he did, although he received little support. Leek was well held by Peter Swan, Jones only occasionally threatened with his pace and Vernon was stifled in midfield. The Welsh half-back line was very ineffective.

After the interval, England continued to hold all the aces. In the 61st minute they scored their fourth goal. Lovely interplay down the left between Haynes and Charlton ended with Haynes shooting fiercely past Kelsey with his right foot. That goal capped a marvellous performance by the England skipper.

Nine minutes later, Greaves scored a magnificent fifth goal. Picking the ball up following a four-man move, he strode majestically past several desperate Welsh challenges before finishing with a devastating shot from an almost impossible angle. The goal brought the crowd to their

feet. Indeed, the quality of all the goals had been a feature of the match.

Near the end, Wales did manage a consolation goal after Alan Hodgkinson had dropped a high cross from Woosnam straight to the feet of Leek, who made no mistake from close range. That was an annoying end for England in an otherwise faultless display.

71st match v Wales.

England v Scotland Home Championship

Played on Saturday, 15 April 1961 at Wembley Stadium.

England: R.D.G.Springett (Sheffield Wed); J.C.Armfield (Blackpool), M.McNeil (Middlesbrough), R.W.Robson (West Brom), P.Swan (Sheffield Wed), R.Flowers (Wolves), B.Douglas (Blackburn R), J.P.Greaves (Chelsea), R.A.Smith (Spurs), J.N.Haynes (Fulham, captain), R.Charlton (Man Utd).
Scotland: F.Haffey (Celtic); R.Shearer (Rangers), E.Caldow (Rangers), D.C.Mackay (Spurs), W.McNeill (Celtic), R.J.McCann (Motherwell), J.M.McLeod (Hibernian), D.Law (Man City), I.St John (Motherwell), P.Quinn (Motherwell), D.Wilson (Rangers).

Half-time 3-0   Full-time 9-3
Ref: M.Lequesne (France)   Att: 97,350

HER Majesty, Queen Elizabeth II and His Royal Highness the Duke of Edinburgh were welcome guests at this England-

Scotland clash and if it was goals that the Royal couple liked best in football, then they could not have picked a better match. Two records were broken on the day, first by the margin of England's victory over their old enemy, and also by the fact that never before has Wembley seen as many goals in a single game.

The sun shone on a marvellously colourful sight as the fans waited in eager anticipation of this annual clash. Johnny Haynes won the toss and the England attack swiftly turned on the style that has been so effective in recent internationals.

After ten minutes they were in the lead. Brilliant work by Jimmy Greaves eventually allowed him to feed a pass to Bobby Robson in a good position. The first-time shot put in by the West Brom player gave Haffey no chance to save. Greaves himself was the next to score some nine minutes later, latching on to a Bobby Smith through-ball to hit a splendid shot accurately placed beyond the unfortunate Haffey.

Scotland, who had started brightly, were now in deep trouble and on the half-hour it was that man Greaves again who proved the thorn in their side. A pin-point pass by the inspirational Haynes — so much of the game revolved around the England skipper — found Smith. He made ground down the right wing before putting over a dangerous centre. Haffey managed a touch but, typically, Greaves was in the right place at the right time to push home the loose ball. Given half a chance, Greaves would punish the opposition so lethally.

Mackay had worked so hard for the besieged Scottish team and Law and Wilson had shown up well. Wilson, in

Jimmy Greaves meets HRH the Duke of Edinburgh before the England-Scotland match at Wembley in April 1961.

England's first goal, scored by Bobby Robson after only ten minutes.

Jimmy Greaves scores England's third goal and the second of his hat-trick.

fact, had a goal disallowed by the French referee Monsieur Lequesne. But that was a rare threat to England and had they showed a little more steadiness in front of goal, then they might easily have doubled their half-time lead. The army of Scottish fans had had little to cheer in that first period, but within ten minutes of the restart they were in a frenzy of excitement.

On 48 minutes they pulled a goal back, not surprisingly through Mackay. His fierce low free-kick took a deflection off of England's defensive wall and left Ron Springett helpless. It was just the tonic Scotland needed and seven minutes later Wilson dived horizontally to get his head to McLeod's cross to close the gap further. Suddenly there was a real match on.

Alas for the visiting fans, their ecstacy lasted barely a minute as England went straight up to the other end to score a decisive fourth goal. Again a free-kick set it up as quick thinking by Greaves saw him flick the ball through a gap for Bryan Douglas to score off of Haffey's fingertips again. Scotland protested about the speed the kick was taken but the referee would have none of it.

Scotland were still able to produce some lovely football at times but they never had a Greaves to finish off their good approach play. In the last 15 minutes, the Scots were left shell-shocked as England stepped up the pace to crush them. It began to rain goals!

Haffey's nightmare continued thus. On 75 minutes Smith, who had previously been kept quiet by McNeill, suddenly popped up to score number five after a Greaves pass had set him up. Scotland perked up for a minute as Quinn received a pass from Mackay and fired in a shot. It passed through a forest of legs before trickling, oh so slowly, past Springett. If that was the end of Scotland's scoring, it certainly was not the end of England's.

Incredibly, in the last 11 minutes they added a further four goals! Haynes scored twice in the 79th and 81st minutes before Greaves in the 82nd and Smith in the 85th finished the rout.

The Queen, for the first time, presented the Home International trophy to the winning captain and for Haynes it was the icing on the cake to end a magnificent

England players are presented to HM The Queen after their sensational 9-3 victory over the Scots.

Skipper Johnny Haynes is chaired by his colleagues as England parade the Home International trophy.

afternoon. Meanwhile, spare a thought for poor Haffey in the Scottish goal. He trudged off, a forlorn figure, devastated by some very high-calibre finishing especially from the magical Greaves.

78th match v Scotland.
Hat-trick by Greaves.
Biggest-ever win over Scotland.

England v Mexico

Friendly

Played on Wednesday, 10 May 1961 at Wembley Stadium.

England: R.D.G.Springett (Sheffield Wed); J.C.Armfield (Blackpool), M.McNeil (Middlesbrough), R.W.Robson (West Brom), P.Swan (Sheffield Wed), R.Flowers (Wolves), B.Douglas (Blackburn R), D.T.Kevan (West Brom), G.A.Hitchens (Aston Villa), J.N.Haynes (Fulham, captain), R.Charlton (Man Utd).

Mexico: A.Mota (Oro); G.Peña (Oro), I.Jáuregui (Atlas), R.Cardenas (Zacatepec), G.Sepúlveda (Guadalajara), A.Portugal (América), A.Del Aguila (Toluca), S.Reyes (Guadalajara), C.Gonzalez (Tampico), F.Flores (Guadalajara), S.Mercado (Toluca).
Sub: Reynoso (Necaxa) for Flores.

Half-time 4-0   **Full-time 8-0**

Ref: R.H.Davidson (Scotland) Att: 76,000

ENGLAND'S magnificent run continued, thanks to a breathtaking performance against Mexico. The visitors from Central

Bobby Charlton (arms raised) celebrates a brilliant goal against Mexico to make it 2-0.

America, on a European tour, had only recently narrowly lost 2-1 to the strong Czechoslovakia side and had beaten the Dutch by the same score, so they arrived at Wembley full of confidence.

On this day, though, they were annihilated by a brilliant blend of short and long passing from England's now familiar 4-2-4 formation. It was a tremendous revenge for the defeat they suffered in Mexico two years earlier, especially for the five survivors of that team. It was also wonderful fare for the 76,000 crowd basking in gloriously sunny weather.

England settled quickly and Johnny Haynes soon stamped his immense authority on the game. His, now almost telepathic, partnership with the immaculate Bobby Robson dominated the midfield from start to finish.

Lovely passing movements abounded as England hit four first-half goals. Fullback Jimmy Armfield was always prominent, linking up well down the right wing with Bryan Douglas. Gerry Hitchens scored the first and then set up Bobby Charlton for a thunderbolt volley which flew past Mota before the goalkeeper could move.

Robson scored number three and then Douglas nipped in for a fourth. Mexico had no answer to all this superb football, although Del Aguila showed some skill at outside-right. Even the substitution of Reynoso for Flores just before half-time failed to stem the tide.

Charlton had a particularly memorable game and every time he gained possession a loud buzz went around this famous old stadium. The collective shout of 'Shoot' was usually the crowd's response as soon as he was anywhere within 40 yards of goal!

The second half was just as one-sided. Steadily, the goal tally rose with the fifth being a penalty, somewhat harshly awarded after a foul on Hitchens. Ron Flowers duly smashed home the spot-kick. Then Charlton scored again with another tremendous 30-yard drive before he went on to complete his hat-trick, following the best move of the match.

Fast flowing passing began with Armfield, was carried on by Robson and involved no less than eight players linking up to take the ball the whole length of the lush green Wembley turf. At the end of all that, Charlton was there to slide home Douglas' flick.

It was vintage football and Mexico were outclassed. Their tip-tap passing game floundered and they made no impact on the strong England defence. Once, near the end, Reyes did hit a post with Ron Springett for once beaten, but generally it was one-way traffic towards the Mexican goal for the rest of the game.

More splendid work by Charlton down the left gave Douglas the chance to end the scoring with the eighth goal, but one wonders what the score might have been had Jimmy Greaves been playing instead of Derek Kevan, for the West Brom player missed several good chances. The injured Bobby Smith must also have wished he could have been playing but, to be fair, Hitchens slotted in superbly and enjoyed a fine game, as indeed did the whole side.

2nd match v Mexico.
Debut goal for Hitchens.
Hat-trick by Charlton.
Penalty by Flowers.

Gerry Hitchens (not in picture) marks his debut by putting England ahead in the first minute against Mexico.

Portugal v England World Cup Qualifier

Played on Sunday, 21 May 1961 in the National Stadium, Lisbon.

Portugal: A.Costa-Pereira (Benfica); M.Lino (Sporting Lisbon), H.de Conceição (Sporting Lisbon), F.Mendes (Sporting Lisbon), G.Figueiredo (Benfica), F.Cruz (Benfica), J.A.Almeida (Benfica), J.Santana (Benfica), J.Aguás (Benfica), M.Coluña (Benfica), D.Gomes (Benfica).

England: R.D.G.Springett (Sheffield Wed); J.C.Armfield (Blackpool), M.McNeil (Middlesbrough), R.Robson (West Brom), P.Swan (Sheffield Wed), R.Flowers (Wolves), B.Douglas (Blackburn R), J.P.Greaves (Chelsea), R.A.Smith (Spurs), J.N.Haynes (Fulham, captain), R.Charlton (Man Utd).

Half-time 0-0   **Full-time 1-1**
Ref: P.Bonetto (Italy)   Att: 65,000

A WIN in this match would go a long way towards securing a place in the finals of the 1962 World Cup. That was what was drummed into the England players before the game. They knew that with two second-leg ties against both Luxembourg and Portugal to come at home, with a good result here their qualification would be almost guaranteed.

The game, played in the excessive heat of the National Stadium, was full of twists and turns, and although England never reproduced the form of some of their recent internationals, they did compete well and had several outstanding individuals. However, whether it was the heat or the extra pressure of the occasion, one could not be sure, but Bobby Smith and Jimmy Greaves never looked as sharp on the day and it made an important difference.

The first half was fairly even but Ron Springett had to make a superb save when Aguás was put clean through after some careless play by Bobby Robson and Bobby Charlton. England, though, at times played some lovely football and might have done even better had they not just overdone things in the Portuguese penalty area. Ron Flowers was a tower of strength for England and he scarcely put a foot wrong. Charlton showed glimpses of his phenomenal talent and Bryan Douglas flicked and tricked his way down the right wing with great heart. Sadly for England, the searing heat had an overall effect on their game and they found it difficult to pace themselves.

Three good chances came England's way in the last ten minutes of the first half. First, Pereira made a superb diving save from a typical Charlton thunderbolt, then Smith headed just past a post and finally, just before the interval, Charlton shot over after a brilliant through-ball played by the masterly Johnny Haynes.

England did not have it all their own way, however, as Portugal worked very hard. Fifteen minutes after the break their effort was rewarded when they sensationally took the lead. Augusto broke down the right and passed the ball inside. Robson intercepted and tried to pass back to Springett. The goalkeeper unfortunately misjudged the bounce and Aguás nipped in smartly to prod the ball home. The goal triggered huge celebrations on the terraces.

At this point England were struggling but suddenly they found inspiration through their skipper, Haynes. The inside-left took the game by the scruff of the neck and inspired his teammates to a late effort in the final third of the match. Charlton looked more dangerous again, Greaves was livelier and the whole side was pushed forward from the back by the displays of Flowers and Jimmy Armfield. Armfield showed incredible stamina as he continually supported his forwards as well as defending soldily against the lively Cavem.

The extra effort was very worthwhile and in the last half-hour England dominated. The increasing pressure on the Portuguese goal had to tell and in the 82nd minute England scored their much deserved equalizer. Haynes was fouled by Mendes on the edge of the box and when the England captain tapped the free-kick sideways, man-of-the-match Flowers crashed in an unstoppable low shot from 20 yards.

In the last eight minutes England came so very close to snatching victory. Lino cleared off the line from Smith and then Pereira saved bravely at the Tottenham player's feet when a goal seemed certain. Finally, in the very last minute, a superb move between Armfield, Charlton and Haynes ended with Greaves' shot being brilliantly turned away by Pereira.

So, England had to be content with the draw. It has set things up nicely for the two home games.

> 6th match v Portugal.
> Portugal's de Conceição also known as 'Hilario'; Figueiredo as 'Germano'; Almeida as 'Jose Augusto'; Gomes as 'Cavem'.

Italy v England
Friendly

Played on Wednesday, 24 May 1961 in the Olympic Stadium, Rome.

Italy: L.Buffon (Inter-Milan); G.Losi (AS Roma), S.Castelletti (Fiorentina), B.Bolchi (Inter-Milan), S.Salvadore (Milan AC), G.Trapattoni (Milan AC), B.Mora (Juventus), F.R.Lojacono (AS Roma), S.Brighenti (Sampdoria), O.E.Sivori (Juventus), M.Corso (Inter-Milan).
Sub: G.Vavassori (Juventus) for Buffon.

England: R.D.G.Springett (Sheffield Wed); J.C.Armfield (Blackpool), M.McNeil (Middlesbrough), R.W.Robson (West Brom), P.Swan (Sheffield Wed), R.Flowers (Wolves), B.Douglas (Blackburn R), J.P.Greaves (Chelsea), G.A.Hitchens (Aston Villa), J.N.Haynes (Fulham, captain), R.Charlton (Man Utd).

Half-time 1-1   Full-time 2-3
Ref: N.Latychev (USSR)   Att: 82,000

ENGLAND followed up their draw in the World Cup match in Lisbon against

Gerry Hitchens heads England into the lead against Italy.

Jimmy Greaves (8) hits England's winner in Rome.

Portugal with this confidence-boosting win in Rome. It was a thrilling game, full of incident and excitement with England putting up a splendid performance.

It was a glorious day in a glorious setting as the teams took to the field to a roar from the 82,000 crowd. Both sides quickly went on to the attack and both goals had narrow escapes early on. There were many outstanding individuals in the game but it was soon clear that Sivori for Italy and Johnny Haynes for England were going to be the chief playmakers. Ron Springett and Buffon also had superb games in their respective goals though both had luck on their side at times.

Lojacono hit England's crossbar from a free-kick and Brighenti was desperately unlucky to head against a post from the rebound. Springett then brought off a brilliant save from Mora at full stretch. But it was not all Italy. England, with their more open passing style, created some fine openings. Defence splitting through passes by Haynes and Bryan Douglas twice sent Jimmy Greaves clear but on each occasion the agile Buffon made super saves.

The game had to see some goals with all this attacking football on show and with six minutes to go before half-time England took the lead. A long cross by the outstanding Jimmy Armfield was met by the powerful head of Gerry Hitchens and the ball flashed into the top corner with Buffon, for once, well beaten.

The goal was greeted by a deafening silence but within four minutes the silence turned to rejoicing as Italy equalized. Sivori, producing some breathtaking skills, conjured up a stunning goal. Taking a square pass from Castelletti he swivelled, slid past a tackle and then thumped home a left-foot shot to the top corner of Springett's net.

After the break, the game twisted and turned at regular intervals. On 55 minutes there was a dramatic moment as Buffon was injured, diving at the feet of Haynes following a brilliant interchange with Hitchens. The goalkeeper was carried off with a bloodied face and he was replaced by Vavassori.

But around this time Sivori began to take over. Playing magnificently he inspired his colleagues into some fine play. His passing brought the wingers into play more and more giving Brighenti a superb service. England were saved at this point by Springett. He saved wonderfully well from Sivori and Brighenti and then turned another Brighenti shot on to the bar and over. The centre-forward missed one sitter but immediately made up for it by giving the Italians the lead. Again Sivori was the architect and again, of course, the crowd went wild with delight.

During this 20-minute spell of Italian pressure, Springett, Peter Swan, Armfield and Mick McNeil were all magnificent and kept England in the match, a match that turned on its head in the last ten minutes.

England stunned the crowd once again by immediately equalizing Brighenti's goal. Sivori, for once, was hustled into a mistake. From the resultant throw-in, Greaves broke to the left, put Hitchens clear and the centre-forward hit a firm left-foot shot through Vavassori's legs and into the Italian net.

The final twist in this magnificent match came with five minutes to go. Haynes intercepted a pass by Trapattoni and put through a reverse angled pass that once again sent Greaves away in full cry. This time the Chelsea player made no mistake and the finish was as lethal as any of his League goals in the season just ended, a perfect left-foot shot inside the far post.

> 8th match v Italy.

Austria v England
Friendly

Played on Saturday, 27 May 1961 in the Prater Stadium, Vienna.

Austria: G.Fraydl (Grazer AK); H.Trubrig (Linzer ASK), E.Strobl (FK Simmering), G.Hanappi (Rapid Vienna), K.Stotz (Austria Vienna), K.Koller (1.Vienna FC),

Following a good centre by Bobby Charlton, Greaves hits England's only goal in the Prater Stadium in May 1961.

H.Nemec (Austria), E.Hof (Sportklub), H.Buzek (1.Vienna FC), H.Senekowitsch (1.Vienna FC), F.Rafreider (FC Dornbirn).
England: R.D.G.Springett (Sheffield Wed); J.C.Armfield (Blackpool), J.Angus (Burnley), B.G.Miller (Burnley), P.Swan (Sheffield Wed), R.Flowers (Wolves), B.Douglas (Blackburn R), J.P.Greaves (Chelsea), G.A.Hitchens (Aston Villa), J.N.Haynes (Fulham, captain), R.Charlton (Man Utd).

Half-time 2-1   Full-time 3-1
Ref: K.Galba (Czechoslovakia)   Att: 90,000

A LONG, hard but entertaining international season ended for England with their first defeat for a year. It also brought an end to their European tour, a tour full of valuable lessons for the following year's World Cup, should they make it.

Ninety thousand people packed the Prater Stadium to see two in form sides battle it out for current supremacy. If possession had been the key to winning, then England would have won by a mile. But, alas, football goes much deeper than just keeping the ball and in the end it is goals that matter most. Austria had beaten Scotland, Norway, Russia, Spain, Italy, Sweden and Switzerland in the past year with their only defeat coming in Hungary. So England had a mammoth task with the heat, hard pitch and probably the most fervently patriotic crowd of the tour all against them.

The game began badly for England and never really got any better. Austria took only two minutes to open the scoring as a quick break by the veteran Hanappi sent Nemec down the right. He found Koller, who in turn gave it to Hof. The inside-right wasted no time and fired in a 15-yard snap shot wide of Ron Springett's dive.

To England's credit they fought back well and after a quarter of an hour they managed to get back on terms. A fiery surge by Bobby Charlton down the left wing ended with a good centre from the by-line. Bryan Douglas just failed to connect but when the ball ran on to Jimmy Greaves, the Chelsea player made no mistake and hit it into the roof of the Austrian net.

The goal gave England confidence and they were now finding their form under the leadership of Johnny Haynes. For 20 minutes it was one-way traffic towards Fraydl's goal. Unfortunately all the promise fell flat in the confines of the Austrian penalty area. The powerful Stotz marshalled his mass of defenders expertly to deny England any space in which to take advantage. And always there was the vastly experienced Hanappi to clear up any loose balls that might have fallen to English forwards.

Despite all the possession England enjoyed it was the Austrians who scored next. The goal came in the 25th minute and fittingly it was Hanappi who began the move deep in his own half. His pass forward found Senekowitsch who moved the ball on swiftly to Rafreider and then Nemec. The right winger burst through the middle in his more accustomed centre-forward position and beat off weak challenges from Jimmy Armfield and Peter Swan. A rebound still gave Nemec possession and in a flash the ball was past Springett and into the England net.

Still England dominated the play. Fraydl somehow kept out fierce shots by Greaves and Charlton but over-elaboration by Greaves, Douglas and especially Charlton prevented further chances in the first half.

However, the shots ratio for the second half, England 15 Austria 4, told its own story of how the match continued. The new caps, John Angus and Brian Miller, had satisfactory debuts but Miller never quite revealed the penetrating work of Bobby Robson as Haynes' partner.

The goal that clinched the result came with only ten minutes left. Again Hanappi slipped the ball out of defence. Buzek then sent a long through-pass into the heart of England's defence. Swan headed away, but only as far as Hof, and like lightning Hof set up Senekowitsch and Springett was beaten by a low shot.

It was a sad end to a marvellous season for England. Seven wins, one draw and just the one defeat here added up to a memorable season. On this day, fatigue at having to play three games in seven days finally caught up with them, but care must be taken not to take anything away from Austria who meticulously planned this victory in every detail.

> 10th match v Austria.
> Debuts for Angus and Miller.

England v World Cup Qualifier
Luxembourg

Played on Thursday, 28 September 1961 at Arsenal Stadium, London.

England: R.D.G.Springett (Sheffield Wed); J.C.Armfield (Blackpool, captain), M.McNeil (Middlesbrough), R.W.Robson (West Brom), P.Swan (Sheffield Wed), R.Flowers (Wolves), B.Douglas (Blackburn R), J.Fantham (Sheffield Wed), R.Pointer (Burnley), D.S.Viollet (Man Utd), R.Charlton (Man Utd).
Luxembourg: P.Steffen (Jeunesse Esch); E.Brenner (Stade Dudelange), J.Hoffman (Avenir Beggen), J.Zambon (Alliance Dudelange), F.Brosius (Spora Luxembourg), F.Konter (Chiers Rodange), C.Dimmer (Red Boys Differdange), H.Cirelli (Alliance Dudelange), J.Hoffman (CS Grevenmacher), R.Schneider (US Luxembourg), A.Schmit (Fola Esch).

Half-time 3-0   Full-time 4-1
Ref: G.Ver Syp (Belgium)   Att: 29,000

THICK London fog had delayed this World Cup second-leg tie against Luxembourg for 24 hours. Long before the end of the 90 minutes, the 29,000 Highbury crowd had resorted to that now growing bad habit of the slow handclap. But one had to sympathise with them after a dismal and disjointed performance by a somewhat unfamiliar-looking England team.

Without Johnny Haynes to control the 4-2-4 line-up England never really got going and Bobby Robson looked lost without his skipper and midfield partner. Jimmy Armfield took over the captaincy and it was a frustratingly long time before the breakthrough came. Steffen had an inspired night in the Luxembourg goal and despite England's other failings, he still had plenty to do.

Ironically, the first clear chance fell to centre-forward Hoffman and only a desperate dive by Ron Springett at his feet saved England from acute embarrassment. The crowd quickly sided with the underdogs, as is often the case for an English audience, and just when it seemed that the visitors were comfortable the home side broke the deadlock.

Thirty-five minutes had elapsed when Bryan Douglas broke away to centre from the right. When the cross reached the middle, Ray Pointer side-footed the first goal. England then quickly and clinically turned the screw.

A second goal soon followed when Pointer's shot was acrobatically saved by Steffen, only for Dennis Viollet to follow up and score. Before the break Bobby Charlton took a Douglas pass in his stride and hit home a screamer for goal number three. At last the fans had something to cheer.

Steffen made a series of fine saves in the second half, although it must be said that England were guilty of some awful finishing. Charlton, Pointer and John Fantham all put in wild shots from good positions and there was little shape in the general display with Robson particularly disappointing, repeatedly making mistakes. To his credit, though, he refused to hide and was never afraid to shoot.

Luxembourg packed their defence, sometimes having seven or eight players in their penalty area. But midway through the half, the whole of the visiting team jumped for joy as Dimmer's free-kick beat Springett to give them a goal. The crowd were delighted for them and made their feelings clear. Near the end, though, Charlton restored the three-goal advantage with another well-taken goal, but when the referee blew the final whistle there was a feeling of relief all round as it ended a poor match overall.

The hopes were that Johnny Haynes, Jimmy Greaves and Gerry Hitchens would all be back when England took on Portugal the following month.

> 3rd match v Luxembourg.
> Debuts for Fantham and Pointer.
> Debut goal for Pointer.
> Armfield captained England for the first time.

Wales v
England　Home Championship

Played on Saturday, 14 October 1961 at Ninian Park, Cardiff.

Wales: A.J.Kelsey (Arsenal); A.C.Harrington (Cardiff C), S.G. Williams (West Brom), M.Charles (Arsenal), W.J.Charles (Juventus), V.H.Crowe (Aston Villa), C.W.Jones (Spurs), A.P.Woosnam (West Ham), D.Ward (Cardiff C), I.J.Allchurch (Newcastle Utd), G.G.Williams (Swansea T).
England: R.D.G.Springett (Sheffield Wed); J.C.Armfield (Blackpool), R.Wilson (Huddersfield T), R.W.Robson (West Brom), P.Swan (Sheffield Wed),

Above: Ray Wilson, who made 63 appearances for England. *Below:* John Connelly, who played 20 times.

R.Flowers (Wolves), J.M.Connelly (Burnley), B.Douglas (Blackburn R), R.Pointer (Burnley), J.N.Haynes (Fulham, captain), R.Charlton (Man Utd).

Half-time 1-1　　Full-time 1-1

Ref: H.Phillips (Scotland)　　Att: 61,500

AFTER the dismal showing in their previous match against Luxembourg, England were determined to do much better in this annual clash against the Welsh. They certainly played their hearts out and with a little luck could easily have won. With John Connelly back on the right wing, England's attack had a bit

more penetration about it. Connelly ran Stuart Williams ragged, failing only in his lack of confidence to finish off the approach play.

Bryan Douglas missed a sitter early on and then Ray Pointer's close-range stab hit Kelsey when the goalkeeper knew little about it. On the half-hour, however, Wales took the lead. Ward's ungamely challenge on Peter Swan left the England centre-half with one boot missing, and in the confusion Graham Williams scored to send the near 62,000 crowd wild with delight. The crowd already held high hopes, especially as the prodigal son of Wales, John Charles, was back in the side.

Generally, though, England were on top and they did not deserve to be behind. Johnny Haynes and Bobby Robson were outstanding in midfield, although the real heroes were probably Ray Wilson and Ron Flowers. They had the pleasure of marking the two best Welsh players in Jones and Woosnam and they did it with an assurity that kept England well on top. Douglas couldn't believe his eyes when somehow Harrington deflected a goalbound shot wide. Then there was an amazing let-off for the Welshmen.

Four shots in as many seconds, by Pointer, Bobby Charlton and Haynes, were kept out by the huge figures of Kelsey and John Charles. The excitement was reaching fever pitch. But, at last, with virtually the last kick of the first half, England deservedly found an equalizer. A lovely move, at pace, between Ron Springett, Haynes, Charlton, Haynes again and Connelly ended with Douglas nipping in to score from the winger's centre.

Sadly, the second half was not a very good one and will be mainly remembered for a series of injuries rather than the football. But England remained in control without threatening in the vital area.

Charlton tried his best and he continually peppered Kelsey's goal with some long-range screamers. Pointer did a lot of strong running off the ball in that familiar stooped style, taking defenders out of position but the other England players could not take advantage. The goalscoring power of the previous season's team would have finished off the Welsh. On the plus side, though, Swan blotted out Ward effectively and Wilson continued to impress, with his speed more than a match for Jones. England were handicapped in the final ten minutes when Jimmy Armfield was reduced to hobbling up and down the wing after an injury.

It did not affect the result, though, and both teams had to be content with the draw. Despite failing to press home their superiority, England could go into their vital World Cup tie with Portugal confident in the knowledge that they had given a much more encouraging performance in Cardiff.

> 72nd match v Wales.

England v
Portugal　World Cup Qualifier

Played on Wednesday, 25 October 1961 at Wembley Stadium.

England: R.D.G.Springett (Sheffield Wed); J.C.Armfield (Blackpool), R.Wilson (Huddersfield T), R.W.Robson (West Brom), P.Swan (Sheffield Wed),

Ray Pointer (on ground) just beats his Burnley colleague John Connelly to the ball and gives England a 2-0 lead over Portugal at Wembley in October 1961.

R.Flowers (Wolves), J.M.Connelly (Burnley), B.Douglas (Blackburn R), R.Pointer (Burnley), J.N.Haynes (Fulham, captain), R.Charlton (Man Utd).

Portugal: A.Costa-Pereira (Benfica); M.Lino (Sporting Lisbon), H.de Conceição (Sporting Lisbon), J.Pérides (Sporting Lisbon), L.Soares (Sporting Lisbon), V.Lucas (Belenenses), A.Fernandes (Belenenses), E.Fereira (Benfica), J.Águas (Benfica), M.Coluña (Benfica), D.Gomes (Benfica).

Half-time 2-0   Full-time 2-0

Ref: M.Bois (France)   Att: 98,750

A NEAR-100,000 people paid record receipts of £52,500 for this vital World Cup second-leg match against Portugal. In the end, although the game itself had not been particularly inspiring, the result certainly gave value for money. England could now settle and prepare for the finals in Chile the following year after reaching the last 16 with this win.

Despite a strong wind and a sun that could not make up its mind whether to come out or stay in, the Wembley pitch looked immaculate. The recent heavy rain had not had any effect on the lush green turf and the natural passing styles of both sides was perfectly suited. The crowd were certainly treated to an exciting opening as in the first ten minutes England built up a two-goal lead.

The first came after only five minutes. Ray Wilson took a free-kick on the left and the Portuguese defenders failed to clear properly. John Connelly sharply latched on to the loose ball and hit a good shot past Costa-Pereira.

Four minutes later one of many lovely passes by Johnny Haynes split the Portugal defence. The Burnley pair of Connelly and Ray Pointer raced after the ball with Pointer winning the race to hit a splendid right-foot shot into the top of the net.

What a tremendous start for England, but unfortunately for the watching thousands it proved to be the end of any real excitement. After the goals the match settled into a midfield battle and most of the play was confined to between the penalty areas. As soon as the attackers reached the box they were tackled strongly by resolute defenders.

Peter Swan, Ron Flowers and Jimmy Armfield were particularly effective. For Portugal, the right-half Pérides was the visitor's outstanding performer and he was continually in the action. Águas, Coluña and Eusébio showed some lovely inter-passing skills but only Eusébio, the new rising star of world football from Mozambique, looked a danger to Ron Springett's goal.

That was especially so after the half-time break and Eusébio twice fired in shots that cannoned back off the posts with Springett floundering.

Águas also hit the woodwork as Lady Luck continued to smile on England but having said that the home side also had their moments.

Haynes, the best passer on view, always looked cool and assured at the heart of England's performance but there was a distinct lack of thrust up front. Bobby Charlton had a rare off day and Pointer, despite his goal, offered little. Bryan Douglas, too, was very ineffective.

The game was played in a good spirit, despite what was at stake and Portugal won a lot of friends with their attitude.

7th match v Portugal.
Portugal's de Conceição also known as 'Hilario'; Soares as 'Lúcio'; Lucas as 'Vicenté'; Fernandes as 'Yauca'; Fereira as 'Eusébio'; Gomes as 'Cavem'.

England v Home Championship
Northern Ireland

Played on Wednesday, 22 November 1961 at Wembley Stadium.

England: R.D.G.Springett (Sheffield Wed);

Ray Crawford, the Ipswich centre-forward who was capped twice for England.

J.C.Armfield (Blackpool), R.Wilson (Huddersfield T), R.W.Robson (West Brom), P.Swan (Sheffield Wed), R.Flowers (Wolves), B.Douglas (Blackburn R), J.J.Byrne (Crystal P), R.Crawford (Ipswich T), J.N.Haynes (Fulham, captain), R.Charlton (Man Utd).

Northern Ireland: V.Hunter (Coleraine); E.J.Magill (Arsenal), A.R.Elder (Burnley), R.D.Blanchflower (Spurs), W.J.T.Neill (Arsenal), J.J.Nicholson (Man Utd), W.L.Bingham (Everton), H.H.Barr (Linfield), W.J.McAdams (Bolton W), J.McIlroy (Burnley), J.C.McLaughlin (Swansea T).

Half-time 1-0   Full-time 1-1

Ref: L.Callaghan (Wales)   Att: 30,000

Bryan Douglas (7) turns away after a shot from Bobby Charlton (not pictured) beats Northern Ireland's goalkeeper Hunter at Wembley in November 1961.

FOR the Portugal game the previous month, Wembley Stadium was full but on a lovely spring-like day for the visit of Northern Ireland, barely 30,000 were present. It was the lowest crowd ever for such a match.

England had the most disjointed of openings and looked like a team who had never played with each other before. It was most disconcerting as during this spell, the Irish could have scored twice with both McLaughlin and McAdams going very close. The laboured approach play of the English was easily held by a solid Irish defence and in midfield Danny Blanchflower, who was celebrating his 50th International cap, quietly but effectively stamped his authority on the game.

However, after 15 minutes, England had a great chance to score. Johnny Haynes missed a sitter, shooting straight at Hunter, and when the rebound came out Magill headed over his own crossbar. At last, one thought, England would settle down, and five minutes later it looked even brighter as Bobby Charlton produced one of his specials. A lovely crossfield move involved Ray Crawford twice, Bryan Douglas and Haynes before being ended by a rocket from Charlton, who had cut inside to set up the angle for his shot.

Despite the goal England continued with their slow sideways build up, they used the width of the pitch well but failed to go forward with any conviction. The longer the game went on the more Blanchflower and McIlroy took control. Having said that, England still created the game's best opening seven minutes into the second half which could have wrapped up the result.

A long pass by Haynes set Charlton free. His cross was flicked on by debutant Johnny Byrne and Crawford was left with a gaping goal in front of him. He had all the time in the world but held his head in dismay as his shot cannoned back off the crossbar.

Byrne was the one forward who continually shone and he must have been disappointed at the service he received, despite his excellent off the ball running. He also had three good goal attempts before half-time, one of which was an outstanding effort. Showing brilliant control, he chested down a deep cross from Haynes and hit a shot on the half-volley

Crystal Palace forward Johnny Byrne, capped 11 times after making his debut against Northern Ireland.

which Hunter saved more by instinct than anything else.

The Irish goalkeeper often showed his inexperience but saves like that justified his inclusion in the team. The England players seemed to play with an attitude of thinking that they only had to turn up to win.

All credit to the Irish, though. Having had only one win in their previous 11 outings, they refused to give up and thanks mainly to the efforts of Blanchflower they were always in the game. With seven minutes to go, they gained their reward for their gutsy performance. An excellent move involving Elder, Nicholson and McAdams ended with McIlroy shooting past Ron Springett to equalize. It was no more than they deserved but it did put the 'tin lid' on a disappointing England display.

With the trip to Chile getting ever nearer, everyone hoped for a big improvement all round.

69th match v Northern Ireland.
Debuts for Byrne and Crawford.

England v Austria
Friendly

Played on Wednesday, 4 April 1962 at Wembley Stadium.

England: R.D.G.Springett (Sheffield Wed); J.C.Armfield (Blackpool), R.Wilson (Huddersfield T), S.Anderson (Sunderland), P.Swan (Sheffield Wed), R.Flowers (Wolves), J.M.Connelly (Burnley), R.Hunt (Liverpool), R.Crawford (Ipswich T), J.N.Haynes (Fulham, captain), R.Charlton (Man Utd).
Austria: G.Fraydl (FK Austria); H.Trubrig (Linzer ASK), E.Hasenkopf (Sportklub), R.Oslanski (Sportklub), K.Stotz (FK Austria), K.Koller (1.Vienna FC), A.Knoll (Sportklub), E.Hoff (Sportklub), H.Buzek (1.Vienna FC), E.Fiala (FK Austria), F.Rafreider (FC Dornbirn).
Sub: R.Flögel (Rapid Vienna) for Fiala.

Half-time 2-0   Full-time 3-1
Ref: P.Schwinte (France)   Att: 45,500

ENGLAND made three changes for this interesting international at Wembley and, in the end, they reversed the scoreline of the match in Vienna 11 months earlier. It was a competent display from them and included some very encouraging performances from the two new caps in the team. It was a nasty, wet and miserable day which kept the crowd down to around 45,000, but the way the home side played lifted the gloom.

In the first half England put together some good football. Johnny Haynes, outstanding throughout, found the answer to the kind of defensive play typical of continental sides. He released the ball quickly and effectively giving the likes of Roger Hunt and Ray Crawford the chance to break clear of defenders. Bobby Charlton and John Connelly also made several darting runs and always looked dangerous.

In the eighth minute, England took the lead. A magnificent run and shot by Haynes cannoned back off a post, but Crawford reacted quickly to meet the rebound and fired in a shot which beat Fraydl with the help of a deflection off Trubrig.

A period of frustration for the home fans

Top: Johnny Haynes and Austria's skipper pictured before the start of the game at Wembley in April 1962. *Bottom:* England's defence scrambles the ball away from an Austrian attack.

followed the goal. England had plenty of the possession and several good chances to add to their score but along the way the finish was not quite there. Connelly, Hunt, Crawford and Charlton all missed inviting targets and good defensive play by Stotz and Oslanski especially combined to keep the score down to the single goal.

It took a somewhat fortuitous penalty award by the French referee to extend England's lead. Connelly, who had actually lost control of the ball, was then bundled over and the Austrians should kick themselves for giving away such a silly spot-kick. Ron Flowers dispatched the penalty fiercely past Fraydl.

Just before the break Austria made a substitution when the ineffective Fiala was replaced by Flögel. As a result the second half saw an improvement by the visitors and they visibly quickened their pace. Haynes, however continued to run the midfield with his astute play and he was ably assisted by the impressive Stan Anderson. Jimmy Armfield and Flowers were outstanding at the back and it came as no real surprise when England scored a third goal in the 67th minute.

Good play between Armfield and Connelly forced a corner with Connelly taking it short for Haynes. The skipper's pin-point centre was nodded in by Hunt and the Liverpool player was delighted.

After that, Anderson created two super chances for Crawford and Hunt but alas both went begging and the situation cried out for a Jimmy Greaves or a Gerry Hitchens to finish off the Austrians. Near the end, Buzek cut England's lead with a diving header but by that time the game was virtually over with the home side in almost total command.

11th match v Austria.
Debuts for Anderson and Hunt.
Debut goal for Hunt.
Penalty by Flowers.

Scotland v England Home Championship

Played on Saturday, 14 April 1962 at Hampden Park, Glasgow.

Scotland: W.D.F.Brown (Spurs); A.W.Hamilton (Dundee), E.Caldow

(Rangers), P.T.Crerand (Celtic), W.McNeill (Celtic), J.C.Baxter (Rangers), A.S.Scott (Rangers), J.A.White (Tottenham H), I.St John (Liverpool), D.Law (Torino), D.Wilson (Rangers).

England: R.D.G.Springett (Sheffield Wed); J.C.Armfield (Blackpool), R.Wilson (Huddersfield T), S.Anderson (Sunderland), P.Swan (Sheffield Wed), R.Flowers (Wolves), B.Douglas (Blackburn R), J.P.Greaves (Spurs), R.A.Smith (Spurs), J.N.Haynes (Fulham, captain), R.Charlton (Man Utd).

Half-time 1-0   Full-time 2-0

Ref: L.Horn (Holland)   Att: 132,441

AT last, for the first time since 1937, Scotland managed a home victory over the Auld Enemy from England — and they managed it in style. What a pity that this Scottish side was not going to Chile as, on this display, they would have given an excellent account of themselves. Their game had everything and but for a fine display by Ron Springett, they would surely have had a hatful of goals.

Right from the start Scotland put the England defence under extreme pressure. Law, White, Baxter and Crerand set up wave after wave of attacks as the blue shirts swept forward. Apart from Springett, Ray Wilson and Ron Flowers also gave sterling service but poor Peter Swan had a game he would quickly want to forget.

The inevitable opening goal came in the 13th minute and it was a beautifully contrived effort. Crerand passed to Law who, with superb control, left Swan for dead and then moved out to the right drawing Springett from his goal. At the perfect moment Law then chipped the ball back into the middle to Davie Wilson, who shot home with Swan vainly trying to recover.

Johnny Haynes and Stan Anderson were under continual pressure from Baxter, Crerand and White. To his credit, Haynes played his heart out and he saw one shot blocked on the line by Caldow just before the interval.

England were very lucky to only be the one goal down at the break and Springett had been their saviour with some very alert goalkeeping. With Law the inspiration for the Scots, and Baxter their driving force, the home side were giving their best display against England for a very long time. The second half continued in the same pattern.

Midway through the half, after long spells of Scottish pressure, Haynes produced a fine effort which struck the crossbar and bounced down, seemingly over the line. But despite English protests, the referee, Holland's Leo Horn, waved play on. Several of the England players were convinced that the ball had crossed the line and after the game even Scotland's Caldow said it had gone in, but to be fair, England hardly deserved it as Scotland had dominated.

Springett continued to shine as the mighty roar of a huge crowd grew to a crescendo, but with two minutes to go Scotland clinched the result with a deserved second goal. Law again began the move and when Swan handled St John's flick, the referee awarded a penalty. Caldow stepped up and sent Springett the wrong way to set up a never-to-be-forgotten roar of approval.

So, a sad day for England. Bobby Charlton, Bryan Douglas and Bobby Smith were largely anonymous and Jimmy Greaves seldom threatened. True, Greaves tried all his tricks to break free from the tough-tackling defenders and once he had Brown stretching full length to save a shot just inside the post. In the end, however, Scotland had proved too much for their guests and delighted in that first win at Hampden against England for 25 years. To make it a double celebration, it clinched the Home Championship for them for the first time in 11 years.

79th match v Scotland.
50th cap for Haynes.
Penalty by Caldow for Scotland.
"It's a special atmosphere playing at Hampden."
Bryan Douglas.

England v Switzerland   Friendly

Played on Wednesday, 9 May 1962 at Wembley Stadium.

England: R.D.G.Springett (Sheffield Wed); J.C.Armfield (Blackpool), R.Wilson (Huddersfield T), R.W.Robson (West Brom), P.Swan (Sheffield Wed), R.Flowers (Wolves), J.M.Connelly (Burnley), J.P.Greaves (Spurs), G.A.Hitchens (Inter-Milan), J.N.Haynes (Fulham, captain), R.Charlton (Man Utd).

Switzerland: A.Pernumian (FC Luzern); P.Roesch (Servette FC), E.Tacchela (Lausanne-Sports), A.Grobéty (Lausanne-

Sports), H.Schneiter (Young Boys), H.Weber (FC Basel), C.Antenen (La Chaux de Fonds), R.Vonlanthen (Lausanne-Sports), N.Eschmann (Stade Francais), A.Allemann (Mantova), R.Dürr (Lausanne-Sports).
Sub: K.Stettler (FC Basel) for Pernumian.

Half-time 3-1   Full-time 3-1

Ref: D.M.Zariquiegui (Spain) Att: 41,000

A LOT of unanswered questions remained after this England performance, the latest friendly international, and although the result went their way, the manner in which it was achieved left a good deal to be desired. With the World Cup in Chile now only a couple of weeks away, England were looking for confidence-boosting performances in their remaining friendlies.

It all began well enough and in the first 20 minutes, all seemed fine. Johnny Haynes immediately took control of the midfield and soon England were ahead. Haynes tapped a free-kick sideways to Ron Flowers, who cracked in a fierce shot which took a slight deflection on its way past Pernumian and into the Swiss net.

Shortly afterwards it looked even better as Gerry Hitchens expertly converted a Bobby Charlton pass. A loss in concentration then allowed Switzerland the chance to pull a goal back, Allemann scoring for them, but then John Connelly restored the two-goal advantage by heading in a long cross from Flowers. With Hitchens and Jimmy Greaves both hitting the woodwork, there seemed little room for complaint.

Inexplicably, it was about this time, with ten minutes of the first half still to go, that England began to struggle. Bobby Robson looked a pale shadow of his former self and that left far too much for Haynes to do. As a result, the Swiss team gained in confidence and began to win most of the midfield possession. They ended the half well on top, making a mockery of the 3-1 scoreline.

Watching from an England point of view the second half seemed uncomfortably endless. The team just could not get going. Peter Swan struggled, Charlton mixed the brilliant with the abysmal and the whole side looked jaded and tired. Perhaps the early two-goal lead had made the players lose their grip but whatever it was it must be corrected before the following month's big tournament.

There were some good performances from the home players and Ron Springett was outstanding. He made brilliant

Ron Springett is well beaten by a shot from Switzerland's Allemann, the man of the match at Wembley in May 1962.

second-half saves from Vonlanthen, Allemann, Eschmann and Allemann again, all from close range. Allemann was, without doubt, the man-of-the-match and was a constant thorn in the England defence.

Switzerland also played better after Stettler had substituted for Pernumian in goal, and their neat, clever play gave England many problems. Another near miss came when Jimmy Armfield cleared a shot of the line.

Apart from Springett, Flowers and Ray Wilson were in splendid form and always tackled tigerishly. It was just as well because the way the home team wearily trudged off at the end, it would seem that any thoughts of winning the World Cup at this moment should have been totally forgotten.

7th match v Switzerland.

Gerry Hitchens, scored four goals in seven games for England.

Peru v
England
Friendly

Played on Sunday, 20 May 1962 at the National Stadium, Lima.

Peru: R.Bazan (Alianza); W.Fleming (Alianza), J.Donaire (Sporting Cristal), R.Guzman (Alianza), J.De La Vega (Alianza), M.Grimaldo (Alianza), V.Zegarra (Alianza), R.Neiri (Sporting Cristal), H.Labotan (Alianza), L.Zevallos (Universitario), H.Montalvo (Universitario).
Sub: A.Mosquera (Universitario) for Zegarra.
England: R.D.G.Springett (Sheffield Wed); J.C.Armfield (Blackpool), R.Wilson (Huddersfield T), R.F.C.Moore (West Ham), M.Norman (Spurs), R.Flowers (Wolves), B.Douglas (Blackburn R), J.P.Greaves (Spurs), G.A.Hitchens (Inter-Milan), J.N.Haynes (Fulham, captain), R.Charlton (Man Utd).

Half-time 0-4   Full-time 0-4
Ref: E.Hieger (Austria)   Att: 58,000
THIS friendly was arranged as part of the build up for the World Cup which started

in a week's time. After their poor showing against the Swiss at Wembley, England were looking for a morale booster from this fixture. They blooded two newcomers to the international scene, Maurice Norman and Bobby Moore, and both did very well on their debuts.

Johnny Haynes won the toss and with the setting sun at their backs. England were soon on the attack and Bazan was out quickly to save at the feet of Jimmy Greaves in the second minute. Two minutes later, Greaves again nearly broke through. Peru could muster only a few attacks in the opening quarter, although Labotan once beat Norman to shoot wide and Neiri saw a hard drive saved by Ron Springett.

After 14 minutes, Gerry Hitchens missed a fine chance from Greaves' pass but a minute later England finally took the lead. Guzman fouled Bryan Douglas as the winger danced through the Peruvian defence and the referee awarded a penalty. Ron Flowers made no mistake and sent the ball high into the right-hand corner of the net.

England were well on top by this time and Bobby Charlton was only just thwarted in time as Bazan dispossessed him as he was about to shoot. In the 24th minute, though, Charlton, beating Fleming, sent a ground pass through to Greaves who cleverly flicked it into the net.

Haynes went off for treatment to an ankle injury after 33 minutes but after he returned England quickly added two more goals. Ray Wilson's pass gave Greaves his second goal and Haynes then set the England number eight up for his hat-trick. That gave England a handsome lead and it could have been more but for their over-eagerness in front of goal.

Peru came more into things after the interval and after 51 minutes they should have pulled a goal back. Jimmy Armfield was adjudged to have fouled Mosquera, who had come on in place of Zegarra, and the referee again awarded a penalty. Montalvo took the kick but shot weakly, straight at Springett, and England escaped.

The remainder of the game was a comfortable exercise for the visitors and with a little more accuracy in front of goal their victory could have been even more overwhelming. The frustrations did get the better of one Peruvian, though, when Grimaldo incurred the wrath of the referee by speaking out of turn. It was enough for the official to send him off.

2nd match v Peru.
Debuts for Moore and Norman.
Hat-trick by Greaves.
Penalty by Flowers.
Penalty missed by Montalvo for Peru.
Grimaldo of Peru sent off.
"I was surprised at being selected, but it was an absolute delight and a tremendous thrill."
Bobby Moore.

World Cup Finals

Hungary v
England
Group Four

Played on Thursday 31 May 1962 at the Braden Stadium, Rancagua, Chile.

Hungary: G.Grosics (Tatabánya);

S.Mátrai (Ferencváros), L.Sárosi (Vasas), E.Solymosi (Újpesti Dózsa), K.Mészöly (Vasas), F.Sipos (MTK Budapest), K.Sándor (MTK Budapest), G.Rákosi (Ferencváros), F.Albert (Ferencváros), L.Tichy (Honvéd), M.Fenyvesi (Ferencváros).
England: R.D.G.Springett (Sheffield Wed); J.C.Armfield (Blackpool), R.Wilson (Huddersfield T), R.F.C.Moore (West Ham), M.Norman (Spurs), R.Flowers (Wolves), B.Douglas (Blackburn R), J.P.Greaves (Spurs), G.A.Hitchens (Inter-Milan), J.N.Haynes (Fulham, captain), R.Charlton (Man Utd).

Half-time 1-0   Full-time 2-1
Ref: L.Horn (Holland)   Att: 7,938

AT last, the much talked about World Cup finals were under way, but alas for England it began with a disappointing result. Less than 8,000 people were dotted about the stadium in Rancagua to see a match that, had it been held in Europe, would surely have attracted a sell-out crowd. Heavy drizzle filled the air and dark skies greeted the teams as they came out.

The high regard which both these sides held for each other made for a very nervous opening quarter of an hour. Both teams were testing each other out as the defences looked to consolidate. But after this opening sparring round it was Hungary who took an unexpected lead.

Tichy, making what seemed an aimless run, suddenly cut inside to unleash a superb 20-yard shot that beat Ron Springett. It was a bitter blow for England but they quickly struck back. Bobby Charlton made a good run and cross which Gerry Hitchens went for. The centre-forward clashed with Grosics and in the collision the goalkeeper was knocked out. Hungary held their lead, despite England enjoying long periods of domination. Unfortunately England's passing was not as acurate as it should have been and Hungary still looked the smoother of the sides, playing with more rhythm.

Bryan Douglas missed a good chance after lovely play by Charlton and Hitchens when he headed wide from a good position. Jimmy Armfield linked well in attacking runs down the right but England's crosses were easily dealt with by the tall Hungarian defenders. In an isolated attack by Hungary, they won a dangerous free-kick after Ron Flowers had fouled Tichy but the defensive wall held firm and blocked the kick. Just before half-time, Springett made a fine double save from Tichy and Sandor. Tichy's shooting was always a threat but on the whole England were a little unfortunate to be behind at the interval.

The second half began with a more open attacking look to it. England were soon pushing forward and Grosics made a brave dive at Jimmy Greaves' feet to stop a certain goal. A blatant piece of obstruction by Sandor then stopped Charlton and also brought a severe reprimand from the referee. But that was an isolated incident in an otherwise splendidly sporting match which was worthy of such a worldwide stage. Sandor then redeemed himself somewhat with some lovely play which ended with Springett scrambling across goal, desperately to save at the foot of the post.

England then produced their most determined spell of attacking and it culminated in a deserved equalizer.

Hitchens challenges the Hungarian goalkeeper Grosics during the World Cup match at Rancagua in May 1962.

Johnny Haynes and Argentina's skipper Navarro before the match at Rancagua during the 1962 World Cup finals.

R.Flowers (Wolves), B.Douglas (Black-burn R), J.P.Greaves (Spurs), A.Peacock (Middlesbrough), J.N.Haynes (Fulham, captain), R.Charlton (Man Utd).

Half-time 0-2   Full-time 1-3
Ref: N.Latychev (USSR)   Att: 9,794

ENGLAND produced a much more positive showing in the second of their Group Four games and deservedly beat the ruthless massed defensive formation of the Argentinians. With a win being vital if they wanted to progress, England soon took up the attacking initiative.

On 17 minutes they took the lead. A fine run and cross by Bobby Charlton found new cap Alan Peacock's head and the ball was goal-bound until centre-half Navarro prevented it from crossing the line with his hand. Penalty! So, for the second game running, a defender had prevented an England forward from scoring by foul means. Once again Ron Flowers made no mistake and it was 1-0.

Bobby Moore was playing superbly at the heart of the defence and his immaculate use of the ball was highly impressive. His co-defenders held the feeble Argentinian attacks confidently and comfortably and as a result the game moved on in a rather tame and unexciting way. Just before the break, though, all that changed.

First of all, Jimmy Armfield made one of his now familiar charges down the right wing and he was desperately unlucky to see his rasping drive hit a post. But England were not to be denied and before half-time they added a second goal with a Charlton special. Picking up possession in the middle of the pitch, he made a typical surging run forward veering to the left before cutting back inside to hit the perfect 20-yard shot low inside the far post. It was an understandably jubilant England side that went in as the half-time whistle blew.

Not surprisingly there was a good deal of caution in England's second-half display. After all, they hardly wanted to throw their advantage away. Rather than push forward in search of more goals and leave themselves open to the dangerous breakaway, they preferred to play carefully and in control. On the hour, an impassioned appeal for handball against Moore was turned down by the Russian referee and six minutes later, England sealed their win with a typical piece of poaching by Jimmy Greaves.

Bryan Douglas made a jinking run before firing in a fierce cross-shot. Goalkeeper Roma successfully punched out, only to find Greaves lurking and then putting the ball in the net like lightning. It was Greaves at his best, although it was probably the only good thing he did in the match, but then, that was Greaves!

The game was now all over bar the shouting except that a silly defensive lapse gave Argentina a goal ten minutes from the end. Four England defenders surrounded Sanfillipo but still the Argentine number-ten managed to poke a slow trickling shot past Ron Springett. It was a disappointing end to an otherwise convincing victory.

Douglas crossed the ball and as Hitchens and Grosics clashed in mid-air it ran loose to Greaves, who shot at the open net. The only way that Sárosi could keep the ball out was to use his hands and that is exactly what he did. Flowers stepped up and coolly scored from the resultant spot-kick, leaving England with everything to play for.

The action continued to be lively and Springett made another fine save, although Fenyvesi was found to be offside. Then, tragically for England, Hungary regained the lead. Flowers seemed to have a pass covered but inexplicably he slipped, giving possession to Albert. The graceful centre-forward quickly homed in on goal, rounded the advancing Springett and guided the ball through the narrowest of gaps left by Ray Wilson's desperate lunge.

It was very disappointing for the England players and although they showed admirable zest and spirit in the final quarter of an hour, they failed to break down the strong Hungarian defence. In fact, a breakaway by Sándor almost produced a third goal for Hungary.

Overall, Hungary's extra cohesion probably meant a deserved victory and England would need to improve their passing if they were to progress any further in the competition.

> 9th match v Hungary.
> Penalty by Flowers.

Argentina v England   Group Four

Played on Saturday, 2 June 1962 at the Braden Stadium, Rancagua, Chile.

Argentina: A.Roma (Boca Juniors); R.Navarro (Independiente), S.Marzolini (Boca Juniors), V.Cap (River Plate), F.Sacchi (Racing Club), R.Páez (San Lorenzo), J.Oleniak (Argentinos Juniors), A.U.Rattín (Boca Juniors), R.Sosa (Racing Club), J.Sanfillipo (San Lorenzo), R.Belén (Racing Club).

England: R.D.G.Springett (Sheffield Wed); J.C.Armfield (Blackpool), R.Wilson (Huddersfield T), R.F.C.Moore (West Ham), M.Norman (Spurs),

> 3rd match v Argentina.
> Debut for Peacock.
> Penalty by Flowers.

Bulgaria v England Group Four

Played on Thursday, 7 June 1962 at the Braden Stadium, Rancagua, Chile.

Bulgaria: G.S.Naidenov (CSKA Sofia); D.Takov (Spartak Plovdiv), D.Zechev (Spartak Sofia), D.Kostov (Slavia Sofia), I.Dimitrov (Lokomotiv Sofia), N.Kovatchev (CSKA Sofia), A.D.Kostov (Levski Sofia), P.Velitchkov (Slavia Sofia), G.Sokolov (Botev Plovdiv), I.Kolev (CSKA Sofia), D.Dermendiev (Trakia Plovdiv).

England: R.D.G.Springett (Sheffield Wed); J.C.Armfield (Blackpool), R.Wilson (Huddersfield T), R.F.C.Moore (West Ham), M.Norman (Spurs), R.Flowers (Wolves), B.Douglas (Blackburn R), J.P.Greaves (Spurs), A.Peacock (Middlesbrough), J.N.Haynes (Fulham, captain), R.Charlton (Man Utd).

Half-time 0-0 Full-time 0-0

Ref: A.Blavier (Belgium) Att: 5,700

THE first-ever meeting between these two sides produced one of the worst internationals ever seen. The only saving grace was that the draw enabled England to progress to the next stage, although after this performance it was difficult to see them go on from there. Neither side showed any urgency to win and although England knew that a draw would be enough, people expected more from them.

On a grey, bitterly cold day, a meagre crowd of less than 6,000 people turned up to watch. After the game those were regarded as the unlucky ones! The Bulgarians defended strongly and in depth from the first whistle and in the first five minutes Jimmy Greaves was twice crowded out on the point of shooting. With 15 minutes gone, England had not played well and, ominously, Ron Springett dropped a right-wing cross from Aleksandar Kostov. Luckily, the ball was cleared and from the breakaway in the 19th minute Greaves was through. He rounded Naidenov as the goalkeeper came out but then hit the post from the tightest of angles.

England were certainly more direct but their passing was once again below par and their was little cohesion within their play. Bobby Charlton gave Greaves another half-chance but it was smothered and then a good move involving Bryan Douglas and Johnny Haynes ended with Greaves offside and so the half finished goalless.

Unfortunately for those watching, the second half proved to be just as uninspiring as the first had been. England created few clear chances and it was Bulgaria who went close with Kolev shooting over on 50 minutes. Haynes replied with a similar effort after a lovely reverse pass by Douglas and the England right winger was always in the thick of the action, despite being remorselessly hounded by Kovatchev, who upended him at regular intervals.

With an hour gone good play by Ron Flowers set up Alan Peacock but his header just scraped the wrong side of the post. All of the time there was the danger of England conceding a silly goal and when Aleksandar Kostov headed Kolev's centre over an open goal, they breathed a huge sigh of relief.

In the last third of the game, England's play became more and more ragged and their passing was awful. Bulgaria were no better and both sides seemed content with the goalless scoreline long before the end. Only Charlton's fierce cross shot relieved the gloom, but it was well reached by Naidenov. The many Argentinians in the crowd barracked both teams as they could see their country's chances of qualifying evaporating in a dire match which, from their point of view, Bulgaria had to win to let Argentina in at England's expense. Judging by their performance, Bulgaria won few friends amongst the South Americans.

England now looked towards Viña del Mar, where they faced the mighty Brazilians.

> First match v Bulgaria.
> First goalless draw England had been involved in since the 0-0 draw with Brazil in the 1958 World Cup in Sweden.

Brazil v England Quarter-final

Played on Sunday, 10 June 1962 in the Sausalito Stadium, Viña del Mar, Chile.

Brazil: G.dos Santos (Santos); D.Santos (Palmeiras), R.de Oliveira (Santos), Z.Alves (Bangu), N.Santos (Botafogo), J.E.Miranda (Santos), M.F.Santos (Botafogo), W.Pereira (Botafogo), E.Neto (Palmeiras), A.Tavares (Botafogo), M.J.Zagalo (Botafogo).

England: R.D.G.Springett (Sheffield Wed); J.C.Armfield (Blackpool), R Wilson (Huddersfield T), R.F.C.Moore (West Ham), M.Norman (Spurs), R.Flowers (Wolves), B.Douglas (Blackburn R), J.P.Greaves (Spurs), G.A.Hitchens (Inter-Milan), J.N.Haynes (Fulham, captain), R.Charlton (Man Utd).

Half-time 1-1 Full-time 3-1

Ref: P.Schwinte (France) Att: 17,736

THE lovely Sausalito Stadium was shrouded in a drifting sea mist from the Pacific Ocean as these two famous teams took to the field for this vital quarter-final tie in the World Cup. England sprang a selection surprise when Gerry Hitchens ran out in place of Alan Peacock. Peacock had suffered from a slight stomach upset overnight and as a result was left out. Brazil were at full strength.

England began confidently and were soon attacking. Bobby Charlton started a good move which ended with Jimmy Greaves volleying high over the bar. Greaves had more luck a few moments later when a stray dog ran on to the pitch. To the amusement of the crowd the number-eight managed to catch the animal and escort it from the field. Five minutes had elapsed when Brazil's midfield star Didí clashed with Ron Flowers and had to go off for treatment. Whilst he was gone, Brazil looked nervous as England played coolly and with composure. But Didí was soon back and gradually Brazil settled.

There was some lovely open play from both sides as the temperature rose. Maurice Norman made a fine tackle on the dangerous Garrincha, and then another break by the Brazilian right winger almost brought a goal. A fast cross went between Ron Springett's legs, only for Jimmy Armfield to save the day with a goal-line clearance. That was a desperate moment for England as Didí and Zito were gaining ominous superiority in midfield. So far, though, the English players were giving as good as they got in the end-to-end play.

Didí slid a superb pass to Amarildo, who forced Springett into a marvellous full-length save. Then Greaves responded with a brilliant run and shot which Gilmar turned over. Flowers joined in the action by shooting just wide and Springett continued to perform well making fine saves from Garrincha and Didí. All this action had come in the first half-hour and in the 32nd minute the first breakthrough came. A corner by Zagalo was met by a full-blooded header by Garrincha and this time Springett had no chance.

Amarildo went very close to adding a second as the mist thickened, but England battled on manfully and in the 38th minute they scored an equalizer. Johnny Haynes put in a free-kick which Greaves, so unluckily, headed against the crossbar. Despair quickly turned to joy as Hitchens was on the spot to head home the rebound.

Charlton and Norman had been England's outstanding first-half players and the side left the field happy with their efforts.

After the interval, Brazil came out even more determined and began the half like an express train. Vava had a goal disallowed, Garrincha's cross was headed straight at Springett by Amarildo, but then after 53 minutes the extra pressure finally told. A thundering free-kick by Vavá flashed past the English defensive wall. Springett understandably failed to hold this rocket and as the ball bounced up, Vavá followed up to head the loose ball home.

Still England bravely attacked but six minutes later, Garrincha scored a memorable goal which effectively ended the contest. He hit an incredible swerving shot from some 25 yards, beating Springett all ends up.

That was virtually that, although Amarildo swerved another blistering shot just over and then Haynes was unlucky to see one good effort punched over by Gilmar. By the end of the game Brazil were in full control and the samba rhythm beat out from the fans. For England, at least, there was satisfaction in the knowledge that they had given their all. Sadly, on the day the South Americans had just a little too much for them.

> 4th match v Brazil.
> Brazil's dos Santos also known as 'Gilmar'; Miranda as 'Zito'; de Oliveira as 'Mauro'; Alves as 'Zózimo'; M.F.Santos as 'Garrincha'; Pereira as 'Didí'; Neto as 'Vavá'; Tavares as 'Amarildo'.

England v France European Nations Cup

Played on Wednesday, 3 October 1962 at Hillsborough, Sheffield.

England: R.D.G.Springett (Sheffield Wed); J.C.Armfield (Blackpool, captain),

Jimmy Armfield, took over the England captaincy for the European Nations game against France at Hillsborough in October 1962. Armfield played 43 times for England.

R.Wilson (Huddersfield T), R.F.C.Moore (West Ham), M.Norman (Spurs), R.Flowers (Wolves), M.S.Hellawell (Birmingham C), C.Crowe (Wolves), R.O.Charnley (Blackpool), J.P.Greaves (Spurs), A.T.Hinton (Wolves).

France: P.Bernard (Nimes Olympique); J.Wendling (Stade de Reims), A.Chorda (Girondins Bordeaux), M.Synakowski (FC Sedan), A.Lerond (Stade Francais), R.Ferrier (AS St-Etienne), L.Robuschi (Girondins Bordeaux), J.Bonnel (US Valenciennes), R.Kopa (Stade de Reims), Y.Goujon (Stade de Rennes), P.Sauvage (Stade de Reims).

Half-time 0-1   Full-time 1-1
Ref: F.Hansen (Denmark)   Att: 35,500

FROM the World Cup to the European Nations Cup, such was the way that competition at international level was developing in the 1960s. England entertained France at Hillsborough with an almost totally new forward line and four new caps in the side. Alas, because there were so many new faces, the England performance was very poor and long before the end the crowd, kept down to just over 35,000 because of a rail strike, were showing their displeasure.

Right from the start it was obvious there would be no cohesion in this England side as they struggled to find any shape and after only eight minutes France took the lead. Raymond Kopa (as he was known), the European Cup legend, set up Goujon, who easily beat Ron Springett.

From that moment England were battling to get on terms, not only with the French, but also with themselves. The half-back line found it difficult to cope with the close passing of France and the forward line ended the night the same strangers that they had been at the beginning. Only Ray Wilson and Jimmy Armfield came out of the game with some credit, although winger Mike Hellawell showed some promise. All too often, though, the England number-seven was blatantly body checked by the uncompromising French defenders.

For France, Wendling attacked well from the full-back position and Ferrier showed up well as the midfield link. And always there was the veteran Kopa. Still able to produce moments of magic, he gave Maurice Norman a torrid time. England created few scoring opportunities and rarely looked likely to threaten Bernard's goal. That they finally gained an equalizer at all owed a good deal to

a rather dubious piece of refereeing after an hour's play. A pass from Alan Hinton found Jimmy Greaves. His low shot was parried by Bernard but as Ray Charnley went for the rebound, the goalkeeper and Wendling obstructed him. Even the Yorkshire fans found it hard to believe when the referee awarded a penalty to England. There was pandemonium amongst the French players, but the referee was adamant and, unmoved by the mayhem around him, Ron Flowers stayed ice-cool to calmly score from the spot-kick.

This was a significant match in England's history as France were to be the last foreign opposition in Walter Winterbottom's reign as England coach. It was a shame for him that it was such a poor display and it also seemed that for the home World Cup of 1966, the England team would have little to offer unless a new formula was found.

15th match v France.
First European Championship match for England.
Debuts for Hellawell, Crowe, Charnley and Hinton.
Penalty by Flowers.
For France Kopa's full name Kopaszewski; Synakowski also known as 'Maryan'.

Northern Ireland v England   Home Championship

Played on Saturday, 20 October 1962 at Windsor Park, Belfast.

Northern Ireland: R.J.Irvine (Linfield); E.J.Magill (Arsenal), A.R.Elder (Burnley), R.D.Blanchflower (Spurs), W.J.T.Neill (Arsenal), J.J.Nicholson (Man Utd), W.M.Humphries (Coventry C), H.H.Barr (Coventry C), S.McMillan (Man Utd), J.McIlroy (Burnley), W.L.Bingham (Everton).

England: R.D.G.Springett (Sheffield Wed); J.C.Armfield (Blackpool, captain), R.Wilson (Huddersfield T), R.F.C.Moore (West Ham), B.L.Labone (Everton), R.Flowers (Wolves), M.S.Hellawell (Birmingham C), F.Hill (Bolton W), A.Peacock (Middlesbrough), J.P.Greaves (Spurs), M.O'Grady (Huddersfield T).

Half-time 0-1   Full-time 1-3
Ref: J.Barclay (Scotland)   Att: 53,750

THIS was England's first Home Championship victory since April 1961, but even though they won the manner in which they achieved it was not wholly satisfying. On a sunny afternoon England blooded three more new caps but took a large part of the game before they finally got their act together.

After quickly assuming command the visitors took the lead in the eighth minute. Jimmy Greaves, giving his best England display for many months, seized on a rebound to head past Irvine. The number ten was outstanding and continually kept the Irish defence on their toes with his constant probing and lightning strikes. Several of his shots were blocked and he brought the best out of Irvine.

Despite the liveliness of Greaves, there was a general lack of pattern about England's play. Their defence looked sound enough around the new centre-half, Brian Labone, and Freddie Hill showed some lovely flair in midfield. However, judging it on the high standards of international football it must be said that the general approach play was weak. Mike Hellawell showed flashes of his terrific speed down the wing but Alan Peacock and Mike O'Grady looked uninspired.

The big crowd urged Ireland on but, despite good work by Nicholson, Blanchflower and McIlroy in midfield, the game tended to drift along aimlessly. However, all that changed after an hour's play. McIlroy's cross-field pass seemed to be covered by Ron Springett but Jimmy Armfield, under severe pressure from Barr, diverted the ball into his own net to give the Irish their equalizer. That suddenly brought the crowd to life again and they roared their approval. Despite a lot of pressure, though, the England defence remained solid with Bobby Moore looking particularly impressive.

After this bout of Irish dominance, England gradually pulled themselves together again and in the last quarter of an hour, after resuming control, they surged forward to snatch victory. A superb match-winning pass through the centre by Greaves put O'Grady clear. The English winger with the Irish-sounding name celebrated his debut with a lovely strike wide of Irvine.

Moments later England went 3-1 up. O'Grady was again the goalscorer, taking a pass from Peacock before shooting into the Irish net. That settled the result but England's mixed performance had given plenty of food for thought during the coming months. There were some plusses, though, and Hill looked extremely promising. He was, on one occasion, desperately unlucky not to score when his 20-yard drive thudded against a post before being cleared.

> 70th match v Northern Ireland.
> Debuts for Labone, Hill and O'Grady.
> Two debut goals for O'Grady.
> Own-goal by Armfield.

England v Wales   Home Championship

Played on Wednesday, 21 November 1962 at Wembley Stadium.

England: R.D.G.Springett (Sheffield Wed); J.C.Armfield (Blackpool, captain), G.L.Shaw (Sheffield Utd), R.F.C.Moore (West Ham), B.L.Labone (Everton), R.Flowers (Wolves), J.M.Connelly (Burnley), F.Hill (Bolton W), A.Peacock (Middlesbrough), J.P.Greaves (Spurs), R.V.Tambling (Chelsea).
Wales: A.H.Millington (West Brom); S.G.Williams (Southampton), C.R.Sear (Man City), W.T.Hennessey (Birmingham C), M.T.G.Nurse (Middlesbrough), P.M.Lucas (Leyton O), B.S.Jones (Swansea T), I.J.Allchurch (Cardiff C), K.Leek (Birmingham C), T.R.Vernon (Everton), T.C.Medwin (Spurs).

Half-time 2-0   Full-time 4-0
Ref: S.Carswell (Northern Ireland)
Att: 27,500

THE smallest crowd ever to attend a full international at Wembley were dotted about the stadium in between the cranes and builder's materials being used to put the new roof on in time for the following spring. England produced a performance more than good enough to beat Wales but

Retiring England manager Walter Winterbottom receives a set of glassware subscribed for by 131 international footballers who played under him since 1946. Also pictured are (left to right) Alan Peacock, Jimmy Armfield, England selectors Joe Mears and Joe Richards, Jimmy Greaves, trainer Harold Shepherdson and Ron Springett.

it still left a few question marks over certain players. They were forced into two late changes with Graham Shaw replacing Ray Wilson, and Bobby Tambling coming in for Mike O'Grady. Both of these new players made satisfactory appearances and neither weakened the structure of the side.

After a night of sleet it was cold but fine by the time the match started and from the moment England took the lead after only ten minutes, there was only ever going to be one result. The two stars of the game immediately stood head and shoulders above their colleagues, Jimmy Greaves for England and Allchurch for Wales.

It was Greaves who created the first goal. A tremendous piece of acceleration through a gap in the Welsh defence ended with a rasping shot which cracked against Millington's crossbar. John Connelly was first to react to the rebound and quickly shot home with the help of a deflection.

Allchurch then did his best to inspire his team, giving a talented midfield display. Unfortunately, all too frequently, he found little support forthcoming and the solid defensive play of Bobby Moore, Ron Flowers and Brian Labone snuffed out any danger. Wales did create two chances on the half-hour but both Vernon and Medwin failed to take them.

They were to rue these misses as in the 35th minute their goalkeeper Millington made the first of two mistakes which probably cost Wales the game. Alan Peacock, who failed to really impress, fired in an angled swinging shot which the goalkeeper, in trying to save, succeeded only in palming the ball into his own net. Peacock's goal but with a large 'assist' from Millington.

Soon after half-time, Allchurch missed the best Welsh chance from point-blank range. On the hour Millington made a terrible hash of a short goal-kick to Williams, giving Peacock the chance to pounce eagerly for his free gift and England's third goal. Connelly and Tambling showed some nice touches as

England dominated the latter stages but Freddie Hill, after a bright opening, faded into anonymity.

With darkness setting in it was left to Greaves to produce the game's outstanding moment. Near the end he picked the ball up and cut inside from the right. He skipped past three desperate Welsh challenges before hitting a magnificent shot into the far top corner.

It was a fitting end, not only to this match, but also to the distinguished career of Walter Winterbottom, whose reign as England's coach had now come to an end. In the dressing-room afterwards there was a presentation to him, subscribed to by the 131 players who had played under him in his 16 years in charge. In response to this gesture he said, "It underlines the bond of friendship between the international players and myself. Today showed that England have the material for a good side. With the support they merit, and playing in England, we must have a great chance of winning the World Cup in 1966."

> 73rd match v Wales.
> Debut for Tambling.
> Walter Winterbottom's last match in charge of team affairs.

France v England   European Nations Cup

Played on Wednesday, 27 February 1963 at the Parc des Princes Stadium, Paris.

France: P.Bernard (Nimes Olympique); J.Wendling (Stade de Reims), B.Rodzik (Stade de Reims), M.Synakowski (FC Sedan), A.Lerond (Stade Francais), R.Herbin (AS St-Etienne), M.Wisnieski (RC, Lens), J.Bonnel (US Valenciennes), Y.Goujon (Stade de Rennes), Y.Douis (AS Monaco), L.Coussou (AS Monaco).
England: R.D.G.Springett (Sheffield Wed); J.C.Armfield (Blackpool, captain), R.P.Henry (Spurs), R.F.C.Moore (West

Ham), B.L.Labone (Everton), R.Flowers (Wolves), J.M.Connelly (Burnley), R.V.Tambling (Chelsea), R.Smith (Spurs), J.P.Greaves (Spurs), R.Charlton (Man Utd).

Half-time 3-0   Full-time 5-2

Ref: J.Kandlbinder (West Germany)

Att: 24,000

WHAT A start for new team manager, Alf Ramsey! Out of the Nations Cup, conceding five goals for the first time since May 1958, and giving a general display that would give Ramsey many headaches. In fact, the scoreline is a little misleading, and it was all a bit closer than at first you would believe.

The first half was a complete disaster from England's viewpoint. As early as the third minute France were a goal up. A flick by Goujon was turned in by the outside-right Wisnieski. On the half-hour it was 2-0 when Wisnieski turned goal maker as his cross was turned in by the star of the night, Douis. The French inside-left took a grip on the match early on and never let go. His artistry was most impressive.

England worked hard enough but there was little evidence of teamwork. Bobby Charlton and Jimmy Greaves showed flashes of their individual skills but there was no cohesion as Ron Flowers, Bobby Moore and Bobby Smith all did their own thing. John Connelly and Bobby Tambling were rarely in the game at all.

Whilst all this was going on Ron Springett, so often the saviour for his side, was enduring a nightmare in England's goal. Several moments of indecision had given his defence a scare and just before the interval he made another costly error. Goujon's cross was totally lost by Springett and Coussou was able to take advantage to score with ease. It was a very dejected England side that trooped off at half-time.

Somewhere under the stands of the Parc des Princes stadium, Mr Ramsey must have had plenty to say to the players at the interval. It was obvious his words must have had an effect because after the play restarted England, at last, began to turn their undoubted hard work into more tangible reward. Almost immediately

Greaves was unlucky when his shot hit the French post following a cross by Bobby Moore. England kept improving and on the hour they pulled a goal back.

It was a good goal too, with Smith rising well to head Greaves' cross wide of Bernard. Fifteen minutes later what had seemed impossible suddenly seemed probable as England reduced the arrears further. Charlton took a corner from the left and up went Tambling to make his one telling contribution scoring with a neat header.

At this point it seemed odds on that this tremendous recovery would be completed. Alas for England, France had other ideas and at last woke up again to the dangers they faced. Within moments of Tambling's goal, the score went from 2-3 to 2-5 and again, sadly, Springett must take most of the blame. A shot from Wisnieski rebounded from the England 'keeper's body to Coussou who returned it to Wisnieski who then had another try. This time he was successful. Within seconds it was five as this time Coussou took a pass from the intelligent Douis to flick it over Springett and lob France to a slightly flattering scoreline.

England, despite a considerable amount of possession, lacked enough thought in the vital areas and on the day they had a goalkeeper who had one of those days all goalkeepers dread.

> 16th match v France.
> Debut for Henry.

England v Scotland Home Championship

Played on Saturday, 6 April 1963 at Wembley Stadium.

England: G.Banks (Leicester C); J.C.Armfield (Blackpool, captain), G.Byrne (Liverpool), R.F.C.Moore (West Ham), M.Norman (Spurs), R.Flowers (Wolves), B.Douglas (Blackburn R), J.P.Greaves (Spurs), R.A.Smith (Spurs), J.J.Melia (Liverpool), R.Charlton (Man Utd).

Scotland: W.D.F.Brown (Spurs); A.W.Hamilton (Dundee), E.Caldow (Rangers), D.C.Mackay (Spurs), J.F.Ure (Dundee), J.C.Baxter (Rangers), W.Henderson (Rangers), J.A.White (Spurs), I.St John (Liverpool), D.Law (Rangers), D.Wilson (Rangers).

Half-time 0-2   Full-time 1-2

Ref: L.Horn (Holland)   Att: 98,606

THIS was Scotland's day as at last they won a famous victory at Wembley, their first on English soil since 1951. A full house paid record receipts (for any game in Britain) of £76,000 for the privilege and the many Scots in the audience made the afternoon their own with their vociferous support. Wembley, looking spick and span with its new roof, braced itself for the invasion of the marauding army.

The match started tragically for Scotland. After only five, a fierce collision between Bobby Smith and Caldow ended with the Scottish captain being stretchered off to hospital with a fractured leg. But far from giving England the edge, it seemed to inspire the Scots to a very high level of skill and endeavour.

Wilson moved to left-back and the Scotland midfield of Baxter, White and Mackay rolled up their sleeves and knuckled down to take a grip on the game. England seemed bereft of ideas. Bobby Moore and Ron Flowers never used the ball constructively and Jimmy Melia was too predictable in all that he did. Up front Bobby Charlton flitted in and out of the game and Jimmy Greaves had a day he would soon like to forget.

The first goal came after half an hour. Henderson put in a deep cross which Jimmy Armfield collected and seemed to have under control. Unfortunately for him, the England skipper tried to dribble the ball clear of his own penalty area and was caught in possession by Baxter. The elegant Scottish number-six strode forward and gave Gordon Banks no chance with a crisp shot.

The goal was no more than Scotland deserved and was a fitting reward for their enterprise and skill. Baxter was a revelation and had a dream match. Memories of the Hungarian, Bozsik, came flooding back as Baxter's presence dominated the play.

Within two minutes, Scotland were two up. Henderson, who gave Gerry Byrne a torrid time throughout, darted through a gap but was brought down, sandwich-style by Flowers and the bewildered Byrne. 'Penalty'!, screamed the Scots.

The referee agreed and the super confident Baxter duly obliged from the spot-kick. It was the first penalty he had ever taken, but on a day when he could have practically walked on water there was never going to be any other volunteer.

From then on it was a story of Scotland controlling what little England could muster. There was one lively spell midway through the second half when England could have come right back into things. Four times Greaves found himself in excellent positions, only to head wide on each occasion. In another attack, Greaves turned sharply and this time brought the best out of his Spurs clubmate, Brown, in goal. With ten minutes to go, and with Scotland understandably tiring, England finally pulled a goal back. The visitors' centre-half, Ian Ure, a tower of strength at the heart of their defence, made his only mistake when he missed a cross by Smith, allowing Bryan Douglas the chance to shoot past Brown.

Yves Douis scores France's second goal in Paris in February 1963 as England go tumbling out of the Nations Cup.

The last word went to Scotland though and Mackay made Banks' crossbar shudder after a blistering free-kick. So Scotland deservedly held on and the deafening roar of their supporters at the final whistle almost lifted the new roof off the stand before it had time to settle!

It was a brave performance by Scotland but one consolation for the home side was the splendid form shown by their new goalkeeper Gordon Banks. He looked safe and sure and was full of confidence.

> 80th match v Scotland.
> Debuts for Banks, Byrne and Melia.

England v Brazil
Friendly

Played on Wednesday, 8 May 1963 at Wembley Stadium.

England: G.Banks (Leicester C); J.C.Armfield (Blackpool, captain), R.Wilson (Huddersfield T), G.Milne (Liverpool), M.Norman (Spurs), R.F.C.Moore (West Ham), B.Douglas (Blackburn R), J.P.Greaves (Spurs), R.A.Smith (Spurs), G.E.Eastham (Arsenal), R.Charlton (Man Utd).

Brazil: G.dos Santos (Santos); A.S.Lima (Santos), R.Costa (Botafogo), J.Ferreira (Palmeiras), E.Bento (Corinthians), R.Dias (São Paulo), D.Rodrigues (Santos), M.Figueiro (Santos), A.Wilson Hondrio (Santos), A.Tavares (Botafogo), J.Macia (Santos).
Sub: O.Ney (Corinthians) for Tavares.

Half-time 0-1   Full-time 1-1
Ref: L.Horn (Holland)   Att: 93,500

THE visit of the current World Champions Brazil to Wembley filled a 93,500 crowd with excitement and expectation. But there was some disappointment for them as before the match it was announced that Pelé, Garrincha and Zito would all be missing from Brazil's line-up. However, there was still an awful lot to admire in the Brazilian team and England had to work very hard to keep them in check.

England, though, made a bright start and Gilmar had to make three great saves in the first 15 minutes. Bobby Smith, Bryan Douglas and Bobby Charlton were all foiled by the goalkeeper, frustrating the home fans.

That frustration became all the more evident when, with virtually their first attack, Brazil opened the scoring after 20 minutes. With the 'banana kick' expert Garrincha missing from the side, nobody, least of all Gordon Banks it seemed, expected the sort of goal scored by Pepe. He produced an incredible bending shot from a free-kick that had Banks groping, first one way, then the other.

After the goal, England continued to work hard, especially new cap Gordon Milne, who did a lot of effective work in his midfield role. Defensively, too, England looked solid, but up front, despite some good running by Charlton and Jimmy Greaves, the final ball always seemed to be the high cross from the wings.

For Brazil, Zequinha and Mengalvio were the stars with the latter a typical Brazilian ball artist. Before half-time, the South Americans made a substitution, taking off Amarildo their World Cup star

Jim Baxter (not pictured) beats debutant Gordon Banks to give Scotland the lead at Wembley in April 1963.

Jimmy Armfield and Gilmar of Brazil before the game at Wembley in May 1963.

and bringing on Ney. At the break they still held their lead.

Straight after the restart, England were desperately unlucky. Within five minutes, Charlton had headed Douglas' right-wing cross against a post with Gilmar beaten and seconds later Charlton was again so

unlucky when he saw another effort headed off the goal-line by Rildo.

For a while after those misses, it seemed England would never work out a route to goal. George Eastham spread some nice passes around the pitch but the attack lacked the imagination needed and Gil-

Bobby Charlton gets in a header against Brazil but the ball hit a post and rebounded clear. Tottenham centre-forward Bobby Smith looks on.

mar was rarely threatened. Bobby Moore and Maurice Norman performed very well at the back and the defence could not be faulted.

The crowd were occasionally stirred by near misses. Ray Wilson kicked off the line an effort by Pepe and Dorval shot just past Banks' post. Then, with just five minutes left and England looking less and less likely to score, Jimmy Armfield joined the attack with a strong break down the right. A cross came over, it was flicked on by Charlton and there was little Douglas in the right place to stab the ball home. The crowd roared their delight and on the whole it was no more than England deserved.

> 5th match v Brazil.
> Debuts for Milne and Eastham.
> Brazil's dos Santos also known as 'Gilmar'; Costa as 'Rildo'; Ferreira as 'Zequinha'; Bento as 'Edwards'; Rodrigues as 'Dorval'; Figueiro as 'Mengalvio'; Hondrio as 'Coutinho'; Tavares as 'Amarildo'; Macia as 'Pepe'.

Czechoslovakia v England   Friendly

Played on Wednesday, 29 May 1963 at the Na Tehelnem poli Stadium, Bratislava.

Czechoslovakia: V.Schroif (Slovan Bratislava); J.Lála (Slavia Prague), L.Novák (Dukla Prague), S.Pluskal (Dukla Prague), J.Popluhár (Slovan Bratislava), J.Masopust (Dukla Prague), J.Štribrányi (Spartak Trnava), A.Scherer (Inter Bratislava), J.Kadraba (SONP Kladno), A.Kvašnák (Sparta Prague), V.Mašek (Sparta Prague).
Sub: T.Bubernik (Inter Bratislava) for Masopust.

England: G.Banks (Leicester C); K.J.Shellito (Chelsea), R.Wilson (Huddersfield T), G.Milne (Liverpool), M.Norman (Spurs), R.F.C.Moore (West Ham, captain), T.L.Paine (Southampton), J.P.Greaves (Spurs), R.A.Smith (Spurs), G.E.Eastham (Arsenal), R.Charlton (Man Utd).

Half-time 0-1   Full-time 2-4
Ref: B.Lööw (Sweden)   Att: 50,000

FROM World Cup winners to World Cup runners-up, that was how England's fixture list worked out. On the first leg of a three-match summer tour of Europe, England took on Czechoslovakia, who lost 3-1 in that famous Final the previous year. As it turned out, England produced one of their best performances for a long time and, indeed, one of their best ever on foreign soil.

With Jimmy Armfield injured the captaincy fell on the young shoulders of Bobby Moore, who became England's youngest-ever captain. How the young man rose to the challenge. He was magnificent and inspired his team.

England withstood tremendous pressure in the first quarter of an hour, mainly thanks to a tactical plan built around a cleverly retreating defence. For years, England's forwards have been frustrated by such defensive methods. Now, thanks to Alf Ramsey, it was Czechoslovakia's turn to be frustrated. By soaking up the pressure and breaking quickly with lightning attacks, usually started by George Eastham, England took a great stride towards winning the match.

After that early burst by the Czechs, England made a stunning reply on 18 minutes. Moore intercepted a pass in midfield and found Bobby Smith. A lovely wall pass and Jimmy Greaves was through. The Tottenham star shimmied and wriggled past three defenders, drew the goalkeeper skilfully and placed the

ball into the net before turning with one arm raised to receive the congratulations of his delighted teammates.

It was typical Greaves and the home crowd and team were suitably stunned into disbelief. Worse was to follow for them two minutes from half-time when their idol and the star of the side, Masopust was taken off to be replaced by Bubernik.

Within a minute of the second half starting, England, unbelievably, went 2-0 up. A scintillating move down the left involving Gordon Milne, Bobby Charlton and Greaves ended with Smith having the easiest of chances from close range.

England were now in a commanding position but for the next 20 minutes after the interval it was backs-to-the-wall as Czechoslovakia fought back. An unfortunate misunderstanding between Moore and Gordon Banks enabled the home side to pull a goal back. Moore lobbed the ball towards his own goal as Banks came out. Banks managed to get a hand to it but as it ran loose, Scherer was on hand to nod it into the empty net.

There then followed some intense pressure. Bubernik crashed a header against a post, Kvašnák then slashed the rebound on to the crossbar before England desperately managed to scramble the ball clear. Throughout this period, Moore, Maurice Norman and the rest of the defence held firm showing great determination and they were rewarded when England came up with the perfect response to the pressure. Greaves set Eastham free on the left and the Arsenal player sent over a deep centre. Terry Paine pulled the ball back from the opposite by-line, it was blocked, ran loose and there was Bobby Charlton roaring in to crash home England's third goal.

Before the relief of that goal had the chance to settle on the England players Czechoslovakia came straight back again to reduce the arrears once more. Kadraba seemed to impede Banks before he was able to head the loose ball home to put the visitors under fierce pressure yet again. With the Czechs pressing hard, it seemed that all England's valiant efforts were to be denied at the death, but with 20 minutes to go, a fourth goal finally sealed victory — and what a beauty it was.

Smith found Paine who, not for the first time, beat his marker before crossing the ball from the by-line. Greaves was there as ever to produce his own special brand of magic as he pulled the ball down with his left foot and shot home devastatingly with his right.

In the remaining minutes, England stroked the ball around arrogantly, keeping possession and drawing applause from even the patriotic home fans. It was a memorable display, well planned tactically and carried out to the letter by a fine team performance. Moore and Norman were the heroes in defence with Milne, Eastham, Greaves, Charlton and Paine all making telling contributions.

It was England's first victory on foreign soil since they beat Italy in Rome in 1961.

> 3rd match v Czechoslovakia.
> Debuts for Shellito and Paine.
> Moore captain for the first time and the youngest ever for England.
> *"I was very proud and thankful that I had achieved my ambition to play for England."*
> Terry Paine

East Germany v England
Friendly

Played on Sunday, 2 June 1963 in the Zentral Stadium, Leipzig.

East Germany: H.Fritsche (Motor Jena); K.Urbanczyk (Chemie Halle), D.Krampe (Vorwärts), M.Kaiser (SCW Karl-Marx-Stadt), W.Heine (BFC Dynamo), K.Liebrecht (Lokomotive Stendahl), R.Nachtigall (Vorwärts), H.Frenzel (Lokomotive Leipzig), P.Ducke (Carl Zeiss Jena), J.Nöldner (Vorwärts), R.Ducke (Carl Zeiss Jena).

England: G.Banks (Leicester C); J.C.Armfield (Blackpool, captain), R.Wilson (Huddersfield T), G.Milne (Liverpool), M.Norman (Spurs), R.F.C.Moore (West Ham), T.L.Paine (Southampton), R.Hunt (Liverpool), R.A.Smith (Spurs), G.E.Eastham (Arsenal), R.Charlton (Man Utd).

Half-time 1-1   Full-time 1-2
Ref: K.Zecević (Yugoslavia)   Att: 90,000

ENGLAND'S summer tour continued with this, their first-ever meeting with East Germany. They suffered a real blow before the match when Jimmy Greaves dropped out of the side with tonsillitis. Liverpool's Roger Hunt came in as his replacement and did very well.

The visitors made a sluggish start to the game and the Germans took a first-half lead. P.Ducke, their roving centre-forward, rounded Maurice Norman and Jimmy Armfield cleverly but could get in only a weak shot. Somehow, though, Gordon Banks misjudged it and allowed the ball to go under his body and into the net, a rare mistake from the goalkeeper.

Twice England nearly scored as they

fought back well. Bobby Smith was only just wide with a shot from the edge of the German penalty area, leaving goalkeeper Fritsche rooted to the spot. Then George Eastham made a fine run which ended with a 25-yard drive which struck a post. On the stroke of half-time, however, England finally scored the goal their play deserved. It was a real beauty too.

The always dangerous Terry Paine made the opening and when his pass came inside Hunt met the ball on the run to hit a ferocious shot from 20 yards that flashed past Fritsche before the goalkeeper could move.

After the break, England continued to make all the running as they took control of the match. Gordon Milne and Eastham worked hard and as the East Germans began to tire, England found more and more chances came their way. Paine had his marker, Krampe in all sorts of trouble with his trickery and the Southampton winger seemed able to pass him at will. Bobby Charlton, on the left also had a good game and it was he who gave England the lead and ultimate victory.

A scramble developed in the German penalty area as Paine tried a shot from ten yards out. The shot was charged down and Smith then tried desperately to get to the loose ball, only to fall over the goalkeeper in his haste. Still the ball ran loose and this time Charlton was there to hammer home a shot from six yards.

Banks had to make some good saves in this half as the Germans tried to come back but he was not altogether convincing as he mishandled some seemingly harmless shots. Ray Wilson was his usual immaculate self and Armfield played well upon his return to the team.

It was another excellent victory, although manager Alf Ramsey was not over-impressed. "Our passing was erratic and careless," he said, "And we lacked a good deal of urgency in our play."

Mr Ramsey, it seemed, was a perfectionist.

> 1st match v East Germany.

Switzerland v England
Friendly

Played on Wednesday, 5 June 1963 in the St Jakob Stadium, Basle.

Switzerland: K.Stettler (FC Basel); A.Grobéty (Lausanne-Sports), E.Tacchella (Lausanne-Sports), H.Weber (FC Basel), H.Schneiter (Young Boys), W.Leimgruber (FC Zürich), A.Allemann (FC Mantova), K.Odermatt (FC Basel), J.Kuhn (FC Zürich), H.Bertschi (La Chaux de Fonds), P.Pottier (Stade Francais).

England: R.D.G.Springett (Sheffield Wed); J.C.Armfield (Blackpool, captain), R.Wilson (Huddersfield T), A.H.Kay (Everton), R.F.C.Moore (West Ham), R.Flowers (Wolves), B.Douglas (Blackburn R), J.P.Greaves (Spurs), J.J.Byrne (West Ham), J.J.Melia (Liverpool), R.Charlton (Man Utd).

Half-time 1-3   Full-time 1-8
Ref: I.Zsolt (Hungary)   Att: 36,000

A MAGNIFICENT summer tour came to an end in a real firework display of goals

in Basle. This new-look, confident England side continued from where they left off in Leipzig, despite several team changes. Alf Ramsey decided to give some of his reserves a chance, bringing in five players including one for the first time, Tony Kay. They responded superbly and England ripped Switzerland apart.

After the two tough fixtures on this tour, this match by comparison must have seemed like a practice match. True, the tricky footwork of Bertschi and Pottier gave England some early difficulties but from the moment England took the lead after 19 minutes, there was only ever going to be one outcome.

A pass through the middle from Jimmy Melia gave Kay possession just inside the Swiss half. The highly promising wing-half then timed the perfect pass inside the full-back for Bobby Charlton to run on to and crack into the roof of the net from a tight angle.

Switzerland came back briefly when a shot by Kuhn struck the England post, but it was only delaying the inevitable as England were aleady dominating. Charlton was in particularly devastating form and his bursts brought two more goals for England before half-time.

On the half-hour, Johnny Byrne celebrated his call up by converting Charlton's pass, and then 12 minutes later, Bryan Douglas thumped in the third, again after a flowing run by Charlton. An isolated raid and sloppy defensive work gave Switzerland a goal by Bertschi before the break, but in the second half the floodgates really opened up.

Playing relaxed and positive football, England tore into the Swiss. Bobby Moore was immaculate at the heart of their defence, Charlton running like the wind, Jimmy Greaves darting here, there and everywhere and Byrne giving a display that augers well for the future. The whole team played their part and soon the goals began to flow.

Byrne and Charlton added numbers four and five and then a lovely move between Charlton, Melia and Greaves set up Kay for the best goal of the match. Melia then scored following a pass by Douglas and then Charlton ended the scoring with his third of the game.

Despite the humiliating scoreline, the Swiss crowd loved every minute and screamed for more as they appreciated what a fine display England had put on for them. They gave England a standing ovation at the end.

> 8th match v Switzerland.
> Debut goal for Kay.
> Hat-trick by Charlton.

Wales v England
Home Championship

Played on Saturday, 12 October 1963 at Ninian Park, Cardiff.

Wales: D.M.Hollins (Newcastle Utd); S.G.Williams (Southampton), G.E. Williams (West Brom), W.T.Hennessey (Birmingham C), H.M.England (Blackburn R), A.D.Burton (Newcastle Utd), L.Allchurch (Sheffield Utd), T.R.Vernon (Everton), R.W.Davies (Bolton W), I.J.Allchurch (Cardiff C), C.W.Jones (Spurs).

England: G.Banks (Leicester C); J.C.Armfield (Blackpool, captain),

Bobby Smith gets in a spectacular diving header but Rest of the World goalkeeper Lev Yashin saved his effort.

R.Wilson (Huddersfield T), G.Milne (Liverpool), M.Norman (Spurs), R.F.C.Moore (West Ham), T.L.Paine (Southampton), J.P.Greaves (Spurs), R.A.Smith (Spurs), G.E.Eastham (Arsenal), R.Charlton (Man Utd).

Half-time 0-1   Full-time 0-4

Ref: W.Brittle (Scotland)   Att: 48,250

THIS was the 18th occasion since the war that these two sides had met and the pattern of this game went the same way as many of the others. The passion and fire of the Red Dragons was in full evidence at the start and Wales gave their full commitment early on. England, meanwhile, fresh from their triumphant summer tour, had the perfect start to quell the excitement of the crowd.

Jimmy Greaves made a clean break down the left and eventually put over a centre beyond Hollins to Bobby Smith, who headed home with ease. The goal had come after five minutes and was a bitter disappointment to the fervent Welsh crowd. To their credit, however, they got behind their favourites and inspired their team to an hour of pressure.

Ivor Allchurch was the man at the heart of Welsh play and his promptings almost produced goals for Jones and Len Allchurch. Gordon Banks was in great form for England and his fine saves kept the lead intact.

Jones was very unlucky when one shot on the turn cannoned back off a post and Jimmy Armfield then rescued England with a fine saving tackle on Ivor Allchurch. Maurice Norman saved with his head from Jones again, the big centre-half being felled by the ferocity of the shot, but at half-time England still clung on to their lead.

Straight after the break, another near miss came for Wales when Vernon had a shot saved by the outstretched foot of Banks. England did have their moments in amongst this Welsh pressure, and Bobby Charlton, seeking the English scoring record, came close with a 20-yard screamer saved at full stretch by Hollins.

Jones had been a constant thorn to Armfield all afternoon and Ivor Allchurch

had controlled things but with 25 minutes to go, England produced the moment that turned the match their way. Norman cleared to George Eastham who, at last, began to put some thought into his passing. A lovely long diagonal pass found Smith who drew the last defender before squaring the ball inside to Greaves, who made it 2-0.

Inside 90 seconds England scored again. Gordon Milne passed to Greaves who glided to the right before laying on another easy goal for Smith. The Tottenham understanding that these two have was never more in evidence in international football than here.

The Welsh crowd were now silent and to rub salt into the wound, Charlton duly beat the record of Nat Lofthouse and Tom Finney by scoring his 31st England goal near the end. Charlton had several goes in a goalmouth scramble before finally lashing home at the third attempt. Finney, as it happens, was watching and applauded generously as his record went.

Until Ivor Allchurch tired, it had been a close-run thing but in the end heart and passion were not enough.

74th match v Wales.
Charlton's goal beat Lofthouse and Finney's total for his 31st goal.

England v Rest of the World Friendly

Played on Wednesday, 23 October 1963 at Wembley Stadium.

England: G.Banks (Leicester C); J.C.Armfield (Blackpool, captain), R.Wilson (Huddersfield T), G.Milne (Liverpool), M.Norman (Spurs), R.F.C.Moore (West Ham), T.L.Paine (Southampton), J.P.Greaves (Spurs), R.A.Smith (Spurs), G.E.Eastham (Arsenal), R.Charlton (Man Utd).

Rest of the World (FIFA): L.Yashin (USSR); D.Santos (Brazil), K.H.Schnellinger (West Germany), S.Pluskal (Czechoslovakia), J.Popluhár (Czechoslovakia), J.Masopust (Czechoslovakia), R.Kopaszewski (France), D.Law (Scotland), A.Di Stefano (Argentina, Colombia & Spain), E.Ferreira (Portugal),

F.Gento (Spain).
Subs: M.Šoškić (Yugoslavia) for Yashin; L.Eyzaguirre (Chile) for Santos; J.C.Baxter (Scotland) for Masopust; U.Seeler (West Germany) for Kopa; F.Puskás (Hungary & Spain) for Ferreira.

Half-time 0-0   Full-time 2-1

Ref: R.H.Davidson (Scotland) Att: 100,000

THE 100,000 people who attended this FA Centenary celebration match, witnessed a spectacle that was a fitting tribute to the occasion. The stars came from all over the world to show the English fans all that is best in this wonderful game, a game that England taught the world all those years ago. The Duke of Edinburgh and the Duke of Gloucester were the Royal guests and everything was set up for a perfect day.

Right from the kick-off all the players settled down to enjoy the game. Subtle skills and magical touches were soon in abundance and the crowd were revelling in the atmosphere. England rose to the occasion with a fine performance and no player impressed more than the enigmatic Jimmy Greaves. Three times in the first-half he tested the man who was arguably the greatest goalkeeper in the world, Yashin, to the full. Each time the big Russian's reflexes were equal to the shot.

Ray Wilson and Jimmy Armfield showed their class, resource and superb timing against the high talent of Kopa and Gento, whilst Gordon Milne covered acres of Wembley's lush turf linking with George Eastham.

The first half was goalless but certainly not without thrills. One superb moment came when Greaves, Bobby Charlton and Bobby Smith combined beautifully for Greaves to take Smith's wall pass perfectly, thread his way through the FIFA defence before firing a shot into the roof of the net from the narrowest of angles. It would have been one of the finest goals ever seen at Wembley but for one snag. The referee had whistled just before for an infringement and all that England got was a free-kick on the edge of the area.

The nearest that the visitors came to scoring was when the great Di Stefano

England players applaud the Rest of the World team after the FA Centenary game at Wembley in October 1963.

somehow contrived to miss a sitter from right in front of Gordon Banks. It was a miss that proved that even the greatest players are human.

Di Stefano held his head disbelievingly. If there was a flaw in the FIFA side it was in their finishing, but Greaves almost put England into the lead right on half-time, only for his left-foot shot to be nonchalantly punched away by Yashin.

After the break the FIFA side made five substitutions but with quality replacing quality there was no let up in the entertainment, although the crowd had to wait until the 70th minute before they at last saw a goal. It came after a Smith centre from the right found Greaves darting in to fire in a shot which was blocked. From the rebound Terry Paine reacted quickly and shot past Šoškić to a tumultuous roar of approval from the crowd.

There were more narrow squeaks at either end before, with just seven minutes to go, Law, combining brilliantly with Di Stefano and Puskás, turned sharply to shoot past Banks to make it 1-1. England then pushed forward, a Charlton special hit the post and Greaves chipped the ball over Šoškić, only to see his shot scrape the angle of post and crossbar. It was thrilling stuff and with three minutes left England made one final push to score a goal that gave them a famous and richly deserved victory.

Again Charlton hit a dipping, swerving shot, and although Šoškić parried the ball, he failed to hold it. That was fatal as it gave Greaves just the chance he needed to nip in and put the loose ball into the net. It was typical Greaves and rounded off a magnificent display which proved, in such company, that he was truly world class. Mind you, in this match everything was world class!

Footnote: Port Vale were 45 minutes late for their League game at Reading that evening. They had watched the match at Wembley and were then held up in a traffic jam on their way to Elm Park.

3rd match v FIFA.

England v Home Championship
Northern Ireland

Played on Wednesday, 20 November 1963 at Wembley Stadium.

England: G.Banks (Leicester C); J.C.Armfield (Blackpool, captain), R.A.Thomson (Wolves), G.Milne (Liverpool), M.Norman (Spurs), R.F.C.Moore (West Ham), T.L.Paine (Southampton), J.P.Greaves (Spurs), R.A.Smith (Spurs), G.E.Eastham (Arsenal), R.Charlton (Man Utd).

Northern Ireland: H.Gregg (Man Utd); E.J.Magill (Arsenal), J.Parke (Hibernian), M.Harvey (Sunderland), W.J.T.Neill (Arsenal), W.J.McCullough (Arsenal), W.L.Bingham (Port Vale), W.Humphries (Coventry C), S.J.Wilson (Falkirk), J.A.Crossan (Sunderland), M.J.Hill (Everton).

Half-time 4-1   Full-time 8-3
Ref: L.Callaghan (Wales)   Att: 53,000

THIS was England's sixth win in a row

since May and they treated the crowd to an exhilarating display of 'goal-power' football. All credit to the Irish, though, as despite the scoreline they contributed much to a first-class night of entertainment.

England continued where they had left off against the FIFA side with Gordon Milne and George Eastham masterly in the midfield of their 4-2-4 formation. The home side took the lead after just 100 seconds. Bobby Moore gave Bobby Charlton a pass from deep in his own half and the Manchester United man set off along the inside-right channel. He feinted and checked and beat two men before laying the perfect pass to Terry Paine, who beat Gregg with an angled shot with ease. It was a fine goal and one that set the pattern of the match.

Soon afterwards Jimmy Greaves hit a post before Wilson forced Gordon Banks into a good save at the other end. At this stage Ireland were making a fight of it and they nearly levelled the scores when Wilson latched on to a bad back-pass by Maurice Norman, only to be thwarted by

Northern Ireland goalkeeper Harry Gregg fails to stop Jimmy Greaves scoring one of his four goals during the Home International match at Wembley in November 1963.

new cap Bobby Thomson. (Yet another Bobby in a team that already had three; a good job Bobby Robson wasn't playing!)

The heavy rain was now causing the lush, green turf to cut up but on 20 minutes it did not stop England scoring again. A flowing move across the whole forward line ended with Greaves superbly beating Gregg with a good shot, a clever change of feet completely deceiving the goalkeeper. By now, Gregg was more and more involved in the action as the pressure mounted on his goal. After half an hour some wing wizardry by Paine ended with a deep cross to the far post. There, yet again, was Greaves, who trapped the ball, aimed one way and shot the other to beat Gregg all ends up. It was vintage stuff with Greaves at his most deadly in front of goal.

On 37 minutes, England made it 4-0 with another marvellous goal. This time Eastham flowed down the left, centred, and there was Paine to volley in a splendid shot. The crowd were revelling in all the excitement but they reserved their biggest cheer for just before half-time when Crossan's horizontal header past Banks' fingertips from Magill's cross pulled a goal back for Ireland.

After the break the flood continued, in goals and rain. Immediately Milne put Paine away and Bobby Smith headed a fifth goal. The Irish refused to surrender and Wilson hammered a fierce shot past Banks from Harvey's pass to make it 5-2. England were not to be denied, though, and turned on more power with half an hour to go. Milne and Eastham combined again to set Greaves away and once more another rocket zoomed into the roof of Gregg's net. Straight away Eastham and Jimmy Armfield traced an opening for Paine to score again, and then a lovely move between Moore, Paine and Smith enabled Greaves to score England's eighth and his own fourth.

The Irish did have one last word to say when Wilson forced the ball through a mass of England defenders following a corner, but on a night to remember England continued the revival that their fans are loving.

> 71st match v Northern Ireland.
> Debut for Thomson.
> Hat-trick by Paine
> Four goals for Greaves.
> *"My favourite memory of playing at Wembley was scoring a hat-trick against Northern Ireland."*
> Terry Paine

Scotland v England Home Championship

Played on Saturday, 11 April 1964 at Hampden Park, Glasgow.

Scotland: C.Forsyth (Kilmarnock); A.W.Hamilton (Dundee), J.Kennedy (Celtic), J.Greig (Rangers), W.McNeill (Celtic), J.C.Baxter (Rangers), W.Henderson (Rangers), J.A.White (Spurs), A.J.Gilzean (Dundee), D.Law (Man Utd), D.Wilson (Rangers).
England: G.Banks (Leicester C); J.C.Armfield (Blackpool, captain), R.Wilson (Huddersfield T), G.Milne (Liverpool), M.Norman (Spurs), R.F.C.Moore (West Ham), T.L.Paine (Southampton), R.Hunt (Liverpool),

Willie Henderson leads Scotland's lap of honour after England's 1-0 defeat at Hampden in April 1964.

J.J.Byrne (West Ham), G.E.Eastham (Arsenal), R.Charlton (Man Utd).

Half-time 0-0   Full-time 1-0
Ref: L.Horn (Holland)   Att: 133,245

THE huge crowd present at this game cheered ecstatically at 4.40pm after Scotland had beaten the Auld Enemy for the third time running. It had been a wet and stormy afternoon but the enthusiasm just could not be dampened. After all the lean years since 1947, it warmed the hearts of all true Scotsmen to see this victory.

There was a slow start to the game with both sides feeling their way. However, two excellent chances fell England's way in the first ten minutes. Both times Roger Hunt had the opening but alas, both times he wasted the opportunity. Each of those chances had been cleverly created and if either had gone in, then the whole complexion of the game may have altered.

As it was, Scotland grew in stature as play progressed. Baxter and Law gradually took command of their midfield battle with the predictable George Eastham and Gordon Milne, whilst Henderson caused Ray Wilson all sorts of problems down the Scottish right flank. The winger's trickery was a delight for the fans.

Early promise from Bobby Charlton and Terry Paine soon faded and, in fact, Charlton had one of those ineffectual games that tends to frustrate the onlooker. But England held on until the break with Bobby Moore in his most immaculate form. More than once the path to England's goal was blocked by one of Moore's timely interceptions and he was given good support by Maurice Norman.

After the interval, Scotland's possession and pressure increased. Baxter, polished and unhurried, controlled the pace of the game with Law his unrelenting partner. Gilzean, always a threat, looked increasingly dangerous and Davie Wilson was giving Jimmy Armfield as torrid a time as Henderson was giving his marker. Still, though, the clever play of Moore and Norman managed to nurse England through 72 minutes of Scottish pressure.

At that moment, the English armour was finally pierced.

Twice earlier, England had escaped penalty appeals against Ray Wilson and Moore, and they were again lucky when Gilzean appeared to be impeded by Armfield. But instead of getting a free-kick on the edge of the area the Dutch referee awarded Scotland a corner. Davie Wilson curled in the kick and, appropriately, Gilzean leapt high to beat Gordon Banks and Norman to the ball to head home. The Hampden Roar was deafening.

A last-minute header by Norman from Paine's cross almost made a mockery of the result which Scotland thoroughly deserved. England's only other worthwhile chance had come midway through the half. Johnny Byrne's quick throw enabled Paine to get to the by-line for the one and only time of the match. He pulled the ball back to Charlton, who just delayed his shot a fraction allowing McNeill the chance to block. It was a richly deserved victory for Scotland.

> 81st match v Scotland.

England v Uruguay Friendly

Played on Wednesday, 6 May 1964 at Wembley Stadium.

England: G.Banks (Leicester C); G.R.Cohen (Fulham), R.Wilson (Huddersfield T), G.Milne (Liverpool), M.Norman (Spurs), R.F.C.Moore (West Ham, captain), T.L.Paine (Southampton), J.P.Greaves (Spurs), J.J.Byrne (West Ham), G.E.Eastham (Arsenal), R.Charlton (Man Utd).
Uruguay: W.Taibo (Wanderers); W.Martinez (Rampla Juniors), N.Diaz (Wanderers), H.Cincunegui (Danubio), A.Pereira (Cerro), R.Pavoni (Defensor), N.Flores (Defensor), J.C.Cortés (Cerro), A.Spencer (Peñarol), R.Gil (Rampla Juniors), J.Pintos (Cerro).

Half-time 1-0   Full-time 2-1
Ref: I.Zsolt (Hungary)   Att: 54,000

England skipper Bobby Moore and Uruguay's Martinez before the match at Wembley in May 1964. Two years later the sides would open the World Cup finals in England.

THIS was England's first-ever victory over Uruguay, but this Wembley match should have been won more convincingly by the home team. Uruguay were a pale shadow of some of their illustrious predecessors and were on their best behaviour after their violent match in Belfast seven days earlier.

Both sides began cautiously and although the Uruguayans produced attractive approach play, the final thrust was not there. Pereira was at the hub of most of the visitor's best attacks and he worked hard for his team.

But in the 20th minute, a lovely move between Bobby Moore and Bobby Charlton gave Jimmy Greaves the chance to fire in a good shot. It looked a goal all the way until Pavoni appeared from nowhere to head the ball away. A short while later, Pavoni was there again blocking a goal-bound shot by Johnny Byrne after a clever flick by Greaves. Byrne then saw another effort tipped against the crossbar and the centre-forward was enjoying a lively game.

There were other close calls under the Uruguayan crossbar before, at last, two minutes before the interval, England made the breakthrough their play deserved. Greaves, inevitably perhaps, showed some lovely footwork before putting an inch perfect pass through to Terry Paine. Paine flicked it first time inside and there was Byrne with the most delicate of touches to glide the ball past Taibo for a delightful goal.

Almost immediately after the break England went two up. Charlton centred,

Johnny Byrne scores the first of his two goals against the Uruguayans.

Greaves pulled the ball down with consummate ease, before allowing Byrne, on the half-turn, to score with his left foot.

England continued to press, although their attacks continually broke down because the final pass went astray. They also persisted in feeding the wrong type

of passes into the inside trio of Greaves, Byrne and George Eastham. With three small players such as these, it was no use putting in a continuous stream of high balls, which is what England kept doing. Also, Paine tended to overdo the dribbling and Pavoni had the beating of him.

With 20 minutes to go, Uruguay stepped up their pace and began a fight-back. Spencer, a lazy looking long-legged player in the mould of Portugal's Eusébio, took a flick from the hard-working Cortés, only to head straight at Gordon Banks. At the other end, Greaves almost made it 3-0 but he just failed to reach Paine's cross as England responded.

But in the 75th minute, Uruguay did pull a goal back. A lovely triangular move between Cortés, Gil and Spencer ended with the latter scoring.

In the end, England held on to win and although on paper it looks a close game, they had more in hand than the score suggested. Having said that, it was not one of their most convincing displays, despite some good individual performances and a promising start to the international career of full-back George Cohen.

3rd match v Uruguay.
Debut for Cohen.
50th cap for Charlton.

Portugal v England   Friendly

Played on Sunday, 17 May 1964 at the National Stadium, Lisbon.

Portugal: A.Costa Pereira (Benfica); A.Festa (FC Porto), F.Cruz (Benfica), M.Coluña (Benfica), G.Figueiredo (Benfica), V.Lucas (Belenenses), J.A.Almeida (Benfica), E.Ferreira (Benfica), J.Torres (Benfica), C.Pinto (FC Porto), A.Simões (Benfica).
Sub: H.da Silva (FC Porto) for Pinto.

England: G.Banks (Leicester C); G.R.Cohen (Fulham), R.Wilson (Huddersfield T), G.Milne (Liverpool), M.Norman (Spurs), R.F.C.Moore (West Ham, captain), P.Thompson (Liverpool), J.P.Greaves (Spurs), J.J.Byrne (West Ham), G.E.Eastham (Arsenal), R.Charlton (Man Utd).

Half-time 1-2   Full-time 3-4
Ref: J.Gardeazabal Garay (Spain)
                          Att: 46,000

THIS special match between these two firm friends of international football was organised to help celebrate the 50th Anniversary of the Portuguese FA. To do full justice to the occasion, both sides produced a marvellous display of open, attacking football.

It was some 17 years earlier that Messrs Matthews, Finney, Lawton, Mannion and Co hit ten goals in this same glorious setting of Lisbon's National Stadium. From the first whistle, the game was a thriller with England showing some exceptional flair.

Young Peter Thompson, winning his first cap, was a lively and enterprising winger who turned Cruz inside out. Gordon Milne, his Liverpool teammate, was a tireless provider in midfield, and George Eastham combined that with some superb imagination in his play. Even the Portuguese fans were to acclaim some of Eastham's touches.

The match exploded into goal action in the 17th minute. A corner by Simões was headed down by the giant Torres and Gordon Banks dived but could not hold

the ball. In rushed Torres to follow up and shoot home.

Almost at once England were level. A clever move between Jimmy Greaves and Johnny Byrne gave Thompson the chance to go outside Cruz and centre for Bobby Charlton to roar in and shoot his 32nd goal for England, a new record.

The action continued at a frantic pace and just before the half-hour, Banks turned away a powerful header by Eusébio. England responded immediately to that with a superb attack. Milne, Greaves and Eastham combined effectively and when Greaves chipped the ball finally to Byrne, the West Ham player calmly stroked it wide of Costa Pereira to give his team a 2-1 half-time lead. Byrne had missed an identical chance early on, but had really impressed with his play and poor Germano had had a torrid time trying to contain him.

When Portugal reappeared for the second half, Hernani had been brought on as a replacement for Pinto, and soon the game exploded again with another burst of goals.

Simões put in a cross and Torres leapt, apparently into the clouds, to head the ball past Banks. Maurice Norman was no midget, but Torres towered over the Spurs man. Soon afterwards, Portugal regained the lead following a mistake by Banks. The goalkeeper missed a cross by Augusto and Eusébio crashed in Torres's side flick to make it 3-2. At this stage Portugal had upped their pace with Eusébio and Coluna gaining command of the midfield.

With the temperature now in the upper '70s, the situation called for all of England's fighting qualities. They responded to the challenge magnificently as Milne and Eastham fought for every ball like tigers. A move they had started ended with George Cohen centring from the right in the 60th minute. Once again, there was Byrne, sharp as a nail, to shoot home.

Three-all and everything to play for. Almost at once, Portugal went close again with the ever-dangerous Torres sweeping a shot against Banks' post. As it happened, though, that was the last threatening moment to the English goal as the visitors, showing remarkable resilience, had the better of the latter stages of this superb game.

Charlton missed a sitter but with only two minutes left on the watch the Manchester United man left his mark again when his miscued shot rebounded to Byrne. The centre-forward was hemmed-in on all sides by defenders, but showing great awareness he coolly chipped a shot into the top corner to complete his own marvellous hat-trick and clinch the result for England.

The style of this match brought the memories flooding back and Stan Matthews and Tom Finney would definitely have approved. Every England player could be proud of his part in an exhilarating international.

8th match v Portugal.
Debut for Thompson.
Hat-trick by Byrne.
Portugal's Figueiredo also known as 'Germano'; Lucas as 'Vicente'; Almeida as 'José Augusto'; Ferreira as 'Eusébio'; da Silva as 'Hernani'.

Republic of Ireland v England   Friendly

Played on Sunday, 24 May 1964 at Dalymount Park, Dublin.

Republic of Ireland: N.M.Dwyer (Swansea T); A.P.Dunne (Man Utd), N.Cantwell (Man Utd), F.Strahan (Shelbourne), W.Browne (Bohemians), M.McGrath (Blackburn R), M.J.Giles (Leeds Utd), M.A.McEvoy (Blackburn R), E.Bailham (Shamrock R), P.Ambrose (Shamrock R), J.Haverty (Millwall).
Sub: R.Whelan (St Patrick's) for Haverty

England: A.K.Waiters (Blackpool); G.R.Cohen (Fulham), R.Wilson (Huddersfield T), G.Milne (Liverpool), R.Flowers (Wolves), R.F.C.Moore (West Ham, captain), P.Thompson (Liverpool), J.P.Greaves (Spurs), J.J.Byrne (West Ham), G.E.Eastham (Arsenal), R.Charlton (Man Utd).

Half-time 1-2   Full-time 1-3
Ref: R.H.Davidson (Scotland) Att: 45,000

THIS was a very different style of match to England's previous game, in Portugal, being scrappy and disjointed. They never reached the same dizzy heights in Dublin as they had in Lisbon, but they always had enough to beat the battling Irishmen.

England now had to adapt to a far more traditional opponent and gone was the continental man-to-man play favoured last weekend. Having said that, there was still enough to encourage England fans into believing the side was beginning to knit together.

The Irish began like demons. Roared on by their passionate crowd they tore into England's defence. Unaffected by a third-minute ankle injury to Haverty, which necessitated him being replaced by Whelan, they put all the pressure on England. However, the visitors responded perfectly to this pressure by scoring in the eighth minute with their first positive attack on Dwyer's goal.

A shot by the previous week's hat-trick hero, Johnny Byrne, was blocked but George Eastham was on the spot to volley home the rebound. That gave England the tonic they needed and the three inside-forwards, in particular, were prominent.

Browne had terrible problems in containing the lively Byrne and after 22 minutes the centre-forward scored England's second goal. Gordon Milne put Jimmy Greaves clear on the left and when the centre came over, Byrne scored, although it took him three attempts before he finally forced the ball past Dwyer.

This goal prompted the Irish to make a tactical switch, moving Browne to full-back and Cantwell to the middle of the defence. Some of the England approach play was a joy to watch at this stage with Milne, Greaves, Byrne and Eastham always involved. Unfortunately, with a two-goal lead behind them, they tended to relax and dwell on the ball for too long. Peter Thompson was guilty of this and as the game wore on Bobby Charlton too often wandered into the middle causing the team to lose its shape.

What was really needed was for Charlton to stay wide and therefore stretch the home defence using the whole width of the pitch.

As a result of this tactical error the Irish were allowed to claw their way back into

Tony Waiters, played the first of his five games for England at Dalymount Park, Dublin.

USA v England
Friendly

Played on Wednesday, 27 May 1964 at Randall's Island, New York.

USA: U.Schwart (New York Hota); I.Borobiak (Ukranian Nationals, Philadelphia), A.Racz (Ukranian Nationals, Philadelphia), H.Rick (New York Hota), J.Garcia (New York Hota), C.Horvath (New York Hungaria), M.Noha (Ukranian Nationals, Philadelphia), W.Chyzowych (Ukranian Nationals, Philadelphia), A.Maté (New York Hungaria), E.Murphy (Chicago Maroons), R.Wild (New York Hota).

England: G.Banks (Leicester C); G.R. Cohen (Fulham), R.A.Thomson (Wolves), M.A.Bailey (Wolves), M.Norman (Spurs), R.Flowers (Wolves, captain), T.L.Paine (Southampton), R.Hunt (Liverpool), F.Pickering (Everton), G.E.Eastham (Arsenal), P.Thompson (Liverpool).
Sub: R.Charlton (Man Utd) for Eastham.

Half-time 0-3   Full-time 0-10
Ref: R.Morgan (Canada)   Att: 5,062

BARELY 5,000 fans were gathered in the Randall's Island Stadium to see England try for more revenge against the USA for that infamous defeat in the 1950 World Cup at Belo Horizonte, Brazil. This time those fans were to witness what the fans all those years ago were expected to see, England trouncing the opposition.

The States team was a real hotch-potch of nationalities with only Chyzowych, a born and bred American. From the first whistle, though, England tore them apart. Alf Ramsey had made several changes for the game, but after only three and a half minutes they opened the scoring when Liverpool's Roger Hunt scored.

One of the new caps, Fred Pickering of Everton, made it 2-0 after six minutes and that Liverpool rivalry went down well with one small section of the crowd. About a dozen crew members of the Liverpool registered *RMS Sylvania* jumped for joy as they screamed the names of their 'local' lads! The ship was docked in New York.

Before half-time, Hunt had added a third goal. That came in the 22nd minute but it was after the break that the real goal avalanche began. On 47 minutes, Pickering scored to make it 4-0, and 2-2 between the Merseyside rivals. Terry Paine then weighed in with a goal two minutes later before Hunt completed his hat-trick after 53 minutes.

The USA had no answer to it all and George Eastham, in particular, had a field day, dominating the midfield play. Sadly, Eastham had to go off injured midway through the half and Bobby Charlton was able to join the action, immediately settling into the rhythm of the game.

Hunt made it 7-0 in the 64th minute and then Charlton got in to the scoring act with a goal four minutes later. One more minute had elapsed when Paine took the score on to 9-0. There was still 16 minutes to go, when Pickering put the score into double figures and a new international scoring record looked very much on for this rampant England team. Alas, despite several near-misses and good attempts, it was not to be and the English

Above: Bobby Thomson, the Wolves full-back who played eight times for England. *Below:* Roger Hunt, Liverpool's great striker who scored four goals for England in New York.

lads were bitterly disappointed afterwards at not beating the record.

All credit must go to the Americans as at no time did they completely surrender and once or twice they had Gordon Banks hopping about on his goal-line. Garcia was their best player but it really was men against boys and the ghost of 1950 was definitely laid to rest this time once and for all . . .or was it?

By the way, you will have noticed that Hunt won the private battle of Merseyside with Pickering by four goals to three.

4th match v USA.
Debuts for Bailey and Pickering.
Debut hat-trick by Pickering.
Four goals for Hunt.
Flowers captain for first time.

---

the match and more was now seen of their attack. England's defence was often caught too square and three minutes from half-time, Strahan moved through to pull a goal back. The wing-half picked the ball up inside his own half and ran at England's defenders. Ron Flowers, Bobby Moore and Ray Wilson all back-peddalled without making a challenge and they were punished when Strahan fired in his shot. He miscued his effort but luck was on his side as the ball squirmed past new cap Tony Waiters.

After the interval, Ireland again began the half in storming fashion. Strahan twice more went close as the shirt-sleeved crowd revelled in the action and the warmth of the day. But as in the first half, England came up with the perfect response.

Probably the best move of the match was begun by Milne in the 55th minute. His pass to Thompson set the move in motion down the right. The ball flowed back to Milne, inside to Byrne and on to Eastham, who had moved out to the right. When Eastham's cross came over, Greaves was there to apply the finishing touch in his best style.

For the rest of the match, other chances fell England's way with George Cohen shooting just wide and Greaves spurning two easy chances with his head. There was a general air of frustration at these unconvincing attacks, but England gave little away at the back. Flowers, on his recall, despite a lot of effort, never looked comfortable as Moore's partner.

England now went on to a four-match summer tour of the Americas where, amongst others, they faced mighty Brazil.

5th match v the Republic of Ireland.
Debut for Waiters.

Brazil v
England Four-Team Tournament

Played on Saturday, 30 May 1964 in the Maracana Stadium, Rio de Janeiro.

Brazil: G.dos Santos (Santos); C.A.Torres (Santos), R.Costa (Botafogo), J.Camargo (Santos), H.Brito (Vasco da Gama), R.Dias (São Paulo), J.Botelho (Palmeiras), G.Oliveira (Botafogo), E.Neto (Palmeiras), E.Arantes (Santos), R.L.Amorim (Palmeiras).

England: A.K.Waiters (Blackpool); G.R.Cohen (Fulham), R.Wilson (Huddersfield T), G.Milne (Liverpool), M.Norman (Spurs), R.F.C.Moore (West Ham, captain), P.Thompson (Liverpool), J.P.Greaves (Spurs), J.J.Byrne (West Ham), G.E.Eastham (Arsenal), R.Charlton (Man Utd).

Half-time 1-0   Full-time 5-1
Ref: P.Schwinte (France)   Att: 110,000

IN a four-team tournament to celebrate the 50th anniversary of the Brazilian FA, England were faced with the daunting task of taking on the host nation in front of well over 100,000 people in the magnificent Maracana Stadium. For an hour they more than held their own but in the final third of the game they fell to the superb magic of a man called Pelé at his extraordinary best.

England began confidently and with Maurice Norman, Bobby Moore and Ray Wilson in outstanding form they contained the Brazilians in some style. Johnny Byrne showed some lovely touches, although he did miss a couple of good chances from George Eastham's promptings. These were vital misses and probably the key to the eventual downfall of the visitors.

Peter Thompson, Bobby Charlton and Jimmy Greaves all performed well and Gordon Milne was always in the thick of the action. But just before the interval, Pelé began to make his mark by setting up the new brilliant young winger, Rinaldo, to shoot past Tony Waiters. It was a blow for England, losing a goal so close to half-time, especially as they had played their hearts out. But undaunted they came straight back after the interval to equalize through Jimmy Greaves. A typical piece of opportunism gave him his goal.

The next few minutes saw England pushing forward well. Eastham fired in a fine shot, only to see Gilmar push the ball on to the crossbar, and then twice more Byrne and Greaves came within a whisker of snatching the lead. Alas, all this was but a dream as in a devastating 15-minute spell which began on the hour, Brazil, and in particular, Pelé, took the game by the scruff of the neck. The Brazilian legend was unbelievable.

First he fed a pass to Rinaldo again and a cracking left-foot shot left Waiters groping at thin air as the ball flew into the top corner. Before Pelé could inflict more damage, England made a spirited attack that almost brought another equalizer. Thompson's fierce shot was blocked by Gilmar and the ball rebounded to Greaves. The Spurs striker got in a shot but somehow the Brazilians scrambled it from the line. From the clearance, the ball fell at Pelé's magical feet and the number-

ten set off on an amazing dribble that went fully 40 yards before he finished off in style with a rasping shot wide of Waiters. It was a memorable goal.

Straight away, George Cohen was fouled as he broke down the right. The free-kick was blocked, Pelé broke away again and gave Julinho the pass to make it 4-1. It must be said that Julinho looked blatantly offside and the free-kick which started it all should never have been awarded as Cohen would have had a vital advantage had the referee played on. But there was no denying the deadly breakaway instigated by Pelé.

The 'Black Pearl' continued to shine brightly and in the last minute the England defence, by now in a desperate state, up-ended Pelé on the edge of the area and from the free-kick Dias chipped in the fifth goal.

Though the scoreline slightly flatters Brazil the scintillating play of Julinho, Dias, Gerson, Rinado and of course Pelé, was always going to make it tough for England. In the final analysis though the main difference between the sides had to be Pelé. The man was a marvel and on this form he could take on the world. Some of his play was sheer poetry.

> 6th match v Brazil.
> Brazil's dos Santos also known as 'Gilmar'; Torres as 'Carlos Alberto'; Costa as 'Rildo'; Camargo as 'Joel'; Botelho as 'Julinho'; Oliveira as 'Gerson'; Neto as 'Vavá'; Arantes as 'Pelé'; Amorim as 'Rinaldo'.
> *"One of the funniest incidents in my time with the squad came at a swimming pool in Rio when some of the players threw Jimmy Greaves in, only to find he couldn't swim!"*
> Terry Paine

Portugal v
England Four-Team Tournament

Played on Thursday, 4 June 1964 at the Pacaembu Stadium, São Paulo, Brazil.

Portugal: A.Lopes (FC Porto); A.Festa (FC Porto), P.Gomes (Sporting Lisbon), F.Mendes (Sporting Lisbon), J.A.Baptista (Sporting Lisbon), J.C.Silva (Sporting Lisbon), J.A.Almeida (Benfica), E.Ferreira (Benfica), J.Torres (Benfica), M.Coluña (Benfica), F.Peres (Belenenses). Sub: V.Lucas (Belenenses) for Mendes.

England: G.Banks (Leicester C); R.A.Thomson (Wolves), R.Wilson (Huddersfield T), R.Flowers (Wolves), M.Norman (Spurs), R.F.C.Moore (West Ham, captain), T.L.Paine (Southampton), J.P.Greaves (Spurs), J.J.Byrne (West Ham), R.Hunt (Liverpool), P.Thompson (Liverpool).

Half-time 1-0   Full-time 1-1
Ref: A.Marques (Brazil)   Att: 70,000

PLAYING against Portugal at Wembley or even in Lisbon had always been a pleasurable occasion for England, but here in the volatile atmosphere amongst Portugal's South American ancestors it was a very different proposition. Also, the Pacaembu Stadium has probably the worst pitch ever to have staged a full international. As a result the game never flowed and in fact the stadium erupted

Ron Flowers, scored an unfortunate own-goal for Portugal in Brazil.

20 minutes from the end when Portugal had a goal disallowed.

But we are jumping ahead of ourselves. In the first half, England saw plenty of the ball and had the better chances. Roger Hunt had a goal disallowed after 15 minutes for offside and Jimmy Greaves was desperately unlucky when his brilliant shot struck the crossbar.

Unfortunately the midfield subtlety of George Eastham was missed and the link between defence and attack was not there. But there was plenty of heart, though, with both full-backs looking solid, Maurice Norman in commanding form and Ron Flowers always a powerhouse in midfield. Greaves was sharp up front but chances were once again lost at vital times.

Portugal, meanwhile, brought on Vicente for Mendes after half an hour's play and just before the interval they opened the scoring, albeit against the general run of play.

As Johnny Byrne was undergoing repairs on the touch-line for an injury, a quick throw-in caught England napping. A fast attack developed and Peres fired in a speculative shot. Unfortunately, for England the ball struck Flowers and was deflected into the net for an own-goal. The crowd went wild and rockets illuminated the night sky.

After the break, England battled on. Terry Paine was very unlucky when he, too, saw a shot strike the Portuguese crossbar and with all their attacks coming to nothing it seemed that England would never find a way through. But on the hour their good play deservedly gave them some reward. A super move began with Gordon Banks finding Byrne. He, in turn, passed to Greaves and then a lovely long through-ball was swept home by Hunt for an excellent goal. It was met by a stunned silence from the crowd.

Everything now to play for, but on 70 minutes came the incident that won few friends for Portugal and did their image no good at all. Coluña, quite rightly, had a goal disallowed for offside by the excellent Brazilian referee. Sadly, the Portuguese players took exception to his decision and went berserk. They hounded and chased the unfortunate referee for a full five minutes whilst a barrage of fireworks and noise erupted from the terraces.

As a result of all this mayhem Torres was sent off for manhandling the official and this only added fuel to the already ugly mood of the crowd. Luckily, there was high wire fencing keeping the crowd away from the pitch, otherwise the situation would have been even more nasty.

When play finally restarted, the atmosphere was very tense. Byrne had a 'goal' disallowed five minutes from the end but, as in Hunt's case, earlier the England lads took it in a sporting manner.

> 9th match v Portugal.
> Own-goal by Flowers.
> Torres sent off for Portugal.
> Portugal's Lopes also known as 'Americo'; Silva as 'José Carlos'; Ferreira as 'Eusébio'; Lucas as 'Vicente'.

Argentina v England Four-Team Tournament

Played on Saturday, 6 June 1964 at the Maracana Stadium, Rio de Janeiro, Brazil.

Argentina: A.Carrizo (River Plate); C.Simeone (Boca Juniors), R.Viertez (River Plate), A.U.Rattín (Boca Juniors), J.Ramos-Delgado (River Plate), J.Vidal (Huracán), D.Onega (River Plate), A.Rendo (San Lorenzo), J.Prospitti (Independiente), Angel Rojas (Boca Juniors), R.Telch (San Lorenzo).
Sub: N.Chaldu (Benfield) for Prospitti.

England: G.Banks (Leicester C); R.A.Thomson (Wolves), R.Wilson (Huddersfield T), G.Milne (Liverpool), M.Norman (Spurs), R.F.C.Moore (West Ham, captain), P.Thompson (Liverpool), J.P.Greaves (Spurs), J.J.Byrne (West Ham), G.E.Eastham (Arsenal), R.Charlton (Man Utd).

Half-time: 0-0   Full-time: 1-0
Ref: L.Horn (Holland)   Att: 95,000

ARGENTINA made sure of winning this four-nation tournament when they beat England by the only goal. It was a narrow victory, won with a goal which looked offside, and disappointing for an England side who could have won, had they taken their chances.

In the opening half, England put in many positive attacks but their finishing did not match their good approach play. Peter Thompson, the one big England success of the tournament, had another fine game and repeatedly turned Viertez inside out. The crowd loved him and were chanting, 'Garrincha, Garrincha', after some of his spectacular runs. That was in honour of Brazil's legendary flying winger. Alas, England could not apply the finishing touch to the many centres that Thompson put over with Jimmy Greaves in particular the chief culprit.

In fact, all three inside-men, Greaves, Johnny Byrne and George Eastham, had poor games, probably an effect of a long, hard season. Bobby Charlton made some spirited dashes down the other wing but again there was no reward from his efforts. Argentina based their game on a rock solid defence in which Rattín and goalkeeper Carrizo were outstanding.

All this proved frustrating for England and the crowd alike who wanted an English victory to help Brazil win the tournament. And it was not just a dream, England created their chances, none more so than the gem that presented itself seven minutes into the second half.

A quick, clever more down the right put Thompson clear. The Argentine defence was split but when Thompson's cross came over, it was Greaves, of all people, who fluffed a golden chance with the goal gaping. If England had scored then, they probably would have gone on to win. It was a mighty let-off for the Argentinians but to rub salt into the wound they then scored what proved to be the winning goal with just 15 minutes to go.

A quick break from defence enabled the clever master technician and tactician, Rendo to set Chaldu, an early substitute for Prospitti, free down the left wing. If he was not offside then Rojas certainly was when he was found with the final pass. Alas, play was not stopped on either occasion and Rojas went on to score. England now looked tired and dispirited because, despite all their hard work, they had failed in the most vital area and if one lesson has to be learned from this tour then it was to take the chances when they come along. For the rest of this match the Argentines were content to play the ball around in small triangles as England gamely tried to regain possession. At the final whistle, as Argentina did a lap of honour, England trudged wearily off.

Their long season was now over and they could reflect on what they had learned from the trip. If nothing else it was all good experience.

> 4th match v Argentina.

Northern Ireland v England Home International

Played on Saturday, 3 October 1964 at Windsor Park, Belfast.

Northern Ireland: P.A.Jennings (Spurs); E.J.Magill (Arsenal), A.R.Elder (Burnley), M.Harvey (Sunderland), W.J.T.Neill (Arsenal), W.J.McCullough (Arsenal), G.Best (Man Utd), J.A.Crossan (Sunderland), S.J.Wilson (Falkirk), J.C.McLaughlin (Swansea T), R.S.Braithwaite (Middlesbrough).

England: G.Banks (Leicester C); G.R.Cohen (Fulham), R.A.Thomson (Wolves), G.Milne (Liverpool), M.Norman (Spurs), R.F.C.Moore (West Ham, captain), T.L.Paine (Southampton), J.P.Greaves (Spurs), F.Pickering (Everton), R.Charlton (Man Utd), P.Thompson (Liverpool).

Half-time 0-4   Full-time 3-4
Ref: W.Brittle (Scotland)   Att: 58,000

THE phrase, 'a game of two halves', is often used in football reporting but never has it been more apt than in this international at Windsor Park. For the first

Jimmy Greaves, another England hat-trick, this time against Northern Ireland at Windsor Park.

45 minutes it was all England. Ireland could do nothing against the lethal finishing of Jimmy Greaves as the visitors rattled in four goals in the first 27 minutes. It looked like a massacre was on the cards, but after the break it was all so very different.

England scored early on when Fred Pickering showed his mobility by shooting home from Terry Paine's cross. The build-up had been excellent starting with George Cohen, before moving on sweetly to Paine, Gordon Milne, Bobby Charlton, Milne again and then to Paine. Then, in a superb 12-minute spell of intense England pressure the score went from 1-0 to 4-0 with a magnificent Greaves hat-trick.

First of all he stole in, typically, to poach a goal out of nothing after he had taken a headed pass from Pickering, strode through the middle, and shot past Jennings. Then Greaves pounced on a mistake by Neill to steal another goal, and finally he was on the end of another Paine-Milne combination to score his 35th international goal and thus regain the record currently held by Charlton.

It was a superb burst by the Spurs star and the quickness of his feet sometimes deceives the eye. The Irish were stunned and as they trooped off at half-time they looked down and out.

But what a transformation in the second half! The Irish fought back splendidly aided and abetted by some slackness in England's play. Early in the half they pulled a goal back. Crossan's centre from the right was met by a flashing header from Wilson which flew past Gordon Banks and into the top corner. It was just the tonic that the home side needed and from that moment it was all Ireland.

Banks suddenly found that he was the busiest player on the field as his defenders crumbled around him. The mercurial Best began to cast his spell on the game, Crossan and Harvey captured the midfield from the previously dominant Charlton and Milne, and McLaughlin became a bundle of energy and mischief to the England defence.

England did make things worse for themselves with some uncharacteristic defensive blunders and on the hour, Milne's mistake was fully punished by McLaughlin. Now the Irish really had their tails up and with 15 minutes to go it seemed as though the whole of Ireland erupted as a third goal was pulled back.

Again it was McLaughlin, and again it was a mistake, this time by Banks, that brought about the goal. It was Banks' one error in an otherwise fine display but it gave Ireland just the impetus they needed for a final assault. Somehow, though, England held on, mainly thanks to Banks, and Northern Ireland's brave fight-back was finally halted by the referee's closing whistle.

The tactical change that Ireland had made at half-time, that is switching Wilson into a more deep-lying role, certainly had the right effect and poor Maurice Norman had a nightmare second half. Even the usually super-cool Bobby Moore had had his feathers ruffled as the Best-inspired Irish side came within a whisker of a most famous comeback.

> 72nd match v Northern Ireland.
> Hat-trick by Greaves.

England v Belgium
Friendly

Played on Wednesday, 21 October 1964 at Wembley Stadium.

England: A.K.Waiters (Blackpool); G.R.Cohen (Fulham), R.A.Thomson (Wolves), G.Milne (Liverpool), M.Norman (Spurs), R.F.C.Moore (West Ham, captain), P.Thompson (Liverpool), J.P.Greaves (Spurs), F.Pickering (Everton), T.F.Venables (Chelsea), A.T.Hinton (Nottm Forest).
Belgium: J.Nicolay (Standard Liège); G.Heylens (RSC Anderlecht), J.Cornelis (RSC Anderlecht), G.Sulon (RFC Liège), L.Vebiest (RSC Anderlecht), J.Plaskie (RSC Anderlecht), F.Vermeyen (Lierse SK), J.Jurion (RSC Anderlecht), P.Van Himst (RSC Anderlecht), P.Van den Berg (Union, Bruxelles), W.Puis (RSC Anderlecht).

Half-time 1-2   Full-time 2-2
Ref: C.Lobello (Italy)   Att: 45,000

THIS was a disappointing display by England, who came very close to defeat against a much-improved Belgium side. The Belgians showed some lovely skills and at times they had England rocking but, alas for the visitors, they failed in their finishing and let their hosts off the hook.

Right from the start, the visitors looked more organised and their fluent 4-2-4 formation proved effective. Their play revolved around the two midfield stars, the bespectacled captain Jurion and the clever Sulon. By comparison, England seemed to have no real plan and it came as no surprise when Belgium took the lead with a well-worked goal.

Cornelis came through from the back on a long and complicated, but controlled run. After he played a one-two with Van den Berg, his shot smashed into the roof of Tony Waiters' net before the goalkeeper could move. It was no more than Belgium deserved.

At this point, Waiters was the hero for England making fine saves from Jurion, Vermeyen and Van Himst. The latter was an artist and he gave Maurice Norman another very difficult night. Van den Berg gave him good support and both the wingers looked good. However, on the half-hour — and totally against the run of play — England drew level with an excellent goal.

There was a quick break from defence as Terry Venables won a midfield tackle and cleverly found Jimmy Greaves. Greaves passed to Fred Pickering, who at first lost control but recovered quickly to shoot home high past Nicolay. It was a tonic England badly needed but they still could not find any rhythm and just before the interval Belgium deservedly regained the lead. This time Van Himst hit a shot past Waiters, although there was a deflection off George Cohen.

The second half continued in the same vein with Belgium showing all the class and guile. England struggled continually to find a pattern with only Venables occasionally looking as though he could match the Belgians' craft. His vision was there for all to see, but unfortunately his teammates failed to come up with the necessary support. For a while it looked as if Belgium would become the third continental side to win at Wembley.

But suddenly, with 20 minutes to go, England somehow found another equalizer. Fittingly, Venables was at the start of the move which a clever pass which set Alan Hinton free. The outside-left moved forward and cracked in a shot which flew past Nicolay after taking a deflection off of Vebiest.

It was a slightly fortunate goal to earn an even more fortunate draw. The cold night air had kept the crowd down to 45,000. It was probably just as well, as England were a long way from their best.

> 15th match v Belgium.
> Debut for Venables.

England v Wales
Home Championship

Played on Wednesday, 18 November 1964 at Wembley Stadium.

England: A.K.Waiters (Blackpool); G.R.Cohen (Fulham), R.A.Thomson (Wolves), M.A.Bailey (Wolves), R.Flowers (Wolves, captain), G.M.Young (Sheffield Wed), P.Thompson (Liverpool), R.Hunt (Liverpool), F.Wignall (Nottm Forest), J.J.Byrne (West Ham), A.T.Hinton (Nottm Forest).
Wales: A.H.Millington (Crystal P); S.G.Williams (Southampton), G.E.Williams (West Brom), W.T.Hennessey (Birmingham C), H.M.England (Blackburn R), B.G.Hole (Cardiff C), R.R.Rees (Coventry C), R.T.Davies (Norwich C), R.W.Davies (Bolton W), I.J.Allchurch (Cardiff C), C.W.Jones (Spurs).

Half-time 1-0   Full-time 2-1
Ref: T.Mitchell (Northern Ireland)
                              Att: 40,000

ONLY 40,000 people turned up for this home international and the half-empty terraces made for a distinct lack of atmosphere. The teams served up a poor match for the faithfuls who did attend and England, in particular, appeared to have mounting problems.

A very experimental side looked just that as England struggled to find the rhythm and cohesion so often missing recently. Mike Bailey looked the most impressive of the players that came into the team and he worked tirelessly to try to inject some pattern into England's play. Unfortunately, he could have made good use of the injured Terry Venables, had he been available. As it was, playing Johnny Byrne at inside-left seemed to have no improving effect on the side.

England did manage to take the lead after 18 minutes. Bailey did well, stretching the whole Welsh defence with a lovely long pass from right to left. The ball reached Alan Hinton and the winger moved forward at speed and fired in a shot. The ball came back off a defender and Hinton was able to have another go. Again the ball was deflected, but this time Frank Wignall was there to divert it past Millington with his head.

Drab England managed to increase their lead after 60 minutes when again Wignall was in the right place to head home Hinton's cross.

Wignall had taken both his goals well and had answered his critics in the best possible way. For Wales, who were now up against it, Hennessey had performed well and Allchurch had shown glimpses of his undoubted class. Jones, too, was always a handful and with a quarter of an hour to go a good pass from Ron Davies sent the flying winger away to pull a good goal back.

Near the end, Wales missed a glorious opportunity when Ron Davies shot straight at Waiters from a clear position and England escaped.

> 75th match v Wales.
> Debuts for Young and Wignall.
> Two debut goals for Wignall.

Holland v England
Friendly

Played on Wednesday, 9 December 1964 at the Olympic Stadium, Amsterdam.

Holland: E.L.Pieters-Graafland (Feyenoord); F.A.Flinkevleugel (DWS Amsterdam), C.P.Veldhoen (Feyenoord), M.D.Israël (DWS Amsterdam), D.C.Schrijvers (DWS Amsterdam), P.J.Fransen (GVAV Groningen), K.Nuninga (Ajax Amsterdam), B.Muller (Ajax Amsterdam), H.Van Nee (Heracles), F.Bouwmeester (Feyenoord), C.Moulijn (Feyenoord).
England: A.K.Waiters (Blackpool); G.R.Cohen (Fulham), R.A.Thomson (Wolves), A.P.Mullery (Spurs), M.Norman (Spurs), R.Flowers (Wolves, captain), P.Thompson (Liverpool), J.P.Greaves (Spurs), F.Wignall (Nottm Forest), T.F.Venables (Chelsea), R.Charlton (Man Utd).

Half-time 0-0   Full-time 1-1
Ref: J.Hannet (Belgium)   Att: 57,500

HOLLAND invited England to take part in this match to help celebrate the 75th

Anniversary of the Dutch FA. Unfortunately, the game did not live up to the occasion and the standard of football was of a very poor quality. When last these two sides, met in 1947, England had won by 8-2, but now the Dutch have caught us up somewhat in terms of football ability.

The first half was a virtual non-event with neither side looking likely to score. Muller and Fransen worked hard for an opening for Holland and they constantly fed the ball to Moulijn and Bouwmeester. These two left-sided attackers looked the most likely, of all the forwards on view, to break the deadlock. But in all honesty both defences found it easy to cope with the feeble offerings of their opponents, and on a dark and windy December night one had to feel sorry for the 57,500 capacity crowd that turned out to see such fare.

At half-time, the players were presented to Prince Bernhardt and this was the first time the crowd had stirred since the start. Both sides tried hard to up the tempo after the interval but still the game tended to plod along in an uninspiring way. England did have a good chance straight after the restart when Terry Venables fierce shot struck the crossbar, bounced down and was then sliced wide by Frank Wignall who was following up.

Now and again Bobby Charlton threatened something with his quick flowing dashes and Jimmy Greaves' form, too, brought hope. For 77 minutes the crowd had waited patiently for some positive goal action and at that moment they finally had their wish come true. The little, but lively Bouwmeester gained possession and found left winger Moulijn with a good pass. He cut inside George Cohen and beat Tony Waiters with a fine strike which flew into the top corner. Needless to say, the crowd went wild with delight.

England were now in imminent danger of a very worrying defeat but with just four minutes to go they dashed all the Dutch hopes of victory with an equalizer. Alan Mullery fed Venables and the England inside-left moved forward and put a lovely pass through for Greaves. The little striker showed all his lethal finishing skills by turning sharply to beat Schrijvers before shooting wide of Graafland.

England certainly escaped defeat by the skin of their teeth in this match, but at least they did not lose. That was one thing in their favour at this time; despite their other failings they were proving a very difficult side to beat.

> 3rd match v Holland.
> Debut for Mullery.

England v Scotland Home Championship

Played on Saturday, 10 April 1965 at Wembley Stadium.

England: G.Banks (Leicester C); G.R.Cohen (Fulham), R.Wilson (Everton), N.P.Stiles (Man Utd), J.Charlton (Leeds Utd), R.F.C.Moore (West Ham, captain), P.Thompson (Liverpool), J.P.Greaves (Spurs), B.J.Bridges (Chelsea), J.J.Byrne (West Ham), R.Charlton (Man Utd).
Scotland: W.D.F.Brown (Spurs); A.W.Hamilton (Dundee), E.G.McCreadie

England manager Alf Ramsey talking to new caps Barry Bridges, Jack Charlton and Nobby Stiles.

Bobby Charlton (not pictured) gives England the lead against Scotland at Wembley in April 1965.

(Chelsea), P.T.Crerand (Man Utd), W.McNeil (Celtic), J.Greig (Rangers), W.Henderson (Rangers), R.Y.Collins (Leeds Utd), I.St John (Liverpool), D.Law (Man Utd), D.Wilson (Rangers).

Half-time 2-1   Full-time 2-2
Ref: I.Zsolt (Hungary)   Att: 98,199

AN incident-packed match at Wembley saw England emerge the heroes after a spirited rearguard action following injury to two of their players. Scotland must have been kicking themselves for not taking advantage of the situation as they had a golden chance to win the game.

At the start there was a torrential downpour, the like of which Wembley has rarely seen. Some parts of the pitch were awash but gradually the sun came through and the ground began to dry out. Henderson was showing some clever pace in the first 20 minutes but Scotland's inside trio

of Law, St John and Collins were very disappointing, so there was little punch up front.

England meanwhile played confidently and after almost half an hour they took the lead. The goal came from a typical surge by Bobby Charlton, who moved forward before hitting a swerving shot into the corner of Brown's net. The goalkeeper might have done better but nobody could deny Charlton his goal.

Soon afterwards England went 2-0 up with a fine goal by Jimmy Greaves. Again Bobby Charlton was heavily involved and his superb defence-splitting pass sent Greaves in for a fine piece of opportunism so typical of the player. It was odds-on an England victory at this stage. However, fate always has a habit of raising its head, especially at Wembley, and especially involving goalkeepers.

Brown had already received criticism over England's first goal and this time it

Jimmy Greaves (8) turns away to celebrate his goal which gave England a 2-0 lead. Scotland, though, drew level.

was Gordon Banks' turn to incur the wrath of the crowd. Scotland, seemingly out of it, launched an attack just before the interval. Banks got himself into a terrible tangle trying to save a low Law shot. Whether he was deceived by the speed or whatever one could not judge, but in trying to save with his feet he succeeded only in helping the ball into his own net.

The goal had a dramatic effect on the game as Scotland, who had been down and almost out before, were suddenly given the lifeline to get back into the match. Coupled with the fact that England lost Ray Wilson with strained muscles in his side just before half-time, it gave Scotland even more of an edge. If that wasn't enough, just after the break Johnny Byrne was reduced to a hobbling passenger by suspected ligament trouble.

It seemed that Scotland must now surely go on to win with England in such dire straights. But when a determined defensive action was called for then, there was no better team than England to do it. And that is just what happened. Bobby Charlton moved into the role of emergency left-back and gave a magnificent performance. His brother Jack, playing for the first time, also performed heroically, and Bobby Moore set a captain's example with an impeccable display. George Cohen and Nobby Stiles also revelled in the extra pressure and both were very cool. Banks, too, made up for his earlier error by saving brilliantly on two or three occasions.

Scotland did manage to draw level when St John headed home in the 60th minute but after that the visitors failed to find the necessary imagination to beat a determined and sturdy defence. Crerand was Scotland's best player but the front men never gelled at all.

For England a special mention for Bobby Charlton's brilliant display and praise must go to Greaves, Peter Thompson and Barry Bridges, who ran themselves into the ground to support their defence trying to relieve some pressure during that second half. So England once again won the Home Championship. Each of their three games had been close but they

remained unbeaten, a positive sign for Alf Ramsey.

82nd match v Scotland.
Debuts for Stiles, J.Charlton and Bridges.

England v Hungary   Friendly

Played on Wednesday, 5 May 1965 at Wembley Stadium.

England: G.Banks (Leicester C); G.R.Cohen (Fulham), R.Wilson (Everton), N.P.Stiles (Man Utd), J.Charlton (Leeds Utd), R.F.C.Moore (West Ham, captain), T.L.Paine (Southampton), J.P.Greaves (Spurs), B.J.Bridges (Chelsea), G.E.Eastham (Arsenal), J.M.Connelly (Man Utd).

Hungary: J.Gelei (Tatabánya); S.Mátrai (Ferencváros), L.Sarosi (Vasas), I.Nagy (MTK), K.Mészöly (Vasas), F.Sipos (Honvéd), J.Göröcs (Újpesti Dózsa), Z.Varga (Ferencváros), F.Bene (Újpesti Dózsa), F.Nógrádi (Honvéd), M.Fenyvesi (Ferencváros).

Half-time 1-0   Full-time 1-0
Ref: P.Schwinte (France)   Att: 52,000

THIS was the first time for 30 years and the first time in five meetings since the war that England had beaten Hungary. Both sides were a pale shadow of their famous predecessors, but England at least were now building a solid-looking defence and the framework for an interesting side.

England began promisingly on a sunny but blustery day and in the first half put together some lovely football. Nobby Stiles and George Eastham linked up well and some of the approach play was excellent. In the 17th minute, England took the lead with a fine goal. Eastham, who was the main England playmaker, this time fed Terry Paine down the right. As three Hungarian defenders were pulled out of position, Paine slipped a diagonal pass inside for Jimmy Greaves, at full stride, to collect and shoot home brilliantly inside Gelei's near post.

The goal was of the highest quality but afterwards the play became tedious and

Fenyvesi, Hungary's outside-left, in a tussle with George Cohen at Wembley in May 1965.

over-elaborate. True, there were plenty of fine passing movements but the finishing, especially England's, was woeful.

One miss, ironically by Greaves, was amazing. Finding himself with only Gelei to beat at close range, he somehow managed to lose the chance — most un-Greaves like. Barry Bridges and Eastham also missed sitters for England, whilst at the other end Bene once completely missed his kicked in front of goal following Nógrádi's pass.

Only a great save by Gordon Banks prevented Bene from making amends just before the interval. The centre-forward turned brilliantly after feinting past four England defenders. Banks then made another fine stop from Nagy in the second

Jack Charlton and Barry Bridges battle it out with a Hungarian forward.

half. Nagy had looked a very good player, linking well with Nógrádi and also trying to set the forwards free.

The game continued as a story of missed chances. John Connelly, Paine, Bridges and Greaves again were all off target from good positions as England tried, sometimes desperately, to add to their single-goal advantage. Luckily, Bobby Moore was again in masterly form at the heart of the defence and with Charlton and Banks also on top of their game, the defence had settled into a comforting solid look about it.

10th match v Hungary.

Yugoslavia v England
Friendly

Played on Sunday, 9 May 1965 at the Red Star Stadium, Belgrade.

Yugoslavia: Z.Škorić (Dinamo Zagreb); V.Durković (Red Star Belgrade), F.Jusufi (Partizan Belgrade), R.Bečejac (Partizan Belgrade), V.Vasović (Partizan Belgrade), V.Popović (Red Star Belgrade), V.Lukaric (NK Rijeka), S.Zambata (Dinamo Zagreb), V.Kovačević (Partizan Belgrade), M.Galić (Partizan Belgrade), D.Džajić (Red Star Belgrade).
Sub: S.Takač (Vojvodina Novi Sad) for Lukaric.
England: G.Banks (Leicester C); G.R.Cohen (Fulham), R.Wilson (Everton), N.P.Stiles (Man Utd), J.Charlton (Leeds Utd), R.F.C.Moore (West Ham, captain), T.L.Paine (Southampton), J.P.Greaves (Spurs), B.J.Bridges (Chelsea), A.J.Ball (Blackpool), J.M.Connelly (Man Utd).

Half-time 1-1   Full-time 1-1
Ref: G.Gere (Hungary)   Att: 60,000

THIS was the day that Yugoslavia celebrated the 21st anniversary of their liberation in World War Two. What the Yugoslavs did not bargain for was that England might just have the gall to ruin the party. But the spirited English all but

did just that with an excellent display that deservedly gained an even share of the honours.

England knew before the game that they had a difficult task. On their previous visits, 1939, 1954 and 1958, they had been well beaten. This time, in a stadium that was still under construction, 60,000 people witnessed a much better display from their visitors.

Mind you, the start that England had could not have been worse as very early on a long through-pass from Kovačević caught the defence on the wrong foot and Galić raced clear. Luckily, Gordon Banks read the situation superbly to make a fine save. But it was only a brief respite as a minute later, worse was to follow. This time a long cross from Popović beat everyone and reached Kovačević, who volleyed in a superb goal.

It was a dream start for the Yugoslavs but England hit back immediately and dampened thoughts of another defeat by scoring a fine equalizer. A corner was taken by Terry Paine and his kick was met brilliantly by Barry Bridges, whose glancing header found the top corner of Škorić's net. It was Bridges' first goal for his country and one that his illustrious predecessors would have been proud of. It was also the first time an England goal had been seen in Yugoslavia since Frank Broome's effort in 1939.

After the goals the game settled down and the excitement went away for a while. After the interval it was England who gained the upper hand and could have gone on to win. Two left-foot shots by Jimmy Greaves flashed narrowly wide and Paine also went close.

A lovely cross by the tireless Ray Wilson almost found the head of Bridges and England were now well on top. At the back Bobby Moore was absolutely magnificent. Setting a captain's example, he seemed to read the Yugoslavs' minds and blotted out all their best attacks with consummate ease. Jack Charlton and the rest of the defence also performed heroically and this is certainly one of the best defensive set-ups England had enjoyed for a long time. Not only did they have Kovačević, Galić, Zambata, Džajić and Takač (substitute for the injured Lukaric just before half-time) totally in their pockets, they also found time to give their colleagues a stream of good passes out of defence.

The only thing lacking was that final finish. This was highlighted on the hour when they had their best chance of the half. A fine move between Nobby Stiles, Paine and Greaves ended with Bridges shooting straight at Škorić's legs from close range. It was a clear chance and one that should have been taken.

But let us not take too much away from what was a superb performance. England's challenge for the 1966 World Cup looked to be taking shape with the defence now settled, Stiles, a combative little terrier, and Alan Ball, despite a nervous beginning, gradually warming to the task. If Bobby Charlton had played then perhaps the extra finishing could have been provided.

Ironically, Yugoslavia almost stole it with just four minutes to go. Takac beat Ray Wilson for probably the only time and pulled the ball back from the by-line. Zambata met it with a spectacular diving header. Thankfully for England, the ball

struck the base of the post. Although Zambata was unlucky, it would have been a terrible injustice had England lost.

7th match v Yugoslavia.
Debut for Ball.
"My feeling on my debut was one of immense pride."
Alan Ball

West Germany v England
Friendly

Played on Wednesday, 12 May 1965 at the Städtisches Stadium, Nuremberg.

West Germany: H.Tilkowski (Borussia Dortmund); J.Piontek (Werder Bremen), H.D.Höttges (Werder Bremen), W.Schulz (Schalke '04), K.Sieloff (VfB Stuttgart), M.Lorenz (Werder Bremen), K.H.Thielen (1.FC Cologne), W.Krämer (MSV Duisburg), W.Rodekamp (Hanover '96), W.Overath (1.FC Cologne), H.Hornig (1.FC Cologne).
England: G.Banks (Leicester C); G.R.Cohen (Fulham), R.Wilson (Everton), R.Flowers (Wolves), J.Charlton (Leeds Utd), R.F.C.Moore (West Ham, captain), T.L.Paine (Southampton), A.J.Ball (Blackpool), M.D.Jones (Leeds Utd), G.E.Eastham (Arsenal), D.W.Temple (Everton).

Half-time 0-1   Full-time 0-1
Ref: I.Zsolt (Hungary)   Att: 67,000

THIS was the tenth meeting between these two old adversaries and West Germany were still searching for their first victory. At the final whistle they were still searching as England produced a marvellous defensive display, coupled with a superb goal to clinch a well-deserved win.

With Jimmy Greaves dropping out in the morning, Alf Ramsey brought in two new caps. Mick Jones of Leeds and Derek Temple of Everton came in to give the attack a slightly odd look about it.

But under the clear night sky, England were quickly into their stride. After only two minutes, Mick Jones had the ball in the German net. Unfortunately for Jones and England, the referee had spotted another player in an offside position and the goal was disallowed. Then Jones continued his spectacular start by taking a fine pass from Alan Ball and forcing Tilkowski, in the German goal, into a brilliant leaping tip-over save.

England sustained their fine opening and in the 35th minute they went ahead. Temple, who had already shown great promise, beat his full-back and ran to the by-line. He pulled the ball back accurately to Terry Paine, who made no mistake from seven yards out. It was a goal of superb quality and richly deserved.

The Germans, as they so often do, hit back at once and Krämer headed against the crossbar. But the England players were calmed by the immaculate display of their skipper Bobby Moore. Once again he was in superb form and he marshalled his defenders brilliantly. Alongside him there was the massive presence of the giant Jack Charlton. The Leeds United player was simply magnificent and in only his fourth international he proved beyond doubt that he would play a major role in England's World Cup preparations.

To top all this defensive quality,

Gordon Banks had probably his best game in an England jersey and the Germans just could not find a way round this impregnable defensive barrier.

The second half saw the Germans throw everything at the England defence in a bid to salvage the game. But Moore stood firm, ably supported by his co-defenders. The full-backs were also in top form and in the midfield the recalled George Eastham worked tirelessly. It was all inspiring stuff.

The 67,000 crowd did their best to encourage their team and the roar was at times deafening, but the nearest they came to an equalizer was when Krämer hit a good shot which struck a post. But England remained calm under this intense pressure and stuck rigidly to their task. In the end they held on to their lead, drawing generous applause from the appreciative crowd.

The red-shirted Englishmen can be justifiably proud of their display and they now travelled to Sweden, hoping to complete the tour on an even higher note.

> 6th match v West Germany.
> Debuts for Jones and Temple.

Sweden v England   Friendly

Played on Sunday, 16 May 1965 in the Ullevi Stadium, Gothenburg.

Sweden: A.Arvidsson (Djurgårdens IF); H.Rosander (IFK Norrköping), L.Wing (Örgryte IS), H.Mild (Djurgårdens IF), O.Bergmark (Örebro SK), B.Nordqvist (IFK Norrköping), L.Eriksson (Djurgårdens IF), H.Larsson (IF Elfsborg), A.Simonsson (Örgryte IS), B.Carlsson (AIK Stockholm), Ö.Persson (Örgryte IS).
England: G.Banks (Leicester C); G.R.Cohen (Fulham), R.Wilson (Everton), N.P.Stiles (Man Utd), J.Charlton (Leeds Utd), R.F.C.Moore (West Ham, captain), T.L.Paine (Southampton), A.J.Ball (Blackpool), M.D.Jones (Leeds Utd), G.E.Eastham (Arsenal), J.M.Connelly (Man Utd).

Half-time 1-1   Full-time 1-2
Ref: H.Faucheux (France)   Att: 18,000

ENGLAND ended their 1965 summer tour on a very high note, winning here in Sweden for the first time since the war. It was not an especially memorable game but England came to do a job and they did it most effectively. Both teams had leading players out with injuries and with the game being televised live coupled with a miserably cold, wet and grey day, the crowd was kept down to a mere 18,000 brave souls.

England quickly assumed command as the match began with Nobby Stiles, George Cohen, Bobby Moore and Jack Charlton dominant. When they eventually took the lead with a fine goal on 18 minutes, it seemed only a matter of how many they would win by. England had already come very close to scoring moments earlier when a super move involving Alan Ball, Terry Paine and the tireless Stiles ended with Arvidsson turning away a cracking shot by Ball.

Seconds later the goal did come. Moore had taken a long free-kick and young centre-forward Mick Jones leapt high above the experienced Bergmark to touch

it on for Ball to run in on the blind side and blast it past the goalkeeper for his first international goal.

The crowd, dotted around the stadium under black umbrellas, were silenced by the goal and as the match wore on it seemed that England would surely add to their lead. But just when it seemed that Gordon Banks would be unemployed for the whole ninety minutes a rare mistake by Moore let in Sweden for an equalizer. It was the 38th minute when a cross from the left by Persson floated in. Moore tried to collect the ball on the half-turn but it slipped away from him and there, suddenly, was Eriksson nipping in to put the ball into England's net with Banks helpless.

It was an amazing situation as England had had more than enough chances to have made the game safe by now, but here they were leaving the field at half-time all square.

To the credit of their professionalism, England began the second half in a very determined mood and as the half progressed, they totally dominated the Swedes. Chances came and went and once Paine made a sparkling run, flying past Nordqvist and Wing only to be unceremoniously up-ended by the left-back for what appeared to be an obvious penalty.

To everyone's amazement, though, the French referee waved play on and the disgusted England players had to look elsewhere for a goal. The pressure they were exerting had to tell, though, and with just over a quarter of an hour left it did, with another well-taken effort.

Cohen, always lively in his support of his forwards, received the ball from Banks and moved it swiftly on to Paine. The winger hit a first-time centre into the middle, where John Connelly came inside to apply a deft touch to send the ball past Arvidsson.

For the remainder of the match England continued to pepper the Swedish goal with good shots. Stiles, always at the heart of the action, Ball and Eastham went very close to adding to the scoreline, but in the end England had to be content with

the 2-1 win. Obviously it was very disappointing to have so much of the game without emphasising their superiority with more goals, but nothing could detract from the fact that England had now completed a very successful and satisfying tour.

> 8th match v Sweden.

Wales v England   Home Championship

Played on Saturday, 2 October 1965 at Ninian Park, Cardiff.

Wales: G.Sprake (Leeds Utd); P.J.Rodrigues (Cardiff C), C.R.Green (Birmingham C), W.T.Hennessey (Birmingham C), H.M.England (Blackburn R), B.G.Hole (Cardiff C), R.R.Rees (Coventry C), T.R.Vernon (Stoke C), R.W.Davies (Bolton W), I.J.Allchurch (Swansea C), G.I.Reece (Sheffield Utd).
England: R.D.G.Springett (Sheffield Wed); G.R.Cohen (Fulham), R.Wilson (Everton), N.P.Stiles (Man Utd), J.Charlton (Leeds Utd), R.F.C.Moore (West Ham, captain), T.L.Paine (Southampton), J.P.Greaves (Spurs), A.Peacock (Leeds Utd), R.Charlton (Man Utd), J.M.Connelly (Man Utd).

Half-time 0-0   Full-time 0-0
Ref: A.F.Webster (Scotland)   Att: 30,000

FOR the first time in 33 years, England failed to score against Wales. On a day when they were looking to put on a good show in preparation for the fast-approaching World Cup competition the following July, everything fell decidedly flat as they produced an inept display.

It was a terrible day with heavy rain continually pouring down. And it was the Welsh who took all the playing honours, being unlucky not to achieve victory. The veteran Ivor Allchurch was still a key figure in their side. Now 35 years old and playing in the Third Division with

Ray Wilson wins this tussle against Wales at Ninian Park in October 1965.

Swansea, Allchurch was still able to outshine the likes of Jimmy Greaves, Bobby Charlton and Nobby Stiles.

England almost scored in the first minute. Terry Paine took a quick throw-in which sent Greaves streaking past the Welsh defenders, but Sprake was alert and managed to smother the final shot. Hole had a storming game for Wales, as did Reece and Davies. The centre-forward gave Jack Charlton a very hard match, although eventually the towering defender won that personal battle.

One Allchurch cross was met by Davies and his fine header hit the angle of Ron Springett's post and crossbar. Both sides had other chances before the interval, notably when Greaves sent Alan Peacock clear only for Sprake to rescue Wales again by saving with his legs.

England's midfield had struggled in the first half with Stiles and Bobby Charlton never really coming to grips with either their opposite numbers or the appalling conditions. There was no lack of effort in their play, but there was a distinct lack of imagination.

The second half was much the same as the first, with Wales just about having the edge. Reece was a constant threat and he stretched George Cohen's powers of recovery to the full. Indeed, Reece was the surprise success for the Welsh and his clever footwork brightened up a dull afternoon. The one big success for England was goalkeeper Ron Springett.

Recalled to the side for the first time in three years he performed with all the assurance that his experience gave him and his handling of the greasy ball was impeccable.

Right at the death, England nearly snatched victory. Bobby Charlton, at last showing some of his blistering acceleration, attacked down the right wing. He centred perfectly for Greaves to come in and head fiercely at goal. The Spurs striker was desperately unlucky to see the ball rebound back from Sprake's crossbar. That would have been the winner but in all honesty it would have been a travesty if this brave Welsh challenge had ended with nothing. For a team fielding six players from outside the First Division, they had played with great skill and passion. Only a goal was missing.

76th match v Wales.

England v Austria
Friendly

Played on Wednesday, 20 October 1965 at Wembley Stadium.

England: R.D.G.Springett (Sheffield Wed); G.R.Cohen (Fulham), R.Wilson (Everton), N.P.Stiles (Man Utd), J.Charlton (Leeds Utd), R.F.C.Moore (West Ham, captain), T.L.Paine (Southampton), J.P.Greaves (Spurs), B.J.Bridges (Chelsea), R.Charlton (Man Utd), J.M.Connelly (Man Utd).

Austria: G.Fraydl (Wacker Innsbruck); R.Sara (FK Austria Wein), W.Stamm (Admira Wein), E.Ullmann (Rapid Wein), J.Frank (SC Schwechat), W.Ludescher (Wacker Innsbruck), A.Fritsch (Rapid Wien), H.Buzek (FK Austria Wein), F.Hasil (Rapid Wien), R.Flögel (Rapid Wien), A.Macek (Austria Salzburg).

John Connelly scores England's second goal against Austria at Wembley in October 1965.

Fritsch scores the winner for Austria with a brilliant 30-yard shot.

Sub: A.Dirnberger (FK Austria Wein) for Frank.

Half-time 1-0   Full-time 2-3
Ref: P.Schwinte (France)   Att: 65,000

WHAT a disappointment this game turned out to be for England. A goal up twice and seemingly in control, they lost two goals in the last nine minutes to give the game on a plate to Austria. Thus, the Austrians became only the third foreign side to win at Wembley.

England, who had gone nine games without defeat, began well enough and scored after only three minutes play. Terry Paine intercepted a bad pass by the Austrian centre-forward, Hasil, before threading a superb pass through for Bobby Charlton to take in his stride at top speed. The home number-ten moved forward and drilled a lovely shot wide of Fraydl.

It was the perfect opening and just the start that the continental sides did not like against England at Wembley. It should have been better still for England. After ten minutes, Jack Charlton came up for

a corner, outjumping everyone only to see his effort hit the bar. When the rebound came out, Jimmy Greaves moved in to begin a catalogue of missed chances. With the open goal yawning in front of him, it needed only the nod of his head but somehow Greaves succeeded in heading against a red-shirted defender and the ball was eventually cleared.

For 45 minutes, England directed this one-way traffic towards Fraydl's goal. Greaves saw a shot saved, as did John Connelly and Barry Bridges. Austria could find no response and the nearest they came to a goal in this half was when Ron Springett had to turn over the bar a back-pass from George Cohen. Greaves was then put through by Connelly for another clear chance and this time the little striker hit the post when it seemed easier to score.

At this point the Austrians replaced Frank, who had suffered a facial injury, with Dirnberger. Almost immediately, though, Greaves missed another golden chance when he hesitated fatally after receiving Connelly's inch perfect cross. On another day Greaves would surely have had a hat-trick by now.

So, at half-time England were only the one goal ahead, it could so easily have been four or five.

After the break the England performance fell apart. The midfield began to lose their grip and all the rhythm went from their play. Austria, meanwhile, played a lot better. Hasil, playing a deep-lying centre-forward role, began to exploit the oceans of room he was suddenly given. Nine minutes into the half the Austrians, incredibly, were level. Hasil miscued a shot but the ball ran kindly for Flögel and suddenly Springett was picking it out of his net.

The crowd grew restless for a positive response and on the hour a good run and cross by Cohen enabled Connelly to score to make it 2-1. It seemed that England had woken up again but in the last 15 minutes the alarm bells once more began to ring. Buzek, the Austrian captain, fired a shot past the defensive wall from a free-kick, bringing a full-length save from Springett. Unfortunately, the goalkeeper could not hold the ball and the nippy Fritsch whipped the rebound in for another equalizer.

Then, with nine minutes left, came the final straw for this inept second-half display by England. Nobby Stiles, who had a poor game, was caught in possession by Fritsch and the winger ran on for 20 yards before unleashing a 30-yard shot which flew into the top corner, catching Springett too far off his line and hopelessly beaten.

That goal highlighted the complete transformation in fortunes and gave Austria a win they barely deserved or looked like getting in the first half. But England had only themselves to blame and now looked to improve in the remaining fixtures before the World Cup finals.

> 12th match v Austria.

England v Home Championship
Northern Ireland

Played on Wednesday, 10 November 1965 at Wembley Stadium.

England: G.Banks (Leicester C); G.R.Cohen (Fulham), R.Wilson (Everton), N.P.Stiles (Man Utd), J.Charlton (Leeds Utd), R.F.C.Moore (West Ham, captain), P.Thompson (Liverpool), J.H.Baker (Arsenal), A.Peacock (Leeds Utd), R.Charlton (Man Utd), J.M.Connelly (Man Utd).

Northern Ireland: P.A.Jennings (Spurs); E.J.Magill (Brighton), A.R.Elder (Burnley), M.Harvey (Sunderland), W.J.T.Neill (Arsenal), J.J.Nicholson (Huddersfield T), J.McIlroy (Stoke C), J.A.Crossan (Man City), W.J.Irvine (Burnley), A.D.Dougan (Leicester C), G.Best (Man Utd).

Half-time 1-1   Full-time 2-1

Ref: L.Callaghan (Wales)   Att: 71,000

ALTHOUGH this win enabled England to draw level with Northern Ireland at the top of the Home Championship table, there was little for their fans to enthuse over. It was a drab game with England, still struggling to find the right blend,

The Charlton brothers, Bobby (right) and Jack, who were about to share in World Cup glory.

looking solid enough at the back but lacking any real flair in midfield.

They opened brightly and after 23 minutes took the lead. Joe Baker, back in the side for the first time in five years, celebrated his recall by popping up to score after a flick on by Alan Peacock. But just when one thought that England had earned themselves a nice platform to build on, they suddenly gave away an equalizer.

The usually reliable Bobby Moore inexplicably allowed Best to get the better of him and the Manchester United star gave Irvine the chance to level matters. That was a bitter blow for England but it must be said that Best was certainly the most thrilling player on view, always in the action, showing terrific skills and generally giving the England defence a torrid time.

Behind Best, the veteran Jimmy McIlroy showed he had lost none of his astute footballing brain and some of his passing was a delight to watch. For England, though, the midfield guile was lacking. Nobby Stiles worked his heart out as ever but his link with Bobby Charlton never worked and the pair failed to create enough of a supply for the front men.

Despite his well-taken goal, Baker

looked ill at ease in his inside-forward role. He was unaccustomed to the position and it showed. By the time the half-time whistle blew, the crowd were beginning to turn against England and one could understand the frustrations of the fans as their side had not performed well. After the break, though, that same crowd played a big part in encouraging the home side to victory.

The one thing Alf Ramsey's team did not lack was strength and this, coupled with their better teamwork, helped to gradually wear the battling Irish down in the second half. After several promising attacks, they finally regained the lead in the 73rd minute when Peacock's spectacular overhead kick found the net.

Overall it was a win that England just about deserved but the manager still had some way to go before he found the right blend to enable a real challenge to be mounted on the rest of the world.

> 73rd match v Northern Ireland.

Spain v England
Friendly

Played on Wednesday, 8 December 1965 at the Santiago Bernabéu Stadium, Madrid.

Spain: J.A.Iribar (Athletic Bilbao); S.Reija (Real Zaragoza), M.Sanchís (Real Madrid), J.Glaría (Atlético Madrid), F.Olivella (FC Barcelona), I.Zoco (Real Madrid), J.A.Ufarte (Atlético Madrid), A.Rodriguez (Atlético Madrid), F.Ansola (Real Betis), M.Martinez (Real Zaragoza), C.Lapetra (Real Zaragoza).
Sub: N.Martin (Pontevedra) for Lapetra.

England: G.Banks (Leicester C); G.R.Cohen (Fulham), R.Wilson (Everton), N.P.Stiles (Man Utd), J.Charlton (Leeds Utd), R.F.C.Moore (West Ham, captain), A.J.Ball (Blackpool), R.Hunt (Liverpool), J.H.Baker (Arsenal), G.E.Eastham (Arsenal), R.Charlton (Man Utd).
Sub: N.Hunter (Leeds Utd) for Baker.

Half-time 0-1   Full-time 0-2
Ref: C.Lo Bello (Italy)   Att: 25,000

THIS was the best England performance for a long time and the perfect way to go into a New Year that could be so important for English football. Alf Ramsey decided to try a new and effective 4-4-2 formation. Dispensing with traditional wingers, he played with four players across the middle and allowed each of the four a free hand in supporting the front runners.

It proved to be classic stuff and within 20 minutes of the start it was obvious which team would win.

England began superbly and after ten minutes they took a deserved lead. A clever free-kick movement involving Bobby Charlton, George Eastham and Ray Wilson ended with the left-back whipping over a centre which was cleverly touched home by Joe Baker.

The number-nine was then desperately unlucky to pull a leg muscle on the half-hour and he limped off to be replaced by debutant Norman Hunter. Thankfully, the changes did not have an adverse effect on the England display and throughout the remainder of the first half they showed all the pace, quality and ideas.

The bemused Spaniards tried desperately to work out what was happening. The full-backs, Reija and Sanchís, were particularly baffled at having no wingers to mark. Incidentally, Spain, too, were trying to rebuild a side, having lost 'superstar' players like Di Stefano, Gento and others. Losing quality like that was a big blow and one from which they were struggling to recover.

Before half-time Spain brought on Neme for outside-left Lapetra but England were full value for their one-goal lead and their only disappointment was that they did not have more goals to show for their superiority.

The second half continued in the same vein with England comfortably controlling the play. Several chances came and went before they deservedly sealed the game with a second goal. It came on the hour and ended a fine move between Bobby Moore, George Cohen and Moore again. The captain's final square pass was turned in by Roger Hunt and the mesmerized Spaniard's resistance was finally over.

England swarmed around the Spanish goal in the remaining half-hour and could have had several more goals. Hunt missed twice and Alan Ball who covered every blade of this Madrid grass, came so close to making it 3-0.

It really was a heartwarming end to the year and England could now move with confidence into 1966.

> 8th match v Spain.
> Debut for Hunter (substitute).
> Spain's Rodriguez also known as 'Adelardo'; Martinez as 'Marcelino'; Martin as 'Neme'.
> *"I'll never forget the faces of the two Spanish full-backs when facing 4-4-2 for the first time. We had no winger so they just stood in space whilst we all piled up the middle."*
> Bobby Charlton

England v Poland
Friendly

Played on Wednesday, 5 January 1966 at Goodison Park, Everton.

England: G.Banks (Leicester C); G.R.Cohen (Fulham), R.Wilson (Everton), N.P.Stiles (Man Utd), J.Charlton (Leeds Utd), R.F.C.Moore (West Ham, captain), A.J.Ball (Blackpool), R.Hunt (Liverpool), J.H.Baker (Arsenal), G.E.Eastham (Arsenal), G.Harris (Burnley).

Poland: M.Szeja (Zagłębie Walbrzych); J.Gmoch (Legia Warsaw), S.Oślizło (Górnik Zabrze), A.Rewilak (Cracovia Kraków), H.Brejza (Odra Opole), P.Suski (LKS Lódź), J.Galéczka (Zagłębie Sosnowiec), Z.Szmidt (GKS Katowice), J.Sadek (LKS Lódź), Jan Wilim (Szombierki Bytom), J.Kowalik (Cracovia Kraków).
Sub: J.Banaś (Polonia Bytom) for Wilim.

Half-time 0-1   Full-time 1-1
Ref: J.Hannet (Belgium)   Att: 47,750

AFTER the euphoria that followed the previous month's splendid victory in Madrid against Spain, England came back down to earth with a bump as a young Poland side gave a fine defensive performance to earn a draw.

This was the first meeting between the two countries and the first full international at Goodison Park for 13 years. The conditions were not good as early evening rain had left the pitch saturated. The heavy conditions hampered England's style and play was bogged down regularly in a sea of mud.

Right from the kick-off, the determination of the Polish side was there for all to see. They employed a five-man defensive barrier, superbly marshalled, and extremely effective. When England did get through, they found Szeja in unbeatable form.

Roger Hunt twice went close and George Eastham and Nobby Stiles also put in goal attempts. Alan Ball was magnificent and covered every inch of the Goodison pitch in setting up all the most positive of England's play. Stiles and Bobby Moore gave him good support but the attack was not firing on all cylinders. Gordon Harris, in for Bobby Charlton, gave plenty of effort but lacked that certain something that separates the good players from the very good.

Joe Baker, after a lively opening, faded as the game wore on and Hunt was guilty of some bad misses from chances he would probably have gobbled up, had they been across Stanley Park at Anfield. But Poland must not have any credit taken away from them. Their defence was outstanding both in the air and on the ground, and the red shirts battled for every loose ball. Just before the break they snatched a surprise lead.

Moore, clearing too casually, had his pass blocked by Banaś, who had only just come on to the field to replace Wilim. The new man ran on and reached the by-line. He crossed low and hard and there was Sadek, a classy centre-forward, to turn the ball sharply past Gordon Banks. All through the match, Jack Charlton had his hands full with Sadek and the number-nine deserved his goal.

Hunt still found time to head Baker's cross wide before the break but Poland's lead stayed intact. They began the second half in a very determined mood and they had the scent of a famous victory. However, England kept plugging away and the crowd roared them on. Again chances were missed as England laid siege on the Polish goal, but Szeja stood firm.

With 15 minutes to go, England at last found the inspiration to equalize. It came from an unlikely quarter. George Cohen made a barnstorming run down the right,

Bobby Moore (out of picture) scores England's equalizer against Poland at Goodison Park in January 1966.

crashing through some hefty challenges from three defenders before sending over a delightful cross to the far post. A tactical switch had pushed Moore forward and the England skipper met the cross with a good header, his joy at scoring plain for all to see.

This tactic almost paid higher dividends right near the end when Ball, still buzzing around tirelessly, centred from the left and Moore again stormed in from the right to power a header towards goal. This time, though, the ball thudded against the crossbar and Poland escaped.

England had to be content with a draw in the end but it must be said that Poland definitely deserved a share of the spoils.

> 1st match v Poland.
> Debut for Harris.
> Moore's goal one of only two he scored for England in 108 appearances.

England v West Germany   Friendly

Played on Wednesday, 23 February 1966 at Wembley Stadium.

England: G.Banks (Leicester C); G.R.Cohen (Fulham), K.R.Newton (Blackburn R), R.F.C.Moore (West Ham, captain), J.Charlton (Leeds Utd), N.Hunter (Leeds Utd), A.J.Ball (Blackpool), R.Hunt (Liverpool), N.P.Stiles (Man Utd), G.C.Hurst (West Ham), R.Charlton (Man Utd).
Sub: R.Wilson (Everton) for Newton.
West Germany: H.Tilkowski (Borussia Dortmund); F.Lutz (Eintracht Frankfurt), M.Lorenz (Werder Bremen), W.Schulz (Hamburger SV), W.Weber (1.FC Cologne), H.Szymaniak (Tasmania Berlin), W.Kramer (MSV Duisburg), F.Beckenbauer (Bayern Munich), S.Held (Borussia Dortmund), G.Netzer (Borussia Mönchengladbach), H.Hornig (1.FC Cologne).
Sub: A.Heiss (Munich 1860) for Hornig.

Half-time 1-0   Full-time 1-0
Ref: P.P.Roomer (Holland)   Att: 75,000

THIS was the 12th meeting — and the seventh full international — between these countries since their first in 1908 and the Germans had still to taste victory. But although that was satisfying from an England point of view, it did not hide the fact that this was a very disappointing international.

Alf Ramsey brought in a couple of new faces as the build-up to July continued, but the game was made up of too much midfield football and not enough positive goal attempts.

England had the better of the game and began well. In the first half they created several good chances. Early on, Alan Ball headed straight at Tilkowski from an excellent position and that was a bad miss from a player who went on to be man of the match with his all-action display.

The home side persevered with their new 4-3-3 formation but it resulted in the play being confined down the centre of the pitch rather than making full use of the width. Geoff Hurst, Ball and Roger Hunt never exploited the wide open spaces of the wings but then the passing of the men behind them did not encourage that.

Gradually the pressure increased on the German goal. Hurst also headed straight at the goalkeeper from Ball's perfect centre, and then a clever move involving Hurst and Nobby Stiles ended with Ball again missing the target.

The play continued to be crab-like in appearance but eventually England took the lead just before half-time. Bobby Moore and Norman Hunter combined well in midfield before bringing George Cohen into play down the right flank. The full-back made another splendid run as he did the previous month against Poland, and ended it with a perfect cross to the middle.

Hunt headed the ball goalwards, but not cleanly. Tilkowski partially saved but the ball stopped almost on the goal-line. The player who followed up first was Stiles who, appropriately enough, as he was wearing the number-nine shirt, rammed the ball home from almost on the goal-line.

There was still time before the interval for two substitutions to be made. Keith Newton was desperately unlucky to damage his shin on his first appearance and leave the field on a stretcher. Ray Wilson came on for him and immediately the Germans withdrew Hornig with a head injury, replacing him with Heiss.

In the second half there were other chances, notably a lobbed volley by the industrious and fiery Ball. This time Tilkowski leapt superbly to turn the effort away. England still looked laboured in their build up, though, despite having a lot of the play and with a quarter of an hour to go the Germans upped their pace. Held, Beckenbauer and Kramer suddenly looked dangerous, and Netzer started to put through some clever passes.

Cohen and Hunter held England together at this stage with some excellent defending, but from one move Kramer crossed from the left, Held nodded the ball on and Heiss' volley zipped past the helpless Gordon Banks. To England's relief the referee had spotted a linesman's flag. After consultation he awarded the Germans a corner, so England breathed again.

Before the end a glancing header by Hunt from Moore's cross hit the bar and a left-footed volley by a strangely subdued Bobby Charlton was blocked. Ball then put Hunt clean through but the Liverpool player missed wildly when he should have done better.

Once again it was the right result for England but a less than convincing performance.

> 7th match v West Germany.
> Debuts for Newton and Hurst.

Scotland v England   Home Championship

Played on Saturday, 2 April 1966 at Hampden Park, Glasgow.

Scotland: R.Ferguson (Kilmarnock); J.Greig (Rangers), T.Gemmell (Celtic), R.Murdoch (Celtic), R.McKinnon (Rangers), J.C.Baxter (Sunderland), J.Johnstone (Celtic), D.Law (Man Utd), W.S.B.Wallace (Heart of Midlothian), W.J.Bremner (Leeds Utd), W.Johnston (Rangers).
England: G.Banks (Leicester C); G.R.Cohen (Fulham), K.R.Newton (Blackburn R), N.P.Stiles (Man Utd), J.Charlton (Leeds Utd), R.F.C.Moore (West Ham, captain), A.J.Ball (Blackpool), R.Hunt (Liverpool), R.Charlton (Man Utd), G.C.Hurst (West Ham), J.M.Connelly (Man Utd).

Half-time 1-2   Full-time 3-4
Ref: H.Faucheux (France)   Att: 133,000

ENGLAND received the boost of going into the World Cup in three months time with the Home Championship under their belts after this seven-goal thriller at Hampden. With 133,000 people packed into this famous old stadium the noise and atmosphere was superb and England began the game in a determined mood.

Once again they used the 4-3-3 formation, but this time with much more conviction. Bobby Charlton was particularly effective and was always available and involved. He showed his best Manchester United form throughout the match, something he hasn't done for England for a while.

The visitors took the lead after 20 minutes. Alan Ball intercepted a casual crossfield pass by Baxter before breaking quickly with Roger Hunt and Geoff Hurst alongside him. When the pass came inside, Hurst had plenty of time to pick his spot to score with ease.

Six minutes later, another intercepted pass brought England a second goal. This time Nobby Stiles cut out Bremner's pass and again the break moved swiftly to Hurst and then on to Hunt, who fired a left-footed cross shot into the far corner. Ferguson might have done better as England gained this unexpected lead.

That silenced the huge crowd but just before the interval they burst into life after a Scottish goal. Johnston took a corner and Law leapt to send a flashing header past Gordon Banks. The Scots went in at half-time right back in the match.

The second half was a see-saw of action and excitement with both defences making mistakes. In the opening seconds, the England players screamed for a penalty when McKinnon palmed the ball out from under his own crossbar after a Bobby Charlton cross. Amazingly, the only person not to see the incident was the referee, who waved play on despite frantic appeals.

England continued to make the running and another quick pass from Ball sent Hunt away again. He ran on and hit another fierce cross shot past Ferguson for number three. On the hour, though, Scotland hit back with Law again in the thick of the action.

He played a one-two with Johnstone but not before he had ridden two ferocious challenges by Ball and Bobby Moore. At the end of it all, Johnstone's acute shot left Keith Newton and Banks stranded.

There was more to come. Bobby Charlton capped his fine performance with a surging run and shot from 25 yards which left Ferguson flat-footed, thinking perhaps that the shot was going wide. How wrong he was.

So, it was 4-2, but again the Scots hit back and with ten minutes to go Law and Baxter combined at a free-kick to give Johnstone the chance to hit his second goal. Again the shot was from an acute angle as it went in off the crossbar. Moore and Newton had stood transfixed whilst all this was going on.

In the last few minutes, England withstood heavy pressure with Johnstone giving Newton a torrid time on the right wing with an inspired spell. Indeed, in the very last minute Stiles became England's hero with a headed goal-line clearance following a shot by Wallace.

Overall England deserved their win. They were more organised, more disciplined and clinical with the chances that came their way.

> 83rd match v Scotland.

England v Yugoslavia
Friendly

Played on Wednesday, 4 May 1966 at Wembley Stadium.

England: G.Banks (Leicester C); J.C.Armfield (Blackpool, captain), R.Wilson (Everton), M.S.Peters (West Ham), J.Charlton (Leeds Utd), N.Hunter (Leeds Utd), T..L.Paine (Southampton), J.P.Greaves (Spurs), R.Charlton (Man Utd), G.C.Hurst (West Ham), R.V.Tambling (Chelsea).

Yugoslavia: M.Šošić (Partizan Belgrad); V.Kuci (Hajduk Split), Ž.Jevtić (Red Star Belgrade), R.Bečejac (Partizan Belgrade), B.Rašović (Partizan Belgrade), V.Vasović (Partizan Belgrade), S.Samardžić (OFK Belgrade), D.Mušović (NK Sarajevo), V.Melić (Red Star Belgrade), J.Skoblar (OFK Belgrade), D.Džajić (Red Star Belgrade).

Half-time 2-0   Full-time 2-0
Ref: J.Malka (West Germany) Att: 54,000

THIS was England's last home game before the World Cup began and the players responded with an excellent performance against very good opponents. It was a severe test of England's defence as the lively Skoblar, Mušović and Samardžić posed plenty of problems for Jack Charlton and company. But it was England who had a magnificent start to the game.

Straight from the opening whistle Bobby Charlton, who had another super game, put Jimmy Greaves away down the right with one of those long, raking passes that were his trademark. Greaves quickly put over a centre and there was Geoff Hurst to head just over. It would have been a classic goal but England did not have to wait too much longer to open their account. This time Terry Paine provided the cross and Greaves was on the end of it to head cleanly past Šošić. It was the little master's 39th goal for his country and one superbly taken.

Other goals should have followed. A great move begun by Bobby Charlton was carried on down the left by Ray Wilson and Greaves, this time centring from the left wing, found Bobby Tambling. Unfortunately, Tambling's volley from close in flew over the bar. Immediately, though, Greaves saw a fine header well saved by Šošić, that came after another clever and intricate move involving Martin Peters, Bobby Charlton and Wilson.

By now the match could have been all over but it was England had to wait until ten minutes from the interval before they increased their lead. It was a goal out of this world and one that the Wembley crowd would remember for a long time. It came from Bobby Charlton. Collecting the ball some 40 yards out, he moved forward majestically, searching for an opening. Then suddenly he changed direction, quickened his pace and let fly a screamer into the top corner. Poor Šošić, a world-class goalkeeper, was dumbfounded. It was a goal in a thousand and the crowd roared their approval. It left Charlton on 37 goals for England and a ding-dong struggle for top dog was now raging between him and Greaves.

Two goals down, Yugoslavia decided to up the pace of their game but as they came at England they left more gaps at the back and it was at their end that most of the chances fell.

Once, Peters sold a beautiful dummy and instead of passing to Tambling he let fly himself a super shot which Šošić brilliantly turned away. Peters could be justifiably proud of his first display at this level and he contributed much to the night's entertainment. Other chances also came and went. A snap shot by Greaves flew just over, Peters narrowly missed with a diving header following a cross by Paine, and Greaves again shot over, this time from a Tambling pass. Super work by Peters and Wilson then set up Greaves again but again the Tottenham striker missed what was a clear chance.

Finally, another fine save by Šošić prevented Tambling scoring after Bobby Charlton and Wilson had opened up the defence again. Despite plenty of Yugoslav attacks, their forwards rarely troubled Gordon Banks and the only disappointing aspect of the game was England's failure to convert more of the goal chances that came their way.

> 8th match v Yugoslavia.
> Debut for Peters.

Finland v England
Friendly

Played on Sunday, 26 June 1966 in the Olympic Stadium, Helsinki.

Finland: M.Halme (Valkeakosken Haka); P.Mäkipää (UP Lahti), R.Aho (TPS Turku), S.T.Kautonen (Reipas Lahti), R.Kanerva (UP Lahti), S.Kilponen (OPS Oulu), M.Kumpulampi (UP Lahti), M.Mäkelä (UP Lahti), M.Hyvärinen (KuPS Kuopio), A.Laine (AIFK Turku), A.Hyttinen (MiPK Mikkeli).

England: G.Banks (Leicester C); J.C.Armfield (Blackpool, captain), R.Wilson (Everton), M.S.Peters (West Ham), J.Charlton (Leeds Utd), N.Hunter (Leeds Utd), I.R.Callaghan (Liverpool), R.Hunt (Liverpool), R.Charlton (Man Utd), G.C.Hurst (West Ham), A.J.Ball (Blackpool).

Bobby Charlton (9, extreme right) wheels away after scoring England's second goal against Yugoslavia at Wembley in May 1966.

Half-time 0-2   Full-time 0-3

Ref: F.Hansen (Denmark)   Att: 10,500

ENGLAND'S Scandinavian tour was arranged as a final warm-up before the World Cup finals started the following month. With games to follow in Norway and Denmark, England were determined to get off to a winning start here in Helsinki. This was not the most inspiring of matches, though, and England struggled for much of the time.

They were presented with a golden opportunity early on when the referee awarded them a penalty. Alan Ball was entrusted with the kick but watched in despair as Halme made a fine diving save. It was not the sort of start England wanted and they laboured from that moment on. Encouragingly, despite their other failings, the chances were still being created but for a long time the finish was not there.

Ball, Martin Peters, who had another impressive match, Geoff Hurst and Roger Hunt all put in goal attempts that were blocked in one way or another. It was frustrating for the players and left Finland in the match with a chance. One cunning cross by Kumpulampi gave England problems until Norman Hunter cleared the danger. Hunter was in dominating form in what was, thankfully, a strong England defence. Jack Charlton won everything in the air and Ray Wilson's fierce tackling contributed much to the solidity of the defensive unit.

For the first half-hour, England scratched around trying to find an opening. Despite their goal chances, they looked decidedly ragged and the sparse crowd sensed that it would not take too much from Finland to throw England deeper into confusion. But with the giant clock by the score-board showing the first half nearly over, the visitors came up with a memorable goal.

Hurst took the ball down the left touchline before sending in a short centre which Peters met superbly to flick past Halme with the outside of his right boot. It was a brilliant piece of positioning and finishing.

There was still time for England to score again before the interval and this time it was an even better goal. Hunt, so full of running, found Ball, who slipped a telling pass to Ian Callaghan. The winger made ground before his long centre cleared several blond Finnish heads for Hunt to arrive at the far post to end the move he had started with a lovely header past Halme. If the first goal had belonged to West Ham then the second definitely belonged to Liverpool. One would have to go a long way to see Hunt's effort bettered.

So, what a transformation. England, for so long looking strained and disjointed, suddenly found themselves totally in control. They could even have had a third goal in the dying seconds of the half but Hunt's effort was disallowed by the referee.

Despite lots of effort and possession in the second half England never looked fully convincing. They had to wait until the very last minute of the match before they scored their elusive third goal. It came in extraordinary fashion as Jack Charlton, up with the attack for the umpteenth time, shot from almost on the by-line. The ball somehow screwed into the net off the boot of Kautonen for a scrappy goal. Somewhat

dubiously the official verdict gave the goal to Charlton.

England now looked to improve in their game in Norway, aiming to show more venom in their finishing as well as their general play.

> 3rd match v Finland.
> Debut for Callaghan.
> Penalty miss by Ball.

Norway v England   Friendly

Played on Wednesday, 29 June 1966 at the Ullevaal Stadium, Oslo.

Norway: S.Andersen (Viking Stavanger); R.Johansen (Fredrikstad FK), A.Mathisen (Vålerengens IF), A.Pedersen (Fredrikstad FK), F.Thorsen (Skeid Oslo), E.Stakseth (Steinkjer IFK), H.Sunde (Nidelr Trondheim), O.Stavrum (SFK Lyn), H.Berg (SFK Lyn), O.Nilsen (Viking Stavanger), E.Johansen (Gjövik Lyn).
Sub: K.Kaspersen (Skeid Oslo) for Andersen.
England: R.D.G.Springett (Sheffield Wed); G.R.Cohen (Fulham), G.Byrne (Liverpool), N.P.Stiles (Man Utd), R.Flowers (Wolves), R.F.C.Moore (West Ham, captain), T.L.Paine (Southampton), J.P.Greaves (Spurs), R.Charlton (Man Utd), R.Hunt (Liverpool), J.M.Connelly (Man Utd).

Half-time 1-5   Full-time 1-6

Ref: H.Carlsson (Sweden)   Att: 29,500

THIS was just the boost the England team wanted before their World Cup challenge and it was all inspired by the irrepressible Jimmy Greaves. The Spurs striker gave a superb performance, netting four of the six goals and running the poor Norwegians ragged.

Ironically, it all began so disastrously for England. After only four minutes an appalling back-pass by Ron Flowers left Ron Springett stranded and gave Sunde the simplest of scoring chances. For the next quarter of an hour England struggled to sort themselves out but on the 19th minute, Greaves began his night of glory. Roger Hunt broke down the right and his sharp cross was headed home by the England number-eight.

Now the floodgates opened and within three more minutes it was 3-1 to England. The second goal came after a Greaves run took him half the length of the field. Under pressure from defenders all the way, Greaves remained cool as he drew the goalkeeper and gently placed the ball wide of him. Within seconds, Greaves was on target again, this time with a typical piece of poaching after John Connelly and the 'keeper had collided. The ball ran loose and whilst others watched and waited, Greaves pounced like a hungry tiger.

It was all vintage stuff and England's all-round performance was now carving the Norwegians apart. It was football worthy of any pitch, on any occasion and soon Greaves was adding a fourth goal, shooting home from a tight angle after good work by Terry Paine and Connelly had set him up. Before half-time, England made it 5-1 when the skipper Bobby Moore moved forward positively and drilled a spectacular 25-yard shot past Andersen.

England went through the second half content with the lead they had, but continuing with a brand of football that gave Norway no chance of a recovery. Bobby Charlton showed some lovely touches in what was a flawless display.

They did manage one goal in this half, when Bobby Charlton twisted magnificently and tapped a pass through a defender's legs for Connelly to shoot home the sixth goal.

The England players had been threatening a big score for a while and Norway could count themselves unlucky to have been on the receiving end, for on the day everything came together for England and Greaves made it 43 goals in 49 internationals with one of his sharpest performances.

> 4th match v Norway.
> Four goals for Greaves.

Denmark v England   Friendly

Played on Sunday, 3 July 1966 at the Idraetspark, Copenhagen.

Denmark: L.Nielsen (BK Frem); J.Hansen (Vejle BK), L.Hartwig (Odense BK 09), J.Petersen (Hvidovre IF), H.Boel (Ikast FS), N.Møller (KB København), B.Schmidt-Hansen (Horsens fS), J.Steen Olsen (Hvidovre IF), H.Enoksen (Aarhus GF), T.Søndergaard (B93 København), U.Le Fevre (Vejle BK).
England: P.P.Bonetti (Chelsea); G.R.Cohen (Fulham), R.Wilson (Everton), N.P.Stiles (Man Utd), J.Charlton (Leeds Utd), R.F.C.Moore (West Ham, captain), A.J.Ball (Blackpool), J.P.Greaves (Spurs), G.C.Hurst (West Ham), G.E.Eastham (Arsenal), J.M.Connelly (Man Utd).

Half-time 0-1   Full-time 0-2

Ref: R.Morgan (Canada)   Att: 32,000

ENGLAND rounded off their Scandinavian tour with another competent if unspectacular win. It was not a good game and was played on a very poor pitch. England's players had to battle hard, none more so than Alan Ball whose fiery display more than once incurred the wrath of the referee as well as the crowd.

Early on England made several openings. Ball completely miskicked, and Jimmy Greaves trod on the ball when well placed. Poor Greaves, four nights earlier he had almost single-handedly destroyed Norway, but here in Denmark he hardly got a kick.

The game was very physical but England had plenty of players well equipped to meet such a challenge. Nobby Stiles, Jack Charlton and Ball were always in the thick of things and in Peter Bonetti they had a very confident goalkeeper. His one difficult save of the match from Enoksen early in the second half was outstanding and one could see why he is known as 'The Cat'.

That save protected the lead given to England by Jack Charlton in the 43rd minute. The big centre-half came up as usual for a corner, but this time John Connelly's kick cleared even Charlton's large frame. But it reached Ball, who quickly lobbed it back and this time Charlton made no mistake with a firm header.

England squad before the game in Copenhagen in July 1966. From left to right: Jack Charlton, Peters, Flowers, Hurst, Moore, Hunter, Banks, Bonetti, Byrne, Springett, Armfield, Hunt, Bobby Charlton, Cohen, Paine, Connelly, Wilson, Greaves, Ball and Stiles.

The goal prevented any embarrassment England might have felt at half-time, of being held by the amateurs of Denmark for so long. The fact was, though, that they had not been in any trouble despite their inability to score. After Bonetti's save, England consolidated their position and took a firm grip on the game. On the hour it culminated in a match-clinching second goal.

It came from George Eastham and was a carefully placed shot between goalkeeper Nielsen and Hartwig, the full-back. There was no further scoring, although England did create several more chances without being able to finish them. Again, as in the Finland match England finished with a 'could have done better' feeling, but 11 goals for and only one against in three matches, gave them a superb platform for their next important games.

5th match v Denmark.
Debut for Bonetti.
50th cap for Greaves.

Poland v England
Friendly

Played on Tuesday, 5 July 1966 at the Slaski Stadium, Chorzów.

Poland: M.Szeja (Zagłębie Walbrzych); H.Brejza (Odra Opole), R.Strzalkowski (Zagłębie Sosnowiec), Z.Anczok (Polonia Bytom), J.Gmoch (Legia Warsaw), W.Winkler (Polonia Bytom), J.Galeczka (Zagłębie Sosnowiec), W.Lubański (Górnik Zabrze), P.Suski (LKS Lódź), J.Liberda (Polonia Bytom), J.Kowalik (Cracovia Kraków).
Sub: Jerzy Wilim (Szombierki Bytom) for Lubański.
England: G.Banks (Leicester C); G.R.Cohen (Fulham), R.Wilson (Everton), N.P.Stiles (Man Utd), J.Charlton (Leeds Utd), R.F.C.Moore (West Ham, captain), A.J.Ball (Blackpool), J.P.Greaves (Spurs), R.Charlton (Man Utd), R.Hunt (Liverpool), M.S.Peters (West Ham).

Half-time 0-1   **Full-time 0-1**
Ref: I.Zsolt (Hungary)   Att: 70,000

THE final test before the World Cup started in a week's time could not have given England a stiffer task than this. Playing Poland in the grey industrial city of Chorzów in front of a fiercely partisan crowd was a severe test for all the players. They came through it magnificently.

After their usual indifferent opening, England took the lead after 13 minutes with as good a goal as one is likely to see anywhere. Roger Hunt, so often underrated, picked up a fine pass from Bobby Charlton, took half-a-dozen strides and suprised Szeja with a terrific 25-yard shot high and wide of the goalkeeper.

From that moment, England were superb with their defence absolutely outstanding. The effort that all the team put in was phenomenal. The full-backs were as solid as rocks, Jack Charlton and Bobby Moore were so dependable and in midfield Nobby Stiles and Martin Peters were tireless workers. Peters had surely won a place in the World Cup line-up after this display. He was everywhere and was always available when his colleagues found themselves in trouble. Two terrific shots by the West Ham player had Szeja leaping about his goal and he showed real world class in everything else he did.

Poland rarely created anything worthwhile, so stifled were they by the supreme England teamwork. There was only the occasional moment of alarm on Gordon Banks' goal. A rare mistake by Moore led to a chance which Suski ballooned over the bar, and then a miskick caused a spinning ball to deceive Banks but the tiny terrier from Manchester United, Nobby Stiles, rescued England with one of his timely interceptions.

Jimmy Greaves had another quiet game and although for much of the time he was hustled out of the action, one moment of sheer magic late in the game took him past three defenders, only to be stopped just short of what would have been one of his greatest-ever goals. Alf Ramsey's late decision to switch Bobby Charlton to the forward line and bring in Peters to the midfield certainly paid off and this performance silenced a huge crowd in this magnificent stadium.

The warning had gone out after this tour that England's defence would give nothing away and the rest of world soccer now knew that they would have to work very hard in the coming weeks.

2nd match v Poland.

England v Uruguay
Group One

Played on Monday, 11 July 1966 at Wembley Stadium.

England: G.Banks (Leicester C); G.R.Cohen (Fulham), R.Wilson (Everton), N.P.Stiles (Man Utd), J.Charlton (Leeds Utd), R.F.C.Moore (West Ham, captain), A.J.Ball (Blackpool), J.P.Greaves (Spurs), R.Charlton (Man Utd), R.Hunt (Liverpool), J.M.Connelly (Man Utd).
Uruguay: L.Mazurkiewicz (Peñarol); H.Troche (Cerro), J.Manicera (Nacional), L.Ubiñas (Rampla Juniors), N.Gonçálves (Peñarol), O.Caetano (Penarol), J.Cortés (Peñarol), M.Viera (Nacional), H.Silva (Peñarol), P.Rocha (Peñarol), D.Pérez (Nacional).

Half-time 0-0   **Full-time 0-0**
Ref: I.Zsolt (Hungary)   Att: 87,148

AT last, after years of planning and months of preparation, the great day had arrived when the 1966 World Cup finals began. After Her Majesty the Queen had completed the opening ceremony and all the pre-match ballyhoo was over, the serious business got under way. The first match was between England, the hosts, and one of the South American giants, Uruguay.

Sadly, the game was something of an anticlimax and proved to be very disappointing for the fans present. Gate receipts of £85,000 were taken but few of the spectators would claim that they had value for money.

The pattern of play which followed was something that England would have to get used to over the coming weeks. A massed defence of sometimes eight or nine players were determined not to lose, to give the hosts a problem they must solve. On this night they failed.

The expectancy at the beginning was soon gone as the Uruguayans negatively began their campaign. True, they had players of skill and Rocha, Silva and Viera all showed their qualities. Early on a fierce long-range shot from Cortés was turned away for a corner by Gordon Banks, but that proved a rare moment of aggression by Uruguay and possession was mainly England's.

Bobby Charlton and Alan Ball worked hard for the openings but apart from long-range shots by Bobby Charlton, Jimmy Greaves and Roger Hunt, few clear chances were created. At half-time the players trooped off and the crowd were left with a feeling of boredom uppermost in their minds.

After the break, the determination improved but still a goal could not be found. With 25 minutes to go, Ray Wilson crossed from the left, Greaves headed backwards and a left-foot shot by Bobby Charlton was diverted by a flick from John Connelly's boot. But Mazurkiewicz, a very able goalkeeper, turned the ball brilliantly around a post.

Time after time Wilson and George Cohen made lung-bursting runs down the wings to support their forwards and they must have been exhausted at the end. England went close again when with a quarter of an hour to go Greaves, for once, outpaced the defenders to run on to Ball's pass, only to see his cross picked off Connelly's head by Mazurkiewicz. With the crowd willing them on to the one goal they needed, England went desperately close twice in the last five minutes.

Connelly headed a flick by Jack Charlton against the Uruguayan crossbar, held his head in his hands, and then found he had been given offside anyway. Then, in the very last moments, a fine move begun by Jack Charlton enabled Ball to find Greaves on the right. Big Jack followed up to receive the ball from Greaves and his headed square pass was back-heeled inches wide by Connelly.

That was England's last chance and the evening ended with everyone being totally frustrated by the game. Needless to say, the Uruguayans were jumping for joy at the end. At least they had achieved what they wanted.

> 4th match v Uruguay.

England v Mexico   Group One

Played on Saturday, 16 July 1966 at Wembley Stadium.

England: G.Banks (Leicester C); G.R.Cohen (Fulham), R.Wilson (Everton), N.P.Stiles (Man Utd), J.Charlton (Leeds Utd), R.F.C.Moore (West Ham, captain), T.L.Paine (Southampton), J.P.Greaves (Spurs), R.Charlton (Man Utd), R.Hunt (Liverpool), M.S.Peters (West Ham).

Mexico: I.Calderón (Guadalajara); G.Peña (Oro), G.Hernández (Atlas), A.Chaires (Guadalajara), J.Del Muro (Vera Cruz), I.Jáuregui (Monterrey), I.Diaz (Guadalajara), G.Núñez (Zacatepec), E.Borja (Universidad de Mexico), S.Reyes (Guadalajara), A.Padilla (Universidad de Mexico).

Half-time 1-0   Full-time 2-0
Ref: C.Lo Bello (Italy)   Att: 92,570

ENGLAND'S vitally important second Group One match again pitted them up against a South American team. This time the plum-red shirts of the Mexicans provided the defensive barrier England had to penetrate. As against Uruguay in their opening fixture, they again found it difficult to unlock an eight or nine man defence, which Mexico employed.

England made a couple of changes, bringing in Terry Paine and Martin Peters and the latter was an immediate success. Gordon Banks had one of his easiest internationals and his £60 match fee could hardly have said to be earned. A few goal-kicks and only one real save to make, such was the sum total of Mexico's attacking ideas. Borja and Padilla showed some flair but generally they were a poor outfit.

Unfortunately, despite a fair amount of huffing and puffing by the England players, there was still very little end product to worry Calderón in the Mexico goal. It was all England, but it was not until the 38th minute that the piece of sheer magic so desperately required arrived. It came courtesy of Bobby Charlton.

Peters intercepted a Mexican pass and moved the ball on to Roger Hunt. A quick switch inside gave Bobby possession just inside his own half. With his thinning hair streaming in the wind, he dribbled free down the centre at pace. A jink left and then right, before his right-foot exploded a blockbuster into the top corner with Calderón hopelessly beaten from 25 yards.

It was a vintage piece of Charlton and the huge sigh of relief could be heard not only in the stadium but up and down the country by the millions watching on television. At last the crowd began to get behind the players and England's World Cup challenge was suddenly awake.

The second half was controlled by England. Although the play was largely dull and unimaginative, the precious goal was enough to appease the large crowd. With a quarter of an hour to go, the stadium erupted again. Once more Peters began the build-up. He combined with Bobby Charlton before putting Jimmy Greaves away with a perfect pass. When

Greaves put in a cross shot, Calderón could only palm the ball away and there on the spot was Hunt to score easily, due reward for some tireless if sometimes vain running.

The crowd were by now delighted. It was only England's fourth victory in the final stages of a World Cup competition, in 16 attempts. But they now had the lead in Group One and, barring accidents, should qualify for another quarter-final.

3rd match v Mexico.

"Bobby Charlton's goal was the best England goal I ever saw but the worst moment of my international career also came in this match when I was concussed."
Terry Paine

"Without doubt Bobby Charlton's goal was the best I have ever seen. Given the occasion and the importance of the match it has to be one of the greatest moments in sporting history too."
The Author

England v France   Group One

Played on Wednesday, 20 July 1966 at Wembley Stadium.

England: G.Banks (Leicester C); G.R.Cohen (Fulham), R.Wilson (Everton), N.P.Stiles (Man Utd), J.Charlton (Leeds Utd), R.F.C.Moore (West Ham, captain), I.R.Callaghan (Liverpool), J.P.Greaves (Spurs), R.Charlton (Man Utd), R.Hunt (Liverpool), M.S.Peters (West Ham).

France: M.Aubour (Olympique Lyonnais); J.Djorkaeff (Olympique Lyonnais), B.Bosquier (FC Sochaux), R.Herbin (AS St-Etienne), M.Artelesa (AS Monaco), R.Budzinski (FC Nantes), Y.Herbet (UA Sedan), J.Bonnel (US Valenciennes), P.Gondet (FC Nantes), J.Simon (FC Nantes), G.Hausser (RC Strasbourg).

Half-time 1-0   Full-time 2-0
Ref: A.Yamasaki Maldonado (Peru)
Att: 98,270

A CROWD of over 98,000, the highest of the tournament so far, greeted these teams at the start, with England getting a wonderful reception. At the end, those same people cheered long into the night as England duly clinched their place in the quarter-finals.

The game was a good one, although England were still not firing on all cylinders. France, trying for their first win of the competition, played some attractive football but finally succumbed after giving their hosts a tough match.

England began well with Martin Peters again the focal point of their midfield. He was so heavily involved in the action, forcing Bobby Charlton to move forward with the venom he showed against Mexico. An early injury to Herbin hampered the French somewhat and they had to reorganise. Herbin went up front with Gondet on the right and Herbet dropping back.

On the half-hour England found the net. Ian Callaghan picked up a Nobby Stiles miscued shot and centred for Peters to head it square for Jimmy Greaves to side foot home. Unfortunately the offside flag was up and the goal was disallowed.

Mexico's goalkeeper Ignacio Calderon dives too late to stop Roger Hunt putting England 2-0 ahead at Wembley during the 1966 World Cup finals.

England line up before the World Cup game against France. From left to right: Moore, Cohen, Banks, Callaghan, Hunt, Wilson, Stiles, Bobby Charlton, Peters, Greaves and Jack Charlton.

Peruvian referee Arturo Yamasaki points to the centre as Roger Hunt gives England the lead against France.

But the home side's increasing pressure had to pay off and with five minutes to go before half-time they made the breakthrough. A short corner was worked between Greaves and Stiles. The Manchester United midfielder lost the ball but recovered quickly to win it back. He then centred for Jack Charlton to nod the ball back for Roger Hunt to head home, to a huge roar from the crowd. It was the perfect end to the half and just the tonic England needed.

In the first 15 minutes after the restart, France went at England ferociously and now the strong home defence was able to show its mettle. The blue shirts of France moved relentlessly forward in search of an equalizer. Ray Wilson read a through-pass intended for Gondet perfectly to cut out imminent danger and then Bosquier fired a 40-yard drive just over Gordon Banks' crossbar.

Shortly after that, George Cohen emulated Wilson by intercepting another very dangerous pass by Gondet. To end this attacking burst, Banks made a fine full-length save from the tireless Simon, whose header from Bosquier's chip almost got through at the inside of the post.

It was all a bit hectic but with Jack Charlton dominating and Bobby Moore immaculate, England's defence safely withstood its sternest test of the tournament so far.

After this 15-minute spell by the French, it was England's turn to put on the pressure. Another goal was disallowed when Peters headed Callaghan's cross across goal for Bobby Charlton to volley home. Amidst a storm of booing, it was found that the Peruvian referee had ruled out the goal. Nobody was quite sure why.

England continued to increase the pressure pounding away at the French defence, and with a quarter of an hour to go they, at last, sealed victory. With Simon injured and prostrate, Artelesa tried a bicycle-kick to attempt to clear his lines. Sadly for France, he miscued. Greaves picked the ball up and quickly passed to Callaghan on the right. Over came another perfect cross and there was his Liverpool teammate Hunt to head his second goal of the night.

England, now more relaxed, went close again as Aubour twice saved brilliantly from Peters. France then hit back with a final gesture of defiance and only a superb

save by Banks prevented Hausser's drive from succeeding.

So England now moved on to a quarter-final match against Argentina at Wembley, where a capacity crowd was a certainty.

17th match v France.

England v Argentina   Quarter-final

Played on Saturday, 23 July 1966 at Wembley Stadium.

England: G.Banks (Leicester C); G.R.Cohen (Fulham), R.Wilson (Everton), N.P.Stiles (Man Utd), J.Charlton (Leeds Utd), R.F.C.Moore (West Ham, captain), A.J.Ball (Blackpool), R.Hunt (Liverpool), R.Charlton (Man Utd), G.C.Hurst (West Ham), M.S.Peters (West Ham).

Argentina: A.Roma (Boca Juniors); R.Ferreiro (Independiente), S.Marzolini (Boca Juniors), A.U.Rattín (Boca Juniors), R.Perfumo (Racing Club), J.Albrecht (San Lorenzo), E.Onega (River Plate), J.Solari (River Plate), L.Artime (Independiente), A.González (Boca Juniors), O.Mas (River Plate).

Half-time 0-0   Full-time 1-0

Ref: R.Kreitlein (West Germany)

Att: 90,584

SOMETIMES a football match is remembered for its outstanding goals, sometimes for a great save or other individual contribution. This match against the volatile Argentinians will always be remembered for the terrible scenes of mayhem after Antonio Rattín was sent off for continually breaking the rules.

Indeed, the loser in this match was the game of football.

From the first attack, when Martin Peters was felled by a blatant body check, it was obvious that Argentina were out to stop England at all costs. Pushing, jostling, chopping, holding and tripping was the order of the day as the West German referee struggled to keep a grip of the proceedings. England were not blameless and in the first half probably conceded more free-kicks.

Goal attempts were few and far between. The undoubted skill of the South Americans was to the fore when a lovely pass by Onega found Mas and his shot flew just past Gordon Banks's post. At the other end, Geoff Hurst, in for Jimmy Greaves, watched in disbelief as Roma made a magnificent save from him. As tempers rose, the referee's pencil worked overtime. Rattín, Artime and Solari were all booked and with ten minutes of the half remaining, all hell broke loose.

With the ball well away from Rattín everyone was amazed to see the referee point to the dressing-room, having sent the Argentine captain off. For the next seven minutes there was bedlam. Players and officials jostled on the pitch and at one point it seemed that the whole Argentinian team would go off. Eventually, with the crowd keeping their good humour remarkably well, order was restored and the game, such as it was, moved on.

In the second half, the ten-man Argentine side battled on. Ferreira and Perfumo were added to the referee's list of bookings and the Charlton brothers joined them later on. Through this shambles it was clear that England's defence was in superb form with Bobby Moore in his usual immaculate mood. But in midfield and up front England struggled.

Argentina has such obvious football talent that it seems a crying shame that their energies have to be channelled in the wrong direction like this.

The game desperately needed a goal. Roger Hunt was easily held and Alan Ball and Bobby Charlton had poor games in midfield. But with just 13 minutes to go the vital breakthrough was achieved. Ray Wilson fed a pass to Peters down the left and the star of the England side put over the most telling and tantalising of centres.

For a split second it seemed to hang in the air, and on the end of it was Hurst, who flicked the ball wide of the crestfallen Roma with the most perfect of glancing headers. The goal was majestic and more than justified Hurst's selection. His teammates were jubilant.

England held on to see that justice was done and they now met the challenge of the Portuguese team in the semi-final. Despite the joy at reaching the next round, the occasion was spoilt for many by the bitter taste of all that went on before in this notorious match. Alf Ramsey, afterwards, was most scathing in his criticism of the Argentinian tactics.

> 5th match v Argentina.
> *"Geoff Hurst's goal was the best England goal I ever saw in my time with the squad. An unstoppable cross and header."*
> Bobby Charlton

Argentina protest but Herr Kreitlein is adamant and Rattín has to go.

Geoff Hurst's 'unstoppable' header which beat Argentina, glanced in from a Peters cross.

England v Portugal
Semi-final

Played on Tuesday, 26 July 1966 at Wembley Stadium.

England: G.Banks (Leicester C); G.R.Cohen (Fulham), R.Wilson (Everton), N.P.Stiles (Man Utd), J.Charlton (Leeds Utd), R.F.C.Moore (West Ham, captain), A.J.Ball (Blackpool), R.Hunt (Liverpool), R.Charlton (Man Utd), G.C.Hurst (West Ham), M.S.Peters (West Ham).

Portugal: J.Pereira (Belenenses); A.Festa (FC Porto), H.de Conceicão (Sporting Lisbon), J.Graça (Vitória Setúbal), J.A.Baptista (Sporting Lisbon), J.C.Silva (Sporting Lisbon), J.A.Almeida (Benfica), E.Ferreira (Benfica), J.A.Torres (Benfica), M.Coluña (Benfica), A.Simões (Benfica).

Half-time 1-0   Full-time 2-1

Ref: P.Schwinte (France)   Att: 94,493

ENGLAND had done it! After a magnificent game and superb performance they had reached the World Cup Final for the first time.

What a contrast to the débâcle of the Argentine game. Fine sporting football played by two teams determined to win — and full marks to Portugal, who contributed so much to a fabulous night's entertainment for the crowd in the stadium and the millions watching on television. It was a joy to watch with,

England manager Alf Ramsey does not want George Cohen to swap his England shirt after the controversial match against Argentina.

thankfully, hardly an interruption from the referee's whistle.

The first half clearly belonged to England. Good approach play by Martin Peters, Bobby Charlton and Alan Ball set up some half-chances, notably to Geoff Hurst. Three times the West Ham player was in a good position but failed with

the finish. The Portuguese defenders were unsure under pressure and Pereira had to be on his toes at all times as England came forward. Nobby Stiles was assigned the task of a man-to-man marking job on the silky skilled Eusébio and did his job well as the Portuguese danger man was kept quiet for long spells.

Bobby Charlton lets fly a right-foot shot for England's second goal against Portugal in the 1966 World Cup semi-final at Wembley.

After 30 minutes play England got their noses in front with a splendid goal. The move began with Ray Wilson's long forward pass being chased by the ever-willing Roger Hunt. Pereira came roaring out of goal to meet Hunt and blocked the ball with his knees, but in a flash the ball ran out to Bobby Charlton and the England maestro cleverly first-timed it through the gap, along the ground and into the empty net. The crowd went wild with delight.

England then had to consolidate, led by Bobby Moore at his assured best. Jack Charlton played well against the giant Torres and both George Cohen and Ray Wilson were solid and dependable full-backs. The half ended with England still a goal up.

If the first half had been England's then the second belonged to Portugal.

Fine play by Graça, Coluña, Augusto and Simoẽs pinned England back for a long spell and Eusébio and Torres began to cause problems. Portugal had one real flaw in their play, though, and that was to take just a little too much time on the ball. It gave England the vital time to fall back and cover in depth with Peters and Ball doing their fair share of defending.

But the red tide of Portuguese attacks kept coming and although they rarely threatened, the relief of a second England goal with ten minutes to go was felt all round. The build-up was excellent as Jack Charlton passed to Ball, on to Moore and then Cohen. The full-back then sent a long ball forward into the inside-right position for Hurst to chase. Hurst cleverly gained possession and waited for support. He did not have to wait long, for there was Bobby Charlton roaring in.

Hurst laid the ball perfectly into his path and wham! It flew past Pereira and all the England players leapt in the air with delight.

There was a lovely moment as the players went back to the middle for the kick-off. As Bobby Charlton approached Augusto, the Portuguese player held his hand out warmly to congratulate the scorer. It emphasised the spirit in which the game was played.

With only ten minutes to go, one could forgive the fans for thinking that the game was won, but far from it! Two minutes later Portugal set up a grandstand finish by pulling a goal back. Torres outjumped everyone to send a header goalwards and only Jack Charlton's hand could prevent the goal. Penalty! Up stepped Eusébio and Gordon Banks was given no chance, beaten for the first time in this World Championship. Seconds later Simoẽs seemed certain to score after another Torres header, but from nowhere the little terrier Stiles came to make a magnificent tackle to save the day.

Torres then shot wide after Jack Charlton and Wilson had collided, and a rocket by Eusébio bounced out of Banks' arms for Stiles to hack away for a corner.

The suspense was agonising and there was still time for one last attack. Eusébio, with lovely skills, slid dangerously towards goal before sending a square pass to Coluña. The Portuguese skipper hit a screamer that arrowed towards the top corner. For a split second England's hearts were in their mouths, but spectacularly, Banks flew across goal leaping upwards to make a superb tip-over save to keep England's lead intact.

It was a magnificent climax to a magnificent match. The final whistle blew shortly afterwards and the joyous scenes will live long in the memory. It was sad that somebody had to lose but Portugal won many friends after this display and everyone in the stadium felt sympathy for Eusébio. One of the world's greatest players left the field in tears as he was overcome with emotion.

But it was tears of joy all the way for England and now they faced the mighty West Germans in the Final.

10th match v Portugal.
Penalty by Eusébio for Portugal.
50th cap for Wilson.
Portugal's Conceicão also known as Hilario; J.C.Silva as 'José Carlos'; Almeida as 'José Augusto'; Ferreira as 'Eusébio'.

England v West Germany   Final

Played on Saturday, 30 July 1966 at Wembley Stadium.

England: G.Banks (Leicester C); G.R.Cohen (Fulham), R.Wilson (Everton), N.P.Stiles (Man Utd), J.Charlton (Leeds Utd), R.F.C.Moore (West Ham, captain), A.J.Ball (Blackpool), R.Hunt (Liverpool), R.Charlton (Man Utd), G.C.Hurst (West Ham), M.S.Peters (West Ham).

West Germany: H.Tilkowski (Borussia Dortmund); H.D.Höttges (Werder Bremen), K.H.Schnellinger (Milan AC), F.Beckenbauer (Bayern Munich), W.Schulz (Hamburger SV), W.Weber (1.FC Cologne), H.Haller (Bologna), W.Overath (1.FC Cologne), U.Seeler (Hamburger SV), S.Held (Borussia Dortmund), L.Emmerich (Borussia Dortmund).

Half-time 1-1   Full-time 4-2 aet (90 minutes, 2-2)

Ref: G.Dienst (Switzerland)   Att: 96,924

THE World Cup had come home at last! England, the pioneers of organised football were the new World Champions after an afternoon of high excitement, emotion, tension and drama that Wembley Stadium had never seen the like of before.

From early in the morning, the atmosphere was electric. The crowd flocked to Wembley from all corners of the world and at kick-off time on a day of squally showers and bright sunshine, the stadium was a sea of waving flags. As the teams marched into the arena, the emotion of the occasion made even the most hardened spectator clear the lump from his throat. It was a magical moment in the history of English football.

The noise was deafening and from high in the stand there came a beating of a drum, a deep pulsating throb that lasted throughout the game. Her Majesty the Queen and the Duke of Edinburgh were introduced to the teams and after all the preliminaries were over, Gottfried Dienst,

England and West Germany players line up before the start of the 1966 World Cup Final.

Bobby Moore and West Germany's captain Uwe Seeler watch as referee Gottfried Dienst of Switzerland tosses the coin.

the referee from Switzerland, blew the opening whistle.

Both sides tentatively felt each other out in the early stages and they found the pitch treacherous after two heavy showers had fallen just before the start. It was ripe for error. That statement proved fatally correct in the 13th minute when Ray Wilson misjudged a headed clearance from Seeler's deep cross. The ball dropped straight at Haller's feet and the German forward wasted no time in hitting a shot into the far corner of Gordon Banks' goal. One could feel the wave of disappointment that swept from the terraces, at least from the English contingent. But thankfully, the home supporters did not have to wait long for a reply.

Only six minutes after the goal, England equalized. Overath unfairly tackled Bobby Moore and the captain quickly spotted a gap in the German rearguard. His instant free-kick floated beautifully 35 yards to the middle and there was Geoff Hurst leaping unchallenged to direct a downwards header to the right of the flat-footed Tilkowski. It was a vital goal.

So, all-square and plenty to play for. Near-misses came at both ends. Banks made two saves in as many seconds from Overath and Emmerich, whilst at the other end Tilkowski parried a left-foot rocket from Roger Hunt after a good pass by Martin Peters. The goalkeeper then needed treatment after a 20-yard fizzer by Bobby Charlton beat his dive but struck

the post and bounced back into Tilkowski's face before being cleared.

The half ended at one goal each and both sets of players walked off to get fresh inspiration from their respective managers. When the teams reappeared, more slanting rain fell, glinting through the watery sunshine. The half opened with some cagey play from both sides. Each sought a chink in the armour of the other's defence and the game went into a relatively quiet spell. The referee annoyed the crowd with some irritating decisions and goal chances were few and far between.

A deep cross by Peters out on the left was met by Bobby Charlton and another fierce shot went only just wide. As the game wore on, both teams tensed up not

Left: Geoff Hurst heads England's equalizer. *Right:* Martin Peters (16) throws his arms in the air after giving England the lead.

Left: Football's most controversial goal? Geoff Hurst's shot in extra-time hits the crossbar and bounces down. *Right:* Nobody seems quite certain but after consulting with a linesman, the referee allowed the goal and England were 3-2 ahead.

Left: The goal which led to extra-time when Wolfgang Weber sidefooted home with 30 seconds remaining. *Right:* Geoff Hurst has just completed his historic hat-trick and England are World Champions.

daring to make the mistake that might settle the issue. But with 13 minutes to go, the stadium erupted.

Alan Ball, who showed boundless energy throughout and covered every blade of this Wembley turf, now forced a corner on the right. He took the kick himself and the ball eventually reached Hurst. Hurst aimed a rather speculative shot goalwards but Höttges deflected it into the path of Peters and Jack Charlton. Peters was there first and his bundled shot billowed the West German net to roars of delight from the crowd.

We thought that was it, but these Germans were not beaten until the very last whistle sounded. Reinforced by Schnellinger and with the tireless efforts of Haller, Overath, Held and Beckenbauer, they kept pushing forward. Moore

and Nobby Stiles were masterly in defence, but with the last minute unwinding, and with Moore's hands all but on the trophy, the Germans found a sensational equalizer.

A somewhat harsh decision gave the Germans a free-kick against Jack Charlton. With everyone back behind the ball, Emmerich blasted the kick against the English wall. The ball rebounded to Held, who blazed wildly sending it across goal. There was a suspicion of handball against Schnellinger but eventually it ran wide and in came Weber to stun the whole of England by crashing the ball past Banks' despairing dive.

England just had time to kick-off again before the referee blew his whistle for the end of 90 minutes. Alf Ramsey came on, as did most of the England World Cup party, and his first task was to get the

players on their feet ready for the extra-time period. Many sides would have folded after having had victory snatched from their grasp in such dramatic fashion, but not England. They rolled up their sleeves and rolled down their socks and prepared for battle all over again.

The energy-sapping pitch was having dire consequences and many players were suffering from cramp. England stuck to the pattern which had served them so well. Stiles and Moore mopped up the Germans' central thrusts, Bobby Charlton and Peters provided from midfield, Ball scurried here, there and everywhere and up front Hurst and Hunt battered away at the German defences.

Extra-time approached its half-way stage as Stiles sent Ball on another lung-bursting run to a through-ball. The fiery

Bobby Moore with the World Cup as England parade around Wembley after their victory in the 1966 Final.

red-haired number-seven collected and put in an instant centre. Hurst trapped the ball with his back to goal, swivelled, and crashed a tremendous shot which thudded against the bar, bounced down and was then headed clear by Weber.

"Goal," shouted Hunt, who turned immediately to salute Hurst's shot. The Germans disagreed, convinced the ball had not crossed the line. The England fans bayed as the referee trotted over to the Russian linesman, Tofik Bakhramov. There was an agonising wait as the two engaged in a tense conversation. But at the end of it all, Mr Dienst pointed to the middle and the English celebrations began in earnest. The Germans argued but the record book had been written and at half-time in extra-time, the score was 3-2 to England.

How the two sides managed to see out the last stage of this two-hour epic was beyond praise and marvellous testament to the wonderful level of fitness, the two

squads had reached. The minutes ticked away, England feared another German comeback, but then, finally, with seconds left, the greatest day in the history of English football was sealed by a fourth goal.

Moore, in majestic form even at this late stage, put another superb defence-splitting pass through the wide open spaces of the German defence, exposed by their desperate attacking commitment. On to it ran Hurst and the West Ham combination reached a remarkable climax as a rasping shot from Hurst's left foot flew into the top corner of Tilkowski's net. A hat-trick for Hurst and the first time that a player had achieved that feat in a World Cup Final.

Seconds later, the whistle blew to end a passionate afternoon. Ball leapt on Hurst, Jack Charlton sank to the floor in sheer fatigue and unashamed joy, whilst brother Bobby's face just crumpled into a flood of tears. The scenes were marvellously unforgettable.

The walk up the steps for the team to receive the trophy was a proud moment and when Moore lifted the World Cup to the heavens, the roar could be heard for miles around. And who will ever forget Nobby Stiles, doing his victory jig on the lap of honour, his toothless smile an image that would be on the front pages of every newspaper the following day.

England were World champions and worthy winners.

> 8th match v West Germany.
> Hat-trick by Hurst.

Northern Ireland v England Home Championship & European Nations Cup

Played on Saturday, 22 October 1966 at Windsor Park, Belfast.

Northern Ireland: P.A.Jennings (Spurs); J.Parke (Sunderland), A.R.Elder (Burnley), S.J.Todd (Burnley), M.Harvey (Sunderland), W.J.McCullough (Millwall), W.Ferguson (Linfield), J.A.Crossan (Man City), W.J.Irvine (Burnley), A.D.Dougan (Leicester C), G.Best (Man U).
Sub: W.S.McFaul (Linfield) for Jennings.
England: G.Banks (Leicester C); G.R.Cohen (Fulham), R.Wilson (Everton), N.P.Stiles (Man Utd), J.Charlton (Leeds Utd), R.F.C.Moore (West Ham, captain), A.J.Ball (Everton), R.Hunt (Liverpool), R.Charlton (Man Utd), G.C.Hurst (West Ham), M.S.Peters (West Ham).

Half-time 0-1   Full-time 0-2
Ref: R.H.Davidson (Scotland) Att: 48,500

ENGLAND proudly paraded their World Cup trophy in front of an enthusiastic crowd at Windsor Park, before going on to beat the Irish clearly if not convincingly. The match had extra incentives this year as the winners of the Home Championship over the next two seasons would automatically qualify for the 1968 European Nations Championship.

Obviously everyone wanted to beat the new World Champions from now on, and Northern Ireland started in typical boisterous mood. Right from the first whistle, it was also obvious that George Best would be the player England would have to contain. The Manchester United wing wizard paraded all his skills and England worked desperately hard to keep him in check. Clubmate Nobby Stiles had a torrid time trying to mark him and more than once incurred the wrath of the crowd with his challenges.

The game was full of fiery tackles and Stiles and Dougan were booked after one skirmish. All the time, though, it was noticed that England were still moving in that familiar well-tuned way of theirs. Bobby Moore and Jack Charlton were dominant at the back, Bobby Charlton, Martin Peters and Alan Ball controlled the midfield, and up front the tireless running of Geoff Hurst and Roger Hunt always caught the eye.

Ironically, Ireland had a fine chance to score before England when Crossan missed an easy opportunity after Gordon Banks had made a superb double save from Dougan. On 15 minutes, Hunt touched the ball into the Irish net after Jennings had parried a fierce Bobby Charlton shot, but the referee disallowed the goal for an offside decision. But after 40 minutes, England broke the deadlock and nosed their way in front.

A throw-in was taken by Hurst to Peters, who advanced down the right before whipping over a fine cross which Hunt hit on the half-volley on the turn past the stranded Jennings. It was a splendid goal and just reward for some unselfish running by the Liverpool player. Within moments of the goal, Ball went very close to making it 2-0 when he hit the bar from close range.

After the interval, Best continued to shine, although his petulance at some of the hard tackling left a lot to be desired. He still remained Ireland's best hope of a comeback, though, as Ireland searched for a goal.

England were again showing the teamwork which had proved so successful last July and, as a unit, could not be faulted.

With 30 minutes left, they clinched the match with a second goal. Again Peters and Hurst combined with the latter heading the former's left-wing cross against the bar. Ireland cleared, but England were back quickly with Bobby Charlton centring again, this time from the right. Peters was on the end of it to head a beautiful goal past substitute goalkeeper McFaul. The new 'keeper had come on to replace the injured Jennings shortly before.

Other chances fell to Hurst, Bobby Charlton and Ball as England controlled the later stages but Crossan probably had the best chance when he missed a sitter laid on for him by Dougan and Irvine.

The fiery tackling that had gone on throughout the game continued and in the end the referee lost his patience and sent Ferguson off for a dangerous tackle on Ball. A few moments later, Best was lucky not to follow his teammate after another bad foul on Ball.

So England marched on, now unbeaten in their last 17 matches and losing only once in their last 28. Alf Ramsey's tactics seemed to be very effective.

74th match v Northern Ireland.
Ferguson sent off for the Irish.

England v Czechoslovakia Friendly
Played on Wednesday, 2 November 1966 at Wembley Stadium.

England: G.Banks (Leicester C); G.R.Cohen (Fulham), R.Wilson (Everton), N.P.Stiles (Man Utd), J.Charlton (Leeds Utd), R.F.C.Moore (West Ham, captain), A.J.Ball (Everton), R.Hunt (Liverpool), R.Charlton (Man Utd), G.C.Hurst (West Ham), M.S.Peters (West Ham).
Czechoslovakia: I.Viktor (Dukla Prague); J.Lála (Slavia Prague), J.Popluhár (Slovan Bratislava), V.Táborský (Sparta Prague), A.Horváth (Slovan Bratislava), J.Geleta (Dukla Prague), A.Kvašňák (Sparta Prague), F.Veselý (Slavia Prague), J.Skikora (Inter Bratislava), E.Schmidt (Spartak Hradec Králové), J.Adamec (Spartak Trnava).
Sub: L.Kuna (Spartak Trnava) for Schmidt.

Half-time 0-0   Full-time 0-0
Ref: P.P.Roomer (Holland) Att: 75,000

THIS was a disappointing goalless draw, played out in the same setting that had seen so much joy only three months ago. It was a very negative performance from both sides with the solid Czech defenders winning the few honours that were going.

England began like steam trains, throwing everything at the visitors in the first ten minutes. Geoff Hurst, Roger Hunt, Alan Ball and Martin Peters all might have scored the early goal, that the game probably needed but when they did hit the target they found goalkeeper Viktor in inspired form, hurling himself about his goal with great athleticism.

The home side played well, up to a point. They used Wembley's vast open spaces with Bobby Moore, Bobby Charlton, Nobby Stiles and Peters all putting probing passes around the pitch. But each

time a promising opening was made, the finishing let the team down. On the night, Hunt and Hurst just could not find their shooting boots.

Just before the interval, with the crowd doing their best to lift England, Viktor produced an outstanding punching save after a double-barrelled header by first Hurst and then Jack Charlton. Then, moments later, Bobby Charlton made one of his famous flowing runs, only to shoot a fraction wide of the target with Viktor this time beaten. The Czechs made a substitution just before half-time when Kuna came on for Schmidt.

The first 20 minutes of the second half brought another barrage of pressure by England, who laid siege on the Czechoslavakian goal. Always, though, the attack petered out in the vital area. Bobby Charlton saw another thunderous shot brilliantly saved again by Viktor whilst other chances came and went.

The best opportunity of all fell to Hunt with only five minutes to go. He was in a fine position as a cross came over to him, but he missed his volley completely, despite the fact that he had all the time in the world.

However, the chance was lost and it sort of summed up the game. England were never in top form and the crowd left in a disappointed mood. For the record, this was only the second goalless draw in 58 full internationals at Wembley since the war. The other was the World Cup match against Uruguay.

4th match v Czechoslovakia.

England v Wales Home Championship & European Nations Cup
Played on Wednesday, 16 November 1966 at Wembley Stadium.

England: G.Banks (Leicester C); G.R.Cohen (Fulham), R.Wilson (Everton), N.P.Stiles (Man Utd), J.Charlton (Leeds Utd), R.F.C.Moore (West Ham, captain), A.J.Ball (Everton), R.Hunt (Liverpool), R.Charlton (Man Utd), G.C.Hurst (West Ham), M.S.Peters (West Ham).
Wales: A.H.Millington (Peterborough Utd); C.R.Green (Birmingham C), G.E.Williams (West Brom), W.T.Hennessey (Nottm Forest), H.M.England (Spurs), B.G.Hole (Blackburn R), R.R.Rees (Coventry C), R.T.Davies (Southampton), R.W.Davies (Newcastle Utd), A.L.Jarvis (Hull C), C.W.Jones (Spurs).

Half-time 3-1   Full-time 5-1
Ref: T.Wharton (Scotland) Att: 76,000

ALTHOUGH England ended with an emphatic win over Wales, this scoreline in no way reflects the way this dual-purpose international went. With both the Home Championship and qualification for the European Championship at stake, there was a lot of added spice to this annual fixture.

On a bitterly cold night when the wind was so biting, some 76,000 brave souls enjoyed a very entertaining game. For a while, England carried on where they left

A hobbling Jack Charlton scores for England against Scotland at Wembley in April 1967, but the World Champions were beaten by their old enemy.

off against Czechoslovakia two weeks earlier. Geoff Hurst was the chief culprit missing three good chances in the opening 20 minutes.

Wales had come, European style, to contain rather than attack and they left only two forwards up. Rees and Jones, did work hard down the flanks and the two Davies always carried a threat. Having said that, the England defence maintained the tight discipline that we have now come to expect of them and they coped fairly easily with the Welsh attacks.

Bobby Moore and Jack Charlton were again very prominent and after half an hour, England were celebrating a goal. Martin Peters put a good pass to Hurst, who quickly fired in a shot which was diverted, unluckily for the Welsh, by Roger Hunt's shoulder. The ball flew past Millington and the goal was credited to Hurst.

That settled England down and three minutes later they scored again with a peach of a goal. Hole's hurried clearance was picked up by Nobby Stiles and he put over a perfect centre which Hurst met with a scorching header. There was no disputing that goalscorer.

It was looking good for England, but Wales quickly came back into the match and moments later it was 2-1. A cross by Ron Davies was flicked home by Wyn Davies to reduce the arrears. That was the first goal attempt the Welsh had put in but it counted with deadly effect.

England, undaunted, kept to their now familiar pattern meticulously, and before half-time they regained their two-goal advantage. Peters this time fed a square pass to Bobby Charlton, who fired in a fierce shot from 20 yards. Millington could perhaps have done better but another deflection meant that the goalkeeper allowed the ball to slip through his grasp, much to his obvious annoyance. Charlton, however, was delighted and had now scored 41 goals for his country.

England had looked very effective in the first half and they now seem to have telepathic powers, so good was the understanding that Alf Ramsey had cultivated. Despite this dominance, Wales

still battled bravely on. A lovely move, one of the best of the match, ended with Ron Davies hitting a stinging shot which thudded against the post before being cleared.

That certainly was a let-off for England but they then pressed home their obvious superiority with two more goals in the last ten minutes. On 80 minutes, Hennessey was in the wrong place at the wrong time to turn a Hunt chip wide of his own goalkeeper for number four; five minutes later, Jack Charlton completed the scoring when he headed in Hurst's centre from the right.

It was an entertaining match, played in a good spirit, with the valiant Welshmen never giving up despite the scoreline.

> 77th match v Wales.
> 50th cap for Moore.
> Own-goal by Hennessey.

England v Scotland Home Championship & European Nations Cup

Played on Saturday, 15 April 1967 at Wembley Stadium.

England: G.Banks (Leicester C); G.R.Cohen (Fulham), R.Wilson (Everton), N.P.Stiles (Man Utd), J.Charlton (Leeds Utd), R.F.C.Moore (West Ham, captain), A.J.Ball (Everton), J.P.Greaves (Spurs), R.Charlton (Man Utd), G.C.Hurst (West Ham), M.S.Peters (West Ham).

Scotland: R.C.Simpson (Celtic); T.Gemmell (Celtic), E.G.McCreadie (Chelsea), J.Greig (Rangers), R.McKinnon (Rangers), J.C.Baxter (Sunderland), W.S.B.Wallace (Celtic), W.J.Bremner (Leeds Utd), J.McCalliog (Sheffield Wed), D.Law (Man Utd), R.Lennox (Celtic).

Half-time 0-1   Full-time 2-3

Ref: G.Schulenberg (West Germany)

Att: 99,063

THE rewards at stake for winning this match were enormous and the pre-match

build up added to the atmosphere of another big Wembley occasion. England began as favourites but at the end trudged off disappointed at losing their long and proud unbeaten record.

The highlight for any Scotland team is to beat the Auld Enemy, but to do it when England were the current World Champions gave them much satisfaction.

The game was not a particularly good one, although it was to have an explosive finish. Scotland made a thrilling start and were making an impact as soon as the first whistle went. Law, Baxter, Bremner and McCalliog all played as though their lives depended on it, but the early pressure paid off when they opened the scoring just before the half hour was up.

Law, showing typically sharp reflexes after a rebound from Wallace's shot reached him, fired past Gordon Banks to send the excitable Scottish fans wild with delight. Wembley was a sea of tartan.

To be fair, England were handicapped by a nasty early injury to big Jack Charlton. He injured a toe — suspectedly broken — in a tackle on Lennox and was forced to hobble painfully but bravely on the right wing. He later moved to centre-forward.

England's attack, with the recalled Jimmy Greaves, never really got to grips with the strong Scottish defence and only Bobby Charlton looked dangerous. The Manchester United star had a fine game and his flowing runs were the feature of England's play.

The home side certainly had their fair share of injuries in this match. Apart from Jack Charlton's toe, Greaves' effectiveness was reduced by a swollen ankle and Ray Wilson was reduced to half-pace by a knock he received. It was a punishing game but all those excuses did not hide the fact that Scotland wanted to win more than England seemed to.

The second half was an even contest with the Scots seemingly content with Law's goal, but with ten minutes to go they sealed the result with a second, decisive goal. Nobby Stiles missed a lob forward from Gemmell and Lennox was there to score easily.

Everyone thought that that would be the end, but suddenly England produced a rousing finale. In the last five minutes there were three more goals. Jack Charlton, still hobbling valiantly, managed to poke the ball home after an Alan Ball pass. That pulled one back but almost immediately a clever one-two between Wallace and the impressive McCalliog ended with the latter celebrating his debut with a goal. England still refused to surrender and before the final whistle, Geoff Hurst headed a Bobby Charlton cross past Simpson.

So, England's 19-match unbeaten run which has stretched since October 1965 had finally come to an end. Circumstances were such that not much went England's way on the day but all credit to the Scots, who produced a passionate performance which deservedly gave them victory. The win clinched the season's Home Championship and kept them in the lead for that place in the 1968 European Nations finals. The eventual qualifiers, based on two years Home Championships, would probably be decided by the following February's clash of these two teams at Hampden Park.

> 84th match v Scotland.

England v Spain
Friendly

Played on Wednesday, 24 May 1967 at Wembley Stadium.

England: P.Bonetti (Chelsea); G.R.Cohen (Fulham), K.R.Newton (Blackburn R), A.P.Mullery (Spurs), B.L.Labone (Everton), R.F.C.Moore (West Ham, captain), A.J.Ball (Blackpool), J.P.Greaves (Spurs), G.C.Hurst (West Ham), R.Hunt (Liverpool), J.W.Hollins (Chelsea).

Spain: J.A.Iribar (Athletic Bilbao); M.Sanchís (Real Madrid), S.Reija (Real Zaragoza), J.Glaría (Atlético Madrid), F.Fernandez (FC Barcelona), J.L.Violeta (Real Zaragoza), A.Amaro (Real Madrid), J.M.Sánchez (Real Madrid), R.M.Grosso (Real Madrid), J.M.Garcia (RCD Español), F.Gento (Real Madrid)

Half-time 0-0   Full-time 2-0
Ref: I.Zsolt (Hungary)   Att: 75,000

ALF Ramsey brought several new faces for the visit of the current European Champions, Spain. For various reasons, six of England's World Cup winning side were missing but Ramsey now had the chance to have a look at a few of the understudies.

The game was a tactical battle and took a long time to produce a goal with neither side seemingly able to outsmart the other. Spain played in their normal style, despite previous rumours of new tactics whilst England stuck rigidly to their 4-3-3 formation. The technical ability of both sides could not be questioned and the professionalism shone through. But the spectators were looking to see just a little piece of flair in the pattern to inspire them.

Goal attempts were few and far between in the first half and the interval score of 0-0 was most predictable. It was not until the 70th minute that the match finally awoke from the chess-like action. There was the most tremendous downpour as the heavens opened and for some inexplicable reason it seemed to lift England.

Jimmy Greaves collides with a Spanish defender at Wembley in May 1967 and Roger Hunt appeals for a free kick.

John Hollins, making an impressive debut, began a move down the left with Alan Mullery. Mullery's return pass was carried almost to the corner-flag by Hollins before a delightful centre found Alan Ball's red head. Ball nodded it back across goal for Roger Hunt to fire in a shot on the turn. Iribar saved well but could not hold the shot and Jimmy Greaves, looking much sharper by the minute, pounced like a hungry panther to shoot home the first goal.

That was just the tonic England needed and soon afterwards Greaves forced a fine save from Iribar with another crashing shot which resulted in a corner. The bombardment was now rocking Spain back on their heels as England found new zest in their play. The pressure on the Spanish defenders was intense and on 75 minutes by a lovely move started by Bobby Moore left Geoff Hurst free on a clever run. The West Ham striker crossed from the right and there was Hunt, completely unmarked, to head past Iribar.

That, as they say, was that. Near the end, Spain almost gained a consolation goal when Amancio, their most dangerous forward, fired in a fierce shot which beat Bonetti and crashed into the net. However, a sharp-eyed linesman had noticed that flying winger Gento's cross had been made from the wrong side of the goal-line.

> 9th match v Spain.
> Debut for Hollins.
> Spain's Fernandez also known as 'Gallego'; Amaro as 'Amancio'; Sánchez as 'Pirri'; Garcia as 'José Maria'.

Austria v England
Friendly

Played on Saturday, 27 May 1967 at the Prater Stadium, Vienna.

Austria: I.R.Pichler (Rapid Wien); H.Wartusch (Wacker Innsbruck), W.Glechner (Rapid Wien), E.Fak (Rapid Wien), R.Eschelmüller (Wacker Innsbruck), G.Sturmberger (LASK Linz), H.Köglberger (LASK Linz), F.Wolny (Wacker Innsbruck), H.Siber (Wacker Innsbruck), P.Schmidt (SK Wien), T.Parits (FK Austria Wien).

England: P.P.Bonetti (Chelsea); K.R.Newton (Blackburn R), R.Wilson (Everton), A.P.Mullery (Spurs), B.L.Labone (Everton), R.F.C.Moore (West Ham, captain), A.J.Ball (Everton), J.P.Greaves (Spurs), G.C.Hurst (West Ham), R.Hunt (Liverpool), N.Hunter (Leeds Utd).

Half-time 0-1   Full-time 0-1
Ref: M.Kitabdjian (France)   Att: 85,000

AFTER Celtic's win in the European Cup Final, England completed a fine week for British football by gaining a very creditable win against the tough Austrian side. This game was a poor one, though, with neither side coming to grips with a difficult, bumpy pitch in the Prater Stadium. The referee, too, had a detrimental effect with his over-officious style.

There were very few moments of the match worth recalling. However, Alan Ball was the undoubted hero of England. The Everton star was everywhere and inspired his colleagues with an all-action display. Austria had their moments, especially when Siber, Köglberger and Parits pressed forward. But their midfield of Eschmuller and Schmidt did not have the flair to conjure up the magic that was needed to break down England's well-organised defence which was superbly marshalled by the immaculate Bobby Moore.

Despite the Austrian dominance, England always seemed to be one step ahead of their opponents and in the 20th minute they expertly snatched the lead. Ball showed fine control to expertly kill a long pass from Alan Mullery. Then he beat Glechner on the turn and stroked the awkwardly bouncing ball past Pichler's dive. It was a fine strike and due reward for Ball's enthusiasm.

After the goal, the game continued in a drab way with neither team able to take a firm grip on the play. Both Roger Hunt and Jimmy Greaves missed badly when well placed and Pichler made some good saves from other chances that fell to England.

The second half was quite forgettable. England continued to be the more organised of the two sides and their superior teamwork gave them a definite edge. In the end they comfortably held on to their one goal advantage and deservedly so, much to the annoyance of the home supporters.

Some of the England players now went to play in Canada under the guise of an FA XI, as part of that country's celebrations for Expo 67. It would be a pleasant way for them to end a very good year of international football.

13th match v Austria.

Wales v England Home Championship & European Nations Cup

Played on Saturday, 21 October 1967 at Ninian Park, Cardiff.

Wales: G.Sprake (Leeds Utd); P.J.Rodrigues (Leicester C), C.R.Green (Birmingham C), W.T.Hennessey (Nottm Forest), H.M.England (Spurs), B.G.Hole (Blackburn R), R.R.Rees (Coventry C), W.A.Durban (Derby Co), J.F.Mahoney (Stoke C), T.R.Vernon (Stoke C), C.W.Jones (Spurs).

England: G.Banks (Stoke C); G.R.Cohen (Fulham), K.R.Newton (Blackburn R), A.P.Mullery (Fulham), J.Charlton (Leeds Utd), R.F.C.Moore (West Ham, captain), A.J.Ball (Everton), R.Hunt (Liverpool), R.Charlton (Man Utd), G.C.Hurst (West Ham), M.S.Peters (West Ham).

Half-time 0-1   Full-time 0-3
Ref: J.R.Gordon (Scotland)   Att: 45,000

WHAT a vital win this would turn out to be in England's quest for a European Championship place. A surprising defeat for Scotland by Northern Ireland now left England one point clear at the top of the two-year table. However, the scoreline here did tend to flatter them somewhat and the Welshmens' brave challenge should not be underestimated. Only Gordon Banks at his brilliant best prevented some reward for the home side. Let the story unfold. On a grey afternoon, full of drizzle, England's defence gave an unusually jittery performance. George Cohen looked heavy footed, Jack Charlton was never his usual dominant self, and Alan Mullery, despite his obvious enthusiasm, lacked the guile of Nobby Stiles. It all made for an uncomfortable afternoon for the defence in general, although as the game wore on, Bobby Moore's calming influence steadied things down.

Two players stood head and shoulders above the rest. Banks, with three vital saves that were all world class, and Bobby Charlton, the maestro in all that he did.

In the first half, Banks made a brilliant reflex save from Vernon on 30 minutes after Rodrigues had put in a wicked cross. Somehow Banks managed to beat away Vernon's effort, even though Jones was also bearing down on the goalkeeper. The timing of that save was spot on as only three minutes later, England took the lead.

Bobby Charlton was spraying passes all over the field in an effort to inspire his colleagues and one such pass found Geoff Hurst down the right. A superb blind-sided run by Martin Peters enabled him to shoot home Hurst's clever pass, leaving four Welsh defenders helpless. It was a fine goal and very typical of the Peters trademark.

Despite the Welsh determination, England held the control of the midfield and, apart from the odd attack, also were more dangerous up front. They should have scored again when Peters put the pass of the match through for Hurst to run on to just before the break. In a one-against-one situation, one would normally back Hurst to score, but this time Sprake made a fine save from a rising shot.

By now Bobby Moore and his men had settled into the economical rhythm so typical under Alf Ramsey. Bobby Charlton was simply superb and only the solid defensive work of Mike England, outstanding at the heart of the Welsh defence, aided and abetted by Hennessey's fine support, prevented total domination by the visitors.

The second half was a much different story. Wales came out with a new fire and wrestled the midfield away from England's clutches. Alan Ball went through a nightmare patch and suddenly the Welsh, with Vernon, Rees and Jones prominent, rocked England back on their heels. For half an hour, the white shirts looked decidedly wobbly. Banks made a fine last ditch save from Mahoney's burst as the pressure increased.

It was obvious that the home side had a weakness at centre-forward and how they must have wished that one of their regular choices had been available. England held on at this stage with some desperate defending at times. But just as an equalizer looked likely they came back with the perfect answer, a double knock-out blow.

Again it followed straight on from a magnificent save by Banks. The Stoke goalkeeper looked beaten when Rees' shot arrowed towards the top corner, but Banks leapt spectacularly to save and break the Welsh hearts. That incident came with only five minutes remaining and as the seconds ticked away, Ball found Peters who then rolled the ball invitingly into Bobby Charlton's path. Bobby needed no second invitation and Sprake could only have seen the left foot draw back before he realised the ball had rocketed past him into the roof of the net.

It was a killer blow for the luckless Welsh and to rub salt into the wound, seconds later, Hennessey brought down Ball and England had a penalty. Ball himself took the spot-kick, duly scored, and that was the end of that.

78th match v Wales.
Penalty by Ball.

England v Northern Ireland Home Championship & European Nations Cup

Played on Wednesday, 22 November 1967 at Wembley Stadium.

England: G.Banks (Stoke C); G.R.Cohen (Fulham), R.Wilson (Everton), A.P. Mullery (Spurs), D.Sadler (Man Utd), R.F.C.Moore (West Ham, captain), P.Thompson (Liverpool), R.Hunt (Liverpool), R.Charlton (Man Utd), G.C.Hurst (West Ham), M.S.Peters (West Ham).

Northern Ireland: P.A.Jennings (Spurs); J.Parke (Sunderland), A.R.Elder (Stoke C), A.Stewart (Glentoran), W.J.T.Neill (Arsenal), M.Harvey (Sunderland), W.G.Campbell (Dundee), W.J.Irvine (Burnley), S.J.Wilson (Dundee), J.J. Nicholson (Huddersfield T), D.Clements (Coventry C).

Half-time 1-0   Full-time 2-0
Ref: L.Callaghan (Wales)   Att: 83,000

NORTHERN Ireland were badly hit by the pre-match news that their two best players, Best and Dougan, would be missing from their line-up for this international at Wembley. It was to prove a major blow to them, as with the extra fire-power of those two players, the crowd might just have witnessed a real shock.

Terry Neill clears from Martin Peters as Pat Jennings prepares to block the ball during the European Nations Cup game against Northern Ireland at Wembley in November 1967.

In the first half, the Irish took nearly all the honours. Campbell was a lively winger, Nicholson a battling midfield star and above all Clements, playing a withdrawn midfield role, controlled the Irish attacks with a cool authority. Several times they came perilously close to taking the lead. A bad mistake by Bobby Moore let in Irvine, who fired into the side netting of Gordon Banks' goal when really he ought to have done better.

Another chance then fell to Irvine after a miscued back-pass by Bobby Charlton. Only Banks' alert dive kept out Irvine's cross shot before Charlton redeemed himself with a goal-line clearance. Almost immediately, Parke crossed from the right and as Banks and Irvine jumped together the goalkeeper dropped the ball where this time David Sadler emerged to clear from the line.

Somehow England hung on with their players seemingly all at sixes and sevens. Charlton worked hard but without penetration, and Peter Thompson promised much without fulfilling the expectation. He had so much talent and was so close to being an outstanding player and yet he still left a niggling doubt about his game.

Ironically, with the Irish virtually dominating the half, it was England who went in at the break with a 1-0 lead. The goal came in the 44th minute and was beautifully taken. A short corner by Charlton to Alan Mullery was squared into the middle for Geoff Hurst to meet it with a ferocious volley which whistled past Jennings. So, poor Northern Ireland, after all their fine work, found themselves a goal down. It must have been a bitter psychological blow.

Predictably perhaps, the second-half performance from the Irish never quite matched the first, although all the players continued to play their hearts out. But

England gradually allowed their extra experience to calm the situation with Banks, Mullery, Ray Wilson and debutant Salder particularly impressive.

All through the second 45 minutes, the extra class was used to knock the fight out of the Irish and on 65 minutes the result was settled beyond doubt by a second England goal.

It was a brilliantly executed goal as a speedy move between Hurst, Mullery and Roger Hunt ended with a rising shot from the latter. The ball was blocked but a clever back-heel by Martin Peters gave Charlton an easy chance which he duly accepted.

It must have been very disappointing for the brave Irish lads in their emerald green, as they never again threatened Banks' goal. But they can be proud of their performance and in the end can take consolation from the fact that in this game the breaks went England's way. Everything was now set for the final group showdown at Hampden Park in February against the Scots.

> 75th match v Northern Ireland.
> Debut for Sadler.

England v USSR
Friendly

Played on Wednesday, 6 December 1967 at Wembley Stadium.

England: G.Banks (Stoke C); C.B.Knowles (Spurs), R.Wilson (Everton), A.P.Mullery (Spurs), D.Sadler (Man Utd), R.F.C. Moore (West Ham, captain), A.J.Ball (Everton), R.Hunt (Liverpool), R.Charlton (Man Utd), G.C.Hurst (West Ham), M.S.Peters (West Ham).

USSR: Y.Pshenichnikov (Pakhtakor Tashkent); Y.Istomin (CSKA Moscow), A.Shesterniev (CSKA Moscow), M.Khurtsilava (Dinamo Tbilisi), V.Anichkin (Dinamo Moscow), I.Sabo (Dinamo Kiev), V.Voronin (Torpedo Moscow), I.Chislenko (Dinamo Moscow), A.Banishevski (Neftchi Baku), E.Streltsov (Torpedo Moscow), E.Malofeev (Dinamo Minsk).

Half-time 1-2   Full-time 2-2

Ref: R.Kreitlein (West Germany)

Att: 93,000

SOME 93,000 spectators converged on Wembley for this attractive international and at the end of a bitterly cold night they went home more than happy with a game of high entertainment. The teams were greeted with a light fall of snow which gave Wembley an unusual but appropriate look as the green carpet suddenly turned white.

Both sides played good football, despite the tricky surface and it was obvious from the early stages that one of the men of the match would be the Soviet goalkeeper, Pshenichnikov. Brought in especially for his extra strength in the air, he fully justified his selection with a succession of saves and catches from all angles. After 25 minutes, though, England did find a way past him.

Good work by Geoff Hurst and Martin Peters ended with a low hard shot by Peters. Pshenichnikov got down well but could not hold the shot and quick as a flash, Alan Ball was there to tap home the rebound.

This Soviet side then showed exactly what rapid strides they had made in international terms. Added to the expected discipline and regimentation of their game comes a new-found awareness of flair. Varonin, Sabo and Streltsov gave a fine display in midfield and close to half-time the elusive right winger Chislenko, appropriately also an expert ice-hockey

Martin Peters, half hidden by the Soviet Union's Sabo, watches his header beat Pshenichnikov for the equalizer at Wembley in December 1967.

player, crashed in a 20 yarder past the startled Gordon Banks.

The goal followed some lovely play by Anichkin and Voronin. England were stunned and seconds later it was even worse for them as new cap Cyril Knowles was caught out by Banishevski, who quickly fed a delightful pass through for Chislenko to score a second well-taken goal. So, from a position of looking to build on their one-goal lead England trudged off at half-time 2-1 down.

The second half continued to delight. Open, attractive football played in a marvellous spirit brought a welcome change from all the recent knocks that the game has endured. The referee, Rudolf Kreitlein, had a vastly different task than when he had been here for the infamous Argentinian World Cup match.

England kept plugging away with Alan Mullery, Bobby Charlton, David Sadler and Ball all giving everything. Each time it looked as though an equalizer would come Pshenichnikov with his agility and sure handling foiled them. The goal-keeper was very reminiscent of his great predecessor, Lev Yashin. Knowles, after his earlier error, settled in well and really you could find little fault with any of the England players.

With a quarter of an hour to go, England were finally rewarded with a deserved goal. A late tackle on Roger Hunt by Khurtsilava gave them a free-kick and from that Bobby Moore found Ray Wilson. The full-back then centred from the left and there was Peters with a superb flashing header which brought the house down as it nestled in the Soviet net.

In the last 15 minutes, only Pshenich-nikov's brilliance kept England at bay and in the last five he was particularly effective. Somehow he kept out tremendous shots from Charlton, Peters and Hunt. How-ever, it was probably right that England did not get a winner as the Soviet display deserved a share of what was a magnificent game.

> 5th match v USSR.
> Debut for Knowles.
> *"I'll never forget my goal against Russia at Wembley. It was from all of one yard!"*
> Alan Ball

Martin Peters' shot flashes past Ronnie Simpson for the first goal of the Scotland-England game at Hampden in February 1968.

Celtic's John Hughes (10) levels the scores after fine work by Charlie Cooke. Hughes had earlier squandered a great chance to equalize.

Scotland v England
Home Championship & European Nations Cup

Played on Saturday, 24 February 1968 at Hampden Park, Glasgow.

Scotland: R.C.Simpson (Celtic); T.Gemmell (Celtic), R.McKinnon (Rangers), W.McNeill (Celtic), E.G. McCreadie (Chelsea), J.Greig (Rangers), W.J.Bremner (Leeds Utd), C.Cooke (Chelsea), W.Johnston (Rangers), J.Hughes (Celtic), R.Lennox (Celtic).

England: G.Banks (Stoke C); K.Newton (Blackburn R), R.Wilson (Everton), A.P.Mullery (Spurs), B.L.Labone (Everton), R.F.C.Moore (West Ham, captain), A.J.Ball (Everton), G.C.Hurst (West Ham), M.G.Summerbee (Man City), R.Charlton (Man Utd), M.S.Peters (West Ham).

Half-time 1-1   Full-time 1-1
Ref: L.Van Ravens (Holland) Att: 134,000

ENGLAND went into this vital match knowing that a draw would be enough to see them through as the group winners of the European Nations Championship matches. Of course, it would also win them the Home Championship, so there was much at stake.

As in any England-Scotland clash there was no quarter given nor received and right from the off it was an all-out battle. But, after the initial exchanges, England scored the goal they needed. It came with 20 minutes gone and was a beauty. It began with a bad throw out by Simpson. Ray Wilson won the ball in the air, beating Johnston, and Mike Summerbee then flicked it sideways to Martin Peters. The England number-11 once again showed his vision by being in the right place at the right time to flash home a superb cross shot into the top corner of Simpson's net from the edge of the box.

The goal put England well and truly into the driving seat and they had chances to sew the game up in the next ten minutes. Playing open attacking football

and allowing the ball to do the work, their tactics were superior than the Scots' close-dribbling game. Unfortunately, Peters and others let the chances slip by and it gave Scotland the chance to fight back.

The man who did as much as anyone to revitalise Scotland was the midfield player Charlie Cooke. For the quarter of an hour before the interval, he turned on the style and dazzled the crowd with some superb skills. First, he bemused an uncertain Gordon Banks with a wicked corner which left Hughes with the simplest scoring chance which, to the dismay of the crowd, he squandered. Then Cooke combined with Greig to tie Keith Newton into knots before the ball found Lennox. The winger centred and there was Hughes to atone for his earlier miss by heading past the scrambling Banks.

The morning rain on top of the bone-hard pitch certainly made the conditions difficult but Cooke's inspiration almost brought another goal when his superb through-pass found Greig. Fortunately for England, the Scotland skipper shot just wide. England, after their fine start, were relieved to reach the interval without further mishap. The break helped them enormously as in it they discussed the problem of Cooke's promptings and found an answer.

In the second half Cooke was continually boxed in by England players and was gradually forced square. As a result he was far less effective. The Scottish forwards were starved of service and faded, giving England the chance to reassert themselves. This time they held on to the initiative. Bobby Moore dominated at the back, Alan Mullery was aggressive in midfield and Bobby Charlton exciting in his unique and graceful way.

Alan Ball was tireless and Peters ever dangerous when making openings for himself. Peters was desperately unlucky when one fine shot cannoned back off a post. Overall, England deserved the draw they wanted but doubts about the jittery performances of Banks, Newton and Brian Labone left a few questions for Alf Ramsey to answer.

England now went on to play a two-legged quarter-final against Spain.

> 85th match v Scotland.
> Debut for Summerbee.

England v Spain
European Nations Cup Quarter-final First Leg

Played on Wednesday, 3 April 1968 at Wembley Stadium.

England: G.Banks (Stoke C); C.B.Knowles (Spurs), R.Wilson (Everton), A.P.Mullery (Spurs), J.Charlton (Leeds Utd), R.F.C.Moore (West Ham, captain), A.J.Ball (Everton), R.Hunt (Liverpool), M.G.Summerbee (Man City), R.Charlton (Man Utd), M.S.Peters (West Ham).
Spain: S.Sadurni (FC Barcelona); J.I.Saez (Athletic Bilbao), J.M.Canos (FC Elche), J.Martinez (Real Madrid), F.Fernandez (FC Barcelona), I.Zoco (Real Madrid), M.Polinario (Valencia CF), A.Amaro

(Real Madrid), F.Ansola (Valencia CF), R.M.Grosso (Real Madrid), J.Claramunt (Valencia CF).

Half-time 0-0   Full-time 1-0
Ref: G.Droz (Switzerland)   Att: 100,000

A FULL house at Wembley greeted the teams for this European Nations cup quarter-final first-leg match and the England fans had to endure a long wait before their team gained the vital breakthrough.

England began in determined fashion and almost immediately Martin Peters had the ball in the net. Unfortunately, the referee spotted an infringement against Mike Summerbee and the goal was disallowed. The Spaniards then defended stoutly with the dominating Zoco a fine central defender. He and Gallego won everything in the air as England pumped cross after cross into the Spanish goal area. The attack had chances, though, with two clear misses by Summerbee and another by Alan Mullery irritating the crowd. The England pressure really should have brought a goal and the Spaniards must have been delighted with their resolute defending.

Peters went close, as did Alan Ball, and when these two combined to give Summerbee another chance, the Manchester City player shot just wide when he ought to have at least hit the target. As the first half wore on, the mental sharpness of England's players began to dull. They became laboured and predictable and at half-time it had all become just a little frustrating.

After the interval Spain began to show everyone their obvious attacking ability as they became more adventurous. Catching England on the break, they began to look menacing. Only a fine save by Gordon Banks prevented the dangerous Amancio scoring after a lovely dummy had exposed the whole English defence. Pirri, too, caused problems and the counter-attacking of the visitors kept Bobby Moore's men on their toes.

England had desperately needed an early goal. That they didn't get one began to show later as several of the players, notably Peters and Bobby Charlton, looked jaded after their long, hard season.

Just as it seemed that the goalless scoreline would remain, England at last found a goal. It came in the 85th minute and began with a free-kick given for a foul by Zoco on Jack Charlton. Moore tapped the ball to his right and Bobby Charlton summoned up some reserves of strength to skip around one defender, veer round the defensive wall and fire a low hard cross shot into the far corner.

Needless to say the relief of the crowd was obvious. Even then, though, England had Banks to thank for another splendid save. This time he dived brilliantly to stop Grosso's clever back heel at the foot of his post.

So the game ended with England able to take a narrow lead to Madrid the following month for the second leg.

> 10th match v Spain.
> Spain's Martinez also known as 'Pirri'; Fernandez as 'Gallego'; Polinario as 'Poli'; Amaro as 'Amancio'.

Spain v England
Quarter-final Second Leg

Played on Wednesday, 8 May 1968 in the Santiago Bernabéu Stadium, Madrid.

Spain: S.Sadurni (FC Barcelona); J.I.Saez (Athletic Bilbao), F.Fernandez (FC Barcelona), J.M.Canos (Elche CF), J.Martinez (Real Madrid), I.Zoco (Real Madrid), J.Rife (FC Barcelona), A.Amaro (Real Madrid), R.M.Grosso (Real Madrid), M.Velazquez (Real Madrid), F.Gento (Real Madrid).
England: P.P.Bonetti (Chelsea); K.R.Newton (Blackburn R), R.Wilson (Everton), A.P.Mullery (Spurs), B.L.Labone (Everton), R.F.C.Moore (West Ham, captain), A.J.Ball (Everton), M.S.Peters

Bobby Charlton's low cross-shot finds the far corner of Sadurni's net for England's winner in the European Nations Cup semi-final first leg against Spain at Wembley in April 1968.

(West Ham), R.Charlton (Man Utd), R.Hunt (Liverpool), N.Hunter (Leeds Utd).

Half-time 0-0   Full-time 1-2

Ref: J.Krnavek (Czechoslovakia)

Att: 120,000

WHAT a tremendous victory this was by a depleted England side. Without five of their World Cup-winning team, they defied all the odds to come home with the prize of a semi-final place in the European Nations Championship. It was a triumph of guts, endeavour and no little amount of skill.

In a torrid atmosphere with 120,000 hot-blooded Spaniards baying for the scalps of the English, the visitors' temperament was thoroughly tested. Two things were in England's favour though, typical English weather and the form of their skipper Bobby Moore. His was the ice-cool head that carried them through the ferocious early stages and then on past further mountains to their final goal.

England survived some very hairy moments early on. Twice goalkeeper Peter Bonetti failed to dominate his six-yard area as crosses came in. He was lucky to get away with his errors of judgement, but gradually Moore sorted out the defensive problems, calming things down in that unfussy style of his. With Brian Labone giving solid support at the heart of the defence, Spain searched in vain for an opening.

The big danger to England was the superb Amancio, who was always in the thick of the action. Of course, he was the darling of the home crowd but England remained in control and they reached half-time with their one-goal lead from the first leg still intact.

The two contrasting styles saw England in their 4-3-3 formation with Spain preferring 4-2-4. Midfielders Pirri and Grosso kept things buzzing for Spain and only three minutes into the second half, the stadium erupted. The move began with a bad cross-field pass by Norman Hunter. The ball was intercepted and moved on at speed by Gento. He skipped around Keith Newton's tackle and squared the ball to Amancio, who joyfully hit a shot past Bonetti.

For a moment the Spanish tails were up and it looked ominous for England but Alf Ramsey's sides have never buckled under pressure and six minutes after Amancio's goal the visitors deservedly equalized.

Roger Hunt's fine shot, after good work by Hunt and Martin Peters, was tipped away for a corner by Sadurni, and from Alan Ball's kick, Peters stormed in to outleap everyone to head home. The goal was greeted by a deafening silence and England were back in the driving seat. Their somewhat predictable game was nevertheless extremely effective with Alan Mullery tireless, along with Ball, and the front men always prepared to chase. Amancio was finally stifled by the combined efforts of Peters, Hunter and Moore. Bobby Charlton still looked jaded but did just enough, and the icing on the cake came with only eight minutes to go.

A long throw by Mullery sent the ever-willing Hunt chasing away down the right wing. He worked his way forward before pulling the ball back diagonally. It ran behind Charlton but there was Hunter, steaming in, to crash a shot wide

of the helpless Sadurni.

England still had to survive some narrow squeaks as Spain tried desperately in the remaining minutes but they had earned the right to a share of good fortune. Their economical movement and pattern had suited the night better and they ran out worthy winners. Now England went to Italy to meet the semi-final challenge from Yugoslavia.

> 11th match v Spain.
> Spain's Martinez also known as 'Pirri'; Fernandez as 'Gallego'; Amaro as 'Amancio'.

England v Sweden   Friendly

Played on Wednesday, 22 May 1968 at Wembley Stadium.

England: A.C.Stepney (Man Utd); K.R.Newton (Blackburn R), C.B.Knowles (Spurs), A.P.Mullery (Spurs), B.L.Labone (Everton), R.F.C.Moore (West Ham, captain), C.Bell (Man City), M.S.Peters (West Ham), R.Charlton (Man Utd), R.Hunt (Liverpool), N.Hunter (Leeds Utd).
Sub: G.C.Hurst (West Ham) for Charlton.
Sweden: S.G.Larsson (Örebro SK); J.Carlsson (Jönköping SIF), K.Kristensson (Malmö FF), B.Nordqvist (IFK Norrköping), R.Grip (AIK Stockholm), L.Eriksson (IK Sirius), B.Larsson (VfB Stuttgart), T.Nordahl (Örebro SK), I.Ejderstedt (Östers IF), S.Lindman (Djurgårdens IF), Ö.Persson (Rangers).
Subs: R.Andersson (Hammarby IF) for Ejderstedt and N.Hult (Malmö FF) for S.G.Larsson.

Half-time 2-0   Full-time 3-1

Ref: O.Huber (Switzerland)   Att: 72,500

ANOTHER efficient and deserved victory for England added to their superb run of only two defeats in 40 internationals. Only Austria and Scotland had beaten them over the previous four years and Sweden never looked like repeating their win of nine years earlier in this very stadium.

The match was never a classic. England played cool and dominating football without setting the pulse racing too fast. Sweden had to rely on the occasional breakaway and Alex Stepney celebrated

his debut with a splendid save from Nordahl midway through the first half.

It was not long, however, before England emphasised their superiority with a goal. It came in the 36th minute and began with a short corner between Roger Hunt and Bobby Charlton. A deflected centre was then met brilliantly by Martin Peters, who dived to head home from six yards. It was a superbly taken goal and showed Peters' knack of being in the right place at the right time.

Two minutes later, England added a second with as fine a goal as you could wish to see. Bobby Moore sent Charlton away with a lovely through-pass. Charlton, in that elegant, flowing stride of his, jinked inside two defenders and let fly a right-foot thunderbolt which roared into the top corner. It was a gem of a goal and how appropriate that such a magnificent effort should enable him to overhaul Jimmy Greaves' record total of 44 international goals. Charlton now had 45 in his 85 appearances.

Sweden struck back bravely and Ejderstedt volleyed just past the post. Shortly afterwards Stepney made another fine save as Nordahl all but broke through. But at half-time it was very clear who held the aces.

England continued to call the tune throughout the second half, although Colin Bell struggled to adjust to this higher level of football in the midfield. However, with 20 minutes to go, England clinched victory with a third goal. Good work by both full-backs, Keith Newton and Cyril Knowles, saw a run by the former and a shot against the bar by the latter. When the rebound came out, the ever-alert Hunt nipped in to poach a typical goal.

With five minutes to go Sweden suffered a cruel blow. Goalkeeper Larsson bravely dived at the feet of Mullery, but in so doing received a serious injury, later diagnosed as a fractured skull. He was replaced by substitute Hult.

Sweden did manage a consolation when another second-half substitute, Andersson, who came on for Ejderstedt, scored with the last kick of the match. It followed a mistake by Norman Hunter but had little effect on England's overall dominance. England also used a substitute when Geoff Hurst came on for Charlton, who had

Roger Hunt nets England's third goal against Sweden at Wembley in May 1968, after Knowles' shot rebounded off the woodwork.

received a slight knock. When the Manchester United ace left the field the crowd gave him rapturous applause and those that were there will never forget his magical goal.

> 9th match v Sweden.
> Debuts for Stepney and Bell.

West Germany v England
Friendly

Played on Saturday, 1 June 1968 at the Niedersachsen Stadium, Hanover.

West Germany: H.Wolter (Eintracht Braunschweig); H.H.Vogts (Borussia Mönchengladbach), M.Lorenz (Werder Bremen), L.Müller (1.FC Nuremberg), K.Fichtel (Schalke '04), W.Weber (1.FC Cologne), B.Dörfel (Hamburger SV), F.Beckenbauer (Bayern Munich), J.Löhr (1.FC Cologne), W.Overath (1.FC Cologne), G.Volkert (1.FC Nuremberg).
England: G.Banks (Stoke C); K.R.Newton (Blackburn R), C.B.Knowles (Spurs), N.Hunter (Leeds Utd), B.L.Labone (Everton), R.F.C.Moore (West Ham, captain), A.J.Ball (Everton), C.Bell (Man City), M.G.Summerbee (Man City), G.C.Hurst (West Ham), P.Thompson (Liverpool).

Half-time 0-0   Full-time 1-0
Ref: L.Van Ravens (Holland) Att: 79,250

THIS match, arranged as a warm-up for the forthcoming European Nations Cup semi-final against Yugoslavia, proved to be a very disappointing exercise for an England team looking jaded and unenthusiastic. The Germans, who had never beaten England in their previous 12 encounters, were anxious to avenge the famous game two years ago when England became World Champions.

This match, however, was a poor one played on a hot, humid and thundery day. Although both sides had key players missing, the football was tedious and even verged on the boring. There were several Union Jacks dotted around the crowd but the Brits had little to cheer.

England tried hard with Alan Ball lively throughout. Colin Bell also worked hard and their two best chances fell to Bell. On both occasions, though, the Manchester City player squandered the openings after fine prompting by Geoff Hurst. Apart from those incidents, the German goal was rarely threatened, but it must be said that the home side fared little better.

Beckenbauer looked a class above his teammates but all too often impressive build-ups petered out on the edge of the box. Lorenz gave good support as did Vogts and Dörfel, who was very quick down the right wing, but goal attempts were very rare at Gordon Banks' end as well.

In the end the goal that finally settled an almost forgettable match came with only nine minutes to go. Beckenbauer, who had been at the heart of most of the best German play, tried a speculative shot from 25 yards. It would have been easily covered but a wicked deflection off Brian Labone left Banks helpless and the goalkeeper watched in dismay as the ball went into the net.

The goal really summed up the game.

> 9th match v West Germany.

England's squad pictured before the game against Scotland at Hampden in February 1968. Back row (left to right): Stepney, Summerbee, Moore, Bailey, Newton, Wright, Thompson, Bobby Charlton, Wilson. Middle row: Stiles, Hunt, Smith, Hunter, Bell, Banks, Harold Shepherdon (trainer). Front row: Bonetti, Hurst, Mullery, Labone, Osgood, Knowles, Ball.

European Nation Finals

Yugoslavia v England
European Nations Cup Semi-final

Played on Wednesday, 5 June 1968 at the Stadio Comunale, Florence, Italy.

Yugoslavia: I.Pantelić (Vojvodina Novi Sad); M.Fazlagić (FK Sarajevo), M.Damjanović (Partizan Belgrade), B.Paunović (Partizan Belgrade), M.Pavlović (Red Star Belgrade), D.Holcer (Hajduk Split), I.Petković (OFK Belgrade), I.Osim (FK Željezničar), V.Musemić (FK Sarajevo), D.Trivic (Vojvodina Novi Sad), D.Džajić (Red Star Belgrade).
England: G.Banks (Stoke C); K.R.Newton (Blackburn R), R.Wilson (Everton), A.P.Mullery (Spurs), B.L.Labone (Everton), R.F.C.Moore (West Ham, captain), A.J.Ball (Everton), M.S.Peters (West Ham), R.Charlton (Man Utd), R.Hunt (Liverpool), N.Hunter (Leeds Utd).

Half-time 0-0   Full-time 1-0
Ref: J.M.Ortiz de Mendibil (Spain)
Att: 40,000

ENGLAND crashed to defeat in this bruising battle and so lost the chance of reaching the European Nations Cup Final. Their dream died with only four minutes of the match to go and the critics who said that England's World Cup win was down to the fact that it was played at Wembley, now had more ammunition for this argument.

The 40,000 crowd, largely Yugoslavian, roared their side on passionately and it took all of the experience of the senior England players to hold the team together in this stifling atmosphere.

The tackling left little to the imagination and the Spanish referee was constantly blowing his whistle. England shared the blame for the tough approach the teams had and as early as the fifth minute, Norman Hunter's fearsome tackle left Yugoslavia's star schemer Osim injured and reduced to a virtual passenger

for the remainder of the match. The histrionics shown by some of the Slavs after being tackled made things look much worse, but to their credit at least England were not guilty of these dramatic performances.

Indeed, in terms of possession and teamwork, England probably had the edge. Keith Newton and Ray Wilson, as well as helping the immaculate Bobby Moore, were always prepared to make forward runs in support of the attack. But England relied on only Roger Hunt as an out-and-out striker with Alan Ball, Bobby Charlton, Alan Mullery and Martin Peters as well as Hunter packing the midfield. The game as a result produced few goalmouth thrills.

For Yugoslavia, Petković and Džajić were lively wingers and Musemić and Trivic were also a handful for the English defence. Half-time arrived with no score and Ball the pick of the England side. His energy seemed endless and he worked so hard to find an opening.

After the break Charlton, looking tired and not 100 per cent fit after his groin strain, suddenly found his shooting boots. A 40-yard weaving run ended with a rocket shot which only just went wide. Then, with 15 minutes to go, he linked well with Moore and Ball to shoot wide once again.

But in the 86th minute, England received a severe blow. Trivic and Holcer combined well and when the centre came in, Džajić roared through to beat Moore to the ball and crash his shot past Banks. It was a disaster and England had little chance to come back.

In the end all their frustration boiled over. Trivic, not for the first time, chopped Mullery with a wild tackle. Mullery, in his exasperation and anger, turned and aimed a kick at his assailant and was sent off to a crescendo of whistles.

It was the first time an England player had been sent off in a full international and that was the final disappointment of a disastrous day.

> 9th match v Yugoslavia.
> Mullery was the first England player to be sent off in a full international.

England v USSR
European Nations Cup Third & Fourth Place Play-off

Played on Saturday, 8 June 1968 at the Olympic Stadium, Rome, Italy.

England: G.Banks (Stoke C); T.J.Wright (Everton), R.Wilson (Everton), N.P.Stiles (Man Utd), B.L.Labone (Everton), R.F.C.Moore (West Ham, captain), N.Hunter (Leeds Utd), R.Hunt (Liverpool), R.Charlton (Man Utd), G.C.Hurst (West Ham), M.S.Peters (West Ham).
USSR: Y.Pshenichnikov (CSKA Moscow); V.Afonin (CSKA Moscow), Y.Istomin (CSKA Moscow), G.Logofet (Spartak Moscow), A.Shesterniev (CSKA Moscow), V.Kaplichni (CSKA Moscow), G.Evriuzhikan (Dinamo Moscow), A.Lenev (Torpedo Moscow), A.Banichevski (Neftchi Baku), A.Bishovets (Dinamo Kiev), E.Malofeev (Dinamo Minsk).

Half-time 1-0   Full-time 2-0

Ref: I.Zsolt (Hungary)   Att: 80,000

WITH Alan Mullery suspended due to his sending off against Yugoslavia, Sir Alf Ramsey decided to recall Nobby Stiles after an absence of 14 months and the tigerish Manchester United midfield star immediately made an impact. With Geoff Hurst in for the injured Alan Ball, and Tommy Wright making his debut at right-back, England looked a little different from the side that lost to the Yugoslavs.

This match was a curtain-raiser for the European Nations Cup Final between Yugoslavia and the host country, Italy. Ironically, of the four sides on view this day, England looked by far the best.

This was a much better showing and a fine team effort. In the first half, England attacked the Soviets hard. Hurst showed much of his old power and Bobby Charlton was at his most graceful.

It was Charlton who gave England a first-half lead after 39 minutes. A slick move involving Bobby Moore, Martin Peters and Hurst ended with Charlton running in to shoot the awkwardly bouncing ball down and beyond Pshenichnikov.

One of the most noticeable aspects of the game was the sporting manner in which it was played. The Russians as they showed at Wembley before last Christmas, played it hard but fair, but on this occasion England out-thought and out-manoeuvred their Soviet opponents. Thankfully, there was no repeat of the tantrums and the histrionics shown by Yugoslavia in the previous game.

Charlton might have had a hat-trick as two other good efforts went perilously close. With Wright — now there is a name that conjures up memories — settling in most effectively and Hurst always dangerous, England continued to hold the aces after the break.

The Soviets had little to offer, although Bishovets was always impressive and Gordon Banks was forced into a brilliant save from a Logofet header. Six minutes afterwards, though, England added a second goal. Peters fired in a shot which was blocked and Hurst moved in to dribble past the goalkeeper and score.

England seemed to have gained a reputation for rough, physical play, yet against a side who were prepared to play good football, there was only one very short stoppage, and that whilst Banks received treatment.

Ten minutes from the end, England should have had a penalty when Peters was tripped in the area by Shesterniev but the Hungarian referee, István Zsolt waved play on.

So England finished in third place in the European Championships, a disappointment in many respects but they could also feel proud of their achievement and now had to look towards Mexico in 1970 for their next big challenge.

> 6th match v USSR.
> Debut for Wright.

Romania v England
Friendly

Played on Wednesday, 6 November 1968 at the Stadium of the 23 August, Bucharest.

Romania: G.Gornea (UT Arad); L.Sătmăreanu (Steaua Bucharest), I.Barbu (FC Argeş Piteşti), C.Dinu (Dinamo Bucharest), M.Mocanu (Petrolul Ploieşti), V.Ghergheli (Dinamo Bucharest), G.Petescu (Steaua Bucharest), I.Pîrcălab (Dinamo Bucharest), N.Dobrin (FC Argeş Piteşti), F.Dumitrache (Dinamo Bucharest), M.Lucescu (Dinamo Bucharest).
Subs: F.Domide (UT Arad) for Dobrin and R.Nunweiller (Dinamo Bucharest) for Petescu.
England: G.Banks (Stoke C); T.J.Wright (Everton), K.R.Newton (Blackburn R), A.P.Mullery (Spurs), B.L.Labone (Everton), R.F.C.Moore (West Ham, captain), A.J.Ball (Everton), R.Hunt (Liverpool), R.Charlton (Man Utd), G.C.Hurst (West Ham), M.S.Peters (West Ham).
Sub: R.McNab (Arsenal) for Wright.

Half-time 0-0   Full-time 0-0

Ref: R.Fiala (Czechoslovakia) Att: 62,000

BUCHAREST on a cold, grey and damp November afternoon is not exactly the most inspiring place and it was no real surprise that these sides produced a dreary international which gave the crowd precious little to cheer.

Romania, an up-and-coming side, began well and in the first 20 minutes should have scored at least one goal, such was their pressure. Pîrcălab missed one fine chance and Gordon Banks had to be on his toes on several other occasions. However, once Bobby Moore had found his feet, the England defence settled down and gradually took the steam out of the home side's initial burst.

Brian Labone had a superb game at the heart of the defence and England did remarkably well to overcome a very unfortunate early injury to Tommy Wright. Arsenal's Bob McNab came on as substitute and made an immediate impact when given his unexpected chance.

England soaked up the pressure from Romania and then counter attacked at great speed. Unfortunately, the twin strike force of Geoff Hurst and Roger Hunt were strangely subdued and as a result England lacked penetration.

The game was almost entirely confined to the midfield area and made watching it a real struggle for the spectators. Straight after the interval, though, England created two good chances. Both came from swift breaks from the back as first Hunt and then Alan Ball missed the target when well positioned. These was their best openings and they should have been taken.

Romania continued to work hard with Ghergheli and Petescu giving Pîrcălab fine support from midfield. However, Banks rarely had a direct shot to deal with and only a few dangerous crosses kept him alert. Labone shone brightest for England, whilst Ball worked tirelessly covering every blade of grass in an effort to inspire the weak English attack. The distinct lack of goals lately was a worrying trend with some very important games coming up.

> 2nd match v Romania.
> Debut as substitute for McNab.

England v Bulgaria
Friendly

Played on Wednesday, 11 December 1968 at Wembley Stadium.

England: G.West (Everton); K.R.Newton (Blackburn R), R.McNab (Arsenal), A.P.Mullery (Spurs), B.L.Labone (Everton), R.F.C.Moore (West Ham, captain), F.H.Lee (Man City), C.Bell (Man City), R.Charlton (Man Utd), G.C.Hurst (West Ham), M.S.Peters (West Ham).
Sub: P.Reaney (Leeds Utd) for Newton.
Bulgaria: S.Simeonov (Slavia Sofia); S.Peshev (Levski Sofia), I.Dimitrov (Akademik Sofia), B.Gaganelov (CSKA Sofia), D.Penev (CSKA Sofia), D.Zhechev (Levski Sofia), G.Popov (Trakia Plovdiv), K.Bonev (Lokomotiv Plovdiv), G.Asparoukhov (Levski Sofia), D.Yakimov (CSKA Sofia), D.Dermendiev (Trakia Plovdiv).
Sub: P.Zhekov (CSKA Sofia) for Popov.

Half-time 1-1   Full-time 1-1

Ref: M.Kitabdjian (France) Att: 80,000

EIGHTY-thousand people went to Wembley to see England take on the unknown talents of the Bulgarians. At the end of the evening they must have left with mixed feelings, enjoying a good game but wondering how on earth the home side didn't win. The only other time these two sides had met was in Chile during the 1962 World Cup, so this was Bulgaria's first visit to Wembley.

Straight away the skill of the Eastern Europeans was eye-catching. England, however, were soon on the attack and within a couple of minutes Simeonov was saving well from Martin Peters. For the next 20 minutes, England put together some superb football, only to be thwarted time and again by the goalkeeper or Zhechev's brilliant defensive play. Bobby Charlton had an especially frustrating night and one typical effort in the first-half was somehow tipped around a post by the inspired Simeonov. So often visiting goalkeepers seemed to reserve their best performances for Wembley.

England were so much on top, yet it was Bulgaria who made a swift break to open the scoring. It came just after the half-hour with a brilliant piece of play by the very impressive Asparoukhov. He beat Brian Labone to a high ball in the centre-circle and then produced an explosive change of pace. His long-legged style

Geoff Hurst (10) levels the scores as the Bulgarian goalkeeper Simeonov is stranded at Wembley in December 1968.

took him clear of the defence and he ran on some 40 to 50 yards before evading Keith Newton's desperate challenge. With expert precision, he then shot low and hard past Gordon West's left hand for a magnificent goal.

So England, after several missed chances, found themselves a goal down. But this was only to spur them on and shortly afterwards they were level again. A scramble in the Bulgarian goalmouth saw several shots blocked but as the ball ran wide, there was Geoff Hurst to hook it home from an acute angle.

At half-time England could easily have been well ahead, but once again missed chances had cost them dearly. Bulgaria, though, were no mugs and in Yakimov, Bonev and Penev they had some class players. Asparoukhov and Popov also showed exceptional talent, although Popov had to be replaced by Jekov for the second half after suffering an injury.

England continued to press after the interval but once again found Simeonov in superb form and the crowd wondered just how he managed to keep out a couple of Charlton thunderbolts. The second effort was right out of the top drawer and had Charlton holding his head in disbelief.

New cap Francis Lee gave a good display, always looking dangerous and full of running. Apart from his shooting, Charlton also had a fine game with some of his characteristic long, raking passes a delight to watch. They were his trademark and looked so good at Wembley. But, despite their territorial advantage and their excellent build-ups, England failed too often in the vital last third of the pitch. True, the Gods seemed to be against them and the inspired form of Simeonov kept them out, but in all honesty they must have felt extremely disappointed at not winning.

> 2nd match v Bulgaria.
> Debuts for West, Lee and Reaney (sub).

England v Romania
Friendly

Played on Wednesday, 15 January 1969 at Wembley Stadium.

England: G.Banks (Stoke C); T.J.Wright (Everton), R.McNab (Arsenal), N.P.Stiles (Man Utd), J.Charlton (Leeds Utd), N.Hunter (Leeds Utd), J.Radford (Arsenal), R.Hunt (Liverpool), R.Charlton (Man Utd, captain), G.C.Hurst (West Ham), A.J.Ball (Everton).

Romania: G.Gornea (UT Arad); L.Sătmăreanu (Steaua Bucharest), A.Boc (Dinamo Bucharest), A.Deleanu (Politehnica Timișoara), D.Anca (U.Cluj-Napoca), C.Dinu (Dinamo Bucharest), E.Dembrowski (Dinamo Bacău), F.Domide (UT Arad), F.Dumitrache (Dinamo Bucharest), R.Nunweiller (Dinamo Bucharest), M.Lucescu (Dinamo Bucharest).

Half-time 1-0   Full-time 1-1
Ref: J.Callaghan (Scotland)   Att:77,000

THIS was the first time that Romania had visited Wembley and of the 77,000 crowd, almost all hoped that the visitors would be the sacrificial lambs to the slaughter. Unfortunately for England, though, things did not work out like that and the fans were in for a frustrating night as once again the old forward failing let England down.

On a heavy pitch saturated by incessant rain, England always dominated the game territorially, but against a side hell bent on defending they had neither the craft nor the guile to find a route to goal. So often against continental opposition, an early strike was necessary and it almost came when Alan Ball had a shot cleared off the line by Deleanu. That was a near miss but, undeterred, England pressed forward. Bobby Charlton fired in a couple of scorchers which Gornea did well to keep out, but Geoff Hurst and Roger Hunt were less effective as the main strike force.

Romania relied on the occasional quick breakaway and Dumitrache, a quality player, was always dangerous. Anca, Dinu and Nunweiller played some clever stuff in midfield and Dembrovschi gave Dumitrache good support at the front.

On the half-hour, though, England deservedly took the lead. A corner by Bobby Charlton was headed in by big brother Jack, who outjumped the defenders. From then on it seemed only a matter of time before they would score again. Bobby Charlton hit a post and had yet another fine shot saved, but his were the only worthwhile chances worth recording as all the others went begging. The close in chances were wasted and although new cap John Radford fired in a couple of good efforts, the goalkeeper was equal to them. Gornea did elect to punch more often than he should have but England failed to punish him when the punch went astray.

Alan Ball gave his usual all-action performance and Bob McNab made excellent use of the left wing in supporting runs. Bobby Charlton, captain for the first time, was always dangerous.

The second half was again dominated by England but the crowd became increasingly irritated by their failure to make all the possession tell in front of goal. More chances were created and lost, and with monotonous regularity the attacks fell predictably short of Romania's goal. It was most frustrating as the gap in quality was obvious but this goalscoring famine was becoming a real crisis.

With 15 minutes to go, Romania were handed a gift. Jack Charlton, twice in quick succession lunged at Nunweiller blocking his shots, but after the second one the Scottish referee amazed everyone by awarding a penalty for what one can only presume was hands. It was hardly deserved but the confident Dumitrache stepped up to calmly score and send his teammates wild with delight at their equalizer.

England were left regretting all the missed chances and, with some very important games coming up, they now looked for a striker who could convert the many goal opportunities their approach play created.

> 3rd match v Romania.
> Debut for Radford.
> Bobby Charlton captain for the first time.
> Penalty for Romania by F.Dumitrache.

England v France
Friendly

Played on Wednesday, 12 March 1969 at Wembley Stadium.

England: G.Banks (Stoke C); K.R.Newton (Blackburn R), T.Cooper (Leeds Utd), A.P.Mullery (Spurs), J.Charlton (Leeds Utd), R.F.C.Moore (West Ham, captain), F.H.Lee (Man City), C.Bell (Man City), G.C.Hurst (West Ham), M.S.Peters (West Ham), M.O'Grady (Leeds Utd).

France: G.Carnus (AS St-Etienne); J.Djorkáeff (Olympique Marseille), J.P.Rostagni (AS Monaco), B.Bosquier (AS St-Etienne), R.Lemerre (FC Sedan), H.Michel (FC Nantes), Y.Herbert (FC Sedan), J.Bonnel (Olympique Marseille),

Geoff Hurst scores from the penalty-spot with French 'keeper Georges Carnus unable to reach the ball at Wembley in March 1968.

C.Loubet (OGC Nice), J.Simon (Girondins Bordeaux), G.Bereta (AS St-Etienne).

Half-time 1-0   Full-time 5-0
Ref: I.Zsolt (Hungary)   Att: 83,000

AT last, England found their goal touch. After having scored only four goals in their previous six internationals, they made eight changes for this game and showed a new determination.

Yet for half an hour there seemed little change as the same pattern emerged of steroetyped football, slow build-up and electing to go from side to side instead of forward. Another excellent crowd of 83,000 people were just beginning to grow restless when England scored a superb goal.

Terry Cooper, who made a very impressive debut as an attacking full-back, combined well with Mike O'Grady and Martin Peters before putting in a fine cross from the left, deep to the far post. Geoff Hurst headed the ball back square and O'Grady met it with a brilliant right-foot volley which rocketed into the French net. It was a goal that even Bobby Charlton would have been proud to score.

From that moment the result was never in doubt as England gradually got their act together. Other chances went begging but France rarely threatened, except when Gordon Banks stopped a shot by Loubet early on, and near the end of the half the 'keeper did well again to thwart the same player.

In the second half, the real fruit blossomed as England powered into France with a new confidence. In the 48th minute England won a penalty. Hurst crossed from the right, O'Grady's right-foot volley was saved full length by Carnus, and as Peters came in on the rebound, he was brought down by Bosquier. Hurst hit home the spot-kick with enormous power.

That goal opened the floodgates and two minutes later, Bobby Moore crossed from the left and Hurst hit a shot into the top corner, the ball taking a deflection

off Michel. By now England were all over the French. Moore was magnificent even on this quagmire of an unfamiliar Wembley pitch. The heavy rain had left puddles glinting in the floodlights, but still the England skipper controlled the play, switching the point of attack regularly.

Francis Lee was particularly lively and had an outstanding game. With 15 minutes to go, he scored a terrific individual goal after a lightning dash and splendid low shot. The crowd were delighted with that goal and shortly afterwards they were on their feet again after Rostagni had up-ended Colin Bell to give Hurst, not only his second penalty, but a goal to complete his hat-trick, his first since that famous one of the World Cup Final in 1966. Two other records made it a very happy night for England. It was their 100th victory against foreign opposition at Wembley, whilst Hurst's first goal was their 200th at the stadium.

> 18th match v France.
> Debut for Cooper.
> Hat-trick for Hurst (2 penalties).

Northern Ireland v England   Home Championship

Played on Saturday, 3 May 1969 at Windsor Park, Belfast.

Northern Ireland: P.A.Jennings (Spurs); D.J.Craig (Newcastle Utd), M.Harvey (Sunderland), S.J.Todd (Burnley), W.J.T.Neill (Arsenal), J.J.Nicholson (Huddersfield T), A.S.McMordie (Middlesbrough), T.A.Jackson (Everton), A.D.Dougan (Wolves), W.J.Irvine (Preston NE), G.Best (Man Utd).
Sub: A.R.Elder (Stoke C) for Harvey.

England: G.Banks (Stoke C); K.R.Newton (Blackburn R), R.McNab (Arsenal), A.P.Mullery (Spurs), B.L.Labone (Everton), R.F.C.Moore (West Ham, captain), A.J.Ball (Everton), F.H.Lee (Man City), R.Charlton (Man Utd), G.C.Hurst (West Ham), M.S.Peters (West Ham).

Half-time 0-1   Full-time 1-3
Ref: W.J.Mullen (Scotland)   Att: 24,500

FOR the first time the Home Championship was condensed into one week and England got off to a flying start by winning in Belfast. Although England's extra power told, it was not without hiccups along the way, however.

The Irish roared into their customary passionate opening spell and in the first 15 minutes they could have sewn up the game as a succession of chances went begging. Three times Irvine shunned clear openings after clever flicks by Best and Dougan had set him up. Best was prominent early on but as the game wore on, Bobby Moore's mastery at the back sealed up the holes.

The combination of Francis Lee and Bobby Charlton in midfield gave England a refreshing look and many of their attacks were much more direct than of late. As the sides settled down England, having withstood the early charge, began to take a grip on the game, and with five minutes of the first half remaining they took the lead. Lee was brought down by Harvey and Martin Peters met Lee's free-kick with a downwards header to score.

After the break Ireland tried hard to come back into things and after exerting some good pressure they equalized on the hour. A fine piece of skill by the irrepressible Best set up the other lively winger, McMordie and his shot beat Gordon Banks. For a short while, the 24,500 crowd anticipated an Irish celebration of a possible victory. Irvine missed another excellent chance and a superb save from Banks thwarted a fine effort by Ireland's best player, Jimmy Nicholson.

A minute later and Lee stunned the crowd into silence with a brilliant individual goal to cap a fine display by him. The Manchester City player was still not finished and near the end he was sent crashing to the ground in the penalty area to give Geoff Hurst the chance to thunder home the spot-kick.

So, England ended with a convincing scoreline, although it must be said that they enjoyed a little of the 'luck of the Irish', luck that the Irish didn't seem to have on this particular day! Some positions were still giving cause for concern to Sir Alf Ramsey who still had plenty to do in the coming months. Indeed, many felt that some new blood would be necessary before England went to Mexico to defend the World Cup.

> 76th match v Northern Ireland.
> Penalty scored by Hurst.

England v Wales   Home Championship

Played on Wednesday, 7 May 1969 at Wembley Stadium.

England: G.West (Everton); K.R.Newton (Blackburn R), T.Cooper (Leeds Utd), R.F.C.Moore (West Ham, captain), J.Charlton (Leeds Utd), N.Hunter (Leeds Utd), F.H.Lee (Man City), C.Bell (Man City), J.Astle (West Brom), R.Charlton (Man Utd), A.J.Ball (Everton).

Wales: G.S.Sprake (Leeds Utd); P.J.Rodrigues (Leicester C), R.J.Thomas

Jack Charlton (left) and Jeff Astle are jubilant because the ball is in the Welsh net. But the whistle had already sounded for a penalty – which Francis Lee missed – at Wembley in May 1969.

Hurst hammers home another penalty, beating Scotland goalkeeper Jim Herriot at Wembley in May 1969.

(Swindon T), W.A.Durban (Derby Co), D.Powell (Sheffield Utd), A.D.Burton (Newcastle Utd), B.S.Jones (Cardiff C), R.T.Davies (Southampton), J.B.Toshack (Cardiff C), R.W.Davies (Newcastle Utd), G.Moore (Charlton A).

Half-time 0-1   Full-time 2-1

Ref: J.Adair (Northern Ireland) Att: 72,000

THIS really was one of the best England-Wales clashes for many years and England had to use all of their experience and knowhow to defeat the challenge of the Welsh Dragon.

In the first-half Wales pushed forward relentlessly with Jones and Graham

Moore outstanding in midfield. Their clever touches and astute passes had England chasing shadows at times. Up front the two Davieses and Toshack gave the home defenders a torrid time and after several near misses, Wales deservedly took the lead in the 18th minute. The goal came after a splendid build up involving Powell, Ron Davies, Jones and then a cross from the right by Rodrigues which Ron Davies, following up, leapt high to head home brilliantly under pressure from Jack Charlton and Norman Hunter.

After the goal Wales continued to dictate with Moore their most influential player. Moments later, though, they had an amazing let-off. A header by Jeff Astle

was handled on the line by Rodrigues, and although Astle followed up to score from the rebound, the referee had already ordered a penalty to be taken. Up stepped Francis Lee, usually a sure shot from the spot, but his kick this time crashed against the bar before being cleared. There seemed no justice in the incident from England's point of view.

Two fine saves from Sprake, first from a header by Lee and then from a rocket by Bobby Charlton, kept the lead intact and deservedly so. Wales had played very well and despite England's near misses, they had more than held their own. Their pressure had forced Gordon West and his defenders into many anxious moments.

The second half saw a complete change round, however. England were somehow revitalised after the break with Bobby Charlton inspiring from the front. In the space of five minutes he fired in a tremendous shot from Colin Bell's pass which crashed against the crossbar. That was from 20 yards and shortly afterwards a lovely combination with Lee gave the Manchester United player another right-footer which this time found the top corner of Sprake's net in similar whizz-bang fashion.

The delighted England fans hardly had time to savour that gem when they were applauding another fine move. Bobby Charlton, Alan Ball, Lee, Bell and Ball again, set up Charlton to fire in yet another right-foot thunderbolt. But this time Sprake made a wonderful save as he turned the ball on to a post and away. Moments later the goalkeeper was in action again, saving once more from Charlton, who seemed hell bent on creating a scoring record in one match.

It was all thrilling action but it was far from over. With 18 minutes left, another central thrust came with Bobby Charlton at the helm. The move also involved Ball and Bell and the latter put in a cross which was headed at the Welsh goal by Astle. Although Sprake blocked the effort, the ball ran free and Lee roared in to crash home the rebound to atone for his penalty miss.

The goal turned out to be the winner in a game that was a delight to watch for all at the stadium and the millions viewing on television. The important difference between the sides was Bobby Charlton. He was quite simply magnificent and his goal would be long remembered as the pearl on a night of high entertainment.

> 79th match v Wales.
> Debut for Astle.
> Lee missed a penalty for England.

England v Scotland Home Championship

Played on Saturday, 10 May 1969 at Wembley Stadium.

England: G.Banks (Stoke C); K.R.Newton (Blackburn R), T.Cooper (Leeds Utd), A.P.Mullery (Spurs), B.L.Labone (Everton), R.F.C.Moore (West Ham, captain), F.H.Lee (Man City), A.J.Ball (Everton), R.Charlton (Man Utd), G.C.Hurst (West Ham), M.S.Peters (West Ham).

Scotland: J.Herriot (Birmingham C); E.G.McCreadie (Chelsea), T.Gemmell (Celtic), R.Murdoch (Celtic), W.McNeill

HRH The Duchess of Kent shakes skipper Bobby Moore's hand before the game against Scotland at Wembley in May 1969.

(Celtic), J.Greig (Rangers), W.Henderson (Rangers), W.J.Bremner (Leeds Utd), C.Stein (Rangers), A.J.Gilzean (Spurs), E.Gray (Leeds Utd).
Sub: W.S.B.Wallace (Celtic) for Gilzean.

Half-time 2-1   Full-time 4-1

Ref: R.Helies (France)   Att: 89,902

A marvellous performance by England in front of a good crowd at Wembley and the millions watching on television. It rounded off a very successful tournament which England had now won with maximum points from their three games. It was a night to savour as England's all-round strength, coupled with some outstanding individual displays, tore the Scots apart. The visitors did not play that badly, but England in this mood were too good for them.

The game was won and lost in the midfield area where Bobby Charlton, Alan Ball, Martin Peters and Alan Mullery won total dominance from Scotland's Bremner and company. With Bobby Moore and Brian Labone also outstanding, the whole side was able to play with a cool composure safe, in the knowledge that everyone was doing their job.

The first goal came after 15 minutes. It began with a lovely move out of defence involving Charlton, Francis Lee, Ball and Keith Newton before Peters took Newton's pass and hit a cross shot wide of the diving Herriot. Four minutes later they added a second goal and this one was a real beauty. Lee, who had been a revelation since coming into the side, took a pass from Charlton and made rapid strides down the left wing. He hurdled over a challenge from McNeill before hitting the ball square and low for Geoff Hurst to touch home superbly.

Despite Bremner's tireless running and Gray's promise, Scotland struggled to make an impact on England's solid defence, so it came as something of a surprise when they pulled a goal back just before the interval. Gray's deep cross from the left was met with a magnificent header by Stein, a bustling, old-fashioned type of centre-forward, and the ball sailed into the far corner with Gordon Banks well beaten. With Charlton and his fellow midfielders stroking the ball around majestically, it was only a matter of time before other goals arrived.

On the hour the result was settled. Another telling thrust by Charlton and Ball ended with a shot rebounding to Peters. As the West Ham player aimed to shoot, his legs were whipped from under him by Greig for what was an obvious penalty. Up stepped Hurst and he almost decapitated Herriot with the ferocity of his shot that made it 3-1. England were now well on top and another thrilling move brought them a fourth goal.

A lovely triangular passing movement between Lee, Ball and Peters ended with the latter side-footing the ball with supreme accuracy past the bamboozled Scottish defenders and wide of the goalkeeper. It rounded off a superb exhibition by England and Sir Alf Ramsey must have been delighted with his side's current form. They now embarked on a fact-finding summer tour of South America in preparation for the following year's defence of the World Cup in Mexico. They certainly must have departed in high spirits.

86th match v Scotland.
50th cap for Banks.
Penalty scored for England by Hurst.

Mexico v England   Friendly

Played on Sunday, 1 June 1969 in the Azteca Stadium, Mexico City.

Mexico: F.Castrejón (América); J.M.Alejándrez (Cruz Azul), G.Peña (Cruz Azul), G.Núñez (América), M.Pérez (América), J.L.González (Universidad), A.Munguia (Cruz Azul), F.Bustos (Cruz Azul), E.Borja (América), L.Estrada (CSD León), C.Victorino (Cruz Azul).

England: G.West (Everton); K.R.Newton (Blackburn R), T.Cooper (Leeds Utd), A.P.Mullery (Spurs), B.L.Labone (Everton), R.F.C.Moore (West Ham, captain), F.H.Lee (Man City), A.J.Ball (Everton), R.Charlton (Man Utd), G.C.Hurst (West Ham), M.S.Peters (West Ham).
Sub: T.J.Wright (Everton) for Newton.

Half-time 0-0   Full-time 0-0

A.Tejeda (Peru)   105,000

ENGLAND had their first experience of the task that faced them the following summer when they took on Mexico in the Azteca Stadium in the first game of their South American tour. The management were anxious to see how the players reacted to the rarefied air of this city. Long before the end it was clear that only detailed preparation would help England in 1970.

The first-half went well with England creating some good chances. Castrejón saved twice from Geoff Hurst and Francis Lee as the goalmouth incidents developed, and then the goalkeeper made the save of the match when he turned a Hurst header on to the bar before desperately reaching out to prevent the rebound rolling over the line. The header was a result of a splendid move involving Hurst and Alan Ball.

Shortly before that incident, Mexico missed a sitter at the other end. Brian Labone completely missed a pass from Bustos which Estrada took to the by-line. When the centre came over it seemed certain that Victorino would score, but he blazed his shot wildly over Gordon West's goal, much to England's relief.

West then made two fine saves from long-range efforts by Pérez and Gonzáles. Their 25-yard drives flew through the thin air at exceptional speed, something else that England's players would have to get used to. The visitors performed well in the opening half though and at times made Mexico look very ordinary. With skipper Bobby Moore in his usual immaculate form and Keith Newton, until he was injured, and Terry Cooper giving excellent support from full-back, the England defence comfortably held the Mexican attack. This despite West and Labone not looking 100 per cent confident.

In the second half, however, the trying conditions began to have an effect on England. Players became drawn and were fighting for breath, especially after bursts of speed or long runs. Bobby Charlton had the most difficult role, being the hub of the midfield. As the game wore on, even he began to make mistakes as the strength drained from his gaunt-looking body.

Mexico missed another fine chance on the hour. This time Borja, who had to go off to have his left ear taped and patched after having been accidentally kicked, left Labone stranded and made for goal completely in the clear. As West came out to narrow the angle and a pack of players snapping at his heels, Borja lost his nerve a little, shot too early and watched in dismay as the ball rolled tantalisingly the wrong side of the post.

So, England escaped and, although the playing and physical conditions made things increasingly difficult for them, one player stood head and shoulders above all others. The superb Moore was outstanding in all that he did. Other players to shine were Hurst, with some intelligent running, Lee, with his quick bursts and effervescent style, and the two full-backs. The match was an extremely useful experience for the whole England party and, hopefully, many lessons had been learned. When they returned for a month's acclimatisation in 1970, just prior to the tournament, they would have the chance to get it absolutely right. In the circumstances, the draw here was an honourable result.

4th match v Mexico.

Uruguay v England   Friendly

Played on Sunday, 8 June 1969 in the Centenario Stadium, Montivideo.

Uruguay: L.Maidana (Cerro); L.Ubínas (Nacional), A.Anchetta (Nacional), J.C.Paz (Rampla Juniors), J.Mujica (Nacional), J.Montero-Castillo (Nacional), J.Cortés (Peñerol), L.Cubilla (Nacional), R.Matosas (Peñarol), H.Silva (Peñarol), J.C.Morales (Nacional).

England: G.Banks (Stoke C); T.J.Wright (Everton), K.R.Newton (Blackburn R), A.P.Mullery (Spurs), B.L.Labone (Everton), R.F.C.Moore (West Ham, captain), F.H.Lee (Man City), C.Bell (Man City), G.C.Hurst (West Ham), A.J.Ball (Everton), M.S.Peters (West Ham).

Half-time 0-1   Full-time 1-2

A.Marques (Brazil)   Att: 55,000

AFTER an extra representative match against a Mexico XI had given England more valuable experience of the conditions, and a 4-0 victory, the squad moved on for this game in Uruguay. The venue was the Centenario Stadium which was also the venue for the very first World Cup Final held in 1930. It was England's second visit, having been beaten here in 1953. This time, though, England performed heroically and registered a famous victory.

They began the game brilliantly and scored an early goal through Francis Lee. It was just the start they needed and in the first half especially, they played some delightful football. The pitch was very poor but the England side, superbly marshalled by Bobby Moore, looked in total command for long spells. Brian Labone's strong tackling and the tireless running of Colin Bell and Alan Ball kept the possession England's, whilst up front Lee was sharp and penetrating.

The pitch cut up badly during the half and although the sun shone, conditions under foot deteriorated rapidly. However, England comfortably held their lead at the interval.

When the teams re-emerged after the break, the Uruguayan crowd whipped up a frenzy of excitement as their team improved at the start of the second half. They equalized early on and the crowd went wild with delight. The goal came from a free-kick, not the first given against the visitors. This time Tommy Wright was penalised after a tackle on the tricky Morales. Mujica took the free-kick on the left and Cubilla was on the spot to head past Gordon Banks.

For half an hour England had worked very hard to protect their lead but the equalizer had given Uruguay new confidence and now the South Americans were in command. Moore and his men worked overtime to repel their eager attack and during this spell it looked odds-on a home victory. But this England side were never more dangerous than when under the cosh and that was just how it proved. With ten minutes to go they scored a magnificent goal to win the match.

From deep in defence the ball moved swiftly to Bell. The Manchester City man was running his heart out and he continued the move with a pass to Ball. The red-haired terrier from Everton then fed Lee, who was sprinting down the right. Over came the cross and there, steaming in, was Geoff Hurst who hit a tremendous volley wide of Maidana. It was a copybook goal and it stunned the crowd into silence.

England remained calm and in control through the last few minutes to clinch a super win made all the sweeter by the standing ovation they received as they left the field. It was a terrific performance.

5th match v Uruguay.

Brazil v England   Friendly

Played on Thursday, 12 June 1969 in the Maracana Stadium, Rio de Janeiro.

Brazil: G.dos Santos (Santos); C.A.Torres (Santos), R.Costa (Santos), C.Tavares (Santos), D.Dias (Santos), J.Camargo (Santos), J.Ventura (Botafogo), G.Oliveira (Botafogo), E.Goncalves (Cruzeiro), E.Arantes (Santos), J.E.America (Santos).
Sub: P.C.Lima (Botafogo) for America.

England: G.Banks (Stoke C); T.J.Wright (Everton), K.R.Newton (Blackburn R), A.P.Mullery (Spurs), B.L.Labone (Everton), R.F.C.Moore (West Ham, captain), A.J.Ball (Everton), C.Bell (Man City), R.Charlton (Man Utd), G.C.Hurst (West Ham), M.S.Peters (West Ham).

Half-time 0-1   Full-time 2-1

Ref: R.Barreto (Uruguay)   Att: 125,000

THIS was carnival night in Rio, a night of never-to-be-forgotten atmosphere, and at the end of it all England were so unlucky not to have a result to take home with them.

With 125,000 football crazy people crammed into the magnificent Maracana Stadium, the teams took the field to a crescendo of drums and samba beat throbbing across the night air. Rockets were fired and in the distance the floodlit statue of Christ looked down on it all from the top of the Corcavado mountain.

After all the pre-match rituals, the game finally got under way. With 15 minutes gone, England, sensationally, took the lead. A flowing move involving Bobby Moore, Colin Bell, Geoff Hurst and Martin Peters ended when Peters' left-wing cross swung into the middle of the Brazilian penalty area. Bobby Charlton dived forward and although he missed the ball, it did enough to divert the defenders eyes and in moved Bell to shoot into the roof of the net.

England then defended superbly for the next 65 minutes. Gordon Banks and Moore were outstanding as the samba rhythm inspired Brazil to wave after wave of exciting attacking moves. Alan Mullery, Keith Newton, Tommy Wright, Bell and Alan Ball all worked tirelessly as the whole team showed all the discipline and teamwork that had stood them in such good stead for such a long time. Brazil tried everything they knew. Tostão and Gérson were supreme in midfield and the man they call 'the new Garrincha', Jairzinho, was a constant danger with his long legged style. Pelé, meanwhile, was simply . . .Pelé! Although well covered for much of the game by England, he still managed some magical moments. But despite all this good play, Brazil just could not pull the goal back.

Just after the interval Charlton missed a fine chance and if England had scored then, the victory might have been theirs. Still the visitors held on comfortably to their precious lead and fought like tigers to preserve it. Tragically, all of their hard work went out of the window with only ten minutes to go when Brazil turned the match upside down.

When a loose ball spun away from Peters on the edge of the England penalty area, four players swooped on it. Brian

Labone and Mullery were in there, but suddenly Tostão thrust out his left foot and the ball crept slowly past Banks who had for so long been the hero. The crowd went berserk and the musical accompaniment seemed to rise several decibels. England were stunned, but not nearly as stunned as they were to be after Brazil's next attack.

Hardly had the cheers died down when Tostão dummied his way around Newton on the right. A swift, low, diagonal pass across the face of the goal and there was the dangerous Jairzinho lurking in just the right spot to glance the ball past Banks.

So there it was. One minute England were looking forward to all the plaudits of a sensational win, the next it was all over for them as Brazil, quite simply, snatched the game from out of England's grasp.

> 7th match v Brazil.
> Brazil's dos Santos also known as 'Gilmar'; Torres as 'Carlos Alberto'; Costa as 'Rildo'; Tavares as 'Clodoaldo'; Camargo as 'Joel'; Ventura as 'Jairzinho'; Oliveira as 'Gérson'; Goncalves as 'Tostão'; Arantes as 'Pelé'; America as 'Edú'; Lima as 'Paulo Cesar'.

Holland v England
Friendly

Played on Wednesday, 5 November 1969 in the Olympic Stadium, Amsterdam.

Holland: E.W.Treijtel (Feyenoord); E.Drost (FC Twente), M.D.Israël (Feyenoord), J.A. Eijkenbroek (Sparta); R.M.Krol (Ajax Amsterdam), W.H.Veenstra (PSV Eindhoven), W.Van Hanegem (Feyenoord), N.J.Rijnders (Ajax Amsterdam), H.J.Cruyff (Ajax Amsterdam), J.Mulder (RSC Anderlecht), P.R.Rensenbrink (FC Brugge).
Subs: D.W.J.Van Dijk (Ajax Amsterdam) for Veenstra and G.D.M.H.Mühren (Ajax Amsterdam) for Van Hanegem.
England: P.P.Bonetti (Chelsea); T.J.Wright (Everton), E.W.Hughes (Liverpool), A.P.Mullery (Spurs), J.Charlton (Leeds Utd), R.F.C.Moore (West Ham, captain), F.H.Lee (Man City), C.Bell (Man City), R.Charlton (Man Utd), G.C.Hurst (West Ham), M.S.Peters (West Ham).
Sub: P.Thompson (Liverpool) for Lee.

Half-time 0-0   Full-time 0-1
Ref: P.Khazakov (USSR)   Att: 40,000

THE fifth of November but certainly no fireworks from this England display. This was a poor game, relieved only by the fact that they managed to win it. They brought in new cap Emlyn Hughes for this friendly international, a game to be used as part of the build-up towards the World Cup finals in Mexico in 1970. Hughes turned out to be one of the few successes of the night.

The game was one of highly complicated and laborious passing movements with very little thrust on the end of it all. Geoff Hurst and Francis Lee were too often left on their own up front and the Dutch found it easy to contain them. However, England's trademark of spirited teamwork was very much in evidence and

there was certainly no lack of effort from Sir Alf Ramsey's players.

Although the usual ultra-efficiency was not 100 per cent apparent, Bobby Moore was assured, Peter Bonetti made some acrobatic interceptions and Hughes positively revelled in playing for his country. But goal chances were few and far between and the 300 or so England fans, reinforced by members of the Portland Squadron of the Royal Navy, which had just put in at Rotterdam, had very little to excite them.

Just before the interval, Colin Bell had Treijtel beaten with a header from Hurst's cross but the ball thumped against the bar before being cleared. A quarter of an hour into the second half, Bell had another clear opening after a cross from Martin Peters. Alas, he missed again.

Holland, with Cruyff their main threat, came back strongly as the game progressed. He and Rijnders created all the Dutch team's best attacks. With 15 minutes to go, Holland began to turn the screw in their quest for victory. Substitute Van Dijk shot straight at Bonetti from a good position, and then a dazzling run by Cruyff, which left four England defenders in his wake, ended with another shot straight at the goalkeeper.

With the klaxons and rockets roaring from a crowd which sensed a possible win, England, not for the first time in recent internationals, came back with the perfect answer, even if it was somewhat fortuitous. Only five minutes remained on the clock when Bobby Charlton gained possession. He miscued his attempted shot, but the ball ran invitingly into the path of Bell some ten yards from goal. The Manchester City man's third chance of the night had this time fallen just right and he hit an unstoppable shot past Treijtel and into the roof of the net.

It was a dramatic ending to a game too often stifled by the technicalities of the play, plus two very efficient defences. An interested spectator was the Brazilian manager João Saldanha, who was on a spying tour of Europe. He did see some things to admire and also, much to the joy of the British sailors, signed their Royal Ensign in a bar before the game.

> 4th match v Holland.
> Debut for Hughes.
> *"My debut for England was the greatest moment of my football career."*
> Emlyn Hughes

England v Portugal
Friendly

Played on Wednesday, 10 December 1969 at Wembley Stadium.

England: P.P.Bonetti (Chelsea); P.Reaney (Leeds Utd), E.W.Hughes (Liverpool), A.P.Mullery (Spurs), J.Charlton (Leeds Utd), R.F.C.Moore (West Ham, captain), F.H.Lee (Man City), C.Bell (Man City), J.Astle (West Brom), R.Charlton (Man Utd), A.J.Ball (Everton).
Sub: M.S.Peters (West Ham) for Bell.
Portugal: J.H.Rodrigues (Benfica); J.Conceiçao (Vitória Setúbal), C.Cardoso (Vitória Setúbal), J.C.José (Sporting Lisbon), A.Murca (Belenenses), F.Tomé (Vitória Setúbal), A.Oliveira (Benfica),

J.Graça (Benfica), F.Guerreiro (Vitória Setúbal), M.A.Silva (Académica Coimbra), J.João (Vitória Setúbal).
Subs: E.Figueredo (Vitória Setúbal) for Graca and M.Campos (Académica Coimbra) for Graça.

Half-time 1-0   Full-time 1-0
Ref; R.Mouthon (France)   Att: 100,000

THIS match turned into an inconclusive performance by England who were now developing another problem in the goals-coring positions. True, they never looked like losing and had most of the play, but their inability to score was now making games closer than they should be.

For the first half-hour, England peppered the Portuguese goal. Their goalkeeper, Henriqué, worked overtime to keep his side in the match and one sensed that an early goal would have put a different complexion on the result. Portugal came to Wembley with their national football in dire straits and they were but a poor shadow of their illustrious predecessors from 1966, a side that came so close to glory on that summer night three years earlier in this very stadium. The current side feared a thrashing on this trip and, quite frankly, they should have got one.

A super move involving Bobby Moore, Alan Ball, Bobby Charlton and Francis Lee ended with Colin Bell's shot grazing the crossbar. Other chances came and went with Lee, Bobby Charlton and Ball all bringing the best out of Henriqué. Then, on 24 minutes, England did score and it came courtesy of the Charlton brothers. England's fifth corner was taken by Bobby and brother Jack rose at the near post to head in.

Perhaps, one thought, that would be the beginning of a goal rush but, alas, it did not turn out that way, much to the frustration of the crowd. Ten minutes before half-time, another swift move between Ball, Alan Mullery and Lee saw a Bobby Charlton shot hit the post. Peter Bonetti had been little more than a spectator throughout the first half and it was remarkable to think that England had only the one goal to show for their superiority.

The second half was no better. In fact, if anything it was worse for England. Portugal's confidence grew, although England still dominated. Jeff Astle's shot was blocked on the line by Cardoso but goal chances were less frequent. Bonetti had to earn his keep with a splendid save from a bending free-kick by the lanky João, and then another free-kick from Toni was saved low down after Jack Charlton had handled on the edge of the box.

With 20 minutes to go, there came the half's most dramatic moment. Martin Peters came on as substitute for Bell, who had dislocated his shoulder. Straight away Peters sent Astle away with a lovely pass. As the centre-forward swerved around the goalkeeper, looking a certain scorer, Henriqué brought him down for an obvious penalty. The Portuguese players erupted and the referee was besieged by gesticulating protestors. It was pandemonium. Carlos and Graça were booked and when eventually the commotion died down, Lee was poised to take the spot-kick. The whole affair had a distinct taste of gamesmanship and it obviously had an

Jeff Astle bursts through the Portuguese defence at Wembley in December 1969. Astle was brought down but Lee missed from the spot.

effect on Lee. His penalty kick was so wide it almost hit the corner flag.

That dramatic incident ended a disappointing showing by England and the one goal was no reward for the efforts of Ball, Bell, Lee, Bobby Charlton and Mullery. The only consolation comes from the fact that at least they continued the good habit of winning.

> 11th match v Portugal.
> Penalty kick missed by Lee.
> Portugal's Rodrigues also known as 'Henriqué'; José as 'José Carlos'; Oliveira as 'Toni'; Silva as 'Antonio'.

England v Holland
Friendly

Played on Wednesday, 14 January 1970 at Wembley Stadium.

England: G.Banks (Stoke C); K.R.Newton (Blackburn R), T.Cooper (Leeds Utd), M.S.Peters (West Ham), J.Charlton (Leeds Utd), N.Hunter (Leeds Utd), F.H.Lee (Man City), C.Bell (Man City), M.D.Jones (Leeds Utd), R.Charlton (Man Utd, captain), I.Storey-Moore (Nottm Forest). Subs: A.P.Mullery (Spurs) for Lee and G.C.Hurst (West Ham) for Jones.

Holland: J.Van Beveren (Sparta); E.Drost (FC Twente), M.D.Israël (Feyenoord), J.A.Eijkenbroek (Sparta), R.M.Krol (Ajax Amsterdam), W.M.A.Jansen (Feyenoord), R.N.J.Rijnders (Ajax Amsterdam), D.W.J.Van Dijk (Ajax Amsterdam), H.J.Cruyff (Ajax Amsterdam), W.Van Hanegem (Feyenoord), P.J.Keizer (Ajax Amsterdam). Subs: G.D.M.H.Mühren (Ajax Amsterdam) for Rijnders and W.H.Veenstra (PSV Eindhoven) for Van Hanegem.

Half-time 0-0   Full-time 0-0
Ref: H.Siebert (West Germany) Att: 75,000

SIR Alf Ramsey made seven changes from England's previous match as he experimented and searched for the right blend for Mexico. On this night's evidence he still had a lot more to do. This was a poor game and the crowd of 75,000 showed their frustration at England's inability to score by several times breaking out into a slow handclap. The artistic Dutchmen showed a lot of skill with some fine touches by Cruyff, Van Dijk and Jansen, but they, too, suffered from a lack of finish.

Goal chances were rare, but in the 25th minute England did find the net. A free-kick by Bobby Charlton was headed square by Mick Jones and there was Ian Storey-Moore to glance a header past Van Beveren. Alas, the referee had spotted an offside and the goal was ruled out.

Van Beveren made some excellent saves at this stage of the game to take the sting out of England. A few minutes after the disallowed goal, he tipped another Storey-Moore header over the bar after an overhead flick by Bobby Charlton. More good work by Jones gave first Bobby Charlton a shot, and then Storey-Moore again, but both times Van Beveren beat away the shots.

On the wet, holding pitch the Dutch were the better ball players and a marvellous swinging free-kick by Keizer almost caught Gordon Banks napping and the goalkeeper did exceptionally well to keep the shot out. Holland had certainly made rapid strides in international football over recent years and they were no longer an easy touch for opponents.

For the rest of the game it was frustration all the way. England's passing was

poor, they failed to stamp any authority on the midfield and they created few clear scoring attempts. On the plus side they have now gone 13 games unbeaten at Wembley and Storey-Moore and Jones both had lively matches. When Jones was substituted by Geoff Hurst, the crowd certainly let the England manager know that they disapproved of his decision to take the Leeds man off.

The final irony came right at the final whistle as the game ended in total confusion. Bobby Charlton hit a good shot into the net, only to find that the referee had blown the final whistle a fraction before the ball had gone in. As they left the ground, the crowd were not quite sure if England had won or drawn! The only other fact worth mentioning was that Bobby Charlton was playing his 98th international and the 68th against foreign opposition, thus beating the record of 67 set by Billy Wright.

> 5th match v Holland.
> Debut for Storey-Moore.

Belgium v England
Friendly

Played on Wednesday, 25 February 1970 at the Astrid Park, Brussels.

Belgium: J.Trappeniers (RSC Anderlecht); G.Heylens (RSC Anderlecht), N.Dewalque (Standard Liège), L.Jeck (Standard Liège), J.Thissen (Standard Liège), W.Van Moer (Standard Liège), J.Dockx (Racing White), O.Polleunis (St Truiden VV), L.Semmeling (Standard Liège), J.Devrindt (RSC Anderlecht), P.Van Himst (RSC Anderlecht).

Sub: J.Verheyen (Beershot VAV) for Polleunis.

England: G.Banks (Stoke C); T.J.Wright (Everton), T.Cooper (Leeds Utd), E.W.Hughes (Liverpool), B.L.Labone (Everton), R.F.C.Moore (West Ham, captain), F.H.Lee (Man City), A.J.Ball (Everton), P.L.Osgood (Chelsea), G.C.Hurst (West Ham), M.S.Peters (West Ham).

Half-time 0-1   Full-time 1-3

Ref: A.S.Bardella (Italy)   Att: 20,500

THIS was a real confidence booster for England on a night of high entertainment in appalling conditions between two sides who went at each other relentlessly from first whistle to last.

After the introduction of several positional changes, England looked much more balanced than of late and Peter Osgood as a roving centre-forward made an auspicious debut. With the sleet slanting down on to a mudheap of a pitch, good football looked distinctly unlikely. Yet that proved an incorrect assumption. The closed in surroundings of Anderlecht's stadium and a fervent, partisan crowd added to England's problems and they made a shaky start as a result. Belgium, also eager to impress with the World Cup only a few months away, opened strongly, quickly winning the early midfield battle and forcing England into errors. Van Moer, Van Himst, Devrindt and Semmeling all went close with goal attempts at Gordon Banks.

But suddenly, after 29 minutes, came the moment that completely changed the game. Osgood picked up the ball from Tommy Wright and cut inside a defender before passing to Martin Peters. The West Ham player slid a perfect pass into the path of Alan Ball and without having to alter his pace, Ball fired a fierce shot past Trappeniers. It was a magnificent goal and one could visibly detect the confidence suddenly return to England's play.

Belgium still fought hard though and fine tackles from Wright and Bobby Moore prevented the dangerous Van Himst from breaking through. At half-time England were still hanging on to their slender lead.

After the break, with the weather getting worse, the battle continued in a blaze of excitement. By now, Ball and Peters had wrestled the midfield away from Belgium and on 55 minutes England scored a second goal. Another fine move across the mud involving Ball, Emlyn Hughes and Peters ended with a cross by the latter. In came Geoff Hurst like an express train and his header gave the goalkeeper no chance.

Almost immediately, though, the Belgians pulled a goal back. Moore, magnificent throughout, was somewhat harshly penalised for handball on the edge of the area. From the free-kick, Dockx drilled his shot through the wall to make it 2-1. Many sides might have faltered at this point, but not England. Within a minute they had restored their two-goal advantage. Terry Cooper moved down the left and crossed to the middle, Hurst flicked it on and although Jeck headed the ball out, it dropped invitingly for the human dynamo Ball, who promptly whacked it back past Trappeniers.

That left the visitors with 30 minutes to negotiate, and led by Moore they clamly repelled all the Belgian efforts in this closing period of the match. Cooper, Hughes and Osgood all looked good and it was satisfying to see Peters back to his best in midfield. A fine victory.

> 16th match v Belgium.
> Debut for Osgood.

Wales v England   Home Championship

Played on Saturday, 18 April 1970 at Ninian Park, Cardiff.

Wales: A.H.Millington (Swansea C); P.J.Rodrigues (Leicester C), R.J.Thomas (Swindon T), W.T.Hennessey (Derby Co), H.M.England (Spurs), D.Powell (Sheffield Utd), R.L.Krzywicki (Huddersfield T), W.A.Durban (Derby Co), R.T.Davies (Southampton), G.Moore (Charlton A), R.R.Rees (Nottm Forest).

England: G.Banks (Stoke C); T.J.Wright (Everton), E.W.Hughes (Liverpool), A.P.Mullery (Spurs), B.L.Labone (Everton), R.F.C.Moore (West Ham, captain), F.H.Lee (Man City), A.J.Ball (Everton), R.Charlton (Man Utd), G.C.Hurst (West Ham), M.S.Peters (Spurs).

Half-time 1-0   Full-time 1-1

Ref: T.Wharton (Scotland)   Att: 47,000

Championship took England to Cardiff and on a blustery day, honours were shared. The game was a poor one and though England had the edge it took a late equalizer to prevent embarrassment after Wales had gone ahead.

The early skirmishes produced few goalmouth incidents, although Bobby Charlton fired a shot against a post in one attack. Another long range shot, this time by Martin Peters, also went close, whilst at the other end Davies powered his way through, only for Gordon Banks to make a brave stop at his feet.

The game went through a certain amount of tedium in the first half and neither side looked likely to break the deadlock. However, with five minutes to go before the interval, a Welsh goal suddenly lifted the tempo. Durban intercepted a pass from Peters and ran 50 yards with the England defence back-pedalling. Durban timed his pass forward to Krzywicki perfectly and the front man beat the square defence to shoot past Banks. It lifted the crowd, it lifted the Welsh team and, in the second half, it had the effect of lifting England.

Knowing they had to come forward, England showed much more enterprise with Peters outstanding. Wales defended doggedly, though, and managed the occasional breakaway. Davies gave Brian Labone a hard time in the air and Hennessey matched Peters for determination. However, an equalizer was always on the cards in this half and it came as no surprise when England grabbed that goal on 70 minutes. And what a spectacular goal it was too!

Charlton and Alan Ball combined to give Francis Lee possession on the left. He cut inside Rodrigues and from the angle of the penalty area, he hit a screamer into the far top corner before Millington could move. It was a superb strike and by now certainly no less than England deserved.

After the goal, England pressed forward in search of a winner and they almost managed it when Charlton's shot flew just too high. But a goal then would have been unfair on the Welsh who overall just about deserved a share of the spoils. For them Hennessey, Durban, Rees, Krzywicki and Davies were the stars, whilst for England, Charlton, Ball, Alan Mullery, Lee and especially Peters caught the eye.

> 80th match v Wales.

England v   Home Championship
Northern Ireland

Played on Tuesday, 21 April 1970 at Wembley Stadium.

England: G.Banks (Stoke C); K.R.Newton (Everton), E.W.Hughes (Liverpool), A.P.Mullery (Spurs), R.F.C.Moore (West Ham), N.P.Stiles (Man Utd), R.Coates (Burnley), B.Kidd (Man Utd), R.Charlton (Man Utd, captain), G.C.Hurst (West Ham), M.S.Peters (Spurs).
Sub: C.Bell (Man City) for Newton.

Northern Ireland: P.A.Jennings (Spurs); D.J.Craig (Newcastle Utd), D.Clements (Coventry C), W.J.O'Kane (Nottm Forest), W.J.T.Neill (Arsenal), J.J.Nicholson (Huddersfield T), A.S.McMordie (Middlesbrough), G.Best (Man Utd), A.D.Dougan (Wolves), A.O'Doherty (Coleraine), R.J.Lutton (Wolves).
Subs: J.Cowan (Newcastle Utd) for O'Doherty and S.Nelson (Arsenal) for Lutton.

Half-time 1-0   Full-time 3-1

Ref: V.G.Pintado (Spain)   Att: 80,000

THIS was a very sentimental and momentus international for Bobby Charlton of England. One of the most popular footballers of all time now shared the distinction, with Billy Wright, of winning 100 caps for his country, a very exclusive club. Captain for the night, Charlton led England out to a rapturous welcome from the big crowd. Before the kick-off he was presented with a silver salver by the FA chairman, Dr Andrew Stephen inscribed with the flags of the 31 nations that he has played against during his majestic and memorable career to date. And if all that was not enough, he then led England to a good win against a spirited Northern Ireland side.

Yet for an hour, the Irish looked the better team, despite the fact that England scored after only six minutes. Charlton started the move with one of his characteristic long passes which Geoff Hurst moved on to new cap Ralph Coates, who won a corner. From Charlton's corner, Martin Peters ghosted in typically to head past his new clubmate, Pat Jennings.

England's two new caps did well. Brian Kidd used the ball well and Coates impressed with some fine play. Ireland, with Best and Dougan prominent and Nicholson and Clements putting in some excellent work down the left, pressed hard. Their approach play was sometimes outstanding, only for their finishing to let them down. Dougan gave Bobby Moore one of his most difficult internationals and Gordon Banks did well to smother a shot by Best. But the goal that Ireland's general play deserved did come five minutes into the second half.

A great crossfield pass by Clements gave possession to Best. His sharp turn beat

100 caps – Bobby Charlton sets out his haul of caps after completing a century of appearances against Northern Ireland at Wembley in April 1970, an occasion he marked with one of England's three goals.

Nobby Stiles and a burst of speed left Emlyn Hughes struggling. As Banks advanced, Best cooly slipped the ball home with a low left-foot shot.

The Irish had worked so hard for their goal so what happened next must have been particularly annoying for them. Charlton, who in the first half had perhaps let the occasion somehow stifle his natural game, began to get to grips with the heavy pitch. Only five minutes after the Irish equalizer he sent Keith Newton away down the right. The full-back carried the ball to the by-line before his slightly deflected cross was headed in by Hurst.

After that goal there was never going to be any other result than an England win as the extra class began to tell. Charlton inspired another fine move and after Peters had centred both Hurst and then Kidd rattled the visitor's crossbar with headers. The pressure continued and as the Irish struggled, they brought on two substitutes to try and stem the tide. However, it had no effect and with just ten minutes to go the stadium erupted at the moment almost everyone had hoped for.

Yet another good move involving Coates, Kidd, Alan Mullery and Hughes ended with Jennings pawing at Hughes' left-wing centre without catching it. The ball ran free and in slid Charlton to score his 48th international goal. Rarely has the Wembley cheers been louder for a Charlton goal.

As the players trooped off after their satisfying performance the electronic scoreboard lit up with a good luck message to the England team as they left Wembley for the last time before embarking on their forthcoming adventure in Mexico. For Charlton, especially, it was a night he would never forget.

77th match v Northern Ireland.
Debut for Coates and Kidd.
Bobby Charlton's 100th cap.

Scotland v England   Home Championship

Played on Saturday, 25 April 1970 at Hampden Park, Glasgow.

Scotland: J.Cruickshank (Heart of Midlothian); T.Gemmell (Celtic), W.Dickson (Kilmarnock), J.Greig (Rangers), R.McKinnon (Rangers), R.Moncur (Newcastle Utd), J.Johnstone (Celtic), D.Hay (Celtic), C.Stein (Rangers), J.O'Hare (Derby Co), W.M.Carr (Coventry C).
Sub: A.J.Gilzean (Spurs) for Moncur.
England: G.Banks (Stoke C); K.R.Newton (Everton), E.W.Hughes (Liverpool), N.P.Stiles (Man Utd), B.L.Labone (Everton), R.F.C.Moore (West Ham, captain), P.Thompson (Liverpool), A.J.Ball (Everton), J.Astle (West Brom), G.C.Hurst (West Ham), M.S.Peters (Spurs).
Sub: A.P.Mullery (Spurs) for Thompson.

Half-time 0-0   Full-time 0-0

Ref: G.Schulenberg (West Germany)

Att: 137,438

A WINDSWEPT Hampden Park produced the first goalless draw between these sides since their first meeting way back in 1872. It was a game dominated by Scotland, but despite having 90 per cent of the possession, they created very few clear chances.

With Stein and Johnstone in sharp form, Scotland pushed forward from the start. Always though they reached a brick wall in the form of an efficient England defence. It was testament to their skill that Gordon Banks was not tested until late on. Yet England were very lucky just before the interval, when Stein burst into the penalty area, only to go sprawling over Brian Labone's outstretched leg. It seemed a certain penalty but to the dismay of the packed house, the referee waved play on.

After an uneventful first half, apart from that incident, the crowd looked to an improvement in the second half. England

continued to soak up lots of Scottish pressure but refused to concede anything. There was nobody on the end of a dangerous Johnstone cross and then O'Hare missed a fine chance, hooking wide from a good position. Johnstone, Greig, Hay and Carr set up attack after attack, but all too often it petered out before entering the danger zone.

Emlyn Hughes made a saving lunge from Hay and then Stiles intercepted a dangerous O'Hare centre. But it was not until the last moments that Scotland finally forced Banks into a save, a double one at that. Fierce shots by Stein and Johnstone were saved at full length as Scotland pushed desperately for the goal they wanted. But they could not break through and the game ended goalless. However, it was not before two other controversial incidents.

Scotland again screamed for a penalty after Stein was tripped a second time, by Stiles, but again the referee would have none of it. Then, as England awoke from their defensive slumbers and put together a late attack, a goal by Geoff Hurst's header from Martin Peters cross in the dying seconds was ruled out by a mystifying offside decision. Had that goal stood then the referee would probably have never been able to leave the ground!

Perhaps it was poetic justice, but at the end of it all the Home Championship ended in a three-way tie with England, Scotland and Wales all ending with four points.

87th match v Scotland.

Colombia v England   Friendly

Played on Thursday, 21 May 1970 in the Campin Stadium, Bogotá.

Colombia: U.Quintana (Atlético); A.Segovia (América), H.Segrera (Depor-

tivo Cali), D.Lopez (Cristal Caldas), O.Lopez (Deportivo Cali), G.Hernandez (Atlético), A.Paz (Independiente Santa Fe), M.Canon (Unión Magdalena), A.Brand (Nacional), J.Gallegos (Deportivo Cali), O.Garcia (Cristal).
Subs: M.Arango (Millionarios) for Paz and C.Araujo (Unión Magdalena) for Brand.

England: G.Banks (Stoke C); K.R.Newton (Everton), T.Cooper (Leeds Utd), A.P.Mullery (Spurs), B.L.Labone (Everton), R.F.C.Moore (West Ham, captain), F.H.Lee (Man City), A.J.Ball (Everton), R.Charlton (Man Utd), G.C.Hurst (West Ham), M.S.Peters (Spurs).

Half-time 0-2   Full-time 0-4
Ref: R.Barrios (Venezuela)   Att: 28,000

THE quest for World Cup glory began here, 8,600 feet up in the towering Andes mountains. After a long journey from home, England's acclimatization period includes this game and another in Ecuador. Here was a colourful scene to greet England with the many multi-coloured ponchos amongst the crowd, the throbbing music from the Mariachi bands and a full-scale turn out by the military academy in their distinctive uniforms.

When the game started, England got off to a flying start. On a wet, uneven pitch they were quickly into their stride and after only three minutes they took the lead. A corner by Bobby Charlton was flicked on by Geoff Hurst and in came Martin Peters to head a fine goal.

From that moment England took command. Playing lovely controlled football and pacing themselves perfectly, they easily held the Colombian team. Bobby Moore, captain supreme, was at his most elegant best and he was always there when danger threatened the England goal. Peters, too, had a fine match, always involved, always dangerous and always ready to have a shot at goal.

Colombia relied on the short-passing game but it was slow and laboured and England had little trouble dealing with it. After other near-misses, England increased their lead on the stroke of half-time. Another corner by Charlton and another superb header by Peters after Hurst's decoy run had opened the way.

Ten minutes after the interval, Charlton added a third, a thumping right-foot rocket from the edge of the area which gave the goalkeeper no chance. It was Charlton's 49th goal — and, as it turned out, last — for his country and it finally settled the result.

Peters, Alan Ball and Alan Mullery strutted around the midfield totally in control. Hurst was twice unlucky not to score, Francis Lee buzzed around effectively and Moore was outstanding at the heart of England's defence.

Ball was everywhere and his perpetual motion style impressed everyone and it was fitting that he should score the last goal just before the end when his fiery red head got on the end of a Terry Cooper cross.

This performance was a real confidence booster for the games ahead. The Colombians were quite simply outplayed and outclassed.

1st match v Colombia.

Ecuador v England   Friendly
Played on Sunday, 24 May 1970 at the Atahualpa Stadium, Quito.

Ecuador: E.Mejia (Emelec); L.Utreras (Deportivo Quito), C.Campoverde (Nueve De Octubre), E.Portilla (LDU Quito), J.Valencia (América), W.Cardenas (Barcelona), J.Bolaños (América), W.Muñoz (Barcelona), G.Peña-Herrera (Nueve De Octubre), P.Carrera (LDU Quito), C.Larrea (LDU Quito).
Subs: V.Cabezas (Emelec) for Munoz and T.Rodriguez (Nacional) for Carrera.
England: G.Banks (Stoke C); K.R.Newton (Everton), T.Cooper (Leeds Utd), A.P.Mullery (Spurs), B.L.Labone (Everton), R.F.C.Moore (West Ham, captain), F.H.Lee (Man City), A.J.Ball (Everton), R.Charlton (Man Utd), G.C.Hurst (West Ham), M.S.Peters (Spurs).
Subs: B.Kidd (Man Utd) for Lee and D.Sadler (Man Utd) for Charlton.

Half-time 0-1   Full-time 0-2
Ref: A.Tejeda (Peru)   Att: 22,250

ENGLAND travelled even higher for their next warm-up friendly when this game was played some 9,300 feet above sea level, and again the morale and spirit of an excellent England squad was lifted even further by another good win.

As in Colombia, the match was preceded by a reserve England XI winning against a local side. When the main meal was served, England began in the confident way that we had come to expect. Another early goal gave England the start they wanted. On another uneven pitch and in a warm temperature, Bobby Moore and Alan Mullery combined in midfield to feed Keith Newton on the right wing. When the cross came over, Francis Lee was at the far post to flick the ball home.

Ecuador were a better team than Colombia and Peña-Herrera, Carrera and Larrea were particularly skilful. They, too, played the short-passing game but England had now learned how to deal with this style. Bobby Charlton, Alan Ball and Martin Peters always kept the attack well supplied and up front, Lee and Geoff Hurst were always sharp.

A bad mistake by Ball almost gave Ecuador an equalizer when he allowed Peña-Herrera a clear run at goal. But Gordon Banks, so impressive, rushed out and blocked his shot with a fine diving save at his feet. Ball then almost made amends before the break when he dived headlong at a cross by Lee. The ball flew just over the bar with the Ecuador defence flat-footed.

After the interval both sides made two substitutions with Rodriguez and Cabezas coming on for the home side and Brian Kidd and David Sadler replacing Lee and Charlton respectively. Charlton had run himself out. Kidd, who was out of the final 22-man squad for the World Cup, immediately made his mark and in the 75th minute he scored the decisive second goal when he dived bravely to head home a Peters centre.

Earlier Ecuador had put some pressure on England with Peña-Herrera lobbing just over and Banks making another world class save from substitute Rodriguez.

The two friendlies were an excellent test for England and they had come through

with flying colours. The preparation had gone very well and they were now ready for their first game in the Mexico World Cup finals.

1st match v Ecuador.

World Cup Finals

Romania v England   Group Three
Played on Tuesday, 2 June 1970 in the Jalisco Stadium, Guadalajara, Mexico.

Romania: S.Adamache (Red Flag, Braşov); L.Salmareanu (Steaua Bucharest), N.Lupescu (Rapid Bucharest), C.Dinu (Dinamo Bucharest), M.Mocanu (Petrolul Ploieşti), I.Dumitru (Rapid Bucharest), R.Nunweiller (Dinamo Bucharest), E.Dembrowski (Dinamo Bacău), G.Tataru (Steaua Bucharest), F.Dumitrache (Dinamo Bucharest), M.Lucescu (Dinamo Bucharest).
Sub: A.Neagu (Rapid Bucharest) for Tataru.
England: G.Banks (Stoke C); K.R.Newton (Everton), T.Cooper (Leeds Utd), A.P.Mullery (Spurs), B.L.Labone (Everton), R.F.C.Moore (West Ham, captain), F.H.Lee (Man City), A.J.Ball (Everton), R.Charlton (Man Utd), G.C.Hurst (West Ham), M.S.Peters (Spurs).
Subs: T.J.Wright (Everton) for Newton and P.L.Osgood (Chelsea) for Lee.

Half-time 0-0   Full-time 0-1
Ref: V.Loraux (Belgium)   Att: 50,000

ENGLAND at last began their defence of the World Cup exactly four weeks after having arrived in Mexico for acclimatization. The pre-tournament friendlies had gone very well and now the important games began. Bobby Moore led his men out and so England fans who had made the long journey roared their approval. The red, white and blue Union Flags were much in evidence.

The opening exchanges were lively to say the least and when Bobby Charlton and Francis Lee played a wall pass on the edge of the area, Charlton was hooked up in the penalty area as he went for the return. Unfortunately the referee waved play on.

With only five minutes gone, Romania almost scored when Nunweiller began a good move which sent the dangerous Dumitrache away. He beautifully dummied Brian Labone and Keith Newton before sending an inch-perfect cross to the far post. In came Tataru from behind Terry Cooper but he miscued his volley wide of the target.

The game settled down after that incident and was constantly interupted by the referee's whistle. The Romanians resorted to less than fair means to stop the England players but to their everlasting credit there was no retaliation from the holders and they could be proud of their faultless temperament.

Dumitrache was a real handful and another superb run in the 23rd minute had Moore and Cooper in trouble before Alan Mullery came across to quell the danger with a fierce challenge.

England grew in confidence as they warmed to the task. Newton and Cooper

Hurst gets his head to a cross but Romanian goalkeeper Adamache grabs the ball during the 1970 World Cup finals.

England and Brazil line up before the start of their World Cup game in Guadalajara.

made some good runs and Moore, Charlton, Alan Ball and Mullery began to drive them forward. Charlton fired in two of his specials and both went close. With ten minutes of the half left, Cooper put in yet another cross after beating Salmareanu, and Lee darted in only to be desperately unlucky enough to see his snapshot strike the bar. Moments later, Martin Peters headed just over from Newton's cross.

The second half saw England tighten up at the back but continue to push forward. On 65 minutes they finally found a way through. Ball put in a deep cross to the far post. Geoff Hurst trapped the ball, skipped around a defender brilliantly in a tight situation and then slammed in a fine shot from an acute angle.

The goal was well received by England and from then on their controlled, thoughtful play took all the sting out of Romania. The Romanians were too defensive in their approach and their cynical play also left a lot to be desired.

When the referee signalled the end of the game, the match-winner had been the same in this game as he had been four years earlier against the West Germans.

A good omen perhaps? It was certainly a satisfactory opening for England and they now moved on to the big one, a match against mighty Brazil.

4th match v Romania.

Brazil v England   Group Three

Played on Sunday, 7 June 1970 in the Jalisco Stadium, Guadalajara, Mexico.

Brazil: F.Mielli (Fluminense); C.A.Torres (Santos), E.Marques (Gremio), C.Tavares (Santos), H.Brito (Flamengo), W.Piazza (Cruzeiro), J.Ventura (Botafogo), P.C.Lima (Botafogo), E.Goncalves (Cruzeiro), E.Arantes (Santos), R.Rivelino (Corinthians).
Sub: R.Lopes (Botafogo) for Goncalves.

England: G.Banks (Stoke C); T.J.Wright (Everton), T.Cooper (Leeds Utd), A.P.Mullery (Spurs), B.L.Labone (Everton), R.F.C.Moore (West Ham, captain), F.H.Lee (Man City), A.J.Ball (Everton), R.Charlton (Man Utd), G.C.Hurst (West Ham), M.S.Peters (Spurs).

Subs: J.Astle (West Brom) for Lee and C.Bell (Man City) for Charlton.

Half-time 0-0   Full-time 1-0
Ref: A.Klein (Israel)   Att: 66,750

LADY Luck did not smile on England in their vital match against their illustrious opponents from Brazil in what was a superb international. England replaced the injured Keith Newton with Tommy Wright in an otherwise unchanged side.

For the opening ten minutes England dictated and Martin Peters, Alan Ball and Francis Lee kept Felix on his toes, but typically, and without warning, Brazil suddenly struck with a venomous attack in the 11th minute. The dangerous and skilful Jairzinho outpaced Terry Cooper and pitched a superb centre into the middle about seven yards out. Up went Pelé to meet it with a powerful downward header. It looked a goal all the way but somehow Gordon Banks not only reached the ball with his dive but also managed to flick it up and over the crossbar. It was a magical moment and the whole stadium rose to applaud.

The boiling heat of the midday sun in

Guadalajara was a very different atmosphere to that of a grey November day at Wembley, but England adapted well to their task. Brian Labone kept a firm hold on Tostão and Alan Mullery was doing a fine containing job on Pelé.

The best chance of a pulsating half for England came when Lee had a double effort saved by Felix. Half-time was reached with the game delicately poised.

In the early part of the second half, Brazil stepped up a gear and produced a dazzling spell which stretched England to the limit. With clever passing movements and lightning pace, they suddenly found some gaps in the English defence. A long-range shot by Paulo Cesar was tipped around the post by Banks, and then Pelé set up Jairzinho, only for Banks to beat him to the pass.

Brazil, and especially Pelé, began to turn the screw and a superb run which took him past four defenders was stopped only by a brilliant tackle by Mullery. Then Banks again saved well when he fisted away a rocket shot by Rivelino.

This pressure had to tell, and on the hour the Brazilians finally broke through. Paulo Cesar gave Tostão possession and at first it seemed Tostão had nowhere to go as the England defenders closed in, but some clever footwork and tricky body-swerves gave him space to turn 180 degrees and chip a square ball to Pelé. The magnificent number-ten was soon surrounded but he just held the ball long enough to allow Jairzinho to move up on his right. At the perfect moment, Pelé slid the ball into Jairzinho's path and this time Banks had no chance to save.

It was a tremendous goal and delighted most of the crowd but to England's eternal credit they came back strongly after this set-back and in the final half hour were desperately unlucky not to equalize. Sir Alf Ramsey tried new tactics, bringing on Colin Bell and Jeff Astle and then pumping long high crosses to the far post. The tactic worked and it put Brazil under new pressure. Astle climbed to meet the crosses, nodding them down to oncoming players and creating several chances. Ball

completely missed his kick from a clear opening and then the best chance of the match fell to Astle. How he missed with only the 'keeper to beat from 12 yards out, no one could imagine, but miss he did and several of the England players held their heads in disbelief.

The final disappointment came with ten minutes to go when Ball hit a glorious shot which cannoned back off the cross-bar. So Brazil ended 1-0 winners. It was a fine game played in a superb spirit and there was so much mutual respect on the faces of the players as they swapped shirts at the end of the match.

8th match v Brazil.
Brazil's Mielli also known as 'Felix'; Torres as 'Carlos Alberto'; Marques as 'Everaldo'; Tavares as 'Clodoaldo'; Ventura as 'Jairzinho'; Lima as 'Paulo Cesar'; Goncalves as 'Tostão'; Arantes as 'Pelé'; Lopes as 'Roberto'.
"I always enjoyed playing against Brazil the most because they were so individually talented — and the best."
Bobby Moore

Czechoslovakia v England Group Three

Played on Thursday, 11 June 1970 in the Jalisco Stadium, Guadalajara, Mexico.

Czechoslovakia: I.Viktor (Dukla Prague); K.Dobiáš (Spartak Trnava), V.Hrivnák (Slovan Bratislava), V.Migas (Sparta Prague), V.Hagara (Spartak Trnava), J.Pollák (VSS Košice), L.Kuna (Spartak Trnava), L.Petráš (Inter Bratislava), J.Adamec (Spartak Trnava), Ja Čapkovič (Slovan Bratislava), F.Veselý (Slavia Prague).
Sub: K.Jokl (Slovan Bratislava) for Čapkovič.

England: G.Banks (Stoke C); K.R.Newton (Everton), T.Cooper (Leeds Utd), A.P.Mullery (Spurs), J.Charlton (Leeds Utd), R.F.C.Moore (West Ham, captain), C.Bell (Man City), R.Charlton (Man Utd),

J.Astle (West Brom), A.J.Clarke (Leeds Utd), M.S.Peters (Spurs).
Subs: A.J.Ball (Everton) for R.Charlton and P.L.Osgood (Chelsea) for Astle.

Half-time 0-0   Full-time 0-1
Ref: R.Mâchin (France)   Att: 49,000

IF England's game against Brazil had been one of the best games of the 1970 World Cup so far, then this one must have been one of the worst.

England took the field with an unfamiliar look about them. Sporting a new all light-blue strip and showing five changes from the team which started against Brazil, they played in an untypical way.

They were disjointed from the first whistle and took a long time to get their game together. It was certainly England's poorest performance for some considerable time. There were few goal attempts worth recording, despite the fact that both sides enjoyed plenty of possession. Allan Clarke of Leeds was making his debut, whilst at the other end of the spectrum Bobby Charlton was making a record-equalling 105th appearance, thus sharing the accolade with Billy Wright.

With England needing only one point to qualify for the quarter-finals there was no reason to make silly errors and with Czechoslovakia having little to offer, the spectators were left with a tedious match. After a non-event of a first-half England began the second with an early goal. Forty-nine minutes had gone when they scored what proved to be the only goal of the match.

It was Colin Bell who made the positive burst into the penalty area, only to be unceremoniously brought down by a Czech defender who then handled the ball for good measure! Penalty! With Geoff Hurst and Francis Lee out of the side, the kick was surprisingly entrusted with the new boy Clarke. But there was no hint of nerves as he showed exceptional coolness to calmly place his shot well out of Viktor's reach.

England's only other worthwhile scoring attempt came midway through the

Gordon Banks makes a magnificent save from Pelé. It was shown again and again on television and was perhaps the most famous goalkeeping save of all time.

half when Alan Ball hit a fine shot which hit the bar. Czechoslovakia then almost made England blush by nearly scoring an equalizer. Adamec's shot deceived Gordon Banks and the ball slipped through the goalkeeper's grasp. The ball hit the woodwork before England's defenders hacked it away to safety. England escaped and, despite this stuttering performance, had made their way safely through to a quarter-final showdown against West Germany. What an ironic twist that was.

5th match v Czechoslovakia.
Debut goal for Clarke (penalty).

West Germany v England   Quarter-final

Played on Sunday, 14 June 1970 in the Guanajuato Stadium, León, Mexico.

West Germany: J.Maier (Bayern Munich); H.H.Vogts (Borussia Mönchengladbach), H.D.Höttges (Werder Bremen), F.Beckenbauer (Bayern Munich), K.Fichtel (FC Schalke 04), K.H.Schnellinger (Milan AC), R.Libuda (FC Schalke 04), U.Seeler (Hamburger SV), G.Müller (Bayern Munich), W.Overath (1.FC Cologne), J.Löhr (1.FC Cologne).
Subs: W.Schulz (Hamburger SV) for Höttges and J.Grabowski (Eintracht Frankfurt) for Libuda.
England: P.B.Bonetti (Chelsea); K.R.Newton (Everton), T.Cooper (Leeds Utd), A.P.Mullery (Spurs), B.L.Labone (Everton), R.F.C.Moore (West Ham, captain), F.H.Lee (Man City), A.J.Ball (Everton), R.Charlton (Man Utd), G.C.Hurst (West Ham), M.S.Peters (Spurs).
Subs: C.Bell (Man City) for Charlton and N.Hunter (Leeds Utd) for Peters.

Half-time 0-1   Full-time 3-2 aet (90 minutes, 2-2)

Ref: A.N.Coerezza (Argentina)   Att: 23,250

THE Jules Rimet trophy finally slipped from England's grasp after this epic match ended in the most dramatic fashion imaginable. Things began to go wrong before the match even started when it was announced that Gordon Banks had gone down with a stomach bug and would not play. That meant that Peter Bonetti had to come in for his first taste of World Cup action. Remembering the superb form of Banks in the previous games, it was indeed a bitter blow.

Now, let the story unfold. England took the field in red shirts and it was shades of the 1966 Final all over again. Five men from each side had survived the interim years and the occasion had added spice for Bobby Charlton as he was celebrating setting up a new appearance record by winning his 106th cap. The scene was set with two similar sides ready to do battle in the hot sun of León.

The opening exchanges saw the Germans looking to wrestle the midfield power away from England. Beckenbauer, Overath and Seeler versus Charlton, Alan Ball, Alan Mullery and Martin Peters. The extra man advantage did not necessarily give England the edge, but they did break quickly and effectively from defence, pushing the Germans back on their heels. In the 31st minute, from one such break,

England opened the scoring with a magnificent goal.

Mullery began the move with a long pass to Keith Newton from midfield. Both players moved forward at speed and when Newton's pass came back into the middle, Mullery was following up to sweep an unstoppable shot past Maier. That gave England control and with Bobby Moore holding the Germans with his customary grace and skill, they reached half-time without mishap.

At the start of the second half, the Germans brought on Schultz to replace Höttges but it had little effect and four minutes into the half, England scored again. A brilliant tackle by Moore robbed Seeler and he found Ball with a good pass. He quickly moved it on to Geoff Hurst and then to Newton, who was again galloping up the right wing. The full-back crossed to the far post and there was Peters, ghosting in to head home in that unique way of his.

At that moment the game looked all over. England two goals up and in control, 'You'll Never Walk Alone' ringing out from the stands.

But Germany refused to lie down. Sir Alf Ramsey obviously felt very confident, though, and brought off Charlton and Peters, obviously with a view that they should be rested for the semi final. Unfortunately it was a move that did not work out for him. The West Germans were far from finished and 20 minutes from the end, Beckenbauer picked up a rebound off Francis Lee, went past Terry Cooper and hit a low cross shot which deceived Bonetti and nestled in the far corner.

Despite some doubt creeping into England's play, they had no need to panic as they still looked in good order. On 78 minutes, another fine move almost settled the match. Peters, Ball and Colin Bell combined, and Bell's cross was met by a diving header by Hurst. The ball rolled agonisingly slowly, just the wrong side of Maier's far post, and the Germans escaped. That was a crucial moment as four minutes later, Fichtel crossed diagonally from the left and there was Seeler who jumped, connected with a slightly fortuitous back-header and watched in almost disbelief as the ball looped up and over the badly-positioned Bonetti.

The Germans brave fight-back was almost complete as the two sides now had to face extra-time, something that seemed unthinkable some 20 minutes earlier. As in 1966, the drama was far from over.

The first half of the extra period was fairly innocuous with few attacks of note. But five minutes after the change of ends, the moment came that the whole of England dreaded. Substitute Grabowski made a good run down the right wing, beating Cooper for pace and going around him on the outside. His cross was deep, beating Newton, but nodded back into the middle by Löhr. Poor Bonetti was chasing shadows and the one person to fear when the ball is in the six-yard box was Müller. The German striker as ever, was prowling and he moved like lightning to volley the ball home from three yards out. The joy of the Germans was in distinct contrast to the absolute despair of the England team.

To their credit England, in the remaining minutes, tried desperately to salvage something. But although Mullery and Newton both shot narrowly over and Ball

miscued a shot after Hurst had headed down to him, the damage had already been done. Eventually the referee blew the final whistle to end this remarkable match.

10th match v West Germany.
Bobby Charlton's 106th cap, a new record, and also his last.

Bobby Moore and the East German skipper exchange pennants before the game at Wembley in November 1970.

England v East Germany   Friendly

Played on Wednesday, 25 November 1970 at Wembley Stadium.

England: P.L.Shilton (Leicester C); E.W.Hughes (Liverpool), T.Cooper (Leeds Utd), A.P.Mullery (Spurs), D.Sadler (Man Utd), R.F.C.Moore (West Ham, captain), F.H.Lee (Man City), A.J.Ball (Everton), G.C.Hurst (West Ham), A.J.Clarke (Leeds Utd), M.S.Peters (Spurs).
East Germany: J.Croy (Motor Zwickau); L.Kurbjuweit (Carl Zeiss Jena), P.Rock (Carl Zeiss Jena), K.Sammer (SG Dynamo Dresden), F.Ganzera (SG Dynamo Dresden), M.Strempel (Carl Zeiss Jena), H.Stein (Carl Zeiss Jena), H.Irmscher (Carl Zeiss Jena), P.Ducke (Carl Zeiss Jena), H.J.Kreische (SG Dynamo Dresden), E.Vogel (FC Karl-Marx-Stadt).
Sub: H.Frenzel (Lokomotive Leipzig) for Strempel.

Half-time 2-1   Full-time 3-1

Ref: R.Schürer (Switzerland)   Att: 93,000

EAST Germany arrived at Wembley with four consecutive wins and a goal difference of 16-0 behind them, so they were going to provide stiff opposition for an England side still smarting over the devastating defeat against West Germany in Mexico. Manager, Sir Alf Ramsey, brought in a new goalkeeper in Peter Shilton and recalled Allan Clarke to the attack to add a subtle touch to the powerful running of Francis Lee and Geoff Hurst.

England began well and one mighty clearance by Shilton almost brought a goal on ten minutes. Clarke headed the

Francis Lee takes the ball around the grounded Croy to score against East Germany. England won 3-1.

Allan Clarke scores England's third goal against the East Germans.

match with a superb goal. Their captain, Stein, found Vogel with a good pass and Vogel's tremendous 25-yard dipping shot caught Shilton a little too far off his line and a bit late with his leap.

That goal took some of the sting out of England and in the first 15 minutes after half-time it was East Germany who dominated. They played fast, fluent and open attacking football making the most of the skills of Sammer, Kreische, Ducke and Vogel. Their long-range shooting was very dangerous and Vogel hit another screamer from 25 yards which Shilton only just managed to tip over at the last second. The goalkeeper saved England again a moment later when he bravely blocked a close range effort from Ducke.

Gradually the fluency of the first half came back into England's game and Peters, Ball and Alan Mullery began to win back the midfield supremacy. Midway through the half they finally wrapped up the result with a decisive third goal. Lee again provided the pass which was superbly read by the impressive Clarke, and the way Clarke tucked away his chance augered well for the progress of his international career.

Peter Shilton, on the eve of his international debut against East Germany.

So England had made a good start to their rebuilding programme. This was an impressive victory and with one or two other adjustments they could look forward to a better future.

> 2nd match v East Germany.
> Debut for Shilton.

clearance square and Lee struck a first-time shot which was brilliantly saved by Croy. Two minutes later, the move was repeated and this time the touch was by Hurst. He found Lee again and the Manchester City striker cleverly side-stepped Strempel and the advancing goalkeeper to stroke the ball home.

The England pressure continued with the East Germans struggling to keep the home forwards at bay. On 20 minutes, England deservedly added a second goal. Sammer, an outstanding player, was left with only one option when trying to stop David Sadler's long dribble and he took it by bringing the centre-half down with a trip. Alan Ball's free-kick was breasted down by Hurst and Martin Peters was there to shoot home an innocuous-

looking left-foot half-volley past the rooted Croy. The goalkeeper looked as though he was unsighted, and by his lack of action it was obvious he never saw the shot coming.

England, now playing with an enjoyable relaxed style, piled on the pressure. Twice they came desperately close to increasing their lead with more exciting play. Lee missed an open goal and then, after Bobby Moore's superb pass, good running and passing between Clarke, Hurst and Lee ended with the latter's shot striking Croy from close range before being hacked clear.

It was one-way traffic as the German defenders chased shadows. But then, on the half-hour and quite unexpectedly, the visitors clawed their way back into the

Malta v England
European Championship Qualifier

Played on Wednesday, 3 February 1971 in the National Stadium, Ta'Qali.

Malta: A.Mizzi (Hibernians); J.Grima (Floriana), A.Mallia (Tarxien Rainbows),

Maltese skipper Joe Cini and England's Alan Mullery exchange pennants before the game in Ta'Qali in February 1971.

A.Camilleri (Floriana), E.Micallef (Sliema Wanderers), E.Darmanin (Sliema Wanderers), R.Cocks (Sliema Wanderers), W.Vassallo (Floriana), J.Cini (Hibernians), E.Theobald (Hibernians), L.Arpa (Floriana).

England: G.Banks (Stoke C); P.F.Reaney (Leeds Utd), E.W.Hughes (Liverpool), A.P.Mullery (Spurs, captain), R.L.McFarland (Derby Co), N.Hunter (Leeds Utd), A.J.Ball (Everton), M.H.Chivers (Spurs), J.Royle (Everton), J.C.Harvey (Everton), M.S.Peters (Spurs).

Half-time 0-1   Full-time 0-1

Ref: F.Marschall (Austria)   Att: 20,000

WHEN the England players walked on to the pitch at the National Stadium, they could not believe their eyes to see not a blade of grass but a surface to rival a sandy parade ground. Sir Alf Ramsey made several changes, bringing in four new caps, Colin Harvey, Roy McFarland (who replaced the injured Labone), Joe Royle and Martin Chivers. With this pitch and all these new faces it was hardly surprising that the game was a poor one.

Alan Mullery, captain for the match, proudly tossed up and England began their European challenge. Obviously the support for the underdogs was loud and passionate and Theobald and Cocks showed some creative talent in a match that was largely devoid of such luxuries. The pitch immediately had an effect as the ball bounced high and erratically making good control virtually impossible. it was also very narrow and the game was

repeatedly held up for throw-ins as passes were constantly over-hit. To cap it all the goal-posts were painted with black and white stripes!

Still the game moved on and a full house cheered their favourites under the fierce Mediterranean sun. Malta's defence played well with Micallef, Camilleri and Mallia all performing admirably. England looked disjointed with only Martin Peters showing good form. And it was Peters who broke the deadlock. Thirty-five minutes had gone when Norman Hunter's pass found the Tottenham man. Peters shot first time, low to the goalkeeper's left and beat Mizzi, who dived late being possibly unsighted.

Other goal chances were few and far between. Before the goal, Chivers had headed narrowly over the bar following a Peters free-kick, and another concerted attack saw Peters and Alan Ball shoot wide. Royle had an effort cleared off the line by Micallef and Emlyn Hughes did likewise at the other end, although the referee had already blown for an infringement by Cini on Gordon Banks.

England produced a thoroughly professional performance in the second half and largely controlled the proceedings. Playing at their own pace, they always held the upper hand despite the hard-working Maltese players giving their all. Mallia chased everything and Cini kept on nagging at McFarland's heels. Near the end, a clever pass by Cocks for once beat McFarland and Hunter and only a quick brave dive by Banks at Cini's feet averted the danger. In an awkward away game

it was pleasing to see England come away with the points to put them in second position in their group.

> 1st match v Malta.
> Debuts for McFarland, Chivers, Royle and Harvey.
> Mullery captain for the first time.

England v Greece
European Championship Qualifier

Played on Wednesday, 21 April 1971 at Wembley Stadium.

England: G.Banks (Stoke C); P.E.Storey (Arsenal), E.W.Hughes (Liverpool), A.P.Mullery (Spurs), R.L.McFarland (Derby Co), R.F.C.Moore (West Ham, captain), F.H.Lee (Man City), A.J.Ball (Everton), M.H.Chivers (Spurs), G.C.Hurst (West Ham), M.S.Peters (Spurs).
Sub: R.Coates (Burnley) for Ball.

Greece: N.Khristidis (Aris Thessalonikis); G.Gaitatzis (Olympiakos), N.Stathopoulos (AEK Athens), A.Spyridon (Aris Thessalonikis), A.Toskas (AEK Athens), D.Kabas (Panathinaikos), G.Koudas (PAOK Thessalonikis), T.Synetopoulos (Olympiakos), G.Dedes (Panionios), D.Papaioannou (AEK Athens), M.Kritikopoulos (Ethnikos).
Subs: S.Khaitas (Panionios) for Cambas and G.Delikaris (Olympiakos) for Dedes

Half-time 1-0   Full-time 3-0

Ref: M.Hirviniemi (Finland)   Att: 60,000

Martin Chivers blasts home England's first goal against Greece at Wembley in April 1971.

ENGLAND continued their quest for European Championship glory with this easy victory over an outclassed Greek side. The home team rarely inspired, but efficiently disposed of this latest challenge.

The first-half was a drab affair with England in command but failing to turn their possession into goals. Bobby Moore's return added a calm assurance to the defence and Roy McFarland supported his captain superbly. Alan Mullery and Martin Peters also looked good, but all too often the ball went square instead of forward.

In the 23rd minute, though, England scored with a well-taken goal. A good move between Francis Lee and Peters ended with a pass to Martin Chivers. The big centre-forward powered past two Greek challenges before surging on to lash home a left-foot shot out of the reach of Khristidis. It was a fine goal but the only really worthwhile memory of a disappointing half.

After the interval, Lee pushed forward more often and the pressure gradually increased. Khristidis began to earn his wages with fine saves from Peters and Lee. Lee put in several good attempts and was by now England's most dangerous forward, but in the 70th minute a cross by Peters was flicked on by Chivers and in came Geoff Hurst to nod home an overdue second England goal.

Both sides made substitutions with Ralph Coates coming on for Alan Ball. He made an immediate impact with his fresh attacking approach and combined with new cap Peter Storey, he layed on a splendid goal for Lee near the end. When Storey's final cross came over, Lee dived horizontally to head spectacularly past the by now overworked Khristidis.

The game was watched by some 60,000 people, the lowest crowd at Wembley since the 1966 World Cup, but they at least had three good goals to savour. As for the rest, well, the Greeks had little to offer except heart and determination. Papaioannou impressed with his tireless midfield work and Koudas showed some lovely close control. Dedes also looked quite useful but despite this, it must be said that Gordon Banks did not have a single direct shot to save in the whole 90 minutes. That highlighted the gulf between the sides.

1st match v Greece.
Debut for Storey.

Francis Lee (extreme left) heads England's second goal against Malta at Wembley in May 1971.

England v Malta
European Championship Qualifier

Played on Wednesday, 12 May 1971 at Wembley Stadium.

England: G.Banks (Stoke C); C.Lawler (Liverpool), T.Cooper (Leeds Utd), E.W.Hughes (Liverpool), R.L.McFarland (Derby Co), R.F.C.Moore (West Ham, captain), F.H.Lee (Man City), R.Coates (Spurs), M.H.Chivers (Spurs), A.J.Clarke (Leeds Utd), M.S.Peters (Spurs).
Sub: A.J.Ball (Everton) for Peters.

Malta: V.Borg Bonaci (Valletta FC); L.Pace (Valletta FC), J.Grima (Floriana), A.Camilleri (Floriana), E.Darmanin (Sliema Wanderers), A.Delia (Hibernians), R.Cocks (Sliema Wanderers), W.Vassallo (Floriana), J.Bonnett (Sliema Wanderers), E.Theobald (Hibernians), L.Arpa (Floriana).
Sub: A.Mizzi (Hibernians) for Bonaci.

Half-time 2-0   Full-time 5-0
Ref: E.Röed (Norway)   Att: 36,500

ONLY 36,500 people turned up to see what was promised as lambs to the slaughter with Malta visiting Wembley for the first time. With England still chasing Switzerland at the top of the group they were looking, not only to win, but also to score as many goals as possible.

As expected, the pattern was set from the start with play situated almost exclusively in Malta's half. England immediately peppered the Maltese goal with shot after shot. But a combination of weak finishing, desperate defending and good goalkeeping kept England at bay for half an hour. They did eventually, however, make the breakthrough when Martin Peters floated in a free-kick and Martin Chivers headed in. Shortly before the half-time break, England made it 2-0 following a corner. Ralph Coates took the kick and when Peters flicked it on, Francis Lee was on the spot to nod the ball home.

The scoreline in no way reflected England's dominance which was so complete that Gordon Banks' action was limited to two back-passes. In the second-half, he didn't even get that much to do.

Within three minutes of the restart, the score went to 4-0. A hand-ball by Darmanin in the penalty area gave Allan Clarke the chance to score from the spot and straight after that, Peters again put in a good cross which Chivers headed in well. It was all over now as the Maltese manfully packed their penalty area, trying desperately to prevent further goals. Sheer numbers of defenders and England's shortcomings in front of goal saw to it that Malta did get away rather more lightly than they should have done.

However, there were still quite a few chances created. Lee and Peters went very close and then England gained another penalty on the hour. Alan Ball had come on for Peters and immediately fired in a terrific volley from Lee's cross, only for a Maltese defender to block it on the line with his hand. Up stepped Clarke again but this time he blazed his shot hopelessly wide.

England soon redeemed themselves somewhat with a fifth goal in the 75th minute. Chris Lawler, making a steady debut, emphasised his superb reputation as a goalscoring full-back by picking a pass up some 35 yards from goal, moving forward ten yards and unleashing a fierce dipping shot that beat the overworked goalkeeper all ends up.

For Banks it was a match memorable only for his lack of action.

> 2nd match v Malta.
> Debut goal for Lawler.
> Clarke scored one penalty for England and missed another.

Northern Ireland v England Home Championship

Played on Saturday, 15 May 1971 at Windsor Park, Belfast.

Northern Ireland: P.A.Jennings (Spurs); P.J.Rice (Arsenal), S.Nelson (Arsenal), W.J.O'Kane (Nottm Forest), A.Hunter (Blackburn R), J.J.Nicholson (Huddersfield T), B.Hamilton (Linfield, Belfast), A.S.McMordie (Middlesbrough), A.D.Dougan (Wolves), D.Clements (Coventry C), G.Best (Man Utd).
Sub: T.Cassidy (Newcastle Utd) for McMordie.
England: G.Banks (Stoke C); P.E.Madeley (Leeds Utd), T.Cooper (Leeds Utd), P.E.Storey (Arsenal), R.L.McFarland (Derby Co), R.F.C.Moore (West Ham, captain), F.H.Lee (Man City), A.J.Ball (Everton), M.H.Chivers (Spurs), A.J.Clarke (Leeds Utd), M.S.Peters (Spurs).

Half-time 0-0   Full-time 0-1
Ref: A.MacKenzie (Scotland)   Att: 33,500

ALTHOUGH England emerged the winners in this opening match of the Home Championship, their performance was far from convincing and in the end they could consider themselves very fortunate. The Irish, with their usual effervescent style, ended with nothing to show for all their effort. Yet all the best attacks came from them and only a brilliant display from Gordon Banks kept England's goal intact.

On 11 minutes came the game's first crucial talking point. Banks gathered and as he threw the ball up to kick clear, Best put his foot up to flick it up and over the goalkeeper. The tricky winger then ran on to nod the loose ball home. To Best's utter displeasure, the referee disallowed the goal for dangerous play. It incensed Best, it incensed the crowd, but surely it was the correct decision.

England continued with a solid defensive look about them but the midfield and front men lacked cohesion and flair as the Irish easily held their flimsy attack. Bobby Moore and Terry Cooper caught the eye and Paul Madeley looked efficient on his debut despite Best's magic on the wing. Sir Alf Ramsey put Peter Storey on the Manchester United star, but Best was far too quick and elusive for the Arsenal man.

Banks made three outstanding saves as the Irish did everything but score and it was a surprise to find the game still scoreless at the break. England played with much more urgency after the interval, but they still had to work very hard to subdue Ireland. Dougan gave Roy McFarland a difficult time and Best continued to be a threat. However, the immaculate Moore was always there, inevitably, and Banks was in outstanding form when the ball did reach the goalkeeper.

The decisive strike came with ten minutes to go. Again it proved a crucial moment tinged with controversy. A high pass by O'Kane was blocked in front of Francis Lee's face by the Manchester City man's hands. Whilst the crowd screamed for hand-ball, Lee ran on determinedly before putting Allan Clarke clean through with a lovely pass. Jennings came out quickly and parried Clarke's first effort but the striker regained possession and coolly slotted home the rebound wide of the goalkeeper. It was a bitter blow to the Irish made all the worse by the dubious decision to allow Lee to continue after it appeared to everyone that he had handled the ball.

But all credit to England, who coped admirably with all the Irish had to offer, and in the remaining minutes the Irish never threatened to save the game despite the tireless work of Nicholson. England won the points but it must be said that on the day the luck of the Irish certainly deserted the green-shirted team.

> 78th match v Northern Ireland.
> Debut for Madeley.
> 50th cap for Alan Ball.

England v Wales Home Championship

Played on Wednesday, 19 May 1971 at Wembley Stadium.

England: P.L.Shilton (Leicester C); C.Lawler (Liverpool), T.Cooper (Leeds Utd), T.Smith (Liverpool), L.V.Lloyd (Liverpool), E.W.Hughes (Liverpool), F.H.Lee (Man City), A.J.Brown (West Brom), G.C.Hurst (West Ham), R.Coates (Spurs), M.S.Peters (West Ham, captain).
Sub: A.J.Clarke (Leeds Utd) for Brown.
Wales: G.Sprake (Leeds Utd); P.J.Rodrigues (Sheffield Wed), R.J.Thomas (Swindon T), E.G.James (Blackburn R), J.G.Roberts (Arsenal), T.C.Yorath (Leeds Utd), L.Phillips (Car-

diff C), W.A.Durban (Derby Co), J.B.Toshack (Liverpool), R.T.Davies (Southampton), G.I.Reece (Sheffield Utd).
Sub: R.R.Rees (Nottm Forest) for Reece.

Half-time 0-0   Full-time 0-0
Ref: M.Wright (Northern Ireland)
                              Att: 70,000

SIR Alf Ramsey decided on wholesale changes for the second of England's three Home Internationals but the performance against Wales reflected the disorganisation this caused. Wales, on their limited resources, played well as a team and thoroughly deserved their draw.

England almost made a disastrous start when Larry Lloyd nearly put through his own goal as he and Peter Shilton struggled to strike an understanding. Lloyd's attempted clearance sliced dangerously close to goal as Shilton desperately tried to intercept. Another new cap, Tony Brown, headed over from a good position with virtually his first touch, so the new players were quickly finding out what life is like at international level.

Brown's effort was a rare clear chance for the home side and it was Wales who proved to be the more dangerous, especially with Davies and Reece working so hard. When these two combined with Toshack in an excellent move, only a brave dive by Shilton halted Toshack's bustling run.

As the half progressed the unexpectedly large crowd of 70,000 became restless at England's lack of cohesion, but just before the interval two good attacks gave them hope. First Francis Lee was very unlucky when he fired in a fine shot which hit the back of the net, only for the effort to be ruled out because Brown was stood in an offside position. Shortly afterwards Martin Peters headed a lovely Terry Cooper cross straight into Sprake's arms as England ended the half on a high note.

Unfortunately, the momentum was not maintained after the interval. The big Welsh defenders kept a tight rein on England's lacklustre attack and even in defence the home side did not show their usual authority, especially with Bobby Moore absent. Lee and Geoff Hurst spoiled another good opening with their hesitancy as England stumbled on.

Ramsey sent on Allan Clarke to try to inject some much needed fire into the attack and it almost worked when his first touch produced a fine shot that flew just wide. By this time, however, a goalless scoreline was almost inevitable. Wales deserved their point for a well-organised defensive display, although this was probably England's most ineffective display since the 1966 World Cup.

> 81st match v Wales.
> Debut for Smith, Lloyd and Brown.
> Peters captain for the first time.

England v Scotland Home Championship

Played on Saturday, 22 May 1971 at Wembley Stadium.

England: G.Banks (Stoke C); C.Lawler (Liverpool), T.Cooper (Leeds Utd),

P.E.Storey (Arsenal), R.L.McFarland (Derby Co), R.F.C.Moore (West Ham, captain), F.H.Lee (Man City), A.J.Ball (Everton), M.H.Chivers (Spurs), G.C.Hurst (West Ham), M.S.Peters (Spurs).
Sub: A.J.Clarke (Leeds Utd) for Lee.

Scotland: R.B.Clark (Aberdeen); J.Greig (Rangers), J.Brogan (Celtic), W.J.Bremner (Leeds Utd), F.McLintock (Arsenal), R.Moncur (Newcastle Utd), J.Johnstone (Celtic), D.T.Robb (Aberdeen), H.P.Curran (Wolves), A.Green (Blackpool), P.B.Cormack (Nottm Forest).
Subs: F.M.Munro (Wolves) for Curran and A.Jarvie (Airdrie) for Green.

Half-time 3-1   Full-time 3-1

Ref: J.F.Dorpmans (Holland) Att: 91,469

THIS was much better from England and once again they overcame the Scots at Wembley with an exhillarating performance. Indeed, in the first half, both sides produced international football of the highest quality.

Early goals set the scene. After only nine minutes, Alan Ball's corner was flicked on by Martin Chivers and Martin Peters roared in to head goalwards. Greig, standing on the goal-line, instinctively thrust his arm upwards pushing the ball on to the bar and out again. The Dutch referee made an instant decision, saw no need for a penalty, and ruled that the ball had already crossed the line.

Hardly had the English cheers died down when the Scottish hordes were waving their yellow banners in celebration of an equalizer. It was two minutes after Peters' goal when Ball made a dreadful hash of an attempted back-pass to Gordon Banks for Curran to nip in smartly to intercept and slide the ball past the goalkeeper's dive.

For the next half-hour it was cut and thrust as both teams searched for the advantage. England played some lovely football during this spell and they frequently carved large holes in the Scotland defence. Francis Lee and Ball failed with their shooting when presented with good chances but the crowd seemed to sense that a goal would come. Sure enough, with five minutes of the half remaining, England regained the lead. One of many exciting bursts by Lee had Robb and Brogan in a tangle and when the ball rebounded off Brogan and into the path of Chivers, the big Spurs striker thundered home a splendid 20-yard shot which beat Clark handsomely.

By this time, Ball and Peters were completely in control of the midfield and it came as no real surprise that England still had time to increase their lead before the break. Again it was Chivers who this time beat Moncur to Chris Lawler's pass to cleverly chip the ball over the advancing Clark.

After the change of ends Scotland came into the game a little more but they rarely managed to threaten Gordon Banks in the England goal. It was England who came closest to adding to the scoreline and on four occasions they should have scored.

It had been a week of patchy form by England but they had at least won the Home Championship yet again and ended very much on a high.

> 88th match v Scotland.

Martin Peters heads England into the lead against Scotland at Wembley in May 1971.

Switzerland v England
European Championship Qualifier

Played on Wednesday, 13 October 1971 in the St Jakob Stadium, Basle.

Switzerland: M.Kunz (FC Basel); P.Ramseier (FC Basel), P.Stierli (FC Zürich), A.Weibel (FC Sion), P.Chapuisat (Lausanne-Sports), J.Kuhn (FC Zürich), W.Balmer (FC Basel), K.Odermatt (FC Basel), F.Künzli (FC Zürich), R.Blättler (FC Basel), D.Jeandupeux (FC Zürich).
Subs: G.Perroud (Servette FC) for Chapuisat and K.Müller (Grasshoppers) for R.Blättler.

England: G.Banks (Stoke C); C.Lawler (Liverpool), T.Cooper (Leeds Utd), A.P.Mullery (Spurs), R.L.McFarland (Derby Co), R.F.C.Moore (West Ham, captain), F.H.Lee (Man City), P.E.Madeley (Leeds Utd), M.H.Chivers (Spurs), G.C.Hurst (West Ham), M.S.Peters (Spurs).
Sub: J.Radford (Arsenal) for Hurst.

Half-time 2-2   Full-time 2-3

Ref: V.Loraux (Belgium)   Att: 58,000

THIS vital European Championship match ended in a splendidly hard-earned victory for England, which meant a giant step towards their target of reaching the final stages of the tournament the following year.

England made a dramatic start to their night with a goal in 55 seconds. Alan Mullery's free-kick found Martin Chivers, who cleverly lobbed a dangerous centre into the area. Geoff Hurst burst into the box to dive headlong and score with a brave and spectacular header. The Swiss goalkeeper, Kunz, seemed to be slow to react and only grabbed the ball after it had crossed the line. It was just the sort of start that England wanted although it was not very long before Switzerland showed what an improved side they were.

After ten minutes, the home team levelled the scores. Kuhn sent a crossfield pass to Jeandupeux, who cleverly held off Mullery's challenge before hitting a 25-yard shot into the roof of Gordon Banks' net.

The goal action continued almost immediately with England dramatically regaining the lead only two minutes later. This time a good move between Paul Madeley, Mullery and Francis Lee gave Chivers possession. His strength took him past Ramseier before he hit a left-foot shot into the far top corner from an acute angle. Again the goalkeeper might have done better but all credit to Chivers for taking his chance well.

So England were now back in the driving seat after that breathless opening, but for the next 30 minutes, up to the break, Switzerland dominated the game. Kuhn, Odermatt and Blättler did some super work in midfield and constantly had the England players chasing shadows. Through it all, though, Bobby Moore kept his cool and held his side together. With Madeley giving excellent support it seemed as though England would weather the storm. Kuhn hit a post as the pressure mounted and then, just before the interval, the Swiss scored a brilliant second equalizer.

Künzli began the move with a pass to Odermatt. Play then continued through Kuhn and Stierli. Stierli overlapped down the left before putting over a fine cross which found Künzli following up to score with a glorious header which gave Banks no chance. The goal rounded off a good spell by the Swiss and they went in, after an eventful half, with their tails up.

The second half belonged to England, though. They tightened up all round and showed a much better approach to defending. With Moore a commanding captain, Madeley battling in midfield, and Lee and Chivers always dangerous up front, the game gradually drifted England's way. The extra teamwork, fitness and general know-how began to pay dividends and after several chances went begging they finally regained the lead again ten minutes from the end.

It was Chivers again who made the decisive run, working his way down the right and hitting a low cross straight into the path of Weibel, who could do no more than turn the ball into his own net.

After that, the Swiss were right out of it in every sense and England could even afford the luxury of bringing on substitute John Radford for Hurst. The win put England on top of their group.

> 9th match v Switzerland.
> 50th cap for Peters.
> Own-goal by Weibel for England.

England European Championship
v Switzerland Qualifier

Played on Wednesday, 10 November 1971 at Wembley Stadium.

England: P.L.Shilton (Leicester C); P.E.Madeley (Leeds Utd), T.Cooper (Leeds Utd), P.E.Storey (Arsenal), L.V.Lloyd (Liverpool), R.F.C.Moore (West Ham, captain), M.G.Summerbee (Man City), A.J.Ball (Everton), G.C.Hurst (West Ham), F.H.Lee (Man City), E.W.Hughes (Liverpool).
Subs: M.H.Chivers (Spurs) for Summerbee and R.W.Marsh (QPR) for Lee.

Switzerland: M.Prosperi (FC Lugano); P.Ramseier (FC Basel), P.Stierli (FC Zürich), G.Perroud (Servette FC), P.Chapuisat (Lausanne-Sports), J.Kuhn (FC Zürich), W.Balmer (FC Basel), K.Odermatt (FC Basel), F.Künzli (FC Zürich), R.Blättler (FC Basel), D.Jeandupeux (FC Zürich).
Sub: P.Meier (Grasshoppers) for Jeandupeux.

Half-time 1-1   Full-time 1-1
Ref: C.Barbulescu (Romania) Att: 98,000

BARRING a disaster in Greece the following month, England now looked certain to qualify for the quarter-finals of the European Championships. This after making somewhat heavy weather of holding the attractive Swiss side to a draw at Wembley. As in Basle, the Swiss played some lovely football at times but after half-time the part-timers once again faded badly as England took control in the later stages.

The home side, with several team changes, were soon in front. The goal came after only nine minutes play and came courtesy of a couple of Swiss errors. A short corner by Francis Lee enabled Emlyn Hughes to chip a centre into the danger area. The goalkeeper came out, only for Ramseier to beat him to the ball and get his head to it. The attempted clearance by the full-back was not a good one and the ball looped up for Mike Summerbee to jump and sent a looping header of his own over Prosperi and into the net.

Also as in Switzerland the previous month, the Swiss greeted the English goal with a fierce spell of pressure. Playing some attractive football, Kuhn, an outstanding player, and Odermatt excelled with their fine understanding. On 26 minutes, these two combined to score a deserved equalizer. Kuhn passed to Odermatt and he fired in a brilliant 'banana' shot on the run from 25 yards out which left Peter Shilton groping. The goalkeeper

Mike Summerbee (7) soars above the Swiss defence to head England's only goal of the match at Wembley in November 1971.

got a touch but could do no more than help the ball into the net.

England then tried hard to come back and Peter Storey had a shot turned onto the bar by Prosperi. Generally, though, the Swiss maintained control up to half-time without finding the necessary punch in the vital goal area.

After the interval, one of England's best moves saw Lee beat two men in a thrilling and aggressive run before shooting right-footed from 20 yards. The ball scraped the outside of a post and Lee could consider himself unlucky not to score after this fine effort.

As the game wore on, the Swiss began to tire but England still could not find a way past a packed defence. Martin Chivers was sent on for Summerbee and towards the end, Sir Alf Ramsey responded to the crowd's chant of, 'Rodney, Rodney,' by bringing on Rodney Marsh to replace Lee. In the end, though, it was all to no avail and England had to be content with the draw. And it could have been worse had not Shilton managed to turn another bending free-kick by Odermatt over the crossbar, but overall the draw was perhaps the fairest result.

England therefore retained the lead in the group table and only a defeat by four or more goals in Greece would now cost them a place in the quarter-finals.

> 10th match v Switzerland.
> Debut, as substitute, for Marsh.

Greece v European
England Championship Qualifier

Played on Wednesday, 1 December 1971 in the Karaiskari Stadium, Pireus.

Greece: N.Khristidis (Aris Thessalonikis); T.Pallas (Aris Thessalonikis), T.Angelis (Olympiakos), A.Toskas (AEK Athens), A.Kapsis (Panathinaikos), K.Elevtherakis (Panathinaikos), G.Koudas (PAOK Thessalonikis), K.Nikolaidis (AEK Athens), A.Adoniadis (Panathinaikos), M.Domazos (Panathinaikos), D.Papaioannou (AEK Athens).
Subs: M.Kritikopolous (Ethnikos) for Koudas and K.Davourlis (Panahaiki) for Nikolaidis.

England: G.Banks (Stoke C); P.E.Madeley (Leeds Utd), E.W.Hughes (Liverpool), C.Bell (Man City), R.L.McFarland (Derby Co), R.F.C.Moore (West Ham, captain), F.H.Lee (Man City), A.J.Ball (Everton), M.H.Chivers (Spurs), G.C.Hurst (West Ham), M.S.Peters (Spurs).

Half-time 0-0   Full-time 0-2
Ref: J.M.Ortiz de Mendibil (Spain)
Att: 42,000

WITH this splendid win in Pireus England duly qualified for the quarter-finals of the European Championships. It was not a vintage display by England but it was a hard-working, wholly committed and thoroughly professional performance that subdued and then finally killed off the lively Greek team.

Greece looked much better organised than they had been at Wembley the previous April. Thanks for that must go to Irishman Billy Bingham, who now managed the Greek national team. It was obvious from the start that this would be no push-over for the visitors as the Greeks began confidently and, urged on by their skipper Domazos, they pushed England back. Domazos was the hub of the side and all the best moves revolved around him or his Panathinaikos clubmate Elevtherakis. With Nikolaidis giving good support, England were under constant pressure. However, with Bobby Moore producing all his calm assurance and Roy McFarland playing extremely well beside him, the defence held very firm.

As the game progressed the English

Greek goalkeeper Khristidis is helpless as Geoff Hurst hammers the ball into the net in Pireus in December 1971.

midfield began to assert itself. Alan Ball, Colin Bell and Martin Peters began to gel effectively. Bell's contribution was immense and it gave Ball more freedom to move forward. The grip became established as Francis Lee twice brought full-length diving saves from Khristidis and then with seven minutes of the first-half left, Bell shot home from Ball's pass, only for the goal to be rightly ruled out for offside.

After the break England continued to keep a firm hold on the game. Greece's earlier burst had now evaporated and with just over half an hour to go, England found the way through they deserved. And what a gem it was too.

Bell found Geoff Hurst with a ground pass, Hurst veered to his right and from outside the area he hit a tremendous shot past Khristidis. It was a superb goal and full reward for England's play. The Greeks tried hard to come back and they sent on two substitutes to try to inject some extra freshness into their play. But England never wavered and instead created further chances which Martin Chivers, Lee and others wasted.

In the end, though, England did manage another goal and it came almost on 90 minutes when Chivers ran on to a lovely through pass from Paul Madeley and slotted it past Khristidis with great confidence.

2nd match v Greece.

England v West Germany European
Championship Quarter-final 1st leg

Played on Saturday, 29 April 1972 at Wembley Stadium.

England: G.Banks (Stoke C); P.E.Madeley (Leeds Utd), E.W.Hughes (Liverpool), C.Bell (Man City), R.F.C.Moore (West Ham, captain), N.Hunter (Leeds Utd), F.H.Lee (Man City), A.J.Ball (Arsenal), M.H.Chivers (Spurs), G.C.Hurst (West Ham), M.S.Peters (Spurs).
Sub: R.W.Marsh (Man City) for Hurst.

West Germany: J.Maier (Bayern Munich); H.D.Höttges (Werder Bremen), P.Breitner (Bayern Munich), G.Schwarzenbeck (Bayern Munich), F.Beckenbauer (Bayern Munich), H.Wimmer (Borussia Mönchengladbach), J.Grabowski (Eintracht Frankfurt), U.Hoeness (Bayern Munich), G.Müller (Bayern Munich), G.Netzer (Borussia Mönchengladbach), S.Held (Kickers Offenbach).

Half-time 0-1   Full-time 1-3
Ref: R.Helies (France)   Att: 95,000

THE pre-match build up to this international was intense, such was the interest in it, but on the night the 'match of the century' turned out to be an acute disappointment to all England's fans. The West Germans were sharp and technically more aware than England and in the end, it must be said, deserving of their victory.

It was a fine game played on a rain-sodden pitch and if there were any neutrals in the capacity crowd then they certainly had value for money. Right from the start, though, it was obvious that England were going to have a tough time. The Germans had a fine midfield trio in Netzer, Hoeness and Wimmer and their two direct wingers, Grabowski and Held, were always dangerous. England's build-up was far too slow and often went sideways instead of forwards, contrary to the incisive approach of the visitors.

The home side had plenty of the possession but the majestic Beckenbauer calmly seemed to spot any danger before it actually happened. The class and skill of the Germans was apparent in the 26th minute when they took the lead. Uncharacteristically, it was a mistake by Bobby Moore which led to the goal. He tried to

dribble clear of his own penalty area, only to be caught in possession by Hoeness who then hit a deflected shot wide of Gordon Banks.

England swept forward after this set-back but time and time again they were foiled by Maier's exceptional goalkeeping. His handling of the greasy ball was impeccable. Alan Ball, Colin Bell and Martin Peters worked hard enough in midfield but without Alan Mullery's bite, the Germans were far superior in this department.

After half-time, England continued to have most of the possession but they could not find a way through the well-drilled German defence. Always, too, they had to guard against the lightning breakaways that the Germans were capable of. To their credit and despite the fact that several players were not at their best England kept battling away. With 15 minutes to go they gained their reward with an equalizer.

An excellent move down the right between Peters and Bell ended with a good shot by Bell. For once Maier failed to hold it and Francis Lee followed up to force home the loose ball. England had worked very hard for the goal, but in the last six minutes all that effort was thrown away.

Once again the culprit was Moore. The England skipper never looked happy on this night and his poor form was emphasised when he was beaten for pace by Held's dash. Moore's mistimed tackle clipped Held's legs and the referee awarded a penalty. Netzer took the kick and although Banks made a superlative effort to save it, the ball went in off the post, much to the goalkeeper's dismay.

Although the goal had an element of luck about it no one could deny that the Germans had looked by far the better all-round side and moments later they rubbed salt into the wound by adding a third goal. It was the irrepressible Müller who spun sharply to shoot home after a clever reverse pass by Hoeness had given him just a sniff

Francis Lee scores England's only goal against West Germany at Wembley in April 1972.

Gordon Banks got to Netzer's penalty but the ball rebounded off a post and into the net.

Maier collects the ball as England attack in Berlin's Olympic Stadium in May 1972.

of a chance. That, sadly from England's point of view, was all that Müller needed.

The scoreline mades the second leg in Berlin look a very difficult task for England.

> 11th match v West Germany.
> Penalty scored by Netzer for West Germany.
> *"Gerd Müller was my most difficult opponent at international level as he was always looking for the opportunity to score a goal."*
> Emlyn Hughes

West Germany v England European Championship Quarter-final 2nd leg

Played on Saturday, 13 May 1972 in the Olympic Stadium, Berlin.

West Germany: J.Maier (Bayern Munich); H.D.Höttges (Werder Bremen), P.Breitner (Bayern Munich), G.Schwarzenbeck (Bayern Munich), F.Beckenbauer (Bayern Munich), H.Wimmer (Borussia Mönchengladbach), U.Hoeness (Bayern Munich), H.Flohe (1.FC Cologne), G.Müller (Bayern Munich), G.Netzer (Borussia Mönchengladbach), S.Held (Kickers Offenbach).
Sub: J.Heynckes (Borussia Mönchengladbach) for Hoeness.

England: G.Banks (Stoke C); P.E.Madeley (Leeds Utd), E.W.Hughes (Liverpool), P.E.Storey (Arsenal), R.L.McFarland (Derby Co), R.F.C.Moore (West Ham, captain), A.J.Ball (Arsenal), C.Bell (Man City), M.H.Chivers (Spurs), R.W.Marsh (QPR), N.Hunter (Leeds Utd).
Subs: M.G.Summerbee (Man City) for Marsh and M.S.Peters (Spurs) for Hunter.

Half-time 0-0   Full-time 0-0
Ref: M.Gugolović (Yugoslavia) Att: 75,000

THE Olympic Stadium in West Berlin was lashed by incessant rain before, during and after this vital match which England had to win, and most of the 75,000 crowd must have been drenched at the end. England made several team changes and Sir Alf Ramsey surprisingly decided on a defensive 4-4-2 formation giving Peter Storey the job of man-to-man marking the dangerous Netzer. With the Germans holding a 3-1 advantage, the odds were stacked against the visitors.

The game was very physical and several times the tackling became just a little too strong. Indeed, some of the England players could count themselves very lucky not to have got into serious trouble with the lenient referee.

All this physical play stifled any real chance of an open game, although England went very close to scoring the early goal they so desperately wanted. It was the seventh minute when Alan Ball took a corner and after Rodney Marsh's flick was saved by Maier, Martin Chivers' follow-up header was blocked on the line by Höttges.

Had England scored then it might have made things different but as it was West Germany began to get into their cool, somewhat arrogant stride. Always dictating the pattern of the game was the masterly Beckenbauer. He would always do just enough in each situation and his control was superb. England, despite all their huffing and puffing, had little to offer. Marsh rarely shone and Chivers, despite that early chance, was very ineffective. To be fair to the front players, England's style on the day did not lend itself too well for attack and in many ways it made it easy for the Germans.

The match was devoid of any real excitement and was particularly notable for the lack of shots on target. Neither goalkeeper was seriously tested and with the rain continually falling, the crowd became understandably restless.

Held did hit one ferocious early shot which crashed against the bar, but that was the only strike the Germans had worthy of the name. For the rest it was a story of cool control by the Germans and desperate but ineffective attacks by England. Mike Summerbee showed some spirit after coming on as a substitute and he made some nice breaks down the right. However, again the threat never developed into goals and for the second time in two international tournaments, England had been knocked out by West Germany.

12th match v West Germany.

Wales v England   Home Championship

Played on Saturday, 20 May 1972 at Ninian Park, Cardiff.

Wales: G.Sprake (Leeds Utd); P.J.Rodrigues (Sheffield Wed), R.J.Thomas (Swindon T), W.T.Hennessey (Derby Co), H.M.England (Spurs), J.G.Roberts (Arsenal), T.C.Yorath (Leeds Utd), R.T.Davies (Southampton), R.W.Davies (Man City), J.B.Toshack (Liverpool), W.A.Durban (Derby Co). Sub: G.I.Reece (Sheffield Utd) for Roberts.
England: G.Banks (Stoke C); P.E.Madeley (Leeds Utd), E.W.Hughes (Liverpool), P.E.Storey (Arsenal), R.L.McFarland (Derby Co), R.F.C.Moore (West Ham, captain), M.G.Summerbee (Man City), C.Bell (Man City), M.I.Macdonald (Newcastle Utd), R.W.Marsh (Man City), N.Hunter (Leeds Utd).

Half-time 0-1   Full-time 0-3
Ref: W.J.Mullan (Scotland)   Att: 33,000

THIS was a much better performance by England earning them a deserved win by a clear margin. It was a match full of ideas and attacking football, mostly from the visitors, and it gave them the perfect start to the Home Championship.

It took England 25 minutes to open their account and it was the effervescent Emlyn Hughes who scored his first international goal. Rodney Marsh showed some lovely touches and it was his headed flick that combined with Hughes to split the Welsh defence. When Colin Bell's shot was parried by Sprake, Hughes continued his run to follow up and shoot home. Judging by his expression, there were not many players who enjoyed scoring as much as Hughes did.

England employed the 4-3-3 formation and employed it very effectively, although the Welsh side did not put them under much pressure. Only Rodrigues and Mike England produced any real form for the home side as the rest of the team struggled. For the visitors, Roy McFarland had a

splendid game and his power in the air stifled the aerial threat of the two Davies's and Toshack.

Malcolm Macdonald made a lively debut and was always in the thick of the action as England dictated play for long periods. Bell and Mike Summerbee were also in good form and they continually posed problems for the Welsh defence, but try as they might England failed to add to their goal, despite their dominance in this first-half.

It was the same pattern after the break with England enjoying the bulk of the possession. Gradually the Welsh challenge evaporated and midway through the half, it was totally extinguished when England scored twice in a minute.

The first of these came after a good run and cross by Peter Storey. Macdonald provided a back header which beautifully teed-up a 15-yard volley for the enterprising Marsh to whack past Sprake. Almost immediately, England went 3-0 up. This time the Manchester City pair of Bell and Summerbee combined brilliantly as Bell superbly flicked in Summerbee's cross to finally crush the Welsh.

England were able to play out the remainder of the game at a leisurely pace thus gaining two points in their quest for the Championship.

82nd match v Wales.
Debut for Macdonald.

England v   Home Championship
Northern Ireland

Played on Tuesday, 23 May 1972 at Wembley Stadium.

England: P.L.Shilton (Leicester C); C.Todd (Derby Co), E.W.Hughes (Liverpool), P.E.Storey (Arsenal), L.V.Lloyd (Liverpool), N.Hunter (Leeds Utd), M.G.Summerbee (Man City), C.Bell (Man City, captain), M.I.Macdonald (Newcastle Utd), R.W.Marsh (Man City), A.W.Currie (Sheffield Utd). Subs: M.H.Chivers (Spurs) for Macdonald and M.S.Peters (Spurs) for Currie.
Northern Ireland: P.A.Jennings (Spurs); P.J.Rice (Arsenal), S.Nelson (Arsenal), W.J.T.Neill (Hull C), A.Hunter (Ipswich T), D.Clements (Sheffield Wed), D.Hegan (Wolves), A.S.McMordie (Middlesbrough), A.D.Dougan (Wolves), W.J.Irvine (Brighton & HA), T.A.Jackson (Nottm Forest).

Half-time 0-1   Full-time 0-1
Ref: W.J.Gow (Wales)   Att: 43,000

SOME 43,000 people watched this match and saw the gallant Irish gain their first victory over England at this stadium since 1957. It was a deserved and historic win and delighted the large contingent of Irish fans present.

England brought in two new caps, Colin Todd and Tony Currie, with Colin Bell taking over the captaincy in the absence of the injured Bobby Moore. As soon as the game started, though, it was obvious that this England performance was not going to inspire much confidence. True, they had plenty of the play but all their moves were predictable and the Irish looked far more dangerous when they attacked. In midfield Bell, Currie and

Peter Storey were out-manoeuvred by the clever play of McMordie, Hegan and Clements. And when England did find a way through, the ever-reliable Jennings showed his class in goal.

The conditions were perfect for football so there was no excuse for the home side. Two players escaped criticism, Emlyn Hughes and Rodney Marsh. Hughes put his heart and soul into the game and was an inspiration to his lacklustre colleagues. As for Marsh, it was he alone who showed the necessary flair to ruffle the Irish defenders. And it was Marsh who set up Malcolm Macdonald for the best of England's chances, but the number-nine blazed wide with the goal at his mercy. That was to prove a costly mistake as five minutes later, the Irish took the lead.

A breakaway attack won a corner. Hegan took it and Peter Shilton was forced into dropping the ball by Irvine's strong challenge. The loose ball fell, McMordie nodded back across goal and there was Neill, celebrating his 51st cap, to ram home the goal from close range. It was the Irish team's first positive attack of the game but it certainly proved effective.

England plodded on and continued to have most of the pressure. Alas, they could not find the necessary guile to break down the visiting defence.

Marsh seemed the only player who looked able to improvise, but all of his best moments needed the help of his less accomplished teammates.

In an attempt to generate some life out of England, manager Ramsey brought on Martin Peters for Currie and Martin Chivers for Macdonald, but the pattern did not change and the Irish ended with a very famous victory under their belt.

79th match v Northern Ireland.
Debuts for Todd and Currie.
Bell captain for the first time.

Scotland v England   Home Championship

Played on Saturday, 27 May 1972 at Hampden Park, Glasgow.

Scotland: R.B.Clark (Aberdeen); J.Brownlie (Hibernian), W.Donachie (Man City), W.J.Bremner (Leeds Utd), W.McNeill (Celtic), R.Moncur (Newcastle Utd), P.Lorimer (Leeds Utd), A.Gemmill (Derby Co), L.Macari (Celtic), D.Law (Man Utd), R.A.Hartford (West Brom). Subs: A.Green (Newcastle Utd) for Donachie and J.Johnstone (Celtic) for Gemmill.
England: G.Banks (Stoke C); P.E.Madeley (Leeds Utd), E.W.Hughes (Liverpool), P.E.Storey (Arsenal), R.L.McFarland (Derby Co), R.F.C.Moore (West Ham, captain), A.J.Ball (Arsenal), C.Bell (Man City), M.H.Chivers (Spurs), R.W.Marsh (Man City), N.Hunter (Leeds Utd). Sub: M.Macdonald (Newcastle Utd) for Marsh.

Half-time 0-1   Full-time 0-1
Ref: S.Gonella (Italy)   Att: 119,325

THIS latest battle in the world's oldest international fixture was ruined by both teams seemingly intent on wanting to kick each other instead of the ball. The first half especially was riddled with fouls and

England players form a defensive wall during training at Middlesbrough in 1972.

it culminated in the referee calling both captains together in an attempt to cool the tempers. England must take a good deal of the blame. They brought in Peter Storey and Norman Hunter into their midfield and this pair did not stand on ceremony. The Scottish players were incensed by some of the challenges and in the end began to retaliate. It all went into producing a bad-tempered game which did little to entertain the huge crowd.

To rub salt into the wound for the home fans, when the football was played it was England who looked the more lively of the two sides. Early on they soaked up heavy Scottish pressure, breaking sharply whenever they had the opportunity. The small Scottish trio of Bremner, Hartford and Gemmill were outpowered in midfield and as a result, the visitors held a firm grip.

Scotland did see one shot cleared off the line by Storey, but in the 28th minute it was England who took the lead. A good move began with Alan Ball. He passed inside to Colin Bell, who quickly switched it to Martin Chivers. The centre-forward played the ball first-time back into the path of Bell, who stabbed a shot wide of Clark's desperate dive.

Half-time was reached after more crude challenges had gone largely unpunished, although Ball, McNeill and Hartford were all booked. Thankfully, after the break, things cooled down somewhat, allowing England to show that they could play some good football. Ball, Bell and Chivers were full of running and Chivers gave McNeill a nightmare afternoon as his powerful running turned the Celtic man inside out.

England's breaks were economical and positive and with better finishing they could and should have added to their score. A good shot by Bell, from Chivers' pass, struck the post with Clark beaten, and Rodney Marsh twice went close. At the other end, a typical Law header was blocked on the line by Hughes and Gordon Banks made two excellent saves from Hartford and Macari. Both these Scottish chances had come from mistakes by Roy McFarland, the first a deflection

and the second a woeful attempted back-pass. McFarland, however, enhanced his growing reputation with an otherwise solid display, as did Paul Madeley and Hughes. In the end, England just about deserved their victory, which also gave them a share of the Championship, ironically, with Scotland.

89th match v Scotland.

England v Yugoslavia   Friendly

Played on Wednesday, 11 October 1972 at Wembley Stadium.

England: P.L.Shilton (Leicester C); M.D.Mills (Ipswich T), F.R.G.Lampard (West Ham), P.E.Storey (Arsenal), J.P.Blockley (Arsenal), R.F.C.Moore (West Ham, captain), A.J.Ball (Arsenal), M.R.Channon (Southampton), J.Royle (Everton), C.Bell (Man City), R.W.Marsh (Man City).

Yugoslavia: E.Marić (Velež Mostar); P.Krivokuća (Red Star Begrade), D.Stepanović (OFK Belgrade), M.Pavlović (Red Star Belgrade), J.Katalinski (Željezničar), B.Paunović (Partizan Belgrade), I.Petković (OFK Belgrade), J.Aćimović (Red Star Belgrade), D.Bajević (Velež Mostar), F.Vladić (Velež Mostar), D.Džajić (Red Star Belgrade).
Subs: D.Holcer (Radnički Niš) for Katalinski and L.Rajković (Hajduk Split) for Pavlović.

Half-time 1-0   Full-time 1-1
Ref: A.Angonese (Italy)   Att; 50,000

ENGLAND fielded four new caps in a newly-shaped side disrupted by club calls and injuries. Jeff Blockley, Frank Lampard, Mick Mills and Mike Channon all came in, whilst an injury to Gordon Banks meant another cap for Peter Shilton.

The match was a very entertaining one but with two consecutive defeats at Wembley behind them, England were looking for a confidence booster before the vital World Cup tie against Wales the

following month. They began purposefully and Joe Royle's header was only foiled by a fine save from Marić early on. Channon and Rodney Marsh also went very close and then Royle again as the exuberance of youth swept England forward. At the other end, Shilton was only called upon once and that was to turn away a scorcher from Vladić.

England's pressure was deserving of a goal and they finally got one five minutes from half-time. It was an excellent move with Colin Bell breaking down the left. His pass reached Channon after the Southampton player had beaten the goalkeeper to the ball on the edge of the area. Channon fell but quickly recovered to pass to Alan Ball, who in turn teed-up a super chance for Royle. The young Everton centre-forward thundered in a shot off the underside of the crossbar to a huge roar from the crowd. A fine goal and one that pushed England's confidence sky-high as they left the field at half-time.

Unfortunately, the experienced Yugoslavs came back strongly after the interval and within five minutes of the restart had found an equalizer. Petković crossed from the right, Bajević headed downwards and with Blockley and the other defenders nowhere, Vladić was on hand to nod home.

That was a bitter disappointment for England but shortly afterwards they produced one of their best moves of the night. Flowing passes between Marsh, Ball and Channon set up Bell, who shot just wide of the far post. With half an hour to go, it looked like England had regained the lead when Ball volleyed a good shot past Marić. But, sadly the referee had spotted an offside in the crowded goalmouth and the goal was ruled out. After that incident the Yugoslavs took control as their extra experience began to tell on some of the younger home players.

Poor Mills had a nightmare debut as the outstanding Džajić turned him inside-out with some superb skills and attacking know-how. One of Europe's top players, he chipped a lovely shot just over the far angle as Shilton clawed thin air. Then, as Yugoslavia, with two fresh substitutes, pushed forward, the England 'keeper

Bobby Moore and Yugoslavia's skipper Džajić before the 1-1 draw at Wembley in October 1972.

made brilliant saves from Holcer and Vladić. The second of those was a brave dive at Vladić's feet after Bobby Moore had been caught in possession.

Džajić continued to be the big danger though and another of his shots rifled into the side netting. With Bajević, Aćimović and Stepanovic also outstanding, it was clear that England had done very well to hold this talented team. With only two minutes left, Džajić exploded another ferocious shot which cannoned back off Shilton's crossbar. That was the last real chance of an absorbing game.

England had had the first-half honours but the second half belonged almost entirely to the visitors. At least the home side had the consolation of some good things from the game with the combination of Channon and Royle particularly promising.

> 10th match v Yugoslavia
> Debuts for Mills, Lampard, Blockley and Channon.
> "I felt a sense of great pride and achievement on being selected. Mind you, my first opponent, Dragon Džajić, turned out to be my most difficult opponent in my England career. It was four years before I was chosen again."
> Mick Mills

Wales v
England　World Cup Qualifier

Played on Wednesday, 15 November 1972 at Ninian Park, Cardiff.

Wales: G.Sprake (Leeds Utd); P.J.Rodrigues (Sheffield Wed), R.J.Thomas (Swindon T), W.T.Hennessey (Derby Co), H.M.England (Spurs), T.J.Hockey (Sheffield Utd), L.Phillips (Cardiff C), J.F.Mahoney (Stoke C), R.W.Davies (Man Utd), J.B.Toshack (Liverpool), L.James (Burnley).
Sub: G.I.Reece (Cardiff C) for Rodrigues.

England: R.N.Clemence (Liverpool); P.E.Storey (Arsenal), E.W.Hughes (Liverpool), N.Hunter (Leeds Utd), R.L.McFarland (Derby Co), R.F.C.Moore (West Ham, captain), J.K.Keegan (Liverpool), C.Bell (Man City), M.H.Chivers (Spurs), R.W.Marsh (Man City), A.J.Ball (Arsenal).

Half-time 0-1　　Full-time 0-1
Ref: W.J.Mullan (Scotland)　Att: 39,000

BEFORE this vital World Cup group match, Sir Andrew Stephen, Chairman of the Football Association, presented Sir Alf Ramsey with a beautiful silver salver to commemorate his 100th international since taking over as manager of England in 1963. The salver was inscribed with the flags of all the countries England had played against in those ten years, and an inscription which read: 'Presented to Sir Alf Ramsey by the Council of the Football Association as a token of esteem and appreciation to mark the 100th occasion on which he has acted as team manager to the England team.'

After those pleasant formalities, the team then had to get down to the serious business of qualifying for the World Cup

finals to be held in Munich in 1974. The game was not a good one. Players on both sides seemed tense at the importance of the match and both teams lacked the necessary flair to beat well-organised defences. What attacking moves there were usually came from England, although the first half saw precious few goal attempts.

However, on 35 minutes England made one attack count. There had been a lot of tentative play before England finally put an excellent move together. Alan Ball and Norman Hunter combined with Ball's low diagonal cross from the by-line reaching Colin Bell at the far post. The Manchester City player slotted the ball past Sprake with the minimum of fuss and the lead was with England.

That goal was one of the few positive moments that the 39,000 crowd had cheered in a disappointing first half. Most of the play went sideways so, not surprisingly, frustration amongst the supporters of both teams was evident.

Peter Storey did an excellent man-to-man marking job on the Welsh danger-man, Leighton James, and totally blotted out the threat from the flying winger. Mahoney and Phillips worked tirelessly for Wales but the visitors always seemed to have control.

In the second half, England might well have had more goals. Martin Chivers put Ball through, only for Sprake to save the shot which was straight at him. That was on 55 minutes and moments later Ray Clemence was called upon to make his first real save by diving low to a Mahoney effort. Ball set up Bell, who shot just wide

England line up before the World Cup qualifier against Wales at Wembley in January 1973. From left to right are Moore, Marsh, Clemence, McFarland, Hunter, Ball, Storey, Keegan, Chivers, Bell, Hughes.

of the far post, and then Rodney Marsh forced Sprake into the save of the night with a superb right-footer.

Bobby Moore and Roy McFarland played brilliantly at the heart of the England defence and in the dying moments, Marsh came desperately close to scoring after Emlyn Hughes had cleverly set him up. When, in the last seconds, Ball put Kevin Keegan through, it seemed that the Liverpool star would celebrate his debut with a goal. Unfortunately, though, Keegan made a mess of trying to dribble around Sprake and the chance was lost.

So in the end, England might have had a clear win against this disappointing Welsh side, but the one goal still proved enough and it gave them great confidence for the future group matches.

83rd match v Wales
Debuts for Clemence and Keegan.
"On my debut I was excited and nervous."
Ray Clemence

England v Wales   World Cup Qualifier

Played on Wednesday, 24 January 1973 at Wembley Stadium.

England: R.N.Clemence (Liverpool); P.E.Storey (Arsenal), E.W.Hughes (Liverpool), N.Hunter (Leeds Utd), R.L.McFarland (Derby Co), R.F.C.Moore (West Ham, captain), J.K.Keegan (Liverpool), C.Bell (Man City), M.H.Chivers (Spurs), R.W.Marsh (Man City), A.J.Ball (Arsenal).
Wales: G.Sprake (Leeds Utd); P.J.Rodrigues (Sheffield Wed), R.J.Thomas (Swindon T), T.J.Hockey (Sheffield Utd), H.M.England (Spurs), J.G.Roberts (Birmingham C), L.James (Burnley), T.C.Yorath (Leeds Utd), J.B.Toshack (Liverpool), J.F.Mahoney (Stoke C), B.C.Evans (Swansea C).
Sub: M.E.Page (Birmingham C) for Rodrigues.

Half-time 1-1   Full-time 1-1
Ref: M.Wright (Northern Ireland)
                              Att: 73,000

THIS was a disappointing result for England in their quest to win qualification to the World Cup finals, and once again they paid the price for not finding the positive form they needed on the night. The spirited Welsh side gave an excellent performance and thoroughly deserved their point.

Right from the start it was obvious that this was not to be England's night. Slow and laborious in their build-up and lacking in imagination and punch up front, they rarely looked like scoring. The early exchanges were nothing more than sparring rounds as both teams sought openings, but in the 23rd minute Wales really put the cat amongst the pigeons by taking the lead.

Evans won the ball with fierce determination and then Yorath and James carried the move on. James evaded Roy McFarland's somewhat clumsy attempt to play him offside and moved to the right by-line before crossing low into the area, where Toshack joyfully touched home from close range.

At this point one expected the England side to up their tempo, spurred on by the fact that they were in trouble. But it never materialised. Wales, with Thomas, Mike England and Roberts looking solid, easily held the powder-puff home attacks so it came as a distinct surprise when the home side equalized.

The goal came four minutes from the interval. Colin Bell made a break down the right and hit a fierce, low cross into the penalty area. Toshack was back helping his defence and deflected the ball away from goal. It ran out of the area but Norman Hunter came roaring in to hit a scorching shot from 25 yards out that arrowed its way into the top corner with Sprake hopelessly beaten by his Leeds clubmate. The goal came as a real surprise to the home fans, who had begun to despair at England ever scoring. Martin Chivers, who had missed a half-chance earlier when his reactions were too slow, then forced Sprake into a fine save as England ended the half on a high note.

Sadly, England flattered to deceive in those closing minutes of the first-half and the second 45 minutes were again played out in a tedious manner. The England fans showed their disapproval on several

occasions with a slow handclap and that hardly encouraged the England team. With Mahoney a busy little terrier in midfield and the Welsh defenders having an easy task coping with England's muted attacks, the game died on its feet.

Chivers again forced a good save out of Sprake and midway through the half, Bell headed a cross from the impressive Emlyn Hughes against the crossbar. That was about it from the home side. Yorath was booked for time-wasting but as far as the Welsh were concerned, that was a small price to pay for such a precious point.

84th match v Wales

Scotland v England   Friendly

Played on Wednesday, 14 February 1973 at Hampden Park, Glasgow.

Scotland: R.B.Clark (Aberdeen); A.Forsyth (Man Utd), W.Donachie (Man City), W.J.Bremner (Leeds Utd), E.P.Colquhoun (Sheffield Utd), M.M.Buchan (Man Utd), P.Lorimer (Leeds Utd), K.Dalglish (Celtic), L.Macari (Man Utd), G.Graham (Man Utd), W.Morgan (Man Utd).
Sub: C.Stein (Coventry C) for Morgan.
England: P.L.Shilton (Leicester C); P.E.Storey (Arsenal), E.W.Hughes (Liverpool), C.Bell (Man City), P.E.Madeley (Leeds Utd), R.F.C.Moore (West Ham, captain), A.J.Ball (Arsenal), M.R.Channon (Southampton), M.H.Chivers (Spurs), A.J.Clarke (Leeds Utd), M.S.Peters (Spurs).

Half-time 0-3   Full-time 0-5
Ref: R.Wurtz (France)   Att: 48,470

WHEN the Scottish FA decided to invite England to Hampden Park to launch their Centenary celebrations, little did they realise what was in store for their team. It was a bitterly cold night and Hampden's pitch had a light covering of snow, but this certainly did not affect England who produced their best display for some considerable time.

Appropriately enough, the visitors had

England in May 1973. Back row (left to right): Hunter, Blockley, Summerbee, Clarke, Hughes, Clemence, Parkes, Shilton, Bell, McFarland, Moore, Chivers, Peters, Harold Shepherdson (trainer). Front row: Madeley, Macdonald, Storey, Ball, Channon, Richards, Nish, Keegan, Currie.

their own centenary celebrations for Bobby Moore was leading out his side for his 100th appearance, thus becoming the third England player to reach that particular landmark. It was a marvellous achievement for this superb player and it was fitting that it should be against Scotland. After the pleasantries and presentations, Moore proceeded to lead his side into a tremendous performance.

It took England just six minutes to take the lead. A fine move built up down the right between Colin Bell and Allan Clarke. Clarke eventually put in a cross and both Mike Channon and Lorimer went for it with the Scot getting the final touch with his head for an own-goal. Before Scotland could recover, Emlyn Hughes pumped a long, high pass through the middle. Channon outjumped Colquohoun and Clarke slid in to touch Channon's cross-shot past his namesake in the home goal.

Sixty seconds later, with still only 15 minutes gone, Scotland's defence was again caught flat-footed. This time Martin Chivers lined up near the corner-flag to take one of his long throw-ins. The Scottish players seemed oblivious to the dangers and their marking was non-existent. As a result the ball reached an unmarked Channon and the Southampton player volleyed it superbly past Clark from a narrow angle. It was a well-taken goal but the Scots had made it much easier for him with their slack defensive play.

So, effectively the match was over. With Channon and Clarke giving England much more zest in attack, and the recalled Martin Peters adding a greater fluency to the midfield, the visitors looked far more positive than of late and were able to create an abundance of goal chances. The shell-shocked Scots were torn to ribbons and had no answer to it all.

Understandably, perhaps, the game died a little with England so much in control, but there were plenty of other chances. Chivers headed against a post and both Channon and Clarke missed virtual open goals. Scotland's only hope came from substitute Stein. He had come on for the injured Morgan and looked the only player capable of salvaging something for the sad hosts.

Before the end though England added two more goals which only emphasised their overall superiority. The first came after a terrible back-pass by Colquohoun with 15 minutes to go. Chivers latched on to it and thumped home England's fourth goal. To round it all off nicely, Clarke punished a mistake by Donachie to shoot a fifth from a sharp angle. The partnership of Channon and Clarke was tremendous with Channon in particular a real livewire.

With Bremner, Graham and the rest totally outclassed, Scotland finished their night of celebration with absolutely nothing at all to celebrate.

> 90th match v Scotland.
> 100th cap for Moore.
> Lorimer scored an own-goal for England.

Northern Ireland v England   Home Championship

Played on Saturday, 12 May 1973 at Goodison Park, Liverpool.

Northern Ireland: P.A.Jennings (Spurs); P.J.Rice (Arsenal), D.J.Craig (Newcastle Utd), W.J.T.Neill (Hull C), A.Hunter (Ipswich T), D.Clements (Sheffield Wed), B.Hamilton (Ipswich T), T.A.Jackson (Nottm Forest), S.J.Morgan (Port Vale),

M.H.M.O'Neill (Nottm Forest), T.Anderson (Man Utd).

England: P.L.Shilton (Leicester C); P.E.Storey (Arsenal), D.J.Nish (Derby Co), C.Bell (Man City), R.L.McFarland (Derby Co), R.F.C.Moore (West Ham, captain), A.J.Ball (Arsenal), M.R.Channon (Southampton), M.H.Chivers (Spurs), J.P.Richards (Wolves), M.S.Peters (Spurs).

Half-time 1-1   Full-time 1-2

Ref: C.Thomas (Wales)   Att: 32,000

WITH the political troubles in Northern Ireland meaning that their soccer team had to play their home game against England at Goodison Park, it was not surprising that there was a certain lack of atmosphere for this Home Championship international. The match reflected this and proved to be drab and lifeless.

England brought in two new caps in David Nish at full-back and John Richards up front and the 'visitors' also scored the early goal that every side wants. A free-kick by Alan Ball was met by a glancing header by Martin Chivers. It seemed an easy save for Jennings but, inexplicably and uncharacteristically, the goalkeeper allowed the ball to go under his body and creep into the net. This bright start by England continued until the 20th minute when everything began to go wrong.

At that moment Peter Storey lost his head and a terrible tackle brought down Morgan to give Ireland a penalty. Clements scored from the spot and England had thrown away their advantage. From then on they also lost control of the midfield that they had held up until then. Colin Bell and Martin Peters were badly off form and Ball, despite his usual industry, was not effective. Meanwhile,

Bobby Moore, Kevin Keegan and Sir Alf Ramsey. Moore joined the '100 caps club', appropriately enough, in the centenary match against Scotland.

the Irish trio of Clements, Jackson and Hamilton were far more positive, although it must be said that Ireland still created few clear chances to score.

New cap Nish showed style and Richards, despite playing out of his normal position of attack leader, did well enough to suggest another chance. Mike Channon was undoubtedly the best England forward on show and the most dangerous. But all the main honours went to the Irish.

Their team was largely made up of players from the lower divisions but they did have the one player on view who showed flair. Trevor Anderson gave an excellent performance and his style and appearance drew comparisons with the legendary George Best. However, despite all of Ireland's promise and possession they threw it all away seven minutes from the end by conceding another soft goal. Again it was Chivers the scorer and again it stemmed from an Irish mistake, this time when Neill stumbled over a flick by Richards to let the big centre-forward in.

It was an undeserved end for the bitterly disappointed Irish team. As for England, there was room for improvement in all areas of the side and it was obvious that the long season just gone has taken its toll on some of their players.

> 80th match v Northern Ireland.
> Debuts for Nish and Richards.
> Penalty for Northern Ireland scored by Clements.

England v
Wales Home Championship

Played on Tuesday, 15 May 1973 at Wembley Stadium.

England: P.L.Shilton (Leicester C); P.E.Storey (Arsenal), E.W.Hughes (Liver-

pool), C.Bell (Man City), R.L.McFarland (Derby Co), R.F.C.Moore (West Ham, captain), A.J.Ball (Arsenal), M.R.Channon (Southampton), M.H.Chivers (Spurs), A.J.Clarke (Leeds Utd), M.S.Peters (Spurs).
Wales: T.J.S.Phillips (Chelsea); P.J.Rodrigues (Sheffield Wed), R.J.Thomas (Swindon T), T.J.Hockey (Norwich C), H.M.England (Spurs), J.G.Roberts (Birmingham C), L.James (Burnley), J.F.Mahoney (Stoke C), J.B.Toshack (Liverpool), M.E.Page (Birmingham C), B.C.Evans (Swansea C).
Subs: D.F.Roberts (Oxford Utd) for England and W.J.Emmanuel (Bristol C) for Page.

Half-time 2-0   Full-time 3-0
Ref: J.W.Paterson (Scotland) Att: 39,000

AT LAST — an English victory at Wembley. For the first time in two years and five matches England overcame the nervousness that they seem to have at playing at their national stadium. It was a good performance, too, with three excellent goals and several other near misses. A small crowd of 39,000 enjoyed the game and were particularly impressed with the home attack which seemed to have now settled down to the three 'Cs', Mike Channon, Martin Chivers and Allan Clarke. The latter was especially sharp and he had an outstanding game.

England began positively and broke the deadlock after 25 minutes. Emlyn Hughes centred from the left and Channon headed back for Chivers to hit a low right-foot shot which flew past Phillips. Eight minutes later, England added a second goal and that was a real gem. Alan Ball's pass gave Channon possession and the Southampton star took on and outpaced both John Roberts and Thomas before hitting a superb shot diagonally into the far corner, again giving Phillips no chance to save.

By now England were well on top and they were desperately unlucky when an offside decision ruled out what would have been a magnificent goal for Clarke. A brilliant ground passing movement at speed involving Ball, Chivers, Clarke, Channon and Clarke again, ended with a marvellous shot high into the roof of the net. But to England's disappointment, the referee ruled the goal out for that offside decision.

Apart from the terrier-like running of Hockey and Mahoney, Wales had little to offer. England meanwhile, although still not firing on all cylinders, were much better than in their recent game against the Irish at Goodison Park and after half-time they continued to have much the better of this match. Chivers also had a goal ruled out for offside and other clear chances were missed by Channon, Chivers and Colin Bell.

But the much deserved third goal did finally arrive and, again, it was a beauty. Seventy-five minutes had been played when Ball again sent Channon sprinting away with a fine long pass. Channon moved quickly, beat Roberts and then passed the ball square to Clarke who, in turn, set up a fine strike by Martin Peters from 20 yards out. The ball flew into the top corner to put the icing on the cake for a much improved England display.

> 85th match v Wales

England v
Scotland Home Championship

Played on Saturday, 19 May 1973 at Wembley Stadium.

England: P.L.Shilton (Leicester C); P.E.Storey (Arsenal), E.W.Hughes (Liverpool), C.Bell (Man City), R.L.McFarland (Derby Co), R.F.C.Moore (West Ham, captain), A.J.Ball (Everton), M.R.Channon (Southampton), M.H.Chivers (Spurs), A.J.Clarke (Leeds Utd), M.S.Peters (Spurs).
Scotland: A.Hunter (Celtic); W.A.Jardine (Rangers), D.McGrain (Celtic), W.J.Bremner (Leeds Utd), J.A.Holton (Man Utd), D.Johnstone (Rangers), W.Morgan (Man Utd), L.Macari (Man Utd), K.Dalglish (Celtic), D.Hay (Celtic), P.Lorimer (Leeds Utd).
Subs: J.Jordan (Leeds Utd) for Macari and C.Stein (Coventry C) for Lorimer.

Half-time 0-0   Full-time 1-0
Ref: K.Tschenscher (West Germany)
Att: 95,950

SCOTLAND, determined to avenge their 5-0 humiliation by England the previous February, went to Wembley with a side packed with players suited more to a physical game. As a result of some weak refereeing, the match was played in a fiercely competitive spirit which frequently overlapped into violent conduct. Both sides were guilty of some questionable tackling and the first half was littered with free-kicks.

England tried hard to put some football together, although their midfield of Colin Bell, Alan Ball and Martin Peters never imposed their skills enough. The build-up was slow and laborious and, despite some good running by Mike Channon,

Martin Chivers and Allan Clarke, the forwards had little chance to score. For Scotland, Hay played the sweeper role and the whole side was brilliantly marshalled by the busy Bremner. Holton and Johnstone were strong defenders and Hunter looked safe and sure in goal.

After only three minutes Macari sent Lorimer away and Peter Shilton did very well to turn his angled shot away to safety. When England then hit back with a flowing move, a rarity in this game, a swift passing exchange involving Shilton, Emlyn Hughes, Bell and Channon ended with a Clarke shot going just wide.

On the half-hour Ball's free-kick was met by a powerful Chivers header, only for Hunter to make a tremendous tip-over save. That was the last of the serious goal attempts of the first half but with only ten minutes of the second half gone, England took the lead. Inevitably, perhaps, the goal came from a free-kick. Ball took it and Peters headed in cleverly at the far post after Chivers had made an excellent dummy run, taking defenders out of position.

The Scots tried hard to come back and the strong-arm stuff worsened, but the visitors lacked the necessary thrust up front and only towards the end did they bring on the more powerful duo of Jordan and Stein to replace Macari and Lorimer.

With five minutes to go, the Scots almost scored and only a magnificent save by Shilton prevented an equalizer. A cross came over and was only half cleared. As the ball dropped just outside the left of the penalty area, Dalglish met it with a sweet left-foot volley which arrowed towards the top left-hand corner of Shilton's goal. It looked a goal all the way but somehow the goalkeeper leapt to his left to claw the ball away with his right hand. It was a stunning save and left Dalglish holding his head in disbelief. The Scottish fans couldn't believe it either, but for Shilton it was the high spot of a superb performance and it now looked as though he had secured his place in goal for some time to come.

This result meant that England had won the Home Championship title for the 29th time and they now moved on for a tour which included a vital World Cup match in Poland.

> 91st match v Scotland.

Czechoslovakia v England   Friendly

Played on Sunday, 27 May 1973 in the Letna Stadium, Prague.

Czechoslovakia: I.Viktor (Dukla Prague); J.Pivarník (Slovan Bratislava), L.Zlocha (Slovan Bratislava), V.Samek (Dukla Prague), V.Hagara (Spartak Trnava), Bičovský (Union Teplice), L.Kuna (Spartak Trnava), I.Novác (Tatran Prešov), B.Veselý (Sparta Prague), Z.Nehoda (Dukla Prague), P.Stratil (Union Teplice).

England: P.L.Shilton (Leicester C); P.E.Madeley (Leeds Utd), P.E.Storey (Arsenal), C.Bell (Man City), R.L.McFarland (Derby Co), R.F.C.Moore (West Ham, captain), A.J.Ball (Arsenal), M.R.Channon (Southampton), M.H.Chivers (Spurs), A.J.Clarke (Leeds Utd), M.S.Peters (Spurs).

Half-time 0-0   Full-time 1-1

Ref: R.Glöckner (East Germany)

Att: 25,000

THIS was another disappointing performance by England, who had yet to find the right blend in midfield. Once again only Alan Ball emerged with any real credit as England wove patterns which succeeded only in confusing themselves.

As early as the second minute, Peter Shilton was brilliantly saving point-blank from Stratil but then could only watch as Nehoda miscued the rebound wide of an open goal. The Czechs were encouraged by this near miss and pushed England back for long spells. The home side were searching to improve on a poor run of five matches without a win and had made several changes in an effort to alter their fortunes.

Vesely gave Peter Storey a torrid time and Roy McFarland often struggled. Luckily for England, Bobby Moore and Paul Madeley were in fine form and held the defence together along with Shilton's solidity. Czechoslovakia's chief playmaker was Kuna, who controlled the midfield from his deep-lying 'centre-forward' position. Bičovský and Novák gave tireless support and the fair haired Pivarník made some brilliant overlap runs down the right.

England held on until the 55th minute when the Czechs finally found a way past Shilton. The goal came following a corner and a short sideways pass by Hagara gave Novák the chance to ram a fierce left-foot shot through a crowded penalty area and wide of Shilton's left hand.

Although their attacks were few and far between, England almost equalized immediately but the 'goal' Mike Channon headed in from Martin Peters cross was ruled out for an offside decision. That was an isolated raid though by an attack that was very ineffective, but one could hardly blame the forwards because the service they received from midfield was so poor.

The Czechs pushed forward after their goal and forced Shilton into two more outstanding saves. First he saved brilliantly from Pivarník and then he thwarted Stratil with a similar piece of fine goalkeeping. Stratil had certainly been impressive.

So, on a gloriously sunny day and on a lush green pitch, the result looked to be slipping away from England. But, as the referee's watch moved into its last minute, out of the blue the visitors somehow found an equalizer. Madeley gave Clarke a precise short pass and the number-ten promptly hit a first-time shot into the top corner of Viktor's net.

The goal spared England's blushes but failed to hide the glaring weaknesses in some areas of the team and they would have to do much better in the forthcoming World Cup match against Poland.

> 6th match v Czechoslovakia.

Poland v England   World Cup Qualifier

Played on Wednesday, 6 June 1973 at the Slaski Stadium, Chorzów.

Poland: J.Tomaszewski (LKS Lódź); K.Rześny (Stal Mielec), J.Gorgoń (Górnik

Zabrze), A.Musiał (Wisla Kraków), M.Bulzacki (LKS Lódź), J.Kraska (Gwardia Warsaw), J.Banaś (Górnik Zabrze), L.Ćmikiewicz (Legia Warsaw), K.Deyna (Legia Warsaw), W.Lubański (Górnik Zabrze), R.Gadocha (Legia Warsaw).
Sub: J.Domarski (Stal Mielec) for Lubański.

England: P.L.Shilton (Leicester C); P.E.Madeley (Leeds Utd), E.W.Hughes (Liverpool), P.E.Storey (Arsenal), R.L.McFarland (Derby Co), R.F.C.Moore (West Ham, captain), A.J.Ball (Arsenal), C.Bell (Man City), M.H.Chivers (Spurs), A.J.Clarke (Leeds Utd), M.S.Peters (Spurs).

Half-time 1-0   Full-time 2-0

Ref: P.Schiller (Austria)   Att: 118,000

SIR Alf Ramsey decided on a 4-4-2 formation for this vital World Cup clash and he made it perfectly clear from the start that England had come to Poland for a point. Alas, all his pre-match plans came woefully unstuck after only seven minutes.

Roy McFarland was somewhat harshly adjudged to have stopped Lubański unfairly down the left flank by the Austrian referee. The free-kick was taken by Gadocha, who hit it low and hard to the near post. It hit Bobby Moore and then Peter Shilton's hands as the goalkeeper tried unsuccessfully to keep it out. It was a bitter blow to England and although one expected a change in their tactics there was little alteration in the first half.

England did get a fine chance to equalize only three minutes after the goal, but Martin Peters headed straight at Tomaszewski from very close range. Peters really should have scored and England were to regret his miss. Their only other good chance of the first half came on the half-hour. A fine move involving Peter Storey, Allan Clarke and Colin Bell split the Polish defence and Martin Chivers was left with the final shot which he rocketed over the bar from some 12 yards out.

For the most part of the half, England had persisted with the negative, containing tactics they had employed from the start. It often left Chivers and Clarke ploughing lonely furrows up front. Territorially, England probably had the better of the half but, for all they saw of the ball, the fact was that they could not score.

Just as England had made a disastrous start to the first half, then so they did at the start of the second. Only one minute had elapsed after the change round when skipper Moore tried to dribble around Lubański. Disastrously, he lost possession to the Polish striker and with England's defence now wide open, Lubański roared on towards Shilton and hit a fierce low shot past the 'keeper and in off the near post. The massive crowd screamed their delight and the 2-0 scoreline seemingly put the game out of England's reach.

As the game wore on, there was no sign of an improvement and the result drifted further and further away from England. They never managed to create another worthwhile chance and it was surprising that the manager did not attempt to use any of his substitutes in trying to rescue the cause. Instead, he persisted with his 4-4-2 formation and ended with nothing.

The final nail in the coffin came near the end of a bad tempered second half. Ćmikiewicz had already upset Peters and when he then clashed with Ball the fiery England midfielder was sent off for violent conduct.

Alan Ball is sent off by Austrian referee Paul Schiller during the World Cup qualifier in Poland in June 1973. Other England players look on in disbelief.

Peter Storey was the star of a very disappointing performance as he covered every blade of grass in his efforts. Clarke, too, showed some silky skills and Madeley also showed his class, but other than that there was little to remember about this showing.

> 3rd match v Poland.
> Ball, second England player to be sent off in an international.

USSR v England
Friendly

Played on Sunday, 10 June 1973 in the Lenin Stadium, Moscow.

USSR: E.Rudakov (Dinamo Kiev); S.Olashanskiy (Spartak Moscow), M.Khurtsilava (Dinamo Tbilisi), E.Lovchev (Spartak Moscow), V.Kuznetsov (Zarya Voroshilovgrad), V.Kaplichniy (CSKA Moscow), V.Muntyan (Dinamo Kiev), V.Papa'ev (Spartak Moscow), A.Andriasyan (Ararat Erevan), V.Onishenko (Zarya Voroshilovgrad), O.Blokhin (Dinamo Kiev). Subs: V.Fedotov (CSKA Moscow) for Kuznetsov, Y.Vasenin (Zarya Voroshilovgrad) for Papa'ev and V.Kozlov (Dinamo Moscow) for Andriasyan.
England: P.L.Shilton (Leicester C); P.E.Madeley (Leeds Utd), E.W.Hughes (Liverpool), P.E.Storey (Arsenal), R.L.McFarland (Derby Co), R.F.C.Moore (West Ham, captain), A.W.Currie (Sheffield Utd), M.R.Channon (Southampton), M.H.Chivers (Spurs), A.J.Clarke (Leeds Utd), M.S.Peters (Spurs). Subs: M.G.Summerbee (Man City) for

Channon, M.I.Macdonald (Newcastle Utd) for Clarke and N.Hunter (Leeds Utd) for Peters.

Half-time 0-1   Full-time 1-2
Ref: W.R.Riedel (East Germany)

Att: 85,000

ENGLAND bounced back superbly from the disappointments of Poland to record a splendid victory in the massive Lenin Stadium in Moscow. The win was all the more impressive in the oppressive heat and humidity of late afternoon which would have sapped the energy of lesser teams.

The boost of an early goal gave England a good start. Ten minutes had gone when a quick, smooth move began with Mike Channon and ended when Martin Peters sent a header over the Russian defensive wall for Martin Chivers, his back to goal, to sweep the awkwardly bouncing ball over his right shoulder and into the far corner of Rudakov's net.

After the goal England took command. Bobby Moore, equalling Bobby Charlton's 106 appearances record, was immaculate, Roy McFarland tenacious and Emlyn Hughes and Peter Storey tireless workers. Other chances were created and England were unlucky when Channon hit the inside of the far post with Rudakov beaten. Later, Tony Currie missed a fine opportunity, shooting wide from close range after Paul Madeley's pass had given him a gilt-edged opening.

The Soviets also had their moments, especially when Onishenko was clean

through only for Peter Shilton to make a brilliant point-blank save two minutes after England's goal. But Currie looked very impressive in only his second game and he showed tremendous flair and skill. Play was hard but always fair and, despite a number of strong tackles, there was no complaint from either side.

England opened the second half just as brightly and again it took them ten minutes to score a well-deserved second goal. A corner was taken on the left by Channon and, after Peters had dummied over the ball, the hapless Khurtsilava was unlucky enough to divert it into his own net.

It was annoying for England when almost immediately Russia pulled a goal back from the penalty-spot by Muntyan after Storey had upended Onishenko. That goal raised the young Russian side's spirits and for the next 25 minutes they upped the tempo and tore into the tiring England players. Fedotov, twice, Vasenin, Kozlov and Blokhin all came within a whisker of equalizing and then a brilliant run by Blokhin set up a score by Kozlov, only for the referee to disallow the goal for offside. The crowd roared their disapproval at the decision whilst England breathed a sigh of relief.

Blokhin, who had been described as 'a poor man's Tom Finney', was the big danger to England in the closing stages and it was with some difficulty that he was contained. At the end, though, England thoroughly deserved their success and Moore and his sweat soaked teammates walked off with a feeling of great satisfaction at a job well done. If only the same form had been shown in Poland.

7th match v USSR.
Own-goal scored by Khurtsilava for England.
Muntyan scored a penalty for Russia.
Bobby Moore equalled Bobby Charlton's 106 cap record.

Italy v England
Friendly

Played on Thursday, 14 June 1973 at the Comunale Stadium, Turin.

Italy: D.Zoff (Juventus); G.Sabadini (Milan AC), G.Facchetti (Inter-Milan), R.Benetti (Milan AC), F.Morini (Juventus), T.Burgnich (Inter-Milan), A.Mazzola (Inter-Milan), F.Capello (Juventus), P.Anastasi (Juventus), G.Rivera (Milan AC), P.Pulici (Torino).
Subs: M.Belluci (Inter-Milan) for Morini and F.Causio (Juventus) for Pulici.

England: P.L.Shilton (Leicester C); P.E.Madeley (Leeds Utd), E.W.Hughes (Liverpool), P.E.Storey (Arsenal), R.L.McFarland (Derby Co), R.F.C.Moore (West Ham, captain), A.W.Currie (Sheffield Utd), M.R.Channon (Southampton), M.H.Chivers (Spurs), A.J.Clarke (Leeds Utd), M.S.Peters (Spurs).

Half-time 1-0   Full-time 2-0
Ref: T.Stanev (Bulgaria)   Att: 52,000

FOR 40 years and in eight previous meetings, the Italians had tried desperately to beat England, and now, at the ninth attempt, they succeeded.

England opened the match brightly and for the first half-hour they controlled proceedings. Mike Channon, Martin Chivers and Emlyn Hughes all went close with good efforts but gradually the tall, elegant Facchetti snuffed out the threat from Channon, and Sabadini and Morini did likewise to Allan Clarke and Chivers. It then became a typical Italian performance as their tight defence refused to give anything away, combining clever tactical play with their usual mixture of strong tackling and blatant body checking.

Before half-time, Italy added the extra mountain for England to climb by opening the scoring. Rivera put Pulici clean through the middle and the latter sped towards goal. Out came Peter Shilton, who dived bravely and brilliantly at the winger's feet. Alas for England, lady luck refused to smile on them as the ball ran loose to Anastasi, who shot home low and hard and through Bobby Moore's legs as the England skipper tried desperately to get back to cover.

The second half was only six minutes old when Italy scored again. Another devastatingly quick break saw the ball move swiftly between Rivera, Anastasi and Pulici, who then crossed for Capello to score with a flashing header. England seemed to have a very good case for offside but their appeals fell on deaf ears as the stadium erupted into a crescendo of noise.

Italy then showed what marvellous football they can produce when they are on song. Superb passing and quick breaks had England's beleaguered defence at full stretch. Hughes brought down Pulici with a crude tackle and Rivera rattled the England crossbar from the free-kick. Then Shilton made a fine save from Anastasi as the Italians pushed forward relentlessly.

Roy McFarland takes the ball away during the game in Turin in June 1973.

Now Bobby Moore goes away from the Italians. Moore topped Bobby Charlton's record of 106 caps in this match.

England tried everything they knew but on the day it was just not good enough and, indeed, they did well to prevent further goals from the rapant Italians. Moore, who was celebrating beating Bobby Charlton's record appearance total by winning his 107th cap, Peter Storey, Paul Madeley, Channon and Currie all produced some bright moments but the extra passion of Anastasi, Rivera, Capello and Mazzola made sure that Italy gained the win they so desperately wanted.

9th match v Italy.
Bobby Moore's 107th cap, a new record.

England v Austria
Friendly

Played on Wednesday, 26 September 1973 at Wembley Stadium.

England: P.L.Shilton (Leicester C); P.E.Madeley (Leeds Utd), E.W.Hughes (Liverpool), C.Bell (Man City), R.L.McFarland (Derby Co), N.Hunter (Leeds Utd), A.W.Currie (Sheffield Utd), M.R.Channon (Southampton), M.H.Chivers (Spurs), A.J.Clarke (Leeds Utd), M.S.Peters (Spurs, captain).

Austria: F.Koncilia (SW Innsbruck); R.Sara (FK Austria), E.Krieger (FK Austria), J.Schmidradner (Offenbach Kickers), J.Eigenstiller (SW Innsbruck), R.Hattenberger (SW Innsbruck), A.Starek (Rapid Vienna), H.Ettmayer (VfB Stuttgart), W.Kreuz (Sparta Rotterdam), J.Krankl (Rapid Vienna), K.Jara (Valencia CF).
Subs: W.Kriess (SW Innsbruck) for Eigenstiller and F.Gombasch (SW Innsbruck) for Hattenberger.

Half-time 3-0   Full-time 7-0
Ref: C.G.Corver (Holland)   Att: 48,000

Mike Channon (centre) scores the first of England's seven goals against Austria at Wembley in September 1973.

AS A warm up exercise for the forthcoming World Cup tie against Poland the following month, this friendly with Austria proved to be the perfect build-up — a much improved confidence-building performance, a hatful of goals, and little to criticise.

Austria came to Wembley with a good pedigree. Excellent draws against Brazil and Hungary and a narrow defeat against the strong Sweden side meant the prospect of a difficult match for England. But right from the start the home side quickly stamped their authority on the game. They soon took the lead. In the tenth minute, Martin Peters crossed and Martin Chivers jumped with a posse of defenders leaving Mike Channon free to score as the ball came to him. He cleverly flicked it in with his heel.

England continued to press home their advantage and on 30 minutes they increased their lead with a fine goal by Allan Clarke. Trapping a centre form Tony Currie, he sold a brilliant dummy to full-back Sara before turning inside and hitting a superb left-foot shot into the far corner.

For a while after that goal England slipped into a sloppy spell but on the stroke of half-time they snapped out of it to score goal number-three. Again it was Clarke the executioner, this time superbly taking a cross from Colin Bell before shooting home at the second attempt after his first effort had been blocked.

After half-time England completely dominated and further goals came at regular intervals. Clarke came desperately close to scoring a hat-trick, but saw his shot kicked on to a post by a defender. When the ball bounced out, Channon pounced and cracked it back into the net. Currie, so often at the heart of all the good things England did, made the fifth goal with a fast, low centre which was flicked past Koncilia by Chivers.

Apart from the hard working Starek and Ettmayer, Austria had little to offer in response to this slaughter and on the hour England hit the goal trail again with a real beauty. This time a lob by Channon was met on the volley with a brilliant shot into the top corner by Currie. That was particularly well deserved for the Sheffield United player. Austria were by now completely overrun and three minutes from the end, England rounded things off. Currie, Channon, Chivers and Clarke all featured in a lovely move which ended with Bell hitting a fast, low cross-shot past Koncilia. The goalkeeper's nightmare was now complete.

14th match v Austria.

England v Poland World Cup Qualifier

Played on Wednesday, 17 October 1973 at Wembley Stadium.

England: P.L.Shilton (Leicester C); P.E.Madeley (Leeds Utd), E.W.Hughes (Liverpool), C.Bell (Man City), R.L.McFarland (Derby Co), N.Hunter (Leeds Utd), A.W.Currie (Sheffield Utd), M.R.Channon (Southampton), M.H.Chivers (Spurs), A.J.Clarke (Leeds Utd), M.S.Peters (Spurs, captain).
Sub: K.J.Hector (Derby Co) for Chivers.

Poland: J.Tomaszewski (LKS Lódź); A.Szymanowski (Wisla Kraków), A.Musial (Wisla Kraków), M.Bulzacki (LKS Lódź), J.Gorgoń (Górnik Zabrze), H.Kasperczak (Stal Mielec), G.Lato (Stal Mielec), L.Cmikiewicz (Legia Warsaw), K.Deyna (Legia Warsaw), J.Domarski (Stal Mielec), R.Gadocha (Legia Warsaw).

Half-time 0-0   Full-time 1-1
Ref: V.Loraux (Belgium)   Att:100,000

ENGLAND would not be going to the World Cup finals in 1974. That was the cold, hard fact left after this breathtaking match had run its course. It was a tragedy for the players who gave so much and at the end they could perhaps blame 'Lady Luck' for their demise.

With 100,000 people packed into Wembley, England began like a train and immediately tore into the opposition. Poland, superbly marshalled by Deyna, had to defend continuously as Tony Currie, Colin Bell and Martin Peters seized control of the midfield. Mike Channon was in sparkling form up front, but

Left: **Domarski beats Shilton with a wicked drive at Wembley in October 1973.** *Right:* **Norman Hunter is consoled by Bobby Moore and Harold Shepherdson after England crashed to the Poles.**

Allan Clarke sends Tomaszewski the wrong way from the penalty-spot but it is not enough to save England.

Martin Chivers always struggled and never provided the necessary thrust down the middle.

The hero for Poland was undoubtedly Tomaszewski in goal. He had an inspired night as he repeatedly foiled shot after shot that rained in on him. At times he hardly knew anything about it as the ball bounced off his body, but credit where credit is due, he also made some outstanding saves and probably did not deserve Brian Clough's accolade in judging him 'a clown'.

On 19 minutes, he dived to save at the foot of the post from Allan Clarke and just before half-time he produced the save of the night, going full length to foil Currie. Poland rarely attacked, although brief glimpses of their undoubted skill did shine through the barrage of England attacks produced. The atmosphere was electric as the crowd sensed an England

goal but to their frustration half-time arrived goalless.

England still kept up the incessant attacking after the break but Poland still remained firm with Tomaszewski seemingly unbeatable. The crowd played their part in trying to inspire England and a roar of 'England, England' came from the terrraces. It seemed impossible to think at this stage that it was still goalless.

Then, with an hour gone, came the unthinkable as Poland, in what was probably their first real attack, went ahead. England were attacking, but a long pass out of the packed Polish defence was aimed at Gadocha out on the left wing and on the half-way line. Over came Norman Hunter to cover what seemed an easy ball for him to clear. He could have put it anywhere but inexplicably his feet got in a tangle and Gadocha was suddenly clear of the England defence. Emlyn

Hughes tried desperately to get back as Gadocha sped towards goal, but as Hughes was drawn to the tackle the winger coolly laid it inside where Lato and Domarski were all alone. The pass found Domarski who wasted no time in hitting a wicked, low shot which deceived Peter Shilton and flew under the goalkeeper's dive. Shilton might have done better but the real blame had to lay with Hunter, which was ironic since Bobby Moore had committed a similar error against the Poles in Chorzów.

England, to their credit, were not unduly affected by the goal and still pushed forward relentlessly. Clarke saw a goal disallowed but six minutes after Poland's goal, England equalized. Martin Peters was blatantly pushed in the penalty area and the referee awarded a spot-kick. One cannot imagine the tension that must have been on Clarke's shoulders but he

Four Derby County players in the England squad, from left to right, are Kevin Hector, Roy McFarland, Colin Todd and David Nish.

coolly stepped up and easily beat Tomaszewski.

Now, one thought, perhaps the floodgates would open. Sadly it was not to be, despite a furious onslaught by England. Clarke, Channon and Currie were all thwarted by Tomaszewski's heroics, saving with his body, hands and even feet. Sir Alf Ramsey's substitution of Chivers should surely have been done earlier with Kevin Hector's appearance coming only two minutes from the end. Even then, Hector saw a header from Currie's corner kicked off the line in the last seconds. How near the Derby man came to becoming a national hero overnight.

So England were out of the World Cup and as they trooped dejectedly off of Wembley's lush turf, the roar of 100,000 fans was testament to the undoubted effort they had given and came as some consolation. However, in the cold light of day, the fact still remained that they were not going to Munich and questions were to be asked as to why.

4th match v Poland.
Debut for Hector as substitute.
Penalty scored for England by Clarke.
"When Poland scored it was the worst moment of my international career."
Emlyn Hughes

England v Italy
Friendly

Played on Wednesday, 14 November 1973 at Wembley Stadium.

England: P.L.Shilton (Leicester C); P.E.Madeley (Leeds Utd), E.W.Hughes (Liverpool), C.Bell (Man City), R.L.McFarland (Derby Co), R.F.C.Moore (West Ham, captain), A.W.Currie (Sheffield Utd), M.R.Channon (Southampton), P.L.Osgood (Chelsea), A.J.Clarke (Leeds Utd), M.S.Peters (Spurs).
Sub: K.J.Hector (Derby Co) for Clarke.
Italy: D.Zoff (Juventus); L.Spinosi (Juventus), G.Facchetti (Inter-Milan), R.Benetti (Milan AC), M.Bellugi (Inter-Milan), T.Burgnich (Inter-Milan), F.Causio (Juventus), F.Capello (Juventus), G.Chinaglia (Lazio), G.Rivera (Milan AC), L.Riva (Cagliari).

Half-time 0-0   Full-time 0-1
Ref: F.Marques Lobo (Portugal) Att: 95,000

THE disappointments of the Poland match a month earlier still loomed large as England went into this friendly against old adversaries, Italy. This was now a World Cup warm-up for the Italians, but not for England who now had to concentrate on regrouping, rebuilding and rethinking.

On a damp night, Italy proved more than capable of holding the home attack. Their defensive attitude had seen them go ten matches without a goal against and all the time their lightning breaks were so dangerous. England did not play that badly and produced some good moments in the first half. Emlyn Hughes and Colin Bell went close and the impressive Tony Currie twice forced Zoff into outstanding saves. Zoff carried on where Poland's Tomaszewski left off and Wembley was fast becoming a favourite venue for visiting goalkeepers, Herr Koncilia of Austria excepted, of course.

The slippery pitch caused both sides problems, although Peter Osgood and the brilliant Rivera showed how easy it could be as they gracefully strutted around the lush turf. Osgood did well and so, too, did Currie, who showed some marvellous vision and creativity. Goal chances at either end were rare, though, as the two defences held their grip on the game. Italy saw much less of the possession but with Causio, Riva, Chinaglia and especially Rivera all in superb form the dangerous breakaways by the visitors kept England continually on their toes.

With the game slowly drifting into a goalless draw, one of those Italian breaks suddenly paid off. Only three minutes were left when Capello fed a pass to Chinaglia down the right. Bobby Moore came across to cover but Chinaglia outpaced him before firing the ball in from the by-line. Peter Shilton beat it out but Capello, following up, seized on the rebound to score.

There were a lot of Italian supporters in the Wembley crowd and they went wild with delight as England tried desperately to salvage something in the remaining minutes. But Italy were not about to let anything slip at this late stage and they comfortably held on to their one goal advantage. They had been controlled by the immaculate Rivera, whose talent shone through the drizzle all night.

10th match v Italy.
Bobby Moore's 108th and last international.

Italian goalkeeper Dino Zoff makes a flying save at Wembley in November 1973.

Portugal v England Friendly

Played on Wednesday, 3 April 1974 in the Stadium of Light, Lisbon.

Portugal: V.Damas (Sporting Lisbon); F.Rebelo (Vitória Setúbal), A.Correia (Benfica), A.Oliveira (Benfica), H.Coelho (Benfica), J.Mendes (Vitória Setúbal), R.Jordão (Benfica), O.Machado (Vitória Setúbal), V.Baptista (Benfica), A.Silva (CUF, Coimbra), J.Joao (Vitória Setúbal). Subs: V.Costa (Barreirense) for Oliveira, R.da Silva (Vitória Setúbal) for Baptista, V.Pereira (CUF, Coimbra) for A.Silva.
England: P.B.F.Parkes (QPR); D.J.Nish (Derby Co), M.Pejic (Stoke C), J.M.Dobson (Burnley), D.V.Watson (Sunderland), C.Todd (Derby Co), S.Bowles (QPR), M.R.Channon (Southampton), M.I.Macdonald (Newcastle Utd), T.D.Brooking (West Ham), M.S.Peters (Spurs, captain). Sub: A.J.Ball (Arsenal) for Macdonald.

Half-time 0-0   Full-time 0-0

Ref: E.Guruceta (Spain)   Att: 15,000

THE dawn of a new era, or to put it more truthfully, the very late evening of a new era. Portugal liked to kick-off their evening games at 10pm, so it was a late start for England and the six new faces in their side. Sir Alf Ramsey had decided to bring in some new blood and the young players obliged with some excellent play in the opening half-hour.

After two minutes Malcolm Macdonald was within a whisker of beating the home goalkeeper to a through-ball from Mike Pejic. Then, three minutes later, a short corner between Stan Bowles and Trevor Brooking ended with Mike Channon heading against the Portuguese crossbar. Still England kept pressing and they came close again when a lovely, flowing move involving Colin Todd, Brooking and Macdonald ended with Martin Dobson's header flying just over.

Unfortunately it was a start that England could not sustain. The late kick-off and the inexperience of youth probably had some bearing on the alarming way the visitors faded away. They seemed content to coast through the latter stages of the game against a Portugal side which was but a pale shadow of their illustrious predecessors. There was little threat from the home attack. Joao was their outstanding player and at the hub of all their best work, but with Dave Watson and Todd having excellent games, goal chances were at a premium. The best of Portugal's efforts came in the second half when Octavio brought a flying save out of Phil Parkes.

Brooking also looked good for England and Pejic did little wrong after his late call-up due to Peter Storey's injury. Despite the bulk of the possession being with Portugal, the England team held firm and there was a solid look about the defence. Portugal never really looked like scoring.

There was a sad postscript to this match, which came at the end of April 1974 when Sir Alf Ramsey was sacked from his position as team manager. It was a very sad end for the man who kept his promise and brought the World Cup to England in 1966. Alas, because of the way of things in England, his failures would probably

be as well remembered as his successes. Yet his overall results whilst in charge were tremendous and, for the record, look like this:

P	W	D	L	F	A
113	69	27	17	224	98

> 12th match v Portugal.
> Debuts for Parkes, Pejic, Dobson, Watson, Bowles and Brooking.
> Sir Alf Ramsey's last match in charge of the team.
> Portugal's Correia also known as 'Artur'; Oliveira as 'Toni'; Coelho as 'Humberto'; Machado as 'Octavio'; A.Silva as 'Arnaldo'; Costa as 'Valtir'; da Silva as 'Romeu'.

Wales v England Home Championship

Played on Saturday, 11 May 1974 at Ninian Park, Cardiff.

Wales: T.J.S.Phillips (Chelsea); P.S.Roberts (Portsmouth), J.G.Roberts (Birmingham C), D.F.Roberts (Oxford Utd), R.J.Thomas (Derby Co), T.C.Yorath (Leeds Utd), J.F.Mahoney (Stoke C), A.K.Villars (Cardiff C), G.I.Reece (Cardiff C), R.T.Davies (Portsmouth), L.James (Burnley). Subs: L.Cartwright (Coventry C) for P.Roberts and D.P.Smallman (Wrexham) for Davies.
England: P.L.Shilton (Leicester C); D.J.Nish (Derby Co), M.Pejic (Stoke C), E.W.Hughes (Liverpool, captain), R.L.McFarland (Derby Co), C.Todd (Derby Co), J.K.Keegan (Liverpool), C.Bell (Man City), K.Weller (Leicester C), S.Bowles (QPR), M.R.Channon (Southampton).

Half-time 0-1   Full-time 0-2

Ref: R.McFadden (Northern Ireland)
Att: 26,000

WITH caretaker manager Joe Mercer at the helm, England began the Home Championship with a difficult match in Cardiff. The game began in a scrappy fashion and there were few chances in the early stages.

However, once England had settled into a rhythm the promise began to show through. Good, direct football made a refreshing appearance and Wales struggled to resist the England surges. Mike Channon looked particularly lively and he was a constant thorn to the home rearguard. With Keith Weller settling into a midfield role there was much more purpose in the visitors' attack.

The vital breakthrough came in the 35th minute and it was a fine move that led to the goal. Colin Todd, looking distinctly classy in the Bobby Moore mould, began the move by finding Weller down the right. A lovely one-two with Channon enabled Weller to reach the by-line before he centred hard and low. Phillips palmed the ball out, but Stan Bowles was on the spot to score from the rebound.

Wales gave their usual display full of heart and passion, but on this occasion they lacked any real authority or penetration. England's back-four looked very solid with both full-backs giving excellent displays.

The second half belonged almost

entirely to England. Colin Bell missed two good chances from close range and England still had to see the best of the Manchester City star at this level. Channon and Bowles both forced Phillips into full-length saves and, as Wales retaliated, their best player, Mahoney, brought the best out of Peter Shilton. The goalkeeper brilliantly turning over Mahoney's superb 20-yard volley.

That save had come moments after England had added a deserved second goal. It came in the 55th minute and was somewhat fortuitous. Bowles played a short corner back to David Nish and the full-back's long cross deceived the Welsh defence. Kevin Keegan got a touch which completely fooled Villars, who was standing on the goal-line. The Cardiff player missed with his attempted clearance and the ball trickled slowly over the line.

It was nice for Joe Mercer to start with a win and already his style had shone through in the positive way that England had gone about their business.

> 86th match v Wales.
> Debut for Weller.
> Hughes captain for the first time.
> Joe Mercer's first match as temporary manager.

England v Home Championship Northern Ireland

Played on Wednesday, 15 May 1974 at Wembley Stadium.

England: P.L.Shilton (Leicester C); D.J.Nish (Derby Co), M.Pejic (Stoke C), E.W.Hughes (Liverpool, captain), R.L.McFarland (Derby Co), C.Todd (Derby Co), J.K.Keegan (Liverpool), C.Bell (Man City), M.R.Channon (Southampton), S.Bowles (QPR), K.Weller (Leicester C). Subs: N.Hunter (Leeds Utd) for McFarland and F.S.Worthington (Leicester C) for Bowles.
Northern Ireland: P.A.Jennings (Spurs); P.J.Rice (Arsenal), S.Nelson (Arsenal), W.J.O'Kane (Nottm Forest), A.Hunter (Ipswich T), T.Cassidy (Newcastle Utd), B.Hamilton (Ipswich T), D.Clements (Everton), S.J.Morgan (Aston Villa), S.B.McIlroy (Man Utd), R.C.McGrath (Spurs). Subs: T.A.Jackson (Nottm Forest) for O'Kane and M.H.M.O'Neill (Nottm Forest) for Hamilton.

Half-time 0-0   Full-time 1-0

Ref: R.H.Davidson (Scotland) Att: 47,000

NORTHERN Ireland, fresh from their 1-0 win over Scotland, went to Wembley determined as ever to take something home from the game. They certainly made it hard for the England lads with Jennings, especially, in fine form. The new, adventurous England carried on where they had left off against Wales and were soon putting the Irish under pressure.

Mike Channon was again the driving force in an otherwise disappointing attack, Kevin Keegan buzzed around continuously but Stan Bowles never quite got going, despite some nifty footwork at times. Jennings made a brilliant save from Colin Bell on the half-hour, after a lovely

Keith Weller turns away to celebrate his goal against Northern Ireland at Wembley in May 1974.

pass by Channon had set up the Manchester City man. That was a good chance, but although Keith Weller, Bell and Emlyn Hughes worked hard, goal efforts were kept to a minimum by two tight defences.

After the break, England produced a master-stroke. Ten minutes into the half, Joe Mercer took off Bowles and sent on Frank Worthington. Suddenly, the attack looked more threatening as the tactic of using a bigger and stronger front man started to pay off. Yet it was the Irish who should have gone ahead just after Worthington's arrival on the scene. A long free-kick by Alan Hunter was misjudged by his namesake Norman Hunter, another substitute. The latter, knowing he was beaten, blatantly pulled the ball down with his left hand for what looked to everyone an obvious penalty. There was hardly a person in the stadium who could not believe it when the referee allowed play to carry on.

If the Irish thought that was bad, then they were bitterly disappointed some ten minutes later when England took the lead. Worthington was at the hub of the goal. A lovely pass to Channon on the left and then Worthington followed up to get on the end of Channon's cross to nod back across goal where Weller was on hand to head home from close range.

The goal effectively ended the Irish challenge and the last 20 minutes belonged to England with only Jennings standing in the way of a massacre. A

superb double save from Channon brought the house down and then the goalkeeper turned a brilliant Mike Pejic free-kick away from danger. Near the end, Jennings foiled the impressive Worthington with another fine diving save.

In the final analysis it had been Worthington who had made the difference and his introduction was the turning point. Ireland were well served by Clements, McGrath, Cassidy, Alan Hunter and the irrepressible Jennings. All in all an entertaining international which meant that England needed only to draw their match against Scotland to win the title yet again.

> 81st match v Northern Ireland.
> Debut as substitute for Worthington.

Scotland v England Home Championship

Played on Saturday, 18 May 1974 at Hampden Park, Glasgow.

Scotland: D.Harvey (Leeds Utd); W.A.Jardine (Rangers), D.McGrain (Celtic), W.J.Bremner (Leeds Utd), J.A.Holton (Man Utd), J.Blackley (Hibernian), J.Johnstone (Celtic), K.Dalglish (Celtic), J.Jordan (Leeds Utd), D.Hay (Celtic), P.Lorimer (Leeds Utd).

England: P.L.Shilton (Leicester C); D.J.Nish (Derby Co), M.Pejic (Stoke C), E.W.Hughes (Liverpool, captain),

N.Hunter (Leeds Utd), C.Todd (Derby Co), M.R.Channon (Southampton), C.Bell (Man City), F.S.Worthington (Leicester C), K.Weller (Leicester C), M.S.Peters (Spurs).
Subs: D.V.Watson (Sunderland) for Hunter and M.I.Macdonald (Newcastle Utd) for Worthington.

Half-time 2-0   Full-time 2-0
Ref: L.W.Van der Kroft (Holland)
Att: 94,487

IN the pouring rain of Glasgow, Scotland deservedly beat England, but they did not score the goals without a good deal of help from the visiting defenders.

England made a disastrous start to the game. After only four minutes, a swift Scotland move ended with an angled shot from Jordan being deflected past Peter Shilton by the outstretched leg of Mike Pejic. The goal gave Scotland the impetus to take control and in their midfield Bremner, Dalglish and the tireless Hay outplayed their counterparts in the England side. Only Colin Bell looked in good form in the visitors' engine-room as Keith Weller, Emlyn Hughes and Martin Peters tried to blend together.

The other big plus for Scotland was the form of their impish winger, Jimmy Johnstone. He was a thorn to all the England defenders, although Pejic stuck to his task well in trying to deal with him. A move involving the winger brought Scotland's second goal on the half-hour.

Johnstone, Bremner and Lorimer exchanged passes and the move ended with a shot by Dalglish. Again Shilton had the initial shot covered, but again the ball took a wicked deflection off a defender, this time Colin Todd. The goalkeeper must have thought that there was some sort of conspiracy going on, although on both occasions there was an element of misfortune for the 'scorer'.

So, 2-0 down and both goals scored by their own players, England tried hard to come back with Mike Channon the most dangerous of their front runners. But with their midfield so ineffective, the forwards were starved of any real service. Ironically, their two best chances fell to Hughes just before the break, but on both occasions the opportunities were squandered as the England captain fired his shots too high.

At half-time, Joe Mercer decided to replace the struggling Norman Hunter with Dave Watson to try to put a grip on the dangerous Jordan. Then, midway through the half, the manager tried to add some pep to the attack by withdrawing Frank Worthington, who had not played that badly, and sending on Malcolm Macdonald.

But it was Shilton who was still the busier of the two goalkeepers. He made many fine saves as the Scots tried to press home their overall superiority. The home crowd were delighted by their team's display and Hampden was a sea of yellow and blue banners at times. Hay, Lorimer, Jordan, Dalglish and Johnstone all forced Shilton into superb action whilst England hardly raised an attack at the other end.

Bell continued to work tirelessly, with Pejic and Channon also giving a good account of themselves. In the cold light of day, though, it was Shilton who had been the star performer as Scotland prepared for their forthcoming World Cup challenge by obtaining the scalp they preferred above all others. Beating England, for them, sometimes becomes over important and now they had to turn their thoughts quickly to the much more crucial games against Brazil, Yugoslavia and Zaïre in Germany.

92nd match v Scotland.
Own-goals scored by both Pejic and Todd for Scotland, although some sources credit Jordan with Pejic's goal.

England v Argentina   Friendly

Played on Wednesday, 22 May 1974 at Wembley Stadium.

England: P.L.Shilton (Leicester C); E.W.Hughes (Liverpool, captain), A.Lindsay (Liverpool), C.Todd (Derby Co), D.V.Watson (Sunderland), C.Bell (Man City), J.K.Keegan (Liverpool), M.R.Channon (Southampton), F.S.Worthington (Leicester C), K.Weller (Leicester C), T.D.Brooking (West Ham).
Argentina: D.Carnevali (Las Palmas); R.Perfumo (Cruzeiro), F.Sá (Independiente), R.Glaria (San Lorenzo), R.Telch (San Lorenzo), A.Bargas (FC Nantes), A.Balbueno (Independiente), M.Brindisi (Huracán), M.Kempes (Rosario Central), C.Squeo (Racing Club), R.Ayala (Atlético Madrid).
Subs: E.Wolff (River Plate) for Glaria and R.Houseman (Huracán) for Brindisi.

Mike Channon turns away after scoring England's first goal against Argentina at Wembley in May 1974.

Half-time 1-0   Full-time 2-2
Ref: A.Ithurralde (Argentina) Att: 68,000

WHEN this international was arranged it was agreed by the sides that the game would have an Argentinian referee. This was on condition that if England played in Buenos Aires the following summer, then that game would have an English official. Such were the strained relationships between the two Football Associations and after the end of the 90 minutes at Wembley, England might have been regretting the decision to agree to this, as the official at Wembley had a vital bearing on the result.

The match began with both sides testing each other cautiously. England's style of long passes out of defence contrasted interestingly with the more closely woven play of their South American visitors.

As England settled, the midfield play of Colin Bell and Keith Weller showed up well, whilst Mike Channon, Kevin Keegan and Frank Worthington were constantly on the move in attack, giving the Argentinian defenders all sorts of problems. In fact, the whole England side were playing some very good football and right on half-time they took a well-deserved lead with a goal of the highest quality.

Big Dave Watson, a tower of strength throughout, won the ball on the left and passed it square inside to Bell, who then pushed it through a gap in the defence and there was Channon, as sharp as a razor, to guide it past Carnevali and into the net at the far post.

Some strange decisions by the referee angered the crowd and on the field the tempers simmered just below the surface. Before the interval, Hughes clashed with Perfumo and Glaria punched the England skipper in retaliation. Glaria was very lucky not to be sent off and only a diplomatic substitution at half-time, prevented further confrontations. As it was it seemed that England had made the game safe in the 55th minute when they scored a second goal.

A surging run by Bell ended with a crashing shot against the bar. When the ball bounced down, Worthington reacted quickly to hook the ball into the net. It seemed all over but the Argentinians had other ideas. Within two minutes of Worthington's goal they pulled one back. Ayala broke quickly down the right, over came his cross which Peter Shilton could only palm out to Kempes. The long-haired centre-forward wasted no time and promptly hit the ball straight back into the net.

The game was really buzzing now and England so nearly scored again straight from the restart. A fine move down the left by Keegan and Alec Lindsay saw the full-back centre. Once again it was Bell who roared in to hit a splendid volley which struck Carnevali in the chest before being scrambled away. The goalkeeper knew little about the shot and could count himself very lucky to have kept it out.

Argentina kept going with determination but incurred the wrath of the crowd with some of their antics. Amongst all this skullduggery, though, there was the undoubted footballing talent of the Latins. Once, Lindsay did well to clear a goalbound shot from Ayala off his own goal-line. But with only five minutes to go, the referee made the decision which cost England the win they deserved.

A cross came in from the left and Hughes tackled Kempes. The Argentine striker went down, making a meal of a fairly innocuous challenge, and the referee immediately pointed to the penalty-spot. Despite English protests, the kick was taken and Kempes beat Shilton with ease. The crowd were disgusted and the visitors left the field at the end to a crescendo of boos as well as the now infamous chant of 'Animals, Animals' inspired by the antics of the 1966 Argentinian side.

It was disappointing for England, who had given an excellent performance.

6th match v Argentina.
Debut for Lindsay.
Penalty scored for Argentina by Kempes.

East Germany v England
Friendly

Played on Wednesday, 29 May 1974 at the Central Stadium, Leipzig.

East Germany: J.Croy (Motor Zwickau); J.Fritsche (Lokomotive Leipzig), B.Bransch (Carl Zeiss Jena), K.Weise (Carl Zeiss Jena), S.Wätzlich (Dynamo Dresden), J.Pommerenke (1.FC Magdeburg), H.Irmscher (Carl Zeiss Jena), W.Löwe (Lokomotive Leipzig), J.Streich (Hansa Rostock), J.Sparwasser (1.FC Magdeburg), E.Vogel (Carl Zeiss Jena). Sub: M.Hoffmann (1.FC Magdeburg) for Vogel.

England: R.N.Clemence (Liverpool); E.W.Hughes (Liverpool, captain), A.Lindsay (Liverpool), C.Todd (Derby Co), D.V.Watson (Sunderland), J.M.Dobson (Burnley), J.K.Keegan (Liverpool), M.R.Channon (Southampton), F.S.Worthington (Leicester C), C.Bell (Man City), T.D.Brooking (West Ham).

Half-time 0-0   Full-time 1-1
Ref: G.Müncz (Hungary)   Att: 100,000

ENGLAND gained an extremely creditable draw in front of 100,000 people in Leipzig in the first of their three-match summer tour. There were several stories within the story of an always interesting international which was played on a pitch sodden by heavy rain before the kick-off.

The visitors started like an express train. They put together some super attacking football and, with a little more luck, could easily have had two or three goals. Trevor Brooking, Martin Dobson and Mike Channon all hit the German woodwork as England tried desperately to press home their first-half advantage. Dobson was outstanding and Brooking and Frank Worthington were also in fine form. When Channon missed an absolute sitter from five yards out, after an attempted cross-shot by Dave Watson found the Southampton striker, it seemed that England would never score and they looked dejected as they trooped off at the interval. They knew that they should have had some reward for all their good play.

Channon and Kevin Keegan ran their hearts out in their search for a breakthrough but the ball just would not run kindly for them in the vital area. This England dominance continued for 15 minutes after the restart. In that time, Colin Bell had fired in another great shot which again hit the upright and the first goal they so richly deserved would not come.

Then, midway through the second half, the inevitable happened. With England so much on top it had to be the Germans who would score first and sure enough it happened like that. Wätzlich and substitute Hoffmann worked a lovely move down the left. Hoffmann's cross was misheaded by Alec Lindsay and there was Streich to seize on to the mistake and hit a left-foot shot wide of Ray Clemence's desperate dive and into the top corner.

Streich was a very impressive player and his goal showed England how to do it, because within a minute the visitors were level. Brooking was fouled on the edge of the box and England were awarded a free-kick. Channon took it and his low

20-yard drive flashed into the net leaving Croy helpless. It was a fine goal and one they thoroughly deserved, but the effort England had put in over the first 75 minutes began to tell. As they tired the Germans stepped up a gear and in the last 15 minutes they controlled the game.

Sparwasser and Irmscher took over the midfield and orchestrated some superb swift attacks. The dangerous Streich was brilliantly supported by Löwe and they forced Clemence into three magnificent saves as the goalkeeper suddenly found himself working overtime to preserve the draw.

England's adventurous approach to the whole game could be applauded but now, as players were being caught out of position, questions had to be asked.

3rd match v East Germany.

Bulgaria v England
Friendly

Played on Saturday, 1 June 1974 in the Vassil Levski Stadium, Sofia.

Bulgaria: R.Goranov (Lokomotiv Sofia); I.Zafirov (CSKA Sofia), D.Zhechev (Levski Spartak), S.Velitchkov (CSKA Sofia), B.Kolev (CSKA Sofia), D.Penev (CSKA Sofia), V.Voinov (Levski Spartak), K.Bonev (Lokomotiv Plovdiv), A.Mikhailov (Lokomotiv Sofia), K.Borisov (Lokomotiv Sofia), G.Denev (CSKA Sofia). Subs: M.Vassilev (Akademik Sofia) for Voinov and P.Panov (Levski Spartak) for Denev.

England: R.N.Clemence (Liverpool); E.W.Hughes (Liverpool, captain), A.Lindsay (Liverpool), C.Todd (Derby Co), D.V.Watson (Sunderland), J.M.Dobson (Burnley), J.K.Keegan (Liverpool), M.R.Channon (Southampton), F.S.Worthington (Leicester C), C.Bell (Man City), T.D.Brooking (West Ham).

Half-time 0-1   Full-time 0-1
Ref: R.Nyhus (Norway)   Att: 70,000

THE improvement England have so obviously made under Joe Mercer's temporary leadership was again evident in this fine win in the Levski Stadium. Against another of the World Cup qualifiers and in front of a fanatical Bulgarian crowd, England once more showed a refreshing willingness to attack.

However, it was the Bulgarian side that had much the better of the opening 20 minutes. Bonev and Kolev put in some sterling work in their midfield and stretched England with their probing passes. Their best scoring effort, in fact, came from Bonev. The number-eight took a free-kick some 20 yards out and hit his shot superbly, only to see it dip and swerve before striking the bottom of Ray Clemence's upright.

For the remainder of the half, though, England gained a grip on the game. Gradually their extra power and skill took over, with Colin Bell outshining all the other excellent individual displays. His country was at last seeing him the way that the supporters at Maine Road, Manchester saw him week in and week out. In this game Bell was magnificent.

Ten minutes from the end of the first half, England gained the perfect psycho-

logical boost with a well-taken goal by Frank Worthington. That goal meant that the visitors could go into the second half with the confidence that had held them in good stead so often in their recent games. Indeed, in this half they should have had more goals. Mike Channon twice put in good attempts which deserved a better fate. first a superb run saw him leave defenders trailing in his wake before shooting against the far post with goalkeeper Garanov stranded. Then, in another attack, he combined with the classy Worthington to open up a gap in the Bulgarian defence. He crossed to the middle where Martin Dobson roared in to head straight at Garanov.

If England had converted these two chances they would have been marvellous goals but it did emphasise the fine form that Channon had shown in recent internationals. He had now hit the woodwork in three consecutive games and must have wondered what he had to do to score.

England still had one problem to cure. If they could find a top notch goalscorer to finish off all the chances they created, then they would indeed have been a formidable force..

3rd match v Bulgaria.

Yugoslavia v England
Friendly

Played on Wednesday, 5 June 1974 at the Red Star Stadium, Belgrade.

Yugoslavia: E.Marić (Velež Mostar); P.Krivokuća (Red Star Belgrade), I.Buljan (Hajduk Split), V.Bogičević (Red Star Belgrade), J.Katalinski (FK Željezničar), D.Mužinić (Hajduk Split), I.Petković (FC Troyes), B.Oblak (Hajduk Split), I.Šurjak (Hajduk Split), J.Aćimović (Red Star Belgrade), D.Džajić (Red Star Belgrade). Subs: E.Hadziabdić (FK Željezničar) for Krivokuća and D.Bajević (Velež Mostar) for Mužinić.

England: R.N.Clemence (Liverpool); E.W.Hughes (Liverpool, captain), A.Lindsay (Liverpool), C.Todd (Derby Co), D.V.Watson (Sunderland), J.M.Dobson (Burnley), J.K.Keegan (Liverpool), M.R.Channon (Southampton), F.S.Worthington (Leicester C), C.Bell (Man City), T.D.Brooking (West Ham). Sub: M.I.Macdonald (Newcastle Utd) for Worthington.

Half-time 1-1   Full-time 2-2
Ref: S.Gonella (Italy)   Att: 90,000

ENGLAND completed their tour of Eastern Europe with another superb team performance against yet another World Cup qualifier. Yugoslavia were a tough nut and a passionate crowd made it a real test for the new spirit of this England side.

The visitors made a fine start, taking the lead after only six minutes. A corner by Kevin Keegan reached Dave Watson and then on to Trevor Brooking. Brooking then fired in a shot which was blocked on the line, but Mike Channon was razor-sharp to knock in the rebound and emphasise what a fine tour he had enjoyed.

Yugoslavia were spurred into action by the goal and they were inspired by their brilliant skipper Džajić. The left winger, not for the first time against England, was in fine form and his educated left-foot produced an equalizer on 23 minutes. His fine cross was headed out by Dave Watson to Colin Bell, who was a little slow to react. The Yugoslavs needed no second look at an error and Šurjak picked up the ball, crossed to the far post and Petkovic headed in.

It was nip and tuck for the remainder of the half. Colin Todd and Watson were superb at the heart of the defence and Bell covered every inch of the Red Star stadium. Both teams played some exhillarating football and it certainly was an international of the highest quality. Yugoslavia were served spendidly by Bogicevic and Acmovic in midfield and Šurjak was a constant danger alongside the irrepressible Džajić.

Seven minutes after the interval, the crowd erupted as Yugoslavia took the lead. Again Watson headed out from his area but this time the ball dropped for Oblak some 30 yards out. The number-eight let fly without hesitation and it could have gone anywhere, but Oblak had hit it perfectly and the ball arrowed right into the top corner of Ray Clemence's net with the goalkeeper helpless. It was a marvellous strike and a super goal.

England refused to give up, though, and with Channon and Keegan chasing everything the least they deserved was an equalizer. Fifteen minutes from the end they gained their due reward. Emlyn Hughes and Alec Lindsay combined for the substitute Malcolm Macdonald to nodd the ball forward. As it dropped, there was Keegan diving headlong amongst the Yugoslavs' feet to bravely head home.

Right near the end, England almost snatched a winner. Lindsay sent a long through-pass forward which split the defence and left Macdonald with a clear run at goal. With only Maric to beat, he drew the goalkeeper, took careful aim, but just sent his shot the wrong side of the left-hand post. It would have been an incredible win, but having said that, in many ways the draw was the right result.

It certainly was a splendid way for Joe Mercer to end his brief, but always entertaining, handling of the national side. It only remained to be seen if new man Don Revie could continue his good work.

> 11th match v Yugoslavia.
> Joe Mercer's last match as temporary manager.

England European Championship
v Czechoslovakia Qualifier

Played on Wednesday, 30 October 1974 at Wembley Stadium.

England: R.N.Clemence (Liverpool); P.E.Madeley (Leeds Utd), E.W.Hughes (Liverpool, captain), J.M.Dobson (Burnley), D.V.Watson (Sunderland), N.Hunter (Leeds Utd), G.C.J.Francis (QPR), C.Bell (Man City), F.S.Worthington (Leicester C), M.R.Channon (Southampton), J.K.Keegan (Liverpool).
Subs: T.D.Brooking (West Ham) for Dobson and D.Thomas (QPR) for Worthington.
Czechoslovakia: I.Viktor (Dukla Prague); J.Pivarník (Slovan Bratislava), V.Varadin (Spartak Trnava), P.Bičovský (Union

Kevin Keegan looks on as Mike Channon (hidden) beats the Czech defence to score at Wembley in October 1974.

Colin Bell is flat out after scoring England's second goal against Czechoslovakia at Wembley.

New manager Don Revie with Liverpool's Emlyn Hughes before the game against the Czechs.

Teplice), Jo.Capcović (Slovan Bratislava), A.Ondruš (Slovan Bratislava), M.Masný (Slovan Bratislava), I.Pekárik (Slovan Bratislava), J.Švehlík (Slovan Bratislava), M.Gajdůšek (Dukla Prague), P.Stratil (Union Teplice).
Subs: R.Vojáček (Baník Ostrava) for Capkovic and L.Kuna (Spartak Trnava) for Bičovský.

Half-time 0-0   Full-time 3-0
Ref: M.Kitabdjian (France)   Att: 85,000

A NEW manager, a new strip and a new challenge as England set off on their European Championship quest with a convincing victory over Czechoslovakia. Don Revie has been given the reins after

England players wave to the crowd after beating Czechoslovakia 3-0 before 85,000 fans.

Joe Mercer's cameo rule and his first move was to give England a new outfit. Still white shirts and blue shorts, but each with a red, white and blue stripe down the sides. Very bright and a marketing man's dream!

As for the game, England took a long time to settle it after missing several good chances early on. Three times in the opening 15 minutes the home side should have scored. Mike Channon, twice, and Frank Worthington both missed from good positions and all too often the frustrations built up as the Czechs doggedly held out. Channon's two efforts were bad misses as he headed and then volleyed over the bar from close in after being set up by lovely crosses from Worthington. Worthington himself then went close when his header hit the upright after a corner by Emlyn Hughes. Even then, Channon might have scored from the rebound.

The match could and should have been all over by half-time, but as it was England had to wait until the 65th minute to finally reach the turning point. Revie made a double substitution, bringing on Dave Thomas and Trevor Brooking, and it proved a master-stroke.

Immediately the pair made their presence felt and within five minutes, Thomas made the first goal. The winger soon started to give his marker Varadin problems, and one run down the right ended with the defender tripping the England man. Thomas took the free-kick himself and floated the ball in for Channon to

atone for his earlier misses by leaping high to head past Viktor.

That goal was just the lift England badly needed at that stage and within ten minutes of the opening goal they had another to celebrate. A break by the ever-willing Channon ended with a superb diagonal cross which Kevin Keegan dummied cleverly, allowing Bell to come in with a beautifully guided low shot. Almost at once it was 3-0. Again the Bell-Channon combination did the trick, first when Bell sent Channon galloping down the left, and then when Channon's cross came over for Bell to follow up at high speed to head home a magnificent goal.

Bell had gained his reward in his best game for England so far, and with the solid Dave Watson and the promising Gerry Francis also giving fine displays then it all augered well for the future. Needless to say Revie could barely hide his delight, and neither could the crowd.

> 7th match v Czechoslovakia.
> Debuts for G.Francis and, as substitute, D.Thomas.
> Don Revie's first match in charge.

England v Portugal
European Championship Qualifier

Played on Wednesday, 20 November 1974 at Wembley Stadium.

England: R.N.Clemence (Liverpool);

P.E.Madeley (Leeds Utd), T.Cooper (Leeds Utd), C.Bell (Man City), D.V.Watson (Sunderland), E.W.Hughes (Liverpool, captain), G.C.J.Francis (QPR), M.R.Channon (Southampton), A.J.Clarke (Leeds Utd), T.D.Brooking (West Ham), D.Thomas (QPR).
Subs: C.Todd (Derby Co) for Cooper and F.S.Worthington (Leicester C) for Clarke.
Portugal: V.Damas (Sporting Lisbon); A.Soares (Benfica), F.Sardinha (Vitória Guimarães), A.Teixeira (FC Porto), H.Coelho (Benfica), C.Alinho (Sporting Lisbon), T.Néné (Benfica), J.Alves (Boavista), V.Martino (Benfica), O.Machado (Vitória Setúbal), F.Faria (Sporting Lisbon).
Subs: A.Oliveira (FC Porto) for Néné and R.da Silva (Vitória Guimarães) for Faria.

Half-time 0-0   Full-time 0-0
Ref: A.Buchelli (Swizerland)   Att: 70,750

DON Revie discovered just how hard international football could be after this visit by Portugal to Wembley. The opposition came intent on not losing and showed precious little inclination to go forward. On a rainy night it was obvious from the start just how Portugal wanted to play.

Funneling everyone back into defence every time England had possession, they frustrated the home side with some fierce tackles and some unceremonious clearances. When England did find a way through the defensive barrier, they then came up against yet another continental goal-

Left: **Action in the Portuguese goalmouth at Wembley in November 1974.** *Right:* **Mick Channon rides a tackle from Coelho.**

keeper who saved a good performance for Wembley.

In the 20th minute, a fine move down the right between Colin Bell, Trevor Brooking and Mike Channon ended when a close-range shot by Dave Thomas was somehow kept out by a spectacular leap from Damas. That goal attempt was a rare moment of excitement as usually, England's efforts were bogged down in midfield.

The second half was almost as bad with no significant improvement. The England forwards repeatedly, and somewhat annoyingly, fell into the Portuguese offside trap, thus irritating the crowd. England had no one prepared to hold the ball and try to dribble at the defence.

Terry Cooper was unlucky in his comeback match, his first for two years, as he lasted only 25 minutes. A hard tackle left him limping and he had to leave the field.

All through the second half, goal chances were at a premium, although Damas saved well from Channon five minutes from the end after Frank Worthington's header from a Thomas cross had set him up. Portugal's only threat came from the lively Néné but his good moments were few and far between and all too often he was left on his own upfield.

> 13th match v Portugal.
> Portugal's Soares also known as 'Artur'; Sardinha as 'Osvaldinho'; Coelho as 'Humberto'; Machado as 'Octavio'; Faria as 'Chico'; da Silva as 'Romeu'.

England v West Germany   Friendly

Played on Wednesday, 12 March 1975 at Wembley Stadium.

England: R.N.Clemence (Liverpool); S.J.Whitworth (Leicester C), I.T.Gillard (QPR), C.Bell (Man City), D.V.Watson (Sunderland), C.Todd (Derby Co), A.J.Ball (Arsenal, captain), M.R.Channon (Southampton), M.I.Macdonald (Newcastle Utd), A.A.Hudson (Stoke C), J.K.Keegan (Liverpool).

West Germany: J.Maier (Bayern Munich); R.Bonhof (Borussia Mönchengladbach),

England skipper Alan Ball and the great Franz Beckenbauer of West Germany exchange pennants before the game at Wembley in March 1975.

H.H.Vogts (Borussia Mönchengladbach), K.H.Körbel (Eintracht Frankfurt), F.Beckenbauer (Bayern Munich), B.Cullmann (1.FC Cologne), M.Ritschel (Kickers Offenbach), H.Wimmer (Borussia Mönchengladbach), E.Kostedde

Above: Colin Bell (arms raised) has just scored England's first goal against the West Germans. *Below:* Alan Ball seems upset at the end of the game. Alan Hudson is the other England player.

(Kickers Offenbach), H.Flohe (1.FC Cologne), B.Hölzenbein (Eintracht Frankfurt).
Subs: H.Kremers (FC Schalke 04) for Wimmer and J.Heynckes (Borussia Mönchengladbach) for Kostedde.

Half-time 1-0   Full-time 2-0

Ref: A.Schaut (Belgium)   Att: 98,000

ENGLAND celebrated their 100th international at Wembley Stadium by beating the World Champions, West Germany. It was their first victory over their old enemies since that famous day in July 1966. England played very well and produced some terrific football. Despite the dreadful weather the stadium was nearly full and the 98,000 people thoroughly enjoyed the rain-soaked night.

The Germans were missing some of their star players with the likes of Müller, Grabowski, Overath, Breitner, Netzer and Hoeness, all out for various reasons, but right from the start it was England who made all the running. New cap Alan Hudson made a sensational debut in midfield and he looked as though he was a seasoned international as he strode majestically through his task. He slowed things down to just the pace he wanted and sprayed delightful passes all over the lush Wembley turf. At the back Colin Todd was outstanding and, along with the rock-like Dave Watson, bottled up the German attack with ease. The other big hit on the night was Kevin Keegan. He was everywhere and had his best game yet for his country.

England took the lead in the 25th minute. Another of the night's successes, Steve Whitworth, made a positive run down the right wing, only to be upended by Bonhof's tackle. Hudson took the free-kick and cleverly flighted the ball into the middle for Colin Bell to hit a splendid volley past Maier, albeit with the help of a deflection. It was a goal England thoroughly deserved and they nearly added others as attack followed attack. A rocket shot by Malcolm Macdonald, from Keegan's pass, was brilliantly saved by Maier. Shortly afterwards Macdonald put in another good effort when he chipped just over after a lovely through-pass by Hudson.

The Germans made little impact on the first half, although near the break an attack ended with a double effort by Holzenbein and Ritschel. The first shot was blocked by Ian Gillard and then the rebound shot was blocked inadvertently by a German defender before being cleared.

After the break, England continued to hold all the aces. Bell went close with one good effort and so did Gillard. Bell and Alan Ball provided endless running and boundless energy to give England the edge, although the Germans, never easy to beat, also had good service from Cullmann and Flohe, but the immaculate Beckenbauer was not quite the force he has been in previous encounters.

Midway through the second half, England clinched the result with a decisive second goal. Mike Channon flicked the ball to Ball advancing to the right by-line. Ball, revelling in being made captain, centred to the far post where Macdonald leapt high to head his first goal for his country. The crowd's jubilation was obvious and in the last minute Keegan came desperately close to scoring the goal his performance so richly deserved, but his brilliant chip shot hit the crossbar before being hacked away by the Germans.

The Germans' substitution of Kremers and Heynckes for Wimmer and Kostedde made little difference and the visitors ended up a well-beaten side.

> 13th match v West Germany.
> Debuts for Whitworth, Gillard and Hudson.
> England's 100th match at Wembley.

Malcolm Macdonald celebrates one of his five goals against Cyprus at Wembley in April 1975.

England v Cyprus
European Championship Qualifier

Played on Wednesday, 16 April 1975 at Wembley Stadium.

England: P.L.Shilton (Stoke C); P.E.Madeley (Leeds Utd), T.K.Beattie (Ipswich T), C.Bell (Man City), D.V.Watson (Sunderland), C.Todd (Derby Co), A.J.Ball (Arsenal, captain), M.R.Channon (Southampton), M.I.Macdonald (Newcastle Utd), A.A.Hudson (Stoke C), J.K.Keegan (Liverpool).
Sub: D.Thomas (QPR) for Channon.

Cyprus: M.Alkiviadis (EPA Larnaca); K.Kovis (Anorthosis Famagusta), K.Kureas (Olympiakos, Greece), N.Stefanos (Apoel Nicosia), N.Pantziaras (Apoel Nicosia), D.Kitzas (Paralimni), N.Kharalambous (Omonia Nicosia), G.Savva (Omonia Nicosia), M.Markou (Apoel Nicosia), L.Theodorou (EPA Larnaca), A.Styliandou (Apoel Nicosia). Subs: A.Konstantinou I (AEL Limassol) for Alkiviadis and A.Konstantinou II (Paralimni) for Kharalambous.

Half-time 2-0   Full-time 5-0
Ref: M.Hirviniemi (Finland) Att: 65,000

THIS was a night to remember for Malcolm Macdonald as the Newcastle centre-forward scored all five of England's goals, a post-war record. It was an easy victory for England and consolidated their position at the top of their group.

Cyprus had little to offer and right from the start it was all England as wave after wave of attacks swept forward. Unfortunately, there was a certain predictability about England's play and they lacked the necessary guile to really ram home their superiority. However, they were soon in front and only two minutes had gone when Kevin Keegan was brought down. Alan Hudson flighted in the free-kick and in came Macdonald with a powerful downward header wide of the flat-footed Alkiviades.

It would have seemed that England had gained the perfect start but they tended to slip back into their frustrating ways of not being able to break down a massed defence, which was all that Cyprus had to offer. True, chances were created but the midfield failed to punish the Cypriots to the full. But luck was on the side of Alkiviades, who made some incredible saves, usually without knowing too much about them.

Mike Channon and Colin Bell both missed narrowly and Macdonald himself missed one open goal. But then, after 35 minutes, England found another way through, as Bell's cross was met by a thumping left-foot shot by Macdonald.

By half-time, though, the crowd had become a little impatient at England not asserting the superiority they had so obviously enjoyed. But their frustration was eased somewhat in the 53rd minute when Macdonald brought the house down by completing his hat-trick. Paul Madeley, so often helping the attack, swung over yet another centre which Keegan switched back across goal for Macdonald to kneel down and nod the ball into the net.

Kevin Beattie then saw a goal disallowed after putting the ball in the net. He had injured the goalkeeper in the process and Cyprus had to bring on a replacement, but the new goalkeeper had little chance with the two goals that followed. England also made a substitution, bringing on Dave Thomas for Channon, and his first touch laid on goal number-four for both Macdonald and England. It was a cracker too as the centre-forward powered in another fine header from Thomas' perfect cross. To finish off the night, the same combination gave England their fifth goal with yet another Macdonald header.

So, it was a personal triumph for Macdonald, who had set up a post-war record. Indeed, only four other players

have scored five for England in one match. Howard Vaughton in 1882, Steve Bloomer in 1896, G.O.Smith in 1899 and Willie Hall in 1938. 'Super Mac' therefore joined a very exclusive club.

As for England, there was certainly some justifiable criticism of their performance, but a 5-0 win in any international must be considered a good result. It certainly enhanced their chances of qualifying for the finals of this competition.

> 1st match v Cyprus.
> Debut for Beattie.
> Five goals for Macdonald equalled the record in one match.
> Cyprus' Kovis also known as 'Nikolau'; Stefanos as 'Michael'; Savva as 'Gregory'.

Cyprus v England
European Championship Qualifier

Played on Sunday, 11 May 1975 in the Tsirion Stadium, Limassol.

Cyprus: A.Konstantinou I (AEL Limassol); K.Kovis (Anorthosis Famagusta), N.Pantziaras (Apoel Nicosia), M.Stefanos (Apoel Nicosia), S.Stylianov (AEL Limassol), D.Kitzas (Panathinaikos), N.Kharalambous (Omonia Nicosia), G.Savva (Omonia Nicosia), T.Konstantinou (AEK Athens), A.Panayotou (EPA Larnaca), A.Miamiliotis (Apoel Nicosia). Subs: A.G.Kokos (Omonia Nicosia) for Panayotou and K.Papettas (Olympiakos Nicosia) for Miamiliotis.

England: R.N.Clemence (Liverpool); S.J.Whitworth (Leicester C), T.K.Beattie (Ipswich T), C.Bell (Man City), D.V.Watson (Sunderland), C.Todd (Derby Co), A.J.Ball (Arsenal, captain), M.R.Channon (Southampton), M.I.Macdonald (Newcastle Utd), J.K.Keegan (Liverpool), D.Thomas (QPR). Subs: E.W.Hughes (Liverpool) for Beattie and D.Tueart (Man City) for Thomas.

Half-time 0-1 **Full-time 0-1**

Ref: T.Stanev (Bulgaria) Att: 21,000

ENGLAND travelled to Cyprus for this European Championship match which coincided with the opening of the new Tsirion Stadium in Limassol. It was a full house as 21,000 people packed into it with 5,000 of them being British troops stationed on the island, so there was no lack of support. Everything was set as they all basked under a glorious Meditteranean sun waiting in anticipation of what they hoped would be a fine international. Sadly, the game did not live up to their expectations.

The new pitch was barely playable. Bumpy and heavily sanded, it meant that the ball rarely ran true and England found it very difficult to master the awkward conditions. However, they did manage a fine start as after only six minutes Kevin Keegan forced a corner on the left. Dave Thomas took it and there was Keegan leaping high to direct a fine header into the far top corner.

It should have been the tonic England needed but, alas, they were unable to build on it. Cyprus, with Stefanos, Tasos Konstantinou and Savva all prominent, tackled with determination and stifled the best of a limited England attack. Malcolm Macdonald, trying to repeat his sensational feat against Cyprus at Wembley, saw a shot hacked off the line and the same fate happened to a Mike Channon shot. These positive moments became less frequent as the game wore on and at half-time there had been no change in the scoreline.

Kevin Beattie was injured just before the break and Emlyn Hughes replaced him. After half-time, Channon and Thomas switched wings in an effort to spice up the attack and it almost worked when a typical Channon run ended with a shot against a post. The midfield players worked tremendously hard, but the forwards too often lost control at the vital moment.

Ray Clemence had been little more than a spectator as Colin Todd and Dave Watson coped easily with the poor Cypriot attack and the nearest we came to a goal in the second-half was when Macdonald's back header was again cleared off the line, this time by full-back Kovis.

Dennis Tueart replaced Thomas for the last quarter of an hour to win his first cap, but it made little difference to the pattern of a poor game. Nevertheless, England were now three points clear at the top of their group with games in Czechoslovakia and Portugal to come in the autumn.

> 2nd match v Cyprus.
> Debut for Tueart, as substitute.
> Cyprus' Kovis also known as 'Nikjolau'; Stefanos as 'Michael'; Savva as 'Gregory'; T.Konstantinou as 'Tasos'.

Northern Ireland v England Home Championship

Played on Saturday, 17 May 1975 at Windsor Park, Belfast.

Northern Ireland: P.A.Jennings (Spurs); P.J.Rice (Arsenal), W.J.O'Kane (Nottm Forest), C.J.Nicholl (Aston Villa),

A.Hunter (Ipswich T), D.Clements (Everton), B.Hamilton (Ipswich T), M.H.M.O'Neill (Nottm Forest), D.W.Spence (Bury), S.B.McIlroy (Man Utd), T.A.Jackson (Nottm Forest).
Sub: T.Finney (Sunderland) for Hamilton.

England: R.N.Clemence (Liverpool); S.J.Whitworth (Leicester C), E.W.Hughes (Liverpool), C.Bell (Man City), D.V.Watson (Sunderland), C.Todd (Derby Co), A.J.Ball (Arsenal, captain), C.Viljoen (Ipswich T), M.I.Macdonald (Newcastle Utd), J.K.Keegan (Liverpool), D.Tueart (Man City).
Sub: M.R.Channon (Southampton) for Macdonald.

Half-time 0-0 **Full-time 0-0**

Ref: T.H.Reynolds (Wales) Att: 36,000

THIS was England's first visit to Belfast in nearly five years and the 36,000 crowd were very generous in their applause as the teams walked out on to the Windsor Park pitch. Political unrest has left the people of Northern Ireland with a passion to see top international sport and their relief at England's visit was plain to see and hear. Sadly, they were deserving of a much better game than this.

The ground looked a picture at the kick-off, with a lush green pitch ready for action. Both sides struggled to get going, however, and the play quickly slipped into mediocrity. In midfield, Colin Bell, Alan Ball and new cap Colin Viljoen tried hard for England, but their play was too predictable. The flair and penetration was missing from this vital area and, as a result, the forward line had little effective service.

Kevin Keegan buzzed around up front and was England's most dangerous player. Bell produced some good work in the first half and Colin Todd did little wrong at the back. The problem with England's approach play was that it was too laborious, too often going square instead of forwards, an old failing that, alas, kept recurring.

The Irish also had their problems. Indeed, it was not until after half-time that they began to find their feet. Suddenly realising that England were there for the taking, they piled on the pressure. The tall, blond Spence caused havoc with his ungainly style, and McIlroy and Clements took control of the midfield. But it was all to no avail as the final finish was not there to capitalise on good approach play.

Twice McIlroy missed close-range chances after Spence had set him up, and then Spence headed inches wide after crosses by Clements and Rice. Losing Hamilton, injured by a tackle by Dennis Tueart, upset Ireland's rhythm a little and gradually the pressure eased on the England defence.

For the rest the game drifted into obscurity with neither side either capable of or deserving of victory.

> 82nd match v Northern Ireland.
> Debut for Viljoen.

England v Wales Home Championship

Played on Wednesday, 21 May 1975 at Wembley Stadium.

England: R.N.Clemence (Liverpool);

S.J.Whitworth (Leicester C), I.T.Gillard (QPR), G.C.J.Francis (QPR), D.V.Watson (Sunderland), C.Todd (Derby Co), A.J.Ball (Arsenal, captain), M.R.Channon (Southampton), D.E.Johnson (Ipswich T), C.Viljoen (Ipswich T), D.Thomas (QPR).
Sub: B.Little (Aston Villa) for Channon.

Wales: W.D.Davies (Everton); R.J.Thomas (Derby Co), M.E.Page (Birmingham C), J.F.Mahoney (Stoke C), J.G.Roberts (Birmingham C), L.Phillips (Aston Villa), A.T.Griffiths (Wrexham), B.Flynn (Burnley), D.P.Smallman (Everton), J.B.Toshack (Liverpool), L.James (Burnley).
Sub: D.Showers (Cardiff C) for Smallman.

Half-time 1-0 **Full-time 2-2**

Ref: J.W.Paterson (Scotland) Att: 51,000

A CROWD of 51,000 people, which included Prime Minister Harold Wilson, turned up at Wembley on a lovely early summer's evening to enjoy a good game which Wales came so close to winning.

England began well enough and there was no hint of the drama to come later. They took the lead as early as the tenth minute when a good cross-field pass by Colin Todd was picked up by Gerry Francis. He moved forward before releasing the ball to Colin Viljoen, who made a brilliant burst forward, taking possession and firing a fierce shot which hit Phillips and rebounded perfectly for David Johnson to score easily with a close-range header.

So, England had the boost of an early goal and they confidently kept control as the half wore on. Despite Alan Ball and Francis both trying to play their club role of central midfielder, and sometimes getting in each other's way, England attacked frequently and Johnson came desperately close to making it 2-0 after another splendid Viljoen run had set him up for a header.

At this stage everything pointed to an easy win for England. At half-time they were still in command and should have had more goals to show for their dominance. After the break, though, the game changed direction. Wales suddenly came to life following a corner won by Toshack. James took the kick, Smallman flicked it on and Griffiths headed towards goal. That effort was blocked, but after a terrific scramble Toshack was there to thump a shot into the roof of the net.

That goal was a blow to England but lifted Wales completely. Curiously, the Welsh then sent on Showers for Smallman, a move that might have upset their rhythm, but it had little effect and midway through the half, after another defensive blunder by England, Wales scored a second goal. James took a long throw from the right, Toshack and Dave Watson went for it and the ball bounced off Ian Gillard's thigh before dropping just right for Griffiths to jubilantly put his side ahead.

The Welsh were delighted at England's generosity and sensed a Wembley victory for the first time. But on 70 minutes, England brought on Brian Little to replace Mike Channon and the Aston Villa player was soon making his presence felt with a penetrating run and shot through the middle. It was the cue for England to up their tempo and they looked far more dangerous. With only five minutes to go and with Wales so close to an historic victory, Little gained possession and made

John Toshack has just scored for Wales at Wembley in May 1975.

David Johnson heads home against the Welsh, one of his two debut goals.

a fine run down the right, outpacing Page. He then centred perfectly to the far post and in came Johnson to rescue England with a flashing header.

It was tough on Wales, who in the second half had heroes in Mahoney, Flynn, James and Toshack, but overall there was no denying England's right to a share of the spoils.

87th v Wales.
Debuts for Johnson and, as substitute, Little.
Two debut goals for Johnson.

England v
Scotland Home Championship

Played on Saturday, 24 May 1975 at Wembley Stadium.

England: R.N.Clemence (Liverpool); S.J.Whitworth (Leicester C), T.K.Beattie (Ipswich T), C.Bell (Man City), D.V.Watson (Sunderland), C.Todd (Derby Co) A.J.Ball (Arsenal, captain), M.R.Channon (Southampton), D.E. Johnson (Ipswich T), G.C.J.Francis (QPR), J.K.Keegan (Liverpool).
Sub: D.Thomas (QPR) for Keegan.
Scotland: S.Kennedy (Rangers); W.A.Jardine (Rangers), D.McGrain (Celtic), F.M.Munro (Wolves), G.McQueen (Leeds Utd), B.D.Rioch (Derby Co), K.Dalglish (Celtic), A.Conn (Spurs), D.Parlane (Rangers), E.J.MacDougall (Norwich C), A.Duncan (Hibernian).
Subs: L.Macari (Man Utd) for MacDougall and T.Hutchison (Coventry C) for Duncan.

Half-time 3-1   Full-time 5-1
Ref: R.Glöckner (East Germany)
Att: 98,241

ON YET another splendid Wembley occasion, England produced their best display for some months, although it must be said that the Scots, and goalkeeper Kennedy in particular, contributed to their own downfall.

Scotland made a disastrous opening. On five minutes Gerry Francis played a couple of one-twos with David Johnson and Mike Channon and then let fly from 25 yards. It was a good shot but it seemed a fairly comfortable save for Kennedy. But for some inexplicable reason the goalkeeper

stood rooted to the spot as the ball sped past him. It was a real blow to the visitors and they were visibly shaken. Within two minutes things got worse for them. Francis and Alan Ball combined to set Kevin Keegan away down the right. Over came a lovely centre to the far post and in roared the powerful Kevin Beattie to head home. Kennedy must again take some of the blame as he was caught in no man's land as the cross came over.

With England in command so early they were able to continue with relaxed and enjoyable football, settling into a good rhythm. Francis, Colin Bell and Ball revelled in their domination of the midfield and clever running by all the front players pulled Scotland all over the place. Francis was outstanding as he probed every avenue through the visitors' defence. It was Francis who created a third goal in the 40th minute. Playing another series of one-twos, the move ended when Bell hit a super 20-yard rising shot past Kennedy.

The match looked all over, but immediately Scotland were given a chance to get back into it. Colin Todd was somewhat harshly penalised for hand-ball to give the Scots a slightly fortunate penalty. Rioch's lethal left foot duly converted the spot-kick and Scotland left the field at half-time with some hope to cling to.

The visitors did work harder after the interval and for awhile quelled the rampaging English. McQueen and McGrain tried to tighten the defence with some good play and Conn showed some clever footwork when Scotland put an attack together. But midway through the half, England put an end to this attempted Scottish fight-back. A free-kick was cleverly put through Bell's legs by Ball so that Francis could fire in another long range shot. This time Kennedy was beaten by a deflection and what little confidence was left in the goalkeeper had now evaporated.

Scotland made another token rally as both Parlane and Duncan fired in shots that brushed the outside of Ray Clemence's posts, but England were not to be denied and their fine team performance was completed with a fifth goal. Keegan's header was touched on to the crossbar by the luckless Kennedy only for Johnson to net from the rebound in the ensuing scramble.

After the recent poor displays by England it was refreshing to see everyone contributing effectively. It also meant that England took the Home Championship.

93rd v Scotland.
Rioch scored a penalty for Scotland.

Switzerland v
England   Friendly

Played on Wednesday, 3 Sepember 1975 at the St Jakob Stadium, Basle.

Switzerland: E.Burgener (Lausanne-Sports); J.Stohler (FC Basel), P.Fischbach (FC Zürich), S.Trinchero (FC Sion), G.Guyot (Servette FC), R.Hasler (FC Basel), H.J.Pfister (Servette FC), H.Schild (Young Boys), K.Müller (Servette FC), R.Botteron (FC Zürich), D.Jeandupeux (Girondins Bordeaux).
Sub: R.Elsener (Grasshoppers) for Schild.

Acrobatics by Kevin Beattie, Ted MacDougall and Colin Todd at Wembley in May 1975. England hammered the Scots 5-1.

England: R.N.Clemence (Liverpool); S.J.Whitworth (Leicester C), T.K.Beattie (Ipswich T), C.Todd (Derby Co), D.V.Watson (Man City), G.C.J.Francis (QPR, captain), C.Bell (Man City), M.R.Channon (Southampton), D.E. Johnson (Ipswich T), A.W.Currie (Sheffield Utd), J.K.Keegan (Liverpool). Sub: M.I.Macdonald (Newcastle Utd) for Johnson.

Half-time 1-2   Full-time 1-2
Ref: W.Eschweiler (West Germany)
Att: 25,000

DESPITE a sparkling first 25 minutes, England had a disappointing night in Basle after the Swiss took the initiative on the half-hour. True, they held on for a win but once again many questions were left unanswered.

After only seven minutes England took the lead. Kevin Keegan picked up possession in the centre of the field and hit a good long pass down the right to Mike Channon. The Southampton player outpaced the left-back and then aimed a firm shot to the far post. Burgener did well to get his hands to the ball but could only parry it for Keegan, following up, to shoot home. It was the perfect start for England and for a short while they threatened to tear Switzerland apart.

Five minutes after that goal, Colin Bell's superb pass sent David Johnson clear of the square defence with only the goalkeeper to beat. Burgener came out to meet the striker and clumsily brought him down for a definite penalty. Up stepped Keegan but, alas, justice was not seen to be done as the Liverpool player's shot was saved by Burgener, diving to his right. Keegan had also missed a penalty for his club in the League the previous Saturday.

Despite this set-back, England were still very much in command and almost immediately they scored a second goal. This time a bad pass by Trinchero was intercepted by Johnson, who quickly released a pass that again split the square

defence for Channon to run on to. Channon scored with the minimum of fuss and things looked set for a resounding victory. What went wrong afterwards cannot be easily explained, but from the moment, on the half-hour when Müller headed in a corner by Pfister, after Ray Clemence had completely missed the ball in the air, the Swiss dominated the proceedings.

Clemence had a night he will quickly want to forget and on three other occasions he misjudged crosses from the wings. He also nearly handed Switzerland an equalizer by losing possession to Jeandupeux, only for Dave Watson to save the day with a clearing header.

The Swiss made clever use of their two wingers with Pfister on the right and Jeandupeux on the left a constant menace. In the middle, Müller was always dangerous and Botteron, the star of the night, and Hasler worked so hard to take the initiative away from England. All too often Channon and Johnson were frustratingly caught offside and Clemence continued to make his colleagues' hearts flutter.

However, England's back-four held firm with Colin Todd outstanding and Steve Whitworth, Watson and Kevin Beattie giving excelllent support. England's best player on the night, though, was undoubtedly Bell who covered every blade of grass trying to inspire his teammates. It was Switzerland who created the best second-half chances with Müller, twice, Botteron and Pfister all going close. Pfister's shot at last brought the best out of Clemence.

Tony Currie often looked impressive, but the overall team performance overshadowed his own display. Near the end, England nearly scored a third goal. Substitute Malcolm Macdonald was put through by Keegan, but weight of numbers of Swiss defenders finally edged the Newcastle player out.

11th match v Switzerland.
Keegan missed a penalty for England.
Francis captain for the first time.

Czechoslovakia v England
European Championship Qualifier

Played on Thursday, 30 October 1975 in the Slovan Poli Stadium, Bratislava.

Czechoslovakia: I.Viktor (Dukla Prague); J.Pivarník (Slovan Bratislava), L.Jurkemik (Inter Bratislava), A.Ondruš (Slovan Bratislava), K.Gögh (Slovan Bratislava), P.Bičovský (Union Teplice), L.Knapp (Baník Ostrava), J.Pollák (VSS Košice), M.Masný (Slovan Bratislava), P.Gallis (VSS Košice), Z.Nehoda (Dukla Prague). Sub: K.Dobiaš (Spartak Trnava) for Gögh.

England: R.N.Clemence (Liverpool); P.E.Madeley (Leeds Utd), I.T.Gillard (QPR), C.Todd (Derby Co), R.L.McFarland (Derby Co), G.C.J.Francis (QPR, captain), C.Bell (Man City), M.R.Channon (Southampton), M.I.Macdonald (Newcastle Utd), A.J.Clarke (Leeds Utd), J.K.Keegan (Liverpool). Subs: D.V.Watson (Sunderland) for McFarland and D.Thomas (QPR) for Channon.

Half-time 1-1   Full-time 2-1
Ref:A.Michelotti (Italy)   Att: 45,000

THIS match proved most disappointing for England. Abandoned early the previous night because of thick fog descending on the stadium, the re-run started brightly but ended in failure that would prove costly in the final group analysis.

The first half went so well for England, too. Playing controlled and positive football they dictated so much of the game. Kevin Keegan, Colin Todd and Colin Bell were outstanding and the defenders always kept the Czechs at bay. On the half-hour, England took a deserved lead. Keegan made it with a sparkling run in which he beat two men, slipped a couple of clumsy tackles by Pollák and then cleverly lobbed the ball to Mike Channon, standing at the far post. Channon coolly pulled the ball down and chipped it brilliantly over Viktor and into the net for a fine goal.

The Czechs found it difficult to make any impression on the strong England defence, although Bobby Charlton look-alike, Pollák, was undoubtedly their star as he was always at the hub of everything his side did and looked very impressive. England should have capitalised on their excellent approach play but, alas, their finishing, with Malcolm Macdonald and Alan Clarke both off form, lacked the necessary sharpness. Not adding to their goal was to prove costly to the visitors as, just on the stroke of half-time, the home side equalized.

Masný took a corner and Nehoda came in like an express train to head home at the near post. The crowd were delighted and cheered their team off at the interval. The cheers had hardly subsided after the restart when the Czechs took the lead. Masný, always a threat down the flank, reached the by-line, not for the first time, and centred perfectly for Gallis to tuck away a lovely glancing header.

That was a bitter blow for England but they tried manfully to come back. Bell covered every blade of grass, Keegan chased and harried and Channon ran until exhaustion got the better of him, allowing Dave Thomas to come on for the last quarter of an hour. Unusually, the normally impeccable behaviour of the Czechs was not in evidence. Knapp was continually stopping Bell by unsavoury methods, elbows, pushing, shirt-tugging etc., in fact, anything that would stop the England dynamo. Gögh was booked, and his second-half replacement, Dobiaš, had little intention of playing the ball, rather the man. To sum up the Czech's bad behaviour, even their reserve goalkeeper, Vencel, was dismissed from the substi-tutes' bench after he manhandled the referee. It was all very ugly and clearly had an effect on England as they faded badly before the game ended.

The group table was now wide open and both sides now had fixtures to come in Portugal. They held the key as to who would qualify.

8th match v Czechoslovakia

Portugal v England
European Championship Qualifier

Played on Wednesday, 19 November 1975 at the José Alvalade Stadium, Lisbon.

Portugal: V.Damas (Sporting); F.Rebelo (Vitória Setúbal), R.Rodrigues (Vitória Guimarães), F.Freitas (Belenenses), A.Soares (Benfica), O.Machado (FC Porto), J.Alves (Boavista), A.Oliveira (Benfica), T.Néné (Benfica), V.Batista (Benfica), M.Moinhos (Benfica).
Subs: A.Lima (Boavista) for Rebelo and A.Carolino (Boavista) for Rodrigues.
England: R.N.Clemence (Liverpool); S.J.Whitworth (Leicester C), T.K.Beattie (Ipswich T), P.E.Madeley (Leeds Utd), D.V.Watson (Man City), C.Todd (Derby Co), J.K.Keegan (Liverpool), M.R.Channon (Southampton), M.I.Macdonald (Newcastle Utd), G.C.J.Francis (QPR, captain), T.D.Brooking (West Ham).
Subs: D.Thomas (QPR) for Madeley and A.J.Clarke (Leeds Utd) for Macdonald.

Half-time 1-1   Full-time 1-1
Ref: E.Linemayr (Austria)   Att: 30,000

THE current limitations in the English game were again evident in England's performance in this vital European Championship match. They needed a win to put pressure on Czechoslovakia for their final game in Cyprus four days later, but failed. And in the first-half especially, they looked a poor side.

Portugal, led impressively from mid-field by Alves, Octavio and Toni, began well and all the early pressure came from them. On 15 minutes they took the lead. Paul Madeley fouled Néné 25 yards out to give away a free-kick. Up stepped Rodrigues to bend a superb shot around the defensive wall and into the top corner with Ray Clemence left groping. It was a disastrous start for England and things could have been made much worse over the next 20 minutes.

Colin Todd missed a cross from Batista, leaving Toni with a glorious chance which he squandered, and then a superb through-ball by Toni sent Alves clear, only for the forward's shot to go over. Had those two chances been taken, then England's European Championship hopes would have been all over. But fortune was on their side and slowly but surely they began to come to terms with things. With five minutes of the half to go, Portugal paid the price of some unfair tactics on the edge of their area.

Mike Channon was fouled as he went for a chip by Madeley and from the free-kick, Gerry Francis backheeled to Chan-non and his deflected shot found the net. That goal gave England a much-needed boost as they had struggled for much of the half. Todd was still obviously suffer-ing from his niggling groin injury and Kevin Beattie also had a torrid time.

After the interval, though, England played much better and they looked the most likely team to score. In the first 20 minutes of the second half they missed three clear chances. First, Beattie's long pass sent Malcolm Macdonald away. He seemed certain to score but lost control carelessly and ended with a feeble shot. He should have done better. Next, a crossfield pass from Francis found Trevor Brooking, who centred perfectly for Channon. Alas, the Southampton man shot over with his left foot from close range. Finally, a long pass from Madeley found Brooking again. Brooking's flick left Kevin Keegan bearing down on goal, but when Francis was given the shooting chance, the ball flew over the bar.

The remainder of the game was played out with a lot of effort but few oppor-tunities. Brooking's clever vision was prominent and he and Francis were always probing the Portuguese defence with some raking passes. Todd and Beattie had much better second halves and the Portuguese attack was easily held. Their stars were the three midfield men already mentioned, whilst the tiny Alves rekindled memories of his grandfather by similarly wearing gloves during play.

Now England had to hope that Cyprus could prevent Czechoslovakia from win-ning their final game. It was a forlorn hope that should have been unnecessary.

14th match v Portugal.
Portugal's Soares also known as 'Artur', Oliveira as 'Toni', Machado as 'Octavio' and Lima as 'Tai'.

Wales v England
Friendly

Played on Wednesday, 24 March 1976 at the Racecourse Ground, Wrexham.

Wales: B.W.Lloyd (Wrexham); M.E.Page (Birmingham C), J.P.Jones (Liverpool), T.C.Yorath (Leeds Utd), L.Phillips (Aston Villa), I.P.Evans (Crystal Palace), C.S.Harris (Leeds Utd), B.Flynn (Burn-ley), A.T.Curtis (Swansea C), J.G.Roberts (Birmingham C), A.T.Griffiths (Wrexham).
England: R.N.Clemence (Liverpool); T.J.Cherry (Leeds Utd), P.G.Neal (Liver-pool), M.D.Mills (Ipswich T), P.B.Thompson (Liverpool), M.Doyle (Man City), J.K.Keegan (Liverpool, cap-tain), M.R.Channon (Southampton), P.J.Boyer (Norwich C), T.D.Brooking (West Ham), R.Kennedy (Liverpool).
Subs: D.T.Clement (QPR) for Cherry and P.J.Taylor (Crystal Palace) for Channon.

Half-time 0-0   Full-time 1-2
Ref: I.M.Foote (Scotland)   Att: 21,000

IT WAS no real surprise to see a disjointed display from both sides in this interna-tional which was arranged as part of the Welsh FA's Centenary celebrations. Both sides were largely experimental, having been badly hit by late injuries and withdrawals. England, in fact, took the field with no less than six new caps, and then added two more when Dave Clement and Peter Taylor came on as substitutes. Wales, too, were lacking some key players and they missed the dangerous Toshack more than anyone else.

The first-half was largely devoid of any exciting incident. Both teams struggled to find any rhythm, although England definitely had the better of the half. New captain Kevin Keegan celebrated his appointment with a fine display, and in the midfield he was well supported by Ray Kennedy and Trevor Brooking. Overall, although more organised, England lacked the finish to their attacks.

Phil Boyer missed a good chance on 20 minutes, after Trevor Cherry's cross had eluded Lloyd, and then, for Wales, two long-range shots from their danger man, Harris, brought Ray Clemence into the action. The nearest either team came to scoring, though, was when Keegan dived full length to head a Mick Mills cross just wide.

After the break both sides found some sort of rhythm that had been missing in the first half. Don Revie made two substitutions and in the 71st minute England finally achieved the break-through. Taylor, on for Mike Channon, combined well with Brooking to create an opening for Ray Kennedy to explode a fierce left-foot shot which crashed into the roof of the net. Ten minutes later it was 2-0. Again Brooking made the goal, wrong-footing the Welsh defenders with a clever cross from which Taylor ran in to score.

And that was virtually that until the battling Welsh pulled a goal back in the very last minute. Curtis gained some reward for a hard working display by shooting through a crowd of players.

The game was very much an experi-mental one for England, but at least Don Revie has now had the opportunity to see a few of the fringe players available to him.

Welsh goalkeeper Dai Davies punches clear from an England attack at Cardiff in May 1976. The other Welsh defender is Ian Evans.

88th match v Wales.
Debuts for Cherry, Neal, Doyle, Thompson, Boyer, Kennedy and, as substitutes, Clement and Taylor.
Debut goals for Kennedy and Taylor.
Keegan captain for the first time.
"I was totally elated to make my debut and very proud to pull on the white jersey."
Phil Neal

Wales v
England Home Championship

Played on Saturday, 8 May 1976 at Ninian Park, Cardiff.

Wales: W.D.Davies (Everton); R.J. Thomas (Derby Co), M.E.Page (Birmingham C), J.F.Mahoney (Stoke C), L.Phillips (Aston Villa), I.P.Evans (Crystal Palace), A.T.Curtis (Swansea C), B.Flynn (Burnley), T.C.Yorath (Leeds Utd), J.B.Toshack (Liverpool), L.James (Derby Co).
Subs: D.E.Jones (Norwich C) for Thomas and A.T.Griffiths (Wrexham) for Curtis.
England: R.N.Clemence (Liverpool); D.T.Clement (QPR), M.D.Mills (Ipswich T), B.Greenhoff (Man Utd), R.Kennedy (Liverpool), J.K.Keegan (Liverpool), G.C.J.Francis (QPR, captain), J.S.Pearson (Man Utd), M.A.Towers (Sunderland), P.J.Taylor (Crystal Palace).

Half-time 0-0   Full-time 0-1
Ref: R.H.Davidson (Scotland) Att: 24,500

THERE were more new faces in the England line-up for the return trip to Wales for the annual Home Championship clash. Three more debutants were put in by Don Revie and eight of the side had a total of only ten caps between them, so once again it was a very experimental team.

Early on, Wales took the initiative and, but for the brilliant form of Ray Clemence, England would have been dead and buried by the end of the first half-hour. The sun shone brightly on a shirt-sleeved crowd and they roared their delight as Yorath, Mahoney and Flynn controlled the midfield. England's defence was under a constant barrage and Clemence made three outstanding saves from close-range headers as Toshack, Curtis and James were all thwarted. It seemed odds on that Wales would score, but Clemence's heroics coupled with some determined defensive play meant England were able to go in at half-time still on level terms.

The second half began in the same pattern, but despite Curtis' tireless probing, Toshack's power and Flynn's prompting, the Welsh still could not find a way to goal. As so often happens when a team is on top, the other side then snatch a goal. And this is just what happened on the hour when England took the lead.

The goal came out of nothing. A pass by Gerry Francis found Peter Taylor on the edge of the area. Taylor fired in a snap-shot immediately which flew low into the net with Davies beaten. Although Wales battled hard and came back strongly, they could not break down the visitors' resistance. Toshack gave Brian Greenhoff and Phil Thompson a torrid time in the air and James and Curtis did some fine work, but at the final hurdle they always found Clemence in top form.

The new England players were still taking time to settle and they could consider themselves lucky to have won this game. As for Wales, they failed to take advantage of their midfield dominance and lacked the ability to finish off all their good approach play, although for that they could mostly blame Ray Clemence.

89th match v Wales
Debuts for Greenhoff, Pearson and Towers.

England v Home Championship
Northern Ireland

Played on Tuesday, 11 May 1976 at Wembley Stadium.

England: R.N.Clemence (Liverpool); C.Todd (Derby Co), M.D.Mills (Ipswich T), P.B.Thompson (Liverpool), B.Greenhoff (Man Utd), R.Kennedy (Liverpool), J.K.Keegan (Liverpool), M.R.Channon (Southampton), J.S.Pearson (Man Utd), G.C.J.Francis (QPR, captain), P.J.Taylor (Crystal Palace).
Subs: J.Royle (Man City) for Keegan and M.A.Towers (Sunderland) for Taylor.
Northern Ireland: P.A.Jennings (Spurs); P.J.Rice (Arsenal), S.Nelson (Arsenal), C.J.Nicholl (Aston Villa), A.Hunter (Ipswich T), D.Clements (New York Cosmos), B.Hamilton (Everton), S.B.McIlroy (Man Utd), D.W.Spence (Bury), T.Cassidy (Newcastle Utd), D.McCreery (Man Utd).
Sub: P.W.Scott (York City) for Nelson.

Half-time 2-0   Full-time 4-0
Ref: C.Thomas (Wales)   Att: 48,000

WEMBLEY Stadium was only half full for this Home International, but the England fans that were there enjoyed a good performance from their team which, after a poor start, developed into a convincing victory.

For half an hour, England struggled to find a pattern. They were disjointed and lacked understanding, rarely looking like breaking down the determined Irish defence. It was not until their first breakthrough that England began to find their feet. This came in the 35th minute and began with the ball moving out of defence with Mick Mills. His long pass over the Irish defenders was brilliantly dummied by Mike Channon, leaving Gerry Francis a simple tap-in chance which he duly converted.

That goal gave England the confidence to settle down after their shaky start and 60 seconds later they were two up. This time Channon was fouled by Cassidy in the area and the referee awarded a penalty. Channon himself took the kick and scored with consummate ease. Now England were in complete command and they were revelling in the perfect conditions of

Kevin Keegan gets past a despairing lunge from Northern Ireland's Allan Hunter at Wembley in May 1976.

Wembley. Colin Todd, in an unaccustomed right-back position, looked good and both he and Mills were able to push forward in support of the attack. By now, the Irish looked a poor side with only Cassidy, Hamilton and McIlroy impressing.

After half-time it was a similar story as England continued to hold all the aces. Jennings, celebrating a new Irish record of 60 caps, proved his worth with several top-class saves but after 65 minutes he was powerless to stop England's third goal. Phil Thompson started the move with a long pass to club colleague Ray Kennedy out on the left. The Liverpool connection continued with a pass to Kevin Keegan, who crossed to the centre. Peter Taylor headed the ball down, Kennedy followed up to shoot, the shot was blocked but Stuart Pearson followed up to lash home the rebound. Taylor received a knock for his part in the goal and immediately went off to be replaced by Tony Towers. The Irish, too, made a substitution, sending on Peter Scott for Nelson.

It was now all England and with 15 minutes to go, they scored a fourth goal. A quick burst by Todd saw him reach the by-line and centre. The ball reached Channon and a fierce shot crashed into the roof of the Irish net with Jennings well beaten. That goal effectively ended the positive action and now England went

to Scotland, brim full of confidence and looking to extend their unbeaten run. For Northern Ireland, it was a battle with Wales to avoid the wooden spoon.

83rd match v Northern Ireland. Penalty scored for England by Channon.

Scotland v England Home Championship

Played on Saturday, 15 May 1976 at Hampden Park, Glasgow.

Scotland: A.Rough (Partick T); D.McGrain (Celtic), W.Donachie (Man City), T.Forsyth (Rangers), C.Jackson (Rangers), B.D.Rioch (Derby Co), K.Dalglish (Celtic), D.S.Masson (QPR), J.Jordan (Leeds Utd), A.Gemmill (Derby Co), E.Gray (Leeds Utd).
Sub: D.Johnstone (Rangers) for Gray.

England: R.N.Clemence (Liverpool); C.Todd (Derby Co), M.D.Mills (Ipswich T), P.B.Thompson (Liverpool), R.L.McFarland (Derby Co), R.Kennedy (Liverpool), J.K.Keegan (Liverpool), M.R.Channon (Southampton), J.S.Pearson (Man Utd), G.C.J.Francis (QPR, captain), P.J.Taylor (Crystal Palace).
Subs: M.Doyle (Man City) for McFarland and T.J.Cherry (Leeds Utd) for Pearson.

Half-time 1-1   Full-time 2-1
Ref: K.Palotai (Hungary)   Att: 85,165

ON A dull wet Hampden Park afternoon, these two old enemies once again fought out the destination of the Home Championship. At the end of it all, Scotland came away with a victory much to their passionate fans' delight.

England made a good start opening with some bright attacks. Stuart Pearson looked sharp and lively early on and after only ten minutes, England were ahead. The goal was created by Roy McFarland as he put in a low centre which was met by a spectacular diving header by Mike Channon which gave Rough no chance. At that moment. one could have heard a pin drop in Hampden, but it wasn't too long before the tartan flags were waving again.

Masson, Gemmill and Rioch soon took over the midfield and the Scots began to put England under pressure. Dalglish was in fine form and it was only seven minutes after England's goal that the Scots equalized. A corner by Gray was met by a Masson header and it was 1-1. From then on, Scotland remained in command and right on the stroke of half-time they were denied what looked like a certain penalty. Dalglish, on a splendid run, went past several defenders and when Ray Clemence came out to dive at the Scot's feet, the goalkeeper succeeded only in bringing the forward down to a unanimous roar of 'Penalty!'.

Alas for Scotland, and to the relief of Clemence and England, the referee refused the claim, saying that he had already blown for half-time. There were a few Scots in the crowd who might just have disagreed with him!

However, if Clemence escaped that time, then four minutes into the second half, fate conspired against the England 'keeper. A good run by Jordan, who outpaced McFarland and Colin Todd, ended with a centre to Dalglish. He controlled it quickly and shot low, but with no great power, past Mick Mills. Clemence, at the near post, seemed to have it well covered but inexplicably the ball eluded his grasp, went through his legs and nestled neatly in the English net. The roar could have been heard on Hadrian's Wall and poor Clemence wished at that moment that the ground would open up and swallow him. His only excuse might have been that he was still groggy after a terrible back-pass by Ray Kennedy had led to him being hurt diving at Dalglish's feet.

Scotland remained on top after that goal as Masson, McGrain, Dalglish and Jordan stretched the England defence time and again. They failed to add to their goal tally, though, and near the end only a brilliant saving tackle by Forsyth prevented Channon from salvaging an undeserved draw. England did have some plus marks with Channon, Kevin Keegan, Gerry Francis and Todd working tremendously hard, but too often some of their colleagues were not showing the same effort. Kennedy, Mills and Peter Taylor had poor games and, as a result, the left-hand side of England's formation was very vulnerable.

With a tough summer tournament in America coming up, there was much work to be done to get the team firing on all cylinders.

Trevor Brooking in a battle with Zico of Brazil during the USA Bicentennial tournament in Los Angeles in May 1976.

94th match v Scotland.
"The worst moment of my international career was letting the ball between my legs against Scotland at Hampden in 1976."
Ray Clemence

Brazil v England
USA Bicentennial Tournament

Played on Sunday, 23 May 1976 in the Coliseum Stadium, Los Angeles, USA.

Brazil: E.Leão (Palmeiras); O.Pereira (América), M.A.Feliciano (Vasco da Gama), P.R.Falcão (Internacional), M.Ferreira Pereira (Fluminense), J.J.A.dos Santos (Guarani), G.Alves (Fluminense), A.Antunes Coimbra (Flamengo), A.N.Ferreira (Gremio), R.Rivelino (Fluminense), L.Pinto Neto (Internacional).
Subs: F.C.Marinho (Botafogo) for Feliciano; H.F.Beto (Gremio) for dos Santos; C.R.Oliveira (Vasco da Gama) for A.N.Ferreira.
England: R.N.Clemence (Liverpool); C.Todd (Derby Co), M.D.Mills (Ipswich T), P.B.Thompson (Liverpool), M.Doyle (Man City), T.J.Cherry (Leeds Utd), J.K.Keegan (Liverpool), M.R.Channon (Southampton), J.S.Pearson (Man Utd), T.D.Brooking (West Ham), G.C.J.Francis (QPR, captain).

Half-time 0-0   Full-time 1-0
H.J.Weyland (West Germany) Att: 32,495

ENGLAND opened this special tournament with a game against the mighty Brazilians. With an enthusiastic crowd present, it was a largely experimental Brazil line-up with only a handful of the established names in the side.

In the first half, England had a good deal of the possession. Their hard-working style contrasted vividly with the loping, lazy, deceptively casual style of the Brazilians and they forced Brazil back with some spirited attacks. England used the width of the pitch much better than in recent games and Trevor Brooking made an immediate impact with his vision and awareness. This gave England more options and they came close to scoring several times.

Mike Channon, a lively raider, twice made fine diagonal runs which stretched the Brazilian defence. His first ended with a shot blocked on the goal-line and the second with a shot tipped away by Leão. It all looked very encouraging. Kevin Keegan also appeared sharp and he fired in two very dangerous crosses which Stuart Pearson and Channon both came close to deflecting into the net. Towards the end of the half, though, Brazil conjured up some typical magic to remind England of their power.

Zico, the man they called the 'new Pelé', left the whole England defence looking in several different directions as he moved in to fire in the best shot of the half. Ray Clemence had to be at his most agile best to keep it out and made a fine save, but the warning was there for all to see. Nevertheless, England were able to go off at the interval more than happy with their efforts and they reappeared in confident mood.

Shortly after the restart Brazil brought on Roberto and Marinho and it was the latter who made the greater mark on the game. Almost immediately he glided through to hit a screaming 35-yard shot which crashed against the crossbar before Clemence had moved. Marinho looked every inch the typical Brazilian player — tremendous pace, vicious shooting power and yet with a delicacy about his touch.

Just when it seemed that England had reached a safe stage of the match, the Brazilians struck a killer blow. Channon was back to head clear a corner, but succeeded only in finding Gil. The number-nine quickly turned the ball back across goal and in came substitute Roberto to push it in at the far post. It was a bitter disappointment for England to lose it at such a late stage, but at least they had built up some confidence with a spirited team effort.

9th match v Brazil
Brazil's Peirera also known as 'Orlando'; Feliciano as 'Marcus Antonio'; M.Ferreira Pereira as 'Miguel'; dos Santos as 'Amaral'; Alves as 'Gil'; Antunes as 'Zico'; A.N.Ferreira as 'Neca'; Pinto Neto as 'Lula'; Oliveira as 'Roberto'.

Italy v England
USA Bicentennial Tournament

Played on Friday, 28 May 1976 in the Yankee Stadium, New York, USA.

Italy: D.Zoff (Juventus); G.Facchetti (Inter-Milan), F.Rocca (AS Roma),

M.Roggi (Fiorentina), R.Benetti (Milan AC), M.Bellugi (Bologna), G.Antognoni (Fiorentina), F.Capello (Juventus), F.Graziani (Torino), F.Causio (Juventus), P.Pulici (Torino).
Subs: A.Maldera (Milan AC) for Roggi, R.Zaccerelli (Torino) for Benetti and C.Sala (Torino) for Causio.
England: J.J.Rimmer (Arsenal); D.T. Clement (QPR), P.G.Neal (Liverpool), M.Doyle (Man City), P.B.Thompson (Liverpool), M.A.Towers (Sunderland), R.C.Wilkins (Chelsea), M.R.Channon (Southampton, captain), J.Royle (Man City), T.D.Brooking (West Ham), G.A.Hill (Man Utd).
Subs: T.J.Corrigan (Man City) for Rimmer and M.D.Mills (Ipswich T) for Neal.

Half-time 2-0   Full-time 2-3

H.J.Weyland (West Germany) Att: 40,750

ON A poor pitch usually used for baseball, these sides produced a memorable match and at the end of it all, England's superb second-half fight-back had been a real delight.

England opened the game brightly. They attacked the Italians with some positive football and were unlucky not to score in the first quarter of an hour. A glorious move brought a super save from Zoff. Gordon Hill began the move, finding Mike Channon who cleverly beat Roggi and then brought Tony Towers into the play. Towers found Hill again and the Manchester United winger swept past his marker, only for his shot to bring the best out of Zoff. Almost immediately a bad mistake by Mike Doyle gave possession to Pulici. In a flash, so typical of Italian football, the ball had gone to Causio who set up Graziani and it was 1-0.

After their poor start, the Italians suddenly had their tails up. A dazzling exchange between Capello and Causio on the right led to a cross by Benetti. England failed to clear and Graziani pounced for his and Italy's second goal.

It hardly seemed fair on England who had certainly not looked two goals worse than Italy. True, the Italians moved gracefully but the high standard of play came from both teams and made nonsense of the sandy, bumpy pitch. Zoff had to make other good saves from Hill and a deflected shot by Towers, and England might have had a penalty when Facchetti brought Channon down in full flight. There was no love lost between these two and it showed in the heated exchange after that tackle.

So, at half-time England seemed in a hopeless position, 2-0 down against one of the world's meanest defences. However, one thing England were not short of was guts and within two minutes of the restart they were sensationally level.

Substitutes Joe Corrigan and Mick Mills came on and England were quickly on the attack. Trevor Brooking went past Rocca and found Joe Royle with a good pass. Royle shot powerfully and this time Zoff failed to hold it, enabling Channon to dart in to shoot home the loose ball. In the very next minute Hill took a corner from the right and there was Phil Thompson coming from nowhere to flick the ball perfectly wide of Zoff and into the far corner. It was stirring stuff and six minutes later England went one better and took the lead.

Channon sent Brooking away and ran for the return to belt in the third goal to send his teammates wild with delight. What a transformation! Italy were stunned and Channon might have completed a memorable hat-trick but after bursting clear his shot struck a post.

Italy tried to come back but their petulance was hampering their play now and they looked very ruffled. Corrigan saved from Antognoni and then, near the end, a brave but correct decision by the referee ruled out Facchetti's goal after he had fouled Corrigan.

A splendid game ended in an exciting victory. What a shame it all happened in such a second-class tournament.

> 11th match v Italy.
> Debuts for Rimmer, Wilkins, Hill and, as substitute, Corrigan.
> Channon captain for first time.
> *"My debut was one of the most emotional times for me and a nerve tingling experience."*
> Ray Wilkins

Finland v England   World Cup Qualifier

Played on Sunday 13 June 1976 at Olympic Stadium, Helsinki.

Finland: G.Enckelman (TPS Turku); E.Vihtilä (Ilves Tampere), A.Mäkynen (VPS Vassa), A.Tolsa (Beerschot), E.Ranta (Valkeakosken Haka), P.Jantunen (Reipas Lahti), J.Suomalainen (KTP Kotka), E.Heiskanen (KuPS Kuopio), A.Heiskanen (KTP Kotka), D.Rissanen (KuPS Kuopio), M.Paatelainen (Valkeakosken Haka).
Sub: S.Pyykkö (OPS Oulu) for Suomalainen.
England: R.N.Clemence (Liverpool); C.Todd (Derby Co), M.D.Mills (Ipswich T), P.B.Thompson (Liverpool), P.E.Madeley (Leeds Utd), T.J.Cherry (Leeds Utd), G.C.J.Francis (QPR, captain), M.R.Channon (Southampton), J.S.Pearson (Man Utd), T.D.Brooking (West Ham), J.K.Keegan (Liverpool).

Half-time 1-2   Full-time 1-4

Ref: A.Delcourt (Belgium)   Att: 24,500

AFTER a long and exhausting domestic season, plus a tour of North America, the England party now had to knuckle down to the most important of jobs, a World Cup qualifier. It was always going to be an awkward fixture but in the end the result went well for them.

The Olympic Stadium pitch was in poor condition, being patchy and bumpy, and England, playing in red shirts, quickly realised that it was down the wings that all the best attacks would come. Early on Finland announced their intentions with some crude challenges on Stuart Pearson, Mike Channon and Kevin Keegan. The England players showed remarkable restraint though and almost opened the scoring when Pearson headed past Enckelman, only for the goal to be disallowed.

If that was disappointing it also proved the incentive that England needed and a few minutes later they did get their deserved breakthrough. One of many free-kicks given away by Finland saw Phil Thompson find Trevor Brooking out wide. Brooking drove in a deep centre to Keegan who headed back across goal for Pearson to flick the ball home, this time legitimately.

The Finns relied on the occasional breakaway to relieve the pressure and from one such attack they gave England a scare when Rissanen broke clear of the defence to fire in a powerful shot. Ray Clemence saw it late but dived brilliantly to hold the ball in horizontal flight. The warning was not heeded by England and a few minutes later, Gerry Francis lost possession to Rissanen. The Finnish danger man moved wide and then centred for Paatelainen to head down against the foot of the post. Somehow the ball spun behind Clemence and over the line for an equalizer.

It was a blow for England but, with Brooking taking up some lovely positions and Keegan and Channon always able to find space, it was not too long before the lead was regained. Once again the weak Finnish left flank was exposed as Pearson got behind the defenders to centre for Keegan to head a magnificent goal from a difficult angle. The half-time lead was well deserved.

With Brooking and Francis always looking to create openings, England were desperate to put some space between the teams. On the hour the decisive goal came. It was Francis who put a lovely pass through the static Finland defence. Several forwards could have got to it, but Channon was first to react. Half-hearted offside appeals were waved away as Channon moved forward, his first shot struck Enckelman but when he picked up the rebound, he coolly side-stepped the 'keeper and this time made no mistake.

Four minutes later, England scored again when Thompson's pass, somewhat fortuitously thanks to an error by Tolsa, found the effervescent Keegan. The Liverpool star ran forward some 20 yards and clipped a fine shot wide of the goalkeeper for a lovely individual goal.

Other chances went missing as England dominated the remaining time, especially when Channon, hampered by a cold, wildly blazed the ball over from close range. Then Trevor Cherry hit the foot of a post in the last few minutes with Pearson narrowly failing in the follow-up attempt. Those misses were to be regretted in the final analysis with Italy the main rivals in the group.

> 5th match v Finland.

England v   Friendly Republic of Ireland

Played on Wednesday, 8 September 1976 at Wembley Stadium.

England: R.N.Clemence (Liverpool); C.Todd (Derby Co), T.J.Cherry (Leeds Utd), B.Greenhoff (Man Utd), R.L.McFarland (Derby Co), P.E.Madeley (Leeds Utd), J.K.Keegan (Liverpool, captain), R.C.Wilkins (Chelsea), J.S.Pearson (Man Utd), T.D.Brooking (West Ham), C.F.George (Derby Co).
Sub: G.A.Hill (Man Utd) for George.
Republic of Ireland: M.Kearns (Walsall); P.M.Mulligan (West Brom), J.P.Holmes (Coventry C), M.P.Martin (West Brom),

Kevin Keegan, England's captain, and Paddy Mulligan of the Republic of Ireland during the game at Wembley in September 1976.

Channon's skill around goal but they were well served by Todd, Keegan and Trevor Brooking. George, brought in to try and add zest to the attack, was very disappointing and it was a sad sight to see him replaced in the second half by Gordon Hill and then watch as he trudged dejectedly back to the dressing-rooms. He knew in his heart that he had not produced his best, not a new thing to happen for a player when he pulls on that famous white shirt of England.

> 6th match v Republic of Ireland.
> Debut for George.
> Penalty scored for the Republic of Ireland by Daly.

England v Finland   World Cup Qualifier

Played on Wednesday, 13 October 1976 at Wembley Stadium.

England: R.N.Clemence (Liverpool); C.Todd (Derby Co), T.K.Beattie (Ipswich T), P.B.Thompson (Liverpool), B.Greenhoff (Man Utd), R.C.Wilkins (Chelsea), J.K.Keegan (Liverpool, captain), M.R.Channon (Southampton), J.Royle (Man City), T.D.Brooking (West Ham), D.Tueart (Man City).
Subs: M.D.Mills (Ipswich T) for Brooking and G.A.Hill (Man Utd) for Tueart.

Finland: G.Enckelman (TSP Turku); T.Heikkinen (OPS Oulu), E.Vihtilä (Ilves Tampere), A.Mäkynen (VPS Vaasa), E.Ranta (Valkeakosken Haka), P.Jantunen (Reipas Lahti), J.Suomalainen (KTP Kotka), M.Toivola (HJK Helsinki), J.Nieminen (HJK Helsinki), A.Heiskanen (KTP Kotka), M.Paatelainen (Valkeakosken Haka).
Subs: E.Heiskanen (KuPS Kuopio) for Jantunen and S.Pyykkö (OPS Oulu) for Suomalainen.

Half-time 1-0   Full-time 2-1
Ref: U.Eriksson (Sweden)   Att: 87,000

ENGLAND went into this match knowing that a convincing victory would put all the pressure on Italy in their group, but on the night their familiar failure to finish off inferior teams reared its head again. A crowd of 87,000 people packed into Wembley ready to give the vociferous support that was needed. At the end of the evening, though, it was obvious from the jeers that they were none too satisfied at what they had seen. It all began so well, too.

Right from the kick-off England swept forward to win three early corners. From the third of these, taken by Trevor Brooking, Phil Thompson flicked the ball on and Joe Royle headed it into a cluster of players. The ball was cleared with what looked suspiciously like Ranta's hand, only for Dennis Tueart to celebrate his recall to the side by prodding home the rebound.

One thought that the goal would set England up but, alas, try as they might the expected deluge of goals did not materialise. True, they had 95 per cent of the possession and true, Enckelman was on top of his game in the Finnish goal, but really no amount of excuses can hide the inadequacies of the home attack.

Royle and Mike Channon both glanced Brooking centres too near the goalkeeper

D.A.O'Leary (Arsenal), W.L.Brady (Arsenal), G.A.Daly (Man United), G.A.Conroy (Stoke C), S.D.Heighway (Liverpool), M.J.Giles (West Brom), D.J.Givens (QPR).

Half-time 1-0   Full-time 1-1
Ref: H.Alexander (Scotland)   Att: 51,000

AGAINST a typically determined and stubborn Irish side, England made heavy weather of this friendly international at Wembley and at the end the team from the Republic deserved their draw.

There was some promise about England's play early on with the back-four playing well, interchanging positions with a natural fervour, and using the full-backs to good effect when going forward. Colin Todd was particularly sharp and put over some dangerous crosses. Ray Wilkins settled quickly into his midfield role and made some good early breaks. Chances were created for Stuart Pearson, new cap Charlie George and captain Kevin Keegan as England put on some pressure. In each case, though, the opening was lost.

For the Irish, Brady and Giles worked well together and Givens was always a handful up front. Heighway also looked sharp and Ray Clemence had to make several saves from Givens. The Republic

team showed a lot of character and had they taken a little more care about their finishing, then they might well have had a goal or two. As it was, a minute before half-time, England opened the scoring with a well-taken goal.

George found Keegan with a neat pass and his centre from the right was met with a firm side-footed volley by Pearson and the power of the shot enabled it to go in off Kearns' body. The goal gave England a distinct psychological advantage as the sides went in at the break, but to their credit the Irish refused to panic, beginning the second half with the same calm composure that had stood them in good stead for the first 45 minutes.

The Republic worked hard and deserved some reward for all their attractive approach play. It came as no real surprise then when they scored an equalizer. Heighway burst in from the wing and Todd nudged him off balance before Wilkins brought him down completely. Penalty! Daly took the spot-kick and scored with the minimum of fuss. It was ironic because Todd and Wilkins had been England's best players.

Heighway, Givens and Conroy worked themselves to a standstill in an effort to gain the lead but England defended well. Up front though the home side showed very little. They badly missed Mike

Joe Royle heads goalwards against Finland at Wembley in October 1976.

England's second and winning goal against the Finns, scored by Joe Royle after Channon had pulled the ball back.

and then Enckelman saved brilliantly from Tueart and Brooking. Colin Todd, Kevin Beattie and Brian Greenhoff all reinforced the attack whenever possible but England could not add to their goal tally. Indeed, towards the end of the half Finland made a rare breakaway attack which almost brought an equalizer. Ray Clemence came out to meet Nieminen and brought him down outside the area for a free-kick which came to nothing, but earned Clemence a booking.

Three minutes after the interval Finland produced another break which this time did prove positive. Ray Wilkins allowed Heiskanen too much room in midfield and when Nieminen received the pass he coolly side-footed the ball past Clemence to equalize.

That goal might do untold damage to England's World Cup challenge in the long run but at least they did recover things somewhat four minutes later. Kevin Keegan found Channon, who beat three players in the area before pulling the ball back for Royle to hit home what proved to be the winner.

Despite that goal, the crowd became increasingly frustrated with England especially when only two fine saves by Clemence prevented another equalizer. Substitute Esa Heiskanen and his brother Aki Heiskanen both saw shots saved and then Don Revie did nothing to calm the crowd when he decided to take off one of their best players, Brooking, and bring on Mick Mills. That seemed a curious decision and made no difference to England's play.

For the remainder of the second half England's game just went to pieces as Finland came more and more into the picture and but for the inspired goalkeeping of Clemence the visitors would surely have gained the draw they deserved. The Finns were justly proud of their performance especially as only five weeks earlier they had been hammered 6-0 by Scotland.

By the time the referee blew for time, the crowd's patience had gone and the players left the field to a crescendo of jeers.

5th match v Finland.

Italy v England   World Cup Qualifier

Played on Wednesday, 17 November 1976 at the Olympic Stadium, Rome.

Italy: D.Zoff (Juventus); A.Cuccureddu (Juventus), M.Tardelli (Juventus), R.Benetti (Juventus), C.Gentile (Juventus), G.Facchetti (Inter-Milan), F.Causio (Juventus), F.Capello (Milan AC), F.Graziani (Torino), G.Antognoni (Fiorentina), R.Bettega (Juventus).

England: R.N.Clemence (Liverpool); D.T.Clement (QPR), M.D.Mills (Ipswich T), B.Greenhoff (Man Utd), R.L.McFarland (Derby Co), E.W.Hughes (Liver-

Roberto Bettega scores Italy's second goal against England in the Olympic Stadium, Rome, in November 1976.

pool), J.K.Keegan (Liverpool, captain), M.R.Channon (Southampton), S.Bowles (QPR), T.J.Cherry (Leeds Utd), T.D. Brooking (West Ham).
Sub: T.K.Beattie (Ipswich T) for Clement.

Half-time 1-0   Full-time 2-0
Ref: A.Klein (Israel)   Att: 70,750

THE cauldron of the Olympic Stadium in Rome was not for the faint-hearted as England took on Italy in this vital World Cup match. Don Revie made six changes plus two other positional changes for the game, a fact which hardly inspired continuity for such an important occasion.

For 20 minutes England played a cautious, containing game and in fact made a fair share of the attacks. Brian Greenhoff instigated most of these from his new role in midfield, although there was little penetration to be seen from the front men. Italy, typically, soaked these attacks up comfortably and they gradually began to assert themselves on the game. It was Causio who turned the match ominously towards the Italians. A mistake by Mick Mills let him in for a 40-yard run which ended with a shot just over, but the warning to England was clear.

Bettega and Graziani upped the tempo and Bettega only just missed with a header before Tardelli made Ray Clemence's fingers sting with a fierce shot. England, meanwhile, persisted with the fruitless ploy of a long cross into the penalty area. Stan Bowles hardly got a kick and it was left to Dave Clement to go closest when he headed Trevor Brooking's centre just over. England's only real hope was to frustrate Italy long enough to upset their fragile composure, but just as it seemed that might be on the cards, the Italians scored.

It was the 36th minute when England gave away a dangerous free-kick on the edge of the box. Causio tapped it to one side and Antognoni drove in a shot which deflected off of Kevin Keegan and left Clemence helpless.

After half-time, England tried hard without ever looking convincing and they never threatened Zoff's goal. The Italians were in command of the midfield and should really have turned their superiority into goals. As it was a fine move involving Antognoni. Graziani and Benetti ended with Bettega just failing to reach the cross.

Italy's second and decisive goal was delayed until the 77th minute by brave England resistance. Benetti began the move, linking well with Causio before finding Benetti taking a return pass wide on the left. Causio again came in on the move and took over, sending in a hard, low centre which Bettega met with a superb diving header for a magnificent goal.

But for Roy McFarland's superb defensive play in the remaining minutes, Italy would surely have added further goals to emphasise their dominance. As it was, the result still left England with everything to play for in their remaining group matches, but there was no doubt that this defeat was a big set-back.

12th match v Italy.

England v Holland   Friendly

Played on Wednesday, 9 February 1977 at Wembley Stadium.

England: R.N.Clemence (Liverpool); D.T.Clement (QPR), T.K.Beattie (Ipswich T), M.Doyle (Man City), D.V.Watson (Man City), P.E.Madeley (Leeds Utd), J.K.Keegan (Liverpool, captain), T.J.Francis (Birmingham C), B.Greenhoff (Man Utd), S.Bowles (QPR), T.D.Brooking (West Ham).
Subs: J.S.Pearson (Man Utd) for Madeley and C.Todd (Derby Co) for Greenhoff.

Holland: P.Schrijvers (Ajax Amsterdam); W.L.J.Suurbier (Ajax Amsterdam), H.Hovenkamp (AZ 67 Alkmaar), W.Rijsbergen (Feyenoord), R.M.Krol (Ajax Amsterdam), J.Neeskens (FC Barcelona), J.Peters (NEC Nijmegen), W.van de Kerkhof (PSV Eindhoven), H.J.Cruyff (FC Barcelona), W.J.Rep (Valencia CF), P.R.Rensenbrink (RSC Anderlecht).
Sub: K.Kist (AZ 67 Alkmaar) for Rep.

Half-time 0-2   Full-time 0-2
Ref: W.Eschweiler (West Germany)
                          Att: 90,000

THIS was the best performance by a visiting team to Wembley since the infamous match against the Hungarians in 1953. England, hoping to rebuild their dented confidence after the Italy game, were given a football lesson by a Cruyff inspired Dutch side.

Don Revie again made many changes and it showed early on as Holland ripped England apart with some superb football. Rensenbrink shot just over after fine work by Hovenkamp, Peters continually found Cruyff in acres of space and Neeskens always looked dangerous with typical bursts from midfield. England continued with their infuriating habit of pumping long high balls into the middle, hoping that Kevin Keegan would somehow get on the end of them. The fact that he was one of the shortest men on the pitch seemed to be ignored by the England management.

The only surprising thing was that Holland took 29 minutes to score. A square pass by Cruyff gave Neeskens possession and he had time to spot Peters running into the area. For a fraction of a second it looked as though Neeskens' pass was too far ahead of Peters but the number seven reached out a foot to clip it over Ray Clemence and into the net.

Despite spirited running by Dave Clement and especially Brian Greenhoff, England had neither the skill nor the know-how to break down the Dutch defence. It was a bitter blow when Greenhoff had to go off with an arm injury as with him went England's only hope.

Holland continued to show England the way, stroking the ball around Wemb-

Jan Peters, scorer of two goals against England at Wembley in February 1977, this time fails to connect with the ball.

This time Peters is on target, hitting home his side's second goal.

Kevin Keegan heads England's first goal against Luxembourg at Wembley in March 1977.

ley's lush surface with the arrogance of thoroughbreds. On 39 minutes they scored a long overdue second goal. Again the build-up was majestic. Cruyff, at the heart of every attack, combined well with Krol to release Hovenkamp. He made ground before slipping a lovely pass inside to Peters who once again had taken up a good position in front of goal. This time Peters calmly took his time before putting his shot wide of Clemence.

Even the English crowd, so disappointed with their own team's performance had to concede the magnificence of the Dutch and they gave excellent applause as they went off at half-time.

After the break England did fractionally better and Trevor Francis suggested that he might have something to offer in the future. One shot brought a good save from Schrijvers but it did not disguise the overall dominance of the Dutch. Another superb piece of play by Cruyff gave Peters the chance of a memorable hat-trick but this time Clemence saved.

Revie brought on an extra forward when Stuart Pearson replaced Paul Madeley but it made little difference and at the end the England confidence had taken another battering.

6th v Holland.
Debut for Francis.

England v World Cup Qualifier
Luxembourg

Played on Wednesday, 30 March 1977 at Wembley Stadium.

England: R.N.Clemence (Liverpool); J.Gidman (Aston Villa), T.J.Cherry (Leeds Utd), R.Kennedy (Liverpool), D.V.Watson (Man City), E.W.Hughes (Liverpool), J.K.Keegan (Liverpool, captain), M.R.Channon (Southampton), J.Royle (Man City), T.J.Francis (Birmingham C), G.A.Hill (Man Utd).
Sub: P.Mariner (Ipswich T) for Royle.

Luxembourg: R.Zender (Red-Black Pfaffenthal); R.Fandel (Aris Bonnevoie), J.L.Margue (Progres Niedercorn), L.Mond (Jeunesse Esch), L.Pilot (Racing, Brussels), J.Zuang (Stade Dudelange), M.Di Domenico (Red Boys Differdange), G.Dresch (Avenir Beggen), N.Braun (FC Metz), P.Philipp (Royale Union), G.Dussier (AS Nancy-Lorraine).
Sub: N.Orioli (Alliance Dudelange) for Di Domenico.

Half-time 1-0   Full-time 5-0

Ref: P.Bonett (Malta)   Att: 78,000

ON A night when England had to win, and win by a hatful of goals, Don Revie decided yet again to make many changes

to the side. As a result, despite a bright start, England looked disjointed and struggled with the determined man to man marking by Luxembourg. Only the inferior fitness of the visitors brought about their downfall.

England's positive opening was capped on ten minutes by a goal from skipper Kevin Keegan. John Gidman made one of many dashing runs down the right before crossing deep to the far side of the penalty area. Joe Royle controlled the ball for Dave Watson to gently float it back across the area for Keegan to jump high and head home. That goal should have been the springboard for all-out assault on the Luxembourg goal, but although Watson hit a shot against the post shortly after the goal, the remainder of the half was a succession of predictable play which even Luxembourg had little trouble containing.

Goalkeeper Zender did make some good saves but England lacked the ruthlessness they needed. By the time Trevor Francis headed Royle's short cross on to the crossbar half-time was beckoning and as the teams went off, sections of the crowd were screaming for Paul Mariner who was on the substitute's bench. After the interval they got their wish as Mariner replaced Royle and the Ipswich player was soon in the action forcing a fine save from Zender after an excellent turn and shot from Francis' pass.

With the realisation that goals were the order of the day, England finally heeded the message on the hour and started the avalanche that they so desperately needed. A corner by Gordon Hill was only half cleared and Watson headed back for Francis to ram the ball in from close range.

At last England began to get it together. With Luxembourg visibly tiring, more excellent work by Francis produced a third goal in the 65th minute.

His fine run and cross found Ray Kennedy at the far post and he squeezed the ball in from a difficult angle. Four minutes later, another Hill corner was met by Mike Channon and although Zender made a brave effort to save, the referee ruled that Channon's header was over the line.

Trevor Cherry then missed a simple chance before the referee awarded England a penalty after Channon had gone down. It was a dubious decision and not nearly as clear cut as perhaps other challenges had been. Nevertheless, Channon himself stepped up to score from the spot-kick and England had gone some way to salvaging some of the confidence lost in their previous two matches.

Three minutes from the end of the match Luxembourg had Dresch sent off for a foul on Channon, his second bookable offence.

4th v Luxembourg.
Debuts for Gidman and, as substitute, Mariner.
Penalty scored for England by Channon.
Dresch of Luxembourg sent off.

Northern Ireland v England Home Championship

Played on Saturday, 28 May 1977 at Windsor Park, Belfast.

Northern Ireland: P.A.Jennings (Spurs); J.M.Nicholl (Man Utd), P.J.Rice (Arsenal), T.Jackson (Man Utd), A.Hunter (Ipswich T), B.Hamilton (Everton), R.C.McGrath (Man Utd), S.B.McIlroy (Man Utd), G.Armstrong (Spurs), D.McCreery (Man Utd), T.Anderson (Swindon T).
Subs: M.H.O'Neill (Nottm Forest) for Armstrong and D.W.Spence (Blackpool) for Anderson.
England: P.L.Shilton (Stoke C); T.J.Cherry (Leeds Utd), M.D.Mills (Ipswich T), B.Greenhoff (Man Utd), D.V.Watson (Man City), C.Todd (Derby Co), R.C.Wilkins (Chelsea), M.R.Channon (Southampton, captain), P.Mariner (Ipswich T), T.D.Brooking (West Ham), Tueart (Man City).
Sub: B.E.Talbot (Ipswich T) for Wilkins.

Half-time 1-1   **Full-time 1-2**
Ref: B.R.McGinlay (Scotland) Att: 34,000

WITH THE five Liverpool players in the England squad rested following their magnificent European Cup triumph three days ago, it was another much-changed side that travelled to Windsor Park for the first match in this year's Home Championship. It did mean a recall however for Peter Shilton who, at his own request, had been left out of the side. His decision to play again for the national team must have delighted the England manager.

Mind you, after only four minutes of this game Shilton must have wondered what he had come back to as Northern Ireland took the lead. Jackson made a surging run before passing to Armstrong. Armstrong then fired in a shot which Shilton could only block and McGrath had the simplest of task to score from the rebound.

It was a bad start by England but on a day when the weather was oppressive and the players weary after a long hard season they showed considerable character in fighting back. Mike Channon, captain again, was the game's most lively forward and although he missed chances he was always involved, unlike the ineffective Paul Mariner who was most disappointing.

Ireland attacked with their customary enthusiasm, although it must be said they lacked their usual flair. On 27 minutes, England equalized with a well-taken goal by Channon. A superb positive run by Colin Todd ended with a quick pass which set up Channon, who guided a right-foot shot wide of Jennings. Before half-time Channon missed two other fine chances when he headed crosses by Mariner and Trevor Brooking wide. If those efforts had been made to count, the game would have been beyond an Irish comeback, but the second half gave the battling home team hope as McIlroy and Anderson, especially, threatened to give them their first home victory over England for 50 years.

The game was definitely swinging the way of the Irish and they were on top but unfortunately for them they failed to create any real scares for England's defence. The visitors worked hard and when Brian Talbot replaced the disappointing Ray Wilkins in the 65th minute, their midfield had a more solid look about it. Indeed, Talbot almost scored in the 76th minute when his powerful shot was superbly saved by Jennings. Good displays by Brian Greenhoff and Brooking kept England going and with four minutes remaining they stunned the home crowd by snatching the lead.

Again Talbot was prominent as he made a determined run down the right before putting over a centre. The cross was at an awkward height and Dennis Tueart did very well, going down on his knees to head home. Shortly afterwards the match ended.

It was perhaps a little unfair on the luckless Irish but overall an England victory was just about deserved.

84th match v Northern Ireland.
Debut as substitute for Talbot.

England v Wales Home Championship

Played on Tuesday, 31 May 1977 at Wembley Stadium.

England: P.L.Shilton (Stoke C); P.G.Neal (Liverpool), M.D.Mills (Ipswich T), B.Greenhoff (Man Utd), D.V.Watson (Man City), E.W.Hughes (Liverpool), J.K.Keegan (Hamburger SV), M.R.Channon (Southampton), J.S.Pearson (Man Utd), T.D.Brooking (West Ham), R.Kennedy (Liverpool).
Sub: D.Tueart (Man City) for Brooking.
Wales: W.D.Davies (Everton); R.J.Thomas (Derby Co), J.P.Jones (Liverpool), J.F.Mahoney (Stoke C), L.Phillips (Aston Villa), I.P.Evans (Crystal Palace), P.A.Sayer (Cardiff C), B.Flynn (Burnley), T.C.Yorath (Coventry C), N.S.Deacy (PSV Eindhoven), L.James (Derby Co).
Sub: D.F.Roberts (Oxford Utd) for Phillips.

Half-time 0-1   **Full-time 0-1**
Ref: J.R.Gordon (Scotland)   Att: 48,000

AT last, after many years of trying, the Welsh finally tasted victory against England at Wembley. It was a very satisfying moment for them, but for England all sorts of questions were once again raised by a very disappointing display. With the Liverpool players available again, England made five changes from the Northern Ireland match.

The game started badly for the home side and they rarely put together a decent move in the opening half. For their first

Mick Channon tries a shot against Wales at Wembley in June 1977. The Welsh defenders are Joey Jones, Terry Yorath and Brian Flynn.

real chance by either side, we had to wait until the 38th minute which showed how dull the first half was. Then James sent Sayer away down the left and his cross found Deacy. He should have done better than he did and it all ended with a pass back to Yorath who shot over. Actually, Yorath was the outstanding Welshman on view and despite a booking early on for a foul on Brian Greenhoff, he showed all the fire and passion so typical of Welsh players.

Twice Wales showed up the vulnerability of the centre of the England defence with dangerous attacks but this went unheeded by England and with a minute of the half left, Wales made the breakthrough. Yorath's pass should have been intercepted by Emlyn Hughes but a misunderstanding between him and Peter Shilton gave James the chance of possession. Taken by surprise Shilton could only dive desperately, bringing James down in the process. The referee did not hesitate and awarded Wales a penalty from which James sent Shilton the wrong way.

At least the goal had the effect of livening up the lacklustre England attack with Kevin Keegan in particular seeing more of the ball after the break. He headed narrowly wide from a Ray Kennedy centre and his running also enabled Stuart Pearson to win more freedom from tight marking. It was Pearson who almost forced an equalizer. A long pass left him free and as he pushed the ball around Davies, the goalkeeper appeared to bring him down.

Despite frantic appeals from players and crowd alike the referee refused the penalty claims and the Welsh team breathed again.

The England attacks grew more desperate as the minutes ticked away, with Mike Channon going closest when he was foiled by a good save from Davies after a fine run and shot. Dennis Tueart replaced Brooking in a fruitless substitution and in the end Wales held on comfortably to celebrate a famous victory. Nothing could deny them their moment of glory.

90th match v Wales.
Penalty scored for Wales by James.

England v
Scotland Home Championship

Played on Saturday, 4 June 1977 at Wembley Stadium.

England: R.N.Clemence (Liverpool); P.G.Neal (Liverpool), M.D.Mills (Ipswich T), B.Greenhoff (Man Utd), D.V.Watson (Man City), E.W.Hughes (Liverpool, captain), T.J.Francis (Birmingham C), M.R.Channon (Southampton), J.S.Pearson (Man Utd), B.E.Talbot (Ipswich T), R.Kennedy (Liverpool).
Subs: T.J.Cherry (Leeds Utd) for Greenhoff and D.Tueart (Man City) for Kennedy.
Scotland: R.Rough (Partick Th); D.McGrain (Celtic), W.Donachie (Man City), T.Forsyth (Rangers), G.McQueen (Leeds Utd), B.D.Rioch (Everton), D.S.Masson (QPR), K.Dalglish (Celtic), J.Jordan (Leeds Utd), R.A.Hartford (Man City), W.Johnston (West Brom).
Subs: A.Gemmill (Derby Co) for Masson and L.Macari (Man Utd) for Jordan.

Half-time 0-1   Full-time 1-2

Ref: K.Palotai (Hungary)   Att: 100,000

Dave Watson gets above Scotland's Kenny Dalglish at Wembley in June 1977.

ENGLAND suffered their third defeat in their last four games at Wembley when the rampaging Scots duly clinched the Home Championship with a 2-1 win. The scenes of mayhem at the end as the unruly and over exuberant Scottish fans literally tore Wembley apart raised many questions and brought fencing at future such fixtures a stage closer.

The game itself began evenly. Both sides worked hard with Jordan missing with a header from a Masson free-kick, whilst Brian Greenhoff and Ray Kennedy both put in good efforts for England. Rough saved well from Greenhoff's shot and Kennedy headed just wide. Throughout the half it was cut and thrust as each side searched for the advantage. Eventually the pendulum swung Scotland's way in the last five minutes of the half.

Concerted pressure on the England goal saw Phil Neal being hustled by Dalglish. It seemed that Neal might have been fouled but in the scuffle for possession the ball was handled by the England full-back and the Hungarian referee gave a free-kick

to Scotland. It was not the first strange decision he had made in the match and certainly not the last. To rub salt into England's wound, when the free-kick was taken, Hartford's cross found McQueen's head and Ray Clemence was left helpless in goal as the ball flew past him. The goal had come at just the right time for Scotland and they walked off shortly afterwards at half-time with a distinct psychological advantage.

At the start of the second half England tried hard to make some impression but the determined Scots were like tigers as they confidently protected their lead. They also looked dangerous themselves when they attacked and on the hour virtually settled the match with a second goal. It was a fine move started when Hartford played a lovely pass to Johnston. The winger sped down the left before sending over a deep, searching cross to the far side.

Rioch was there to head back across goal and Macari, Mick Mills and Dalglish all threw themselves at the ball. It was Dalglish who made the decisive touch and at the second attempt he stabbed the ball home.

With McGrain and McQueen towers of strength in the Scottish defence, there seemed no way back for England. They looked jaded and disjointed as they tried in vain to get back into the game. They had little to offer and rarely troubled the visitors' defence. In fact it was not until three minutes from the end that they finally gained some consolation.

Trevor Francis was pulled down in the area and Mike Channon took the chance to score from the penalty-spot. Really, though, that goal gave a false impression to the scoreline and the Scots won with embarrassing ease, much to the delight of their fans who made Wembley look more like Hampden Park on the day. What a shame that they did not contain their celebrations a little bit more at the end.

95th match v Scotland.
Penalty scored for England by Mike Channon.

Brazil v England

Friendly

Played on Wednesday, 8 June 1977 at the Maracana Stadium, Rio de Janeiro.

Brazil: E.Leão (Palmeiras); J.M.Rodrigues (Corinthians), J.Rodrigues Neto (Botafogo), A.C.Cerezo (Atlético Mineiro), E.N.Filho (Fluminense), J.J.A.dos Santos (Guarani), G.Alves (Botafogo), A.Antunes Coimbra (Flamengo), C.R.Oliveira (Vasco da Gama), R.Rivelino (Fluminense), P.C.Lima (Flamengo).
Sub: J.M.Picasso (Botafogo) for Alves.
England: R.N.Clemence (Liverpool); P.G.Neal (Liverpool), T.J.Cherry (Leeds Utd), B.Greenhoff (Man Utd), D.V.Watson (Man City), E.W.Hughes (Liverpool), J.K.Keegan (Hamburger SV, captain), T.J.Francis (Birmingham C), J.S.Pearson (Man Utd), R.C.Wilkins (Chelsea), B.E.Talbot (Ipswich T).
Subs: M.R.Channon (Southampton) for Pearson and R.Kennedy (Liverpool) for Wilkins.

Half-time 0-0   Full-time 0-0
Ref: A.Ducatelli (Argentina)   Att: 77,000

THE FIRST match of this demanding summer tour of South America was in the Maracana Stadium against the mighty Brazilians. One could not have a more difficult fixture at the end of a long hard English season and yet this is what England had to face. And at the end of the 90 minutes they came away with all the honours after holding their illustrious opponents to a goalless draw.

With the news filtering through that Italy had beaten Finland 3-0 in England's World Cup group, adding further disappointment to the team, it would not have been a surprise had their been a less than committed approach. How wrong we were as England took the first half by storm. As early as the fifth minute they almost took the lead. Kevin Keegan made the first of many fine runs, reaching the by-line before crossing to Brian Greenhoff. His header was knocked down to Stuart Pearson who was unlucky to see Leão save with his legs.

With England's 4-4-2 formation spear-

headed by the tireless Keegan and Brian Talbot, the Brazilians found it difficult to win the ball. Their midfield, even with the likes of Zico and Rivelino, could not get to grips with England and midway through the half Trevor Francis shot wide after great work by Phil Neal and Talbot. A third clear chance was created shortly before the interval when Leão's mistake let in Keegan, but again the shot went the wrong side of the post.

At half-time Brazil's manager, Claudio Coutinho obviously gave his team a real rollicking and it seemed to work as after the interval, Brazil were a different kettle of fish. Suddenly they took control of the midfield as the England lads tired somewhat. It was now that the visitors' defence won the accolades. With Trevor Cherry outstanding at left-back and Dave Watson a tower of strength at the heart of the defence, England withstood all that is best from Brazilian football. The silky skills, the lightning pace and the frightening shooting power was suddenly there for all to see. And nobody saw it better than England's goalkeeper Ray Clemence.

Clemence was magnificent in the second half. He dashed out of his goal to save brilliantly at Gil's feet and then blocked another shot from Cerezo. By this time Rivelino, Zico and Cerezo were dominating the game and they combined superbly at times. Phil Neal had a nightmare task against Paulo Cesar and struggled to hold him. But Cherry continued his outstanding performance, making one brilliant saving tackle when Paulo Cesar seemed certain to score. He followed that up with two goal-line clearances after Clemence, at last, was beaten. The goalkeeper then made breathtaking saves from Paulo Cesar and Roberto before topping the lot with an amazing save from Gil after Zico had set the centre-forward up.

England tried to stem the tide a little by introducing two fresh faces, Ray Kennedy and Mike Channon coming on as substitutes, but the second half belonged to Brazil. In the end though the tenacity of the England players deservedly gained them a share of the spoils. It was the first time an English side had held the Brazilians on their own soil, a heartening achievement.

10th match v Brazil.
Brazil's J.M.Rodrigues also known as 'Zé Maria'; Filho as 'Edinho'; dos Santos as 'Amaral'; Alves as 'Gil'; Antunes as 'Zico'; Oliveira as 'Roberto'; Lima as 'Paulo Cesar I'; Picasso as 'Zimario'.
"One of the funniest things I ever saw whilst I was with the squad was seeing a couple of England players chatting up some transvestites in Rio!"
Steve Coppell

Argentina v England

Friendly

Played on Sunday, 12 June 1977 at La Bombonera Stadium, Buenos Aires.

Argentina: H.Baley (Huracán); D.P.Killer (Racing Club), A.C.Tarantini (Boca Juniors), V.Pernia (Boca Juniors), A.Gallego (Newells Old Boys), D.Passarella (River Plate), D.R.Bertoni (Independiente), O.C.Ardíles (Huracán),

L.J.Luque (River Plate), R.Bochini (Independiente), O.Ortiz (River Plate).
Subs: O.Larrosa (Independiente) for Bochini and J.R.Rocha (Newell's Old Boys) for Ortiz.
England: R.N.Clemence (Liverpool); P.G.Neal (Liverpool), T.J.Cherry (Leeds Utd), B.Greenhoff (Man Utd), D.V.Watson (Man City), E.W.Hughes (Liverpool), J.K.Keegan (Hamburger SV, captain), M.R.Channon (Southampton), J.S.Pearson (Man Utd), R.C.Wilkins (Chelsea), B.E.Talbot (Ipswich T).
Sub: R.Kennedy (Liverpool) for Greenhoff.

Half-time 1-1   Full-time 1-1
Ref: R.Barreto (Uruguay)   Att: 60,000

THIS was a potentially volatile fixture for England, who were visiting Buenos Aires for the first time since their infamous meeting at Wembley in 1966 caused so much bad feeling between the countries. But any hint of trouble was quickly nipped in the bud by the referee's firm control and the fact that England scored an early goal.

A packed crowd at the imposing home ground of Boca Juniors were baying for the home side when after only three minutes England took the lead. Stuart Pearson and Mike Channon were both brought down by heavy challenges and from the quickly taken free-kick, Brian Greenhoff found Channon galloping away down the right. Channon turned a neat cross to the near post and Pearson nipped in to flick a fine goal wide of Baley. At that moment the silence was uncanny.

Unfortunately England could only hold the lead for 12 minutes. Argentina upped their tempo in the midfield and in one attack, Greenhoff brought down Bertoni in a dangerous position on the edge of the area. From the free-kick, Bertoni curled his shot around the wall and beyond Ray Clemence's despairing leap.

For a while Ardíles, Gallego and Bochini controlled proceedings, but England held firm and, without too many scares, reached half-time comfortably level. There was one near miss when Clemence dropped a fierce shot from Luque but Watson came to the rescue with a goal-line clearance.

After the break the game deteriorated with both sides seemingly content with a draw. Argentina only put in three worthwhile attempts at goal, all of which were easily dealt with by Clemence. At the other end Greenhoff's withdrawal meant that substitute Ray Kennedy was able to bolster the England midfield allowing Brian Talbot to move into a more central position which suited him better. But the visitors rarely threatened Baley's goal and the most memorable incident of the second half came with ten minutes to go.

Cherry put in a mild tackle on Bertoni from behind and as the Leeds player backed away Bertoni turned and punched him, knocking out two of Cherry's front teeth. For the first time in the match the referee was not on the spot and had to consult his linesman for advice. After this he showed the red card to Bertoni and then, to the astonishment of the whole England party, did the same thing to Cherry.

It was a ludicrous decision and totally unjust on Cherry. One could perhaps understand the diplomacy of the decision

Daniel Bertoni's free-kick sails over Ray Clemence's head in Buenos Aires in June 1977.

but there was no justice at all. As Don Revie said later, "Cherry was the unluckiest player in the world to be sent off!"

Cherry was only the third England player ever to be sent off in a full international. The only other incident of the half worth recalling was when Emlyn Hughes cleared a shot off the goal-line, but anything other than at least a share of the spoils would have been as unfair on England as Cherry's dismissal was.

> 7th match v Argentina.
> Cherry sent off.
> Bertoni (Argentina) sent off.

Uruguay v England   Friendly

Played on Wednesday, 15 June 1977 in the Centenary Stadium, Montevideo.

Uruguay: N.Clavijo (Defensor); R.Rivadavia (Rampla Juniors), J.Salomon (Defensor), A.de los Santos (Nacional), A.Peyreyra (Danubio), B.Javier (Defensor), R.B.Rodríguez (Defusàr), J.Carrasco (Rampla Juniors), J.Santelli (Defensor), I.Maneiro (Peñarol), W.Oliveira (Wanderers).
Subs: S.Muletahler (Wanderers) for Oliveira.
England: R.N.Clemence (Liverpool); P.G.Neal (Liverpool), T.J.Cherry (Leeds Utd), B.Greenhoff (Man Utd), D.V.Watson (Man City), E.W.Hughes (Liverpool), J.K.Keegan (Hamburger SV, captain), M.R.Channon (Southampton), J.S.Pearson (Man Utd), R.C.Wilkins (Chelsea), B.E.Talbot (Ipswich T.).

Half-time 0-0   Full-time 0-0
Ref: M.Comesena (Argentina) Att: 36,000

ENGLAND completed their South American tour by preserving their unbeaten

record with this goalless draw. But this was the most disappointing of their three games and with a little more enterprise they could, and should have won it.

The match was a poor one with the bumpy pitch and lightweight ball causing many errors in control and passing. England had been forewarned about the tough Uruguayan tackling and Mike Channon was soon feeling the full force as he was hauled down three times in the early stages. From one free-kick against Pereira, Ray Wilkins' shot was easily cleared and then another effort by Trevor Cherry was saved by the none too confident Clavijo in goal. Ray Clemence saved elegantly from Oliveira at the other end, but then for a while the goal chances dried up.

England's midfield performed well with Wilkins and Brian Talbot always prominent. However, Kevin Keegan and Brian Greenhoff looked less effective with Keegan being seemingly wasted in this role. Wilkins put over one teasing cross which Channon came desperately close to converting and then Stuart Pearson headed wide from Phil Neal's cross.

After that, goal chances became extremely rare and the game drifted into mediocrity. The only relief came from Wilkins who was unlucky with a speculative 35-yard shot which only just flew over the bar. Uruguay had a chance when Maneiro's chip left Oliveira free in front of goal but the number-11 lifted his shot far too high. Uruguay suffered through their abyssmal passing and they were, without doubt, the worst side England had faced for many months.

Though it would have perhaps been a slightly unsatisfying way of winning England should really have had a penalty near the end when Santos raised his hand to pull down a cross by Wilkins. It seemed an obvious penalty but the referee waved play on and the Uruguayan crowd breathed a sigh of relief. This continent

certainly seemed to have a different set of rules from the rest of football sometimes! At least, though England, for the first time, completed a South American tour undefeated.

> 6th match v Uruguay.

England v Switzerland   Friendly

Played on Wednesday, 7 September 1977 at Wembley Stadium.

England: R.N.Clemence (Liverpool); P.G.Neal (Liverpool), T.J.Cherry (Leeds Utd), T.McDermott (Liverpool), D.V.Watson (Man City), E.W.Hughes (Liverpool, captain), J.K.Keegan (Hamburger SV), M.R.Channon (Southampton), T.J.Francis (Birmingham C), R.Kennedy (Liverpool), I.R.Callaghan (Liverpool).
Subs: G.A.Hill (Man Utd) for Channon and R.C.Wilkins (Chelsea) for Callaghan.
Switzerland: E.Burgener (Lausanne-Sports); S.Trinchero (Servette FC), P.Fischbach (FC Zürich), L.Bizzini (Servette FC), P.Chapuisat (FC Zürich), R.Hasler (Neuchâtel Xamax), H.Barberis (Servette FC), R.Elsener (Grasshoppers), J.Küttel (Young Boys), Demarmels (FC Basel), R.Botteron (FC Zürich).
Subs: J.Brechbühl (Young Boys) for Hasler, B.Rieder (Etoile Carouge) for Elsener, C.Sulser (Grasshoppers) for Küttel and A.Von Wartburg (FC Basle) for Demarmels.

Half-time 0-0   Full-time 0-0
Ref: G.Konrath (France)   Att: 43,000

AFTER A summer of controversy over Don Revie's sudden resignation from the position of team manager, the FA offered Ron Greenwood the temporary position

For Liverpool and England. Left to right are Ian Callaghan, Terry McDermott, Ray Clemence, Phil Neal, Ray Kennedy and Emlyn Hughes.

Ray Kennedy hammers in a shot against the Swiss at Wembley in September 1977.

quarter of an hour with England just failing to find the necessary finish. In one last desperate attack, Kennedy controlled a difficult bouncing ball and fired in a powerful shot which Burgener brilliantly parried. That was the last chance and in the end the crowd left very disappointed at England's inability to break down the well-organised Swiss defence. It was becoming a frequent problem at Wembley for the national side. Full credit to Switzerland, though, for an excellent performance.

12th match v Switzerland.
Debut for McDermott.
First match in charge for Ron Greenwood.

Luxembourg v England World Cup Qualifier

Played on Wednesday 12 October 1977 at the Stade de Ville in Luxembourg.

Luxembourg: J.Moes (Avenir Beggen); M.Barthel (Red Boys Differdange), R.Fandel (Aris Bonnevoie), L.Mond (Jeunesse Esch), N.Rohmann (Jeunesse Esch), J.Zuang (Stade Dudelange), R.Michaux (Red Boys Differdange), P.Philipp (Royale Union), G.Dussier (Lille OSC), V.Monacelli (Stade Dudelange), N.Braun (FC Metz).
Sub: J.Zangerle (US Luxembourg) for Fandel and M.Di Domenico (Red Boys Differdange) for Braun.

England: R.N.Clemence (Liverpool); T.J.Cherry (Leeds Utd), E.W.Hughes (Liverpool, captain), D.V.Watson (Man City), R.Kennedy (Liverpool), I.R.Callaghan (Liverpool), T.McDermott (Liverpool), R.C.Wilkins (Chelsea), P.Mariner (Ipswich T), T.J.Francis (Birmingham C), G.A.Hill (Man Utd).
Subs: T.K.Beattie (Ipswich T) for Watson and T.J.Whymark (Ipswich T) for McDermott.

Half-time 0-1   Full-time 0-2
Ref: A.Jargusz (Poland)   Att: 9,250

ANOTHER frustrating day for England and their supporters. Once again goals, and lots of them, were the order of the day but once again, against mediocre opposition, England were unable to deliver the goods. With England's only realistic hope of edging out Italy from their group depending on the goals they could score in this game in Luxembourg, one expected all out assault from the start.

In fact England were lucky to keep their goal intact as several very dangerous breaks by the home side almost brought them a goal or two. Obviously England had most of the possession but their old failing in front of goal once again let them down. Trevor Francis made one early break that forced Moes into a good interception, but Francis was too often alone in finding any sort of imagination.

Paul Mariner was particularly disappointing in his support and one glaring miss on 20 minutes after lovely play by Francis, brought jeers from the home crowd. Gordon Hill then produced a good save from Moes who turned his 25-yard drive on to the crossbar and away to safety.

The home side broke cleverly at times and one such move involving Mond, Michaux and Braun ended with first Ray

for three games. For his first game against the Swiss, he turned to the successful European Cup winning Liverpool side for his selections, using seven of the team that beat Borussia Mönchengladbach. It was in an effort to bring some continuity to the team but, alas, on this occasion they could not beat a hard-working Swiss side.

As so often happens at Wembley, a visiting team raised their game to a level way beyond their normal. But this was without doubt the best Swiss team that England have ever played against and in the first half the visitors could easily have been two or three goals up.

After an early miss by Ray Kennedy when he headed into the goalkeeper's hands, the Swiss suddenly looked dangerous as they broke swiftly. Küttel sent Hasler away, only for his shot to go a foot wide, but these two combined again shortly afterwards when Küttel just missed a dangerous centre from Hasler. England, meanwhile, were well held with Kevin Keegan being closely marked. The most impressive player on the pitch was Elsener, playing on the left side of the Swiss attack. His change of pace was particularly eye-catching.

England's best and most attractive movements invariably began at the feet of the evergreen Ian Callaghan. Recalled to the side for the first time since 1966, he used all his experience, and his delightful passing deserved better support from his colleagues. One long ball from him almost brought about a fortunate goal when Hasler, thinking wrongly that he was under pressure, almost put through his own goal but Burgener dived to save.

After the interval Gordon Hill came on for Mike Channon and he did manage to add some zest to the England attack, but it was the Swiss who almost scored an early second-half goal. Both Barberis and Küttel had successive close range shots blocked before England at last took a grip on the play. From that moment play was almost entirely at the Swiss end.

Hill made some lively runs down the left but all too often found his colleagues closely marked by some positive Swiss defending. Burgener was a highly competent goalkeeper and pulled off several good saves with one notable effort from Hill after Trevor Francis had sent the substitute clear.

This pressure intensified over the last

Clemence blocking Michaux's shot and then Emlyn Hughes hacking the ball away for a corner. On the half-hour England, at last, got the breakthrough they needed. Rohmann and Mariner challenged for an Ian Callaghan cross and Mariner was able to knock it down for Ray Kennedy to latch on to it and drive a good shot wide of Moes.

Unfortunately the goal did not bring the expected avalanche, instead, all of England's efforts fell short, usually around Rohmann's broad shoulders as the home centre-half won everything in the air.

England made two second-half substitutes with Trevor Whymark and Kevin Beattie coming on but there was little improvement. Only Francis and Ray Wilkins showed anything of their international pedigree and it was bitterly disappointing to see such a poor side as Luxembourg hold England with such ease. Mariner had a case for a penalty after a challenge by Fandel but it was not until injury time that England scored again. The goal was similar to the first one with some of the roles reversed. This time it was Kennedy who headed down Callaghan's cross for Mariner to shoot home.

All in all though a poor performance by England.

> 5th match v Luxembourg.
> Debut, as substitute, for Whymark.

England v Italy   World Cup Qualifier

Played on Wednesday, 16 November 1977 at Wembley Stadium.

England: R.N.Clemence (Liverpool); P.G.Neal (Liverpool), T.J.Cherry (Leeds Utd), R.C.Wilkins (Chelsea), D.V.Watson (Man City), E.W.Hughes (Liverpool, captain), J.K.Keegan (Hamburger SV), S.J.Coppell (Man Utd), R.D.Latchford (Everton), T.D.Brooking (West Ham), P.S.Barnes (Man City).
Subs: T.J.Francis (Birmingham C) for Keegan and J.S.Pearson (Man Utd) for Latchford.
Italy: D.Zoff (Juventus); M.Tardelli (Juventus), C.Gentile (Juventus), R.Benetti (Juventus), R.Mozzini (Torino), G.Facchetti (Inter-Milan), F.Causio (Juventus), R.Zaccarelli (Torino),

F.Graziani (Torino), G.Antognoni (Fiorentina), R.Bettega (Juventus).
Subs: A.Cuccureddu (Juventus) for Facchetti and C.Sala for Graziani (Torino).

Half-time 1-0   Full-time 2-0

Ref: K.Palotai (Hungary)   Att: 92,000

THE best England performance for two years: that was how best to describe this fine win over Italy, and although qualification for the World Cup finals was still only a formality for the Italians, England, at least, gave some cause for optimism for the future. Italy now required just a 1-0 victory in their remaining group match, at home to Luxembourg, and England knew, barring a miracle, their World Cup challenge was over for another four years. Italy won the group on goal-difference, which was a shame because on the evidence of this game, England had much to offer world football.

Ron Greenwood picked two wingers in Steve Coppell and Peter Barnes and went into the match determined to attack Italy down their flanks. It was a good tactical decision which on the day paid off handsomely. Right from the start there was a real passion about England's play and they quickly won over the 92,000 crowd. As early as the 11th minute they took the lead. Trevor Brooking, outstanding throughout, roamed out to space on the right to send over one of many accurate crosses. Kevin Keegan met it superbly and his firm glancing header looped over Zoff

With a superb header, Kevin Keegan heads England's first goal against Italy at Wembley in November 1977.

Trevor Brooking slots the ball wide of Dino Zoff after a brilliant pass from Keegan.

to nestle in the far corner of the Italian's net.

The goal gave England a great incentive and for a while they tore into Italy. You could see the nervousness oozing from the visitors as Coppell, Barnes, Brooking and Keegan searched busily for the vital second goal.

For the remainder of the half the Italians looked anything but confident. They resorted to their usual unfair methods with Benetti and Gentile both having their names taken by the referee as desperate tackles went in. Barnes was particularly lively and although he missed two good chances from Coppell's promptings he brought the crowd to its feet with one brilliant dribble that ended with Zoff saving low down at the foot of the post.

Despite all this passion, though, England failed to score again before the half-time whistle sounded, much to Italy's obvious relief.

Obviously Italy's manager, Enzo Bearzot, had harsh words with his players at the interval and his new instructions were soon apparent at the restart. Keegan and Brooking were allowed less room and gradually the play went the way Italy wanted it to. They were also now able to counter-attack more often and there was less pressure on their back four. However, England still played with commendable spirit and no little amount of skill but Keegan was now tiring and the close marking of Benetti was getting to him. It cost the England star a booking after he understandably retaliated to a particularly crunching tackle from the Italian.

In the end, though, Keegan had the last laugh as with ten minutes left he put a brilliant pass through for Brooking and the West Ham player, finding himself clear, coolly slotted the ball wide of Zoff. One more goal would really have put some pressure on Italy for their game with Luxembourg, but with Keegan being replaced by Trevor Francis and Italy tightening up even more at the back, England rarely looked like adding to their two goals.

England could take great heart from this display and it augered well for the future, perhaps for the first time for some years.

13th match v Italy.
Debut for Coppell, Latchford and Barnes.
50th cap for Hughes.
"It is always difficult to describe your feelings on your debut for your country, but obviously I was very proud and delighted."
Steve Coppell

West Germany v England
Friendly

Played on Wednesday, 22 February 1978 in the Olympic Stadium, Munich.

West Germany: J.Maier (Bayern Munich); H.H.Vogts (Borussia Mönchengladbach), H.Zimmermann (1.FC Cologne), R.Rüssmann (FC Schalke 04), G.Schwarzenbeck (Bayern Munich), R.Bonhof (Borussia Mönchengladbach), R.Abramczik (FC Schalke 04), H.Neumann (1.FC Cologne), B.Hölzenbein (Eintracht Frankfurt), H.Flohe (1.FC Cologne), K.H.Rummenigge (Bayern Munich).
Subs: B.Dietz (MSV Duisburg) for Neumann, R.Worm (MSV Duisburg) for Holzenbein and M.Burgsmüller (Borussia Dortmund) for Flohe.
England: R.N.Clemence (Liverpool); P.G.Neal (Liverpool), M.D.Mills (Ipswich T), R.C.Wilkins (Chelsea), D.V.Watson (Man City), E.W.Hughes (Liverpool, captain), J.K.Keegan (Hamburger SV), S.J.Coppell (Man Utd), J.S.Pearson (Man Utd), T.D.Brooking (West Ham), P.S.Barnes (Man City).
Sub: T.J.Francis (Birmingham C) for Keegan.

Half-time 0-1   Full-time 2-1
Ref: F.Wöhrer (Austria)   Att: 78,000

WITH Ron Greenwood now in control on a full-time basis the first test for his new regime couldn't have been more difficult. An away match against the current World Champions! But hard as this might be for the new manager, then if England were to build on their excellent victory over the Italians these were just the sort of games he needed.

England began confidently. Ray Wilkins and Trevor Brooking controlled the midfield and the all action approach of the visitors contrasted rather vividly with the somewhat over casual attitude of the Germans. They seemed content to just sit back and let England do all the attacking. Peter Barnes had a fine first half and his wing play was a feature of England's display. With Steve Coppell also playing well the German defence was frequently pulled out of position. In the 16th minute, Barnes produced a dazzling run and so nearly scored with his final shot.

Kevin Keegan was also in outstanding form and England continued to make all the running. A Barnes centre was headed weakly at goal by Stuart Pearson as the pressure increased and the first time that Ray Clemence was tested came as late as the 26th minute when Bonhof's free-kick was deflected by Rummenigge on to the woodwork. Despite having so much of the game, England created few clear openings but in the 41st minute they finally found a way through.

A good pass by Wilkins sent Phil Neal away on the right. The full-back sent it on to Coppell and the winger centred for Pearson to outjump Rüssman and head in off of a post. It was a good goal and one that lifted the England team's confidence to an even higher level.

Early in the second half, West Germany stepped up the pace. They pushed forward more frequently but with Dave Watson and Emlyn Hughes looking solid in defence, the Germans looked far from convincing and England held their lead comfortably. Attacks came and went before the home side sent on Worm, Dietz and Burgsmüller as substitutes. Worm had played the previous night in the corresponding 'B' international and scored Germany's goal. Within minutes of coming on here he had done it again. It was Dietz who could have scored but instead he laid the ball square to Worm, who equalized with a shot that Clemence got a hand to but could not stop.

The goal had come with just ten minutes to go and was a bitter disappointment for England, but there was still hope that they could hold on for an honourable draw for the remainder of the game. Keegan went off, exhausted after covering every blade of grass, and the Hamburger

SV star received a very warm round of applause from his adopted fans.

At that point the game seemed to be drifting towards a draw but, with only five minutes left, all of England's good work came undone. Watson gave away a dangerous free-kick on the edge of the area and Bonhof's fierce shot pierced the defensive wall to beat Clemence.

England were desperately unlucky to lose this game but they could take consolation from another very much improved performance in what was a difficult match.

14th match v West Germany.

England v Brazil
Friendly

Played on Wednesday, 19 April 1978 at Wembley Stadium.

England: T.J.Corrigan (Man City); M.D.Mills (Ipswich T), T.J.Cherry (Leeds Utd), B.Greenhoff (Man Utd), D.V.Watson (Man City), A.W.Currie (Leeds Utd), J.K.Keegan (Liverpool, captain), S.J.Coppell (Man Utd), R.D.Latchford (Everton), T.J.Francis (Birmingham C), P.S.Barnes (Man City).
Brazil: E.Leão (Palmeiras); J.M.Rodrigues (Corinthians), E.N.Filho (Fluminense), A.C.Cerezo (Atlético Mineiro), A.C.da Silva (Vasco da Gama), J.J.Amaral (Guarani), G.Alves (Botafogo), A.Antunes Coimbra (Flamengo), J.B.Nunes (Santa Cruz), R.Rivelino (Fluminense), D.J.Guimaraes (Vasco da Gama).
Sub: J.B.da Silva (Internacional) for Nunes.

Half-time 0-1   Full-time 1-1
Ref: C.G.Corver (Holland)   Att: 92,000

WHEN one thinks of Brazilian teams over the years, words such as flair, skill, power, brilliance and magical all flow from the tongue freely. But after their display at Wembley, then a few more less familiar words must be used to describe them. Physical would probably be the most polite description as Brazil used every means possible to stop this injury-hit England side. For real *aficionados* of the Brazilian game it was a sad night.

A packed Wembley roared England on, but right from the start Brazil made their intentions clear. Edinho scythed into Brian Greenhoff and then Abel slid into the heels of Trevor Francis. It was all far removed from what everyone expected. After ten minutes, though, Brazil showed something of the better side of their game. A stunning six-man move orchestrated by Rivelino ended with Gil, looking for all the world as though he was going to pass, instead fired a vicious shot inside Joe Corrigan's near post for a superb goal.

England were not put off by this early set-back at all and they pushed the Brazilians back with some positive and controlled football. Kevin Keegan, despite being continually fouled, was joining the attack at every opportunity and he was unlucky with a header from Peter Barnes' cross which went over. Francis, too, had a couple of clear chances, which he narrowly missed, and then Mick Mills joined in to hit a fine shot just over after Tony Currie had linked up with the full-back.

Kevin Keegan celebrates his goal against Brazil at Wembley in April 1978.

The Brazilians reacted to this stream of attacking football with some ruthless defending. Ze Maria was booked for a terrible challenge on Keegan, and four of his colleagues joined him later in the referee's notebook.

The game degenerated after the interval as England, too, gave away their fair share of free-kicks. Play was confined to the midfield and goal chances were very rare. It seemed that only an England goal would prevent the match from sinking without trace and on 70 minutes that is exactly what happened. For the umpteenth time Cerezo committed a foul, this time bringing down Francis on the edge of the Brazilian penalty area. The wall lined up but Keegan stepped up to bend a lovely shot around it and beyond Leão.

It was no more than England deserved and it was fitting that Keegan should score the goal. The crowd tried everything to spur their players on to further reward but the remaining minutes had very little in the way of excitement and in the end they had to be content with the 1-1 draw.

11th match v Brazil.
Brazil's Rodrigues also known as 'Ze Maria'; Filho as 'Edinho'; A.C.da Silva as 'Abel'; Alves as 'Gil'; Antunes Coimbra as 'Zico'; Guimaraes as 'Dirceu'; J.B.da Silva as 'Batista'.

Wales v
England   Home Championship

Played on Saturday, 13 May 1978 at Ninian Park, Cardiff.

Wales: W.D.Davies (Wrexham); M.E.Page (Birmingham C), J.P.Jones (Liverpool),

Phil Dwyer heads Wales' only goal against England at Ninian Park in May 1978.

L.Phillips (Aston Villa), D.E.Jones (Norwich C), T.C.Yorath (Coventry C), C.S.Harris (Leeds Utd), B.Flynn (Leeds Utd), A.T.Curtis (Swansea C), P.J.Dwyer (Cardiff C), M.R.Thomas (Wrexham).
Subs: G.Davies (Wrexham) for D.Jones and J.P.Mahoney (Middlesbrough) for Yorath.
England: P.L.Shilton (Nottm Forest); M.D.Mills (Ipswich T, captain), T.J.Cherry (Leeds Utd), B.Greenhoff (Man Utd), D.V.Watson (Man City), R.C.Wilkins (Chelsea), S.J.Coppell (Man Utd), T.J.Francis (Birmingham C), R.D.Latchford (Everton), T.D.Brooking (West Ham), P.S.Barnes (Man City).
Subs: A.W.Currie (Leeds Utd) for Cherry and P.Mariner (Ipswich T) for Latchford.

Half-time 0-1   Full-time 1-3

Ref: M.Moffatt (Northern Ireland)
                                    Att: 17,750

ENGLAND began the 1978 Home Championship with a hard-fought victory in

Cardiff. On a bumpy pitch, which made good football very difficult, both sides put in a fully committed performance and what the game lacked in finesse it more than made up for with incident.

The visitors dominated the early exchanges. Ray Wilkins and Trevor Brooking looked sharp in midfield and Bob Latchford was a lively front man. So it was not too surprising when England opened the scoring in the eighth minute. A move built up from the back with Mick Mills moving the ball on to Brooking. Brooking, then crossed and seemed to have overhit the centre, but it was well collected by Peter Barnes who then centred perfectly for Latchford to head in brilliantly at the near post.

England were then hit by two pieces of bad luck for which the pitch must take a share of the blame. First of all, in the 16th minute Trevor Cherry, leaping high, fell awkwardly. He had to go off immediately with what later proved to be a broken collarbone. It was a blow to England and necessitated a reorganisation. Tony Currie came on as substitute, allowing Wilkins to drop back to right-back with Mills switching to the left. It was doubly disappointing as Wilkins had looked good up to then but lost his effectiveness after his change of position.

But at least it allowed Currie to come on and it was soon evident that he had a natural pedigree at this level. England were then further hampered, though, when Latchford pulled a muscle and had to limp off to be replaced by Paul Mariner. Again, it was a shame because the goalscorer had looked good whilst he was on. All these changes unsettled England and the rhythm went out of their game for a while. But Wales had little to offer in the first half, so the lead was held comfortably.

After the break Wales looked a sharper team. Harris was their main hope and his pace and trickery led to many good attacks. Peter Shilton showed some vulnerability in the air but his groundwork was first class. He once dived amongst the flailing boots to grab Thomas' cross-shot. But this improved Welsh play then brought them an equalizer. Brooking was caught in possession by Mahoney, who quickly sent Harris away on another run. The winger outpaced Mills before crossing for Phil Dwyer to head home.

For a while after the goal Wales pegged England back but good solid defending and clever play gradually took the steam out of the Welsh who faded over the last 15 minutes. With ten minutes left, England scored a gem of a goal to regain the lead. Currie picked up possession on the half-way line and ran over 25 yards before unleashing a spectacular curling shot from 30 yards which beat Dai Davies all ends up.

It was a fine goal reminiscent of Bobby Charlton and signalled the end of the Welsh resistance. With a minute to go, a good move down the left involving Steve Coppell ended with a cross to the middle where Barnes was on hand to crash home a shot from just inside the penalty area.

> 91st match v Wales.
> Mills captain for first time.

England v Home Championship
Northern Ireland

Played on Tuesday, 16 May 1978 at Wembley Stadium.

England: R.N.Clemence (Liverpool); P.G.Neal (Liverpool), M.D.Mills (Ipswich T), B.Greenhoff (Man Utd), D.V.Watson (Man City), E.W.Hughes (Liverpool, captain), S.J.Coppell (Man Utd), R.C.Wilkins (Chelsea), J.S.Pearson (Man Utd), A.W.Currie (Leeds Utd), A.S.Woodcock (Nottm Forest).
Northern Ireland: J.A.Platt (Middlesbrough); J.M.Nicholl (Man Utd),, P.W.Scott (York C), B.Hamilton (Millwall), C.J.Nicholl (Southampton), S.B.McIlroy (Man Utd), D.McCreery (Man Utd), M.H.O'Neill (Nottm Forest), T.Anderson (Peterborough Utd), G.Armstrong (Spurs), R.C.McGrath (Manchester Utd).
Sub: G.T.Cochrane (Burnley) for McGrath.

Half-time 1-0   **Full-time 1-0**
Ref: J.R.Gordon (Scotland)   Att: 48,000

Ray Wilkins beats Chris Nicholl to get in a cross against Northern Ireland at Wembley in May 1978.

A BATTLING Northern Ireland side never looked like winning this Home Championship international but they worked tirelessly to make things very difficult for England. Overall the game was a poor one with both sides finding it hard to raise play above the boredom level.

In a humid atmosphere and with a small crowd, England played a 4-3-3 formation but found scoring chances down to a minimum, especially in the first half. The Irish offered virtually no threat to the home defence and Mick Mills, Phil Neal and especially Dave Watson, were all able to push up regularly to help the attack. Several times Watson found himself in the thick of the action but with Scott and Chris Nicholl playing particularly well the ball was cleared with monotonous regularity. Emlyn Hughes and Watson coped easily at the back despite the midfield promptings of McIlroy, McCreery and O'Neill.

England experimented with only one winger in Steve Coppell, but keen tackling kept him in check. Newcomer Tony Woodcock was also held so few clear-cut chances were created. But a minute before the interval, England found a way through. Watson, yet again up with the attack, controlled a corner by Ray Wilkins and cleverly backheeled it to Neal, who drove a firm shot through a cluster of legs and beyond Platt.

It was the perfect psychological boost for England and after the break they restarted in positive fashion. A long pass by Mills sent Woodcock on a chase and only a brave stop by Platt prevented a score. Then Wilkins struck a good shot which hit the side netting before two fine efforts by Watson almost brought a second goal. His first header was blocked on the line by Scott and then a second header was saved by Platt. Watson was desperately unlucky that he did not score.

England were now well in command, although they continued to miss chances failing to find the finish their approach play deserved. Tony Currie did some lovely work in the midfield especially as the Irish lads faded, and for the visitors only an Armstrong shot straight at Ray Clemence lifted their gloom. In many scrambles around the Irish goal, the ball often bounced loose but it never found an English boot to finish it off. Stuart Pearson missed a couple of good chances and ironically, near the end, it was Clemence who had to make the best save of the match when an isolated raid saw a good shot by Anderson well held by the England goalkeeper.

A final flurry of activity almost gave Woodcock a debut goal. First he beat Platt, only for Hamilton to clear off the line and then Platt made the last of his many saves by pushing Woodcock's shot around a post.

Steve Coppell (far right) scores England's winner against Scotland at Hampden Park in May 1978.

In the end England had won with ease but they had never inspired the confidence that they should have done. Perhaps a few more goals might have done that for them.

> 85th match v Northern Ireland.
> Debut for Woodcock.

Scotland v England   Home Championship

Played on Saturday, 20 May 1978 at Hampden Park, Glasgow.

Scotland: A.Rough (Partick Thistle); S.Kennedy (Aberdeen), W.Donachie (Man City), T.Forsyth (Rangers), K.Burns (Nottm Forest), B.D.Rioch (Derby Co), D.S.Masson (Derby Co), K.Dalglish (Liverpool), J.Jordan (Man City), R.A.Hartford (Man City), W.Johnston (West Brom).
Subs: A.Gemmill (Nottm Forest) for Rioch and G.J.Souness (Liverpool) for Masson.
England: R.N.Clemence (Liverpool); P.G.Neal (Liverpool), M.D.Mills (Ipswich T), R.C.Wilkins (Chelsea), D.V.Watson (Man City), E.W.Hughes (Liverpool, captain), S.J.Coppell (Man Utd), A.W.Currie (Leeds Utd), P.Mariner (Ipswich T), T.J.Francis (Birmingham C), P.S.Barnes (Man City).
Subs: B.Greenhoff (Man Utd) for Hughes and T.D.Brooking (West Ham) for Mariner.

Half-time 0-0   Full-time 0-1
Ref: G.Konrath (France)   Att: 90,000

SCOTLAND were looking to leave for Argentina and the World Cup finals with a victory over the Auld Enemy to inspire them to even greater heights. As it occurred they left with the memory of another defeat at the hands of England and many unanswered questions about their best line-up.

Territorially Scotland had much the better of this game. Rioch, Masson and Hartford dominated the midfield, but for all their possession they created few clear chances for their forwards. Johnston gave Phil Neal a difficult time but Jordan was completely mastered by England's star, Dave Watson. The Manchester City man had a fine game, dominating in the air and holding England together when the Scots were at their most potent in the first half.

Hartford was Scotland's main threat. As well as prompting many attacks he also twice nearly scored himself. One shot scraped a post and then after a Johnston cross he lobbed a shot on to the bar. There was another scare for England when Emlyn Hughes appeared to handle a header by Dalglish but the French referee ignored all the passionate pleas by the Scots. It was significant that Scotland, despite their overall superiority, had not forced Ray Clemence into one save and it summed up their performance.

The second half continued in the same vein with Scotland continually pushing forward, only to keep hitting a wall of white England shirts. The visitors remained calm under intense pressure from both the Scottish players and the vociferous home crowd. England can be proud of that.

Substitutes were used by both sides in an effort to pep up their play, but it had little effect on Scotland. Then, with just seven minutes remaining, England scored. Paul Mariner was immediately in the action, beginning the move which led to a cross from Peter Barnes. Trevor Francis jumped with Rough and the 'keeper dropped the ball under pressure straight to the feet of Steve Coppell, who promptly thumped it into the net for a goal which stunned the crowd into silence.

England held out comfortably for the win over the remaining minutes and although the home fans gave Scotland a rousing send-off at the end, their hopes and expectations had taken a battering after this defeat by their arch enemy. The England players, meanwhile, took a great deal of pride out of their visit.

> 96th match v Scotland.

England v Hungary   Friendly

Played on Wednesday, 24 May 1978 at Wembley Stadium.

England: P.L.Shilton (Nottm Forest); P.G.Neal (Liverpool), M.D.Mills (Ipswich T), R.C.Wilkins (Chelsea), D.V.Watson (Man City), E.W.Hughes (Liverpool, captain), J.K.Keegan (Hamburger SV), S.J.Coppell (Man Utd), T.J.Francis (Birmingham C), T.D.Brooking (West Ham), P.S.Barnes (Man City).
Subs: B.Greenhoff (Man Utd) for Watson and A.W.Currie (Leeds Utd) for Coppell.
Hungary: S.Gujdár (Honvéd); P.Török (Vasas), I.Kocsis (Honvéd), J.Tóth (Újpesti Dózsa), S.Zombori (Vasas), Z.Kereki (Haladás VSE), L.Fazekas (Újpesti Dózsa), T.Nyilasi (Ferencváros), A.Törőcsik (Újpesti Dózsa), S.Pintér (Honvéd), L.Nagy (Újpesti Dózsa).
Sub: K.Csapó (Tatabánya) for Fazekas.

Peter Barnes (far left) scores the first of the four goals that destroyed Hungary at Wembley in May 1978.

Half-time 3-0   Full-time 4-1
Ref: R.Vigliani (France)   Att: 74,000

TWENTY-FIVE years had passed since the Hungarians came to Wembley and gave England a football lesson but their 1978 counterparts found just the opposite as England gave their best display yet under Ron Greenwood's charge. Playing some delightful football they tore into the bewildered Hungarians throughout the first half.

England were ahead as early as the 11th minute with a fine goal. Goalkeeper Gujdár kicked clear but Dave Watson met it with a full-blooded header, sending it back deep into Hungary's half. Kevin Keegan chased enthusiastically, brought the ball under control and then turned it inside for Peter Barnes to prod into the net. England's confidence soared and they were soon back again. The inventiveness of Ray Wilkins and Trevor Brooking were the outstanding features of the home display and Keegan and Trevor Francis were a formidable combination up front. The whole side played with style and imagination and on the half-hour they increased their lead.

Again Barnes was involved, taking the ball down the wing to the by-line before putting over a good centre. The Hungarian defender intercepted the ball with his arms and the referee had no hesitation in giving England a penalty. Phil Neal stepped up, making no mistake, and Hungary were now really up against it. There was little to enthuse over in their team and almost immediately they were 3-0 down.

A long pass by Francis found Keegan but the goalkeeper raced out of his area and brought him down. Brooking sent the free-kick into the middle, where Dave Watson touched the ball on for Francis to finish with a powerful header. It was magnificent stuff and England could have had other goals, notably after Keegan's brilliant backheel set up Brooking. The West Ham player shot but alas it was too close to Gujdár and the 'keeper saved.

At half-time, though, the crowd gave a huge ovation to their side whilst the Hungarians trooped off in a very dejected state of mind.

After the interval England, understandably perhaps, could not quite sustain their earlier dominance and this allowed Hungary the chance to show their undoubted talent. Törőcsik began to look a very good player and Nyilasi showed some silky skills in the midfield. Their attacks were still limited, though, and England continued to hold the upper hand. But on the hour, a slip by Neal let in Nyilasi. He quickly found Nagy, who hit a fine shot past Peter Shilton.

For a few minutes after the goal, Hungary looked the better side and only a fine save by Shilton from Törőcsik's shot prevented them pulling back a second goal. However, England then steadied themselves and regained the initiative. With ten minutes to go they sealed their victory with another goal. Barnes again made the play and his cross was slightly deflected by Brooking. The ball ran free to an incoming Tony Currie who drove in an unstoppable shot.

That ended a splendid night for England and their fans went home delighted at what they had seen.

> 11th match v Hungary.
> Penalty scored for England by Neal.

Denmark v England
European Championship Qualifier

Played on Wednesday, 20 September 1978 at the Idraetspark, Copenhagen.

Denmark: B.Jensen (FC Brugge); F.Nielsen (OB Odense), S.Lerby (Ajax Amsterdam), P.Roentved (Werder Bremen), H.Munk-Jensen (AaB Aarlborg), S.Lerby (Ajax Amsterdam), F.Arnesen (Ajax Amasterdam), F.Lund (Fortuna Düsseldorf), C.Nielsen (Borussia Mönchenglabach), A.Simonsen (Borussia Mönchengladbach). B.Nielsen (Ande-

rlecht), J.Kristensen (Naestved IF). Sub: A.Hansen (Tennis FC) for B.Neilsen.

England: R.N.Clemence (Liverpool); P.G.Neal (Liverpool), M.D.Mills (Ipswich T), R.C.Wilkins (Chelsea), D.V.Watson (Man City), E.W.Hughes (Liverpool, captain), J.K.Keegan (Hamburger SV), S.J.Coppell (Man Utd), R.D.Latchford (Everton), T.D.Brooking (West Ham), P.S.Barnes (Man City).

Half-time 2-2   Full-time 3-4
Ref: A.Prokop (East Germany) Att: 48,000

THIS seven-goal thriller had everything, good goals, bad errors, fierce tackling, fine skills, all in fact the neutral observer could wish for in a football match. Unfortunately, from a purely professional point of view it was a disappointing performance from an England side who had too many players off form.

To begin their European challenge with this difficult away match meant that England had to be at their best. Denmark, with lots of skill and determination, gave everything although, thankfully, their defence was worse than England's. Early on both sides set the pattern by dishing out some rough tackles. Kevin Keegan spent all night trying to escape the crude challenges of Lund, and Denmark's star player Simonsen received similar treatment from Mick Mills. In attack England had the better of the early exchanges. Steve Coppell shot just wide in one raid before, on 14 minutes, Keegan almost gave England the lead when, after a good move involving Peter Barnes and Ray Wilkins, he hit the post with a good shot.

Three minutes later the breakthrough did come. Keegan was again fouled by Lund and from the free-kick Trevor Brooking floated the ball towards Keegan and his carefully guided header looped over goalkeeper Jensen and in under the crossbar.

The lively Simonsen was only just stopped by Dave Watson's foul after Emlyn Hughes had been beaten and England cleared the free-kick and broke away dangerously themselves. Another

Keegan heads past Danish goalkeeper Birger Jensen in Copenhagen in September 1978.

free-kick was awarded and Brooking again crossed. This time Watson got a touch on and in came Keegan to throw himself headlong to score number two.

Denmark were now committed to all-out attack and a minute later, with England's defence looking more and more ragged, they won a penalty. Phil Neal was often at full stretch and it came as no surprise when he fouled Lerby in the area. Simonsen coolly slotted home the spot-kick and the 48,000 crowd roared Denmark on. By this time excitement was at fever pitch and shortly afterwards the Danes equalized. A lovely through-pass by Kristensen sent Arnesen away and his shot flew past Ray Clemence.

The home side now had their tails up and England struggled to contain them. Their breaks from midfield were not being picked up and the visitors were glad to hear the half-time whistle. After the break Ron Greenwood dropped Keegan back to try to stem the flow of that Danish midfield. It worked because on 51 minutes England regained the lead. Brooking, who had a fine match throughout, won a corner. He took the kick himself only for the ball to bounce back to him. This time he sent in a low cross which Keegan just missed but Bob Latchford followed in to force the ball over the line.

Although back in the lead England still struggled in defence. They just could not come to terms with the speed of the Danes and they were very lucky when C.Nielsen was left unmarked in front of goal only for him to head yards wide. There was no let up in the fierce pace or the goalmouth action, but as the game wore on the extra quality of England began to show. Brooking was superb and his link-up with Keegan was almost telepathic. Wilkins cracked a shot against the bar after a cross by Barnes but then Denmark hit back with a substitute Hansen scraping the outside of a post in the 70th minute. Almost immediately the same player missed a glorious chance to equalize.

England escaped and with six minutes to go, Neal moved forward to hit a fine shot into the roof of the net to give the visitors a two-goal cushion again. This brought some relief to the away side but there was still time for Roentved to crash home a centre from Lund to make it 4-3 to England.

In the end the more controlled play of the last 20 minutes had given England the edge they just about deserved. An entertaining game and a satisfying victory.

> 6th match v Denmark.
> Penalty scored for Denmark by Simonsen.

Republic of Ireland v England European Championship Qualifier

Played on Wednesday, 25 October 1978 at Dalymount Park, Dublin.

Republic of Ireland: M.Kearns (Walsall); P.M.Mulligan (West Brom), J.P.Holmes (Spurs), M.T.Lawrenson (Brighton & HA), D.A.O'Leary (Arsenal), W.L.Brady (Arsenal), G.A.Daly (Derby Co), A.P.Grealish (Orient), P.G.McGee (QPR), G.J.Ryan (Brighton & HA), D.J.Givens (Birmingham C).
Subs: F.A.Stapleton (Arsenal) for McGee and E.Gregg (Bohemians) for O'Leary.

England: R.N.Clemence (Liverpool); P.G.Neal (Liverpool), M.D.Mills (Ipswich T), R.C.Wilkins (Chelsea), D.V.Watson (Man City), E.W.Hughes (Liverpool, captain), J.K.Keegan (Hamburger SV), S.J.Coppell (Man Utd), R.D.Latchford (Everton), T.D.Brooking (West Ham), P.S.Barnes (Man City).
Sub: P.B.Thompson (Liverpool) for Watson and A.S.Woodcock (Nottm Forest) for Barnes.

Half-time 1-1   Full-time 1-1

Ref: H.Aldinger (West Germany) Att: 48,000

ENGLAND'S second difficult away tie in their European Championship group took them to Dublin. They gave a mixed performance but in the end were probably satisfied with a point.

They began well and quickly stamped their authority on the game. After only eight minutes they took the lead when Bob Latchford headed home cleverly from a Trevor Brooking corner. The ball had been deflected into Latchford's path. Three minutes later, England came desperately close to scoring again. Another Brooking corner was headed clear by Givens, only for Steve Coppell to lash a volley goalwards. The Manchester United player was very unlucky to see his fine effort cannon back off the crossbar.

England kept up the pressure and were denied what looked a penalty when Lawrenson held back Kevin Keegan. The referee refused England's appeals and after this incident the Irish side began to fight back. They began to win the midfield battle with Brady being the central linchpin. One lovely pass by him almost let in McGee only for Dave Watson to clear desperately. In the 22nd minute, England were hampered when Watson had to go off with a leg injury. The commanding centre-half was replaced by Phil Thompson.

The gradual Irish improvement was completed when, after 26 minutes, a neat free-kick by Brady was fired home by Daly. O'Leary and Lawrenson used their height well and Keegan and Latchford were well held. Coppell was the main England threat and his runs always caused problems for Holmes. Brooking, too, showed his quality but defensively England did not look too good.

The second half saw the home side start well but then, as the game wore on, England began to regain control and it was the visitors who created the better chances. Ray Wilkins miskicked when well-placed Latchford was prevented from scoring a certain goal by a desperate late saving tackle by O'Leary. Coppell then

Peter Shilton makes a fine diving save against Czechoslovakia at Wembley in November 1978.

Steve Coppell pounces to give England victory over the Czechs after the European Champions' goalkeeper failed to hold a cross from Tony Currie.

giving England top-class opposition. The result was a big confidence booster but they had a magnificent display by Peter Shilton to thank for their win.

The Czechs took the initiative from the start adapting to the tricky conditions better than England and they were soon attacking forcefully. The dangerous Masný brought the first of many saves from Shilton when his low shot was well held by the 'keeper. Then the brilliant Nehoda broke down the right, shooting wide when perhaps a pass to Štambachr might have produced better results for them. Nehoda was looking very good and Trevor Cherry had his work cut out in trying to shut him down. More good work by Nehoda then gave Štambachr a chance, but again Shilton saved, albeit with some difficulty.

England found it very hard to make headway as the Czech's bold attacking play forced them back for long spells. Kevin Keegan was tightly marked and Tony Woodcock and Peter Barnes were also well held. All through England were frustrated by the good play of the visitors. Only one clear chance came England's way in the first half, but an awkward bounce took the ball away from Keegan. After 36 minutes Vojáček bundled Woodcock down and the England striker had to go off to be replaced by Bob Latchford.

Shilton continued to keep England in it and he made two superb saves from Kozák and then Nehoda enabling his team to go in at half-time still on level terms.

The game pattern did not change too much in the second half, although England did come more into things. Viv Anderson had a comfortable debut and it was he who started the move on 68 minutes which brought the goal. He made ground on the right before finding Tony Currie

saw a fine shot brilliantly saved at full stretch by Kearns.

England pressed hard for a winner with the Republic managing to relieve the pressure only with the occasional break-away. Near the end both, Kearns and Mulligan cleared off the line and the ball just would not go in for England. However, overall a draw was probably about right and both teams seemed happy at the final whistle.

7th match v Republic of Ireland.

England v Czechoslovakia Friendly

Played on Wednesday, 29 November 1978 at Wembley Stadium.

England: P.L.Shilton (Nottm Forest); V.A.Anderson (Nottm Forest), T.J.Cherry (Leeds Utd), P.B.Thompson (Liverpool), D.V.Watson (Man City), R.C.Wilkins (Chelsea), J.K.Keegan (Hamburger SV, captain), S.J.Coppell (Man Utd), A.S.Woodcock (Nottm Forest), A.W.Currie (Leeds Utd), P.S.Barnes (Man City).
Sub: R.D.Latchford (Everton) for Woodcock.

Czechoslovakia: P.Michalík (Baník Ostrava); J.Barmoš (Inter Bratislava), R.Vojáček (Baník Ostrava), L.Jurkemik (Inter Bratislava), K.Gögh (Slovan Bratislava), F.Štambachr (Dukla Prague), J.Kozák (Lokomotiva Košice), M.Gajdušek (Dukla Prague), K.Jarušek (Zbrojovska Brno), M.Masný (Slovan Bratislava), Z.Nehoda (Dukla Prague).
Sub: A.Panenka (Bohemians Prague) for Jarušek.

Half-time 0-0   Full-time 1-0

Ref: E.Linemayr (Austria)   Att: 92,000

IT was a bone-hard, frosty surface that greeted the teams for this Wembley friendly international with the reigning European Champions, Czechoslovakia

Viv Anderson, the first black footballer to be capped at senior level for England, enjoyed a fine debut against the Czechs.

to take it on. Currie hit it low into the goalmouth and with Michalík and Jurkemik getting in each other's way Steve Coppell pounced to walk the ball in over the icy goalmouth. It was a rather fortunate break for England but they followed it with their best spell of the match. They still created few chances though and towards the end the Czechs again came at England strongly.

With only a few minutes to go Panenka bent a free-kick narrowly wide as Shilton scrambled across his goal and that was virtually the Czechs' last chance. They had played well but had met Shilton on one of his unbeatable nights.

> 9th match v Czechoslovakia.
> Debut for Anderson, who thus became the first black player to represent England at this level.

England v Northern Ireland

European Championship Qualifier

Played on Wednesday, 7 February 1979 at Wembley Stadium.

England: R.N.Clemence (Liverpool); P.G.Neal (Liverpool), M.D.Mills (Ipswich T), A.W.Currie (Leeds Utd), D.V.Watson (Man City), E.W.Hughes (Liverpool, captain), J.K.Keegan (Hamburger SV), S.J.Coppell (Man Utd), R.D.Latchford (Everton), T.D.Brooking (West Ham), P.S.Barnes (Man City).

Northern Ireland: P.A.Jennings (Arsenal); P.J.Rice (Arsenal), S.Nelson (Arsenal),

Kevin Keegan jumps over Northern Ireland's Pat Jennings and Sammy Nelson after scoring in the match at Wembley in February 1979.

J.M.Nicholl (Man Utd), C.J.Nicholl (Southampton), D.McCreery (Man Utd), M.H.O'Neill (Nottm Forest), S.B.McIlroy (Man Utd), G.Armstrong (Spurs), W.T.Caskey (Derby Co), G.T.Cochrane (Middlesbrough).
Subs: R.C.McGrath (Man Utd) for Coch-

rane and D.W.Spence (Blackpool) for Caskey.

Half-time 1-0   **Full-time 4-0**

Ref: U.Ericsson (Sweden)   Att: 92,000

ENGLAND leap-frogged over the North-

Mick Mills leads the England celebrations after Dave Watson's goal against the Irish.

ern Ireland side to top the group one table after this emphatic, if not totally convincing victory. The Irish had come to Wembley as group leaders after their unexpected win in Bulgaria and they were full of confidence. But it all went out of the window as England overpowered them.

It took England a while to settle down and in the first quarter of an hour their defence looked decidedly shaky. But as soon as they took the lead in the 25th minute there was never any real doubt about the outcome. Steve Coppell put in a cross and Kevin Keegan beat Jennings to the ball and his header found the net.

That goal lifted England and Keegan had a splendid night. He was everywhere and with so much room given to him by the overworked Irish defenders he revelled in it. The midfield of Trevor Brooking, Tony Currie and Coppell played superbly well and were much too good for McIlroy, O'Neill and McCreery. There was one awkward moment for Ray Clemence when McIlroy's free-kick rebounded from the crossbar but that was an isolated threat. By half-time the only thing lacking from England's dominance was more goals.

Three minutes after the interval that problem was solved as the home side scored two quick goals. Keegan, always involved, sent a cross to the far post where Bob Latchford brushed aside a challenge and headed through the hands of Jennings. Before the Irish could recover from that set-back England scored a third goal. Again Keegan was involved as he and Brooking forced Ireland to concede a corner. Brooking took the kick and in came the powerful Dave Watson to crash home an unstoppable header.

The Irish were now right out of it and England tore their defence apart. Rice, Nelson and the two Nicholls were pulled all over Wembley by the tremendous running of Keegan, Latchford and Brooking. All three were outstanding and all three had a hand in the fourth goal on 63 minutes. Brooking took yet another corner, Keegan nodded it on and Latchford turned the ball past Jennings for a fine goal.

The Irish manager, Danny Blanchflower was not impressed by the physical side of England's game but it did not hide the fact that his side were outclassed. Currie and Brooking looked superb, especially in the second half, and Keegan was world class. His spell in the German League for Hamburger SV had certainly enhanced his reputation.

86th match v Northern Ireland.

Northern Ireland v England Home Championship

Played on Saturday, 19 May 1979 at Windsor Park, Belfast.

Northern Ireland: P.A.Jennings (Arsenal); P.J.Rice (Arsenal), S.Nelson (Arsenal), J.M.Nicholl (Man Utd), C.J.Nicholl (Southampton), V.Moreland (Derby Co), B.Hamilton (Swindon T), S.B.McIlroy (Manchester Utd), G.Armstrong (Spurs), W.T.Caskey (Derby Co), G.T.Cochrane (Middlesbrough).
Subs: R.C.McGrath (Man Utd) for Moreland and D.W.Spence (Blackpool) for Cochrane.

England: R.N.Clemence (Liverpool); P.G.Neal (Liverpool), M.D.Mills (Liverpool, captain), P.B.Thompson (Liverpool), D.V.Watson (Man City), A.W.Currie (Leeds Utd), S.J.Coppell (Man Utd), R.C.Wilkins (Chelsea), R.D.Latchford (Everton), T.McDermott (Liverpool), P.S.Barnes (Man City).

Half-time 0-2   Full-time 0-2
Ref: I.M.Foote (Scotland)   Att: 34,000

ENGLAND'S opening Home Championship fixture ironically took them to Windsor Park, Belfast only three months after their 4-0 drubbing of the Irish at Wembley. Both sides were eager to gain the psychological advantage to take with them into the return European Championship fixture in the October. On this day though it was the English who won with plenty to spare.

As usual the Irish team opened strongly in the early stages and only a fine tackle by Ray Wilkins prevented McIlroy from scoring in the fourth minute. But once England had settled the game swung regularly towards Jennings's goal. By the time sixteen minutes had elapsed the visitors were two goals up.

The first came after nine minutes. Nelson fouled Peter Barnes on the right hand edge of the area, Steve Coppell took the free-kick and in roared Dave Watson to send a firm header wide of Jennings. Seven minutes later a lovely four man move involving Terry McDermott, Bob Latchford, Wilkins and Coppell ended with the latter scoring from Wilkins a pass.

England might have increased their lead shortly afterwards but Latchford missed a good chance by not putting enough power into a header which allowed Chris Nicholl the time to clear from the line. It was difficult to see how the Irish could recover from this two-goal deficit especially as their midfield was totally overrun by the England trio of McDermott, Wilkins and Tony Currie. McIlroy did manage a volley which went just over and then Ray Clemence saved easily when Cochrane cut inside and shot.

There was much more purpose about England's attack and they looked dangerous every time they went forward. Coppell was particularly lively and he gave Rice a difficult game. Latchford too, had a good match and the Irish defenders were often at sixes and sevens in coping. Only McIlroy looked dangerous for Ireland and only the quickness of Clemence averted an awkward situation after McIlroy had got past Phil Thompson. Clemence then went down to easily save another shot from McIlroy before England regained their rhythm of the first half and all the pressure was on Ireland.

Rice somehow blocked a shot by Currie and other chances began to threaten Jennings goal. With Clemence now virtually a spectator it was all England and their best chance of adding to their goal tally fell to Barnes after Wilkins had set him up in front of goal with only Jennings to beat. The huge, and deserved, reputation of the big Irish goalkeeper must have upset Barnes because the England winger totally miskicked the ball to waste a glorious opportunity.

Nevertheless, despite missing several chances, England won and won with ease,

and, in doing so, put the pressure on the Irish for the October clash.

87th match v Northern Ireland.

England v Wales Home Championship

Played on Wednesday, 23 May 1979 at Wembley Stadium.

England: T.J.Corrigan (Man City); T.J.Cherry (Leeds Utd), K.G.Sansom (Crystal Palace), A.W.Currie (Leeds Utd), D.V.Watson (Man City), E.W.Hughes (Liverpool, captain), J.K.Keegan (Hamburger SV), R.C.Wilkins (Chelsea), R.D.Latchford (Everton), T.McDermott (Liverpool), L.P.Cunningham (West Brom).
Subs: T.D.Brooking (West Ham) for Currie and S.J.Coppell (Man Utd) for Latchford.
Wales: W.D.Davies (Wrexham); W.B.Stevenson (Leeds Utd), J.P.Jones (Wrexham), J.F.Mahoney (Middlesbrough), P.J.Dwyer (Cardiff C), L.Phillips (Swansea C), T.C.Yorath (Coventry C), B.Flynn (Leeds Utd), R.M.James (Swansea C), J.B.Toshack (Swansea C), A.T.Curtis (Leeds Utd).
Sub: C.S.Harris (Leeds Utd) for Toshack.

Half-time 0-0   Full-time 0-0
Ref: M.Moffatt (Northern Ireland)
Att: 70,250

ENGLAND fielded two new faces for this difficult game with Kenny Sansom and Lawrie Cunningham gaining their first caps. In a hard but always interesting encounter, Wales deserved their point but some poor England finishing helped their cause considerably.

Laurie Cunningham gets in a tackle on Joey Jones of Wales.

Both sides began brightly with Cunningham and Kevin Keegan looking sharp for England. Joe Corrigan saved an early shot from Curtis and then dealt confidently with a Toshack long-range effort. At the other end, Keegan twice went close and on the half-hour Terry McDermott

Steve Coppell beats George Wood to score England's second goal against Scotland at Wembley in May 1979.

was desperately unlucky when his fine shot scraped the outside of a Welsh post.

Corrigan continued his confident display when he raced from goal to powerfully head clear after finding himself outside his area. Big Dave Watson would have been proud of that header himself! Meanwhile, Cunningham hit a fierce shot just over and then saw a good cross go tantalisingly wide of the upright with no England forward able to get a touch.

It was now a question of who would be able to last the pace the better. As the game wore on it was obvious that England would finish the stronger. Jones saw one shot blocked but generally Wales made little impression on the solid England back line. With 20 minutes of the match left England made the first of two substitutions which almost turned the result their way. First Trevor Brooking replaced Currie and then Steve Coppell came on for the disappointing Bob Latchford.

Both the fresh players made an immediate impact. With Keegan's sparkle stifled by the close marking of Phillips, the attack needed a boost and Coppell came very close when he intercepted a back-pass and shot from a narrow angle. But the angle proved too great and the chance was lost. Then in the final hectic last few minutes, Keegan was in the thick of a scramble but twice England saw efforts by Trevor Cherry and Coppell cleared from the line.

A goal then would have been unfair on the battling Welsh who had given their usual hard-working performance led by Terry Yorath, John Mahoney and especially little Brian Flynn. For England, it was a case of building gradually the side that Ron Greenwood would like to see performing regularly.

92nd match v Wales.
Debuts for Sansom and Cunningham.

England v Scotland Home Championship

Played on Saturday, 26 May 1979 at Wembley Stadium.

England: R.N.Clemence (Liverpool); P.G.Neal (Liverpool), M.D.Mills (Ipswich T), P.B.Thompson (Liverpool), D.V.Watson (Man City), R.C.Wilkins (Chelsea), S.J.Coppell (Man Utd), J.K.Keegan (Hamburger SV, captain), R.D.Latchford (Everton), T.D.Brooking (West Ham), P.S.Barnes (Man City).

Scotland: G.Wood (Everton); G.E.Burley (Ipswich T), F.T.Gray (Leeds Utd), J.Wark (Ipswich T), G.McQueen (Man Utd), P.Hegarty (Dundee Utd), K.Dalglish (Liverpool), G.J.Souness (Liverpool), J.Jordan (Man Utd), R.A.Hartford (Man City), A.Graham (Leeds Utd).

Half-time 1-1   Full-time 3-1

A.J.Garrido (Portugal)   Att: 95,000

AS so often happens Scotland came to Wembley determined to put all their many troubles behind them by winning the one fixture that really mattered to them in their soccer calendar. They produced a revitalised performance which was way above their recent showings. It contributed to a super game, but in the end class told.

The first half was an absorbing battle. Scotland tore into England and Souness, Hartford and Wark won the midfield tussle hands down in the early stages. Up front Jordan, Dalglish and Graham caused all sorts of problems for England. Meanwhile Bob Latchford had an early 'goal' cancelled out because of a foul on Wood before Scotland quickly struck back. Wark shot just over after a clearance by Mick Mills had dropped at his feet. Three minutes later, Graham gave Phil Neal the slip and seemed certain to set

up a goal as a sea of blue shirts waited for the expected cross. Somehow, though, Mills blocked Dalgish's shot and then the defence deflected a Souness shot just wide.

The corner which followed was met by McQueen and Ray Wilkins did well to head the effort off the line. But all this pressure had to pay off and in the 21st minute the visitors took the lead. Jordan's strong run was halted but the ball ran for Graham. He put in a fierce centre and Dalglish was at the far post to control and pass square for Wark to score easily. At that stage the Scots were firmly in control of the match but England showing revived spirits under Ron Greenwood, cleverly fought their way back. The turning point probably came after a wonderful save by Ray Clemence.

Jordan hit a fine shot from 20 yards which took a wicked deflection off of Dave Watson's head. With Clemence already committed one way, he performed a miracle to somehow twist and push his right hand out to deflect the ball for a corner. It was one of the most remarkable saves ever seen at Wembley.

The Scots continued to dominate for a while but, with half-time imminent, England found a way back. Watson, Peter Barnes and Kevin Keegan combined to give Barnes possession 20 yards out. The winger cleverly flicked the ball up before hitting a low half-volley wide of Wood in the Scottish goal. It was a goal out of the blue and hardly deserved.

Despite this set-back, Scotland started in lively fashion after the interval with Graham having a shot saved only at the second attempt by Clemence, and then Watson almost put through his own goal when clearing Wark's dangerous cross away for a corner. Scotland were playing with great determination but England were definitely more in the game than they had been in the first half. On 62 minutes they really upset the Scots by taking the lead.

Dave Watson hooks the ball away from Bulgaria's Zhelyazkov in Sofia in June 1979.

Bulgaria v England
European Championship Qualifier

Played on Wednesday, 6 June 1979 at the Vassil Levski Stadium, Sofia.

Bulgaria: Y.Filipov (CSKA Sofia); N.Grancharov (Levski Spartak), K.Ivkov (Levski-Spartak), G.Bonev (Lokomotiv Sofia), I.Iliev (Slavia Sofia), R.Zoravkov (Lokomotiv Sofia), V.Voynov (Levski Spartak), K.Borisov (Levski Spartak), (Slavia Sofia), A.Zhelyazkov (Slavia Sofia), P.Panov (Levski Spartak), C.Tsvetkov (Slavia Sofia).
Subs: T.Barzov (Levski Spartak) for Zarovkov and R.Gotchev (Levski Spartak) for Voinov.

England: R.N.Clemence (Liverpool); P.G.Neal (Liverpool), M.D.Mills (Ipswich T), P.B.Thompson (Liverpool), D.V.Watson (Man City), R.C.Wilkins (Chelsea), J.K.Keegan (Hamburger SV, captain), S.J.Coppell (Man Utd), R.D.Latchford (Everton), T.D.Brooking (West Ham), P.S.Barnes (Man City).
Subs: T.J.Francis (Nottm Forest) for Latchford and A.S.Woodcock (Nottm Forest) for Barnes.

Half-time 0-1   Full-time 0-3

Ref: E.Dörflinger (Switzerland)   Att: 50,000

ENGLAND took a giant step towards the 1980 European Championship Finals in Italy with this magnificent win in Sofia against a solid Bulgarian side. Ron Greenwood asked Kevin Keegan to drop back and play a deeper midfield role to counter the anticipated threat from Bulgaria's strong midfield challenge. It worked a treat.

But early on, only a brilliant save by Ray Clemence prevented Borisov from scoring following a free-kick taken by Tsvetkov. The Bulgarians held the upper hand for a short while and stretched the visitors' defence on one or two occasions. But England, too, looked capable of stealing a goal and they almost did so when Keegan, at the near post, flicked on a corner in the 12th minute for Dave Watson to power in a header from close range which crashed against the crossbar. Runs by Peter Barnes and Keegan also came close to producing a goal and in the 33rd minute England finally made the breakthrough.

Watson and Ray Wilkins combined to put Trevor Brooking away and the West Ham man's final pass found Keegan perfectly placed to rifle home a good shot. The goal gave England a much-needed boost as the stifling heat was making life very uncomfortable.

Immediately, England should have scored a second goal when first Bob Latchford failed to beat Filipov when clean through, and then, after the ball had bounced to Barnes, the winger hit the post before finally Latchford's second attempt was cleared from the line. Bulgaria hit back but Clemence made another good stop from Zhelyazkov and England were able to hold on to their precious half-time lead.

At this point the game was still evenly balanced but England restarted with a fresh determination. Bulgaria, never afraid to dish out some rough treatment, were soon stopping Barnes by unfair means. Brooking's free-kick eluded everyone although both Watson and Latchford were desperately close to getting a

The goal followed a lovely flowing move. Coppell began it, combining with Keegan to send Latchford away down the left. Latchford laid the ball back to Barnes who then fed the overlapping Mills with a good pass. Mills, who had another fine game, sent a superb long pass across to Wilkins who controlled it well, turned inside a defender and fired in a shot. Wood failed to hold it and Coppell pounced on the mistake to score.

Watson then almost scored, at the right end this time, when his deflected shot looped over the bar, Keegan also shot over and Watson again went close with a header just wide. By now England were exerting all the pressure and after 69 minutes they scored another gem of a goal.

Coppell was again heavily involved, winning the ball superbly in his own half playing a one-two and then setting Keegan striding towards goal. Keegan reached the edge of the area and then played another brilliant one-two with Trevor Brooking before firing the perfect shot under Wood's diving body. It was a magnificent goal and one that silenced the hordes of travelling Scottish fans.

England played out the last 20 minutes with great authority and only a swift break by Dalglish which was thwarted by Clemence produced an anxious moment. The transformation in England's second-half performance was quite extraordinary.

97th match v Scotland.

touch. However, the second goal that England wanted soon arrived, and in fact they killed the game stone dead by scoring two goals in a minute.

A corner taken by Brooking in the 53rd minute reached Watson and this time the big defender made no mistake with a firm header. Sixty seconds later it was 3-0 as England scored a superb goal. Once again Brooking was the instigator, sending Coppell free on the right. The far post cross was inch-perfect and in came Barnes to score with a header, a rare feat for the winger.

England were now well on top and they used the opportunity to give Trevor Francis and Tony Woodcock some more international experience with Francis, in particular, giving the Bulgarian defenders even more problems with his electric pace. One dazzling run should have given England at least a penalty. Filipov brought him down blatantly with a minute to go, but the referee waved play on.

Bulgaria almost pulled one back when Borisov's shot hit the woodwork but England ran out worthy winners and went off at the end with loud applause ringing out from the sporting Bulgarian supporters.

4th match v Bulgaria.

Sweden v England
Friendly

Played on Sunday, 10 June 1979 in the Råsunda Stadium, Solna.

Sweden: J.Möller (Malmö FF); H.Borg (Eintracht Brunswick), I.Erlandsson (Malmö FF), H.Arvidsson (Östers IF), R.Åman (Djurgårdens IF), C.Torstensson (Åtvidabergs FF), A.Linderoth (Marseille), M.Nordgren (Östers IF), T.Cervin (Malmö FF), A.Grönhagen (Djurgårdens IF), S.Johansson (Halmstads BK).
Subs: K.Johansson (Hammarby IF) for Erlandsson and P.Nilsson (Östers IF) for S.Johansson.

England: P.L.Shilton (Nottm Forest); V.A.Anderson (Nottm Forest), T.J.Cherry (Leeds Utd), T.McDermott (Liverpool), D.V.Watson (Man City), E.W.Hughes (Liverpool, captain), J.K.Keegan (Hamburger SV), T.J.Francis (Nottm Forest), A.S.Woodcock (Nottm Forest), A.W.Currie (Leeds Utd), L.P.Cunningham (West Brom).
Subs: R.C.Wilkins (Chelsea) for McDermott, P.B.Thompson (Liverpool) for Watson and T.D.Brooking (West Ham) for Currie.

Half-time 0-0   Full-time 0-0
Ref: E.Linemayr (Austria)   Att: 35,691

IN a game organised to help celebrate the Swedish FA's Diamond Jubilee, both sides used the opportunity to take a look at the potential of several fringe players. The crowd of 35,691 saw a match which never rose to any great heights but always remained absorbing.

Peter Shilton had to be alert to punch away an early corner from Sweden and then Lawrie Cunningham made a good run for England as the sides felt each other out. It took about 20 minutes for the pattern of the game to evolve with England playing a controlled and patient

Viv Anderson on the ball against Sweden at Solna in June 1979.

build up. It gave them the slight edge but they had to remain alert to the sharp counter attacks of the talented Swedes.

Good chances were created at both ends with Trevor Francis mistiming a header from Terry McDermott's cross, and then the impressive Emlyn Hughes made a typically surging run forward which ended with a right-foot shot that bounced back off the crossbar, with Francis just failing to reach the rebound. S.Johansson then put in a good effort which brought Shilton into the action again before Cunningham went close for England.

The visitors had struggled somewhat to win the midfield battle before half-time and at the break Ray Wilkins was sent on to replace McDermott. Three minutes into the second half, Wilkins set up Francis with a fine chance which the Nottingham Forest player squandered by shooting wide of the far post. After that miss there was a spell of Swedish pressure although they did not create a clear chance of a breakthrough and it was England who came close again. It was Möller who had to move swiftly off his line to block another effort by Francis after a fine run and cross by Cunningham. Tony Woodcock almost set up his Forest colleague again with clever use of his chest, and then Wilkins miscued after Francis had found the Chelsea man with a good cross.

In a final flurry England brought on Trevor Brooking and they almost broke the deadlock when Kevin Keegan side-footed the ball just the wrong side of a post from a good position. Following that incident the game petered out and although neither side looked particularly impressive, some lessons were learned. A word of praise must go to Hughes, who had an outstanding game. If only he could have illuminated his display with a goal from that shot just before half-time. Alas, the woodwork had the final say.

10th match v Sweden.

Austria v England
Friendly

Played on Wednesday, 13 June 1979 in the Prater Stadium, Vienna.

Austria: F.Koncilia (RSC Anderlecht);

R.Sara (FK Austria Wien), E.Obermayer (FK Austria Vienna), E.Baumeister (FK Austria Vienna), B.Pezzey (Eintracht Frankfurt), R.Hattenberger (VfB Stuttgart), K.Welzl (AZ 67 Alkmaar), H.Prohaska (FK Austria Vienna), W.Kreuz (SK VÖEST), K.Jara (MSV Duisburg), G.Jurtin (SK Sturm Graz).
Sub: W.Schachner (FK Austria Vienna) for Welzl.

England: P.L.Shilton (Nottm Forest); P.G.Neal (Liverpool), M.D.Mills (Ipswich T), P.B.Thompson (Liverpool), D.V.Watson (Man City), R.C.Wilkins (Chelsea), J.K.Keegan (Hamburger SV, captain), S.J.Coppell (Man Utd), R.D.Latchford (Everton), T.D.Brooking (West Ham), P.S.Barnes (Man City).
Subs: R.N.Clemence (Liverpool) for Shilton, T.J.Francis (Nottm Forest) for Latchford and L.P.Cunningham (West Brom) for Barnes.

Half-time 3-1   Full-time 4-3
Ref: A.Ponnet (Belgium)   Att: 31,000

ENGLAND'S 1979 summer tour ended in glorious defeat here at the Prater Stadium but the side won many new friends in the 31,000 crowd as they served up a wonderful exhibition of attacking football. The last time these two teams met England won 7-0 but now the seven goals were shared more evenly and both teams were deserving of credit for what was a magnificent international.

It was obvious from the start that this Austrian side were a different proposition to that of 1973. They attacked in waves and showed exceptional pace and skill. As early as the second minute, Baumeister hit a 20-yarder just wide of Peter Shilton's left-hand post and Austria took an early grip of the midfield. Jara, Prohaska and Kreuz dominated the middle of the pitch and England's defence was continually ripped apart by the lightening raids of Welzl and Jurtin. Dave Watson was lucky not to concede a penalty when he brought Kreuz down clumsily, but Austria never let the incident upset them and they continued to dominate the game.

On 20 minutes they took a deserved lead. Kreuz took a short corner to Jara via Barmeister. The cross then came over perfectly for Pezzey to head spectacularly past Shilton. England were at sixes and sevens again eight minutes later, although it was an unlucky rebound off Kevin Keegan which gave Jara the chance to feed Jurtin who, in turn, moved it on to Welzl and again Shilton had no chance to save. The excitement was unrelenting with this time England coming back. The team showed great determination as Keegan sent Steve Coppell away. The winger did really well to go round a defender before finding Keegan with a good cross. The Hamburg star headed home superbly to pull a goal back.

The goal lifted England and Bob Latchford should have done better with a header from Trevor Brooking's cross, but soon it was Austria who were on top again. Poor Shilton must have wondered why he had chosen the first half to keep goal as Ron Greenwood had promised him and Ray Clemence 45 minutes each, especially when Austria made it 3-1 on 39 minutes. It was a real cracker, too, as Jurtin broke quickly from defence and passed to Welzl after brilliantly losing Mick Mills. Welzl turned inside Phil Thompson and hit an unstoppable left-foot shot past Shilton's

Kevin Keegan beats Birger Jensen to score the only goal of the European Championship game against Denmark at Wembley in September 1979.

right hand. Rarely under Greenwood's reign had England been so shell-shocked at half-time as they were on this day in Vienna.

To their eternal credit, however, England resumed in determined fashion and within two minutes of the restart they were back to 3-2 as Koncilia fumbled Keegan's shot to allow the alert Coppell to shoot home the loose ball. The goal gave England even greater belief that they could salvage something and Austria faded a little after Welzl was substituted by Schachner in the 55th minute.

England were searching for goals and in the 63rd minute they sensationally equalized. Peter Barnes's fine run found substitute Trevor Francis, who in turn found Coppell. The winger centred and Ray Wilkins shot home superbly from the edge of the area to the delight of his teammates. For a few minutes it looked as though England could pull off a dramatic victory as they surged forward. But, alas, in the 70th minute, a lapse in concentration allowed Sara's free-kick to find Pezzey's head and this time Clemence was the 'keeper well beaten. The free-kick had been a harsh decision against Coppell but there was no denying the header from the impressive Pezzey.

England still fought hard and they were desperately unlucky when Keegan's shot struck the post following Brooking's free-kick. Coppell also went close and Keegan almost converted another Brooking cross. Alas, 'Lady Luck' would not smile on England in the later stages and Austria held on for their victory. It was harsh on the visitors but they had more than played their part in a tremendous match.

15th match v Austria.
First time England had conceded more than three goals in a match since they lost to Brazil in Rio in May 1964.

England v Denmark
European Championship Qualifier

Played on Wednesday, 12 September 1979 at Wembley Stadium.

England: R.N.Clemence (Liverpool); P.G.Neal (Liverpool), M.D.Mills (Ipswich T), P.B.Thompson (Liverpool), D.V.Watson (Werder Bremen), R.C.Wilkins (Man Utd), T.McDermott (Liverpool), S.J.Coppell (Man Utd), J.K.Keegan (Hamburger SV, captain), T.D.Brooking (West Ham), P.S.Barnes (West Brom).

Denmark: B.Jensen (FC Brügge); O.Højgaard (KB København), S.Busk (MVV Maastricht), S.Ziegler (Hvidovre IF), M.Olsen (RWD Molenbeek), F.Arnesen (Ajax Amsterdam), H.Jensen (Ajax Amsterdam), S.Lerby (Ajax Amsterdam), B.Nielsen (RSC Anderlecht), A.Simonsen (FC Barcelona), P.Elkjaer (SK Lokeren).

Subs: J.J.Bertelsen (Esbjerg BK) for Nielsen and O.F.Bjerg (AaB Aarlborg) for Elkjaer.

Half-time 1-0   Full-time 1-0
Ref: C.Dias-Curreia (Portugal) Att: 82,000

ENGLAND edged a little closer to the European Championship Finals with this Wembley win against the improving Danish side. It was a victory gained without being altogether convincing and England still had a few problems with some positions.

Their midfield of Ray Wilkins, Terry McDermott and Steve Coppell soon got to grips with their job and as a result of their good play Denmark's midfield never created the mayhem as they had done in the match in Copenhagen 12 months earlier. Sadly, though, England never found the penetration they needed to break down the solid visiting defence. Having

said that, they did manage one breakthrough and it proved conclusive.

The goal came in the 18th minute and it was Phil Neal who broke down the right before centering. Wilkins and Coppell both let it go and in roared Kevin Keegan to joyfully smash the ball into the roof of the net with his left foot. The England skipper had justified the faith Ron Greenwood had put in him by making him the lone striker as England packed their midfield. Peter Barnes and Coppell were supposed to operate down the flanks but they were always too deep to be fully effective as attackers.

The Danes put the lanky Busk on Keegan throughout the 90 minutes, but Keegan was always a threat and was the real success of this England performance. For Denmark, the skilful Simonsen was the main threat and everytime he received the ball the crowd sensed the danger. But on the night the visitors failed to find the cutting edge to some excellent approach play. H.Jensen and Elkjaer, especially, failed to hit the target from good positions despite their good support play to Simonsen.

As the second half wore on and with England unable to add to their slender lead one continually felt that the Danes were capable of pulling the game around. However, the solid defensive play of Dave Watson and his fellow defenders, coupled with the poor finishing of Denmark, meant that the lead was perhaps more safe than it looked. Ray Clemence's most anxious moment came from an Elkjaer header but the goalkeeper made a fine save to end that particular threat.

In fact, a better chance fell to the substitute Bertelsen who had come on for Neilsen. It came with ten minutes to go as he found himself with the ball at his feet and the goal at his mercy. Luckily for England, though, instead of scoring, he put his shot wide of the far post.

For England Trevor Brooking had missed an earlier chance with a header and then in the 77th minute, a desperate goalmouth scramble ended with Phil Thompson's shot being blocked by Jensen and Keegan's effort from the rebound being hacked off the line.

It was not the best England performance but at least they had gained the result they needed.

7th match v Denmark.

Northern Ireland v
England European Championship
Qualifier

Played on Wednesday, 17 October 1979 at Windsor Park, Belfast.

Northern Ireland: P.A.Jennings (Arsenal); P.J.Rice (Arsenal), S.Nelson (Arsenal), J.M.Nicholl (Man Utd), A.Hunter (Ipswich T), D.McCreery (QPR), T.Cassidy (Newcastle Utd), S.B.McIlroy (Man Utd), G.J.Armstrong (Spurs), T.Finney (Cambridge Utd), V.Moreland (Derby Co).
Subs: P.Rafferty (Linfield) for Hunter, W.T.Caskey (Derby Co) for McCreery.
England: P.L.Shilton (Nottm Forest); P.G.Neal (Liverpool), M.D.Mills (Ipswich T), P.B.Thompson (Liverpool), D.V.Watson (Southampton), R.C.Wilkins (Man Utd), J.K.Keegan (Hamburger SV, captain), S.J.Coppell (Man Utd), T.J.Francis (Nottm Forest), T.D.Brooking (West Ham), A.S.Woodcock (Nottm Forest).
Sub: T.McDermott (Liverpool) for Brooking.

Half-time 0-2   **Full-time 1-5**
Ref: A.Ponnet (Belgium)   Att: 55,000

ON a dull, wet afternoon in Belfast, England, barring a mathematical nightmare, virtually assured themselves of a place in the 1980 European Championship finals in Italy. And they did it in style, too, giving the Irish a real lesson in the art of finishing.

After a quiet start with both sides probing each other's defences, the game was transformed by a stunning goal by England. Ray Wilkins, from deep inside his own half, sent a superb 40-yard pass to Trevor Francis. The Nottingham Forest striker showed his tremendous pace to leave the Irish defenders trailing in his wake. He drew Jennings from goal and then coolly placed the ball wide of the 'keeper and into the net. The goal was just the boost that England needed and they then enjoyed a prolonged spell of pressure which culminated in a second goal on 33 minutes.

This time it was Dave Watson who hit a long ball out of defence to Francis. The forward had acres of space down the left and, after a quick burst of speed, he crossed from the by-line and clubmate Tony Woodcock stabbed the ball home from close range. England remained on top until half-time and at the break the Irish brought on the local Linfield player, Rafferty, to replace Hunter, much to the delight of the crowd. For a while it had the desired effect of tightening up Ireland's defence. Indeed, early in the second half they even managed to pull a goal back when Mick Mills was adjudged to have

fouled McIlroy in the area. Moreland beat Peter Shilton from the penalty-spot and suddenly Ireland were back in the game. They pushed forward for the equalizer, roared on by the crowd. McIlroy was a constant danger to England and Shilton had to be at his best to make a fine diving save from him. That was to prove a vital moment as, soon afterwards, the Woodcock-Francis partnership exploded again.

It was on the hour when Steve Coppell made a splendid run down the right. He cleverly beat Nelson before crossing to Woodcock at the far post. Woodcock turned the ball towards goal and Francis was in like lightning to push it past Jennings. That goal really knocked the stuffing out of the Irish and 11 minutes later England had another.

Again Francis was at the hub as he centred superbly from the right with uncanny accuracy to find Woodcock diving forward to head home a magnificent goal. The combination of these two players had proved most profitable and both had turned in magnificent performances. Ireland were, by now, well out of it and England rubbed salt into their wounds in the 83rd minute with a fifth goal. Woodcock found Phil Neal who hammered a probing ball into the middle and the unfortunate Nicholl turned it past his own goalkeeper.

England played out the remaining minutes in total command and a fine all-round performance came to an end. Fine service from their midfield players and the outstanding displays from Francis and Woodcock were the main feature of their super victory.

88th match v Northern Ireland.
Penalty scored for Northern Ireland by Moreland.
Own-goal scored by Nicholl.

England v European
Bulgaria Championship Qualifier

Played on Thursday, 22 November 1979 at Wembley Stadium.

England: R.N.Clemence (Liverpool); V.A.Anderson (Nottm Forest), K.G.Sansom (Crystal Palace), P.B.Thompson (Liverpool, captain), D.V.Watson (Southampton), R.C.Wilkins (Man Utd), K.P.Reeves (Norwich C), G.Hoddle (Spurs), T.J.Francis (Nottm Forest), R.Kennedy (Liverpool), A.S.Woodcock (1.FC Cologne).
Bulgaria: K.Khristov (Pirin Blagoevgrad); R.Karakolev (Marek Stanke Dimitrov), B.Dimitrov (Lokomotiv Sofia), G.Bonev (Lokomotiv Sofia), I.Iliev (Slavia Sofia), G.Dimitrov (CSKA Sofia), T.Barzov (Levski Sparrak), P.Markov (CSKA Sofia), A.Zhelyazkov (Slavia Sofia), B.Velichkov (Lokomotiv Sofia), I.Tsvetkov (Slavia Sofia).
Subs: K.F.Manolov (Trakia Provdiv) for Velichkov and K.Kostadinov (Trakia Provdiv) for Tzvetkov.

Half-time 1-0   **Full-time 2-0**
Ref: E.Frederiksen (Sweden)   Att: 72,000

FOR the first time ever, a Wembley international had to be postponed because of adverse weather conditions, but the dense fog that shrouded the stadium 24 hours earlier had lifted in time for the game to finally get under way. Some 72,000 people still managed to reach the stadium for this re-run and they were rewarded with an interesting international capped by two fine goals.

Unfortunately, the day's delay had robbed England of the services of Kevin Keegan as the Hamburg player had to return to his club commitments but it did allow Kevin Reeves to win his first cap. Continuing Ron Greenwood's policy of

Kevin Reeves looks on as a header from Dave Watson (not in picture) crosses the line against Bulgaria at Wembley in November 1979.

Glenn Hoddle scores England's second goal against the Bulgarians – a great way to celebrate his debut.

blooding new and exciting players, the manager also selected Glenn Hoddle for his debut. Right from the start England's intentions were obvious.

In the very first minute they roared forward only for Dave Watson to rocket a shot over the top from six yards. It was to prove the first of many wasted chances. Hoddle had a shot charged down as the pressure mounted and after nine minutes England took a deserved lead. A Tony Woodcock corner was only half cleared and from the edge of the box, Hoddle curled in a fine centre for Watson to head home powerfully, thus atoning for his earlier miss.

Throughout the first half it was one-way traffic towards the Bulgarian goal. Khristov, in the visitors' goal, produced save after save as the home attack, inspired by Ray Wilkins, found many gaps to exploit. Bulgaria were desperate not to be heavily beaten and they defended passionately. For all their pressure, though, England could not find another way to goal and trooped off at half-time disappointed at only having the one goal to show for all their dominance. Ray Clemence had only one save to make in the half and that was as late as the 42nd minute.

At the interval, Bulgaria brought on Kostadinov but although his busy style put more pep into their play, they still failed to create any real threat. Instead England continued to dominate. Trevor Francis produced a brilliant turn and cross which Tony Woodcock failed to take advantage of, and Hoddle should have done better when Viv Anderson's cross found him right in front of goal. Unfortunately he delayed his shot too long and was robbed by a defender.

Two rare breakaways from Bulgaria threatened to make a mockery of the scoreline but in the 70th minute England at last scored the long overdue second goal. Anderson's cross was cleared to Wilkins, who turned it immediately into the danger area. Francis knocked it back and Hoddle showed all his undoubted skill by side-footing powerfully into the top corner

from 20 yards. It was a wonderful way of celebrating his first international, but all through the game Hoddle showed some lovely touches and his obvious talent should have made him a regular for many years to come.

Other goals should have been scored, especially when Wilkins' shot was saved by the overworked Khristov. Even in the last few seconds, the goalkeeper thwarted Francis. England were now officially through to the European Championships and the confidence throughout the team at that moment was making other nations take note of their form.

> 5th match v Bulgaria.
> Debuts for Reeves and Hoddle.
> Debut goal for Hoddle.
> Thompson captain for the first time.

England v Republic of Ireland

European Championship Qualifier

Played on Wednesday, 6 February 1980 at Wembley Stadium.

England: R.N.Clemence (Liverpool); T.J.Cherry (Leeds Utd), K.G.Sansom (Crystal Palace), P.B.Thompson (Liverpool), D.V.Watson (Southampton), B.Robson (West Brom), J.K.Keegan (Hamburger SV, captain), T.McDermott (Liverpool), D.E.Johnson (Liverpool), A.S.Woodcock (1.FC Cologne), L.P.Cunningham (Real Madrid).
Sub: S.J.Coppell (Man Utd) for Johnson.
Republic of Ireland: G.Peyton (Fulham); C.Hughton (Spurs), A.A.Grimes (Man Utd), D.A.O'Leary (Arsenal), W.L.Brady (Arsenal), G.A.Daly (Derby Co), A.P.Grealish (Luton T), S.D.Heighway (Liverpool), F.A.Stapleton (Arsenal), F.O'Brien (Philadelphia Fury).
Subs: R.Healey (Cardiff C) for Peyton and P.O'Leary (Shamrock Rovers) for D.O'Leary.

Half-time 1-0   Full-time 2-0
Ref: K.Scheurell (East Germany)
Att: 90,250

ENGLAND completed the formality of their European Championship group matches by beating the Republic of Ireland at Wembley, thanks mainly to the goalscoring power of their captain, Kevin Keegan. A debut was given to the West Bromwich Albion midfield player Bryan Robson, and it was also the first time that all the players attached to continental clubs were available at the same time.

After a slow start Robson's first serious touch almost put Keegan in with a chance but the pass was not quite good enough. On ten minutes Lawrie Cunningham put in the first of many dangerous corners with the outside of his right foot. The ball bounced around the goalmouth without any England player making the vital contact and eventually it was cleared. Peyton was having difficulty with crosses as England kept up the pressure and David Johnson's pace was also causing the Irish problems. Two centres by Johnson caused confusion in the visitor's defence and Cunningham headed just wide from one of them. Tony Woodcock had a disappointing match though and found it difficult to shake off the tight marking of O'Leary and Lawrenson.

In the end, predictably perhaps, it was left to Keegan to provide the breakthrough for England after 35 minutes play. It was the Hamburg star who began the move, passing to Terry McDermott on the right. Over came a deep cross to the far post, Johnson headed it back and there was Keegan, following up, to shoot home powerfully past Peyton. It was a well-taken goal and Keegan went on to enjoy a wonderful performance.

The Republic's only worthwhile effort of the first half came in the 40th minute when Stapleton's header bounced around the goalmouth dangerously before Ray Clemence eased the situation with a good catch. After the interval the visitors enjoyed their best spell of the match. Liam Brady moved forward with effect and another Stapleton header went close. Then a surging run by Lawrenson almost set O'Brien up before a nasty accident upset the rhythm of the game.

Keegan put over another telling cross and Johnson roared in to meet it. Unfortunately, he and Peyton collided and there was a nasty clash of heads. Both players had to leave the field and the long delay upset everyone.

Healey replaced Peyton and with ten minutes left he was beaten by a truly brilliant goal by Keegan. Moving down the left he received possession, looked up and carefully measured a delightful chip over the onrushing defenders and goalkeeper before seeing the ball drop gently into the far corner of the Irish net. The crowd erupted and rarely has a better goal been seen at Wembley.

O'Leary, who had been limping for some time, finally had to go off but in so doing he created an interesting fact as he was replaced by his brother. By this time the game had virtually died on its feet but Robson raised a cheer when he almost notched a debut goal, but his 15-yard shot was deflected narrowly wide.

England, without reaching any dizzy heights, won the match and the group.

They could be proud of their record in this tournament and Italy beckoned with the side full of confidence. As for Keegan, two words summed up his display: world class!

8th match v Republic of Ireland.
Debut for Robson.

Spain v England
Friendly

Played on Wednesday, 26 March 1980 in the Nou Camp Stadium, Barcelona.

Spain: L.Arconada (Real Sociedad); S.Urquiaga (Athletic Bilbao), M.Bianqueti (FC Barcelona), R.Gordillo (Real Betis), J.Alexanco (Athletic Bilbao), A.Guisasola (Athletic Bilbao), D.Ruiz (Athletic Bilbao), E.Saura (Valencia CF), J.Satrustegui (Real Sociedad), J.Alvarez (Sporting Gijon), J.Gomez (Real Madrid). Subs: A.Olmo (FC Barcelona) for Alesanco, F.Carrasco (FC Barcelona) for Saura and J.Diego (Real Sociedad) for Juanito.
England: P.L.Shilton (Nottm Forest); P.G.Neal (Liverpool), M.D.Mills (Ipswich T), P.B.Thompson (Liverpool), D.V.Watson (Southampton), R.C.Wilkins (Man Utd), J.K.Keegan (Hamburger SV, captain), S.J.Coppell (Man Utd), T.J.Francis (Nottm Forest), R.Kennedy (Liverpool), A.S.Woodcock (1.FC Cologne). Subs: E.W.Hughes (Wolves) for Neal and L.P.Cunningham (Real Madrid) for Francis.

Half-time 0-1   Full-time 0-2
Ref: R.Roth (West Germany) Att: 29,500

IT took England only 25 seconds to warn Spain that they were in for a tough night in this friendly international in Barcelona. At that moment Kevin Keegan forced Arconada into the first of many fine saves. It gave England the initiative that they never lost.

After three minutes Ray Kennedy set up Tony Woodcock, only for the shot to go just wide. The pace of Trevor Francis and Woodcock was setting Spain all sorts of problems and although Peter Shilton had to deal with an awkward cross by Urquiaga, the pressure was all one-way. A brilliant run by Francis was only stopped at the expense of a free-kick. He then fired in a fierce shot which Arconada failed to hold, but Phil Thompson's follow-up shot flew over the crossbar.

Francis then missed a fine chance in the 13th minute after a superb move between Woodcock, Mick Mills and Keegan. It seemed that this blistering start just had to bring a goal and sure enough, on 16 minutes, England made the breakthrough. Steve Coppell's flick sent Woodcock away on a long chase. The defenders converged and Arconada raced out of his goal but Woodcock somehow kept his nerve to steer the ball home with a brave stretch. He was hurt in the process but resumed after treatment to the congratulations from his teammates.

Spain tried desperately to come back, but by half-time England were back on top again creating chance after chance. Keegan, Ray Wilkins, Coppell, Woodcock and Francis all went close and really England should have had more goals to

David Johnson, wearing an England shirt for the first time in five years, challenges Fulham's Gerry Peyton during the game against the Republic of Ireland at Wembley in February 1980.

show for their superiority. The only threat to their own goal came after a tackle on Saura by Dave Watson which certainly seemed to justify the crowd's call for a penalty.

After the break, Spain made some tactical switches and the introduction of Carrasco gave them more bite. They tightened up all round and certainly did not hold back in their tackles. Woodcock, in particular, was brutally treated and eventually Alexanco was booked for a blatant foul on the England player. Uria put in a good effort for Spain and Diego was a lively substitute after replacing Juanito. Despite this brief flurry by Spain, England still maintained control and one screaming shot by Wilkins brought another brilliant save out of Arconada. On 64 minutes though England clinched the game with a decisive second goal, and what a beauty it was too!

Thompson headed out of defence to Wilkins, who sent Coppell away down the right. Sheer persistence enabled the winger to hold off a challenge before putting in a great pass to Francis. It was just the sort of pass Francis thrived upon, running on to the ball and outpacing the chasing defenders. As the goalkeeper advanced towards him, Francis hit a splendid shot into the far corner in convincing style. A superb goal.

Unfortunately, the Spanish players then resorted to some crude tackles on the visitors and it was to England's credit that they showed remarkable restraint, not allowing themselves to be drawn into a brawl.

12th match v Spain.
50th cap for Keegan.
Spain's Alvarez also known as 'Uria'; Bianqueti as 'Migueli'; Gomez as 'Juanito'; Ruiz as 'Dani'.

England v Argentina
Friendly

Played on Tuesday, 13 May 1980 at Wembley Stadium.

England: R.N.Clemence (Liverpool); P.G.Neal (Liverpool), K.G.Sansom (Crystal Palace), P.B.Thompson (Liverpool), D.V.Watson (Southampton), R.C.Wilkins (Man Utd), J.K.Keegan (Hamburger SV, captain), S.J.Coppell (Man Utd), D.E.Johnson (Liverpool), A.S.Woodcock (1.FC Cologne), R.Kennedy (Liverpool). Subs: T.J.Cherry (Leeds Utd) for Neal, G.Birtles (Nottm Forest) for Johnson and T.D.Brooking (West Ham) for Kennedy.
Argentina: U.M.Fillol (River Plate); J.Van Tuyne (Rosario Central), A.Tarantini (River Plate), J.Olguín (Independiente), A.Gallego (Newell's Old Boys), D.Passarella (River Plate), S.Santamaria (Newell's Old Boys), J.A.Barbas (Racing Club), L.Luque (River Plate), D.A.Maradona (Argentinos Juniors), D.Valencia (Talleres Córdoba). Subs: R.Díaz (River Plate) for Santamaria, J.Simon (Newell's Old Boys) for Van Tuyne and C.Ischia (Velez Sarsfield) for Barbas.

Half-time 1-0   Full-time 3-1
Ref: B.R.McGinlay (Scotland) Att: 90,000

WHAT a superb international! England went into this match against the reigning World Champions full of confidence after an excellent run of results. It showed in their play when, on the night, the whole side played brilliantly and the Argentinians were well beaten.

Right from the start the excitement was continuous with chances falling at either end. Dave Watson, whose power in the air always troubled the visiting defence, came up for one attack and headed down for Kevin Keegan to drive a shot inches wide. At the other end the new wonder boy of world football, Maradona, made his mark with a dazzling run which left several defenders trailing in his wake. Again the ball trickled agonisingly wide of the post, but the crowd, basically hostile to the Argentinians as a team, applauded loudly the run of Maradona. It was breathtaking.

It was nip and tuck for much of the first half with both sides giving as good as they got. The visitors came close twice as Kenny Sansom cleared off the line, but just before the interval England found a goal. Steve Coppell did exceptionally well

David Johnson celebrates scoring England's first goal against Argentina at Wembley in May 1980.

to pull back a cross from the by-line and David Johnson jumped well to thump home a powerful header. It was the Liverpool player's fourth goal in his fifth game and was a real tonic to the home players who had played very well throughout the first half.

Within six minutes of the restart the crowd were on their feet again as England made it 2-0. Ray Kennedy made ground down the left before shooting towards the far post. Fillol could only parry the ball up in the air and Johnson moved smartly again to tap home the rebound to add to his already impressive record.

The game continued in a high-class vein. Argentina were full of very talented individuals but lacked the teamwork shown by the England lads. However, on 54 minutes the visitors found a lifeline. Maradona went on another of his mazy dribbles, only for Sansom to unbalance the superbly gifted 19-year-old, bringing him down. Penalty! Up stepped skipper Passarella who powered his shot high past Ray Clemence's left hand. For a moment it looked as though a repeat of the 2-2 draw here in 1974 might well be on the cards, but England's captain had other ideas. Johnson was again involved, receiving from Keegan down the left before passing to Coppell. The Manchester United winger delicately laid the ball into the path of Keegan, who flashed it past Fillol to restore England's two goal advantage.

Ron Greenwood made three substitutions with Trevor Brooking, Trevor Cherry and Garry Birtles coming on. Brooking and Birtles joined in with the theme of the night by adding even more quality to a pitch already overloaded with skill. The game continued to the end in

the same wonderful pattern with every player deserving the standing ovation from the capacity crowd as they left the arena.

8th match v Argentina.
Debut, as substitute, for Birtles.
50th cap for Watson.
Penalty scored for Argentina by Passarella.
"The best England international I have ever seen."
The Author

Wales v England Home Championship

Played on Saturday, 17 May 1980 at the Racecourse Ground, Wrexham.

Wales: W.D.Davies (Wrexham); P.T.Price (Luton T), J.P.Jones (Wrexham), P.Nicholas (Crystal Palace), D.E.Jones (Norwich C), M.R.Thomas (Man Utd), B.Flynn (Leeds Utd), T.C.Yorath (Spurs), I.P.Walsh (Crystal Palace), D.C.Giles (Swansea C), L.James (Swansea C). Sub: K.Pontin (Cardiff C) for D.Jones.

England: R.N.Clemence (Liverpool); P.G.Neal (Liverpool), T.J.Cherry (Leeds Utd), P.B.Thompson (Liverpool, captain), L.V.Lloyd (Nottm Forest), G.Hoddle (Spurs), T.D.Brooking (West Ham), R.Kennedy (Liverpool), S.J.Coppell (Man Utd), P.Mariner (Ipswich T), P.S.Barnes (West Brom). Subs: K.G.Sansom (Crystal Palace) for Neal and R.C.Wilkins (Man Utd) for Lloyd.

Half-time 2-1   Full-time 4-1

Ref: M.Foote (Scotland)   Att: 24,250

ENGLAND, fielding a much-changed side, lost in Wales for the first time since 1955. It had to go down as one of their worst performances, although nothing could be taken away from the Welsh, who thoroughly deserved their victory. Yet in the early stages of the match there was no hint of what was to be the final outcome.

England began well and on 15 minutes they took the lead. Trevor Cherry did well down the left and centred for Peter Barnes to fire in a shot. On the end of it was Paul Mariner, who managed to deflect it and the ball flew into the net. All was going well up to then, but the Welsh then came back with a vengeance.

Five minutes after England's goal, the Welsh danger man, James, sent over a good cross which Walsh headed back. Thomas had time and room to fire in the knockdown from close range. Worse was to come for the visitors as Wales, inspired by their goal, attacked furiously. Phil Neal limped off to be replaced by Kenny Sansom, who slotted in on the left allowing Cherry to move over to the right, but it was Larry Lloyd in the middle who had the most torrid time of it.

Time and again James pulled the big defender out of position and after half an hour, Wales took the lead. James went around Lloyd on the right and chipped a perfect cross to the far post where Walsh rose high to head past Ray Clemence. Lloyd's frustrations earned him a booking before half-time as England battled back into it. They almost equalized when Barnes put in a good shot, only for a slight deflection by a defender preventing the goal.

Glenn Hoddle showed some good form as England pressed hard but on the hour, another defensive blunder sealed the result for Wales. Joey Jones picked up the ball just inside England's half and set off on a surging run. He went past Phil Thompson and let fly. Clemence failed to hold the shot and James followed up to head the rebound into the net. England's embarrassment continued when, after 66 minutes, Wales netted a fourth goal. With Trevor Brooking trying vainly to stop the lively Giles by unfair means, the referee allowed the Welshmen to play on and Giles's shot was diverted past Clemence by Thompson for an own-goal. The final humiliation!

Just to end a miserable day for Lloyd, the big centre-half hobbled off with ten minutes to go with an ankle injury. He, more than most, would not forget this international as he was never selected to represent his country again. Wales, meanwhile, savoured the moment with pride.

93rd match v Wales.
Own-goal scored for Wales by Thompson.

England v Home Championship Northern Ireland

Played on Tuesday, 20 May 1980 at Wembley Stadium.

England: T.J.Corrigan (Man City); T.J.Cherry (Leeds Utd), K.G.Sansom (Crystal Palace), T.D.Brooking (West Ham), D.V.Watson (Southampton), E.W.Hughes (Wolves, captain), T.McDermott (Liverpool), R.C.Wilkins

David Johnson and Noel Brotherston are both flat out as England's goal goes in against Northern Ireland at Wembley in May 1980.

(Man Utd), D.E.Johnson (Liverpool), K.P.Reeves (Man City), A.E.Devonshire (West Ham).
Sub: P.Mariner (Ipswich T) for Reeves.
Northern Ireland: J.A.Platt (Middlesbrough); J.M.Nicholl (Man Utd), M.M.Donaghy (Luton T), S.B.McIlroy (Man Utd), C.J.Nicholl (Southampton), J.P.O'Neill (Leicester C), N.Brotherston (Blackburn R), T.Cassidy (Newcastle Utd), T.Finney (Cambridge Utd), G.J.Armstrong (Spurs), W.R.Hamilton (Burnley).
Subs: D.McCreery (QPR) for Cassidy and G.T.Cochrane (Middlesbrough) for Hamilton.

Half-time 0-0   Full-time 1-1

Ref: G.P.Owen (Wales)   Att: 32,000

AFTER England's dismal showing in Wales, Ron Greenwood again made several changes, nine in all, to try to see as many players as possible before the following month's European Championship finals. Again, though, it showed in England's play and it was another disjointed and disappointing performance.

The greasy surface made control difficult but England made a promising start. Dave Watson saw a good header well saved by Platt and then David Johnson did extremely well to reach a skidding long pass before setting up new cap Alan Devonshire with a chance. Unfortunately, the West Ham player shot over. England continued this early pressure, with Ray Wilkins hitting a good shot just over before the industrious Trevor Cherry put over a tantalising cross which created problems for the Irish defence before eventually being cleared.

Sadly, all this sharp early play from England flattered to deceive and soon the game drifted into a midfield stalemate with

little to entertain the small crowd. Both Johnson and Kevin Reeves struggled to make an impact, despite the promptings of Wilkins and Trevor Brooking. Northern Ireland faired even worse and Joe Corrigan did not have a single shot to save in the first-half. Only McIlroy looked dangerous for the visitors. Because they had so few defensive duties, Watson and Cherry were continually able to push forward and in the last few seconds of the half, Cherry found himself in front of goal staring at a golden chance, but sadly for England, Jimmy Nicholl cleared from the goal-line.

The monotonous pattern continued into the second half with play mostly in the Irish half, but with no real conviction from the home attack. One good chance fell to Brooking shortly after the restart, after good work by Reeves had given him the opportunity on a plate. Once more, though, the opening was wasted as Brooking lifted his shot way over the top.

Throughout this half there were long periods of inactivity as the game stopped and started. Ireland relied on the occasional breakaway and England suffered from a distinct lack of ideas. At last, though, in the 81st minute, the home fans had something to cheer. A centre by Emlyn Hughes was helped on by Kenny Sansom and as the ball ran to the far post, Johnson nipped in to beat Brotherston and score.

The jubilation lasted barely two minutes however as the Irish snatched an equalizer from one of their breaks. A long pass by Jimmy Nicholl eventually found substitute Cochrane and the Middlesbrough player hit home a fine shot to stun the crowd into silence.

89th match v Northern Ireland.
Debut for Devonshire.

Scotland v England   Home Championship

Played on Saturday, 24 May 1980 at Hampden Park, Glasgow.

Scotland: A.Rough (Partick Thistle); D.McGrain (Celtic), I.Munro (St Mirren), P.Hegarty (Dundee Utd), A.McLeish (Aberdeen), W.Miller (Aberdeen), G.D.Strachan (Aberdeen), R.S.Aitken (Celtic), K.Dalglish (Liverpool), J.Jordan (Man Utd), A.Gemmill (Birmingham C).
Subs: G.E.Burley (Ipswich T) for Munro and A.M.Gray (Wolves) for Aitken.
England: R.N.Clemence (Liverpool); T.J.Cherry (Leeds Utd), K.G.Sansom (Crystal Palace), P.B.Thompson (Liverpool, captain), D.V.Watson (Man City), R.C.Wilkins (Man Utd), S.J.Coppell (Man Utd), T.McDermott (Liverpool), D.E.Johnson (Liverpool), P.Mariner (Ipswich T), T.D.Brooking (West Ham).
Sub: E.W.Hughes (Wolves) for Mariner.

Half-time 0-1   Full-time 0-2

Ref: A.J.Garrido (Portugal)   Att: 85,000

SOME 85,000 people came to Hampden hoping that Scotland could gain the draw or win that would condemn England to the wooden spoon in the Home Championship. Most of them left bitterly disappointed after a hard-working performance gave the visitors a deserved victory.

The Scottish defence looked vulnerable from the start and England scored after only eight minutes play. Terry McDermott began the move, sending his Liverpool colleague David Johnson off on a run. Johnson crossed deep to the far post where Paul Mariner headed the ball across goal, giving a simple tap in chance for Trevor Brooking. It was a blow to Scotland but they hit back strongly. The impressive Jordan began to make his presence felt and he was well supported by Dalglish.

Gemmill was Scotland's other star and he almost set up a goal for Dalglish, only for Ray Clemence's brave diving stop to save the day. As the half wore on, most of the play was towards the England goal but the visitors did produce a near thing when Mariner headed a Brooking corner goalwards. Luckily for Scotland, Munro was there to clear off the line. Shortly afterwards Ray Wilkins went close again. He did very well to control Mariner's cross, beat McGrain, and then shoot, but Rough got down well to push the ball around a post.

At the other end Clemence made a similar save after Dalglish's fine run ended with a good shot. Then Jordan, having an excellent match, shot just wide after Dalglish had set him up, making it another chance Scotland had wasted. All through the half, Scotland had been let down by an inconsistent midfield in which Aitken and McLeish never contributed enough.

After the interval England immediately went on the attack. Five minutes after the restart Coppell, who was England's best player, found Johnson. He cut across the Scottish goal before shooting. The ball was blocked and Mariner hit a follow-up shot that just scraped the outside of the post. At this point, Scotland took off the ineffective Aitken and brought on Gray to try to pep up the home attack. Dalglish moved back to midfield, which upset his good partnership with Jordan, but desperate measures were required by Scotland in an effort to save the match. Little progress was made, however, as England comfortably held on to their lead.

In the 70th minute, England, somewhat surprisingly, brought on Emlyn Hughes for the lively Mariner. The substitution was irrelevant, however as five minutes later the visitors added goal number-two. Johnson sped away down the left before finding Brooking. The ball moved on sweetly to Coppell, who hit a good shot goalwards. Rough blocked it but could not hold on to the ball and Coppell followed up to joyfully tap home the rebound. That goal clinched the result and in the remaining minutes the game petered out.

So, England, by winning, handed the wooden spoon to the Scots, much to the disgust of their fans! England also recovered some of their faltering confidence after poor performances against the Welsh and Irish. A win in Scotland is always special and was a real boost for the difficult games ahead in Italy.

> 98th match v Scotland.

Australia v England
Friendly

Played on Saturday, 31 May 1980 at the Cricket Ground, Sydney.

Australia: G.Woodhouse (Leichardt APIA); S.Perry (Brisbane C), I.Prskalo (Marconi), J.Muir (Marconi), J.Tansey (Heidelberg Utd), J.Yzendoorn (Heidelborg Utd), A.Henderson (Marconi), J.Rooney (Heidelberg Utd), M.Jankovics (Marconi), G.Cole (Heidelberg Utd), K.Boden (Sydney C).

Subs: P.Sharne (Marconi) for Boden and I.Selemidis (Heidelberg Utd) for Rooney.
England: T.J.Corrigan (Man City); T.J.Cherry (Leeds Utd, captain), F.R.G.Lampard (West Ham), B.E.Talbot (Ipswich T), R.C.Osman (Ipswich T), T.I.Butcher (Ipswich T), B.Robson (West Brom), A.Sunderland (Arsenal), P.Mariner (Ipswich T), G.Hoddle (Spurs), D.Armstrong (Middlesbrough).
Subs: B.Greenhoff (Leeds Utd) for Robson, P.D.Ward (Brighton & HA) for Sunderland and A.E.Devonshire (West Ham) for Armstrong.

Half-time 0-2   Full-time 1-2
Ref: T.Boskovic (Australia)   Att: 26,750

ENGLAND made the long trip to Sydney in Australia for a specially arranged friendly international to help celebrate the Centenary of the Australian FA. Many a cricket Test match has been played between the two countries but this was the first occasion that they had met to play soccer, and on a cricket ground! Some notable names were conspicuous by their absence, but it did give Ron Greenwood an opportunity to look at a few of the fringe players under senior conditions.

Australia began in lively fashion but England's defence, marshalled well by acting skipper Trevor Cherry, soon snuffed out any early threat to Joe Corrigan's goal. The midfield of Bryan Talbot, Brian Robson, Glenn Hoddle and David Armstrong were far too strong for the Australians and England were soon pressing. They scored early on when Hoddle struck home a good shot from 20 yards and then seemed set for a big score when Terry Butcher put his Ipswich teammate Paul Mariner through for a well-taken second goal after 24 minutes. Somehow, though, England lost their way a little. True, they dominated the first half but after the break they sat back on their lead and allowed Australia to come at them.

The home side showed great determination and put England's defence under some considerable pressure. If Rooney or Jankovics had taken chances that came their way, then the visitors could have been in trouble. Good defending from all the back-four players kept England in control, despite persistent attacks.

With only two minutes to go the Australians scored the goal their hard work deserved. An infringement in the area gave the home team a penalty and Cole, a school teacher by profession, was given the task which he duly completed.

> 1st match v Australia.
> Debuts for Osman, Butcher, Sunderland, Armstrong and, as substitute, Ward.
> Cherry captain for the first time.
> Penalty scored for Australia by Cole.
> *"My feelings on my international debut were of pride, euphoria and a sense of responsibility, especially the latter, as there had been so many good and exciting players to have played before me. My main focal point, when the National Anthem was playing, was of my wife Rita and my own family back home, especially my parents, who I knew were so proud of me."*
> Terry Butcher

European Championship Finals

Belgium v England
Group Two

Played on Tuesday, 12 June 1980 in the Stadio Comunale, Turin, Italy.

Belgium: J.M.Pfaff (SK Beveren); E.Gerets (Standard Liège), L.Millecamps (KSV Waregem), W.Meeuws (FC Brugge), M.Renquin (Standard Liège), J.Cools (Beerschot VAV), F.Van der Eycken (FC Brugge), W.Van Moer (Beringen FC), F.Van der Elst (New York Cosmos), Vandenbergh (Lierse SK), J.Ceulemans (FC Brugge).
Sub: R.Mommens (SC Lokeren) for Van Moer.
England: R.N.Clemence (Liverpool); P.G.Neal (Liverpool), K.G.Sansom (Crystal Palace), P.B.Thompson (Liverpool), D.V.Watson (Southampton), R.C.Wilkins (Man Utd), J.K.Keegan (Hamburger SV, captain), S.J.Coppell (Man Utd), D.E.Johnson (Liverpool), T.D.Brooking (West Ham), A.S.Woodcock (1.FC Cologne).
Subs: T.McDermott (Liverpool) for Coppell and R.Kennedy (Liverpool) for Johnson.

Half-time 1-1   Full-time 1-1
Ref: H.Aldinger (West Germany) Att: 15,250

THE European Championship finally got under way after all the weeks of anticipation. England's first match was against the dangerous Belgium side in Turin, but alas, the game will be remembered for all the wrong reasons. It was ruined by the antics of some of the so-called English fans, who reacted badly to a Belgian equalizer and prompted the Italian police to resort to tear gas to quell a threatened riot.

The match had begun promisingly for England as they looked sharp in the early stages. Kevin Keegan was soon making those darting runs of his and his team enjoyed the bulk of the possession. Belgium relied on a strong, well-organised defence, a clever offside trap and the occasional dangerous breakaway. After eight minutes, Ray Wilkins sent in an accurate centre which Tony Woodcock headed wide when perhaps he should have done better. That was the first of many fine passes by Wilkins, who had a good game. Belgium nearly made England pay for that miss shortly afterwards, though, and only a superb save by Ray Clemence prevented Van der Eycken's shot counting.

The Belgian tackling was fierce, to say the least, and Woodcock and David Johnson took a real buffeting from Millecamps in particular. Keegan, who was shadowed throughout by Van der Eycken, continually had his ankles tapped to hinder his progress. But attacks came in at either end, with Keegan caught just offside following a Trevor Brooking free-kick for England, and then Ceulemans hit a free-kick which again brought the best out of Clemence. Renquin volleyed narrowly wide before England retaliated with Kenny Sansom finding Woodcock, who centred just too high for the stretching Johnson.

There was a vital moment in the 22nd minute when Keegan pounced to shoot

Gerets of Belgium is bowled over by Dave Watson in the European Championship game in Turin in June 1980.

home a Dave Watson headed pass. Unfortunately, and controversially, the referee gave an offside decision against Woodcock seconds earlier in the move. The disappointment at that decision did not last long, though, as three minutes later England were ahead with a quite brilliant goal from Wilkins.

The midfield player picked up the ball in the middle and as the defence converged, he lobbed it over them. Running on to his own pass, he then spotted Pfaff just off his line and lobbed the ball again, this time over the goalkeeper and into the net. It was a marvellous goal and sent the English fans wild with delight.

Unfortunately the lead did not last long and four minutes later the Belgians hit back. England failed to clear Van Moer's corner-kick and the ball ran loose for Ceulemans to score easily from close range. This was the signal for the English section of the crowd to turn nasty. Annoyed by Italian supporters cheering the Belgian goal, they decided that they would try and do something about it. Trouble flared and the Italian police charged, using tear gas to calm the near riot. But the wind blew the gas across the pitch and several players were affected by it, especially Clemence. On appeal from the players and the manager Ron Greenwood the referee suspended play for ten minutes.

When the game finally restarted, the heart had gone and the high standard of play before the Belgian goal was never reached again. England kept falling into the Belgian offside trap with perhaps Johnson having the best of the opportunities, but alas he delayed his shot too long and lost the chance.

> 17th match v Belgium.
> 50th cap for Clemence.

Italy v England   Group Two

Played on Sunday, 15 June 1980 in the Stadio Comunale, Turin, Italy.

Italy: D.Zoff (Juventus); C.Gentile (Juventus), F.Collovati (Milan AC), G.Scirea (Juventus), G.Oriali (Inter-Milan), R.Benetti (AS Roma), M.Tardelli (Juventus), G.Antognoni (Fiorentina), F.Causio (Juventus), F.Graziani (Torino), R.Bettega (Juventus).
Sub: G.Baresi (Inter-Milan) for Causio.

England: P.L.Shilton (Nottm Forest); P.G.Neal (Liverpool), K.G.Sansom (Crystal Palace), P.B.Thompson (Liverpool), D.V.Watson (Southampton), R.C.Wilkins (Man Utd), J.K.Keegan (Hamburger SV, captain), S.J.Coppell (Man Utd), G.Birtles (Nottm Forest), R.Kennedy (Liverpool), A.S.Woodcock (Nottm Forest).
Sub: P.Mariner (Ipswich T) for Birtles.

Half-time 0-0   Full-time 1-0

Ref: N.Rainea (Romania)   Att: 59,750

SOME tough tackling in the early stages set the pattern for this crucial game in England's group. A victory against the host nation in front of almost 60,000 people, mostly passionate Italians, seemed a daunting task. In the end it proved to be just out of England's reach.

Italy showed how dangerous they could be when going forward and Bettega's cross skidded off a defending head. Fouls continually interrupted the flow of play and after only nine minutes, both Benetti and Tardelli had received yellow cards, with Kevin Keegan and Tony Woodcock the target for their tackling. Half-way through the first 45 minutes, England looked in control as they confidently coped with the situation. Indeed, it was going so well that the scent of victory was wafting under their noses. Woodcock was putting in some tireless running and a through-ball by Ray Kennedy was headed on by Gary Birtles for Woodcock. His final cross was too long but shortly afterwards he robbed Scirea before being stopped, predictably, by a foul. From the free-kick, Woodcock's shot hit the defensive wall and Keegan did the same with a shot from the rebound. Zoff then saved bravely at Keegan's feet after Birtles and Phil Neal had combined to set up the England skipper.

Italy took a while to put in a serious goal attempt and when they did, they missed a golden chance. Antognoni and Oriali combined well to give Graziani an opening right in front of goal. The number-ten completely miskicked, though, and it gave Peter Shilton the chance to dive courageously amongst the legs to smother the ball. The home fans could not believe the miss and they let Graziani know of their feelings in no uncertain terms.

After half-time Italy stepped up the pace and the second half was superb entertainment as both sides searched for a breakthrough. Italy were much more positive now and looked a much better side for it, England were now struggling to hold them. Oriali's cross was met by Scirea who shot just who shot just wide and then Shilton made a good save from Graziani.

Bettega's header narrowly missed before England bravely hit back. Dave Watson headed Ray Kennedy's free-kick just wide of the far post and minutes later England were desperately unlucky not to score. Ray Wilkins, playing splendidly again, centred and Keegan cleverly dummied to allow the ball to run on to Kennedy. He flipped it up and hit a stunning half-volley which crashed against a post with Zoff beaten.

The excitement continued as that incident shook Italy back into action. Another attack ended with Shilton saving from Scirea with his feet. At the other end another good effort by Keegan brought a fingertip save from Zoff to raise English hopes again, but after 78 minutes play the decisive strike came.

Antognoni passed to Graziani out on the left. Neal came to tackle but missed and was beaten by Graziani's pace. Over came the cross and although Watson and Keegan were there, the ball ran between them and Tardelli joyfully volleyed home.

Eleven minutes were left but it was too late for England to find a way round such a mean defence. It effectively ended England's chance to qualify for the next stage of the competition and it was sad, after so much effort, that they ended with nothing.

> 14th match v Italy.

Spain v England   Group Two

Played on Wednesday, 18 June 1980 in the San Paolo Stadium, Naples, Italy.

Spain: L.Arconada (Real Sociedad); J.Alvarez (Sporting Gijon), J.Alexanco (Athletic Bilbao), A.Olmo (FC Barcelona), S.Suarez (Sporting Gijon), J.Gomez (Real Madrid), R.Gordillo (Real Betis), E.Saura (Valencia CF), J.Cardenosa (Real Betis), J.Zamora (Real Sociedad), C.Alonso (Real Madrid).
Subs: D.Ruiz (Athletic Bilbao) for Juanito and F.Carrasco (FC Barcelona) for Cardenosa.

England: R.N.Clemence (Liverpool); V.A.Anderson (Nottm Forest), M.D.Mills (Ipswich T), P.B.Thompson (Liverpool), D.V.Watson (Southampton), R.C.Wilkins (Man Utd), J.K.Keegan (Hamburger SV, captain), T.McDermott (Liverpool), A.S.Woodcock (1.FC Cologne), T.D.Brooking (West Ham), G.Hoddle (Spurs).
Subs: T.J.Cherry (Leeds Utd) for Ander-

son and P.Mariner (Ipswich T) for Hoddle.

Half-time 0-1   Full-time 1-2

Ref: E.Linemayr (Austria)   Att: 14,500

SEVERAL team changes caused England to feel their way into this match carefully. They knew they had to win, and win well to have an outside chance of qualifying for the third-place Final, so they took few chances in the early stages.

However, England still had the better of the first exchanges although Spain's Zamora headed wide from a Saura cross. Terry McDermott then sent England away with a long forward pass. Arconada fumbled the ball but Kevin Keegan's back header was cleared off the line. From then on the game developed into a midfield contest with England building their attacks slowly, whilst Spain relied on the swift counter-attack. One such break was stopped only by a clever Viv Anderson interception in the 13th minute, but five minutes later it was England that edged their noses in front.

Cundi was shadowing Keegan everywhere, regularly bringing him down. From one of many free-kicks England produced a sparkling move involving Glenn Hoddle, Trevor Brooking and McDermott. The latter player sent over a long centre to the far post where Ray Wilkins did extremely well to head across goal for Brooking to slide home.

The goal gave England control of the match for a while and they should have added further goals. However, the best two chances fell to Spain with Santillana shooting over from a great position and Ray Clemence saving well with his feet from Zamora. Hoddle was beginning to stretch the Spanish with his graceful long passes and from one of them Wilkins hit a powerful snap shot which ripped into the side-netting.

Straight after half-time the referee gave Spain a way back into the game with what can only be described as a terrible decision. Zamora and Santillana played a one-two in the area and as Clemence came out to dive at Zamora's feet, the Spaniard went down despite the fact that Clemence clearly won the ball fairly with both hands. To the disgust of the England players and Clemence in particular, the referee awarded Spain a penalty. Dani took the kick and further infuriated Clemence by checking his stride when running up to the ball before shooting into the net. The referee ignored this infringement and allowed the goal to stand.

Six minutes later there was more drama. Dave Watson twice challenged Saura in a crowded penalty area and the referee decided the second challenge was unfair and awarded Spain a second penalty. Again Dani took the kick and again he stopped in his run-up to the ball before shooting past Clemence. This time, though, the referee took action and awarded the spot-kick to be retaken. Dani then placed his second shot the opposite way to the first and Clemence dived splendidly low to his right to save. It seemed justice had prevailed.

On the hour England made them pay and scored what proved to be the decisive goal. Anderson centred and Arconada was forced to tip the ball over for a corner. Brooking took the kick and, spotting

McDermott lurking unmarked on the edge of the box, pulled the ball back towards him. McDermott met it with the sweetest of volleys but Arconada pulled off a superb save. Unfortunately for the goalkeeper, he could not hold the ball and Tony Woodcock darted in to score from the rebound.

Clemence made some good saves in the remaining half-hour but England, too, had their moments. They knew that their only hope of qualifying for another match was to win this game by several goals, but alas Belgium's unexpected 0-0 draw with Italy put paid to England's hopes of further progress. It was Belgium who had effectively ended England's hopes with their draw against them in the first match, but they proved it was no fluke by now qualifying for the Final.

For England, some satisfaction came from the tournament but once again they missed out when it mattered most.

13th match v Spain.
One penalty scored and one missed by Dani of Spain.
Spain's Alvarez also known as 'Uria'; Suarez as 'Cundi'; Gomez as 'Juanito'; Alonso as 'Santillana'; Ruiz as 'Dani'.

England v Norway World Cup Qualifier

Played on Wednesday, 10 September 1980 at Wembley Stadium.

England: P.L.Shilton (Nottm Forest); V.A.Anderson (Nottm Forest), K.G.Sansom (Crystal Palace), P.B.Thompson (Liverpool, captain), D.V.Watson (Southampton), E.L.Gates (Ipswich T), T.McDermott (Liverpool), P.Mariner (Ipswich T), A.S.Woodcock (1.FC Cologne), G.Rix (Arsenal).

Norway: T.R.Jacobsen (Vålerengens IF); B.Berntsen (Viking Stavager), T.Kordahl (Lillestrøm SK), E.Aas (Bayern München), S.Grøndalen (Rosenberg BK), R.Albertsen (Den Haag), Å.F.Hareide (Molde FK), A.Dokken (Lillestrøm SK), A.Larsen-økland (Bayer 04 Leverkusen), P.Jacobsen (Hankameratene), R.Ottesen (Bayer 04 Leverkusen).
Sub: A.Erlandsen (Lillestrøm SK) for Ottersen.

Tony Woodcock scores England's second goal against Norway at Wembley in September 1980.

Half-time 1-0   Full-time 4-0

Ref: M.van Langenhove (Belgium)
Att: 48,250

IN the aftermath of a disappointing European Championship, England had to lift themselves quickly to begin their World Cup challenge for the 1982 tournament in Spain. This first match in their group brought the Norwegians to Wembley where the Scandinavians gave a good account of themselves, making life far from easy for their hosts.

There were two more new caps in the home side with Eric Gates and Graham Rix taking on midfield roles. The disappointments of the previous summer was reflected by lots of empty spaces in the stands and it was a disjointed opening half that England served up for the remaining loyalist fans. Rix made an early impact with a couple of penetrating passes, but on the whole England found it hard to get into any sort of rhythm. Norway offered plenty of physical power and their midfield were quickly into the tackle. Their technical know-how was of a high standard and it was obvious from the first whistle that England would have difficulty breaking them down.

The first real chance of the game fell to Norway and Peter Shilton had to move smartly to turn Hareide's header over the bar in the 17th minute. England retaliated immediately with Tony Woodcock putting in a shot which T.Jacobsen scrambled around a post. England were not playing well, though, and the ease in which Norway found gaps in the home defence alarmed the Wembley crowd. The service to Woodcock and Paul Mariner dried up despite the early promise from Rix and Bryan Robson.

However, England did find a goal before half-time, mainly due to the sharpness of Terry McDermott. Rix sent in a free-kick to the far side of the penalty area and McDermott met the ball on the volley to hit a splendid shot into the far corner of the Norwegian net. It was a fine goal but the lead was fragile and England still looked out of sorts as they trooped off at half-time.

After the break, Norway continued to defend resolutely, always managing to block the England scoring attempts. But in the 66th minute the home side found another way through. A centre by Phil Thompson, deep to the far post, cleared the defence for Mariner to head down to Tony Woodcock, who wasted no time in stabbing the ball past the goalkeeper. That looked curtains for Norway but they refused to give in and showed considerable skill and tenacity as they hit back with a couple of dangerous attacks. P.Jacobsen put in a fine run and shot which only just failed and a goal then might have made England struggle even more than they were doing.

With the match still not settled, England were then very fortunate to score a third goal. They actually put together an excellent move which ended with Gates putting his Ipswich colleague away through the middle with a penetrating pass. Mariner sped into the area but was tackled by Aas. It seemed to everyone that the challenge had been a fair one but inexplicably the referee found it necessary to award England a penalty. It seemed a harsh decision, but not looking a gift-horse in the mouth, (especially after what had happened against Spain in the June), McDermott stepped up to thump home the spot-kick. The game was now effectively over with the Norwegians understandably bitterly disappointed.

With five minutes to go, England made the scoreline even more flattering with a fourth goal, albeit the best of the match. Mariner gained possession and made positive strides into the area again. As two defenders converged, the Ipswich striker showed some lovely footwork and control to lose them before shooting past goalkeeper Jacobsen.

Hence the new World Cup campaign started with a result that was much better than the performance.

> 5th match v Norway.
> Debuts for Gates and Rix.
> Penalty scored for England by McDermott.

Romania v England   World Cup Qualifier

Played on Wednesday, 15 October 1980 in the 23 August Stadium, Bucharest.

Romania: V.Iordache (Steaua Bucharest); N.Negrila (Universitatea Craiova), I.Munteanu (Sportul Studenţesc Bucureşti), S.Sames (Steaua Bucharest), C.Stefanescu (Universitatea Craiova), A.Beldeanu (Universitatea Craiova), Z.Crişan (Universitatea Craiova), A.Iordanescu (Steaua Bucharest), R.Camataru (Universitatea Craiova), A.Ticleanu (Universitatea Craiova), M.Raducanu (Steaua Bucharest).
Sub: I.Dumitru (Politehnica Timişoara) for Ticleanu.
England: R.N.Clemence (Liverpool); P.G.Neal (Liverpool), K.G.Sansom (Crystal Palace), P.B.Thompson (Liverpool, captain), D.V.Watson (Southampton), B.Robson (West Brom), G.Rix (Arsenal), T.McDermott (Liverpool), G.Birtles (Nottm Forest), A.S.Woodcock (1.FC Cologne), E.L.Gates (Ipswich T).
Subs: L.P.Cunningham (Real Madrid) for Birtles and S.J.Coppell (Man Utd) for Gates.

Half-time 1-0   Full-time 2-1

Ref: U.Ericsson (Sweden)   Att: 81,000

Dave Watson in action against Romania in Bucharest in October 1980.

THIS match was always going to be one of the most difficult for England in their group and that was just how it turned out to be. They were completely outplayed in the first 45 minutes and, despite a much better second-half showing, they ended the game well beaten.

Romania made their intentions clear right from the start and it was a full minute into the match before an England player even touched the ball. The quick, neat passing of the home side set the pattern with the visitors struggling to hold them. The Romanians plan was to feed their brilliant winger Raducanu as much as possible. He soon made his mark and so did the giant, but deceptively mobile centre-forward, Camataru. He gave Dave Watson a torrid time and England's normally dependable centre-half had an unhappy game. In one Romanian attack the big defender was very fortunate not to give away a penalty when he brought Camataru down with a desperate tackle.

With England pinned back in defence it was virtually impossible for them to push forward. Bryan Robson looked sharp, though, and it was he who put in their first serious shot which Iordache saved with some difficulty. A low cross by Graham Rix was also grabbed by the goalkeeper as Eric Gates came in. These were isolated raids however and Romania were in command.

Raducanu switched to the right, then left with equal effect and was the instigator of the opening goal which came after 34 minutes. In a superb flowing move he combined with Negrila, Crişan, Ticleanu and Beldeanu with deadly one-touch passes, finally setting himself up in the heart of the England penalty area with only Phil Thompson in front of him. Two more strides by Raducanu and Thompson was taken out of the game before the Romanian confidently swept the ball wide of Ray Clemence.

It was a well-deserved goal as England's defence had failed to cope from the outset. This meant that the midfield were unable to feed their forwards any sort of service as they were fully employed helping the defence. All the players worked hard though and Tony Woodcock looked their most effective attacker, doing well on

several occasions. Garry Birtles gave him some useful support at times, but there was little chance for either to score. Indeed, the last chance of the first half fell to Camataru, who went very close to increasing Romania's lead. They must have felt disappointed at half-time as the scoreline gave little indication of their domination.

Ron Greenwood replaced Gates with Steve Coppell at the start of the second half and the visitors looked more composed than they had earlier. Romania seemed content to sit on their lead, allowing England to move forward more often. Watson tried to atone for his defensive frailties by frequently joining the attack. To illustrate the difference it took Romania another 14 minutes after the restart to have a shot at goal. That was when Iordanescu hit a shot which grazed the bar.

This complacent attitude of the Romanians offered England a lifeline and they quickly seized the initiative. This more positive approach paid off for the visitors when they equalized. Woodcock robbed Stefanescu and passed to Birtles. The Cologne striker invited the return pass which was played perfectly by Birtles for Woodcock to burst through hitting a firm shot past Iordache.

It seemed England now had a real chance. The tiring Birtles, who had worked hard, was replaced by Lawrie Cunningham and the momentum was kept up, but in the 76th minute the Swedish referee brought England's brave fight-back to an abrupt halt.

Several times the Romanians appeared to be playing for a penalty and had already appealed for two or three without success. This time, though, after Crişan went down, they were successful. Both Robson and Kenny Sansom should have put in more positive tackles but it seemed that neither had made the sort of challenge that produced the dramatic tumble of Crişan. Unfortunately the referee saw it differently and Iordanescu scored from the spot-kick.

England's disappointment was clear for everyone to see.

> 5th match v Romania.
> Penalty scored for Romania by Iordanescu.

England v Switzerland
World Cup Qualifier

Played on Wednesday, 19 November 1980 at Wembley Stadium.

England: P.L.Shilton (Nottm Forest); P.G.Neal (Liverpool), K.G.Sansom (Arsenal), B.Robson (West Brom), D.V.Watson (Southampton), M.D.Mills (Ipswich T, captain), S.J.Coppell (Man Utd), T.McDermott (Liverpool), P.Mariner (Ipswich T), T.D.Brooking (West Ham), A.S.Woodcock (1.FC Cologne).
Sub: G.Rix (Arsenal) for Brooking.

Switzerland: E.Burgener (Lausanne-Sports); R.Wehrli (Grasshoppers), H.Hermann (Grasshoppers), H.Lüdi (FC Zürich), A.Geiger (FC Sion), U.Barberis (AS Monaco), H.J.Pfister (Grasshoppers), M.Tanner (FC Basel), R.Schönenberger (Young Boys), R.Elsener (FC Zürich), R.Botteron (1.FC Cologne).
Subs: A.Egli (Grasshoppers) for Tanner and P.Marti (FC Basel) for Schonenberger.

Half-time 2-0   Full-time 2-1

Ref: J.N.Keizer (Holland)   Att: 69,000

A MUCH changed England side took the field against Switzerland determined to put behind them the defeat suffered in Romania the previous month, but after a good first half they allowed their visitors to come back strongly.

The first 45 minutes was almost exclusively played in the Swiss half. The experience of the selected side shone through and in the early minutes Terry McDermott twice went close with good shots. Trevor Brooking and Steve Coppell made intelligent use of the wings and Mick Mills was an inspirational captain. It was Mills' interception that almost gave Tony Woodcock a goal but Switzerland were saved by Lüdi's headed clearance. Woodcock's pace was a constant problem for the Swiss and their defence struggled to keep him in check.

England swept forward and wave upon wave of attacks peppered the beleaguered Burgener. The goalkeeper strove manfully to stem the tide and made several good saves. McDermott flicked Brooking's cross just over and Coppell shot wide after a fine pass from Mills. The Swiss, meanwhile, relied heavily on the pace and skill of the lively Botteron, but their attacks were rare in the face of this onslaught by England.

All the home side needed was goals and on 22 minutes the deserved breakthrough came. Again Mills was heavily involved, taking advantage of McDermott's clever decoy run to bring Coppell into play. The winger moved forward and fired a hard, low centre diagonally across goal. Phil Neal lunged at it but he was beaten to the ball by the Swiss defender, Tanner, who then had the misfortune to deflect it into his own net. The goal put England more at ease and they began to play some delightful football. Other chances were created with Brooking and Coppell both having headers saved by Burgener.

The goalkeeper kept the Swiss in the match at this stage and he cleverly pushed away Mariner's well-directed header. The Swiss also continually played the offside trap and the linesman's flag often saved them. It did so when Woodcock saw his goal ruled out. On the half-hour, though,

Mick Mills gives Paul Mariner a hug after Mariner's goal against Switzerland in the World Cup qualifier at Wembley in November 1980.

England made it 2-0. Brooking's free-kick from the left was glanced home brilliantly by Mariner with Burgener, for once, well beaten.

England had dominated the half and could easily have had more goals, so it was therefore somewhat annoying for the home fans when the Swiss were allowed to come back strongly in the second period. True, the Swiss played much better and they broke much more positively into attack. Botteron and Pfister were always dangerous and on 77 minutes they deservedly pulled a goal back. Barberis and Wehrli combined well on the left and when Wehrli passed inside to Pfister, the striker fired in a superb first-time shot that left Peter Shilton with no chance.

England were left with an awkward quarter of an hour to hold on to their lead, a ludicrous situation considering their earlier dominance.

13th match v Switzerland.
Own-goal scored for England by Switzerland's Tanner.

England v Spain
Friendly

Played on Wednesday, 25 March 1981 at Wembley Stadium.

England: R.N.Clemence (Liverpool);

P.G.Neal (Liverpool), K.G.Sansom (Arsenal), B.Robson (West Brom), R.C.Osman (Ipswich), T.L.Butcher (Ipswich T), J.K.Keegan (Southampton, captain), T.J.Francis (Nottm Forest), P.Mariner (Ipswich T), T.D.Brooking (West Ham), G.Hoddle (Spurs).
Subs: P.S.Barnes (West Brom) for Francis and R.G.Wilkins (Man Utd) for Brooking.
Spain: L.Arconada (Real Sociedad); J.A.Camacho (Real Madrid), R.Gordillo (Real Betis), A.Macedo (Sporting Gijon), M.Tendillo (Valencia CF), J.Gomez (Real Madrid), Alonso (Real Zaragoza), J.Alonso (Sporting Gijon), J.Satrustegui (Real Sociedad), J.Zamora (Real Sociedad), M.Alonso (Real Santander).
Subs: R.Montero (Sevilla FC) for V.Alonsa and D.Ruiz (Athletic Bilbao) for Juanito.

Half-time 1-2   Full-time 1-2
Ref: W.Eschweiler (West Germany)

Att: 71,750

THIS was as vital a match for Spain as much as it was for England, and on a wet Wembley night the visitors proved deserved victors. As hosts of the following year's World Cup, Spain were experimenting with their side to try and find the right blend. On the night they looked to have found it. Ron Greenwood, too, brought in some fresh faces in an effort to raise English spirits after a series of indifferent performances.

The pattern of the game was clear after only a few minutes. England pushed forward from the first whistle to put pressure on the Spanish defence. But the visitors broke from defence to attack at breathtaking speed and with superb skill.

Terry Butcher was soon up supporting his attack, but it left Russell Osman somewhat exposed and that was just the chink in the armour that Spain were looking for. Three times in the first three minutes the nervous Osman made mistakes and from the third, Spain took the lead. Zamora raced across the saturated turf, drew Ray Clemence from goal and then slipped a pass to Satrustegui who was left with an easy task to score.

To give continental sides an early goal like that is always asking for trouble and England never fully recovered. Spain now had their tactics sewn up and they filed back into defence as soon as there was any hint of danger. As usual their tackling left a lot to be desired with Macedo being booked for a reckless challenge that sent Paul Mariner crashing to the ground. Kevin Keegan was also closely marked and the England captain had no room at all. Meanwhile, Spain found plenty of freedom to break quickly into attack with Satrustegui allowed a free header after a mix up between Clemence and Phil Neal. The Spaniard missed that time, but Spain still looked dangerous and soon a cross by Juanito was met by Gordillo whose shot deflected off Neal, on to the crossbar, and away to safety.

England were now in deep trouble. Mariner and Keegan were having no success, despite some good prompting by Bryan Robson, but Glenn Hoddle, on the international stage once more, was having a quiet match. However, the class of the Tottenham star was soon in evidence as he suddenly struck a surprise equalizer after 28 minutes. He picked up a clearance to fire a superb volley wide of the highly rated Arconada.

Despite the goal, England still looked very vulnerable to the swift counter attack. Six minutes later they were behind again. Poor defensive play left Zamora alone in the area to receive Juanito's pass and he was easily able to beat Clemence. There had been a hint of offside in Juanito's original run but the officials allowed play to go on.

After the break England, to their credit, attacked furiously. Spain, without looking entirely convincing, defended stubbornly. They certainly enjoyed a helping of good fortune and Arconada was very lucky when Robson shot straight at him from eight yards when it seemed easier to score. The ball constantly flew across the Spanish goal area with the greasy conditions causing more than one Spanish heart to flutter. Trevor Brooking, Mariner and Keegan all went within a whisker of an equalizer, and substitutes Ray Wilkins and Peter Barnes were brought on without success. Always, though, England had to guard against the lightning breakaways and Satrustegui should have scored with a header from Zamora's centre. The ball went wide.

The remaining minutes were all England but could not score again as they recorded their first home defeat since the Dutch won in 1977. It was also the first time that Ron Greenwood had tasted defeat at Wembley.

> 14th match v Spain.
> Spain's V.Alonso also known as 'Victor'; Gomez as 'Juanito'; J.Alonso as 'Joaquin'; M.Alonso as 'Marcos'; Ruiz as 'Dani'.

England v
Romania World Cup Qualifier

Played on Wednesday, 29 April 1981 at Wembley Stadium.

England: P.L.Shilton (Nottm Forest); V.A.Anderson (Nottm Forest), K.G.Sansom (Arsenal), B.Robson (West Brom), D.V.Watson (Southampton, captain), R.C.Osman (Ipswich T), R.C.Wilkins (Man Utd), T.D.Brooking (West Ham), S.J.Coppell (Man Utd), T.J.Francis (Nottm Forest), A.S.Woodcock (1.FC Cologne).
Sub: T.McDermott (Liverpool) for Brooking.
Romania: V.Iordache (Steaua Bucharest); N.Negrila (Universitatea Craiova), I.Munteanu (Sportul Studenţesc Bucureşti), S.Sames (Steaua Bucharest), C.Stefanescu (Universitatea Craiova), A.Beldeanu (Universitatea Craiova), Z.Crisan (Universitatea Craiova), A.Iordanescu (Steaua Bucharest), R.Camataru (Universitatea Craiova), T.Stoica (Steaua Bucharest), I.Balaci (Universitatea Craiova).

Half-time 0-0   Full-time 0-0
Ref: H.Aldinger (West Germany)

Att: 63,000

ENGLAND went into this vital World Cup match hit by injury which robbed them of four players. It meant making six changes in all, so it was hardly surprising that the performance was somewhat disappointing.

Early on England played some clever and constructive football with Trevor Brooking imposing himself on the match as the playmaker-in-chief. Roaming around cleverly, he crossed from both wings in that familiar outswinging style of his to lay on several chances for the forwards. Promising moves developed especially one that involved Viv Anderson, Bryan Robson and Steve Coppell. When Coppell's cross finally came over, Brooking's header lacked both power and direction and the chance was lost.

Romania were looking to break quickly from defence as the Spaniards had done last month, but they were not as skilful and rarely threatened the England goal. England's midfield of Ray Wilkins, Robson and Brooking were showing some good imagination but in the Romanian

Bryan Robson is tightly marked by Romania's Stefan Sames at Wembley in November 1981.

penalty area, the attacks usually floundered around the big defenders, Sames and Stefanescu. Neither Trevor Francis nor Tony Woodcock could make much impression on them, although Woodcock put in a volley with which he could and should have done better. Iordache made several saves notably from Francis, Woodcock and Russell Osman. Osman also shot wide after another attacking sortie.

The one real chance that came Romania's way in the first half came courtesy of an almost nightmare moment for Peter Shilton. Balaci's high long-range header seemed easy for the goalkeeper but Shilton slipped as he went for it and had to scramble desperately to claw the ball away from the goal-line.

Two minutes after the interval, a roar went up from the disappointingly low crowd. Robson, running in to meet Coppell's centre, took possession, waltzed around Iordache and planted the ball into the net. Alas, the West Bromwich Albion star was given offside and one could imagine that the groan could almost be heard in Birmingham. Francis showed some lovely touches but he was too often blocked before he could put in one of those electrifying bursts that England so badly needed.

Obviously patience was of the essence but the crowd was becoming increasingly restless with England's inability to score. The tiring Brooking was replaced by Terry McDermott, a fruitless substitution, as England sought new ideas. Wilkins shot wide, and then Iordache made a very brave save at the feet of Coppell. Near the end, only a brilliant saving tackle by Osman prevented the embarrassment of defeat after Crisan had raced upfield on a breakaway.

At the final whistle, the huge Romanian entourage leapt up from the bench as though they had won the World Cup itself. As for England, they went off to a chorus of booing, pondering their next two World Cup games, difficult away ties in Switzerland and Hungary.

6th match v Romania.
Watson captain for the first time.

England v Brazil   Friendly

Played on Tuesday, 12 May 1981 at Wembley Stadium.

England: R.N.Clemence (Liverpool, captain); P.G.Neal (Liverpool), K.G.Sansom (Arsenal), B.Robson (West Brom), A.E.Martin (West Ham), R.C.Wilkins (Man Utd), S.J.Coppell (Man Utd), T.McDermott (Liverpool), P.Withe (Aston Villa), G.Rix (Arsenal), P.S.Barnes (West Brom).
Brazil: V.Peres (São Paulo); E.Freitas (Fluminense), L.L.Junior (Flamengo), A.C.Cerezo (Atlético Mineiro), J.O.Bernadi (São Paulo), L.C.Ferreira (Atlético Mineiro), P.I.de Jesus (Gremio), S.B.S.S.F.Oliveira (Corinthians), J.R.Lima (Atlético Mineiro), A.Antunes Coimbra (Flamengo), E.A.de Assis (Atlético Mineiro).

Half-time 0-1   Full-time 0-1

Ref: E.Linemayr (Austria)   Att: 75,000

ENGLAND'S preparations for the forthcoming World Cup matches were again hit by injuries and absenteeism and it was a patchwork side that took the field for the prestigious friendly against the mighty Brazilians. Having said that, the home side surprised everyone with a gutsy display that really set the crowd alight, and they were desperately unlucky not to get a result.

The rhythm of the samba pounded across Wembley as Brazil quickly settled into that familiar flowing pattern. In the first ten minutes they threatened to tear the red-shirted England team apart. Socrates thumped a shot against Ray Clemence's chest and then it looked as though Eder would convert Reinaldo's clever pass until Terry McDermott made a vital tackle to clear the danger. It was powerful stuff and after 11 minutes the pressure told. Edevaldo burst through from midfield before putting the ball into the England penalty area. Kenny Sansom tried to clear, but he and Zico connected with the ball almost simultaneously and it flew past Clemence for a very fortunate goal.

It had been a harrowing opening for this unfamiliar looking home side but gradually England began to make some progress. They found that when they were in possession they had much more room than in recent internationals. Peter Barnes showed some thrilling form down the wing and regularly skipped past defenders. Steve Coppell's long passes were also a bright feature.

Mind you, the Brazilians were still well on top and Alvin Martin was very fortunate when he impeded Reinaldo, only for the Brazilian to go on and shoot past Clemence. Martin's luck came in the fact that the referee had already blown for a foul. The free-kick came to nothing and England escaped.

Brazil showed the crowd the whole repertoire of tricks and skills but there was some reservations after an ugly tackle by Eder on Barnes reminded the spectators of the seedier side of their game, much in evidence on their last visit to Wembley. At half-time England could be pleased at only being the one goal down.

After the break England's self confidence grew and they competed with renewed vigour. Barnes, in top form, sprinted down the right before bringing Valdir Peres to a good save at the near post, and then a brilliant move involving Bryan Robson, Coppell and Peter Withe ended with Graham Rix shooting over.

Robson was the driving force for England as they pushed Brazil back for long spells. Still, though, Brazil were dangerous on the break and Eder clipped Clemence's crossbar with a spectacular long-range shot. New caps Martin and Withe had nervous first games, although Withe had suffered through a lack of support. The England attitude was so much better in this half and it was reflected in the superb encouragement given by the crowd as the match built up into a crescendo of excitement.

The pressure grew on the Brazilian goal as England searched desperately for an equalizer and the crowd were on the edge of their seats in the final minutes. Coppell's brilliant shot was tipped over by Peres and, then right at the end, it seemed that Withe had surely equalized when his volley hit the post, ran along the line, only for the linesman's flag to rule out any chance anyway by giving him offside. The crowd's response to England's super effort was to applaud them from the field, a rare occurrence in some barren years.

12th match v Brazil.
Debuts for Martin and Withe.
Brazil's Freitas also known as 'Edevaldo'; Bernadi as 'Oscar'; Ferreira as 'Luisinho'; de Jesus as 'Pavio Isidoro'; Oliveira as 'Socrates'; Lima as 'Reinaldo'; Antunes Coimbra as 'Zico'; de Assis as 'Eder'.
"My favourite memory of playing at Wembley was captaining England against Brazil."
Ray Clemence

England v Wales   Home Championship

Played on Wednesday, 20 May 1981 at Wembley Stadium.

England: T.J.Corrigan (Man City); V.A.Anderson (Nottm Forest), K.G.Sansom (Arsenal), B.Robson (Man Utd), D.V.Watson (Southampton, captain), R.C.Wilkins (Man Utd), S.J.Coppell (Man Utd), G.Hoddle

Alvin Martin takes the ball away from Brazil's Reinaldo at Wembley in May 1981.

(Spurs), P.Withe (Aston Villa), G.Rix (Arsenal), P.S.Barnes (West Brom).
Sub: A.S.Woodcock (1.FC Cologne) for Withe.
Wales: W.D.Davies (Wrexham); K.Ratcliffe (Everton), J.P.Jones (Wrexham), P.Nicholas (Arsenal), L.Phillips (Swansea C), P.T.Price (Luton T), C.S.Harris (Leeds Utd), B.Flynn (Leeds Utd), I.P.Walsh (Crystal Palace), M.R.Thomas (Man Utd), L.James (Swansea C).
Subs: D.C.Giles (Swansea C) for Harris and I.J.Rush (Liverpool) for James.

Half-time 0-0   Full-time 0-0
Ref: B.R.McGinlay (Scotland) Att: 34,250

THIS disappointing result gave England two unwanted records as their important World Cup ties loomed. They had never, until then, gone three games without scoring since internationals began, and it was also four games since they last won at Wembley.

England began confidently enough and were looking to build on the improved display against Brazil a fortnight earlier. Glenn Hoddle showed some early promise and some good attacks were built up from midfield. One lovely move involving Ray Wilkins and Peter Barnes ended when Phillips cleared the ball away from danger. The best chance of Wales scoring seemed to be from the carelessness of England's defenders. Some indecisive play following two crosses by Harris and Thomas almost caused Joe Corrigan some embarrassment especially when Kenny Sansom sliced the ball over his own crossbar whilst attempting to clear.

After this bright start the game fell into a subdued period which made the atmos-

phere at Wembley almost non-existent. Only some 34,000 people attended the match and they had precious little to entertain them. The game was crying out for some inspiration, but although Hoddle sprayed some lovely passes around and Bryan Robson and Viv Anderson made some positive forward runs, there was little service to the strike force which consisted of only Peter Withe.

There was little Withe could do on his own although, as usual, he gave 100 per cent effort. Steve Coppell went close with a header and a minute before the interval, after a comfortable save by Corrigan, Anderson again made a move down the right. When the final pass came in, Barnes' shot was blocked by Flynn.

After the break there was little change in the monotony. England, generally moving forward, never looked to have the imagination to beat the well-organised Welsh defence. Phillips and Price played very well but had little to mark with Withe, and then later, Tony Woodcock, struggling to find their form. England's full-backs impressed and did as much as anyone to provide attacking support. Hoddle showed glimpses of his undoubted class, although he suffered through a lack of vision from his colleagues.

Withe wasted a half-chance and was immediately replaced by Woodcock. The home side continued to search for a goal and Sansom was unlucky to see his effort cleared from the goal-line by the head of Phillips. With eight minutes to go, Wales almost snatched the win that would have been a travesty. Nicholas hit a long pass for Giles, a substitute, to run on to. Dave Watson chased him but was outpaced. Fortunately for England, Giles sent his weak shot wide of Corrigan's goal, much

to the relief of the sparse crowd.

The alarming deficiency in the goal department had been most worrying at this time, and Ron Greenwood knew he needed maximum effort from England's players over the important coming weeks.

94th match v Wales.

England v Scotland Home Championship

Played on Saturday, 23 May 1981 at Wembley Stadium.

England: T.J.Corrigan (Man City); V.A.Anderson (Nottm Forest), K.G.Sansom (Arsenal), R.C.Wilkins (Man Utd), D.V.Watson (Southampton, captain), B.Robson (West Brom), S.J.Coppell (Man Utd), G.Hoddle (Spurs), P.Withe (Aston Villa), A.S.Woodcock (1.FC Cologne), G.Rix (Arsenal).
Subs: A.E.Martin (West Ham) for Watson and T.J.Francis (Nottm Forest) for Woodcock.

Scotland: A.Rough (Partick Thistle); D.McGrain (Celtic), F.T.Gray (Leeds Utd), D.Provan (Celtic), A.McLeish (Aberdeen), W.Miller (Aberdeen), R.S.M.Stewart (West Ham), R.A.Hartford (Everton), J.Jordan (Man Utd), S.Archibald (Spurs), J.N.Robertson (Nottm Forest).
Subs: P.Sturrock (Dundee Utd) for Provan and D.Narey (Dundee Utd) for Hartford.

Half-time 0-0   Full-time 0-1
Ref: R.Wurtz (France)   Att: 90,000

THE annual clash between these two old enemies once more produced much

Trevor Francis tries to get in a cross as Willie Miller comes thundering in during the England-Scotland match at Wembley in May 1981.

concern over England's current form. They failed to score yet again and, despite a lot of possession, did not inspire any confidence for the immediate future.

England began quite well and were soon creating chances. After only seven minutes, Steve Coppell shot over the bar from a great position. It was the first of many missed chances on a day which highlighted the severe problem affecting England in recent internationals. Ray Wilkins and Bryan Robson were working hard in midfield but Graham Rix and Glenn Hoddle only flitted in and out of the game.

Scotland had few clear-cut chances in the first half, although Hartford forced a fine diving save from Joe Corrigan with one good shot. Corrigan looked very solid in goal and England continued to create the better scoring opportunities. After 17 minutes, Rix shot wide from a good position and three minutes from the interval Coppell centred, only for Rix to miss again, heading over an open goal.

It was obvious that England's continual failure to score was beginning to have a dire affect on their confidence. They still enjoyed most of the possession, but another chance went begging in the 62nd minute. A fine ball from Coppell sent Kenny Sansom away. Sansom lobbed the ball perfectly for Peter Withe to head goalwards, but it lacked power and Miller was able to scramble the ball off the goal-line. Again, it really should have been a goal and England were made to pay two minutes later when Scotland took the lead.

Jordan found Provan who sent Archibald racing away. The Spurs striker had already shown some good form and this time he was clear, but as he reached the penalty area he was stopped by Robson's desperate tackle. Penalty! Up stepped Robertson for the kick and it was 1-0.

England were now in deep trouble and Corrigan twice had to save well from the dangerous Archibald. There were few scares for the Scottish defence in the remaining minutes, although England made some claims for a penalty themselves

when Miller seemed to pull back Francis with seven minutes to go.

England had to put away some of the numerous chances they were creating, otherwise they could forget all about qualifying for the World Cup. Goals win matches, not mere possession.

99th match v Scotland.
Penalty scored for Scotland by Robertson.

Switzerland v England World Cup Qualifier

Played on Saturday, 30 May 1981 in the St Jakob Stadium, Basle.

Switzerland: E.Burgener (Lausanne-Sports); H.Hermann (Grasshoppers), G.Zappa (FC Zürich), A.Egli (Grasshoppers), H.Lüdi (FC Zürich), R.Wehrli (Grasshoppers), U.Barberis (AS Monaco), R.Botteron (1.FC Cologne), F.Scheiwiler (FC St Gallen), C.Sulser (Grasshoppers), R.Elsener (FC Zürich).
Subs: M.Weber (Young Boys) for Hermann and E.Maissen (FC Basel) for Elsener.

England: R.N.Clemence (Liverpool); M.D.Mills (Ipswich T), K.G.Sansom (Arsenal), R.C.Wilkins (Man Utd), D.V.Watson (Southampton), R.C.Osman (Ipswich T), S.J.Coppell (Man Utd), J.K.Keegan (Southampton, captain), P.Mariner (Ipswich T), T.J.Francis (Nottm Forest), B.Robson (West Brom). Subs: P.S.Barnes (West Brom) for Watson and T.McDermott (Liverpool) for Francis.

Half-time 2-0   Full-time 2-1

Ref: A.Prokop (East Germany)   Att: 40,000

ANOTHER unhappy day for the England team. Not only did they lose against the unfancied Swiss but their so-called supporters caused mayhem on the terraces with some disgraceful scenes of violence.

Once again it had all started quite brightly with England settling down

nicely, playing neat and constructive football. They even threatened to score on a couple of occasions. After 11 minutes, England might have had a penalty when Trevor Francis's shot appeared to touch a Swiss hand before Zappa almost sliced the ball into his own net, only for the alert Burgener to dive and save. Just as it looked as if England would break their goalscoring duck which has stretched through four games, they suddenly threw the match away in a few careless minutes.

The game had reached the 28th minute when Zappa moved out of defence finding Scheiwiler with a good pass. On reaching the England penalty area Scheiwiler played a neat one-two with Sulser before smashing a shot past Ray Clemence. Moments later, Sulser, a real livewire, was sent sprinting away following a free-kick which left Dave Watson stranded. Sulser powerfully swept past Russell Osman and then evaded a desperate lunge by Kenny Sansom before shooting into the left-hand corner of the goal.

At this point the trouble began to flare up on the terraces and soon tempers reached boiling point. The game was inadequately policed, the mood was ugly and once again tear-gas was brought in to try to calm things down. Even after that though there was still more fighting on a day that once again tarnished the worsening record of English football hooligans.

Back on the field England were stunned by the two goals and the uncertainty crept back into their play. Watson was shaky at the back, Bryan Robson and Ray Wilkins in midfield failed to match the extra skills of Botteron and Barberis, and Paul Mariner, up front, had little effect on the well-organised home defence.

After half-time, Ron Greenwood brought on Terry McDermott for the disappointing Francis and nine minutes into the second half the Liverpool player gave England a tonic by scoring a splendid goal. Steve Coppell robbed Hermann and gave a pass to McDermott. The substitute moved forward and hit a fine low shot

Switzerland's Sulser sweeps past Russell Osman to put his side 2-0 ahead in Basle in May 1981.

Hungary's Garaba (on ground) brings down Kevin Keegan during the World Cup qualifier in Budapest in June 1981.

Keegan himself took the penalty and although Katzirz went the right way, the ball still eluded him and finished up in the back of the net.

into the same corner that Sulser had found earlier.

McDermott shot just wide later in the half and right at the end, Robson almost made up for his poor display by hitting a ground shot from long range which looked a goal, but Burgener dived superbly to thrust out a hand to save.

This defeat had almost fatally damaged England's hopes of qualifying for the finals of the competition and was a very poor performance. Only a miracle could save them from World Cup exit now and even a win in Hungary the following week would not necessarily save them, reliant as they now were on other results.

14th match v Switzerland.

Hungary v
England   World Cup Qualifier

Played on Saturday, 6 June 1981 in the Nep Stadium, Budapest.

Hungary: B.Katzirz (Pécsi MSC); G.Martos (Waterschei Thor), L.Balint (FC Brugge), I.Garaba (Honvéd), J.Varga (Honvéd), S.Müller (R Antwerp FC),

T.Nyilasi (Ferencváros), J.Mucha (Ferencváros), L.Fazekas (Antwerp FC), L.Kiss (Vasas), A.Törőcsik (Újpesti Dózsa).
Subs: A.Komjati (Vasas) for Müller and B.Bodonyi (Honvéd) for Fazekas.

England: R.N.Clemence (Liverpool); P.G.Neal (Liverpool), M.D.Mills (Ipswich T), P.B.Thompson (Liverpool), D.V.Watson (Southampton), B.Robson (West Brom), J.K.Keegan (Southampton, captain), S.J.Coppell (Man Utd), P.Mariner (Ipswich T), T.D.Brooking (West Ham), T.McDermott (Liverpool).
Sub: R.C.Wilkins (Man Utd) for Brooking.

Half-time 1-1   Full-time 1-3
Ref: P.Casarin (Italy)   Att: 70,000

THEY say that football is an unpredictable game and never has that saying been more apt than after this magnificent victory by England in Hungary. England went into the match given little chance of improving on a dismal run of six matches without a win and with only one goal in the process. They were visiting a city where they had not won since 1909 and a city where memories were still vivid of a 7-1 mauling in 1954 at the hands of

the Puskás-inspired Magyars of yesteryear.

The game began at a cracking pace and Hungary were soon breathing down on Ray Clemence's goal. They missed chances in that opening spell, misses that were to cost them dearly. On 13 minutes Fazekas set up a golden opportunity for Nyilasi, who looked a certain scorer. But the shot was poor and straight at Clemence so England escaped. Four minutes later, a fine move involving Balint, Fazekas and Nyilasi was ended only by a superb tackle from the much-improved Dave Watson. Regained confidence in Watson's game was inspired by the recalled Phil Thompson's majestic performance in the England defence. The Liverpool man had rarely played better for his country.

So England rode this opening storm and gradually began to assert themselves on to the game. On 18 minutes they surprised everyone including, probably, themselves by scoring the opening goal. Kevin Keegan found Bryan Robson, who in turn set Steve Coppell on a typically eager run. Coppell then found Phil Neal on the right, who crossed into the middle. Coppell followed it up and flicked it to Terry McDermott. The ball was quickly moved on to Trevor Brooking, who ended the move by drilling a low hard shot between post and goalkeeper. It was a beautifully worked goal and was ultimately the inspiration for victory. The silence from the big crowd was deafening.

Hungary came back strongly with Clemence saving a header by Kiss with some difficulty. England then seemed to be denied a possible penalty after shots by Keegan and then McDermott were blocked. Fazekas then shot at Clemence after a move orchestrated by Törocsik had opened England up and then Hungary almost equalized when Niyilasi thundered in a header which crashed against the crossbar. With only a minute to go before the break Hungary finally scored that elusive goal. The aggressive Garaba made the decisive break, bursting from defence to set Kiss on his way. The ball moved on to Törocsik and although Clemence dived bravely at his feet, the ball fell loose for Garaba to follow up and score. The psychological effect must have been devastating, as seconds later the half-time whistle went.

But not to be dismayed England continued to play well after the restart. They contained Hungary and then, on the hour, they sensationally regained the lead. This time the polished Neal passed to Keegan, who quickly moved it on to Brooking. The West Ham man cut in from the right and arrowed a terrific shot into the top corner where the ball dramatically wedged in the net stanchion.

A minute later, Paul Mariner missed a golden chance as the marauding McDermott sent him clear with only the goalkeeper to beat. Mariner, though, could only hit his shot straight at Katzirz and the ball was cleared. With 16 minutes to go, though, England did score again. This time the Italian referee could not refuse the penalty claims when Garaba chopped down Keegan after Mariner had put him through. Keegan converted the kick himself and the lead was now safe.

So, this unexpected lifeline gave England an outside chance of qualification for the World Cup after all seemed lost a week ago. But they deserved that chance after a memorable display. Brooking was the man of the match, although he had to go off near the end following Bodonyi's crude challenge which sent him flying. By then, though, he had done enough.

12th match v Hungary.
Penalty scored for England by Keegan.
"I had a number of favourite players during my time with the squad, but I think Trevor Brooking stands out as a player of elegance."
Ray Wilkins

Norway v England World Cup Qualifier

Played on Tuesday, 9 September 1981 in the Ullevaal Stadium, Oslo.

Norway: T.Antonsen (Hamarkameratene); B.Berntsen (Viking Stavanger), Å.F.Hareide (Molde FK), E.J.Aas (Nottm Forest), S.Grøndalen (Moss FK), R.Albertson (KFC Winterslag), A.Giske (SK Brann), H.Thoresen (PSV Eindhoven), A.Larsen-Økland (Bayer 04 Leverkusen), P.Jacobsen (Vålerengens IF), T.Lund (Lillestrøm SK).

Subs: A.Dokken (Panathinaikos) for Lund and T.Pedersen (IK Start) for Thoresen.
England: R.N.Clemence (Liverpool); P.G.Neal (Liverpool), M.D.Mills (Ipswich T), P.B.Thompson (Liverpool), R.C.Osman (Ipswich T), B.Robson (West Brom), J.K.Keegan (Southampton, captain), T.J.Francis (Man City), P.Mariner (Ipswich T), G.Hoddle (Spurs), T.McDermott (Liverpool).
Subs: P.Withe (Aston Villa) for Mariner and P.S.Barnes (Leeds Utd) for Hoddle.

Half-time 2-1   Full-time 2-1
Ref: J.Kacprzak (Poland)   Att: 22,000

THE stuttering of England in their World Cup quest seemed to have all but come to a standstill after this disastrous defeat in Norway. After the euphoria of England's win in Hungary in the June, it seemed a formality that they would overcome the mostly part-timers of this Scandinavian country.

It started well enough and both Trevor Francis and Paul Mariner had half-chances in the Norwegian penalty area which they failed to take. On 17 minutes, though, England took a deserved lead. Mariner, out on the left, centred towards Kevin Keegan. The England skipper flicked it on and Bryan Robson, running from deep, latched on to it, skipped around a couple of challenges and shot past Antonsen from an almost sitting position. It was just the tonic England needed, or so it appeared.

Norway, improving their game like so many other smaller nations, were playing with a lot of determination. They gave England plenty of warning of their capabilities, notably when Hareide headed Grondalen's free-kick powerfully, only for Ray Clemence to save well at the foot of the left-hand post. On 37 minutes, though, Clemence was left helpless as Norway found an equalizer.

Lund took a corner on the right, collected a rebound and then centred dangerously. The ball deflected off of Mick Mills and Albertsen ran in to shoot under Clemence. Five minutes later another disaster hit England. This time Larsen-Økland's cross looked easy for Terry McDermott to clear but he inexplicably allowed the ball to go past him, setting up an easy goal for Thoresen.

So, at half-time England trailed by 2-1. It was an unimaginable situation, but one that had to be met square on. Early in the second half Mariner flicked a Keegan cross wide when perhaps a headed pass would have been better. Glenn Hoddle saw his strong shot deflected over and then Mills had a shot deflected into the side netting. The more desperate England became, the more difficult it was for them to score. The Norwegian penalty area was very congested at times, so Ron Greenwood replaced Hoddle with Peter Barnes to try and give his side a bit of width. Later he swapped Mariner for Peter Withe but it was all to no avail and Norway were delighted at the final whistle recording their first-ever win over England.

For the visitors it seemed that all that was left amongst the ruins of their group matches were a few prayers. They certainly needed some help from elsewhere.

6th match v Norway.

England v Hungary World Cup Qualifier

Played on Wednesday, 18 November 1981 at Wembley Stadium.

England: P.L.Shilton (Nottm Forest); P.G.Neal (Liverpool), M.D.Mills (Ipswich T), P.B.Thompson (Liverpool), A.E.Martin (West Ham), B.Robson (Man Utd), J.K.Keegan (Southampton, captain), S.J.Coppell (Man Utd), P.Mariner (Ipswich T), T.D.Brooking (West Ham), T.McDermott (Liverpool).
Sub: W.A.Morley (Aston Villa) for Coppell.

Hungary: F.Meszáros (Sporting Lisbon); G.Martos (Waterschei Thor), L.Bálint (Toulouse FC), J.Tóth (Újpesti Dózsa), S.Müller (Hércules Alicante), I.Garaba (Honvéd), L.Fazekas (R Antwerp FC), K.Csapó (Tatabánya), A.Törocsik (Újpesti Dózsa), L.Kiss (Vasas), S.Sallai (Debreceni BSC).
Subs: G.Kerekes (Debreceni BSC) for Fazekas and G.Szántó (Ferencváros) for Csapo.

Half-time 1-0   Full-time 1-0
Ref: G.Konrath (France)   Att: 92,000

IT was official! England could now make their plans for Spain. After 14 months of what can only be described as indifferent World Cup action, England managed to scratch together enough points to finish second in their group. The other teams helped their cause by taking points off each other, but England at least have the satisfaction of two good wins against the eventual group winners, Hungary.

This Hungarian side were a pale shadow of some of their illustrious predecessors, but England still had to play well. Backed by a vociferous full-house at Wembley they made a positive start. Kevin Keegan was soon in the action. A quick free-kick by Steve Coppell found Keegan's head after the Southampton star had lost his marker, Sallai. The header lacked power, though, and Meszáros saved easily. Keegan was shadowed everywhere by Sallai but the England captain still buzzed around in that effervescent style of his.

The atmosphere at Wembley was electric and England kept up the pressure. Phil Neal hit a good cross-shot just wide and after Meszáros had punched out a Mick Mills cross, Terry McDermott also pulled a shot wide. This good start was at last rewarded 16 minutes into the game. Alvin Martin challenged for a McDermott cross and the ball dropped for West Ham clubmate Trevor Brooking to try a shot. It was a mis-hit effort but fell perfectly for Paul Mariner to ram home. The crowd were delighted and really the celebrations could have started at that point.

Hungary, already assured of their place in the finals, never seriously threatened Peter Shilton's goal. They missed the exciting Nyilasi and as a result their attack could not get going. England continued to push forward with McDermott hitting a volley just over and Keegan twice going very close.

After the break England coolly controlled the game. Shilton made his only saves of the night from Balint and Kiss without too much difficulty, whilst at the other end Mariner might have secured a hat-trick had he been sharper with his finishing. One header which flew wide

Above: **Paul Mariner (9) scores the only goal of the game against Hungary at Wembley in November 1981. There can have been few more vital goals for England – it sent them through to the World Cup finals in Spain.** *Below:* **Mariner celebrates with the help of Phil Neal and Terry McDermott.**

had him holding his head in horror.

An injury to Steve Coppell gave Tony Morley his first cap and he almost celebrated it immediately. Only a superb save by Meszáros prevented what would have been a brilliant goal by the Aston Villa winger. Keegan saw another effort hacked off the line by Sallai and England could not quite manage a deserved second goal.

However, with Robson in command of the midfield and Martin and Phil Thompson dominant at the back England's victory was complete. At the final whistle the jubilant crowd roared their approval and the players did a well deserved lap of honour.

It had been a long, hazardous journey to Spain but now having clinched the tickets, Ron Greenwood began his preparations in earnest.

13th match v Hungary.
Debut, as substitute, Morley.
"My injury against Hungary was without doubt the worst moment of my international career."
Steve Coppell

England v
Northern Ireland Home

Championship

Played on Tuesday, 23 February 1982 at Wembley Stadium.

England: R.N.Clemence (Liverpool); V.A.Anderson (Nottm Forest), K.G.Sansom (Arsenal), R.C.Wilkins (Man Utd), D.V.Watson (Southampton), S.B.Foster (Brighton & HA), J.K.Keegan (Southampton, captain), B.Robson (Man Utd), T.J.Francis (Man City), G.Hoddle (Spurs), W.A.Morley (Aston Villa).
Subs: C.Regis (West Brom) for Francis and A.S.Woodcock (1.FC Cologne) for Morley.
Northern Ireland: P.A.Jennings (Arsenal); J.M.Nicholl (Sunderland), S.Nelson (Brighton & HA), M.M.Donaghy (Luton T), C.J.Nicholl (Southampton), J.P.O'Neill (Leicester C), M.H.O'Neill (Norwich C), S.B.McIlroy (Stoke C), W.R.Hamilton (Burnley), G.J.Armstrong (Watford), N.Brotherston (Blackburn R).
Subs: D.McCreery (Tulsa Roughnecks) for M.O'Neill and G.T.Cochrane (Middlesbrough) for Brotherston.

Half-time 1-0   Full-time 4-0
Ref: G.P.Owen (Wales)   Att: 55,000

ENGLAND made a dream start to this, the first Home Championship match of the season. Within 44 seconds the ball was in the back of the Irish net, put there by Bryan Robson. England kicked off and quickly won a free-kick. Viv Anderson sent Trevor Francis away and the striker turned on the speed and zoomed past Nelson to reach the by-line. Over came the cross and Robson was left with the simple task of scoring. It was one of the quickest goals ever seen at Wembley and, despite a stuttering performance, England never looked in danger.

Ron Greenwood experimented by using Ray Wilkins as an extra defender sweeping behind the back four. The plan worked quite well in this match, but against sterner opposition the tactic would face tougher examination. With Wilkins committed at the back it meant that Robson and Glenn Hoddle saw little of the ball in midfield, leaving England unable to get forward in numbers.

For a while the Irish took the initiative and showed some of the form and confidence that had seen them also qualify for the World Cup in Spain in the coming summer. McIlroy was a constant threat, clipping the bar with a corner and then missing a good chance after robbing debutant Steve Foster, running clear, only to shoot straight at Ray Clemence. Neither goalkeeper was severely tested again in a first half largely devoid, apart from the early goal, of any real excitement.

England caught the Irish cold at the start of the second half as well. Again Anderson freed Francis, and again Francis supplied the cross, this time a high curling one. In the middle was Kevin Keegan, who had time and room to pick his spot with a good header. This spelt the end for the Irish who visibly wilted after the goal. England took command and, after Francis had limped off to be replaced by Cyrille Regis, the attack livened up even more.

Regis could and should have scored with a header, that was disappointing but his all-round display was very impressive and he certainly gave Chris Nicholl a hard time whilst he was on. Tony Woodcock also came on as substitute and the Irish also made two changes but the pattern remained the same with England pushing the Irish back continuously.

At the end, with Ireland now tiring, England rammed home their superiority with two more goals in the last five minutes. Wilkins moved forward from his defensive duties and hit a superb 25-yarder which zipped past Jennings. Then Woodcock made a good break and crossed for Kenny Sansom. The Arsenal full-back turned sharply in the box and fired in his shot. Jennings managed to parry it but only into the path of Hoddle who applied the finishing touch.

The win was well deserved although both teams looked to have future events on their minds.

90th match v Northern Ireland.
Debut for Foster and, as substitute, Regis.

Wales v
England Home Championship

Played on Tuesday, 27 April 1982 at Ninian Park, Cardiff.

Wales: W.D.Davies (Swansea C); C.Marustik (Swansea C), K.Ratcliffe (Everton), P.Nicholas (Arsenal), N.C.A.Stevenson (Swansea C), J.P.Jones (Wrexham), A.T.Curtis (Swansea C), B.Flynn (Leeds Utd), I.J.Rush (Liverpool), M.R.Thomas (Brighton & HA), R.M.James (Swansea C).
Subs: C.S.Harris (Leeds Utd) for Flynn and L.James (Swansea C) for Thomas.
England: T.J.Corrigan (Man City); P.G.Neal (Liverpool), K.G.Sansom (Arsenal), P.B.Thompson (Liverpool, captain), T.I.Butcher (Ipswich T), B.Robson (Man Utd), R.C.Wilkins (Man Utd), T.J.Francis (Man City), P.Withe (Aston Villa), G.Hoddle (Spurs), W.A.Morley (Aston Villa).
Subs: C.Regis (West Brom) for Francis and T.McDermott (Liverpool) for Hoddle.

Half-time 0-0   Full-time 0-1
Ref: O.Donnelly (Northern Ireland)
Att: 50,000

England line up before the game against Wales at Ninian Park in April 1982. From left to right are Peter Withe, Trevor Francis, Terry Butcher, Bryan Robson, Phil Neal, Glenn Hoddle, Tony Morley, Ray Wilkins, Kenny Sansom, Joe Corrigan and Phil Thompson.

Phil Neal clears the ball watched by Holland's Arnold Muhren.

ANOTHER morale-boosting victory for England, who were putting an impressive run together. They controlled this match in Cardiff for long spells, inspired by a rock solid back-four in which Phil Thompson and Terry Butcher were outstanding.

In the first half particularly, England probed the Welsh defence, led by a strong midfield of Bryan Robson, Glenn Hoddle and Ray Wilkins. Two chances were created by the silky skills of Hoddle, first in the 15th minute when he provided the cross for Robson to head just wide. Then 17 minutes later, he sent a great pass to Trevor Francis whose shot was deflected on to a post before being cleared.

Joe Corrigan, winning only his eighth cap in five years, had little to do in the opening half but was called upon in the second half on several occasions as Wales hit back. The period just after the break was the best spell for the Welsh and Rush forced one fine save from the England goalkeeper.

The game was more evenly contested in this half and the substitution of Leighton James for Thomas led to new encouragement for the Welsh. England, meanwhile, had to contend with two nasty injuries. Robson eventually had six stitches in a facial wound and then Hoddle's game was brought to an abrupt end by a cynical tackle by Nicholas. The Spurs star limped off to be replaced by Terry McDermott.

Curtis and Rush both made dangerous breaks but with Phil Neal and Kenny Sansom supporting their central defensive partners well, Corrigan had plenty of cover. The goal that nipped the Welsh pressure in the bud came in the 74th minute. Debutant Stevenson, climbed all over Peter Withe in a challenge five yards outside the penalty area. Robson and Wilkins tapped the free-kick to each other

before Francis stepped up to lash home a fierce shot that flew into the top left-hand corner of Davies' goal.

It was a strike worthy of a better match and gave Francis his first England goal for two years. But it was enough to win the match and keep up England's improved run of results.

95th match v Wales.

England v Holland
Friendly

Played on Tuesday, 25 May 1982 at Wembley Stadium.

England: P.L.Shilton (Nottm Forest, captain), P.G.Neal (Liverpool), K.G.Sansom (Arsenal), P.B.Thompson (Liverpool), S.B.Foster (Brighton & HA), B.Robson (Man Utd), R.C.Wilkins (Man Utd), A.E.Devonshire (West Ham), P.Mariner (Ipswich T), T.McDermott (Liverpool), A.S.Woodcock (1.FC Cologne).
Subs: G.Rix (Arsenal) for Devonshire and P.S.Barnes (Leeds Utd) for Mariner.
Holland: H.Van Breukelen (DOS Ultrecht); M.Van de Korput (Torino), J.A.B.Metgod (AZ 67 Alkmaar), E.Ophof (Ajax Amsterdam), R.M.Krol (Napoli), P.Boeve (Ajax Amsterdam), S.La Ling (Ajax Amsterdam), J.Peters (AZ 67 Alkmaar), W.Kieft (Ajax Amsterdam), A.J.M.Mühren (Ipswich T), S.Tahamata (Standard Liège).
Subs: F.Rijkaard (Ajax Amsterdam) for Metgod, K.Van Kooten (Go Ahead Eagles) for La Ling and R.Van der Kerkhof (PSV Eindhoven) for Peters.

Half-time 0-0   Full-time 2-0
Ref: P.Bergamo (Italy)   Att: 69,000

THIS match gave England an excellent opportunity to try to extend their recent

run of improved performances when they took on one of the best teams in the world at that time.

The early moments saw both teams feeling each other out cautiously. It was soon evident that Holland would be pushing their full-backs into attack as much as possible, but England counteracted this well by filling the midfield with as many players as possible. Bryan Robson and Ray Wilkins worked tirelessly for possession, despite the attentions of the powerful Krol. As the pattern developed, England found space behind the attacking midfield of the Dutch, space which they began to exploit as the game progressed.

Wilkins put in a curling long range shot which Van Breukelen saved and then after 20 minutes the goalkeeper did even better after Paul Mariner had put the lively Tony Woodcock through. Alan Devonshire was making some excellent runs at the Dutch and had the beating of Ophof. One lovely cross gave Mariner a free header but the Ipswich man wasted the opportunity by heading straight into the goalkeeper's hands.

By now England held the upper hand and before the break they created another good chance. Devonshire was again prominent sending a fine pass to Wilkins. A delicate chip to Mariner at the far post was only just thwarted by the outstretched fingers of Van Breukelen. It looked as though a goal just had to come and moments later it almost did, but at the other end. A centre by Peters cleared the static Steve Foster and Kieft headed at goal. Thankfully, Peter Shilton was alert to the danger and made a good save.

At half-time the unfortunate Devonshire had to withdraw due to injury and he was replaced by Graham Rix, but England's growing domination of the match continued unaffected. Indeed, Rix was prominent as the home side suddenly took a stranglehold on the game. Three minutes after the restart, a probing right-wing cross by Phil Thompson had Van Breukelen groping under pressure from Mariner. The ball broke invitingly and Woodcock had time and space to pick his spot to score.

Five minutes later England effectively sealed the victory by scoring a second goal. Rix was again the provider, fooling the Dutch defence with a clever pass to Mariner. The Ipswich striker turned sharply and hit a fine shot past Van Breukelen.

The match was won and lost in those five minutes. Rix and Wilkins remained in control of the midfield and, despite several substitutions, the Dutch rarely looked like pulling anything back. One player did catch the eye and that was the 19-year-old Rijkaard, who looked a very good prospect when he came on. England now travelled to Hampden Park needing only a point from the Scots to win the Home Championship. A confident mood was assured after this fine win.

7th match v Holland.
Shilton captain for the first time.

Scotland v England Home Championship

Played on Saturday, 29 May 1982 at Hampden Park, Glasgow.

Scotland: A.Rough (Partick Thistle); G.E.Burley (Ipswich T), D.McGrain (Celtic), A.D.Hansen (Liverpool), A.Evans (Aston Villa), D.Narey (Dundee Utd), K.Dalglish (Liverpool), G.J.Souness (Liverpool), J.Jordan (Milan AC) R.A.Hartford (Man City), A.B.Brazil (Ipswich T).
Subs: P.Sturrock (Dundee Utd) for Jordan and J.N.Robertson (Nottm Forest) for Hartford.
England: P.L.Shilton (Nottm Forest); M.D.Mills (Ipswich T), K.G.Sansom (Arsenal), P.B.Thompson (Liverpool), T.I.Butcher (Ipswich T), B.Robson (Man Utd), J.K.Keegan (Southampton, Captain), S.J.Coppell (Man Utd), P.Mariner (Ipswich T), T.D.Brooking (West Ham), R.C.Wilkins (Man Utd).
Subs: T.McDermott (Liverpool) for Keegan and T.J.Francis (Man City) for Mariner.

**Half-time 0-1	Full-time 0-1**
Ref: J.Redelfs (West Germany)	Att: 80,500

THIS was the 100th official international between these old rivals and it was, therefore, fitting that the sides should be led out by two of the game's greatest stars, George Young for Scotland and Tom Finney for England. Finney would certainly have been happier with the eventual outcome, although it was always going to be a good omen for England with him representing them as England never lost an international here when the Preston North End wizard was in the team.

With the World Cup just around the corner, the game took on an even more important look than usual, but despite great Hampden Roar from 80,500 people present, it was England who started the better. Trevor Brooking, who was at his most elegant throughout, hit a volley that

was well saved by Rough, Terry Butcher just missed from close range and then Paul Mariner headed wide with a glancing header from Brooking's cross.

This impressive opening was rewarded after 14 minutes when England took the lead. Brooking sent in a corner, Bryan Robson headed it back, Butcher headed against the bar, and then Mariner dived bravely to head the rebound into the net. The visitors had thoroughly deserved that goal as they had looked much the better team. Scotland, experimenting with a sweeper, just could not get their game together and their manager, Jock Stein, had plenty of problems to sort out before his team took on the might of the Brazilians and Russians in Spain.

They worked hard enough and in one spell Peter Shilton had to make three saves in a minute as first Brazil put in a shot, then Phil Thompson's back-header caused his own goalkeeper severe problems, before Souness hit a shot following a corner which Shilton did well to hold. Generally, though, the Scots were weak in midfield and it was in that area that Brooking excelled.

At half-time Scotland made a few tactical changes and for a while their play improved. Evans went close with a header from Brazil's cross, but such openings were rare as Thompson and Butcher stood like rocks at the heart of England's defence. Butcher was outstanding and had rarely played better for his country. As the game went on, it was England who finished the stronger. In the last ten minutes, Trevor Francis did very well to beat a man and shoot inches wide, and then substitute Terry McDermott was only inches away from another cross-cum-shot by Francis. Robson remained busy and effective in midfield and Brooking was superb as England recorded yet another victory on this, the oldest of their away venues. Their 100 cent record in the Home Championship gave them the title once more.

100th international against Scotland.

Iceland v England Friendly

Played on Wednesday, 2 June 1982 in the Laugardalsvöllur Stadium, Reykjavik.

Iceland: G.Baldursson (Fram); O.Oskarsson (IBV Vestmannaeyjar), M.Geirsson (Fram), S.Jónsson (FC Brugge), T.Haraldsson (Fram), K.Thordjarson (Stade Lavallois), J.Gudjlaugsson (1.FC Cologne), A.Edjvaldsson (Fortuna Düsseldorf), A.Gudjohnsén (SK Lokeren), P.Thordjarson (RC Lens), L.Gudjmundsson (Waterschei Thor).
Subs: P.Ormsleu (Fortuna Düsseldorf) for Gudjohnson and S.Grétasson (UBK) for Gudmundson.
England: T.J.Corrigan (Man City); V.A.Anderson (Nottm Forest), P.G.Neal (Liverpool, captain), D.V.Watson (Southampton), R.C.Osman (Ipswich T), T.McDermott (Liverpool), G.Hoddle (Spurs), A.E.Devonshire (West Ham), P.Withe (Aston Villa), C.Regis (West Brom), W.A.Morley (Aston Villa).
Subs: S.J.Perryman (Spurs) for Devonshire and P.Goddard (West Ham) for Regis.

**Half-time 1-0	Full-time 1-1**
Ref: I.Nielsen (Denmark)	Att: 9,000

THIS was the first full international that England had ever played against Iceland and manager Ron Greenwood used the opportunity to have a look at a few of the fringe members of his squad who were seeking a place in the final 22 selected for the World Cup finals in Spain. As a result it was a very different-looking England side that took the field in Reykjavik. The weather was cold, keeping the crowd down to around 9,000 and the pitch was bumpy and bare, hardly the setting for any player to impress the England manager.

England took a while to settle but Glenn Hoddle's free-kick was only saved with some difficulty by Baldursson. Very few chances were created in a sterile first-half but the Icelanders surprised everyone in the 23rd minute when they took the lead. Edjvaldsson's low cross found Gudjohnsén and the centre-forward shot past Joe Corrigan from close range. It was a shock and a set-back for England and they received another blow when Cyrille Regis had to go off with a recurrence of a troublesome groin injury.

For a while it looked as though a major upset was on the cards, but gradually England began to assert themselves. They had most of the possession and either side of half-time they began to find gaps in the home defence. However, goalkeeper Baldursson was rarely troubled and it was not until the 69th minute that England finally found a way through.

Hoddle, who had been at the heart of all of England's better play, set up a chance for Regis's replacement Paul Goddard, and the West Ham man celebrated his international debut by joyfully scoring the equalizer.

Not the most inspiring of performances by England's 'reserves' but one or two players would have jogged Greenwood's thoughts, especially Hoddle.

1st match v Iceland.
Debuts, as substitutes, for Goddard and Perryman.
Debut goal for Goddard.
Neal captain for the first time.

Finland v England Friendly

Played on Thursday, 3 June 1982 in the Olympic Stadium, Helsinki.

Finland: P.Alaja (Malmö FF); A.A.Lahtinen (Notts Co), J.Ikäläinen (Örgryte IS), M.Granskog (IFK Nörrkoping), E.Pekonen (Kuusysi Lahti), H.Turunen (KPT Kotka), K.Haaskivi (Edmonton Drillers), P.Rautiainen (Werder Bremen), J.Himanka (Lillestrøm SK), T.Ismail (HJK Helsinki), J.Nieminen (AIK Stockholm).
Subs: O.Huttunen (Valkeakosken Haka) for Alaja, P.Kymäläinen (TPS Turku) for Turunen and A.Valvee (Valkeakosken Haka) for Nieminen.
England: R.N.Clemence (Liverpool); M.D.Mills (Ipswich T), K.G.Sansom (Arsenal), P.B.Thompson (Liverpool), A.E.Martin (West Ham), B.Robson (Man Utd), J.K.Keegan (Southampton, captain), S.J.Coppell (Man Utd), P.Mariner (Ipswich T), T.D.Brooking (West Ham), R.C.Wilkins (Man Utd).
Subs: G.Rix (Arsenal) for Robson, T.J.Francis (Man City) for Coppell and A.S.Woodcock (1.FC Cologne) for Brooking.

Paul Mariner heads a consolation goal for England in the Olympic Stadium, Helsinki, in June 1982.

Half-time 0-2   Full-time 1-4

Ref: R.Jushka (USSR)   Att: 21,500

ENGLAND totally dominated this, their last international before the World Cup began two weeks later. It was a good work out and continued England's excellent run up to the finals. This match was arranged as part of the celebrations for the 75th anniversary of the Finnish Football Association and the crowd was particularly delighted that Kevin Keegan was fit to play.

The visitors were soon on the attack. Bryan Robson and Trevor Brooking had oceans of room down the left-hand side of the pitch and were exploiting it well. Robson saw Ikäläinen clear his shot off the line early on, then Alaja saved well from a Brooking effort. It was not too long before England did find the net. It was in the 14th minute, when Brooking put in the first of many dangerous corners, Paul Mariner met the ball unchallenged to head home. After a further 13 minutes another Brooking corner found Robson. His initial header struck the goalkeeper but cannoned back to him and this time the Manchester United ace powered it into the net with his left foot.

England were at this stage on the rampage, although Ray Clemence had to make one excellent save from the Finnish danger man, Ismail, following a good breakaway attack by the hosts. Before the interval, Keegan found the net, again following a Brooking cross, but this time the referee ruled it out for offside. But 15 minutes into the second half, the Finns were reeling again as Robson struck once more. The midfield player burst through from the middle on his own to shoot brilliantly past Alaja. Robson sustained

an injury to his foot in the process of scoring and as a precaution he was immediately taken off.

It made little difference though as England continued to dominate. Two minutes later they went 4-0 up as Brooking, once more the provider, found Mariner with a lovely cross from the left. Mariner emphasised his recent scoring form by heading the ball firmly into the net.

For the remainder of the match, England relaxed somewhat. Trevor Francis and Tony Woodcock replaced Steve Coppell and Brooking, but with the game won they then conceded only their second goal in nine months. Graham Rix made a seemingly innocuous challenge on Himanka but the referee saw fit to award Finland a penalty and Haaskivi duly scored from the spot.

One last coincidence regarding the visit to Helsinki came in the fact that in 1966 England won here 3-0. Six weeks later they had won the World Cup! An omen perhaps?

6th match v Finland.
Penalty scored for Finland by Haaskivi.

World Cup Finals

France v England

Group Four
Phase One

Played on Wednesday, 16 June 1982 in the San Mamés Stadium, Bilbao, Spain.

France: J.L.Ettori (AS Monaco); P.Battiston (AS St-Etienne), M.Trésor (Bordeaux), C.Lopez (AS St-Etienne), M.Bossis (FC Nantes), J.F.Larios (AS St-

Etienne), R.Girard (Bordeaux), A.Giresse (Bordeaux), D.Rocheteau (Paris St-Germain), M.Platini (AS St-Etienne), G.Soler (Bordeaux).
Subs: J.Tigana (Bordeaux) for Larios and D.Six (VfB Stuttgart) for Rocheteau.

England: P.L.Shilton (Nottm Forest); M.D.Mills (Ipswich T, captain), K.G.Sansom (Arsenal), P.B.Thompson (Liverpool), T.I.Butcher (Ipswich T), B.Robson (Man Utd), S.J.Coppell (Man Utd), T.J.Francis (Man City), P.Mariner (Ipswich T), G.Rix (Arsenal), R.C.Wilkins (Man Utd).
Sub: P.G.Neal (Liverpool) for Sansom.

Half-time 1-1   Full-time 1-3

Ref: A.J.Garrido (Portugal)   Att: 40,500

ENGLAND made the most sensational start to their World Cup challenge by scoring the quickest goal ever seen in the tournament's 52-year history. The searing heat and the importance of the match made the occasion almost unbearably tense, but within 27 seconds of the first whistle the England players and fans were jumping for joy.

From the kick-off, England won a throw-in on the right wing. Steve Coppell's long throw into the French penalty area was flicked on by Terry Butcher, across goal. It ran free and there was Bryan Robson coming in all on his own. The midfield star did really well to hook a waist-high bouncing ball down and beyond the bemused Ettori in the French goal. What a start!

In the absence of the injured Kevin Keegan, England were captained by Mick Mills and the Ipswich man must have been delighted and amazed by this opening. Both sides then had to settle down though and it was not easy in the 91 degrees heat.

Bryan Robson heads home a magnificent second goal against France in England's opening game of the 1982 World Cup finals.

England, playing in unfamiliar red shirts, could afford to contain rather than push forward too much, as the goal had given them a cushion. This was not altogether wise however as it allowed the French to gather their thoughts and their skills.

Platini was their playmaker combining effectively with Larios and Giresse. They concentrated most of their attacks down the middle, probing the relative inexperience of Butcher. Trevor Francis and Coppell operated down the flanks for England with Graham Rix looking to release them with some long passes. This chess-like situation went on for 25 minutes with each side probing the other. But it was at this point that France drew level. Francis lost possession and allowed Larios to find Soler. Soler's burst of speed left his marker, Butcher, and Peter Shilton was then beaten by a crisp shot.

With France employing the sweeper system, England were forced to shoot from long range. Phil Thompson's effort only just went wide and Coppell forced a save from Ettori with another. France's only worthwhile reply came from a dangerous Platini free-kick.

Mercifully the half-time also coincided with the temperature dropping as evening fell in Bilbao. This gave England the chance to use their running strength. Francis began to examine the French defenders with his pace and early in the second half Ray Wilkins came desperately close to scoring after one fine Francis run and shot had rebounded to him from Ettori's knees. Wilkins chested it down and lobbed the ball goalwards only to see it drop the wrong side of the crossbar.

Again England had started the half well and it continued with Francis heading a

Mills' cross over the bar before having another go from a Rix pass. Once more the shot went over but in the 66th minute England deservedly regained the lead. Again Francis was involved, bursting clear down the right before putting over a centre for Robson, who came from nowhere, to head home a magnificent goal. It was reminiscent of the kind of finishing for which Martin Peters was famous.

Crowd trouble briefly threatened on the terraces giving cause for concern, but the Spanish police acted quickly and soon got the situation under control and the football, happily, took preference.

By now France were looking desperate. They were wilting under the heat, still in the 80s, and their two substitutions seemed to be their last throw of the dice. It had no effect on England's immaculate defenders and it came as no real surprise when they increased their lead. Coppell crossed deep to the far side where Wilkins tapped the ball to Francis who quickly fired in a shot. It was blocked but bounced up and lobbed perfectly to Mariner, who half-volleyed a firm shot past Ettori. It was the fifth consecutive international that Mariner had hit the net, a marvellous record.

> 19th match v France.
> Robson scored quickest goal in World Cup history.
> *"Bryan Robson's goal after 27 seconds was the best England goal I remember. Steve Coppell's long throw hit my head, dropping for Bryan to score. It was such a feeling, all the hard work prior felt worth it."*
> Terry Butcher

Czechoslovakia v England Group Four Phase One

Played on Sunday, 20 June 1982 in the San Mames Stadium, Bilbao, Spain.

Czechoslovakia: S.Seman (Lokomotiva Košice); J.Barmos (Inter Bratislava), J.Fiala (Dukla Prague), L.Radimec (Baník Ostrava), R.Vojaček (Baník Ostrava), L.Jurkemik (Inter Bratislava), P.Chaloupka (Bohemians Prague), L.Vizek (Dukla Prague), J.Berger (Sparta Prague), P.Janečka (Zbrojovska Brno), Z.Nehoda (Dukla Prague). Subs: K.Stromsik (Dukla Prague) for Seman and M.Masny (Slovan Bratislava) for Janečka.

England: P.L.Shilton (Nottm Forest); M.D.Mills (Ipswich T, captain), K.G.Sansom (Arsenal), P.B.Thompson (Liverpool), T.I.Butcher (Ipswich T), B.Robson (Man Utd), S.J.Coppell (Man Utd), T.J.Francis (Man City), P.Mariner (Ipswich T), G.Rix (Arsenal), R.C.Wilkins (Man Utd). Sub: G.Hoddle (Spurs) for Robson.

Half-time 0-0   Full-time 0-2
Ref: C.Corver (Holland)   Att: 36,000

ENGLAND qualified for the second-phase matches by virtue of this win against the disappointing Czechoslovakia side. Although both England goals were slightly fortuitous, there was no denying England their right to join Brazil in the next stage of the competition, the only two sides so far definitely through.

This was a very different match from the one against France where England had to overcome the flair of the attractive

Trevor Francis hammers England into the lead against Czechoslovakia in Bilbao during the early stages of the 1982 World Cup finals.

French team. This time it was the dour, disciplined organisation of a typical Iron Curtain side. Marshalled from the back by their captain, Vojaček, the Czechs were resolute and very strong in the tackle. Having said that, England could have been three up after the first ten minutes.

Steve Coppell sent over a wicked cross that so outfoxed Seman that the goalkeeper could only watch as the ball ran along the face of the crossbar before being cleared. Paul Mariner saw a header hacked off the line and then Ray Wilkins hit a superb volley which the 'keeper knew little about as it cannoned back off his body with Mariner just failing to reach the rebound. This blistering start cooled a little over the next minutes but England always held the upper hand. One Czech attack did see Vizek's cross almost converted but this was an isolated raid.

Mariner was soon back testing the big Czech defenders. His delicate flick was all but converted by Bryan Robson, who just got underneath the ball before lifting it just over the bar. Another good attack soon followed with Graham Rix rounding Barmos, and putting over a cross, only for Robson to head just wide. The Czechs were growing desperate in thought and deed with Chaloupka being booked for a nasty tackle on Trevor Francis. It was disappointing for England not to be well in front at half-time especially after having had so much of the game. During the interval Robson was withdrawn after a groin injury had hampered him and it gave Glenn Hoddle the chance to be seen on a world stage.

After the break England pushed forward relentlessly. With Vojaček and his central defenders so strong in the middle the attacks came more frequently down the

flanks. There was still a feeling that if England could score, then it would be all over. And that, as they say, is exactly what happened.

Just over an hour of the match had elapsed. Mariner and Rix both went close to scoring and England were awarded a corner. The kick was taken by Wilkins and looked easy for an unchallenged Seman in the Czech goal. The goalkeeper, who had looked shaky from the start, inexplicably allowed the ball to slip through his fingers and it dropped straight at the feet of Francis, who was standing alone. The England striker could not believe his luck and promptly volleyed it into the empty net, much to the delight of his teammates.

At last the Czechoslovakian defence had been breached and within three minutes England were two up. Francis, sharp and lively throughout, combined with Mariner. The number-nine looked to return a pass into the path of Francis, only for Barmos to intercept and slide the ball into his own net for an own-goal. Seman promptly gave way to Stromsik after the former had broken a finger to complete a miserable match for the 'keeper.

England ended the game in total control

10th match v Czechoslovakia.
Own-goal scored for England by Barmos.
"I remember a very amusing incident on an evening during the 1982 World Cup. Four hooded members of the squad lifted an immaculately dressed secretary of the FA off the tennis court and put him into the swimming pool. Ron Greenwood's permission was granted beforehand, though!"
Mick Mills

and they went into the match against Kuwait comforted by the knowledge that they were already through to the next stage. They also had a record of nine wins and one draw over the previous ten games.

Kuwait v England
Group Four
Phase One

Played on Tuesday, 25 June 1982 in the San Mamés Stadium, Bilbao, Spain.

Kuwait: A.Al Tarabulsi (Kuwait); N.Saed Mubarak (Tadhamon), A.Ma'Yoof (Kasmah), M.Mubarak (Salmiya), W.Al Jasem (Kuwait), A.Al Buloushi (Al-Arabi), S.Al Houti (Kuwait), F.Kameel (Tadhamon), A.Al Anbari (Kuwait), F.Al Dakhil (Al-Qadsia), Y.Al Suwaayed (Kasmah).
Sub: H.Al Shemmari (Kasmah) for Al Jasem.

England: P.L.Shilton (Nottm Forest); P.G.Neal (Liverpool), M.D.Mills (Ipswich T, captain), P.B.Thompson (Liverpool), S.B.Foster (Brighton & HA), G.Hoddle (Spurs), S.J.Coppell (Man Utd), T.J.Francis (Man City), P.Mariner (Ipswich T), G.Rix (Arsenal), R.C.Wilkins (Man Utd).

Half-time 0-1   Full-time 0-1

Ref: G.Aristizabal (Colombia) Att: 39,700

IT was difficult for England to motivate themselves for the last of their first phase matches, knowing that they had already qualified for the second phase. This might help to explain the reason for such a disappointing display. Ron Greenwood made three changes, leaving out Kenny Sansom, Terry Butcher and Bryan Robson. This gave Phil Neal, Steve Foster and Glenn Hoddle the chance to impress.

But the game was a poor one. Kuwait were delighted to be playing against the mighty England and they ran their hearts out in trying to contain their illustrious opponents. But England were always in command and pushed forward with the same confidence that they had shown in their earlier matches. This time, though, the finishing was missing.

Several chances were lost before England took the lead in the 27th minute. Again it was the Paul Mariner-Trevor Francis partnership that came up trumps. Peter Shilton punted a long kick forward and the ball was superbly brought under control by Mariner. A clever back-heel played the ball into Francis' path and a lovely turn of speed took him clear of Mubarak's sliding tackle. On went the England striker, drawing the goalkeeper off his line before coolly slotting the ball wide of Al Tarabulsi's right hand for a superbly taken goal.

Unfortunately, that was the last real highlight of the game. Play became scrappy and disjointed, although England should have had more goals. Both Mariner and Francis missed good chances and Steve Coppell, Graham Rix and Hoddle all put in goal attempts. But England did not add to their single-goal lead, although not worrying too much as it was all rather academic.

By virtue of topping their group they went on to meet West Germany and Spain in the second phase, two old adversaries.

> 1st match v Kuwait.
> After drawing 1-1 with Iceland on 2 June 1982, this was the last match in a run of nine consecutive wins for England.

West Germany v
England   Group 'B' Phase Two

Played on Tuesday, 29 June 1982 at the Santiago Bernabéu Stadium, Madrid, Spain.

West Germany: H.Schumacher (1.FC Cologne); M.Kaltz (Hamburger SV), K.H.Förster (VfB Stuttgart), U.Stielike (Real Madrid), B.Förster (VfB Stuttgart), H.Müller (VfB Stuttgart), P.Breitner (Bayern Munich), W.Dremmler (Bayern Munich), H.P.Briegel (1.FC Kaiserslautern), K.H.Rummenigge (Bayern Munich), U.Reinders (Werder Bremen).
Subs: K.Fischer (1.FC Cologne) for Müller and P.Littbarski (1.FC Cologne) for Reiners.

England: P.L.Shilton (Nottm Forest); M.D.Mills (Ipswich T, captain), K.G.Sansom (Arsenal), P.B.Thompson (Liverpool), T.I.Butcher (Ipswich T), B.Robson (Man Utd), S.J.Coppell (Man Utd), T.J.Francis (Man City), P.Mariner (Ipswich T), G.Rix (Arsenal), R.C.Wilkins (Man Utd).
Sub: A.S.Woodcock (1.FC Cologne) for Francis.

Half-time 0-0   Full-time 0-0

Ref: A.C.Coelho (Brazil)   Att: 75,000

MANY of the previous clashes between these two old rivals had been memorable. This time, though, the game was instantly forgettable. The Germans were determined not to lose at any cost and therefore produced an ultra-cautious display.

Brian Rix brings down Briegel in the Bernabéu Stadium, Madrid, as the two great rivals, England and West Germany, fight out a goalless draw.

England, for their part, had neither the flair nor the ideas to find a way through.

Neither side wanted to risk losing this vital game and it quickly showed in the pattern of play. Most of the early passes went sideways or backwards, although one cross by Steve Coppell had Schumacher stretching. England definitely had the better of the first 20 minutes. Ray Wilkins hit a good shot from 25 yards, which the goalkeeper again saved, and another attack saw Bryan Robson almost put his header over the advancing 'keeper after Paul Mariner had flicked the ball on. The main danger to England came from the Germans' lightning breakaways. The speed at which they could turn defence into attack was ominous, although they did it so infrequently that England were able to cope comfortably.

Breitner looked sharp and his cross from the right, low and hard, was almost touched by Rummenigge, although Peter Shilton looked unruffled. Another positive burst by Breitner left Phil Thompson standing, but the angle became too tight for the final shot and Shilton saved. The German sweeper system stifled most of the England attacks, so the game drifted into mediocrity.

Little changed after half-time and it was all very chess-like. Briegel marked Mariner out of the game and Karl-Heinz Förster did the same to Francis. This obviously left England few options in attack, although the beaver-like style of Robson threatened to find a way through. But such a move was just what Stielike was there for and he was always alert to any threat. The German sweeper was booked in the second half, stopping Robson unfairly after the Manchester United star looked to have broken through the cordon of white shirts. What the game lacked in inspiration it certainly made up for in terms of defensive effort.

Ron Greenwood sent on Tony Woodcock to use the Cologne player's knowledge of the Bundesliga but it was to no avail and the nearest anyone came to a goal arrived in the 85th minute and nearly ruined all England's defensive qualities.

Rummenigge, who up to then had had a very quiet game, suddenly skipped around Graham Rix and let fly from

outside the area. The ball beat Shilton but crashed back off the crossbar, much to the relief of every English fan watching. That would have been a cruel time to lose a goal and poor reward for some determined defending. The result left everything still to play for when England met the hosts of the tournament, Spain, for a place in the semi-finals.

> 15th match v West Germany.

Spain v
England   Group 'B' Phase Two

Played on Monday, 5 July 1982 at the Santiago Bernabéu Stadium, Madrid, Spain.

Spain: L.Arconada (Real Sociedad); J.Camacho (Real Madrid), R.Gordillo (Real Betis), M.A.Alonso (Real Madrid), M.Tendillo (Valencia CF), J.Alexanço (FC Barcelona), J.Satrustegui (Real Sociedad), J.Zamora (Real Sociedad), S.Urquiaga (Athletic Bilbao), E.Saura (Valencia CF), C.Alonso (Real Madrid).
Subs: A.Macedo (Sporting Gijon) for Tendillo and P.Uraldi (Real Sociedad) for Saura.

England: P.L.Shilton (Nottm Forest); M.D.Mills (Ipswich T, captain), K.G.Sansom (Arsenal), P.B.Thompson (Liverpool), T.I.Butcher (Ipswich T), B.Robson (Man Utd), G.Rix (Arsenal), T.J.Francis (Man City), P.Mariner (Ipswich T), A.S.Woodcock (1.FC Cologne), R.C.Wilkins (Man Utd).
Subs: T.D.Brooking (West Ham) for Rix and J.K.Keegan (Southampton) for Woodcock.

Half-time 0-0   Full-time 0-0

Ref: A.Ponnet (Belgium)   Att: 75,000

WITH West Germany having beaten Spain 2-1, England knew just what they had to do in this match. A win by two clear goals would see them through to the semi-finals and Ron Greenwood brought in Tony Woodcock as an extra striker instead of Steve Coppell, who had been performing predominantly in midfield. So, the intentions were clear and for the first time in the tournament England had the added boost of Kevin Keegan and

Phil Thompson and Ray Wilkins leave the field, heads down, after England failed to beat Spain and advance to the 1982 World Cup semi-finals.

for a wonderful effort. They qualified a little fortuitously from their original group matches but in Spain they easily won their phase one group, conceded only one goal in five games and now left the tournament despite an unbeaten record. The only thing missing was an inspirational world-class figure capable of turning vital matches. Perhaps Keegan might have been that man had not fate so cruelly robbed England of his services. For Ron Greenwood it was farewell to the England scene. His retirement coincided with England's exit, but he could have been proud of his achievements and he deservedly won the support of all his players throughout his time in charge.

> 15th match v Spain.
> Ron Greenwood's last match as team manager.
> Keegan's 63rd and last international.
> Also Brooking's last international (47 caps).
> Spain's C.Alonso also known as 'Santillana'.
> *"Being involved with the World Cup squad of '82 was a very happy memory for me. We had a great atmosphere during the month we had together with lots of laughs."*
> Phil Neal

Denmark v England
European Championship Qualifier

Played on Wednesday, 22 September 1982 in the Idraetspark, Copenhagen.

Denmark: T.Rasmussen (Aarhus GF); I.Nielsen (Feyenoord), S.Busk (KAA Gent), P.Roentved (Randers Freja FC), O.Rasmussen (Hertha BSC), S.Lerby (Ajax Amsterdam), J.J.Bertelsen (FC Seraing), J.Olsen (Ajax Amsterdam), A.Hansen (Hamburger SV), P.Elkjaer (SC Lokeren), L.Bastrup (Hamburger SV).

England: P.L.Shilton (Southampton); P.G.Neal (Liverpool), K.G.Sansom (Arsenal), R.C.Wilkins (Man Utd, captain), R.C.Osman (Ipswich T), T.I.Butcher (Ipswich T), W.A.Morley (Aston Villa), B.Robson (Man Utd), P.Mariner (Ipswich T), T.J.Francis (Sampdoria), G.Rix (Arsenal).
Sub: R.A.Hill (Luton T) for Morley.

Half-time 0-1   **Full-time 2-2**
Ref: C.Corver (Holland)   Att: 44,250

FOR his first match in charge, new manager, Bobby Robson, promised a more positive approach to his selections and he included Tony Morley and Russell Osman as his first significant changes to the side. This was a difficult first fixture in the new European Championship competition as Denmark were beginning to emerge as an exciting and skilful side.

England made a good start and were soon on the attack. Osman pumped a long ball forward and a scramble developed on the edge of the Danish penalty area. Paul Mariner and Bryan Robson battled for possession, before Graham Rix hit a long-range volley which goalkeeper Rasmussen did very well to save. After seven minutes, though, the Danish 'keeper was picking the ball out of his net when Trevor Francis stretched to prod a pass into the area wide of him.

Trevor Brooking amongst their substitutes, although neither was fully fit.

Spain soon made it clear that they would not make it easy for England. Two crunching tackles on Bryan Robson by Tendillo and Miguel Alonso sent more than a few murmurs around this magnificent stadium. Then two mistakes by the normally dependable Kenny Sansom almost brought problems for England, but luckily for them Miguel Alonso hit both chances well wide. Ray Wilkins then fell victim to typical Latin histrionics after his challenge on Camacho left the Spaniard impersonating Davy Crockett's death scene at the Alamo! The referee was suitably fooled enough to book the unfortunate Wilkins.

Sansom then almost made amends for his earlier errors when he shot just wide following a Wilkins free-kick. Most of England's attacks were being built down the left flank with Graham Rix prominent. But few clear chances were created, although both Trevor Francis and Robson had fierce shots saved by Arconada. At the end of a disappointing half, England had not shown the inspiration they so desperately needed to break the deadlock.

Sadly, the pattern showed little signs of alteration after the change of ends and Greenwood let it go on until the hour was up before throwing in his last cards. The familiar figures of Keegan and Brooking came on for Rix and Woodcock and the whole of England was willing the move

to come off. A few minutes later it almost did.

Brooking picked up possession and was allowed to go on by the Spanish defence. Eventually he hit a fierce shot, only for Arconada to produce a fine save, his best of the tournament. What a time for him to pick to make his only world-class save of the competition! By now things were becoming desperate for England with everybody pushing forward.

Then came the moment when it looked as though England, at last, would make the vital breakthrough. Robson, who ran his heart out, made a good break down the left and clipped a delightful centre into the middle, where Keegan looked a certain scorer. The thick mop of black curls met it well enough but, alas, the ball flew the wrong side of the post. It was a tragedy for England and especially for Keegan. The Southampton star would surely have scored had he been fitter and sharper but as it was the chance was gone.

From that moment the heart went out of England's attacks and although they pushed forward until the end the target of two goals was never on. When the final whistle blew, several England players collapsed, more in anguish than fatigue. They had given their all and remained unbeaten but their old failing in front of goal had let them down. No one person can be blamed but if you don't score goals, you don't win matches.

However, all the players deserved credit

Despite the set-back of an early goal against them, it was Denmark who dominated the play over the next phase of the game. Urged on by a powerful midfield, they put Osman and Terry Butcher under almost constant pressure. Elkjaer and Bastrup were quick and lively front runners and several times they broke through the visitors' defence. One break by Elkjaer after an error by Phil Neal saw Osman chasing desperately after the big Danish striker. When both players suddenly crashed to the ground in the penalty area it looked ominous for England, but the referee refused claims for a penalty. Neal then completed a difficult half for himself by being booked for a foul on Lerby.

Early in the second half another challenge by an England defender might have produced a penalty. This time Kenny Sansom and Peter Shilton clashed with Bastrup and once again the referee annoyed the home crowd by waving away frantic appeals for a spot-kick. Lerby protested so strongly that it earned him a booking. The England defence continued to look shaky as Neal's back-pass almost put Shilton in trouble, and then, in the 69th minute, Denmark at last broke through.

Olsen, making another of several penetrating runs, went down in the box after a lunging tackle by Osman. This time, quite rightly, the referee had no hesitation in giving a penalty. There was more than one ironic cheer from the crowd at that decision. Hansen duly scored from the spot and Denmark looked in charge. But ten minutes later, very much against the run of play, England regained the lead. Ray Wilkins, skipper in his 50th appearance and playing with great composure, took a corner on the left and the kick cleared a posse of defenders to drop nicely for Francis to stab the ball home on the half-volley.

It seemed unbelievable that England might win after Denmark had had so much of the play but justice was done with seconds left when the outstanding Olsen weaved past several defenders before sliding the ball under the diving Shilton to equalize.

A mixed result for new boss Bobby Robson, but although England didn't lose and at the end of the day the dropped point proved crucial. The continuing problems seen on the terraces here gave cause for concern. Once more there was trouble amongst the rival fans and the problem seemed to be getting worse.

> 8th match v Denmark.
> Bobby Robson's first match as manager.
> Debut, as substitute, for Hill.
> Penalty scored for Denmark by Hansen.
> 50th cap for Wilkins.
> Wilkins captain for the first time.

England v West Germany   Friendly

Played on Wednesday, 13 October 1982 at Wembley Stadium.

England: P.L.Shilton (Southampton); G.V.Mabbutt (Spurs), K.G.Sansom (Arsenal), P.B.Thompson (Liverpool), T.I.Butcher (Ipswich T), R.C.Wilkins (Man Utd, captain), R.A.Hill (Luton T), C.Regis (West Brom), P.Mariner (Ipswich T), D.Armstrong (Middlesbrough), A.E.Devonshire (West Ham).
Subs: G.Rix (Arsenal) for Armstrong, A.S.Woodcock (Arsenal) for Mariner and L.L.Blissett (Watford) for Regis.

West Germany: H.Schumacher (1.FC Cologne); M.Kaltz (Hamburger SV), G.Strack (1.FC Cologne), K.H.Förster (VfB Stuttgart), B.Förster (VfB Stuttgart), W.Dremmler (Bayern Munich), H.P.Briegel (1.FC Kaiserslautern), N.Meier (Werder Bremen), K.Allofs (1.FC Cologne), K.H.Rummenigge (Bayern Munich), L.Matthäus (Borussia Mönchengladbach).
Subs: H.Hieronymus (Hamburger SV) for K.H.Forster, P.Littbarski (1.FC Cologne) for Meier and S.Engels (1.FC Cologne) for Allofs.

Half-time 0-0   Full-time 1-2
Ref: K.Palotai (Hungary)   Att: 67,500

THIS prestigious friendly against the 1982 World Cup runners-up gave England and Bobby Robson the chance to pit their wits against one of the top sides of world football. The manager had to make several changes, giving new caps to Gary Mabbutt and David Armstrong, and it was a largely inexperienced side that took the field for the home side.

It was soon obvious to all that this new look England team would chase everything to try and overcome the extra class of the Germans. The visitors were unsettled by an early injury to Karl-Heinz Forster, who collided with Ray Wilkins and had to be carried off with a nasty shin wound. This early misfortune gave England the chance to take the initiative, which they held until half-time with some spirited play. Alas, the goals which would have emphasised their superiority would not come, a story so often seen at Wembley games.

Good work by Ricky Hill and Alan Devonshire kept the dangerous Kaltz and Briegel's forward runs in check, but those England players contributions to attack was therefore less productive and as a result chances were rare. On the half-hour mark, England so nearly opened the scoring. Mabbutt, playing with all the maturity of a veteran in his unfamiliar right-back position, found the ball at his feet inside the penalty area. A crisp shot beat Schumacher but cannoned back off the upright before being cleared. The Germans always seemed to have their fair share of such moments, but they were also probably the best side to take advantage of this kind of good fortune.

Mabbutt showed his defensive qualities with a fine tackle that stopped a surging run from the powerful Briegel, and then Peter Shilton made a fine tip over save from Meier's firm header. So, at half-time there was no score, but England were reasonably happy with their showing.

The pressure increased after the interval. A pouncing run by Cyrille Regis almost broke the deadlock, only for Schumacher to save brilliantly at the near post. Shortly afterwards Wilkins chipped a cross from the by-line to Regis. His backward-headed pass looked to be beating the incoming Hill, but the Luton player twisted in the air to flip the ball goalwards. Again Schumacher saved the day with an excellent diving save.

The Germans seemed content to hang on, waiting for any chance to break quickly and dangerously. England were given a warning of this when Allofs hit a vicious long-range shot which tested Shilton. The same player then sent the potentially lethal Rummenigge away, only for Mabbutt to make another timely intervention. It looked like the one goal that was needed would not come either way, but then, suddenly, a ten-minute spell saw England concede two goals to the mercurial Rummenigge.

Littbarski, who had replaced Meier, began to pierce holes in England's defence with some clever footwork. In the 72nd minute, his fine play set up the German captain who cleverly flicked the ball past Shilton with his right foot. Ten minutes later, the same players combined again for a similar goal, again flicked with the outside of Rummenigge's right foot.

To their credit the shell-shocked England side refused to give in and continued to battle with great heart. In the 85th minute they were at last rewarded to some extent when substitute Tony Woodcock swivelled amongst a crowded goalmouth to fire home. The torrential rain and fine opponents made this a baptism of fire for Bobby Robson's new England at Wembley, but although they lost there was a lot to praise. Sad, though, that the 12-match unbeaten run should come to an end.

> 16th match v West Germany.
> Debuts for Mabbutt and, as substitute, Blissett.

Greece v England   European Championship Qualifier

Played on Wednesday, 17 November 1982 in the Kaftatzoglio Stadium, Salonika.

Greece: N.Sarganis (Olympiakos); G.Gounaris (Olympiakos), K.Iosifidis (PAOK Thessalonikis), G.Foiros (Aris Thessalonikis), A.Kapsis (Panathinaikos), S.Livathinos (Panathinaikos), P.Mikhos (Olympiakos), T.Mitropoulos (Olympiakos), N.Anastopoulos (Olympiakos), K.Ardizoglou (AEK Athens), T.Mavros (AEK Athens).
Subs: G.Kostikos (PAOK Thessalonikis) for Ardizoglou and S.Kofidis (Heraklis) for Mavros.

England: P.L.Shilton (Southampton); P.G.Neal (Liverpool), K.G.Sansom (Arsenal), P.B.Thompson (Liverpool), A.E.Martin (West Ham), B.Robson (Man Utd, captain), S.Lee (Liverpool), G.V.Mabbutt (Spurs), P.Mariner (Ipswich T), A.S.Woodcock (Arsenal), W.A.Morley (Aston Villa).

Half-time 0-1   Full-time 0-3
Ref: A.Prokop (East Germany)   Att: 41,500

A MAGNIFICENT victory in the most trying of circumstances: that was how to sum up this European Championship international. Before the match England's chances were virtually written off after they lost at least seven players through injury, travelling with very much a makeshift side.

The rain was lashing down and the wind was very gusty at the kick-off. The Greek crowd had already shown a very hostile attitude towards the visitors, but within 74 seconds of the first whistle they were silenced by an England goal. Phil Neal advanced down the right and chipped a cross to his full-back partner, Kenny Sansom, who had also joined the attack. Sansom flicked the ball on and Tony Woodcock lunged forward to shoot home, despite some fierce challenges by the desperate Greek defenders.

It was a terrific boost for England and it gave them the confidence to settle down into a good rhythm. The midfield of Gary Mabbutt, Sammy Lee, Bryan Robson and Tony Morley kept a tight rein on things and the back-four were in no mood to give anything away at all. Robson did have to clear off the line on one occasion, and Peter Shilton mispunched during another Greek attack, which caused a flutter or two. But generally England looked rock solid and the dangerous Anastopoulos or Mavros had little chance to shine.

After the interval England looked totally in command and threatened to add to their lead on several occasions. Paul Mariner saw a goal ruled out for offside, Robson pulled a shot wide after a dazzling run by the outstanding Woodcock, Mariner then lofted an attempted lob too high and Woodcock's powerful header was saved at the foot of the post. All this attacking had to pay off and on the hour England at last made it 2-0. It was Woodcock who again made the decisive break. His run ended with a superb lob over the goalkeeper.

Five minutes later England did it again with Lee, celebrating a marvellous debut, crashing home from close range after the ball had bounced to him. If that was the end of the scoring it certainly was not the end of England's impressive performance. They had not controlled an away game so well for many years. The full-backs were superb, Robson, after a slow start, was magnificent in his first game as captain, Lee was a revelation and Woodcock demonstrated all his exceptional qualities. Mabbutt, too, deserved much praise as he successfully switched from full-back to midfield in only his second appearance. He looked comfortable in all that he did.

All in all it was a superb win for England and a considerable boost for Bobby Robson with three home games to follow.

3rd match v Greece.
Debut goal for Lee.
Robson's first match as captain.

England v Luxembourg European Championship Qualifier

Played on Wednesday, 15 December 1982 at Wembley Stadium.

England: R.N.Clemence (Liverpool); P.G.Neal (Liverpool), K.G.Sansom (Arsenal), A.E.Martin (West Ham), T.I.Butcher (Ipswich T), B.Robson (Man Utd, captain), G.V.Mabbutt (Spurs), L.L.Blissett (Watford), S.J.Coppell (Man Utd), A.S.Woodcock (Arsenal).
Subs: G.Hoddle (Spurs) for Mabbutt and M.V.Chamberlain (Stoke C) for Coppell.
Luxembourg: J.Moes (Avenir Beggen); J.P.Girres (US Luxembourg), H.Meunier (Progres Niedercorn), M.Bossi (Progres Niedercorn), N.Rohmann (San Diego),

J.Clemens (Spora Luxembourg), G.Hallers (FC Metz), C.Weis (Stade de Reims), G.Dresch (Avenir Beggen), J.B.Reiter (Saarbrücken), M.Di Domenico (Red Boys Differdange).
Sub: A.Nurenberg (Progres Niedercorn) for Di Domenico.

Half-time 4-0   Full-time 9-0
Ref: H.Jönsson (Iceland)   Att: 35,000

THIS was a throw back — some said — to the good old days of regular huge victories that England used to enjoy against inferior opposition. On this night the Luxembourg side were totally overwhelmed and, believe it or not, the scoreline could have been doubled.

Right from the kick-off England surged forward and it looked as though they had scored in the second minute but Moes succeeded with a double save, first pushing Gary Mabbutt's header on to the bar and then blocking Luther Blissett's overhead kick from the rebound. The goalkeeper also did well to save a swerving shot from Bryan Robson and then another header by the busy Mabbutt. The pressure had to tell and in the 21st minute it did.

Robson sent Blissett away down the left and when the cross came in a defender, Bossi deflected the ball wide of Moes for an own-goal. This opened the floodgates and four minutes later it was 2-0 after Steve Coppell nipped smartly between two defenders to head home Kenny Sansom's cross. England's attacks were incessant. Tony Woodcock was brilliant and inspired many of them. Several times Blissett was set up with chances but each time the Watford man squandered the opening.

In the 37th minute England scored again. This time a Coppell corner was headed down by Alvin Martin and Woodcock struck like lightning to glance the ball past the beleaguered goalkeeper. That was England's 14th corner, some indication of the pressure Luxembourg were under. Just before the interval Blissett, at last, found the target. He was left with a simple tap-in which even then he nearly fluffed, and that all came after excellent play by Robson.

England continued to sweep forward pounding relentlessly against Luxembourg's defence. A quarter of an hour into the second half they scored number five. More fine work by Woodcock ended with a shot against the bar. The ball bounced down for Blissett, who scored his second goal. The ease with which England were playing gave Bobby Robson the chance to bring on new cap Mark Chamberlain and the Stoke player scored with virtually his first touch, jumping high to head home Terry Butcher's cross. Luxembourg simply had no answer to it all. Although they had been beaten recently by both Denmark and Greece, the margins were narrow, so this thrashing was all the more satisfying from an England point of view.

The chances continued to flow and they finished with a flourish as three more goals swept past the luckless goalkeeper in the last four minutes. First, Blissett completed his hat-trick after again being set up by the impressive Woodcock. Then Glenn Hoddle, on for the brilliant Mabbutt, scored the goal of the night with a flashing half-volley which went just inside the post. And finally, to complete the rout, Phil Neal, with more of a cross

than a shot, found the net for the ninth goal. The crowd screamed for ten, but Luxembourg managed to avoid that particular embarrassment. It was an excellent result for England and certainly did no harm to their goal-difference.

6th v Luxembourg.
Debut goal for Chamberlain (substitute).
Hat-trick scored by Blissett.
Own-goal scored for England by Bossi.

England v Wales Home Championship

Played on Wednesday, 23 February 1983 at Wembley Stadium.

England: P.L.Shilton (Southampton, captain), P.G.Neal (Liverpool), D.J.Statham (West Brom), S.Lee (Liverpool), A.E.Martin (West Ham), T.I.Butcher (Ipswich T), G.V.Mabbutt (Spurs), L.L.Blissett (Watford), P.Mariner (Ipswich T), G.S.Cowans (Aston Villa), A.E.Devonshire (West Ham).
Wales: N.Southall (Everton); J.P.Jones (Chelsea), K.Ratcliffe (Everton), J.F.Mahoney (Swansea C), P.T.Price (Spurs), K.F.Jackett (Watford), G.J.Davies (Fulham), B.Flynn (Burnley), I.J.Rush (Liverpool), M.R.Thomas (Stoke C), R.M.James (Swansea C).
Subs: G.F.Berry (Wolves) for Jones and L.James (Sunderland) for Mahoney.

Half-time 1-1   Full-time 2-1
Ref: R.B.Valentine (Scotland) Att: 24,000

ONLY 24,000 people, then the lowest crowd ever to attend a full international at Wembley, came to see England attempt to lay the Welsh bogey that had prevented them winning against them for ten years. As it turned out the hoodoo was broken by a penalty with only ten minutes remaining.

The cold weather and frosty pitch made conditions very difficult and helped to produce a scrappy game. England had two early chances, each falling to the two new caps. Both times, though, Southall was there to smother both Derek Statham and Gordon Cowans efforts. After 15 minutes, Wales took the lead against the run of play. Ratcliffe made a decisive break down the more icy part of the pitch. Over came his cross and a miscue by Robbie James left Terry Butcher groping. The ball ran kindly for Ian Rush, who moved forward with that familiar burst of speed of his to hit a good shot between Peter Shilton and the far post. It was a deadly piece of finishing.

It was a fine goal and, ten minutes later, the Liverpool star might have had another. Flynn pierced England's square defence with a good long pass which left Rush running alone towards Shilton with only the goalkeeper to beat. A calculated shot struck the post, came back to Rush again but his second effort was saved by Shilton.

England then began to hit back. Butcher went very close with a header after a fine run and pass by his fellow defender Alvin Martin. That was the first of several near misses as they kept the momentum going. Luther Blissett scraped the outside of a post following a corner, but five minutes from the interval the Watford man had a big say in the eventual equalizer. A superb turn took his marker, Price, out of the game and allowed Alan Devonshire the chance to cross hard and low. Surprisingly, the man on the end of the cross was Butcher, who this time found the target to score his first international goal. It was also England's first against Wales at Wembley since 1975.

The second half was very disappointing and the match deteriorated in quality. Chances were few and far between although Southall was the busier of the two goalkeepers. Statham and Cowans looked good in their respective roles but England had to wait until the 80th minute for the decisive moment.

Cowans cleverly found himself in a great position in the area with the ball at his feet only for Flynn to bring him crashing to the ground for an obvious penalty. Up stepped Phil Neal, who had missed one the previous weekend in an FA Cup tie against Brighton for Liverpool, but this time there was no mistake as he sent Southall the wrong way for the winner.

> 96th match v Wales.
> Debuts for Cowans and Statham.
> Penalty scored for England by Neal.

England v Greece European Championship Qualifier

Played on Wednesday, 30 March 1983 at Wembley Stadium.

England: P.L.Shilton (Southampton, captain); P.G.Neal (Liverpool), K.G.Sansom (Arsenal), S.Lee (Liverpool), A.E.Martin (West Ham), T.I.Butcher (Ipswich T), S.J.Coppell (Man Utd), G.V.Mabbutt (Spurs), T.J.Francis (Samp-

doria), A.S.Woodcock (Arsenal), A.E.Devonshire (West Ham). Subs: L.L.Blissett (Watford) for Woodcock and G.Rix (Arsenal) for Devonshire.

Greece: N.Sarganis (Olympiakos); G.Gounaris (Olympiakos), N.Karoulias (Panathinaikos), G.Galitsios (Larissa), P.Mikhos (Olympiakos), K.Xanthopoulos (Heraklis), V.Kousoulakis (Olympiakos), K.Kousi (Aris Thessalonikis), N.Anastopoulos (Olympiakos), T.Mitropoulos (Olympiakos), G.Kostikos (PAOK Thessalonikis). Subs K.Ardizoglou (AEK Athens) for Anastopoulos and G.Dopas (Panathinaikos) for Mitropoulos.

Half-time 0-0   Full-time 0-0

Ref: D.Krchňak (Czechoslovakia)

Att: 48,500

THE archetypal goalless draw: that was the best way to sum up a quite dreadful match. Totally devoid of any real goal attempts, the game went from bad to worse as the 90 minutes dragged to their conclusion. Long before the end, the crowd were voicing their disapproval and manager Bobby Robson had plenty of work to do in the coming weeks to try to improve things.

Right from the start the Greeks fell back on to the defensive. Nine men, sometimes ten, were herded back behind the ball everytime England had possession, and the home side found it impossible to break them down. Trevor Francis twice went close to scoring the early goal so desperately needed in this sort of match, but generally England were too predictable in their build up. They persisted in sending in long, hopeful balls searching for a target man who was not there. Neither Francis nor Woodcock played that type of game but, to be fair, Francis looked very sharp.

England dominated the possession but

had neither the flair nor the ideas to unlock the stubborn and determined Greek defence. Xanthopoulos shadowed Francis everywhere, continually bringing him down, for which, eventually, he earned himself a deserved booking. Other challenges went unpunished, though, and all the continuity was taken from the game.

It was fully an hour before England created their first worthwhile chance. That came by virtue of a superb run and shot by Francis which brought a good save from Sarganis. Francis had shown such speed and trickery that he had left four defenders in his wake. Sadly, the finish was not there.

Luther Blissett was sent on to replace the ineffective Woodcock and Graham Rix came on for the disappointing Alan Devonshire. But the changes had little effect on England's performance and the game slowly drifted into oblivion. The Greek attack was non-existent and never threatened the home captain, Peter Shilton. In fact, he had what was probably his easiest international, some consolation for England who had never conceded a goal to Greece. However, the Greeks were understandably delighted with their result and they danced with joy at the final whistle.

> 4th match v Greece.

England v Hungary European Championship Qualifier

Played on Wednesday, 27 April 1983 at Wembley Stadium.

England: P.L.Shilton (Southampton, captain); P.G.Neal (Liverpool), K.G.Sansom (Arsenal), S.Lee (Liverpool), A.E.Martin (West Ham), T.I.Butcher (Ipswich T), G.V.Mabbutt (Spurs),

England's team which beat Hungary 2-0 in the 1983 European Championship qualifier at Wembley. Back row (left to right): Peter Withe, Alvin Martin, Terry Butcher, Trevor Francis, Gordon Cowans, Peter Shilton. Front row: Kenny Sansom, Sammy Lee, Phil Neal, Luther Blissett and Gary Mabbutt.

T.J.Francis (Sampdoria), P.Withe (Aston Villa), L.L.Blissett (Watford), G.S.Cowans (Aston Villa).
Hungary: B.Katzirz (Pécsi Munkás SC); G.Martos (Waterschei Thor), I.Kocsis (Lierse SK), J.Tóth (Újpesti Dózsa), P.Hannich (Rába Vasas ETO), I.Garaba (Honvéd), J.Varga (Honvéd), T.Nyilasi (Ferencváros), L.Kiss (Vasas SC), J.Kardos (Újpest Dózsa), G.Hajszán (Rába Vasas ETO).
Subs: G.Burcsa (Rába Vasas ETO) for Martos and A.Töröcsik (Újpesti Dózsa) for Kiss.

Half-time 1-0   Full-time 2-0
Ref: P.D'Elia (Italy)   Att: 54,000

THE unusual sight of two goalkeeping captains tossing the coin and exchanging formalities gave an unfamiliar start to this vital European Championship game. After the bitter disappointment of last month's clash with Greece it was so important that England won this match.

After a tentative opening they began to move forward with purpose. In the 13th minute Luther Blissett had the ball in the Hungarian net, but the goal was ruled out for a foul on Katzirz by the Watford man. The Hungarians then hit back, showing plenty of skill on the ball. Hajszán got through but was given offside and Varga had a shot blocked by a forest of legs in the England penalty area. An astute pass by the ever dangerous Nyilasi almost set up Hungary again, but the player lost control at the vital moment.

On the half-hour, England took the lead. Peter Withe was brought down right near the corner flag. When Gordon Cowans hit a hard, low cross into the middle Trevor Francis flicked it in with his head to score his third goal in three matches under Bobby Robson.

The goal gave England greater confidence and they pushed forward with more authority in search of a second goal. Blissett, who tended to miss more chances than he scored, began a catalogue of bad finishing. First, Kenny Sansom set him up, only for him to pull his shot wide. Then Withe's pass saw Blissett hit the crossbar, although the referee had already blown for offside. And then the striker created a chance for himself only for his shot to be blocked by Katzirz, with Francis hitting a follow up effort wide.

In the second half England remained in control but always keeping a watchful eye on dangerous Hungarian breakaways. Other chances came and went until, in the 70th minute, the long-awaited second goal arrived. Withe, who worked tirelessly throughout, finally broke his international scoring duck by chesting down Sammy Lee's long cross to the far post and thumping home a beautiful half-volley which left Katzirz helpless.

That goal was no less than England deserved as Lee had just previously had a superb shot brilliantly tipped away by the goalkeeper. Hungary rallied briefly and Peter Shilton had to be at his best to push over a vicious dipping volley by Kardos. Even then, though, England were soon pushing forward again and Withe almost added a third goal, but he and Sansom got in each other's way after a mistake by Hannich.

14th match v Hungary.

Northern Ireland v England Home Championship

Played on Saturday, 28 May 1983 at Windsor Park, Belfast.

Northern Ireland: P.A.Jennings (Arsenal); J.M.Nicholl (Toronto Blizzard), M.M.Donaghy (Luton T), J.McClelland (Rangers), C.J.Nicholl (Southampton), M.H.O'Neill (Norwich C), G.Mullan (Glentoran), S.B.McIlroy (Stoke C), G.J.Armstrong (Watford), W.R.Hamilton (Burnley), I.E.Stewart (QPR).
Sub: N.Brotherston (Blackburn R) for Mullan.
England: P.L.Shilton (Southampton, captain); P.G.Neal (Liverpool), K.G.Sansom (Arsenal), G.Hoddle (Spurs), G.P.Roberts (Spurs), T.I.Butcher (Ipswich T), G.V.Mabbutt (Spurs), T.J.Francis (Sampdoria), P.Withe (Aston Villa), L.L.Blissett (Watford), G.S.Cowans (Aston Villa).
Sub: J.C.B.Barnes (Watford) for Blissett.

Half-time 0-0   Full-time 0-0
Ref: H.W.King (Wales)   Att: 28,750

ENGLAND produced a very poor performance in this match at Windsor Park. Against a hard-working Irish side they produced little in the way of inspiration and the game must go down as a complete non-event. Credit to the Irish who hustled and harried England into errors but towards the end even their enthusiasm was dampened by the boredom of it all.

The Irish opened with their usual aggressive running and new cap Graham Roberts had a difficult baptism in the England defence. A long pass out of the Irish defence should have been cut out by Roberts, but Stewart beat him to the ball and, with Armstrong's help, set up half-chances for both Hamilton and Mullen. The danger was cleared that time but a little while later Armstrong's cross was met powerfully by Roberts and only a brilliant save by Peter Shilton prevented a very embarrassing own-goal.

After that crazy incident the Irish took control. They showed more enthusiasm than England with McIlroy and O'Neill willing workhorses. They were helped by some good running from the forwards and some solid defending at the back. This Irish domination of the midfield meant that the England trio of Gary Mabbutt, Glenn Hoddle and Gordon Cowans failed to give their forwards the service they needed. True, Hoddle showed some neat touches but never took the grip on proceedings that his talent demanded. Twice before half-time the Irish nearly scored. First Phil Neal joined Roberts in attempting to beat his own goalkeeper, then Shilton made another marvellous save after a thrilling run and shot by Stewart.

Ireland continued to have the better of things after the interval without creating any clear-cut openings. In fact it was England who almost scored on the hour. Neal made a rare sortie upfield and chipped a lovely ball for Trevor Francis, who was stood near the penalty-spot. Francis headed towards goal and was unlucky to see his effort just clear the crossbar with Jennings helpless.

The remainder of the match was uneventful with Ireland failing to breach the English defence and England, in turn,

showing little appetite for the game. Only Shilton showed true international class, whilst McIlroy and O'Neill shone brightest for the Irish.

91st match v Northern Ireland.
Debut for Roberts and, as substitute, Barnes.

England v Scotland Home Championship

Played on Wednesday, 1 June 1983 at Wembley Stadium.

England: P.L.Shilton (Southampton); P.G.Neal (Liverpool), K.G.Sansom (Arsenal), S.Lee (Liverpool), G.P.Roberts (Spurs), T.I.Butcher (Ipswich T), B.Robson (Man Utd, captain), T.J.Francis (Sampdoria), P.Withe (Aston Villa), G.Hoddle (Spurs), G.S.Cowans (Aston Villa).
Subs: G.V.Mabbutt (Spurs) for Robson and L.L.Blissett (Watford) for Withe.
Scotland: J.Leighton (Aberdeen); C.R.Gough (Dundee Utd), F.T.Gray (Leeds Utd), W.Miller (Aberdeen), A.McLeish (Aberdeen), D.Narey (Dundee Utd), G.D.Strachan (Aberdeen), G.J.Souness (Liverpool), A.M.Gray (Wolves), C.Nicholas (Celtic), E.Bannon (Dundee Utd).
Subs: J.Wark (Ipswich T) for Nicholas and A.B.Brazil (Spurs) for Bannon.

Half-time 1-0   Full-time 2-0
Ref: E.Frederiksson (Sweden) Att: 83,000

ENGLAND duly completed their Home Championship victory by comfortably beating the Scots at Wembley. The game was not exactly a classic, but gave England some good pointers towards their decisive match against Denmark in September which could decide their European Championship fate.

Early attacks gave the many Scottish fans plenty to cheer but they all came to nothing. England suffered an early blow when Bryan Robson stretched for the ball in a tackle with Narey and pulled a muscle in his groin. It was obvious that he was in pain, but he carried on for a while. Trevor Francis and Kenny Sansom went close with good efforts and then in the 13th minute the breakthrough came. Sansom sent in a long throw from the left, Terry Butcher touched it on with his head and in roared Robson to force the ball home. It was a typically gutsy goal despite his obvious discomfort.

Almost immediately McLeish headed desperately over his own crossbar to clear a splendid attack engineered by lovely play between Glenn Hoddle and Gordon Cowans. The Scots were playing with their usual spirit but created few scoring opportunities. Just before the break they managed three half-chances close together, but England's defence cleared the danger. The home side lost a second player through injury at half-time, (Robson had already gone off to be replaced by Gary Mabbutt), when Peter Withe retired with strained knee ligaments.

Luther Blissett was Withe's replacement and he was immediately in the action showing his exceptional pace. McLeish was left standing by one explosive burst of speed from the Watford player, but

Leighton made a good save to stop him scoring. England by now were in control and it came as no surprise when they increased their lead ten minutes into the second half. Francis put in some good work down the right before putting in a centre. A terrific scramble developed in the goalmouth with Cowans and Phil Neal trying to get the vital touch. It eventually came from Cowans, who joyfully lashed home the loose ball to register his first goal for his country.

Much of the remainder of the game was littered with niggly fouls and some of the tackling left a lot to be desired. The Swedish referee struggled to keep control and let far too many challenges go unpunished.

However, it was always England who created the better of the chances. Both Francis and Sammy Lee had goals ruled out and another Francis effort brought a fine save out of Leighton. A Graham Roberts piledriver flew just wide whilst at the other end, Strachan forced a superb save from Peter Shilton who had been largely untroubled up to then. Strachan was Scotland's best player but overall the boys in blue must have been bitterly disappointed with their display. Yet another win over the Auld Enemy for England and once again it clinched the Home Championship for them.

> 101st match v Scotland.
> 50th cap for Shilton.

Australia v England
Friendly

Played on Sunday, 12 June 1983 on the Cricket Ground, Sydney.

Australia: T.Greedy (St George Budapest, Sydney); A.Davidson (South Melbourne Hellas), D.Ratcliffe (St George Budapest, Sydney), S.O'Connor (Sydney City Hakoah), C.Yankos (Heidelberg U), C.Jennings (Sydney Olympic), P.Kethelos (Sydney Olympic), J.Watson (Sydney City Hakoah), J.Cant (Sydney City Hakoah), J.Kosmina (Sydney City Hakoah), P.O'Connor (Woollongong).
Subs: P.Stone (St George Budapest) for Watson and D.Mitchell (Sydney City Hakoah) for P.O'Connor.
England: P.L.Shilton (Southampton, captain); D.J.Thomas (Coventry C), D.J.Statham (West Brom), S.C.Williams (Southampton), R.C.Osman (Ipswich T), T.I.Butcher (Ipswich T), M.F.Barham (Norwich C), J.C.Gregory (QPR), L.L.Blissett (Watford), T.J.Francis (Sampdoria), G.S.Cowans (Aston Villa).
Subs: J.C.B.Barnes (Watford) for Statham and P.A.Walsh (Luton) for Blissett.

Half-time 0-0   Full-time 0-0
Ref: T.Boskovic (Australia)   Att: 27,500

'IT is long way to come for a 0-0 draw!' That was the verdict of one spectator after the opening international in a series of three against Australia. Bobby Robson gave first caps to four new players and the later substitution of Paul Walsh for Luther Blissett made it five. All these changes meant a disjointed and disappointing display from England in what was a very poor game.

The Australians were soon packing their defence inviting England to come

at them. This they did with Mark Barham, Steve Williams and John Gregory showing some nice touches. Danny Thomas, too, showed his class and he was undoubtedly the pick of the side. However, all this reasonable approach play repeatedly broke down in the last third of the field and Mr Greedy in the home goal had little to do. The Trevor Francis-Blissett partnership did not gell so there was no punch up front, whilst at the other end Peter Shilton had to make two good saves from Kosmina and Kethelos as the Australians enjoyed their best spell just before the interval. The England captain was otherwise unemployed in what was a sterile game.

The 27,500 crowd grew more and more restless as the game deteriorated in the second half to an even lower standard of play. There was virtually no goalmouth action and England's best chance came as late as the 90th minute when Gregory headed a corner by Gordon Cowans wide of the post. At the final whistle it was obvious that the home side were delighted at having held their illustrious opponents but the crowd's disappointment was also obvious as they booed both teams off the field.

> 2nd match v Australia.
> Debuts for Thomas, Williams, Barham, Gregory and, as substitute, Walsh.

Australia v England
Friendly

Played on Wednesday, 15 June 1983 at Lang Park, Brisbane.

Australia: T.Greedy (St George Budapest, Sydney); A.Davidson (South Melbourne Hellas), C.Jennings (Sydney Olympic), C.Yankos (Heidelberg U), D.Ratcliffe (St George Budapest, Sydney), S.O'Connor (Sydney City Hakoah), J.Watson (Sydney City Hakoah), J.Cant (Sydney City Hakoah), J.Kosmina (Sydney City Hakoah), P.Kethelos (Sydney Olympic), P.O'Connor (Woollongong).
Subs: K.Murphy (South Melbourne Hellas) for Kethelos and D.Mitchell (Sydney City Hakoah) for P.O'Connor.
England: P.L.Shilton (Southampton, captain); P.G.Neal (Liverpool), D.J.Statham (West Brom), M.F.Barham (Norwich C), R.C.Osman (Ipswich T), T.I.Butcher (Ipswich T), J.C.Gregory (QPR), T.J.Francis (Sampdoria), P.A.Walsh (Luton T), G.S.Cowans (Aston Villa), J.C.B.Barnes (Watford).
Sub: S.C.Williams (Southampton) for Statham.

Half-time 0-0   Full-time 0-1
Ref: P.Rampley (Australia)   Att: 9,750

THE second match of England's Australian adventure saw an improved display that gave their rather battered reputation, after the first game, a much-needed boost. This time they pinned Australia back for long periods and, but for a fine performance by the home goalkeeper, they would surely have registered the expected high-scoring victory.

Right from the start the new partnership of Paul Walsh and Trevor Francis looked sharp and lively. In the seventh

minute Greedy made a brilliant save from Francis after Phil Neal had split the home defence with a fine pass. Neal constantly joined the attack with some surging runs down the right and just before the interval he almost scored when his powerful shot beat Greedy but was cleared off the line by S.O'Connor. Other chances came and went in the first half with Australia's only respite coming from the running of the tricky Kosmina. His impressive play gave Terry Butcher a tough time in the England defence and the home fans loved it when Kosmina had possession.

The second half followed a similar pattern to the first with England pushing forward continuously. In the 57th minute they at last broke the deadlock. The Australian defence could not clear an England attack properly and the ball was picked up by Luther Blissett. He turned it across goal where both Walsh and Butcher just failed to get a touch. But John Gregory managed to retrieve it from the by-line and pulled it back again across goal and this time Walsh reacted like lightning to push the ball past Greedy. Australia protested that the ball had gone out of play, but the referee would have none of it.

Greedy again saved well after Butcher had headed a Gregory cross goalwards and the home side continued to defend stubbornly and with great determination. In the end, though, England were well worth their win and with a little more luck they could have scored many more goals.

> 3rd match v Australia.

Australia v England
Friendly

Played on Sunday, 19 June 1983 at Olympic Park, Melbourne.

Australia: T.Greedy (St George Budapest, Sydney); A.Davidson (South Melbourne, Hellas), C.Jennings (Sydney Olympic), C.Yankos (Heidelberg U), D.Ratcliffe (St George Budapest, Sydney), S.O'Connor (Sydney City Hakoah), J.Watson (Sydney City Budapest), J.Cant (Sydney City Hakoah), K.Murphy (South Melbourne Hellas), J.Kosmina (Sydney City Hakoah), P.O'Connor (Woollongong).
England: P.L.Shilton (Southampton, captain); P.G.Neal (Liverpool), N.Pickering (Sunderland), R.C.Osman (Ipswich T), T.I.Butcher (Ipswich T), S.Lee (Liverpool), J.C.Gregory (QPR), G.S.Cowans (Aston Villa), T.J.Francis (Sampdoria), P.A.Walsh (Luton T), J.C.B.Barnes (Watford).
Subs: N.P.Spink (Aston Villa) for Shilton, D.J.Thomas (Coventry C) for Neal and L.L.Blissett (Watford) for Walsh.

Half-time 1-1   Full-time 1-1
Ref: J.Johnston (Australia)   Att: 22,000

SOME 22,000 people came to this, the third and final match in the triology, hoping that Australia could continue their 'success' of the previous two games against England. Certainly, once again, it was the home side who came away with most of the credit.

For the first 20 minutes, though, it was all England. Greedy, the home goalkeeping hero of the previous matches, again performed brilliantly, cutting out dangerous corners and also saving good shots from Trevor Francis and Gordon Cowans. In the 19th minute, though, the England pressure paid off. Ratcliffe brought Francis down with a crashing tackle and the play was held up for several minutes as the England player received treatment. When the free-kick was finally taken by Cowans, Francis showed no ill effects from the incident by hitting a superb shot wide of the flat-footed Greedy.

Australia continued to show the resilience seen in the other games and they played with commendable determination. They came back strongly after the goal and on 27 minutes they scored a sensational equalizer. Good work by Yankos and Murphy gave Watson possession on the right. He hit over a cross which eluded the jumping Terry Butcher and Kosmina, only for the ball to strike Phil Neal on the chest and deflect past Peter Shilton for an own-goal. It was a bitter blow for England and to be pegged back before half-time after having so much of the half seemed to sap their spirit.

The second half began with England once more pushing forward relentlessly, but it was the home side who almost took the lead in the 62nd minute. Ratcliffe, who had stayed close to Francis all through the game, went up for a corner and only just headed wide from Watson's kick. But England, too, were unlucky when, five minutes later, John Barnes hit a superb shot which struck the crossbar from some 25 yards.

In the 73rd minute, the visitors should have regained the lead. A push by Kosmina on Butcher in the penalty area was seen by the referee and he had no hesitation in awarding a penalty. Francis stepped up for the spot-kick and promptly drilled his shot past Greedy and into the net. Unfortunately the referee spotted something wrong and ordered the kick to be retaken, ruling that Francis had taken the kick too soon. The decision was a strange one and it must have upset Francis as his second attempt flew over the crossbar, much to the delight of the home fans.

The chance of victory went with that miss and although England stayed on top, the Australians held on for the draw their manager was delighted with. For the England players the final whistle brought to an end a long and tiring season.

> 4th match v Australia.
> Debuts for Pickering and, as substitute, Spink.
> Own-goal by Neal for Australia.
> Francis missed a penalty at the second attempt.

John Gregory on the ball against Denmark in September 1983.

Trevor Francis in action against the Danes, who scored a great victory at Wembley.

England v Denmark
European Championship Qualifier

Played on Wednesday, 21 September 1983 at Wembley Stadium.

England: P.L.Shilton (Southampton); P.G.Neal (Liverpool), K.G.Sansom (Arsenal), S.Lee (Liverpool), R.C.Osman (Ipswich T), T.I.Butcher (Ipswich T), R.C.Wilkins (Man Utd, captain), J.C.Gregory (QPR), P.Mariner (Ipswich T), T.J.Francis (Sampdoria), J.C.B. Barnes (Watford).
Subs: L.L.Blissett (Watford) for Lee and M.V.Chamberlain (Stoke C) for Barnes.

Denmark: O.Kjar (Esbjerg BK); O.Rasmussen (Hertha BSC), I.Nielsen (Feyenoord), M.Olsen (RSC Anderlecht), S.Busk (KAA Gent), S.Lerby (Bayern Munich), J.Bertelsen (Seraing), J.Olsen (Ajax Amsterdam), A.Simonsen (Vejle BK), M.Laudrup (Juventus), K.Berggren (Pisa).
Subs: J.Mölby for J.Olsen and P.Elkjaer (SC Lokeren) for Laudrup.

Half-time 0-1   Full-time 0-1
Ref: A.Ponnet (Belgium)   Att: 82,050

DENMARK became firm favourites to qualify from Group Three of the European Championships after this splendid victory at Wembley. They were full value for their win and, despite the narrow scoreline, they were convincingly better than England on the night.

September never seemed a good month for England, as their results in previous years suggested, and it was apparent as early as the first minute how sharp the Denmark forwards were. John Barnes lost possession and Simonsen immediately exposed a lack of pace in England's defence with a lovely chip that sent Laudrup away. Peter Shilton hesitated but the moment was perhaps too much for the 19-year-old Laudrup as the Danish

forward could only hit the side netting with his weak shot.

Almost immediately there was more danger for England as Terry Butcher lost control on the by-line to give Jesper Olsen a free run. The Dane rolled a pass into the path of Berggren and it looked a certain goal until Berggren somehow managed to miss the ball completely. England, meanwhile, showed little penetration against the well-organised Denmark defenders, although Sammy Lee and Trevor Francis made one promising break, only for Ray Wilkins to waste the opportunity with a poor cross.

Denmark were looking sharper and more confident than England and in the 37th minute their good play was rewarded. Laudrup, a constant danger, drew both Butcher and Kenny Sansom out to the right before sending over a good cross. Phil Neal and two Danish attackers went for it and in the ensuing scramble Neal was seen to handle the ball. The referee immediately pointed to the penalty-spot and Simonsen calmly sent Shilton the wrong way from the kick.

There was little improvement from England after the break. Their laborious build up was easily dealt with by Denmark's excellent defenders, with only Francis and Barnes looking even remotely like upsetting the visitors composure. Morten Olsen and Lerby were outstanding and goal attempts from England were few and far between. The Danes cleverly kept possession, passing the ball continuously to thoroughly frustrate England and their fans. Only once did the home side come close to snatching a point and that was in the last few seconds.

Luther Blissett had come on as a late substitution for Lee and suddenly found himself in a good position. He hit his shot well enough but Kjar, although not knowing much about it, saved the ball with his knees. In truth, a goal then would have been an injustice to the classy Danes who thoroughly deserved their victory. They now led the group table whilst England had it all to do to rescue the situation.

> 9th match v Denmark.
> Phil Neal's 50th and last cap.
> Penalty scored by Simonsen for Denmark.
> *"When I realised I had played my last international I felt satisfied that I had done my utmost every time I played for England."*
> Phil Neal

Hungary v England European Championship Qualifier

Played on Wednesday, 12 October 1983 in the Nep Stadium, Budapest.

Hungary: A.Kovacs (Vasas Csepel); G.Sconka (Rába Vasas ETO), J.Kardos (Újpesti Dózsa), J.Varga (Honvéd), I.Garaba (Honvéd), P.Hannich (Rába Vasas ETO), F.Csongrady (Videoton), G.Burcsa (Videoton), L.Dajka (Honvéd), T.Nyilasi (Ferencváros), G.Haisan (Rába Vasas ETO).
Subs: Szokola (Ferencváros) for Hannich and L.Nagy (Honvéd) for Burcsa.
England: P.L.Shilton (Southampton); J.C.Gregory (QPR), K.G.Sansom (Arsenal), T.I.Butcher (Ipswich T), A.E.Martin (West Ham), S.Lee (Liverpool), B.Robson (Man Utd, captain), G.Hoddle (Spurs), P.Mariner (Ipswich T), G.V.Mabbutt (Spurs), L.L.Blissett (Watford).
Sub: P.Withe (Aston Villa) for Blissett.

Half-time 0-3   Full-time 0-3
Ref: B.Galler (Switzerland)   Att: 15,000

ENGLAND, needing nothing less than a win to have any chance of overhauling Denmark at the top of their group, travelled to Budapest determined to give everything, and a dazzling first-half display gave them a marvellous win.

From the opening whistle England went forward positively and it was soon clear who was going to control the game. It was Glenn Hoddle, at last showing some of his outstanding club form at this level. He was certainly the inspiration behind most of England's attacks and on 12 minutes he put his side in front.

Luther Blissett was fouled on the edge of the area by the awkward Kardos. Sammy Lee and Bryan Robson stood over the ball but allowed Hoddle to curl a superb shot into the top left-hand corner of Hungary's goal. Immediately afterwards England were awarded a similar free-kick and

Hoddle went desperately close to making it two goals, only for this effort to be cleared. Then on 18 minutes, Hoddle took a corner which Varga headed clear at the near post. The ball was only cleared as far as Lee, though, and the little midfield player promptly dispatched a fine swerving shot beyond the stunned Kovacs and into the net.

England were cock-a-hoop and continued to press forward confidently. Kardos, who had a nightmare of a match, was lucky to escape punishment when he deliberately handled another probing through pass from Hoddle which would have left Blissett in the clear. The defender was not so lucky shortly afterwards though when he was booked for a foul on Blissett. With four minutes to go before half-time, England virtually sealed the game up with another goal.

Blissett was fortunate when his misplaced cross went well beyond the far post but found the alert Lee. Lee passed to Hoddle, who cleverly beat two defenders before squaring the ball to Paul Mariner who side-footed a simple, but very effective goal.

The Hungarians brought on two substitutes after half-time but found no improvement in their play. England continued to hold all the aces and could easily have added more goals to their tally. Long before the end, the home fans were whistling their derision at the failure of their team. England's missed chances were disappointing in this half but the game had already been won and lost in the first 45 minutes. They now had to beat Luxembourg in their last match and hope for good news from Denmark's last games to see who goes through to the finals.

> 15th match v Hungary.

Luxembourg v England European Championship Qualifier

Played on Wednesday, 16 November 1983 in the City Stadium, Luxembourg.

Luxembourg: J.P.Defrang (US Luxembourg); R.Michaux (Red Boys Differdange), H.Meunier (Jeunesse Esch), G.Dresch (Avenir Beggen), M.Bossi (Progres Niedercorn), N.Wagner (Avenir Beggen), G.Hellers (Standard Liège), T.Malget (FC Wietz), J.P.Barboni (Jeunesse Esch), B.Reiter (FC Chalonnais), R.Langers (FC Metz).
Subs: J.P.Girres (Avenir Beggen) for T.Malget and G.Jeitz (US Rumelange) for J.P.Barboni.
England: R.N.Clemence (Liverpool); M.Duxbury (Man Utd), K.G.Sansom (Arsenal), S.Lee (Liverpool), A.E.Martin (West Ham), T.I.Butcher (Ipswich T), B.Robson (Man Utd, captain), G.Hoddle (Spurs), P.Mariner (Ipswich T), A.S.Woodcock (Arsenal), A.E.Devonshire (West Ham).
Sub: J.C.B.Barnes (Watford) for Woodcock.

Half-time 0-2   Full-time 0-4
Ref: C.Bakker (Holland)   Att: 12,000

THERE was an air of great disappointment after England's easy win here against Luxembourg. That was because of Denmark's win in Greece which enabled them

to pip England for the qualifiers' spot in Group Three of these championships.

England did all they had to do here with Tony Woodcock looking lively in the early stages of the game and twice going close to scoring. As it was, they were soon ahead. Glenn Hoddle took a corner on the right, Terry Butcher and home goalkeeper Defrang both missed it and in came the ever-alert Bryan Robson to sweep the loose ball into the net for a typical goal from the England captain.

On 25 minutes the visitors suffered a blow when Woodcock had to leave the field with a groin injury, but it did not affect their overall superiority. Paul Mariner might have done better after a lobbed pass by substitute John Barnes had set up a chance, but five minutes before the interval Mariner made amends by scoring England's second goal.

Sammy Lee angled a pass into the middle and both Mariner and defender Meunier went for it. It was touch and go as to who made the firmer touch but in the end the goal was credited to Mariner.

After the interval, Luxembourg began to tire. All their earlier running was beginning to take effect on their inferior fitness and England, with Hoddle dictating the play, were in total command. Five minutes after the restart Hoddle crossed to the far post where Barnes got his head to the ball. He didn't connect properly but it ran on kindly for Butcher to score easily from close range. Six minutes later a perfect pass from Hoddle sent Robson clear and he confidently beat Defrang with a crisply hit shot.

Defrang continued to be the best and busiest Luxembourg player and he made superb saves from both Robson and Mariner. His goalkeeping was most impressive throughout. At the other end, only Reiter's industry gave Ray Clemence any anxious moments as England coasted home.

After the match news filtered through that Denmark had beaten Greece and it was therefore a very subdued party that left the ground to return to England.

> 7th match v Luxembourg.
> Debut for Duxbury.

France v England Friendly

Played on Wednesday, 29 February 1984 at the Parc des Princes Stadium, Paris.

France: J.Bats (AJ Auxerre); M.Amoros (AS Monaco), P.Battiston (Bordeaux), M.Bossis (FC Nantes), Y.Le Roux (AS Monaco), L.Fernández (Paris St-Germain), A.Giresse (Bordeaux), M.Platini (Juventus), J.Tigana (Bordeaux), B.Bellone (AS Monaco), J.Touré (FC Nantes).
Subs: T.Tusseau (Bordeaux) for Battiston and D.Rocheteau (Paris St-Germain) for Bellone.
England: P.L.Shilton (Southampton); M.Duxbury (Man Utd), K.G.Sansom (Arsenal), S.Lee (Liverpool), G.P.Roberts (Spurs), T.I.Butcher (Ipswich T), B.Robson (Man Utd, captain), B.Stein (Luton T), P.A.Walsh (Luton T), G.Hoddle (Spurs), S.C.Williams (Southampton).
Subs: J.C.B.Barnes (Watford) for Lee and A.S.Woodcock (Arsenal) for Stein.

Bryan Robson, the England skipper on target against Luxembourg.

Tony Woodcock heads past Jim Platt for the only goal of the Home Championship game against Northern Ireland at Wembley in April 1984.

Half-time 0-0   Full-time 2-0

Ref: M.Van Legenhove (Belgium)

Att: 45,000

THIS match had to go down as one of England's worst performances for a long time. Looking disjointed and lacking in ideas they were easy meat to a French side inspired by Platini. To make it an even worse night there were more ugly disturbances on the terraces which was bound to be met by a barrage of questions back home.

From the first whistle of the game the play was controlled by that man Platini. The current European Footballer of the Year quickly took a hold of the vital midfield area and showed all of his skill and vision. The England defenders scarcely knew how to handle him. However, some of England's early midfield play was quite delightful with Glenn Hoddle, Bryan Robson and Steve Williams showing some nice touches, but always in control was Platini. Several times in the first half the French players split the England defence wide open and from one move Bellone missed a gilt-edged chance when he rounded Peter Shilton but missed the target with his shot. A second miss followed when Shilton had to block another Bellone shot and then Platini ruined a terrific run by Tigana with a poor

finishing attempt. At half-time it was still goalless but England were very lucky to be in that position.

After half-time, France continued to dominate and on the hour they were at last rewarded with a goal. Giresse put in a delightful cross that beat Terry Butcher and found Platini ghosting in behind him to loop a header over Shilton. The goal gave France even more confidence and ten minutes later they scored again. Shilton dashed from goal to foil Touré but in so doing handled the ball outside the area. From the free-kick Platini fired a glorious shot into the top corner with unerring accuracy.

France, who looked a fine side on the night, were now rampant. England battled on manfully but lacked the necessary bite to worry the home defenders. They managed only three half-decent goal attempts throughout the whole match, but Williams, Paul Walsh and Hoddle all saw French goalkeeper Bats easily save their efforts. Hoddle was very disappointing and he could not compete with the outstanding Giresse and Platini. Bobby Robson sent on two substitutes but that move failed to change the pattern of the game and France ended comfortable winners.

If Robson had problems with his team then the FA had even more worries over the fans' behaviour. There were skir-

mishes throughout the night by youths from both countries.

> 20th match v France.
> Debut for Stein.

England v Home Championship
Northern Ireland

Played on Wednesday, 4 April 1984 at Wembley Stadium.

England: P.L.Shilton (Southampton); V.A.Anderson (Nottm Forest), A.P.Kennedy (Liverpool), S.Lee (Liverpool), G.P.Roberts (Spurs), T.I.Butcher (Ipswich T), B.Robson (Man Utd, captain), R.C.Wilkins (Man Utd), A.S.Woodcock (Arsenal), T.J.Francis (Sampdoria), G.Rix (Arsenal).

Northern Ireland: J.A.Platt (Ballymena); J.M.Nicholl (Rangers), M.M.Donaghy (Luton T), J.McClelland (Rangers), G.M.A.McElhinney (Bolton W), M.H.O'Neill (Notts Co), G.J.Armstrong (Real Mallorca), S.B.McIlroy (Stoke C), W.R.Hamilton (Burnley), N.Whiteside (Man Utd), I.E.Stewart (QPR).

Half-time 1-0   Full-time 1-0

Ref: R.Bridges (Wales)   Att: 24,000

WITH the decision to end the Home Championship after this season this game saw a little piece of soccer history pass into oblivion as England played their last Home International at Wembley. As this is the last year of the tournament the Irish and the Welsh were extra determined to do well as theirs was the greater loss, especially in important revenue.

This match was a poor one though with neither side capable of raising their game above the mediocre level, a regular feature in this competition in its twilight years. England had few attacking ideas, despite the excellent prompting from the recalled Ray Wilkins. The Manchester United man had a fine game and was one of England's few successes on the night. Unfortunately, goal chances were rare, although a Bryan Robson volley dipped just over with Platt groping. Ireland also had little to offer and their poor scoring record against England never looked like being improved upon.

The goal that was to prove the match winner came in the 40th minute. Viv Anderson, up with the attack, drove in a fierce shot. Platt failed to hold the ball but pushed it upwards. That left the jumping Tony Woodcock the easiest of tasks to head it into the empty net. On the run of play, the goal was just about deserved but early in the second half the Irish had two golden chances to equalize.

Both openings fell to Hamilton who found himself clear of defenders with free headers at Peter Shilton. Unfortunately for Ireland the striker could only manage to head the ball into Shilton's waiting arms on both occasions. England hit back through Trevor Francis but his shot grazed the outside of a post. Ireland, who always seemed to have the better of the clear chances, failed miserably again when Armstrong found himself clear of the defence and running at Shilton. Anderson had put the Irishman onside, but once again a gilt-edged opening was lost as the goalkeeper pushed aside Armstrong's final shot.

A Graham Rix lob that went over was the only other worthwhile goal attempt as England tried to press home their slim advantage. But play deteriorated to a level far below international quality. The fans in a small crowd had long since lost interest and the final whistle was greeted with almost total silence. Of all the England-Northern Ireland Home Internationals, this one will only be remembered for the fact that it was the last.

92nd match v Northern Ireland.
Debut for Kennedy.

Wales v England Home Championship

Played on Wednesday, 2 May 1984 at the Racecourse Ground, Wrexham.

Wales: N.Southall (Everton); D.O.Phillips (Plymouth A), J.P.Jones (Chelsea), R.M.James (Stoke C), J.Hopkins (Fulham), K.Ratcliffe (Everton), G.J.Davies (Fulham), A.Davies (Man Utd), I.J.Rush (Liverpool), M.R.Thomas (Chelsea), L.M.Hughes (Man Utd).

England: P.L.Shilton (Southampton); M.Duxbury (Man Utd), A.P.Kennedy (Liverpool), S.Lee (Liverpool), A.E.Martin (West Ham), M.Wright (Southampton), R.C.Wilkins (Man Utd, captain), J.C.Gregory (QPR), P.A.Walsh (Luton T), A.S.Woodcock (Arsenal),

D.Armstrong (Southampton).
Subs: T.W.Fenwick (QPR) for Martin and L.L.Blissett (Watford) for Armstrong.

Half-time 1-0   Full-time 1-0
Ref: D.Syme (Scotland)   Att: 15,000

THIS dismal display by England ended in defeat and Wales gained much satisfaction from this, the last of their Home Internationals against their old adversaries. The Welsh were particularly critical over the abolition of the tournament so the victory was savoured with relish. Manager Bobby Robson's England squad was much changed and the quest for continuity is an often almost impossible task for the beleaguered boss as player after player become unavailable for one reason or another. In the end, nine regulars were missing.

Wales began well and the dangerous Rush was soon making his presence felt. He went close early on and was then brought down in the 19th minute, giving Wales a free-kick out on the right. The kick was taken by Alan Davies and he found his Manchester United teammate, Mark Hughes, who cleanly headed past Peter Shilton. It has to be said that England's defenders stood rooted to the spot and allowed Hughes a free header.

The visitors looked disjointed and showed very little in attack. Southall hardly had a shot to save and it was obvious that the many team changes were having a bad effect on England. After the interval the Welsh team continued to control the bulk of the play. Several times they should have added to their slender lead, especially through Gordon Davies who missed two clear chances. Rush, too, failed to show the deadly finishing that had become his hallmark, although near the end Shilton had to be at his best to keep out one of his efforts.

Shilton, in fact, was England's only real success and but for him Wales would have added to their lead. Hughes did put the ball into the net for what looked a second goal but the referee disallowed it for an infringement. So the Welsh ended this fixture with a victory, only their 14th in 97 attempts.

97th match v Wales.
Debuts for Wright and, as substitute, Fenwick.

Scotland v England Home Championship

Played on Saturday, 26 May 1984 at Hampden Park, Glasgow.

Scotland: J.Leighton (Aberdeen); C.R.Gough (Dundee Utd), A.R.Albiston (Man Utd), J.Wark (Liverpool), A.McLeish (Aberdeen), W.Miller (Aberdeen), G.D.Strachan (Aberdeen), S.Archibald (Spurs), M.McGhee (Aberdeen), J.Bett (SC Lokeren), D.Cooper (Rangers).
Subs: P.McStay (Celtic) for Strachan and M.T.Johnston (Watford) for McGhee.

England: P.L.Shilton (Southampton); M.Duxbury (Man Utd), K.G.Sansom (Arsenal), R.C.Wilkins (Man Utd), G.P.Roberts (Spurs), T.W.Fenwick (QPR), M.V.Chamberlain (Stoke C), B.Robson (Man Utd, captain),

A.S.Woodcock (Arsenal), L.L.Blissett (Watford), J.C.B.Barnes (Watford).
Subs: S.K.Hunt (West Brom) for Chamberlain and G.W.Lineker (Leicester C) for Woodcock.

Half-time 1-1   Full-time 1-1
Ref: P.Casarin (Italy)   Att: 73,064

ON a wet but firm Hampden Park pitch, these two sides fought out the last ever Home Championship international. Appropriately enough, the honours were shared.

England began like tigers, dominating the early exchanges. Their attack looked more lively than it had done for a long time, pinning the Scots back into their own penalty area. Bobby Robson decided on a 4-2-4 formation to give his forwards the much needed support so lacking in their recent games. It looked early on that England would record a handsome victory, but as so often before in this fixture, the Scots suddenly took the wind out of England's sails by scoring, totally against the run of play.

Terry Fenwick blocked a shot by McGhee, deflecting the ball for a corner. Cooper took the kick, Peter Shilton punched clear but Strachan regained possession to kick another dangerous ball across goal. It should have been a formality for the defence to clear but, as they did against Wales, the defenders all left it to each other allowing McGhee to score easily with a free header at the far post which went back across goal to beat Shilton. Needless to say the goalkeeper was furious.

England could consider themselves unfortunate to be behind as forwards Tony Woodcock, Luther Blissett and John Barnes had put tremendous pressure on the home defenders. Even experienced men like Miller were hurried into errors. Despite several near misses, England had to wait until the 37th minute before they found an equalizer, and what a gem it was! Mark Chamberlain did well to retrieve the ball from going out and then pass to Woodcock. The Arsenal striker then went for goal, drawing Miller towards him before superbly going around the defender and shooting on the turn with his left foot between Leighton and the right-hand post. A brilliant goal!

It was no less than England deserved and they then held the initiative until Scotland brought on Johnston and McStay. Those players seemed to bring the best out of Cooper and it was the winger who looked Scotland's best hope for victory. One Cooper cross caused havoc in the England penalty area before Graham Roberts rescued the situation by clearing over the bar after a tantalising lob by Betts. A minute later McStay sent Archibald clear with a clever diagonal pass, but Shilton remained alert and managed to parry the shot.

Woodcock was injured and with him went England's best chance. Although Ray Wilkins and Bryan Robson worked tirelessly in midfield the Scots gradually took command. Wark went close from a Cooper corner, forcing a save from Shilton, and the goalkeeper saved England again six minutes from the end with a marvellous moment.

Albiston moved forward to centre for Johnston to meet the ball on the volley. It looked a certain goal but Shilton threw himself at it and turned the shot away. England brought on Steve Hunt and Gary Lineker to try and pep up their attack in the closing minutes, but Scotland were pressing hard for the winner and in the last few seconds McLeish hit another shot that was well held by Shilton. At the final whistle, England were happy with the draw but Scotland's strong finish almost tipped the scales their way.

In the final analysis of the 102 England-Scotland fixtures England won 40, Scotland 39 and 23 were drawn. England scored 183 goals and Scotland 166.

> 102nd match v Scotland.
> Debuts, as substitutes, Hunt and Lineker.
> The last Home Championship international.

England v USSR Friendly

Played on Saturday, 2 June 1984 at Wembley Stadium.

England: P.L.Shilton (Southampton); M.Duxbury (Man Utd), K.G.Sansom (Arsenal), R.C.Wilkins (Man Utd), G.P.Roberts (Spurs), T.W.Fenwick (QPR), M.V.Chamberlain (Stoke C), B.Robson (Man Utd, captain), T.J.Francis (Sampdoria), L.L.Blissett (Watford), J.C.B.Barnes (Watford).
Subs: M.W.Hateley (Portsmouth) for Francis and S.K.Hunt (West Brom) for Barnes.

USSR: R.Dasaev (Spartak Moscow); A.Chivadze (Dinamo Tbilisi), S.Baltacha (Dinamo Kiev), A.Demianenko (Dinamo Kiev), T.Sulakvelidze (Dinamo Tbilisi), S.Aleinikov (Dinamo Minsk), G.Litovchenko (Dnepr Dnepropetrovsk), K.Oganesian (Ararat Erevan), A.Zygmantovich (Dinamo Minsk), S.Rodionov (Spartak Moscow), O.Blokhin (Dinamo Kiev).
Subs: B.Pozdnyakov (Spartak Moscow) for Aleinikov, S.Gotsmanov (Dinamo Minsk) for Zygmantovich and O.Protasov (Dnepr Dnepropetrovsk) for Rodionov.

Half-time 0-0   Full-time 0-2
Ref: M.Vautrot (France)   Att: 38,125

THE regimented warm-up exercises of the Soviets seen before the match were largely laughed at by the home crowd, but at the end of the 90 minutes there were few people who were still smiling.

On a gloriously sunny afternoon, the USSR showed their exceptional pace right from the start and after just three minutes they missed a golden chance. A lovely crossfield pass by Demianenko sent Rodionov away down the left. As the England defenders converged, Rodionov sent in a fine pass to find Litovchenko all alone in front of goal. It looked a certainty that he would score but somehow he pulled his shot wide.

The warning was there for all to see with the Soviets looking good in all departments. Dasaev proved a formidable goalkeeper and he made a fine save from Mark Chamberlain's splendid run and shot in the 18th minute in what was England's best moment of the first half. Towards the end of the first 45 minutes the Russians stepped up a gear. Some superb skills were shown by substitute

Gotsmanov and Oganesian which left Kenny Sansom groping. Thankfully, Peter Shilton was alert to the danger, tipping over Oganesian's fierce shot in fine style. Then, a minute from the break Shilton saved England again, diving bravely at Rodionov's feet after Mike Duxbury was beaten. England still managed an attempt by Luther Blissett but Dasaev saved, somewhat clumsily, leaving the game goalless at the half-way stage.

The first-half honours had all gone to the red-shirted Soviets and eight minutes after the restart their superiority was emphasised with a goal. Duxbury went deep to retrieve a long pass out of the Russian defence, but in trying to control it he fell over his own feet. That left Gotsmanov completely free and with a clear run at goal. This time even Shilton was powerless as Gotsmanov drilled his shot low to the left hand corner.

The veteran Blokhin, still a magnificent player, then produced a superb run and shot which just clipped the outside of a post. The outstanding feature of the Soviet play was their incredible pace. In midfield, England, quite frankly, were overrun. Bryan Robson looked jaded after his long hard season, and it left too much for Ray Wilkins to cover. Steve Hunt and Mark Hateley went on as substitutes as Bobby Robson shuffled his pack to try and rescue the situation. Wilkins created a half-chance for Hateley almost immediately but Dasaev saved and the goalkeeper was there again straight afterwards, when Wilkins himself put in a shot.

Sadly, there was little conviction in England's attacks and it came as no real surprise when, in the last minute, the pace of the Russians once again exposed the ponderous home defenders. Blokhin outpaced them all before hitting a fierce shot at goal. Shilton parried it but looked on in horror as Protasov, who had only been on the field for two minutes, followed up to score a second goal for the Soviet Union. It was certainly no less than the impressive visitors deserved.

> 8th match v USSR.
> Debut, as substitute, for Hateley.

Brazil v England Friendly

Played on Sunday, 10 June 1984 in the Maracana Stadium, Rio de Janeiro.

Brazil: Costa (Vasco da Gama); Leandro (Flamengo), Mozer (Flamengo), Ricardo (Fluminense), Junior (Flamengo), Zenon (Corinthians), Pires (Vasco da Gama), Assis (Gremio), Renato (Gremio), Roberto (Vasco da Gama), Tato (Fluminense).
Subs: Vladmir (Corinthians) for Leandro and Reinaldo (Atlético Mineiro) for Roberto.

England: P.L.Shilton (Southampton); M.Duxbury (Man Utd), K.G.Sansom (Arsenal), R.C.Wilkins (Man Utd), D.Watson (Norwich C), T.W.Fenwick (QPR), B.Robson (Man Utd, captain), M.V.Chamberlain (Stoke C), M.W.Hateley (Portsmouth), A.S.Woodcock (Arsenal), J.C.B.Barnes (Watford).
Sub: C.D.Allen (Spurs) for Woodcock.

Half-time 0-1   Full-time 0-2
Ref: J.Cardelino (Chile)   Att: 56,126

THE magnificent Maracana Stadium was

the setting for this, one of England's greatest ever triumphs. The thrilling way that the visitors set about their illustrious hosts would be talked about for many years to come, as would one of their two goals.

It all began quietly as the England back four nervously repelled the famous early onslaught from the Brazilians. Renato gave Kenny Sansom a hard time with his speed and trickery and only Peter Shilton of the defence was showing his true form in this spell. The goalkeeper saved well from Renato and then made a brilliant stop to prevent Zenon scoring after Assis had miskicked. Renato then missed another chance before England gradually got going.

Ray Wilkins and Bryan Robson were working hard in midfield and eventually Mark Hateley tested Costa with a good header which then led to an England counter-thrust. Hateley found John Barnes with a lovely pass and the winger set off on a fine run which eventually was stopped, although not before the crowd had taken note of the silky skills of the Watford player. Just before the interval even the home fans stood to applaud what will go down as one of the best goals ever scored by an England player.

Hateley again began the move when his challenge for a header eventually led to the ball running to Barnes who was out wide on the left. The England players urged him to run at the defenders and the winger obliged with the most spectacular of dribbles. Cutting inside he took on and beat the entire home defence, one after the other, until his last touch put the ball past the bamboozled goalkeeper. The crowd just could not believe that an Englishman had the cheek to play Brazil at their own game and succeed. It was a wonderful moment that will live in the memory for ever.

Half-time came to give everyone time to catch their breath and after the break the growing confidence could be seen in everything the England players tried. Robson and Wilkins were superb in midfield and though the Brazilians were missing several key players nothing should be taken away from the England performance. They also had the bulk of the second half with Barnes, Mark Chamberlain and Hateley all showing tremendous ability, with the two wingers more than justifying their selection.

Brazil created only one genuine chance in the second half, which was testament to the strength of the England defence, whereas the visitors always looked dangerous when they attacked. Just after the hour they deservedly went further ahead. A lovely flowing move involving Wilkins, Tony Woodcock and Barnes ended with a fine cross deep to the far post. Costa never got near it and in roared Hateley to score with a thumping header. A sensational result was now a distinct probability. Indeed, England could have added to their lead when first Woodcock and then Robson both missed good chances.

Eventually the referee blew his whistle to end the match and England were able to celebrate a very famous victory.

> 13th match v Brazil.
> Debuts for Watson and, as substitute, Allen.

Uruguay v England Friendly

Played on Wednesday, 13 June 1984 in the Centenary Stadium, Montevideo.

Uruguay: R.Rodriguez (Nacional); N.Gutierrez (Peñarol), E.Acevedo (Defensor), N.Montelongo (Peñarol), M.Bassio (Peñarol), D.Martinez (Danubio), C.Aguilera (Nacional), R.Perdomo (Nacional), W.Cabrera (Nacional), J.Carrasco (Nacional), L.Acosta (Wanderers).
Sub: R.Sosa (Danubio) for Acosta.
England: P.L.Shilton (Southampton); M.Duxbury (Man Utd), K.G.Sansom (Arsenal), R.C.Wilkins (Man Utd), D.Watson (Norwich C), T.W.Fenwick (QPR), B.Robson (Man Utd, captain), M.V.Chamberlain (Stoke C), M.W.Hateley (Portsmouth), C.D.Allen (Spurs), J.C.B.Barnes (Watford).
Sub: A.S.Woodcock (Arsenal) for Allen.

Half-time 1-0   Full-time 2-0
Ref: G.Gonzales (Paraguay)   Att: 32,800

THE England players were brought crashing back down to earth by this defeat in Montevideo. After the euphoria of the previous Sunday's victory in Brazil, England were hoping to go on from that thrilling win by beating Uruguay. Alas, it was not to be.

They suffered a dreadful set-back as early as the seventh minute when Mark Hateley, who played so well in Rio, was harshly adjudged to have brought down the flying winger Acosta just inside the penalty area. The referee pointed to the spot much to England's horror and Acosta himself scored from the penalty kick. It was a bitter blow, especially coming so early in the game, but to their credit the visitors knuckled down and were soon fighting back.

Clive Allen will want to forget this match. He had already missed a fine chance in the first minute before he then missed another clear opportunity on the quarter hour. Mark Chamberlain spent much of the match hurdling over some of the outrageous challenges coming in from the Uruguayans, although he did put in one shot that he pulled just wide from a good position. Dave Watson had two good efforts cleared from off the line as England continued a spirited fight-back, and the team also showed commendable restraint after some truly hostile tackles.

On returning to the pitch after half-time England were kept waiting for around five minutes as the Uruguayans kept their guests wondering just when the second half was going to start. The visitors were understandably annoyed at this antic but did not let it upset their game upon the eventual restart. Indeed, had Allen been able to find the finish he had done all season at White Hart Lane, then England could have been well ahead by this time. Hateley flicked on Chamberlain's long throw but Allen's shot was blocked. Then Ray Wilkins' lovely pass gave him a fourth opportunity, which again he squandered.

The Uruguayans, in between the bouts of rough stuff, showed some lovely skills and looked a better side than Brazil on this showing. Acosta, before injury curtailed his game, and Aguilera were full of tricks and were a real handful for the English defenders. The home team's

sharpness was seen to the full on 68 minutes. Perdomo crossed from the right, just over Watson's head, to find Cabrera, who controlled the ball and shot past Peter Shilton all in one movement for a splendidly taken goal.

The unfortunate Allen was substituted by Tony Woodcock before the end but there was then little hope of a comeback. Despite a spirited performance, the earlier missed chances had cost England dearly.

7th match v Uruguay.
Penalty scored for Uruguay by Acosta.

Chile v England Friendly

Played on Sunday, 17 June 1984 in the National Stadium, Santiago.

Chile: R.Rojas (Colo Colo); H.Tabilo (Cobreloa), E.Gomez (Cobreloa), L.Hormazabal (Colo Colo), M.Araya (Cobresal), A.Hisis (Colo Colo), C.Toro (Magallanes), J.Soto (Naval), L.Venegas (Magallanes), J.Aravena (Universidad Catolica), J.Cavarrubias (Cobreloa).
Subs: E.Cofre (Santiago Wanderers) for Toro, L.Rodrigues (Universidad de Chile) for Soto and H.Puebla (Cobreloa) for Cavarrubias.
England: P.L.Shilton (Southampton); M.Duxbury (Man Utd), K.G.Sansom (Arsenal), R.C.Wilkins (Man Utd), D.Watson (Norwich C), T.W.Fenwick (QPR), B.Robson (Man Utd, captain), M.V.Chamberlain (Stoke C), M.W.Hateley (Portsmouth), C.D.Allen (Spurs), J.C.B.Barnes (Watford).
Sub: S.Lee (Liverpool) for Chamberlain.

Half-time 0-0   Full-time 0-0
Ref: L.Felix (Brazil)   Att: 3,876

THE last match of England's South American tour ended with the most disappointing of their three games. The goalless draw with Chile did nothing to maintain England's reputation which had been built on two excellent performances in Brazil and Uruguay. Maybe the subconscious of the players allowed them to relax too much, especially as the pre-match verdict hinted at an easier game against the weakest of the three nations. Whatever the reason England did not play well.

With the snow-capped Andes mountains producing an impressive backdrop to the stadium, England began confidently and were soon creating chances. There was little wrong with their approach play and Bryan Robson and Ray Wilkins were soon in command of the midfield. But once again their problem was up front where nobody was able to cash in on the many chances created.

Chile's goalkeeper, Rojas, was undoubtedly their star as he defied England with a series of fine saves. He tipped over a good shot by Wilkins and then kept out a glancing header by Clive Allen, a shot by John Barnes, a diving header by Wilkins, a ferocious effort from Robson and a chip by Barnes. Chile's only reply came from Aravena, who is reputed to have the hardest shot in the world, but Peter Shilton was alert to the danger. England just could not find a way through. Numerous deflections and scrambles also threatened Rojas's goal but

the one score that probably would have sealed the game just would not come. As the game wore on it became obvious that England would not score the goal their overwhelming superiority deserved. The biggest disappointment was Barnes. He rarely seemed to have an appetite for the game and showed nothing of his finishing power.

Shilton made one other save from Cavarrubias in what was, for the goalkeeper, an easy international. England had only themselves to blame him not ending the tour on a high note but they were not good enough on the day. This disappointed the small crowd who had mostly come to see the English team.

3rd match v Chile.

England v East Germany Friendly

Played on Wednesday, 12 September 1984 at Wembley Stadium.

England: P.L.Shilton (Southampton); M.Duxbury (Man Utd), K.G.Sansom (Arsenal), S.C.Williams (Southampton), M.Wright (Southampton), T.I.Butcher (Ipswich T), B.Robson (Man Utd, captain), R.C.Wilkins (Man Utd), P.Mariner (Ipswich T), A.S.Woodcock (Arsenal), J.C.B.Barnes (Watford).
Subs: M.W.Hateley (Milan AC) for Mariner and T.J.Francis (Sampdoria) for Woodcock.
East Germany: R.Müller (1.FC Lokomotive Leipzig); R.Kreer (1.FC Lokomotive Leipzig), H-J.Dorner (SG Dynamo Dresden), D.Stahmann (1.FC Magdeburg), U.Zotzsche (1.FC Lokomotive Leipzig), R.Troppa (BFC Dynamo), M.Leibers (1.FC Lokomotive Leipzig), W.Steinbach (1.FC Magdeburg), J.Streich (1.FC Magdeburg), R.Ernst (BFC Dynamo), R.Minge (SG Dynamo Dresden).
Sub: H.Richter (1.FC Lokomotive Leipzig) for Streich.

Half-time 0-0   Full-time 1-0
Ref: A.R.Thomas (Holland)   Att: 23,951

LESS than 24,000 people turned up at Wembley to see this international and the empty spaces meant the stadium had very little in the way of atmosphere. As a result the players could not raise their game and the match was a poor one.

For England the same old problem raised its ugly head again, as the attack looked woefully short of ideas. Finishing was a nightmare for them during this time, making it very difficult for them to win games. Again there was no shortage of possession with Ray Wilkins playing superbly in midfield. Unfortunately some of his colleagues rarely showed the form of which they were capable so England, naturally, struggled.

A lovely pass from Wilkins sent Kenny Sansom clear down the left after ten minutes' play. Steve Williams met Sansom's cross with a good header at goal, only for Müller to make a fine tip-over save. But apart from that incident there were few efforts which troubled the German goalkeeper. Paul Mariner twice and Williams again put in other shots but Müller was able to save those easily.

The East Germans seemed to have a very

laid back attitude towards the game and showed little urgency. However, a couple of swift counter attacks had Peter Shilton in the action and their best forward was undoubtedly the outstanding Streich, who became the 12th player to win 100 caps in international football. One of his shots grazed the outside of a post with Shilton scrambling across goal.

After the interval, with England's attack by now almost non-existent, the game looked destined to be goalless. The Germans seemed content just to avoid defeat which would continue their very impressive run of recent results. Bobby Robson, meanwhile, decided to send on Trevor Francis and Mark Hateley for the ineffective Mariner and Tony Woodcock. Immediately there was an improvement. Francis sent Mike Duxbury forward with a good pass and then the move switched across field to the left. Sansom gained possession and hit a deep cross over to the far post, where Wilkins nodded the ball back for Bryan Robson to volley home a superb goal. It was a goal totally out of step with the mediocrity of the match as a whole but it was enough to give England a win.

As for the rest, it was best forgotten.

> 4th match v East Germany.

England v Finland   World Cup Qualifier

Played on Wednesday, 17 October 1984 at Wembley Stadium.

England: P.L.Shilton (Southampton); M.Duxbury (Man Utd), K.G.Sansom (Arsenal), S.C.Williams (Southampton), M.Wright (Southampton), T.I.Butcher (Ipswich T), B.Robson (Man Utd, captain), R.C.Wilkins (Milan AC), M.W.Hateley (Milan AC), A.S.Woodcock (Arsenal), J.C.B.Barnes (Watford).
Subs: G.A.Stevens (Spurs) for Duxbury and M.V.Chamberlain (Stoke C) for Robson.

Finland: O.Huttunen (Valkeakosken Haka); E.Pekonen (Kuusysi Lahti), P.Kymalainen (TPS Turku), A.A.Lahtinen (Notts Co), E.Petaja (TPS Turku), K.Hasskivi (Cleveland Force), L.Houtsonen (KuPS Kuopio), K.Ukkonen (KSV Cercle Brugge), J.Ikalainen (Örgryte IS), P.Rautiainen (Arminia Bielefeld), A.Valvee (Vasalund).
Subs: H.Turunen (KuPS Kuopio) for Haaskivi and A.Hjelm (Ilves Tampere) for Valvee.

Half-time 2-0   Full-time 5-0
Ref: A.Suchanek (Poland)   Att: 47,234

ENGLAND'S new World Cup challenge got off to a flying start with this emphatic win over Finland. The crowd, later announced as the lowest ever for a home World Cup match, were none the less delighted with the performance. Before the game an electrical fault put the Wembley floodlights out, leaving the Finns bemused and bewildered as they tried to warm up. When the game started they were left with the same feelings.

England began slowly in the first half gradually increasing their pressure on Huttunen in the Finnish goal. The goalkeeper did not look particularly safe,

especially with his tendency to punch the ball rather than catch it. Tony Woodcock twice had him in trouble and several other England attempts only just missed. When the first goal did arrive several home players had a foot in it. Steve Williams' free-kick hit the defensive wall, but Terry Butcher fired in the rebound. That hit Woodcock but the ball ran loose for John Barnes to shoot against the bar. From the rebound the ball found Mark Hateley, who shot home from a tight angle. It was a nice way for him to celebrate the visit of his father Tony Hateley, who was at the stadium to see him play.

The second goal followed in the 41st minute and was even more of a scramble. Bryan Robson found Woodcock, but Huttunen blocked the shot. Unfortunately for the goalkeeper the ball rebounded towards the near post. Defenders Pekonen and Kymalainen looked able to clear but inexplicably got in each other's way. This gave Woodcock the chance to follow up to make a decisive second touch. The first half had belonged to England but one dangerous Finnish break saw Ukkonen centre for Houtsonen to head wide.

Bobby Robson decided to switch Mike Duxbury with substitute Gary Stevens and the Spurs defender was soon in action as the second half began. Five minutes into the half, Stevens set up Hateley for a fine 40-yard run. Showing superb control, he beat two defenders and slipped the ball under Huttunen for a fine goal. Hateley continued to impress and in the 70th minute he headed a Barnes cross back towards Woodcock. The Arsenal player miscued but Robson was there to take advantage, prodding home England's fourth goal.

The home side were now in complete control and with two minutes to go Kenny Sansom enjoyed a special moment when he scored his first goal for his country. A low cross from another substitute, Mark Chamberlain, was missed by Woodcock and Hateley as well as all the Finnish defenders. It found Sansom free and keeping his eye firmly on the ball, he joyfully swept a shot past Huttunen. In more ways than one it had been a black night for Finland.

> 7th match v Finland.
> Debut, as substitute, for Stevens.

Turkey v England   World Cup Qualifier

Played on Wednesday, 14 November 1984 in the Inönü Stadium, Istanbul.

Turkey: Yasar Duran (Fenerbahçe); Ismail Kartal (Fenerbahçe), Yusuf Altintas (Galatasaray), Kemal Sardar (Trabzonspor), Cem Pamiroğlu (Fenerbahçe), Rasit Cetiner (Galatasaray), Mujdat Yetkiner (Fenerbahçe), Ridvan Dilmen (Fenerbahçe), Ahmet Keloğlu (Kocaelispor), Ilyas Tufekci (Fenerbahçe), Erdal Keser (Galatasaray).
Sub: Hasan Sengün (Trabzonspor) for Ilyas.

England: P.L.Shilton (Southampton); V.A.Anderson (Arsenal), K.G.Sansom (Arsenal), S.C.Williams (Southampton), M.Wright (Southampton), T.I.Butcher (Ipswich T), B.Robson (Man Utd, captain), R.C.Wilkins (Milan AC), P.Withe

(Aston Villa), A.S.Woodcock (Arsenal), J.C.B.Barnes (Watford).
Subs: G.A.Stevens (Spurs) for Williams and T.J.Francis (Sampdoria) for Withe.

Half-time 0-3   Full-time 0-8
Ref: K.Christov (Czechoslovakia)
Att: 40,000

ON a cold afternoon in Istanbul, England produced a fine exhibition of high-class finishing to totally overwhelm a poor Turkish side. It was their best away win since they beat the USA 10-0 in 1964 and now they were in an excellent position at the head of their qualifying group.

England were on the attack immediately and when they won their first corner on the quarter hour, they soon exposed Turkey's weakness in the air. Ray Wilkins floated in the kick and Terry Butcher beat the groping Yasar to the ball, flicking it on for Viv Anderson to also help it on, into the path of the marauding skipper Bryan Robson who headed a typical goal at the far post. Hardly had the Turks recovered from that blow when four minutes later Butcher tackled Rasit and released Tony Woodcock with a lovely pass. The Arsenal player ran on before beating Yasar with a crisp shot.

There were an unusually high number of left-footed players in the England side, so it was important for Steve Williams to hold his position on the right so that the balance would be there. When he strayed inside manager Bobby Robson was visibly annoyed as he hopped around the touch-line gesticulating at the Southampton star. But right on half-time, Williams created a third goal with a fine run. He almost scored himself after breaking clear but Yasar managed to touch the shot on to a post. The save did not do the goalkeeper much good however as Bryan Robson reacted swiftly to beat Woodcock to the rebound and score.

After the interval it was simply a matter of how many England would score. Only three minutes into the half John Barnes notched his first goal since that memorable effort in Brazil. Soon afterward the Watford man scored again for good measure and then, after a glorious move and combination with the outstanding Wilkins, Robson completed his hat-trick with a brilliant sixth goal. It was seven on the hour as Woodcock, with the help of Anderson and Wilkins, rifled another goal past the, by now, thoroughly despondent Yasar in the Turkey goal.

It was embarrassingly easy for the visitors and umpteen chances went begging. Woodcock twice, and Peter Withe, also twice, could have added to the total, and Gary Stevens had a goal disallowed. Anderson might have had a penalty had he fallen in the area when tripped, but then, with four minutes to go, the Arsenal defender repeated his clubmate Kenny Sansom's feat of the previous match by

> 1st match v Turkey.
> Hat-trick for Robson.
> *"My favourite player of my era was without any doubt Bryan Robson, who in my opinion was one of England's greatest players. He really was inspirational, a great colleague and down to earth. A manager's player and a great professional."*
> Terry Butcher

Bryan Robson (7) opens the scoring against Turkey in Istanbul in November 1984.

scoring his first international goal to make it 8-0.

Bobby Robson's after match quote said it all. "It is not often you score eight and yet feel you have let your opponents off the hook!"

Northern Ireland v England World Cup Qualifier

Played on Wednesday, 27 February 1985 at Windsor Park, Belfast.

Northern Ireland: P.A.Jennings (Arsenal); J.M.Nicholl (West Brom), M.M.Donaghy (Luton T), J.P.O'Neill (Leicester C), J.McClelland (Watford), P.C.Ramsey (Leicester C), G.J.Armstrong (Real Mallorca), S.B.McIlroy (Stoke C), J.M.Quinn (Blackburn R), N.Whiteside (Man Utd), I.E.Stewart (QPR).
England: P.L.Shilton (Southampton); V.A.Anderson (Arsenal), K.G.Sansom (Arsenal), R.C.Wilkins (Milan AC, captain), A.E.Martin (West Ham), T.I.Butcher (Ipswich T), T.M.Steven (Everton), G.A.Stevens (Spurs), M.W.Hateley (Milan AC), A.S.Woodcock (Arsenal), J.C.B.Barnes (Watford).
Sub: T.J.Francis (Sampdoria) for Woodcock.

Half-time 0-0   Full-time 0-1

Ref: V.Roth (West Germany) Att: 28,000

ENGLAND took another giant step towards the Mexico World Cup finals with this win in a difficult fixture in Belfast. Northern Ireland, beaten only once in five years here, were formidable opponents who needed the points as much as their visitors from across the Irish Sea.

There was a mist hanging over the

ground as the crowd gathered for this important match. The game itself, though, was not of the highest international quality but was interesting none the less. England began well with Mark Hateley soon testing goalkeeper Jennings with a good left-foot shot. The goalkeeper was equal to it, however, and was as determined as most to keep his goal intact on what, for him, was a very special night. In winning his 108th cap he was equalling Bobby Moore's British record of appearances.

John Barnes was also effective early on and gave Jimmy Nicholl a roasting as he went both inside and outside the full-back. Unfortunately, this bright start by England faded as the Irish gained momentum. One Armstrong run was only stopped by a crucial interception by Viv Anderson and England's only threat for some time came from a Ray Wilkins chip. The skipper was holding his side together well, showing his usual composure, whilst at the back Terry Butcher was in commanding form. Alvin Martin was not having the best of games though and he was booked for a foul on Whiteside. Moments later the West Ham man was lucky to stay on the field after another badly-timed tackle brought McIlroy down.

Just before half-time England came very close to conceding a goal. Donaghy put in a good centre which was met by Quinn's head. The header beat Peter Shilton all ends up, but crashed against the crossbar before being cleared. That signalled the end of a half that was just edged by Northern Ireland.

Gary Stevens opened the second half with a volley that flew just wide, but it was Quinn again who caused further danger with another header from a Stewart cross. Butcher could only head clear as

far as Armstrong, who then hit a shot which was deflected wide.

Ireland chased everything in a tireless way, but all the time they were pushing forward in search of a winner, there was always the chance that England could snatch something on the break. And that is exactly what happened in the 76th minute. A long clearance from Martin was challenged for by Hateley, who then turned and ran on to the loose ball. With a superb piece of finishing, he then drew Jennings out of goal before hitting a clinical right-foot shot into the net. The goal proved decisive and deserved the title 'matchwinner'. It was also a personal triumph for the man the Milan AC fans had nicknamed 'Attila'.

> 93rd match v Northern Ireland.
> Debut for Steven.

England v Republic of Ireland Friendly

Played on Tuesday, 26 March 1985 at Wembley Stadium.

England: G.R.Bailey (Man Utd); V.A.Anderson (Arsenal), K.G.Sansom (Arsenal), T.M.Steven (Everton), M.Wright (Southampton), T.I.Butcher (Ipswich T), B.Robson (Man Utd, captain), R.C.Wilkins (Milan AC), M.W.Hateley (Milan AC), G.W.Lineker (Leicester C), C.R.Waddle (Newcastle Utd).
Subs: G.Hoddle (Spurs) for Robson and P.Davenport (Nottm Forest) for Hateley.
Republic of Ireland: P.Bonner (Celtic); C.W.G.Hughton (Spurs), J.M.Beglin (Liverpool), M.T.Lawrenson (Liverpool), M.J.McCarthy (Man City), W.L.Brady

Robson in determined action again, this time against Romania in Bucharest in May 1985. The Romanian player is Nicolae Ungureanu.

(Inter-Milan), R.A.Whelan (Liverpool), G.P.Waddock (QPR), E.O'Keefe (Port Vale), F.A.Stapleton (Man Utd), P.McGrath (Man Utd).
Subs: K.O'Callaghan (Portsmouth) for Whelan, J.F.Byrne (QPR) for O'Keefe and D.A.O'Leary (Arsenal) for McGrath.

Half-time 1-0   Full-time 2-1
Ref: G.Smith (Scotland)   Att: 34,793

ENGLAND maintained their winning sequence at Wembley with this victory over the Irish. That made five wins in a row, only tarnished by conceding a late goal, the first they had let in nine hours of football.

It was soon apparent that the game would revolve around two central characters, Ray Wilkins for England and Liam Brady for the Irish. Both players showed the effects of their continental education at that time being enjoyed at their respective clubs, but it was Wilkins who had the better of this personal duel. He was soon involving Trevor Steven and Chris Waddle in some splendid moves and, with Mark Hateley combining well with Gary Lineker, there were plenty of options for England. Brady had no such options with his attack and his best work went unrewarded.

Hateley twice went close and then Kenny Sansom, who was making several fine runs down the left, put in a dangerous cross which Bonner only just scrambled around a post. The full-back then fired in a good right-foot shot before setting up Hateley for another shot which Bonner again saved. Another defender, Terry Butcher, also moved forward when possible and just before half-time his cross brushed Hateley's head before dropping

to Steven, who side-stepped Beglin's challenge and shot home his first goal for his country.

England's tactics were hindered after half-time as Lawrenson stifled Sansom's room down the left by closing him down more. With Bryan Robson then being carried off with a badly bruised ankle after a tackle by O'Keefe and Hateley also having to go off with an injury, it meant that England had to totally reorganise. But Peter Davenport was a lively replacement for Hateley and he was soon helping Lineker to score a marvellous second goal.

Lineker took possession and, veering to the left of goal, he cleverly clipped a fine shot over Bonner for a goal of sheer class. It was a marvellous way for the Leicester City player to open his scoring account for England.

England then lost their overall control and by the latter stages of the game they seemed content to just sit on the two-goal cushion. This gave the Irish the chance to come back into the game, but it was not until the last minute that they were able to pull a goal back. Unfortunately, debutant Gary Bailey was at fault as he fumbled Brady's shot over the line after Ireland's best player had interchanged passes with Stapleton.

9th match v Republic of Ireland.
Debuts for Bailey, Waddle and, as substitute, Davenport.

Romania v England World Cup Qualifer

Played on Wednesday, 1 May 1985 in the 23 August Stadium, Bucharest.

Romania: S.Lung (Universitatea Crai-

ova); N.Negrilă (Universitatea Craiova), C.Ştefănescu (Universitatea Craiova), N.Ungureanu (Universitatea Craiova), M.Rednic (Dinamo Bucharest), G.Iorgulescu (Sportul Studenţesc Bucharesti), M.Coras, (Sportul Studenţesc Bucharest), M.Klein (Cornivul Hunedoara), R.Cămătaru (Universitatea Craiova), L.Bölöni (Steaua Bucharest), G.Hagi (Sportul Studenţesc Bucharesti).
Subs: S.Iovan (Steaua Bucharest) for Iorgulescu and M.Lăcătus, (Steaua Bucharest) for Coras.
England: P.L.Shilton (Southampton); V.A.Anderson (Arsenal), K.G.Sansom (Arsenal), T.M.Steven (Everton), M.Wright (Southampton), T.I.Butcher (Ipswich T), B.Robson (Man Utd, captain), R.C.Wilkins (Milan AC), P.Mariner (Arsenal), T.J.Francis (Sampdoria), J.C.B.Barnes (Watford).
Subs: G.W.Lineker (Leicester C) for Mariner and C.R.Waddle (Newcastle Utd) for Barnes.

Half-time 0-0   Full-time 0-0
Ref: E.Guruceta (Spain)   Att: 70,000

INTERNATIONAL football matches in Romania can be pretty daunting so England's trip to Bucharest for this vital World Cup qualifier was considered the key as to whether they could progress to the finals. Therefore, the hard won point at the end of the day was gratefully received by Bobby Robson and his team.

The first half-hour went particularly well for England. They started positively, keeping possession and marking tightly, giving the Romanians no room to string their moves together. The visitors were also able to mount some excellent attacks themselves. John Barnes was dangerous down the wing and his crosses were exposing Romania's weakness in the air. Trevor Steven, somewhat surprisingly, was the best attacker and he put in two headers, both of which only just missed the target. Then Bryan Robson met a free-kick in typical fashion and was desperately unlucky to see his header strike the angle of the post and crossbar.

Gradually though the good start faded and England's attacks became fewer and fewer. Romania took over the midfield from the previously commanding Robson and Ray Wilkins, and from the moment that the dangerous Hagi thundered a powerful shot into Peter Shilton's arms it was to be a backs-to-the-wall situation. Negrillă fired in two fierce drives and Cămătaru almost broke through with another effort.

The second half was affected by Romania losing their sweeper Iorgulescu to injury five minutes before the interview. He had been the linchpin of the side and they were never as effective after he went off. Despite this, and urged on by a passionate crowd, Cămătaru forced a superb save from Shilton and then Bölöni put in another good shot which was again well saved by Shilton.

England were really up against it now and only 100 per cent effort from the whole side would ensure their goal was kept intact. To this end, Bobby Robson had all his substitutes warming up on the touch-line in an effort to gee up his team. With 20 minutes to go, England almost snatched a goal. Kenny Sansom's long throw was touched on by Terry Butcher and Robson met it to fire in a shot. That was blocked but the ball found Paul Mariner who only had to touch it into the net from close range. To the dismay of his colleagues, he somehow put the ball wide. That was a golden chance of victory for England, and indeed, their last chance of the match, a bad miss by the ineffective Mariner.

Ten minutes later only another brilliant save by Shilton rescued England as Ungureanu set up Hagi. The right-foot shot was well smothered by the 'keeper. When the final whistle blew it came as a great relief for the England players with this result seeing them almost on the plane to Mexico.

> 7th match v Romania.
> Sansom's 50th cap.

Finland v England World Cup Qualifier

Played on Wednesday, 22 May 1985 in the Olympic Stadium, Helsinki.

Finland: O.Huttunen (Valkeakosken Haka); A.Lahtinen (Notts Co), P.Kymalainen (TPS Turku), J.Ikalainen (KuPS Kuopio), J.Nieminen (HJK Helsinki), H.Turunen (KuPS Kuopio), L.Houtsonen (KuPS Kuopio), K.Ukkonen (CS Bruges), M.Lipponen (TPS Turku), P.Rautiainen (Arminia Bielefeld), J.Rantanen (HJK Helsinki). Subs: E.Petäjä (Östers IF) for Lahtinen and A.Hjelm (Ilves Tampere) for Ukkonen.
England: P.L.Shilton (Southampton); V.A.Anderson (Arsenal), K.G.Sansom (Arsenal), T.M.Steven (Everton), T.W.Fenwick (QPR), T.I.Butcher (Ipswich T), B.Robson (Man Utd, captain),

R.C.Wilkins (Milan AC), M.W.Hateley (Milan AC), T.J.Francis (Sampdoria), J.C.B.Barnes (Watford). Sub: C.R.Waddle (Newcastle Utd) for Steven.

Half-time 1-0   Full-time 1-1
Ref: S.Kirschen (East Germany) Att: 30,000

ENGLAND, who had never been beaten by Finland, travelled to Helsinki looking for the two points that would guarantee them a place in the next year's World Cup finals. It was a cold, grey day and within five minutes the weather was the least of England's worries as the Finns, incredibly, took the lead.

They had opened strongly, pinning England back on their heels, and when Lahtinen, the Notts County player, took a long throw, there was total confusion in the visitors' defence. Ikalainen nudged the ball on for Lipponen to put in a header. Peter Shilton managed to deflect it on to the bar, but Rantanen was quickest to meet the rebound and prodded the ball over the line.

It was a dreadful blow to England's hopes and two minutes later it could have been even worse. This time it was a through pass that caught them out and Lipponen was away. He rolled his shot past the advancing Shilton, but as the large frame of Rantanen moved in for the kill a saving tackle from Terry Butcher rescued the situation. That was a crucial moment and it enabled the England players to gather their thoughts and energies. Gradually the opening onslaught by Finland subsided and the visitors began to take command.

Three times Trevor Francis went close to an equalizer and his sharpness was the biggest threat to Finland. But the Finns were not overawed and one break saw Turunen almost punish Viv Anderson's mistake, but his final shot was saved by Shilton. By half-time, the balance of play was edging England's way, although they still had to find a goal from somewhere.

Despite Bryan Robson and Ray Wilkins having largely ineffective games, the persistence of the team was still impressive and had to be admired. Five minutes after the restart England, at last, found their equalizer. Full-back Anderson slipped the ball through the home defence and Mark Hateley lunged forward to beat Huttunen's attempted block to force the ball home.

As the game wore on England assumed almost total control but they just could not find another goal. Francis continued to impress and he forced a good save from Huttunen ten minutes from the end. Substitute Chris Waddle and Francis then combined to give Robson a half-chance. This time, though, the England skipper was crowded out of things by a determined Finland defence. Nieminen fired in a free-kick which tested Shilton, but that was the only other serious threat to England's goal.

In the end, both sides had to be content with the draw but in England's case it was surely a point dropped. However, they were still well placed to qualify in their group and now needed only three points from their three home games to ensure their place in Mexico.

> 8th match v Finland.

Scotland v England Rous Cup

Played on Saturday, 25 May 1985 at Hampden Park, Glasgow.

Scotland: J.Leighton (Aberdeen); C.R.Gough (Dundee Utd), M.Malpas (Dundee Utd), R.S.Aitken (Celtic), A.McLeish (Aberdeen), W.Miller (Aberdeen), G.D.Strachan (Man Utd), G.J.Souness (Sampdoria), S.Archibald (Barcelona), J.Bett (SC Lokeren), D.R.Speedie (Chelsea). Sub: M.MacLeod (Celtic) for Strachan.
England: P.L.Shilton (Southampton); V.A.Anderson (Arsenal), K.G.Sansom (Arsenal), G.Hoddle (Spurs), T.W.Fenwick (QPR), T.I.Butcher (Ipswich T), B.Robson (Man Utd, captain), R.C.Wilkins (Milan AC), M.W.Hateley (Milan AC), T.J.Francis (Sampdoria), J.C.B.Barnes (Watford). Subs: G.W.Lineker (Leicester C) for Hoddle and C.R.Waddle (Newcastle Utd) for Barnes.

Half-time 0-0   Full-time 1-0
Ref: M.Vautrot (France)   Att: 66,489

DESPITE the demise of the Home Championship, the annual fixture between England and Scotland was retained and in this game they were competing for a new trophy, the Rous Cup, named after the famous football dignitary, Sir Stanley Rous. The game, switched from Wembley for mainly political and safety reasons, turned out to be a disappointing affair, although the Scots beat the English at Hampden for the first time in nine years.

On a miserably wet day, both sides had key players missing with England making the early running. Glenn Hoddle's shot was easily saved by Leighton, and Trevor Francis then shot wide, both efforts following good passes from Bryan Robson. Souness was booked for a foul on Francis and then both Ray Wilkins and Steve Archibald followed him into the referee's notebook after a bad-tempered clash on the half-way line.

The first half was very poor and there were few other noteworthy goal attempts. Strachan's fine diagonal pass did set up one chance for Bett, but the big Scot pulled his shot wide. At the other end, the lively Francis set up Mark Hateley but the opening was wasted.

Nine minutes after the break, Viv Anderson made a long and spirited run down the field, only for Aitken to end it by fouling the England player. With England stepping up the pace, it seemed that they might just break the deadlock, especially after Chris Waddle replaced the ineffective John Barnes. In one run Waddle beat Miller with some lovely skills but the final pass was not quite converted into a goal. Just when it looked that the game would go England's way, Scotland surprisingly, took the lead. It was the 70th minute when McLeish loped up from the back to find Bett wide on the left. A deep cross accurately picked out Gough and the ball was headed over Shilton and into the net.

Both sides made further substitutions, but there was little else to excite the large crowd. Some disturbances on the terraces added fuel to the 'ban all English fans' brigade and all in all it was a very dismal afternoon for Bobby Robson and his team.

With Souness now in control of the midfield, Scotland easily held on to their lead.

103rd match v Scotland.

Italy v England Three-Team Tournament
Aztec 2,000

Played on Thursday, 6 June 1985 at the Azteca Stadium, Mexico City, Mexico.

Italy: G.Galli (Fiorentina); G.Bergomi (Inter-Milan), P.Vierchowod (Sampdoria), G.Baresi (Inter-Milan), F.Collovati (Inter-Milan), R.Tricella (Verona), B.Conti (AS Roma), S.Bagni (Napoli), G.Galderisi (Verona), A.Di Gennaro (Verona), A.Altobelli (Inter-Milan).
Subs: F.Tancredi (AS Roma) for Galli, A.Cabrini (Juventus) for Collovati, P.Fanna (Verona) for Conti and M.Tardelli (Juventus) for Galderisi.
England: P.L.Shilton (Southampton); M.G.Stevens (Everton), K.G.Sansom (Arsenal), T.M.Steven (Everton), M.Wright (Southampton), T.I.Butcher (Ipswich T), B.Robson (Man Utd, captain), R.C.Wilkins (Milan AC), M.W.Hateley (Milan AC), T.J.Francis (Sampdoria), C.R.Waddle (Newcastle Utd).
Subs: G.Hoddle (Spurs) for Steven, G.W.Lineker (Leicester C) for Francis and J.C.B.Barnes (Watford) for Waddle.

Half-time 0-0   Full-time 2-1

Ref: A.Marquez (Mexico)   Att: 8,000

THE mean Italian defence, so often a feature of their football, was certainly much in evidence again in this meeting in Mexico City. In front of a crowd numbering around 8,000, (which looked lost in the vast Azteca Stadium), the likes of Bergomi, Baresi and Collovati gave little away. The game was part of a special mini-tournament, and it also gave England the opportunity to get a feel of the conditions here as part of their preparations for their expected participation in the following year's World Cup.

England had approached the game looking to play in short bursts to conserve energy in the rarified air, and for over an hour it worked well. But as a spectacle the first half was very poor. It was not until Bagni's wild shot flew high over the bar in the 23rd minute that either goal had been threatened. The England players were given lots of space in the midfield, but as soon as they reached the penalty area the Italians clamped a vice-like grip around their attack. Terry Butcher and Mark Hateley both went close in England's best two moves with Butcher heading just wide after a Trevor Steven cross and Hateley only inches away from a clever Kenny Sansom centre. Trevor Francis also showed some neat control and Gary Stevens of Everton looked impressive on his debut.

After the interval, the teams continued to probe each other's defences and on 74 minutes it was the Italians who broke the deadlock with a somewhat fortuitous goal. Bagni put in a deep centre from the right and Peter Shilton badly misjudged the flight of the ball. The goalkeeper was horrified to see it drop into the net. Whether the thin air had anything to do with it, one can only wonder. It was most unusual for Shilton to let in a soft goal

Robson is toppled by an Italian defender in the Azteca Stadium.

and all the harder to take when it occurred.

However, almost immediately England equalized. John Barnes crossed and Hateley burst through to bravely head the ball through substitute goalkeeper Tancredi's hands. It was no less than England deserved and for the remainder it looked as though they would earn themselves an honourable draw.

Alas, in the very last minute all their hard work was undone by a terrible refereeing decision. What seemed a perfectly fair tackle by Stevens ended with Vierchwod going down dramatically. Incredibly, the Mexican referee pointed to the penalty-spot despite the anguished protests of the England players. Altobelli converted the kick and England were beaten.

15th match v Italy.
50th cap for Francis.
Penalty scored for Italy by Altobelli.
Debut for Stevens.

Mexico v England Three-Team Tournament
Aztec 2,000

Played on Sunday, 9 June 1985 in the Azteca Stadium, Mexico City.

Mexico: P.Larios (Cruz Azul); M.Trejo (América), F.Quirarte (Guadalajara), F.Bargos, R.Amador, C.Múñoz (UNAM), M.España (UNAM), J.Aguirre (América), M.Negrete (UNAM), M.Boy, L.Flores (UNAM).
Subs: C.De los Cobos for España, C.Hermosillo (América) for Boy and A.Domínguez (América) for Flores.
England: G.R.Bailey (Man Utd); V.A.Anderson (Arsenal), K.G.Sansom (Arsenal), G.Hoddle (Spurs), T.W.Fenwick (QPR), D.Watson (Norwich C), B.Robson (Man Utd, captain), R.C.Wilkins (Milan AC), M.W.Hateley (Milan AC), T.J.Francis (Sampdoria), J.C.B.Barnes (Watford).
Subs: K.M.Dixon (Chelsea) for Hoddle, P.Reid (Everton) for Wilkins and C.R.Waddle (Newcastle Utd) for Barnes.

Half-time 1-0   Full-time 1-0

Ref: V.Roth (West Germany) Att: 15,000

ENGLAND found themselves at the bottom of the table after two games in

this three-team tournament following this defeat by the hosts, Mexico. In a game where they had lots of possession, England were let down by some lacklustre finishing.

Manager Bobby Robson made several changes from the Italy game in an effort to put pressure on the established players before the following year's World Cup. England began well and were soon on the attack, but in the tenth minute Mexico almost capitalised on a mistake by Ray Wilkins. Gary Bailey did well, though, and parried a header by Flores. That was a warning for England which they did not heed. Ten minutes later Wilkins again left Terry Fenwick and Dave Watson exposed and Boy was able to release Flores with a good pass. There was a suspicion of offside but Flores wasted no time before drilling a fierce shot in off the far post.

The first half continued to be played in attractive style with both sides playing open, attacking football. The negative aspects of the other two games played in the tournament so far thankfully did not carry over into this game. However, England's big failing was obvious as their forwards looked unlikely to score if they played all night. Chances were created but Trevor Francis missed a sitter just before Mexico's goal. That chance came after Kenny Sansom's centre was headed down by Bryan Robson straight to Francis' feet. Unfortunately, Francis could only manage a feeble shot and Larios was able to save easily.

Wilkins had a shot cleared off the line after the interval as England tried desperately to pull the goal back. Even the tactical switch to bring on Peter Reid and Kerry Dixon for their first games failed to lift the side.

There was still no punch in attack emphasising England's current goalscoring problem. Only five goals had come in the last seven internationals.

When Viv Anderson outjumped Larios to head into the net it seemed England had equalized, but the referee, somewhat harshly disallowed the goal, saying that Anderson had impeded the goalkeeper.

5th match v Mexico.
Debuts, as substitutes, for Reid and Dixon.

Chris Waddle is on the ball against Mexico. Mark Hateley is the other England player.

West Germany v England
Friendly

Played on Wednesday, 12 June 1985 in the Azteca Stadium, Mexico City, Mexico.

West Germany: H.Schumacher (1.FC Cologne); T.Berthold (Eintracht Frankfurt), A.Brehme (1.FC Kaiserslautern), D.Jakobs (Hamburger SV), M.Herget (Bayer 05 Uerdingen), K.Augenthaler (Bayern Munich), P.Littbarski (1.FC Cologne), L.Matthäus (Bayern Munich), F.Mill (Borussia Mönchengladbach), F.Magath (Hamburger SV), U.Rahn (Borussia Mönchengladbach).
Subs: H.Waas (Bayer 04 Leverkusen) for Littbarski and O.Thon (FC Schalke 04) for Magath.

England: P.L.Shilton (Southampton); M.G.Stevens (Everton), K.G.Sansom (Arsenal), G.Hoddle (Spurs), M.Wright (Southampton), T.I.Butcher (Ipswich T), B.Robson (Man Utd, captain), P.Reid (Everton), K.M.Dixon (Chelsea), G.W.Lineker (Leicester C), C.R.Waddle (Newcastle Utd).
Subs: P.W.Bracewell (Everton) for Robson and J.C.B.Barnes (Watford) for Lineker.

Half-time 0-1   Full-time 0-3
Ref: J.Leanza (Mexico)   Att: 8,000

ENGLAND met West Germany in Mexico City to complete the South American part of their tour. The match was arranged so that both sides could continue to get the feel of the conditions in preparation for the World Cup in 1986. The Germans, who had only two days to acclimatise since arriving, were probably asking too much of their players in view of the huge difference in the playing conditions. In the end it was confirmed by their biggest defeat against England since 1935.

Glenn Hoddle takes the ball away against West Germany in the Azteca Stadium.

Bryan Robson passed a late fitness test and was able to lead his country into battle. He was soon in the thick of things in that famous style of his. Early on, the Germans were having trouble in judging the strength of their passes in the thin air, regularly over-hitting them. But Peter Shilton soon discovered that the Germans still posed a threat with some powerful shooting and had to deal with several good efforts. Glenn Hoddle was England's main architect and he set up a half-chance for Gary Lineker which the striker narrowly failed with.

Then, after almost half an hour's play, Robson should have scored. Peter Reid sent Kenny Sansom away and the cross was met by Robson's outstretched toe, only for the ball to fly over the bar much to Robson's annoyance. A minute later the skipper atoned by giving England the lead. Hoddle chipped the ball towards Kerry Dixon, who chested a pass to Robson. With a controlled strike Robson volleyed the ball past Schumacher.

Seven minutes later, a near disaster almost cost England their deserved lead. Rahn burst through, only to be brought down by Mark Wright's clumsy challenge. It was an obvious penalty and up stepped Brehme for the kick, only for Shilton to dive to his left to make a wonderful tip-around save. That was a body blow for the Germans and it was one they never fully recovered from.

Shilton, meanwhile, was delighted as his record against penalties was none too good normally.

Eight minutes into the second half, England increased their lead. Hesitation by Augenthaler gave Terry Butcher the chance to run for goal. He almost fooled Schumacher but just failed with his effort. However, the rebound fell nicely for Dixon and the Chelsea man scored his first goal for his country.

By this time the Germans were feeling the effects of their late arrival in Mexico and although their long-range shooting was still a threat, Rahn hitting the post with one ferocious drive following a good pass by Matthäus, England were able to control the bulk of the play. It therefore came as no real surprise when they added a third goal after 67 minutes. John Barnes immediately looked lively after he replaced the injured Gary Lineker and it was he who put in a fine cross for Dixon to loop a clever header over the German 'keeper.

> 17th match v West Germany.
> Debut, as substitute, for Bracewell.
> Shilton saved a penalty from Brehme.

USA v
England   Friendly

Played on Sunday, 16 June 1985 in the Coliseum Stadium, Los Angeles.

USA: A.Mausser (unattached); P.Van der Beck (Dallas Sidekicks), M.Windischmann (Adelphi University), D.Canter (Chicago Sting), P.Caligiuri (UCLA), E.Radwanski Uni of N Carolina, Greensboro), K.Crow (San Diego Sockers), J.Kerr (Duke University), H.Perez (San Diego Sockers), R.Davis (St Louis Steamers), B.Murray (Clemson University).
Subs: T.Harris (Los Angeles Lazers) for Mausser, M.Brady (American University) for Canter, T.Synder (Penn State University) for Radwanski, J.Hooker (UCLA) for Kerr and J.Ladouceur (San Diego Sockers) for Murray.
England: C.C.E.Woods (Norwich C), V.A.Anderson (Arsenal), K.G.Sansom (Arsenal), G.Hoddle (Spurs), T.W. Fenwick (QPR), T.I.Butcher (Ipswich T), B.Robson (Man Utd, captain), P.W. Bracewell (Everton), K.M.Dixon (Chelsea), G.W.Lineker (Leicester C), C.R.Waddle (Newcastle Utd).
Subs: D.Watson (Norwich C) for Sansom, T.M.Steven (Everton) for Hoddle, P.Reid (Everton) for Robson and J.C.B.Barnes (Watford) for Waddle.

Half-time 0-2   Full-time 0-5
Ref: E.Codesal (Mexico)   Att: 10,145

ENGLAND ended their tour of the Americas with this easy victory over the United States. In the Coliseum Stadium, Los Angeles, a crowd of just over 10,000 looked lost in the vast bowl that could hold 90,000. Most of the supporters who were there cheering for England who, kitted out in a smart all-white strip, were never in danger against a team totally naïve in the art of tactics.

Chris Woods, making his debut in goal, had to dive sharply at the feet of Radwanski to prevent a shock goal from the Americans, but moments later, in the 13th minute to be exact, England took a deserved lead with a real gem of a goal. A superb chipped pass by Glenn Hoddle was magnificently controlled on his chest and volleyed all in one go by Gary Lineker and the ball flew past the startled Mausser. It was a tremendous piece of finishing that would have graced any stadium in the world.

Two minutes later, Kerry Dixon was brought down in the area only for Hoddle to join the, 'missed a penalty for England' club. Mausser saved the spot-kick but it only delayed the inevitable and on the half-hour the goalkeeper was helpless as Dixon stumbled through a tackle to side-foot home the second goal.

The second half was dominated by England and it was soon 3-0 as Dixon broke down the right before crossing to the far post where Chris Waddle nodded the ball back for Lineker to finish off. Not long afterwards it was Dixon again as substitute goalkeeper Harris could only help the ball in after Dixon's shot from near the penalty shot.

With nine minutes to go England wrapped up a convincing victory with a fifth goal. An acrobatic knock down by Paul Bracewell had set up substitute Trevor Steven for an easy goal, leaving the Americans well beaten. In a match that saw no less than nine substitutions the pride of winning a cap for one's country was somewhat devalued.

> 5th match v USA.
> Debut for Woods.
> Penalty missed for England by Hoddle.

England v
Romania   World Cup Qualifier

Played on Wednesday, 11 September 1985 at Wembley Stadium.

England: P.L.Shilton (Southampton); M.G.Stevens (Everton), K.G.Sansom (Arsenal), T.W.Fenwick (QPR), M.Wright (Southampton), G.Hoddle (Spurs), B.Robson (Man Utd, captain), P.Reid (Everton), M.W.Hateley (Milan AC), G.W.Lineker (Everton), C.R.Waddle (Spurs).
Subs: A.S.Woodcock (Arsenal) for Lineker and J.C.B.Barnes (Watford) for Waddle.
Romania: S.Lung (Universitatea Craiova); N.Negrilă (Universitatea Craiova), C.Ştefănescu (Universitatea Craiova), N.Ungureanu (Universitatea Craiova), M.Rednic (Dinamo Bucharest), S.Iovan (Steaua Bucharest), M.Coraş (Sportul Studenţesc Bucureşti), M.Klein (Corvinul Hunedoara), R.Cămătaru (Universitatea Craiova), L.Bölöni (Steaua Bucharest), G.Hagi (Sportul Studenţesc Bucureşti).
Sub: R.Gabor (Corvinul Hunedoara) for

Coraş and D.Mateuţ (Corvinul Hunedoara) for Klein.

Half-time 1-0   Full-time 1-1
Ref: K.H.Tritschler (West Germany)
     Att: 59,500

ENGLAND were hoping for a win in this match to give them the points they need to guarantee qualification for the World Cup — and but for a linesman's flag they would have had one. As it is they had to wait at least until the Turkey game the following month.

The home side quickly settled into their stride. Peter Reid and Bryan Robson working hard to give Glenn Hoddle the freedom he could exploit. And Hoddle did not disappoint, spraying some lovely passes around the lush Wembley turf. But Romania were a tricky team and still looked dangerous on occasions, especially with their long-range shooting which left the crowd gasping at more than one close call. The main threat came from a little pocket battleship called Hagi. His skill, control and ferocious shooting power gave England plenty to think about.

In ten minutes Hagi almost gave the visitors the lead when he hit a tremendous shot from fully 30 yards which dipped and swerved past Peter Shilton. Luckily for England, the ball rebounded off the crossbar. A short while later Ştefănescu also put in a fierce long-range shot but gradually Reid and Robson began to gain control. After Coraş had been booked for a clumsy challenge on Chris Waddle, Hoddle floated the free-kick on to the head of Terry Fenwick. The Queen's Park Rangers player headed past goalkeeper Lung but the goal was ruled out because Mark Hateley was standing in an offside position. Another lovely piece of play by Hoddle then sent Waddle away and when the cross came in both Hateley and Mark Wright went desperately close to applying the finishing touch.

Midway through the half, England at last got their noses in front. A fine piece of thinking by Kenny Sansom found Hoddle on the left edge of the penalty area. The Spurs player turned elegantly and curled a simple shot around Lung and into the net with the side of his foot. It was a lovely goal and indicative of Hoddle's overall display.

But England were quickly reminded that the game was far from over when Wright's mistake allowed Coraş the chance to feed Hagi. He did everything but score as his shot, clipped over the advancing Shilton, struck the angle of bar and post and England breathed again.

In the second half Romania opened brightly, attacking with purpose in the early exchanges. But England also had their moments and when Lineker chased yet another raking pass from Hoddle, only a fine saving tackle by Bölöni rescued the visitors. Immediately after that near miss the Romanians broke away to equalize. A long pass forward found the tall Cămătaru. He held off Gary Stevens and Wright before shooting past the advancing Shilton.

After their goal, the Romanians seemed content to just shut up shop and allow England no room in or around the penalty area.

> 8th match v Romania.

England v Turkey World Cup Qualifer

Played on Wednesday, 16 October 1985 at Wembley Stadium.

England: P.L.Shilton (Southampton); M.G.Stevens (Everton), K.G.Sansom (Arsenal), G.Hoddle (Spurs), M.Wright (Southampton), T.W.Fenwick (QPR), B.Robson (Man Utd, captain), R.C.Wilkins (Milan AC), M.W.Hateley (Milan AC), G.W.Lineker (Everton), C.R.Waddle (Spurs).
Subs: T.M.Steven (Everton) for Robson and A.S.Woodcock (Arsenal) for Hateley.

Turkey: Yasur Duran (Fenerbahçe); Ismail Demirez (Galatasaray), Yusuf Altinas (Kocaelispor), Rasit Cetiner (Galatasaray), Sedat Ozden (Bursaspor), Abdülkerim Durmaz (Fenerbahçe), Hüseyin Cakiroglu (Fenerbahçe), Mujdat Yetkiner (Fenerbahçe), Şenol Corlu (Fenerbahçe), Hasan Vezir (Trabzonspor), Ünal (Beşiktaş).

Half-time 4-0   Full-time 5-0

Ref: A.Milchenko (USSR)   Att: 52,500

NORTHERN Ireland's magnificent win in Bucharest earlier in the day had given England the qualification they wanted for Mexico even before they had taken the field against Turkey. The afternoon kick-off for the Irish meant that everyone knew the outcome before this game which allowed England to approach it in a relaxed frame of mind.

It soon showed in their play as they repeatedly tore large holes in the weak Turkish defence. As a match it was no contest and England were soon ahead. Gary Lineker saw a shot blocked and Bryan Robson missed a sitter before Chris Waddle broke the deadlock after 15 minutes. Playing in a much more direct manner than of late, the Spurs player set off on a fine run, dragging the ball to his right past two defenders before shooting past Yasar. The goalkeeper might have done better but at least Waddle was off the mark in scoring his first international goal.

Three minutes later it was 2-0 as Glenn Hoddle, revelling in the space he had, sent Gary Stevens away down the right. When the perfect centre came over from the full-back, Lineker had the easiest of tasks to head home.

It was all too easy for England as they pulled the overawed Turkish defenders all over the place. The visitors clung on, sometimes desperately, and it took another 17 minutes before the home side scored again. A lovely pass from Hoddle sent Robson free, the captain firing in a shot which struck a post. A series of rebounds and ricochets returned the ball to Robson again and this time he made no mistake. Then, just before the interval, Lineker was again in the perfect position for another fine cross by Stevens and a powerful header gave Yasar no chance.

Almost immediately after the restart Lineker completed a superb hat-trick by hitting a firm drive wide of the beleaguered goalkeeper. Lineker must have thought it was his birthday as he was left almost totally unmarked. That goal early in the second half should have triggered an avalanche of goals but somehow England lost their way a little. Losing Robson with a pulled hamstring did not help the continuity but the crowd were probably right to feel a little aggrieved that England did not add to their total.

But a win is a win and England could now start planning in earnest for the following summer.

> 2nd match v Turkey.
> Hat-trick for Lineker.

England v World Cup Qualifier Northern Ireland

Played on Wednesday, 13 November 1985 at Wembley Stadium.

England: P.L.Shilton (Southampton); M.G.Stevens (Everton), K.G.Sansom (Arsenal), R.C.Wilkins (Milan AC, captain), M.Wright (Southampton), T.W.Fenwick (QPR), P.W.Bracewell (Everton), G.W.Lineker (Everton), K.M.Dixon (Chelsea), G.Hoddle (Spurs), C.R.Waddle (Spurs).

Northern Ireland: P.A.Jennings (Spurs); C.Nicholl (West Brom), M.M.Donaghy (Luton T), J.P.O'Neill (Leicester C), A.McDonald (QPR), D.McCreery (Newcastle Utd), S.A.Penney (Brighton & HA), S.B.McIlroy (Man City), J.M.Quinn (Blackburn R), N.Whiteside (Man Utd), I.E.Stewart (QPR).
Sub: G.J.Armstrong (West Brom) for Penney and N.Worthington (Sheffield Wed) for Stewart.

Half-time 0-0   Full-time 0-0

Ref: E.Fredriksson (Sweden)   Att: 70,500

WITH England safely qualified for the Mexico finals, the pressure was off them for the visit of Northern Ireland in the last of their Group Three matches. However, for the Irish it was to be a desperate night as they searched for the one point they needed to be sure of accompanying their opponents to South America. At the end of the night there was not one person in the stadium, apart from perhaps the odd Romanian, who begrudged them their reward.

The man largely responsible for the fulfillment of the Irish dream was the big Spurs goalkeeper Pat Jennings. The 40-year-old had a memorable night. The game started quietly. England showed little urgency and the Irish were content to just contain their opponents shutting down early in midfield where the chances are created. Only Glenn Hoddle looked in good form for the home side and most of their better moves stemmed from him. Stewart was assigned to keep him in check and, on the whole, he did a good job. But on the occasions Hoddle escaped the shackles, he created some splendid openings. On the half-hour he all but scored as he moved inside, deliberately curling a superb shot at goal.

Before half-time Hoddle set up Kerry Dixon with a delightful chip that the Chelsea man should have put away. Alas, his header was well wide. It was a bad miss. Then a fine through pass by Ray Wilkins saw Gary Lineker galloping free. Again, though, the shot was wide. The Irish, meanwhile, had shown very little inclination to attack with only Stewart or Quinn creating minor disturbances to the unemployed English defence.

The second half was very poor and the crowd grew restless with England's lack of appetite for the game. As the minutes ticked away the Irish clung on grimly to their precious point although towards the end the tension, for their fans, became almost unbearable. For a split second it seemed that all of their solid and resolute defending had been for nothing when Kenny Sansom's long throw headed for Dixon. McDonald and O'Neill both jumped to challenge and there was what looked a definite hand-ball by one of the defenders. The referee waved aside England's frantic appeals. Then Nicholl almost put through his own goal and with two minutes, left Jennings produced the last of several brilliant saves and it was by far the best.

A cross from Gary Stevens cannoned off the head of Dixon and was looping towards the far side of goal. It looked a certain goal but Jennings adjusted his footing superbly before nonchalently flicking the ball over the bar. The Irishmen in the crowd went wild with delight, but even then Dixon missed another good chance which had the supporters of both sides breathing a heavy sigh, for different reasons. At the final whistle the Irish team were delighted and their resolute defending had earned them their ticket to Mexico. They hoped that Jennings, who was about to retire would postpone his decision until after the finals. Certainly the reception the fans gave him may have swayed his mind.

> 94th match v Northern Ireland.

Egypt v England Friendly

Played on Wednesday, 29 January 1986 in the Nasser Stadium, Cairo.

Egypt: El Batal (Al Ahly); Sidki (Al Ahly), Yassin (Al Ahly), Omar (Ettihad), Saleh (Al Ahly), Ghani (Al Ahly), Majtoub (Al Ahly), Zeid (Al Ahly), Hazem (Ismaili), Abdou (Al Ahly), Yehia (Zamalek).
Subs: G.A.Hamid (Zamalek) for Zeid and Tilissi (Mehalla) for Hazem.

England: P.L.Shilton (Southampton); M.G.Stevens (Everton), K.G.Sansom (Arsenal), G.S.Cowans (Bari), M.Wright (Southampton), T.W.Fenwick (QPR), T.M.Steven (Everton), R.C.Wilkins (Milan AC, captain), M.W.Hateley (Milan AC), G.W.Lineker (Everton), D.Wallace (Southampton).
Subs: C.E.Woods (Norwich C) for Shilton, R.H.Hill (Luton T) for Steven and P.A.Beardsley (Newcastle Utd) for Lineker.

Half-time 0-2   Full-time 0-4

Ref: A.Vasarass (Greece)   Att: 20,000

THIS friendly international saw England visit a foreign land never before visited at this level, so it was quite an adventure for everyone in the party. On a gloriously sunny day and in a big stadium the authorities were disappointed at the poor turn-out of local people. There were about 20,000 in at the start to see the kick-off. In the early stages both teams were cautiously feeling each other out.

But England were soon pushing forward and they took the lead on 15 minutes. Kenny Sansom made a good break inside before slipping a lovely pass to Mark

Hateley on the left. The big centre-forward accelerated and then hit a fierce shot at goal. El Batal managed to parry the effort but only into the path of Trevor Steven who had an easy task to score.

If England then thought that they had an easy game on their hands they were soon having second thoughts. Egypt stormed back and showed just why the emergence of African football was being taken so seriously. But for the outstanding work of England's Peter Shilton they could easily have gone ahead let alone drawn level. Three times Shilton saved, from Hazem's firm header after a cross by Yehia, from Zeid's ferocious close-range effort and finally from Hazem's head again, also following a cross from Yehia.

Hateley relieved the pressure somewhat with two good efforts but it was right on half-time before England scored again. A chip from Ray Wilkins was aimed at Hateley, but the luckless Omar could only deflect his attempted interception wide of his goalkeeper for an own-goal.

If Egypt were looking to fight back in the second half they were soon to be disappointed as England immediately scored a third goal. Wilkins, always in the thick of the action, found Steven with a long pass. Steven made ground before centring for debutant Danny Wallace to fire home an excellent first goal for his country. Shilton then had to be sharp to save two long-range shots from Zeid and Yehia. That was the last contributions from Shilton's great display, as manager Bobby Robson decided to give Chris Woods his second cap, coming on for the last half-hour.

The big blond Norwich goalkeeper was soon bravely diving at the feet of Majtoub after England's back four, not for the first time, had been pierced. Both Mark Wright and Gary Stevens had looked shaky at times and it was certainly a good job that England's goalkeepers had played well.

Peter Beardsley was also given a debut run out, as Gary Lineker limped off, and he quickly got into the action going close with a good start. With ten minutes to go, Gordon Cowans capped a promising display by nonchalently shooting past El Batal from the edge of the area. A late substitution then saw Ricky Hill come on for Steven and Hill almost made it five with a good header which the goalkeeper did well to push on to the bar. El Batal finished the match with another fine save, this time thwarting Wallace.

1st match v Egypt.
Debuts for Wallace and, as substitute, Beardsley.
Debut goal for Wallace.
Own goal scored for England by Omar.

Israel v England　　Friendly

Played on Wednesday, 26 February 1986 in the Ramat Gan Stadium, Tel Aviv.

Israel: A.Ran (Maccabi Haifa); E.Aharoni (Maccabi Haifa), E.Davidi (Hapoel Beer Sheva), M.Ivanir (Maccabi Tel-Aviv), A.Cohen (Maccabi Tel-Aviv), M.Shimonov (Maccabi Tel-Aviv), M.Sinai (Hapoel Tel-Aviv), U.Malmilian (Beitar Jerusalem), Z.Armeli (Maccabi Haifa), R.Turk (Hapoel Tel-Aviv), E.Ohana (Beitar Jerusalem).

Subs: E.Aluf (Bnei Yeuda) for Davidi, E.Cohen (Hapoel Tel-Aviv) for Turk and R.Rosenthal (FC Bruges) for Ohana.
England: P.L.Shilton (Southampton); M.G.Stevens (Everton), K.G.Sansom (Arsenal), R.C.Wilkins (Milan AC), T.I.Butcher (Ipswich T), A.E.Martin (West Ham), B.Robson (Man Utd, captain), G.Hoddle (Spurs), K.M.Dixon (Chelsea), P.A.Beardsley (Newcastle Utd), C.R.Waddle (Spurs).
Subs: C.E.Woods (Norwich C) for Shilton, A.S.Woodcock (Arsenal) for Dixon and J.C.B.Barnes (Watford) for Waddle.

Half-time 1-0　　Full-time 1-2
Ref: A.Mercial (Switzerland)　Att: 15,000

ON A scorching day in Tel Aviv England found life hard in this international arranged to celebrate the opening of this new stadium in the Israeli capital. On a pitch not altogether conducive to good football, the extra experience of the visitors eventually told with an outstanding contribution coming from their captain, Bryan Robson.

An early attack almost brought England a goal as Ran only just beat Kerry Dixon to the ball. Then Davidi floated a back-pass which so nearly beat the goalkeeper, before Robson had a shot deflected just wide. This early pressure from England came to an abrupt end after seven minutes play when a lobbed forward pass by Ivanir caught Terry Butcher and his fellow defenders rather square leaving Ohana a clear run at goal. He eventually shot and although Peter Shilton got a hand to the ball he could not prevent a shock goal for the jubilant Israel team.

Only a desperate intervention by Gary Stevens prevented a similar break by Sinai before England began to cleverly find their way back into the game. They owed much for this to the strong play of their midfield trio of Glenn Hoddle, Robson and Ray Wilkins. Gradually they were able to assert their command on the proceedings. The main source of danger to the Israeli defence came from Peter Beardsley and Robson. Both came close to scoring an equalizer on several occasions before the interval but the final touch could not be found. Dixon, who never really got going, missed probably the best chance of the half and England still trailed at the break.

The Israeli defence still stood firm after half-time with former Liverpool player Avi Cohen the chief organiser. England needed something special to turn their possession into goals and it finally came after 51 minutes. Hoddle, again the playmaker, flighted a fine centre to Robson and the captain volleyed a superb right-foot shot which whistled past Ran, giving the goalkeeper no chance.

Although England were now in control of the game, Israel still looked dangerous when they broke from defence, and when a Stevens error let in Malmilian it looked odds on a goal. But they survived and with Beardsley and Robson still looking the most likely to score, it seemed only a matter of time before England netted again.

Wilkins put in several excellent long-range shots before the balance finally tilted England's way with only four minutes to go. Substitute Tony Woodcock centred from the left and again the ball was met by Robson. This time Avi Cohen denied the Manchester United man a goal

with a hand-ball that prevented the ball crossing the line. Luckily for England it was pretty blatant and an easy decision for the referee to award a penalty. It was Robson himself who appropriately obliged from the spot-kick. After the match some people questioned the wisdom of playing such opposition but the conditions were very similar to what England were to face in Mexico, so it was an excellent experience.

1st match v Israel.
50th cap for Robson.
Penalty scored for England by Robson.

USSR v England　　Friendly

Played on Wednesday, 26 March 1986 in the Dinamo Stadium, Tbilisi.

USSR: R.Dasaev (Spartak Moscow); V.Bessonov (Dinamo Kiev), A.Chivadze (Dinamo Tbilisi), A.Demianenko (Dinamo Kiev), A.Bubnov (Spartak Moscow), O.Kuznetsov (Dinamo Kiev), S.Gotsmanov (Dinamo Minsk), A.Zavarov (Dinamo Kiev), S.Aleinikov (Dinamo Minsk), G.Kondratyev (Guria Lanchkhuti), S.Rodionov (Spartak Moscow).
Subs: O.Blokhin (Dinamo Kiev) for Chivadze, G.Litovchenko (Dinamo Kiev) for Bessonov and I.Dobrovolsky (Dinamo Moscow) for Zavarov.
England: P.L.Shilton (Southampton); V.A.Anderson (Arsenal), K.G.Sansom (Arsenal), R.C.Wilkins (Milan AC, captain), M.Wright (Southampton), T.I.Butcher (Ipswich T), G.Hoddle (Spurs), G.S.Cowans (Bari), G.W.Lineker (Everton), P.A.Beardsley (Newcastle Utd), C.R.Waddle (Spurs).
Subs: S.B.Hodge (Aston Villa) for Cowans and T.M.Steven (Everton) for Waddle.

Half-time 0-0　　Full-time 0-1
Ref: V.Tsonchev (Bulgaria)　Att: 62,500

FACING the might of the Soviet Union in their own land is a daunting enough prospect at any time, but when they had not been beaten at home for two years and not even conceded a goal in 18 matches, then the magnitude of England's task was incredible. But they rose to the occasion superbly.

England settled into their stride quickly despite not being able to field their strongest team. Chris Waddle was prominent and an early centre only just missed after Peter Beardsley had turned it towards goal. Another centre by Waddle flew across goal with Mark Wright desperately close to getting touch. The Soviets, meanwhile, had started nervously and the crowd of over 62,000 had little to cheer and were noticably quiet.

Midway through the half England looked to have won a penalty when Gary Lineker was brought down by the goalkeeper after the striker had run on to a back-pass by Chivadze. But the Bulgarian referee waved away frantic appeals from the England players. Three minutes later the visitors were even more incensed when the referee awarded a penalty against them. Viv Anderson was the culprit having been adjudged to have impeded Gotsmanov. It seemed a very harsh decision and so unjust in relation to the earlier incident when the expected penalty was refused. However, to England's obvious pleasure, Chivadze only succeeded in striking his spot-kick against a post. So perhaps, in the end, justice was seen to be done.

With Russia trying hard to gain the initiative — Zavarov was particularly prominent — play was mainly in the England half, although the visitors strong defence rarely looked in any trouble. Indeed, had Lineker taken advantage of a superb Glenn Hoddle pass then they might even have gained the lead. At half-time it was still goalless and the Russian spectators sensed their team's frustrations when they saw the great Blokhin come out as a second-half substitute. The brilliant front runner had caused a stir by being left out in the first place, so now the crowd had their wish. And he was soon creating havoc. A fast dribble to the by-line and a cross to the middle was met by another substitute, Litovchenko and only a brilliant close-range save by Peter Shilton saved the situation for England.

The goalkeeper had not had much to do up to that moment but the significance of the save was soon evident. Ten minutes later, and with only 20 minutes to go, England scored a golden goal. Chris Waddle aimed a pass into space out on the left. Beardsley chased hard alongside Bubnov and won the race for possession after a good tackle. He then looked up to see Waddle following up, laid the ball into the path of his colleague and watched in delight as Waddle's hard, low left-foot shot zipped past the impressive Dasaev.

Near the end Lineker missed another fine chance following Hoddle's glorious pass, but there was no need to worry too much as the one goal proved enough for a truly magnificent victory and ample revenge for the defeat at Wembley two years earlier.

9th match v USSR.
Debut, as substitute, for Hodge.
Chivadze missed a penalty for Russia.

England v Scotland
Rous Cup

Played on Wednesday, 23 April 1986 at Wembley Stadium.

England: P.L.Shilton (Southampton); M.G.Stevens (Everton), K.G.Sansom (Arsenal), G.Hoddle (Spurs), D.Watson (Norwich C), T.I.Butcher (Ipswich T), R.C.Wilkins (Milan AC, captain), S.B.Hodge (Aston Villa), M.W.Hateley (Milan AC), T.J.Francis (Sampdoria), C.R.Waddle (Spurs).
Subs: P.Reid (Everton) for Wilkins and G.A.Stevens (Spurs) for Hodge.
Scotland: A.Rough (Hibernian); C.R.Gough (Dundee Utd), M.Malpas (Dundee Utd), S.Nicol (Liverpool), A.McLeish (Aberdeen), W.Miller (Aberdeen), G.J.Souness (Sampdoria), R.S.Aitken (Celtic), C.Nicholas (Arsenal), D.R.Speedie (Chelsea), E.J.P.Bannon (Dundee Utd).
Sub: P.K.F.Nevin (Chelsea) for Nicholas.

Half-time 2-0   Full-time 2-1
Ref: M.Vautrot (France)   Att: 68,357

AS usual in these encounters the opening exchanges were at 'gale force' as both sides seeked to gain the upper hand. England, fresh from their triumph in Russia, soon showed the midfield play that had served them so well in that match. Ray Wilkins and Glenn Hoddle attempted to cool the pace of the game down and Steve Hodge looked lively with some decisive breaks down the right. One of his crosses reached Mark Hateley for an early chance but the centre-forward bundled the ball the wrong side of a post.

Unfortunately the tackling became fiercer and the referee, having already booked Dave Watson, was in danger of losing control. But on the half-hour a goal settled things down. It came from England and, not unexpectedly, came from one of the many free-kicks. Miller had flattened Hodge and Hoddle floated the kick deep into the Scotland penalty area. McLeish mis-headed across goal and then Hodge headed the ball back to Terry Butcher who headed past Rough for his first goal in two years. Needless to say the Ipswich player was just a little bit pleased.

England maintained their grip on the game despite a good strike by Souness which Peter Shilton turned around the post. Then with five minutes left before half-time, the home side emphasised their superiority with a second goal. Hoddle, showing all the elegant array of his skills, began the move with a lovely 50-yard pass to full-back Kenny Sansom. The Arsenal player suddenly found himself with an open route to goal, he advanced forward and hit a splendid 30-yard drive which Rough could only push sideways and upwards. The ball was free and who should be there to finish the move with a full-length diving header but Hoddle

England's 1986 World Cup squad. Back row (left to right): Francis, Stevens, Dixon, Hoddle, Martin, Waddle, Watson, Fenwick, Lineker. Middle row: Dr Vernon Edwards (medical officer), Fred Street (physiotherapist), Anderson, Hateley, Shilton, Bailey, Woodcock, Barnes, Don Howe (coach), Norman Medhurst (physiotherapist). Front row: Sansom, Wilkins, Bryan Robson (captain), Bobby Robson (manager), Wright, Steven, Bracewell.

England line up in Mexico. From left to right are Robson, Sansom, Shilton, Stevens, Waddle, Wright, Reid, Hoddle, Dixon, Lineker, Butcher.

who ended the move he had started. An excellent goal and a decisive half-time lead for England.

Eleven minutes into the second half and another fierce tackle resulted in Scotland being given a way back into the match. Butcher's challenge on Nicholas left the Scot writhing in agony on the edge of the area. The referee ordered a penalty, Nicholas was carried off and Souness drilled home the spot-kick.

After that incident the game continued on its frenzied journey. Despite all the huffing and puffing, though, neither side looked like adding to their score. England missed Bryan Robson and Gary Lineker, although Hodge and Hoddle did play well. That is the first time England had won the Rous Cup and it gave them a good send off for their World Cup campaign. Their run of unbeaten games now totalled nine, whilst Scotland's run ended at eight. Both sides could look forward with confidence to the weeks ahead.

104th match v Scotland.
Penalty scored for Scotland by Souness.

Mexico v England　Friendly

Played on Saturday 17 May 1986 in the Coliseum Stadium, Los Angeles, USA.

Mexico: P.Larios (Cruz Azul); M.Trejo (América), A.Manzo (America), M.España (UNAM), C.Hermosillo (América), J.Aguirre (América), F.Cruz (UNAM), L.Flores (UNAM), C.Múñoz (UN León),

R.Servin (UNAM), M.Negrete (UNAM). Subs: F.Quirarte (Guadalajara) for Manzo, A.Dominguez (América) for España and F.Javier Cruz (Monterrey) for Hermosillo.

England: P.L.Shilton (Southampton); V.A.Anderson (Arsenal), K.G.Sansom (Arsenal), G.Hoddle (Spurs), T.W.Fenwick (QPR), T.I.Butcher (Ipswich T), B.Robson (Man Utd, captain), R.C.Wilkins (Milan AC), M.W.Hateley (Milan AC), P.A.Beardsley (Newcastle Utd), C.R.Waddle (Spurs). Subs: G.A.Stevens (Spurs) for Robson, T.M.Steven (Everton) for Wilkins, K.M.Dixon (Chelsea) for Hateley and J.C.B.Barnes (Watford) for Waddle.

Half-time 0-3　Full-time 0-3
Ref: V.Mauro (USA)　　Att: 45,000

ON a sweltering hot day, England began their World Cup adventure with this pre-tournament friendly in the Los Angeles Coliseum Stadium. Some 45,000 people attended the match and they witnessed a fine first-half performance by the men from Europe.

The sun shone through the haze of smog which often pollutes this city, but England quickly adapted to the conditions and they were soon moving forward purposely. Hermosillo fired an early shot for Mexico across goal, but from then until half-time England ripped the Mexicans apart. In the 22nd minute Ray Wilkins tapped a free-kick to Chris Waddle out on the left. The cross came in and Mark Hatelely, stooping very low, headed home. It was a brave header and one too quick for the TV cameramen who missed the action completely.

Peter Beardsley was proving the perfect foil for the dangerous Hateley and some of his touches were a joy to watch. Skilful work from Glenn Hoddle, Wilkins and Bryan Robson kept the Mexican defence at full stretch and on the half-hour Hateley climbed superbly to head home his second goal from Beardsley's fine cross.

Seven minutes later Beardsley himself scored after chesting down a Wilkins free-kick. It was his first goal for his country and one thoroughly deserved for his outstanding first-half display. That goal made it 3-0 to England at half-time and effectively the game had been won and lost at that junction.

The second half was played in oppressive heat and it had a withering effect on the England players. It was especially noticeable that Viv Anderson and Ray Wilkins were struggling. However, the big lead gained in the first period was never in danger of being pulled back by the Mexicans although one save from Cruz by Peter Shilton had to be seen to be believed, world class in every sense. Terry Butcher and Terry Fenwick were also prominent, working well together and showing a good understanding.

6th match v Mexico.

Canada v England　Friendly

Played on Saturday, 24 May 1986 in the Swangard Stadium, Vancouver.

Canada: P.Dolan; R.Lenarduzzi (Tacoma Stars), R.Wilson (unattached), R.Ragan

(unattached), R.Samuel (unattached), T.Moore (Glentoran), G.Gray (Chicago), C.James (Toronto Blizzard), M.Sweeney (Cleveland), I.Vrablic (Golden Bay Earthquakes), C.H.Valentine (unattached).
Subs: J.Lowrey for Gray and D.Mitchell (Tacoma Stars) for Valentine.
Note: Due to the demise of the NASL in 1984, a number of Canadian players were playing in the Major Indoor Soccer League in the USA and thus had no 'outdoor' club affiliation.
England: P.L.Shilton (Southampton); M.G.Stevens (Everton), K.G.Sansom (Arsenal), G.Hoddle (Spurs), A.E.Martin (West Ham), T.I.Butcher (Ipswich T), S.B.Hodge (Aston Villa), R.C.Wilkins (Milan AC, captain), M.W.Hateley (Milan AC), G.W.Lineker (Everton), C.R.Waddle (Spurs).
Subs: C.E.Woods (Norwich C) for Shilton, P.Reid (Everton) for Wilkins, P.A.Beardsley (Newcastle Utd) for Lineker and J.C.B.Barnes (Watford) for Waddle.

Half-time 0-0   Full-time 0-1
Ref: J.Meachin (Canada)   Att: 10,000

AFTER the heat of Los Angeles, England moved to Vancouver to meet Canada on a dull, wet day and gave a performance to match the weather. Indeed, they needed a vast improvement if they were to achieve anything in the following month's World Cup tournament. Mind you, this really was a 'nothing' sort of game and it was hard to consider it as a full international. But it was classed as one and Canada, it must be remembered, were also into the finals, so it should not have been taken lightly.

The first attacks of any note came from the Canadians. Sweeney beat the offside trap in the 24th minute and set up Ragan with a chance but Peter Shilton was alert to the danger and ran out of his goal to kick clear. Sweeney then shot wide from Valentine's right-wing cross and then Gray wasted another good opportunity after a mistake by Ray Wilkins.

For England, Steve Hodge showed some good skills and looked sharp as the replacement for the injured Bryan Robson. Kenny Sansom was immaculate throughout and Terry Butcher was his usual solid self. Up front, Gary Lineker made some dangerous bursts and had one seemingly good goal disallowed. Mark Hateley saw a firm header well saved by Dolan and then Hodge hit a post after good work by Sansom.

In the 60th minute, England scored the goal which settled the match. Hateley, having just previously hit the bar with a header, was on the spot perfectly to cash in after Dolan fumbled a free-kick by Glenn Hoddle. It was a simple tap in chance but it was gratefully received and accepted to spare England's blushes.

> 1st match v Canada.

World Cup Finals

Portugal v England   Group F

Played on Tuesday, 3 June 1986 in the Tecnológico Stadium, Monterrey, Mexico.

Portugal: M.Bento (Benfica); A.M.Magalhaes (Benfica), F.Rosa (Boavista),

J.Oliveira (Benfica), A.Inacio (FC Porto), D.M.F.Miranda (Benfica), A.André (FC Porto), S.Carlos Manuel (Benfica), J.Pacheco (Sporting Lisbon), A.Sousa (Sporting Lisbon), F.Gomes (FC Porto).
Subs: J.Antonio (Belenenses) for Miranda and P.Futre (FC Porto) for Gomes.
England: P.L.Shilton (Southampton); M.G.Stevens (Everton), K.G.Sansom (Arsenal), G.Hoddle (Spurs), T.W. Fenwick (QPR), T.I.Butcher (Ipswich T), B.Robson (Man Utd, captain), R.C.Wilkins (Milan AC), M.W.Hateley (Milan AC), G.W.Lineker (Everton), C.R.Waddle (Spurs).
Subs: S.B.Hodge (Aston Villa) for Robson and P.A.Beardsley (Newcastle Utd) for Waddle.

Half-time 0-0   Full-time 1-0
Ref: V.Roth (West Germany)   Att: 19,998

HAVING just gone 11 games without defeat England went into their first match of this World Cup in Mexico full of confidence. It seemed unthinkable that they might lose to a very ordinary Portugal side, but that is exactly what happened.

The weather, having been perfect for England over recent days, suddenly changed an hour before kick-off and the players took the field in baking hot sunshine. From the start England pressed forward into a defence that was solid. The Portuguese made their intentions obvious, a packed defence with an occasional breakaway when possible.

Early attacks saw dangerous Gary Stevens' crosses find Mark Hateley's head and a typical penalty-box lunge by Bryan Robson, but both efforts missed the target. Robson, thankfully fit again, was making some clever runs into the penalty area giving Portugal more than one anxious moment. But despite their overall superiority, England could not turn their pressure into goals and the longer the game went on the more frustrated they became.

Two minutes into the second half, a fine run by Chris Waddle ended with a hard, low centre. Gary Lineker, who seemed unaffected by his strapped up wrist, lunged forward and only just failed to get a vital touch. Ten minutes later and Lineker went even closer. This time he beat the goalkeeper Bento, only to see Oliveira chase back to hook the ball off the goal-line.

It looked odds on a goalless draw at this stage but with only 15 minutes to go, England met disaster. For once Diamantino got the better of Kenny Sansom and crossed low to the far post. Carlos Manuel was left totally unmarked and had the easiest of tasks to beat Peter Shilton from close range. It was a terrible moment for England and all the millions of fans back home watching anxiously on television. Despite a few close calls, Portugal were able to hang on to their lead to win the game. The mood in their country was in stark contrast to that in England, as the streets of Lisbon were alive with the celebrations of this unexpected victory.

England, meanwhile, had to think again and they met Morocco expected to do a lot better. They could hardly do worse!

> 15th match v Portugal.
> Portugal's Magalhaes also known as 'Álvaro'; Miranda as 'Diamantino'.

Morocco v England   Group F

Played on Friday 6 June 1986 in the Tecnológico Stadium, Monterrey, Mexico.

Morocco: E.Badou; L.Khalifi, M.El Biaz, N.Bouyahyaoui, A.Lamriss, A.Dolmy, M.Merry, A.Bouderbala, M.Timoumi (FAR), A.Khairi, A.Merry (Le Havre AC).
Subs: L.Oudani for Lamriss and A.Souleymani for M.Merry.
Most of the Moroccan club names unknown)
England: P.L.Shilton (Southampton); M.G.Stevens (Everton), K.G.Sansom (Arsenal), G.Hoddle (Spurs), T.W. Fenwick (QPR), T.I.Butcher (Ipswich T), B.Robson (Man Utd, captain), R.C. Wilkins (Milan AC), M.W.Hateley (Milan AC), G.W.Lineker (Everton), C.R.Waddle (Spurs).
Subs: S.B.Hodge (Aston Villa) for Robson and G.A.Stevens (Spurs) for Hateley.

Half-time 0-0   Full-time 0-0
Ref: G.Gonzalez (Paraguay)   Att: 20,200

THE temperature at kick-off time was just on the 100-degree mark, but the heat generated throughout this game by a series of near disasters for England was of melting pot proportions. At the end of it all, England were still in with a chance of qualifying for the later stages but oh, how tough they had made it for themselves.

Morocco opened brilliantly and really could have killed off the game had they taken the chances that came their way. Bouderbala was the main thorn in England's side and he set up Khairi for a shot which Peter Shilton held only at the second attempt. Shortly afterwards Krimau miscued a shot but the ball ran for Bouderbala again and he should have done much better than hit his shot straight at Terry Butcher. Only a desperate tackle by Terry Fenwick prevented another sharp break by the lively Bouderbala from producing fruit. England could make no headway and Mark Hateley, especially, was easily held by the determined Moroccan defenders, so the attack was punchless.

With seven minutes to go before half-time, England suffered a double blow. Bryan Robson went for a ball in typical courageous fashion in the Moroccan penalty area but in so doing fell awkwardly. It was obvious that the captain's suspect shoulder had been badly damaged again. After a few minutes treatment behind the goal he was led away in agony. Most of the agony came from the pain, but Robson also probably realised that his World Cup was most definitely over.

If that was not bad news enough then worse was to follow. Within minutes Ray Wilkins was penalised and in his anger and frustration at the decision he threw the ball towards the referee. The Paraguayan official took a firm line and sent him off the field. It must have been a very stunned dressing-room at half-time.

The second half was largely devoid of any real excitement. England's ten men battled on bravely and, in fact, due to the Moroccans showing a surprising reluctance to come forward, had the better of the attacks. The searing heat was not conducive to playing with anything less than 11 fit men, so credit must be given to the England players who worked so hard in this half. The Moroccans seemed content with their point, so it left England still in with a chance to qualify for the next stage.

> 1st match v Morocco.
> Wilkins sent off for England.
> Morocco's Badou also known as 'Zaki';
> A.Merry as 'Krimau'.
> *"Being sent off in Mexico was without doubt the worst moment of my England career!"*
> Ray Wilkins

Poland v England
Group F

Played on Wednesday, 11 June 1986 in the Universitario Stadium, Monterrey, Mexico.

Poland: J.Mlynarczyk (FC Porto); M.Ostrowski (Pogoń Szczecin), R.Wójcicki (Widzew Lódź), W.Matysik (Górnik Zabrze), J.Urban (Górnik Zabrze), S.Majewski (1.FC Kaiserlautern), W.Smolarek (Widzew Lódź), R.Komornicki (Górnik Zabrze), K.Pawlak (Lech Poznań), Z.Boniek (AS Roma), D.Dziekanowski (Legia Warsaw). Subs: A.Buncol (Legia Warsaw) for Matysik and J.Karaś (Legia Warsaw) for Komornicki.

England: P.L.Shilton (Southampton, captain); M.G.Stevens (Everton), K.G.Sansom (Arsenal), G.Hoddle (Spurs), T.W.Fenwick (QPR), T.I.Butcher (Ipswich T), S.B.Hodge (Aston Villa), P.Reid (Everton), P.A.Beardsley (Newcastle Utd), G.W.Lineker (Everton), T.M.Steven (Everton). Subs: C.R.Waddle (Spurs) for Beardsley and K.M.Dixon (Chelsea) for Lineker.

Half-time 0-3   Full-time 0-3

Ref: A.Daina (Switzerland)   Att: 22,700

IT was all or nothing for England in this match against Poland, their last in Group 'F'. Bobby Robson had delayed announcing his team until an hour before kick-off and with Bryan Robson, Ray Wilkins, Mark Hateley and Chris Waddle all left out or unavailable it was a very different side that eventually took the field.

The pressure on the players was intense as defeat would send them home and the signs looked ominous early in the game as Peter Shilton made two good saves from Smolarek after Peter Reid and Terry Fenwick had lost possession. After the second of those saves, the ball went to Glenn Hoddle. He sent a lovely pass out to the left to the galloping Gary Lineker. His pass inside found Peter Beardsley who, in turn, played it to Trevor Steven. A beautifully timed pass then brought the overlapping Gary Stevens into play and his low, hard cross was swept home by the jubilant Lineker.

At last, after only seven minutes, England were off the mark. It was a fine goal and testimony to the speed and especially the anticipation of Lineker. Poland were stunned and the relief felt by England's team could be almost touched by everyone watching. The nation was alive again!

Seven minutes later it was 2-0 with another magnificent goal. A brilliant pass by Beardsley sent the exciting Steve Hodge away down the left and his superb first-time centre was again swept home by Lineker. The players were overjoyed and

this excitement continued unabated. After 26 minutes, the English voices were shouting again as Steven hit a corner into the box. Mlynarczyk missed it completely and Lineker was there behind him to ram the ball into the roof of the net to complete an amazing hat-trick.

The look of joy on Lineker's face when he scored was so appealing and it really spoke volumes for the whole country's feelings. Even the England players looked stunned as they walked off at half-time, not quite believing what they had achieved in a remarkable 45 minutes. Surely something had to go wrong on this eventful day?

But England had no need to worry. The dangerous Boniek did hit a post in the second half, but steady and solid defensive work by all the players slammed the door shut on any possible way back for the Poles.

The team gave everything that Bobby Robson could have asked for and, at last, England's pride was restored.

> 5th match v Poland.
> Hat-trick for Lineker.

Paraguay v England
Second Round

Played on Wednesday, 18 June 1986 in the Azteca Stadium, Mexico City.

Paraguay: R.Fernández (Cerro Porteño); J.Torales (Libertad), C.Zabala (Cerro Porteño), V.Schettina (Guaraní), R.Delgado (Olimpia), J.Núñez (Cerro Porteño), B.Ferreira (Guaraní), J.C.Romero (Fluminense), R.Cabañas (América Cali), A.Cañete (Talleres Córdoba), A.Mendoza (Olimpia). Sub: J.Guasch (Olimpia) for Torales.

England: P.L.Shilton (Southampton, captain); M.G.Stevens (Everton), K.G.Sansom (Arsenal), G.Hoddle (Spurs), A.E.Martin (West Ham), T.I.Butcher (Ipswich T), S.B.Hodge (Aston Villa), P.Reid (Everton), P.A.Beardsley (Newcastle Utd), G.W.Lineker (Everton), T.M.Steven (Everton). Subs: G.A.Stevens (Spurs) for Reid and M.W.Hateley (Milan AC) for Beardsley.

Half-time 0-1   Full-time 0-3

Ref: J.Al-Sharif (Syria)   Att: 98,728

ENGLAND progressed to the World Cup quarter-finals thanks to a conclusive victory in this, their first international against Paraguay. It was a very colourful scene in the Azteca Stadium as the two sides lined up. The sun was hot and the crowd were buzzing with anticipation.

The first half-hour was fairly even with both teams carefully feeling each other out. Paraguay looked sharp and full of typical South American attributes. Twice they almost took the lead after mistakes by England defenders. First, a badly-headed clearance by Alvin Martin, (in for the suspended Terry Fenwick), fell for Cañete to fire in an instant shot. But thankfully Peter Shilton, as ever, was alert to the danger and made a superb tip-over save. Then Terry Butcher, normally such a rock solid defender, tried to pass back to his goalkeeper, only to give it straight to Cañete. This time the Paraguayan laid the ball into the path of Mendoza who

had what seemed an easy task to score. Unbelievably, though, he miscued his shot and gave Shilton the chance to make an easy save.

As they did against Poland, England then went straight down the other end to score a goal themselves. Glenn Hoddle chipped the ball across goal where Gary Lineker almost got a touch. Instead, it ran on and Steve Hodge latched on to it and sent it back across goal for a second time. Who was there again? Of course, that man Lineker, and this time he turned it into the net. The exciting partnership between Lineker and Peter Beardsley then combined to almost score the goal of the tournament so far, but Lineker's final volley from Beardsley's cross was brilliantly tipped over by Fernández.

As the game went into the second half, the Paraguayans started to show the seedier side of South American soccer with some intimidating challenges. Both Lineker and Martin were caught by flying elbows and for a while these rough-house tactics got worse. But to their eternal credit, England rose above all that and punished Paraguay in the best possible way, scoring two more excellent goals.

Butcher hit a good shot which Fernández saved but failed to hold. The ball ran loose and in ran Beardsley to snap up the half-chance. That was a very popular goal as the little Geordie had been taken to almost every England supporter's heart with his fine play and ebullient character. To put the icing on the cake, Gary Stevens of Spurs, on for the limping Peter Reid, was soon sending in a cross to Lineker who swept home his second goal to make it 3-0. All credit to Lineker who, after a Paraguayan elbow had caught him in the throat, had to be carried off on a stretcher. But after a few minutes, thankfully, he was able to continue, so the goal was particularly satisfying for him.

England went into the quarter-final where they would face Argentina.

> 1st match v Paraguay.

Argentina v England
Quarter-final

Played on Sunday, 22 June 1986 in the Azteca Stadium, Mexico City.

Argentina: N.Pumpido (River Plate); J.L.Cuciuffo (Velez Sarsfield), J.L.Brown (Brest), O.Ruggeri (River Plate), J.J.Olarticoechea (FC Nantes), R.Giusti (Independiente), S.D.Batista (Argentinos Juniors), J.Burruchaga (FC Nantes), H.A.Enrique (River Plate), D.A.Maradona (Napoli), J.Valdano (Real Madrid). Sub: C.Tapia (Boca Juniors) for Burruchaga.

England: P.L.Shilton (Southampton, captain), M.G.Stevens (Everton), K.G.Sansom (Arsenal), G.Hoddle (Spurs), T.W.Fenwick (QPR), T.I.Butcher (Ipswich T), S.B.Hodge (Aston Villa), P.Reid (Everton), P.A.Beardsley (Newcastle Utd), G.W.Lineker (Everton), T.M.Steven (Everton). Subs: C.R.Waddle (Spurs) for Reid and J.C.B.Barnes (Watford) for Steven.

Half-time 0-0   Full-time 2-1

Ref: A.Bennaceur (Tunisia)   Att: 114,580

THE teams walked out into the white-

Gary Lineker celebrates a goal against Paraguay in the Azteca Stadium during the 1986 World Cup.

hot atmosphere of the Azteca Stadium for this quarter-final of the World Cup with the crowd anticipating the action of a clash everyone wanted to see. Peter Reid had recovered from his ankle injury and Bobby Robson also recalled Terry Fenwick after his suspension.

Both players were involved early on with Reid's crunching challenge on Brown certainly testing his ankle to the full, whilst Fenwick's first tackle on Maradona earned him a booking from the Tunisian referee. The first half was a tense and tight affair, few goal chances being

created as both teams searched tentatively for openings. Poor Gary Lineker and Peter Beardsley hardly got a kick, and only Reid looked impressive with his all-action style. The referee had already shown his weakness and that was to worry England with the Argentinians' usual habit of putting doubt into the mind of any weak official. There was not a shot worthy of the name in the opening 45 minutes and it was no surprise to see it scoreless.

Five minutes into the second half, though, the whole complexion of the match changed with one explosvie incident. And it was down to one man . . .Maradona! The little super star suddenly burst into life, picking up the ball just inside the England half. He ran at England's defence looking to play a one-two, but Steve Hodge managed to intercept and flick a looping back-pass towards Peter Shilton. The goalkeeper raced out and seemed to have an easy punched clearance, despite Maradona going for the same ball. The punch came, but not from Shilton! Maradona had beaten Shilton with his hand, pushing the ball into the net. Incredibly, the referee gave a goal.

It was all a nightmare for England as Hodge, Glenn Hoddle, Kenny Sansom and the crestfallen Shilton chased the referee back to the half-way line to plead their case. It was no use, though, and England had to accept the decision. To their eternal credit they knuckled down to their game again despite their obvious dismay.

Four minutes later, it was Maradona again but this time he scored a goal of such brilliance that it will be remembered for being as famous as the first goal will be infamous, for as long as the game is played. Picking up the ball just inside his own half, he skipped away from three England players and ran directly at goal again. Beating off challenges from Reid, Fenwick and Butcher, he paused just a

Diego Maradona and Peter Shilton exchange greetings before the World Cup match in the Azteca Stadium.

fraction to allow Shilton to commit himself before flicking home a devastating goal.

It was the best goal of the tournament so far and it was created at such breathtaking speed that it left England reeling. What a shame that his first goal had left such a bitter taste in the mouth. A gifted player such as Maradona should not have to resort to cheating.

Bobby Robson decided to throw on two substitutes to try and salvage the game and Chris Waddle and John Barnes were ordered to play wide. For a while Argen-

tina were forced back and with nine minutes to go a superb cross from Barnes gave Lineker his sixth goal of the competition as his header beat Pumpido all ends up. The goal meant a nervous last few minutes for the South Americans and they hung on by their fingernails, especially when another Barnes cross was missed by a whisker by the lunging Lineker. Somehow the ball was kept out and it was a mighty relieved Argentine side, who jumped for joy at the sound of the final whistle. They were through to the semi-finals, thanks to one legal goal

The infamous 'Hand of God' goal as Maradona fists the ball past England goalkeeper Peter Shilton.

and another illegal one. No wonder that some of the England fans felt bitter.

So, England's eventful World Cup was over for another four years at least, but they went home with their heads held high. After a false start they could be proud of their achievements in Mexico. Both on and off the field they behaved almost impeccably, and after the dreadful events in the Heysel Stadium the whole squad must take due credit for starting to build bridges.

9th match v Argentina.

Sweden v England   Friendly

Played on Wednesday 10 September 1986 in the Söderstadion, Stockholm.

Sweden: J.Möller (Malmö FF); R.Nilsson (IFK Gothenbug), G.I.Hysén (IFK Gothenbug), P.Larsson (IFK Gothenbug), S.Fredriksson (IFK Gothenbug), U.Erikssson (Hammarby IF), R.Prytz (Young Boys), G.Strömberg (Atalanta), A.Palmér (Malmö FF), J.Ekström (IFK Gothenbug), B.Nilsson (Malmö FF).
Sub: J.Persson (Malmö FF) for Hysen.
England: P.L.Shilton (Southampton, captain); V.A.Anderson (Arsenal), K.G.Sansom (Arsenal), T.M.Steven (Everton), A.E.Martin (West Ham), T.I.Butcher (Rangers), S.B.Hodge (Aston Villa), R.C.Wilkins (Milan AC), K.M.Dixon (Chelsea), G.Hoddle (Spurs), J.C.B.Barnes (Watford).
Subs: C.R.Waddle (Spurs) for Steven and A.R.Cottee (West Ham) for Barnes.

Half-time 0-0   Full-time 1-0
Ref: W.Fockler (West Germany) Att: 15,646

AFTER the triumphs and traumas of the World Cup tournament in Mexico, it was back to the nitty gritty of a cold night in Stockholm for the first match of a new season. Manager Bobby Robson had a few problems and he had to make several changes to the side. Unfortunately, England produced the usual poor September performance.

Sweden soon adapted to the difficult pitch and their early attacks stretched the England defence to the limits. The normally reliable Terry Butcher looked distinctly vulnerable and Alvin Martin, alongside him, also failed to inspire the confidence and authority needed. Maybe this uncertainty also had an effect on Peter Shilton as even he was guilty of some fumbled handling.

England's new attack partnership of Kerry Dixon and John Barnes never gelled, although Barnes did set up Ray Wilkins for a good shot which was deflected over in the 22nd minute. Almost all of the attacking play was coming from the Swedes. Winger Bengt Nilsson's cross almost gave Hysén a goal and corner after corner was forced against the visitors' jittery defence. It was certainly an undistinguished half from England, who were very fortunate to still be level at the break.

Only a few moments into the second half, Sweden came closest yet to seeing a goal. A tremendous shot from Bengt Nilsson beat Shilton, but crashed against a post. The warning was there for all to see but England failed to take heed. Five minutes after the restart Sweden

deservedly took the lead. Prytz's good pass put Ekström into space and Butcher's hesitancy was his downfall as Ekström strode past him to nonchalently fire a shot past Shilton. It was a quality goal from this tall striker and enhanced his already formidable reputation.

Sweden continued to hold all the aces and England soon brought on Tony Cottee for his first cap to replace the very disappointing Barnes. In the Watford player's defence, an early tackle by Roland Nilsson had left Barnes limping and it was noticable that he looked less than 100 per cent fit.

There was a slight improvement from England over the latter stages of the game, but only a Dixon effort troubled the home 'keeper Müller. At the other end, Bengt Nilsson brought the best out of Shilton as Sweden tried to emphasise their superiority with a second goal. There was no doubt that the Swedes deserved their victory and England were very flattered by the final scoreline.

11th match v Sweden.
Debut, as substitute, for Cottee.

England v Northern Ireland

European Championship Qualifier

Played on Wednesday, 15 October 1986 at Wembley Stadium.

England: P.L.Shilton (Southampton); V.A.Anderson (Arsenal), K.G.Sansom (Arsenal), G.Hoddle (Spurs), D.Watson (Everton), T.I.Butcher (Rangers), B.Robson (Man Utd, captain), S.B.Hodge (Aston Villa), P.A.Beardsley (Newcastle Utd), G.W.Lineker (FC Barcelona), C.R.Waddle (Spurs).
Sub: A.R.Cottee (West Ham) for Beardsley.
Northern Ireland: P.A.Hughes (Bury); G.J.Fleming (Nottm Forest), N.Worthington (Sheffield Wed), J.McClelland (Watford), A.McDonald (QPR), M.M.Donaghy (Luton T), S.A.Penney (Brighton & HA), D.A.Campbell (Nottm Forest), C.J.Clarke (Southampton), N.Whiteside (Man Utd), I.E.Stewart (Newcastle Utd).
Sub: S.B.McIlroy (Man City) for Whiteside.

Half-time 1-0   Full-time 3-0
Ref: A.Constantin (Belgium) Att: 35,300

GARY Lineker came back from the 1986 World Cup in the summer as a national hero after his goalscoring exploits in the world's premier football tournament. In England's first group match of the new European Championship, he carried on where he left off in Mexico with a dazzling display.

It was a completely different atmosphere compared to their match against Argentina in Mexico and on a cool Wembley night the stadium was less than half full. The Irish began with five players operating in their midfield and this successfully frustrated England in the opening half-hour. Donaghy's excellent work subdued Bryan Robson's effectiveness, although Glenn Hoddle went close with a clever chipped shot which went just over. Then Hughes dropped a corner,

only to see Chris Waddle's volley ricochet away off of Donaghy's head.

But in the 32nd minute England at last found a way past the stubborn Irish defence. Again Hughes had difficulties from a corner. Dave Watson went up with several defenders and the ball bounced off of him to Lineker, who pounced like a hungry panther to drill home a clinical shot. It was a goal England deserved and despite some spirited defending by Ireland the result afterwards was never seriously in doubt.

Hoddle curled a super shot into the net at the beginning of the second half, only to find that Lineker had strayed offside. Shortly after that Hoddle was again unlucky when he met a Lineker cross to flash a header against a post. Fleming had performed brilliantly in his first game for the Irish and the visitors continued to bravely resist all England's efforts.

But in the last 15 minutes their resistance finally crumbled. Steve Hodge burst into a good position, but his shot was blocked by the knees of Hughes. The ball rebounded to Waddle, who silenced a few of his obvious critics by sweeping it back into the net. The Peter Beardsley and Lineker partnership had not been quite as effective in this game, mainly because Beardsley was still not fully recovered from injury. But near the end, a fine pass from the Newcastle man gave Lineker the chance to make ground. His acceleration was breathtaking and as he approached the Irish penalty area, he looked up and chipped a glorious shot with his left foot which clipped the inside of a post before finding the net.

It was a memorable goal and the crowd were delighted with their favourite striker. Lineker in this mood was true world class. It was an excellent start for England in this European campaign.

95th match v Northern Ireland.

England v Yugoslavia   European Championship Qualifier

Played on Wednesday, 12 November 1986 at Wembley Stadium.

England: C.E.Woods (Rangers); V.A.Anderson (Arsenal), K.G.Sansom (Arsenal), G.Hoddle (Spurs), M.Wright (Southampton), T.I.Butcher (Rangers, captain), G.V.Mabbutt (Spurs), S.B.Hodge (Aston Villa), P.A.Beardsley (Newcastle Utd), G.W.Lineker (FC Barcelona), C.R.Waddle (Spurs).
Subs: R.C.Wilkins (Milan AC) for Hodge and T.M.Steven (Everton) for Waddle.
Yugoslavia: M.Ravnic (NK Rijeka); Zoran Vujović (Bordeaux), M.Baljić (FK Željezničar), R.Šabanadžović (FK Željezničar), M.Elsner (Red Star Belgrade), F.Hadžibegić (Real Betis), S.Katanec (Partizan Belgrade), M.Janković (Red Star Belgrade), H.Škoro (FK Željezničar), B.Sliškovic (Marseille), Zlatko Vujović (Bordeaux).
Subs: S.Tuce (Velež Mostar) for Škoro and P.Jurić (Velež Mostar) for Tuce.

Half-time 1-0   Full-time 2-0
Ref: F.Woehrer (Austria)   Att: 60,000

THE Yugoslav side came to Wembley with a skilful look about their team and

England knew that they were in for a stiff test. The danger showed itself in the visitors' first attack. A lovely 40-yard through ball from Baljic gave Zlatko Vujovic a clear run at goal. He beat Mark Wright with alarming ease, but could not beat Chris Woods who dived to make an excellent save.

England spent the next period trying to gain the upper hand in the midfield area where Gary Mabbutt, Steve Hodge and Glenn Hoddle all worked hard. Peter Beardsley, too, was full of running and it was his clever flick that led to the opening goal. The pass found Hodge wide on the left, who then made ground before seeing his attempted cross blocked and cleared for a corner. From this Hoddle curled a good ball into the area for Mabbutt to rise unchallenged to score his first goal for his country with a firm downwards header.

The Yugoslavs came back and were breaking intelligently and at tremendous speed. Woods again distinguished himself with a fine save from a powerful Škoro shot and then, with Woods for once beaten, Hodge was in the perfect position to clear another effort off the goal-line. At the other end, Gary Lineker, not as sharp as usual, failed to control a superb lobbed pass from Beardsley and so lost an excellent chance.

England tightened up all round at the start of the second half in an effort to cut down the danger from the Yugoslavs. They also attacked well and twice they nearly added to their lead as Radnic saved one Lineker shot at full stretch and then a goal-line clearance prevented yet another Lineker attempt.

In the 57th minute Chris Waddle went down the left flank and curled in a hard, low near-post cross. Of all the England players, the last one you would expect to see popping up to side-foot home was Viv Anderson. But he did just that and the delighted Arsenal full-back was mobbed by his jubilant teammates.

It looked all over bar the shouting at this stage but Yugoslavia refused to give in and the last half-hour sent palpitations through more than one England fan's heart. A mistake by Wright let in Zlatko Vujović, but the highly rated striker missed an excellent opportunity by shooting wide. He did the same again shortly afterwards and then, after a sickening collision between Hodge and Hoddle had left England with ten men, the same player hit a post with another fine shot.

The last ten minutes saw England hanging on to what they had and it came as a welcome relief when the final whistle went. At the end of these group matches, England would look back on this game and realise just how well they had done to win 2-0.

12th v Yugoslavia.
Butcher captain for the first time.
"My feelings upon realising I had played my last international can be summed up in one word — Choked!"
Ray Wilkins

Spain v England
Friendly

Played on Wednesday, 18 February 1987 at the Santiago Bernabéu Stadium, Madrid.

Spain: A.Zubizarreta (FC Barcelona); M.P.Chendo (Real Madrid), J.A.Camacho (Real Madrid), J.C.Arteche (Atlético Madrid), M.Víctor (FC Barcelona), R.Gordillo (Real Madrid), F.J.Carrasco (FC Barcelona), J.M.G.M. del Campo (Real Madrid), E.Butragueño (Real Madrid), R.Gallego (Real Madrid), V.Ramón (Sevilla FC).
Subs: M.Sanchís (Real Madrid) for Zubizarreta, G.Andrinúa (Athletic Bilbao) for Camacho, F.Roberto (Sporting Gijón) for Gordillo and A.Joaquín for del Campo.
England: P.L.Shilton (Southampton); V.A.Anderson (Arsenal), K.G.Sansom (Arsenal), G.Hoddle (Spurs), T.A.Adams (Arsenal), T.I.Butcher (Rangers), B.Robson (Man Utd, captain), S.B.Hodge (Spurs), P.A.Beardsley (Newcastle Utd), G.W.Lineker (FC Barcelona), C.R.Waddle (Spurs).
Subs: C.E.Woods (Rangers) for Shilton and T.M.Steven (Everton) for Waddle.

Half-time 1-2   Full-time 2-4
Ref: C.Pieri (Italy)   Att: 30,000

THESE nations had played many stirring games over the years with England regularly doing well in past encounters. This match was no exception as they turned on the style in the famous Bernabéu Stadium, home of the legendary Real Madrid. The night was also a personal triumph for one man. His name? . . .Of course, Gary Lineker. He had a game he will never forget, especially as this was the land of his latest club side, Barcelona.

A bright start by England gave them three chances to take the lead, all of which were missed in the early minutes. The Spanish defence looked vulnerable but it was at the other end that the first goal came. Kenny Sansom was having a rare off night and Spain were quick to exploit the weakness on the left of England's defence. A pass by the dangerous Butragueño inside the full-back sent Chendo clear. When the cross came in, Butragueño was following up to score. That goal came in the 14th minute but over the next 14, England turned the game upside down.

Glenn Hoddle was showing some lovely touches and he kept his eager front men supplied with the ball. On 24 minutes an equalizer deservedly arrived. Good work by Peter Beardsley and Lineker set up Bryan Robson for a fine shot which curled in but struck a post. The rebound found Hoddle who then had a shot blocked by Zubizarreta. Again the ball came out to Hoddle and this time he clipped it to the far post where Lineker was waiting to pounce.

Four minutes later, Hoddle's free-kick was nodded down by Viv Anderson and Lineker, at full pace, slid in the loose ball. That was 2-1 to England and they continued to play well throughout the remainder of the half and at the start of the second they emphasised their power by making it 3-1. Spain's midfield player Víctor was caught in possession and Lineker sent Beardsley away. A measured shot could only be pushed up by Zubizarreta and in came Lineker to nod the ball into the unguarded net for a clinical piece of opportunism which completed his hat-trick.

The visitors were now rampant with Beardsley, Chris Waddle, Hoddle and Robson all prominent as wave after wave of attacks swept forward. Hoddle's shot just grazed the side netting and then the

same player struck another shot which cannoned back off the crossbar. Another goal had to come and, inevitably perhaps, it was Lineker who scored it in the 56th minute. Again Beardsley was the provider as his lovely inviting pass across the area was seized on by Lineker who drilled a fine shot between goalkeeper and post. It was a superbly taken goal and probably the best of the four.

Bobby Robson brought on Chris Woods for another spell in goal and he saved well from Ramón. In the 76th minute, although Ramón did beat Woods to register Spain's second goal. But that goal was no more than a consolation as England had thoroughly outclassed Spain for most of the match. All the players deserve a mention, with Tony Adams making a very pleasing debut, but the one outstanding player in world football had to be Gary Lineker. In this mood he was lethal!

16th match v Spain.
Debut for Adams.
Four goals for Lineker.
Spain's del Campo also known as 'Míchel'.

Northern Ireland v England
European Championship Qualifier

Played on Wednesday, 1 April 1987 at Windsor Park, Belfast.

Northern Ireland: G.Dunlop (Linfield); G.J.Fleming (Nottm Forest), M.M.Donaghy (Luton T), J.McClelland (Watford), A.McDonald (QPR), P.C.Ramsey (Leicester C), D.A.Campbell (Nottm Forest), D.McCreery (Newcastle Utd), K.J.Wilson (Ipswich T), N.Whiteside (Man Utd), N.Worthington (Sheffield Wed).
Sub: D.J.Wilson (Brighton & HA) for Campbell.
England: P.L.Shilton (Southampton); V.A.Anderson (Arsenal), K.G.Sansom (Arsenal), G.V.Mabbutt (Spurs), M.Wright (Southampton), T.I.Butcher (Rangers), B.Robson (Man Utd, captain), S.B.Hodge (Aston Villa), P.A.Beardsley (Newcastle Utd), G.W.Lineker (FC Barcelona), C.R.Waddle (Spurs).
Sub: C.E.Woods (Rangers) for Shilton.

Half-time 0-2   Full-time 0-2
Ref: E.Aladren (Spain)   Att: 23,000

A BLISTERING start by the Irish threatened to give England a shock in this European Championship international in Belfast. Spurred on by their usual enthusiastic supporters, they rocked the England defence back on its heels.

Worthington looked odds-on to score when he chested down a long cross, only to lose control at the vital moment. Kevin Wilson did reach the loose ball but Peter Shilton was able to save the close range shot. Then an acrobatic header by Worthington only just missed the upright as the pressure increased. At this stage England were in danger of being overrun and just could not get their game together at all. Mark Wright again looked vulnerable and the full-backs were enduring a nightmare in these early stages. The visitors had few attacking ideas but after 15 minutes the whole complexion of the match changed thanks mainly to the inspirational drive of their skipper.

Bryan Robson fired in a fine shot from the edge of the area which only just missed the target, but three minutes later he came up with the perfect foil against all this Irish pressure. Gary Mabbutt's long throw was flicked on by Terry Butcher and Robson was in to glance a header past Dunlop.

The goal was doubly effective. Not only did it have a calming influence on England's play, it also knocked the stuffing out of Ireland. England settled down into their recent good rhythm and Robson came very close to increasing the lead when Chris Waddle centred and the captain, at the second attempt, fired a shot against the legs of Dunlop.

The game had changed dramatically by now and before half-time England did score another goal. Peter Beardsley's good work gave Waddle the ball and the Spurs player cut inside before delivering the perfect curved shot that went around Dunlop to leave the 'keeper helpless. It was a fine goal and virtually ended the contest.

The second half was easy for England. They went about their business in a cool and professional manner. Mabbutt and Robson continued to work well together and Beardsley's industry was top class. Although Wright continued to struggle when the Irish did manage to attack, England were able to cover him quite easily because they were so much on top. The substitution of Chris Woods for Shilton merely emphasised England's second half confidence.

96th match v Northern Ireland.
50th cap for Butcher.

Turkey v England
European Championship Qualifier

Played on Wednesday, 29 April 1987 in the Atatürk Stadium, Izmir.

Turkey: U.Fatih (Samsunspor); D.Ismail (Galatasaray), Y.Semih (Galatasaray), C.Ali (Sariyer), Ö.Erhan (Galatasaray), C.Riza (Beşiktaş), T.Uğur (Galatasaray), K.Erdal (Galatasaray), V.Hasan (Trabzonspor), D.Savaş (Galatasary), G.Iskender (Trabzonspor). Sub: T.Ilyas (Galatasary) for Iskender.
England: C.E.Woods (Rangers); V.A.Anderson (Arsenal), K.G.Sansom (Arsenal), G.Hoddle (Spurs), T.A.Adams (Arsenal), G.V.Mabbutt (Spurs), B.Robson (Man Utd, captain), S.B.Hodge (Spurs), C.D.Allen (Spurs), G.W.Lineker (FC Barcelona), C.R.Waddle (Spurs). Subs: J.C.B.Barnes (Watford) for Hodge and M.W.Hateley (Milan AC) for Allen.

Half-time 0-0   Full-time 0-0
Ref: A.Butenko (USSR)   Att: 25,000

THE bitterly cold wind that blew through the Atatürk Stadium here in Izmir certainly had a chilling effect on England's European Championship hopes. The goalless draw might have had dire consequences when all the totting up in the group was concluded.

The first half was instantly forgettable. Apart from an early Gary Lineker volley from a superbly judged Glenn Hoddle pass, there were few, if any, worthy goal attempts. Clive Allen, a player of similar style to Lineker, did not really hit it off with his co-striker, probably because of that similarity. To be fair, though, they both had a very poor service from a midfield that struggled throughout.

Turkey, who had never managed a goal against England before, put in three useful long-range attempts. Savaş twice, and Erdal tested Chris Woods but each effort was saved without much problem and it was England who generally held the initiative. But it was also a lacklustre performance by the visitors and it took them until the 69th minute before they again threatened Fatih's goal.

At that point Chris Waddle's cross was chested down by Allen and then prodded past Fatih. Unfortunately the goal was ruled out because Allen was adjudged to be offside. It was tough on Allen, who showed his Tottenham form in that one and only moment.

Manager Bobby Robson brought on Mark Hateley and John Barnes to add height and weight to the attack, but despite one clear chance, the move did not work. Near the end, a rare probing pass from Hoddle sent Hateley away and his low cross from the left only just failed to give Lineker yet another international goal.

In all honesty, though, a goal then would have been unfair on the determined Turks and undeserved for England.

3rd match v Turkey.

England v Brazil
Rous Cup

Played on Tuesday, 19 May 1987 at Wembley Stadium.

England: P.L.Shilton (Southampton); M.G.Stevens (Everton), S.Pearce (Nottm Forest), P.Reid (Everton), T.A.Adams (Arsenal), T.I.Butcher (Rangers), B.Robson (Man Utd, captain), J.C.B.Barnes (Watford), P.A.Beardsley (Newcastle Utd), G.W.Lineker (FC Barcelona), C.R.Waddle (Spurs). Sub: M.W.Hateley (Milan AC) for Lineker.
Brazil: Carlos (Corinthians); Josimar (Botafago), Geraldao (Cruzeiro), Ricardo (Guarani), Douglas (Cruzeiro), Nelsinho (São Paulo), Muller (São Paulo), Silas (São Paulo), F.Da Silva (Palmeiras), Edu (Palmeiras), Valdo (Gremio). Subs: Rai Dungha (Vasco da Gama) for Silas and Rai (Botafogo) for Edu.

Half-time 1-1   Full-time 1-1
Ref: M.Vautrot (France)   Att: 92,000

FOR the first time, 1987 saw three teams invited to compete for the Rous Cup, with Brazil accepting the invitation to join England and Scotland. In front of a capacity crowd of 92,000, the Brazilian samba beat echoed around the stadium heralding the visit of arguably the most popular visitors seen at Wembley. When the Brazilians visited, the whole stadium seemed to be electric with anticipation. This side was young and inexperienced, but the skills were all there and were obvious, even in the warm-up.

The first half was full of good football and right from the kick-off England pushed the ball around in confident style. Bryan Robson and Peter Reid, although outnumbered in midfield, worked so hard that the extra number of Brazilians was not noticed. The other player who was prominent was Peter Beardsley. After his recent injury problems he seemed determined to show the world what he could do, and on the night he was outstanding.

He was at the heart of all England's best work and he set up both Terry Butcher and Tony Adams with headers that the confident Carlos saved. The little Geordie then combined with Robson, Gary Stevens and Chris Waddle in separate attacks which all caused panic in the Brazilian defence. England might have had a penalty when Gary Lineker seemed to be held by Nelsinho as he tried to control a delicate chip by Waddle. Almost immediately, though, the goal England had threatened came along.

Inevitably it was Beardsley the instigator as his superb run down the left stretched Brazil to the limits, and when the cross came over Lineker dived to head a fine goal with Carlos hopelessly beaten.

Brazil, who had already shown their incredible speed, struck back straight away. Only 60 seconds after England's goal a cross from the right was swept home by the dangerous Mirandinha, soon to play for Newcastle, for the equalizer. England had been caught out by a lack of concentration after going ahead and they were fully punished. It was a lesson to learn, especially against a side like Brazil.

The second half was nicely set up, but in truth the Brazilians had the better of the match after the break. Their confidence grew and their crisp, rhythmic passing was now stretching England. Muller, who gave Stuart Pearce a tough baptism, was very prominent, with his pace outstanding. Mirandinha almost punished a slip by Pearce but Silas, unmarked at the far post, volleyed wide. Then, only a fine saving tackle by Adams rescued England after another lightening counter attack by Muller.

As the game went on it was Brazil who looked the most likely winners, but credit England, they stuck to their task well and on their first half display alone they deserved their share of the spoils. An entertaining game with Carlos for Brazil looking their best 'keeper since the legendary Gilmar.

14th match v Brazil.
Debut for Pearce.
Brazil's Da Silva also known as 'Mirandinha'.

Scotland v England
Rous Cup

Played on Saturday, 23 May 1987 at Hampden Park, Glasgow.

Scotland: J.Leighton (Aberdeen); C.R.Gough (Spurs), M.MacLeod (Celtic), P.McStay (Celtic), A.McLeish (Aberdeen), W.Miller (Aberdeen), A.M.McCoist (Rangers), R.S.Aitken (Celtic), B.J.McClair (Celtic), N.Simpson (Aberdeen), I.W.Wilson (Leicester C). Sub: C.Nicholas (Celtic) for McClair.
England: C.E.Woods (Rangers); M.G.Stevens (Everton), S.Pearce (Nottm

Forest), G.Hoddle (Spurs), M.Wright (Southampton), T.I.Butcher (Rangers), B.Robson (Man Utd, captain), S.B.Hodge (Spurs), M.W.Hateley (Milan AC), P.A.Beardsley (Newcastle Utd), C.R. Waddle (Spurs).

Half-time 0-0   Full-time 0-0

Ref: D.Pauly (West Germany) Att: 64,713

RARELY has an international between these old adversaries been as devoid of passion and excitement as this one. Both teams looked tired and lacked ideas at the end of a long, hard season.

The first half was particularly bad with the game littered by a succession of misplaced passes that kept giving possession back to the other side. It took Scotland over 30 minutes to produce a worthwhile attack, although that eventually came to nothing. England, meanwhile, were little better. Bryan Robson headed wide from close range and their general play was somewhat more organised, but again bad passing seemed to be the order of the day. Few clear chances were created and the crowd jeered the players from the field after a terrible first 45 minutes.

The second half improved slightly, it could hardly have got worse, but still the goals were rarely threatened. Strong centre-half performances at both ends, McLeish for Scotland and Mark Wright for England, countered the efforts of the opposing forwards, although to be honest there was little good forward play from anyone. Mark Hateley had a particularly poor game and one couldn't help wondering why England manager Bobby Robson did not try a couple of substitutions to try to lift his side. Only one shot was worthy of the name in this half and that was a long-range effort by England's

Terry Butcher shadows Scotland's Ally McCoist at Hampden in 1987.

Charlie Nicholas' shot hits the crossbar as the England defence look on. The ball flew over for a goal-kick.

skipper, Robson, a shot that hit the side netting.

A very poor game and one that everyone present quickly wanted to forget. Just for the record, Brazil won the Rous Cup thanks to their win in Scotland.

105th match v Scotland.

West Germany v England
Friendly

Played on Wednesday, 9 September 1987 in the Rhein Stadium, Düsseldorf.

West Germany: E.Immel (VfB Stuttgart); A.Brehme (Bayern Munich), M.Frontzek (Borussia Mönchengladbach), J.Kohler (1.FC Cologne), M.Herget (Bayer 05 Uerdingen), G.Buchwald (VfB Stuttgart), P.Littbarski (1.FC Cologne), H.Dorfner (Bayern Munich), R.Völler (AS Roma), O.Thon (FC Schalle 04), K.Allofs (Marseille).
Subs: S.Reuter (1.FC Nuremberg) for Brehme and W.Wuttke (1.FC Kaiserslautern) for Völler.

England: P.L.Shilton (Derby Co, captain); V.A.Anderson (Man Utd), K.G.Sansom (Arsenal), G.Hoddle (AS Monaco), T.A.Adams (Arsenal), G.V.Mabbutt (Spurs), P.Reid (Everton), J.C.B.Barnes (Liverpool), P.A.Beardsley (Liverpool), G.W.Lineker (FC Barcelona), C.R.Waddle (Spurs).
Subs: N.J.Webb (Nottm Forest) for Hoddle and M.W.Hateley (AS Monaco) for Waddle.

Half-time 2-1 **Full-time 3-1**
Ref: P.Casarin (Italy) Att: 50,000

ONE sometimes wondered why England played internationals in September because their traditionally poor performances in this month over the years was continued with this alarmingly resounding defeat in West Germany. The Germans, rebuilding after a successful 1986 World Cup, had far too much for the visitors and could have won by more goals.

The Germans started like an express train and they tore into England from the kick-off. Völler's pace exposed the laboured Tony Adams and the sheer speed of thought by West Germany had all the England players looking bewildered. Within six minutes Völler had volleyed a great shot against a post after Kenny Sansom's bad clearance. Urged on by the impressive Frontzek, Germany continued to rip huge holes in the English defence. Thon missed a fine chance when he miscued from close range and Brehme went very close with another effort. The pressure had to tell and when Herget's pass found Littbarski, the little winger struck a 20-yard shot which dipped and swerved to beat Peter Shilton completely.

Straight after the goal, Dorfner sent Völler free again and after evading Sansom's weak challenge the striker's shot was only just scrambled away by Shilton. From the corner, a mistake by Adams gave Völler another gilt-edged chance which somehow he managed to lift over the bar, much to England's relief.

On 35 minutes, yet another corner

produced a second goal for the Germans. Littbarski curled it in wickedly to the near post and, incredibly, Viv Anderson, Sansom and Shilton all failed to keep the ball out and they turned around in disbelief to see it nestling in the far corner of the net.

England were in disarray but a superb piece of opportunism by Gary Lineker then brought them back into the game just before half-time. A crunching tackle on Buchwald by Peter Reid won the ball and the midfield player then found Peter Beardsley. A swift pass to Lineker and the decisive prod of a man, who by now had scored 20 goals in only 21 appearances for his country, found the net.

For a while in the second half England managed to put the Germans under some pressure as they bravely fought their way back into things. John Barnes and Mark Hateley, on for Chris Waddle, both went close as suddenly a few holes appeared in the previously watertight home defence. However, a substitution by manager Franz Beckenbauer was to give the Germans back their superiority. The impressive Völler went off and on came Wuttke, and as so often happened with the Germans, the substitute proved to be just as effective. On 84 minutes Wuttke cut in from the left to hit an unstoppable shot past the groping Shilton. The goalkeeper had no chance and the goal gave the Germans a scoreline more suited to their overall superiority.

18th match v West Germany.
Debut, as substitute, for Webb.
In coming on as substitute, Webb became the 1,000th player used by England in international football.

Lineker chipping the ball over Turkey's Fatih.

England v Turkey
European Championship Qualifier

Played on Wednesday, 14 October 1987 at Wembley Stadium.

England: P.L.Shilton (Derby Co); M.G.Stevens (Everton), K.G.Sansom (Arsenal), T.M.Steven (Everton), T.A.Adams (Arsenal), T.I.Butcher (Rangers), B.Robson (Man Utd, captain), N.J.Webb (Nottm Forest), P.A.Beardsley (Liverpool), G.W.Lineker (FC Barcelona), J.C.B.Barnes (Liverpool).
Subs: G.Hoddle (AS Monaco) for Steven and C.Regis (Coventry C) for Beardsley.

Turkey: U.Fatih (Samsunspor); C.Riza (Beşiktaş), Y.Semih (Galatasaray), Ç.Ali (Karşiyaka), Ö.Erhan (Galatasaray), G.Ali (Galatasaray), T.Uğur (Galatasaray), G.Muhammet (Galatasaray), V.Kayhan Hasan (Rizespor), K.Erdal (Sariyer), S.Iskender (Trabzonspor).
Sub: D.Savaş (Galatasaray) for G.Ali.

Half-time 4-0 **Full-time 8-0**
Ref: A.Thomas (Holland) Att: 42,528

THE poor old Turks must have been sick of playing England. Three years earlier they were beaten on their own ground by 8-0 and now, in the European Championships, they suffered an identical fate at Wembley.

England, unrecognisable from the previous month's game in Germany, went at their visitors from the first whistle. After only two minutes it was new boy Neil Webb who set up the first goal. Trevor Steven, always lively, made a decoy run to Webb's right, taking defenders with him. Webb ignored the obvious pass and

Lineker's second goal, rapped home after his first effort was blocked.

Gary Lineker, with a superb finish, scores against Turkey at Wembley in October 1987.

instead, looked up, before curling a tantalising cross into the area where John Barnes came storming in to hit a splendid half-volley past the stunned goalkeeper. Ironically, it was Barnes' first England goal since that World Cup match in Istanbul, mentioned earlier.

England's confidence soared after that brilliant opening and they proceeded to put together some scintillating football which bewildered Turkey's defenders. On ten minutes, it was 2-0 with the scorer, inevitably perhaps, Gary Lineker. Good work by Kenny Sansom had set the striker up and he scored with a superb finish.

Bryan Robson scores in the eight-goal thrashing of Turkey.

Peter Beardsley (middle) scores against the Turks as England go on a goal spree.

Barnes then shot wide, as did Lineker, and Webb had a goal disallowed. Poor Fatih in goal just did not know which way to turn, and on the half-hour England deservedly increased their lead. A marvellous run by Peter Beardsley set up Barnes again and a clinical shot in off the post ripped into Turkey's net.

The England pressure was relentless with Beardsley going close and Erhan so nearly putting through his own goal when Lineker's low cross was deflected by the defender. Other goals were inevitable and Lineker was again the man of the moment as he rapped in his second and England's fourth just before the break. Barnes, Bryan Robson and Beardsley were all involved in the build up and although Lineker's first shot was blocked on the line, his second was deadly accurate.

After the break England continued to dominate and although a nasty tackle took the impressive Steven out of the game, they were soon adding to their goal tally. Webb shot through a crowd of players and Robson's cheeky back-heel helped it into the net. It was the captain's 20th goal for his country.

Still there was no let up for the Turks and Beardsley brilliantly headed in a delightful chipped pass from substitute Glenn Hoddle. That goal really pleased the crowd as Beardsley had thoroughly deserved it, his first at Wembley by the way. Soon afterwards Robson put a fine through ball which split the Turkish defence for Lineker to run on to. As the goalkeeper came out, Lineker coolly knocked the ball over him to register his own hat-trick and England's seventh goal.

That made a remarkable 23 goals in 22 games for Lineker who by now was one of the hottest properties in world football.

Turkey were by now just going through the motions as England came forward relentlessly. Right near the end, the cheer of the night was reserved for Webb. Another brilliant piece of skill from Hoddle, beating two men and pulling the ball back waist high to Webb, was met by a thunderous volley from the Forest man. That was the icing on the cake as far as England were concerned. Now for the big one in Belgrade the following month.

4th match v Turkey.
Hat-trick for Lineker, his fourth for England.

Yugoslavia v England European Championship Qualifier

Played on Wednesday, 11 November 1987 in the Red Star Stadium, Belgrade.

Yugoslavia: M.Ravnić (NK Rijeka); Zoran Vujović (Bordeaux), M.Baljić (FK Željezničar), S.Katanec (Partizan Belgrade), M.Elsner (OGC Nice), F.Hadžibegić (FC Sochaux), D.Stojković (Red Star Belgrade), M.Mlinarić (Dinamo Zagreb), F.Vokri (Partizan Belgrade), M.Baždarević (FC Sochaux), Zlatko Vujović (Bordeaux). Subs: V.Radača (Rad Belgrade) for Ravnić and M.Janović (Real Madrid) for Elsner.
England: P.L.Shilton (Derby Co); M.G.Stevens (Everton), K.G.Sansom (Arsenal), T.M.Steven (Everton), T.A.Adams (Arsenal), T.I.Butcher (Rangers), B.Robson (Man Utd, captain), N.J.Webb (Nottm Forest), P.A.Beardsley (Liverpool), G.W.Lineker (FC Barcelona), J.C.B.Barnes (Liverpool). Subs: P.Reid (Everton) for Robson and G.Hoddle (AS Monaco) for Webb.

Half-time 0-4   Full-time 1-4

Ref: M.Vantrot (France)   Att: 70,000

THIS match has got to go down as one of the best away victories the England team has ever achieved. All the players were magnificent and in a blistering first half they ripped the heart out of Yugoslavia with four superb goals.

England had never won here before, so prior to the kick-off the odds were heavily stacked towards Yugoslavia, but after only two minutes it was England who took the lead with a brilliant piece of opportunism from Peter Beardsley. A long punt forward by Peter Shilton was met by Hadžibegić, who tried to back-head towards his own goalkeeper. The ball seemed safe enough as Elsner shepherded it back to Ravnić, but hesitancy on the part of both defenders gave Beardsley the chance to nip in with that unique style of his and hook his foot around Elsner before prodding the ball over the goal-line.

It was just the start England wanted and the confidence oozed from their play as they continued to attack. On 16 minutes, incredibly, they went 2-0 up. Once again Elsner and his 'keeper got in a muddle and Ravnić, inexplicably, gave away an indirect free-kick for picking the ball up a second time in the area. Everyone was bewildered by the referee's decision until television playbacks proved him absolutely right. From the kick, Bryan Robson teed the ball up for John Barnes and he hit a screamer into the far corner of the net.

The England fans watching just could not believe it and within eight minutes the game moved into the realms of dreamland for them as England doubled their lead. Both came from corners with Trevor Steven sending over the first, from which Neil Webb dived amongst the flying boots to head forward for Robson to spin round and drive the ball past Ravnić.

Shortly afterwards a corner from the right by Barnes was met by Tony Adams and the big defender was absolutely delighted to head his first goal for his country.

It certainly was a stunned Yugoslav team that walked off at half-time. They had no answer to it all. Mind you, England, too, looked a little stunned as

they walked off, probably because they just couldn't believe what they had achieved in that eventful first 45 minutes.

An injury to Ravnić had forced a substitution for the second half and his replacement, Radača, was soon in the action. In fact, his good saves from both Webb and Barnes seemed to lift his colleagues and they put a lot more effort into their play. England looked very solid, though, and despite the Yugoslavs' extra passion in this half, good defensive work by Terry Butcher and his co-defenders kept goal attempts to a minimum.

With ten minutes to go, Yugoslavia did pull a goal back when a corner was met by Stojković's downwards header which finally beat Shilton. It was no more than a consolation, though, and England could be very proud of their tremendous performance and they have qualified for the European Championship finals in style.

> 13th match v Yugoslavia.
> *"Trying to pick out my most memorable match is very difficult. To have played 77 times, every occasion was memorable in its own right, but this game in Yugoslavia and a match versus Scotland in 1989 really stand out for me."*
> Terry Butcher

Israel v England Friendly

Played on Wednesday, 17 February 1988 in the Ramat Gan Stadium, Tel Aviv.

Israel: B.Ginzburg (Maccabi Tel-Aviv); Avraham Cohen (Beitar Jerusalem), E.Cohen (Hapoel Tel-Aviv), N.Klinger (Maccabi Haifa), Avi Cohen (Liverpool), M.Shimonov (Maccabi Tel-Aviv), N.Alon (Hapoel Petah-Tikvah), U.Malmilian (Beitar Jerusalem), E.Driekes (Maccabi Tel-Aviv), M.Ivanir (Maccabi Tel-Aviv), S.Tikva (Maccabi Natanya). Sub: D.Brailovsky (Maccabi Haifa) for Tikva.
England: C.E.Woods (Rangers); M.G.Stevens (Everton), S.Pearce (Nottm Forest), N.J.Webb (Nottm Forest), D.Watson (Everton), M.Wright (Derby Co), C.D.Allen (Spurs), S.McMahon (Liverpool), P.A.Beardsley (Liverpool, captain), J.C.B.Barnes (Liverpool), C.R.Waddle (Spurs). Subs: T.W.Fenwick (Spurs) for Wright and M.G.Harford (Luton T) for Allen.

Half-time 0-0   Full-time 0-0

Ref: A.Constantin (Belgium)   Att: 6,000

THIS instantly forgettable match was in stark contrast to the euphoria of that magnificent win in Yugoslavia last November. Admittedly there were several team changes for this friendly, but nothing can detract from a poor performance.

The Ramat Gan Stadium was saturated by heavy rain and when play began it was soon obvious that the pitch resembled a lake as the water splashed around each tackle. When Gary Stevens made an early run down the wing, he almost disappeared in a cascade of spray and the game was already nearing farcial conditions. However the referee decided to carry on and

England continued to probe a well organised defence in which Avi Cohen was outstanding as sweeper.

Peter Beardsley, who, due to Bryan Robson's absence, was very proud to join a select band that has captained his country, and Clive Allen were bogged down in the middle and rarely offered a threat. John Barnes and Chris Waddle also had poor games and only Neil Webb and debutant Steve McMahon showed some of their club form. McMahon, especially, revelled in the conditions and he tried hard to inspire his teammates.

After 15 minutes, a low cross-cum-shot from Stuart Pearce whizzed in off the wet turf, only for Klinger to rescue his beaten goalkeeper with a goal-line clearance. Then, with England having the better of play, Waddle headed Beardsley's deflected cross against a post. Just before the break, Ginzburg had a brainstorm, collecting Waddle's through ball but travelling out of his area and giving away a needless free-kick. From the kick Barnes curled in a fine shot which rattled the crossbar before being cleared.

That was the last chance of the half and the last effort of any note for some considerable time as the game became bogged down in a morass of mud.

Israel produced their best moment in the second half when their captain, Malmilian, intercepted McMahon's pass and sent Brailovsky away. The substitute flicked a shot on the run over Chris Woods, but also just over the bar. A late flourish from England in the increasing gloom almost brought a winner as Barnes twice went close. A volley was saved by Ginzburg and a brilliant dribble was ruined by an off-target shot. Another incessant downpour signalled the end of a very poor international.

> 2nd match v Israel.
> Debuts for McMahon and, as substitute, Harford.
> Beardsley captain for the first time.

England v Holland Friendly

Played on Wednesday, 23 March 1988 at Wembley Stadium.

England: P.L.Shilton (Derby Co); M.G.Stevens (Everton), K.G.Sansom (Arsenal), T.M.Steven (Everton), T.A.Adams (Arsenal), D.Watson (Everton), B.Robson (Man Utd, captain), N.J.Webb (Nottm Forest), P.A.Beardsley (Liverpool), G.W.Lineker (FC Barcelona), J.C.B.Barnes (Liverpool). Subs: M.Wright (Derby Co) for Watson, G.Hoddle (AS Monaco) for Webb and M.W.Hateley (AS Monaco) for Beardsley.
Holland: H.van Breukelen (PSV Eindhoven); S.Troost (Feyenoord), S.Silooy (Racing Club de Paris), R.Koeman (PSV Eindhoven), B.van Aerle (PSV Eindhoven), J.Wouters (Ajax Amsterdam), G.Vanenburg (PSV Eindhoven), A.J.H.Muhren (Ajax Amsterdam), J.Bosman (Ajax Amsterdam), R.Gullit (Milan AC), J.van't Schip (PSV Eindhoven). Subs: H.Kruzen (Den Bosch) for Gullit and A.Koot (Feyenoord) for van't Schip.

Half-time 1-2   Full-time 2-2

Ref: A.Prokop (West Germany) Att: 74,590

THIS was a vital friendly for both teams as England and Holland would next resume battle in the European Championship finals in the summer. They were in the same group, so each was looking for a form guide of the other.

England began well and John Barnes got on the end of a good move between Trevor Steven and Gary Stevens and then van Breukelen had to leap spectacularly to save a Barnes header. That came in the opening minute and England kept up the momentum to open the scoring in the 12th minute. Once again the goalscorer was the incredible Gary Lineker. Playing in only his 24th international, his phenomenal scoring rate continued when he beat everyone to a long Stevens pass. Lineker's pace took him clear of the converging defenders and he coolly slotted the ball past the goalkeeper. That was now 24 goals in 24 games, a tremendous record.

It all looked good for England, in fact too good really as suddenly Holland moved up a gear to take over control of the midfield. Gullit, a world star if ever there was one, began to show the packed Wembley stands all the skill that he possessed. His running pulled players out of position and England suddenly looked more vulnerable, especially down the left flank. The Dutch grew increasingly dangerous and in the 21st minute they deservedly equalized. A fine pass by the impressive Koeman sent Wouters down the right and his hard, low cross was turned into his own net by the unfortunate Tony Adams. The Arsenal pair of Adams and Kenny Sansom had struggled throughout the half and seven minutes later Holland took the lead.

Gullit was well forward and jumped for a ball with Sansom. There was such a difference in height and one had to question the England set-up as to why Sansom was jumping with him in such a deep position. The ball fell for van Aerle, who crossed immediately for Bosman to score with a clinical header which gave Peter Shilton no chance. To add to England's problems, Peter Beardsley was hurt after a strong challenge and had to be replaced by Mark Hateley. However a lovely run by Barnes was only stopped at the expense of a corner and it gave England a slight boost just before half-time.

Gullit almost clinched the match for Holland just after the restart but both Wouters and Bosman failed to capitalise on a lovely chipped pass by the star in dreadlocks. On the hour Gullit left the field and it was no coincidence that England equalized as soon as he had gone. A free-kick from Steven came into the area and Adams made up for his earlier error by heading a more acceptable goal, into the Dutch net this time.

The remainder of the game saw England in the ascendency again. Glenn Hoddle, replacing Neil Webb, grabbed the opportunity to again win many friends with his classy touches and several times van Breukelen was put under pressure. But in the end a draw was about right, for both sides had good spells and bad. Now it would be down to the real thing the following summer with England hopefully finding something extra.

8th match v Holland.
Adams scored a goal for each team.

Hungary v England
Friendly

Played on Wednesday, 27 April 1988 in the Nep Stadium, Budapest.

Hungary: J.Szendrei (Malaga); I.Kozma (Újpesti Dózsa), A.Pintér (Ferencváros), J.Sass (Honvéd), T.Balog (Vasas SC), A.Róth (Feyenoord), J.Kiprich (Tatabánya), I.Garaba (Rennes), J.Fitos (Honvéd), L.Détári (Eintracht Frankfurt), I.Vincze (Tatabánya).
Subs: I.Varga (MTK-VM) for Róth and K.Kovács (Honvéd) for Kiprich.
England: C.E.Woods (Rangers); V.A.Anderson (Man Utd), S.Pearce (Nottm Forest), T.M.Steven (Everton), T.A.Adams (Arsenal), G.A.Pallister (Middlesbrough), B.Robson (Man Utd, captain), S.McMahon (Liverpool), P.A.Beardsley (Liverpool), G.W.Lineker (FC Barcelona), C.R.Waddle (Spurs).
Subs: M.G.Stevens (Everton) for Pearce, M.W.Hateley (AS Monaco) for Beardsley, A.R.Cottee (West Ham) for Lineker and G.Hoddle (AS Monaco) for Waddle.

Half-time 0-0   Full-time 0-0
Ref: K-H.Tritschler (West Germany)
Att: 26,500

A SPARSE crowd of under 27,000 watched this friendly international in the famous Nep Stadium in Budapest. They saw a drab game in which an experimental England side probably just about had the edge.

Mind you, the visitors endured a shaky start as their inexperienced back four struggled to get into the rhythm of the game. Hungary, inspired by the skilful Détári, put together some useful attacks and were soon exploiting the nervous Tony Adams. Ironically, new cap Gary Pallister looked the most at ease of the defenders and he made several important tackles. Adams had a nightmare opening half-hour and on 25 minutes his foul on Détári almost produced a goal for Hungary. Détári himself took the free-kick and curled his shot around the wall and against the foot of the post.

However, after that incident England began to settle down and Bryan Robson played a captain's part, covering the whole pitch with his infectious enthusiasm and determination. Gradually his side took command and Chris Woods was never seriously troubled again as the Hungarians faded. Having said that, England still showed very little up front and goal chances were rare. Steve McMahon gave his skipper good support but Peter Beardsley and Gary Lineker had little opportunity to shine.

The first half ended goalless and the second began in the same fashion as the first had ended. By now England's authority had been well and truly stamped on the game, though, and all they needed was a goal. In the last 20 minutes they created several good chances. Substitutes Mark Hateley and Glenn Hoddle stretched goalkeeper Szendrei with good efforts, as did the rampaging Robson. Near the end, Pallister almost crowned a very satisfying debut with a header from Chris Waddle's corner but, much to his annoyance, he put the header wide. Just before the final whistle, a delicate chip by Robson found McMahon but Szendrei rescued his side again by blocking the shot with his knees.

The game could have proved costly as Stuart Pearce left the field with a nasty knee injury and was rated doubtful for the forthcoming European Championship finals. It was also a rare sight to see Lineker substituted. For the record this was the first ever draw between these two countries in 16 meetings.

16th match v Hungary.
Debut for Pallister.

England v Scotland
Rous Cup

Played on Saturday, 21 May 1988 at Wembley Stadium.

England: P.L.Shilton (Derby Co); M.G.Stevens (Everton), K.G.Sansom (Arsenal), N.J.Webb (Nottm Forest), D.Watson (Everton), T.A.Adams (Arsenal), B.Robson (Man Utd, captain), T.M.Steven (Everton), P.A.Beardsley (Liverpool), G.W.Lineker (FC Barcelona), J.C.B.Barnes (Liverpool).
Sub: C.R.Waddle (Spurs) for Steven.
Scotland: J.Leighton (Man Utd); C.R.Gough (Rangers), S.Nichol (Liverpool), R.S.Aitken (Celtic), A.McLeish (Aberdeen), W.Miller (Aberdeen), N.Simpson (Aberdeen), P.McStay (Celtic), A.M.McCoist (Rangers), M.MacLeod (Borussia Dortmund), M.T.Johnston (FC Nantes).
Subs: T.Burns (Celtic) for Simpson and K.W.Gallacher (Dundee Utd) for McCoist.

Half-time 1-0   Full-time 1-0
Ref: J.Quiniou (France)   Att: 70,480

THE final scoreline of this international did not reflect England's superiority, for the home side won with plenty to spare against a poor Scotland side. The Rous Cup was again a triangular tournament with this time Colombia being the invited guests.

An early booking for Dave Watson after a foul on Johnston heralded a slightly shaky start, but England soon settled, with Bryan Robson and Neil Webb again impressing in the midfield. The goal which was to eventually settle the match came as early as the 11th minute and was a pure gem. A throw-in by Gary Stevens found John Barnes who spotted Peter Beardsley's lovely run and flicked a superb pass to his Liverpool colleague. Beardsley controlled the ball brilliantly and then nonchalently chipped it over the advancing Leighton. It was a fine goal and after that England never looked like losing.

Leighton dispelled the myth of Scottish goalkeepers at Wembley by playing a blinder, keeping his side in with a shout throughout the remaining 79 minutes. He made an exceptional save in the first half from Gary Lineker and another from Webb, and he then continued to shine after the interval.

A double save stopped both Lineker and Beardsley and then the goalkeeper produced a brilliant tip-over from a clever chip shot from full-back Kenny Sansom. Eleven minutes from the end, Leighton enjoyed a slice of good fortune when he mispunched a Chris Waddle cross on to the head of Barnes. Unfortunately for England, Barnes' header looped on to the top of the crossbar.

Mark Wright (right) in action against Colombia at Wembley in May 1988.

It would have been a travesty had Scotland's only worthwhile shot counted near the end, but the previously unemployed Peter Shilton managed to block Gallacher's shot with his legs and England cleared the danger. It was pleasing to see Beardsley in such fine form and apart from his goal, he was England's outstanding player of the match.

To win the Rous Cup again, England now needed just a draw against the talented Colombian side when they visited Wembley the following week .

106th match v Scotland.

England v Colombia   Rous Cup

Played on Tuesday 24 May 1988 at Wembley Stadium.

England: P.L.Shilton (Derby Co); V.A.Anderson (Man Utd), K.G.Sansom (Arsenal), S.McMahon (Liverpool), M.Wright (Derby Co), T.A.Adams (Arsenal), B.Robson (Man Utd, captain), C.R.Waddle (Spurs), P.A.Beardsley (Liverpool), G.W.Lineker (FC Barcelona), J.C.B.Barnes (Liverpool).
Subs: G.Hoddle (AS Monaco) for Waddle and M.W.Hateley (AS Monaco) for Barnes.
Colombia: R.Higuita (Nacional); A.Escobar (Nacional), L.Herrera (Nacional), C.Hoyos (Deportivo Cali), J.Arango (Nacional), A.Garcia (Independiente Santa Fe), C.Valderrama (Deportivo Cali), B.Redin (Deportivo Cali), L.Alvarez (Nacional), L.Perea (Nacional), A.Iguaran (Millionarios).
Subs: J.Trellez (Nacional) for Arango and A.Valderrama (Nacional) for Iguaran.

Half-time 1-0   Full-time 1-1
Ref: K.J.Assenmacher (West Germany)
Att: 25,756

LESS than 26,000 people came to Wembley for this international which decided the destination of the Rous Cup. The low turn-out was a shame because the Colombians proved to be attractive opposition and showed all the skills so typical of South American teams.

England looked sharp at the start and were soon attacking. Peter Beardsley shot wide with a volley from Gary Lineker's cross and all looked good for the home side. But Colombia had no little skill and in Carlos Valderrama, a player with a wonderfully eccentric bright orange bushy hair style, they had a world-class performer. He looked like a 'mad professor' but on the field he was the centre point of all Colombia's good ideas and indeed, in some ways he was their professor!

But it was England who scored first. Steve McMahon, working tirelessly with Bryan Robson, fired in a shot which the other eccentric Colombian, goalkeeper Higuita, tipped around the post for a corner. Chris Waddle curled in the cross and Lineker reacted like the superb goalscorer he was — with a perfect glancing header. The goal had come after 22 minutes and was incredibly Lineker's 25th international goal in only 27 games.

The Brazil-like strip of yellow and blue worn by the Colombians inspired them to play like their illustrious neighbours for a while and several times their neat, short, inter-passing game was only a whisker away from breaking through the England defence. Once again the centre-half position looked weak for England without the injured Terry Butcher, and both Mark Wright and Tony Adams rescued themselves from trouble only because of their long legs just reaching dangerous through balls. Higuita, at the other end, spent a great deal of his game outside his area, chesting balls down, heading them away and sweeping like an outfield player. He was not to be beaten again.

Indeed, the impressive play of the South Americans was rewarded in the 67th minute with a deserved equalizer. John Barnes had forced a save out of Higuita and Robson had seen a header deflected wide, but shortly after this, substitute Trellez sent over a corner and Escobar put in a powerful header which went in off the crossbar.

Maybe the result would have been different had Lineker added a second from a good position just after his goal, but no one in the small crowd could deny the visitors their goal especially as it fulfilled a dream for Colombia to score at a stadium they know as 'The Cathedral'.

2nd match v Columbia.
50th cap for Hoddle.

Switzerland v England   Friendly

Played on Saturday, 28 May 1988 in the Stade Olympique, Lausanne.

Switzerland: J.Corminboeuf (Neuchâtel Xamax); A.Geiger (Neuchâtel Xamax), M.Schällibaum (Servette FC), T.Tschuppert (FC Aarau), M.Weber (Young Boys), T.Bickel (FC Zürich), C.Bonvin (FC Sion), P.Perret (Neuchâtel Xamax), H.Hermann (Neuchâtel Xamax), B.Sutter (Neuchâtel Xamax), H-P.Zwicker (FC St Gallen).
Subs: P.Mottiez (Neuchâtel Xamax) for Bickel, K.Turklymaz (AC Bellinzona) for Bonvin and M.Andermatt (Grasshoppers) for Perret.
England: P.L.Shilton (Derby Co); M.G.Stevens (Everton), K.G.Sansom (Arsenal), T.M.Steven (Everton), M.Wright (Derby), T.A.Adams (Arsenal), B.Robson (Man Utd, captain), N.J.Webb (Nottm Forest), P.A.Beardsley (Liverpool), G.W.Lineker (FC Barcelona), J.C.B.Barnes (Liverpool).

Tony Adams clears for England in the 1-1 draw against Colombia.

Subs: C.E.Woods (Rangers) for Shilton, C.R.Waddle (Spurs) for Steven, D.Watson (Everton) for Adams and P.Reid (Everton) for Robson.

Half-time 0-0   Full-time 0-1

Ref: L.Agnolin (Italy)   Att: 10,000

IN this, their last match before the European Championships, England gave an understandably subdued performance, but they did do just enough to win and in fact coasted for much of the game.

They began brightly enough and twice in the first minute they might have gone ahead. Tony Adams found Bryan Robson and a lovely pass then left Gary Lineker with a clear chance. But, for once, Lineker's first touch was poor and Corminboeuf was able to block the shot when he really shouldn't have been given a chance. Almost immediately the goalkeeper was diving to save a John Barnes shot.

Weber then saved the day for the Swiss when he cleared over his own crossbar after the goalkeeper had missed a Lineker cross. England's continued pressure, so nearly brought a reward when a Barnes corner was flicked on by Lineker for Adams to meet with a powerful header. Again, though, Corminboeuf was on top of his job.

Having dominated much of the half without over exerting themselves it was therefore disappointing to find England still level at the break. After the restart the visitors were made to regret their

missed chances for a while as Switzerland put them under some pressure with some sharp attacks. With the impressive Hermann their main play-maker, they mounted a series of good raids on the England goal. However, second-half substitute goalkeeper Chris Woods was rarely troubled.

After 59 minutes England, somewhat against the run of play in this half, took the lead. There was some suspicion of offside as Robson sent Peter Beardsley sprinting away down the left. But there was no whistle and Beardsley's cross was met first time by Lineker and the striker drilled home a clinical shot. The goal, although welcome, did not alter the second-half pattern and the Swiss team continued to have the better of the possession. Sutter and Zwicker showed little penetration though and seemed intent on shooting from long range.

15th match v Switzerland.

European Championship Finals

Republic of Ireland v England   Group Match

Played on Sunday, 12 June 1988 in the Neckar Stadium, Stuttgart, West Germany.

Republic of Ireland: P.Bonner (Celtic);

C.B.Morris (Celtic), C.W.G.Hughton (Spurs), M.J.McCarthy (Celtic), K.B.Moran (Man Utd), R.A.Whelan (Liverpool), P.McGrath (Man Utd), R.J.Houghton (Liverpool), J.W.Aldridge (Liverpool), F.A.Stapleton (Derby Co), A.Galvin (Sheffield Wed).
Subs: N.J.Quinn (Arsenal) for Stapleton and K.M.Sheedy (Everton) for Galvin.

England: P.L.Shilton (Derby Co); M.G.Stevens (Everton), K.G.Sansom (Arsenal), N.J.Webb (Nottm Forest), T.A.Adams (Arsenal), M.Wright (Derby Co), B.Robson (Man Utd, captain), P.A.Beardsley (Liverpool), G.W.Lineker (FC Barcelona), J.C.B.Barnes (Liverpool), C.R.Waddle (Spurs).
Subs: G.Hoddle (AS Monaco) for Webb and M.W.Hateley (AS Monaco) for Beardsley.

Half-time 1-0   Full-time 1-0

Ref: S.Kirschen (East Germany) Att: 53,000

WHAT a disastrous start to England's challenge for the European Championship. Their all-round performance against the Irish side could not have been more disappointing and the stadium was awash with a sea of emerald green at the end.

The tactical battle was waged long before the start with the two managers trying to outdo each other. In the end the Republic's manager Jack Charlton, used Houghton and Galvin to close down the space of England's wide men. Stapleton virtually played as an extra midfield man and England's rhythm was totally upset by the quick tackling Irishmen. As soon as an England player gained possession, a swarm of green shirts would be snapping at his heels.

At the first opportunity, the Irish pumped long balls forward and on 20 minutes, after England had nervously scratched their way along, one of these long passes paid dividends. Moran's long free-kick landed wide of the area and both Gary Stevens and Mark Wright had the chance to clear. But they dawdled and when Kenny Sansom tried to rescue the situation, he only succeeded in hitting the ball straight up into the air. A sideways header by Aldridge, then left Houghton with a simple looping header over Peter Shilton's right hand.

After that the Irish settled into the defensive solidarity that had seen them go eleven games without defeat and England's task was to try and find a way around it. Wright put in one effort in the first half but lifted the shot just too high. Meanwhile, Gary Lineker forced Bonner into the first of several good saves in the 35th minute.

England made some changes after the break but one never felt that they showed the urgency needed against a side like the Republic of Ireland. Sansom's quick pass gave Lineker the sort of half chance he invariably scored from, but after Bonner had blocked his shot Peter Beardsley hit the rebound way over the bar. Beardsley was guilty of another bad miss after Bryan Robson had set him up and both the England strikers showed a distinct lack of sharpness.

Another Lineker miss then followed and only after Glenn Hoddle came on did England look as though they might come back. They increased the pressure on Bonner's goal and the goalkeeper, with a mixture of good skills and perhaps a couple of leprechauns sitting on his crossbar, kept his goal intact. Hoddle's first touch was a free-kick which Bonner fumbled, and then the Monaco player freed Lineker with a lovely pass only for the final shot to go just wide.

Robson hit a screamer which thudded into Bonner's midriff and then Lineker's next attempt cannoned off the goalkeeper's knee as he dived the wrong way. A spectacular volley by Hoddle skimmed the Irish crossbar and finally Bonner made his best save of the game from yet another Lineker effort.

Despite all these goal attempts by England, they were never very convincing. The Irish, meanwhile, showed the tremendous spirit that Charlton has cultivated. They played to their strengths and thoroughly deserved their victory.

> 10th match v Republic of Ireland.

Holland v England Group Match

Played on Wednesday, 15 June 1988 in the Rhein Stadium, Düsseldorf, West Germany.

Holland: H.van Breukelen (PSV Eindhoven); A.van Tiggelen (RSC Anderlecht), R.Koeman (PSV Eindhoven), R.van Aerle (PSV Eindhoven), G.Vanenburg (PSV Eindhoven), A.J.H.Mühren (Ajax Amsterdam), R.Gullit (Milan AC), M.van Basten (Milan AC), E.Koeman (KV Mechelen), F.Rijkaard (Real Zaragoza), J.Wouters (Ajax Amsterdam).

Subs: W.Kieft (PSV Eindhoven) for Vanenburg and W.Suvrijn (Roda JC) for van Basten.

England: P.L.Shilton (Derby Co); M.G.Stevens (Everton), K.G.Sansom (Arsenal), T.A.Adams (Arsenal), M.Wright (Derby Co), T.M.Steven (Everton), B.Robson (Man Utd, captain), G.Hoddle (AS Monaco), P.A.Beardsley (Liverpool), G.W.Lineker (FC Barcelona), J.C.B.Barnes (Liverpool).
Subs: C.R.Waddle (Spurs) for Steven and M.W.Hateley (AS Monaco) for Beardsley.

Half-time 1-0   Full-time 3-1
Ref: P.Casarin (Italy)   Att: 65,000

IT was a day of mixed emotions for England's goalkeeper Peter Shilton, who joined Billy Wright, Bobby Charlton and Bobby Moore as the only players to earn 100 caps for England. Sadly, he was unable to celebrate as England had a disastrous match and bowed out of these championships.

The stark reality of the situation was apparent after a dismal performance against Holland. Admittedly the Dutch were a fine team and England did not enjoy the best of luck, but even allowing for that there was still no excuse for their overall display.

They began well enough and in the seventh minute a mix-up between van Breukelen and Ronald Koeman left Gary Lineker with a chance. Alas, the ball ran wide of goal so when Lineker's shot was finally put in the angle was acute and the ball struck the post before being cleared. The bad luck that plagued England against the Irish reared its ugly head again before half-time. A free-kick taken by Bryan Robson was hit cleanly by Glenn Hoddle, only for the ball to strike the post, run along the goal-line and away to safety.

By this time, though, the Dutch side had begun to show their pedigree and Shilton had to be on his toes to save long-range efforts from Ronald Koeman, Gullit and Wouters. A minute before the break, though, Holland took the lead. Rijkaard robbed Lineker and fed a pass to Gullit. Gary Stevens allowed him far too much room and his cross was controlled by van Basten and, after a sharp turn, was thumped past Shilton with the minimum of fuss. That was a bitter blow for England, coming as it did on the stroke of half-time, and but for a goal-line clearance by Stevens, van Basten would have scored again before the players went off.

England began the second half in very determined mood and equalized early on through the tenacity of their skipper. Peter Beardsley gave Robson possession and after a swift interchange with Lineker he bundled the ball over the diving goalkeeper and into the net. The look of determination and relief on Robson's face said it all.

After that goal England enjoyed a spell of good pressure. Lineker went close and the Dutch, at this point, were distinctly wobbly. But in the space of four minutes the game and the European Championships were ripped out of England's reach. In the 72nd minute Gullit again set up van Basten and he scored his second goal. Four minutes later the same player scored following a corner and the jubilation he felt at scoring a hat-trick against England was obvious for all to see.

England never looked capable of staging a comeback after that burst and at the final whistle they trudged off seemingly in a state of shocked disbelief at their fate in Düsseldorf. Several of their players had not performed as one knew they could and that was the biggest disappointment. They now went on to an academic group match against the USSR where the best they could hope for was to salvage some pride.

> 9th match v Holland.
> 100 caps for Shilton, only the fourth player to reach that milestone for England alongside Billy Wright, Bobby Charlton and Bobby Moore.
> Hat-trick scored for Holland by van Basten.

USSR v England Group Match

Played on Saturday, 18 June 1988 in the Wald Stadium, Frankfurt, West Germany.

USSR: R.Dasaev (Spartak Moscow); V.Khidijatullin (Spartak Moscow), V.Bessonov (Dinamo Kiev), O.Mikhailichenko (Dinamo Kiev), O.Kuznetsov (Dinamo Kiev), V.Rats (Dinamo Kiev), S.Aleinikov (Dynamo Minsk), G.Litovchenko (Dinamo Kiev), A.Zavarov (Dinamo Kiev), I.Belanov (Dinamo Kiev), O.Protasov (Dinamo Kiev).
Subs: V.Pasulko (Spartak Moscow) for Belanov and S.Gotsmanov (Dinamo Minsk) for Zavarov.

England: C.E.Woods (Rangers); M.G.Stevens (Everton), K.G.Sansom (Arsenal), D.Watson (Everton), T.A.Adams (Arsenal), G.Hoddle (AS Monaco), B.Robson (Man Utd, captain), S.McMahon (Liverpool), G.W.Lineker (FC Barcelona), T.M.Steven (Everton), J.C.B.Barnes (Liverpool).
Sub: N.J.Webb (Nottm Forest) for McMahon.

Half-time 2-1   Full-time 3-1
Ref: D.Santos (Portugal)   Att: 53,000

ENGLAND'S last match in the tournament gave them the opportunity to salvage some respect; alas, it all turned out to be a nightmare.

Right from the start the Soviets, showing a confident, flowing style, tore large holes in the English defence. Their pace was exceptional and the England defenders looked like cart-horses in comparison. It took only three minutes for the USSR to take the lead and it was mainly due to a dreadful pass by Glenn Hoddle which was easily intercepted. The ball moved quickly on and Aleinikov was the player who finished the move off. The Russians were soon creating other chances and the England players looked all at sea. It looked as though they could be in for a real trouncing, but a surprise equalizer on the quarter-hour lifted their spirits and brought them back into the match.

Hoddle atoned for his earlier error by floating a free-kick perfectly on to the head of Tony Adams, who headed home powerfully. Nine minutes later England almost took the lead when a rare good run by John Barnes left his marker beaten

Peter Shilton, who celebrated 100 caps when he played against Holland in Düsseldorf.

and sent a fine centre into the middle. Dasaev was struggling as the cross came over but Trevor Steven missed the chance as his downwards header bounced up and away off the crossbar.

These England attacks flattered to deceive, though, and the Russians dominated the remainder of the half. Two very dangerous through passes by the elegant Kuznetsov sent Protosov clear, but on both occasions the forward squandered the chances. Two minutes later, another Russian attack split the defence wide open again. Mikhailichenko hit a lovely diagonal pass out to Zavarov on the left and when the cross came in, Mikhailichenko followed up to head home the return pass.

The heart had gone from England's play in the second half and again the Russians dominated. Protosov was particularly effective with his runs at the plodding England defence. Only a brave save by Chris Woods prevented a goal from one of Protosov's bursts, but there was not a defender in sight when Litovchenko cut the ball back from the left for substitute Pasulko to score unchallenged in the 73rd minute.

England had now lost their third match on the trot, a depressing enough statistic on its own, but what was worse, their confidence had hit rock bottom. The tournament had been nothing short of a nightmare for them.

10th match v USSR.

England v Denmark   Friendly

Played on Wednesday, 14 September 1988 at Wembley Stadium.

England: P.L.Shilton (Derby Co); M.G.Stevens (Rangers), S.Pearce (Nottm Forest), D.Rocastle (Arsenal), T.A.Adams (Arsenal), T.I.Butcher (Rangers), B.Robson (Man Utd, captain), N.J.Webb (Nottm Forest), M.G.Harford (Luton T), P.A.Beardsley (Liverpool), S.B.Hodge (Nottm Forest).
Subs: C.E.Woods (Rangers) for Shilton, D.S.Walker (Nottm Forest) for Adams, A.D.Cottee (Everton) for Harford and P.J.Gascoigne (Spurs) for Beardsley.
Denmark: T.Rasmussen (Aarhus GF); B.Jensen (Brøndby IF), K.Neilsen (Brøndby IF), L.Olsen (Brøndby IF), J.Bertram (Brøndby IF), J.Molby (Liverpool), J.Helt (Lyngby BK), J.Hansen (OB Odense), K.Vilfort (Brøndby IF), L.Elstrup (OB Odense), M.Laudrup (Juventus).
Subs: J.Heintze (PSV Eindhoven) for B.Jensen, B.Kristensen (Aarhus GF) for J.Bertram and K.Jorgensen (Naestved IF) for K.Vilfort.

Half-time 1-0   **Full-time 1-0**
Ref: A.Ponnet (Belgium)   Att: 25,837

ENGLAND were anxious to put the agony of the summer behind them when the attractive Denmark side visited Wembley. It was vital that the home side could produce a performance that would give them some confidence before the difficult home game against Sweden the following month for their first World Cup group match. As it happened this was a much improved display.

Unfortunately the size of the crowd reflected England's recent form and only 25,837 people watched. Therefore, understandably, the atmosphere as the game began was somewhat lacking. Early on it looked as though there was to be no improvement in England's form as the dangerous Laudrup exchanged passes with Elstrup and then rolled a shot past Peter Shilton. Fortunately for England it also rolled past the far post. Another attack then led to a good move between Laudrup and Jensen but this time the defence scrambled the ball clear.

The man who lifted the home side was their effervescent captain Bryan Robson. After curling a brilliant shot just over the Danish crossbar he began to take control of the midfield. He was everywhere, urging on his defenders and backing up his forwards, as well as foraging in midfield for every loose ball. Under his influence England began to find some confidence and on 29 minutes it was all turned into a goal.

After Rasmussen had smothered a shot by Mick Harford, England pressed forward again. A long pass from the back was nodded on by Harford to Robson. With typical determination, the skipper battled hard for possession and Neil Webb was on hand to sweep home the loose ball. Another Robson-inspired move almost brought a second goal just before the interval but Peter Beardsley finished with a weak shot.

The second half proved to be something of an experimental period as manager Bobby Robson introduced two new caps in Des Walker and Paul Gascoigne and also brought on Chris Woods and Tony Cottee. The team changes settled in comfortably and England easily held the best of the Danish attacks whilst putting together some good moves themselves. David Rocastle had an interesting debut and shared in some of England's best moments.

The only real threat to England's lead came 15 minutes from the end after Terry Butcher had gifted a back-pass straight to Laudrup. Somehow, though, as an equalizer seemed certain, the big defender recovered the situation with a masterly saving tackle.

10th match v Denmark.
Debuts for Rocastle and, as substitutes, Gascoigne and Walker.

England v Sweden   World Cup Qualifier

Played on Wednesday, 19 October 1988 at Wembley Stadium.

England: P.L.Shilton (Derby Co); M.G.Stevens (Everton), S.Pearce (Nottm Forest), N.J.Webb (Nottm Forest), T.A.Adams (Arsenal), T.I.Butcher (Rangers), B.Robson (Man Utd, captain), P.A.Beardsley (Liverpool), C.R.Waddle (Spurs), G.W.Lineker (FC Barcelona), J.C.B.Barnes (Liverpool).
Subs: D.S.Walker (Nottm Forest) for Adams and A.D.Cottee (Everton) for Barnes.
Sweden: T.Ravelli (Östers IF); R.Nilsson (IFK Gothenburg), G.Hysén (Fiorentina), P.Larsson (Ajax Amsterdam), R.Ljung (Malmö FF), J.Thern (Malmö FF), G.Strömberg (Atalanta), R.Prytz (Ata-

lanta), J.Nilsson (Malmö FF), H.Holmqvist (Cesena), S.Pettersson (Ajax Amsterdam).
Subs: D.Schiller (Lillestrøm SK) for R.Nilsson and J.Ekström (Bayern Munich) for Holmqvist.

Half-time 0-0   **Full-time 0-0**
Ref: G.Biquet (France)   Att: 65,628

ONCE again it was a bitterly frustrating night at Wembley for England's players, manager and supporters alike as they failed to break down the talented and well organised Swedes. Although the final scoreline was disappointing, it was not as bad as all that because Sweden had several excellent results prior to this game and were a clever team. Unfortunately, though, the Press and public demand more from our national side.

Sweden began in confident form, looking comfortable on the ball and solid at the back. Hysén was in good form and was controlling all around him. The best of the chances in the first half fell to the Swedes, and Peter Shilton had to adjust his footing before pushing Ljung's deceiving shot around a post. England, meanwhile, never really tested Ravelli once, although Chris Waddle had a goal disallowed and John Barnes hit a volley wide. All-in-all, the half had been largely devoid of any real excitement and the crowd grew restless.

Twice early in the second half Shilton had to deal with shots from Thern and Joakim Nilsson. Both times the goalkeeper needed a second attempt at gathering the ball, causing a few flutters amongst the crowd. Gary Lineker, still finding his feet after his recent illness, was not at his sharpest although he still managed to put in the best of England's goal attempts. One looping header went over the bar when normally he might have done better, and then he shot wide after a lovely piece of play by Waddle.

After an early burst in this half, the visitors rarely threatened especially after Des Walker had come on for Tony Adams. The Forest player looked good and countered the threat of Ekström, one of Sweden's substitutes. A rousing finale saw Waddle hit a good shot which shaved a post, and right at the death it appeared that Lineker had broken the deadlock. Unfortunately, as with Waddle earlier, the goal was disallowed. As the players trooped off, the crowd were less than pleased with England's performance and let their feelings be known.

However, there was still a long way to go and at least a draw got England off the mark.

12th match v Sweden

Saudi Arabia v England   Friendly

Played on Wednesday, 16 November 1988 in the King Fahd Stadium, Riyadh.

Saudi Arabia: A.Al-Deayeh; A.Saleh, S.Al-Nuaimah, A.Jameel, M.Jawad, S.Al-Mutiaq, F.Al-Mussibeeh, M.Al-Suwayed, M.Abdullah, S.Mubarek, M.Al-Jaman.
Subs: K.A.L.-Subiani for A.Al-Deayeh, Y.Al-Thinayyan for M.Al-Suwayed and K.Masa'ed for M.Al-Jamaan.
(Club names not available)

England: D.A.Seaman (Arsenal); M.Sterland (Sheffield Wed), S.Pearce (Nottm Forest), M.L.Thomas (Arsenal), T.A.Adams (Arsenal), G.Pallister (Middlesbrough), B.Robson (Man Utd, captain), D.Rocastle (Arsenal), P.A.Beardsley (Liverpool), G.W.Lineker (FC Barcelona), C.R.Waddle (Spurs).
Subs: P.J.Gascoigne (Spurs) for Thomas, A.M.Smith (Arsenal) for Beardsley and B.Marwood (Arsenal) for Waddle.

Half-time 1-0   Full-time 1-1
Ref: J.Mandi (Bahrain)   Att: 8,000

THE Saudi Arabian Football Association had come a long way in the ten years before England stepped out into the magnificent King Fahd Stadium and it was a dream come true for this Middle Eastern country. To be able to entertain the originators of this great game of football was a real boost for them. Ninety minutes after the opening whistle they could easily have been celebrating a famous victory. England produced one of their, now common, poor performances. New faces and reorganised positions meant a disjointed look about the side and the display reflected that.

Within 15 minutes, England were a goal down. Poor defensive play had already been evident and when Stuart Pearce's attempted pass to Bryan Robson hit the referee and rebounded to Abdullah, there was nobody to catch the most noted of the Arabian forwards. He scored despite the attentions of Mel Sterland and David Seaman. The goal was a bitter blow for the visitors and their fans in the crowd were silenced. Not so much by the scoreline, but England's apparent lack of appetite to try and pull the goal back. The rest of the half saw the Saudis comfortably in control.

After a stiff talking-to by manager Bobby Robson, England resumed after the break with much more determination. Both Gary Pallister and Gary Lineker forced saves out of Al-Deayeh and Peter Beardsley also saw an effort stopped by the goalkeeper. The pressure increased until the 54th minute, when England finally grabbed an equalizer. A free-kick was floated into the middle by David Rocastle and his club colleague Tony Adams jumped high at the far post to force home a powerful header.

Everyone thought at this stage that England would go on to record another victory, but play deteriorated and long before the end the game was destined for a draw. Altogether, five new caps were used by the manager but it was never the type of international where their potential could be properly assessed.

1st match v Saudi Arabia.
Debuts for Seaman, Sterland, Thomas and, as substitutes, Smith and Marwood.

Greece v England
Friendly

Played on Wednesday, 8 February 1989 in the Olympic Stadium, Athens.

Greece: S.Ikonomopulos (AEK Athens); Y.Hatziathanassiou (Panathinaikos), G.Kutalis (AEK Athens), K.Mavrides (Panathinaikos), J.Kallitzakis (Panathinaikos), P.Tsalouhidis (Olympiakos), D.Saravakos (Panathinaikos), K.Lagonidis (PAOK Thessalonikis), Y.Samaras (Panathinaikos), N.Nioblias (OFI Kritis), N.Tsiantakis (Olympiakos).
Sub: J.Manolas (AEK Athens) for Hadjithanasiou, S.Borbokis (PAOK Thessalonikis) for Lagondis and N.Kalogeropoulos (Pansserraikos) for Samares.
England: P.L.Shilton (Derby Co); M.G.Stevens (Rangers), S.Pearce (Nottm Forest), D.S.Walker (Nottm Forest), T.I.Butcher (Rangers), B.Robson (Man Utd, captain), D.Rocastle (Arsenal), N.J.Webb (Nottm Forest), A.M.Smith (Arsenal), G.W.Lineker (FC Barcelona), J.C.B.Barnes (Liverpool).
Sub: P.A.Beardsley (Liverpool) for Smith.

Half-time 1-1   Full-time 1-2
Ref: H.Holzmann (Austria)   Att: 6,000

THE wide open space of the huge Olympic Stadium in Athens was sparsely populated for the visit of England in this friendly international, but after only one minute the Greek supporters were wild with delight.

In a disastrous opening Terry Butcher and Gary Stevens got themselves into a tangle over a pass and allowed Saravakos to run free towards goal. Des Walker was caught cold and Butcher's attempt at recovery only resulted in a penalty as his challenge brought the Greek player down. Saravakos himself netted from the spot-kick and thus became the first Greek player ever to score against England.

It was an incredible knock to England's already vulnerable confidence but to their eternal credit they knuckled down to the job and were soon creating chances. Bryan Robson, Neil Webb and David Rocastle were allowed acres of space in the midfield and they were soon taking advantage of it. After six minutes Robson pulled a shot wide after good work by Stuart Pearce, Gary Lineker and Alan Smith. A minute later and it was 1-1. Both Lineker and Smith were taking a buffeting from some close marking and after one such challenge on Smith a free-kick was awarded. John Barnes, so often disappointing at this level, quickly spotted a gap and delicately clipped a fine shot, in off the crossbar and the goalkeeper's back. It was something like his regular form at Liverpool, and it was a treat to see him do it in an England shirt.

Before the interval England had several chances which should have given them the lead. Barnes volleyed wide, a Smith header was touched around the post for a corner and from that kick Butcher's header was cleared off the line. It looked a formality for the second half, but England restarted without any zest in their play and that was disappointing.

A spell of tedious football followed before Peter Shilton was troubled by a shot from Tsiantakis just after the hour mark. Indeed, the Greeks looked more likely to score in this period. Thankfully, though, England woke from their slumbers, undoubtedly geed up by a gesticulating Bobby Robson on the touch-line. In a strong finish they not only scored the winner but looked impressive.

The change coincided with the introduction of Peter Beardsley who replaced Smith. Immediately there was an improvement in England's play and the Liverpool player sent his clubmate Barnes away. Barnes hit over a cross which Lineker nodded down to Robson. The captain fired in a magnificent volley which flashed into the net. It was a goal worthy of winning any game and so it proved in this match. Once again England owed a huge debt of gratitude to their inspiring skipper.

5th match v Greece.
Penalty scored for Greece by Saravakos.

Albania v England
World Cup Qualifier

Played on Wednesday, 8 March 1989 at the Qemal Stafa Stadium, Tiranë.

Albania: H.Mersini (17 Nëntori Tiranë); A.Lekbello (17 Nëntori Tiranë), S.Gega (Partizani Tiranë), S.Hodja (17 Nëntori Tiranë), H.Zmijani (Vilaznia Shkoder), M.Josa (17 Nëntori Tiranë), Z.Millo (Partiznai Tiranë), F.Jera (Vilaznia Shkoder), S.Demollari (Dinamo Tiranë), Y.Shehu (Partizani Tiranë), A.Minga (17 Nëntori Tiranë).
England: P.L.Shilton (Derby Co); M.G.Stevens (Rangers), S.Pearce (Nottm Forest), D.Rocastle (Arsenal), D.S.Walker (Nottm Forest), T.I.Butcher (Rangers), B.Robson (Man Utd, captain), N.J.Webb (Nottm Forest), J.C.B.Barnes (Liverpool), G.W.Lineker (FC Barcelona), C.R.Waddle (Spurs).
Subs: A.M.Smith (Arsenal) for Lineker and P.A.Beardsley (Liverpool) for Waddle.

Half-time 0-1   Full-time 0-2
Ref: J.Blankenstein (Holland) Att: 25,000

ALL the pre-match worries England had about this difficult trip to the unknown territory of Albania were totally unfounded as they won comfortably to go top of their group. Their performance was not outstanding, but more professional and solid than their opponents.

England were very positive from the start, although Peter Shilton had to dive smartly to save from Minga in the opening minute. The English midfielders then began to stamp their authority on the game and stretched the Albanian defence on a number of occasions. In the 18th minute, and not unexpectedly, England took the lead. One of several good moves involving David Rocastle saw the Arsenal player deliver a volleyed pass towards Chris Waddle. Gary Lineker latched on to Waddle's chested pass but was blocked as he shot. The ball ran free and John Barnes was on hand to pop in his eighth goal for his country.

For the next ten minutes England, frustratingly, allowed Albania to come back into the game with some sloppy play. The Albanians mounted a series of good attacks and the visitors' defence looked far from happy under pressure. Minga and Shehu looked lively raiders and for a while it looked ominous. Bryan Robson did well to block Minga, and Shehu should have done better after he had cleverly side-stepped Des Walker. Zmijani then shot just wide following a corner and Shehu brought a marvellous tip-over save from Shilton.

This flurry of activity gradually eased as England, once more inspired by the top form Robson, managed to assert themselves again, not before Shilton had produced another fine save from Millo after a mistake by Gary Stevens, however. Before half-time Robson twice went close as England hit back and Lineker, who was having a lean spell for a change, also had two attempts at ending his scoreless sequence.

What England needed was a vital second goal and it came in the second half. Stuart Pearce had made a typical burst down the left before being fouled. Barnes took the free-kick which curled into the box for Robson to climb highest to head home his 24th international goal. That equalled Geoff Hurst's contribution and it was a nice way for Robson to celebrate his 50th game as captain.

That goal virtually ended Albania's challenge and also gave England the chance to relax and play the football they were capable of. All that was missing was further goals, although there were plenty of opportunities. Stevens missed after Waddle's fine run, Lineker hit a shot into the side netting and even the substitutes combined to miss one, Alan Smith setting up Peter Beardsley for a mishit shot which was cleared off the line. The Albanian crowd politely applauded at the end and England were able to enjoy the success of their difficult trip.

> 1st match v Albania.
> Robson's 50th game as captain.

England v Albania   World Cup Qualifier

Played on Wednesday, 26 April 1989 at Wembley Stadium.

England: P.L.Shilton (Derby Co); M.G.Stevens (Rangers), S.Pearce (Nottm Forest), N.J.Webb (Nottm Forest), D.S.Walker (Nottm Forest), T.I.Butcher (Rangers), B.Robson (Man Utd, captain), D.Rocastle (Arsenal), P.A.Beardsley (Liverpool), G.W.Lineker (FC Barcelona), C.R.Waddle (Spurs).
Subs: P.A.Parker (QPR) for Stevens and P.J.Gascoigne (Spurs) for Rocastle.
Albania: B.Nallbani (Partizani Tiranë); H.Zmijani (Vilaznia Shkoder), A.Bubeqi (Flamurtari Vlorë), S.Hodja (17 Nëntori Tiranë), S.Gega (Partizani Tirana), F.Jera (Vilaznia Shkoder), Y.Shehu (Partizani Tiranë), A.Lekbello (17 Nëntori Tiranë), Z.Millo (Partizani Tiranë), F.Hasanpapa (17 Nëntori Tiranë), S.Demollari (Dinamo Tiranë).
Sub: P.Noga (Partizani Tiranë) for Hasanpapa.

Half-time 2-0   Full-time 5-0
Ref: E.Halle (Norway)   Att: 60,602

OVER 60,000 people stood in silence at the start of this World Cup match in a moving tribute to the tragedy which happened at Hillsborough on 15 April 1989. The England team then returned to the job of beating the Albanians. They achieved this in style and with a thoroughly professional performance.

It took only five minutes for the visiting defence to be pierced and, much to his relief, it was Gary Lineker who broke his barren spell to score. Chris Waddle's cross was met by the heads of David Rocastle and defender Jera, and the ball then bounced kindly for Lineker to nod home

an easy header. That set England on their way and seven minutes later they added a second goal.

This time Gary Stevens sent Lineker scampering away down the right. The striker cleverly waited for Peter Beardsley to make some space before delivering the ball to him. The Liverpool player had no problem in beating the unfortunate Nallbani who had not enjoyed the best start to his international career. At only 17 years of age he was having a daunting baptism.

At this stage England were all over their opponents and a cricket score was in prospect. Terry Butcher set up another chance for Lineker but this time the goalkeeper saved. Bryan Robson then had a header parried and Waddle, after a brilliant run, could not quite find the shot to match his approach play. Before the interval, Robson missed another good chance when he headed wide.

All the Albanians had to offer was plenty of spirit and hard work, and credit must go to them for this. Demollari was desperately disappointed when his goal was disallowed for an offside decision by the Norwegian referee. That incident virtually ended Albania's small threat and three second-half goals from England gave the scoreline a more realistic look.

Neil Webb and Lineker combined to give Beardsley a second goal and then Paul Gascoigne helped Waddle to score the fourth only a few minutes after coming on as substitute for Rocastle.

The evening was sealed when Gascoigne delighted the crowd by scoring a brilliant individual goal for the fifth.

> 2nd match v Albania.
> Debut, as substitute, for Parker.

England v Chile   Rous Cup

Played on Tuesday 23 May 1989 at Wembley Stadium.

England: P.L.Shilton (Derby Co); P.A.Parker (QPR), S.Pearce (Nottm Forest), N.J.Webb (Nottm Forest), D.S.Walker (Nottm Forest), T.I.Butcher (Rangers), B.Robson (Man Utd, captain), P.J.Gascoigne (Spurs), N.H.Clough (Nottm Forest), J.Fashanu (Wimbledon), C.R.Waddle (Spurs).
Sub: A.D.Cottee (Everton) for Fashanu.
Chile: R.Rojas (São Paulo); P.Reyes (Universidad de Chile), L.Contreras (La Serena), H.Gonzalez (Colo Colo), J.Pizzarro (Colo Colo), H.Rubir (Bologna), R.Ormeno (Colo Colo), J.Covarrubias (Cobreloa), F.Astengo (Gremio), R.Espinoza (Colo Colo), O.Hurtado (Universidad Catolica).
Sub: J.Vera (OFI Kritis) for O.Hurtado (Universidad Catolica).

Half-time 0-0   Full-time 0-0
Ref: E.Fredrikson (Sweden)   Att: 15,628

THE smallest crowd ever to attend a full international at Wembley went home disappointed at both the display from England and the unsporting antics of Chile, the latest of the sides to be invited over for this tournament. Once again we were treated to the worst aspects of South American football instead of seeing the

flowing football that all those countries are capable of.

In a match that had little to offer the 15,628 spectators who did turn up, it came as no surprise to see it end goalless. England could find little rhythm and with two new caps and several changes to the side that was not unexpected. Alas, it was in attack where the deficiencies showed up the most. John Fashanu looked way out of his depth in such company and Nigel Clough never reached anywhere near his Nottingham Forest form, although he did work hard.

Chile seemed intent on spoiling any chance of a good football match. Their skills, as ever, were clearly there, but emotionally they showed no control and repeatedly fell after challenges as though they had been felled by a 12-bore shotgun. Rubir and Reyes rightfully received bookings for wild tackles and Fashanu then joined them in the referee's notebook when he retaliated with an elbow in the face of his marker. That completed a miserable debut for him. Goalkeeper Rojas did show his athleticism and made acrobatic saves from Neil Webb and Clough headers.

But the only other incident worthy of note came right near the end when substitute Tony Cottee saw an effort cleared off the line.

> 4th match v Chile.
> Debuts for Clough and Fashanu.

Scotland v England   Rous Cup

Played on Saturday, 27 May 1989 at Hampden Park, Glasgow.

Scotland: J.Leighton (Man Utd); S.McKimmie (Aberdeen), M.Malpas (Dundee Utd), R.S.Aitken (Celtic), A.McLeish (Aberdeen), J.McPherson (Hearts), P.K.F.Nevin (Everton), P.McStay (Celtic), A.M.McCoist (Rangers), R.Connor (Aberdeen), M.T.Johnston (Nantes).
Sub: P.Grant (Celtic) for Connor.
England: P.L.Shilton (Derby Co); M.G.Stevens (Rangers), S.Pearce (Nottm Forest), T.M.Steven (Everton), D.S.Walker (Nottm Forest), T.I.Butcher (Rangers), B.Robson (Man Utd), C.R.Waddle (Spurs), J.Fashanu (Wimbledon), A.D.Cottee (Everton), N.J.Webb (Nottm Forest).
Sub: S.G.Bull (Wolves) for Fashanu and P.J.Gascoigne (Spurs) for Cottee.

Half-time 0-1   Full-time 0-2
Ref: M.Vautrot (France)   Att: 63,282

WITH this hard-fought victory at Hampden Park, England duly won the Rous Cup again, but the Scots must have been kicking themselves for not doing better. They missed a hatful of chances and had only themselves to blame.

In a surprisingly open game, both sides went close early on. It was nip and tuck for the opening phase until England edged their noses in front after 20 minutes with a superb goal. Gary Stevens put over a good cross and Chris Waddle threw himself full length to spectacularly head past Leighton. It was a marvellous moment and one that Waddle really enjoyed.

The goal had come just after Peter Shilton had saved well low to his right from McCoist following a flowing Scottish move. Bryan Robson had also gone close and the skipper was much more aggressive than he had been against Chile. Only a fine save by Jim Leighton prevented a typical goal by his Manchester United colleague.

The Scots stepped up the pressure for an equalizer before the interval but always found Shilton a seemingly impregnable barrier. The goalkeeper had some luck after blocking a McPherson attempt as the ball flew over the bar after hitting him. But the Derby man showed his skill many more times in a very confident display.

John Fashanu suffered an early injury and the Wimbledon player was desperately disappointed at having to come off, he knew in his heart that he had not done himself justice in his two appearances. This injury gave a chance to Steve Bull, though, and when he had an early opportunity to show his paces he made it very clear that just because he played in the Third Division did not mean to say that he was incapable of competing at international level. He started with an impressive lay off and then chased and harried and generally put himself around as any good centre-forward should.

McKimmie was Scotland's big success story and he fired in a long shot early in the second half which Shilton saved. Then the full-back all but set up McCoist, who shot at Shilton but watched in dismay as the rebound flew off his knee and out for a goal kick. Scotland were rampant in this spell and the vociferous crowd were roaring them on. Neil Webb and Robson were being overrun in midfield, but Shilton continued to perform heroics, making another excellent save when he beat away a shot by substitute Grant.

Just as it seemed certain that Scotland would pull the goal back, England broke away to wrap up the result with a second goal. It was a rampaging bull that did the trick, Steve Bull to be precise! He took a long pass from Stevens, spun round McPherson and then fired in a ferocious diagonal shot which left Leighton groping at thin air. The goal was superb and certainly gave Bull the chance to prove a few doubters wrong about him.

A few minutes later he almost repeated the move, shaking off McPherson again, and another defender, only for Leighton to save his final shot. In the dying seconds Leighton saved his side again as he bravely blocked Paul Gascoigne's effort.

So, England once again won at Hampden. They could afford a smile, for without Shilton's saves it might have been a different story.

> 107th match v Scotland.
> Debut, as substitute, for Bull, who also scored a debut goal.

England v Poland World Cup Qualifier

Played on Saturday, 3 June 1989 at Wembley Stadium.

England: P.L.Shilton (Derby Co); M.G.Stevens (Rangers), S.Pearce (Nottm Forest), N.J.Webb (Nottm Forest), D.S.Walker (Nottm Forest), T.I.Butcher (Rangers), B.Robson (Man Utd, captain), C.R.Waddle (Spurs), P.A.Beardsley (Liverpool), G.W.Lineker (FC Barcelona), J.C.B.Barnes (Liverpool).
Subs: D.Rocastle (Arsenal) for Waddle and A.M.Smith (Arsenal) for Beardsley.
Poland: J.Bako (LKS Lódź); R.Wójcicki (Hamburger SV), J.Wijas (GKS Katowice), D.Wdowczyk (Legia Warsaw), D.Lukasik (Lech Poznań), W.Matysik (AJ Auxerre), W.Prusik (Śląsk Wrocław), J.Urban (Górnik Zabrze), K.Warzycha (Ruch Chorzów), J.Furtok (Hamburger SV), M.Leśniak (Bayer 04 Leverkusen).
Sub: R.Tarasiewicz (Śląsk Wrocław) for Urban and R.Kosecki (Legia Warsaw) for Leśniak.

Half-time 1-0   Full-time 3-0
Ref: L.Agnolin (Italy)   Att: 69,203

ENGLAND took a giant step forward in their World Cup challenge with this resounding victory against Poland. They should have had more goals, but there were no real complaints from anyone about that.

Right from the start it was obvious that there was never going to be a repeat of that infamous tie in 1973 when England did everything but win. On that day a goalkeeper named Tomaszewski had the game of his life, but here, his modern-day counterpart, Bako, quickly incurred the wrath of the crowd with a crude challenge on Gary Lineker outside his area. It rightly earned the goalkeeper a booking.

Poland had already shown panic in their defensive ranks with Bryan Robson and Peter Beardsley prominent in early attacks. But a surprise break by Poland ended with Furtok's shot being saved by Peter Shilton, and that was a warning to England. Chris Waddle then almost punished a bad back-pass, but his shot struck Bako and frustration was slightly in the air as 20 minutes of England pressure had gone by without the goal they deserved coming. Urban headed over following a Polish corner, but in the 24th minute England, at last, took the lead.

Breaking quickly, John Barnes, at last showing some of his Liverpool form in an England shirt, made a splendid run before releasing Lineker in the inside-right channel. Instinctively, the striker fired in a shot which Bako saved but could not hold. Lineker followed up and put the ball into the net from a tight angle with his second attempt.

This positive play by England was a tonic and they continued to dominate. A corner by Beardsley was flicked on by Barnes and only a marvellous reflex save by Bako stopped a certain goal from Neil Webb's powerful header. Des Walker was really looking the part and his pace often rescued his side when danger threatened. A booking was the only blemish on a fine performance.

After the interval Poland improved a little and as a result England had cause to regret some of their earlier missed chances. A fine move by Poland ended with a shot from Urban which was deflected around Shilton's left-hand post, but just as the visitors looked in with a chance of salvaging something from the game, England hit with a second goal.

There were 20 minutes remaining when Lineker laid off a good pass to Stevens. The full-back sent over a lovely deep centre and Barnes came roaring in to volley home a glorious goal. He made it look easy but it was anything but that. The goal meant that the win was virtually safe for England as Poland then faded. With seven minutes left, the home side sealed victory completely with another well-taken goal. A terrible back-pass, one of many unforced errors by the Poles, was seized on by Rocastle and he crossed low and hard for Neil Webb to score easily from close range.

A good win but England now faced difficult away games in both Sweden and Poland to determine who progressed to the finals in Italy the following summer.

> 6th match v Poland.
> *"Wembley was the stadium I loved playing in the most because it was our Kingdom, our patch of mighty England! (I used to say this before every game, with a few expletives thrown in!)"*
> Terry Butcher

Denmark v England Friendly

Played on Wednesday, 7 June 1989 in the Idraetspark, Copenhagen.

Denmark: P.B.Schmeichel (Brøndby IF); H.Risom (Vejle BK), K.Nielsen (Brøndby IF), L.Olsen (Brøndby IF), I.Nielsen (PSV Eindhoven), J.Bartram (Bayer ø5 Uerdingen), J.Helt (Lyngby BK), H.Andersen (RSC Anderlecht), L.Elstrup (Odense BK), M.Laudrup (Juventus), B.Laudrup (Brøndby IF).
Subs: J.Larsen (Vejle BK) for I.Nielsen, K.Vilfort (Brøndby IF) for Andersen and P.Rasmussen (OB Odense) for B.Laudrup.
England: P.L.Shilton (Derby Co); P.A.Parker (QPR), S.Pearce (Nottm Forest), N.J.Webb (Nottm Forest), D.S.Walker (Nottm Forest), T.I.Butcher (Rangers), B.Robson (Man Utd, captain), D.Rocastle (Arsenal), P.A.Beardsley (Liverpool), G.W.Lineker (FC Barcelona), J.C.B.Barnes (Liverpool).
Subs: D.A.Seaman (QPR) for Shilton, S.McMahon (Liverpool) for Webb, S.G.Bull (Wolves) for Beardsley and C.R.Waddle (Spurs) for Barnes.

Half-time 0-1   Full-time 1-1
Ref: J.Uilenberg (Holland)   Att: 18,400

THIS friendly international, arranged as part of the celebrations for the Centenary of the Danish Football Association, was one that will be instantly forgotten such was the quality of the game. Neither side showed the urgency in their play, despite the fact that for England it was a perfect warm-up match for the important game in Sweden coming up. There was little, though, for the 18,400 spectators to enthuse over.

As early as the second minute England seemed to have a legitimate claim to a penalty as Kent Nielsen's challenge on Gary Lineker sent the England man sprawling. A lovely pass by Bryan Robson had set up the chance and Lineker was furious with the referee.

Denmark, with their neat approach play, looked a useful side and both the Laudrup brothers were dangerous. Unfortunately for them, though, the Danes tended to over-elaborate their moves and England were able to defend comfortably. In the 26th minute Lineker exacted revenge for the earlier incident by giving England the lead. David Rocastle dispossessed Andersen and fed a pass to Neil Webb. He cleverly side-stepped Andersen, who was trying to recover his mistake, and crossed low from the right. The goal was gaping and Lineker rarely scored a simpler goal for his country.

Peter Shilton had enjoyed a quiet match to celebrate breaking Bobby Moore's England appearance record. The best moment of his 109th appearance came before the start when he picked up a presentation from the Football Association to mark his achievement. His worst moment came in the 54th minute, when Lars Elstrup wriggled free of the defence before planting a shot between Shilton and the near post. Terry Butcher must take some of the blame for the goal but Shilton would have been very disappointed at the way it went in.

At this point, both managers decided to bring on an army of substitutes and with all the changes it was not surprising that the rest of the game degenerated into mediocrity. Neither side looked likely to break the deadlock and in the end everyone was happy to hear the final whistle. It is sad that England managers had agreed to all those substitutions, for it ruined most games and also, more importantly, surely devalued the winning of a cap.

> 11th match v Denmark.
> 109th cap for Shilton, a new record.

Sweden v England World Cup Qualifier

Played on Wednesday, 6 September 1989 in the Råsunda Stadium, Solna.

Sweden: T.Ravelli (IFK Gothenburg); R.Nilsson (IFK Gothenburg), G.I.Hysén (Liverpool), P.Larsson (Ajax Amsterdam), R.Ljung (Young Boys), L.Engqvist (Malmö FF), J.Thern (Benfica), K.Ingersson (IFK Gothenburg), J.Nilsson (Malmö FF), J.Ekström (AS Cannes), M.Magnussen (Benfica).
Subs: G.Strömberg (Atalanta) for Ingesson and A.Limpar (Cremonese) for J.Nilsson.
England: P.L.Shilton (Derby Co); M.G.Stevens (Rangers), S.Pearce (Nottm Forest), D.S.Walker (Nottm Forest), T.I.Butcher (Rangers, captain), S.McMahon (Liverpool), C.R.Waddle (Spurs), N.J.Webb (Man Utd), P.A.Beardsley (Liverpool), G.W.Lineker (Spurs), J.C.B.Barnes (Liverpool).
Subs: P.J.Gascoigne (Spurs) for Webb and D.Rocastle (Arsenal) for Barnes.

Half-time 0-0   Full-time 0-0
Ref: H.Forstinger (Austria)   Att: 38,588

WITH this battling point won in Solna, England edged a fraction nearer the nine-point target which would give them guaranteed entry into the finals in Italy the following year. Traditionally, September is not the month when they are at their best and for such a vital match as this it was not a good sign for their supporters. However, they need not have worried as two of England's greatest campaigners did as much as anyone to give them the point they deserved, Terry Butcher and the ageless Peter Shilton.

The match was an uncompromising affair with tackles going in thick, fast and not always fairly. The Swedes were a hard side and from the moment Gary Lineker was caught by Roland Nilsson in the second minute after the striker had sprinted on to a Steve McMahon pass England knew it was not going to be easy. The visitors attack was not as sharp as of late and both Lineker and Peter Beardsley were off form.

On the other hand Sweden were often dangerous going forward but quality defending by England kept the home side's goal chances to a minimum. In the 26th minute, though, England suffered a sickening blow which almost threatened this defensive stability. Butcher and Ekström both went for a high ball and a clash of heads left blood pouring from the England skipper's head. It looked as though Butcher might have to go off, but he refused to leave the field and swathed in a white bandage that quickly turned blood red he bravely carried on. It was very characteristic of this wholehearted player.

There was a chance at either end just before half-time, with first Lineker seeing a good shot well saved by the impressive Ravelli, and then a superb run by Joakim Nilsson ended with Engqvist having a crisp shot brilliantly saved by Shilton. The goalkeeper had looked supremely safe in the first half and he inspired so much confidence to his colleagues. With Butcher by now soaked in his own blood but manfully playing on, these two were the rocks on which the Swedes kept floundering.

Straight after half-time, though, it was England who nearly took the lead. A fine double save by Ravelli twice prevented Lineker from breaking the deadlock. Later, a Stuart Pearce thunderbolt free-kick was also scrambled away by the 'keeper.

Sweden, despite their dominance of possession, could not turn it into goals as England's stubborn defence refused to yield. In the 74th minute another severe injury robbed the visitors of Neil Webb, who damaged an Achilles tendon in an innocuous incident. All Manchester United fans were to be very disappointed with that news.

In the final five minutes there were two more chances for Sweden to snatch the win and the impressive Des Walker was at the heart of both incidents. First the defender made a crucial interception to deny Magnusson and then a rush of blood saw Walker give a suicidal back-pass straight to the Swede. But once again, England owed a debt of gratitude to Shilton as the goalkeeper stood firm and blocked Magnusson's shot, thus preserving England's vital point.

> 13th match v Sweden.

Poland v England World Cup Qualifier

Played on Wednesday, 11 October 1989 at the Slaski Stadium, Katowice.

Poland: J.Bako (Zagłębie Lubin); P.Cz-
achowski (Stal Mielec), Z.Kaczmarek (Legia Warsaw), D.Wdowczyk (Legia Warsaw), R.Warzycha (Górnik Zabrze), J.Nawrocki (GKS Katowice), B.Tarasiewicz (Neuchâtel Xamax), J.Ziober (LKS Lódź), R.Kosecki (Legia Warsaw), D.Dziekanowski (Celtic), K.Warzycha (Ruch Chorzów).
Sub: J.Furtok (Hamburger SV) for Warzycha.
England: P.L.Shilton (Derby Co); M.G.Stevens (Rangers), S.Pearce (Nottm Forest), S.McMahon (Liverpool), D.S.Walker (Nottm Forest), T.I.Butcher (Rangers), B.Robson (Man Utd, captain), D.Rocastle (Arsenal), P.A.Beardsley (Liverpool), G.W.Lineker (Spurs), C.R.Waddle (Spurs).

Half-time 0-0   Full-time 0-0
Ref: E.Aladren (Spain)   Att: 30,000

IT was official: England had qualified for the World Cup Finals to be held in Italy next summer. That was the outcome of this hard fought draw against Poland where the main hero was, yet again, the incredible Peter Shilton.

Poland looked extremely sharp early on and Celtic's Dziekanowski put in a fourth-minute shot which Shilton comfortably saved. Des Walker and Terry Butcher were given a torrid time by the fast and mobile Polish forwards. In midfield the home side held the initiative for long spells and right-back Czachowski was a constant danger with his close control and positive breaks down the right. Another good shot, this time from Krzystof Warzycha, was well saved by the England goalkeeper and the Poles continually drove forward. A rare shot by England, from Steve McMahon, only briefly relieved the pressure before Shilton produced a marvellous save to deny Dziekanowski a fine header.

The first relief that England had from this onslaught actually came at the moment of the half-time whistle and manager Bobby Robson must have had some stern words with his players at the break. Because after the interval, England did improve somewhat and began to have some say in the midfield battle. Poland, having seen their best efforts thwarted by a superb goalkeeping display, began to lose heart and, as tiredness crept into their play, England started to get on top. Bryan Robson so nearly grabbed a goal in the 62nd minute. Peter Beardsley's corner was met by the skipper's head and only a brilliant save by the giant Bako prevented a goal.

Chris Waddle was the main threat to Poland's goal and one jinking run was ended by a fully stretched catch by the goalkeeper. As time ticked away and England edged nearer the one point they needed to guarantee their place in Italy, possession was the name of the game. England played the ball around desperately trying to stretch the Poles and prevent them from being able to build dangerous attacks.

All credit to Stuart Pearce, Gary Stevens, Walker and Butcher for standing firm in front of Shilton. But in the very last minute the England fans had their hearts in their mouths as a tremendous 35-yard shot from Tarasiewicz crashed against England's crossbar with Shilton, for once, beaten.

At the end of the day, though, everything worked out right and the 40-year-old goalkeeper was one of the happiest men in Poland. He had finally got his own back after that nightmare moment in the 1973 World Cup match at Wembley.

> 7th match v Poland.

England v Italy — Friendly

Played on Wednesday, 15 November 1989 at Wembley Stadium.

England: P.L.Shilton (Derby Co); M.G.Stevens (Rangers), S.Pearce (Nottm Forest), S.McMahon (Liverpool), D.S.Walker (Nottm Forest), T.I.Butcher (Rangers), B.Robson (Man Utd, captain), C.R.Waddle (Marseille), P.A.Beardsley (Liverpool), G.W.Lineker (Spurs), J.C.B.Barnes (Liverpool).
Subs: D.J.Beasant (Chelsea) for Shilton, N.Winterburn (Arsenal) for Pearce, S.B.Hodge (Nottm Forest) for McMahon, M.C.Phelan (Man Utd) for Robson and D.A.Platt (Aston Villa) for Beardsley.
Italy: W.Zenga (Inter-Milan); G.Bergomi (Inter-Milan), P.Maldini (Milan AC), F.Baresi (Milan AC), R.Ferri (Inter-Milan), N.Berti (Inter-Milan), R.Donadoni (Milan AC), F.De Napoli (Napoli), G.Vialli (Sampdoria), G.Giannini (AS Roma), A.Carnevale (Napoli).
Subs: R.Baggio (Fiorentina) for Vialli and A.Serena (Inter-Milan) for Carnevale.

Half-time 0-0   Full-time 0-0
Ref: H.Forstinger (Austria)   Att: 75,000

ENGLAND grew in confidence for their impending World Cup challenge after this morale boosting performance against the Italians at Wembley. True, they never defeated their visitors but they did enough against one of the tournament favourites to suggest they need fear no one.

Immediately Bryan Robson and Steve McMahon imposed themselves on to the midfield and they soon put pressure on the Italian defence. Gary Lineker was felled just outside the area and Stuart Pearce's rocket-like free-kick only just cleared the crossbar. Chris Waddle, who had an excellent game throughout, then combined well with Lineker to set up John Barnes for a header which was saved by goalkeeper Zenga.

Italy were well served by their big goalkeeper although the main organiser of their unyielding defence was Baresi. The Italian captain had a fine match and he used his superb ability of reading a game to full advantage. Despite this typical reliance on defence, Italy still looked dangerous on a couple of breakaways, and with more emphasis on attack would surely be the best in the world on current form.

But credit must also go to England as they impressed everyone watching with their willingness, running power and no little amount of skill. Another chance arrived in the 27th minute when Waddle's free-kick from the left was met by Terry Butcher. The England stalwart should have done better than head wide, especially as Zenga had badly misjudged that situation.

Italy's Carnevale did get the ball into the England net, but the offside whistle saved the day. It was testament to Eng-land's good play that the Italians retreated into defence for long spells and this pattern continued after the break. In the 74th minute, Peter Beardsley saw his shot cleared off the line in what was one of England's best moments and then Lineker was unlucky when his goal was ruled out after an infringement by Butcher was spotted by the referee. That seemed a harsh decision and it angered the home players. A winning goal then would have been a fitting reward for a very good performance.

> 16th match v Italy.
> Debuts, all as substitutes, for Beasant, Phelan, Winterburn and Platt.

England v Yugoslavia — Friendly

Played on Wednesday, 13 December 1989 at Wembley Stadium.

England: P.L.Shilton (Derby Co); P.A.Parker (QPR), S.Pearce (Nottm Forest), M.L.Thomas (Arsenal), D.S.Walker (Nottm Forest), T.I.Butcher (Rangers), B.Robson (Man Utd, captain), D.Rocastle (Arsenal), S.G.Bull (Wolves), G.W.Lineker (Spurs), C.R.Waddle (Marseille).
Subs: D.J.Beasant (Chelsea) for Shilton, A.R.Dorigo (Chelsea) for Pearce, D.A.Platt (Aston Villa) for Thomas, S.McMahon (Liverpool) for Robson and S.B.Hodge (Nottm Forest) for Rocastle.
Yugoslavia: T.Ivković (Sporting Lisbon); V.Stanojković (Partizan Belgrade), P.Spasic (Partizan Belgrade), D.Brnović (FC Metz), F.Hadžibejić (FC Sochaux), Z.Vulić (Real Mallorca), H.Škoro (Torino), S.Susic (Paris St-Germain), R.Mihajlović (Bayern Munich), D.Stojković (Red Star Belgrade), T.Savevski (AEK Athens).
Sub: Petric (Partizan Belgrade) for Spasic, Panadic (Dinamo Zagreb) for Brnović and R.Prosinečki (Red Star Belgrade) for Susic.

Half-time 1-1   Full-time 2-1
Ref: D.Pauly (West Germany) Att: 34,796

CONTINUING their build up for the World Cup, England took on a very good Yugoslavia side at Wembley and produced another encouraging win. Once again, though, they owed an enormous amount to their skipper Bryan Robson. The Manchester United star already held the record for the fastest goal scored in a World Cup finals match and, here, after only 38 seconds, he netted another quick one in near-record time.

As often happens Gary Lineker was fouled in England's first attack. Chris Waddle took the free-kick and the ball cleared the static defence for Robson to head powerfully past the stunned Ivković in the Yugoslav goal. The visitors had been caught cold and not since Jackie Milburn's 45-second goal for Newcastle against Manchester City in the 1955 FA Cup Final had Wembley seen such an explosive start.

Manager Bobby Robson had brought several fringe players in to give them some experience and also the chance for them to make an impact. They were soon learning a great deal about football at this level as the Yugoslavian side came back strongly from their early set-back. Stoj-ković, a very talented player, showed all his skill and in the 18th minute it was he who made the visitor's equalizer. After a Steve Bull shot had been blocked, Stojković gained possession and found Škoro. The England defenders backed off as Škoro ran at them and the winger punished them by hitting a splendid shot from 22 yards which beat the diving Peter Shilton. It was a fine goal and now it was England's turn to be stunned.

With Michael Thomas and David Rocastle finding it difficult to come to terms with this higher grade of football it was left to Robson to hold the midfield together. He did so brilliantly and certainly was an inspiration to the junior members of his side.

The second half was fairly even, but England edged themselves back in front again after 68 minutes. Paul Parker made another of several fine runs from his deep position, exchanged passes with Lineker and then put over a dangerous cross. The ball was flicked on by Bull and there was the irrepressible Robson to drive a left-foot shot home. No wonder the skipper received a standing ovation as he left the field after 75 minutes.

Stuart Pearce was booked as he, too, found the going difficult against this talented side but, thanks to Robson's influence and scoring power, England were able to hold on to their lead and record a very good result.

> 14th match v Yugoslavia.
> Debut, as substitute, for Dorigo.
> Five substitutes used in a match for the first time.

England v Brazil — Friendly

Played on Wednesday, 28 March 1990 at Wembley Stadium.

England: P.L.Shilton (Derby Co); M.G.Stevens (Rangers), S.Pearce (Liverpool), S.McMahon (Liverpool), D.S.Walker (Nottm Forest), T.I.Butcher (Rangers), D.A.Platt (Aston Villa), C.R.Waddle (Marseille), P.A.Beardsley (Liverpool), G.W.Lineker (Spurs), J.C.B.Barnes (Liverpool).
Subs: C.E.Woods (Rangers) for Shilton and P.J.Gascoigne (Spurs) for Beardsley.
Brazil: Taffarel (Internacional); Jorginho (Montpelier), Mozer (Marseille), Galvao (Botafago), Branco (FC Porto), Ricardo (Benfica), Bebeto (Vasco Dagama), Dunga (Fiorentina), Careca (Napoli), Silas (Sporting Lisbon), Valdo (Benfica).
Sub: Aldair (Benfica) for Mozer, Muller (Torino) for Bebeto, Alemao (Napoli) for Silas and Bismark (Vasco da Gama) for Valdo.

Half-time 1-0   Full-time 1-0
Ref: K.Peschel (East Germany) Att: 80,000

WHAT A confidence booster for England — to beat the mighty Brazilians with only 70 days to go before the World Cup finals.

Both teams had regulars missing but the game was a good one and of vital experience to the home players, especially the younger ones. Right from the start it was obvious that the Brazilians possessed all their traditional skills but on the night,

Paul Gascoigne, now establishing himself as one of England's leading stars, was about to have a memorable, if ultimately sad, time in the 1990 World Cup.

England's central defensive partnership of Terry Butcher and Des Walker was magnificent. Walker looked a class player with his speed and confidence on the ball, indeed, he looked more like a Brazilian at times! Early on Mozer put in a cross shot which Peter Shilton saved but in the 12th minute the goalkeeper suffered a badly-cut eye after a collision with Walker and had to be replaced by Chris Woods.

The Rangers 'keeper took his chance well, though, and looked full of confidence. Several times he dealt with free-kicks from Branco who had a go at goal, even from 45 yards range. But in the 37th minute, the capacity crowd of 80,000, now housed in an all-seater stadium, jumped for joy as England took the lead. Peter Beardsley took a corner which was flicked on by John Barnes. The ball flew on to Gary Lineker, who stooped to head it past Tafferel. It was a memorable goal for the supreme England striker as it enabled him to equal the 30-goal total of both Nat Lofthouse and Tom Finney.

The second half was evenly contested with Brazil putting together some exquisite passing movements. The finish wasn't there because their moves usually floundered on the rock-like Butcher and Walker. Brazil were unlucky, though, when substitute Muller went around Woods and fired in a shot which looked to be handled on the line by Stuart Pearce as the full-back cleared. But the referee waved play on amidst a storm of protest by the Brazilians.

Television replays later seemed to uphold Brazil's claim but the referee, unfortunately, does not have that luxury.

Another player who did well for England was Chris Waddle and whenever he gained possession there was a buzz of anticipation from the crowd. David Platt, playing his first full game, found it tough going but did enough to warrant being given another chance. Brazil, meanwhile, had now tightened up their defence considerably and in goalkeeper Tafferel they found an excellent goalkeeper. With two such strong defences on show, it really came as no surprise that there was no further score. It is always nice to beat the Brazilians and England can savour a good victory.

15th match v Brazil.

England v Czechoslovakia Friendly

Played on Wednesday, 25 April 1990 at Wembley Stadium.

England: P.L.Shilton (Derby Co); L.M.Dixon (Arsenal), S.Pearce (Nottm Forest), T.M.Steven (Rangers), D.S.Walker (Nottm Forest), T.I.Butcher (Rangers), B.Robson (Man Utd, captain), P.J.Gascoigne (Spurs), S.G.Bull (Wolves), G.W.Lineker (Spurs), S.B.Hodge (Nottm Forest).
Subs: D.A.Seaman (Arsenal) for Shilton, A.R.Dorigo (Chelsea) for Pearce, M.Wright (Derby Co) for Walker and S.McMahon (Liverpool) for Robson.
Czechoslovakia: L.Mikloško (West Ham); M.Bielik (Sparta Prague), F.Straka (Borussia Mönchengladbach), I.Hašek (Sparta Prague), J.Kocian (St Pauli), V.Kinier (Slovan Bratislava), J.Bílek (Sparta Prague), L.Kubík (Fiorentina),

I.Knoflíček (St Pauli), T.Skuhravý (Sparta Prague), L.Moravčik (Plastika Nitra).
Subs: M.Kadlec (TJ Vitkovice) for Straka and V.Weiss (Inter Bratislava) for Skuhravý.

Half-time 2-1   Full-time 4-2
Ref: M.Girard (France)   Att: 21,342

ENGLAND had found a new star. That was the verdict after this fine victory against another of the World Cup challengers. The man who won the hearts of everyone was Paul Gascoigne. In only his second full game he showed the form he had promised since his Newcastle days and staged a one-man show that had Wembley buzzing.

Yet the night had started badly with the Czechs showing their attacking flair early on. England's defence was exposed by the speed of a break involving Kubík and Knoflíček in the 11th minute. It was from Knoflíček's cross that the tall Skuhravý headed down and beyond the diving Peter Shilton. At this point England were looking for some inspiration and they found it in the ebullient form of Gascoigne. In the 16th minute he stroked a glorious pass with the outside of his boot towards Steve Bull. The big striker let it come over his shoulder, down on to his chest and on to his right foot with superb control before crashing a thumping shot into the roof of Mikloško's net. It was a truly magnificent goal and seven minutes later England took the lead.

Gascoigne's corner was helped on by both Terry Butcher and Gary Lineker and there was Stuart Pearce lunging in to register his first goal for his country. At half-time Bobby Robson brought on substitutes David Seaman, Mark Wright and Tony Dorigo for some vital experience but England stayed in command. Within 11 minutes of the restart, the Gascoigne-Bull partnership struck again. Gascoigne took on two defenders and his confidence showed as he beat them and whipped over a pin-point cross which Bull dispatched with a bullet-like header into the Czech net.

England were now well on top and Bull twice went close to a hat-trick. But in the 81st minute, a lapse in concentration let the Czech side back into the reckoning. Steve Hodge, who had not enjoyed the best of games, gave away a needless free-kick on the edge of the England penalty area. Kubík took the kick and curled a fine shot around the wall and beyond Seaman. It was an irritating goal, carelessly conceded and Gascoigne reacted as though all his good work would be wasted if he did not take a hold of the proceedings again.

So, with just two minutes to go he struck back with a simply magnificent goal. Dorigo and Wright combined to give Gascoigne possession and the star of the night dummied and shuffled past his marker before hitting a fine shot into the roof of the net. It was a goal worthy of an even greater stage and what a pity that only just over 21,000 people were at Wembley to see it. In fact the quality of the goals on this excellent night of football was first class.

Now Bobby Robson had some tough decisions to make because Gascoigne had certainly grabbed his opportunity.

11th match v Czechoslovakia.

England v Denmark Friendly

Played on Wednesday, 15 May 1990 at Wembley Stadium.

England: P.L.Shilton (Derby Co); M.G.Stevens (Rangers), S.Pearce (Nottm Forest), S.McMahon (Liverpool), D.S.Walker (Nottm Forest), T.I.Butcher (Rangers, captain), S.B.Hodge (Nottm Forest), P.J.Gascoigne (Spurs), C.R.Waddle (Marseille), G.W.Lineker (Spurs), J.C.B.Barnes (Liverpool).
Subs: C.E.Woods (Rangers) for Shilton, A.R.Dorigo (Chelsea) for Pearce, D.A.Platt (Aston Villa) for McMahon, D.Rocastle (Arsenal) for Waddle and S.G.Bull (Wolves) for Lineker.
Denmark: P.B.Schmeichel (Brøndby IF); J.Sivebaek (AS St-Etienne), K.Nielsen (Aston Villa), L.Olsen (Brøndby IF), H.Andersen (RSC Anderlecht), J.Bartram (Bayer 05 Uerdingen), J.Jensen (Brøndby IF), K.Vilfort (Brøndby IF), F.Povlsen (PSV Eindhoven), M.Laudrup (FC Barcelona), B.Laudrup (Bayer 05 Uerdingen).
Subs: M.Brunn (Silkeborg) for Povlsen and L.Jakobsen (Odense BK) for Laudrup.

Half-time 0-0   Full-time 1-0
Ref: J.McCluskey (Scotland)   Att: 27,643

DENMARK gave England all sorts of problems in the first half of this friendly international and exposed some of the weaknesses that Bobby Robson would have to work on before June. The Danes attacked in waves and, but for Peter Shilton's outstanding form and the wonderful defensive covering of Des Walker, England would have been in deep trouble.

Great work by Brian Laudrup completely beat Stuart Pearce and his pass set up Andersen, whose shot was beaten away by an alert Shilton. The skill of Michael Laudrup was also evident and only a brilliantly-timed tackle by Walker prevented the Danish star from scoring. Terry Butcher and Pearce were both having an uncomfortable night and Denmark seemed to hold all the aces without finding the net. The experiment of using John Barnes alongside Gary Lineker proved fruitless, although the service these two received from the midfield was very poor so Schmeichel's first half was largely undisturbed.

The second half was much better for England and some substitutions put new vigour into their game. Nine minutes after the restart they took the lead with a fine goal from Lineker. A lovely cross from Hodge was met first time by Lineker and the ball crashed down off the crossbar, but behind the line for a goal. It was the star striker's 31st goal for his country, so he was left a clear third in the all-time list of England goalscorers. Only Jimmy Greaves and Bobby Charlton had more.

Two brave saves by substitute Chris Woods kept the lead intact and eventually, as the time ran out, there was no way back for Denmark. They might have felt a little aggrieved about the result but, as England have found many times to their cost in the past, if you don't score then you have no chance of winning.

Paul Gascoigne did some useful work, but was more defensive than usual mainly due to Denmark's sharp attacking play. But England had now gone 17 matches unbeaten and they were within three of over-hauling the record run of Sir Alf Ramsey's team set up just prior to the 1966 World Cup triumph.

12th match v Denmark.
50th caps for both Waddle and Barnes.

England v Uruguay   Friendly

Played on Wednesday, 22 May 1990 at Wembley Stadium.

England: P.L.Shilton (Derby Co); P.A.Parker (QPR), S.Pearce (Nottm Forest), S.B.Hodge (Nottm Forest), D.S.Walker (Nottm Forest), T.I.Butcher (Rangers), B.Robson (Man Utd, captain), P.J.Gascoigne (Spurs), C.R.Waddle (Marseille), G.W.Lineker (Spurs), J.C.B.Barnes (Liverpool).
Subs: P.A.Beardsley (Liverpool) for Hodge and S.G.Bull (Wolves) for Lineker.
Uruguay: E.Pereira (Nacional); N.Gutierrez (Verona), H.De Leon (River Plate), J.Herrera (Figueras), J.Perdomo (Genoa), A.Dominguez (Peñarol), A.Alzamendi (Logrones), S.Ostolaza (Nacional), E.Francescoli (Marseille), R.Paz (Genoa), R.Sosa (Lazio).
Sub: S.Martinez (Defensor) for Sosa.

Half-time 0-1   Full-time 1-2
Ref: P.D'elia (Italy)   Att: 38,751

WITH England just three days away from departure for the World Cup finals in Italy, they were looking to extend their 17-match unbeaten run. So it came as a big shock to them to lose that proud record at home to Uruguay. That meant the six-year unbeaten home record also came to an end and it was not the best way for the team to leave these shores.

Uruguay came to Wembley with a tarnished reputation after many years of cynical and robust play, but on this night the fans saw the brighter side of their game. Superb skills on the ball, swift inter-passing and deadly strikes on goal made a mockery of their apparent need to resort to their usual unsavoury tactics. Stuart Pearce made one of his fierce early tackles to let the visitors know England could look after themselves but Uruguay hit back with some lovely football. It culminated in them taking the lead after 27 minutes.

Chris Waddle lost possession and his Marseille clubmate, Francescoli, swept the ball out to the left finding Alzamendi. A cross to the middle and Ostolaza looped a header over Peter Shilton and into the net. It looked spectacular, but it was actually slightly fortuitous as Ostolaza had no real control as to where his header would go. Having said that, Shilton was not too pleased with his positioning either.

Just before the goal Paul Gascoigne had been brought down as he burst through looking likely to go all the way. Then Pearce hit a stunning free-kick from 25 yards which Pereira dived full-length to push round a post. Before half-time, a Gascoigne corner almost led to an equalizer but Uruguay eventually scrambled the ball away as John Barnes and Terry Butcher tried to force it over the line.

Six minutes after the restart, though,

England were level. Gascoigne set the move going, finding Pearce with a lovely pass. The full-back crossed and Barnes controlled it brilliantly before hitting a superb shot into the far corner beating Pereira all-ends-up.

England had done very well to come back, but in the 64th minute they fell behind again. Once more Shilton was at fault as Perdomo's long free-kick went through his fingers as he dived to save. Having got to the ball the goalkeeper would feel that he should have kept it out. As the game wore on, one felt that it was not to be England's night.

Two penalty appeals were ignored as Bryan Robson and Barnes went down in the area and the goalkeeper, Pereira, did very well to save a Barnes back header following a Waddle corner. England worked hard to the end, but that elusive goal would not come. The nearest they came was when Pearce burst through only for Pereira to make a fine save to preserve Uruguay's lead.

Perhaps, in some ways, it was a good thing that England's unbeaten run ended before they went to Italy, but it is never very nice to lose at home. Thankfully it does not happen very often.

8th match v Uruguay.
50th cap for Lineker.

Tunisia v England   Friendly

Played on Saturday, 2 June 1990 in the Olympic Stadium, Tunis.

Tunisia: Zitouni; Mbadbi, Neji, Hishiri, Yahia, Mahjoubi, Sellimi, Tarak, Hergal, Rouissi, Khemiri.
Subs: Dermach for Hergal and Rashid for Khemiri.
(Initials and club names untraced)
England: P.L.Shilton (Derby Co); M.G.Stevens (Rangers), S.Pearce (Nottm Forest), S.B.Hodge (Nottm Forest), D.S.Walker (Nottm Forest), T.I.Butcher (Rangers), B.Robson (Man Utd, captain), P.J.Gascoigne (Spurs), C.R.Waddle (Marseille), G.W.Lineker (Spurs), J.C.B.Barnes (Liverpool).
Subs: P.A.Beardsley (Liverpool) for Hodge, M.Wright (Derby Co) for Butcher, D.A.Platt (Aston Villa) for Waddle and S.G.Bull (Wolves) for Lineker.

Half-time 1-0   Full-time 1-1
Ref: R Medjiba (Algeria)   Att: 25,000

ENGLAND'S last international before the game against the Republic of Ireland opened their World Cup campaign in a few days time was largely a non-event as regards building a side capable of winning the trophy. In a hotch-potch of a performance, only a late goal rescued them from the humiliation of defeat.

They should never have been in that position though as many chances went begging. In the 13th minute, Bryan Robson should have done better than head wide from Paul Gascoigne's free-kick. Four minutes later a lovely pass by Robson set up Gary Lineker, who cut inside before hammering in a fierce shot which Zitouni did well to push over. Then, a minute after that, more good work by Gascoigne gave Lineker another chance but again Zitouni saved well.

Lineker was given some rough treatment by the Tunisian defenders, who were well aware of his reputation and Hicheri was rightly booked for one foul on the Spurs player. On 27 minutes, England received a severe blow. A pass by Gascoigne, intended for Gary Stevens, instead found Hergal and from fully 30 yards he hit a superb shot which dipped over Peter Shilton and crashed into the net to give Tunisia a sensational lead. Suddenly England found themselves facing a real problem and they knew they would have to work really hard to get back into the game. After 35 minutes they so nearly equalized but Stuart Pearce's free-kick crashed against a post before being cleared.

After the break England came close to conceding a second goal when Neji almost scored early on, his shot hitting the side netting. The Tunisians did not stand on ceremony with their tackling and both Lineker and Gascoigne received a severe buffeting. Ironically, the only yellow card that the referee produced in this half was aimed at Terry Butcher for an alleged elbow in the face of Dermach, a substitute.

England were still struggling after an hour's play, so manager Bobby Robson decided on a change of tactics to try to rescue things, bringing on Peter Beardsley to partner Lineker and switching John Barnes back to the wing. A good run and shot almost brought Gascoigne a goal and then the Spurs player set up Robson, only for Zitouni to again save the day for the home side. The goalkeeper had had a fine game and a minute later he made another good stop to foil the disappointing Chris Waddle. That was Waddle's last contribution as Steve Bull and David Platt came on with ten minutes to go.

The visitors were becoming desperate as time slipped away, but with only a minute left they finally scored an equalizer. From a clearance by Stevens, Gascoigne picked up the ball and made a long run down the middle. His poorly hit pass managed to find Barnes wide on the left and the winger made ten yards before whipping in a hard waist-high cross. Bull then became the hero, stooping to send a bullet header past Zitouni, much to the relief of his teammates.

1st match v Tunisia.

World Cup Finals

Republic of Ireland v England   Group F

Played on Monday, 11 June 1990 in the Stadio Sant 'Elia, Cagliari, Sardinia.

Republic of Ireland: P.Bonner (Celtic); C.B.Morris (Celtic), S.Staunton (Liverpool), M.J.McCarthy (Millwall), K.B.Moran (Blackburn R), P.McGrath (Aston Villa), R.J.Houghton (Liverpool), A.D.Townsend (Norwich C), J.W.Aldridge (Real Sociedad), A.G.Cascarino (Aston Villa), K.M.Sheedy (Everton).
England: P.L.Shilton (Derby Co); M.G.Stevens (Rangers), S.Pearce (Nottm Forest), D.S.Walker (Nottm Forest), T.I.Butcher (Rangers), B.Robson (Man Utd, captain), C.R.Waddle (Marseille), P.J.Gascoigne (Spurs), J.C.B.Barnes (Liverpool), G.W.Lineker (Spurs),

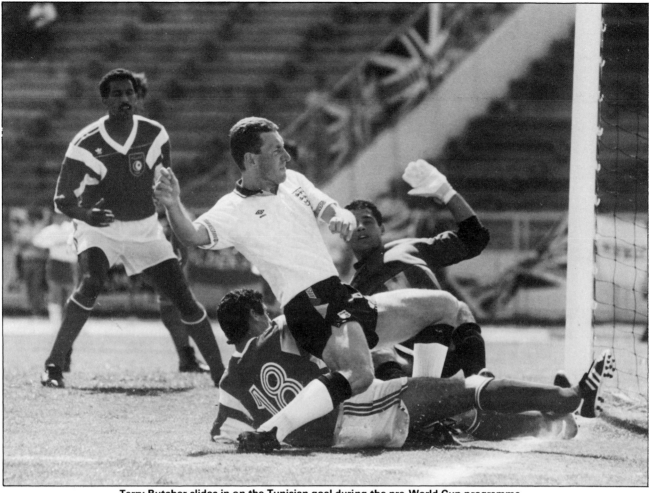

Terry Butcher slides in on the Tunisian goal during the pre-World Cup programme.

P.A.Beardsley (Liverpool).
Sub: S.G.Bull (Wolves) for Lineker.

Half-time 0-1   Full-time 1-1

Ref: A.Schmidhuber (West Germany)

Att: 35,238

ENGLAND'S attempt at revenge for their awful showing against the Republic of Ireland in the 1988 European Championships was only half achieved in this opening match of the World Cup finals in Italy. A stale, unimaginative game was the result and a draw was the obvious result long before the end.

Once again there were precious few moments of good football to appreciate as the ball was pummelled from the edge of one area to the edge of the other. The Irish, playing strictly to their strengths, chased and harried the England players, refusing to let them settle into any kind of rhythm, but on nine minutes England scored a priceless goal. Chris Waddle, who showed flashes of skill throughout, cleverly danced around Staunton before delivering a probing diagonal cross towards the sprinting Gary Lineker. The striker let it bounce on his chest and this deceived McCarthy and Bonner to the extent that the ball ran towards an open goal. Lineker followed up and beat Morris to it to scramble it into the net. There was jubilation on the England bench as the players regrouped to withstand the expected aerial bombardment from the Irish.

Sure enough that ploy was used constantly as the Irish team tried to push

England back. However, Terry Butcher and Des Walker were in fine form and only a McGrath header tested Peter Shilton. England's midfield could not get to grips with the ball as it continually flew over their heads and as a result the game became very scrappy and, indeed, boringly predictable. It cried out for someone to hold the ball, a playmaker. However, at half-time England were satisfied with the position having had few alarms at the back.

When the players re-emerged after the break they were greeted by a torrential electrical storm which swept across the stadium. The game carried on as before with the Irish looking less and less like scoring. With only 25 minutes to go Bobby Robson sent on Steve McMahon in an effort to help bolster the England midfield. It proved to be a tragic mistake.

The Liverpool player had only been on the field for three minutes when he lost possession to Sheedy on the edge of his own penalty area and then watched in horror as the Irishmen crashed in a low shot with that trusty left foot of his. The ball flashed past the diving Shilton to give Ireland the draw and enabled the critics of England to have a field day.

11th match v Republic of Ireland.

Holland v England

Group F

Played on Saturday, 16 June 1990 in the Stadio Sant 'Elia, Cagliari, Sardinia.

Holland: H.van Breukelen (PSV Eindhoven); B.van Aerle (PSV Eindhoven), J.van't Schip (Ajax Amsterdam), R.Koeman (Barcelona), F.Rijkaard (Milan AC), A.van Tiggelen (RSC Anderlecht), J.Wouters (Ajax Amsterdam), R.Gullit (Milan AC), M.van Basten (Milan AC), R.Witschge (Ajax Amsterdam), H.Gillhaus (Aberdeen).
Sub: W.Kieft (PSV Eindhoven) for van't Schip.

England: P.L.Shilton (Derby Co); P.A.Parker (QPR), S.Pearce (Nottm Forest), M.Wright (Derby Co), T.I.Butcher (Rangers), D.S.Walker (Nottm Forest), B.Robson (Man Utd, captain), P.J.Gascoigne (Spurs), C.R.Waddle (Marseille), G.W.Lineker (Spurs), J.C.B.Barnes (Liverpool).
Subs: D.A.Platt (Aston Villa) for Robson and S.G.Bull (Wolves) for Waddle.

Half-time 0-0   Full-time 0-0

Ref: Z.Petrović (Yugoslavia)   Att: 35,267

THIS was a much better performance from England and with a little luck they might have been celebrating a famous victory over the current European Champions. Manager Bobby Robson's tactic of playing Mark Wright as a continental-style sweeper was a resounding success and deserving of further consideration.

After initial teething troubles the players settled down well and the defence looked in top form. Des Walker was soon clamping shut on the dangerous van Basten, whilst Terry Butcher kept a close watch on Gillhaus. Both sides probed each other looking for that vital opening. Paul

Gascoigne had a fine game and his growing confidence came shining through. In a midfield containing Gullit, one of the world's best players, Gascoigne did not look out of place and more than held his own.

England played much more positively in this game and two fine moves within a minute in the first half almost produced goals. Gascoigne to John Barnes, on to Lineker who outpaced van Tiggelen before cutting the ball back. Unfortunately it just eluded Barnes but Gascoigne then centred after wriggling past two defenders and Robson headed just wide at the near post.

England had had a good opening half and the second period belonged to them as well. Lineker again had a chance but blazed over the bar when he found himself in a fine position. That was a bad miss but in another attack Lineker's shot hit van Breukelen before rebounding to the striker, who, this time, put it into the net. But the referee decided controversially that Lineker had controlled the ball with his hand so the goal was ruled out.

Wright had settled into the sweeper's role with consummate ease and the whole performance had the English fans buzzing. Right on the full-time whistle Gascoigne was fouled on the right side of the penalty area. Up stepped Stuart Pearce to take the free-kick and his fierce drive flew across van Breukelen's dive and into the far corner. For a split-second there was euphoria amongst England's supporters. Sadly, the eagle-eyed referee was once again on the spot pointing out to everyone that his arm was raised indicating an indirect free-kick, so, of course, Pearce's shot was ruled out.

It was all very disappointing but it must be said that the referee had a fine game and was the first of the tournament who did not resort to giving a yellow card at the first foul!

After such a promising display it was annoying that England could not get the goal their play deserved. It was also a sad match for England's captain, Bryan Robson, who once again, as in Mexico four years earlier, had to leave the action through injury. Sadly for Robson he was to return home with an Achilles tendon injury. England now had to beat Egypt to be absolutely sure of qualifying for the next stage of the competition, not a formality by any measure.

> 10th match v Holland.

Egypt v England
Group F

Played on Thursday, 21 June 1990 in the Stadio Sant'Elia, Cagliari, Sardinia.

Egypt: A.A.Ahmed Shobier (Al Ahly); Ibrahim Hassan (Al Ahly), Rabie Yassein (Al Ahly), G.Hani Ramzy (Al Ahly), M.Z.Hesham Yakan (Zamalek), M.Ahmed Ramzy (Zamalek), A.Ismail Youssef (Zamalek), S.Magdi Abdelghani (Al Ahly), H.Hossam Hassan (Al Ahly), G.M.Abdel Hamid (Zamalek), A.A.E.K.Ahmed Abdou (Olympic).
Subs: A.K.Abdel Rahman (Zamalek) for Abdel Hamid and M.Tarek Soliman (El Masry) for Ahmed Abdou.
England: P.L.Shilton (Derby Co, captain), P.A.Parker (QPR), S.Pearce (Nottm Forest), P.J.Gascoigne (Spurs), D.S.Walker (Nottm Forest), M.Wright (Derby Co), S.McMahon (Liverpool), C.R.Waddle (Marseille), S.G.Bull (Wolves), G.W.Lineker (Spurs), J.C.B.Barnes (Liverpool).
Subs: D.A.Platt (Aston Villa) for Waddle and P.A.Beardsley (Liverpool) for Bull.

Half-time 0-0   Full-time 0-1
Ref: K.Roethlisberger (Switzerland)
Att: 34,959

IT is always difficult playing against so-called lesser international opposition, especially when you know that a win would put you through to the next round. And so it proved when England met Egypt in Cagliari in their final group match. Egypt, so improved since they were beaten 4-0 in Cairo four years ago, soon let everyone know their intentions. A stream of back-passes to their goalkeeper soon had the crowd whistling their derision and it was obvious that they had little thought of attacking England.

The first half, quite frankly, was awful and was almost devoid of any exciting moments. Paul Parker put in England's only worthwhile shot and the other full-back Stuart Pearce was the only player who looked in good form. Too often the predictable and laboured moves of the England side fell on the tough tackling defence in which Hany Ramzy was superb. Shobeir, in goal, also showed great confidence and it looked for a long time that this match would go the same way as all the other games in this group and end in a draw.

Gary Lineker and Steve Bull struggled as a partnership in this game and often they got in each other's way. Chris Waddle and John Barnes played far too deep and only Paul Gascoigne showed any real flair.

The second half was little better than the first with Egypt content with the scoreline and defending in depth. They wasted as much time as possible causing the referee to book Ibrahim Hassan and Abdelghani, and generally it was a frustrating time for England's players and supporters. Just as it seemed any break through was impossible England finally edged their noses in front. It came after 59 minutes and not surprisingly Gascoigne was at the heart of things. The midfield player flighted a lovely free-kick over from the left touch-line after Des Walker had been fouled. The heads went up and it was Mark Wright who rose above the Egyptian defence to glance his header past the crestfallen Ahmed Shobeir.

The goal meant the Egyptians had to put much more urgency in their play if they were to have any chance. They did push England back for a while and in the last few minutes Peter Shilton dived to his left to save a goalbound shot from Hamid and Egypt's last chance had gone. The great adventure was over for them but the emergence of African football in this tournament had been one of the highlights. For Bobby Robson it meant that his 91st game as manager would not now be his last.

> 2nd match v Egypt.
> "The funniest part of my international career can be summed up in two words — Paul Gascoigne! He was just hilarious to be with!"
> Terry Butcher

Belgium v England
Second Round

Played on Tuesday, 26 June 1990 in the Dall'Ara Stadium, Bologna, Italy.

Belgium: M.Preud'homme (KV Mechelen); E.Gerets (PSV Eindhoven), S.Demol (FC Porto), G.Grün (RSC Anderlecht), M.De Wolf (Kortrijk), L.Clijsters (KV Mechelen), F.Van der Elst (FC Bruges), V.Scifo (AJ Auxerre), B.Versavel (KV Mechelen), M.Degryse (RSC Anderlecht), J.Ceulemans (FC Bruges).
Subs: P.Vervoort (RSC Anderlecht) for Versavel and N.Claesen (R Antwerp FC) for Degryse.
England: P.L.Shilton (Derby Co); P.A.Parker (QPR), S.Pearce (Nottm Forest), M.Wright (Derby Co), D.S.Walker (Nottm Forest), T.I.Butcher (Rangers, captain), S.McMahon (Liverpool), C.R.Waddle (Marseille), P.J.Gascoigne (Spurs), G.W.Lineker (Spurs), J.C.B.Barnes (Liverpool).
Subs: D.A.Platt (Aston Villa) for McMahon and S.G.Bull (Wolves) for Barnes.

Half-time 0-0   Full-time 0-1 aet (90 minutes, 0-0)
Ref: P.Mikkelsen (Denmark)   Att: 34,520

THE magic of the World Cup was epitomised by the drama which unfolded in Bologna between England and Belgium. Rarely has there been such a heart-stopping end to an international in this tournament over the years.

England got off to a bad start and in the first ten minutes the Belgians had three good chances to take the lead. They all came courtesy of bad defensive errors from, in turn, Terry Butcher, Paul Parker and John Barnes. Much to England's relief each opportunity was wasted and eventually they began to settle into a better rhythm. But Belgium were playing neat and controlled football with the technical skills of Scifo and the evergreen Ceulemans much in evidence. Ceulemans, in fact, was unlucky when, after evading Mark Wright's challenge, he crashed a fierce shot against a post with Peter Shilton struggling.

Chris Waddle was England's main hope however and he looked the one player capable of matching the Belgians at their own game. As the half drew to a close England were gaining in confidence and when Stuart Pearce's cross found Barnes it looked odds on a goal. But, alas, Barnes could find none of his Liverpool form out here and he shot tamely wide. Three minutes from half-time Barnes did find the net when he volleyed perfectly past the Belgian goalkeeper after Gary Lineker's cross. But the referee gave offside which, to say the least, was a very dubious decision.

Straight after the interval Scifo again showed how dangerous he could be when he hit a magnificent curling shot which again thudded against Shilton's right-hand post. The shot had come in from fully 30 yards out and it would have been a goal of stunning quality.

However, England came back strongly from that and the best move of the match, involving Lineker and Waddle, ended with Lineker's shot being blocked. The tension on the pitch, and at home amongst the millions watching on television, was almost unbearable, but despite several

Peter Shilton blocks a shot from Cameroon's Biyik in the San Paolo Stadium, Naples.

other near misses, notably when Preud-'homme made fine saves from Lineker and Steve Bull, the deadlock could not be broken in the 90 minutes.

The match then went into extra-time and the two tired teams seemed to be content with the thought of penalties to decide the winner. Both sides were carrying injuries and survival was the name of the game at this point. But then, with only 60 seconds of extra-time to go, there came a moment of extraordinary elation for England.

Gascoigne chipped a delicate free-kick just to the right of the penalty-spot and substitute David Platt allowed the ball to come over his shoulder before hooking an unstoppable volley into the far corner of the net with the goalkeeper caught totally flat-footed.

No one in the stadium, or watching from afar, could quite believe it but the look of absolute joy on the face of Lineker summed up the feelings of a nation. Brilliant!

18th match v Belgium.

Cameroon v England Quarter-final

Played on Sunday, 1 July 1990 in the San Paolo Stadium, Naples, Italy.

Cameroon: T.N'Kono (RCD Español); B.Massing (US Creteil), B.A.Ebwelle (Tonerre Yaoundé), J.E.Kunde (Canon Yaoundé), S.E.Tataw (Tonerre Yaoundé), L.P.M'Fede (Canon Yaoundé), J.C.Pagal (La Roche), T.Libiih (Tonerre Yaoundé), C.T.Makanaky (SC Toulon), F.Oman Biyik (Stade Lavallois), K.Maboang

(Canon Yaoundé).
Subs: E.Ekeke (Valenciennes) for M'Fede and R.Milla (Saint Pierre) for Maboang.
England: P.L.Shilton (Derby Co); P.A.Parker (QPR), S.Pearce (Nottm Forest), M.Wright (Derby Co), D.S.Walker (Nottm Forest), T.I.Butcher (Rangers, captain), D.A.Platt (Aston Villa), C.R.Waddle (Marseille), P.J.Gascoigne (Spurs), G.W.Lineker (Spurs), J.C.B. Barnes (Liverpool).
Subs: T.M.Steven (Rangers) for Butcher and P.A.Beardsley (Liverpool) for Barnes.

Half-time 0-1 Full-time 2-3 aet (90 minutes, 2-2)

Ref: E.Codesal Mendez (Mexico) Att: 55,205

ONE could never imagine that the drama of England's game against Belgium could be surpassed, but in this quarter-final match against Cameroon, the surprise team of the tournament, England experienced every conceivable emotion.

England looked vulnerable early on as the talented Cameroon players chased and harried and showed a great deal of skill. Libiih headed over after one of many good crosses by M'Fede had set him up for a clear chance. It took a little while for England to settle but on 25 minutes they grabbed the lead with a fine goal from the hero of the Belgium game, David Platt. Stuart Pearce made a great run down the left and put over a brilliant cross for Platt to storm in at the far post and send a firm header low to N'Kono's left.

The Africans showed no ill effects after the goal and continued to show up well. They were not at all overawed by the occasion and with Kunde, an effective sweeper, organising everyone around him they had plenty to offer. A rare mistake

by Des Walker left Omam Biyik clear but Peter Shilton was out quickly to block the shot. England were struggling now, mainly because the Cameroon players would not allow them time to settle on the ball. On either side of the interval Cameroon produced some very dangerous attacks. Terry Butcher stopped Massing and Libiih headed over from a good position. But in the 56th minute they deservedly scored an equalizer.

It looked as though Platt was fouled in the Cameroon penalty area but the referee waved play on and the Africans broke quickly. Their 'super sub', 38-year-old Roger Milla, attacked down the right and was sent crashing to the ground by Paul Gascoigne's clumsy challenge. This time the referee did give a penalty, Kunde's kick was emphatic and the Africans now really had their tails up.

Makanaky almost scored another goal and then Cameroon, sensationally, took the lead. Ekeke, another substitute, was sent clear by the incredible Milla and finished with devastating coolness.

England were now in disarray. Pearce had to block another Makanaky shot and Shilton made desperate saves from Omam Biyik and Makanaky again. But England showed great character to keep going and amidst all the mayhem, at least pushed forward continuously. Over 55,000 fans were enthralled by the action and the millions watching at home were willing an equalizer from England. With only eight minutes remaining the persistence of the English players was finally rewarded.

Gary Lineker burst through but was a victim of a wild challenge by a defender. This time there was no doubt about the penalty decision. Imagine, though, the

Gary Lineker scores from the penalty-spot against Cameroon, one of his two spot-kicks against the Africans.

tension of the situation as Lineker lined up to take the spot-kick. Only eight minutes to go and the hopes of his whole country resting on his trusty right foot. There was little sign of worry from the supreme England striker and his shot was true to bring England right back into the match.

A nasty injury to Mark Wright meant a bandaged head for the Derby player but he bravely carried on through the extra period. The injury seemed to upset England's rhythm though as Paul Parker had to move to the middle and Trevor Steven operated as an emergency right-back. The Cameroons had the better of the first half of the extra-time and there were many anxious moments in the England penalty area. In one attack only a brilliant clearance by Steven saved the day.

With this first period of extra-time almost at an end, and England hanging on somewhat, a breakaway gave Gascoigne possession. He released the pass of the game through a square defence for Lineker to sprint on to. As he rounded N'Kono the goalkeeper hauled him down giving England another penalty. Amazing to think that England had not had a penalty given to them for four years and yet suddenly, here they were with two in one game. Lineker, after treatment for injury sustained in the challenge, again showed an icy coolness, although inside he must have been churning! His army of fans need not have worried as he blasted the ball past the goalkeeper to put England ahead for the second time.

During the second half of extra-time England played much better and held on more comfortably that at any other time in the game. Having said that, it was a very relieved set of players that welcomed the final whistle. The Cameroon side had given them a terrific battle and congrat-ulations must go to them for their wonderful tournament. But all credit, too, to the English lads. They never gave up, showed great character and reaped the reward of a semi-final place.

1st match v Cameroon.
Two penalties scored for England by Lineker.
Penalty was also scored for Cameroon, by Kunde.

West Germany v England Semi-final

Played on Wedneday, 4 July 1990 in the Delle Alpi Stadium, Turin, Italy.

West Germany: B.Illgner (1.FC Cologne); J.Kohler (Bayern Munich), K.Augenthaler (Bayern Munich), T.Berthold (AS Roma), G.Buchwald (VfB Stuttgart), O.Thon (Bayern Munich), L.Matthäus (Inter-Milan), T.Hässler (Juventus), A.Brehme (Inter-Milan), J.Klinsmann (Inter-Milan), R.Völler (AS Roma).
Subs: S.Reuter (Bayern Munich) for Thon and K-H.Riedle (Lazio) for Völler.

England: P.L.Shilton (Derby Co); P.A.Parker (QPR), S.Pearce (Nottm Forest), D.S.Walker (Nottm Forest), T.I.Butcher (Rangers, captain), M.Wright (Derby Co), D.A.Platt (Aston Villa), P.J.Gascoigne (Spurs), P.A.Beardsley (Liverpool), G.W.Lineker (Spurs), C.R.Waddle (Marseille).
Subs: T.M.Steven (Rangers) for Butcher.

Half-time 0-0 Full-time 1-1 aet (90 minutes, 1-1)
W.Germany won 4-3 on penalties
Ref: J.Ramiz Wright (Brazil) Att: 62,628

ENGLAND'S charismatic World Cup adventure came to a shattering end here in Turin after a dramatic penalty com-petition went against them. On a night when England did their country and their supporters proud, it was still a bitter pill to swallow.

The England players went into this game with a zest that belied the fact that they had just come through two exhaust-

ing 120-minute matches in the previous two rounds. It certainly said a lot for their fitness but with the giant prize of a World Cup Final place at stake, then perhaps it was not that surprising. Early on England made all the running and it was the Germans who back-pedalled. Peter Beardsley and Gary Lineker made some splendid runs promoted by the fine midfield work of Paul Gascoigne, David Platt and Chris Waddle. With full-backs Paul Parker and Stuart Pearce both able to join the attack, the options were both full and varied.

Despite all this attacking play, though, Illgner was rarely tested, although Waddle almost caught him out with a shot from the half-way line. The referee's whistle had already blown but it was an effort out of the 'Pelé book of football!' Aug-enthaler, Buchwald and Kohler were all stretched to the limit as England's positive play looked so promising. Waddle was having a fine game and sprayed good passes all over the field. A marvellous move involving Gascoigne, Platt, Lineker and Waddle emphasised England's super-iority with only Parker's final header letting them down. A crisp shot by Gascoigne also went close but, ominously, the half had not brought them the goal their play deserved.

After the break the Germans picked their game up and the balance of power slowly began to shift towards them. In the 59th minute they took a somewhat fortuitous lead. Pearce clumsily fouled Hässler and although at first Peter Shilton had Brehme's free-kick covered, the ball took a wicked deflection off Parker and looped agonisingly over the back-pedalling goalkeeper and into the net. It was a tragic goal from England's point of view but it did seem to wake them up again, and Gascoigne especially. Three times he set up openings with his clever play and Beardsley should have done better with the first of them, Wright headed wide from the second and Waddle just failed from the third.

Bobby Robson then sent Trevor Steven on for Butcher to try to go for an even more adventurous look, and in the 80th minute the England fans went wild with delight. Another overlap by Parker enabled him to send over a deep cross which ripped through the heart of the German defence, causing all sorts of confusion, before Lineker whipped in a tremendous left-foot shot into the far corner to give Illgner no chance. That goal was no less than England deserved and it was typical of the absolutely brilliant finishing of the country's number-one striker.

So, once again extra-time was called for. Shilton made a superb save from Klinsmann early on and Waddle hit a fine shot which crashed against the inside of a post narrowly missing Lineker's lunge at the rebound. In between there were the famous tears from Gascoigne as the referee booked him for a challenge on Berthold. The German made the most of it and Gascoigne knew at once that his two bookings from the tournament would automatically keep him out of the Final if England made it. To his credit, he knuckled down, responding to his teammates encouragement, to contribute so much to a great game.

The second period of extra-time was exhausting and with three minutes to go, Buchwald's shot scraped the outside of a post. That would have been a travesty had it gone in, but maybe it would have been a better end than the heartache which followed.

With 120 minutes' football unable to separate the two sides, the dreaded penalty competition was brought into play. It began well enough with Lineker, Beardsley and Platt scoring the first three for England. Unfortunately, so did Brehme, Matthäus and Riedle for the Germans. The next man up was usually one of the surest strikers of a ball in the country, but this time Stuart Pearce's firm shot hit the legs of the diving Illgner and was saved. There were more tears as Pearce, one of England's most passionate players, broke down as he realised the enormity of his miss. Thon then put the Germans 4-3 up and it was left to Waddle to rescue the situation. Sadly, his shot flew high over the bar and England were out of the competition.

It was a desperate moment but England held their heads high. They had given everything and never gave up hope, even when all seemed lost in their earlier games. They had come so very close to making the Final and their spirit and character was second to none. They won many new friends with their performances in Italy and their supporters were very proud of their efforts.

19th match v West Germany.
Match settled by penalty competition.
Lineker, Beardsley and Platt scored for them whilst Pearce and Waddle missed.
Butcher's last international.
"When I realised I had played my last game for England I felt very proud of my achievements, but mostly pleased, because I knew my decision to retire was the correct thing to do. (Nothing like going out at the top!)"
Terry Butcher

Italy v England
Third Place Play-Off

Played on Saturday, 7 July 1990 in the Sant Nicola Stadium, Bari.

Italy: W.Zenga (Inter-Milan); F.Baresi (Milan AC), G.Bergomi (Inter-Milan), C.Ferrara (Napoli), P.Vierchowod (Sampdoria), P.Maldini (Milan AC), G.Giannini (AS Roma), C.Ancelotti (Milan AC), L.De Agostini (Juventus), R.Baggio (Fiorentina), A.Schillaci (Juventus).
Subs: R.Ferri (Inter-Milan) for Giannini and N.Berti (Inter-Milan) for De Agostini.

England: P.L.Shilton (Derby Co, captain); M.G.Stevens (Rangers), A.R.Dorigo (Chelsea), D.S.Walker (Nottm Forest), P.A.Parker (QPR), M.Wright (Derby Co), D.A.Platt (Aston Villa), S.McMahon (Liverpool), P.A.Beardsley (Liverpool), G.W.Lineker (Spurs), T.M.Steven (Rangers).
Subs: C.R.Waddle (Marseille) for Stevens and N.J.Webb (Man Utd) for McMahon.

Half-time 0-0   Full-time 2-1
Ref: J.Quiniou (France)   Att: 51,426

DESPITE the acute disappointment of the host nation's fans at not seeing Italy in the Final, a carnival atmosphere prevailed for this game which decided the third and fourth place in the competition. Both sides brought in reserves, with Italy surprising everyone by playing six defenders in their team.

England opened brightly showing the relaxed form that the occasion seemed to warrant. Gary Stevens tested Zenga with an early shot but, despite some nice touches from David Platt and Trevor Steven, it was the Italians who looked the more likely to score. After 15 minutes Peter Shilton had to save a long shot by Giannini and twice the dangerous Baggio forced the goalkeeper into other good saves. Near the half-hour Shilton palmed a Ferrara shot on to a post after Mark Wright had challenged Baggio, and Salvatore Schillaci, such a hit in the tournament, could not quite get a hold of the rebound which enabled England to clear.

A breakaway attack then took the pressure off for a while as Steven beat De Agostini on the left and crossed. Lineker met the ball with a header which unluckily for England struck the back of an Italian defender. Italy had definitely had the edge in the first half but England had not played badly with Tony Dorigo showing great confidence in linking well with his colleagues.

When the opening goal did come, midway through the second half, it was courtesy of an unfortunate error of judgement by the hitherto immaculate Shilton. Shepherding the ball to safety with his feet, as goalkeepers do these days, he completely failed to see Baggio lurking, ready to pounce. The striker quickly saw his chance and nicked the ball away from Shilton's toes. It ran to Schillaci who neatly side-stepped Des Walker before crossing for Baggio to follow up and score. Shilton was very disappointed, but it gave a lesson to his eventual successor.

England then brought on Chris Waddle and Neil Webb and immediately the latter forced a good save from Zenga. With 11 minutes to go, Steven sent Dorigo galloping away down the left. The full-back sent over a lovely centre which was met by Platt's header from just inside the area. The ball fairly rocketed into the top corner of Zenga's net, giving the goalkeeper absolutely no hope of saving.

Sadly, but in some ways fittingly, it was Italy who then had the last word. Baggio and Schillaci combined on the edge of the England penalty area in the 83rd minute, putting pressure on Paul Parker. The defender seemed to lose his balance, stuck out a leg and brought down Schillaci in the process. A penalty was awarded and the Italian star took the kick himself to give Italy a 2-1 victory.

It had been a great adventure for England but now it was all over. The match ended in a party atmosphere with the teams collecting their medals and then joining in with a 'Mexican Wave' with smiles all round. The England team were given a tumultuous welcome on returning to Luton Airport and then it was announced that they had won the FIFA Fair Play Award which epitomised the way England played its football, strengthening the chances of gaining re-entry for English club sides into European competition.

The only sad aspects of the tournament was the announcement that Peter Shilton and Terry Butcher would be retiring from international football. Shilton had been a magnificent servant to his country and his total of 125 caps will take some beating. It was also farewell to manager Bobby Robson. Although much maligned by some quarters of the Press, he could hardly have got any more from his players. The whole squad had given their all.

17th match v Italy.
Penalty scored for Italy by Schillaci.
Last internationals for Shilton and Bobby Robson, as manager.

England v Hungary
Friendly

Played on Wednesday, 12 September 1990 at Wembley Stadium.

England: C.E.Woods (Rangers); L.M.Dixon (Arsenal), S.Pearce (Nottm Forest), P.A.Parker (QPR), D.S.Walker (Nottm Forest), M.Wright (Derby Co), D.A.Platt (Aston Villa), P.J.Gascoigne (Spurs), S.G.Bull (Wolves), G.W.Lineker (Spurs, captain), J.C.B.Barnes (Liverpool).
Subs: A.R.Dorigo (Chelsea) for Pearce and C.R.Waddle (Marseille) for Bull.

Hungary: Z.Petry (Honvéd); T.Monos (Veszprémi), L.Disztl (MTK Budapest), J.Keller (Ferencváros), Z.Limperger (Ferencváros), I.Garaba (Ferencváros), I.Kozma (Dunfermline), Z.Bucs (Videoton), J.Gregor (Veszprémi), B.Bérczy (MTK Budapest), K.Kovács (AJ Auxerre).
Subs: T.Simon (Ferencváros) for Monos and Z.Aczél (Honvéd) for Garaba.

Half-time 1-0   Full-time 1-0
Ref: E.Fredriksson (Sweden)   Att: 51,459

A NEW season, a new manager and a new captain. Graham Taylor took charge for this game and he immediately selected Gary Lineker as captain. The new skipper responded as only he could by scoring the

Mark Wright and David Platt in action against Hungary at Wembley in September 1990, Graham Taylor's first game in charge of England.

decisive goal in the 44th minute. All in all it proved to be a night full of promise.

England began showing the confidence they had gained from their successful World Cup campaign and tore into the Hungarians from the start. Luckily for the visitors their goalkeeper, Petry, held firm under intense pressure and England could find no way through. John Barnes, looking much more like his Liverpool self, made good use of the free role that Taylor had given him. As early as the first minute his marvellous run set up David Platt for a cross which the Hungarian defence only just managed to clear. Lee Dixon did put in a shot from the clearance but it was a poor one.

Other half-chances were created but the England fans had to wait until just before the break to see a goal. Paul Gascoigne, emerging as the new star of the side, ran cleverly to give Platt a chance to shoot. He hit it well and Petry could only parry the ball and as Gascoigne challenged, it ran kindly for Lineker and that was that, 1-0. It was Lineker's 36th goal for his country and put him in sight of Jimmy Greaves and Bobby Charlton, the only two players ahead of him.

England continued to keep control after the break and Lineker so nearly scored a second when he hit Steve Bull's cross inches wide. Midway through the half Bérczy turned the ball into his own net when under pressure but the referee saw a foul and disallowed it. The home side played some lovely cultured football at times and it was disappointing that they could not find the goals their play merited, something for Graham Taylor to work on in the future.

The Hungarians had Bucs and Simon booked as their frustrations boiled over

and, for England, Chris Woods had a quiet time as the first of Peter Shilton's successors, having to make only one real save of note. However, there were many pleasing aspects of England's play in Taylor's first game in charge.

17th match v Hungary.
Debut for Dixon.
Lineker captain for the first time.
Graham Taylor's first match as manager.

England v Poland
European Championship Qualifier

Played on Wednesday, 17 October 1990 at Wembley Stadium.

England: C.E.Woods (Rangers); L.M.Dixon (Arsenal), S.Pearce (Nottm Forest), P.A.Parker (QPR), D.S.Walker (Nottm Forest), M.Wright (Derby Co), D.A.Platt (Aston Villa), P.J.Gascoigne (Spurs), S.G.Bull (Wolves), G.W.Lineker (Spurs, captain), J.C.B.Barnes (Liverpool).
Subs: C.R.Waddle (Marseille) for Bull and P.A.Beardsley (Liverpool) for Lineker.

Poland: J.Wandzik (Panathinaikos); P.Czachowski (Stal Mielec), D.Wdowczyk (Celtic), R.Szewczyk (GKS Katowice), Z.Kaczmarek (AJ Auxerre), J.Nawrocki (GKS Katowice), R.Tarasiewicz (AS Nancy-Lorraine), R.Warzycha (Górnik Zabrze), J.Furtok (Hamburger SV), R.Kosecki (Legia Warsaw), J.Ziober (Montpellier PSC).
Subs: K.Warzycha (Panathinaikos) for Furtok and D.Kubicki (Lech Poznań) for Kosecki.

Half-time 1-0   Full-time 2-0
Ref: T.Lanese (Italy)   Att: 77,040

ENGLAND took a step towards the European Championship finals to be held in Sweden in 1992 with this vital opening win against Poland at Wembley. The Poles arrived full of confidence and with a useful pedigree. In the first half, especially they made full use of their undoubted skills.

With Kaczmarek operating as a sweeper the England players were well held by their markers. Stuart Pearce caused some early danger with one of his free-kicks. That was off-target but the ball eventually ran to John Barnes who turned it on to Lee Dixon, but he failed with his attempted shot. Dixon then centred for Steve Bull to force a fumbled save from Wandzik.

Poland were breaking cleverly when they saw the chance and Chris Woods did very well with one Tarasiewicz effort. Both Mark Wright and Des Walker had to use their terrific speed to good effect in both defence and when trying to support their midfield. With six minutes of the half left England took a priceless lead. Paul Gascoigne's corner was flicked on by Wright and Gary Lineker, as ever, was there to head goalwards. Nawrocki blocked the ball on the line but unfortunately for his side it was with his hand, so the referee awarded a penalty. Up stepped Lineker and international goal number-37 was duly recorded.

Shortly after the change of ends, Lineker suffered a nasty injury as he bravely dived in amongst the flying boots. After treatment it was decided to take him off and later he had to have eight stitches in a head wound. Graham Taylor made a

Steve Bull's header is saved by Wandzik of Poland at Wembley in October 1990.

Gary Lineker scores from the penalty-spot against the Poles.

Mark Wright tangles with Wandzik during the European Championship qualifying match which England won 2-0.

double substitution as Lineker went off, bringing on Peter Beardsley and Chris Waddle. But it was Poland who then went close when Wdowczyk hit a half volley just wide. Generally though, England were by now in comfortable command, with David Platt and Gascoigne looking particularly good.

The result was finally put beyond doubt in the 89th minute. Beardsley, who looked very sharp after he came on, picked the ball up wide on the right. He advanced forward but began to cut in, spotting

Wandzik slightly out of position. With that Beardsley then struck a brilliant swerving shot with the outside of his right foot which curled away from the goal-keeper and flew into the net. It was a fine goal and gave England just the boost they needed in this competition.

8th match v Poland.
Penalty scored for England by Lineker.

Republic of Ireland v England
European Championship Qualifier

Played on Wednesday, 14 November 1990 at Lansdowne Road, Dublin.

Republic of Ireland: P.Bonner (Celtic); C.B.Morris (Celtic), S.Staunton (Liverpool), M.J.McCarthy (Millwall), D.A.O'Leary (Arsenal), P.McGrath (Aston Villa), R.J.Houghton (Liverpool), R.A.Whelan (Liverpool), N.J.Quinn (Man City), J.W.Aldridge (Real Sociedad), A.D.Townsend (Chelsea).
Subs: A.F.McLoughlin (Swindon T) for Whelan and A.G.Cascarino (Aston Villa) for Quinn.

England: C.E.Woods (Rangers); L.M.Dixon (Arsenal), S.Pearce (Nottm

Forest), T.A.Adams (Arsenal), D.S.Walker (Nottm Forest), M.Wright (Derby Co), D.A.Platt (Aston Villa), G.S.Cowans (Aston Villa), P.A.Beardsley (Liverpool), G.W.Lineker (Spurs, captain), S.McMahon (Liverpool).

Half-time 0-0 Full-time 1-1
Ref: P.D'Elia (Italy) Att: 45,000

ENGLAND manager Graham Taylor took a brave gamble before this match, leaving out Paul Gascoigne and recalling, instead, Gordon Cowans for his first international in over four years. He explained that he felt that Gascoigne's style was not suited to this particular game against this awkward Irish side and so he selected his team on a purely tactical basis. It all made more sense as the game progressed.

With Mark Wright and Tony Adams taking care of the high balls and Des Walker sweeping up anything on the ground the ploy worked well. However, the overall standard of the play was very poor. It was a very windy day and the pitch resembled a ploughed field so perhaps it was too much to expect some good football. Republic of Ireland, when they gained possession, pumped everything long, aiming for the gangly Quinn. Goal chances were few and far between in the first half with only a free-kick by Whelan troubling Chris Woods. There was one other talking point of the half when Lee Dixon's clumsy challenge on Townsend might have produced a penalty.

Poor Gary Lineker had an unenviable task. With Peter Beardsley playing a deeper role it meant that Lineker was left on his own up front. He ran himself to a standstill trying to shut defenders down and also managed to make space for shooting chances. That he was one of England's best performers on the day says a lot for his character and skill. The only blot on him came after he had badly missed an opportunity created by Steve McMahon and Stuart Pearce. But he can surely be forgiven for that slight blemish.

After the break a bizarre shot by McCarthy from two yards inside his own half almost gave Republic of Ireland the lead. The ball was just punted forward but caught on the wind and Woods was very relieved to see it scrape the wrong side of the crossbar. That incident sort of summed up the match. There was no style, it was just a battle to see who could break the other down first.

Then in the 69th minute, a move totally out of character with the scrappiness of the earlier play, brought England a fine goal.

David Platt, Lineker and Pearce built a lovely move down the left before the ball was worked to the right. Full-back Dixon fired in a low cross which Platt met at the far post to bundle home. For a while after the goal it looked as if England were going to avenge the results of the previous two meetings between the sides. But after Cascarino had replaced Quinn in the 74th minute Republic of Ireland began to fight back. England still looked comfortable though so it came as a bitter disappointment to them when Cascarino netted with a header in the 79th minute.

It was a well-taken goal and the 45,000 crowd went wild with delight, urging their team on to a winner. England

David Platt celebrates a goal against the Republic of Ireland in Dublin in November 1990.

deservedly hung on, though, and in the final reckoning they would be pleased with this valuable point.

12th match v Republic of Ireland.

England v Cameroon   Friendly

Played on Wednesday, 6 February 1991 at Wembley Stadium.

England: D.A.Seaman (Arsenal); L.M.Dixon (Arsenal), S.Pearce (Nottm Forest), T.M.Steven (Rangers), D.S.Walker (Nottm Forest), M.Wright (Derby Co), B.Robson (Man Utd, captain), P.J.Gascoigne (Spurs), I.E.Wright (Crystal Palace), G.W.Lineker (Spurs), J.C.B.Barnes (Liverpool).
Subs: G.A.Pallister (Man Utd) for Robson and S.B.Hodge (Nottm Forest) for Gascoigne.

Cameroon: J.A.Bell (Bordeaux); B.A.Ebwelle (Canon Yaoundé), J.E.Kunde (Prevoyance Yaoundé), J.Onana (Canon Yaoundé), S.E.Tataw (Tonnerre Yaoundé), A.Kana Biyik (Le Havre), E.M'Bouh (Vitória Guimarães), L.P.M'Fede (Canon Yaoundé), J.C.Pagal (AS St-Etienne), E.Ekeke (Valenciennes), F.Omam Biyik (Stade Rennes).
Subs: T.Libiih (Tonnerre Yaoundé) for Omam Biyik and G.Tapoko (Peantheare Bajante) for Ekeke.

Half-time 1-0   Full-time 2-0

Ref: J.Balnkenstwein (Holland) Att: 61,075

THE many friends that were won over to the Cameroon players by their perfor-

The scene as the Wembley groundstaff roll up the covers before the game against Cameroon in February 1991, when sub-zero temperatures made it probably the coldest night on which an England home international match was played.

mances in Italy, were glad of another opportunity to see them in action here at Wembley. However, after the game many of those admirers had rather different opinions. On a bitterly cold night where gloves and tights were the rule rather than the exception, Cameroon showed no appetite for attack and also showed a rather surly attitude which did not please the Wembley crowd of just over 61,000.

England made all the early running and Bryan Robson almost scored with a typical header from a corner in the first few minutes. The Cameroon players were

decidedly negative and allowed England the freedom of Wembley in the midfield. David Seaman had nothing to do but watch the game and on 20 minutes his side took the lead. A high cross by Trevor Steven was headed back by debutant Ian Wright and Gary Lineker pounced. As he skipped around goalkeeper Bell he was caught by flailing arms which sent him crashing to the ground. Penalty! Lineker took the kick and added yet another goal to his ever-growing tally.

The goal did draw some response from the Africans but they never troubled the

England defence and most of the play was confined to the visitor's half. Cameroon's robust tackling did not go down too well with either England's players or fans, and everyone was becoming increasingly frustrated by these tactics.

On the hour, England made the game safe with another goal. Lineker forced Tataw into conceding a corner and Stuart Pearce's kick flicked off a headed challenge between Mark Wright and Kunde at the near post, touched Ian Wright on the way for Lineker, who else, to pick up the pieces and score from close range. Graham Taylor then made a couple of substitutions bringing on Steve Hodge and Gary Pallister, the latter only after a shirt had been found for him. He had forgotten to put one on under his tracksuit!

It gave England the chance to try a tactical switch but it had little effect on a drab game. It was a shame that the talented African players had not used the occasion to show off their talents a little more, but in the end they were well beaten. Whether their absent star player, Roger Milla, left out over a wrangle about an appearance fee, could have lifted them will remain a mystery.

> 2nd match v Cameroon.
> Debut for I.Wright.
> Penalty scored for England by Lineker.

England v Republic of Ireland

European Championship Qualifier

Played on Wednesday, 27 March 1991 at Wembley Stadium.

England: D.A.Seaman (Arsenal); L.M.Dixon (Arsenal), S.Pearce (Nottm Forest), T.A.Adams (Arsenal), D.S.Walker (Nottm Forest), M.Wright (Derby Co), B.Robson (Man Utd, captain), D.A.Platt (Aston Villa), P.A.Beardsley (Liverpool), G.W.Lineker (Spurs), J.C.B.Barnes (Liverpool).
Subs: L.S.Sharpe (Man Utd) for Adams and I.E.Wright (Crystal Palace) for Lineker.
Republic of Ireland: P.Bonner (Celtic); D.J.Irwin (Man Utd), S.Staunton (Liverpool), D.A.O'Leary (Arsenal), K.B.Moran (Blackburn R), A.D.Townsend (Chelsea), P.McGrath (Aston Villa), R.J.Houghton (Liverpool), N.J.Quinn (Man City), J.W.Aldridge (Real Sociedad), K.M.Sheedy (Everton).
Sub: A.G.Cascarino (Aston Villa) for Aldridge.

Half-time 1-1   Full-time 1-1
Ref: K.Rothlisberger (Switzerland)
Att: 77,753

ONCE again the Republic of Ireland team proved to be a thorn in England's side, and by virtue of this draw they now looked favourites to go through to the finals in Sweden in 1992.

England were off to a good start as David Platt went close early on. Then in the tenth minute Stuart Pearce was headed away by Staunton only as far as Lee Dixon who hit a first time shot in the general direction of the Irish goal. Whether it would have gone in is debatable but it struck the left knee of

David Seaman punches clear against the Republic of Ireland in the European Championship qualifying match at Wembley in March 1991.

This time Seaman fails to stop a shot by the Republic's Niall Quinn.

Staunton and flew wide of the wrong-footed Bonner. A case for an own-goal maybe, but the official verdict gave it to Dixon.

The Irish responded typically with a barrage of high balls aimed at Quinn. This unsettled England and Tony Adams in particular struggled to contain his former Arsenal colleague. David Seaman also looked uncertain and a week punch out from a cross almost produced an equalizer but Peter Beardsley saved the day by clearing off the goal-line.

In the 28th minute, though, Ireland did find the way back they deserved. Yet another high ball was floated across by McGrath and, with Seaman and Adams both rooted to the spot, Quinn nipped in to glance home a fine header. More defensive errors before the break by England gave manager Graham Taylor a few problems to sort out at half-time and he decided to bring on Lee Sharpe for a debut appearance and put Mark Wright on the dangerous Quinn. This did achieve a tightening up in defence but it was the Irishmen who still created the better chances in the second half.

There were two marvellous opportun-

ities for Sheedy and Houghton but each time the final shot was wayward. Dixon just did enough to distract Sheedy but Houghton's miss, after a Casacarino knock down, was inexcusable and he really should have done better.

England had a poor half and their attack just could not get going. They rarely threatened Bonner's goal and in the end had to be content with only one point.

> 13th match v Republic of Ireland.
> Debut, as substitute, for Sharpe.

Turkey v England
European Championship Qualifier

Played on Wednesday, 1 May 1991 at the Atatürk Stadium, Izmir.

Turkey: D.Hayrettin (Galatasaray); C.Riza (Beşiktaş), T.Ogun (Trabzonspor), K.Gökhan (Beşiktaş), C.Recep (Beşiktaş), A.Muhammet (Galatasaray), K.Ünal (Trabzonspor), D.Ridvan (Fenerbahçe), O.Mehmet (Beşiktaş), C.Tanju (Galatasaray), G.Ali (Beşiktaş).
Sub: U.Feyyaz (Beşiktaş), for Ali.

Goalkeeper Hayrettin falls in front of England's Alan Smith during the European Championship qualifying game in Izmir in May 1991.

Wimbledon striker Dennis Wise scores a debut goal for England in Izmir. It proved to be the winner.

England's managerial duo Graham Taylor and Lawrie McMenemy.

England: D.A.Seaman (Arsenal); L.M.Dixon (Arsenal), S.Pearce (Nottm Forest), D.F.Wise (Chelsea), D.S.Walker (Nottm Forest), G.A.Pallister (Man Utd), D.A.Platt (Aston Villa), G.R.Thomas (Crystal Palace), A.M.Smith (Arsenal), G.W.Lineker (Spurs, captain), J.C.B. Barnes (Liverpool).
Sub: S.B.Hodge (Nottm Forest) for Thomas.

Half-time 0-1   Full-time 0-1
Ref: W-G.Wiesel (West Germany)
Att: 20,000

A VITAL win and a step nearer qualification. That was the outcome of this awkward trip to Turkey, but the manner in which it was achieved left the England supporters disappointed. The days of big victories over small footballing countries are but a dim and distant memory by and large as top coaches spread their organisational abilities around the globe.

But England could never succeed in some people's eyes and when they were faced with this type of fixture, nothing short of a five-goal winning margin would suffice. Of course, it is not that easy but having said that it is unacceptable to everyone if the players do not, apparently, give one hundred per cent effort. Here, once again, several of the established men let themselves down and the new caps were found a little wanting at this higher level.

Turkey, with a little more control in front of goal, might have caused a major upset. England looked disjointed with so many new faces and they could not settle into a rhythm. They did go close to scoring with one first-half effort. Alan Smith pounced to turn Stuart Pearce's cross goalwards only to see the ball strike the crossbar. The rebound was met by the incoming Geoff Thomas, but a fine save from Hayrettin somehow kept the shot out.

Des Walker, with his usual calm authority, held the England defence together, receiving good support from Gary Pallister. But Turkey looked lively and they desperately wanted to register their first goal of the tournament and their first-ever strike against England. Both Ridvan and Tanju should have done

better when they were presented with a clear chance by sheer bad defensive play by England. Twice, also, the Turks had goals disallowed for offside as the pressure increased but when England took the lead in the 32nd minute, it took the heat out of the situation. A long free-kick by Pearce was headed down and across goal by Pallister. The ball fell awkwardly for the tiny Dennis Wise, but he celebrated his first cap by bundling it into the net.

In the 51st minute, Walker was a little lucky to get away with a challenge on Tanju as many referees would have given a penalty. It was just one incident in a half that was best forgotten. Smith and Gary Lineker had very few decent passes from the midfield, although Lineker did bring one excellent save out of Hayrettin from close range. In midfield both Thomas (substituted at half-time) and Wise struggled, and David Platt had a very quiet game by his high standards. John Barnes was in one of his infuriating moods. Occasionally he would show some fabulous skills but generally he contributed very little to the team, a luxury England perhaps were not able to afford much longer.

The closing stages were fraught with danger as the Turks sensed they could save the game. Ridvan, unbelievably outpacing Walker, missing a fine chance and Feyyaz, so nearly beat David Seaman with a header. But England held on and although they set the manager some problems, at least they had the satisfaction of winning.

5th match v Turkey.
Debut for Wise and Thomas.
Debut goal for Wise.

England v USSR The England Challenge Cup

Played on Tuesday, 21 May 1991 at Wembley Stadium.

England: C.E.Woods (Rangers); M.G.Stevens (Rangers), A.R.Dorigo (Chelsea), D.F.Wise (Chelsea), P.A.Parker (QPR), M.Wright (Derby Co, captain), D.A.Platt (Aston Villa), G.R.Thomas (Crystal Palace), A.M.Smith (Arsenal), I.E.Wright (Crystal Palace), J.C.B.Barnes (Liverpool).
Subs: D.Batty (Leeds Utd) for Wise and P.A.Beardsley (Liverpool) for I.Wright.

USSR: A.Uvarov (Dinamo Moscow); A.Chernishov (Dinamo Moscow), V.Kulkov (Spartak Moscow), A.Tsveiba (Dinamo Kiev), D.Galyamin (CSKA Moscow), I.Shalimov (Spartak Moscow), A.Mikhailichenko (Sampdoria), A.Kanchelskis (Man Utd), I.Kolyvanov (Dinamo Moscow), V.Tatarchuk (Dinamo Kiev), D.Kuznetsov (CSKA Moscow).
Subs: I.Korneyev (CSKA Moscow) for Shalimov and A.Mostovoy (Spartak Moscow) for Tatarchuk.

Half-time 2-1   **Full-time 3-1**
Ref: E.Aladren (Spain)   Att: 23,789

ONLY 23,789 people turned up at Wembley for the first of two internationals in an invitation tournament competing for the England Challenge Cup. It was a triangular competition with Argentina the third party. What a pity that so few people were present because the Soviets are attractive opposition, full of strength and skill. England did extremely well in this game, though, and they benefited from a fine display from David Platt, who was now really beginning to establish his growing reputation.

The Soviets were pegged back early on by some swift England attacks. It was obvious from the start that the visitors, and especially goalkeeper Uvarov, were vulnerable under pressure in particular from high balls into the box. Ironically though it was USSR who scored the opening goal. Eleven minutes had gone when Tony Dorigo allowed Kolyvanov to cross from the right. Mikhailichenko chested the ball to Tatarchuck, who instantly shot at goal. Chris Woods looked to have it covered but unfortunately, Mark Wright, who was skipper for the first time, stuck out a foot to deflect it wide of his goalkeeper. This time the official verdict was 'own-goal' which made one wonder if Staunton should have been 'credited' with England's goal against Republic of Ireland in March.

Whatever, with Platt and Geoff Thomas looking lively in midfield England did not let the goal upset them. It took only six minutes for the home side to find the equalizer and inevitably it came from a high ball into the penalty area. Paul Parker's free-kick was only flapped at by Uvarov and the ball went straight to Thomas. His instant shot looked harmless enough until that is, Alan Smith turned it into the net with a clever touch. The goal emphasised the good season he had just enjoyed with League Champions, Arsenal.

John Barnes showed some nice touches as England continued to hold all the aces and it came as no surprise when they took the lead in the 44th minute. A brilliant

Alan Smith and the USSR's Andrei Chernishov in action at Wembley in the England Challenge Cup.

burst through the middle by Platt only ended when Tsveiba brought him down for an obvious penalty. In the absence of Gary Lineker, Platt himself scored from the spot-kick and his first-half display had been very reminiscent of Bryan Robson at his best.

A fine save from Mostovoi's firm header by the largely unemployed Woods, early in the second half, prevented an equalizer by USSR and then Parker was a little fortunate when his foul on the edge of the box against Kolyvanov gave away a free-kick. The ball was only just deflected over when the kick was taken. At this point the Soviets were showing signs of getting on top and Graham Taylor brought on two substitutes, new cap David Batty and the experienced Peter Beardsley. The alterations worked a treat and England were soon asserting themselves again. Smith missed a great chance when a fine run by Barnes created an opening, but with two minutes to go the result was sealed with another fine goal by Platt. A lovely move involving several players ended with Batty finding Platt just outside the area. He side-stepped a Soviet challenge and drove a hard, low shot into the corner. That rounded off a good day for England perfectly.

11th match v USSR.
Debut, as substitute, for Batty.
Mark Wright captain for the first time.
Penalty scored for England by Platt.

England v Argentina
The England Challenge Cup

Played on Saturday, 25 May 1991 at Wembley Stadium.

England: D.A.Seaman (Arsenal); L.M.Dixon (Arsenal), S.Pearce (Nottm Forest), D.Batty (Leeds Utd), D.S.Walker (Nottm Forest), M.Wright (Derby Co), D.A.Platt (Aston Villa), G.R.Thomas (Crystal Palace), A.M.Smith (Arsenal), G.W.Lineker (Spurs, captain), J.C.B. Barnes (Liverpool).
Sub: N.H.Clough (Nottm Forest) for Barnes.

Argentina: S.J.Goycochea (Racing Club); S.Vazquez (Ferro Carril Deste), A.Enrique (River Plate), J.H.Basualdo (River Plate), F.Gamboa (Newell's Old Boys), O.Ruggeri (Velez Sarsfield), C.Garcia (Racing Club), D.Franco (Newell's Old Boys), J.E.Simón (Pisa), G.Marcelloto (Monterrey), A.Boldrini (Newell's Old Boys).
Sub: A.Mohammed (Huracán) for Marellotto.

Half-time 1-0   **Full-time 2-2**
Ref: Z.Petrović (Yugoslavia)   Att: 44,497

Smith outjumps Argentina's Alberto Enrique in the end-of-season Wembley tournament.

ANOTHER entertaining game at Wembley but also a disappointment for England who let a two-goal lead slip against Argentina. The draw was enough to give England the trophy on offer, but after outplaying the South Americans for so long, a victory would have been much more satisfying.

The first hour was dominated by England. Playing fast, open football their neat passing movements repeatedly tore large holes in the Argentine defence. The home side deservedly opened the scoring after 15 minutes when Stuart Pearce's deep free-kick caught out Argentina who tried to push too far forward. It left Gary Lineker the opportunity to steal in and guide a marvellous diving header past Goycochea. It was his 40th goal for England and he now was only four behind the legendary Jimmy Greaves who held second spot in the all-time list of goalscorers.

David Batty tumbles after a tackle by Sergio Vazquez of Argentina at Wembley in May 1991.

Everything looked perfect for England at this point. David Batty was really impressive in his first full game and David Platt was showing some excellent touches. Geoff Thomas completed a very good midfield and the Argentinians had little answer to the play from the home team. Goycochea made a fine save from Platt and then his flying leap prevented John Barnes from curling a wonderful shot into the far corner. It seemed only a question of time before England would score again.

Seven minutes into the second half, Platt duly obliged with a second goal. Again Pearce featured in the move and his fine cross was headed home with some panache by the Aston Villa star. Everyone thought the game was as good as over for Argentina, but how wrong can you be?

With 66 minutes gone, England committed the cardinal sin of letting in a goal from a set-piece. Mohammed's corner found Garcia totally unmarked and he headed home unchallenged. Where all the home defenders were left everyone puzzled and David Seaman's positioning also left much to be desired. Seven minutes later, things went from bad to worse as England did it again. Another corner was met by Franco, who outjumped the defenders to power home an excellent header to equalize.

England were shell-shocked but they gradually settled down again and took the game to the visitors. Sadly, once again the Argentines showed the nasty side of their temperament. Cynical fouls on Lee Dixon and Smith won few friends in the crowd and they became incensed at these antics. Mind you, England were not blameless and a Mark Wright foul deserved a booking. The referee tried to show a leniency but perhaps an earlier yellow card or two might have diffused a volatile situation.

Sad to say the Argentinians walked off the Wembley pitch to a chorus of boos, especially when they removed their shirts and taunted the crowd by waving them in the air. That was very silly.

10th match v Argentina.

Australia v England   Friendly

Played on Saturday, 1 June 1991 in the Sydney Football Stadium, Sydney.

Australia: R.Zabica (Adelaide City); I.Gray (Marconi), D.Kurakovic (South Melbourne Hellas), N.Zelic (Sydney Olympic), A.Tbin (Adelaide City), T.Vidmar (Adelaide City), P.Wade (South Melbourne Hellas), M.Petersen (South Melbourne Hellas), G.Arnold (Roda JC), E.Tapai (Adelaide City), A.Vidmar (Adelaide City).
Sub: G.Brown (Parramatta Eagles) for Tapai.
England: C.E.Woods (Rangers); P.A.Parker (QPR), S.Pearce (Nottm Forest), D.Batty (Leeds Utd), D.S.Walker (Nottm Forest), M.Wright (Derby Co), D.A.Platt (Aston Villa), G.R.Thomas (Crystal Palace), N.H.Clough (Nottm Forest), G.W.Lineker (Spurs, captain), D.E.Hirst (Sheffield Wed).
Subs: D.F.Wise (Chelsea) for Lineker and J.A.Salako (Crystal Palace) for Hirst.

Half-time 0-1   Full-time 0-1

Ref: B.Tasker (New Zealand)   Att: 36,827

DESPITE all the argument and questions on the wisdom of an exhausting tour of Australia at the end of a long and hard

domestic season, England duly arrived in Sydney to play this match and fulfil their obligations. Just as England found eight years earlier the 'Socceroos', as Australia were affectionately known, produced a high level of skill and effort to frustrate the 'Poms'. In fact England had to be thankful that Chris Woods was in fine form in goal.

Early on England were on top and they created several good chances. Mark Wright, Gary Lineker and David Platt all went close in the space of three minutes but the best chance probably fell to Nigel Clough. Alas, his shot from 12 yards was pulled wide. Despite England's overall dominance the Aussies refused to capitulate to the pressure and, indeed, they were quite dangerous in breakaways. A mistake by David Batty left Arnold with a clear opening and only a tremendous save by Woods prevented a goal. Almost immediately the goalkeeper produced an even better save to foil Gray's goalbound header.

On 40 minutes, though, England took the lead. A Stuart Pearce free-kick was drilled into the area and in a scramble to clear the ball Gray put through his own goal. The goal was a little fortuitous, but none the less deserved for England's first-half superiority.

The second half was not a particularly good one. England remained mostly in control, although Australia did produce good efforts from A.Vidmar and Gray as they both came close to wiping out England's lead. Another chance fell to Tapai and he looked a certain scorer as he strode clear of England's defence. But a brilliantly-timed tackle by Paul Parker saved the situation and England were never really threatened again.

Unfortunately England did not look

Australia's Ian Gray heads an own-goal in the Sydney Football Stadium in June 1991. Alas for poor Gray, it proved to be the only goal of the game.

like scoring in this half either and they created not one chance worthy of the name, especially after Lineker had to go off with a leg injury. But the win gave Graham Taylor his ninth unbeaten result since he took charge of the team, a record equalling Don Revie's start in 1974-75.

5th match v Australia.
Debut for Hirst and, as substitute, Salako.

New Zealand v England Friendly

Played on Monday 3 June 1991 in the Mount Smart Stadium, Auckland.

New Zealand: Gosling (Sydney Olympic); Ridenton (Mount Wellington), Gray (Waitakere City), Dunford (Miramar Rangers), C.L.Evans (Oxford Utd), Ironside (Sydney Olympic), McGarry (Christchurch United), Halligan (Christchurch United), D.Edge (Waikato), De Jong (Fortuna Sittard), Ferris (Mount Mauganui).
England: C.E.Woods (Rangers); P.A.Parker (QPR), S.Pearce (Nottm Forest), D.Batty (Leeds Utd), D.S.Walker (Nottm Forest), E.D.Barratt (Oldham A), D.A.Platt (Aston Villa), G.R.Thomas (Crystal Palace), D.F.Wise (Chelsea), G.W.Lineker (Spurs, captain), M.E.Walters (Rangers).
Subs: B.F.Deane (Sheffield Utd) for Batty and J.A.Salako (Crystal Palace) for Walters.

Half-time 0-0   Full-time 0-1
Ref: D.Voutsinas (Australia)   Att: 17,500

JET lag and a dramatic climatic change did not help England's cause in this match in Auckland. It was therefore hardly surprising that the game was a very disappointing one. The match had been arranged as one of two to help celebrate the New Zealand Football Association's

Gary Lineker gets in a header against New Zealand in the Mount Smart Stadium, Auckland, in June 1991.

Centenary. England, with three new caps in the side, never really got going and their best moments were reserved for the final five minutes.

New Zealand offered plenty of spirit and courageously battled away for every loose ball. Goal attempts on this cold and windy day were few and far between and the nearest anyone came to a goal in the first-half was when Chris Woods dropped a corner. The ball fell for Dunford, only

three yards from goal, but somehow he shot over the crossbar. To be fair it looked as though Woods had been impeded but having said that it looked also as though the referee would have given a goal. It certainly was a lucky escape.

Dennis Wise, again looking a little out of his depth in an international jersey, Paul Parker, giving a careless display and Earl Barratt, often struggling, gave England an uninspiring look about them, and but for a fine tackle by Des Walker, De Jong might have scored.

In the second half New Zealand continued to work hard to frustrate England and the visitors found it difficult to break the Kiwis down. But with only five minutes of a drab game remaining, the visitor's attack flickered into action. John Salako, making another lively appearance as substitute, as he had done in Sydney, hit the bar with a good shot. It looked as though that effort would be England's best of the match, but three minutes into injury time Wise sent Parker away and Lineker anticipated the cross brilliantly to sprint in front of his marker to sweep home the last-gasp winner. The goal saw Lineker at his best and was a wonderful piece of opportunism.

It ruined the New Zealand party but set a new record for Graham Taylor as the tenth match without defeat since he replaced Bobby Robson as manager.

1st match v New Zealand.
Debuts for Barrett, Walters and, as substitute, Deane.

John Salako fires past New Zealand goalkeeper Grant Schofield at the Athletic Park, Wellington, during the second game against the Kiwis on England's 1991 Australasian tour.

New Zealand v England
Friendly

Played on Saturday, 8 June 1991 in the Athletic Park, Wellington.

New Zealand: Schofield (Mount Wellington); Ridenton (Mount Wellington), Gray (Waitakere City), Dunford (Miramar Rangers), C.L.Evans (Oxford Utd), Ironside (Sydney Olympic), McGarry (Christchurch United), Halligan (Christchurch United), D.Edge (Waikato), De Jong (Fortuna Sittard), Ferris (Mount Maunganui).
Sub: T.Edge (Waikato) for D.Edge.

England: C.E.Woods (Rangers); G.A.Charles (Nottm Forest), S.Pearce (Nottm Forest, captain), D.F.Wise (Chelsea), D.S.Walker (Nottm Forest), M.Wright (Derby Co), D.A.Platt (Aston Villa), G.R.Thomas (Crystal Palace), B.C.Deane (Sheffield Utd), I.E.Wright (Crystal Palace), J.A.Salako (Crystal Palace).
Sub: D.E.Hirst (Sheffield Wed) for Deane.

Half-time 0-1   Full-time 0-2

Ref: R Lorenc (Australia)   Att: 25,000

GRAHAM Taylor's winning sequence as England's manager continued with another hard fought win against New Zealand in the second of these commemorative games. This was by far the best performance of the three tour games so far and was all the better when one considered the awful conditions that the city of Wellington offered. A howling gale made good football very difficult, but all-in-all it was not a bad match.

Showing far more pace than in the earlier games, England were soon attacking Schofield's goal. An indication of the poor conditions came when the goalkeeper's first goal-kick blew back and landed on the edge of his own area. The early pressure that England exerted paid off for the visitors when they took a 12th-minute lead. John Salako, who played well throughout, made a determined run down the right and centred low and hard. Brian Deane dummied the cross and it left stand-

Substitute David Hirst is congratulated after scoring against the New Zealanders in Wellington.

in skipper Stuart Pearce the chance to lash home a fierce shot from just inside the penalty area.

Salako seemed to be involved in every English attack and he certainly looked to have that something extra that an international needs. On 21 minutes he set up David Platt for an acrobatic kick which sent the ball flashing into the net again. Unfortunately the referee had spotted an offside and the goal was ruled out. Minutes later, Ian Wright put in a wind-assisted cross which Schofield somehow scrambled around a post.

The second half was also controlled by England and only poor finishing prevented them from running up a rugby score, an appropriate idea considering that this is the home of the famous All Blacks!

A great run by Geoff Thomas gave Dennis Wise an easy chance which he squandered and Ian Wright's following up attempt was cleared off the line by Gray. England kept up the pressure and on 50 minutes deservedly increased their lead. Full-back Gary Charles, who made a confident debut, outpaced the home

defenders before driving a low cross to the near post. David Hirst controlled the ball brilliantly before turning sharply to shoot under Schofield's diving body. It was an excellent goal for the substitute, who had replaced Deane at half-time.

The only threats that England had to their lead came when Charles sent a dreadful back-pass straight to McGarry. The New Zealander's shot beat Chris Woods but Des Walker saved Charles's blushes with a frantic clearance. The other chance fell to Declan Edge just after England's second goal, but he blasted the ball over the bar with only Woods to beat.

In the final seconds, another tremendous burst by Salako almost produced another goal. His run and shot was brilliant, Schofield pushed the ball on to a post and the goalkeeper watched in disbelief as Thomas, following up, somehow managed to screw his shot wide of an open goal.

2nd match v New Zealand.
Debut for Charles.
Pearce captain for the first time.

Malaysia v England
Friendly

Played on Wednesday, 12 June 1991 in the Merdeka Stadium, Kuala Lumpur.

Malaysia: Hassan Miskam (Johore); Serbegeth Singh (Kuala Lumpur), Lee Kin Hong (Kedah), Zaid Jamil (Selangor), A.Jayakanthan (Selangor), Chow Siew Yai (Kuala Lumpur), Ahmad Yusof (Panang), Nasir Yusof (Johore), Matlan Marjan (Sabah), Zainal Hassan (Penang), Dollah Salleh (Panang).
Sub: Khairul Azman (Penang) for Hassan.
England: C.E.Woods (Rangers); G.A.Charles (Nottm Forest), S.Pearce (Nottm Forest), D.Batty (Leeds Utd), D.S.Walker (Nottm Forest), M.Wright (Derby Co), D.A.Platt (Aston Villa), G.R.Thomas (Crystal Palace), N.H. Clough (Nottm Forest), G.W.Lineker (Spurs, captain), J.A.Salako (Crystal Palace).

Half-time 0-3   Full-time 2-4
Ref: A.Letchumerabamy   Att: 41,248

ENGLAND'S last match of an exhausting tour took them to Kuala Lumpur where over 41,000 people sweltered in 100 per cent humidity in the Merdeka Stadium. The game was another personal triumph for Gary Lineker, who, having missed the game in Wellington because of club tour committments, returned to the side to score all four goals in a wonderful display in the art of finishing.

The excitement began after only 42 seconds. Geoff Thomas' forward pass released Lineker on the left of goal and a rasping shot left the home goalkeeper, Hassan, helpless. It was a marvellous start for England and one of the best of Lineker's England goals. The visitors pushed forward relentlessly from then on and, midway through the half, a Stuart Pearce corner from the right was flicked on by Mark Wright and Lineker was at the far post to knock the ball into the net. On the half-hour the supreme England striker collected his fifth international hat-trick with a lovely glancing header at the near post after a delicate chip by David Platt.

This burst of goalscoring left Malaysia shell-shocked, but they kept battling away and before half-time Matlan took advantage of some sloppy defensive play by England to score and send the crowd wild with delight. Chris Woods was furious with his defence, particularly as it was the first goal he had conceded on the tour, thus ruining his proud record.

However, this minor blot did not affect England's superiority and they coasted through the second half. On 70 minutes another lovely run from John Salako, the real hit of the tour, ended with a cross from the right which was met with a simple header from that man Lineker again. It was another clinical piece of finishing and a marvellous milestone for the Spurs player. It was his 45th goal for England, thus eclipsing Jimmy Greaves to slip into second place in the all-time list of goalscorers. Only Bobby Charlton, with 49 goals, now lay ahead of Lineker.

The only other black mark on an otherwise good day for England came when Matlan, who was already a hero for scoring one goal in the match, suddenly popped up with a second strike, which

would probably give him immortality amongst his own countrymen.

It had been a long and very tiring tour for England but they ended it with four wins out of four and given Graham Taylor the chance to see one or two fringe players perform in international football. The wisdom of such a tour certainly raised questions, but there was absolutely no question that the public relation exercise proved a huge success and England won many new friends as a result.

> 1st match v Malaysia.
> Four goals for Lineker which was the second time he has scored four. It also included his fifth hat-trick.

England v Germany
Friendly

Played on Wednesday, 11 September 1991 at Wembley Stadium.

England: C.E.Woods (Rangers); L.M.Dixon (Arsenal), A.R.Dorigo (Leeds Utd), D.Batty (Leeds Utd), G.A.Pallister (Man Utd), P.A.Parker (Man Utd), D.A.Platt (Bari), T.M.Steven (Rangers), A.M.Smith (Arsenal), G.W.Lineker (Spurs), J.A.Salako (Crystal Palace).
Subs: P.A.Stewart (Spurs) for Salako and P.C.Merson (Arsenal) for Steven.
Germany: B.Illgner (1.FC Cologne); M.Binz (Eintracht Frankfurt), A.Brehme (Inter-Milan), J.Kohler (Juventus), S.Effenberg (Bayern Munich), G.Buchwald (VfB Stuttgart), A.Möller (Eintracht Frankfurt), T.Hässler (AS Roma), K-H.Riedle (Lazio), L.Matthäus (Inter-Milan), T.Doll (Lazio).
Sub: J.Klinsmann (Inter-Milan) for Doll.

Half-time 0-1   Full-time 0-1
Ref: A.Spirrin (USSR)   Att: 59,493

THE new unified German team provided attractive opposition for England's first international of the new season. Once again the Germans showed the enormous strength of their game and all their stars

looked extremely sharp. But England were not disgraced and in fact played very well. With a little more luck they certainly would not have lost.

The Germans started in their usual confident manner. They moved the ball around Wembley's luscious turf with superb precision. Matthäus was showing his World Cup form and controlling most of their best moves and twice early on they almost took the lead. A corner needlessly given away by Tony Dorigo was taken by Möller. Buchwald met the cross and the ball grazed the outside of a post. Almost at once the Germans again went close. Doll, the only East German in the side, beat David Batty and set up Möller, but his shot flew over the bar.

Gradually, England settled and soon it was the home side who were in control. A Lee Dixon cross was controlled by Gary Lineker and his superb swivel and shot forced Illgner to make a brilliant half-stop. The ball was rolling towards the net with John Salako roaring in, but Effenburg just kept it out with a desperate goal-line clearance. The same defender then gave Lineker possession with a poor back-pass but Kohler rescued his teammate with a timely tackle. Salako switched wings to attack Brehme and from one fine run Alan Smith headed at goal only for Illgner to tip over the bar.

Germany were by now distinctly rattled and when Dorigo's 60-yard pass sent Lineker sprinting clear only a blatant foul by Brehme stopped England's striker. The German defender was very lucky to stay on the field with only a booking to show for his cynicism. He could thank Lineker for that, as the England player's acceptance of a handshake probably swayed the referee's mind towards a yellow card rather than red. A marvellous moment which highlighted the Englishman's sense of fair play.

Lineker was again the victim when Kohler's crude challenge gave him Germany's second booking. Immediately a cross was headed against the bar by David Platt as England desperately searched for

David Batty and Germany's Steffan Effenberg at Wembley in September 1991.

Alan Smith (second left) scores the only goal of the European Championship qualifying game against Turkey at Wembley in October 1991.

a goal and Lineker was also close to snapping up the rebound but he could not quite direct his header on target.

Typically, with England on top, the Germans took the heat out of the situation by scoring a goal in injury-time of the first half. A breakaway by the dangerous Doll showed his immense talent by beating both Salako and Paul Parker before crossing for Riedle to head an easy goal past Chris Woods. So England went in at half-time rocked by this set-back.

After the break they tried their best to recover and put together some excellent football at times. But always, the Germans did just enough to hang on to their lead, a sign of a class side. Indeed, they also had their moments, and fine saves by Woods from Riedle and Matthäus kept England only one behind. The best effort from the home side came when Dixon's deflected shot was brilliantly saved by Illgner.

> 20th match v Germany.
> Debuts, as substitutes, for Stewart and Merson.
> Graham Taylor's first defeat in charge after a record opening run.

England v Turkey
European Championship Qualifier

Played on Wednesday, 16 October 1991 at Wembley Stadium.

England: C.E.Woods (Sheffield Wed); L.M.Dixon (Arsenal), S.Pearce (Nottm Forest), D.Batty (Leeds Utd), D.S.Walker (Nottm Forest), G.V.Mabbutt (Spurs), B.Robson (Man Utd), D.A.Platt (Bari), A.M.Smith (Arsenal), G.W.Lineker (Spurs, captain), C.R.Waddle (Marseille).
Turkey: D.Hayrettin (Galatasaray);

Ç.Recep (Beşiktaş), T.Ogün (Trabzonspor), K.Gökhan (Beşiktaş), K.Tugay (Galatasaray), S.Turhan (Fenerbahçe), U.Feyyaz (Beşiktaş), Ç.Riza (Beşiktaş), K.Ünal (Trabzonspor), Ç.Oğuz (Fenerbahçe), Ç.Orhan (Trabzonspor).
Sub: M.Hami (Trabzonspor) for Feyyaz.

Half-time 1-0   Full-time 1-0

Ref: A.M.Navarette (Spain)   Att: 50,896

NOT a very impressive display but a valuable two points none the less. That was how best to describe this inept display by England against the minnows of the group, Turkey. It put them two points clear of the rest of the group in these Championships but it remained to be seen whether they would reach the finals in Sweden next summer.

A bad foul by Gökhan on Gary Lineker opened the proceedings and the Turkish defender was lucky to only get a yellow card. The best of the early attacking came from the visitors and Chris Woods was soon in action, stopping a header by Feyyaz and a long-range shot from Tugay. The England formation did not seem to inspire the players or the supporters and the recalled Bryan Robson looked strangely out of sorts.

The first decent attempt at goal from England came midway through the first half. David Batty, Alan Smith and Stuart Pearce produced a good move which lacked the finish, but a minute later the breakthrough came. Lee Dixon found Pearce with a rare good pass and the Forest man made ground before curling a superb cross to the far post. Goalkeeper Hayrettin went for the ball but missed it completely and watched in horror as Smith scored with the simplest of headers which he tucked away well.

Turkey, looking much more organised and controlled than on their previous

visits to Wembley, came back strongly from this set-back and Ünal twice forced Woods into outstanding saves to prevent an equalizer. Chris Waddle then hit a purple patch, making some sparkling runs. A stream of good crosses caused confusion in the Turkish defence and from two of them David Platt and Smith had chances. Alas, they were both squandered and the half ended without further addition to the score.

The second half was a complete non-event. England, lacking any positive ideas, could not break down the determined Turkey defence. Lineker and Robson did have half chances following crosses from Waddle and Dixon respectively, but the sharpness was missing and the finish could not be found. Overall then it was a disappointing performance by England and the general lack of urgency was the most worrying aspect that Graham Taylor had to work on.

> 6th match v Turkey.

Poland v England
European Championship Qualifier

Played on Wednesday, 13 November 1991 in the Lech Stadium, Poznań.

Poland: J.Bako (Beşiktaş); R.Warzycha (Everton), T.Waldoch (Górnik Zabrze), R.Soczynski (Fenerbaçhe), R.Szewczyk (GKS Katowice), P.Czachowski (Zagłębie Lubin), R.Kosecki (Galatararay), D.Skrzypczak (Lech Poznań), J.Furtok (Hamburger SV), J.Ziober (Montpellier), J.Urban (CA Osasuna).
Subs: A.Fedoruk (Stal Mielec) for Dzewczyk and M.Rzepka (Lech Poznań) for Kosecki.
England: C.E.Woods (Sheffield Wed); L.M.Dixon (Arsenal), S.Pearce (Nottm Forest), A.A.Gray (Crystal Palace),

Gary Lineker's superb goal against Poland in the November 1991 European Championship qualifying game.

D.S.Walker (Nottm Forest), G.V.Mabbutt (Spurs), D.A.Platt (Bari), G.R.Thomas (Crystal Palace), D.Rocastle (Arsenal), G.W.Lineker (Spurs, captain), A.Sinton (QPR).
Subs: A.M.Smith (Arsenal) for Gray and A.M.Daley (Aston Villa) for Sinton.

Half-time 1-0   Full-time 1-1

Ref: H.Forstineer (Austria)   Att: 15,000

ONCE again, England owe an enormous debt of gratitude to their inspirational captain, as Gary Lineker, the scourge of Poland, scored the spectacular equalizer which takes his team through to the European Championship finals in Sweden next summer. The goal was superb and left the Spurs striker within three of Bobby Charlton's record total of 49.

Early on, though, it was the Poles who seemed destined for the glory. They settled quickly into their rhythm and an eager attack saw Soczynski set up Furtok for a shot on the turn which Chris Woods dived smartly to save at the near post. England also created an early chance with David Platt seeing his shot saved in the 17th minute. In fact, it was England who came closest to a goal when a good run and cross from new cap Andy Sinton was flicked on by Platt to give another debutant, Andy Gray, a fine chance at the far post. Unfortunately, the newcomer snatched at his shot and it hit the side-netting. Gray held his head in his hands, he knew he should have scored.

With just over half an hour gone the Poles, sensationally, took the lead. David

Rocastle, looking confident, was somewhat harshly penalised for a challenge on Ziober. The free-kick was some 35 yards from goal and seemingly not too dangerous, but when Ziober tapped the kick to Szewcyck Woods' safe positioning for the shot was ruined when Gary Mabbutt deflected the shot wide of the goalkeeper. The goal left a tricky period for England to negotiate before half-time but fine play from Des Walker and safe handling by Woods kept Poland at bay.

After the interval England played with much more assurance. Poor Gray had struggled and Alan Smith was sent on as a substitute for the Crystal Palace player. England then dominated for a long spell without gaining due reward, but a further substitution, Tony Daley for Sinton, helped tilt the balance England's way. With 77 minutes gone the visitors found a priceless equalizer.

A corner by Rocastle was headed down by Mabbutt and Lineker, who was stood just to the left of goal, spun round superbly to volley an unstoppable shot into the roof of the Polish net. Joyous scenes of English celebration followed as Lineker, once again, had come up trumps. It was a magnificent goal and one worthy of the rewards it provided.

The defence capably dealt with any further attacks from Poland and England were safely through to the finals, a worthy performance.

9th match v Poland.
Debut for Gray, Sinton and, as substitute, Daley.

England v France
Friendly

Played on Wednesday, 19 February 1992 at Wembley Stadium.

England: C.E.Woods (Sheffield Wed); R.M.Jones (Liverpool), S.Pearce (Nottm Forest, captain), M.R.Keown (Everton), M.Wright (Liverpool), D.S.Walker (Nottm Forest), N.J.Webb (Man Utd), G.R.Thomas (Crystal Palace), N.H.Clough (Nottm Forest), A.Shearer (Southampton), D.E.Hirst (Sheffield Wed).
Sub: G.W.Lineker (Spurs) for Hirst.

France: G.Rousset (Olympique Lyonnais); M.Amoros (Marseille), J.Angloma (Marseille), B.Boli (Marseille), L.Blanc (Napoli), B.Casoni (Marseille), D.Deschamps (Marseille), L.Fernandez (AS Cannes), J-P.Papin (Marseille), C.Perez (Paris St-Germain), E.Cantona (Leeds Utd).
Subs: J-P.Durand (Marseille) for Perez and A.Simba (Paris St-Germain) for Fernandez.

Half-time 1-0   Full-time 2-0

Ref: A.Schmidhuber (West Germany)

Att: 58,723

EYEBROWS were certainly raised when manager Graham Taylor decided to leave out Gary Lineker for this important friendly against France. Eventually, though, the Spurs striker had the last word on the controversial decision.

With France in England's group for the European Championship finals in

Sweden the following June it was important that the psychological advantage should be gained. At the start England looked laboured and struggled to find their rhythm. Passes too often went astray and goal attempts were few and far between. France, meanwhile, were showing the cohesion that had seen them go 19 internationals without defeat which included qualifying for those finals from their group with a 100 per cent record.

It was a most pleasing display from young right-back Rob Jones. His meteoric rise to fame from Crewe Alexandra via Liverpool to this England cap in only a few months was indeed a fairy-story and yet he had taken everything in his stride, giving a cultured performance in this game. The right-back position had been a problem for Taylor but Jones did himself no harm with this display. In fact, it was from one of his many sorties down the right flank that England opened the scoring. There was only a minute to go before the interval when Jones's run won a corner. Nigel Clough's cross was headed down by Mark Wright to where Alan Shearer, standing unmarked, spun 180 degrees to whip home a fierce shot. It was a fine goal and due reward for the Southampton player's contribution. If ever a replacement for Lineker was to be considered then surely Shearer looked to have every chance of making a name for himself.

So, a half-time lead, against the general run of play, but it signalled to the French that England were improving after their poor start. At half-time Taylor decided to take off the ineffective David Hirst and bring on Lineker.

It brought the loudest cheer of the night from the crowd and what followed with Lineker's partnership with Shearer was reminiscent of his earlier link-up with Peter Beardsley. Straight away the French were rattled and their hard man Boli quickly let Gary know that he was around with a scything tackle which sent the England substitute crashing to the ground. Boli deserved his booking.

Lineker's first positive touch was brilliant as a superb through ball sent Geoff Thomas galloping clear of the defence and a goal seemed a formality. Unfortunately for England, Thomas made a complete hash of an attempted chip over the goalkeeper and the ball went out of play near the corner-flag! It was a miss that would haunt Thomas for a very long time. Shearer, looking more lively with the introduction of Lineker to the fray, set up his co-striker for another chip shot. This time it was more measured and only just went wide of the far post.

The England attack continued to press and in the 74th minute they scored a second goal. Again Shearer was the provider when his cross was hit on the volley by Clough. The fierce shot deserved a goal but was parried by Rousset, but Lineker pounced first to first head against the bar, and then score with his second attempt. A sharply-taken goal.

Simba did hit the post with one shot as France tried to recover, but the new partnership of Lineker and Shearer had certainly impressed the watching public and pundits.

> 21st match v France.
> Debuts for Keown, Shearer and Jones.
> Debut goal for Shearer.

Nigel Clough gets in a shot against France at Wembley in February 1992.

Goalscorers Gary Lineker and Alan Shearer after the game against France.

Czechoslovakia v England   *Friendly*

Played on Wednesday, 25 March 1992 in the Strahov Stadium, Prague.

Czechoslovakia: L.Mikloško (West Ham); P.Hapal (Sigma Olomouc), M.Kadlec (1.FC Kaiserslautern), K.Kula (VfB Stuttgart), M.Glonek (Slovan Bratislava), V.Němeček (Sparta Prague), M.Bílek (Real Betis), J.Chovanec (Sparta Prague), L.Kubik (FC Metz), T.Skuhravý (Genoa), I.Knoflíček (Bochum).
Subs: M.Frýda (Sparta Prague) for Kula, J.Němec (Sparta Prague) for Němeček and H.Siegel (Sparta Prague) for Knoflíček.

England: D.A.Seaman (Arsenal); M.R.Keown (Everton), S.Pearce (Nottm Forest, captain), D.Rocastle (Arsenal), D.S.Walker (Nottm Forest), G.V.Mabbutt (Spurs), D.A.Platt (Bari), P.C.Merson (Arsenal), N.H.Clough (Nottm Forest), M.W.Hateley (Rangers), J.C.B.Barnes (Liverpool).
Subs: L.M.Dixon (Arsenal) for Rocastle, G.W.Lineker (Spurs) for Mabbutt,

P.A.Stewart (Spurs) for Clough and A.R.Dorigo (Leeds Utd) for Barnes.

Half-time 1-1   Full-time 2-2
Ref: G.Kapi (Austria)   Att: 12,320

IN THIS, the latest friendly match as part of the preparation for the forthcoming European Championships, England were very lucky to come away from Prague with a draw. Graham Taylor's patched up team gave an indifferent performance and the Czechs could be annoyed with themselves for not winning.

The opening minutes were quite bright from an England point of view but soon the Czechs were stretching the visitors with some good, probing attacks. With danger man Skuhravý looking every inch the star performer, the swift passing movements had England scrambling. The midfield was overrun as John Barnes, Nigel Clough and David Rocastle struggled to find their form. David Platt did his best to hold things together but it was left to Des Walker's outstanding skills to keep the home side at bay.

David Platt battles it out against Czechoslovakia in Prague in March 1992.

On 21 minutes, though, even he was powerless to prevent a goal, and indeed, it came from a free-kick he had conceded. A clumsy challenge gave Chovanec the chance to curl a cross towards the middle, Skuhravý, always alive and sharp around goal, was first to react and his glancing header gave David Seaman little chance to save as the ball nestled in the far corner.

At this point England were struggling but after 28 minutes an excellent move brought them a surprise equalizer. Seaman's throw found Stuart Pearce who, in turn, found Clough. The Nottingham Forest midfield star then produced his best pass in an England shirt to send Mark Hateley away. He passed to Platt on the left who then pulled the ball back across goal. Rather fortiously, it found its way to Paul Merson in the old inside-right position. The Arsenal striker did very well and celebrated his first full appearance with a well struck low shot that beat Mikloško.

Both Kula and Hapal put in shots which the uncomfortable Seaman had struggled to save and the goalkeeper's nightmare continued after Czechoslovakia were awarded a corner in the 60th minute. Chovanec's winger was low but should have been easily cleared. But first, Tony Dorigo and then Seaman, allowed the ball to squirt between their legs and into the net. There was a horrified look on the England players' faces at this wholly embarrassing moment.

Somewhat surprisingly, after a lacklustre display, the visitors were not finished yet. Pearce, characteristically battling for everything, found Martin Keown, of all people, on the left edge of the penalty area. The big defender cut inside before unleashing a fine rising drive which flashed past West Ham's Mikloško for another equalizer. It was a fine goal but one, in all honesty, that England did not deserve. Ironically England might then have even snatched an unlikely victory but Dorigo's good shot was well saved. If that had gone in, England would have been even more embarrassed.

Not the best of exercises as Graham Taylor tried to build his best team, but there is always some good to come out of every game and Merson's display was

particularly satisfying. With Alan Shearer impressing in the previous, then perhaps Gary Lineker's impending retirement would not be the disaster that most people thought.

12th match v Czechoslovakia.

CIS v
England   Friendly

Played on Wednesday, 29 April 1992 in the Central Lenin Stadium, Moscow.

CIS: D.Kharin (CSKA Moscow)); A.Chernishov (Spartak Moscow), K.Tzhadadze (Spartak Moscow), A.Tsveiba (Dinamo Kiev), I.Ledyakhov (Spartak Moscow), I.Shalimov (Foggia), A.Mikhailichenko (Rangers), A.Kanchelskis (Man Utd), I.Kolivanov (Foggia), A.Mostovoy (Benfica), S.Yuran (Benfica). Subs: S.Kiryakov (Dinamo Moscow) for Ledyakhov, V.Karpin (Spartak Moscow) for Kanchelskis, V.Lyuty (MSV Duisburg) for Kolyvanov and V.Onopko (Spartak Moscow) for Yuran.

England: C.E.Woods (Sheffield Wed); M.G.Stevens (Rangers), A.Sinton (QPR), D.S.Walker (Nottm Forest), M.R.Keown (Everton), T.M.Steven (Marseille), D.A.Platt (Bari), C.L.Palmer (Sheffield Wed), A.M.Daley (Aston Villa), G.W.Lineker (Spurs, captain), A.Shearer (Southampton). Subs: A.N.Martyn (Crystal Palace) for Woods, K.Curle (Man City) for Sinton, P.A.Stewart (Spurs) for Steven and N.H.Clough (Nottm Forest) for Shearer.

Half-time 1-1   Full-time 2-2

Ref: P.Werner (Poland)   Att: 18,580

AFTER their rather fortunate 2-2 draw in their last match in Czechoslovakia, England repeated the result when they visited Moscow for a match against the new Commonwealth of Independent States team, in reality the rump of the old Soviet empire. But this time the result was very creditable and was the latest performance in the tough series of friendly internationals leading up to the European Championships. There were more changes forced on Graham Taylor's selection and he brought in Carlton Palmer for his debut and brought back Tony Daley.

In the opening half-hour England looked very comfortable and held the best of the home attacks with ease. The defence, with both full-backs giving confident displays, looked in little trouble and England were able to mount some excellent moves. On 15 minutes they took a deserved lead. Daley, making one of several fine runs, took a pass from Trevor Steven and accellerated to the by-line. His blistering pace left the CIS defenders in his wake before a perfect cross picked out skipper Gary Lineker for a lovely glancing header which gave the ace scorer his 48th and, as it turned out, last international goal, just one short of Bobby Charlton's record total.

Several players impressed during the rest of the half with Andy Sinton having a very good game in his unaccustomed left-back position. He kept the Manchester United winger, Kanchelskis, very quiet and eventually the CIS player was withdrawn. It all looked good for England until one minute before the interval. After

Akhrik Tsveiba of the CIS tries to rob Gary Lineker in the Central Lenin Stadium, Moscow, in April 1992.

Chris Woods had tipped over a long distance shot from Shalimov, the goalkeeper was then beaten when Tshadadze headed home from the resultant corner.

An hour into the match and the CIS side took the lead after a spell of pressure. Tsveiba's shot hit a post and one of the substitutes, Lyuty, headed the rebound to the other substitute, Kiryakov, who scored. England were now struggling after their excellent first half but after a great free-kick by Mikhailichenko narrowly missed the target, Graham Taylor brought on Nigel Clough and Keith Curle to try and change the pattern of the game. Within minutes it was working and both the new players made good contributions as England regained their midfield superiority.

The improvement culminated in an equalizer after Clough's marvellous pass set up Steven who capped a fine game with a very well taken goal. Unfortunately the Rangers player had to leave the field injured shortly after his goal following a shuddering tackle by Tzhadadze.

Although there were no more goals, England continued to play well, due mainly to the much improved passing throughout the team. Near the end they almost regained the lead but Sinton's shot was well saved.

12th match v CIS (Russia)
Debuts for Palmer and, as substitutes, Curle and Martyn.

Hungary v England   Friendly

Played on Tuesday, 12 May 1992 in the Nep Stadium, Budapest.

Hungary: I.Brockhauser (Újpesti Dózsa); T.Simon (Ferencváros), A.Telek (Ferencváros), J.Szalma (Fortuna Sittard), E.Lórincz (Molenbeek), Z.Limperger (Burgos), J.Kiprich (Feyenoord), E.Kovács (Honvéd), I.Pisont (Honvéd), P.Lipcsei (Ferencváros), I.Vincze (Honvéd).
Subs: Z.Kecskes (MTK Budapest) for Szalma and G.Márton (Honvéd) for Lipcsei.

England: A.N.Martyn (Crystal Palace); M.G.Stevens (Rangers), A.R.Dorigo (Leeds Utd), K.Curle (Man City), D.S.Walker (Nottm Forest), M.R.Keown (Everton), N.J.Webb (Man Utd), C.L.Palmer (Sheffield Wed), P.L.Merson (Arsenal), G.W.Lineker (Spurs, captain), A.M.Daley (Aston Villa).
Subs: D.A.Seaman (Arsenal) for Martyn, A.Sinton (QPR) for Curle, D.Batty (Leeds Utd) for Webb, A.M.Smith (Arsenal) for Merson and I.E.Wright (Arsenal) for Daley.

Half-time 0-0   Full-time 0-1
Ref: H.Holzmann (Austria)   Att: 12,500

ANOTHER victory for England as they kept their successful run going in Budapest and continued to build up the confidence before the real action began in Sweden the following month. However, this was not a good game and at times the standard of play fell well below what is expected from international football. Once again though there were some plus points for Graham Taylor amidst a patchy display.

Hungary began as if they meant business and opened huge gaps in the shaky England defence. However, Martin Keown, Des Walker, and Keith Curle held firm, so much so that Nigel Martyn was not troubled until late in the first half. In the midfield the new combination of Neil Webb and Carlton Palmer struggled to make any headway and it was not until Gary Stevens and Tony Dorigo pushed forward that England began to improve.

Lorincz and Limperger made surging runs deep into England territory but Hungary lacked any kind of finish and each time the move fizzled out.

At half-time the manager decided to change England's tactics, bringing on Andy Sinton for Curle and Alan Smith for Paul Merson. The 4-2-4 formation was switched to 4-4-2 and immediately there was an improvement. Keown cleared an attack in the first minute of the second half but after settling into the new pattern, England started to look more confident. In the 56th minute they scored a goal which was in keeping with the rest of this match.

A chipped pass by Sinton sent Gary Lineker free in the box but to the right of goal. The striker hit an instant cross to the far post, where Neil Webb stooped to head towards goal. The ball appeared to be covered by Brochauser but before he could claim it the Hungarian sweeper, Telek, stuck out a foot to divert it into his own net.

Webb soon gave way to David Batty as the substitutions continued to flow and the Leeds man was quickly making his presence felt in that familiar style of his. Lineker was also withdrawn but although his replacement, Ian Wright, worked hard, he had little chance to show his recent club scoring form.

A mistake by David Seaman (another substitute!) almost let in Kiprich but the goalkeeper was rescued by a Gary Stevens clearance. Seaman again showed a nervous hesitancy that is worrying at this level. Still, in the end the clean sheet was preserved and England were able to hold on to their one-goal lead.

18th match v Hungary.

Neil Webb (on ground) swoops to head the winner in the Nep Stadium in May 1992.

England v Brazil
Friendly

Played on Sunday, 17 May 1992 at Wembley Stadium.

England: C.E.Woods (Sheffield Wed); M.G.Stevens (Rangers), A.R.Dorigo (Leeds Utd), C.L.Palmer (Sheffield Wed), D.S.Walker (Nottm Forest), M.R.Keown (Everton), A.M.Daley (Aston Villa), T.M.Steven (Marseille), D.A.Platt (Bari), G.W.Lineker (Spurs, captain), A.Sinton (QPR).
Subs: S.Pearce (Nottm Forest) for Dorigo, P.C.Merson (Arsenal) for Daley, D.Rocastle (Arsenal) for Steven and N.J.Webb (Man Utd) for Sinton.
Brazil: Carlos (Palmeiros); Winck (Vasco da Gama), Mozer (Marseille), Ricardo II (Paris St-Germain), Mauro de Silva (Bragantino), Branco (Genoa), Bebeto (Vasco da Gama), Henrique (Palmeiras), Reato (Botafogo), Rai (São Paulo), Valdo (Paris St-Germain).
Subs: Charles (Flamengo) for Winck, Valdeir (Botafogo) for Henrique, Junior (Flamengo) for Reato and Sergio (Corinthians) for Valdo.

Half-time 0-1   Full-time 1-1
Ref: J.McCluskey (Scotland)   Att: 53,428

THE visit of Brazil to Wembley is always looked upon with eager anticipation, but this game was more subdued than usual. Two reasons for that situation lay in the fact that several of Brazil's top players were unavailable due to club commitments, and also that England were anxious not to lose with the European Championships just around the corner.

Brazil were soon showing the crowd all the best things from their game as some lovely passing movements were put together with the minimum of fuss. But it was England who should have opened the scoring in the tenth minute when they were awarded a penalty. Gary Stevens had fed a fine through ball for Gary Lineker to run onto. The England striker reached the pass before Carlos, but as he attempted to nod the ball around the goalkeeper, Carlos made contact with flapping hands. Lineker went down and the penalty was

given. It looked a harsh decision but it did not matter as, for the first time in an England shirt, Lineker completely fluffed the kick giving Carlos the chance to make an easy save. A wry smile from Lineker showed that he had missed a golden chance to equal that much sought-after record of Bobby Charlton.

The England midfield of Trevor Steven and Carlton Palmer struggled to contain the lively Brazilians. Almost at will they carved great holes in the home defence and Henrique looked an outstanding prospect. Ten minutes after the penalty miss, Brazil took a deserved lead. Renato's cross from the right was missed by Rai who had attempted an overhead kick. Stevens failed to clear and instead the ball ran just right for Bebeto who lashed the ball past Chris Woods.

After the interval Chris Woods, who had already made a couple of excellent saves, had his busiest time in an England shirt. Brazil were always looking to score and the goalkeeper made brilliant saves from Rai and Henrique. But England found an equalizer shortly after the restart which stunned the visitors. Substitute Neil Webb chipped a pass forward in search of Lineker but instead, Brazilian Charles, another substitute, attempted a clearance which only sent the ball across goal and into the path of David Platt. A firm downward volley and Platt scored his first international goal for a year.

The goal did not lift England's performance though, and indeed, Brazil stepped up the pace to put more pressure on Woods. The goalkeeper made several more good saves and once, when he was finally beaten, Stevens cleared off the line with a brave header.

Apart from Woods, it was difficult to say that any of the England players had a good game. Even Des Walker was hurried into uncharacteristic efforts by these quicksilver Brazilians. The South Americans seemed to have abandoned their recent tendency to play a more European style to return to their old ways, lots of flair and simply oozing skill.

> 16th match v Brazil
> Penalty missed for England by Lineker.

Finland v England
Friendly

Played on Wednesday, 3 June 1992 in the Olympic Stadium, Helsinki.

Finland: O.Huttunen (Valkeakosken Haka); J.Rinne (Kuusysi Lahti), P.Järvinen (Kuusysi Lahti), E.Petäjä (Malmö FF), E.Holmgren (GAIS), J.Kinnunen (Kuusysi Lahti), J.Litmanen (MyPa), M.Myyry (SC Lokeren), A.Hjelm (Ilves Tampere), K.Tarkkio (Kuusysi Lahti), J.Huhtamäki (MP Mikkeli).
Subs: J.Van Hala (HJK Helsinki) for Rinne, A.Heikkinen (TPS Turku) for Holmgren, J.Vuorela (HJK Helsinki) for Litmanen and A.Tegelberg (RoPS Rovaniemi) for Tarkkio.
England: C.E.Woods (Sheffield Wed); M.G.Stevens (Rangers), S.Pearce (Nottm Forest), M.R.Keown (Everton), D.S.Walker (Nottm Forest), M.Wright (Liverpool), D.A.Platt (Bari), T.M.Steven (Marseille), N.J.Webb (Man Utd), G.W.Lineker (Spurs, captain), J.C.B. Barnes (Liverpool).
Subs: C.L.Palmer (Sheffield Wed) for Stevens, A.M.Daley (Aston Villa) for Steven and P.C.Merson (Arsenal) for Barnes.

Half-time 1-1   Full-time 1-2
Ref: B.Karlsson (Sweden)   Att: 16,101

THIS was England's last chance of action before the European Championships in Sweden and the game turned out to be something of a nightmare. The performance itself was not too impressive but worst of all was the fact that both John Barnes and Gary Stevens were now out of those championships after sustaining serious injuries.

It was only the 13th minute when Barnes went down clutching his ankle in agony. A ruptured Achilles tendon was eventually diagnosed and the Liverpool player, who had just seen his whole season ruined by a series of injuries, looked crestfallen as he hobbled to the bench. Paul Merson took his place and the Arsenal striker was soon making some interesting runs down the left.

In the 26th minute, England were awarded a corner. Stuart Pearce's kick was cleared and because most of the defenders had gone up to join the attack, only Stevens was left to cover any kind of breakaway. Tarkkio quickly spotted this and ran at the full-back before releasing a good pass to the talented Litmanen. As the Finn entered the area, Trevor Steven, one of a possee of defenders racing back, made a challenge which seemed good but in the process brought down Litmanen. The referee decided it was a foul and ordered a penalty-kick. After some protest by the England players, Hjelm stepped forward to put his side one up.

A couple of good runs by the industrious Steven was the main highlight of England's struggle to come back into the match, and it was not until the last minute of the half that they eventually found an equalizer. Neil Webb won a tackle which gave possession to Steven. He spotted David Platt running in from the left unmarked and sent a perfect pass for the Bari player to beat Huttunen with a well-placed side-footed shot.

Gary Lineker was never given a chance of catching Bobby Charlton's record and

England's Tony Daley (middle) in action against Brazil at Wembley in May 1992.

John Barnes receives treatment during the game against Finland in Helsinki in June 1992.

it was looking more and more elusive for the popular Spurs striker. At least though England did grab the lead just after the hour. A long throw by Carlton Palmer was flicked on by the head of Mark Wright at the near post and once again Platt was on the spot to volley home a very well-taken second goal.

Most of this second half was played at a very leisurely pace with England comfortably containing the weak Finland attack. Indeed, had Pearce's header gone in instead of hitting the post, and had Platt's shot not been brilliantly saved by Huttunen, England's win might have been greater.

Manager Graham Taylor now had several problems in finding his side for the opening game against Denmark the following week and those latest injuries were of no help to him whatsoever.

9th match v Finland.
Penalty scored for Finland by Hjelm.

European Championship Finals

Denmark v England   Group One

Played on Thursday, 11 June 1992 in Malmö, the Malmö Stadium, Sweden.

Denmark: P.B.Schmeichel (Man Utd); J.Sivebaek (AS Monaco), K.Nielsen (Aarhus GF), L.Olsen (Trabzonspor), H.Andersen (1.FC Cologne), K.Christofte (Brøndby IF), J.Jensen (Brøndby IF), F.Povlsen (Borussia Dortmund), B.Laudrup (Bayern Munich), B.Christensen (FC Schalke 04), K.Vilfort (Brøndby IF).
England: C.E.Woods (Sheffield Wed); K.Curle (Man City), S.Pearce (Nottm Forest), M.R.Keown (Everton), D.S.Walker (Nottm Forest), T.M.Steven (Marseille), D.A.Platt (Bari), P.C.Merson (Arsenal), A.M.Smith (Arsenal), G.W.Lineker (Spurs, captain), C.R. Palmer (Sheffield Wed).
Subs: A.M.Daley (Aston Villa) for Curle and N.J.Webb (Man Utd) for Merson.

Keith Curle takes the ball past a grounded Brian Laudrup during the 1992 European Championship finals in Sweden.

Half-time 0-0   Full-time 0-0
Ref: J.Blankenstein (Holland) Att: 26,385

ENGLAND finally began their challenge for the 1992 European Championship in Malmö with this awkward match against Denmark, who were in the competition only because of the late withdrawal of the expelled Yugoslavia team, yet were to become the eventual tournament champions. England were on a hiding to nothing. If they won, it was to be expected. If they lost, then it was a disaster, and if they drew . . . well? . . .

Manager Graham Taylor decided to fill the problem right-back position with Keith Curle, the Manchester City player, but before 12 minutes had elapsed both Curle and Martin Keown had been booked, such was the edginess of England's early play. At no time in the game did they look comfortable and all the players struggled at times.

The first half saw few clear chances created but in the 25th minute, a neat build-up between Paul Merson and Gary Lineker ended with Alan Smith side-footing the ball goalwards. With goalkeeper Schmeichel beaten, the ball

scrapped the outside of the post. Merson also made a couple of good positive runs into the box and from one of them he shot wide when he should have at least found the target. Unfortunately the Arsenal player could not sustain this bright form and England did not threaten Schmeichel's goal nearly enough. The big Manchester United goalkeeper showed some shaky handling, but the England players were unable to apply the necessary pressure to take advantage.

Curle was lucky when he again held back a Danish player, the offence for which he had already been cautioned, but a second challenge by Stuart Pearce luckily caught the eye of the referee, a piece of quick thinking by the England left-back which probably prevented the red card coming out for Curle. When Tony Daley was sent on after the hour, it was no surprise to see Curle taken off. Trevor Steven, probably the pick of the midfield, was switched to right-back and the move almost paid off when Daley burst through to hit a screamer which Schmeichel touched over the bar.

On 65 minutes, England had a lucky escape. A good move by Denmark split the defence and Christensen received Sivebaek's pass before setting up Jensen to the right of goal. Jensen did everything correctly and his shot beat the diving Chris Woods. It looked a certain goal but the ball struck the inside of the far post and bounced across goal where Woods was able to pounce on the rebound, much to his and England's relief.

A further substitution bringing on Neil Webb for Merson did not produce dividends and the game eventually petered out to a dismal goalless draw. Even then Denmark almost snatched victory at the death. It was the last minute when a cross from the left just evaded the lunging Vilfort, a goal then and England would have been virtually out of the reckoning for this tournament.

13th match v Denmark.

France v England   Group One

Played on Sunday, 14 June 1992 in the Malmö Stadium, Malmö, Sweden.

France: B.Martini (AJ Auxerre); M.Amoros (Marseille), L.Blanc (Napoli), B.Boli (Marseille), B.Casoni (Marseille), D.Deschamps (Marseille), F.Sauzée (Marseille), L.Fernandez (AS Cannes), J-P.Durand (Marseille), E.Cantona (Leeds Utd), J-P.Papin (Marseille).
Subs: J.Angloma (Marseille) for Sauzée and C.Perez (Paris St-Germain) for Fernandez.
England: C.E.Woods (Sheffield Wed); A.Sinton (QPR), S.Pearce (Nottm Forest), M.R.Keown (Everton), D.S.Walker (Nottm Forest), C.L.Palmer (Sheffield Wed), D.A.Platt (Bari), D.Batty (Leeds Utd), A.Shearer (Southampton), G.W.Lineker (Spurs, captain), T.M.Steven (Marseille).

Half-time 0-0   Full-time 0-0
Ref: S.Puhl (Hungary)   Att: 26,535

ENGLAND'S progress in this tournament was being hampered by their current

David Batty holds off Jean-Philippe Durand of France in the Malmö Stadium.

inability to score a goal! Once again a sterile, unimaginative game was played with England, at least performing better than they did against Denmark, but lacking the necessary flair to break down a well-organised defence. The game had its moments but the fear of losing stifled any kind of entertainment.

Both sides spent the early part of the game feeling each other out and probing the defences. The first goal attempt took a while to arrive and in fact it was not until the 16th minute that it fell to Jean-Pierre Papin. It was the French star's only real chance of the whole game and came after he beat Martin Keown to flick the ball towards goal. Chris Woods reacted brilliantly, though, and he was quickly down to his left to make a fine one-handed save. England, meanwhile, tried hard to work the ball forward. Both Trevor Steven and David Batty got through a tremendous amount of work but, alas, the guile was not there and only occasionally did they look dangerous.

Alan Shearer, full of running, broke promisingly on the left but instead of making for goal he decided to square the ball to Gary Lineker. Unfortunately the pass was underhit and France cleared the danger. Des Walker was back to his best form in policing the potentially lethal Papin and Carlton Palmer answered a few of his critics with a confident display in his role as sweeper. One lovely moment of skill when he dummied a French attacker to feed the ball safely back to Woods must have given him great satisfaction.

As a spectacle the game was bitterly disappointing. It was all very chess-like with no player from either side capable of showing that special piece of skill to lift the play above the predictable.

In the second half France probably had more of the possession but it was England who had the best of what goal chances there were. Lineker and Shearer both helped on a long clearance and David Platt

volleyed over from the edge of the box. It was close, and a few minutes later England's best move, involving Lineker and Sinton ended when Shearer met Sinton's cross with a diving header to send the ball flashing inches wide.

France carried little threat up front but from one corner the substitute, Angloma, headed powerfully at goal. Woods, for once, was beaten but Sinton was perfectly positioned on the post to clear from the goal-line.

Fernandez and Batty were both booked as the play became even more tense and there was a nasty moment when Stuart Pearce was butted by the French defender Boli. It was as well for the Frenchman that the referee did not spot it as Pearce was left with a nasty gash on his cheek which later needed stitches. The England defender almost gained revenge in the best possible way a few minutes later.

The referee had just ordered him off to receive treatment for his facial wound, but as a free-kick had been awarded against France he was quickly back to take the kick. He hit a beauty and was desperately unlucky to see the ball strike the underside of the crossbar, bounce down and eventually be cleared by a defender.

That would have been a nice way to score what would have almost certainly been a winning goal, but as Denmark found in the previous game, it is no good hitting the woodwork instead of the back of the net.

| 22nd match v France |

Sweden v England
Group One

Played on Wednesday 17 June 1992 in the Råsunda Stadium, Solna.

Sweden: T.Ravelli (IFK Gothenburg); N.L.R.Nilsson (Sheffield Wed), J.Eriksson (IFK Norrköping), P.Andersson (Malmö FF), J.Bjorklund (SK Brann), S.Schwarz (Benfica), K.Ingasson (KV Mechelen), J.Thern (Benfica), A.E.Limpar (Arsenal), T.Brolin (Parma AC), M.Dahlin (Borussia Mönchengladbach).
Sub: J.Ekström (IFK Gothenburg) for Limpar.

England: C.E.Woods (Sheffield Wed); D.Batty (Leeds Utd), S.Pearce (Nottm Forest), M.R.Keown (Everton), D.S.Walker (Sampdoria), C.L.Palmer (Sheffield Wed), A.M.Daley (Aston Villa), N.J.Webb (Man Utd), D.A.Platt (Bari), G.W.Lineker (Spurs, captain), A.Sinton (QPR).
Subs: A.M.Smith (Arsenal) for Lineker and P.C.Merson (Arsenal) for Sinton.

Half-time 0-1   Full-time 2-1
Ref: J.Rosa Dos Santos (Portugal)

Att: 30,126

YET another challenge by England in a major championship fell by the wayside as they were beaten in Stockholm by the host nation. They had the perfect start to the match but, in the end, they were just not good enough.

It all looked very promising early on as England went positively at their opponents. David Batty, filling in admir-

ably in the problem right-back position, was soon helping in an attack down the right. It was the fourth minute when Neil Webb played a delightful pass forward and Batty cleverly flicked the ball to Gary Lineker with his head to leave England's top striker in a good position to centre. The captain looked up and pulled the perfect pass into the path of the incoming David Platt. Although Platt did not make a clean contact he did enough to bundle the ball wide of Ravelli and into the net.

Joyous English scenes greeted the goal and in these early stages the Swedes were really rocking. England then had two great chances to finish the match off. In the 34th minute another fine pass, this time from Platt, left Tony Daley clear of the home defence and making for goal. It seemed an ideal chance for the speedy winger and, had he gone for goal, he would surely have scored. As it was he opted to try and find Lineker coming in at the far side of goal. Alas, the Daley attempt resembled neither a shot at goal nor a pass and the ball passed harmlessly out for a goal-kick. At this level those sort of chances must be taken.

A minute later and Daley had another golden opportunity. Stuart Pearce's perfect cross to the far post found Daley in lots of space and with a free header. Unfortunately the Aston Villa player headed tamely over the bar and the chance was wasted. As the half wore on England played quite well but without dominating and, of course, scoring the goals that would clinch the result. Towards the end of the half there were signs that Sweden were gathering themselves for something of a recovery. Both Brolin and Dahlin were beginning to create problems for the England defence and in one attack Batty almost gave away a penalty as Brolin went down when challenged from behind.

At the interval Sweden made a significant tactical switch. They bought on Ekström to play up front, taking off the ineffective Limpar, and then promptly pumped the ball towards the big striker at every opportunity. It quickly gave Sweden control of the match as England struggled to come to terms with this new ploy. An equalizer became a distinct possibility and it came as no surprise when they finally scored. Once again, and far too often lately, it was a corner that proved to be the downfall of England. Schwarz took the kick and Eriksson met it with a powerful downward header which gave Chris Woods no chance. Goals conceded from corners were becoming a worrying trend of recent England performances and something that Graham Taylor had to stop. Here it cost him the chance of progress.

Worse was to come for the England fans and on 64 minutes their morale hit rock bottom as Lineker was substituted. With his impending self-retirement from the English game, it effectively ended the chance for him to overhaul the England scoring record. It was a very sad moment for one of England's all-time greats.

If that was a sad moment then what happened eight minutes from time finished the England supporters off. Brolin exchanged passes with Ekström and Dahlin before shooting on the run wide of the full-length dive of Chris Woods for the goal of the tournament. That, as they say, was the end of that! England never looked like equalizing and in the end they

David Platt celebrates a goal against Sweden in Solna.

finished well beaten. It was very disappointing, especially as they had made such an encouraging start to the game.

> 14th match v Sweden.
> Lineker's last international.
> 50th cap for Pearce.

Spain v England   Friendly

Played on Wednesday, 9 September 1992 in the El Sardinero Stadium, Santander.

Spain: A.Zubizarreta (FC Barcelona); A.Ferrer (FC Barcelona), A.Muñoz (Atlético Madrid), R.Solozabal (Atlético Madrid), J.M.López (Atlético Madrid), J.Vizcaino (Atlético Madrid), G.Fonseca (RCD Español), M.Gonzalez (Real Madrid), J.Bakero (FC Barcelona), R.Martín Vázquez (Marseilles), G.Amor (FC Barcelona).
Subs: C.Parralo (Real Oviedo) for Muñoz, F.Gomez (Valencia CF) for Fonseca, J.Goicoechea (FC Barcelona) for Gonzalez, A.Perez (Real Madrid) for Bakero and A.Cervera (Valencia CF) for Martín Vázquez.
England: C.E.Woods (Sheffield Wed); L.M.Dixon (Arsenal), S.Pearce (Nottm Forest, captain), P.E.C.Ince (Man Utd), D.S.Walker (Sampdoria), M.Wright (Liverpool), D.White (Man City), D.A.Platt (Juventus), N.H.Clough (Nottm Forest), A.Shearer (Blackburn R), A.Sinton (QPR).
Subs: D.J.Bardsley (QPR) for Dixon, P.C.Merson (Arsenal) for White, B.C.Deane (Sheffield Utd) for Sinton and C.L.Palmer (Sheffield Wed) for Bardsley.

Lopez of Spain and David White of England doing battle in this September 1992 friendly in Santander.

Half-time 1-0   Full-time 1-0
Ref: J.A.Veiga (Portugal)   Att: 22,000

ENGLAND lost in Spain for the first time in 32 years and gave a very disappointing performance. It could have been so different had they taken a very good early chance that came their way. Graham Taylor was looking to his players to put the summer disappointment behind them and start the new season on a winning note. But once again the September jinx struck.

A marvellous pass by Nigel Clough in the second minute set up that early chance which should have enabled England to take the lead. The pass found debutant David White and the Manchester City player, who had been knocking the goals in regularly in the Premier League, fluffed his golden chance allowing Zubizarreta to block his weak shot. Perhaps the chance had come before White had found his international feet but whatever, from that moment Spain took control and nobody impressed more than the £2 million player, Martín Vázquez. His skill was a class above and he was the instigator of most of Spain's best moves. He tormented Arsenal's Lee Dixon throughout the first half, so much so, that Dixon was replaced by David Bardsley at half-time.

The goal that eventually settled the match came in the 11th minute. Des Walker, uncharacteristically looking off form, attempted to give the ball to Mark Wright but only succeeded in giving it to Martín Vázquez. The Spaniard quickly hit a shot at goal and although the ball was deflected, it ran perfectly into the path of Fonseca who calmly slipped a shot wide of Chris Woods.

England had ample time to get back into the match but they never had the guile or effort they needed. With David Platt still not fully fit and nobody of the quality of, say, a Bryan Robson in midfield, the attack was starved of any decent opportunities to shine. Clough, who showed some lovely touches, did not see enough of the ball and Alan Shearer was superbly marked by the outstanding Lopez.

It was not until the 65th minute that England had another worthwhile goal attempt. Carlton Palmer, who replaced the injured Bardsley only 18 minutes after the Queen's Park Rangers player had come on for Dixon, put over a deep cross which Zubizarreta fumbled. The ball fell for White and although he put in a firm shot on target the 'keeper recovered well to make the save.

After that incident there was very little from either side and it was ironic that Spain's success was achieved using a very English style of play. In all truth, the 1-0 scoreline flattered England.

17th match v Spain.
Debuts for Ince, White and, as substitute, Bardsley.
Spain's Gonzalez also known as 'Míchel'; Parralo as 'Cristóbal'; Munõz as 'Toni'; Gomez as 'Fernando'; Cervera as 'Alvaro'; Perez as 'Alfonso'.

England v Norway
World Cup Qualifer
Played on Wednesday, 14 October 1992 at Wembley Stadium.

England: C.E.Woods (Sheffield Wed); L.M.Dixon (Arsenal), S.Pearce (Nottm Forest, captain), D.Batty (Leeds Utd), D.S.Walker (Sampdoria), T.A.Adams (Arsenal), D.A.Platt (Juventus), P.J.Gascoigne (Lazio), A.Shearer (Blackburn R), I.E.Wright (Arsenal), P.E.C.Ince (Man Utd).
Subs: P.C.Merson (Arsenal) for Wright and C.L.Palmer (Sheffield Wed) for Dixon.

Paul Gascoigne bursting through against Norway at Wembley in October 1992.

Norway: E.Thorstvedt (Spurs); R.Nilsen (Viking Stavanger), T.Pedersen (IFK Gothenburg), R.Bratseth (Werder Bremen), S.Bjørnebye (Rosenborg BK), K.Ingebrigtsen (Rosenborg BK), E.Mykland (IK Start), R.Rekdal (Lierse SK), G.Halle (Oldham A), G.Sørloth (Rosenborg BK), J.Jakobsen (Young Boys).
Subs: H.Berg (Lillestrøm SK) for Pedersen and J.Flo (Sogndal) for Mykland.

Half-time 0-0   Full-time 1-1
Ref: A.Brizio Carter (Mexico)   Att: 51,441

ENGLAND came out with a very determined attitude for this vital World Cup qualifier and it will remain a mystery for a very long time as to why they did not beat Norway convincingly after an excellent performance. With Paul Gascoigne back in the side after his lengthy injury problems and pulling all the strings, the home side looked better than for several games.

Three early attacks in the first 15 minutes set the scene with a lovely move down the left involving Stuart Pearce, Alan Shearer and Ian Wright ending with a pass into the path of David Platt. Unfortunately Platt could not quite reach the ball and failed to get any power behind his shot. Then Gascoigne flicked a fine pass out to Platt on the left and a first-time cross was met by Shearer, but his downward header, although firm enough, was too straight and easily saved by Thorstvedt.

A corner then gave England another chance but when Shearer's header found Tony Adams in front of goal, the big Arsenal player elected to head back across goal instead of having a go himself. The ball was cleared.

Still England dominated and a terrible mix-up betwen Bratseth and Nilsen gave Wright a golden chance but alas, he was finding it difficult to open his scoring account at this level and he completely missed his attempted kick. The first half was very good for the home side and all they lacked was a goal. Adams was looking very strong and Paul Ince and David Batty were working so hard. One brilliant pass by Batty set Platt up, but an offside against Wright put a stop to the move. Lee Dixon was the one disappointing player and his distribution was awful as he repeatedly gave the ball away. His crosses, too, were very poor.

Norway only occasionally threatened but Bjørnebye did hit one fine shot from 25 yards which crashed into the side netting with Chris Woods groping.

Woods then had to save at full stretch from a free-kick. Ince was booked for a challenge on Halle but the game as a whole was played in a good spirit.

Probably the best move of the half came just before the interval when Ince fed Wright and the Arsenal striker returned a glorious pass back to Ince, who then passed inside to Platt. Some lovely control then enabled Platt to fire in an overhead shot which Thorstvedt was well positioned to save. The half ended with Gascoigne also being booked for some illegal use of his elbow.

A slow start to the second half was interrupted when Rekdal hit a fierce shot just over for Norway. Batty then shot wide after another Gascoigne lay-off and this attack saw Gascoigne gesticulating to the crowd in an effort to lift the home players. It worked. As the incessant rain poured down England were awarded a free-kick just to the right of the penalty area. Stuart Pearce, at the second attempt, drove in a low cross and Platt completed the well-rehearsed move by stretching to touch the ball past the goalkeeper. It meant that Platt had scored England's last five goals.

The pressure was unrelenting and at this point a home win seemed a certainty. A Gascoigne corner beat Thorstvedt and Shearer's header was goalbound until Mykland popped up to head off the line. Substitute Paul Merson then hit a shot into the side netting and Shearer was guilty of the miss of the match when Gascoigne's superb free-kick was headed wide by the Blackburn striker.

So, after all this pressure and domination what happened next was particularly hard to take. There were 14 minutes left when Jakobsen received a throw-in and pulled the ball back to Rekdal, stood about 25 yards from goal. He took it on his chest and hit a screaming half volley that flew like an arrow into Woods's top left hand corner. A tremendous goal but one the Norwegians hardly deserved.

There were no more clear chances and the visitors were delighted with the result at the final whistle. It left them well clear at the top of the group.

> 7th match v Norway.

England v Turkey   World Cup Qualifier

Played on Wednesday, 18 November 1992 at Wembley Stadium.

England: C.E.Woods (Sheffield Wed); L.M.Dixon (Arsenal), S.Pearce (Nottm Forest, captain), C.L.Palmer (Sheffield Wed), D.S.Walker (Sampdoria), T.A.Adams (Arsenal), D.A.Platt (Juventus), P.J.Gascoigne (Lazio), A.Shearer (Blackburn R), I.E.Wright (Arsenal), P.E.C.Ince (Man Utd).

Turkey: D.Hayrettin (Galatasaray); Ç.Recep (Beşiktaş), K.Bülent (Galatasaray), K.Gökhan (Beşiktaş), T.Ogün (Trabzonspor), C.Orhan (Trabzonspor), M.Hami (Trabzonspor), K.Ünal (Trabzonspor), O.Mehmet (Beşiktaş), C.Oguz (Fenerbahçe), S.Hakan (Galatasaray). Sub: S.Riza (Beşiktaş) for Hami and O.Ersel (Buraspor) for Mehmet.

Half-time 2-0   Full-time 4-0

Ref: B.Karlsson (Sweden)   Att: 42,984

England celebrate Stuart Pearce's goal against Turkey at Wembley in November 1992.

Paul Gascoigne scores his second goal against the Turks, coolly dribbling round Hayrettin to slot the ball into the empty net.

THIS was an excellent victory for England as they confidently began to increase their challenge for World Cup qualification. Not only was it an emphatic scoreline but it was a performance full of class with Paul Gascoigne once again the hub of all England's good play.

After several promising scoring opportunities had just failed in the early stages, notably when Lee Dixon's cross shot hit the far post, England gained the lead in the 19th minute. Paul Ince, having a great season for his club, Manchester United, and now bringing that form into an England shirt, made a sharp challenge on a dawdling Bülent. The Turkish defenders were thrown into a panic and when Gascoigne gained possession, the writing was on the wall. He danced around Gökhan's desperate tackle and slotted the ball wide of Hayrettin for a clinical piece of finishing.

This gave England the platform they needed and they quickly asserted their authority by playing some lovely football.

Ten minutes after Gascoigne's goal they scored another. This time Stuart Pearce slipped a pass to Gascoigne who, in turn, released Ian Wright with a superb flick. The Arsenal player sped down the left, looked up, and put over a fine cross for Alan Shearer to come inside defender Ogün, and score with a glorious diving header. It was a magnificent goal and due reward for the home side's pressure.

Earlier, Turkey had missed a fine chance themselves when Chris Woods saved from Hakan but could not prevent the ball rolling to Ünal who seemed certain to score. But Turkey, who must hate playing at Wembley, failed to register that elusive first goal against England because Ünal's shot crashed against the crossbar.

To be fair, that was an isolated raid by Turkey and came after a rare mistake by Des Walker and Tony Adams. These two were beginning to strike up a fine understanding.

In the second half England continued

to hold all the aces and 15 minutes after the restart, Pearce's free-kick was deflected beyond the reach of Hayrettin for goal number-three. Ersel then came on as substitute and immediately had a great chance to pull one back for Turkey, but that first goal remained elusive as he completely fluffed the opportunity. Shortly after that Hami tried an audacious 40-yard free-kick and brought a fine save out of Woods.

But the final word, appropriately enough, was left for Gascoigne who had looked a class above the rest all night. Walker, making a rare but welcome surge forward, ended his run with a cross towards Shearer in the middle. Under challenge, Shearer missed it but Gascoigne seized on to the ball to coolly dribble around Hayrettin before tucking it into the net. The crowd, as they say, went wild!

> 7th match v Turkey.
> 50th cap for Walker.

David Platt scores England's third goal against San Marino at Wembley in February 1993.

England v San Marino
World Cup Qualifier

Played on Wednesday, 17 February 1993 at Wembley Stadium.

England: C.E.Woods (Sheffield Wed); L.M.Dixon (Arsenal), A.R.Dorigo (Leeds Utd), C.L.Palmer (Sheffield Wed), D.S.Walker (Sampdoria), T.A.Adams (Arsenal), D.A.Platt (Juventus, Captain), P.J.Gascoigne (Lazio), L.Ferdinand (QPR), J.C.B.Barnes (Liverpool), D.Batty (Leeds Utd).

San Marino: P.L.Benedettini (Juvenes); B.Muccioli (Novafeltria), M.Genari (Juvenes), L.Zanotti (Juvenes), C.Canti (Juvenes), W.Guerra (Calcio San Marino), P.Manzaroli (Calcio San Marino), M.Mazza (Cerveteri), N.Bacciocchi (Calcio San Marino), M.Bonini (Bologna), F.Francini (Santarcangiolese).
Subs: P.Mazza (Maremmana) for Bacciocchi and F.Matteoni (Calcio San Marino) for Francini.

Half-time 2-0   Full-time 6-0
Ref: R.Phillippi (Luxembourg)   Att: 51,154

INJURY-HIT England left it very late before finally overcoming the gallant but totally outclassed San Marino side. It was a patchy performance by the home team and many of the surprisingly large crowd of over 51,000 went away slightly disappointed at what they had seen.

After a slow, rather tedious start, England found the net in the 13th minute. A corner by Paul Gascoigne was flicked on by John Barnes at the near post and was met with a downwards header by a leaping David Platt at the far post. It was a well-taken goal and one that enabled Platt to celebrate his appointment as captain in the absence of Stuart Pearce.

The nerves were settled by the goal and England stormed forward in search of the avalanche of goals anticipated before the game. Alas, they found it difficult to overcome a packed defence and some desperate clearances from the San Marino

defenders, but ten minutes later they made it 2-0 when Platt scored with another header. This time David Batty was the provider with a neat cross to the far post for Platt to again leap well to head goalwards. Benedettini clawed the ball out but the referee adjudged that it had already crossed the line and gave the goal. Television replays suggested he might have made a mistake, but there was no denying England's right to the lead.

Other chances came and went before half-time. Gascoigne hit a free-kick inches wide and Tony Dorigo, Platt and Batty all put in goal attempts which narrowly failed to add to the total. Despite this dominance, England rarely looked convincing and there was something lacking in their play.

It took over 40 more minutes for England to finally break the dam of the determined San Marino defenders. True, there were plenty of chances, notably when new cap Les Ferdinand headed Batty's cross just wide when he might have done better. Dorigo shot over, Carlton Palmer, who put in a great deal of effective work on the night, saw a fine shot very well saved by the competent Benedettini. The goalkeeper then scrambled another Ferdinand effort around a post. All this pressure had to bring its reward eventually and in the 66th minute, Dorigo's cross was flicked on by Ferdinand and as the goalkeeper came to claim the ball, Platt nipped in, took possession, went around the keeper and coolly tapped in England's third goal to complete his own hat-trick.

This goal triggered another onslaught from England as the tiring San Marino players finally gave way under the pressure. The best goal of the match came from Palmer in the 78th minute when he dived full length to head home Ferdinand's excellent low cross. All of these headers would have pleased Nat Lofthouse, the watching guest of honour.

At last England were now putting some realism into the scoreline and on 83 minutes it was Platt again. Dorigo's long

pass forward was brilliantly headed on by Ferdinand, Tony Adams took possession to the left of goal and pulled the ball back into the middle. A headed clearance reached Lee Dixon, who then half-hit a shot towards goal. It would have been easily saved but Platt was there to divert the ball wide of the goalkeeper. Frantic appeals for offside were overruled.

Three minutes later Dixon collected a long ball from the left by Palmer and centred for Adams to power in another header which bounced down on to the line from the crossbar. Ferdinand dived forward to head into the net to prevent any argument and thus claimed his first international goal, good reward for a promising debut.

Even then the action was not over as Batty's superb through ball found Dorigo sprinting into the area. Manzaroli bundled the full-back over for what was an obvious penalty. Platt, who had done everything right up to then, took the kick but looked on in horror as Benedettini dived to save. Malcolm Macdonald's post-war record of five goals in a match was safe for a little while longer.

The final flurry had given England the big win they expected but had everyone been on their game, perhaps the long spells of inactivity earlier would have been avoided. Barnes and Gascoigne were both ineffective with Barnes in particular taking a lot of stick from the crowd.

1st match v San Marino.
Debut goal for Ferdinand.
First game as captain for Platt.
Four goals for Platt plus a missed penalty.

Turkey v England
World Cup Qualifier

Played on Wednesday, 31 March 1993 at the Atatürk Stadium, Izmir.

Turkey: I.Engin (Fenerbaçhe); C.Recep

(Beşiktaş), T.Ogün (Trabzonspor), Alli Guncar (Beşiktaş), K.Tugay (Galatasaray), K.Bulent (Galatasaray), U.Feyyaz (Beşiktaş), K.Unal (Trabzonspor), O.Mehmet (Beşiktaş), C.Oguz (Fenerbaçhe), C.Orhan (Trabzonspor).
Subs: D.Hayrettin (Galatasaray) for Engin and M.Hami (Trabzonspor) for Recep.

England: C.E.Woods (Sheffield Wed); L.M.Dixon (Arsenal), A.Sinton (QPR), C.L.Palmer (Sheffield Wed), D.S.Walker (Sampdoria), T.A.Adams (Arsenal), D.A.Platt (Juventus, captain), P.J.Gascoigne (Lazio), J.C.B.Barnes (Liverpool), I.E.Wright (Arsenal), P.E.C.Ince (Man Utd).
Sub: N.H.Clough (Nottm Forest) for Dixon and L.S.Sharpe (Man Utd) for Wright.

Half-time 0-2   Full-time 0-2

Ref: F.Baldas (Italy)   Att: 50,000

ENGLAND faced a stiff task in Izmir in what was a very awkward match in their qualifying group. The Turkish crowd were in a very hostile mood and the England players were hit by objects thrown by the spectators before the start. Manager Graham Taylor had several team selection problems but his first task was to win the match.

Early strong challenges set the pattern but England gained just the start they wanted, when in the sixth minute they took the lead. Tugay fouled Ian Wright out on the right wing and John Barnes floated in a curling free-kick. David Platt reacted quickly and glanced a lovely downwards header under the goalkeeper and into the net. It was the captain's tenth goal in ten matches and his 17th in all, but few were as important as this one.

The game then degenerated into a scrappy affair. The mood of the crowd reached the Turkish players and they put in some very crude challenges on the England players. One, again by Tugay, left Lee Dixon writhing in agony, and although he carried on he was later replaced by Nigel Clough. There were few clear opportunities for either side in the remainder of the first-half. Tony Adams was in outstanding form and he made some tremendous interceptions to frustrate the home side. Chris Woods was rarely called upon and the half looked to be ending with the same scoreline.

The Turkey goalkeeper, Engin, had been injured in collisions with both Adams and Platt and the referee had added on several minutes of injury time at the end of the half and England made full use of that with a second goal. The home side had sent on a substitute goalkeeper, Hayrettin, and the first thing he had to do was pick the ball out of the net. Paul Ince sent a fine cross into the middle and Paul Gascoigne made his one telling contribution with a looping header which dropped over the goalkeeper, much to the England players' delight.

Clough replaced Dixon at half-time and the game continued with England prepared to hang on to what they had. Andy Sinton showed some good control in his unaccustomed left-back position and Adams continued to shine. Woods saved well from both Orhan and Feyyaz as the Turks tried to salvage something, but at the other end Gascoigne made one mazy dribble which set up a chance for Platt again but this time the England skipper volleyed wide. Platt and Orhan were

David Platt scores England's first goal against Turkey at Izmir in March 1993.

England's Chris Woods receivces police protection as the teams leave the field in Izmir.

booked for innocuous incidents and it made a mockery of the referee's handling of the match as many horrendous challenges had gone unpunished.

But at least England came away with the result they wanted and it set them up nicely for the visit of Holland in their next group match.

1st match v Turkey.

England v Holland World Cup Qualifier

Played on Wednesday, 28 April 1993 at Wembley Stadium.

England: C.E.Woods (Sheffield Wed); L.M.Dixon (Arsenal), M.W.Keown (Arsenal), C.L.Palmer (Sheffield Wed), D.S.Walker (Sampdoria), T.A.Adams (Arsenal), D.A.Platt (Juventus, captain), P.J.Gascoigne (Lazio), L.Ferdinand (QPR), J.C.B.Barnes (Liverpool), P.E.C.Ince (Man Utd).
Sub: P.C.Merson (Arsenal) for Gascoigne.
Holland: E.de Goey (Feyenoord); D.Blind (Ajax Amsterdam), F.de Boer (Ajax Amsterdam), J.Wouters (Bayern Munich), R.Witschge (Feyenoord), A.Winter (Lazio), D.Bergkamp (Ajax Amsterdam), F.Rijkaard (Milan AC), J.Bosman (Anderlecht), R.Gullit (Milan AC), M.Overmars (Ajax Amsterdam).
Subs: J.de Wolf (Feyenoord) for Bosman and P.van Vossen (Anderlecht) for Gullit.

Half-time 2-1   Full-time 2-2

Ref: P.Mikkelsen (Denmark) Att: 73,163

THIS was a vital World Cup match for both sides as neither could afford to lose. Despite the huge stakes, though, the game was an excellent one, full of fast attacking football.

England began in brilliant form and they had a dream start. In the very first minute, Paul Ince was fouled right on the edge of the penalty area by Witschge. The kick was just to the right of goal and was taken by John Barnes. The Liverpool player had been given a rough ride by the crowd in England's previous appearance at Wembley, but here he answered them in the best possible way by drilling a left-

Goalscorer John Barnes is buried beneath a mass of England players during the World Cup qualifier against Holland at Wembley in April 1993.

Ian Wright celebrates his goal which levelled the scores against Poland in Katowice in May 1993.

foot shot which flew past de Goey and into the top corner. It was just the tonic both the crowd and the player wanted.

With Carlton Palmer, Ince and Paul Gascoigne all looking good in the midfield, the pressure continued and another run and cross by Barnes almost brought a second goal in the ninth minute, but David Platt's shot from an acute angle hit the side netting. It would have been a fine goal had it gone in, but England did not have to wait much longer to add to their score.

Gascoigne almost set up Platt, but Blind's tackle blocked the home skipper. The ball, however, found Les Ferdinand with a clear chance. The Queen's Park Rangers player kept his cool and hit a fierce shot to the far post. The ball struck the upright, but luck was on England's side as the rebound went straight to Platt, who was still grounded, but managed to score his 18th goal for his country.

Holland were now in trouble but they had already shown glimpses of their potential and when the highly-rated Bergkamp ghosted in towards a cross by Overmars, only a timely and brilliant interception by Des Walker saved the day. Just when it seemed that England were in control, the Dutch pulled a goal back and what a superb goal it was.

Wouters made ground down the middle before chipping a pass forward over Bergkamp's shoulder. As the ball dropped, the blond striker lobbed a volley gently over the crestfallen Chris Woods.

That goal was a blow to the home side, but an even worse blow was in losing Gascoigne at half-time, thanks to a dreadful elbow in the face he received from the unpunished Wouters. Paul Merson replaced the Lazio player.

England still played well after the break but without quite the same conviction, although Holland created few openings to worry a solid rearguard in which Tony Adams and Walker were in top form. A tactical switch by the Dutch brought the fiercesome de Wolfe into their defence and he certainly does not stand on ceremony with his play.

After an entertaining half, it looked as though England would hold on to their deserved lead. But in the 86th minute came disaster. The lively Overmars, who had switched from left wing to right, suddenly burst past Walker, leaving the England defender desperately chasing back. He tugged at the Dutchman's shirt and by the time Overmars fell, he was in the penalty area and the referee had no option but to award a spot-kick. Substitute van Vossen remained super cool as he sent Woods the wrong way to give the Dutch a point they scarcely deserved.

> 11th match v Holland.
> Penalty for Holland scored by van Vossen.

Poland v England World Cup Qualifier

Played on Saturday, 29 May 1993 at the Slaski Stadium, Katowice.

Poland: J.Badko (Beşiktaş); P.Czachowski (Udinese), R.Szewczek (GKS Katowice), M.Kosminski (Udinese), M.Lesiak (Wacker Innsbruck), C.Brzecek (Lech Poznań), L.Swierczewski (GKS Katowice), D.Adamczuk (Eintracht Frankfurt), J.Furtok (Hamburg), R.Kosecki (CA Osasuna), M.Lesniak (Wattenscheld).
Subs: M.Wegrzyn (GKS Katowice) for Lesniak and L.Jalocha (Lech Poznań) for Brzecek.

England: C.E.Woods (Sheffield Wed); D.J.Bardsley (QPR), A.R.Dorigo (Leeds Utd), C.L.Palmer (Sheffield Wed), D.S.Walker (Sampdoria), T.A.Adams (Arsenal), D.A.Platt (Juventus, captain), P.J.Gascoigne (Lazio), E.P.Sheringham (Spurs), J.C.B.Barnes (Liverpool), P.E.C. Ince (Man Utd).
Subs: I.E.Wright (Arsenal) for Palmer and N.H.Clough (Nottm Forest) for Gascoigne.

Half-time 0-1   Full-time 1-1

Ref: S.Muhamenthaler (Switzerland)

Att: 60,000

NOT for the first time England were faced with a difficult World Cup qualifier in Poland for this, the latest of their group matches. Both sides needed the points desperately and it was soon reflecting in the play.

Fierce tackles seemed to be the order of the day with Carlton Palmer and Paul Ince winning several of them. Poland, though, had a glorious early opportunity when Lesniak ran 50 yards unchallenged before he side-footed the easiest of chances wide of the England goal. it had seemed impossible to miss and Chris Woods looked very relieved.

England were enjoying plenty of possession and a fine Paul Gascoigne free-kick had goalkeeper Bako diving at full stretch to push the ball away. Unfortunately that was an isolated goal attempt by the visitors and only a Teddy Sheringham header which flew wide gave Poland any real problem.

As the game wore on Kosecki was seen to be the danger man for the home team. His running down the right put Tony Dorigo under pressure and the full-back was unable to make the forward runs his team had hoped for. England's midfield was disappointing and apart from his free-kick Gascoigne made little impact. The one big success was David Bardsley who had a fine game at right-back as the late replacement for Lee Dixon who had a kidney complaint.

Ten minutes from half-time the Poles opened the scoring. John Barnes, again ineffective, lost possession to Lesniak. The ball was passed forward and Des Walker was again sprinting back towards his own goal. it seemed that Walker was oblivious to Adamczuk's roaring up behind him and before the defender could make up his mind what to do Adamczuk's foot came in to lob the ball over the advancing Woods. It was a bad goal to concede but very well taken by the Polish player.

In the second-half England worked hard to try to salvage something from the game. Their passing improved but they rarely threatened Bako's goal. At one point Woods almost presented Poland with a gift when his attempted clearance from Walker's back-pass was intercepted by Lesniak only 12 yards from goal. Amazingly the striker could not punish the goalkeeper, although to be fair Woods redeemed himself by pushing the shot wide. later the keeper also made a fine save from a fierce shot by Kozminski.

As the time slipped away it looked inevitable that England were heading for defeat but with just six minutes to go they suddenly found an equalizer from an unlikely source. Barnes and Dorigo combined cleverly down the left and Dorigo angled a lovely cross towards the far post. The Polish marking was very poor much to the delight of Ian Wright. The England substitute had only been on for 20 minutes but he hit a sweet half-volley which Bako touched but could not prevent crossing the line. To say that Wright was delighted would be an understatement and he punched the air in celebration. His first goal for his country had been a long time coming but in the end it could prove one of the most vital of his career.

| 10th match v Polland. |
| Debut for Sheringham. |

Norway v England   World Cup Qualifier

Played on Wednesday, 2 June 1993 at the Ulleval Stadium, Oslo.

Norway: E.Thorstvedt (Spurs); G.Halle (Oldham A), T.Pedersen (SK Brann), R.Bratseth (Werder Bremen), S.Bjornebye (Liverpool), O.Leonhardsen (Rosenborg BK), K.Rekdal (SK Lierse), E.Mykland (IK Start), L.Bohinen (Young Boys), J.Flo (Sogndal), J.Fjortoft (Rapid Vienna).
Subs: R.Nilsen (1.FC Cologne) for Bratseth and G.Sorloth (Rosenborg) for Fjortoft.
England: C.E.Woods (Sheffield Wed);

Paul Gascoigne, wearing a mask to protect his injured face, makes his feelings known to the referee in Oslo in June 1993.

L.M.Dixon (Arsenal), G.A.Pallister (Man Utd), D.S.Walker (Sampdoria), T.A.Adams (Arsenal), L.S.Sharpe (Man Utd), D.A.Platt (Juventus, captain), C.A.Palmer (Sheffield Wed), L.Ferdinand (QPR), P.J.Gascoigne (Lazio), E.P.Sheringham (Spurs).
Subs: N.H.Clough (Nottm Forest) for Walker and I.E.Wright (Arsenal) for Sheringham.

Half-time 1-0   Full-time 2-0
Ref: S.Puhl (Hungary)   Att: 22,500

ENGLAND got it all horribly wrong when they travelled to Oslo for this, the most important of their World Cup group matches so far. As a result, at the end of the day they now had to win all three of their remaining fixtures and hope for the failings of others to help their prospects of qualifying for the finals in the United States.

Manager Graham Taylor decided on a totally different tactical plan and made four team changes to accommodate it. He played a back-three formation with Paul Gascoigne being given a free role behind the front three. Sadly, it just did not work. Too many players were off form on the night for the plan to have any chance of succeeding.

Gary Pallister was soon being tormented by the runs of Bohinen and from one early burst a cross was headed at goal by Fjortoft. Chris Woods saved well but Bohinen proved he had the beating of the Manchester United man. England looked ill at ease and the players seemed lost as to what they should be doing. Norway, meanwhile, played as a unit and constantly put the visitor's defence under pressure. The first-half produced nine corners for the home side against none for England, some measure of the dominance of the Norwegians.

In the 43rd minute the inevitable happened. Des Walker, again looking less than comfortable, was penalised for a foul on Fjortoft. Whilst he stood arguing with the referee Halle quickly saw the opportunity to feed the ball through for Fjortoft, who was able, unchallenged, to pull back a cross to the near post. Leonhardsen reacted quicker than Lee Dixon or David Platt and although his shot was deflected past Woods it was a goal Norway deserved for their first-half performance.

Whatever was said by the England management at half-time had little chance to take effect as within three minutes of the restart Norway scored a second goal. Again it was embarrassing how the defence was so easily exposed. A long pass by Mykland found Leonhardsen who was confronted by Walker. The Norwegian easily by-passed the defender with a pass to the overlapping Bohinen. Totally unchallenged, Bohinen was able to cut inside and hit a rasping right-foot shot across Woods and in. Woods must have been disappointed with his attempted save but he would also want to know how Bohinene could be allowed to get so far without a challenge coming from England.

Immediately Les Ferdinand had a golden chance to pull a goal back after Platt's left-wing centre found him right in front of goal. Unfortunately, Ferdinand totally miskicked the ball which went wide and the opportunity was gone. That was England's first and probably best chance to save something from a match that they would quickly want to forget. In all honesty it was Norway who should have had more goals before the end.

The England task would be so much harder now.

> 8th match v Norway.

USA v England
US Cup

Played on Wednesday, 9 June 1993 at the Foxboro Stadium, Boston.

USA: A.Meola (US National Team); D.Armstrong (US National Team), M.Lapper (US National Team), J.Doyle (US National Team), F.Clavijo (US National Team), J.Agoos (US National Team), T.Dooley (1.FC Kaiserslautern), J.A.Harkes (Sheffield Wed), T.Ramos (Real Betis), R.C.Wegerle (Coventry C), E.Wynalda (Saarbrücken).
Subs: E.Stewart (Willem II) for Wynalda and A.Lalas (US National Team) for Dooley.
England: C.E.Woods (Sheffield Wed); L.M.Dixon (Arsenal), A.R.Dorigo (Leeds Utd), D.Batty (Leeds Utd), G.A.Pallister (Man Utd), C.A.Palmer (Sheffield Wed), P.E.C.Ince (Man Utd, captain), N.H. Clough (Liverpool), L.Ferdinand (QPR), J.C.B.Barnes (Liverpool), L.S.Sharpe (Man Utd).
Subs: D.S.Walker (Sampdoria) for Palmer and I.E.Wright (Arsenal) for Ferdinand.

Half-time 1-0   Full-time 2-0
Ref: A.Weiser (Austria)   Att: 37,652

FORTY-three years ago, almost to the day, England suffered their most humiliating defeat of all time at the hands of the United States team of 1950. On another trip to the States in 1993 they suffered a similar experience. After the bitter disappointment of their defeat in Norway the England players were looking for a morale-boosting tournament in the US Cup, especially arranged as part of the preparation for the anticipated qualifica-

tion for next year's World Cup here. On the evidence of their first game in the competition though there would be no repeat trip next year.

England were simply awful. New captain Paul Ince strove manfully to rally his troops but his team lacked confidence and showed no appetite for the fight. The USA side played with great assurance, reinforced by those players playing good football abroad, including Harkes and Wegerle, stars of our own Premier Division.

There were few clear goalscoring opportunities in the early stages but Nigel Clough was only a whisker away from John Barnes's first-minute cross after good work by Ince. But Clough faded from the action from that moment and it was Harkes and Wegerle who looked the most dangerous of the players on view. At the back Gary Pallister and Carlton Palmer's central defensive partnership did not work at all with both players struggling.

Twice the States team squandered clear openings as Wynalda and Dooley wasted their chance. England's best hope seemed to be Lee Sharpe and he made a couple of good runs which almost produced a breakthrough but goalkeeper Meola was always alert and in confident mood. One shot by Lee Dixon did strike the post but there was little conviction about England's attacks.

As a result of all their poor defending it came as no surprise when the States opened the scoring in the 43rd minute. Agoos crossed from the left and England's defence just stood and watched as Ramos brought the ball down with superb control before cutting it back for Dooley to stoop and ram home an unstoppable header.

England rallied for a while after the restart and Meola produced a fine save from Clough's shot and then the goalkeeper repeated his feat from a free-kick, again from Clough. But this mini-revival was short-lived as England slipped back into their abysmal form of the first-half. Ince was lucky not to be booked after a terrible tackle on Dooley but in the end he was punished because after Dooley had gone off the field his replacement, Lalas, promptly scored a decisive second goal. He had only been on the field for four minutes when he met a left-wing corner with a thumping header which left England totally beaten and the American crowd delighted.

Rarely has an England team left a football field with such a dreadful performance behind them. There was nothing more to be said.

> 6th match v USA.
> Ince's first game as captain.

Brazil v England
US Cup

Played on Sunday, 13 June 1993 in the RFK Stadium, Washington.

Brazil: Taffarel (Parma); Jorginho (Bayern Munich), Valber (São Paulo), Marcio Santos (Bordeaux), Nonato (Cruzeiro), Luisinho (Vasco da Gama), Dunga (Pescara), Valdeir (Bordeaux), Rai (São Paulo) Careca (Napoli), Elivelton (São Paulo).
Subs: Cafu (São Paulo) for Nonato,

Palhinha (São Paulo) for Luisinho and Almir (São Paulo) for Valdeir.
England: T.D.Flowers (Southampton); E.D.Barrett (Aston Villa), A.R.Dorigo (Leeds Utd), D.Batty (Leeds Utd), G.A.Pallister (Man Utd), D.S.Walker (Sampdoria), P.E.C.Ince (Man Utd, captain), N.H.Clough (Liverpool), I.E.Wright (Arsenal), A.Sinton (QPR), L.S.Sharpe (Man Utd).
Subs: D.A.Platt (Juventus) for Batty, C.A.Palmer (Sheffield Wed) for Ince and P.C.Merson (Arsenal) for Clough.

Half-time 0-0   Full-time 1-1
Ref: H.Diasusa (USA)   Att: 54,118

WITH England manager Graham Taylor under increasing pressure from the Press and media, and with several players also being hounded mercilessly, it was imperative that England boosted their confidence with a good performance in this game. Brazil, looking as good as they have done for several years, were formidable opponents and it was certainly going to be a tough job. But on this day England rose to the occasion and at last came through with their heads held high.

Brazil were quickly into their stride, showing that slick passing so natural in their play, and in the third minute Careca was ominously outpacing Gary Pallister. But the Manchester United ace timed his tackle to perfection to stifle the danger. It was a lovely moment and set the big defender up for a fine performance. It also had an inspiring effect on his teammates.

In the seventh minute though Brazil missed a simple chance. A long pass by Dunga split the defence, a typical Brazilian flick by Elivelton set up Rai and he was left with just new cap Tim Flowers to beat. It seemed a certain goal but Rai's shot struck the advancing keeper and the ball was cleared.

The midfield was a contrast in styles. Brazil, passing and running off the ball, whilst England harried and tackled with a ferocity that took the edge off the South Americans. In Andy Sinton England had a quality performer and he sensibly filled the gaps left by others. With Paul Ince and David Batty strong in the tackle England were more than holding their own. Up front though Ian Wright was vitually on his own so England's attack was muted. However, on the whole it had been a much improved performance in the first half.

Straight after the break the England fans were jumping for joy as their side took the lead. Taylor had brought on David Platt for Batty to try and pep up the attack and it worked almost immediately as the substitute's first touch brought a goal. Lee Sharpe took a short corner to Sinton who chipped a cross into the area. Platt, in that unique way of his, arrived perfectly to direct a header at goal despite the strong challenge of Marcio Santos. Goalkeeper Tafferel hesitated for a fatal second, wrongly believing the ball to be going wide. By the time he realised the header was past him and went in off the post. It was Platt's 19th goal for his country and one that gave him a good deal of pleasure.

At this point England were content to sit back and deal with each new Brazilian attack. All the players worked their hearts out, a refreshing change after recent performances, and the South Americans

Paul Gascoigne and assistant manager Lawrie McMenemy at Bisham Abbey during an England training session.

were becoming increasingly frustrated. Flowers dealt confidently with everything that came his way and he looked as though he was enjoying every moment of his baptism. The confidence he projected spread to the rest of the side and there was a much more positive display from the team. Even Des Walker was back to his best form and he and Pallister were outstanding at the heart of the defence. But for one slight lapse they would all have been rewarded with a famous victory.

Never bothered by being a goal down, Brazil continued to push forward relentlessly and in the 76th minute they were rewarded. A corner proved to be England's undoing. Almir sent over a cross, Palhina knocked it down and Santos was left unmarked to easily score from close range.

It was very disappointing for England and although Flowers had to make a wonderful reflex save right at the end there was no disputing England's right to a share of the spoils. It had been a much improved display that was widely welcomed.

> 17th match v Brazil.
> Debut for Flowers.

Germany v England   US Cup

Played on Saturday, 19 June 1993 in the Pontiac Silverdome, Detroit.

Germany: B.Illgner (1.FC Cologne); S.Effenberg (Fiorentina), T.Helmer (Bayern Munich), G.Buchwald (VfB Stuttgart), A.Möller (Juventus), L.Matthäus (Bayern Munich), M.Schultz (Borussia Dortmund), C.Ziege (Bayern Munich), T.Strunz (VfB Stuttgart), K-H.Riedle (Lazio), J.Klinsmann (AS Monaco).
Subs: M.Zorc (Borussia Dortmund) for Effenberg and M.Sammer (Borussia Dortmund) for Moeller.

England: A.N.Martyn (Crystal Palace); E.D.Barrett (Aston Villa), A.Sinton (QPR), D.S.Walker (Sampdoria), G.A.Pallister (Man Utd), L.S.Sharpe (Man Utd), D.A.Platt (Juventus, captain), P.E.C.Ince (Man Utd), P.C.Merson (Arsenal), N.H.Clough (Liverpool), J.C.B.Barnes (Liverpool).
Subs: M.R.Keown (Arsenal) for Pallister, I.E.Wright (Arsenal) for Clough and N.Winterburn (Arsenal) for Sharpe.

Half-time 1-1   Full-time 2-1
Ref: E.Philippi Cavani (Uruguay)

Att: 62,126

ENGLAND'S disappointing season ended with another defeat but this match against the high class German side did give some hope for the future. The Germans, by winning this match, won the tournament and in so doing also condemned England to the wooden spoon. But at least the tour ended on a positive note.

Both sides settled quickly with the Germans swift passing and possession football pulling England around. But the English defenders stuck to their task well and only a Riedle header which went just wide and an Effenberg shot which went over gave Nigel Martyn any anxious moments. At the other end only desperate defending cleared Paul Merson's centre from David Platt's head, whilst shots from Nigel Clough and Lee Sharpe were both blocked. Then a fine diving catch at full stretch by Martyn kept Möller's clever effort out.

In the 25th minute the best move of the match almost gave England a goal. Platt started the move with a pass to Clough. He found Merson who hit a long diagonal cross into the middle where Platt had timed his run to perfection. Unfortunately Platt just got underneath the ball and his header went narrowly over the bar instead of into it.

It was a splendid effort but typically of the Germans they then went down to the other end and opened the scoring. Matthäus gained possession and chipped a delightful ball over the defence for Effenberg to run on to. The bounce beat Gary Pallister and it left the German with a clear chance which he tucked under Martyn's dive.

Good pressure was the response from England and Merson, who had an excellent game, brought the save of the match from Illgner with a tremendous volley which the 'keeper tipped over. That only delayed the inevitable though as almost immediately England equalized. Another fine passing move down the left saw Paul Ince play a couple of one-two's with Des Walker and John Barnes, the second of which left him clear of the defence. He hit a low ball to the far post and the ever-ready Platt was there to tap the ball home, his 20th for his country. It was a marvellously worked goal and thoroughly deserved.

In the first few minutes of the second-half Ince almost made it 2-1 with a ferocious shot which Illgner again did really well to tip over. If that had gone in then surely England would have had the confidence to go on and win the match. As it was, in the 53rd minute the Germans regained the lead and this time they were to hold on to it. Barnes made the fatal error when his pass across field was intercepted. From that the ball broke for Riedle to swerve around the defence and shoot low to Martyn's right. The goalkeeper did well to get down and make the save but the ball rolled against the post and Klinsmann was the first to react and he swept it into the empty net.

For the rest it was a question of trying to break down the strong German defence whilst carefully watching the swift breakaways instrumented by Matthäus. In the end England just could not find a way through and although encouraged by the two performances against Brazil and Germany, they would now have to look to plan for the vital games of a new season and the vital games coming up.

> 21st match v Germany.

Paul Bracewell

Steve Coppell

Joe Corrigan

Gordon Cowans

England's Players

Up to and including Germany v England, 19 June 1993

Player	Debut	Last Capped	Total Caps	Player	Debut	Last Capped	Total Caps
A.A'Court	6.11.57	26.11.58	5	S.G.Bull	17.5.89	17.10.90	13
T.A.Adams	18.2.87	2.6.93	26	T.I.Butcher	31.5.80	4.7.90	77
A.Allen	17.10.59	18.11.59	3	G.Byrne	6.4.63	29.6.66	2
C.D.Allen	10.6.84	17.2.88	5	J.J.Byrne	22.11.61	10.4.65	11
R.Allen	28.5.52	1.12.54	5	R.W.Byrne	3.4.54	27.11.57	33
S.Anderson	4.4.62	14.4.62	2	I.R.Callaghan	26.6.66	12.10.77	4
V.A.Anderson	29.11.78	24.5.88	30	H.S.Carter	14.4.34	18.5.47	13
J.Angus	27.5.61	27.5.61	1	M.Chamberlain	15.12.82	17.10.84	8
J.C.Armfield	13.5.59	26.6.66	43	M.R.Channon	11.10.72	7.9.77	46
D.Armstrong	31.5.80	2.5.84	3	G.Charles	8.6.91	12.6.91	2
K.Armstrong	2.4.55	2.4.55	1	J.Charlton	10.4.65	11.6.70	35
G.Astall	20.5.56	26.5.56	2	R.Charlton	19.4.58	14.6.70	106
J.Astle	7.5.69	11.6.70	5	R.O.Charnley	3.10.62	3.10.62	1
J.Aston	26.9.48	7.10.50	17	T.J.Cherry	24.3.76	18.6.80	27
P.J.W.Atyeo	30.11.55	19.5.57	6	A.C.Chilton	7.10.50	3.10.51	2
G.R.Bailey	26.3.85	9.6.85	2	M.H.Chivers	3.2.71	17.10.73	24
M.A.Bailey	27.5.64	18.11.64	2	E.Clamp	18.5.58	15.6.58	4
E.F.Baily	2.7.50	4.10.52	9	D.R.Clapton	26.11.58	26.11.58	1
J.H.Baker	18.11.59	5.1.66	8	A.J.Clarke	11.6.70	19.11.75	19
A.J.Ball	9.5.65	24.5.75	72	H.A.Clarke	3.4.54	3.4.54	1
G.Banks	6.4.63	27.5.72	73	R.Clayton	2.11.55	11.5.60	35
T.Banks	18.5.58	4.10.58	6	R.N.Clemence	15.11.72	16.11.83	61
D.J.Bardsley	9.9.92	29.5.93	2	D.J.Clement	24.3.76	9.2.77	5
M.F.Barham	12.6.83	15.6.83	2	B.H.Clough	17.10.59	28.10.59	2
R.J.Barlow	2.10.54	2.10.54	1	N.H.Clough	23.5.89	19.6.93	14
J.C.B.Barnes	28.5.83	19.6.93	73	R.Coates	21.4.70	19.5.71	4
P.S.Barnes	16.11.77	25.5.82	22	H.Cockburn	28.9.46	3.10.51	13
M.W.Barrass	20.10.51	18.4.53	3	G.R.Cohen	6.5.64	22.11.67	37
E.D.Barrett	3.6.91	19.6.93	3	L.H.Compton	15.11.50	22.11.50	2
D.Batty	21.5.91	13.6.93	14	J.M.Connelly	17.10.59	11.7.66	20
R.L.Baynham	2.10.55	30.11.55	3	T.Cooper	12.3.69	20.11.74	20
P.A.Beardsley	29.1.86	21.5.91	49	S.J.Coppell	16.11.77	30.3.83	42
D.Beasant	15.11.89	13.12.89	2	J.T.Corrigan	18.5.76	2.6.82	9
T.K.Beattie	16.4.75	12.10.77	9	A.R.Cottee	10.9.86	27.5.89	7
C.Bell	22.5.68	30.10.75	48	G.S.Cowans	23.2.83	14.11.90	10
R.T.F.Bentley	13.5.49	22.5.55	12	R.Crawford	22.11.61	4.4.62	2
J.J.Berry	17.5.53	16.5.56	4	C.Crowe	3.10.62	3.10.62	1
G.Birtles	13.5.80	15.10.80	3	L.P.Cunningham	23.5.79	15.10.80	6
L.L.Blissett	13.10.82	2.6.84	14	K.Curle	29.4.92	11.6.92	3
J.P.Blockley	11.10.72	11.10.72	1	A.W.Currie	23.5.72	10.6.79	17
F.Blunstone	10.11.54	28.11.56	5	A.M.Daley	13.11.91	17.6.92	7
P.P.Bonetti	3.7.66	14.7.70	7	P.Davenport	26.3.85	26.3.85	1
S.Bowles	3.4.74	9.2.77	5	B.C.Deane	3.6.91	9.9.92	3
P.J.Boyer	24.3.76	24.3.76	1	N.V.Deeley	13.5.59	17.5.59	2
P.Brabrook	17.6.58	15.5.60	3	A.E.Devonshire	20.5.80	16.11.83	8
P.W.Bracewell	12.6.85	14.11.85	3	J.W.Dickinson	18.5.49	5.12.56	48
G.R.W.Bradford	2.10.55	2.10.55	1	E.G.Ditchburn	2.12.48	5.12.56	6
W.Bradley	6.5.59	28.5.59	3	K.M.Dixon	9.6.85	10.9.86	8
B.Bridges	10.4.65	20.10.65	4	L.M.Dixon	25.4.90	9.6.93	20
P.F.Broadbent	17.6.58	9.4.60	7	J.M.Dobson	3.4.74	30.10.74	5
I.A.Broadis	28.11.51	26.6.54	14	A.R.Dorigo	13.12.89	13.6.93	14
T.D.Brooking	3.4.74	5.7.82	47	B.Douglas	19.10.57	5.6.63	36
J.Brooks	14.11.56	5.12.56	3	M.Doyle	24.3.76	9.2.77	5
A.J.Brown	19.5.71	19.5.71	1	M.Duxbury	16.11.83	17.10.84	10
K.Brown	18.11.59	18.11.59	1	G.E.Eastham	8.5.63	3.7.66	19

Emlyn Hughes

Player	Debut	Last Capped	Total Caps	Player	Debut	Last Capped	Total Caps
W.Eckersley	2.7.50	25.11.53	17	A.A.Hudson	12.3.75	16.4.75	2
D.Edwards	2.4.55	27.11.57	18	E.W.Hughes	5.11.69	24.5.80	62
W.Ellerington	18.5.49	22.5.49	2	L.Hughes	25.6.50	2.7.50	3
W.H.Elliott	18.5.52	26.11.52	5	R.Hunt	4.4.62	15.1.69	34
J.Fantham	28.9.61	28.9.61	1	S.K.Hunt	26.5.84	2.6.84	2
J.Fashanu	23.5.89	27.5.89	2	N.Hunter	8.12.65	30.10.74	28
T.W.Fenwick	2.5.84	17.2.88	20	G.C.Hurst	23.2.66	29.4.72	49
L.Ferdinand	17.2.93	9.6.93	4	P.E.C.Ince	9.9.92	19.6.93	9
T.Finney	28.9.46	22.10.58	76	B.Jezzard	23.5.54	2.11.55	2
R.Flowers	15.5.55	29.6.66	49	D.E.Johnson	21.5.75	12.6.80	8
T.D.Flowers	13.6.93	13.6.93	1	H.Johnston	27.11.46	25.11.53	10
S.B.Foster	23.2.82	25.6.82	3	M.D.Jones	12.5.65	14.1.70	3
W.A.Foulkes	2.10.54	2.10.54	1	R.Jones	20.2.92	20.2.92	1
G.C.J.Francis	30.10.74	13.6.76	12	W.H.Jones	14.5.50	18.5.50	2
T.J.Francis	9.2.77	23.4.86	52	A.H.Kay	5.6.63	5.6.63	1
C.N.Franklin	28.9.46	15.4.50	27	J.K.Keegan	15.11.72	5.7.82	63
J.Froggatt	16.11.49	8.6.53	13	A.P.Kennedy	4.4.84	2.5.84	2
R.Froggatt	12.11.52	8.6.53	4	R.Kennedy	24.3.76	15.6.80	17
T.H.Garrett	5.4.52	10.10.53	3	M.R.Keown	20.2.92	19.6.93	11
P.J.Gascoigne	14.9.88	2.6.93	27	D.T.Kevan	6.4.57	10.5.61	14
E.L.Gates	10.9.80	15.10.80	2	B.Kidd	21.4.70	24.5.70	2
C.F.George	8.9.76	8.9.76	1	C.B.Knowles	6.12.67	1.6.68	4
J.Gidman	30.3.77	30.3.77	1	B.L.Labone	20.10.62	14.6.70	26
I.T.Gillard	12.3.75	30.10.75	3	F.R.G.Lampard	11.10.72	31.5.80	2
P.Goddard	2.6.82	2.6.82	1	E.J.Langley	19.4.58	11.5.58	3
C.Grainger	9.5.56	6.4.57	7	R.Langton	28.9.46	7.10.50	11
A.A.Gray	13.11.91	13.11.91	1	R.D.Latchford	16.11.77	13.6.79	12
J.P.Greaves	17.5.59	27.5.67	57	C.Lawler	12.5.71	13.10.71	4
B.Greenhoff	8.5.76	31.5.80	18	T.Lawton	22.10.38	26.9.48	23
J.C.Gregory	12.6.83	2.5.84	6	F.H.Lee	11.12.68	29.4.72	27
J.Hagan	26.9.48	26.9.48	1	J.Lee	7.10.50	7.10.50	1
J.T.W.Haines	2.12.48	2.12.48	1	S.Lee	17.11.82	17.6.84	14
J.J.Hall	2.10.55	19.5.57	17	A.Lindsay	22.5.74	5.6.74	4
J.Hancocks	2.12.48	22.11.50	3	G.W.Lineker	26.5.84	17.6.92	80
G.F.M.Hardwick	28.9.46	10.4.48	13	B.Little	21.5.75	21.5.75	1
M.G.Harford	17.2.88	14.9.88	2	L.V.Lloyd	19.5.71	17.5.80	4
G.Harris	5.1.66	5.1.66	1	N.Lofthouse	22.11.50	26.11.58	33
P.P.Harris	21.9.49	23.5.54	2	E.Lowe	3.5.47	25.5.47	3
J.C.Harvey	3.2.71	3.2.71	1	G.V.Mabbutt	13.10.82	25.3.92	16
H.W.Hassall	14.4.51	11.11.53	5	T.McDermott	7.9.77	2.6.82	25
M.W.Hateley	2.6.84	25.3.92	32	C.A.McDonald	18.5.88	26.11.58	8
J.N.Haynes	2.10.54	10.6.62	56	M.I.McDonald	20.5.72	19.11.75	14
K.J.Hector	17.10.73	14.11.73	2	R.L.McFarland	3.2.71	17.11.76	28
M.S.Hellawell	3.10.62	20.10.62	2	W.H.McGarry	20.6.54	22.10.55	4
R.P.Henry	27.2.63	27.2.63	1	W.McGuinness	4.10.58	24.5.59	2
F.Hill	20.10.62	21.11.62	2	S.McMahon	17.2.88	14.11.90	17
G.A.Hill	28.5.76	12.10.77	6	R.McNab	6.11.68	3.5.69	4
R.A.Hill	22.9.82	29.1.86	3	M.McNeil	8.10.60	28.9.61	9
A.T.Hinton	3.10.62	18.11.64	3	P.E.Madeley	15.5.71	9.2.77	24
D.E.Hirst	1.6.91	20.2.92	3	W.J.Mannion	28.9.46	3.10.51	26
G.A.Hitchens	10.5.61	10.6.62	7	P.Mariner	30.3.77	1.5.85	35
G.Hoddle	22.11.79	18.6.88	53	R.W.Marsh	10.11.71	24.1.73	9
S.B.Hodge	26.3.86	6.2.91	24	A.E.Martin	12.5.81	10.9.86	17
A.Hodgkinson	6.4.57	23.11.60	5	A.N.Martyn	29.4.92	19.6.93	3
D.A.Holden	11.4.59	24.5.59	5	B.Marwood	16.11.88	16.11.88	1
E.Holliday	17.10.59	18.11.59	3	R.D.Matthews	14.4.56	6.10.56	5
J.W.Hollins	24.5.67	24.5.67	1	S.Matthews	29.9.34	15.5.57	54
E.Hopkinson	19.10.57	28.10.59	14	J.Meadows	2.4.55	2.4.55	1
D.Howe	19.10.57	18.11.59	23	L.D.Medley	15.11.50	28.11.51	6
J.R.Howe	16.5.48	9.4.49	3	J.J.Melia	6.4.63	5.6.63	2

Bobby Moore

Mick Mills

Phil Neal

Phil Parkes, Gordon Banks and Peter Shilton

Player	Debut	Last Capped	Total Caps	Player	Debut	Last Capped	Total Caps
G.H.Merrick	14.11.51	26.6.54	23	G.Robb	25.11.53	25.11.53	1
P.C.Merson	11.9.91	19.6.93	12	G.P.Roberts	28.5.83	2.6.84	6
V.Metcalfe	9.5.51	19.5.51	2	B.Robson	6.2.80	16.10.91	90
J.E.T.Milburn	9.10.48	2.10.55	13	R.W.Robson	27.11.57	9.5.62	20
B.G.Miller	27.5.61	27.5.61	1	D.Rocastle	14.9.88	17.5.92	14
M.D.Mills	11.10.72	5.7.82	42	J.F.Rowley	2.12.48	5.4.52	6
G.Milne	8.5.63	21.10.64	14	J.Royle	3.2.71	30.3.77	6
C.A.Milton	28.11.51	28.11.51	1	D.Sadler	22.11.67	25.11.70	4
R.F.Moore	20.5.62	14.11.73	108	J.A.Salako	1.6.91	12.6.91	4
A.W.Morley	18.11.81	17.11.82	6	K.G.Sansom	23.5.79	18.6.88	86
J.Morris	18.5.49	21.9.49	3	L.Scott	28.9.46	10.11.48	17
S.H.Mortenson	25.5.47	25.11.53	25	D.A.Seaman	16.11.88	12.5.92	9
B.Mozley	21.9.49	16.11.49	2	J.Sewell	14.11.51	23.5.54	6
J.Mullen	12.4.47	20.6.54	12	L.F.Shackleton	26.9.48	1.12.54	5
A.P.Mullery	9.12.64	13.10.71	35	L.S.Sharpe	27.3.91	19.6.93	5
P.G.Neal	24.3.76	21.9.83	50	G.L.Shaw	22.10.58	21.11.62	5
K.R.Newton	23.2.66	14.6.70	27	A.Shearer	20.2.92	18.11.92	6
J.Nicholls	3.4.54	16.5.54	2	K.J.Shellito	29.5.63	29.5.63	1
W.E.Nicholson	19.5.51	19.5.51	1	E.P.Sheringham	29.5.93	2.6.93	2
D.J.Nish	12.5.73	18.5.74	5	P.L.Shilton	25.11.70	7.7.90	125
M.Norman	20.5.62	9.12.64	23	E.Shimwell	13.5.49	13.5.49	1
M.O'Grady	20.10.62	12.3.69	2	R.P.Sillett	15.5.55	22.5.55	3
P.L.Osgood	25.2.70	14.11.73	4	A.Sinton	13.11.91	19.6.93	10
R.C.Osman	31.5.80	21.9.83	11	W.J.Slater	10.11.54	9.4.60	12
S.W.Owen	16.5.54	17.5.54	3	A.M.Smith	16.11.88	17.6.92	13
T.L.Paine	29.5.63	16.7.66	19	L.Smith	15.11.50	18.4.53	6
G.A.Pallister	27.4.88	19.6.93	9	R.A.Smith	8.10.60	20.11.63	15
C.A.Palmer	29.4.92	13.6.93	17	T.Smith (Tommy)	19.5.71	19.5.71	1
P.A.Parker	26.4.89	3.6.91	17	T.Smith (Trevor)	17.10.59	28.10.59	2
P.B.F.Parkes	3.4.74	3.4.74	1	N.P.Spink	19.6.83	19.6.83	1
R.A.Parry	18.11.59	9.4.60	2	R.D.Springett	18.11.59	29.6.66	33
A.Peacock	2.6.62	10.11.65	6	R.Staniforth	3.4.54	1.12.54	8
S.Pearce	19.5.87	18.11.92	53	D.J.Statham	23.2.83	15.6.83	3
J.S.Pearson	8.5.76	16.5.78	15	B.Stein	29.2.84	29.2.84	1
S.C.Pearson	10.4.48	18.5.52	8	A.C.Stepney	22.5.68	22.5.68	1
D.Pegg	19.5.57	19.5.57	1	M.Sterland	16.11.88	16.11.88	1
M.Pejic	3.4.74	18.5.74	4	T.M.Steven	27.2.85	14.6.92	36
W.Perry	2.11.55	14.4.56	3	G.A.Stevens	17.10.84	18.6.86	7
S.J.Perryman	2.6.82	2.6.82	1	M.G.Stevens	6.6.85	3.6.92	46
M.S.Peters	4.5.66	18.5.74	67	P.A.Stewart	11.9.91	29.4.92	3
M.C.Phelan	15.11.89	15.11.89	1	N.P.Stiles	10.4.65	25.4.70	28
L.H.Phillips	14.11.51	1.12.54	3	P.E.Storey	21.4.71	14.6.73	19
F.Pickering	27.5.64	21.10.64	3	I.Storey-Moore	14.1.70	14.1.70	1
N.Pickering	19.6.83	19.6.83	1	B.R.Streten	16.11.49	16.11.49	1
B.Pilkington	2.10.54	2.10.54	1	M.G.Summerbee	24.2.68	10.6.73	8
D.A.Platt	15.11.89	19.6.93	42	A.Sunderland	31.5.80	31.5.80	1
R.Pointer	28.9.61	25.10.61	3	P.Swan	11.5.60	9.5.62	19
J.Pye	21.9.49	21.9.49	1	F.V.Swift	28.9.46	18.5.49	19
A.Quixall	10.10.53	22.5.55	5	B.E.Talbot	28.5.77	31.5.80	6
J.Radford	15.1.69	13.10.71	2	R.V.Tambling	21.11.62	4.5.66	3
A.E.Ramsey	2.12.48	25.11.53	32	E.Taylor	25.11.53	25.11.53	1
P.Reaney	11.12.68	3.2.71	3	J.G.Taylor	9.5.51	19.5.51	2
K.P.Reeves	22.11.79	20.5.80	2	P.H.Taylor	18.10.47	19.11.47	3
C.Regis	23.2.82	14.10.87	5	P.J.Taylor	24.3.76	15.5.76	4
P.Reid	9.6.85	28.5.88	13	T.Taylor	17.5.53	27.11.57	19
D.G.Revie	2.10.54	6.10.56	6	D.W.Temple	12.5.65	12.5.65	1
J.P.Richards	12.5.73	12.5.73	1	D.J.Thomas	12.6.83	19.6.83	2
S.Rickaby	11.11.53	11.11.53	1	D.Thomas	30.10.74	19.11.75	8
J.J.Rimmer	28.5.76	28.5.76	1	G.R.Thomas	1.5.91	20.2.92	9
G.Rix	10.9.80	4.4.84	17	M.L.Thomas	16.11.88	13.12.89	2

Cyrille Regis

Peter Reid

Kenny Sansom

Phil Thompson

Player	Debut	Last Capped	Total Caps	Player	Debut	Last Capped	Total Caps
P.Thompson	17.5.64	5.11.69	16	G.West	11.12.68	1.6.69	3
P.B.Thompson	24.3.76	17.11.82	42	J.E.Wheeler	2.10.54	2.10.54	1
T.Thompson	20.10.51	6.4.57	2	D.White	9.9.92	9.9.92	1
R.Thomson	20.11.63	9.12.64	8	S.J.Whitworth	12.3.75	19.11.75	7
C.Todd	23.5.72	28.5.77	27	T.J.Whymark	12.10.77	12.10.77	1
M.A.Towers	8.5.76	28.5.76	3	F.Wignall	18.11.64	9.12.64	2
D.Tueart	11.5.76	4.6.77	6	R.C.Wilkins	28.5.76	12.11.86	84
D.G.Ufton	21.10.53	21.10.53	1	B.F.Williams	22.5.49	22.10.55	24
T.F.Venables	21.10.64	9.12.64	2	S.C.Williams	12.6.83	14.11.84	6
C.Viljoen	17.5.75	21.5.75	2	A.Willis	3.10.51	3.10.51	1
D.S.Viollet	22.5.60	28.9.61	2	D.Wilshaw	10.10.53	6.10.56	12
C.R.Waddle	26.3.85	16.10.91	62	R.Wilson	19.4.60	8.6.68	63
A.K.Waiters	24.5.64	9.12.64	5	N.Winterburn	15.11.89	19.6.93	2
D.S.Walker	14.9.88	19.6.93	58	D.F.Wise	1.5.91	8.6.91	5
D.L.Wallace	29.1.86	29.1.86	1	P.Withe	12.5.81	14.11.84	11
P.A.Walsh	12.6.83	19.6.83	3	R.E.Wood	2.10.54	20.5.56	3
M.Walters	3.6.91	3.6.91	1	A.S.Woodcock	16.5.78	26.2.86	42
P.D.Ward	31.5.80	31.5.80	1	C.C.E.Woods	16.6.85	9.6.93	42
T.V.Ward	21.9.47	10.11.48	2	F.S.Worthington	15.5.74	20.11.74	8
D.Watson	10.6.84	18.6.88	12	I.E.Wright	6.2.91	19.6.93	13
D.V.Watson	3.4.74	2.6.82	65	M.Wright	2.5.84	9.9.92	43
W.Watson	16.11.49	22.11.50	4	T.J.Wright	8.6.68	7.6.70	11
N.J.Webb	9.9.87	17.6.92	26	W.A.Wright	28.9.46	28.5.59	105
K.Weller	11.5.74	22.5.74	4	G.M.Young	18.11.64	18.11.64	1

Ray Wilkins

Peter Withe

—